POWERS™

VOLUME TWO

D1067030

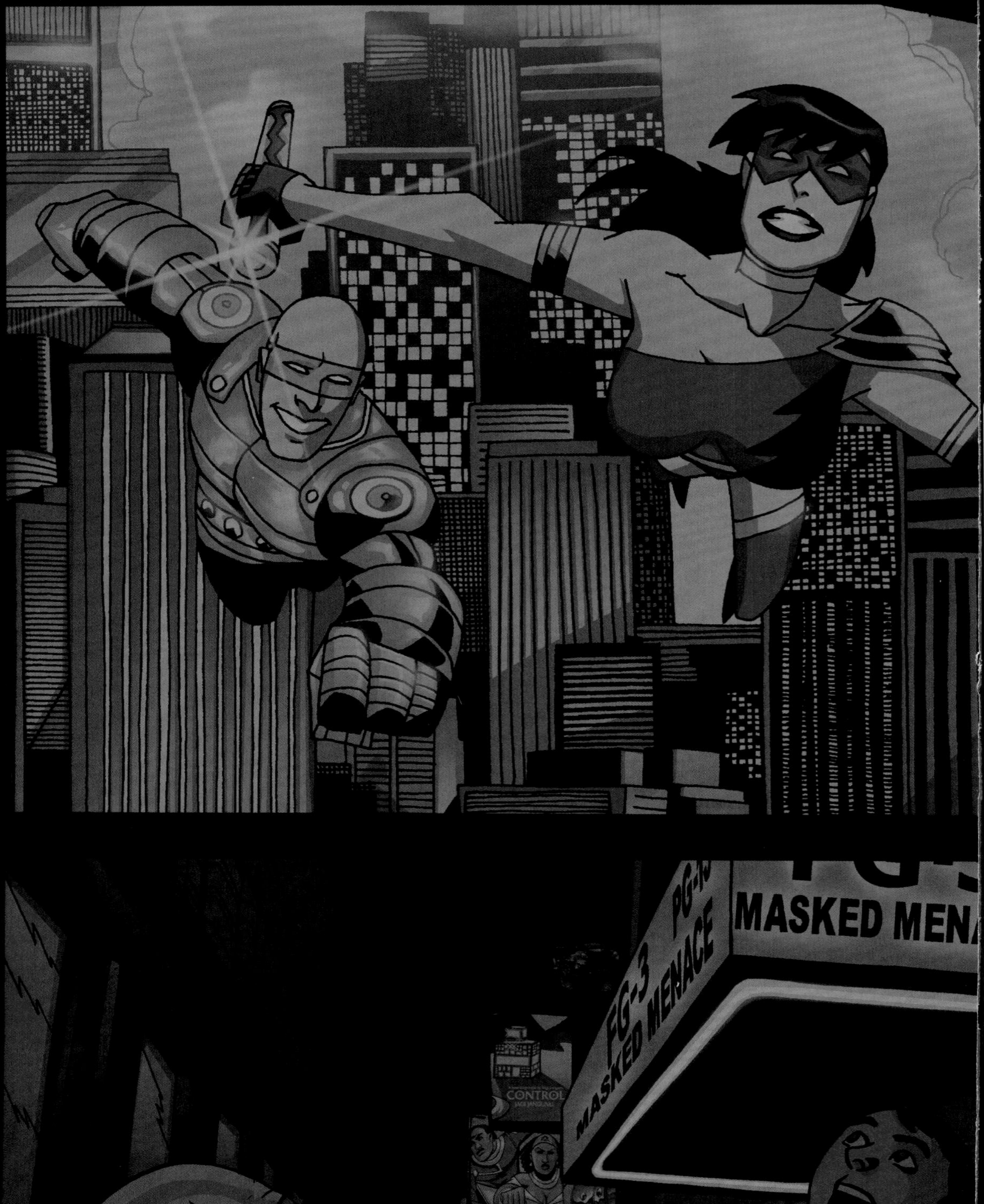
MASKED MENA
FG-3
MASKED MENACE
CONTROL

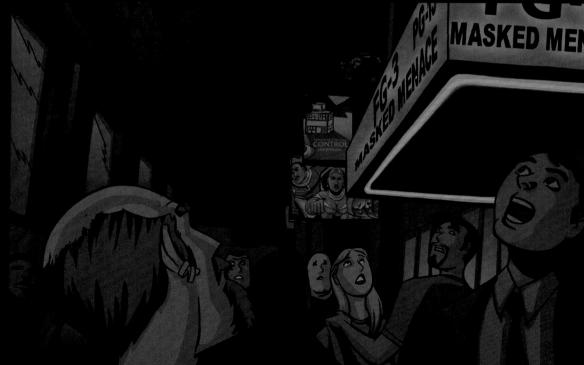

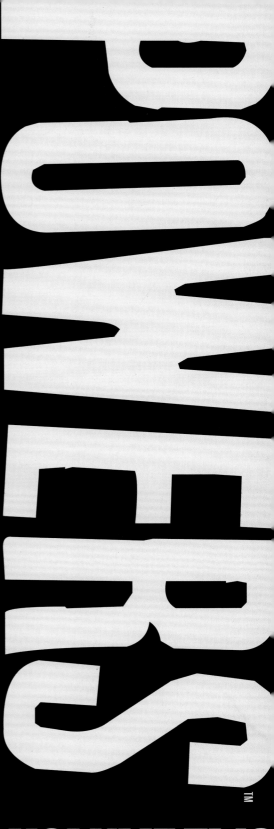

Created by
Brian Michael Bendis and
Michael Avon Oeming

Colored by
Pete Pantazis with
Pat Garrahy and **Brian
Michael Bendis**

Lettered by **Ken Bruzenak**
with **Pat Garrahy** and
Brian Michael Bendis

Art and Cover
Michael Avon Oeming

Dark Horse Books

VOLUME TWO

DARK HORSE
Publisher **Mike Richardson**
Collection Editor **Daniel Chabon**
Assistant Editors **Chuck Howitt-Lease** and **Misha Gehr**

ORIGINAL PRINTING
Publisher **Alisa Bendis**
Editor **Alex Galer**
Publication Design **Curtis King Jr.**

Designer **Kathleen Barnett**
Digital Art Technician **Betsy Howitt**

To find a comics shop in your area, visit comicshoplocator.com.

POWERS Volume Two

Copyright © 2018, 2022 Jinxworld Inc. All rights reserved. Originally
published in single magazine form in *Powers* #12–#24, *Powers Annual*
#1, and *Jinx: True Crime Confessions* #1. Copyright © 2002, 2003, 2009
Jinxworld, Inc. All Rights Reserved. Powers, its logo design, the Jinxworld logo, all characters, their distinctive likenesses and related
elements featured in this publication are trademarks of Jinxworld,
Inc. Dark Horse Books® and the Dark Horse logo are registered trademarks of Dark Horse Comics LLC. All rights reserved. No portion of
this publication may be reproduced or transmitted, in any form or
by any means, without the express written permission of Dark Horse
Comics LLC. Names, characters, places, and incidents featured in this
publication either are the product of the author's imagination or are
used fictitiously. Any resemblance to actual persons (living or dead),
events, institutions, or locales, without satiric intent, is coincidental.

This volume collects *Powers* #12–#24, *Powers Annual* #1, and
Jinx: True Crime Confessions #1, along with all covers and a
sketchbook section.

Published by Dark Horse Books
A division of Dark Horse Comics LLC
10956 SE Main Street
Milwaukie, OR 97222
DarkHorse.com

First edition: December 2022
Ebook ISBN 978-1-50673-034-9
Trade paperback ISBN 978-1-50673-018-9

10 9 8 7 6 5 4 3 2 1
Printed in China

Neil Hankerson Executive Vice President • Tom Weddle Chief
Financial Officer • Dale LaFountain Chief Information Officer •
Tim Wiesch Vice President of Licensing • Vanessa Todd-Holmes
Vice President of Production and Scheduling • Mark Bernardi
Vice President of Book Trade and Digital Sales • Randy Lahrman
Vice President of Product Development and Sales • Ken Lizzi
General Counsel • Dave Marshall Editor in Chief • Davey Estrada
Editorial Director • Chris Warner Senior Books Editor • Cara
O'Neil Senior Director of Marketing • Cary Grazzini Director of
Specialty Projects • Lia Ribacchi Art Director • Michael Gombos
Senior Director of Licensed Publications • Kari Yadro Director
of Custom Programs • Kari Torson Director of International
Licensing • Christina Niece Director of Scheduling

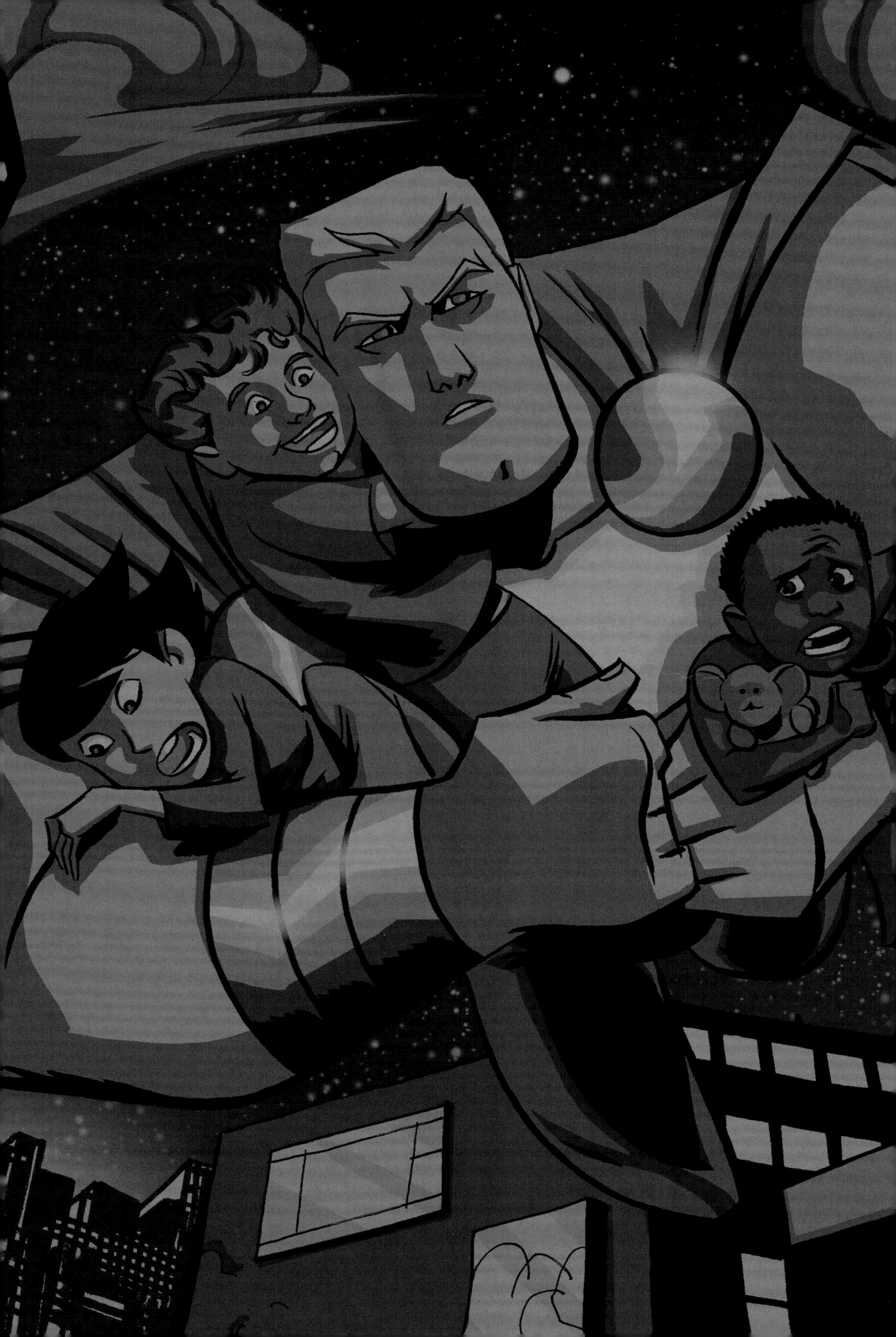

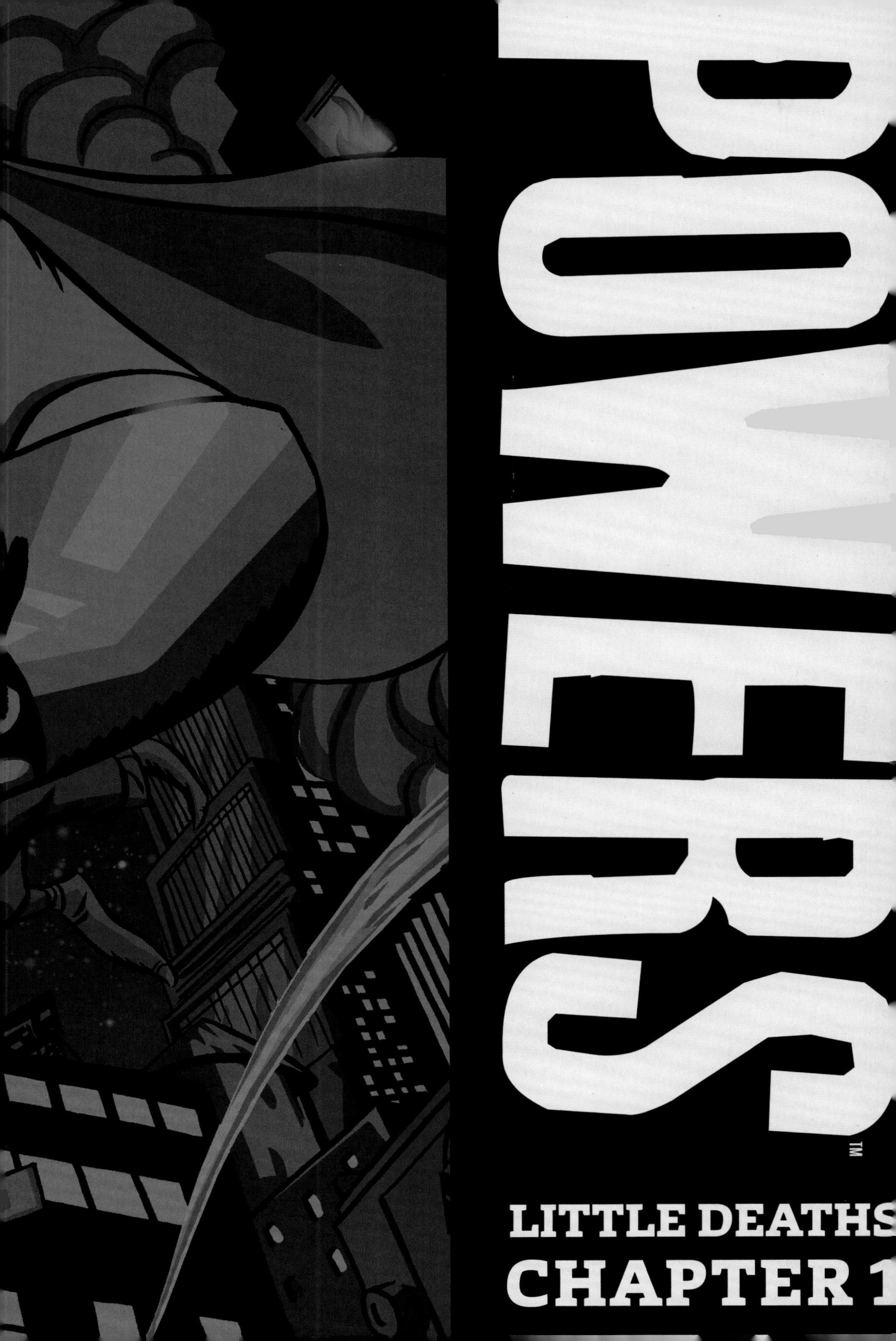

POWERS™

LITTLE DEATHS
CHAPTER 1

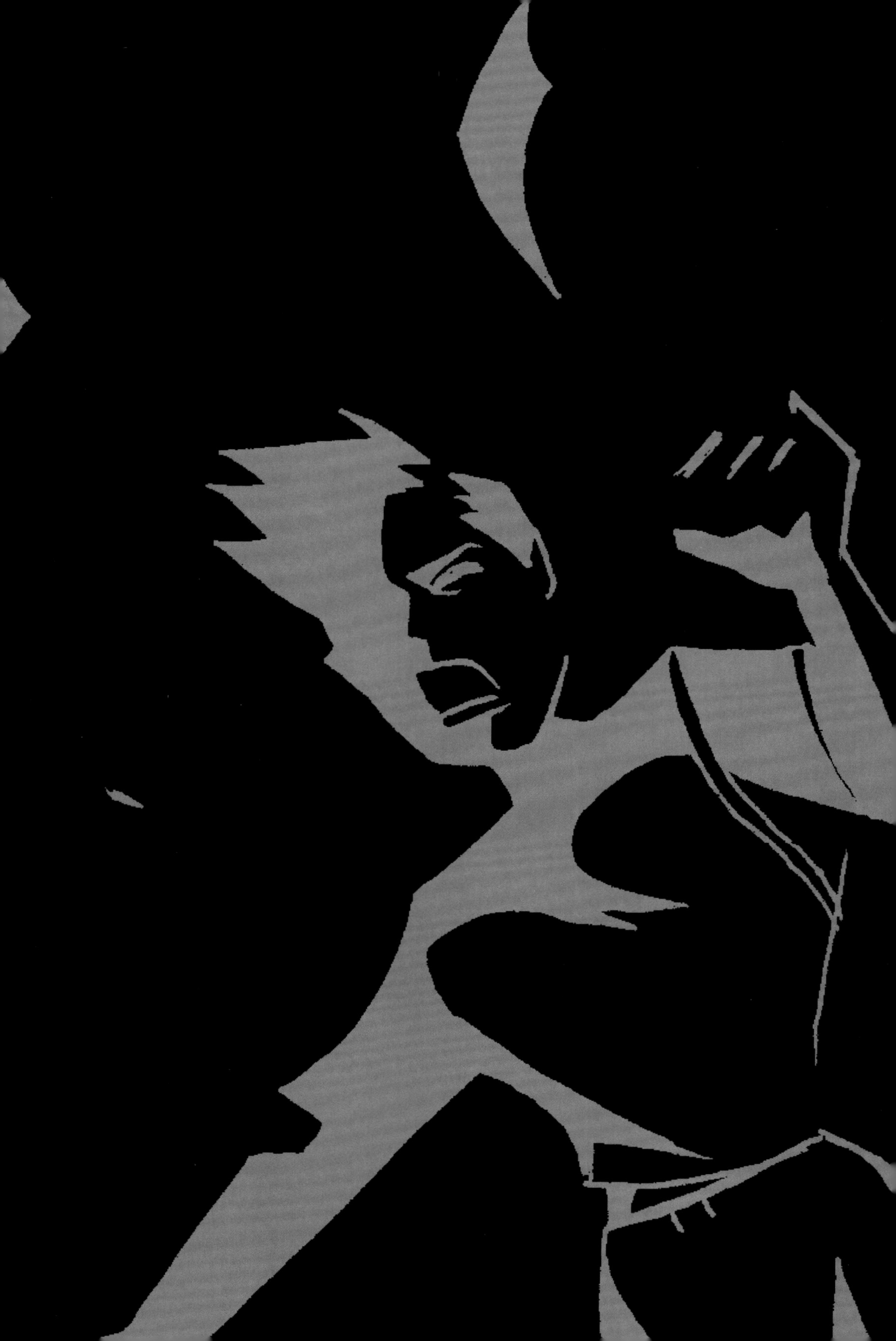

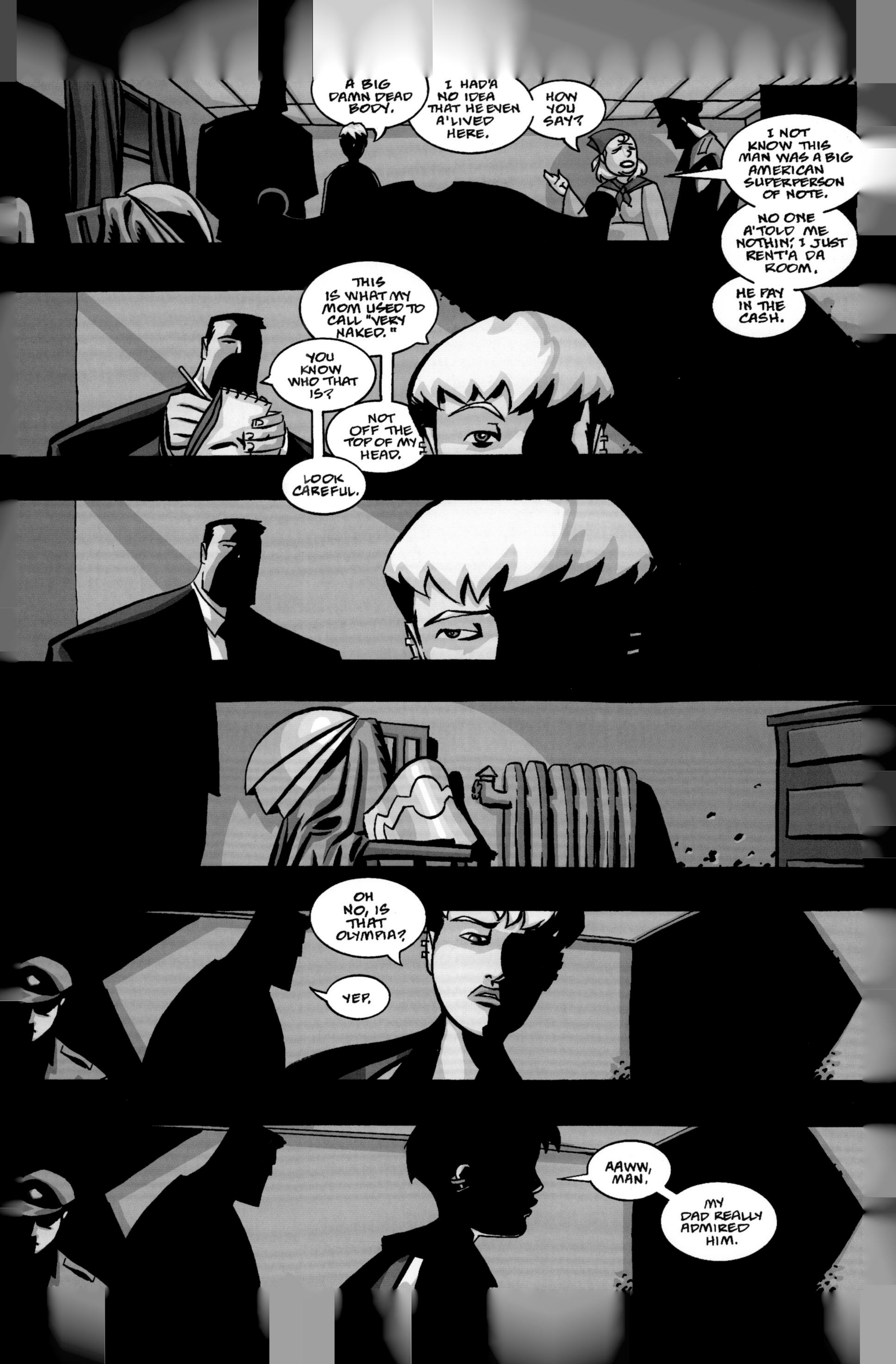
A BIG DAMN DEAD BODY.
I HAD'A NO IDEA THAT HE EVEN A'LIVED HERE.
HOW YOU SAY?
I NOT KNOW THIS MAN WAS A BIG AMERICAN SUPERPERSON OF NOTE.
NO ONE A'TOLD ME NOTHIN'; I JUST RENT'A DA ROOM.
HE PAY IN THE CASH.
THIS IS WHAT MY MOM USED TO CALL "VERY NAKED."
YOU KNOW WHO THAT IS?
NOT OFF THE TOP OF MY HEAD.
LOOK CAREFUL.
OH NO, IS THAT OLYMPIA?
YEP.
AAWW, MAN.
MY DAD REALLY ADMIRED HIM.

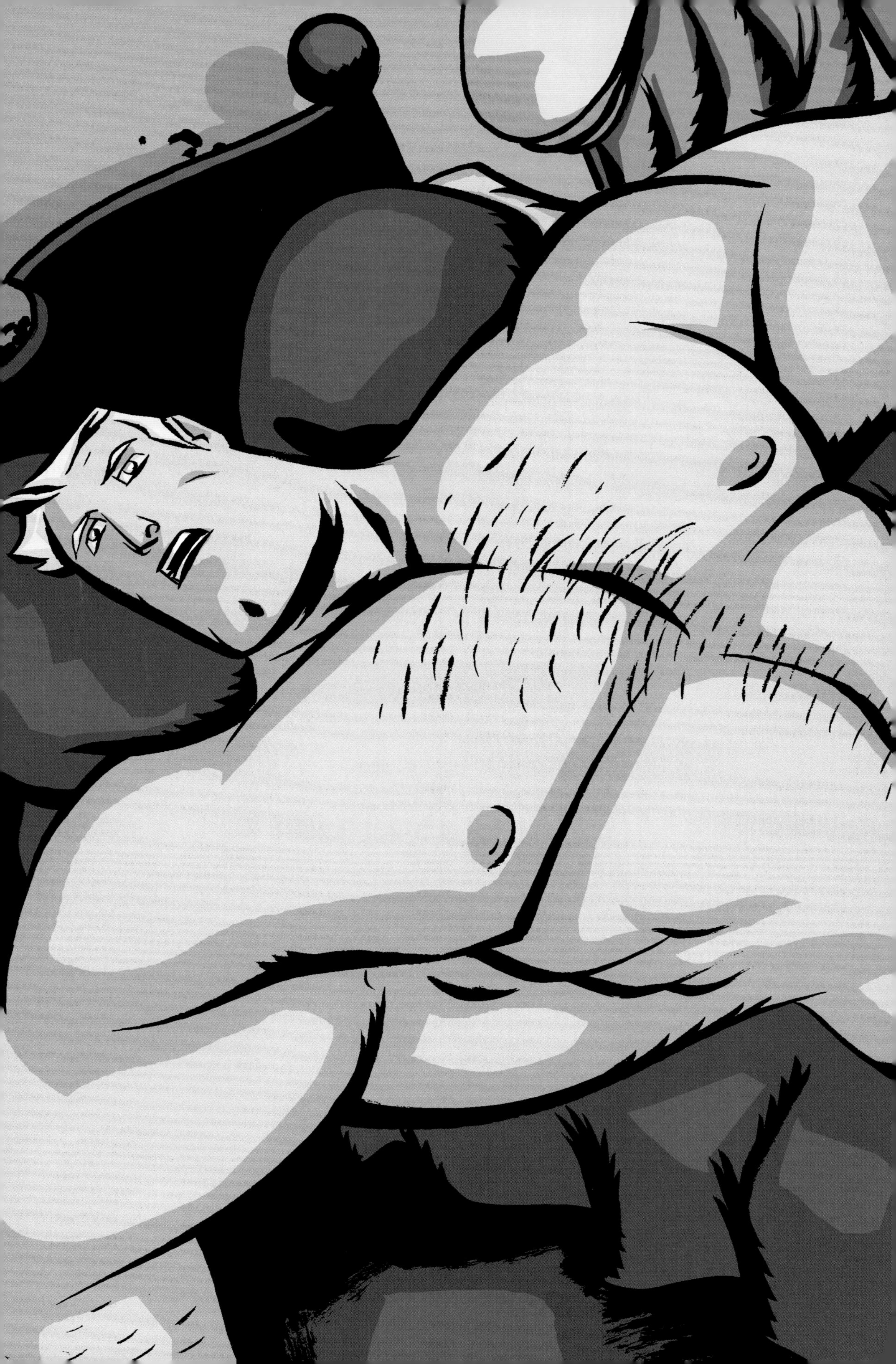

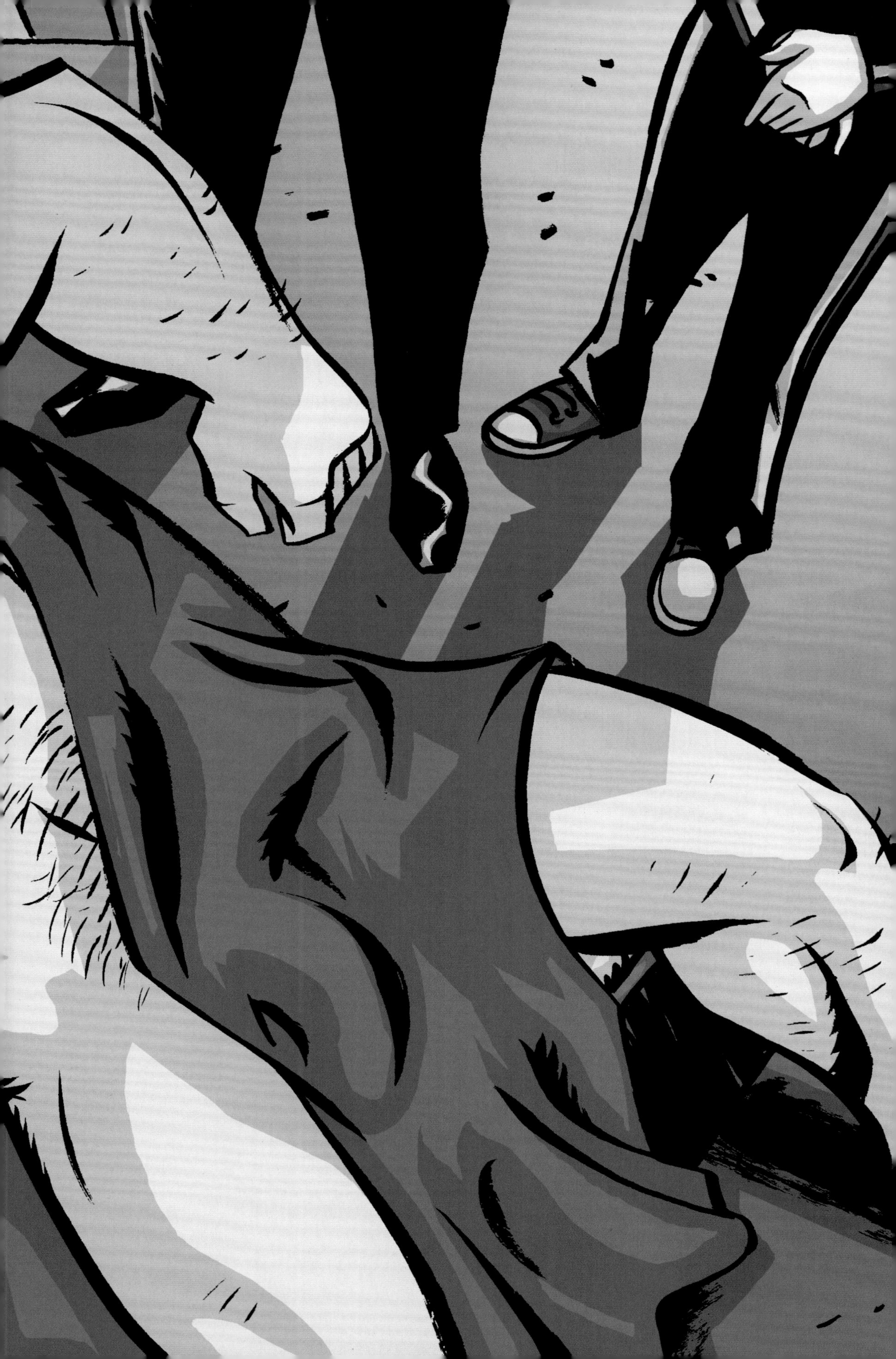

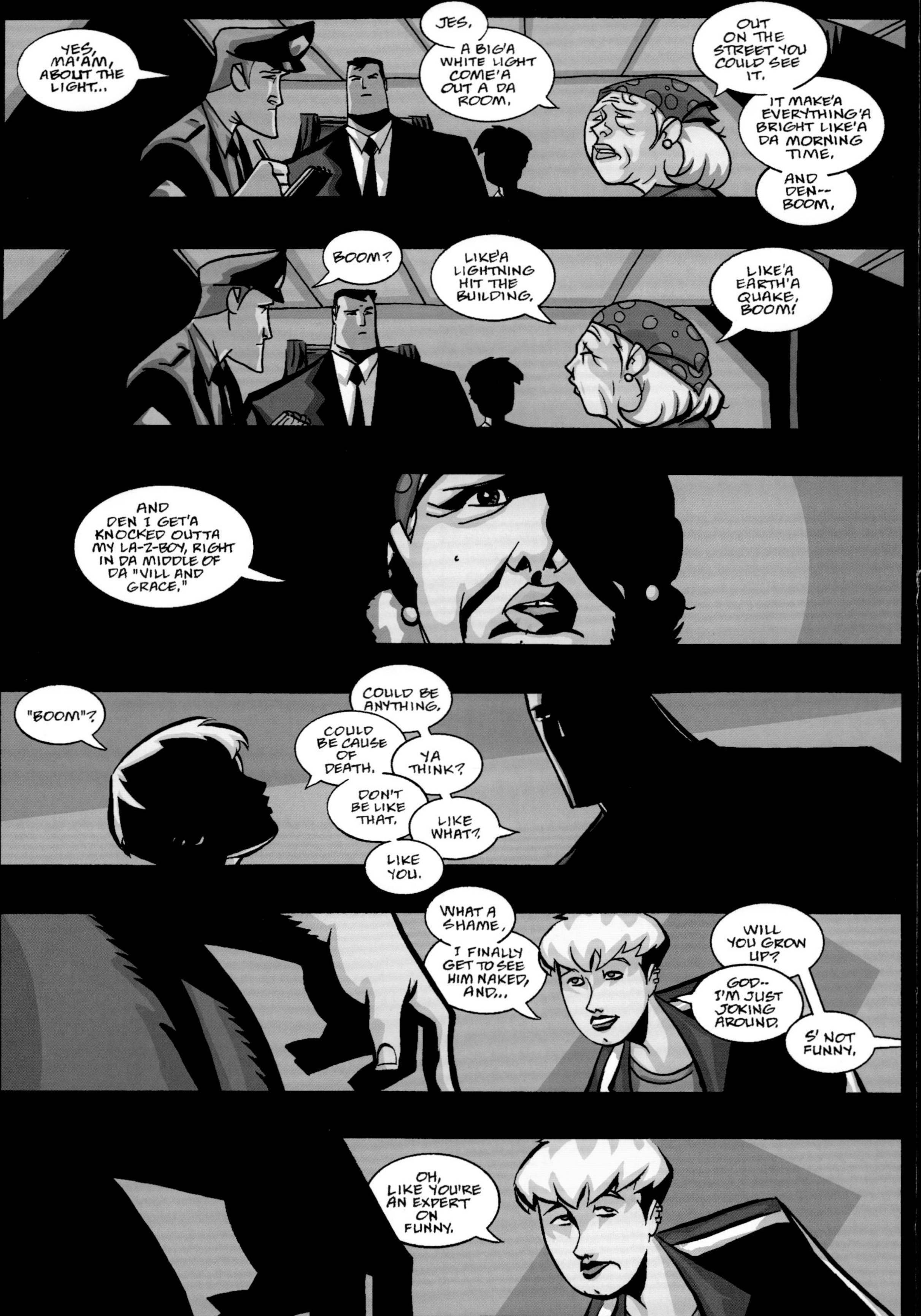
YES, MA'AM, ABOUT THE LIGHT...
JES,
A BIG'A WHITE LIGHT COME'A OUT A DA ROOM.
OUT ON THE STREET YOU COULD SEE IT.
IT MAKE'A EVERYTHING'A BRIGHT LIKE'A DA MORNING TIME.
AND DEN-- BOOM.
BOOM?
LIKE'A LIGHTNING HIT THE BUILDING.
LIKE'A EARTH'A QUAKE, BOOM!
AND DEN I GET'A KNOCKED OUTTA MY LA-Z-BOY, RIGHT IN DA MIDDLE OF DA "VILL AND GRACE."
"BOOM"?
COULD BE ANYTHING.
COULD BE CAUSE OF DEATH.
YA THINK?
DON'T BE LIKE THAT.
LIKE WHAT?
LIKE YOU.
WHAT A SHAME.
I FINALLY GET TO SEE HIM NAKED, AND...
WILL YOU GROW UP?
GOD-- I'M JUST JOKING AROUND.
S' NOT FUNNY.
OH, LIKE YOU'RE AN EXPERT ON FUNNY.

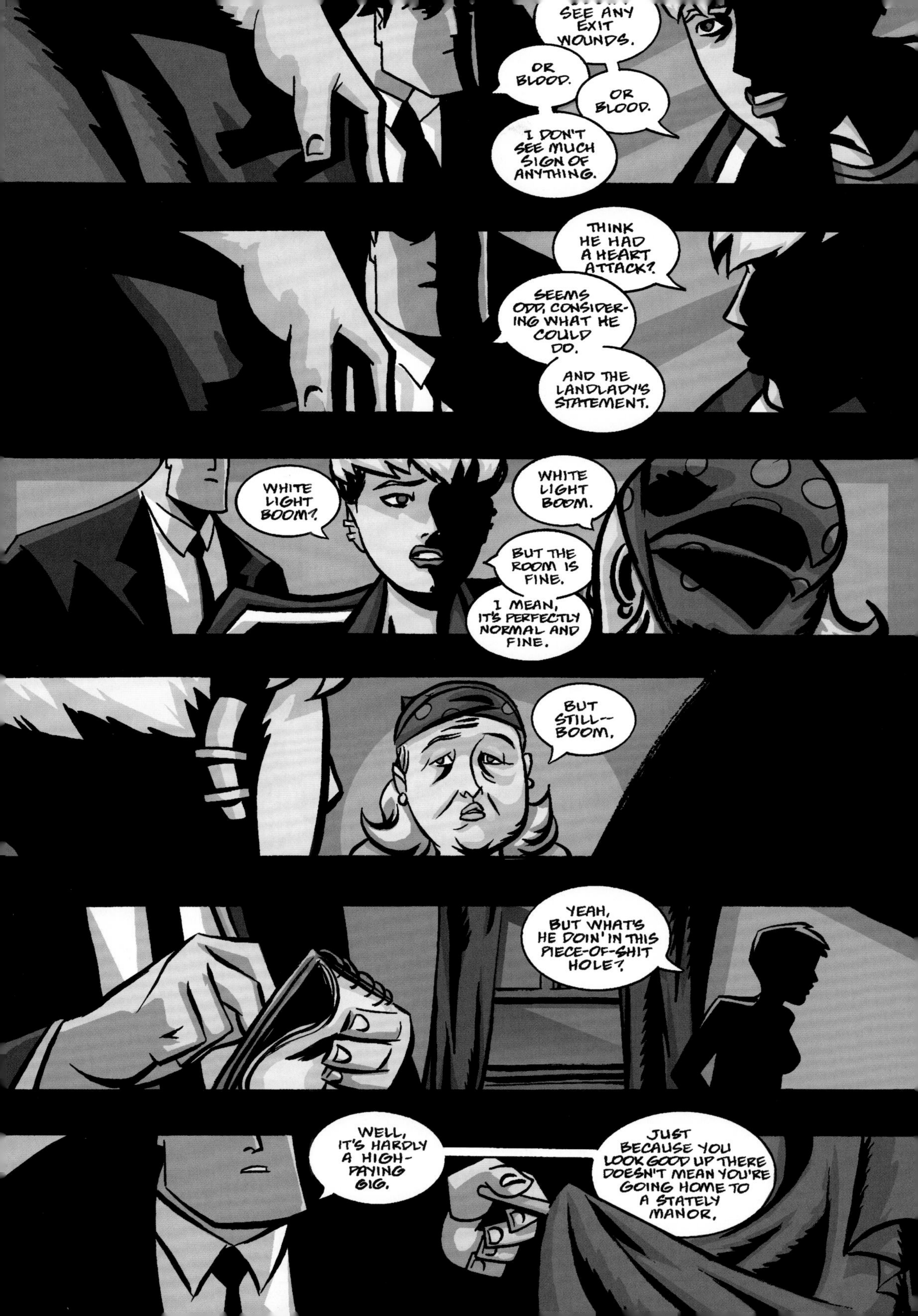
SEE ANY EXIT WOUNDS.
OR BLOOD.
OR BLOOD.
I DON'T SEE MUCH SIGN OF ANYTHING.
THINK HE HAD A HEART ATTACK?
SEEMS ODD, CONSIDER-ING WHAT HE COULD DO.
AND THE LANDLADY'S STATEMENT.
WHITE LIGHT BOOM?
WHITE LIGHT BOOM.
BUT THE ROOM IS FINE.
I MEAN, IT'S PERFECTLY NORMAL AND FINE.
BUT STILL--BOOM.
YEAH, BUT WHAT'S HE DOIN' IN THIS PIECE-OF-SHIT HOLE?
WELL, IT'S HARDLY A HIGH-PAYING GIG.
JUST BECAUSE YOU LOOK GOOD UP THERE DOESN'T MEAN YOU'RE GOING HOME TO A STATELY MANOR.

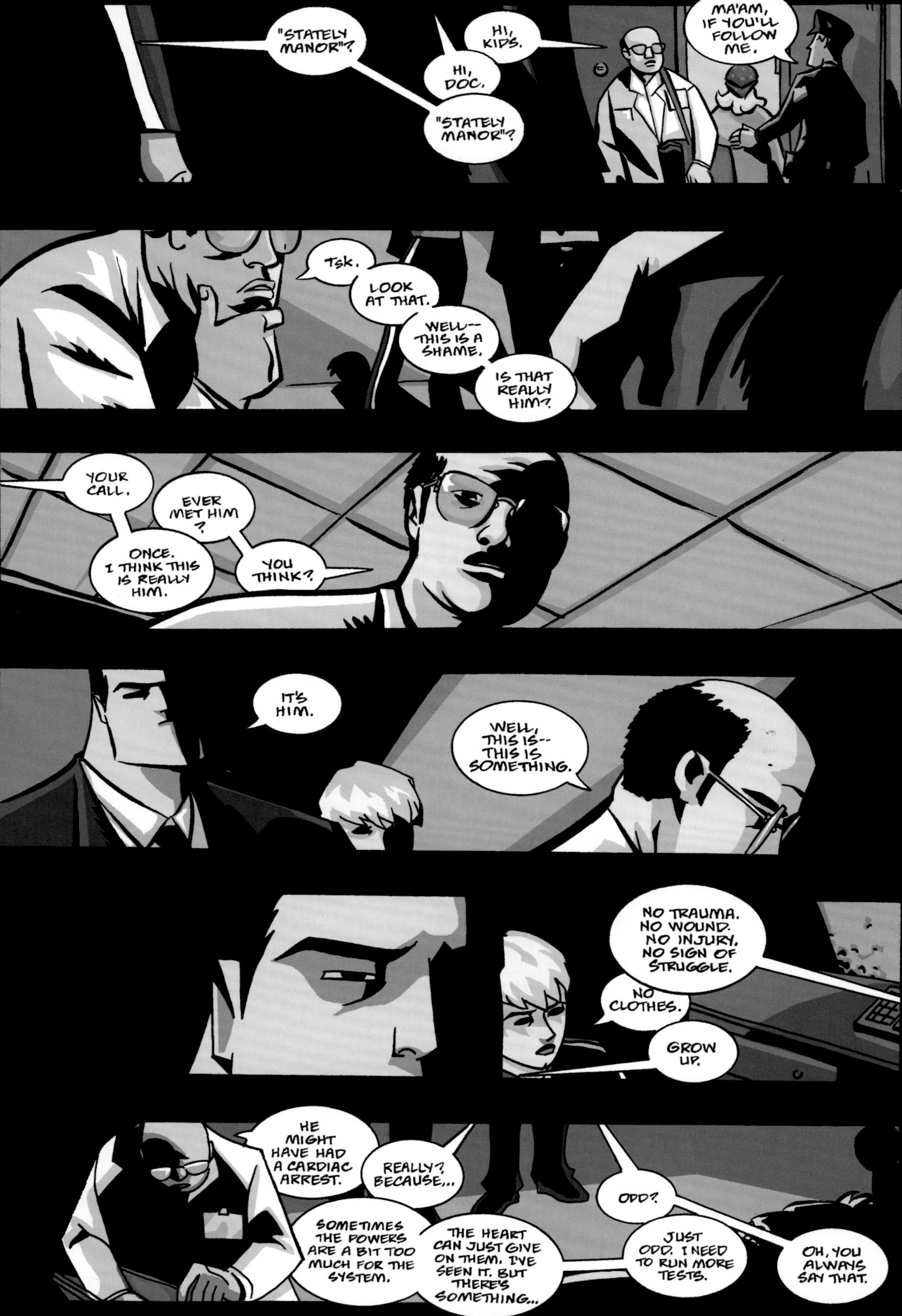
MA'AM, IF YOU'LL FOLLOW ME.
HI, KIDS.
HI, DOC.
"STATELY MANOR"?
"STATELY MANOR"?
Tsk.
LOOK AT THAT.
WELL-- THIS IS A SHAME.
IS THAT REALLY HIM?
YOUR CALL.
EVER MET HIM?
ONCE. I THINK THIS IS REALLY HIM.
YOU THINK?
IT'S HIM.
WELL, THIS IS-- THIS IS SOMETHING.
NO TRAUMA. NO WOUND. NO INJURY, NO SIGN OF STRUGGLE.
NO CLOTHES.
GROW UP.
HE MIGHT HAVE HAD A CARDIAC ARREST.
REALLY? BECAUSE...
SOMETIMES THE POWERS ARE A BIT TOO MUCH FOR THE SYSTEM.
THE HEART CAN JUST GIVE ON THEM. I'VE SEEN IT. BUT THERE'S SOMETHING...
ODD?
JUST ODD. I NEED TO RUN MORE TESTS.
OH, YOU ALWAYS SAY THAT.

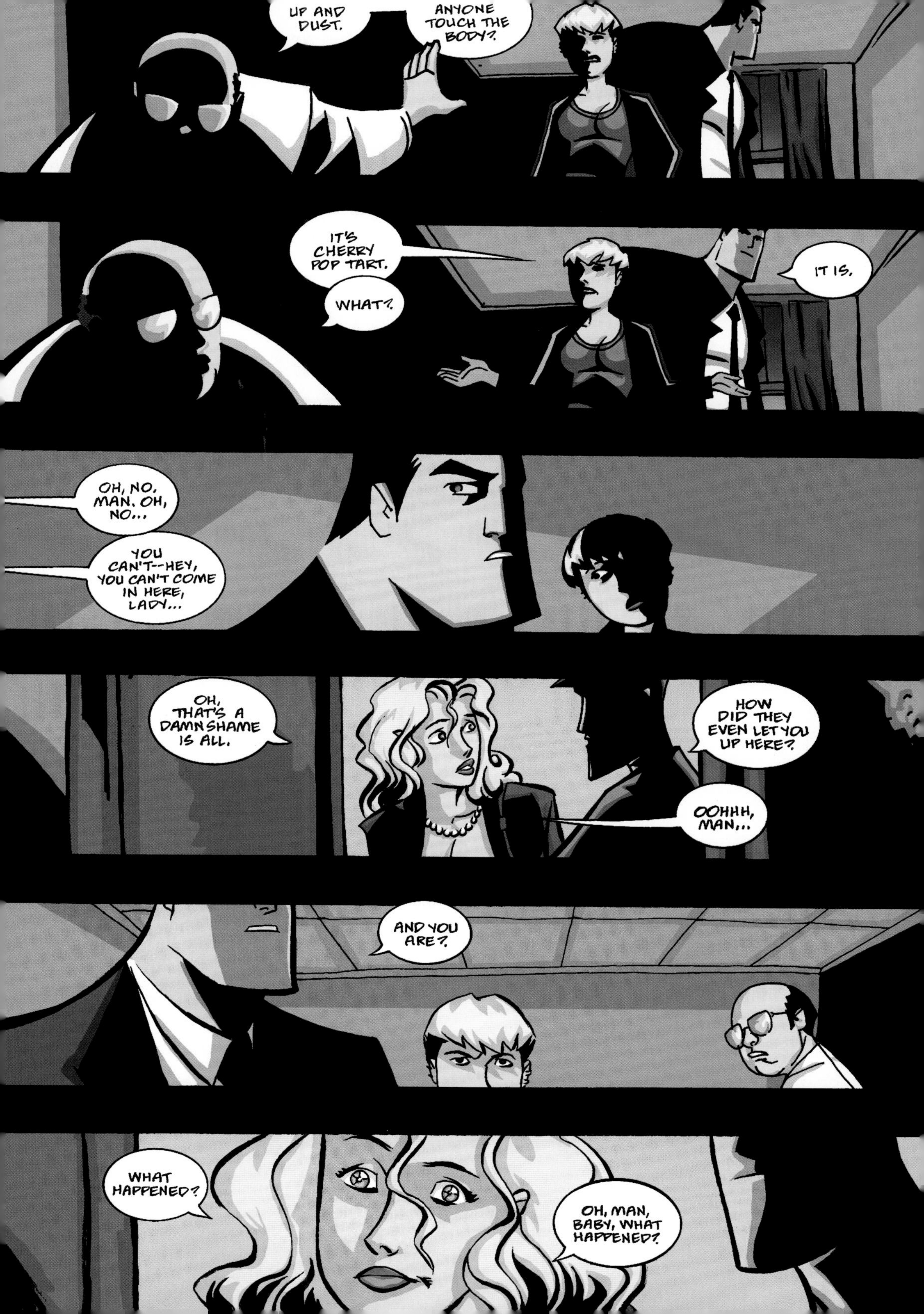
UP AND DUST.
ANYONE TOUCH THE BODY?
IT'S CHERRY POP TART.
WHAT?
IT IS.
OH, NO. MAN. OH, NO...
YOU CAN'T--HEY, YOU CAN'T COME IN HERE, LADY...
OH, THAT'S A DAMN SHAME IS ALL.
HOW DID THEY EVEN LET YOU UP HERE?
OOHHH, MAN...
AND YOU ARE?
WHAT HAPPENED?
OH, MAN, BABY, WHAT HAPPENED?

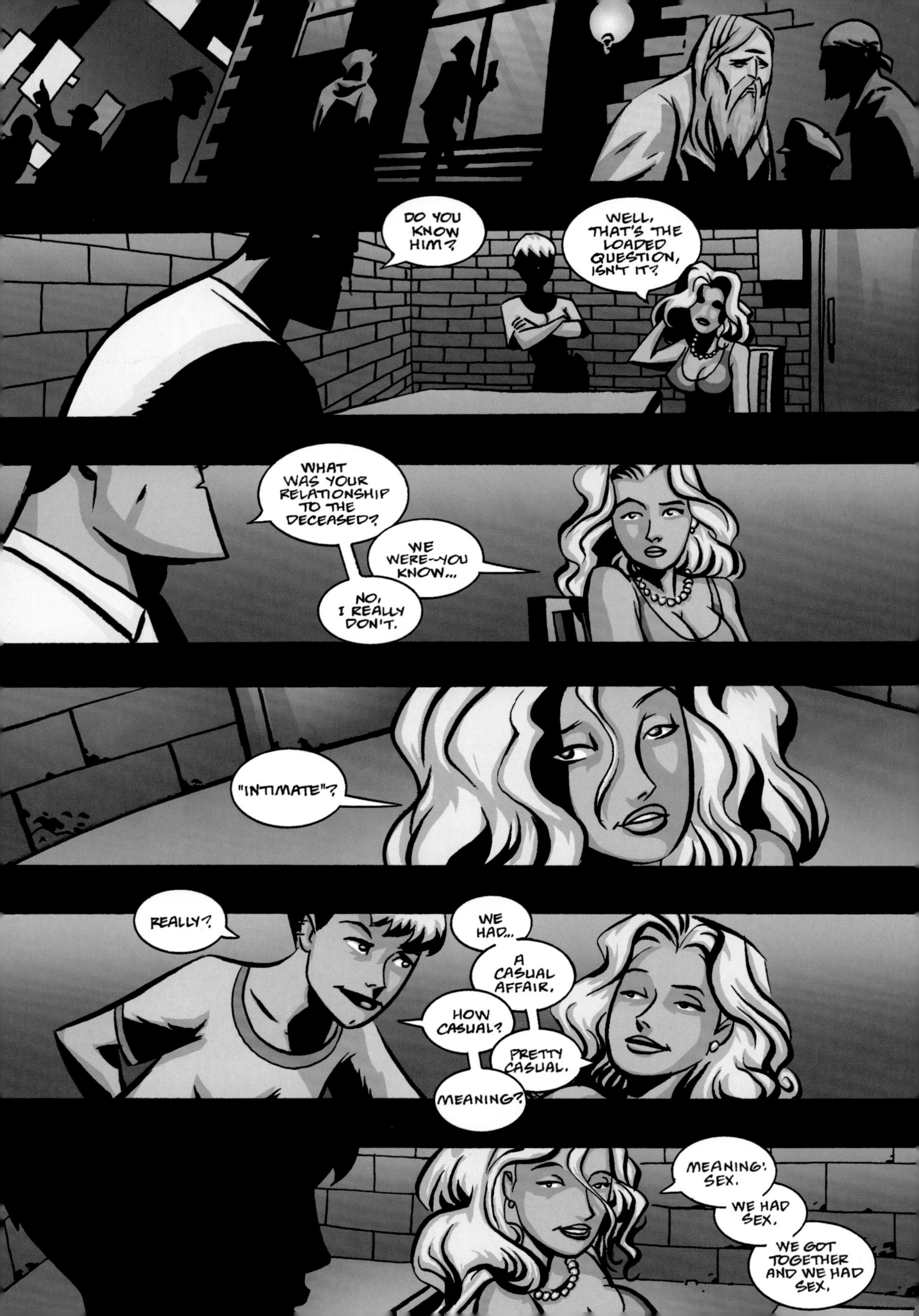

DO YOU KNOW HIM?
WELL, THAT'S THE LOADED QUESTION, ISN'T IT?
WHAT WAS YOUR RELATIONSHIP TO THE DECEASED?
WE WERE--YOU KNOW...
NO, I REALLY DON'T.
"INTIMATE"?
REALLY?
WE HAD...
A CASUAL AFFAIR.
HOW CASUAL?
PRETTY CASUAL.
MEANING?
MEANING: SEX.
WE HAD SEX.
WE GOT TOGETHER AND WE HAD SEX.

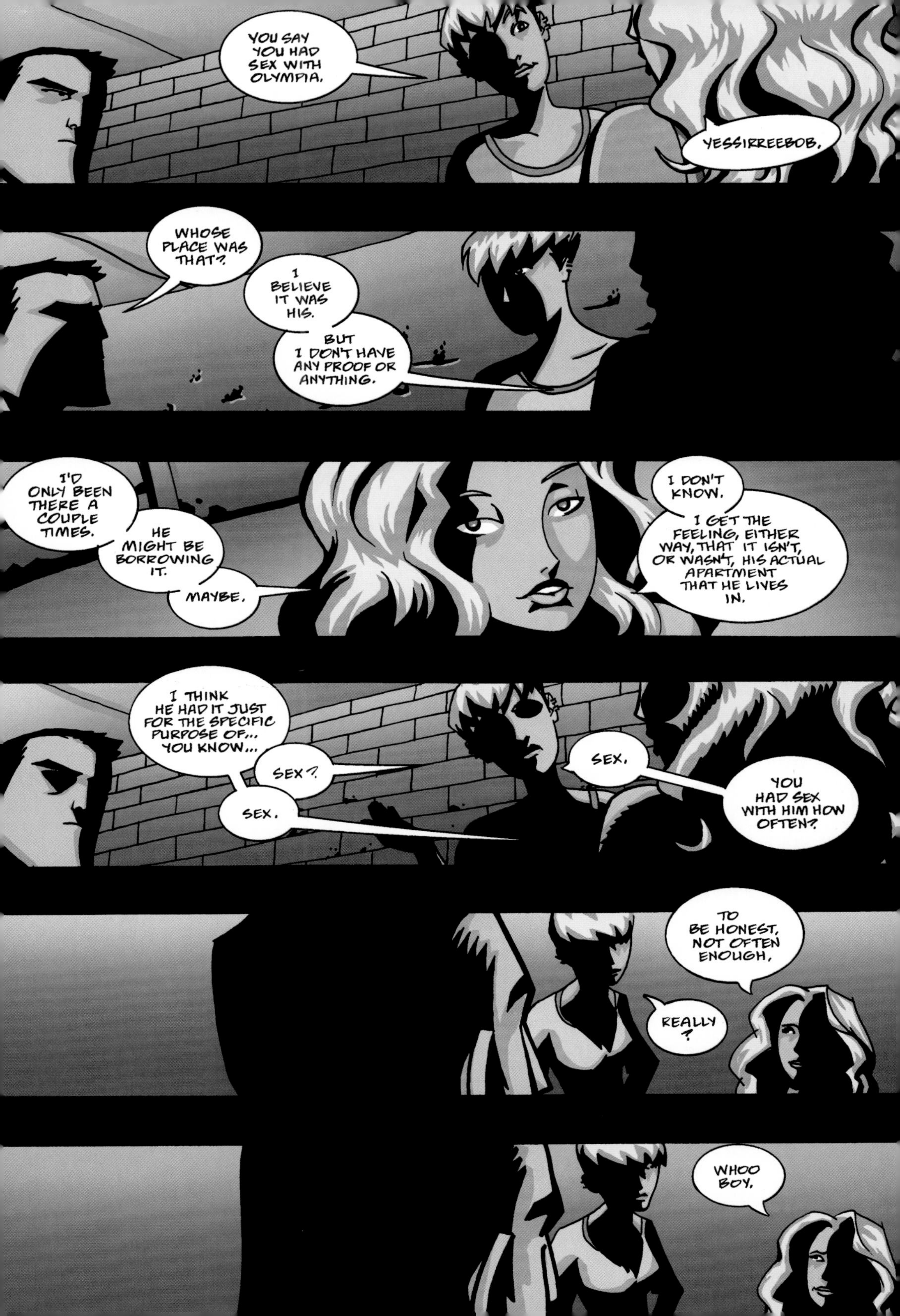
YOU SAY YOU HAD SEX WITH OLYMPIA.
YESSIRREEBOB.
WHOSE PLACE WAS THAT?
I BELIEVE IT WAS HIS.
BUT I DON'T HAVE ANY PROOF OR ANYTHING.
I'D ONLY BEEN THERE A COUPLE TIMES.
HE MIGHT BE BORROWING IT.
MAYBE.
I DON'T KNOW.
I GET THE FEELING, EITHER WAY, THAT IT ISN'T, OR WASN'T, HIS ACTUAL APARTMENT THAT HE LIVES IN.
I THINK HE HAD IT JUST FOR THE SPECIFIC PURPOSE OF... YOU KNOW...
SEX?
SEX.
SEX.
YOU HAD SEX WITH HIM HOW OFTEN?
TO BE HONEST, NOT OFTEN ENOUGH.
REALLY?
WHOO BOY.

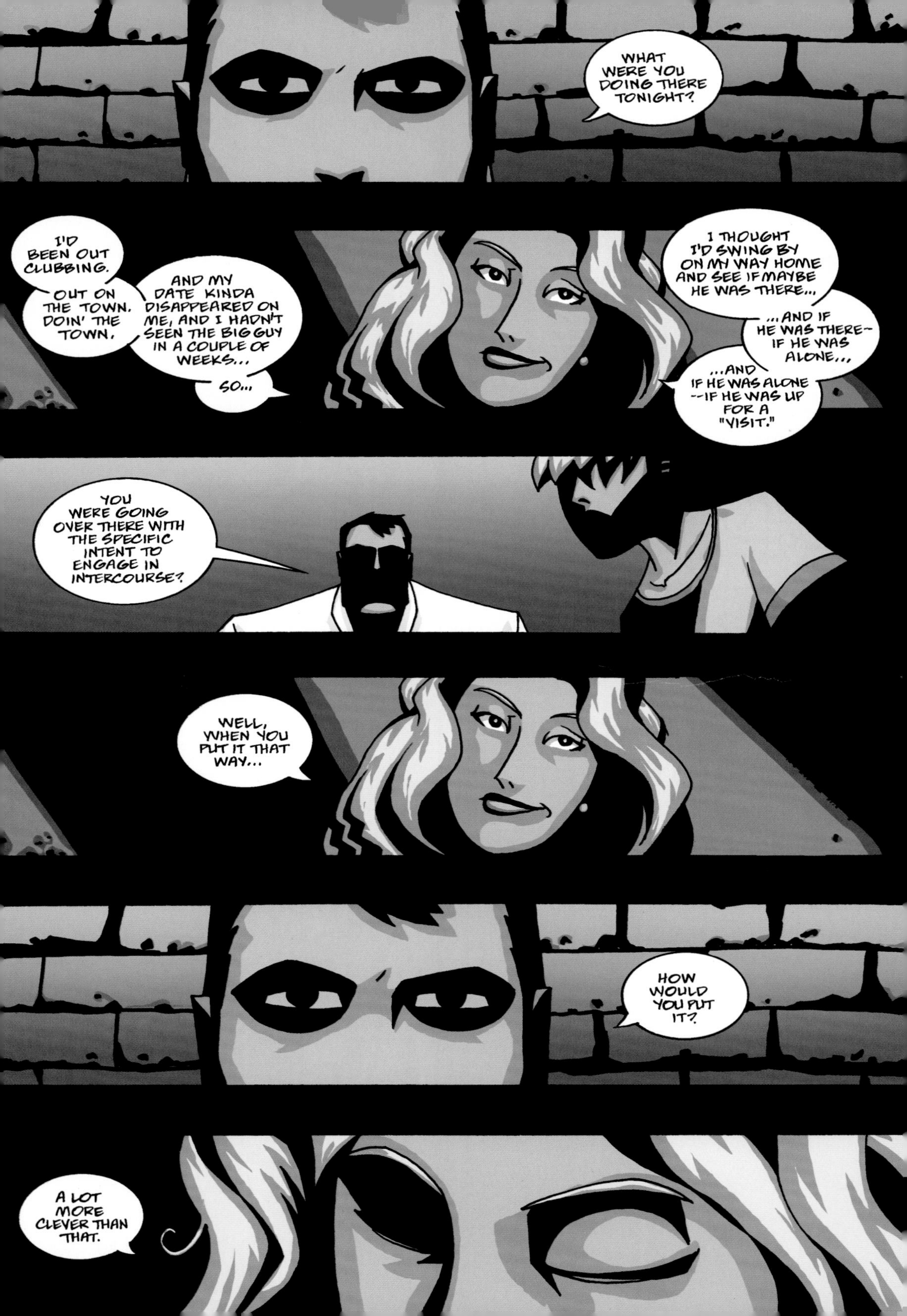
WHAT WERE YOU DOING THERE TONIGHT?
I'D BEEN OUT CLUBBING.
OUT ON THE TOWN. DOIN' THE TOWN.
AND MY DATE KINDA DISAPPEARED ON ME, AND I HADN'T SEEN THE BIG GUY IN A COUPLE OF WEEKS...
SO...
I THOUGHT I'D SWING BY ON MY WAY HOME AND SEE IF MAYBE HE WAS THERE...
...AND IF HE WAS THERE-- IF HE WAS ALONE...
...AND IF HE WAS ALONE --IF HE WAS UP FOR A "VISIT."
YOU WERE GOING OVER THERE WITH THE SPECIFIC INTENT TO ENGAGE IN INTERCOURSE?
WELL, WHEN YOU PUT IT THAT WAY...
HOW WOULD YOU PUT IT?
A LOT MORE CLEVER THAN THAT.

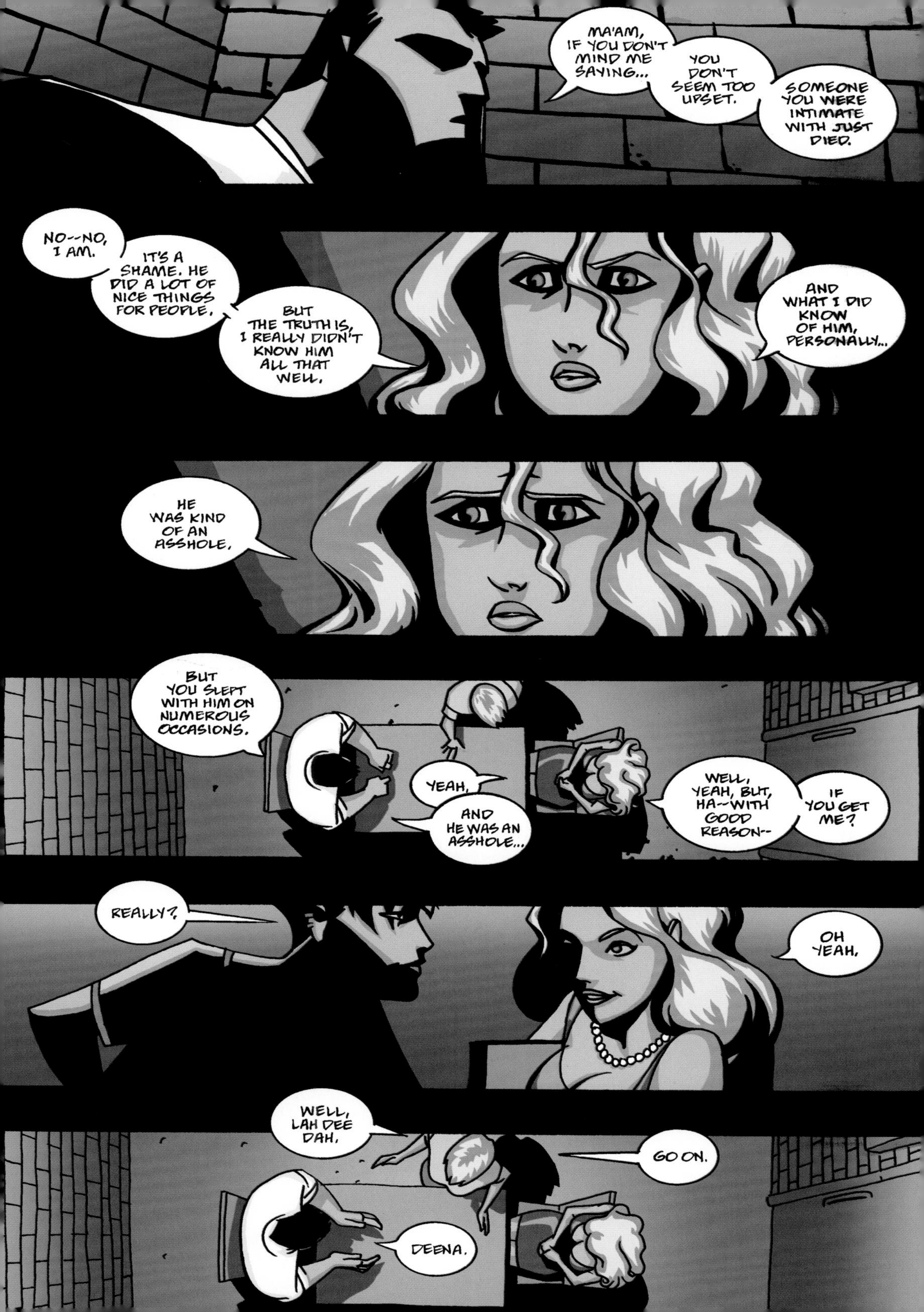
MA'AM, IF YOU DON'T MIND ME SAYING...
YOU DON'T SEEM TOO UPSET.
SOMEONE YOU WERE INTIMATE WITH JUST DIED.
NO--NO, I AM.
IT'S A SHAME. HE DID A LOT OF NICE THINGS FOR PEOPLE.
BUT THE TRUTH IS, I REALLY DIDN'T KNOW HIM ALL THAT WELL.
AND WHAT I DID KNOW OF HIM, PERSONALLY...
HE WAS KIND OF AN ASSHOLE.
BUT YOU SLEPT WITH HIM ON NUMEROUS OCCASIONS.
YEAH,
AND HE WAS AN ASSHOLE...
WELL, YEAH, BUT, HA--WITH GOOD REASON--
IF YOU GET ME?
REALLY?
OH YEAH.
WELL, LAH DEE DAH.
GO ON.
DEENA.

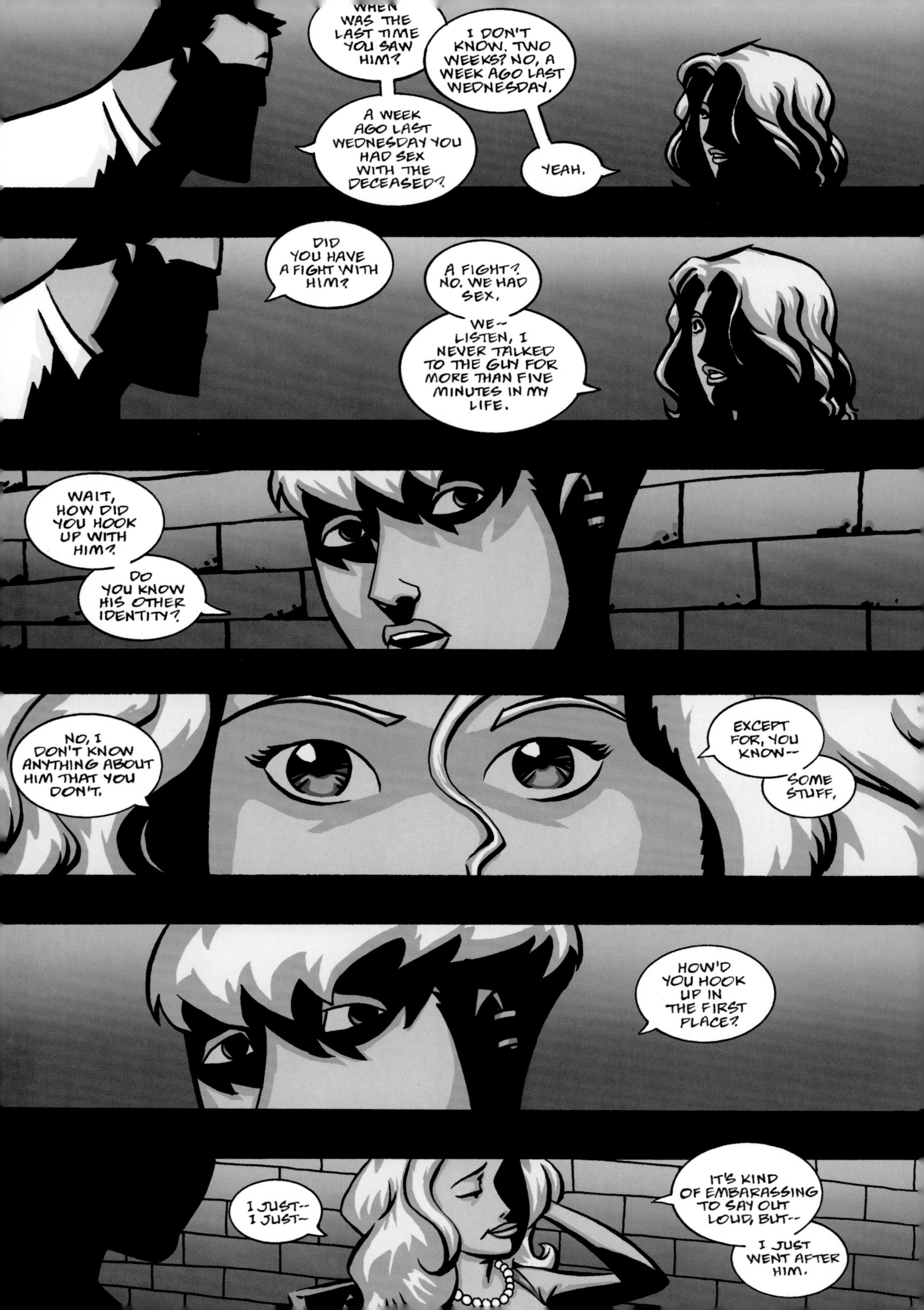
WHEN WAS THE LAST TIME YOU SAW HIM?
I DON'T KNOW. TWO WEEKS? NO, A WEEK AGO LAST WEDNESDAY.
A WEEK AGO LAST WEDNESDAY YOU HAD SEX WITH THE DECEASED?
YEAH.
DID YOU HAVE A FIGHT WITH HIM?
A FIGHT? NO. WE HAD SEX.
WE-- LISTEN, I NEVER TALKED TO THE GUY FOR MORE THAN FIVE MINUTES IN MY LIFE.
WAIT, HOW DID YOU HOOK UP WITH HIM?
DO YOU KNOW HIS OTHER IDENTITY?
NO, I DON'T KNOW ANYTHING ABOUT HIM THAT YOU DON'T.
EXCEPT FOR, YOU KNOW--
SOME STUFF.
HOW'D YOU HOOK UP IN THE FIRST PLACE?
I JUST-- I JUST--
IT'S KIND OF EMBARASSING TO SAY OUT LOUD, BUT--
I JUST WENT AFTER HIM.

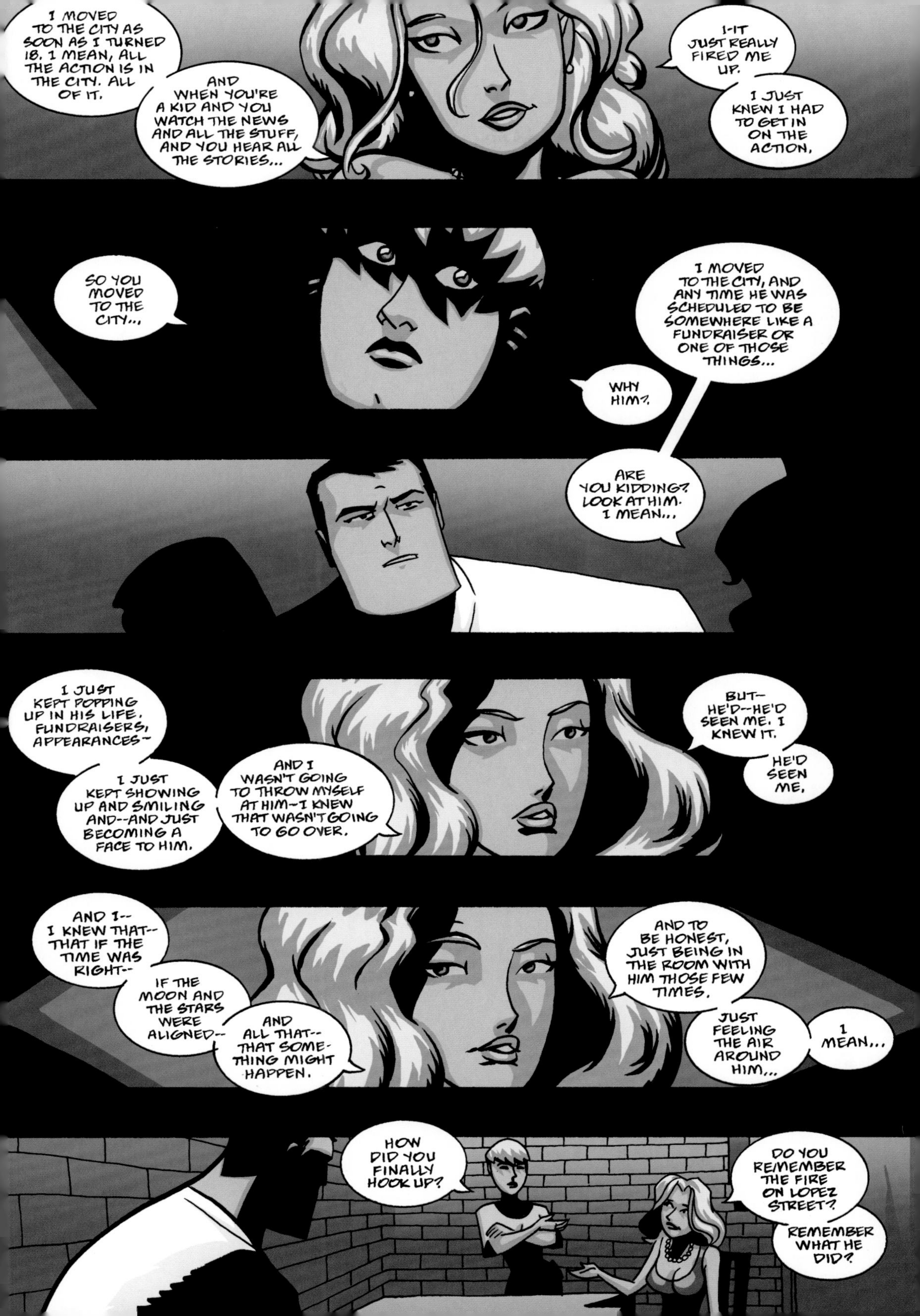
I MOVED TO THE CITY AS SOON AS I TURNED 18. I MEAN, ALL THE ACTION IS IN THE CITY. ALL OF IT.
AND WHEN YOU'RE A KID AND YOU WATCH THE NEWS AND ALL THE STUFF, AND YOU HEAR ALL THE STORIES...
I-IT JUST REALLY FIRED ME UP.
I JUST KNEW I HAD TO GET IN ON THE ACTION.
SO YOU MOVED TO THE CITY...
I MOVED TO THE CITY, AND ANY TIME HE WAS SCHEDULED TO BE SOMEWHERE LIKE A FUNDRAISER OR ONE OF THOSE THINGS...
WHY HIM?
ARE YOU KIDDING? LOOK AT HIM. I MEAN...
I JUST KEPT POPPING UP IN HIS LIFE. FUNDRAISERS, APPEARANCES--
I JUST KEPT SHOWING UP AND SMILING AND--AND JUST BECOMING A FACE TO HIM.
AND I WASN'T GOING TO THROW MYSELF AT HIM--I KNEW THAT WASN'T GOING TO GO OVER.
BUT--HE'D--HE'D SEEN ME. I KNEW IT.
HE'D SEEN ME.
AND I-- I KNEW THAT-- THAT IF THE TIME WAS RIGHT--
IF THE MOON AND THE STARS WERE ALIGNED--
AND ALL THAT-- THAT SOMETHING MIGHT HAPPEN.
AND TO BE HONEST, JUST BEING IN THE ROOM WITH HIM THOSE FEW TIMES.
JUST FEELING THE AIR AROUND HIM...
I MEAN...
HOW DID YOU FINALLY HOOK UP?
DO YOU REMEMBER THE FIRE ON LOPEZ STREET?
REMEMBER WHAT HE DID?

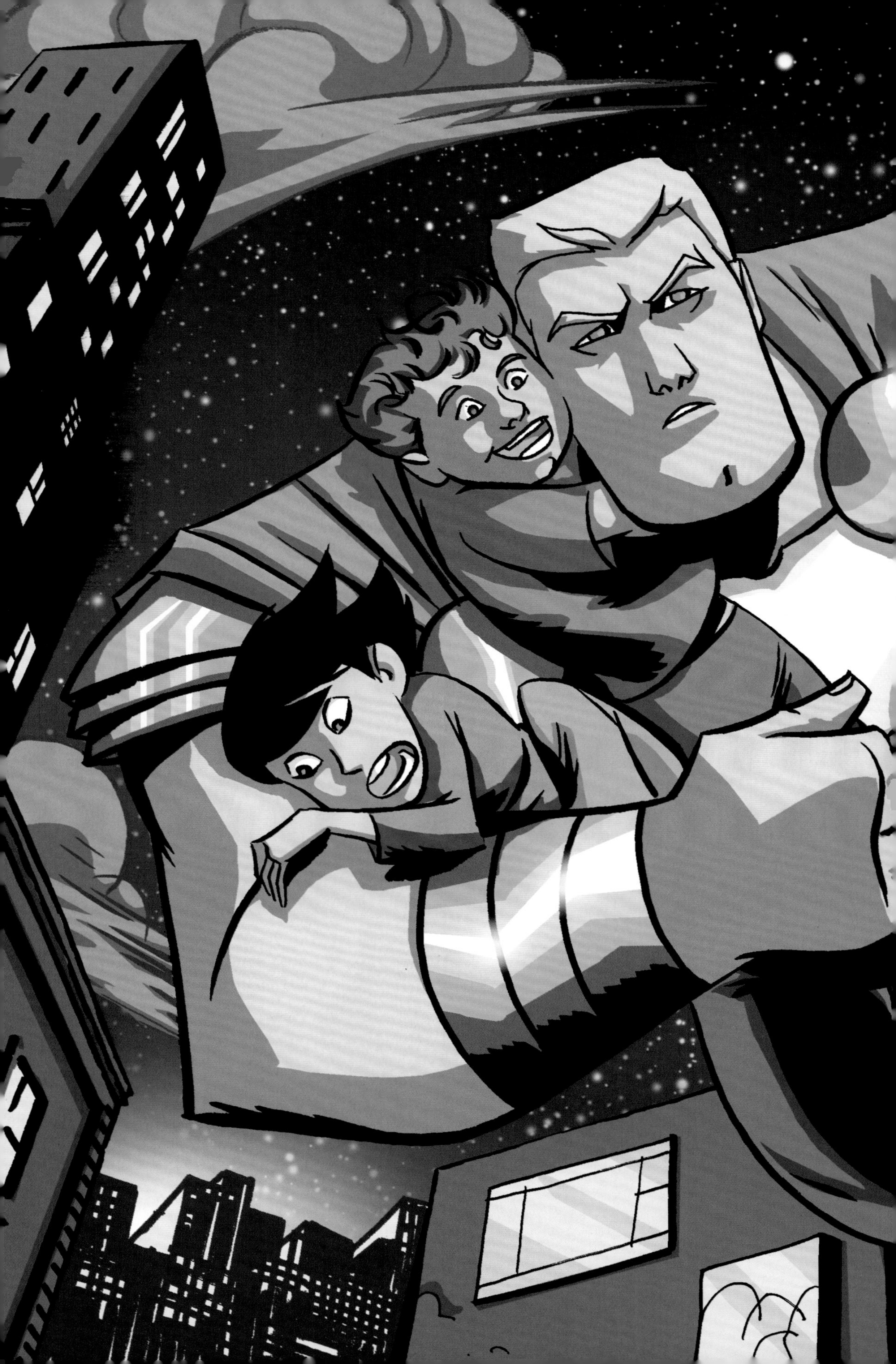

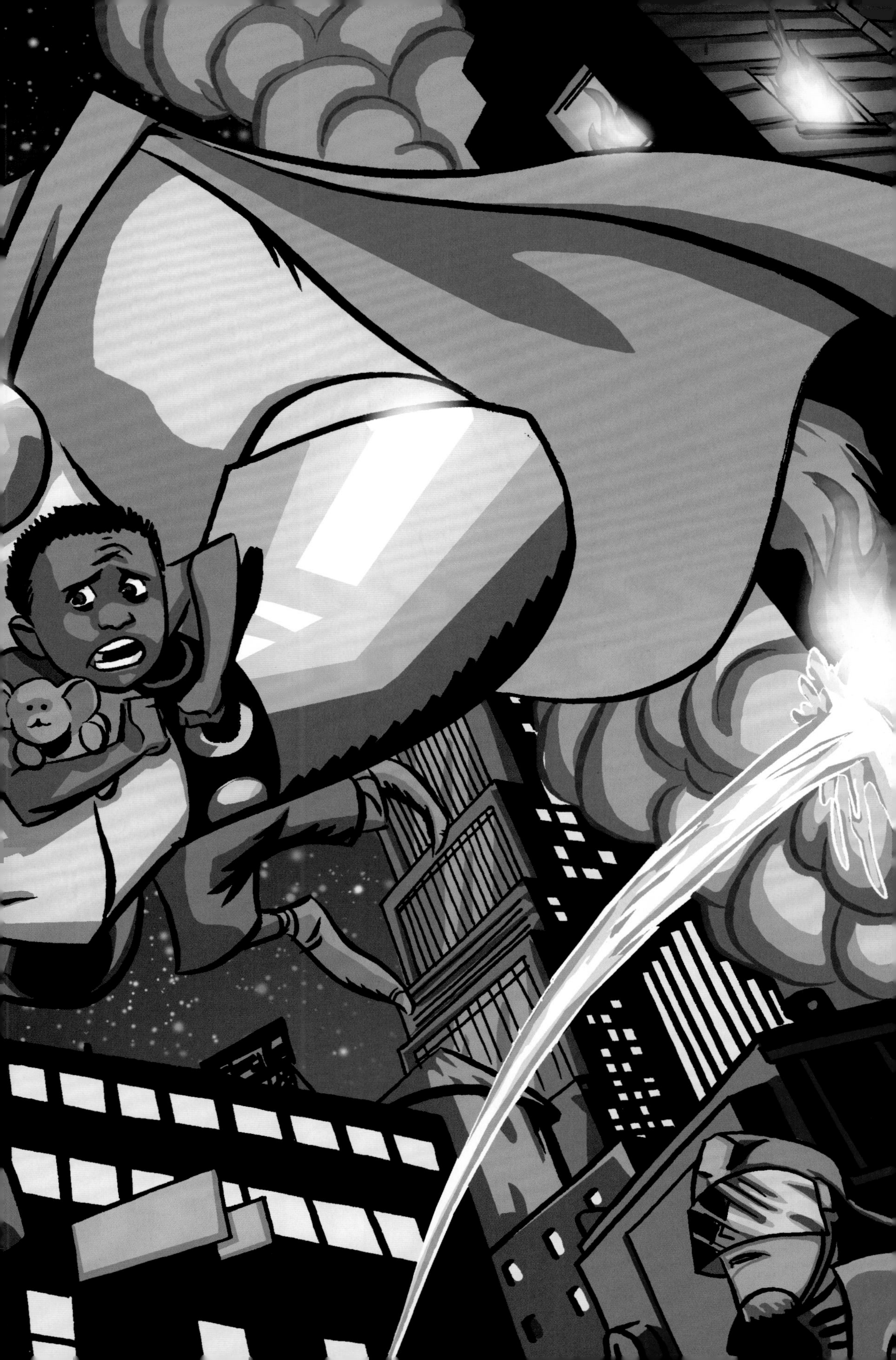

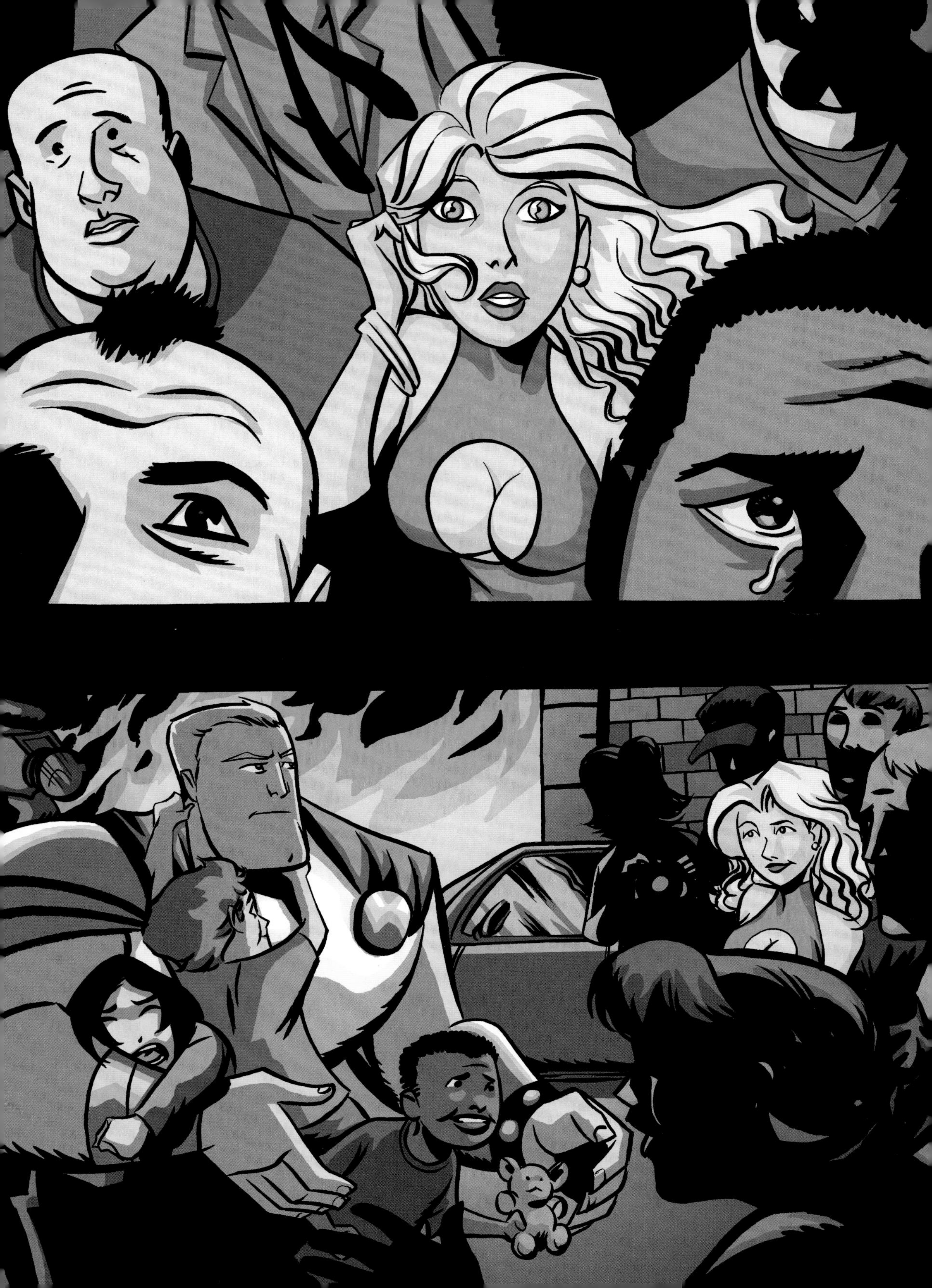

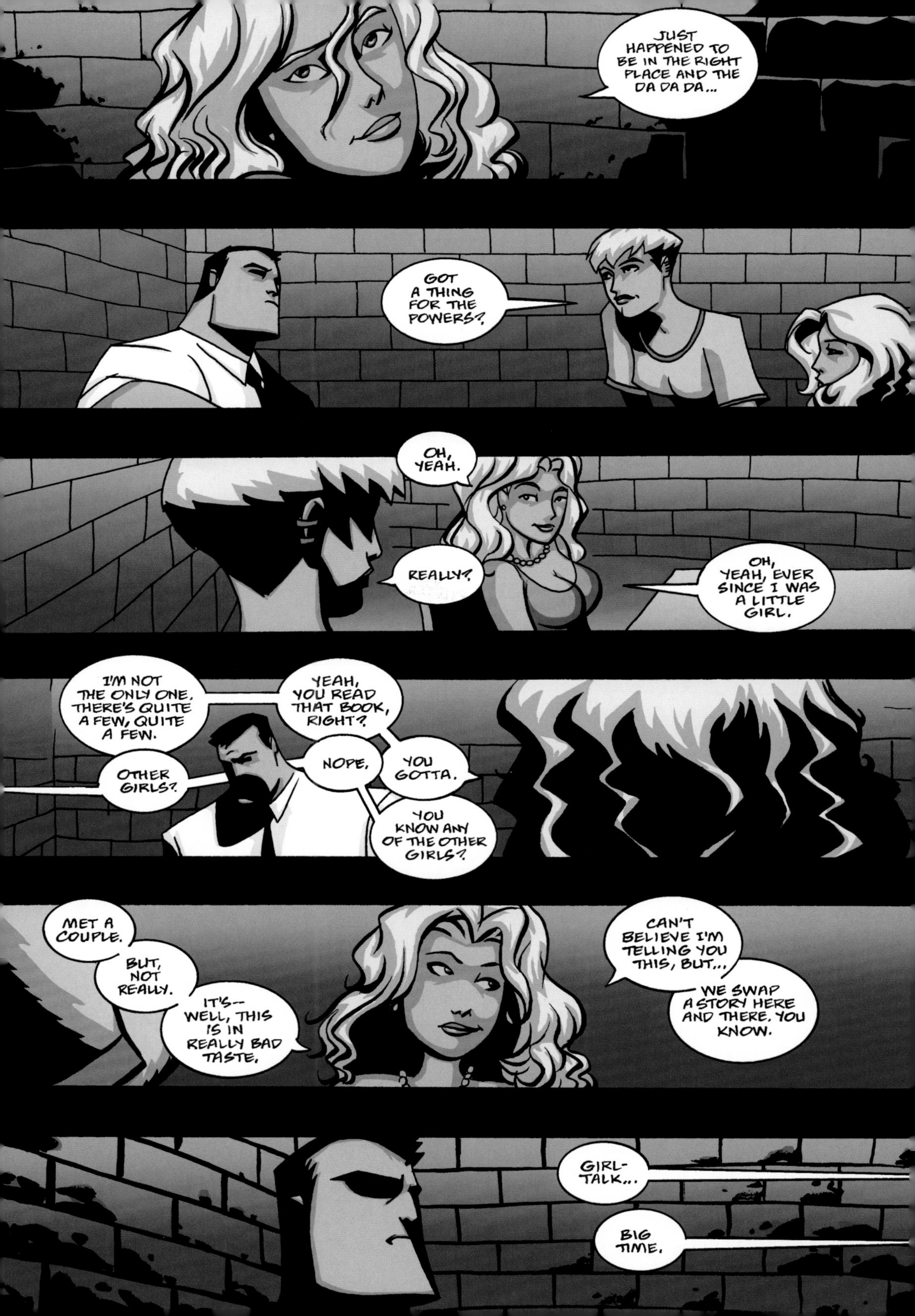
JUST HAPPENED TO BE IN THE RIGHT PLACE AND THE DA DA DA...
GOT A THING FOR THE POWERS?
OH, YEAH.
REALLY?
OH, YEAH, EVER SINCE I WAS A LITTLE GIRL.
I'M NOT THE ONLY ONE. THERE'S QUITE A FEW, QUITE A FEW.
OTHER GIRLS?
YEAH, YOU READ THAT BOOK, RIGHT?
NOPE.
YOU GOTTA.
YOU KNOW ANY OF THE OTHER GIRLS?
MET A COUPLE.
BUT, NOT REALLY.
IT'S-- WELL, THIS IS IN REALLY BAD TASTE.
CAN'T BELIEVE I'M TELLING YOU THIS, BUT...
WE SWAP A STORY HERE AND THERE. YOU KNOW.
GIRL-TALK...
BIG TIME.

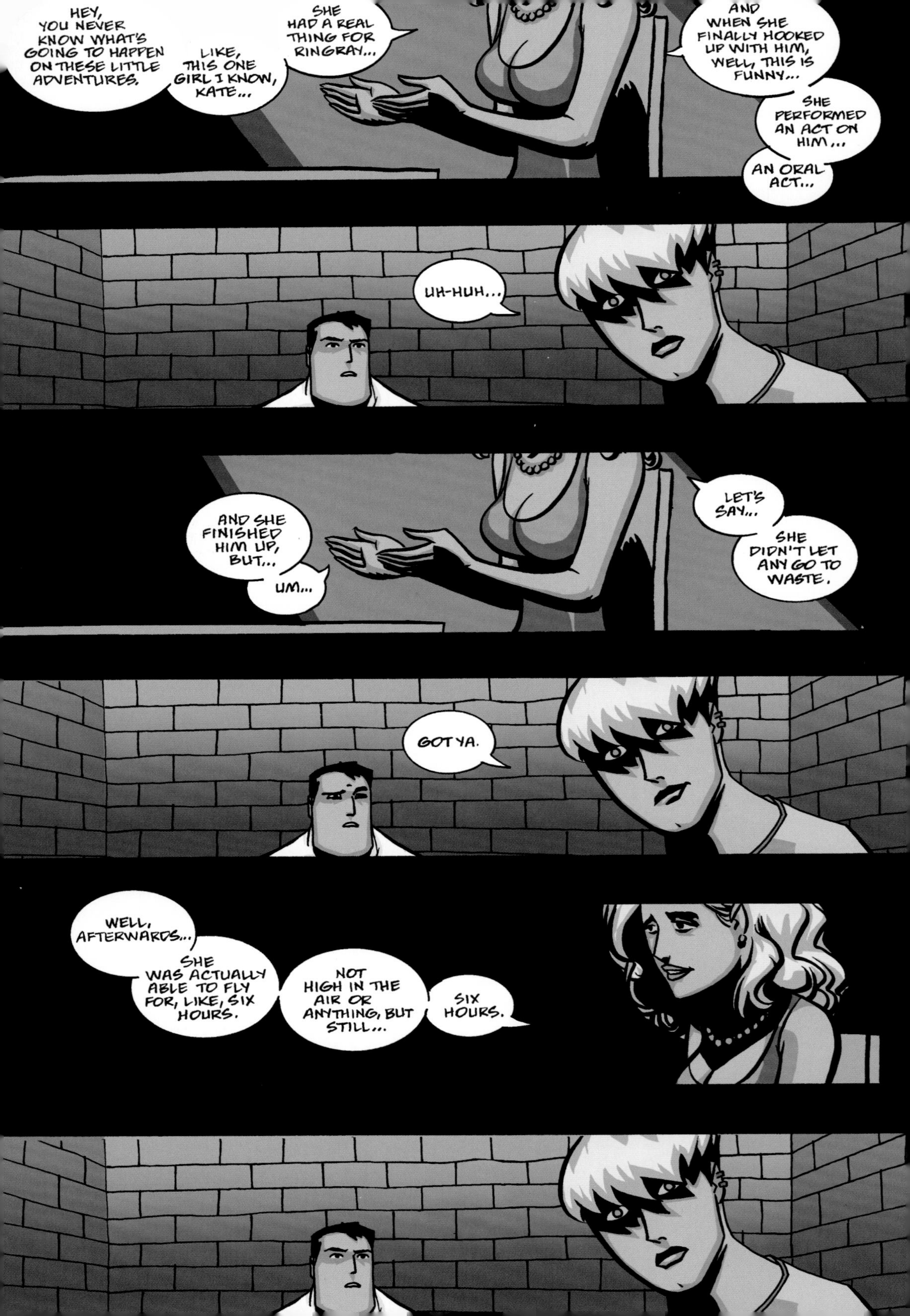
HEY, YOU NEVER KNOW WHAT'S GOING TO HAPPEN ON THESE LITTLE ADVENTURES.
LIKE, THIS ONE GIRL I KNOW, KATE...
SHE HAD A REAL THING FOR RINGRAY...
AND WHEN SHE FINALLY HOOKED UP WITH HIM, WELL, THIS IS FUNNY...
SHE PERFORMED AN ACT ON HIM...
AN ORAL ACT...
UH-HUH...
AND SHE FINISHED HIM UP, BUT...
UM...
LET'S SAY...
SHE DIDN'T LET ANY GO TO WASTE.
GOT YA.
WELL, AFTERWARDS...
SHE WAS ACTUALLY ABLE TO FLY FOR, LIKE, SIX HOURS.
NOT HIGH IN THE AIR OR ANYTHING, BUT STILL...
SIX HOURS.

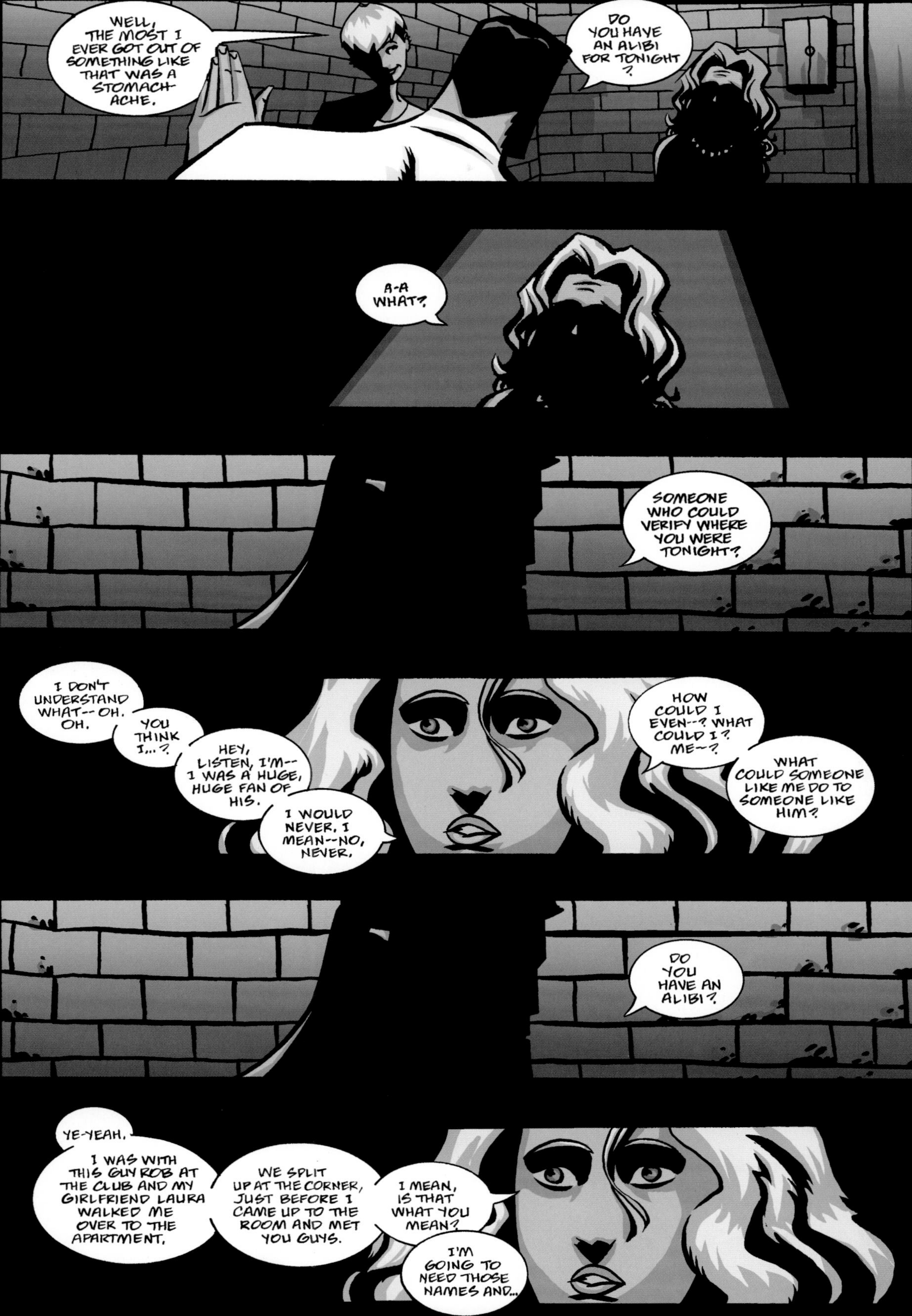
WELL, THE MOST I EVER GOT OUT OF SOMETHING LIKE THAT WAS A STOMACH-ACHE.
DO YOU HAVE AN ALIBI FOR TONIGHT?
A-A WHAT?
SOMEONE WHO COULD VERIFY WHERE YOU WERE TONIGHT?
I DON'T UNDERSTAND WHAT--OH. OH.
YOU THINK I...?
HEY, LISTEN, I'M-- I WAS A HUGE, HUGE FAN OF HIS.
I WOULD NEVER, I MEAN--NO, NEVER.
HOW COULD I EVEN--? WHAT COULD I? ME--?
WHAT COULD SOMEONE LIKE ME DO TO SOMEONE LIKE HIM?
DO YOU HAVE AN ALIBI?
YE-YEAH.
I WAS WITH THIS GUY ROB AT THE CLUB AND MY GIRLFRIEND LAURA WALKED ME OVER TO THE APARTMENT.
WE SPLIT UP AT THE CORNER, JUST BEFORE I CAME UP TO THE ROOM AND MET YOU GUYS.
I MEAN, IS THAT WHAT YOU MEAN?
I'M GOING TO NEED THOSE NAMES AND...

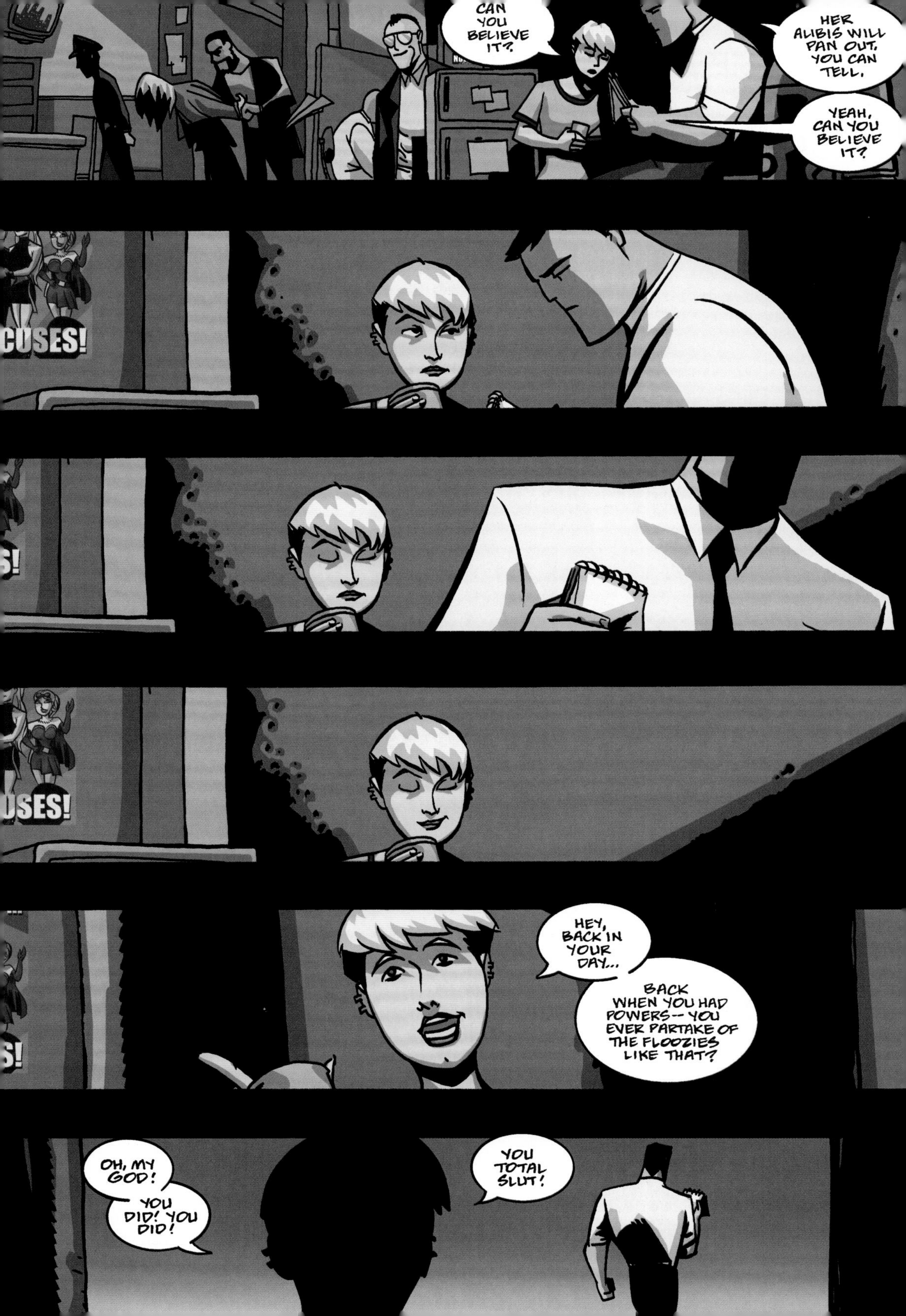
CAN YOU BELIEVE IT?
HER ALIBIS WILL PAN OUT, YOU CAN TELL.
YEAH, CAN YOU BELIEVE IT?
CUSES!
S!
USES!
HEY, BACK IN YOUR DAY...
BACK WHEN YOU HAD POWERS-- YOU EVER PARTAKE OF THE FLOOZIES LIKE THAT?
S!
OH, MY GOD!
YOU DID! YOU DID!
YOU TOTAL SLUT!

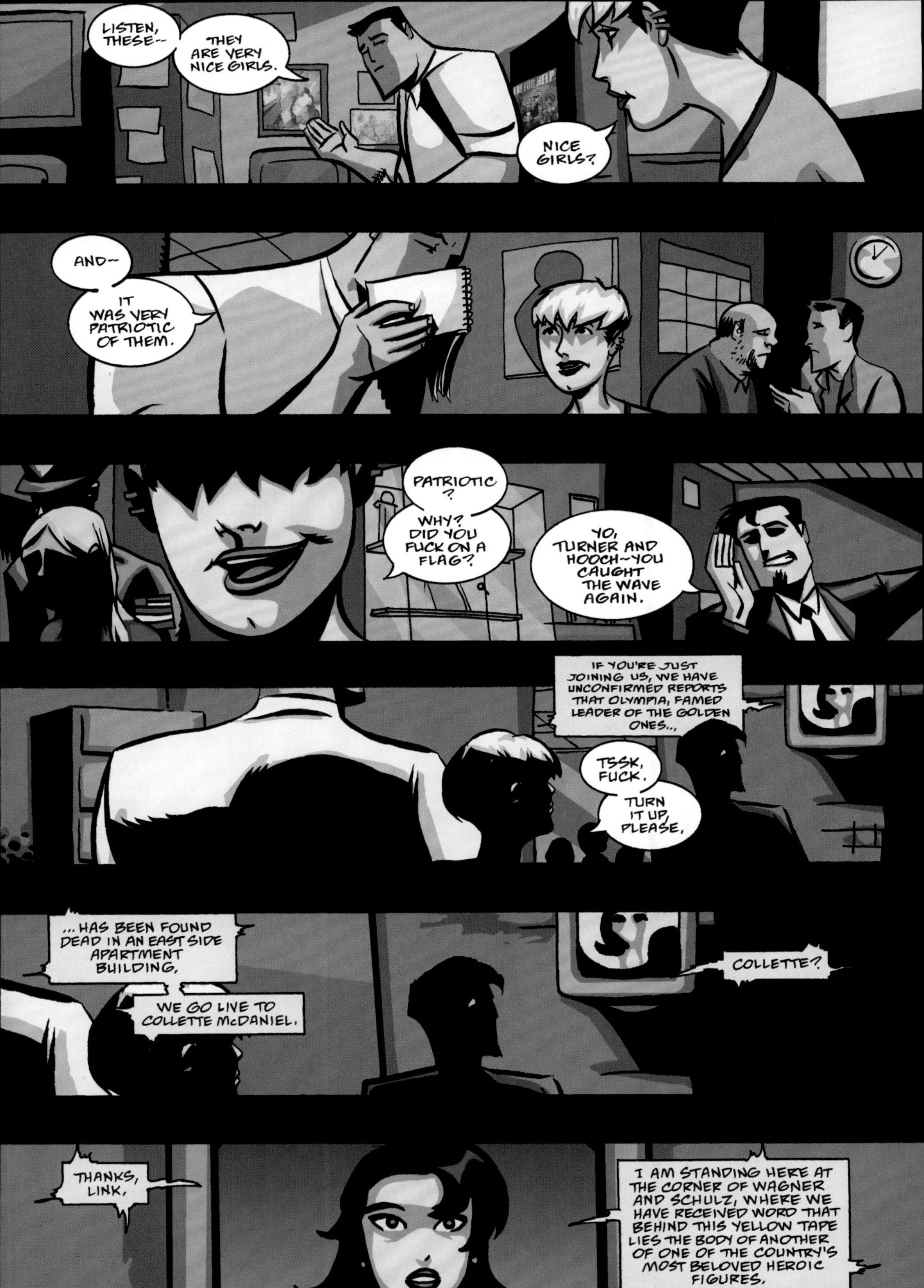

LISTEN, THESE--
THEY ARE VERY NICE GIRLS.
NICE GIRLS?
AND--
IT WAS VERY PATRIOTIC OF THEM.
PATRIOTIC?
WHY? DID YOU FUCK ON A FLAG?
YO, TURNER AND HOOCH--YOU CAUGHT THE WAVE AGAIN.
IF YOU'RE JUST JOINING US, WE HAVE UNCONFIRMED REPORTS THAT OLYMPIA, FAMED LEADER OF THE GOLDEN ONES...
TSSK, FUCK.
TURN IT UP, PLEASE.
...HAS BEEN FOUND DEAD IN AN EAST SIDE APARTMENT BUILDING.
WE GO LIVE TO COLLETTE McDANIEL.
COLLETTE?
THANKS, LINK.
I AM STANDING HERE AT THE CORNER OF WAGNER AND SCHULZ, WHERE WE HAVE RECEIVED WORD THAT BEHIND THIS YELLOW TAPE LIES THE BODY OF ANOTHER OF ONE OF THE COUNTRY'S MOST BELOVED HEROIC FIGURES.

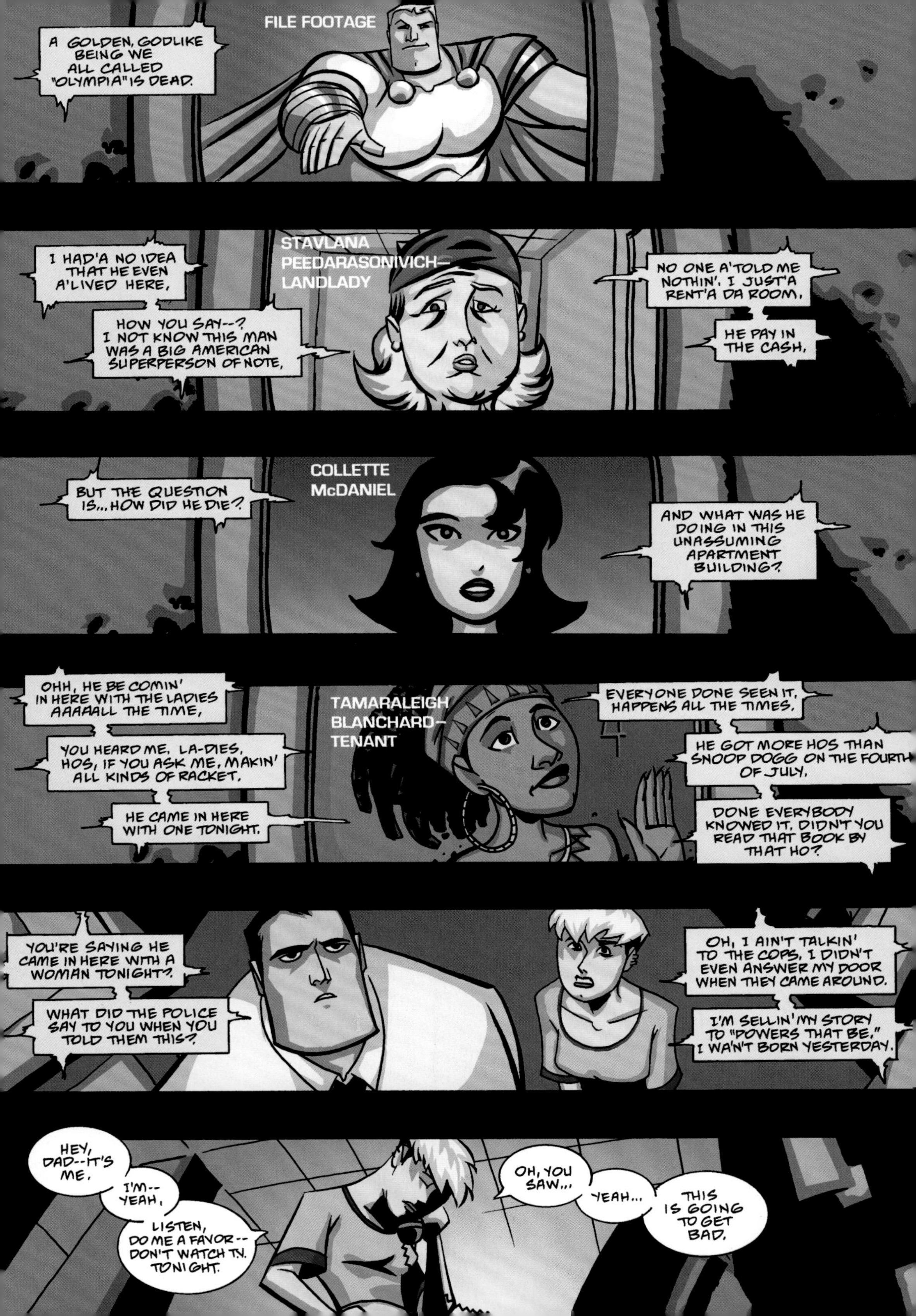
FILE FOOTAGE
A GOLDEN, GODLIKE BEING WE ALL CALLED "OLYMPIA" IS DEAD.
STAVLANA PEEDARASONIVICH—LANDLADY
I HAD'A NO IDEA THAT HE EVEN A'LIVED HERE.
HOW YOU SAY--? I NOT KNOW THIS MAN WAS A BIG AMERICAN SUPERPERSON OF NOTE.
NO ONE A'TOLD ME NOTHIN'. I JUST'A RENT'A DA ROOM.
HE PAY IN THE CASH.
COLLETTE McDANIEL
BUT THE QUESTION IS... HOW DID HE DIE?
AND WHAT WAS HE DOING IN THIS UNASSUMING APARTMENT BUILDING?
TAMARALEIGH BLANCHARD—TENANT
OHH, HE BE COMIN' IN HERE WITH THE LADIES AAAAALL THE TIME.
YOU HEARD ME. LA-DIES. HOS, IF YOU ASK ME. MAKIN' ALL KINDS OF RACKET.
HE CAME IN HERE WITH ONE TONIGHT.
EVERYONE DONE SEEN IT. HAPPENS ALL THE TIMES.
HE GOT MORE HOS THAN SNOOP DOGG ON THE FOURTH OF JULY.
DONE EVERYBODY KNOWED IT. DIDN'T YOU READ THAT BOOK BY THAT HO?
YOU'RE SAYING HE CAME IN HERE WITH A WOMAN TONIGHT?
WHAT DID THE POLICE SAY TO YOU WHEN YOU TOLD THEM THIS?
OH, I AIN'T TALKIN' TO THE COPS. I DIDN'T EVEN ANSWER MY DOOR WHEN THEY CAME AROUND.
I'M SELLIN' MY STORY TO "POWERS THAT BE." I WAN'T BORN YESTERDAY.
HEY, DAD--IT'S ME.
I'M--YEAH.
LISTEN, DO ME A FAVOR--DON'T WATCH T.V. TONIGHT.
OH, YOU SAW...
YEAH...
THIS IS GOING TO GET BAD.

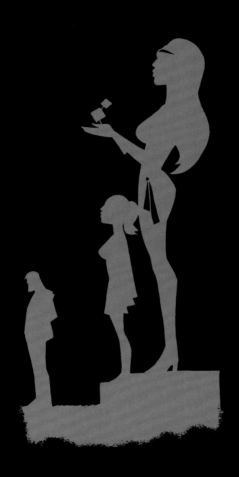

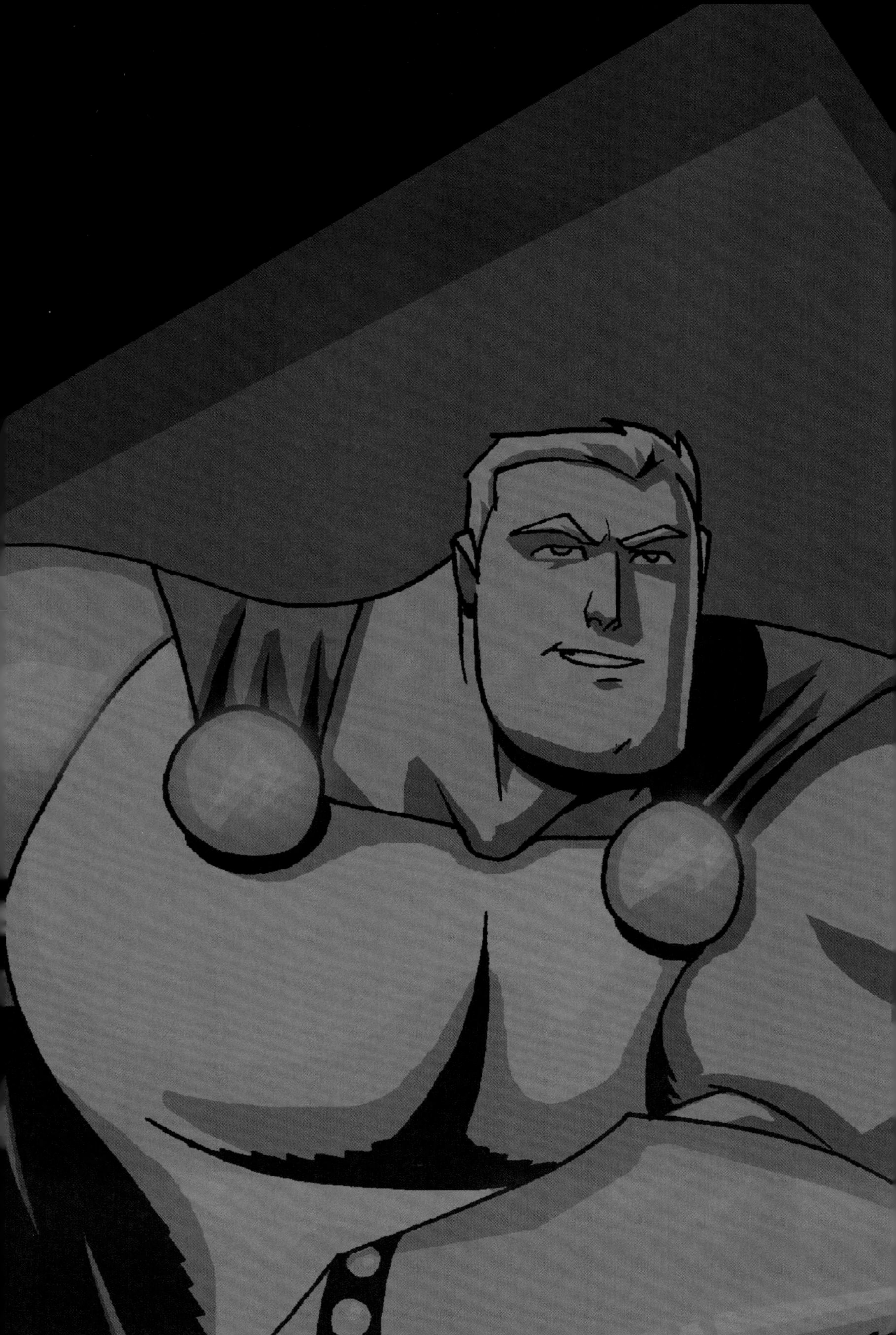

POWERS™

LITTLE DEATHS
CHAPTER 2

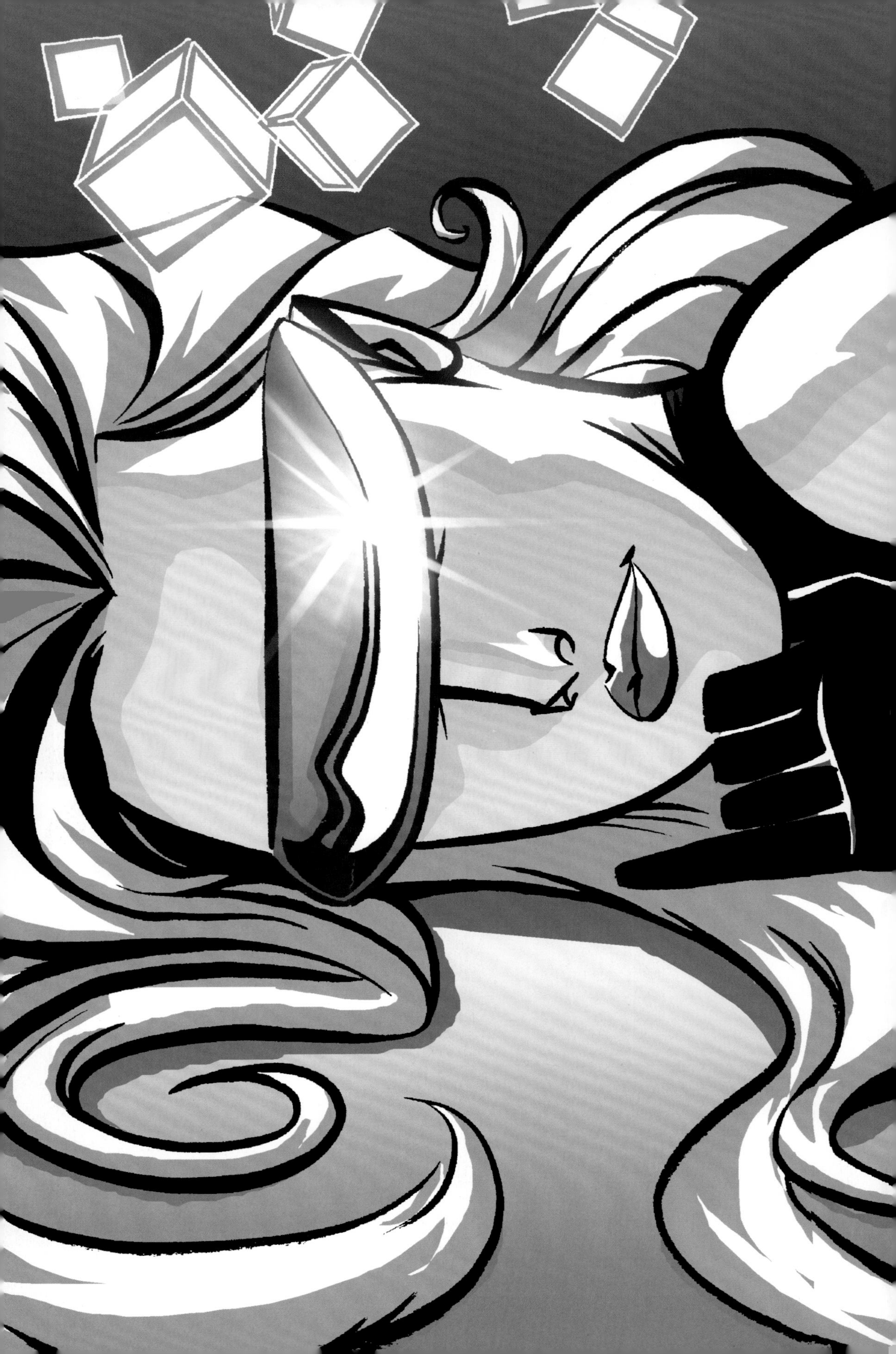

The power of a woman
A new fragrance by Jagi Jangunu
CONTROL
JAGI JANGUNU

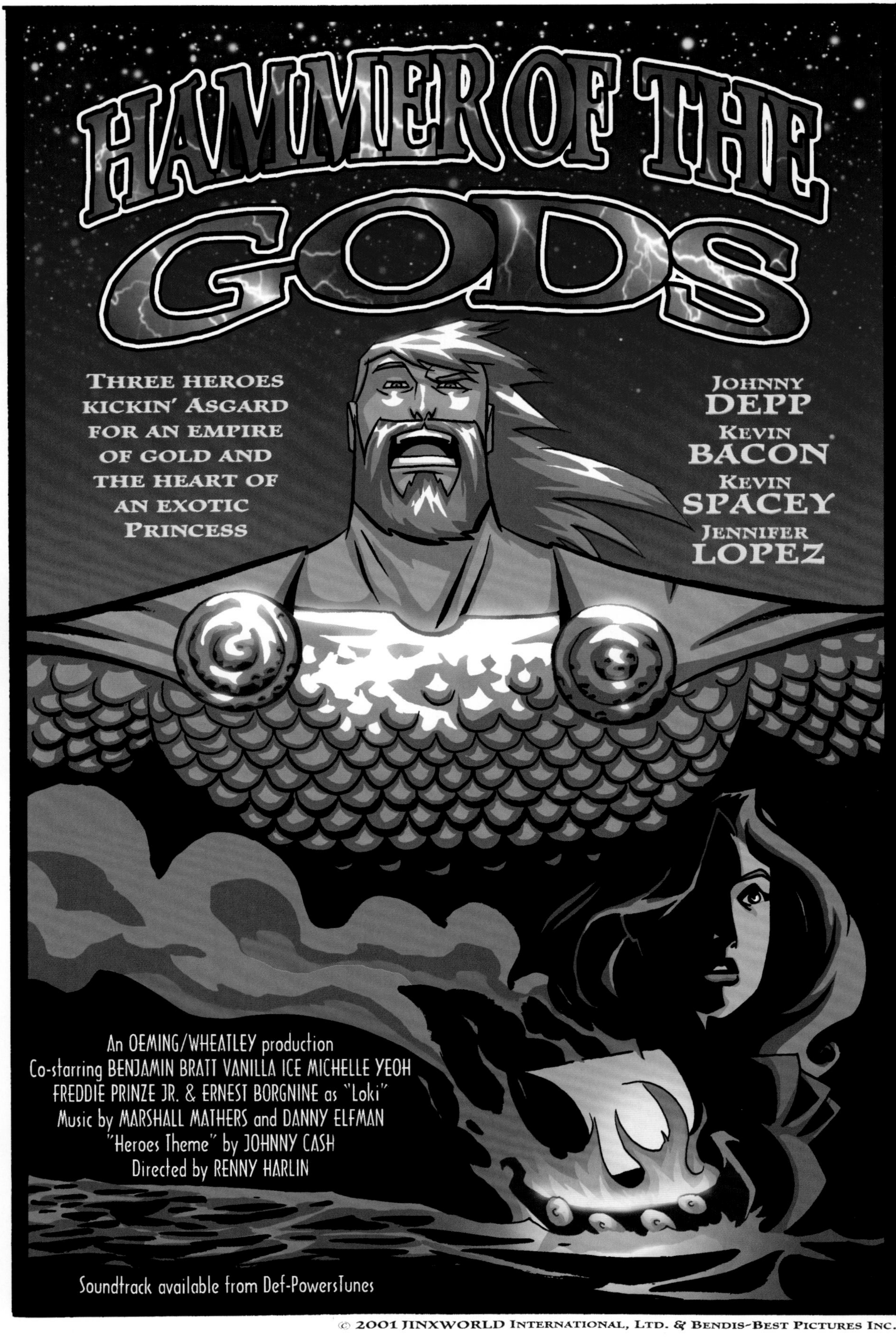

© 2001 JINXWORLD INTERNATIONAL, LTD. & BENDIS-BEST PICTURES INC.

POWERS! INSIDE INFORMATION

www.jinxworld.com

SPUNKY TODD
YOU'RE WATCHING....E!
IS IT ME? OR IS MELISSA RIVERS HOT?
BY BRIAN MICHAEL BENDIS

DIARY OF THE WEEK

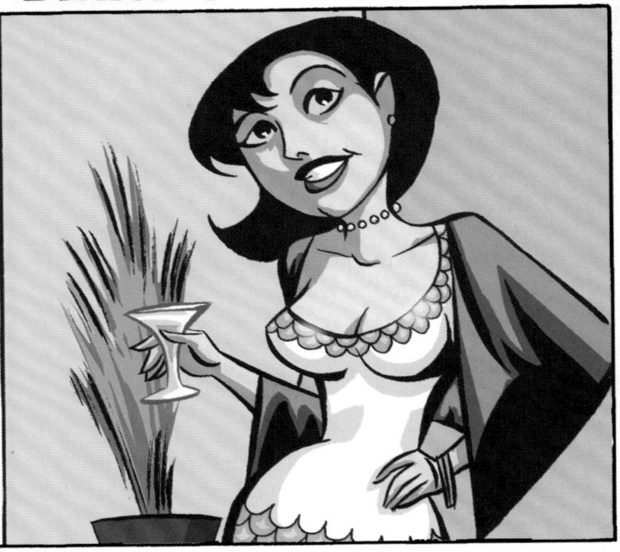

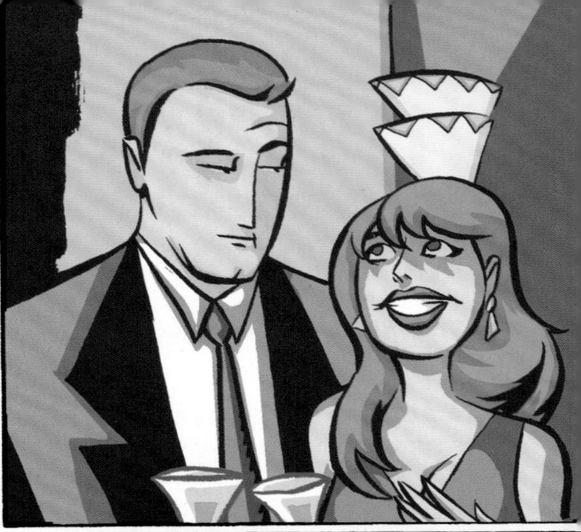

Star reporter Colette McDaniel wowed the crowd with her announcement that portions of the proceeds from her new book: *Who Killed Retro Girl?* Would be going to charity (above). Hunky reporter Rogers Sanders and (Wowsa!) Weather Girl Emma Randle seem awfully chummy for co-workers (above right).

GUESS WHO CAME TO DINNER?

Founders of the Janis Quivers Media Center of the Arts were the brains behind the fund-raising evening at the Broderick Hotel on Benza Island, in aid of the Victims Against Random Super Powered Violence Centre.

Hosted by Channel 5 News, many of the cities top chefs came out to cook for nineteen separate tables of ten guests each. The main courses ranged from jerk chicken pizza to Sashimi salmon torte.

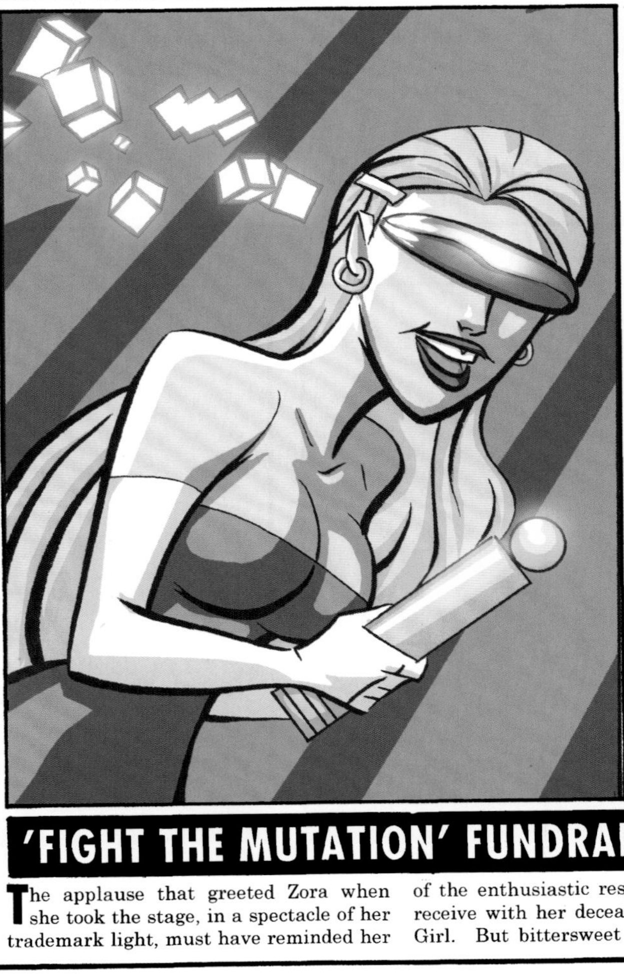

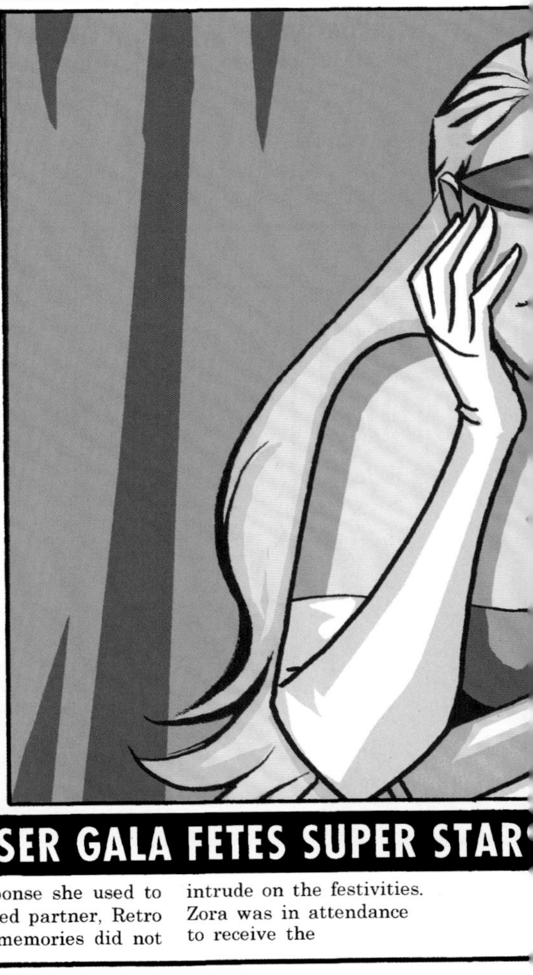

'FIGHT THE MUTATION' FUNDRAISER GALA FETES SUPER STAR

The applause that greeted Zora when she took the stage, in a spectacle of her trademark light, must have reminded her of the enthusiastic response she used to receive with her deceased partner, Retro Girl. But bittersweet memories did not intrude on the festivities. Zora was in attendance to receive the

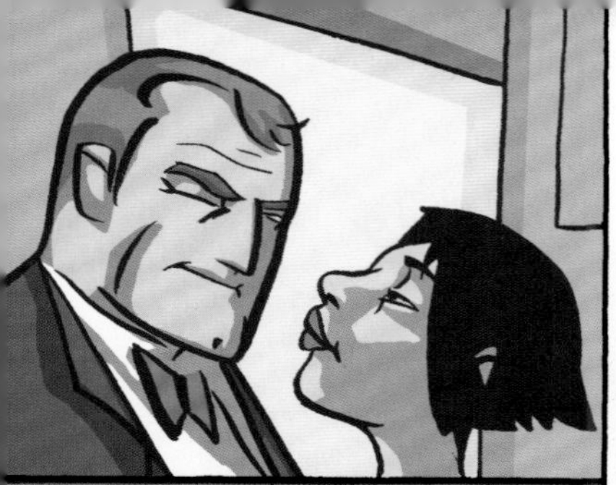

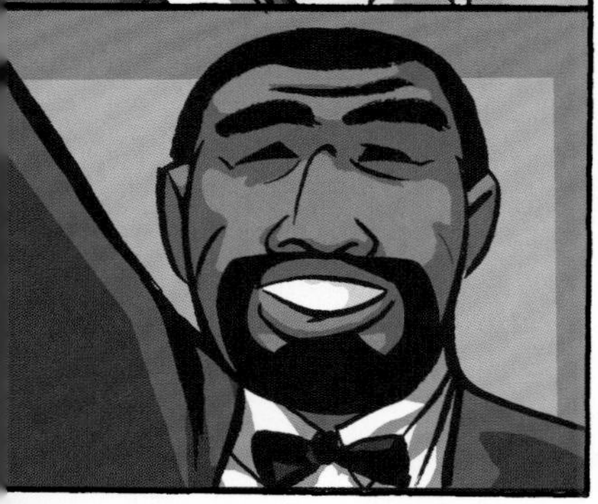

Powers That Be **host Ted Henry popped in with a mystery date (above top). Mayor Washington Lee toasts the room (above).**

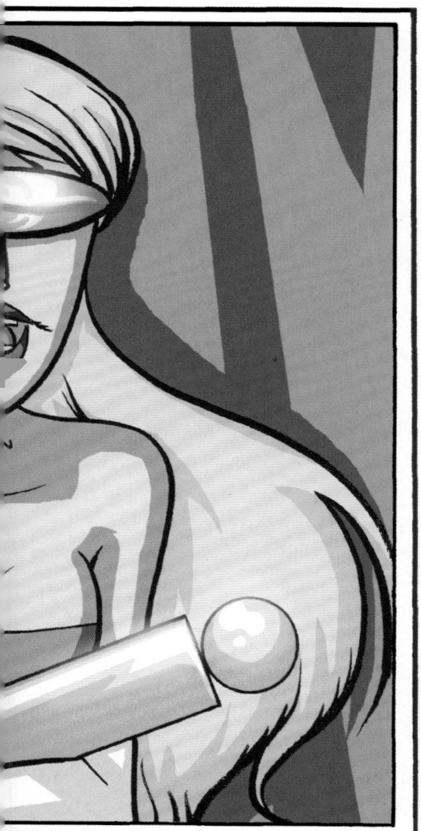

lifetime achievement award for her work against illegal mutation in our city's projects. The gala raised funds to enable children with special abilities to take part in everyday activities with regular children.

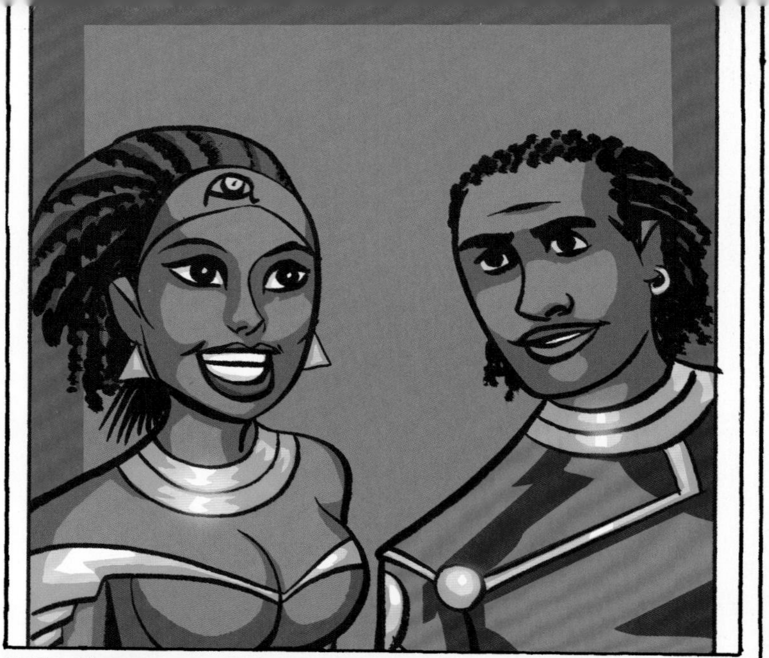

ANNUAL HERO AWARDS HONOR FG-3

Everyone had crossed fingers in hope for the reunion to end all reunions, but it was not to be as Wazz was a no-show when FG-3 teammates Boggiegirl and Benmarley were awarded the Centennial Heroes Award. The gala event was overflowing with Dom Perignon champagne, miniature chocolate Award replicas, and luxury gift baskets for all who attended.

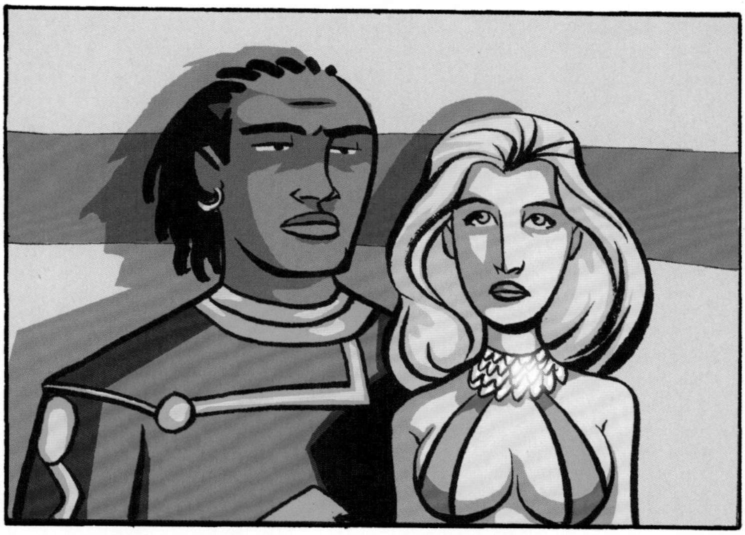

Awards recipients Boggiegirl and Benmarley (top) Benmarly and his date, supermodel Roxanne Plimm (above) Boggie girl and Zora share a hello kiss before the awards (below)

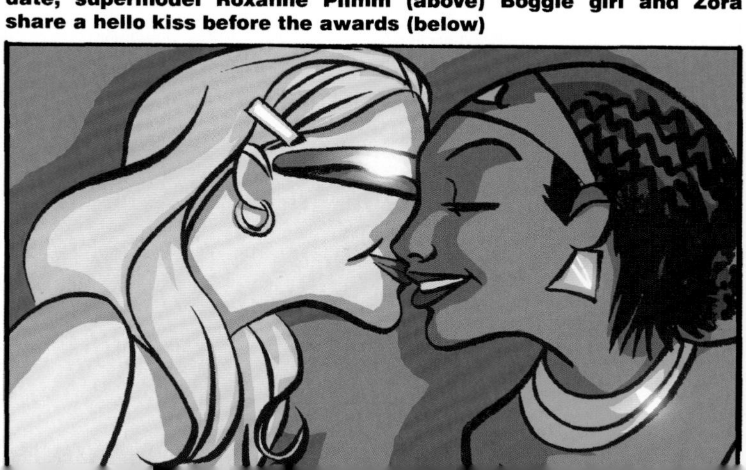

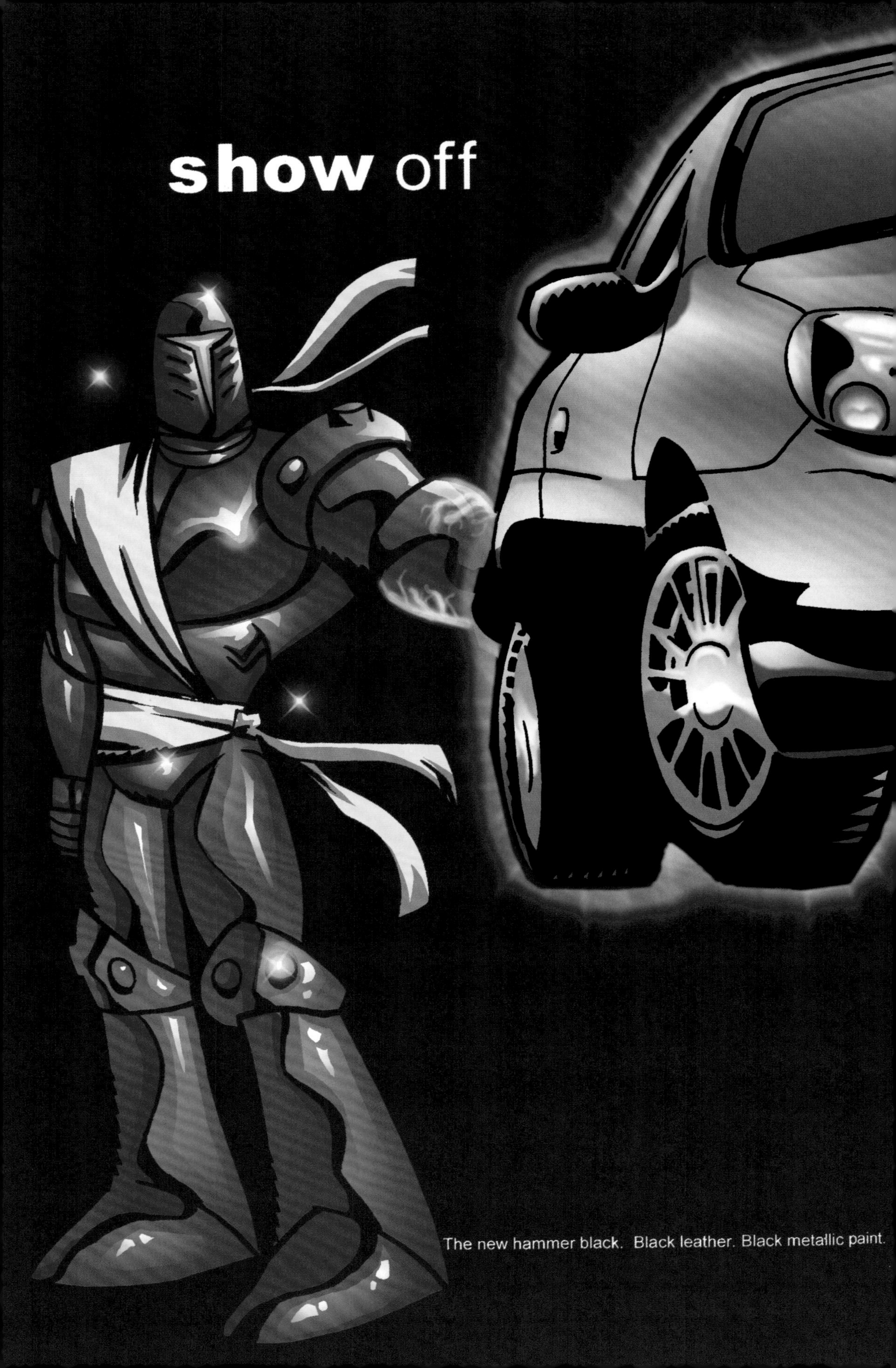
show off
The new hammer black. Black leather. Black metallic paint.

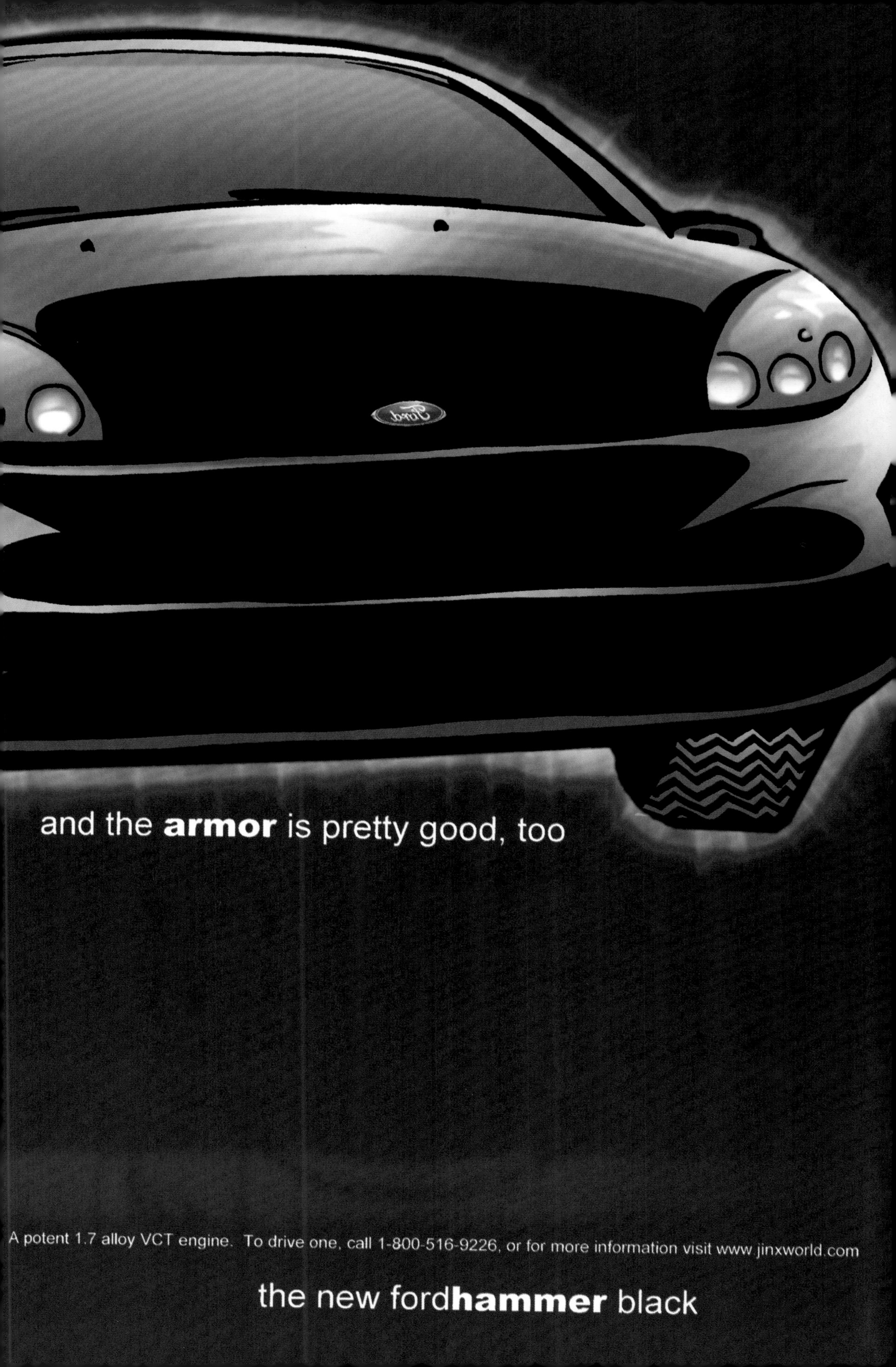
and the **armor** is pretty good, too
A potent 1.7 alloy VCT engine. To drive one, call 1-800-516-9226, or for more information visit www.jinxworld.com
the new ford**hammer** black

OLYMPIA DEAD
Hero found in apartment

Olympia, widely considered to be one of the city's greatest champions, was found dead Saturday night. The police have not ruled out foul play. Official reports so far indicate the police were called after a 'very bright light' burst forth from an apartment at the corner of W75th and Millar Avenue. Olympia was found in the nude, with no signs of a struggle. Police have offered very little information, but admit the case is still open and suspects are being sought for questioning. (For more information, see main article starting on page 10.)

RETRO GIRL
Vandals in mid-town

The newly erected bronze statue of Retro Girl, located in Chaykin Park was vandalized over the past weekend. The words "KAOTIC CHIC" were spray painted on it. The phrase, made popular by the man who confessed to killing Retro Girl, is now an anthem of anarchistic teen movements on the city's East Side. Police are asking citizens with any information regarding this vandalization of city property to call 443-557-8778.

FG-3
Ex-partner sues in court

The supergroup FG-3, which was recently acquitted of intimidation and bribery, charges following a nightclub battle in which three innocent bystanders were injured, is being sued for four million dollars by ex-member Wazz for royalties he says he is contractually owed for merchandising and other related commercial business ventures when he was with the group.

THIS WEEK
A ROUND-UP OF NEWS REPORTS

QUEEN NOIR
To marry ex-nemesis

Queen Noir, the celebrated cult heroine, is set to marry her one-time archenemy, Strike. The pair met during a hostage crisis at the new Federal Aviation Museum ten years ago. Strike served his time and been a reformed man for over a year and a half. Strike is the son of the late super-villain Katmandu, who died of a self-inflicted gunshot wound 17 years ago at the height of his popularity.

ZORA
Single motherhood

Zora has admitted to being a little scared of facing life as a single mother following recent news reports of her adoption of an 11-month-old girl, Katra. In an interview with the magazine *Cape*, the controversial superheroine said she was always full of admiration for single mothers, but now that she herself was one, "It was scary—a whole new path I am about to venture down."

Wazz, whose real name is Sean Wallace, claims that his former team mates Boggie girl and Ben-marley have cheated him out of moneys rightfully owed to him. Wazz left the high profile group after a public argument over the death of their archenemy, Dr. Z.

A member of Wazz's legal team said: "We have no choice but to file suit. FG-3 refuses to address the issue in any other manner."

MOUNTAIN
New career name change

In tune with his new career as spokesperson for Coca-Cola, retired Super Power Mountain has officially changed his street name to " Thirst Quencher." A *Centennial Award* winner, Mountain retired from active status two years ago and has made a name for himself as a spokesman. In a recent interview with *TV Guide*, he stated: "We are all hired monkeys. We all work for as many peanuts as we can. People with powers are no different, and anyone who tells you otherwise is a liar."

SPARKLER
Tops Powers poll

The enduring appeal of Sparkler was proven again last week when the recently deceased hero beat out Retro Girl and Conqueror for the title of "Most Popular Power of the Century." The *Powers of the Century List* was compiled by the BHC Radio2, from the votes of more than 120,000 listeners. Out of the list, only two, Triphammer and Zora, are still alive.

JOHNNY ROYALE
Lawsuit dropped

After months of speculation, the legal firm representing alleged organized crime boss J. "Johnny" Stompinato, a.k.a "Johnny Royale," officially dropped its 150 million dollar lawsuit against the city. Though the murder of Johnny Royale is still under investigation, attorney Robert Evans said that, "further pursuit of the legal action started by our deceased client is at this point a fruitless objective. We hope that this helps the police department find more time to dedicate to our client's mysterious and violent demise."

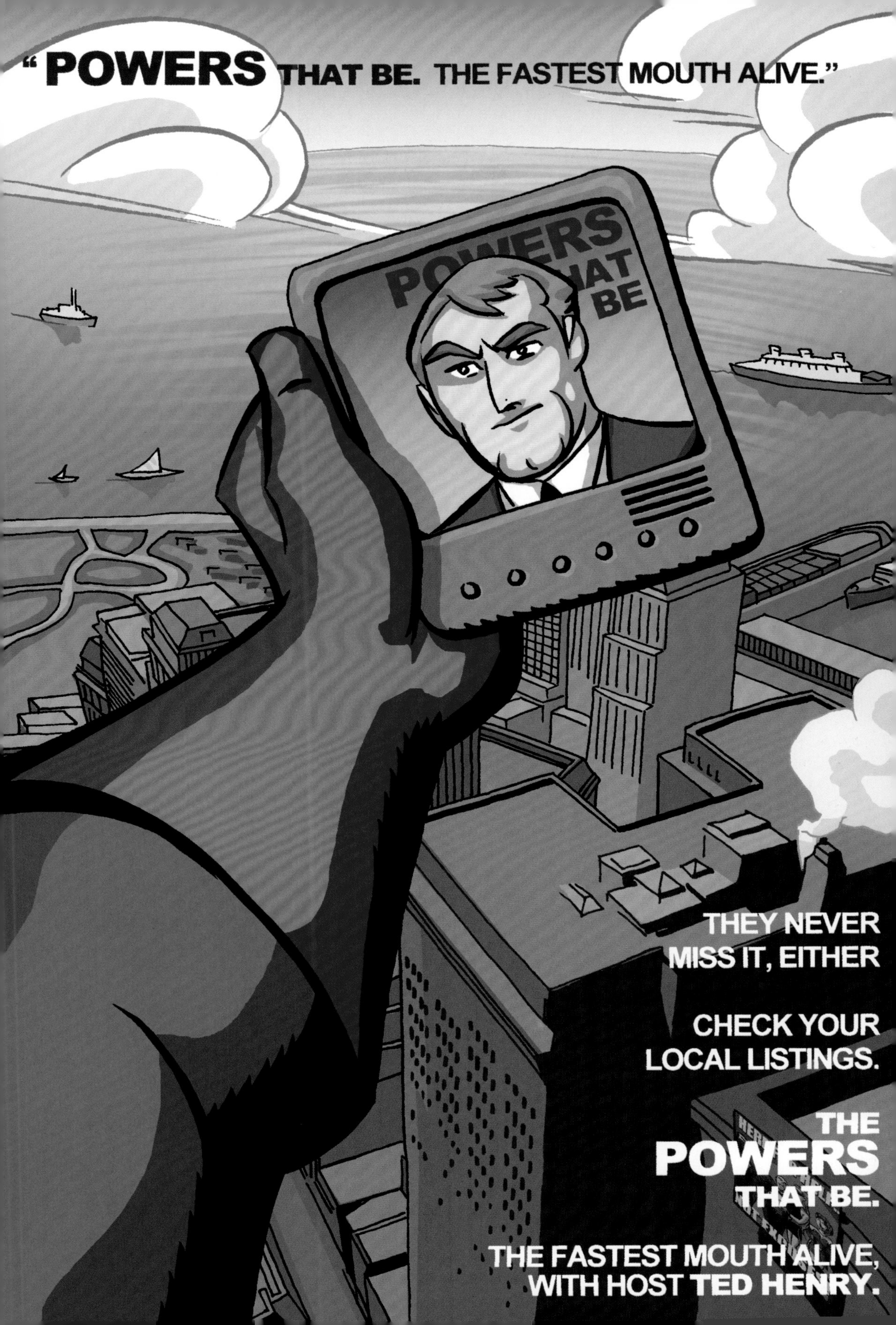

"POWERS THAT BE. THE FASTEST MOUTH ALIVE."
POWERS THAT BE
THEY NEVER MISS IT, EITHER
CHECK YOUR LOCAL LISTINGS.
THE POWERS THAT BE.
THE FASTEST MOUTH ALIVE, WITH HOST TED HENRY.

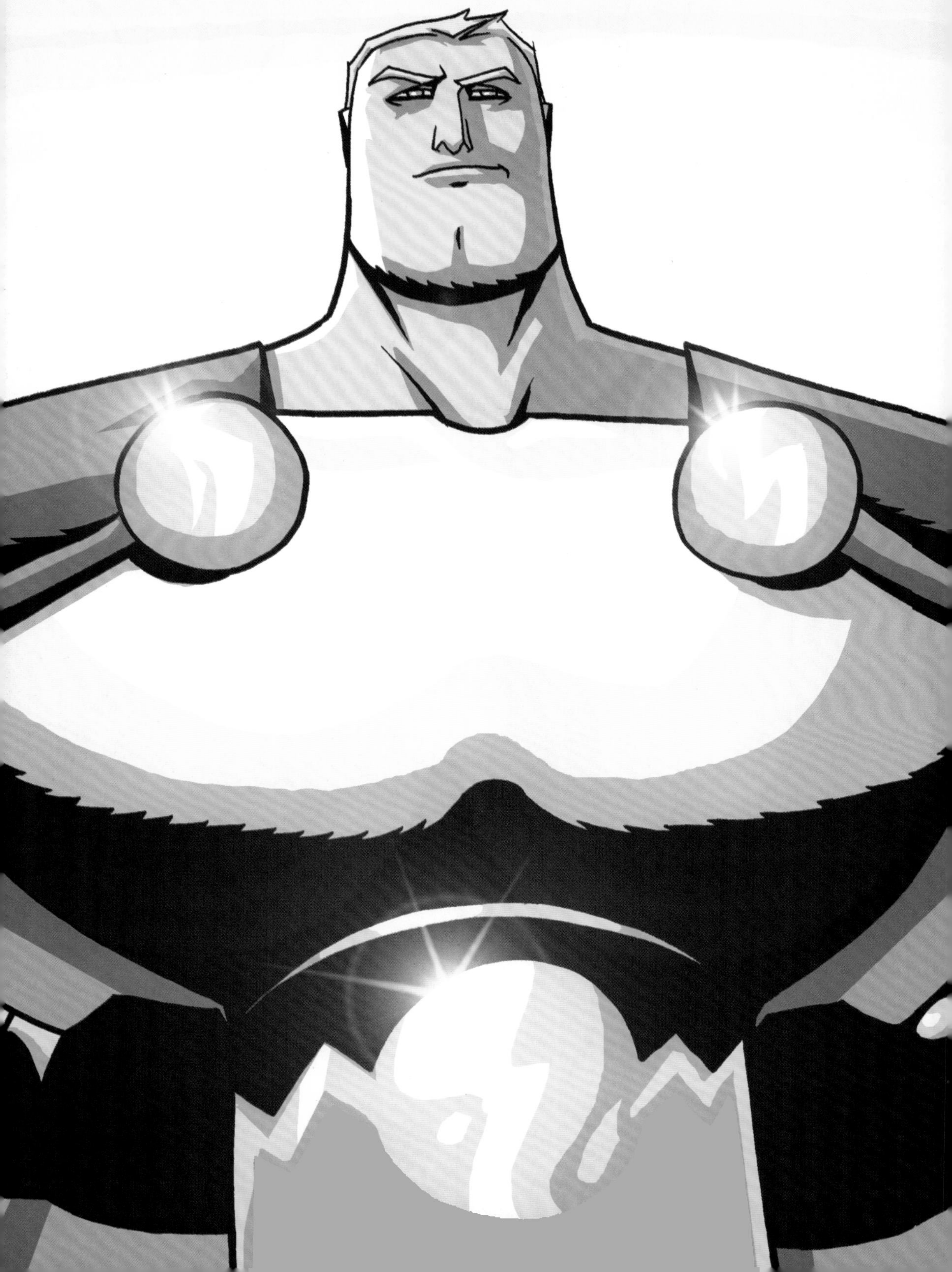

OLYMPIA

LAST INTERVIEW:FACT vs. FICTION

EDITORIAL NOTE: **This interview was conducted two days before the sudden and tragic death of the man known as Olympia. We were going to run an edited version of this interview, but be-cause we believe that this is the last interview he ever gave, we have decided to run it in its entirety. We think this shows a rare glimpse into a man many admired, but few knew anything about.**

Also, legally, we are required to tell you that this rare interview was granted to our magazine in return for us not releasing information that fell into our possession about the man publicly known as Olympia. We will be honoring that agreement.

Olympia. Even his name conjures images of such heroism and self-lessness that immediately fills one's heart with good will towards man, he first came into our lives seven years ago, during the Denver Airport hostage situation--a situation that saved the lives of the President of Mexico and over four hundred civilians.

Olympia then went on to join The Golden Ones, a small band of self-proclaimed heroes that, singly and in groups, have successfully saved the world and mankind from plagues and perils only before imagined in the works of science fiction.

But in recent years, stories have started floating about Olympia alleged sexual transgressions. More than one young woman has come forward with stories of midnight encounters with Olympia. Shocking detail after shock-ing detail has made its way into gossip columns and TV tabloids. ▶

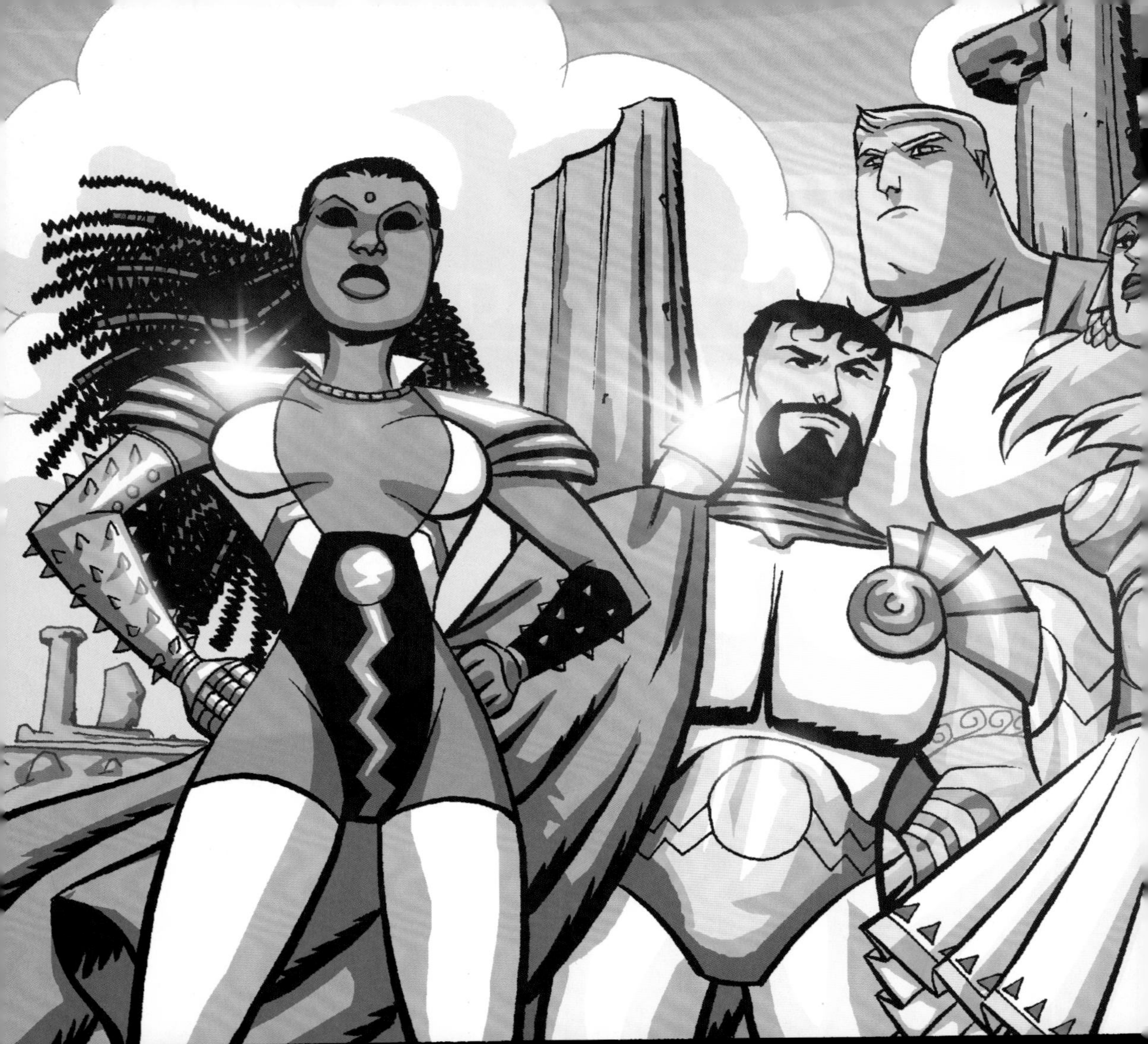

The ***New York Times*** bestseller: *I'm With the Cape*, by self proclaimed groupie Julia Garrison, detailed a three-year affair with a man she wouldn't name by name, described as a "man of incredible power; a golden god among men," and she went on to describe intimate details of their numerous and daring encounters.

Olympia, the man, has never spoken of such matters publicly. Public opinion polls repeatedly show that most Americans don't care what our powered people do in their free time. A whopping 86 percent. But the rumors have plagued Olympia for years, and here, for the first time, he answers such questions.

POWERS: Did you read the book by Julia Garrison?

OLYMPIA: "Wow, you get right to it, don't you?"

Thought you'd appreciate that.

"And I suppose I do."

And?

"And, no, I didn't read it."

But you heard of it?

"Sure, I have a TV. I saw the press."

You have a TV?

(Laughs) "Yes, a big world exclusive. I have a TV."

So you know of the book.

"Sure."

Never even curious about what it said?

"I'll wait for the movie."

That isn't what I asked.

"Good for you. Yes, I was curious, but friends of mine have read certain passages to me. It's a funny book."

Is she talking about you in the book?

"I have no idea."

Really?

"Sure. How do I know what she's doing?"

So, it could be you? You knew her?

"The entire book could be fiction for all we know. She could be having all kinds of fun making up stuff about all kinds of thoughts she's had."

So, you never met her.

"I never said that."

So, you did?

"I didn't say that, either."

Well, either you did or you didn't.

"See, I meet thousands of people every month. I could say I didn't meet her, and then it ends up I did."

But the book details an affair

> "See, I meet thousands of people every month. I could say I didn't meet her, and then it ends up I did."

that lasted over three years.

"Wow."

And it's not with you?

"Again, I haven't read the book."

You had no affair with a woman named Julia Garrison?

"Define affair."

Are you serious?

"Sure. What's an affair? If I was having sexual relations with a woman whose name I didn't even know for over three years, I think I would have to call it something other than 'an affair.'"

What, then? What would you call it?

"I don't know. Is there a name for something like that?"

Not really.

"So there you go."

So, you may or may not have met a woman

Olympia and the Golden Ones became celebrities thanks to their daring feats, but a cloud of impropriety has shadowed them, and lurid sexual innuendoes abound. Rumors of a relationship between Olympia and Retro Girl have titillated fans, particularly in the wake of the superheroine's mysterious death

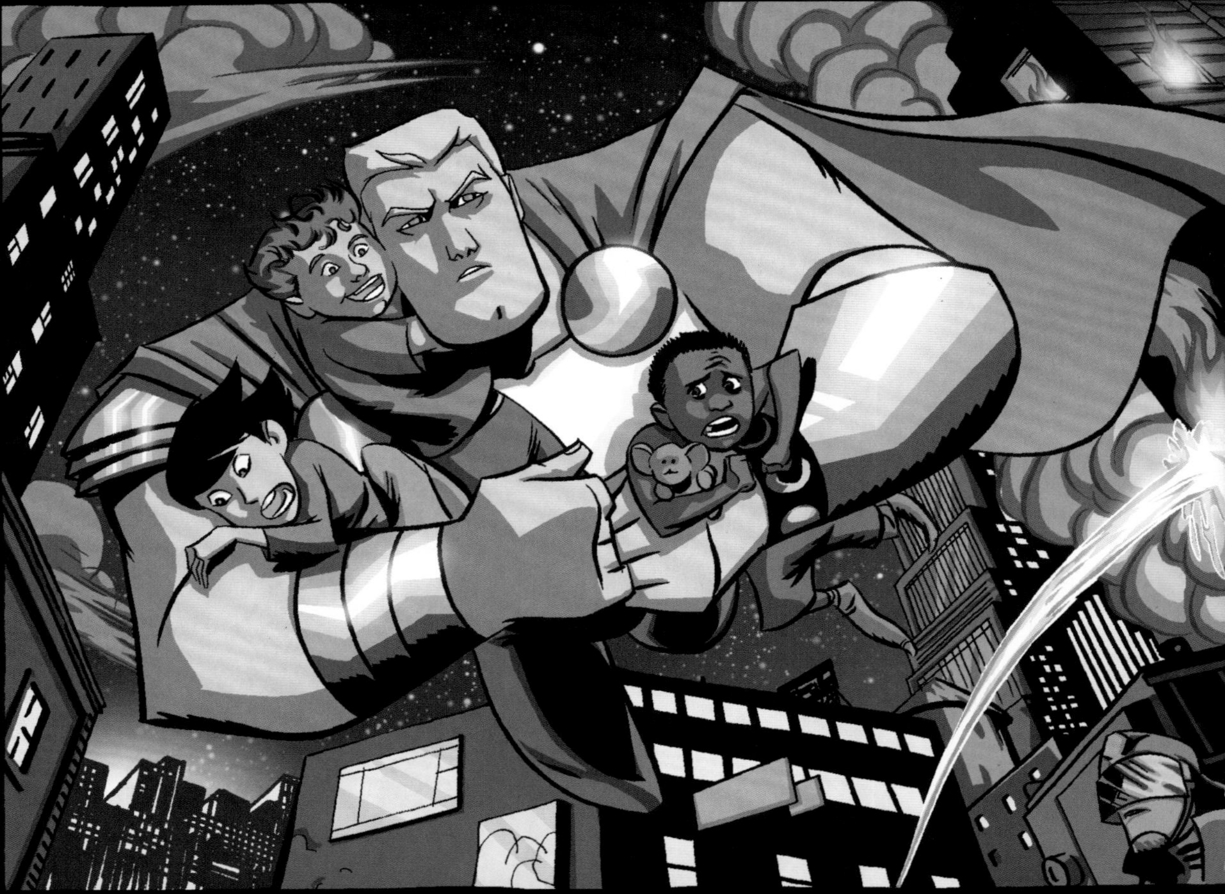

"And I understand what you are trying to accomplish with this interview. But the truth of the matter is, no one cares."

named Julia Garrison, who you may or may not have had a three year relationship with, who wrote a book about someone who may or may not be you, because you didn't read it except for some of it?

"Listen, I understand your job is hard. And I understand what you are trying to accomplish with this interview. But the truth of the matter is, no one cares. First, there's the fact that even if I had a different girlfriend every single night, and engaged in all kinds of who the hell knows what all night long, it's nobody's business. It's not illegal. It's not hurting anyone. And that's what really matters to people. So nobody cares."

Our readers care.

"No, they don't. You're trying to make them care. You want them to care in the worst way. And sure, a GOOD sex story is a good sex story, I'm not denying that. But you people run poll after poll and they tell you—'we don't care.' And I think the only reason you care is because you don't know what is going on. You don't know what the truth is, and you don't know why you can't get to it, and that bothers you."

We have a pretty good idea what the truth is.

"No, you don't. And also, I'm not an elected official. I'm just a guy who lucked into a way of life with these abilities that put me in a *position to help others. Its one of* the greatest things of my life that I'm able to share that gift in a positive way. But, really, I can go on about my business not having to worry about the 'trust of the people,' or whatever."

How did you get that gift? Those powers?

(Laughs) "I can't believe you just asked for my secret origin."

Had to give it a shot.

"Ha, good for you." Laughs "Well, that's not going to happen."

Can I ask why?

"Um—sure. A friend of mine once gave an interview just like this to a fellow like yourself, and he inadvertently gave some information that helped a ▶

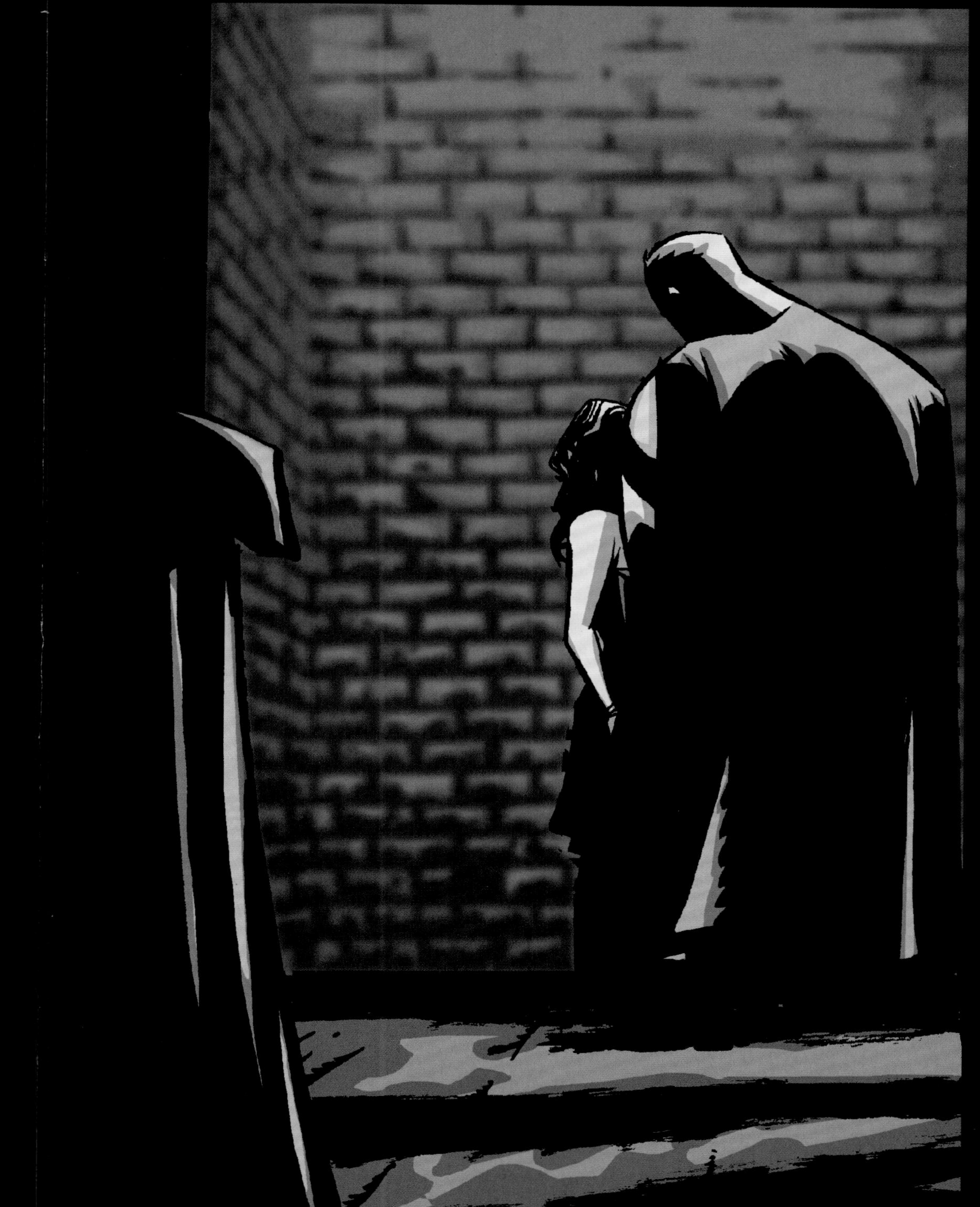

Triumph and tragedy: the public life of a Super Power. Olympia has experienced the full gamut of attention in the press, from heroic adulation to pervasive intrusion during times of sorrow, and now they want to follow him into the bedroom.

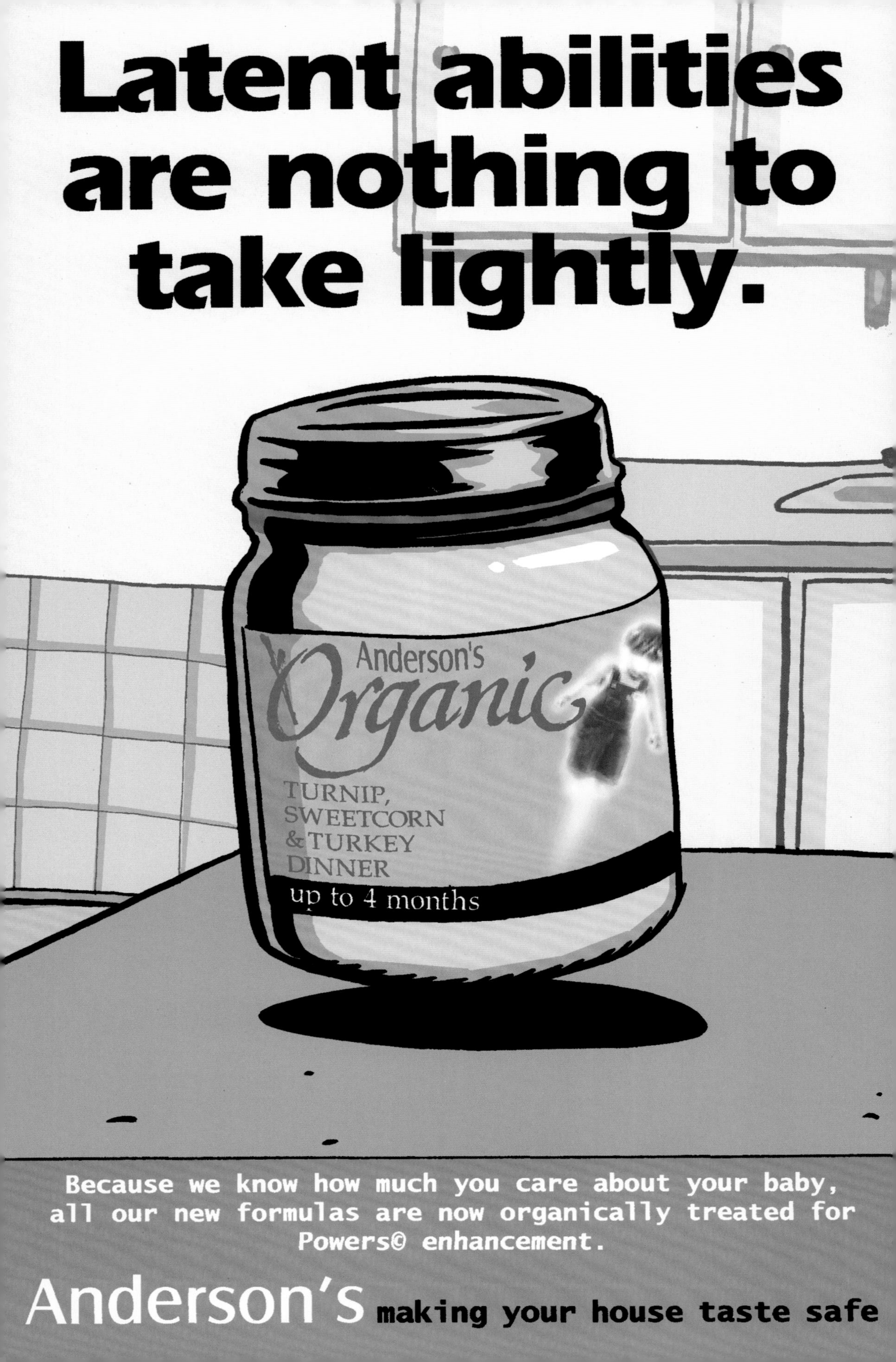
Latent abilities are nothing to take lightly.
Anderson's
Organic
TURNIP, SWEETCORN & TURKEY DINNER
up to 4 months
Because we know how much you care about your baby, all our new formulas are now organically treated for Powers© enhancement.
Anderson's
making your house taste safe

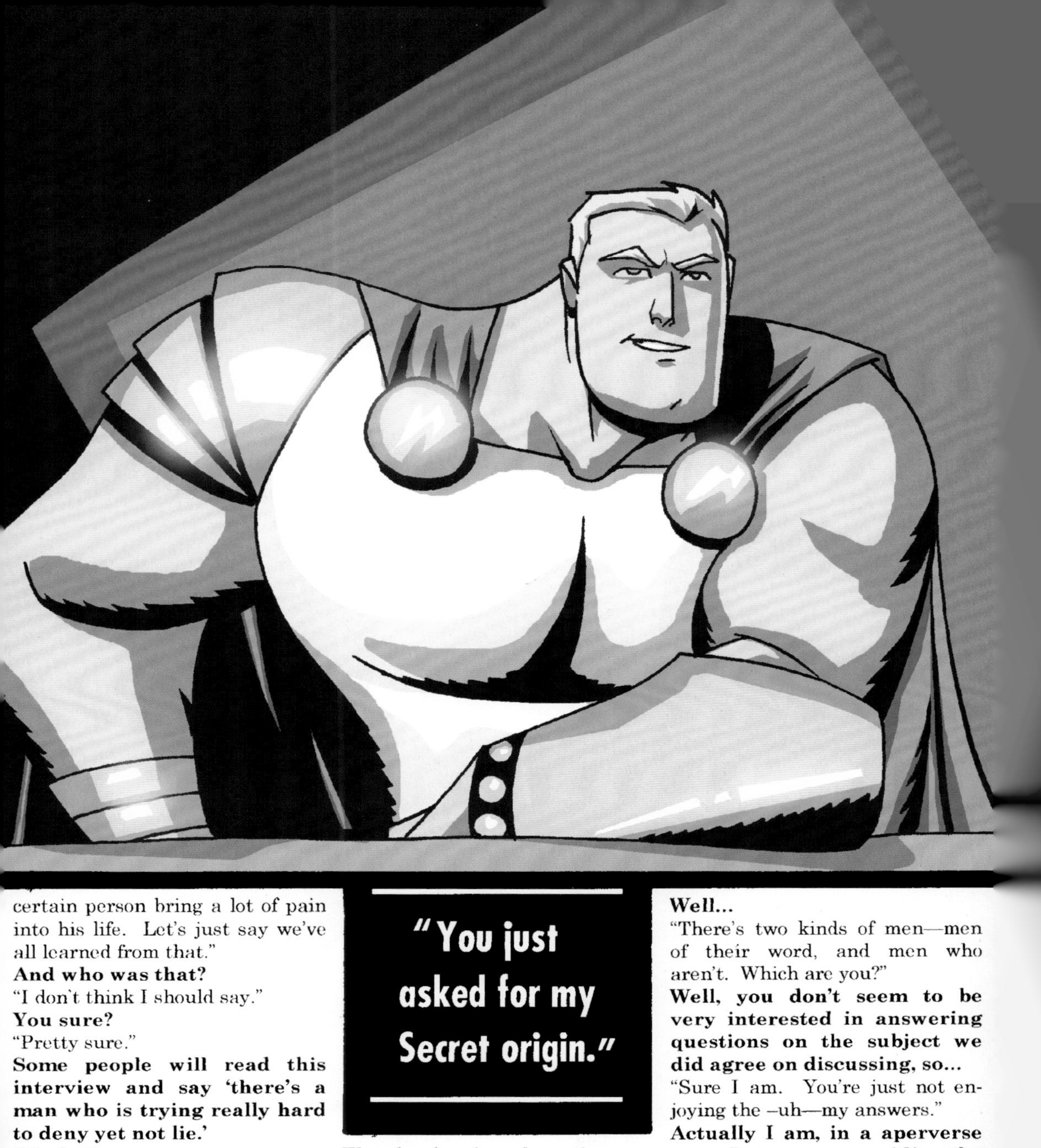

certain person bring a lot of pain into his life. Let's just say we've all learned from that."

And who was that?

"I don't think I should say."

You sure?

"Pretty sure."

Some people will read this interview and say 'there's a man who is trying really hard to deny yet not lie.'

"Maybe."

'There is a guy who is lying by not telling the truth.'

"And, there are those who will say that this interviewer has this chance to sit down with someone with my unique perspective on the world and the only questions he is asking *are* sex questions."

Maybe. Did you attend the funeral of Retro Girl?

"No."

Why?

"I didn't know where it was."

You knew her.

"Yes. Great girl. One of the best."

In the book by Julia

"You just asked for my Secret origin."

The book also describes an affair between characters that strongly resemble you and Retro Girl.

"Come on, the girl is dead."

Yes. Did you have a relationship with her?

"Yes."

Like described in the book?

"I didn't read the book, so."

What kind of relationship did you have?

(Smiles) "A better one than you and I have."

You know what I mean.

"A deaf man knows what you mean. This—uh—isn't what we agreed the interview would be

Well...

"There's two kinds of men—men of their word, and men who aren't. Which are you?"

Well, you don't seem to be very interested in answering questions on the subject we did agree on discussing, so...

"Sure I am. You're just not enjoying the –uh—my answers."

Actually I am, in a aperverse way. But you are avoiding the questions that you are being asked.

"Define avoiding."

See?

"I was joking."

Hmmm...I wonder if you were.

"Now you sound like my therapist."

Ho, you have a therapist?

"Ha! You're good."

Not going to answer?

(Olympia does not answer, but does it with a smile.)

Were you saddened by the death of Retro Girl?

"What kind of question is that? Of course."

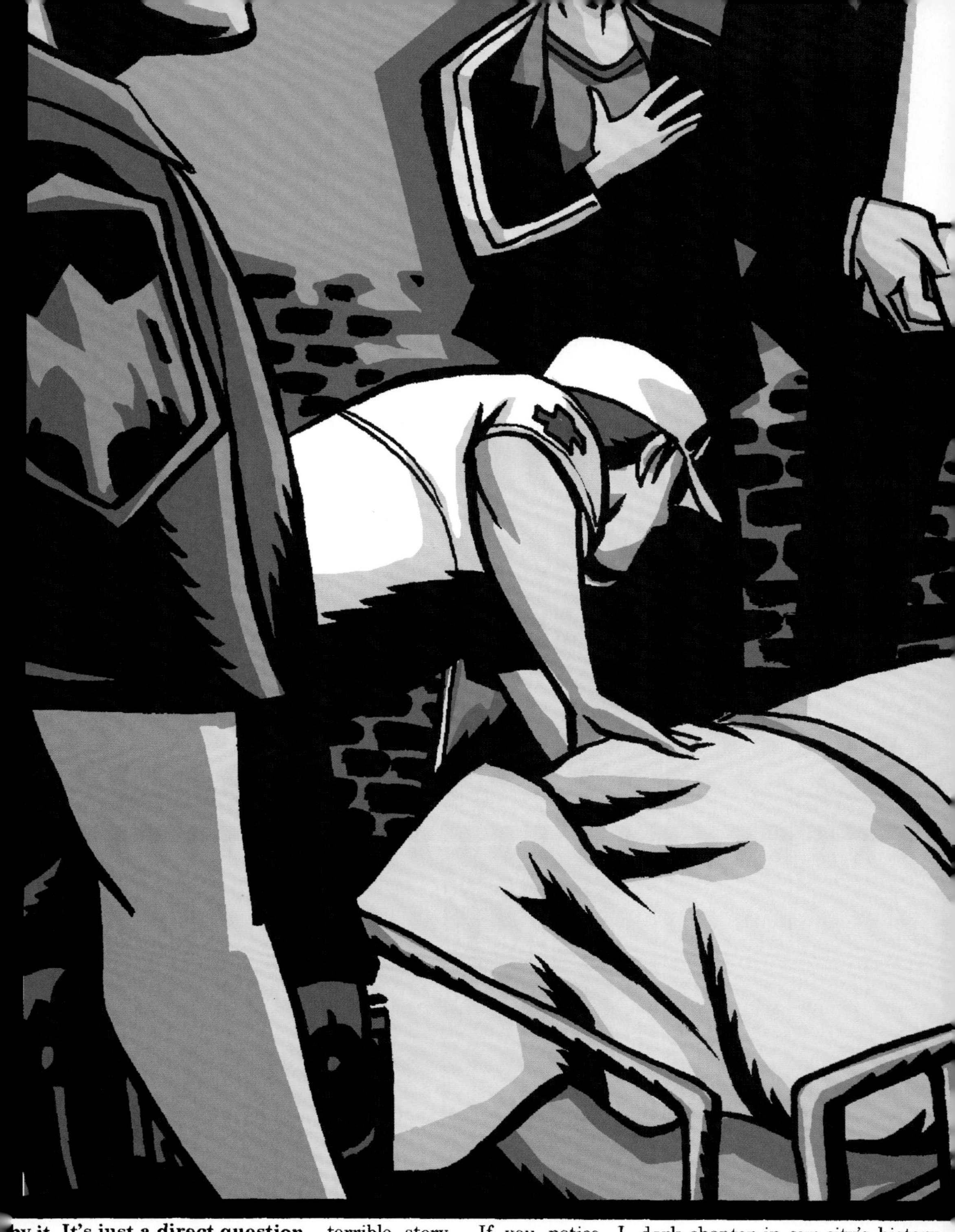

by it. It's just a direct question.
"Lord..."
I thought if I asked you how you felt when you learned of it, that would be more vague and not to your liking.
"Uh-huh. Well, for your information, the whole thing was devastating to me. The death, the whole thing with Triphammer. There were no winners in that terrible story. If you notice, I wasn't around for a while after that. It took a lot out for me to put on my uniform after that..."
Why?
"Just questioning why we do what we do. Is it worth it? Do we make a difference?"
And?
"And I think we do. I think we do in a big way. And though that dark chapter in our city's history will always be there, I just—"(He is visibly shaken by the subject.)
Do you want to continue?
(Pauses) "Uh--not really. Tell you what? You and your magazine can run whatever you want. I don't care. I have no regrets about my life or how I conduct myself. My relationships are my own. My friends know who they

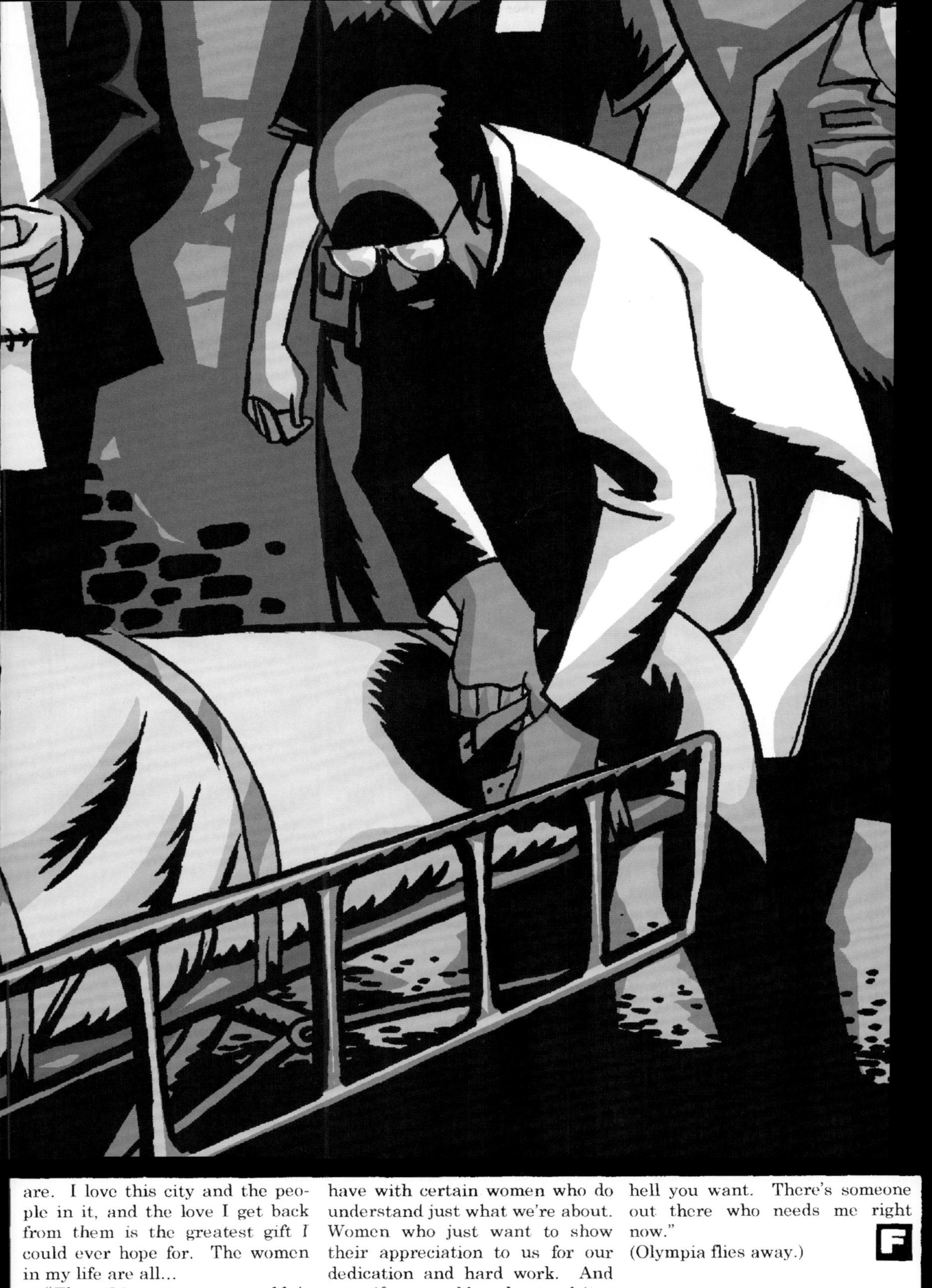

are. I love this city and the people in it, and the love I get back from them is the greatest gift I could ever hope for. The women in my life are all...

"The thing is—you couldn't possibly understand the needs of people like myself. Our appetites, our desires. You couldn't possibly understand the special relationships someone like myself could have with certain women who do understand just what we're about. Women who just want to show their appreciation to us for our dedication and hard work. And even if you could understand it---what difference would it make? Would it make me a worse person? Would it take back any of the sacrifices I've made, or...?

"Just—just print whatever the hell you want. There's someone out there who needs me right now."

(Olympia flies away.)

F

INTERVIEW: MIKE SANGIACOMO
PHOTOS: AVON ARCHIVES

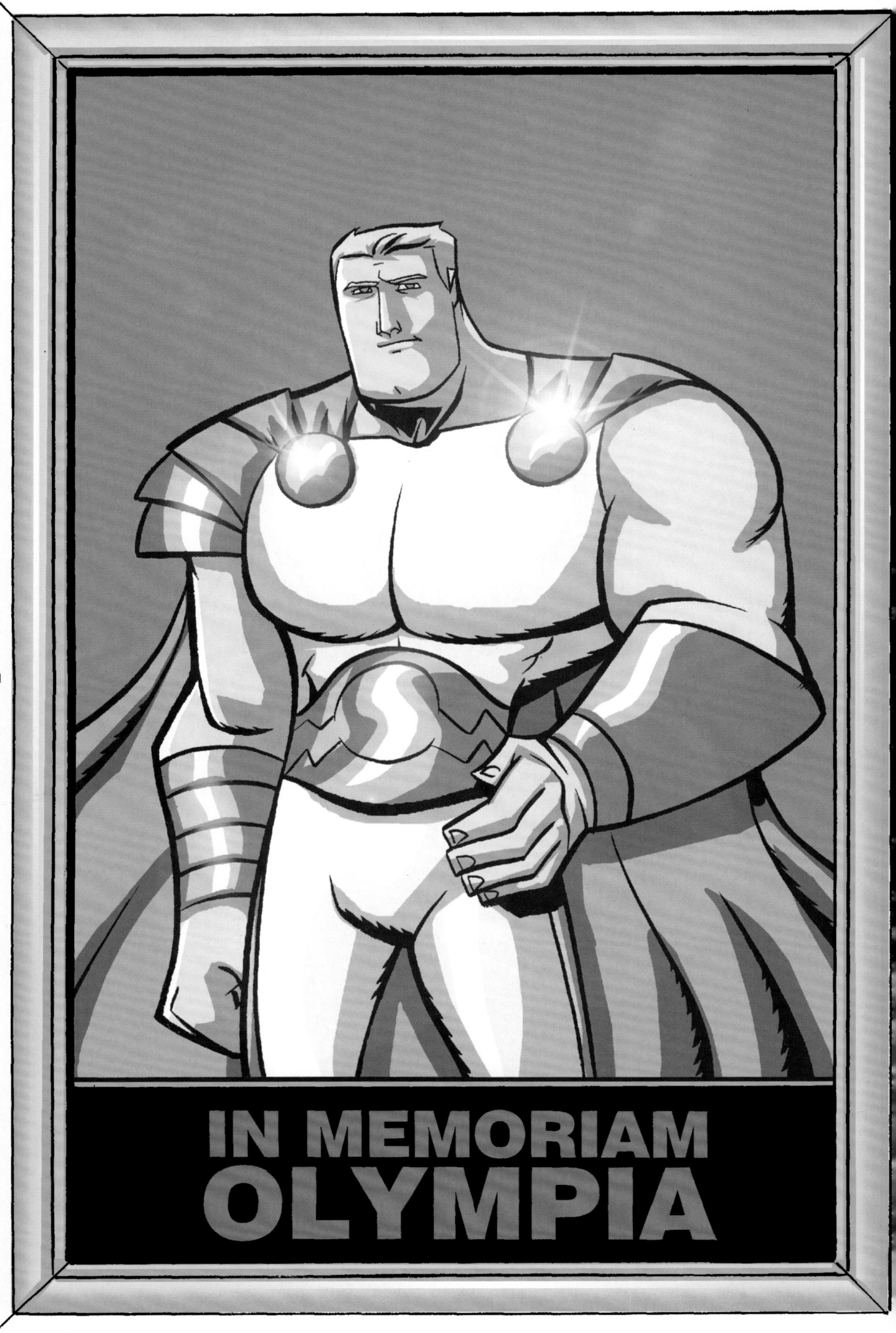
IN MEMORIAM
OLYMPIA

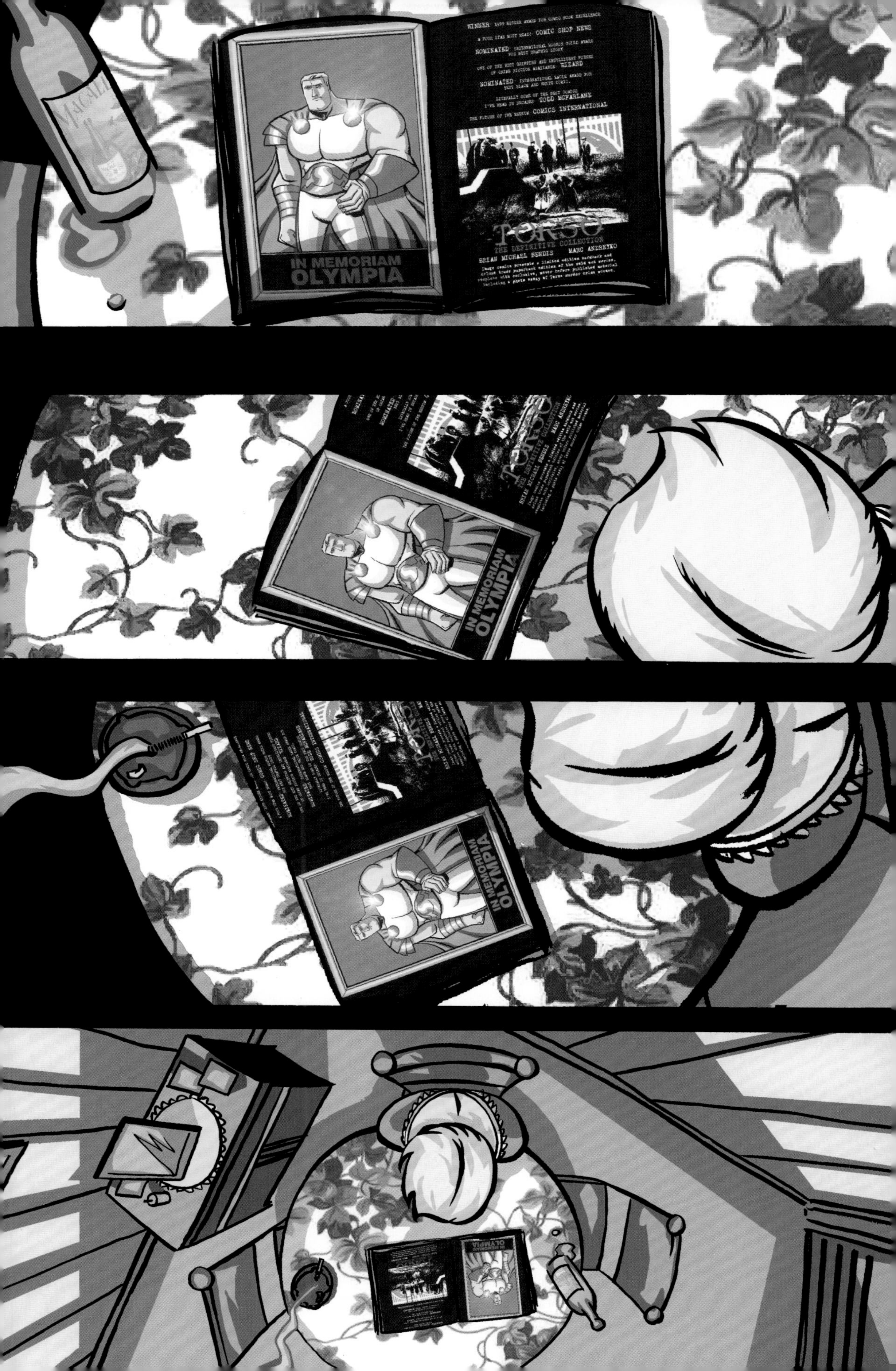
IN MEMORIAM
OLYMPIA
WINNER: 1999 EISNER AWARD FOR COMIC BOOK EXCELLENCE
A FOUR STAR MUST READ! COMIC SHOP NEWS
NOMINATED: INTERNATIONAL HORROR GUILD AWARD FOR BEST GRAPHIC STORY
ONE OF THE MOST GRIPPING AND INTELLIGENT PIECES OF CRIME FICTION AVAILABLE. WIZARD
NOMINATED: INTERNATIONAL EAGLE AWARD FOR BEST BLACK AND WHITE COMIC.
LITERALLY SOME OF THE BEST COMICS I'VE READ IN DECADES. TODD MCFARLANE
THE FUTURE OF THE MEDIUM COMICS INTERNATIONAL
TORSO
THE DEFINITIVE COLLECTION
BRIAN MICHAEL BENDIS
MARC ANDREYKO

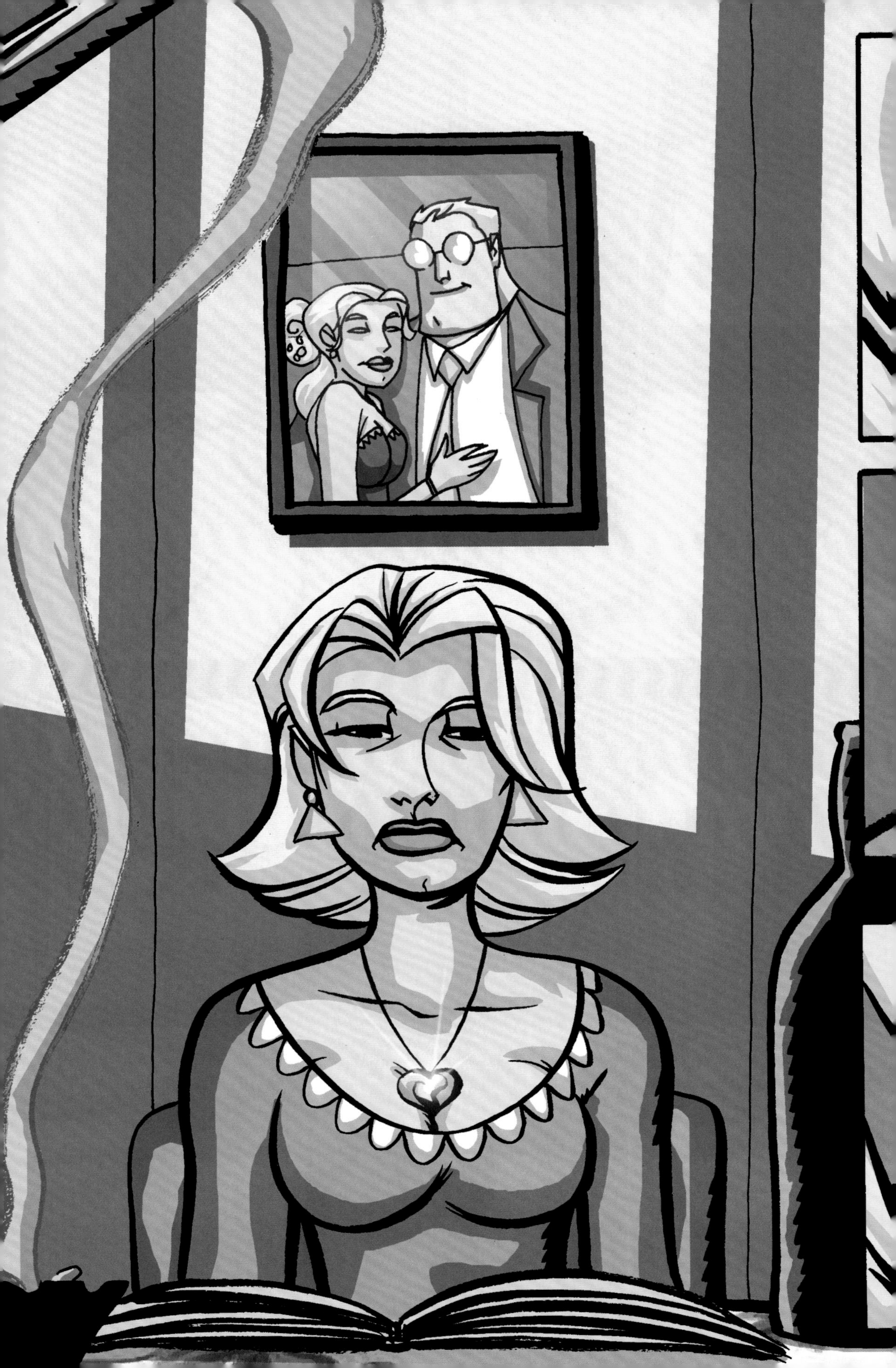

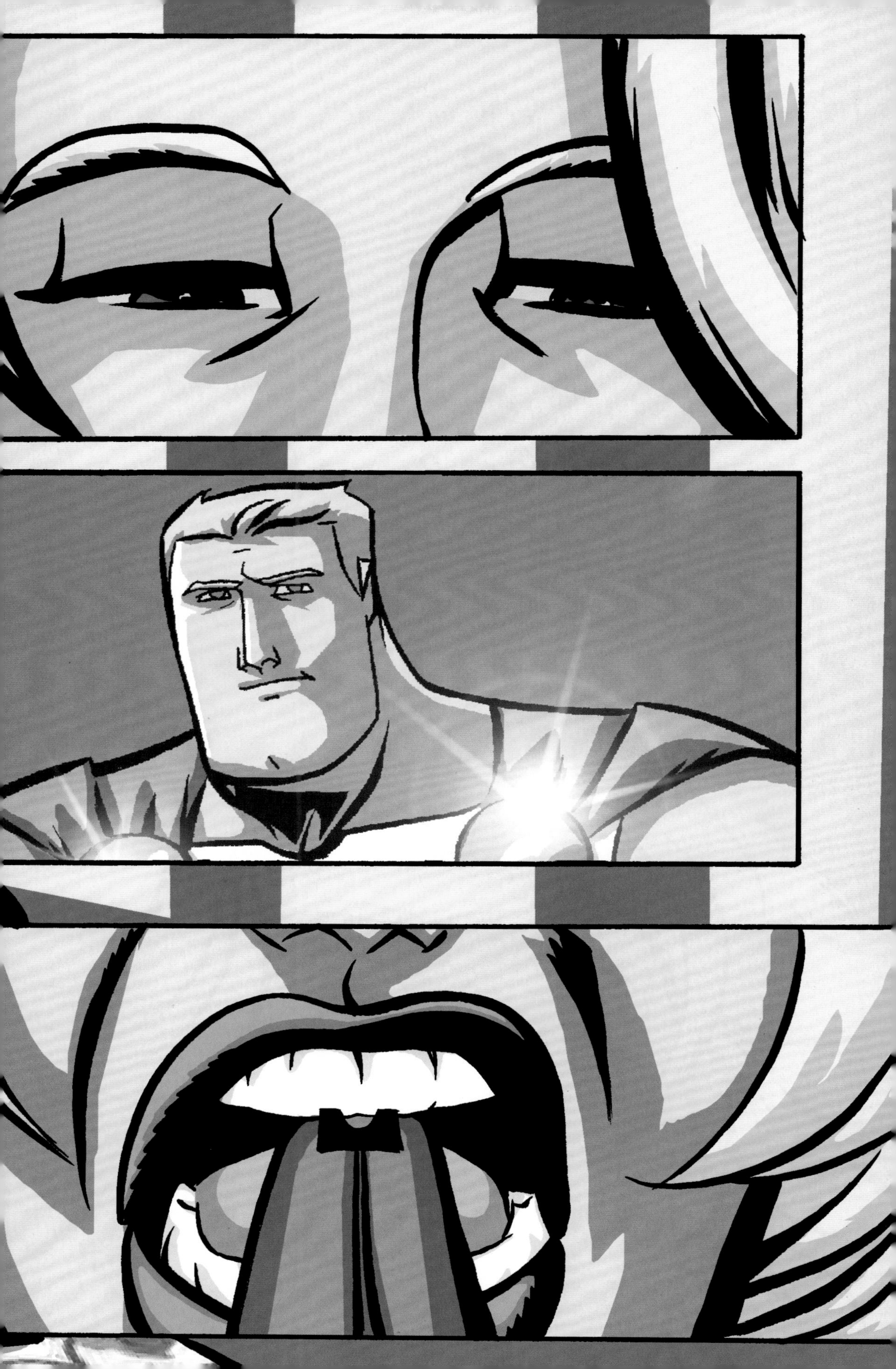

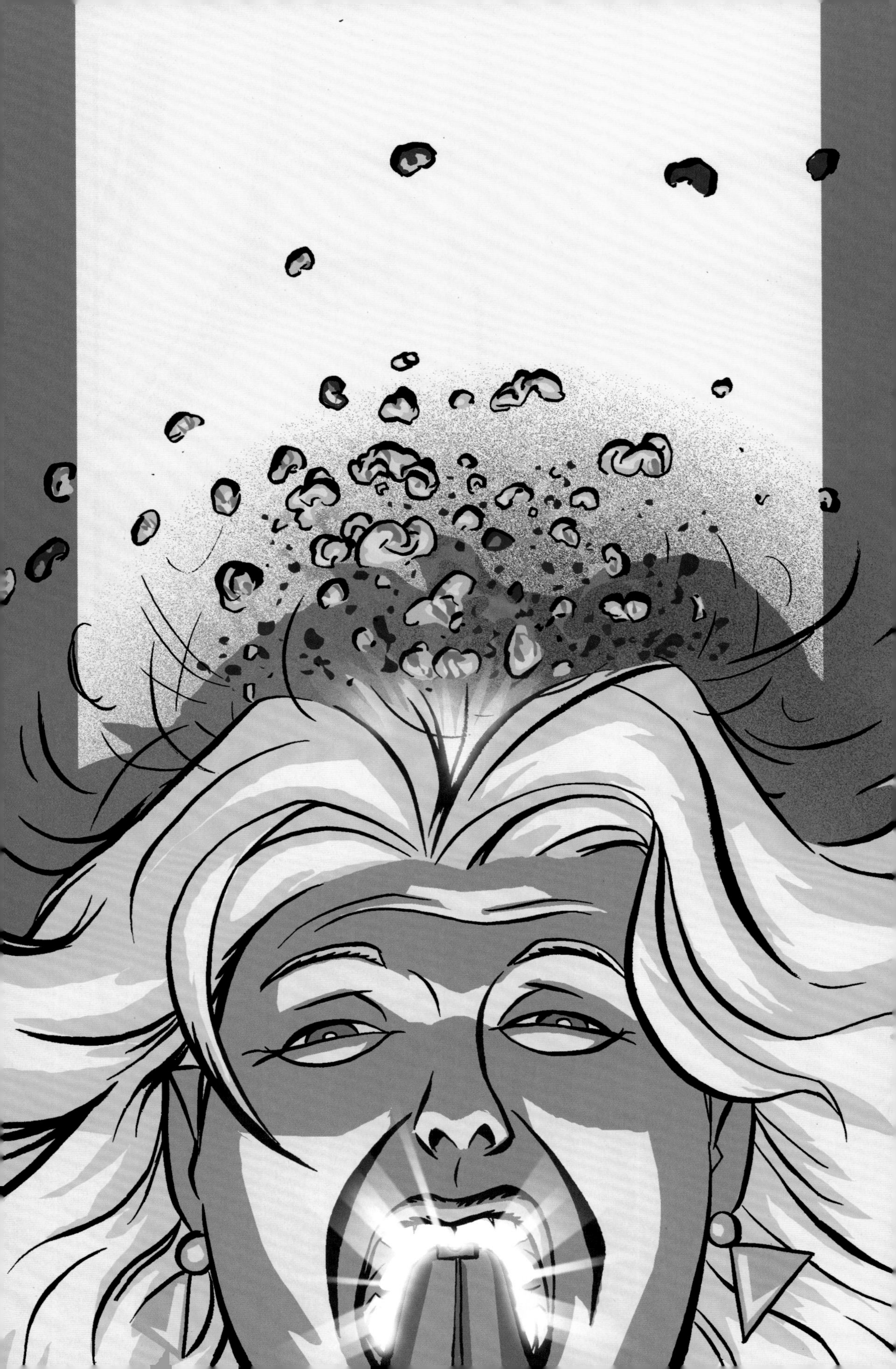

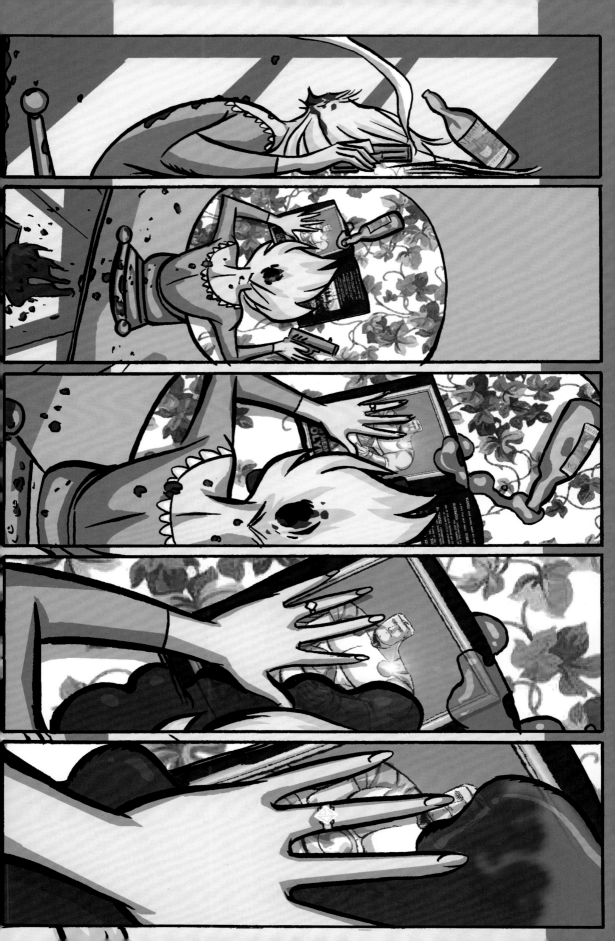

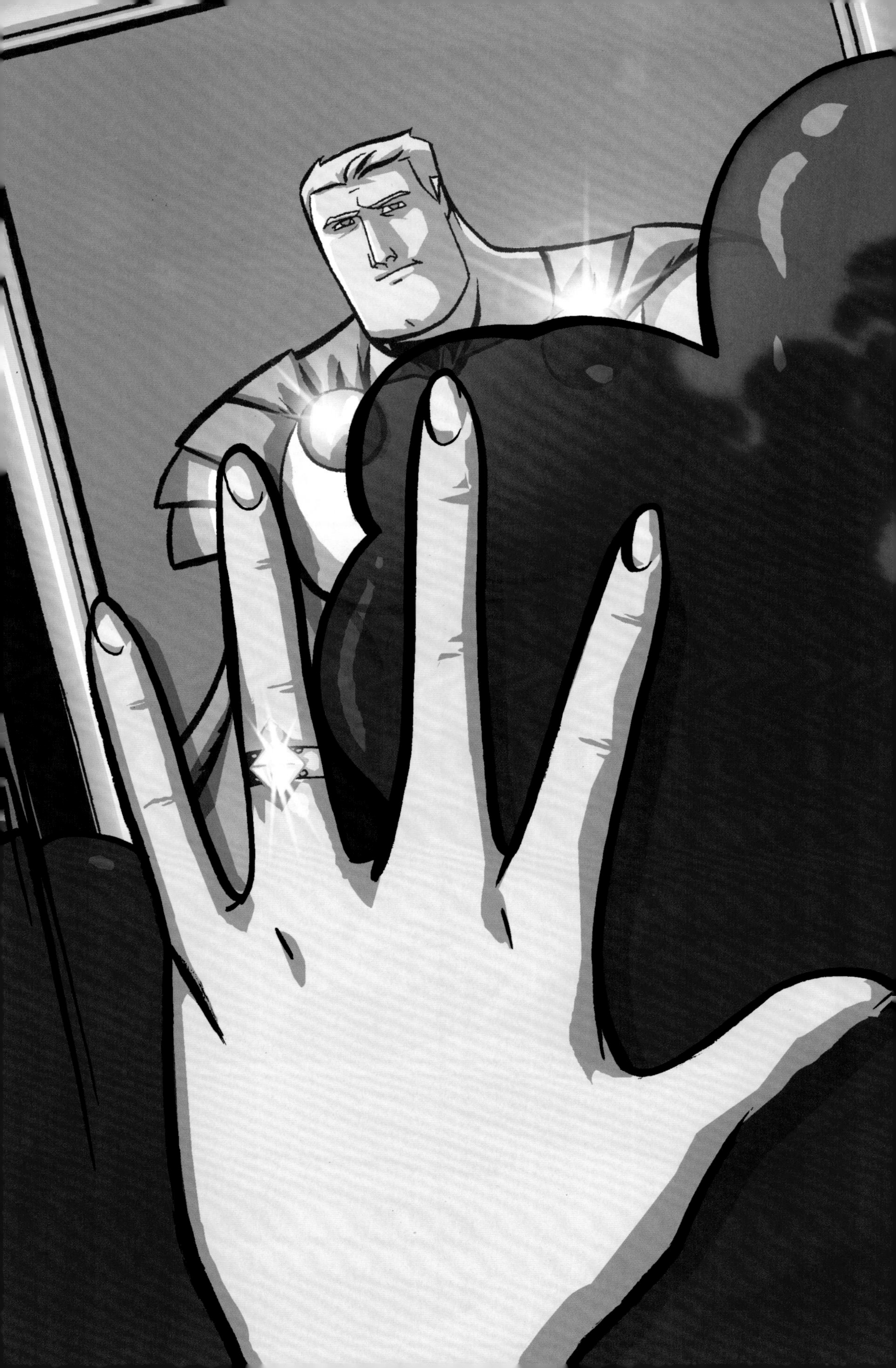

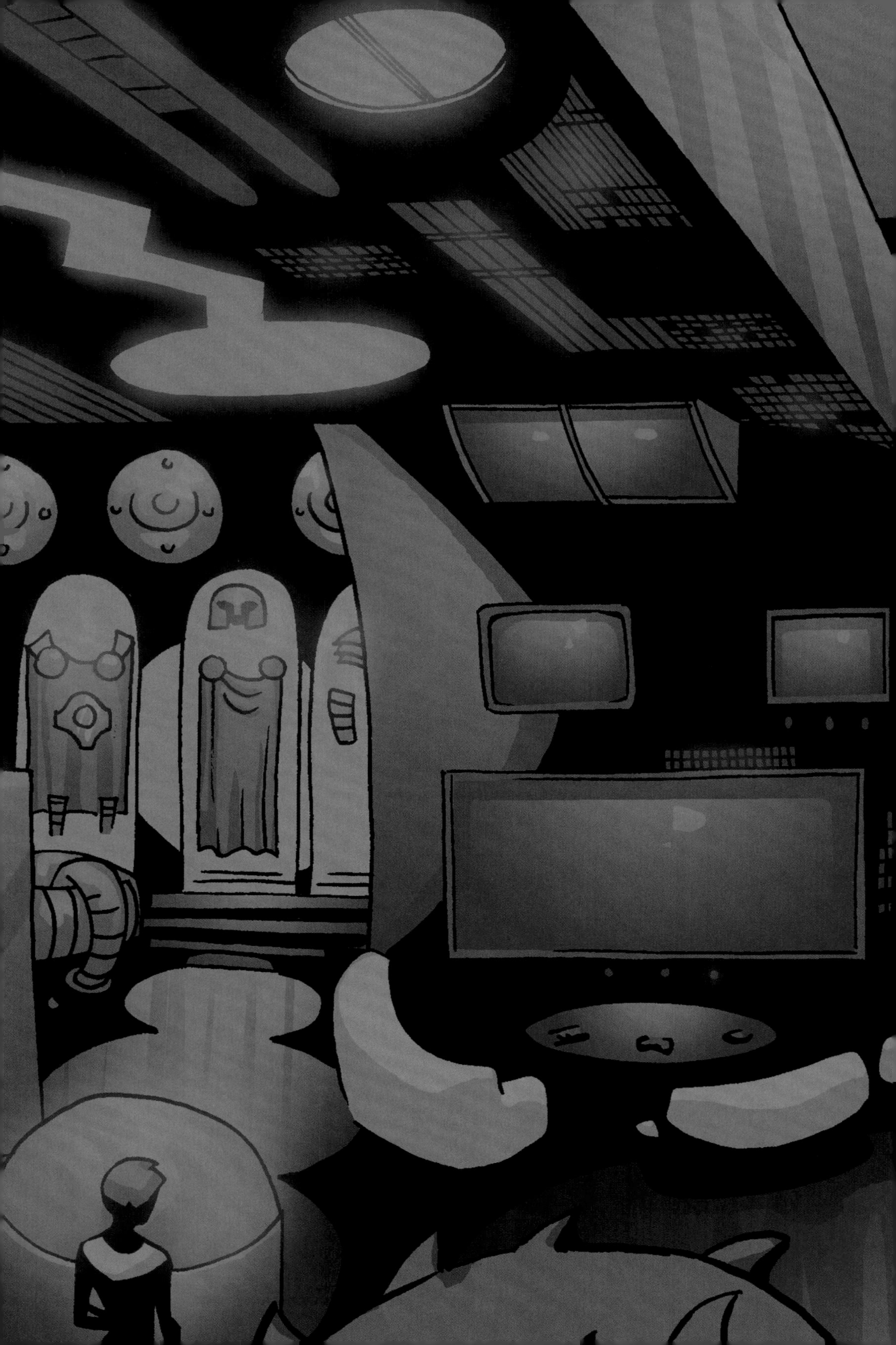

POWERS™

LITTLE DEATHS
CHAPTER 3

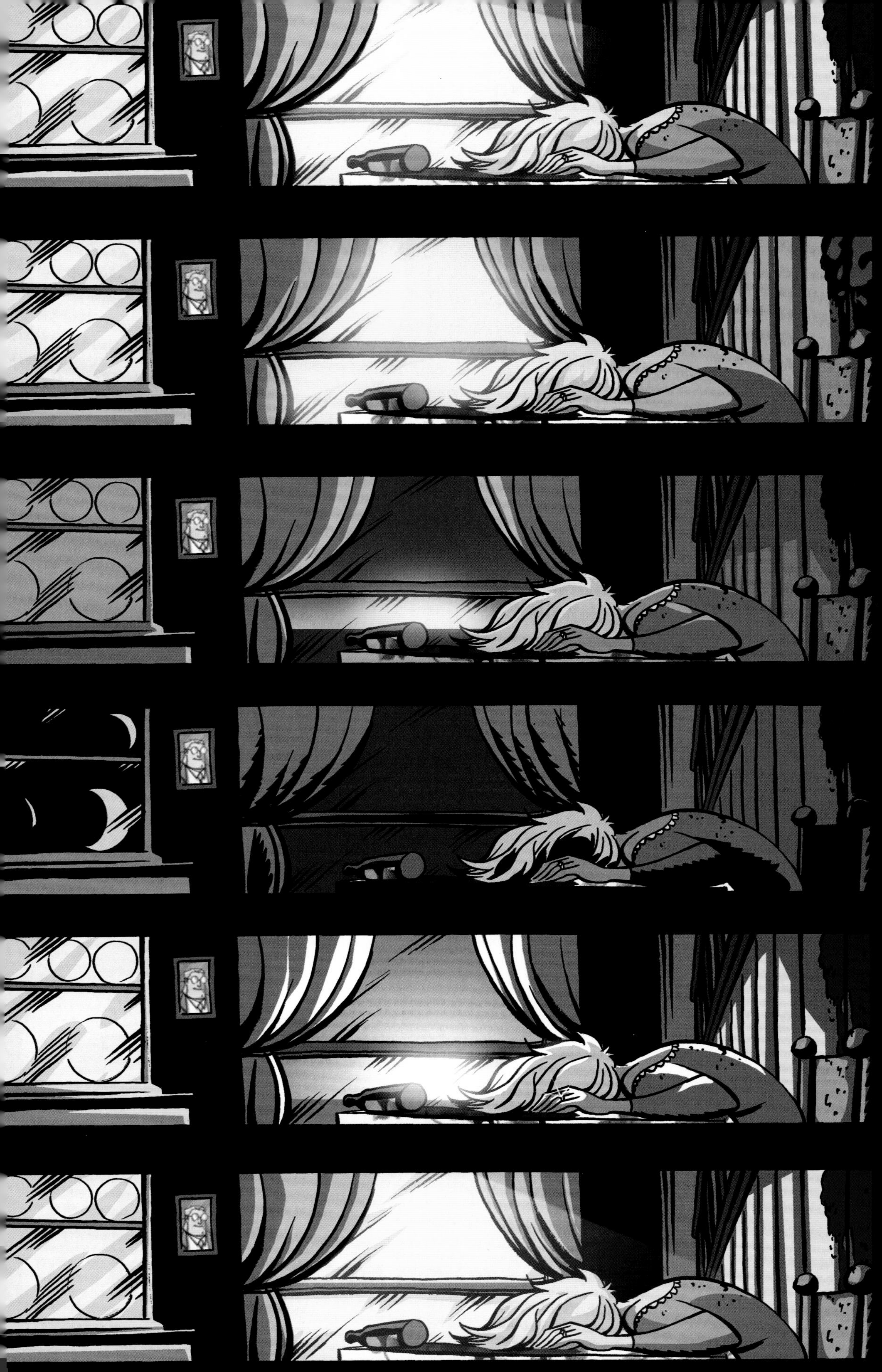

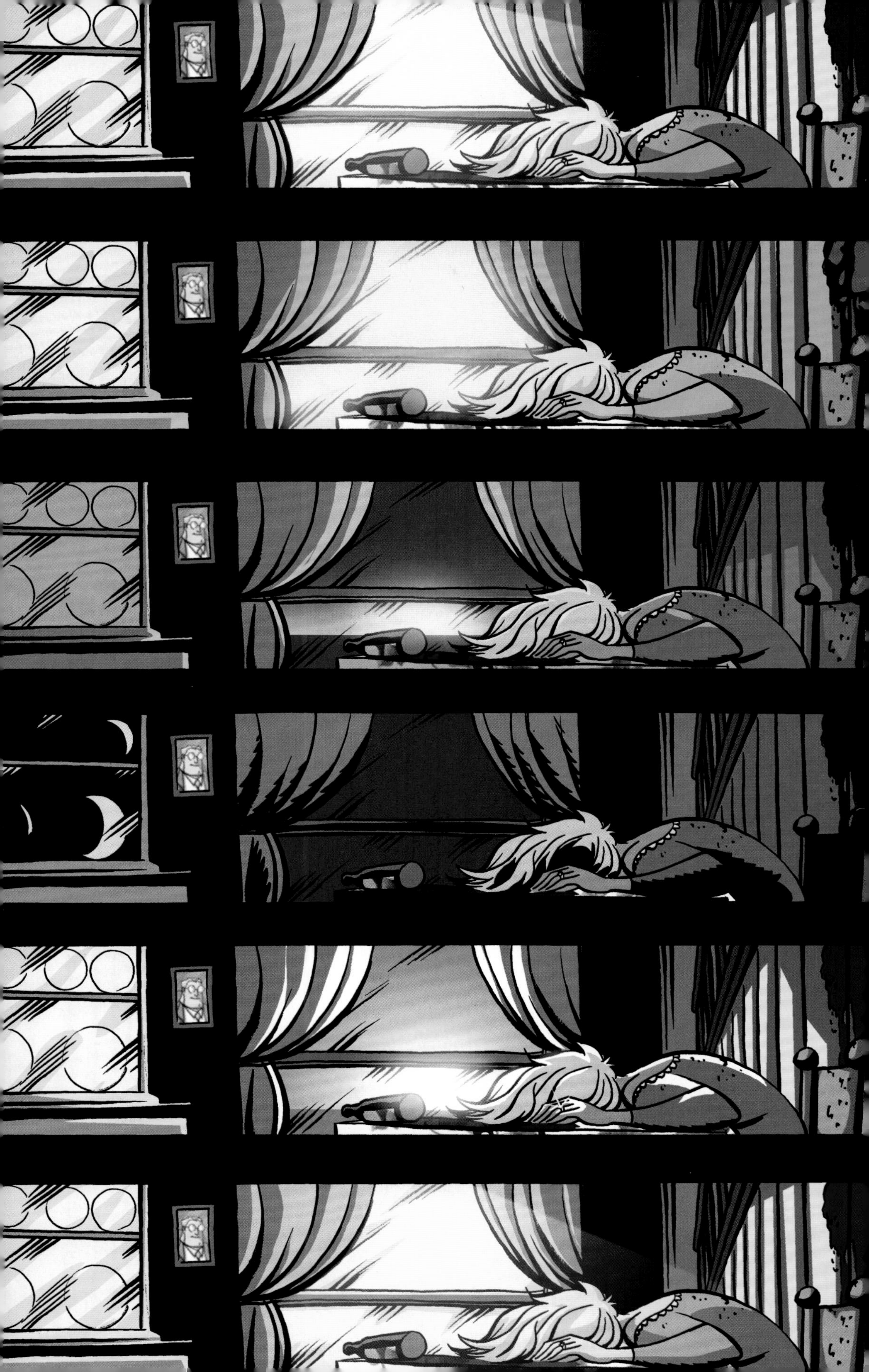

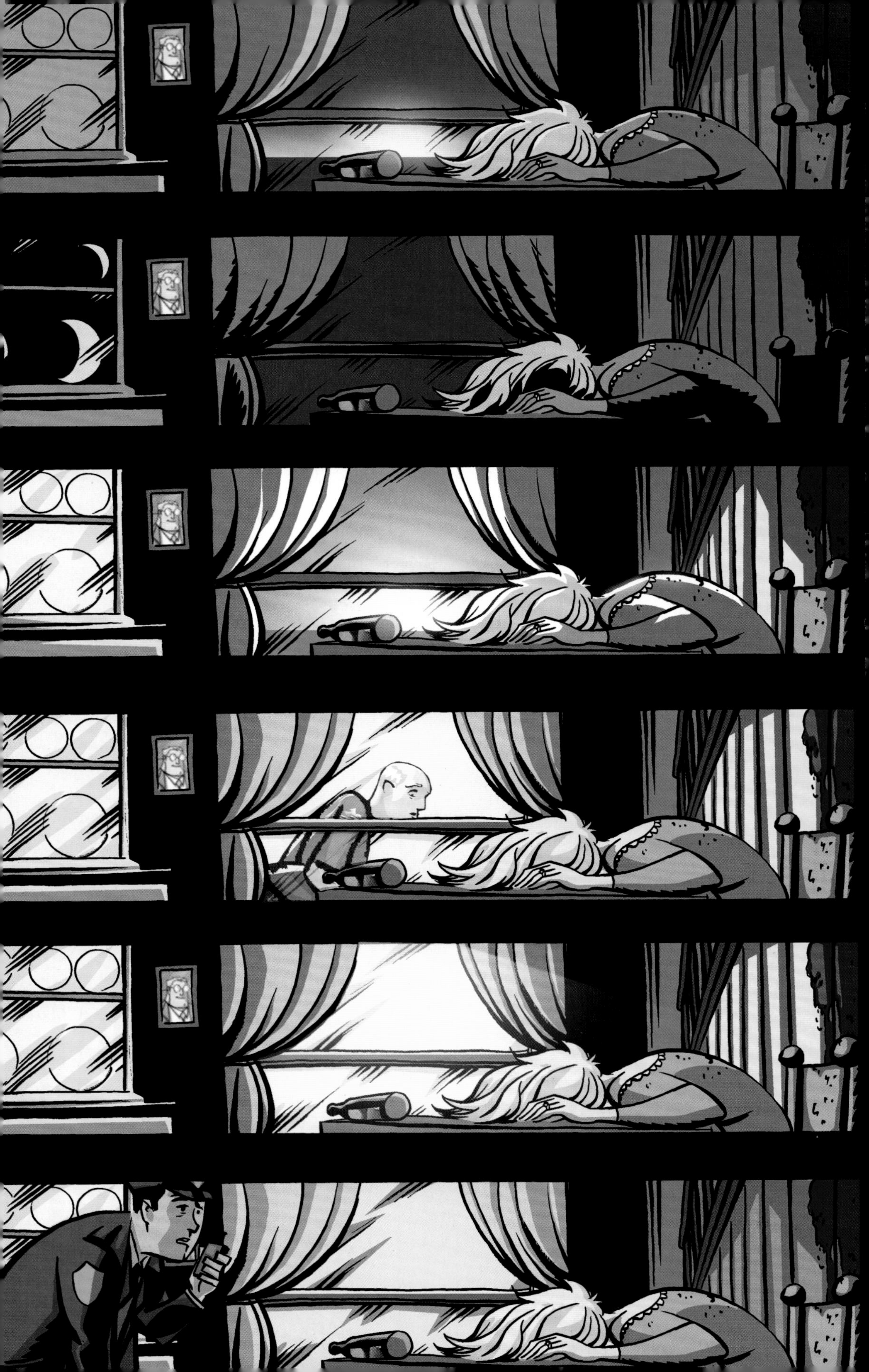

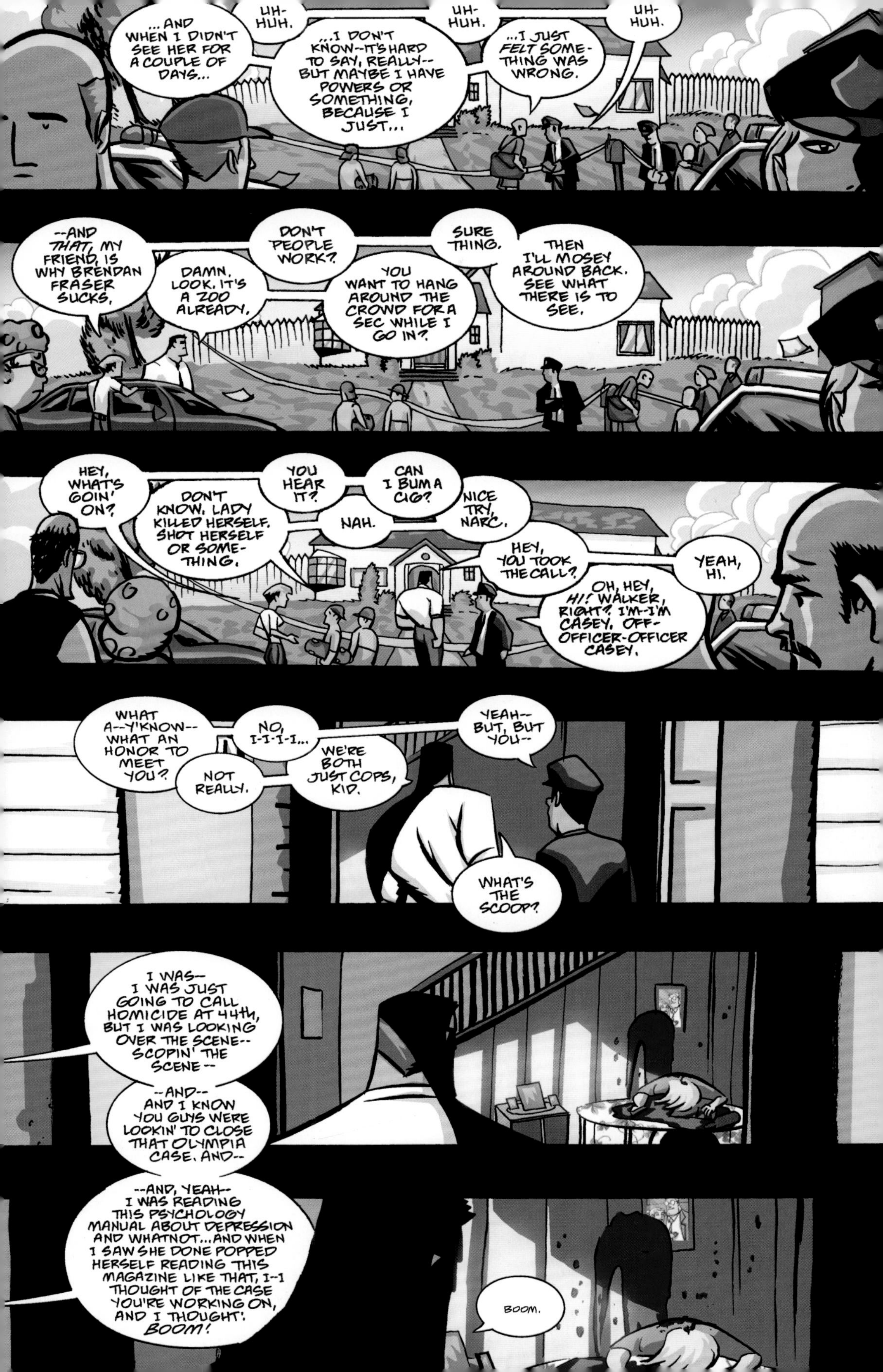
...AND WHEN I DIDN'T SEE HER FOR A COUPLE OF DAYS...
UH-HUH.
...I DON'T KNOW--IT'S HARD TO SAY, REALLY--BUT MAYBE I HAVE POWERS OR SOMETHING, BECAUSE I JUST...
UH-HUH.
...I JUST FELT SOMETHING WAS WRONG.
UH-HUH.
--AND THAT, MY FRIEND, IS WHY BRENDAN FRASER SUCKS.
DON'T PEOPLE WORK?
DAMN. LOOK. IT'S A ZOO ALREADY.
YOU WANT TO HANG AROUND THE CROWD FOR A SEC WHILE I GO IN?
SURE THING.
THEN I'LL MOSEY AROUND BACK. SEE WHAT THERE IS TO SEE.
HEY, WHAT'S GOIN' ON?
DON'T KNOW. LADY KILLED HERSELF. SHOT HERSELF OR SOMETHING.
YOU HEAR IT?
NAH.
CAN I BUM A CIG?
NICE TRY, NARC.
HEY, YOU TOOK THE CALL?
YEAH, HI.
OH, HEY, HI! WALKER, RIGHT? I'M-I'M CASEY. OFF-OFFICER-OFFICER CASEY.
WHAT A--Y'KNOW--WHAT AN HONOR TO MEET YOU?
NOT REALLY.
NO, I-I-I-I...
WE'RE BOTH JUST COPS, KID.
YEAH--BUT, BUT YOU--
WHAT'S THE SCOOP?
I WAS--I WAS JUST GOING TO CALL HOMICIDE AT 44th, BUT I WAS LOOKING OVER THE SCENE--SCOPIN' THE SCENE--
--AND--AND I KNOW YOU GUYS WERE LOOKIN' TO CLOSE THAT OLYMPIA CASE. AND--
--AND, YEAH--I WAS READING THIS PSYCHOLOGY MANUAL ABOUT DEPRESSION AND WHATNOT...AND WHEN I SAW SHE DONE POPPED HERSELF READING THIS MAGAZINE LIKE THAT, I--I THOUGHT OF THE CASE YOU'RE WORKING ON, AND I THOUGHT: BOOM!
BOOM.

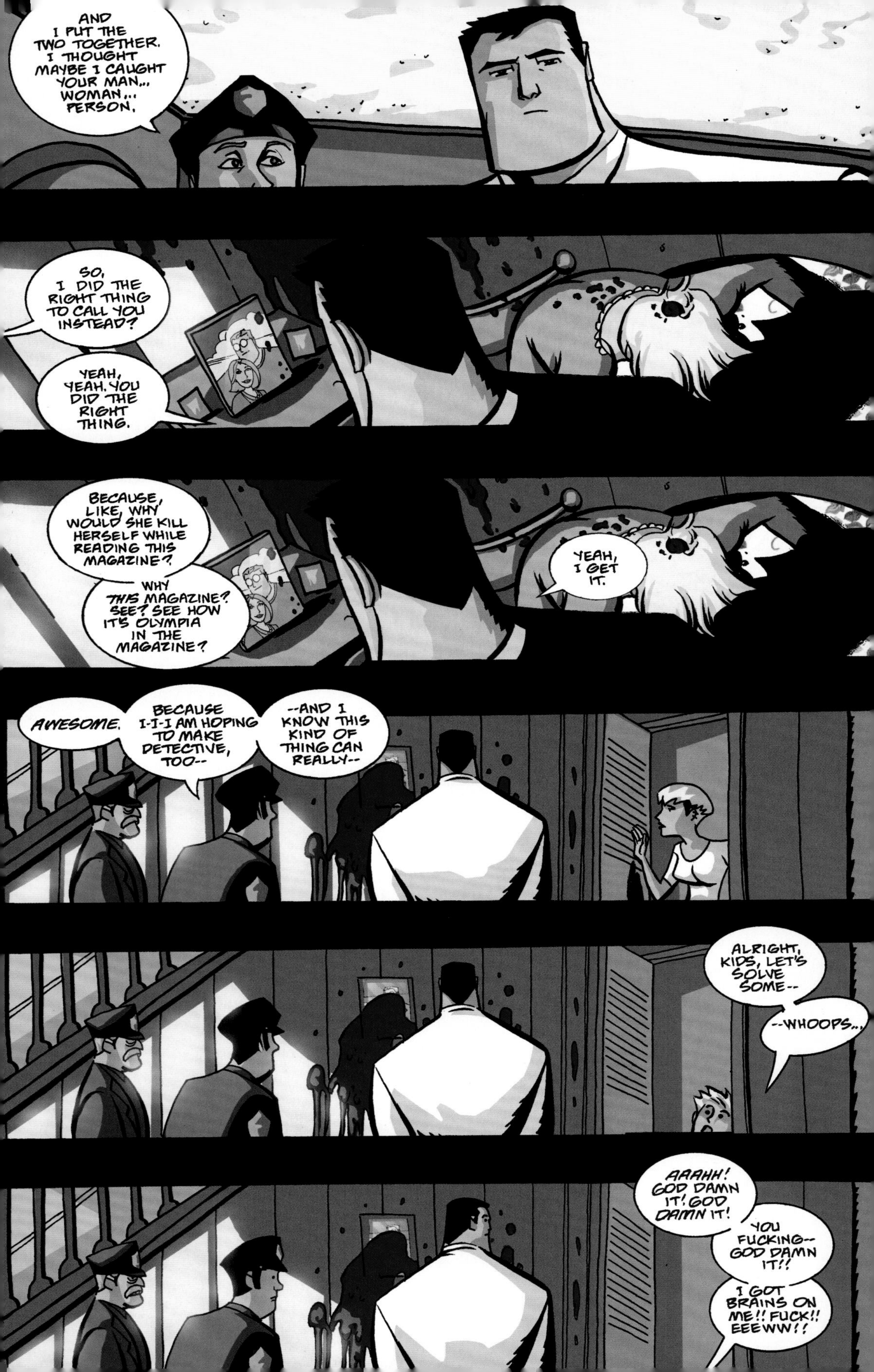
AND I PUT THE TWO TOGETHER. I THOUGHT MAYBE I CAUGHT YOUR MAN... WOMAN... PERSON.
SO, I DID THE RIGHT THING TO CALL YOU INSTEAD?
YEAH, YEAH. YOU DID THE RIGHT THING.
BECAUSE, LIKE, WHY WOULD SHE KILL HERSELF WHILE READING THIS MAGAZINE?
WHY *THIS* MAGAZINE? SEE? SEE HOW IT'S OLYMPIA IN THE MAGAZINE?
YEAH, I GET IT.
AWESOME.
BECAUSE I-I-I AM HOPING TO MAKE DETECTIVE, TOO--
--AND I KNOW THIS KIND OF THING CAN REALLY--
ALRIGHT, KIDS, LET'S SOLVE SOME--
--WHOOPS...
AAAHH! GOD DAMN IT! GOD *DAMN* IT!
YOU FUCKING-- GOD DAMN IT!!
I GOT BRAINS ON ME!! FUCK!! EEEWW!!

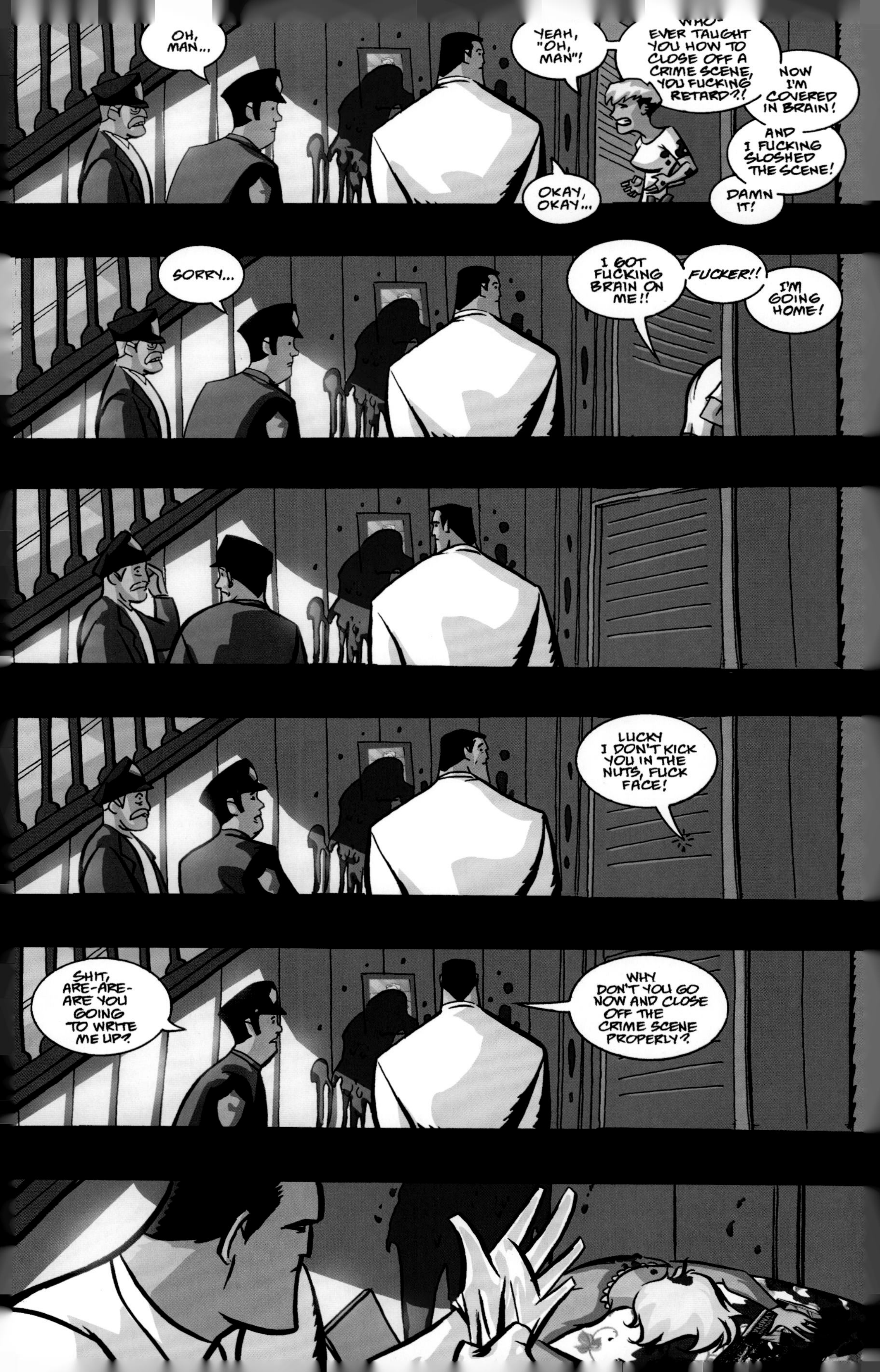
OH, MAN...
YEAH, "OH, MAN"!
EVER TAUGHT YOU HOW TO CLOSE OFF A CRIME SCENE, YOU FUCKING RETARD?!
NOW I'M COVERED IN BRAIN!
AND I FUCKING SLOSHED THE SCENE!
DAMN IT!
OKAY, OKAY...
SORRY...
I GOT FUCKING BRAIN ON ME!!
FUCKER!!
I'M GOING HOME!
LUCKY I DON'T KICK YOU IN THE NUTS, FUCK FACE!
SHIT, ARE-ARE-ARE YOU GOING TO WRITE ME UP?
WHY DON'T YOU GO NOW AND CLOSE OFF THE CRIME SCENE PROPERLY?

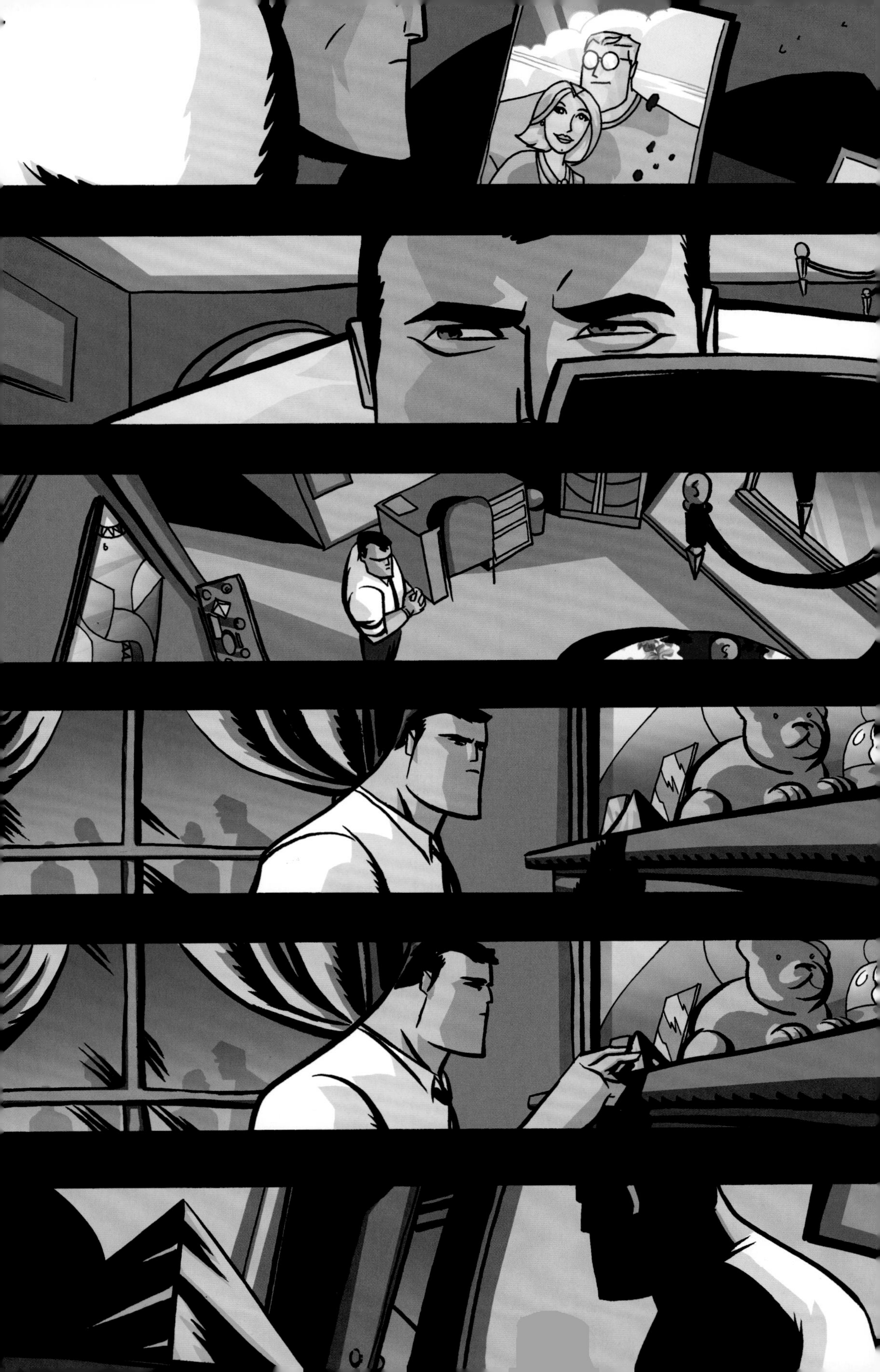

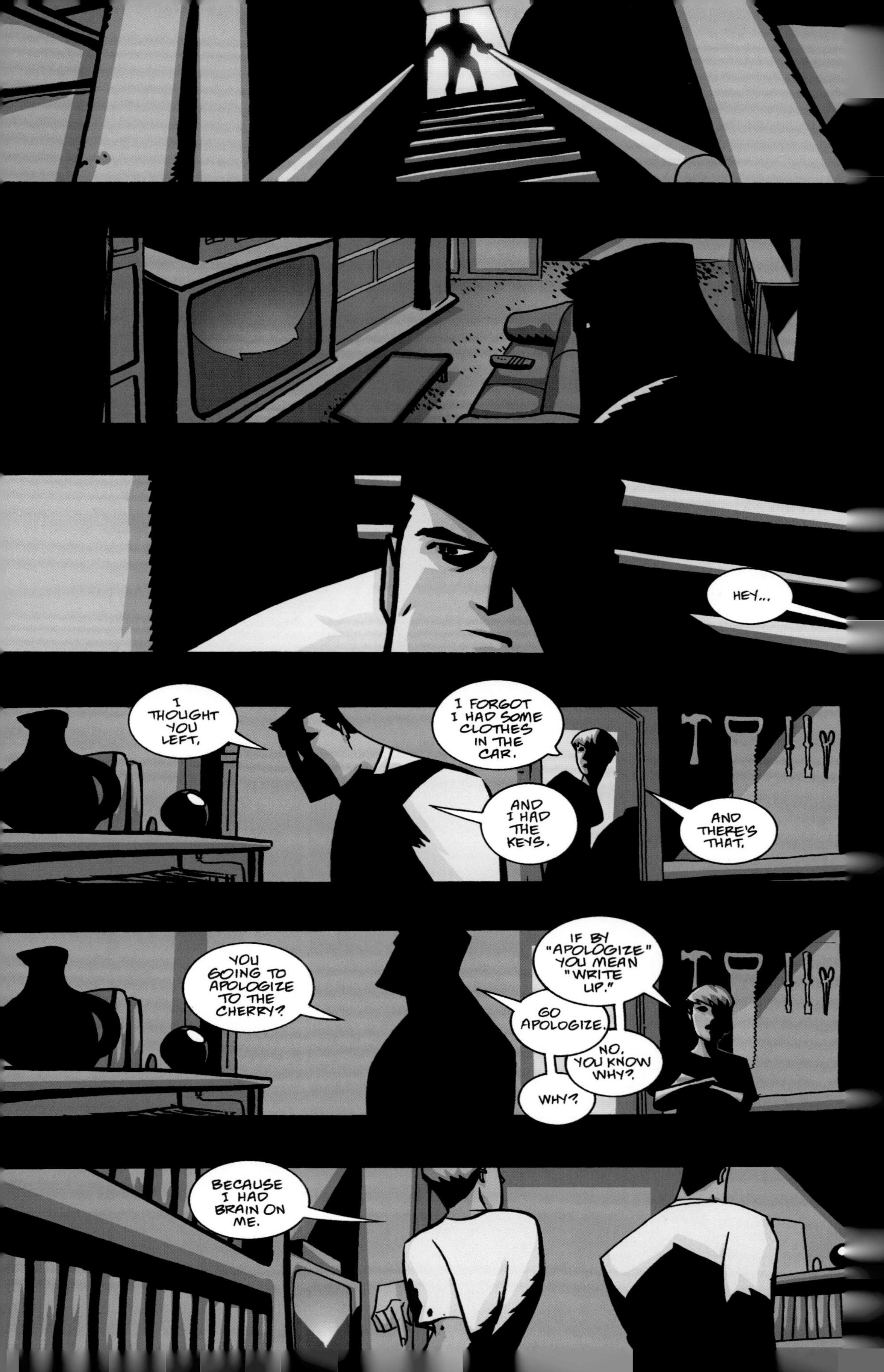
HEY...
I THOUGHT YOU LEFT.
I FORGOT I HAD SOME CLOTHES IN THE CAR.
AND I HAD THE KEYS.
AND THERE'S THAT.
YOU GOING TO APOLOGIZE TO THE CHERRY?
IF BY "APOLOGIZE" YOU MEAN "WRITE UP."
GO APOLOGIZE.
NO. YOU KNOW WHY?
WHY?
BECAUSE I HAD BRAIN ON ME.

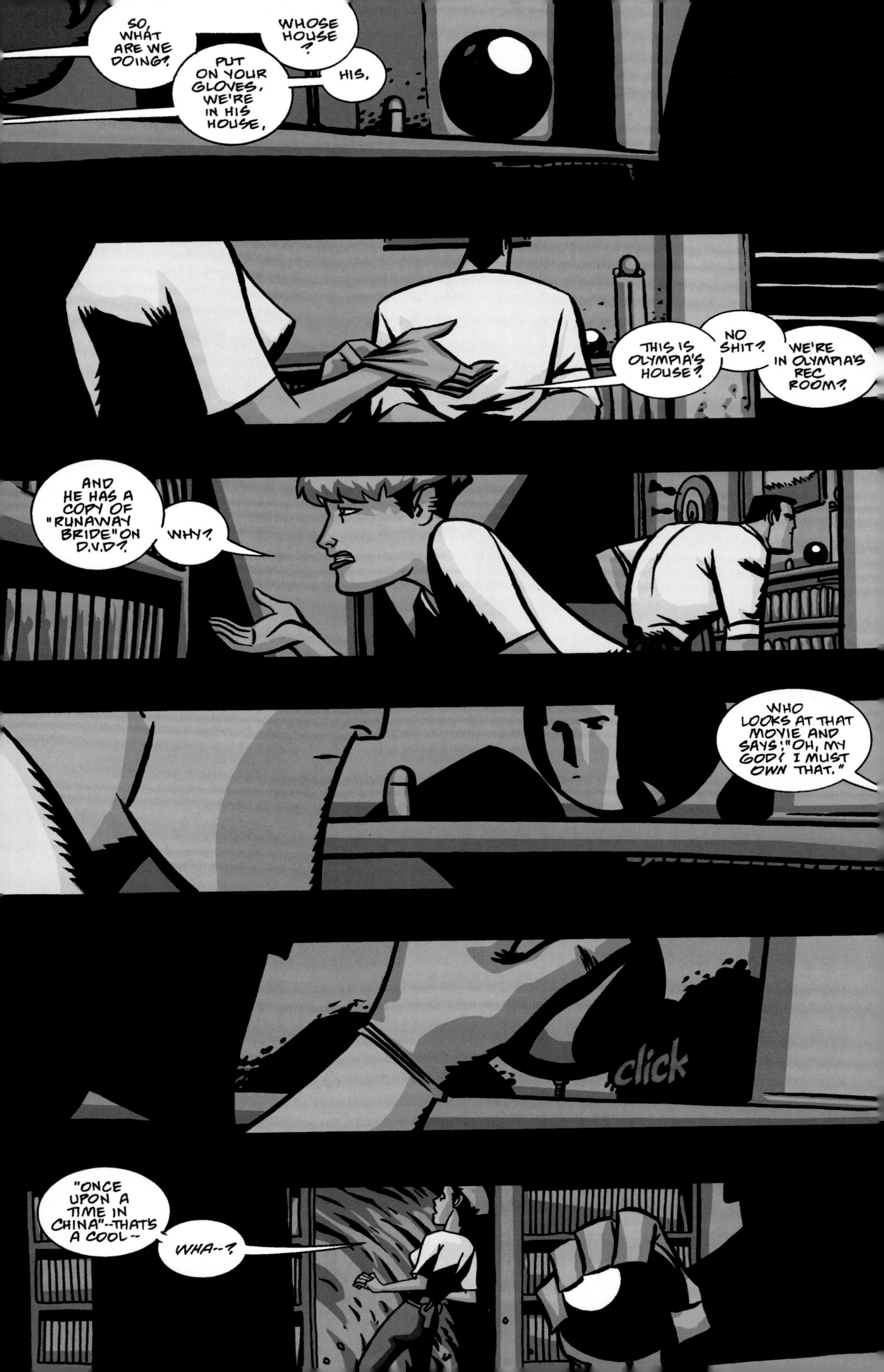
SO, WHAT ARE WE DOING?
WHOSE HOUSE?
PUT ON YOUR GLOVES, WE'RE IN HIS HOUSE.
HIS.
THIS IS OLYMPIA'S HOUSE?
NO SHIT?
WE'RE IN OLYMPIA'S REC ROOM?
AND HE HAS A COPY OF "RUNAWAY BRIDE" ON D.V.D?
WHY?
WHO LOOKS AT THAT MOVIE AND SAYS; "OH, MY GOD! I MUST OWN THAT."
click
"ONCE UPON A TIME IN CHINA"--THAT'S A COOL--
WHA--?

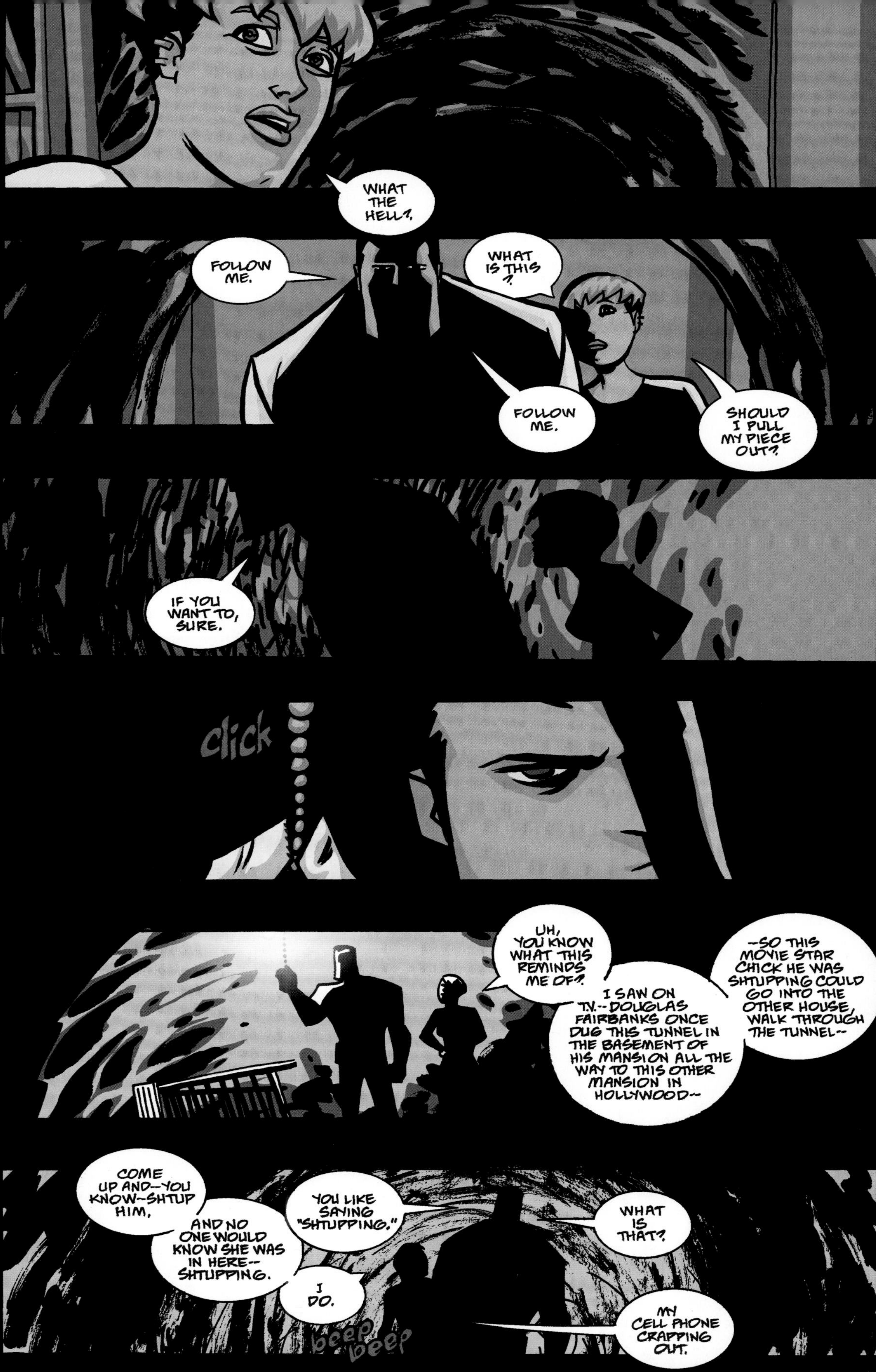
WHAT THE HELL?
FOLLOW ME.
WHAT IS THIS ?
FOLLOW ME.
SHOULD I PULL MY PIECE OUT?
IF YOU WANT TO, SURE.
click
UH, YOU KNOW WHAT THIS REMINDS ME OF?
I SAW ON T.V.--DOUGLAS FAIRBANKS ONCE DUG THIS TUNNEL IN THE BASEMENT OF HIS MANSION ALL THE WAY TO THIS OTHER MANSION IN HOLLYWOOD--
--SO THIS MOVIE STAR CHICK HE WAS SHTUPPING COULD GO INTO THE OTHER HOUSE, WALK THROUGH THE TUNNEL--
COME UP AND--YOU KNOW--SHTUP HIM,
AND NO ONE WOULD KNOW SHE WAS IN HERE--SHTUPPING.
YOU LIKE SAYING "SHTUPPING."
I DO.
WHAT IS THAT?
MY CELL PHONE CRAPPING OUT.
beep beep

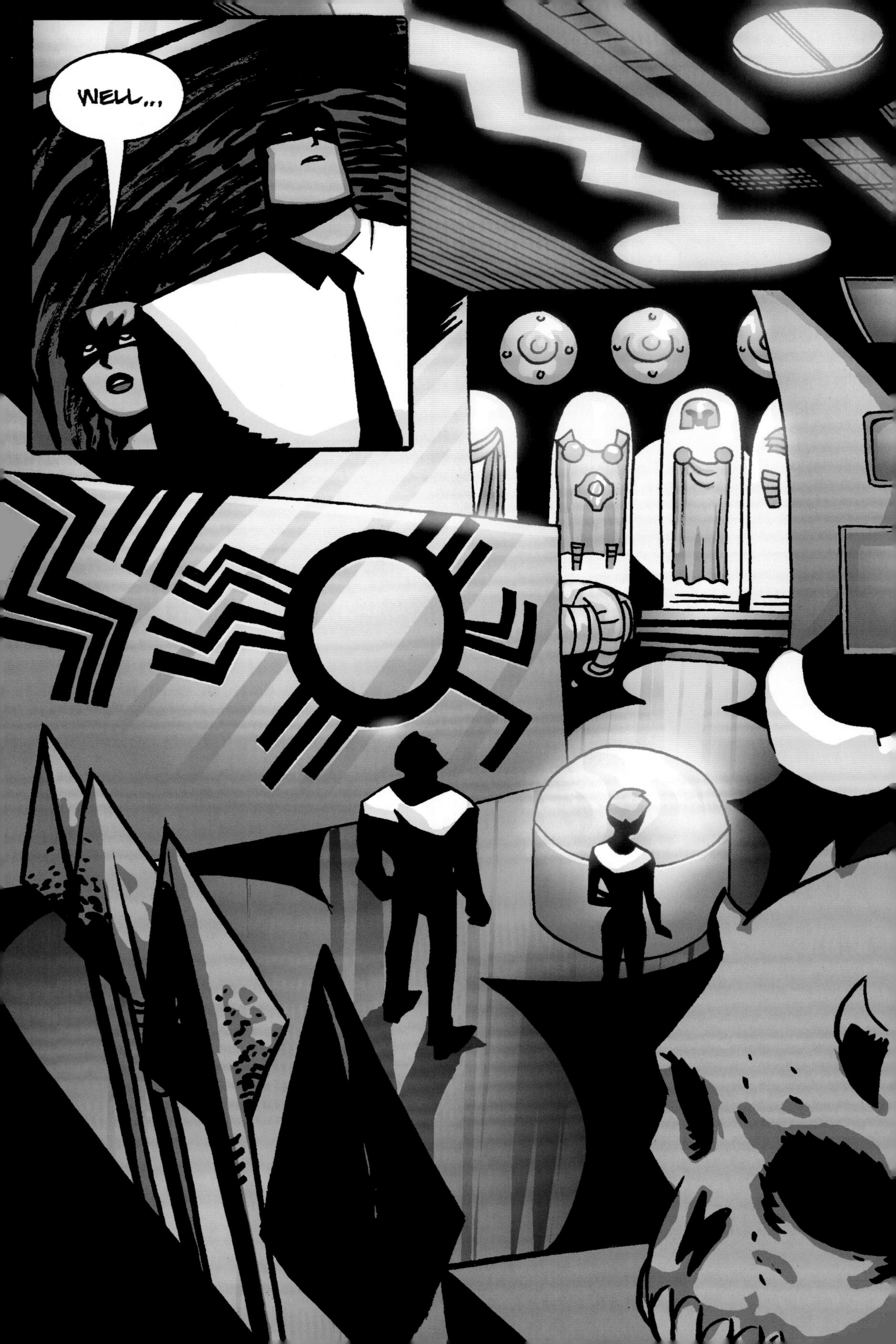
WELL...

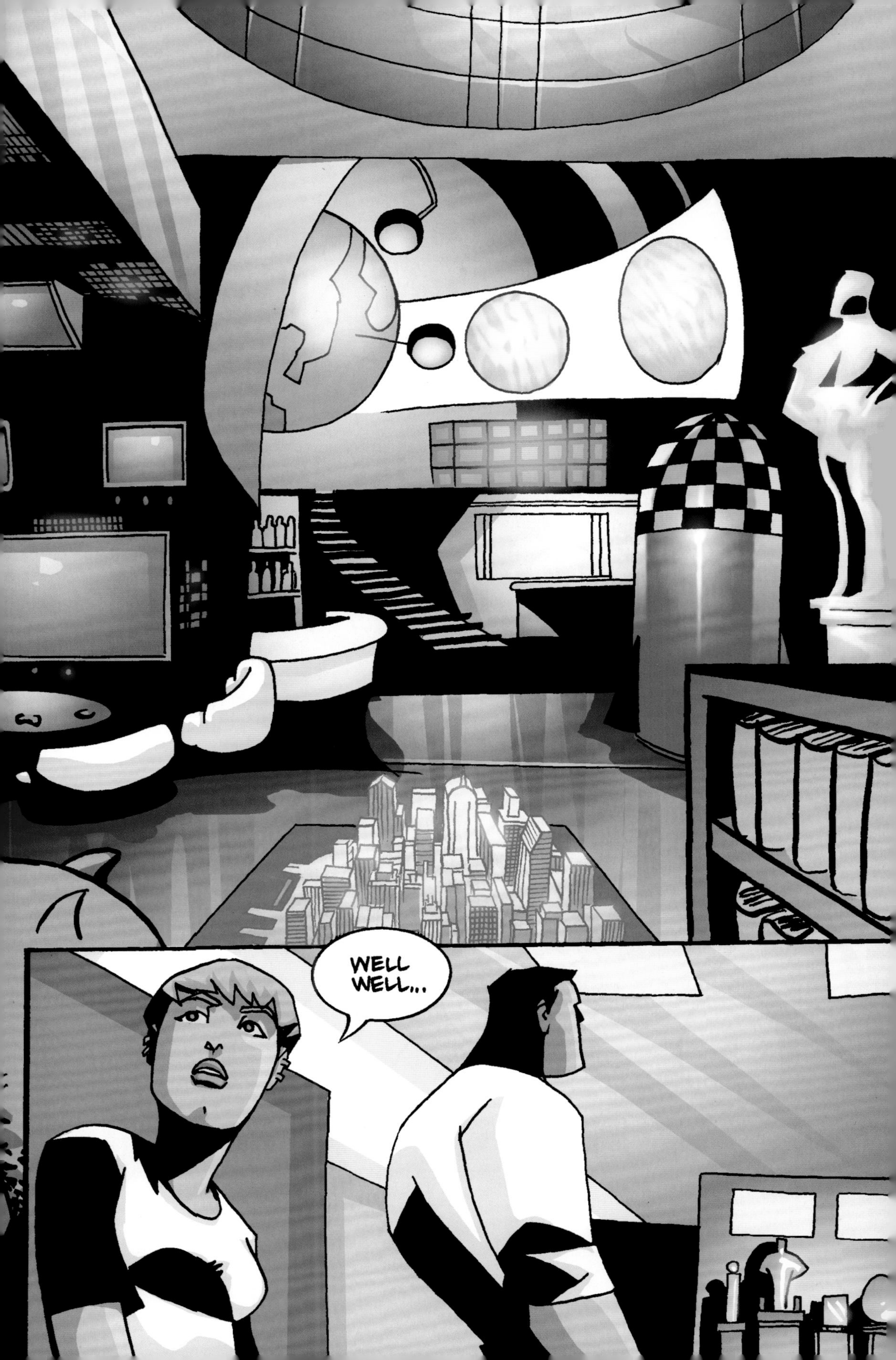
WELL WELL...

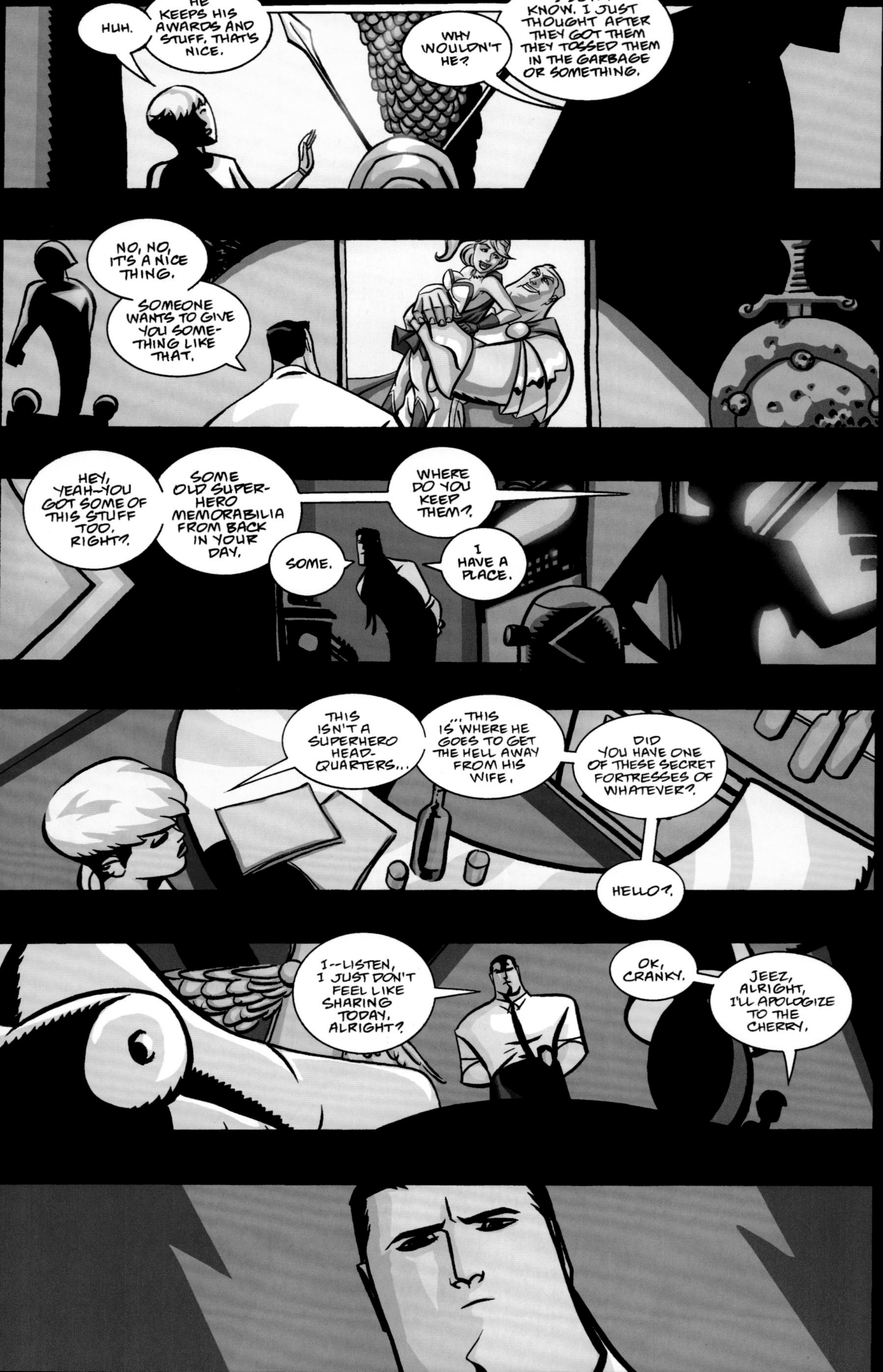
HUH.
HE KEEPS HIS AWARDS AND STUFF. THAT'S NICE.
WHY WOULDN'T HE?
I DON'T KNOW. I JUST THOUGHT AFTER THEY GOT THEM THEY TOSSED THEM IN THE GARBAGE OR SOMETHING.
NO, NO, IT'S A NICE THING.
SOMEONE WANTS TO GIVE YOU SOMETHING LIKE THAT.
HEY, YEAH--YOU GOT SOME OF THIS STUFF TOO, RIGHT?.
SOME OLD SUPERHERO MEMORABILIA FROM BACK IN YOUR DAY.
WHERE DO YOU KEEP THEM?.
SOME.
I HAVE A PLACE.
THIS ISN'T A SUPERHERO HEADQUARTERS...
...THIS IS WHERE HE GOES TO GET THE HELL AWAY FROM HIS WIFE.
DID YOU HAVE ONE OF THESE SECRET FORTRESSES OF WHATEVER?.
HELLO?.
I--LISTEN, I JUST DON'T FEEL LIKE SHARING TODAY, ALRIGHT?
OK, CRANKY.
JEEZ, ALRIGHT, I'LL APOLOGIZE TO THE CHERRY.

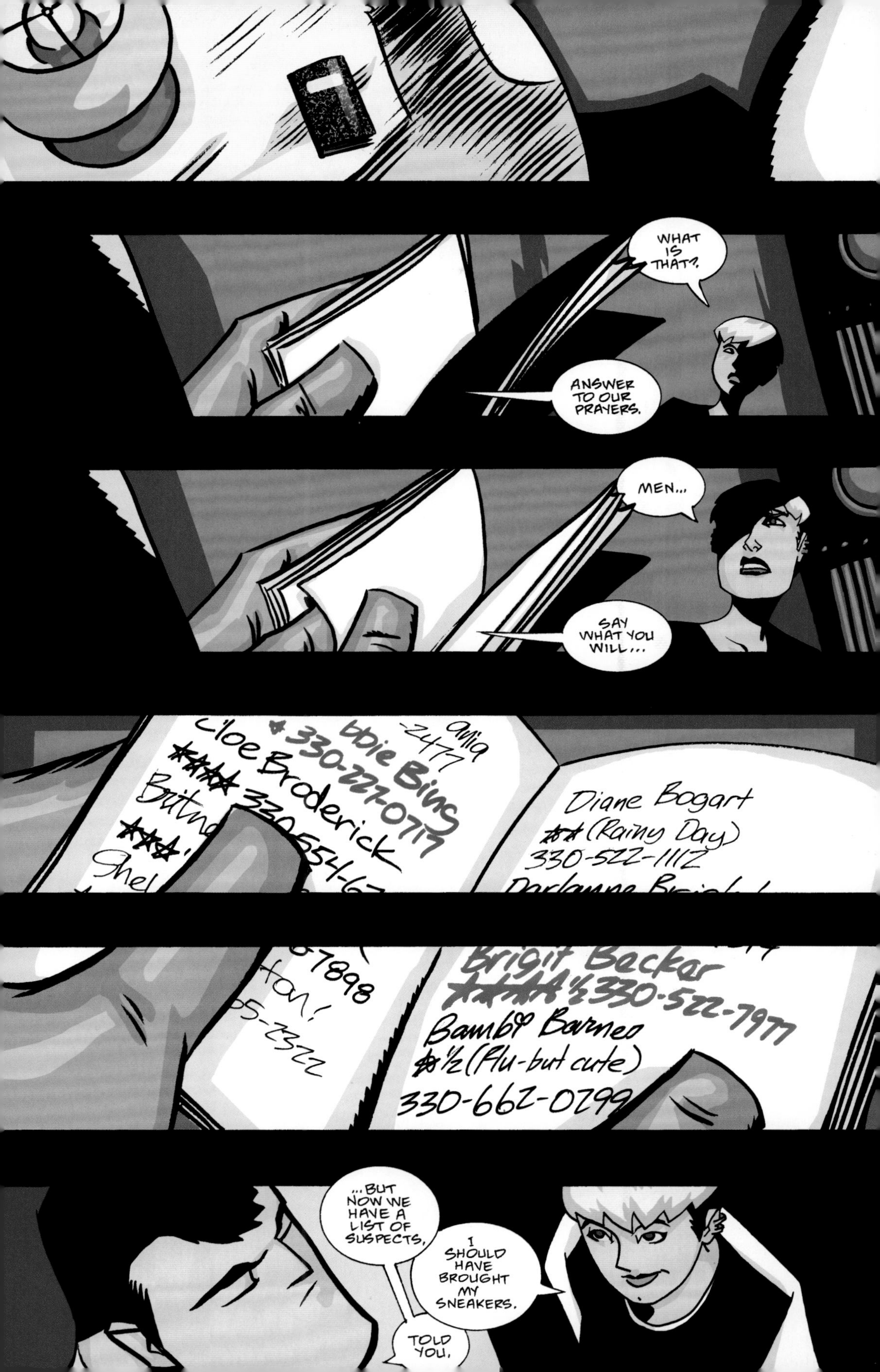
WHAT IS THAT?
ANSWER TO OUR PRAYERS.
MEN...
SAY WHAT YOU WILL...
Cloe Broderick
Diane Bogart
(Rainy Day)
330-522-1112
Brigit Becker
330-522-7977
(Flu-but cute)
330-662-0299
...BUT NOW WE HAVE A LIST OF SUSPECTS,
I SHOULD HAVE BROUGHT MY SNEAKERS.
TOLD YOU.

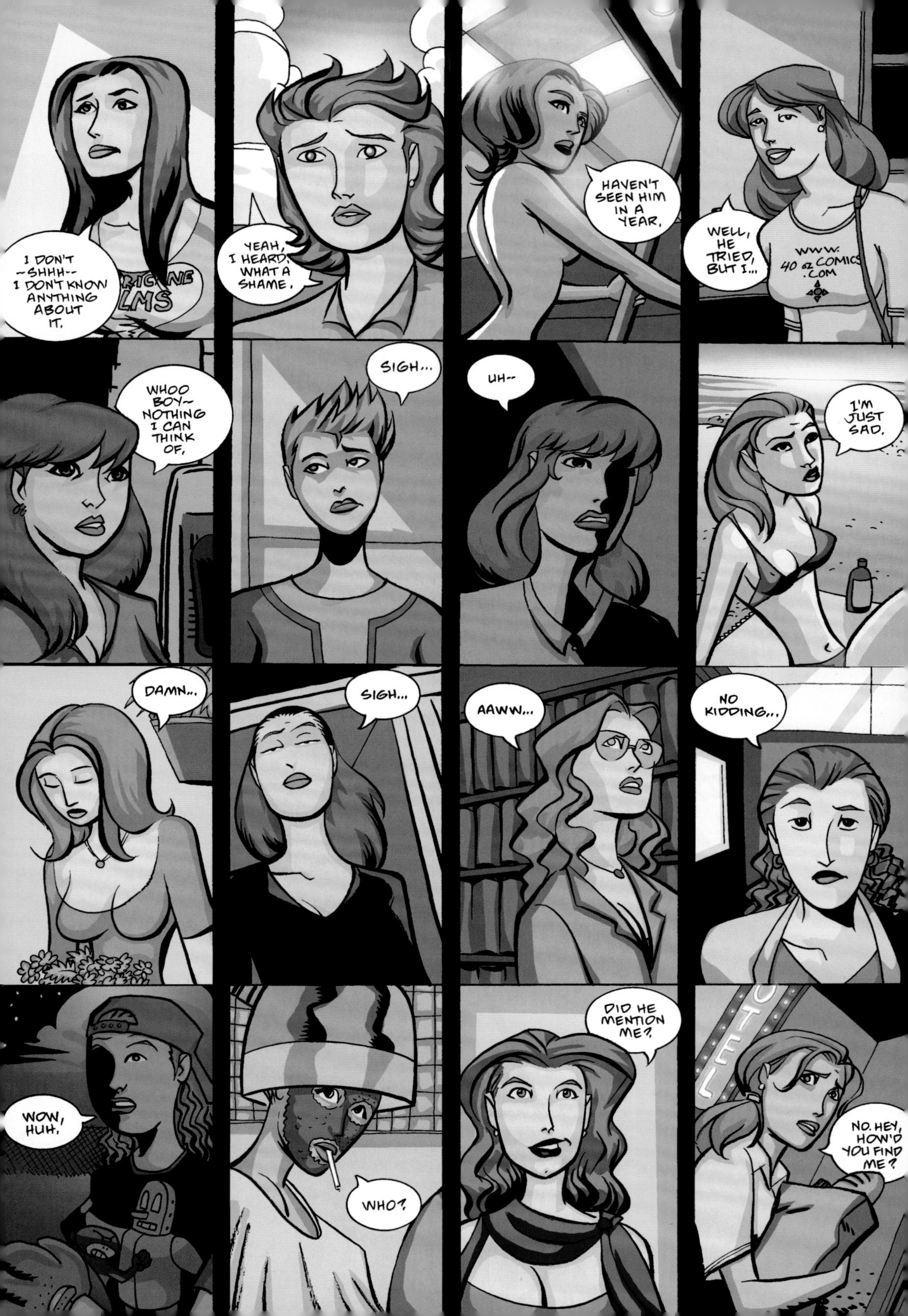
I DON'T --SHHH-- I DON'T KNOW ANYTHING ABOUT IT.
YEAH, I HEARD. WHAT A SHAME.
HAVEN'T SEEN HIM IN A YEAR.
WELL, HE TRIED, BUT I...
WWW. 40 oz COMICS .COM
WHOO BOY-- NOTHING I CAN THINK OF.
SIGH...
UH--
I'M JUST SAD.
DAMN...
SIGH...
AAWW...
NO KIDDING...
WOW, HUH.
WHO?
DID HE MENTION ME?
NO. HEY, HOW'D YOU FIND ME?

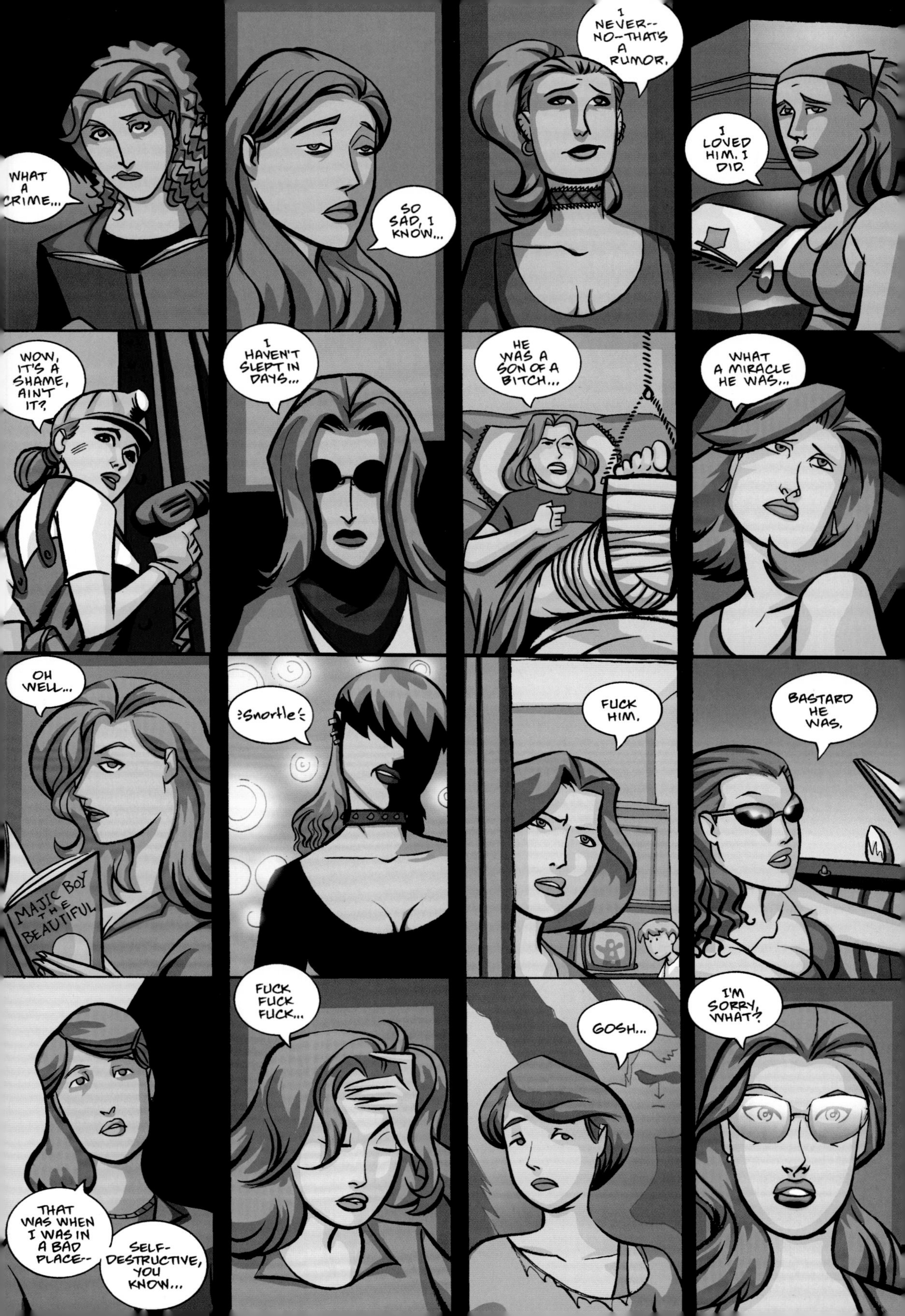
WHAT A CRIME...
SO SAD, I KNOW...
I NEVER-- NO--THAT'S A RUMOR.
I LOVED HIM. I DID.
WOW, IT'S A SHAME, AIN'T IT?
I HAVEN'T SLEPT IN DAYS...
HE WAS A SON OF A BITCH...
WHAT A MIRACLE HE WAS...
OH WELL...
MAJIC BOY THE BEAUTIFUL
Snortle
FUCK HIM.
BASTARD HE WAS.
THAT WAS WHEN I WAS IN A BAD PLACE--
SELF-DESTRUCTIVE, YOU KNOW...
FUCK FUCK FUCK...
GOSH...
I'M SORRY, WHAT?

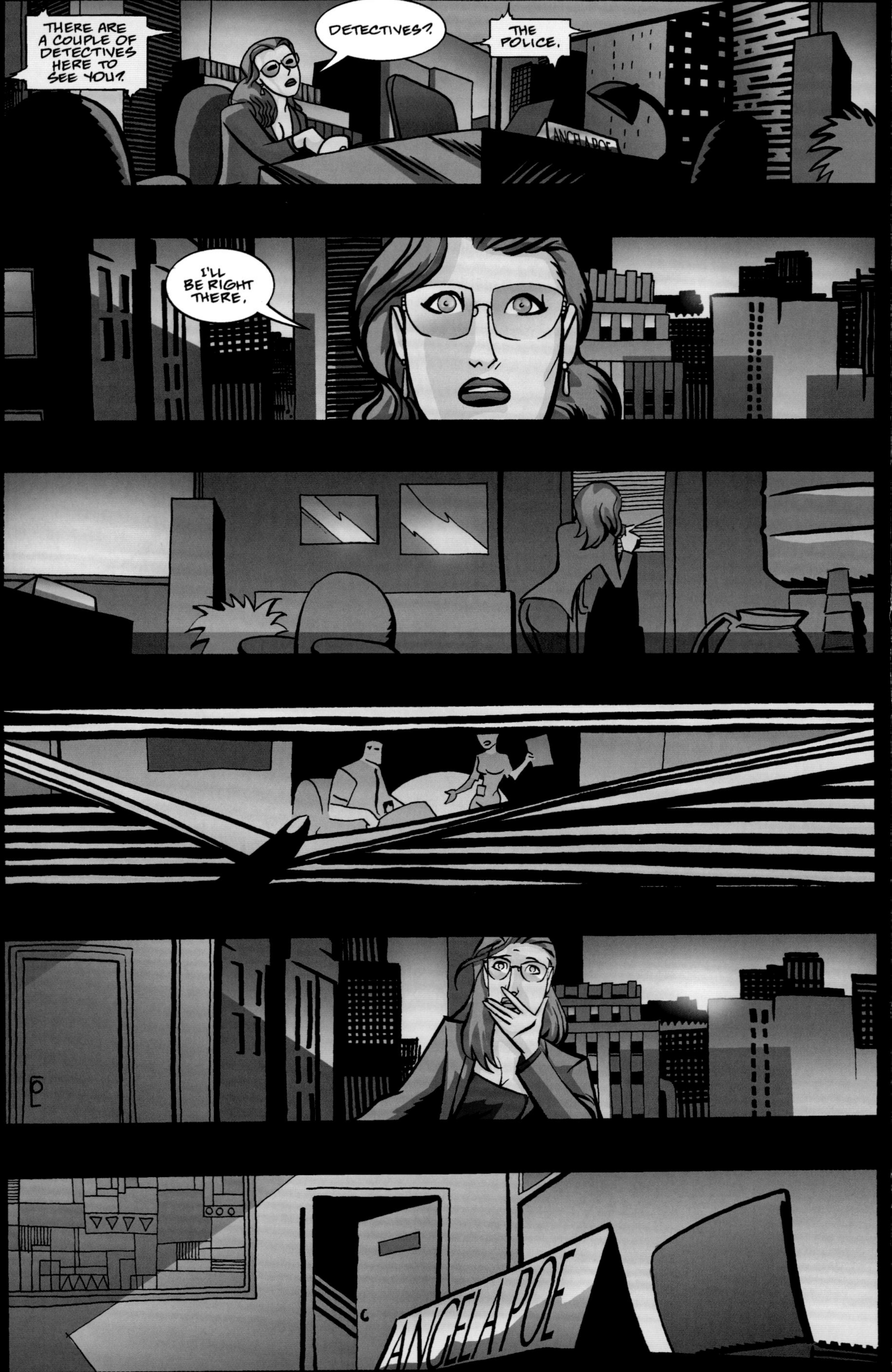
THERE ARE A COUPLE OF DETECTIVES HERE TO SEE YOU?
DETECTIVES?
THE POLICE.
ANGELA POE
I'LL BE RIGHT THERE.
ANGELA POE

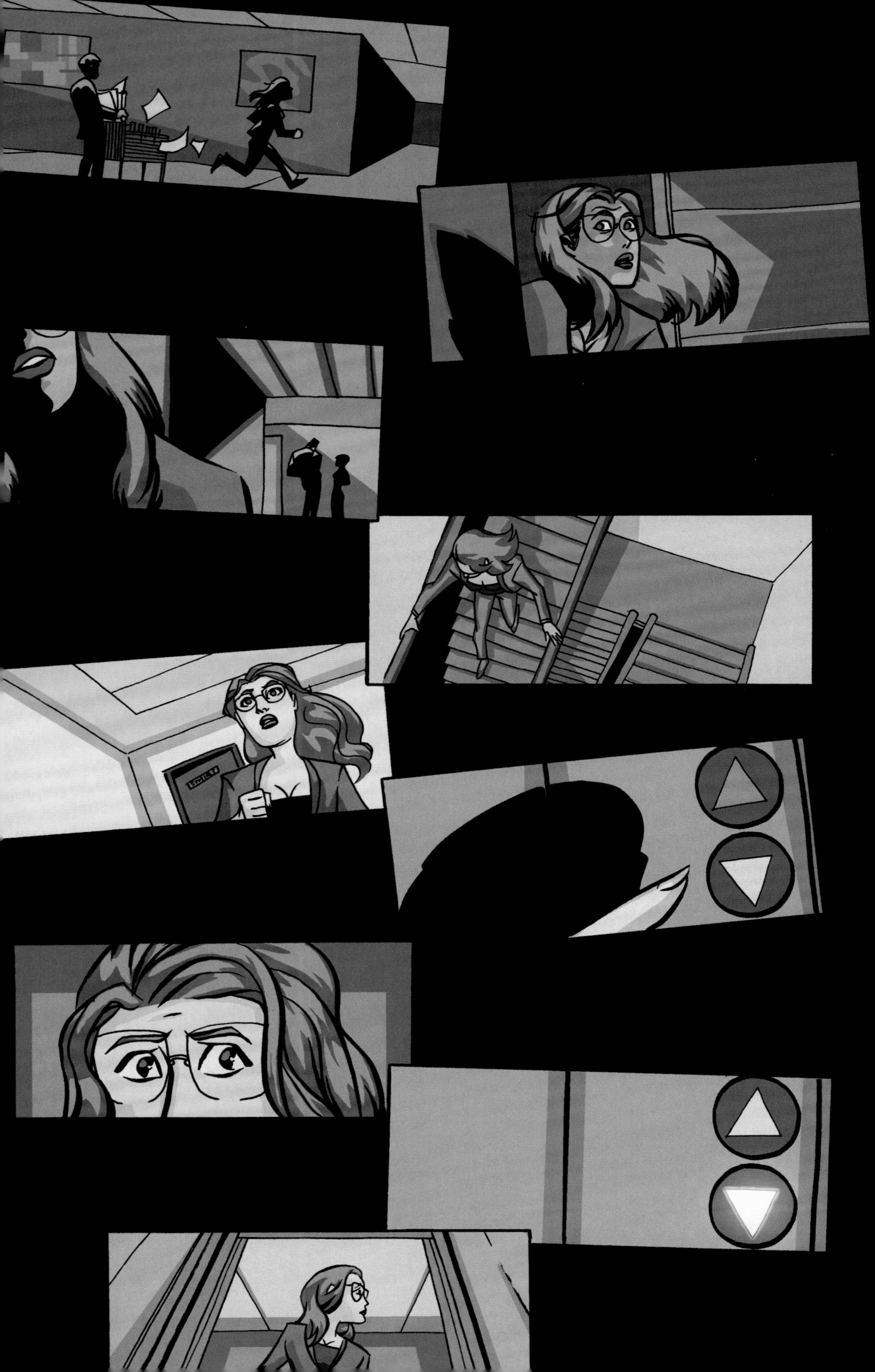

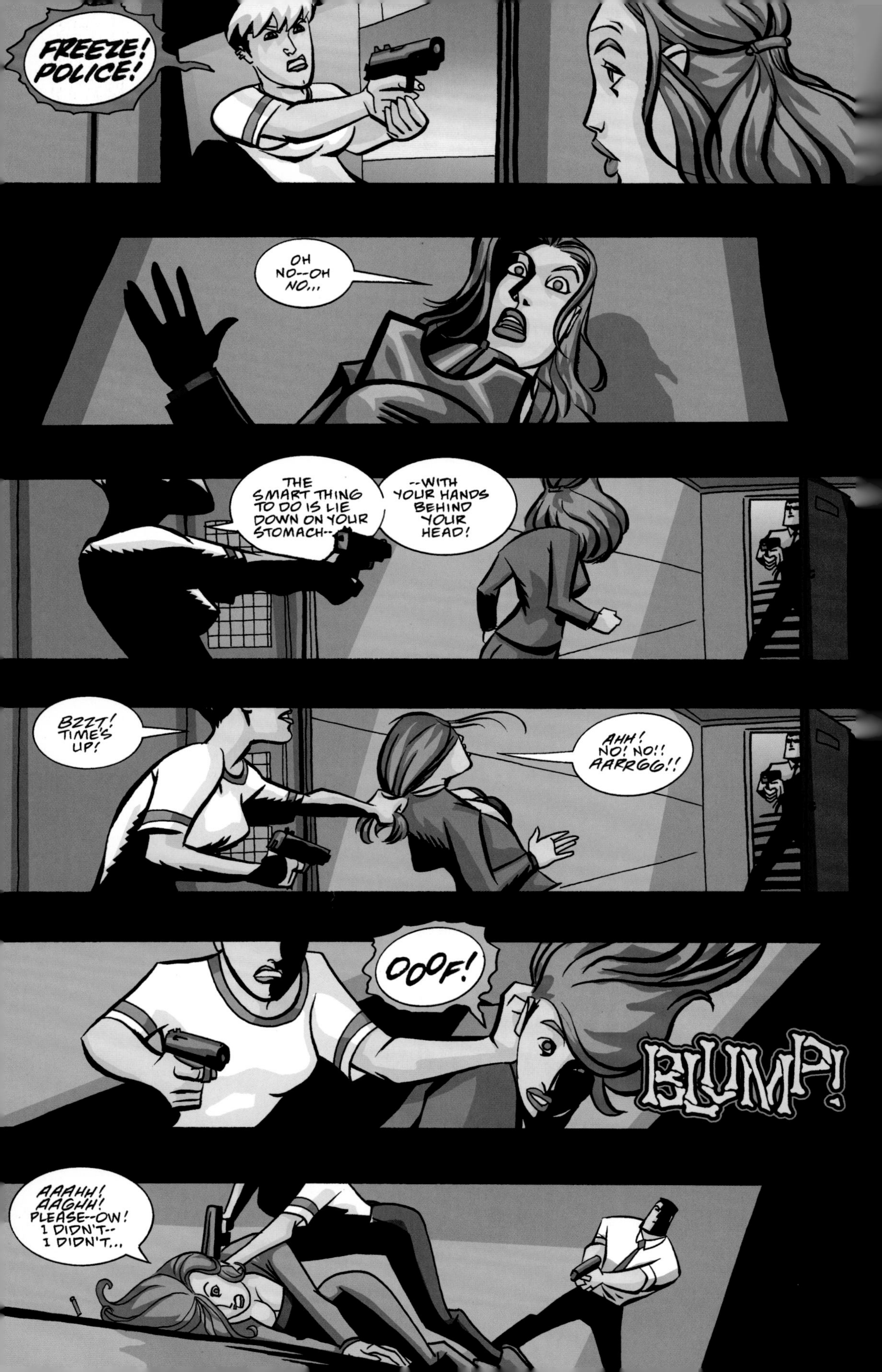
FREEZE! POLICE!
OH NO--OH NO...
THE SMART THING TO DO IS LIE DOWN ON YOUR STOMACH--
--WITH YOUR HANDS BEHIND YOUR HEAD!
BZZT! TIME'S UP!
AHH! NO! NO!! AARRGG!!
OOOF!
BLUMP!
AAAHH! AAGHH! PLEASE--OW! I DIDN'T-- I DIDN'T...

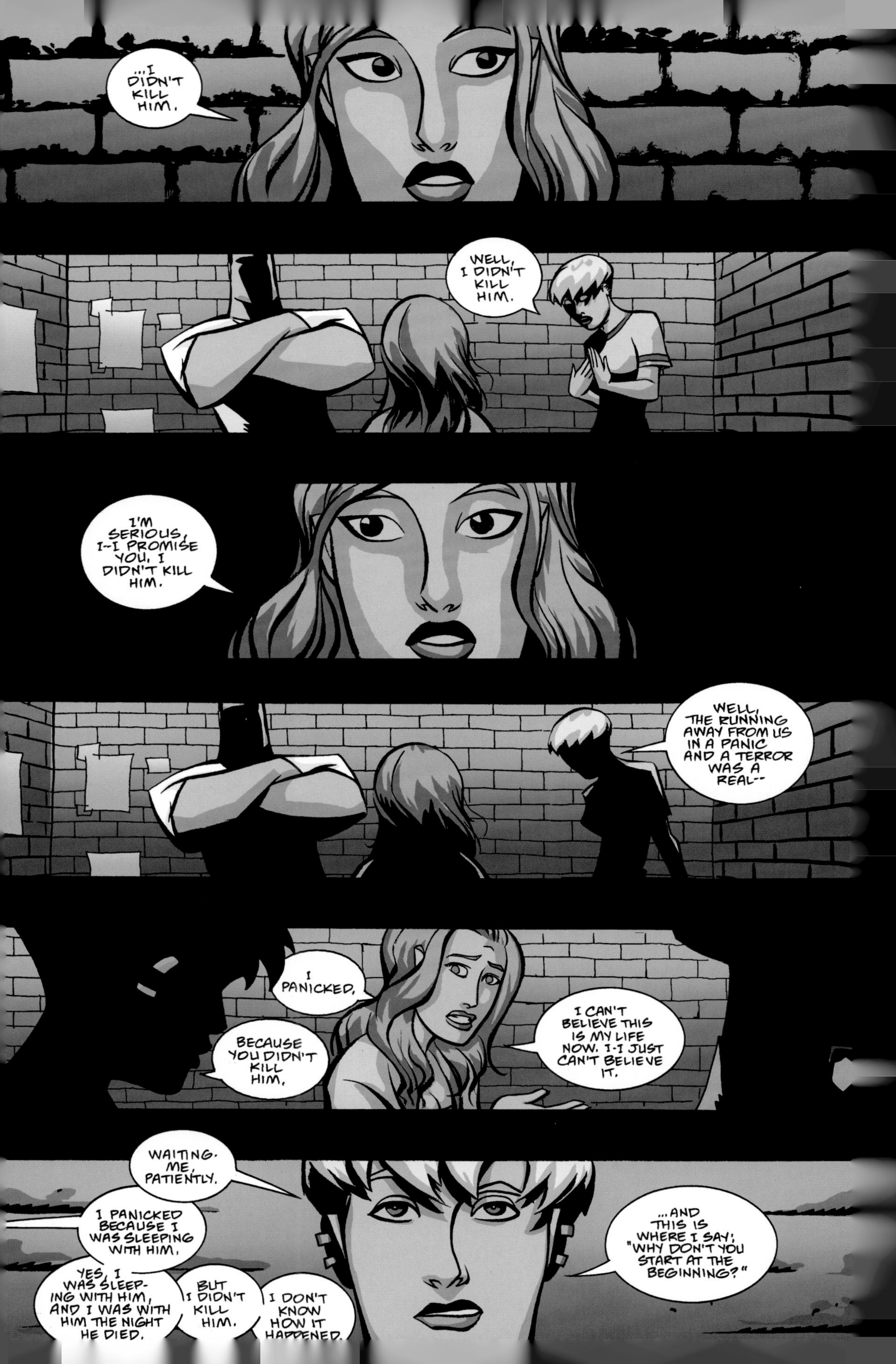
...I DIDN'T KILL HIM.
WELL, I DIDN'T KILL HIM.
I'M SERIOUS, I--I PROMISE YOU, I DIDN'T KILL HIM.
WELL, THE RUNNING AWAY FROM US IN A PANIC AND A TERROR WAS A REAL--
I PANICKED.
BECAUSE YOU DIDN'T KILL HIM.
I CAN'T BELIEVE THIS IS MY LIFE NOW. I-I JUST CAN'T BELIEVE IT.
WAITING. ME, PATIENTLY.
I PANICKED BECAUSE I WAS SLEEPING WITH HIM.
YES, I WAS SLEEP-ING WITH HIM, AND I WAS WITH HIM THE NIGHT HE DIED.
BUT I DIDN'T KILL HIM.
I DON'T KNOW HOW IT HAPPENED.
...AND THIS IS WHERE I SAY; "WHY DON'T YOU START AT THE BEGINNING?"

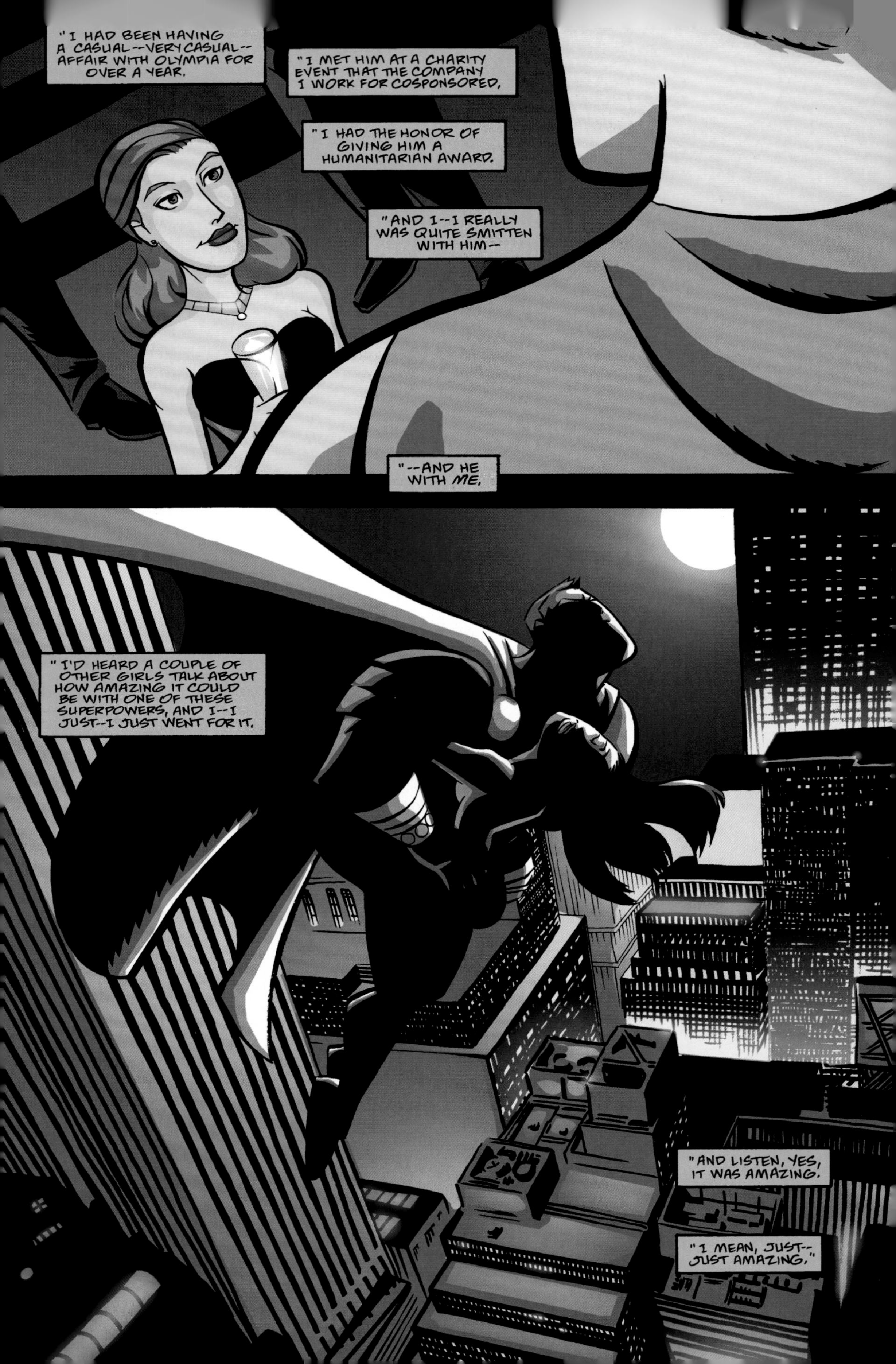
"I HAD BEEN HAVING A CASUAL--VERY CASUAL--AFFAIR WITH OLYMPIA FOR OVER A YEAR.
"I MET HIM AT A CHARITY EVENT THAT THE COMPANY I WORK FOR COSPONSORED.
"I HAD THE HONOR OF GIVING HIM A HUMANITARIAN AWARD.
"AND I--I REALLY WAS QUITE SMITTEN WITH HIM--
"--AND HE WITH *ME*.
"I'D HEARD A COUPLE OF OTHER GIRLS TALK ABOUT HOW AMAZING IT COULD BE WITH ONE OF THESE SUPERPOWERS, AND I--I JUST--I JUST WENT FOR IT.
"AND LISTEN, YES, IT WAS AMAZING.
"I MEAN, JUST--JUST AMAZING."

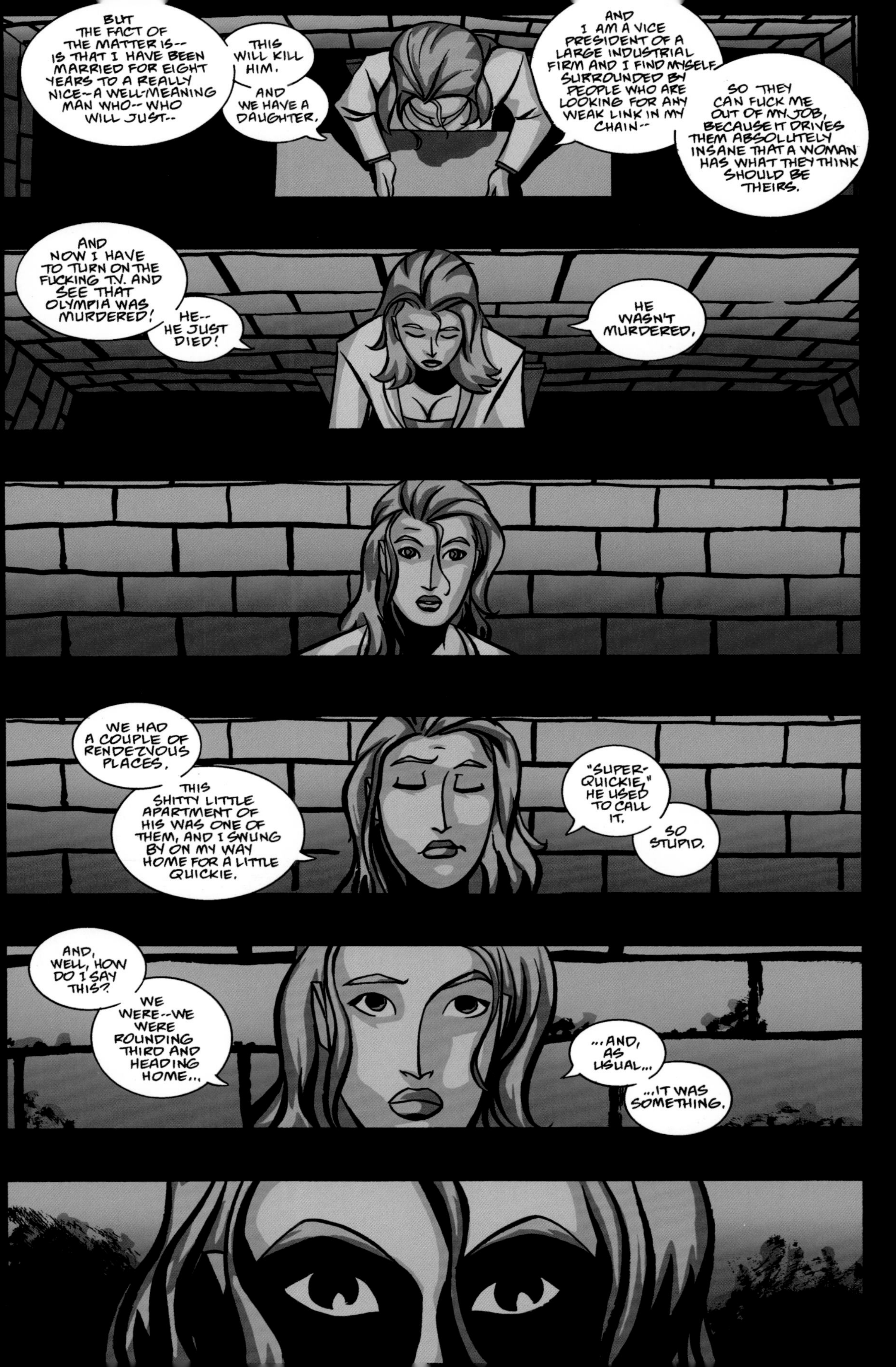
BUT THE FACT OF THE MATTER IS-- IS THAT I HAVE BEEN MARRIED FOR EIGHT YEARS TO A REALLY NICE--A WELL-MEANING MAN WHO--WHO WILL JUST--
THIS WILL KILL HIM.
AND WE HAVE A DAUGHTER.
AND I AM A VICE PRESIDENT OF A LARGE INDUSTRIAL FIRM AND I FIND MYSELF SURROUNDED BY PEOPLE WHO ARE LOOKING FOR ANY WEAK LINK IN MY CHAIN--
SO THEY CAN FUCK ME OUT OF MY JOB, BECAUSE IT DRIVES THEM ABSOLUTELY INSANE THAT A WOMAN HAS WHAT THEY THINK SHOULD BE THEIRS.
AND NOW I HAVE TO TURN ON THE FUCKING T.V. AND SEE THAT OLYMPIA WAS MURDERED!
HE-- HE JUST DIED!
HE WASN'T MURDERED.
WE HAD A COUPLE OF RENDEZVOUS PLACES.
THIS SHITTY LITTLE APARTMENT OF HIS WAS ONE OF THEM, AND I SWUNG BY ON MY WAY HOME FOR A LITTLE QUICKIE.
"SUPER-QUICKIE," HE USED TO CALL IT.
SO STUPID.
AND, WELL, HOW DO I SAY THIS?
WE WERE--WE WERE ROUNDING THIRD AND HEADING HOME...
...AND, AS USUAL...
...IT WAS SOMETHING.

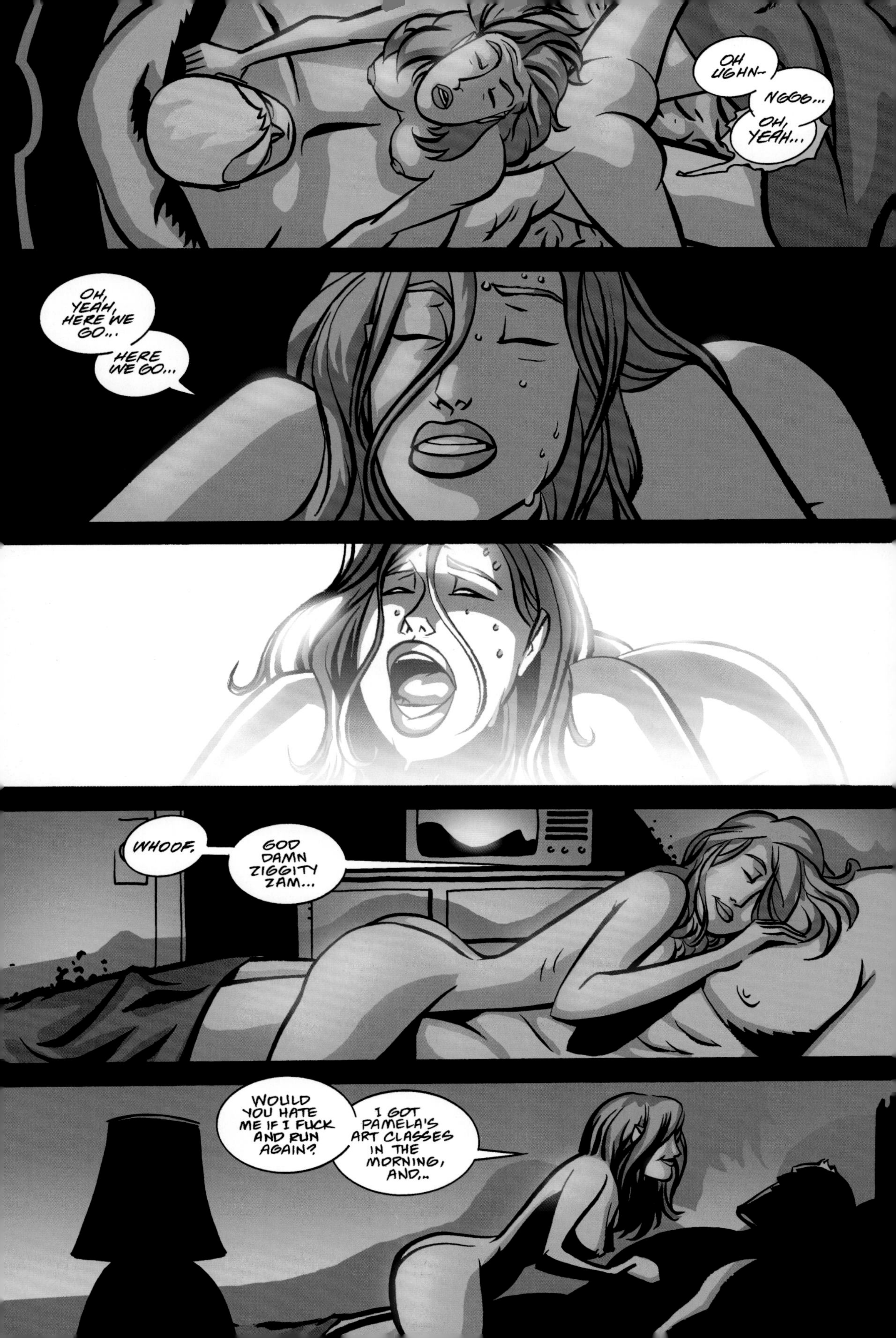

OH UGHN--
NGGG...
OH, YEAH...
OH, YEAH, HERE WE GO...
HERE WE GO...
WHOOF.
GOD DAMN ZIGGITY ZAM...
WOULD YOU HATE ME IF I FUCK AND RUN AGAIN?
I GOT PAMELA'S ART CLASSES IN THE MORNING, AND...

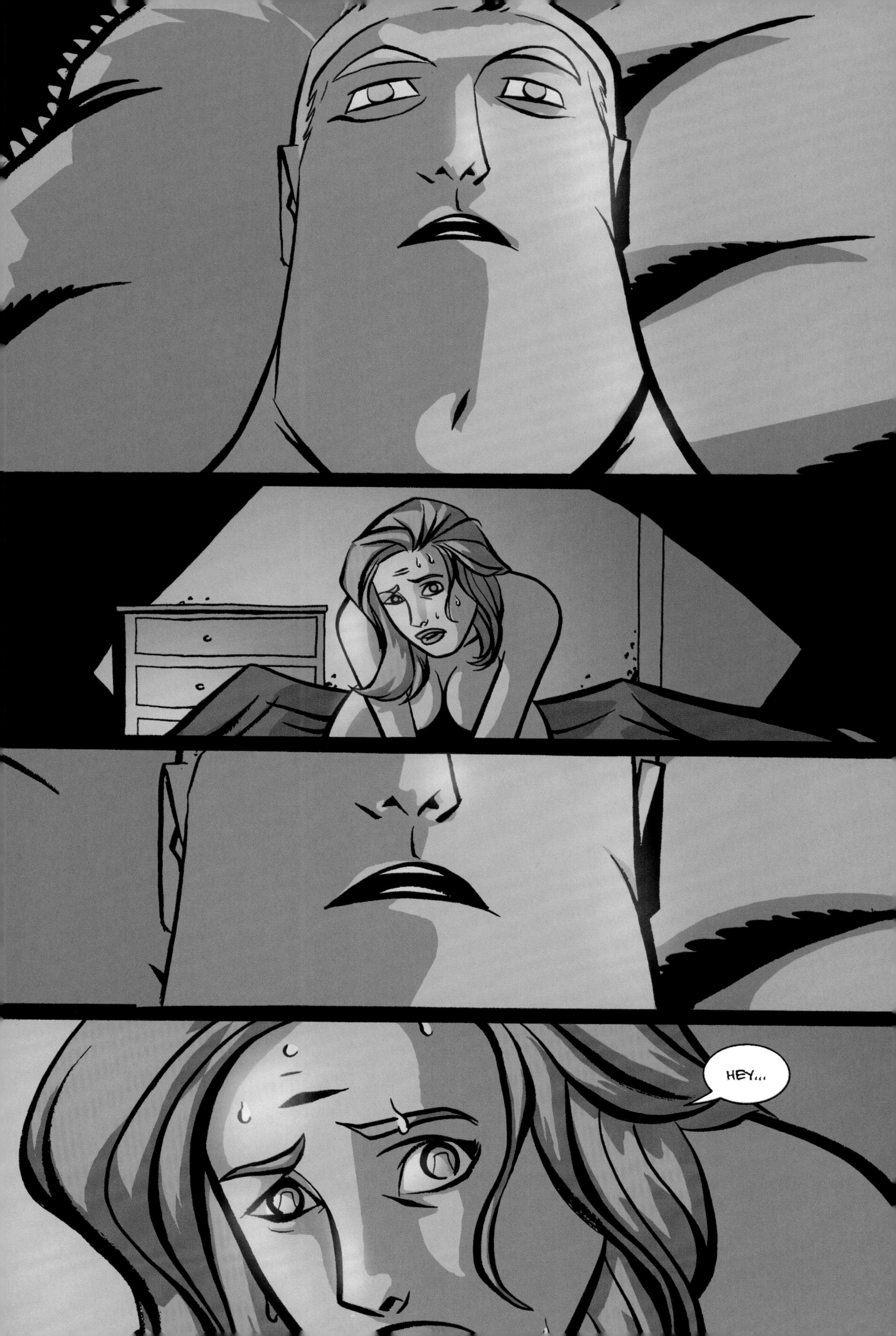
HEY...

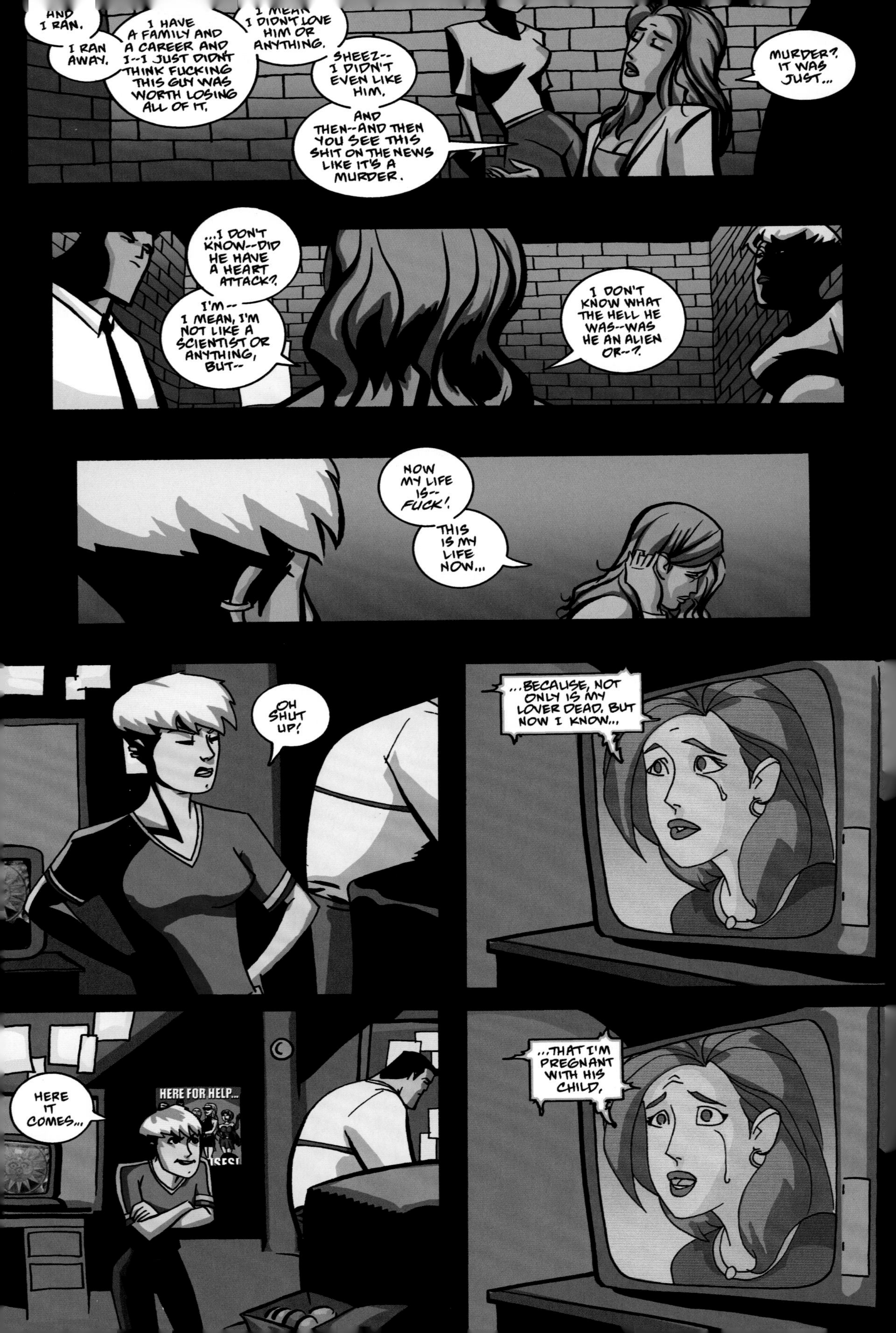
AND I RAN.
I RAN AWAY.
I HAVE A FAMILY AND A CAREER AND I--I JUST DIDN'T THINK FUCKING THIS GUY WAS WORTH LOSING ALL OF IT.
I MEAN I DIDN'T LOVE HIM OR ANYTHING.
SHEEZ-- I DIDN'T EVEN LIKE HIM.
AND THEN--AND THEN YOU SEE THIS SHIT ON THE NEWS LIKE IT'S A MURDER.
MURDER? IT WAS JUST...
...I DON'T KNOW--DID HE HAVE A HEART ATTACK?
I'M-- I MEAN, I'M NOT LIKE A SCIENTIST OR ANYTHING, BUT--
I DON'T KNOW WHAT THE HELL HE WAS--WAS HE AN ALIEN OR--?
NOW MY LIFE IS-- FUCK!
THIS IS MY LIFE NOW...
OH SHUT UP!
...BECAUSE, NOT ONLY IS MY LOVER DEAD, BUT NOW I KNOW...
HERE IT COMES...
HERE FOR HELP...
...THAT I'M PREGNANT WITH HIS CHILD.

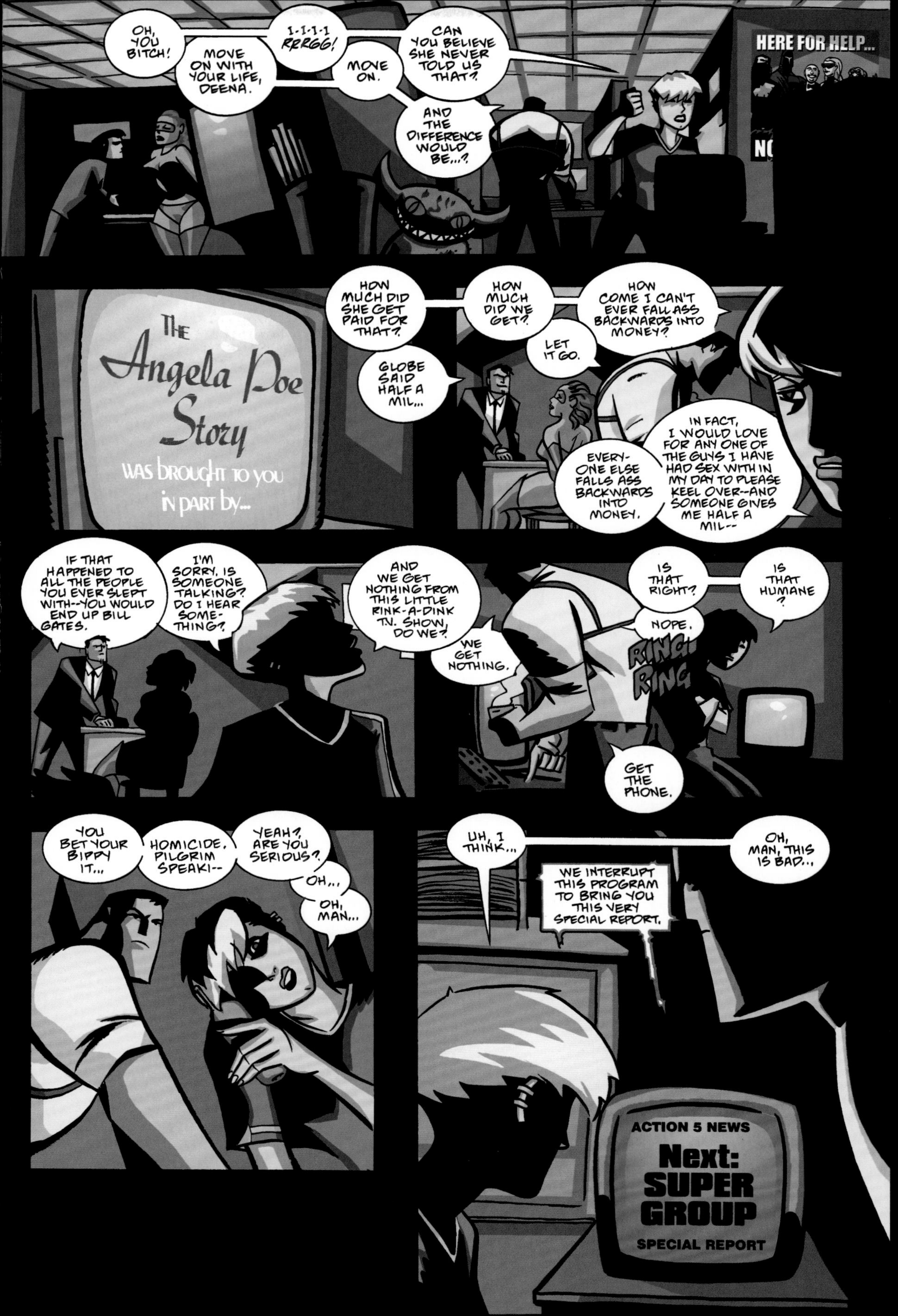
OH, YOU BITCH!
MOVE ON WITH YOUR LIFE, DEENA.
I-I-I-I RRRGG!
MOVE ON.
CAN YOU BELIEVE SHE NEVER TOLD US THAT?
AND THE DIFFERENCE WOULD BE...?
HERE FOR HELP...
The Angela Poe Story was brought to you in part by...
HOW MUCH DID SHE GET PAID FOR THAT?
GLOBE SAID HALF A MIL...
HOW MUCH DID WE GET?
LET IT GO.
HOW COME I CAN'T EVER FALL ASS BACKWARDS INTO MONEY?
EVERY-ONE ELSE FALLS ASS BACKWARDS INTO MONEY.
IN FACT, I WOULD LOVE FOR ANY ONE OF THE GUYS I HAVE HAD SEX WITH IN MY DAY TO PLEASE KEEL OVER--AND SOMEONE GIVES ME HALF A MIL--
IF THAT HAPPENED TO ALL THE PEOPLE YOU EVER SLEPT WITH--YOU WOULD END UP BILL GATES.
I'M SORRY. IS SOMEONE TALKING? DO I HEAR SOME-THING?
AND WE GET NOTHING FROM THIS LITTLE RINK-A-DINK T.V. SHOW, DO WE?
WE GET NOTHING.
IS THAT RIGHT?
IS THAT HUMANE?
NOPE.
GET THE PHONE.
YOU BET YOUR BIPPY IT...
HOMICIDE. PILGRIM SPEAKI--
YEAH? ARE YOU SERIOUS?
OH...
OH, MAN...
UH, I THINK...
WE INTERRUPT THIS PROGRAM TO BRING YOU THIS VERY SPECIAL REPORT.
OH, MAN, THIS IS BAD...
ACTION 5 NEWS
Next: SUPER GROUP
SPECIAL REPORT

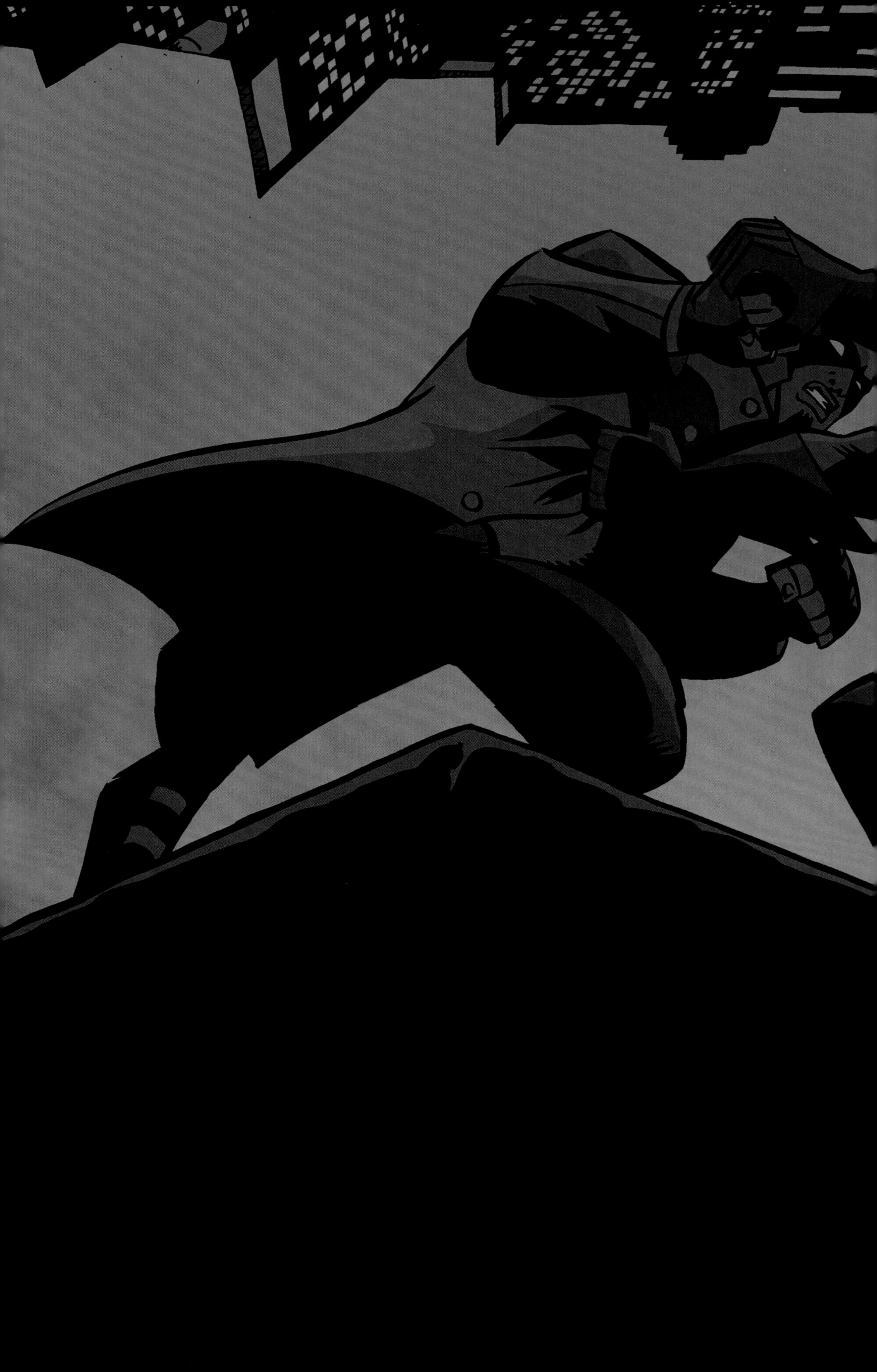

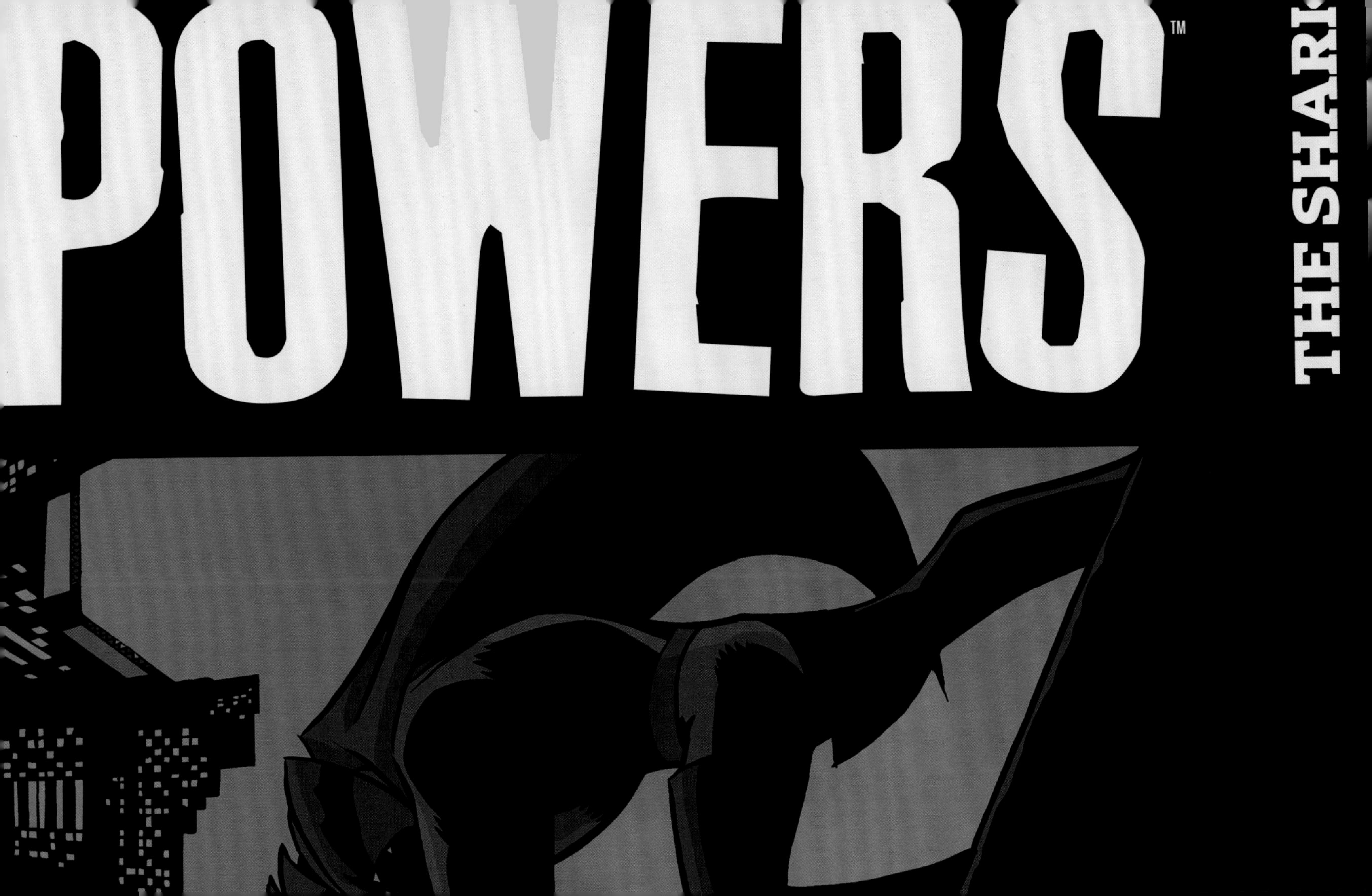
POWERS™
THE SHAR

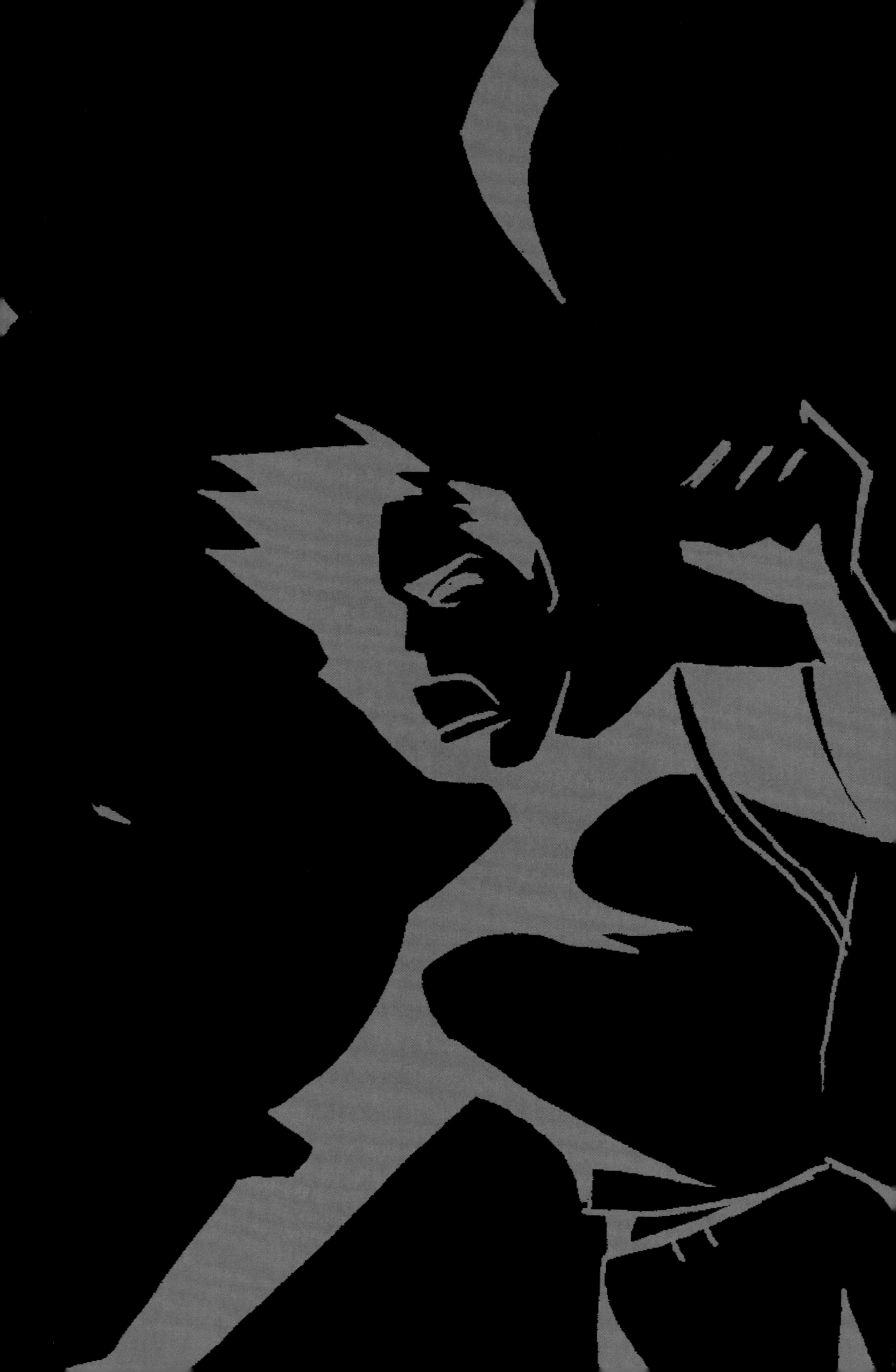

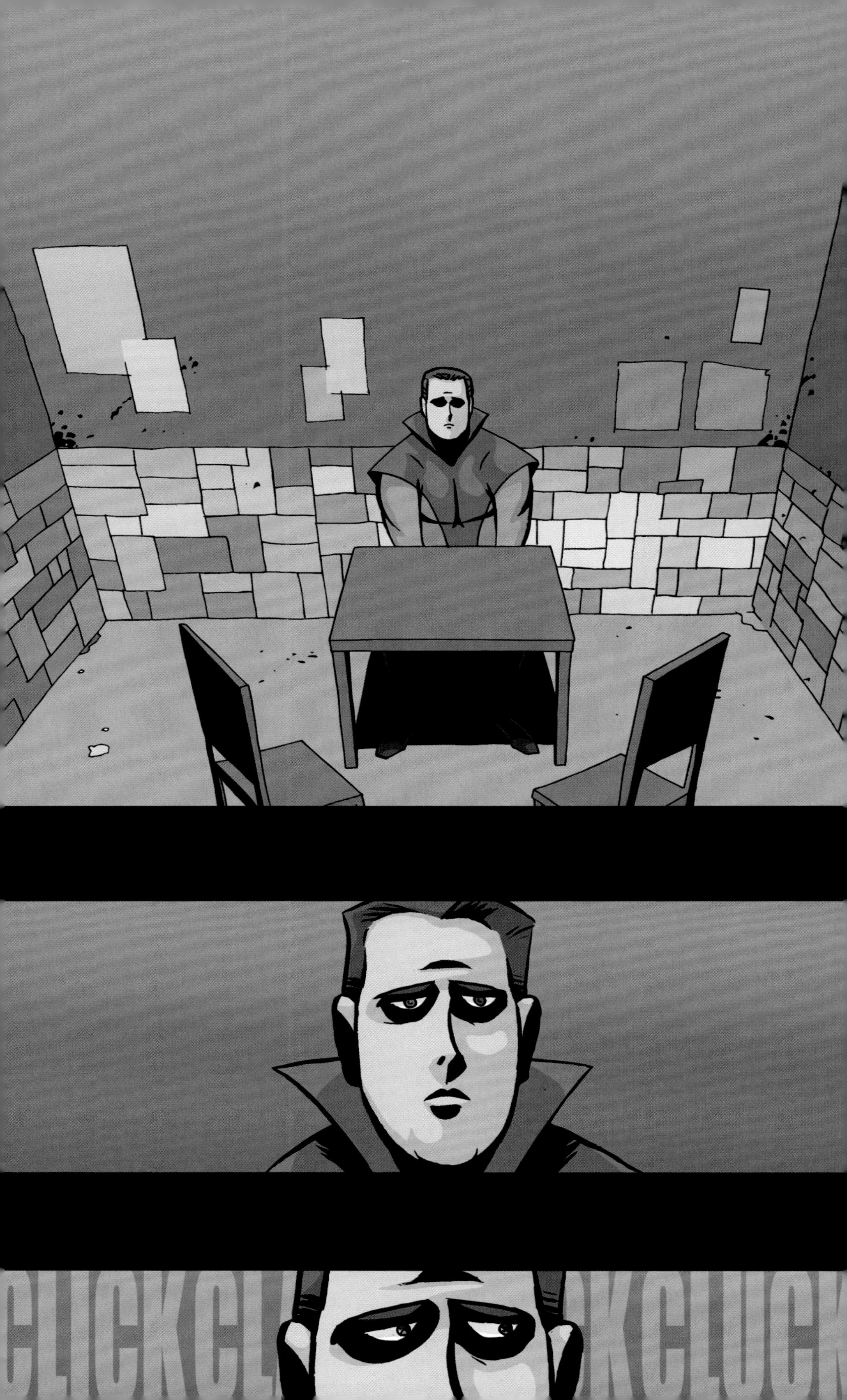
CLICKCL
KCLUCK

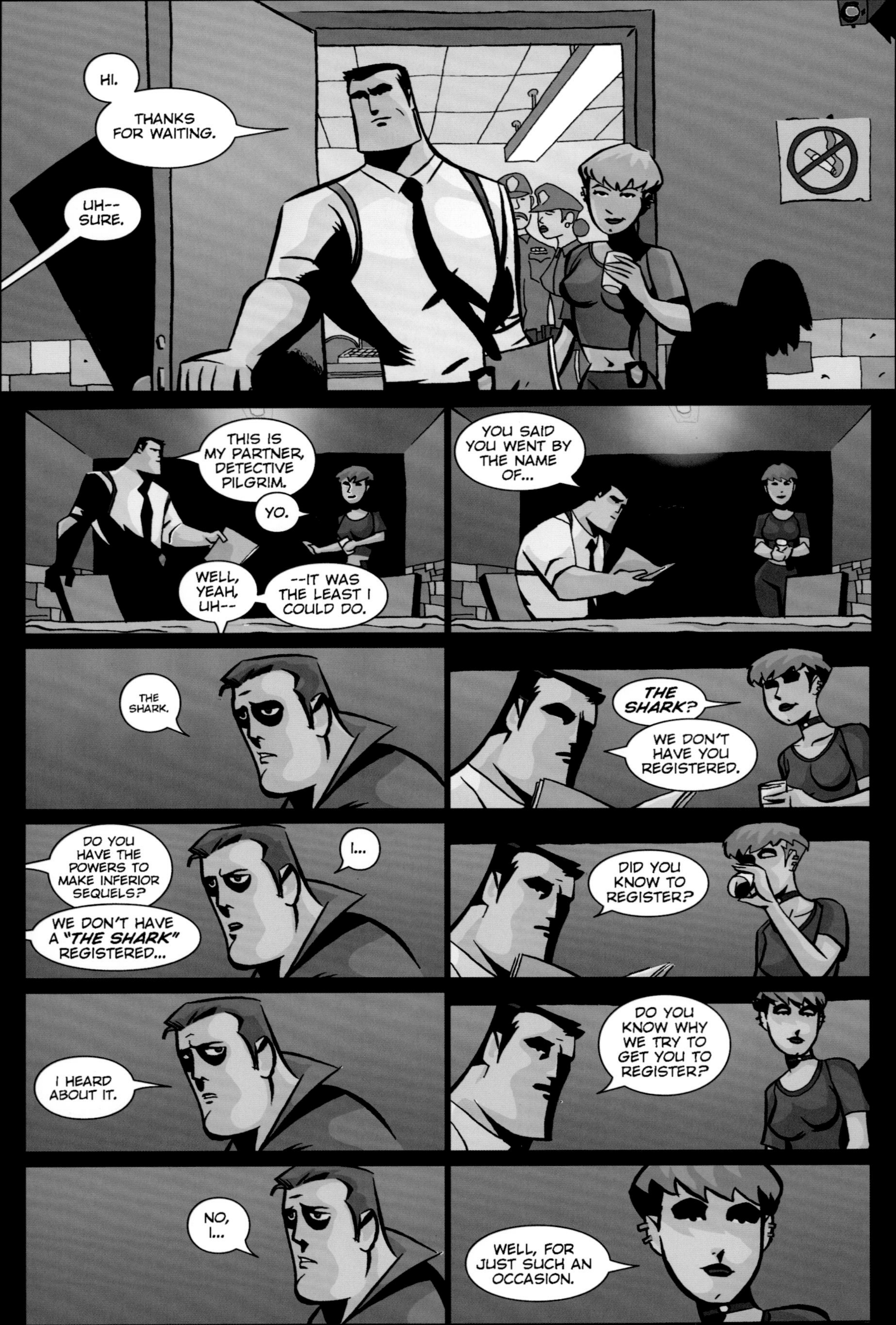
HI.
THANKS FOR WAITING.
UH-- SURE.
THIS IS MY PARTNER, DETECTIVE PILGRIM.
YO.
WELL, YEAH, UH--
--IT WAS THE LEAST I COULD DO.
YOU SAID YOU WENT BY THE NAME OF...
THE SHARK.
THE SHARK?
WE DON'T HAVE YOU REGISTERED.
DO YOU HAVE THE POWERS TO MAKE INFERIOR SEQUELS?
WE DON'T HAVE A *"THE SHARK"* REGISTERED...
I...
DID YOU KNOW TO REGISTER?
I HEARD ABOUT IT.
DO YOU KNOW WHY WE TRY TO GET YOU TO REGISTER?
NO, I...
WELL, FOR JUST SUCH AN OCCASION.

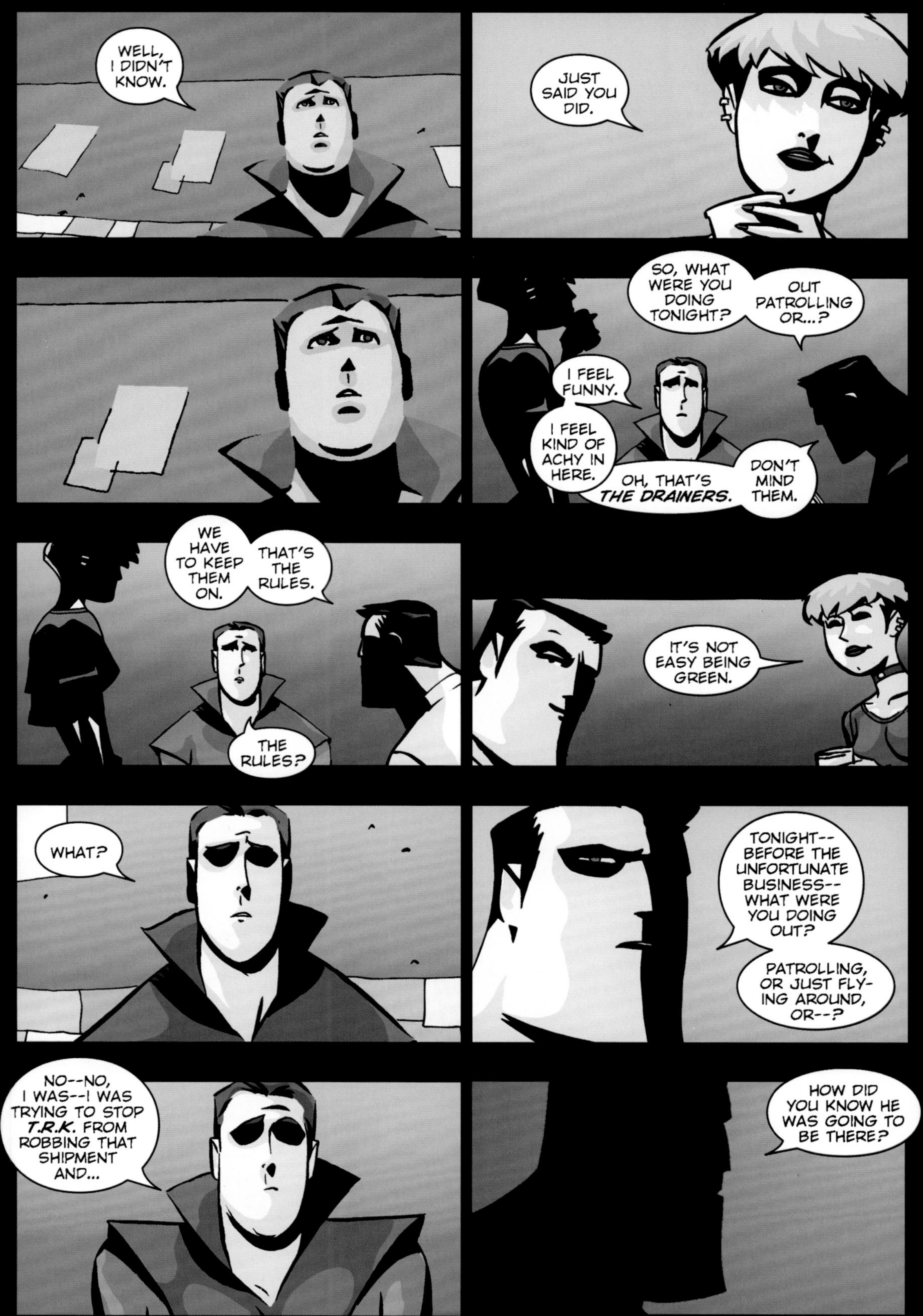
WELL, I DIDN'T KNOW.
JUST SAID YOU DID.
SO, WHAT WERE YOU DOING TONIGHT?
OUT PATROLLING OR...?
I FEEL FUNNY.
I FEEL KIND OF ACHY IN HERE.
OH, THAT'S *THE DRAINERS.*
DON'T MIND THEM.
WE HAVE TO KEEP THEM ON.
THAT'S THE RULES.
THE RULES?
IT'S NOT EASY BEING GREEN.
WHAT?
TONIGHT-- BEFORE THE UNFORTUNATE BUSINESS-- WHAT WERE YOU DOING OUT?
PATROLLING, OR JUST FLY-ING AROUND, OR--?
NO--NO, I WAS--I WAS TRYING TO STOP *T.R.K.* FROM ROBBING THAT SHIPMENT AND...
HOW DID YOU KNOW HE WAS GOING TO BE THERE?

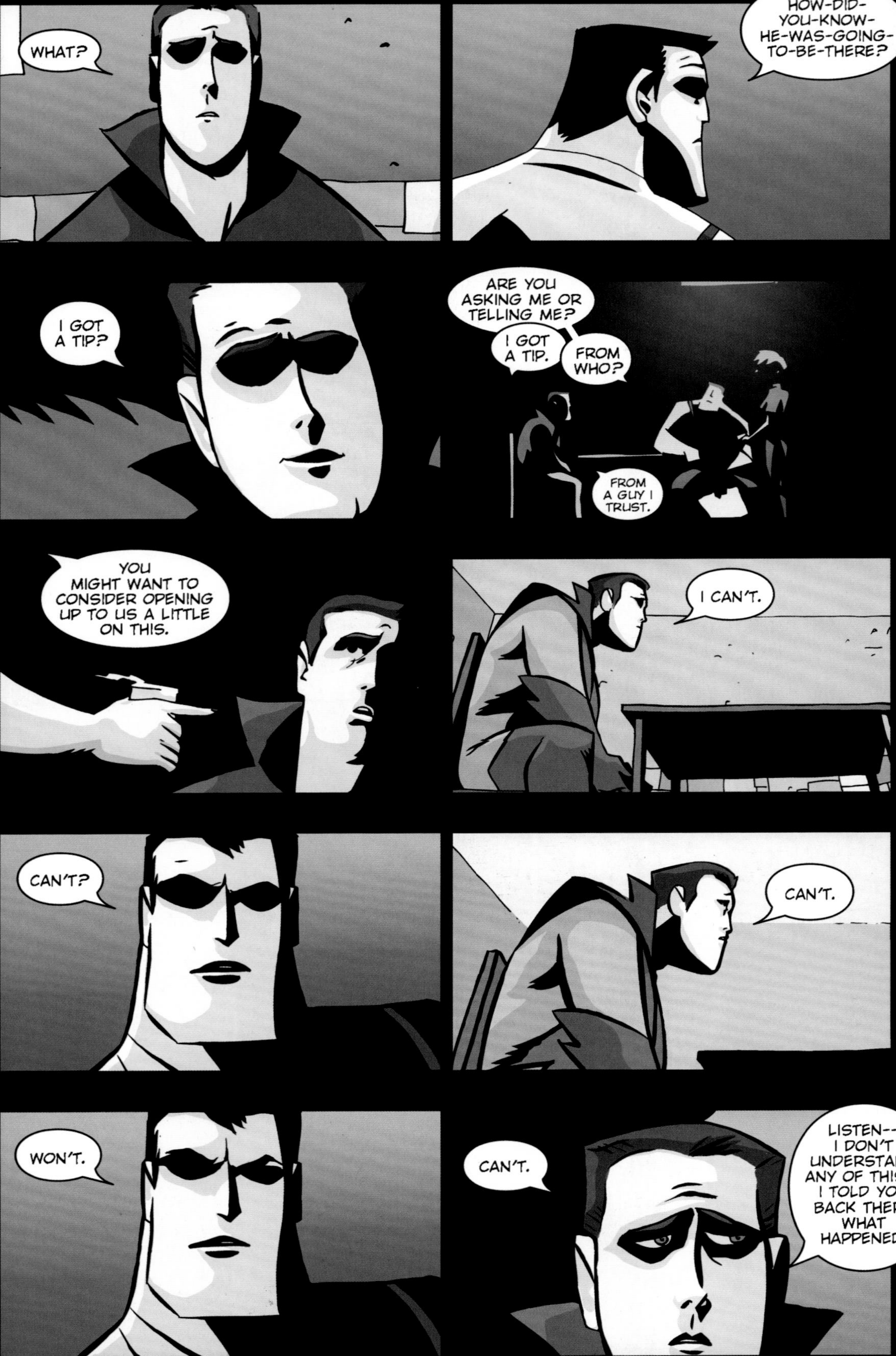

WHAT?
HOW-DID-YOU-KNOW-HE-WAS-GOING-TO-BE-THERE?
I GOT A TIP?
ARE YOU ASKING ME OR TELLING ME?
I GOT A TIP.
FROM WHO?
FROM A GUY I TRUST.
YOU MIGHT WANT TO CONSIDER OPENING UP TO US A LITTLE ON THIS.
I CAN'T.
CAN'T?
CAN'T.
WON'T.
CAN'T.
LISTEN-- I DON'T UNDERSTAND ANY OF THIS-- I TOLD YOU BACK THERE WHAT HAPPENED.

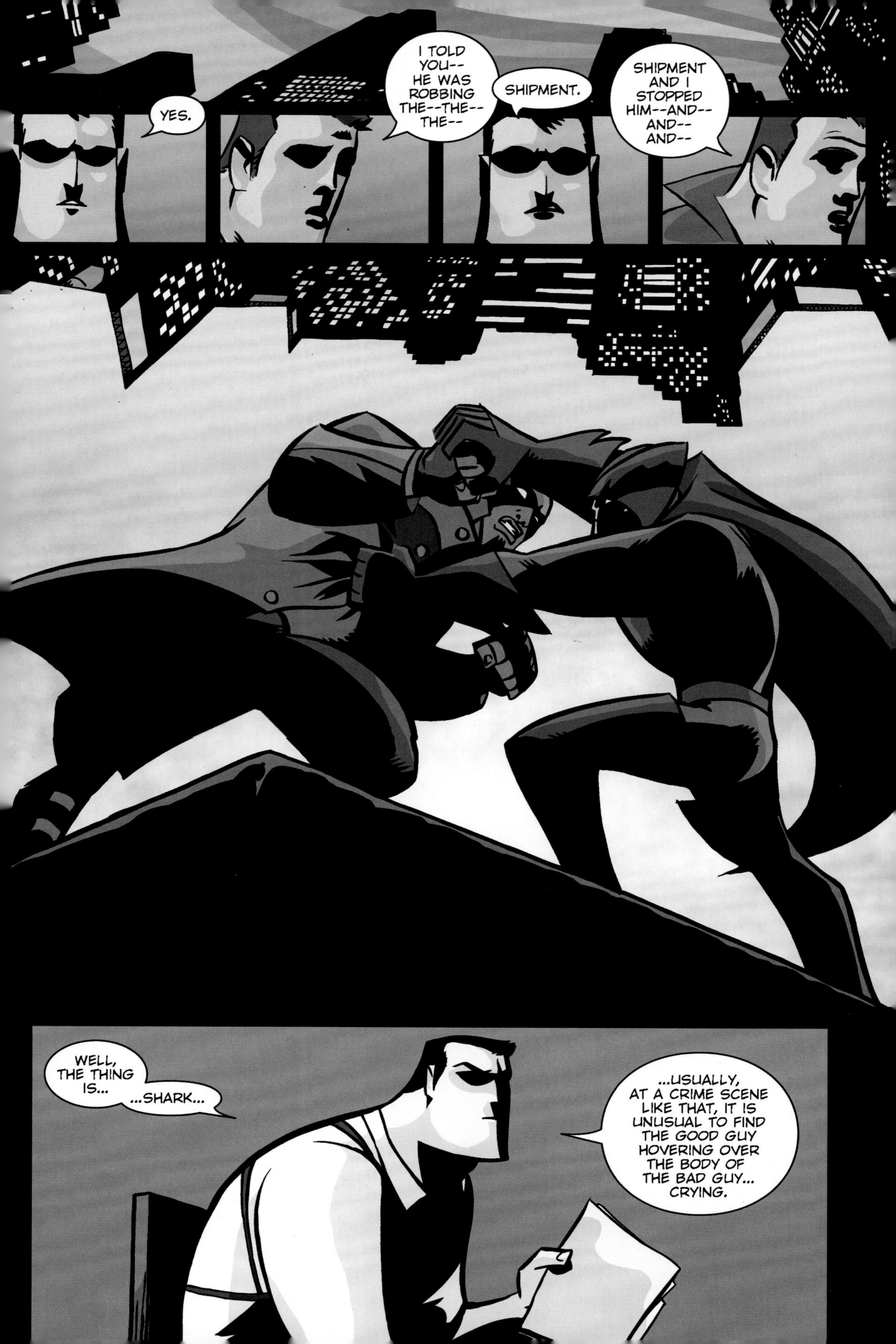
YES.
I TOLD YOU-- HE WAS ROBBING THE--THE-- THE--
SHIPMENT.
SHIPMENT AND I STOPPED HIM--AND-- AND-- AND--
WELL, THE THING IS...
...SHARK...
...USUALLY, AT A CRIME SCENE LIKE THAT, IT IS UNUSUAL TO FIND THE GOOD GUY HOVERING OVER THE BODY OF THE BAD GUY... CRYING.

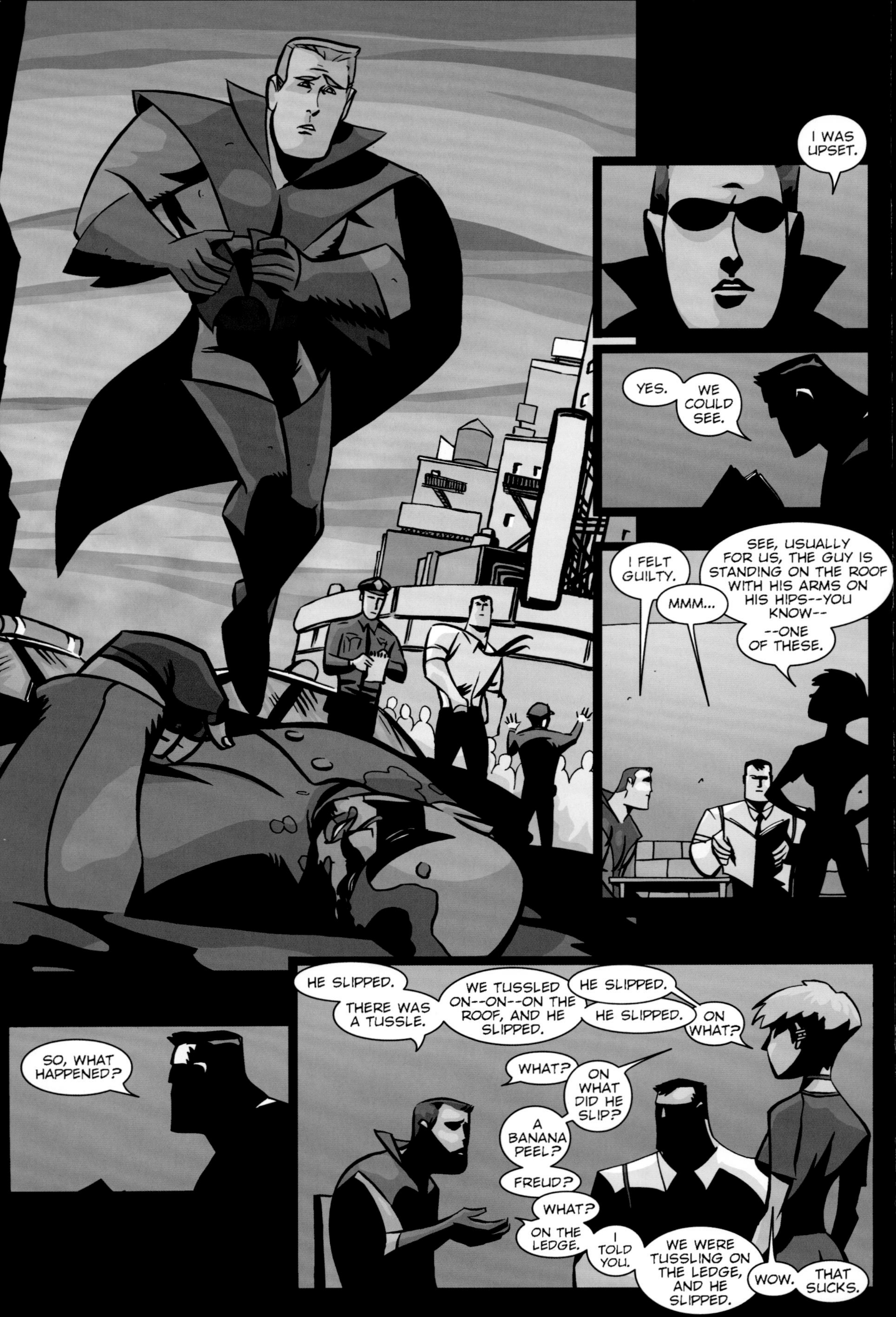
I WAS UPSET.
YES.
WE COULD SEE.
I FELT GUILTY.
MMM...
SEE, USUALLY FOR US, THE GUY IS STANDING ON THE ROOF WITH HIS ARMS ON HIS HIPS--YOU KNOW--
--ONE OF THESE.
SO, WHAT HAPPENED?
HE SLIPPED.
THERE WAS A TUSSLE.
WE TUSSLED ON--ON--ON THE ROOF, AND HE SLIPPED.
HE SLIPPED.
HE SLIPPED.
ON WHAT?
WHAT?
ON WHAT DID HE SLIP?
A BANANA PEEL?
FREUD?
WHAT?
ON THE LEDGE.
I TOLD YOU.
WE WERE TUSSLING ON THE LEDGE, AND HE SLIPPED.
WOW.
THAT SUCKS.

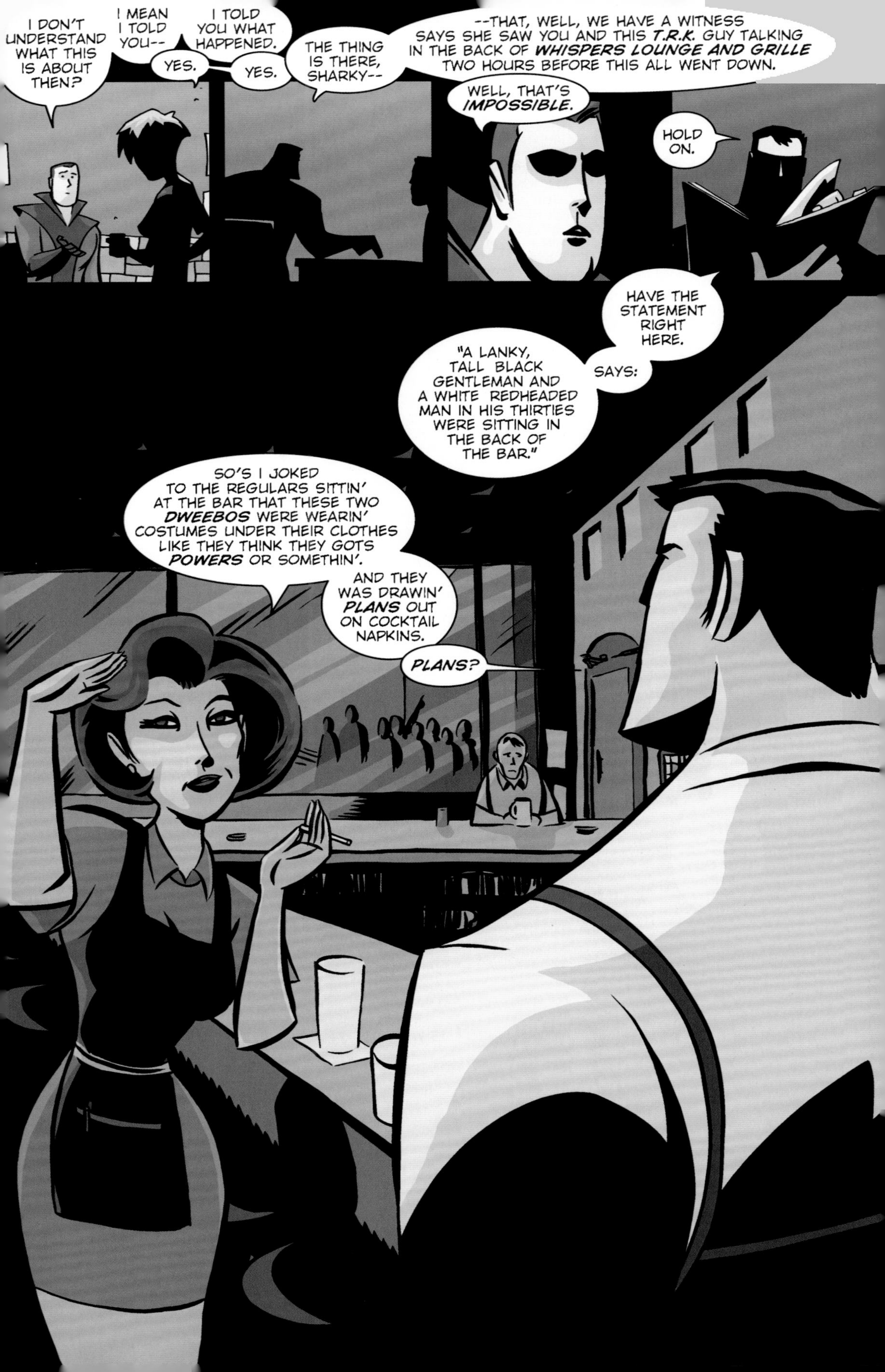

I DON'T UNDERSTAND WHAT THIS IS ABOUT THEN?
I MEAN I TOLD YOU--
YES.
I TOLD YOU WHAT HAPPENED.
YES.
THE THING IS THERE, SHARKY--
--THAT, WELL, WE HAVE A WITNESS SAYS SHE SAW YOU AND THIS T.R.K. GUY TALKING IN THE BACK OF WHISPERS LOUNGE AND GRILLE TWO HOURS BEFORE THIS ALL WENT DOWN.
WELL, THAT'S IMPOSSIBLE.
HOLD ON.
HAVE THE STATEMENT RIGHT HERE.
SAYS:
"A LANKY, TALL BLACK GENTLEMAN AND A WHITE REDHEADED MAN IN HIS THIRTIES WERE SITTING IN THE BACK OF THE BAR."
SO'S I JOKED TO THE REGULARS SITTIN' AT THE BAR THAT THESE TWO DWEEBOS WERE WEARIN' COSTUMES UNDER THEIR CLOTHES LIKE THEY THINK THEY GOTS POWERS OR SOMETHIN'.
AND THEY WAS DRAWIN' PLANS OUT ON COCKTAIL NAPKINS.
PLANS?

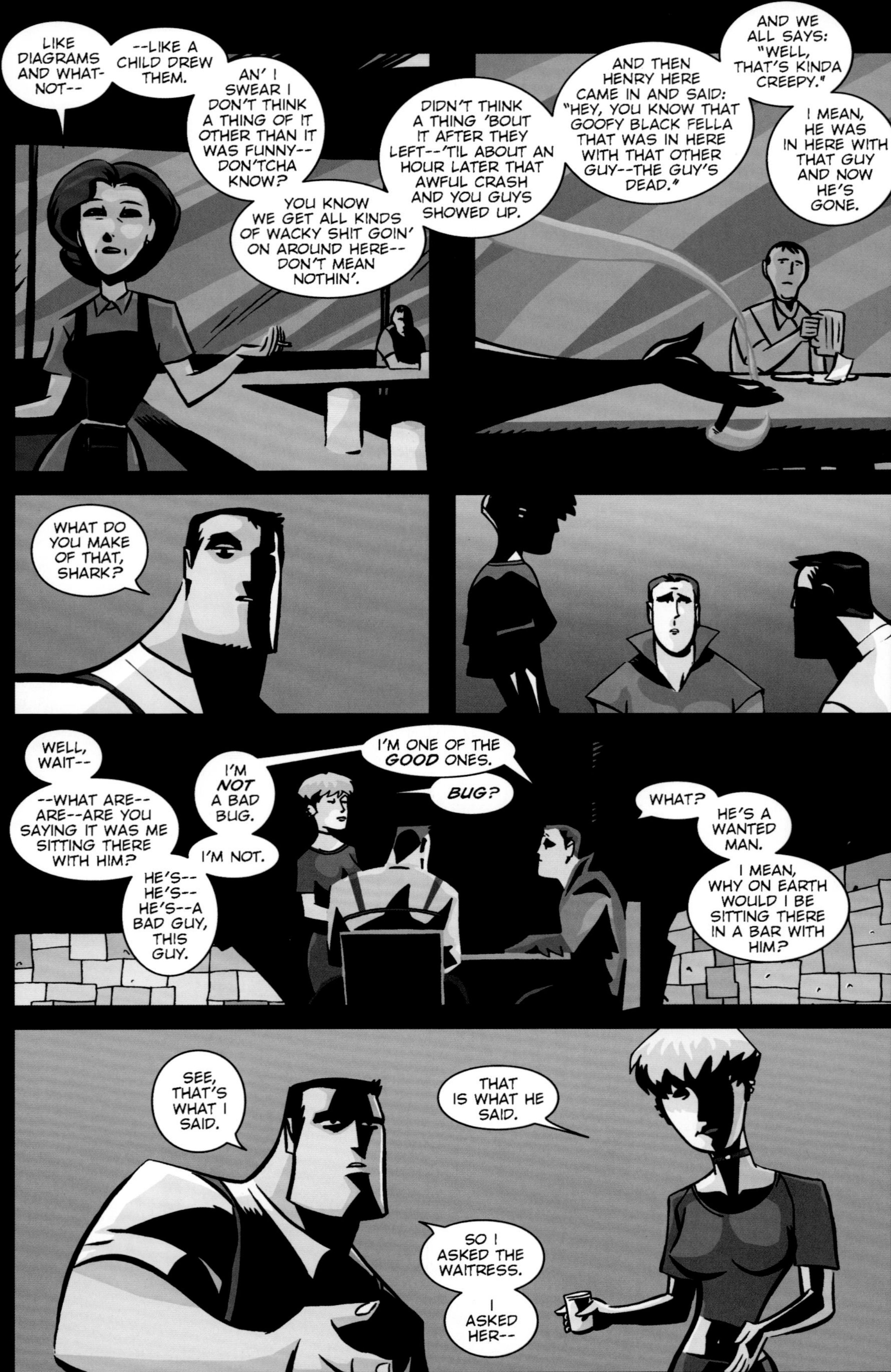
LIKE DIAGRAMS AND WHAT-NOT--
--LIKE A CHILD DREW THEM.
AN' I SWEAR I DON'T THINK A THING OF IT OTHER THAN IT WAS FUNNY-- DON'TCHA KNOW?
YOU KNOW WE GET ALL KINDS OF WACKY SHIT GOIN' ON AROUND HERE-- DON'T MEAN NOTHIN'.
DIDN'T THINK A THING 'BOUT IT AFTER THEY LEFT--'TIL ABOUT AN HOUR LATER THAT AWFUL CRASH AND YOU GUYS SHOWED UP.
AND THEN HENRY HERE CAME IN AND SAID: "HEY, YOU KNOW THAT GOOFY BLACK FELLA THAT WAS IN HERE WITH THAT OTHER GUY--THE GUY'S DEAD."
AND WE ALL SAYS: "WELL, THAT'S KINDA CREEPY."
I MEAN, HE WAS IN HERE WITH THAT GUY AND NOW HE'S GONE.
WHAT DO YOU MAKE OF THAT, SHARK?
WELL, WAIT--
--WHAT ARE-- ARE--ARE YOU SAYING IT WAS ME SITTING THERE WITH HIM?
I'M *NOT* A BAD BUG.
I'M NOT.
HE'S-- HE'S-- HE'S--A BAD GUY, THIS GUY.
I'M ONE OF THE *GOOD* ONES.
BUG?
WHAT?
HE'S A WANTED MAN.
I MEAN, WHY ON EARTH WOULD I BE SITTING THERE IN A BAR WITH HIM?
SEE, THAT'S WHAT I SAID.
THAT IS WHAT HE SAID.
SO I ASKED THE WAITRESS.
I ASKED HER--

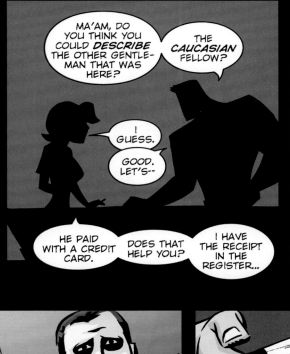

MA'AM, DO YOU THINK YOU COULD *DESCRIBE* THE OTHER GENTLE-MAN THAT WAS HERE?

THE *CAUCASIAN* FELLOW?

I GUESS.

GOOD. LET'S--

HE PAID WITH A CREDIT CARD.

DOES THAT HELP YOU?

I HAVE THE RECEIPT IN THE REGISTER...

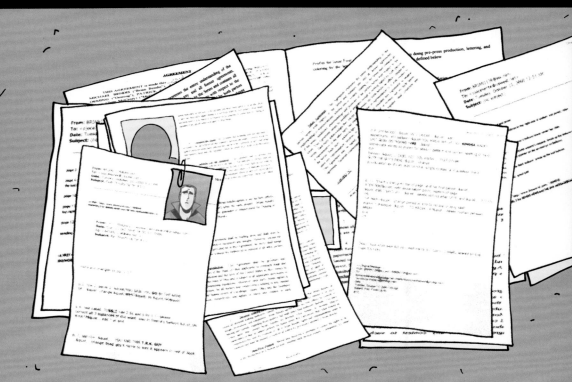

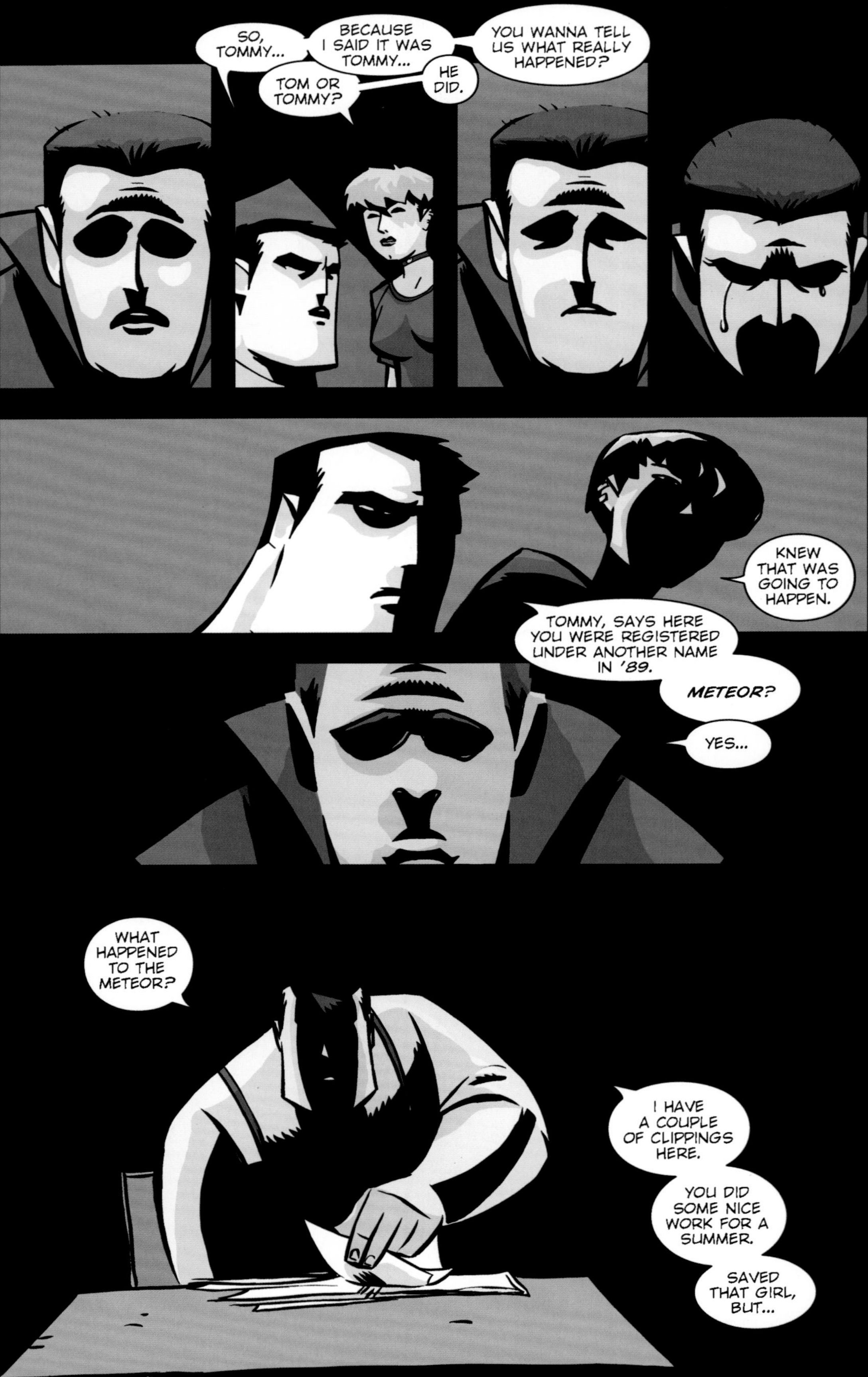
SO, TOMMY...
BECAUSE I SAID IT WAS TOMMY...
TOM OR TOMMY?
HE DID.
YOU WANNA TELL US WHAT REALLY HAPPENED?
KNEW THAT WAS GOING TO HAPPEN.
TOMMY, SAYS HERE YOU WERE REGISTERED UNDER ANOTHER NAME IN '89.
METEOR?
YES...
WHAT HAPPENED TO THE METEOR?
I HAVE A COUPLE OF CLIPPINGS HERE.
YOU DID SOME NICE WORK FOR A SUMMER.
SAVED THAT GIRL, BUT...

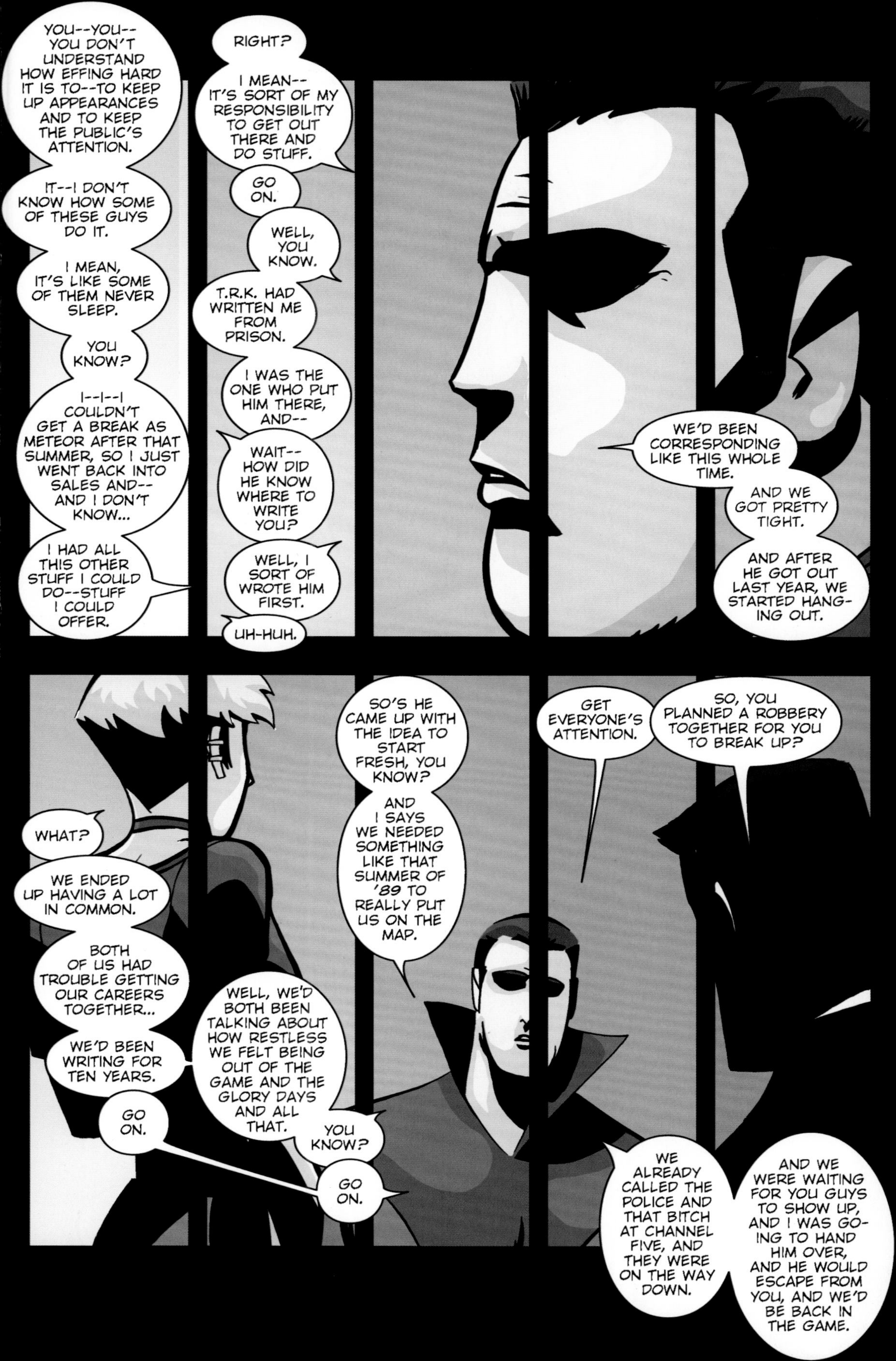
YOU--YOU--YOU DON'T UNDERSTAND HOW EFFING HARD IT IS TO--TO KEEP UP APPEARANCES AND TO KEEP THE PUBLIC'S ATTENTION.
IT--I DON'T KNOW HOW SOME OF THESE GUYS DO IT.
I MEAN, IT'S LIKE SOME OF THEM NEVER SLEEP.
YOU KNOW?
I--I--I COULDN'T GET A BREAK AS METEOR AFTER THAT SUMMER, SO I JUST WENT BACK INTO SALES AND--AND I DON'T KNOW...
I HAD ALL THIS OTHER STUFF I COULD DO--STUFF I COULD OFFER.
RIGHT?
I MEAN--IT'S SORT OF MY RESPONSIBILITY TO GET OUT THERE AND DO STUFF.
GO ON.
WELL, YOU KNOW.
T.R.K. HAD WRITTEN ME FROM PRISON.
I WAS THE ONE WHO PUT HIM THERE, AND--
WAIT--HOW DID HE KNOW WHERE TO WRITE YOU?
WELL, I SORT OF WROTE HIM FIRST.
UH-HUH.
WE'D BEEN CORRESPONDING LIKE THIS WHOLE TIME.
AND WE GOT PRETTY TIGHT.
AND AFTER HE GOT OUT LAST YEAR, WE STARTED HANG-ING OUT.
WHAT?
WE ENDED UP HAVING A LOT IN COMMON.
BOTH OF US HAD TROUBLE GETTING OUR CAREERS TOGETHER...
WE'D BEEN WRITING FOR TEN YEARS.
GO ON.
WELL, WE'D BOTH BEEN TALKING ABOUT HOW RESTLESS WE FELT BEING OUT OF THE GAME AND THE GLORY DAYS AND ALL THAT.
YOU KNOW?
GO ON.
SO'S HE CAME UP WITH THE IDEA TO START FRESH, YOU KNOW?
AND I SAYS WE NEEDED SOMETHING LIKE THAT SUMMER OF '89 TO REALLY PUT US ON THE MAP.
GET EVERYONE'S ATTENTION.
SO, YOU PLANNED A ROBBERY TOGETHER FOR YOU TO BREAK UP?
WE ALREADY CALLED THE POLICE AND THAT BITCH AT CHANNEL FIVE, AND THEY WERE ON THE WAY DOWN.
AND WE WERE WAITING FOR YOU GUYS TO SHOW UP, AND I WAS GO-ING TO HAND HIM OVER, AND HE WOULD ESCAPE FROM YOU, AND WE'D BE BACK IN THE GAME.

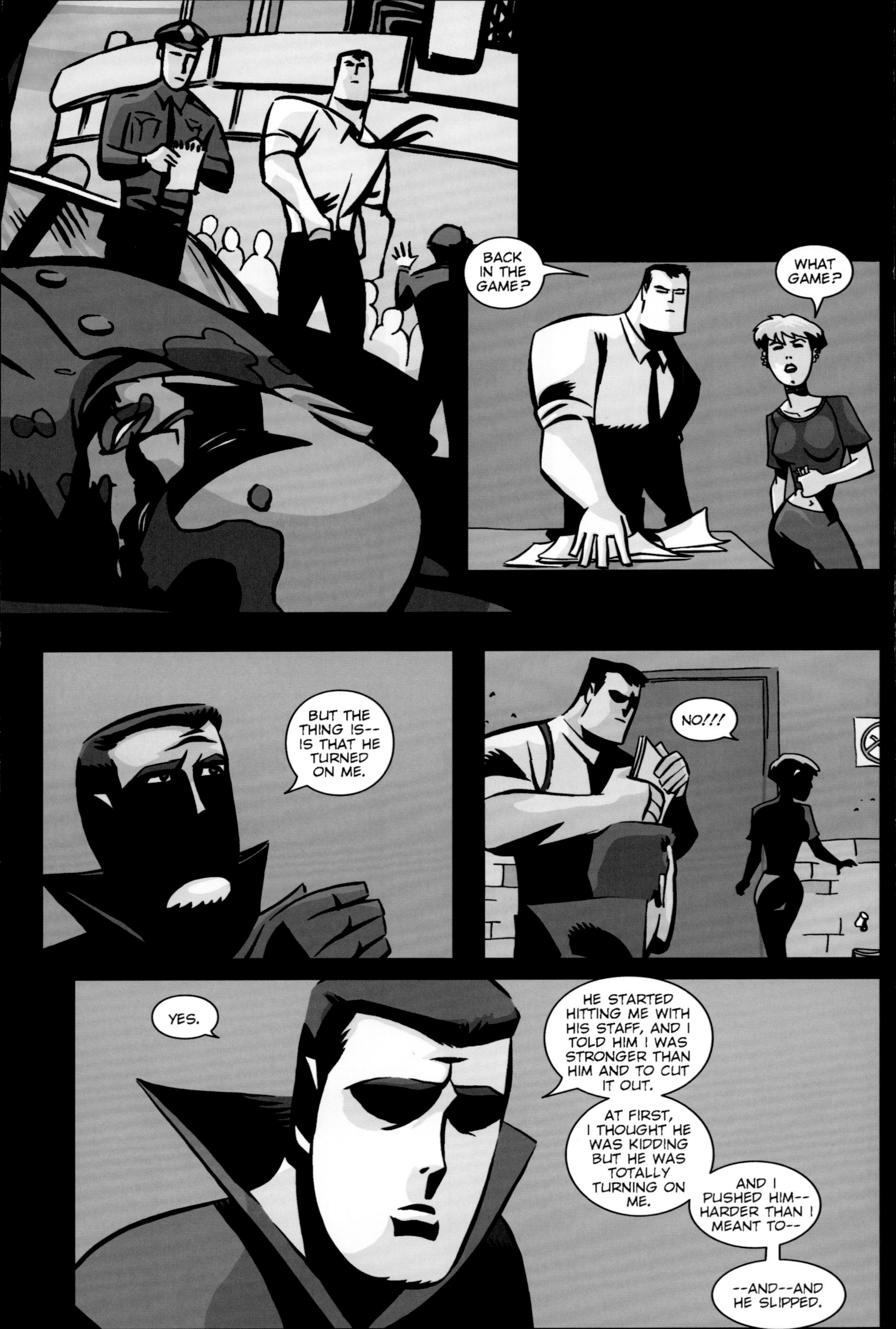

BACK IN THE GAME?
WHAT GAME?
BUT THE THING IS-- IS THAT HE TURNED ON ME.
NO!!!
YES.
HE STARTED HITTING ME WITH HIS STAFF, AND I TOLD HIM I WAS STRONGER THAN HIM AND TO CUT IT OUT.
AT FIRST, I THOUGHT HE WAS KIDDING BUT HE WAS TOTALLY TURNING ON ME.
AND I PUSHED HIM-- HARDER THAN I MEANT TO--
--AND--AND HE SLIPPED.

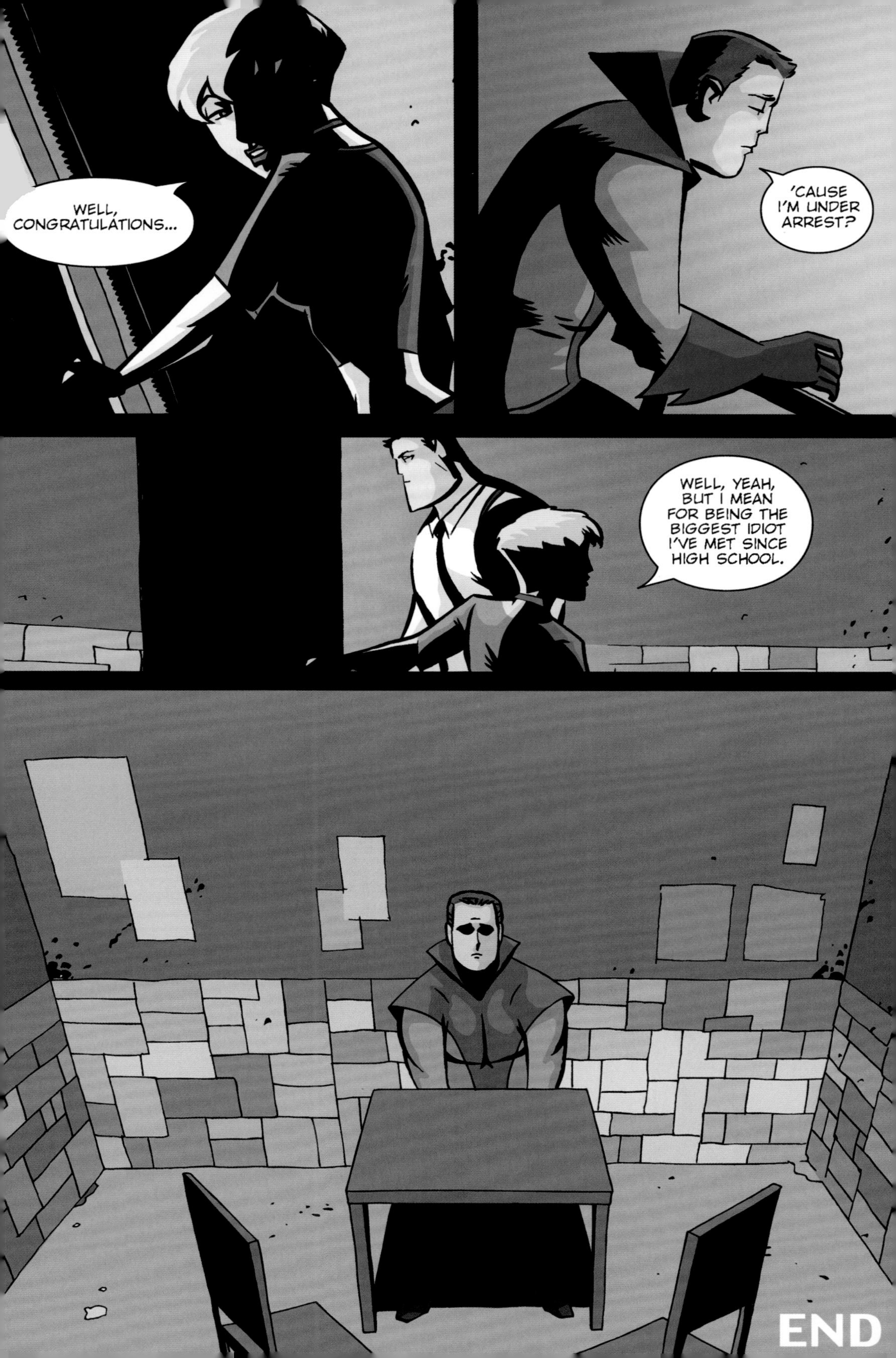
WELL, CONGRATULATIONS...
'CAUSE I'M UNDER ARREST?
WELL, YEAH, BUT I MEAN FOR BEING THE BIGGEST IDIOT I'VE MET SINCE HIGH SCHOOL.
END

PARTIAL TRANSCRIPT FROM COURT DOCKET 55673-2433

THE PEOPLE VS. THOMAS MILLS.

APPEARANCES:

For Plaintiff:

Attorney CLIVE BARROW

For Defendant:

NICHOLAS CORIC District Attorney

JULIET PECK Assistant District Attorney

CSR# 45564

OFFICIAL REPORTER ROBERT STRICT

DATED October 25, 2001   COURTROOM 4

CC: THIS PUPPY OVER TO A DET. DEENA PILGRIM OVER AT HOMICIDE 5TH PR. POWERS DIV.

I have the drawings from channel 5 too - send them as well?

(CONTINUED

CONTINUED:

COURT RESUMES. 10:11 am October 22, 2001

> DEFENSE ATTORNEY CLIVE BARROW
> THE DEFENSE WOULD LIKE TO CALL TO THE
> STAND... MR. THOMAS MILLS.

DEFENDANT THOMAS MILLS TAKES THE STAND. THE BAILIFF
APPROACHES.

> BAILIFF
> DO YOU SWEAR TO TELL THE TRUTH, THE WHOLE
> TRUTH, AND NOTHING BUT THE TRUTH, SO HELP
> YOU GOD?

> TOMMY MILLS
> YES. YES, I DO.

> BAILIFF
> YOU MAY SIT.

DEFENSE ATTORNEY CLIVE BARROW APPROACHES.

> DEFENSE ATTORNEY CLIVE BARROW
> THOMAS...

> TOMMY MILLS
> TOMMY IS OK?

> DEFENSE ATTORNEY CLIVE BARROW
> TOMMY, TELL THE COURT HOW YOU CAME TO
> HAVE POWERS?

> TOMMY MILLS
> WELL, IN COLLEGE I WAS WORKING A- A
> SUMMER CONSTRUCTION JOB. JUST MANUAL
> STUFF. WE WERE MAKING ROOM FOR THIS RIG-
> DIGGING. CLEARING AN AREA OUT FOR IT. AND
> ONE OF THE GUYS HIT ONE OF THE
> UNDERGROUND PIPES- OR WE THOUGHT IT WAS A
> PIPE, BUT IT WAS ACTUALLY THIS METAL
> CANISTER OF SOME KIND. AND WHEN THE GUY-
> SCOTTY- WHEN HE HIT IT WITH HIS SHOVEL-
> THIS GAS CAME SEEPING OUT. IT WAS FULL OF
> THIS BLUEISH GAS. AND EVERYONE AROUND ME.
> WE- WE ALL STARTED CHOKING. I FAINTED. I
> NEVER DID THAT BEFORE, BUT I FAINTED. I
> WAS HOLDING MY EYES. AND WHEN I WOKE UP
> IN THE HOSPITAL, THEY TOLD ME THAT
> EVERYONE ELSE AT THE SITE HAD DIED.
> EVERYONE EXCEPT FOR ME.

> DEFENSE ATTORNEY CLIVE BARROW
> A BLUE-ISH GAS.

(CONTINUED

CONTINUED: (2)

                    TOMMY MILLS
          YES.

                    DEFENSE ATTORNEY CLIVE BARROW
          DID YOU EVER FIND OUT WHAT THE GAS WAS?

                    TOMMY MILLS
          NO, NO BUT I ASKED AROUND. I ASKED THE
          CONSTRUCTION COMPANY I WORKED FOR BUT
          THEY SAID THEY DIDN'T KNOW. SOMEONE TOLD
          ME SOMETHING ABOUT THE F.B.I. BEING
          INVOLVED, BUT I DON'T REALLY KNOW
          ANYTHING BEYOND THAT.

                    PROSECUTOR CORIC
          OBJECTION, HERESY.

                    JUDGE ROLLINS
          SUSTAINED.

                    DEFENSE ATTORNEY CLIVE BARROW
          HOW MANY PEOPLE DIED IN THE ACCIDENT,
          TOMMY?

                    TOMMY MILLS
          UH- TEN. TEN.

                    DEFENSE ATTORNEY CLIVE BARROW
          AND YOU WERE THE SOLE SURVIVOR?

                    TOMMY MILLS
          WELL, SOME OTHER GUYS RAN AWAY BEFORE THE
          GAS REACHED THEM, BUT I WAS THE ONLY ONE
          IN THE IMMEDIATE AREA. YEAH, IT WAS
          REALLY SAD.

                    DEFENSE ATTORNEY CLIVE BARROW
          THE SOLE SURVIVOR.

                    TOMMY MILLS
          I DON'T KNOW WHY? BUT YEAH, I GUESS.

                    DEFENSE ATTORNEY CLIVE BARROW
          AND WHEN YOU RECOVERED YOU FOUND THAT YOU
          HAD POWERS.

                    TOMMY MILLS
          YES, SIR.

                    DEFENSE ATTORNEY CLIVE BARROW
          WHAT POWERS DO YOU HAVE, TOMMY?

(CONTINUED

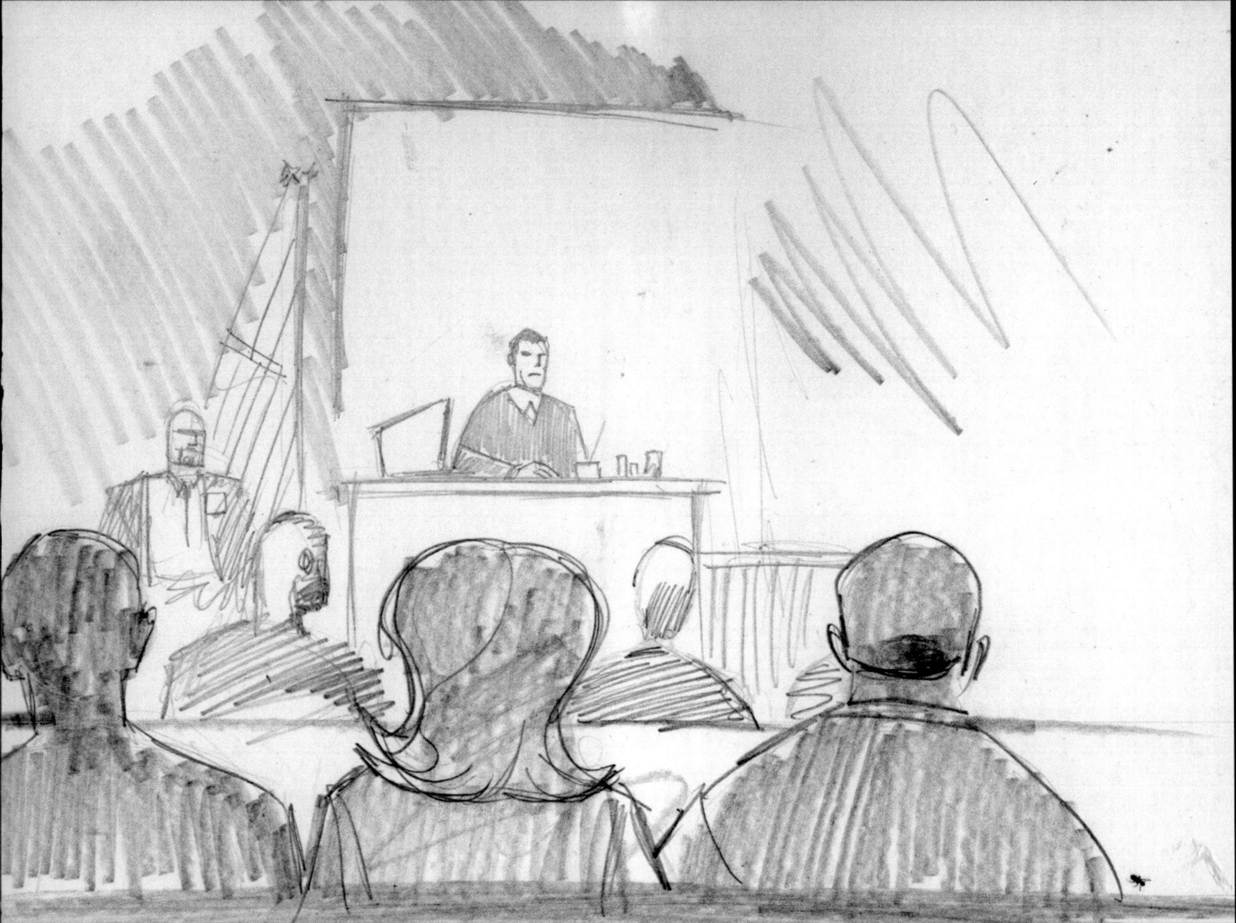

COURTROOM DRAWINGS COURTESY OEMING STUDIOS

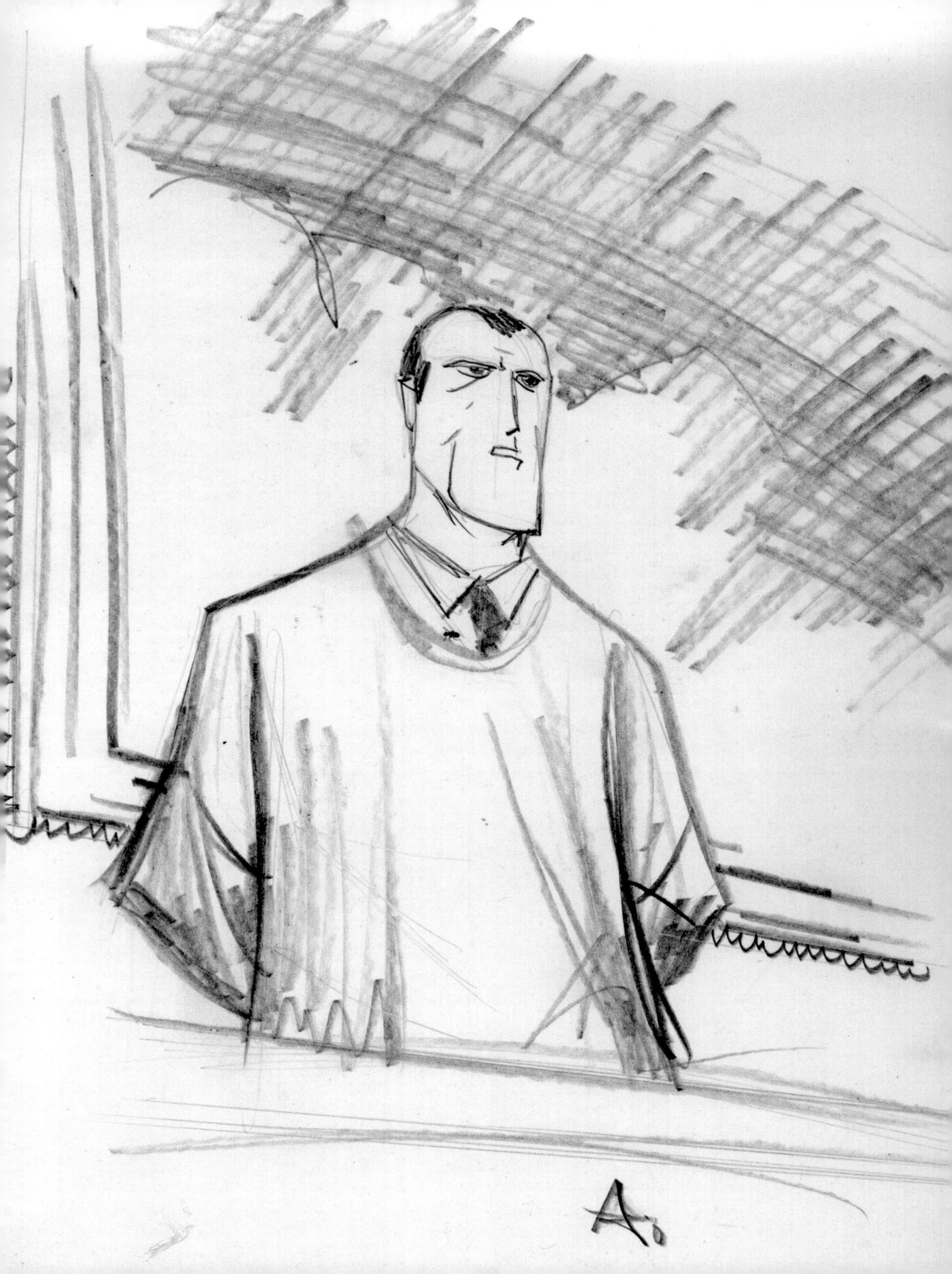
A

                              TOMMY MILLS
          I HAVE - WELL, I'M PRETTY STRONG AND I
          CAN JUMP REALLY HIGH. CAN'T FLY, JUST
          JUMP. AND I'M PRETTY FAST NOW, AND MY
          SKIN IS- IT DOESN'T BREAK THAT EASILY.
          AND MY EYE SIGHT. ALL MY SENSES REALLY-
          THEY'RE REALLY STRONG. I REGISTERED IN AT
          LEVEL FIVE.

                         DEFENSE ATTORNEY CLIVE BARROW
          AND WHEN YOU FOUND YOU HAD THESE POWERS,
          WHAT DID YOU DO?

                              TOMMY MILLS
          I- WELL, IT WAS KIND OF FATE REALLY,
          BECAUSE THAT SAME WEEK I HAPPENED TO WALK
          INTO A CONVENIENT STORE THAN WAS BEING
          HELD UP AND I - I WAS ABLE TO STOP THE
          BURGLARY. NO ONE WAS HURT. IT- IT WAS A
          GOOD FEELING.

                         DEFENSE ATTORNEY CLIVE BARROW
          WOW.

                              TOMMY MILLS
          AND I REALIZED THAT I- I HAD A CALLING-
          THAT I WAS REALLY LUCKY.

                         DEFENSE ATTORNEY CLIVE BARROW
          INDEED.

                              TOMMY MILLS
          SO, I REGISTERED MY COSTUME, GAVE MYSELF
          A NAME.

                         DEFENSE ATTORNEY CLIVE BARROW
          'METEOR?'

                              TOMMY MILLS
          METEOR.

                         DEFENSE ATTORNEY CLIVE BARROW
          WHY METEOR?

                              TOMMY MILLS
          THOUGHT IT SOUNDED PRETTY COOL.

COURTROOM SNICKERS. JUDGE HITS THE GAVEL.

                              JUDGE ROLLINS
          ORDER.

                                                   (CONTINUED

CONTINUED: (4)

> TOMMY MILLS
> WELL, I-I-I DID.

> DEFENSE ATTORNEY CLIVE BARROW
> YOU HAD A PRETTY STRONG START WITH YOUR
> NEW CAREER. A COUPLE OF COLORFUL DISPLAYS
> OF HEROISM.

> TOMMY MILLS
> YES, SIR.

> DEFENSE ATTORNEY CLIVE BARROW
> YOU SAVED THAT GIRL IN THE PARK.

> TOMMY MILLS
> YES, SIR.

> DEFENSE ATTORNEY CLIVE BARROW
> POWERS MAGAZINE FEATURED YOU IN THEIR 'ON
> THE RISE' SIDE BAR

> TOMMY MILLS
> YES, SIR.

> DEFENSE ATTORNEY CLIVE BARROW
> BUT YOU KIND OF FELL OUT OF THE SPOTLIGHT
> AFTER THAT...

> TOMMY MILLS
> YES, SIR.

> DEFENSE ATTORNEY CLIVE BARROW
> WHAT HAPPENED? WHERE'D YOU GO?

> TOMMY MILLS
> WELL, I WAS STILL PRETTY NEW AT ALL OF
> IT, AND I DIDN'T UNDERSTAND, REALLY, HOW
> THE MEDIA WORKED. SO WHEN I WAS ASKED BY
> THIS MAGAZINE SOMETHING ABOUT A POWERED
> PERSONS RESPONSIBILITY IN OUR SOCIETY AND
> IF IT WAS GOOD FOR THE CITY- WELL, I HAD
> MY QUOTE TAKEN OUT OF CONTEXT AND-

> DEFENSE ATTORNEY CLIVE BARROW
> WHAT DID YOU SAY?

> TOMMY MILLS
> I SAID THAT I THOUGHT IT WAS GOOD FOR THE
> CITY TO HAVE PEOPLE WHO WERE WILLING TO
> BE WHERE THE COPS WEREN'T ABLE TO BE OR
> COULDN'T BE. BUT IN THE ARTICLE IT
> SOUNDED WRONG.
> (MORE)

(CONTINUED

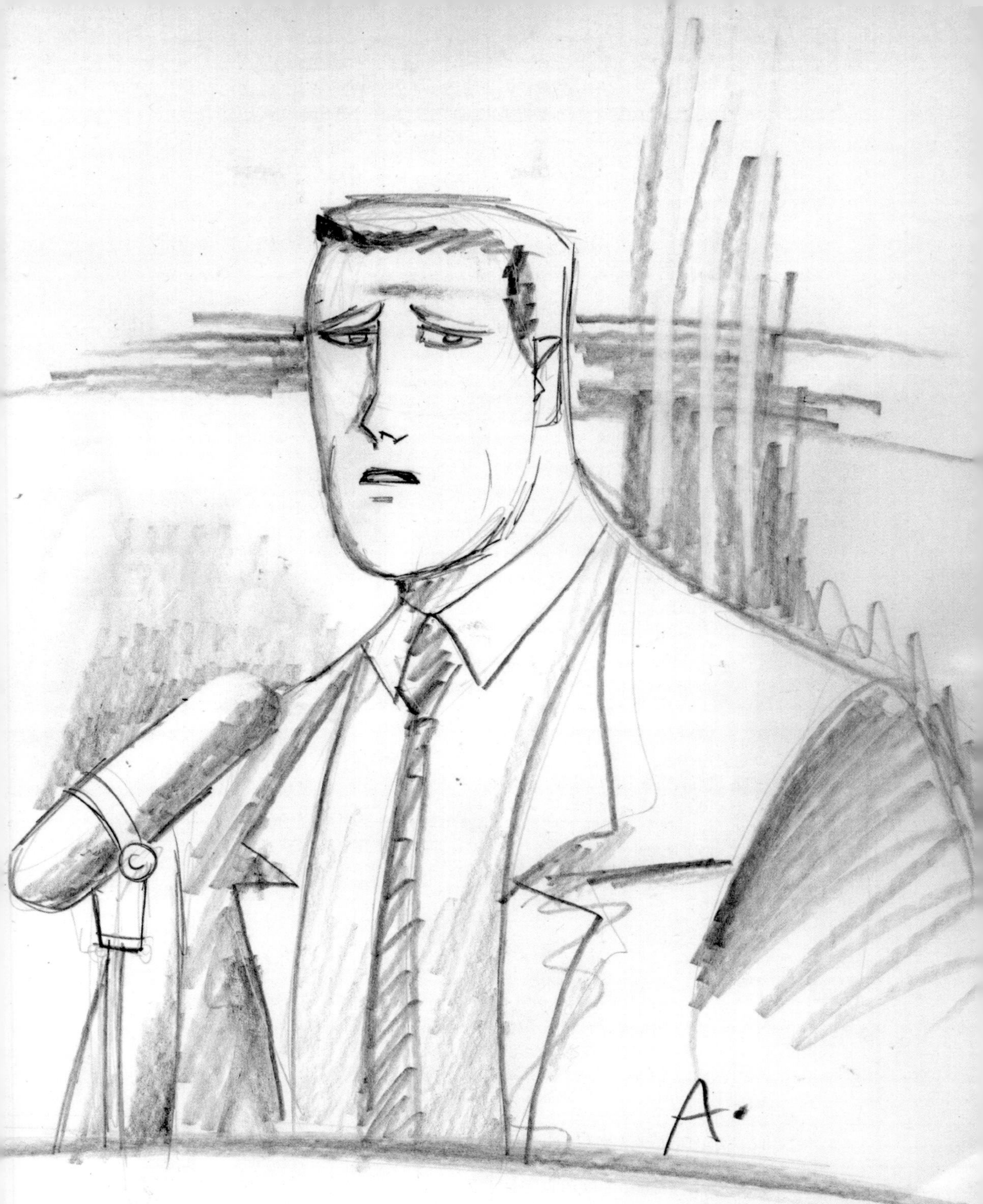
A.

CONTINUED: (5)

                    TOMMY MILLS (CONT'D)
IT SOUNDED IN THE ARTICLE AS IF I THOUGHT
SUPER POWERED PEOPLE WERE DOING THE COPS
JOB FOR THEM. THE TONE OF THE PIECE, IT-
IT WASN'T WHAT I WAS TOLD IT WAS GOING TO
BE.

            DEFENSE ATTORNEY CLIVE BARROW
AND WHERE DID THIS ARTICLE RUN?

                    TOMMY MILLS
IN AIR MAGAZINE.

            DEFENSE ATTORNEY CLIVE BARROW
YOU THINK THE COMMENTS WERE TAKEN OUT OF
CONTEXT?

                    TOMMY MILLS
OH, DEFINITELY. I WASN'T SLAMMING THE
COPS. I ADMIRE THE COPS. I- I WAS TRYING
TO SAY SOMETHING POSITIVE. I THOUGHT IT
WAS NICE THAT WE HAVE THE COPS PLUS WE
ALSO HAVE PEOPLE WHO ARE WILLING TO DRESS
UP AND SYMBOLIZE SOMETHING AND BE
PROACTIVE IN THE COMMUNITY.

            DEFENSE ATTORNEY CLIVE BARROW
'PROACTIVE IN THE COMMUNITY.' WELL SAID.

                    TOMMY MILLS
THANKS, WELL, THIS- THIS ARTICLE WAS LIKE
A DEATH RATTLE FOR MY CAREER AS A SUPER
HERO. ALL THE COPS PUT ME ON THEIR SHIT
LIST OR SOMETHING. EXCUSE MY LANGUAGE. I-
I COULDN'T CATCH A BREAK AFTER THE
ARTICLE. IT WAS WEIRD.

            DEFENSE ATTORNEY CLIVE BARROW
HOW SO?

                    TOMMY MILLS
THE COPS- THE POLICE WOULD IGNORE ME WHEN
THEY SHOWED UP. WHICH IS FINE, I GUESS. I
MEAN, THEY CERTAINLY DON'T OWE ME
ANYTHING. OR- YEAH- OR THEY WOULD TAKE
THE GUY I CAUGHT FOR THEM AND BOOK HIM
WITHOUT GIVING ME ANY CREDIT IN THE
REPORT. AND IN SOME INSTANCES THEY WOULD
JUST LET THE GUY GO. JUST LET HIM GO
RIGHT IN FRONT OF ME.

                 PROSECUTOR CORIC
OBJECTION. MOVE TO STRIKE.

                                    (CONTINUED

CONTINUED: (6)

                    JUDGE ROLLINS
          SUSTAINED. COUNSELLOR? ROUND IT HOME.

                    DEFENSE ATTORNEY CLIVE BARROW
          SO YOU FELT YOUR ACTIONS WERE...?

                    TOMMY MILLS
          I WAS TRYING TO BE HELPFUL. I WAS TRYING
          TO BE PART OF THE COMMUNITY- BUT ITS HARD
          WHEN THE COMMUNITY IS GIVING YOU THE COLD
          SHOULDER. WHEN THE LAW ENFORCEMENT
          OFFICIALS WERE-

                    PROSECUTOR CORIC
          OBJECTION.

                    JUDGE ROLLINS
          SUSTAINED. MOVE FORWARD ON THIS.

                    TOMMY MILLS
          WELL, IT- IT WAS MADE VERY CLEAR AFTER
          THAT ARTICLE THAT THERE WAS LITTLE OR NO
          NEED FOR 'METEOR.' I KNOW WHEN I'M NOT
          WANTED.

                    DEFENSE ATTORNEY CLIVE BARROW
          WHAT DID YOU DO?

                    TOMMY MILLS
          I TOOK THE HINT AND I - I WENT BACK TO MY
          NORMAL LIFE. CIVILIAN LIFE.

                    DEFENSE ATTORNEY CLIVE BARROW
          TELL ME HOW YOU MET REGINALD COPPER WHO
          WE NOW KNOW PUBLICLY AS T.R.K.

                    TOMMY MILLS
          BEFORE I RETIRED, HE TRIED TO ROB THE
          NOZAMACK JEWELRY STORE.

                    DEFENSE ATTORNEY CLIVE BARROW
          THE ONE DOWNTOWN?

                    TOMMY MILLS
          YES. AND I GOT TO HIM BEFORE HE DID ANY
          REAL DAMAGE OR GOT AWAY.

                    DEFENSE ATTORNEY CLIVE BARROW
          AND HE WENT TO JAIL BECAUSE OF THIS.
          BECAUSE OF YOU'RE TIMELY EFFORTS.

                    TOMMY MILLS
          YES.

(CONTINUED

CONTINUED: (7)

                    DEFENSE ATTORNEY CLIVE BARROW
AND YOU WERE IN CONTACT WITH HIM AFTER
THAT?

                    TOMMY MILLS
YES, WE CORRESPONDED.

                    DEFENSE ATTORNEY CLIVE BARROW
BY MAIL.

                    TOMMY MILLS
YES. HE TOLD ME IT WAS PART OF A PROGRAM
IN THE PRISON. A PRISON PROGRAM. THE
PRIEST TOLD HIM TO BREAK DOWN THE WALL
BETWEEN WHERE HE WAS AND HOW HE GOT HERE.

                    DEFENSE ATTORNEY CLIVE BARROW
AND YOU RESPONDED?

                    TOMMY MILLS
YES, IT WAS A HEARTFELT LETTER AND I FELT
WE ACTUALLY HAD A LOT IN COMMON. IT
SEEMED LIKE THE RIGHT THING TO DO.

                    DEFENSE ATTORNEY CLIVE BARROW
AND HE FOUND YOU, HOW?

                    TOMMY MILLS
I ASSUMED HE LOOKED IT UP IN THE BOOK. I-
I REALLY DIDN'T SEE THE REASON FOR A
SECRET IDENTITY.

                    DEFENSE ATTORNEY CLIVE BARROW
WHY NOT?

                    TOMMY MILLS
THEY ALWAYS SEEMED TO ME TO BE KIND OF
LIKE LYING. LYING AND HIDING. JUST DIDN'T
OCCUR TO ME TO DO THAT.

                    DEFENSE ATTORNEY CLIVE BARROW
AND YOU KEPT THIS UP- THIS CORRESPONDENCE
FOR THE ENTIRE NINE YEARS HE WAS IN
PRISON.

                    TOMMY MILLS
YES. ON AND OFF. BUT YES.

                    DEFENSE ATTORNEY CLIVE BARROW
SO, YOU WERE FRIENDS?

                    TOMMY MILLS
I THOUGHT SO, YES.

                                        (CONTINUED

CONTINUED: (8)

                    DEFENSE ATTORNEY CLIVE BARROW
AND IN ALL THAT TIME DID HE EVER TELL YOU
THAT HE PLANNED ON ROBBING AGAIN WHEN HE
GOT OUT?

                    TOMMY MILLS
NO, SIR. NO.

                    DEFENSE ATTORNEY CLIVE BARROW
HE DIDN'T?

                    TOMMY MILLS
NO, NO I WOULD HAVE ENDED THE
CORRESPONDENCE IMMEDIATELY IF THAT HAD
HAPPENED.

                    DEFENSE ATTORNEY CLIVE BARROW
DID YOU EVER TALK ABOUT IT IN THE
HYPOTHETICAL?

                    TOMMY MILLS
NO. NEVER. HE ONLY BROUGHT UP HIS PAST IN
THE CONTEXT OF HIS TALKS WITH THE PRIEST.
HE ALWAYS SOUNDED VERY REMORSEFUL.
ALWAYS.

                    DEFENSE ATTORNEY CLIVE BARROW
AND WHEN HE GOT OUT OF JAIL, YOU SAW EACH
OTHER SOCIALLY?

                    TOMMY MILLS
ONLY A COUPLE OF TIMES. HE WAS ONLY OUT A
FEW MONTHS.

                    DEFENSE ATTORNEY CLIVE BARROW
WHAT DID YOU TALK ABOUT WHEN YOU GOT
TOGETHER?

                    TOMMY MILLS
WELL, LOTS OF STUFF. MOVIES, GIRLS. BUT
WE TALKED A LOT ABOUT HOW HARD IT WAS FOR
HIM TO READJUST TO CIVILIAN LIFE.

                    DEFENSE ATTORNEY CLIVE BARROW
AND WAS IT DURING THESE TALKS THAT HE
BROUGHT UP THE IDEA OF ROBBING THE-

                    PROSECUTOR CORIC
OBJECTION. LEADING.

                    JUDGE ROLLINS
SUSTAINED. CONTINUE.

                                        (CONTINUED

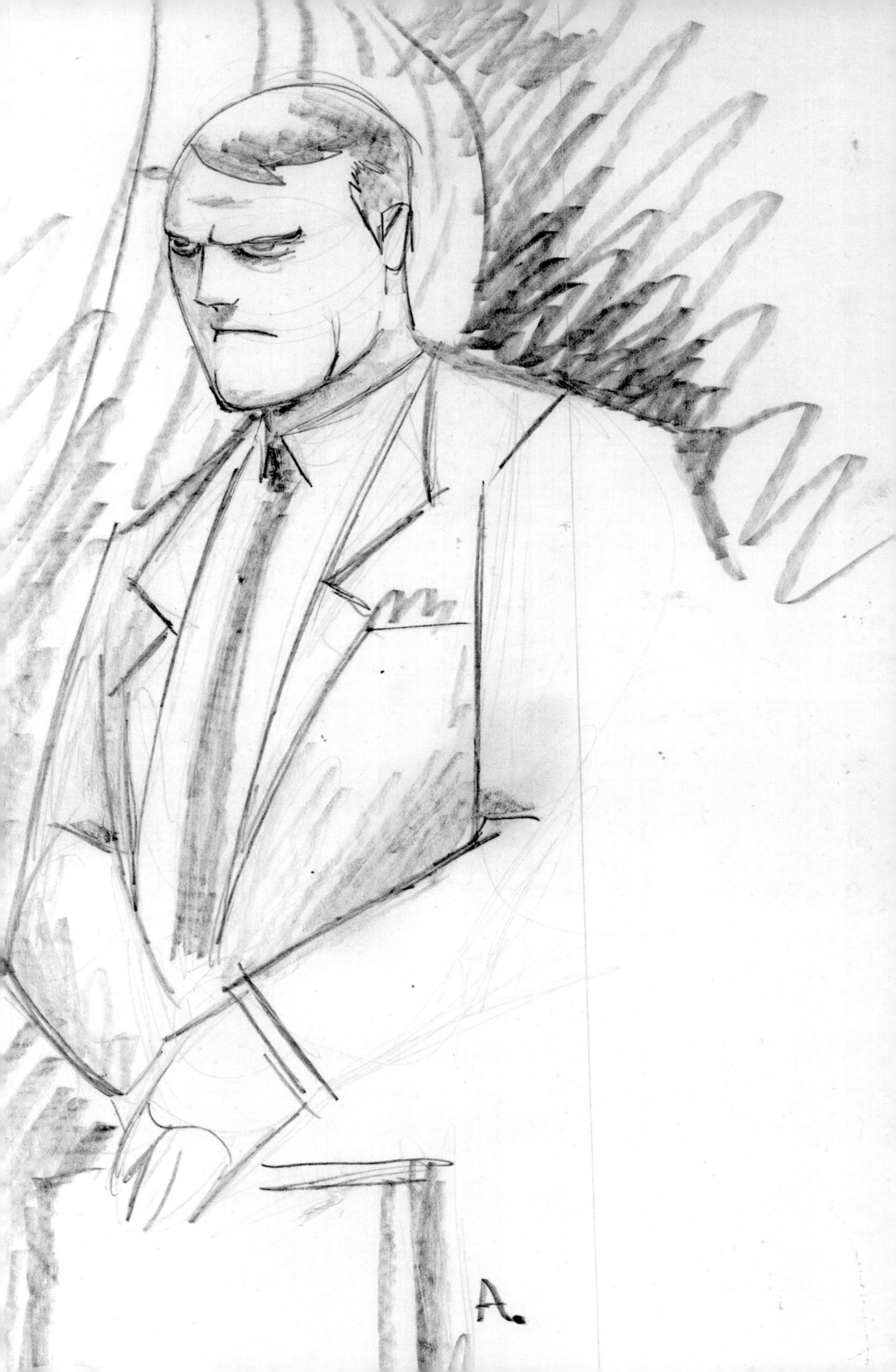

CONTINUED: (9)

                    DEFENSE ATTORNEY CLIVE BARROW
WHEN WAS THE FIRST TIME REGINALD BROUGHT
UP THE IDEA OF THE ROBBERY?

          TOMMY MILLS
THAT DAY. THE DAY HE- HE DIED.

          DEFENSE ATTORNEY CLIVE BARROW
HOW DID IT COME UP?

          TOMMY MILLS
HE STARTED TALKING ABOUT HOW RESTLESS HE
FELT BEING OUT OF 'THE GAME' AND THE
GLORY DAYS AND ALL THAT. YOU KNOW?

          DEFENSE ATTORNEY CLIVE BARROW
UH HUH.

          TOMMY MILLS
HE SAID HE HAD AN IDEA TO START FRESH. HE
SAID WE- WE NEEDED SOMETHING LIKE THAT
SUMMER OF '89 TO REALLY PUT US ON THE MAP
AGAIN. TO GET EVERYONES ATTENTION. HE
SAID HE WAS GOING TO DO THE ROBBERY AND
THAT I SHOULD TRY TO BREAK IT UP, BUT LET
HIM GET AWAY JUST IN THE NICK OF TIME. HE
SAID WE'D BOTH MAKE THE PAPER. I COULDN'T
BELIEVE WHAT HE WAS SAYING.

          DEFENSE ATTORNEY CLIVE BARROW
AND WHAT DID YOU SAY?

          TOMMY MILLS
AT FIRST, I THOUGHT HE WAS JOKING. HE- IT
WAS SO UNLIKE HIM. IT WAS ONLY AFTER HE
STARTED TALKING THIS WAY THAT I REALIZED
THAT HE MIGHT HAVE BEEN DRINKING. HE WAS
QUITE IRRATIONAL AND VERY UNLIKE HIMSELF-
EDGY. AND I - AND I FELT BAD FOR HIM
BECAUSE I KNEW HOW HARD HE HAD TRIED TO
GET HIS LIFE TOGETHER, BUT AT THE SAME
TIME- I WAS, WELL, OVERWHELMED WITH A
FEELING OF DISGUST AND BETRAYAL THAT MY
FRIEND- THIS PERSON I THOUGHT WAS MY
FRIEND- WOULD NOW SOMEHOW TRY TO INVOLVE
ME IN THIS.

          DEFENSE ATTORNEY CLIVE BARROW
SO, YOU TOLD HIM NO.

          TOMMY MILLS
I DID, THEN I PAID THE BILL, GOT UP, AND
I WALKED OUT OF THE DINER.

                              (CONTINUED

CONTINUED: (10)

            DEFENSE ATTORNEY CLIVE BARROW
BUT YOU CAME BACK.

            TOMMY MILLS
IT- IT WAS VERY CLEAR THAT I HAD TO STOP
HIM. THAT I HAD TO COME BACK INTO 'THE
GAME' AND STOP HIM.

            DEFENSE ATTORNEY CLIVE BARROW
WHY DIDN'T YOU CALL THE POLICE?

            TOMMY MILLS
I DID.

            DEFENSE ATTORNEY CLIVE BARROW
YOU DID?

            TOMMY MILLS
I DID. BUT THEY SAID SQUAD CARS WERE
ALREADY ON THE WAY THERE. THEY SAID HE
CALLED IT IN- DARED THEM, TO COME GET
HIM.

            DEFENSE ATTORNEY CLIVE BARROW
SO WHY DIDN'T YOU JUST STAY HOME?

            TOMMY MILLS
I COULDN'T- I KNEW WHAT HE COULD DO TO
THE POLICE OFFICERS. I KNEW WHAT HIS
WEAPONRY COULD DO TO THEM IF THEY WEREN'T
PREPARED. AND I COULD GET THERE IN NO
TIME AT ALL. I FELT A RESPONSIBILITY. TEN
YEARS. HE WAS MY FRIEND.

            DEFENSE ATTORNEY CLIVE BARROW
AND WHEN YOU GOT THERE...

            TOMMY MILLS
HE SAID HE KNEW I WOULD COME, THAT I
WOULDN'T LET HIM DOWN. I TOLD HIM- I SAID
I WASN'T THERE TO HELP. I WAS THERE TO
STOP HIM BEFORE THINGS GOT OUT OF HAND.
BUT HE STARTED LAUGHING AND SWINGING
WILDLY. HE- HE -HE JUST WENT MANIC ON ME.

            DEFENSE ATTORNEY CLIVE BARROW
AND THAT'S WHEN HE SLIPPED.

            TOMMY MILLS
THAT'S WHEN HE SLIPPED.

(CONTINUED

CONTINUED: (11)

                    DEFENSE ATTORNEY CLIVE BARROW
          IN YOUR OPINION, WAS THERE ANYWAY FOR YOU
          TO SAVE HIM?

                    TOMMY MILLS
          DON'T YOU THINK I WOULD HAVE IF I COULD?

                    DEFENSE ATTORNEY CLIVE BARROW
          NO FURTHER QUESTIONS.

PROSECUTOR CORIC APPROACHES.

                    PROSECUTOR CORIC
          MR. MILLS, YOU TOLD THE DETECTIVES WHO
          QUESTIONED AND THEN ARRESTED YOU FOR
          MURDER THAT YOU WERE NOT IN THE DINER
          THAT NIGHT. YOU HELD TO THAT STORY UNTIL
          THEY COULD PROVE TO YOU THAT YOU WERE
          THERE WITH A CREDIT CARD RECEIPT. AND NOW
          YOU SAY YOU WERE THERE- BUT THAT YOU
          QUICKLY LEFT AFTER YOU FOUND OUT THE
          DECEASED HAD A DASTARDLY PLAN.

                    TOMMY MILLS
          YES.

                    PROSECUTOR CORIC
          SO AFTER YOUR FRIEND BETRAYED YOUR TRUST
          AND ADMITTED TO YOU WHAT HIS INTENTIONS
          WERE- YOU STOPPED AND BOUGHT HIM DINNER?

                    TOMMY MILLS
          I-

                    PROSECUTOR CORIC
          YOU DIDN'T JUST WALK RIGHT OUT AND LEAVE
          IN A HUFF. YOU FELT COMPELLED TO SAY:
          I'LL GET THIS ONE?

                    TOMMY MILLS
          I-

                    PROSECUTOR CORIC
          YES?

                    TOMMY MILLS
          I JUST DID.

                    PROSECUTOR CORIC
          MR. MILLS, IN THIS TEN YEARS OF
          CORRESPONDENCE WITH THE DECEASED DID YOU
          EVER KEEP ANY OF THE LETTERS?

                                        (CONTINUED

CONTINUED: (12)

                TOMMY MILLS
NO.

                PROSECUTOR CORIC
NO?

                TOMMY MILLS
NO.

                PROSECUTOR CORIC
WHY NOT?

                TOMMY MILLS
I'M KIND OF A NEAT FREAK. DON'T LIKE-
DON'T LIKE A LOT OF CLUTTER.

                PROSECUTOR CORIC
WOULD IT SURPRISE YOU TO FIND OUT THAT
THE DECEASED, IN FACT, DID?

                TOMMY MILLS
WHAT?

          DEFENSE ATTORNEY CLIVE BARROW
OBJECTION YOUR HONOR!

                PROSECUTOR CORIC
YOUR HONOR I WOULD LIKE TO ENTER INTO
EVIDENCE THIS LOVELY CASE- FULL OF THE
ACTUAL HANDWRITTEN CORRESPONDENCE BETWEEN
THE DEFENDANT AND THE DECEASED AND I
WOULD LIKE TO ENTER IT AS STATES EVIDENCE
C.

          DEFENSE ATTORNEY CLIVE BARROW
OBJECTION!

                JUDGE ROLLINS
OVERRULED.

                TOMMY MILLS
WHAT IS GOING- ?

                PROSECUTOR CORIC
IS THIS YOUR HANDWRITING, SIR?

                TOMMY MILLS
I DON'T KNOW.

                PROSECUTOR CORIC
DID YOU WRITE THIS?

                                        (CONTINUED

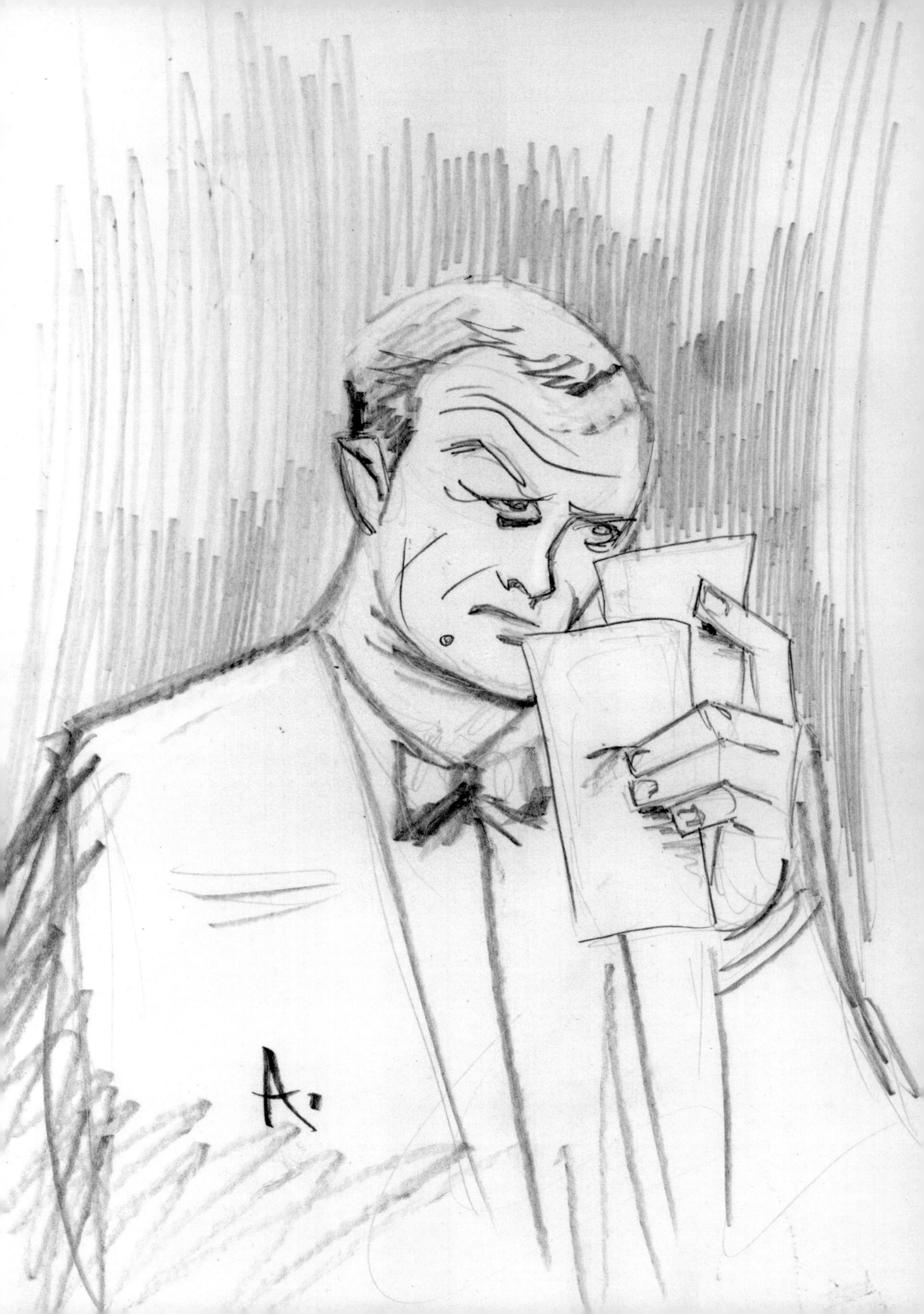

CONTINUED: (13)

                    TOMMY MILLS
I DON'T KNOW.

                    PROSECUTOR CORIC
YOU DON'T KNOW? WELL, THAT'S OK, WE CAN
GET A HANDWRITING EXPERT IN HERE IN A FEW
MINUTES WHO WILL GLADLY TESTIFY THAT IT
IS, IN FACT, YOUR VERY OWN HANDWRITING.
WOULD YOU LIKE A CLOSER LOOK?

                    TOMMY MILLS
NO.

                    PROSECUTOR CORIC
NO? WOW, IF I WAS ON TRIAL FOR MURDER AND
THE PROSECUTOR JUST SHOVED A PIECE OF
PAPER IN MY FACE WHILE I WAS ON THE
STAND... I WOULD WANT A CLOSER LOOK. BUT
THAT'S ME. I'M A FREAK.

                    TOMMY MILLS
IT MIGHT BE MINE.

                    PROSECUTOR CORIC
'MIGHT BE?'

                    TOMMY MILLS
ITS HARD TO SAY.

                    PROSECUTOR CORIC
WELL, READ FOR ME THE HIGHLIGHTED AREA ON
THIS ONE HERE. SEE IF IT RINGS ANY BELLS
FOR YOU. THIS ONE IS DATED 2 YEARS AND 3
MONTHS AGO. READ HERE. YOUR HONOR?

                    JUDGE ROLLINS
MR. MILLS, PLEASE DO WHAT THE PROSECUTOR
ASKS.

                    TOMMY MILLS
'DEAR REG, UCHUM- I- UH- I WAS REALLY
GLAD YOU WROTE BACK TO ME. I BET YOU WERE
SHOCKED TO-'

                    PROSECUTOR CORIC
LOUDER, MR. MILLS.

                    TOMMY MILLS
'I BET YOU WERE SHOCKED TO HEAR FROM ME,
OF ALL PEOPLE, OUT OF THE BLUE. I HAD A
REALLY SHITTY WEEK THIS WEEK.
                    (MORE)

(CONTINUED

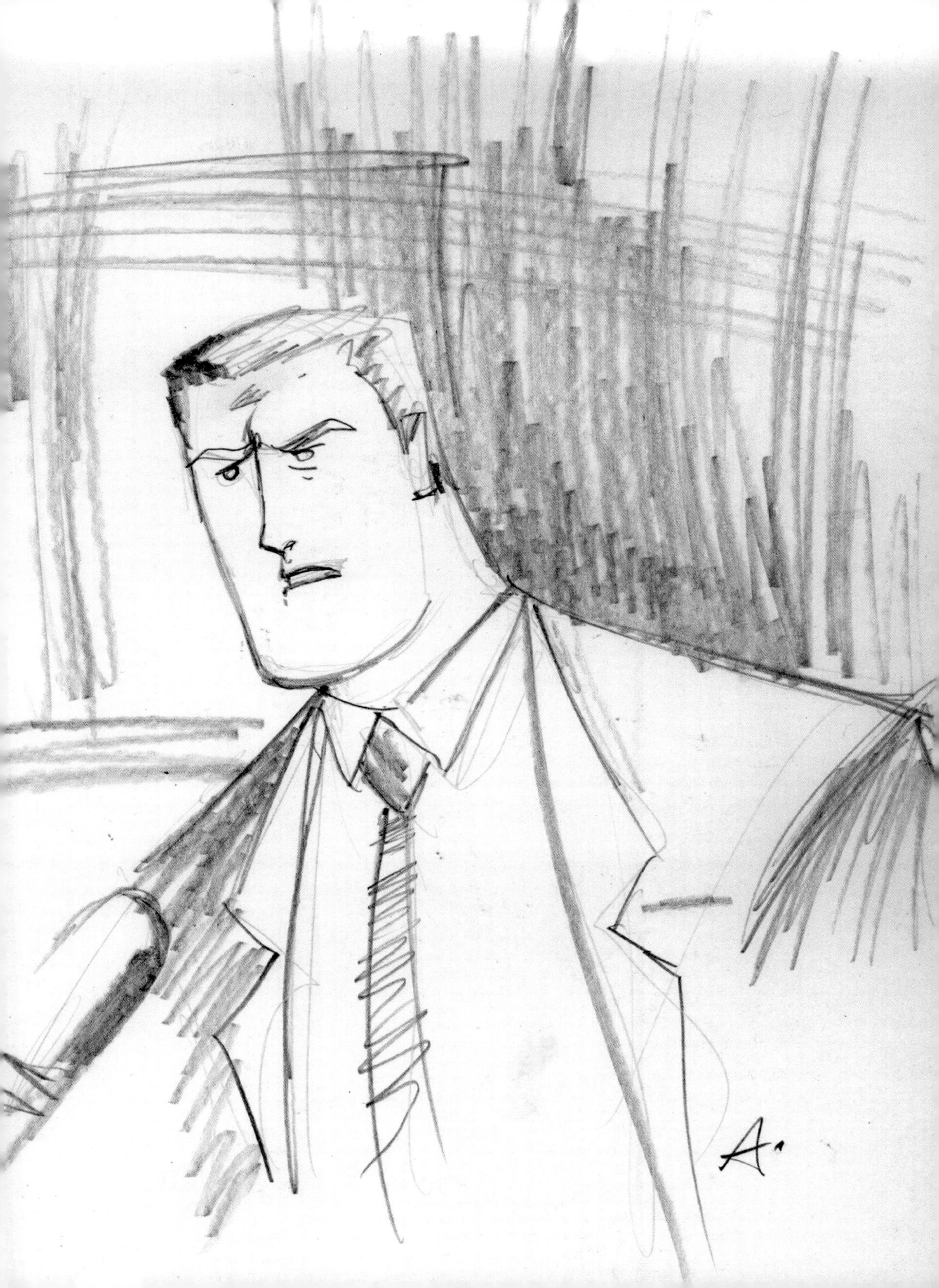

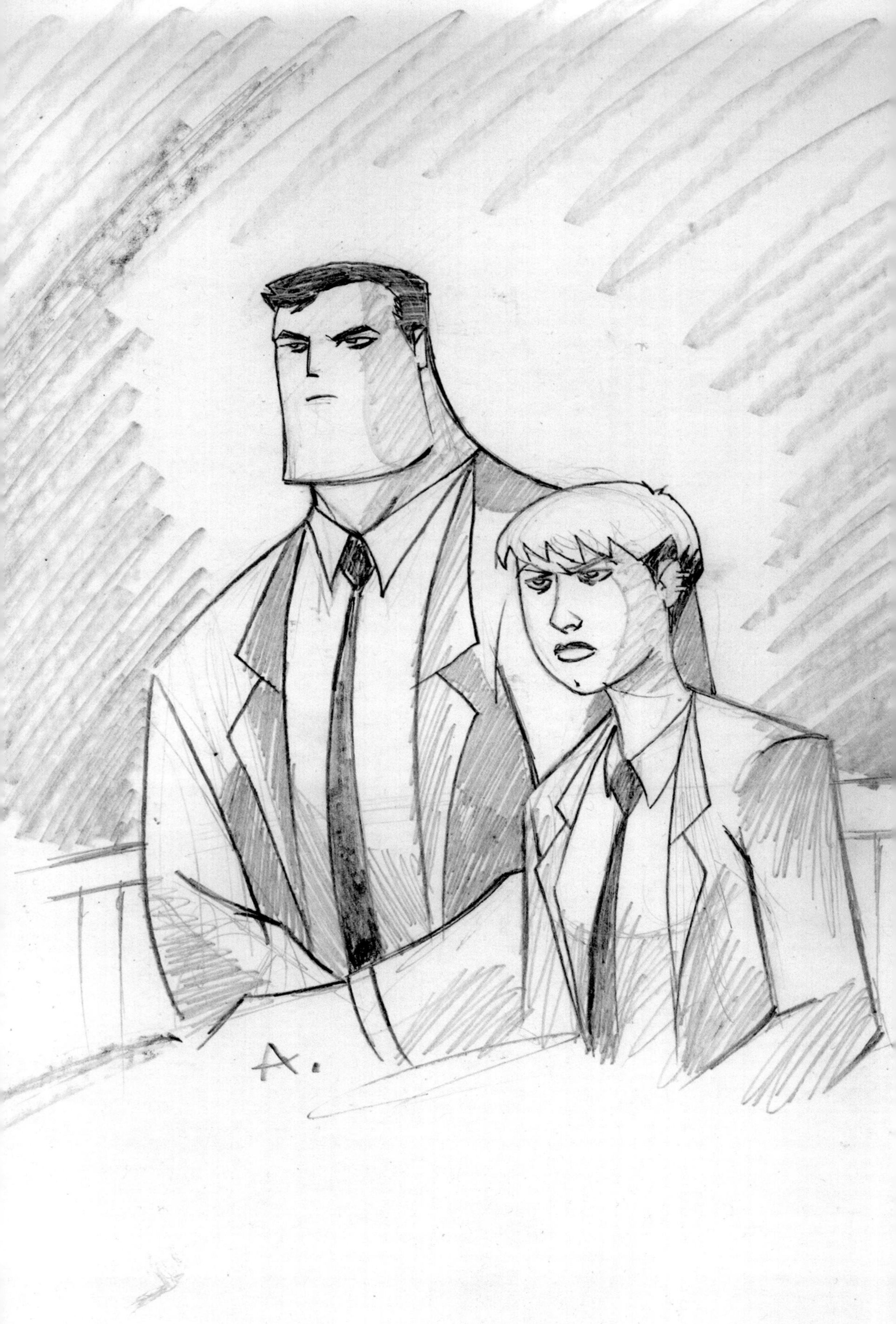

CONTINUED: (14)

                    TOMMY MILLS (CONT'D)
I KIND OF FEEL FUNNY BITCHING ABOUT MY
LIFE CONSIDERING YOUR SITUATION, BUT IT'S
REALLY NOT SO EASY ON THE OUTSIDE WORLD.
I HAVE THIS MENIAL JOB, YET I HAVE ALL
THESE THINGS- THESE POWERS I COULD- UH-
DO. WHEN I THINK OF ALL THOSE UNTALENTED
HACKS WITH ALL THOSE MERCHANDISING DEALS.
AND HERE I AM SITTING IN A CUBICLE HOPING
MY BITCH OF A BOSS DOESN'T BITCH AT ME.
WE GOT FIND A WAY TO... GET BACK IN THE
GAME. I DON'T KNOW ABOUT YOU... BUT I
JUST HAVE TO. ANY IDEAS?'

                    PROSECUTOR CORIC
DID YOU WRITE THAT?

                    TOMMY MILLS
MAYBE.

                    PROSECUTOR CORIC
WELL MR. MILLS, WE WILL HAVE THE
TESTIMONY FROM THE HANDWRITING EXPERT IN
A MINUTE. I HAVE ANOTHER QUESTION: YOU
TOLD THE ARRESTING DETECTIVES THAT THE
DECEASED CONTACTED YOU FROM JAIL FIRST.
THAT HE MADE FIRST CONTACT. WHICH IS IT?

                    TOMMY MILLS
WHAT- WHAT I SAID TODAY-

                    PROSECUTOR CORIC
'WHAT YOU SAID TODAY' WHAT?

                    TOMMY MILLS
WHAT I SAID TODAY- THAT- THAT IS THE
TRUTH.

                    PROSECUTOR CORIC
WILL IT BE THE TRUTH TOMORROW? OR IS WHAT
YOU SAY ONLY TRUE FOR THE DAY...

                    TOMMY MILLS
I...

                    DEFENSE ATTORNEY CLIVE BARROW
OBJECTION!

                    PROSECUTOR CORIC
STRIKE. MR. MILLS, IF, IN FACT, YOU HAD
NO IDEA THAT YOU WERE GOING TO BE GETTING
BACK INTO 'THE GAME' AS YOU SO ELOQUENTLY
COMPLAIN ABOUT IN YOUR MANY, MANY LETTERS
TO YOUR IMPRISONED FRIEND- WHO WAS, IN
FACT, ONCE YOUR ENEMY...
                    (MORE)

                                        (CONTINUED

CONTINUED: (15)

                    PROSECUTOR CORIC (CONT'D)
          HOW IS IT THAT YOU HAD A NEW IDENTITY AND
          COSTUME ALL READY TO GO?

                    TOMMY MILLS
          I DIDN'T SAY-

                    PROSECUTOR CORIC
          WHAT?

                    TOMMY MILLS
          I DIDN'T SAY I DIDN'T WANT TO GET BACK
          INTO 'THE GAME,' I SAID I -

                    PROSECUTOR CORIC
          PLEASE ANSWER THE QUESTION YOU WERE
          ASKED.

                    TOMMY MILLS
          I JUST HAD IT.

                    PROSECUTOR CORIC
          'YOU JUST HAD IT?' WOW. YOU JUST HAD A
          2000 DOLLAR COSTUME MADE. JUST HAPPENED
          TO HAVE IT.

                    TOMMY MILLS
          NO COMMENT.

                    PROSECUTOR CORIC
          NO COMMENT? THIS ISN'T A PRESS
          CONFERENCE. SIR, THIS IS A COURT OF LAW
          AND YOU ARE UNDER OATH.

                    TOMMY MILLS
          I...

                    PROSECUTOR CORIC
          IT'S OK MR. MILLS. I THINK YOU ANSWERED
          THE QUESTION QUITE CLEARLY. I'LL PUT THAT
          ANSWER INTO THE GIANT HOLE IN YOUR STORY
          ALONG WITH THE REST OF THEM.

                    DEFENSE ATTORNEY CLIVE BARROW
          OBJECTION.

                    PROSECUTOR CORIC
          NO FURTHER QUESTIONS.

DEFENSE ATTORNEY CLIVE BARROW APPROACHES.

                    DEFENSE ATTORNEY CLIVE BARROW
          TOMMY, WHEN YOU WERE BEING QUESTIONED BY
          THE POLICE WERE YOU UNDER WHAT THEY CALL:
          A DRAINER?

                                        (CONTINUED

CONTINUED: (16)

                    TOMMY MILLS
          YES, OH YEAH- YES.

                    DEFENSE ATTORNEY CLIVE BARROW
          WAS IT HARD FOR YOU TO THINK UNDER THE
          DRAINER?

                    PROSECUTOR CORIC
          OBJECTION.

                    JUDGE ROLLINS
          OVERRULED.

                    DEFENSE ATTORNEY CLIVE BARROW
          DID YOU COMPLAIN TO THE DETECTIVES THAT
          THE DRAINER WAS MAKING IT HARD TO THINK?

                    TOMMY MILLS
          YES, YES I DID. I TOLD THEM THAT I FELT
          ACHY AND NAUSEOUS, BUT THEY IGNORED ME.

                    DEFENSE ATTORNEY CLIVE BARROW
          THEY IGNORED YOU AGAIN. THESE POLICE.

                    PROSECUTOR CORIC
          OBJECTION YOUR HONOR! DRAINERS IN THE
          POLICE INTERROGATION ROOM ARE STANDARD
          ISSUE AND TOTALLY LEGAL. THEY ARE AN
          INTEGRAL PART OF THE OFFICER'S ARSENAL
          AGAINST PERPS WITH A HIGH FLIGHT RISK,
          LIKE MR. MILLS.

                    JUDGE ROLLINS
          SUSTAINED.

                    DEFENSE ATTORNEY CLIVE BARROW
          LET ME ASK YOU, TOMMY, DID YOU FEEL WHILE
          YOU WERE SITTING UNDER THE DRAINER, THAT
          YOU WERE BEING QUESTIONED IN A SITUATION
          IN WHICH YOU COULD CLEARLY, AND TO THE
          BEST OF YOUR ABILITIES, HELP THE
          DETECTIVES IN THEIR QUEST?

                    TOMMY MILLS
          NO. NO, NOT AT ALL.

                    DEFENSE ATTORNEY CLIVE BARROW
          IN YOUR OPINION, IS THIS THE MAGAZINE
          ARTICLE YOU MENTIONED COMING BACK TO
          HAUNT YOU ALL OVER AGAIN?

                    TOMMY MILLS
          THE THOUGHT DID CROSS MY MIND.

                                        (CONTINUED

CONTINUED: (17)

                    PROSECUTOR CORIC
          OBJECTION!

                    DEFENSE ATTORNEY CLIVE BARROW
          NO FURTHER QUESTIONS YOUR HONOR.

                    JUDGE ROLLINS
          MR. MILLS YOU MAY STEP DOWN. BAILIFF? I
          WOULD LIKE TO SEE COUNCIL IN MY CHAMBERS.
          WE'RE GOING TO TAKE A RECESS UNTIL
          TOMORROW MORNING AT 10 AM. EVERYONE HAVE
          A GOOD NIGHT AND WE WILL SEE YOU
          TOMORROW.

JUDGE DISMISSES JURY.

PARTIAL TRANSCRIPT FROM COURT DOCKET 55673-2433 THE PEOPLE
VS. THOMAS MILLS.

DATED 10:14 am October 23, 2001

                    JUDGE ROLLINS (CONT'D)
          LADIES AND GENTLEMAN OF THE JURY, IT IS
          MY REGRET TO INFORM YOU THAT THIS TRIAL
          HAD ENDED. LAST NIGHT IN HIS HOLDING
          CELL, THE ACCUSED, TOOK HIS OWN LIFE IN A
          VIOLENT MANNER. THIS, OF COURSE, ENDS THE
          PROCEEDINGS AND NULLIFIES ANY JUDGEMENT
          YOU WERE TO BRING FORTH. I HOPE YOU WILL
          ACCEPT MY SINCEREST APOLOGIES FOR THE
          WASTE OF TIME THIS HAS BECOME FOR ALL OF
          US- BUT I DO DECLARE YOUR DUTIES TO THIS
          COURT COMPLETED. CASE DISMISSED.

JURY IS DISMISSED. 10:22 am October 23, 2001

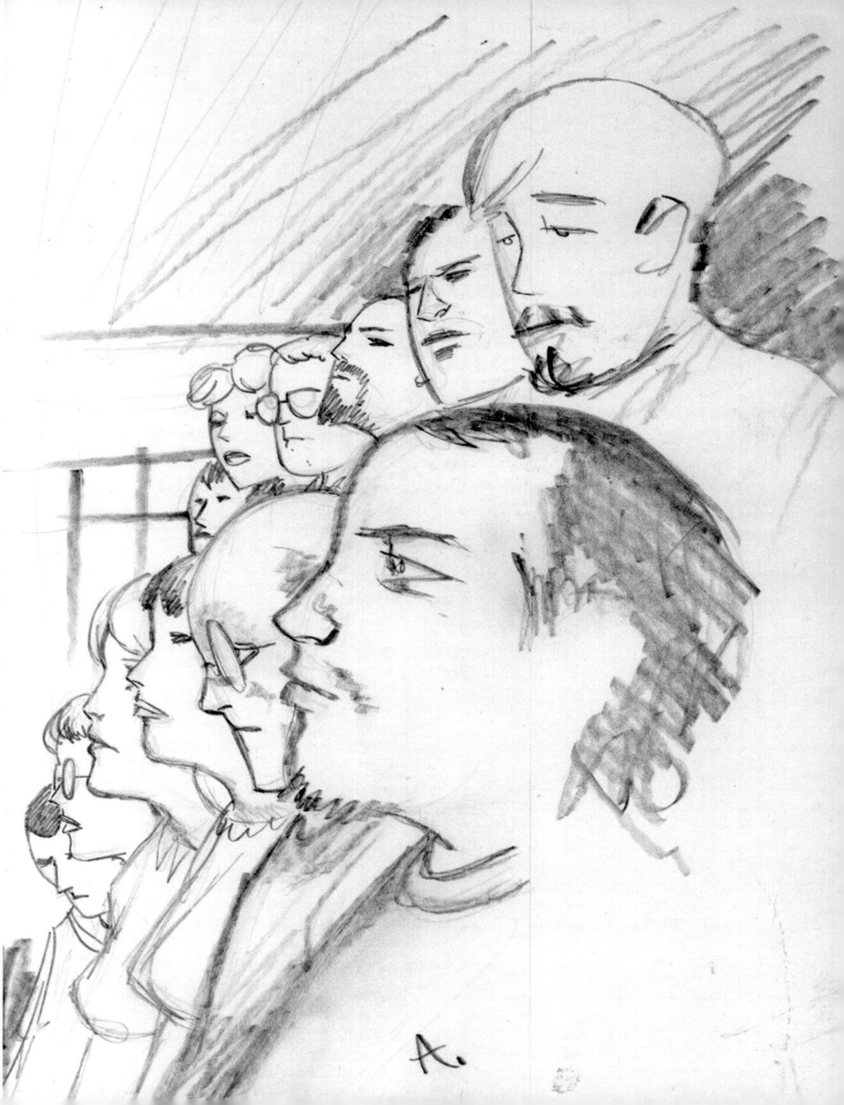
A.

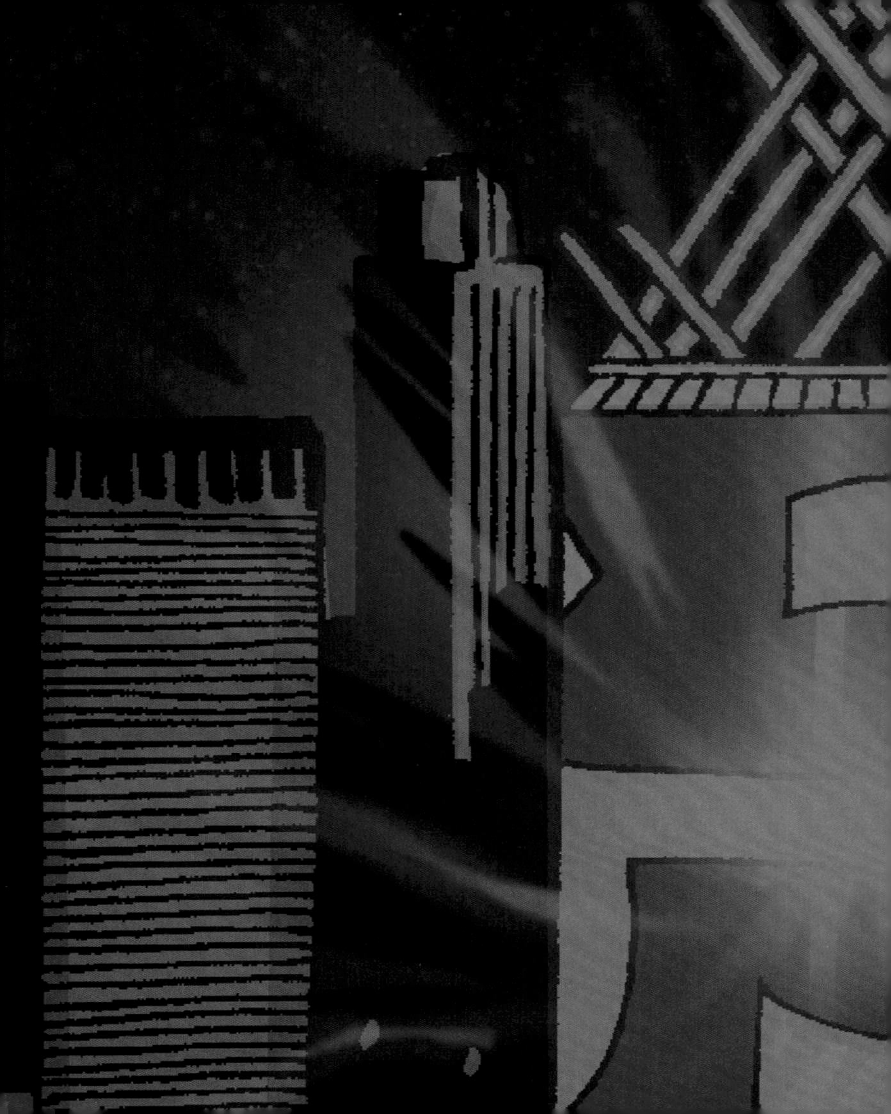

POWERS™

SUPERGROUP
CHAPTER 1

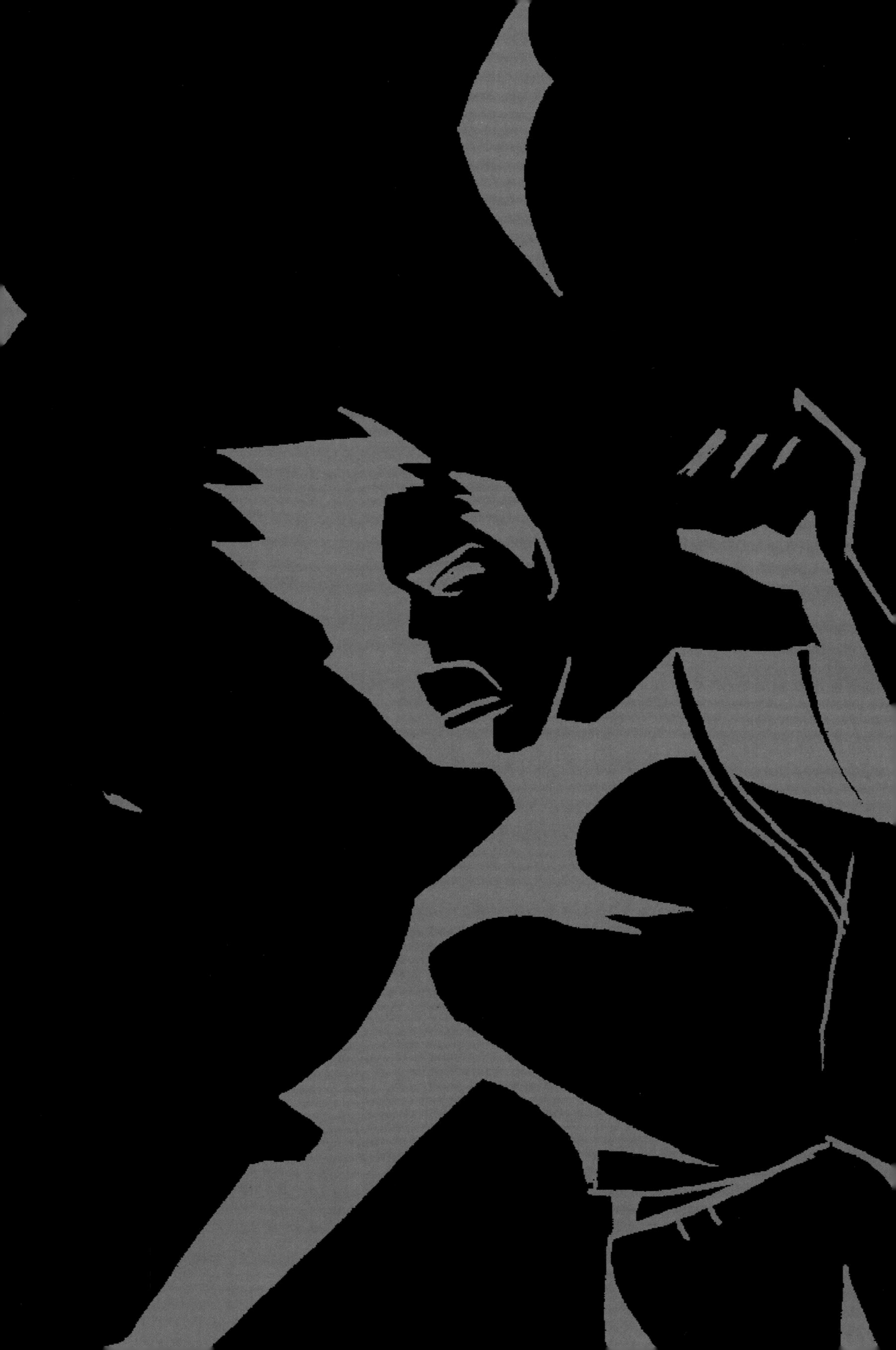

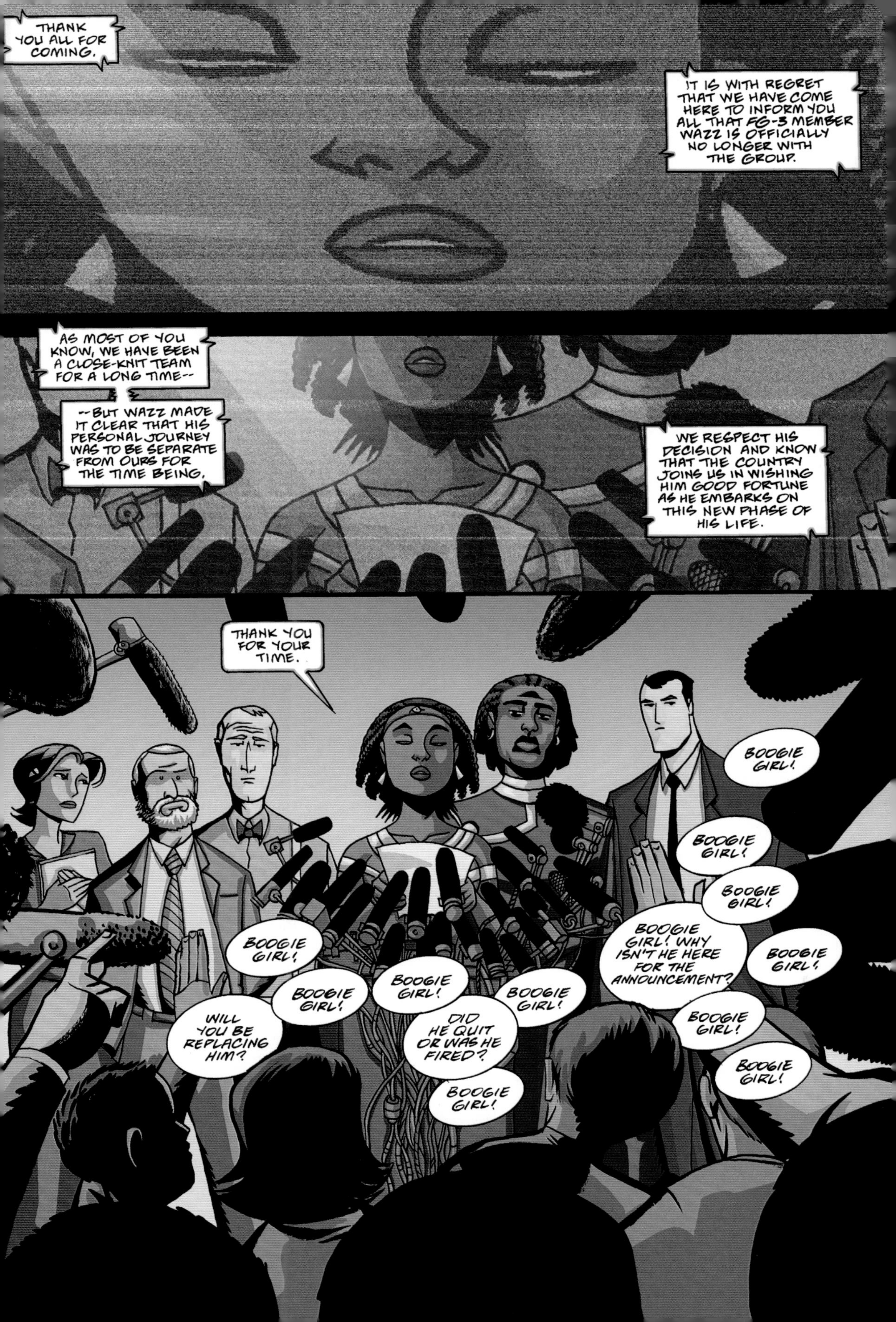
THANK YOU ALL FOR COMING.
IT IS WITH REGRET THAT WE HAVE COME HERE TO INFORM YOU ALL THAT FG-3 MEMBER WAZZ IS OFFICIALLY NO LONGER WITH THE GROUP.
AS MOST OF YOU KNOW, WE HAVE BEEN A CLOSE-KNIT TEAM FOR A LONG TIME--
--BUT WAZZ MADE IT CLEAR THAT HIS PERSONAL JOURNEY WAS TO BE SEPARATE FROM OURS FOR THE TIME BEING.
WE RESPECT HIS DECISION AND KNOW THAT THE COUNTRY JOINS US IN WISHING HIM GOOD FORTUNE AS HE EMBARKS ON THIS NEW PHASE OF HIS LIFE.
THANK YOU FOR YOUR TIME.
BOOGIE GIRL!
BOOGIE GIRL!
BOOGIE GIRL!
BOOGIE GIRL! WHY ISN'T HE HERE FOR THE ANNOUNCEMENT?
BOOGIE GIRL!
BOOGIE GIRL!
BOOGIE GIRL!
BOOGIE GIRL!
BOOGIE GIRL!
WILL YOU BE REPLACING HIM?
BOOGIE GIRL!
DID HE QUIT OR WAS HE FIRED?
BOOGIE GIRL!
BOOGIE GIRL!
BOOGIE GIRL!

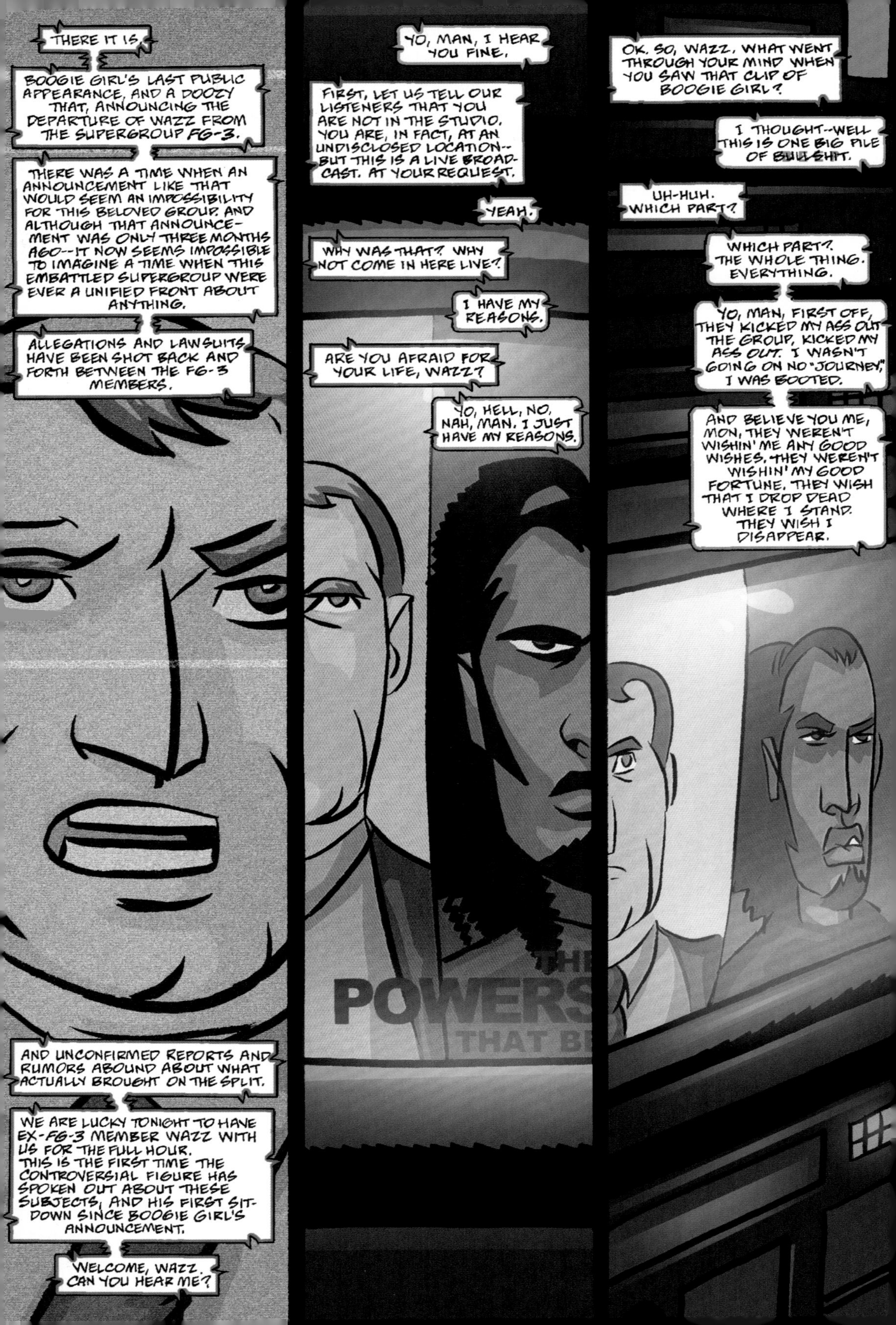
THERE IT IS.
BOOGIE GIRL'S LAST PUBLIC APPEARANCE, AND A DOOZY THAT, ANNOUNCING THE DEPARTURE OF WAZZ FROM THE SUPERGROUP FG-3.
THERE WAS A TIME WHEN AN ANNOUNCEMENT LIKE THAT WOULD SEEM AN IMPOSSIBILITY FOR THIS BELOVED GROUP. AND ALTHOUGH THAT ANNOUNCEMENT WAS ONLY THREE MONTHS AGO--IT NOW SEEMS IMPOSSIBLE TO IMAGINE A TIME WHEN THIS EMBATTLED SUPERGROUP WERE EVER A UNIFIED FRONT ABOUT ANYTHING.
ALLEGATIONS AND LAWSUITS HAVE BEEN SHOT BACK AND FORTH BETWEEN THE FG-3 MEMBERS.
AND UNCONFIRMED REPORTS AND RUMORS ABOUND ABOUT WHAT ACTUALLY BROUGHT ON THE SPLIT.
WE ARE LUCKY TONIGHT TO HAVE EX-FG-3 MEMBER WAZZ WITH US FOR THE FULL HOUR. THIS IS THE FIRST TIME THE CONTROVERSIAL FIGURE HAS SPOKEN OUT ABOUT THESE SUBJECTS, AND HIS FIRST SIT-DOWN SINCE BOOGIE GIRL'S ANNOUNCEMENT.
WELCOME, WAZZ. CAN YOU HEAR ME?
YO, MAN, I HEAR YOU FINE.
FIRST, LET US TELL OUR LISTENERS THAT YOU ARE NOT IN THE STUDIO. YOU ARE, IN FACT, AT AN UNDISCLOSED LOCATION--BUT THIS IS A LIVE BROADCAST. AT YOUR REQUEST.
YEAH.
WHY WAS THAT? WHY NOT COME IN HERE LIVE?
I HAVE MY REASONS.
ARE YOU AFRAID FOR YOUR LIFE, WAZZ?
YO, HELL, NO, NAH, MAN. I JUST HAVE MY REASONS.
THE POWERS THAT BE
OK. SO, WAZZ, WHAT WENT THROUGH YOUR MIND WHEN YOU SAW THAT CLIP OF BOOGIE GIRL?
I THOUGHT--WELL THIS IS ONE BIG PILE OF BULLSHIT.
UH-HUH. WHICH PART?
WHICH PART? THE WHOLE THING. EVERYTHING.
YO, MAN, FIRST OFF, THEY KICKED MY ASS OUT THE GROUP, KICKED MY ASS OUT. I WASN'T GOING ON NO "JOURNEY," I WAS BOOTED.
AND BELIEVE YOU ME, MON, THEY WEREN'T WISHIN' ME ANY GOOD WISHES. THEY WEREN'T WISHIN' MY GOOD FORTUNE. THEY WISH THAT I DROP DEAD WHERE I STAND. THEY WISH I DISAPPEAR.

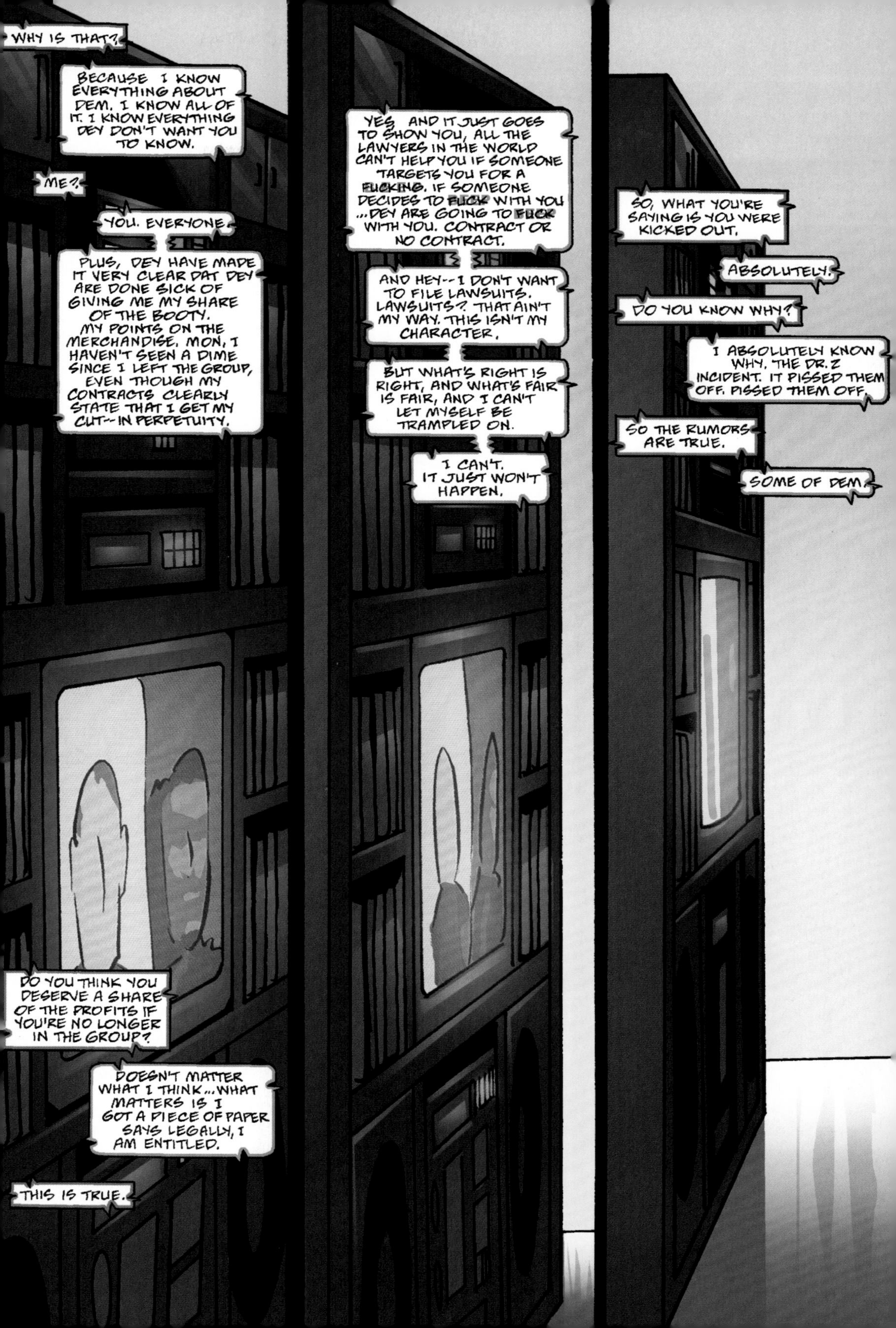
WHY IS THAT?
BECAUSE I KNOW EVERYTHING ABOUT DEM. I KNOW ALL OF IT. I KNOW EVERYTHING DEY DON'T WANT YOU TO KNOW.
ME?
YOU. EVERYONE.
PLUS, DEY HAVE MADE IT VERY CLEAR DAT DEY ARE DONE SICK OF GIVING ME MY SHARE OF THE BOOTY. MY POINTS ON THE MERCHANDISE, MON, I HAVEN'T SEEN A DIME SINCE I LEFT THE GROUP, EVEN THOUGH MY CONTRACTS CLEARLY STATE THAT I GET MY CUT--IN PERPETUITY.
DO YOU THINK YOU DESERVE A SHARE OF THE PROFITS IF YOU'RE NO LONGER IN THE GROUP?
DOESN'T MATTER WHAT I THINK...WHAT MATTERS IS I GOT A PIECE OF PAPER SAYS LEGALLY, I AM ENTITLED.
THIS IS TRUE.
YES AND IT JUST GOES TO SHOW YOU, ALL THE LAWYERS IN THE WORLD CAN'T HELP YOU IF SOMEONE TARGETS YOU FOR A FUCKING. IF SOMEONE DECIDES TO FUCK WITH YOU ...DEY ARE GOING TO FUCK WITH YOU. CONTRACT OR NO CONTRACT.
AND HEY--I DON'T WANT TO FILE LAWSUITS. LAWSUITS? THAT AIN'T MY WAY. THIS ISN'T MY CHARACTER.
BUT WHAT'S RIGHT IS RIGHT, AND WHAT'S FAIR IS FAIR, AND I CAN'T LET MYSELF BE TRAMPLED ON.
I CAN'T. IT JUST WON'T HAPPEN.
SO, WHAT YOU'RE SAYING IS YOU WERE KICKED OUT.
ABSOLUTELY.
DO YOU KNOW WHY?
I ABSOLUTELY KNOW WHY. THE DR. Z INCIDENT. IT PISSED THEM OFF. PISSED THEM OFF.
SO THE RUMORS ARE TRUE.
SOME OF DEM.

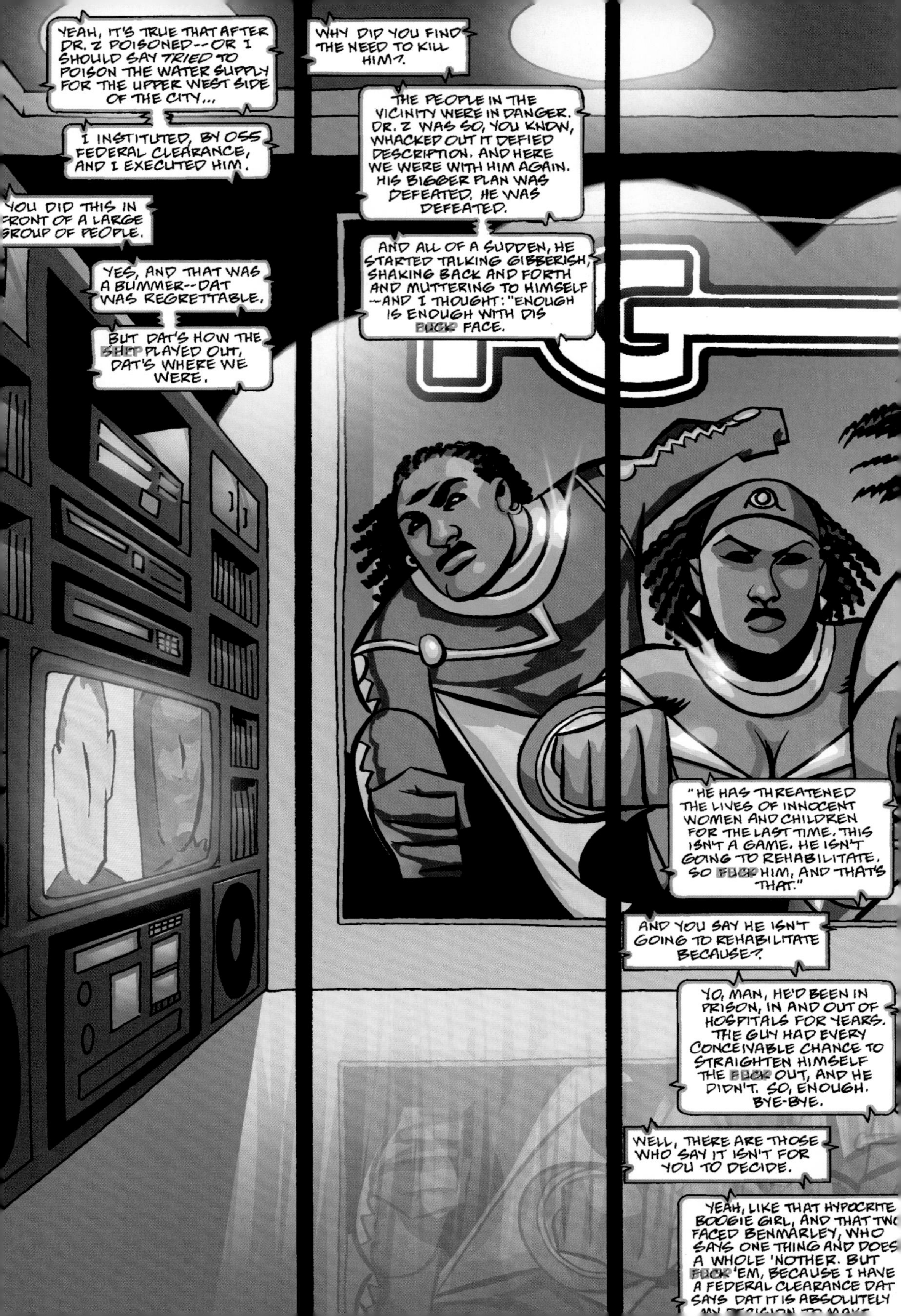

YEAH, IT'S TRUE THAT AFTER DR. Z POISONED--OR I SHOULD SAY *TRIED* TO POISON THE WATER SUPPLY FOR THE UPPER WEST SIDE OF THE CITY...
I INSTITUTED, BY OSS FEDERAL CLEARANCE, AND I EXECUTED HIM.
YOU DID THIS IN FRONT OF A LARGE GROUP OF PEOPLE.
YES, AND THAT WAS A BUMMER--DAT WAS REGRETTABLE.
BUT DAT'S HOW THE SHIT PLAYED OUT, DAT'S WHERE WE WERE.
WHY DID YOU FIND THE NEED TO KILL HIM?
THE PEOPLE IN THE VICINITY WERE IN DANGER. DR. Z WAS SO, YOU KNOW, WHACKED OUT IT DEFIED DESCRIPTION. AND HERE WE WERE WITH HIM AGAIN. HIS BIGGER PLAN WAS DEFEATED. HE WAS DEFEATED.
AND ALL OF A SUDDEN, HE STARTED TALKING GIBBERISH, SHAKING BACK AND FORTH AND MUTTERING TO HIMSELF--AND I THOUGHT: "ENOUGH IS ENOUGH WITH DIS FUCK FACE.
"HE HAS THREATENED THE LIVES OF INNOCENT WOMEN AND CHILDREN FOR THE LAST TIME. THIS ISN'T A GAME. HE ISN'T GOING TO REHABILITATE. SO FUCK HIM, AND THAT'S THAT."
AND YOU SAY HE ISN'T GOING TO REHABILITATE BECAUSE?
YO, MAN, HE'D BEEN IN PRISON, IN AND OUT OF HOSPITALS FOR YEARS. THE GUY HAD EVERY CONCEIVABLE CHANCE TO STRAIGHTEN HIMSELF THE FUCK OUT, AND HE DIDN'T. SO, ENOUGH. BYE-BYE.
WELL, THERE ARE THOSE WHO SAY IT ISN'T FOR YOU TO DECIDE.
YEAH, LIKE THAT HYPOCRITE BOOGIE GIRL, AND THAT TWO FACED BENMARLEY, WHO SAYS ONE THING AND DOES A WHOLE 'NOTHER. BUT FUCK 'EM, BECAUSE I HAVE A FEDERAL CLEARANCE DAT SAYS DAT IT IS ABSOLUTELY

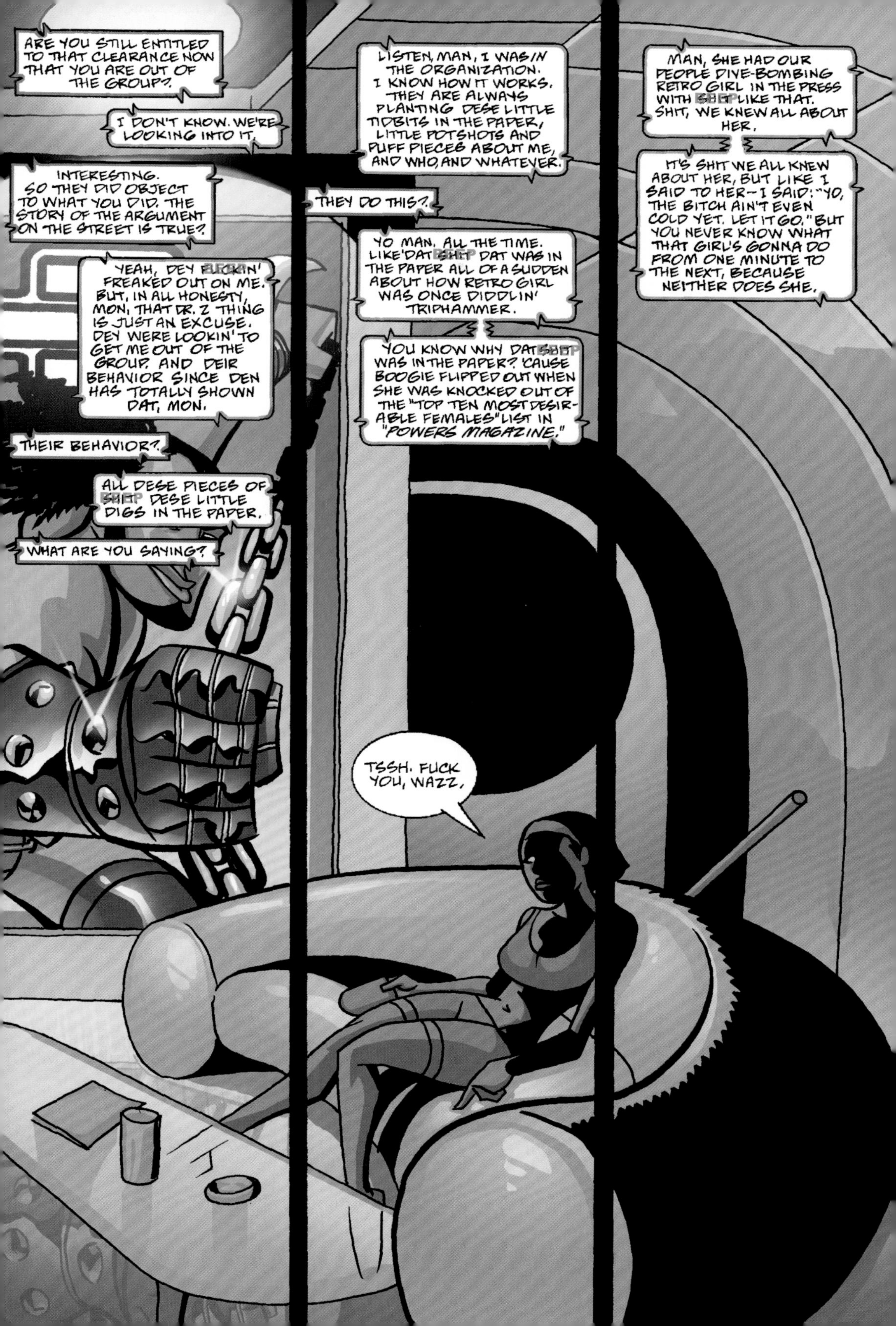
ARE YOU STILL ENTITLED TO THAT CLEARANCE NOW THAT YOU ARE OUT OF THE GROUP?
I DON'T KNOW. WE'RE LOOKING INTO IT.
INTERESTING. SO THEY DID OBJECT TO WHAT YOU DID. THE STORY OF THE ARGUMENT ON THE STREET IS TRUE?
YEAH, DEY BEEPIN' FREAKED OUT ON ME. BUT, IN ALL HONESTY, MON, THAT DR. Z THING IS JUST AN EXCUSE. DEY WERE LOOKIN' TO GET ME OUT OF THE GROUP. AND DEIR BEHAVIOR SINCE DEN HAS TOTALLY SHOWN DAT, MON.
THEIR BEHAVIOR?
ALL DESE PIECES OF BEEP DESE LITTLE DIGS IN THE PAPER.
WHAT ARE YOU SAYING?
LISTEN, MAN, I WAS *IN* THE ORGANIZATION. I KNOW HOW IT WORKS. THEY ARE ALWAYS PLANTING DESE LITTLE TIDBITS IN THE PAPER, LITTLE POTSHOTS AND PUFF PIECES ABOUT ME, AND WHO, AND WHATEVER.
THEY DO THIS?
YO MAN. ALL THE TIME. LIKE 'DAT BEEP DAT WAS IN THE PAPER ALL OF A SUDDEN ABOUT HOW RETRO GIRL WAS ONCE DIDDLIN' TRIPHAMMER.
YOU KNOW WHY DAT BEEP WAS IN THE PAPER? 'CAUSE BOOGIE FLIPPED OUT WHEN SHE WAS KNOCKED OUT OF THE "TOP TEN MOST DESIRABLE FEMALES" LIST IN *"POWERS MAGAZINE."*
MAN, SHE HAD OUR PEOPLE DIVE-BOMBING RETRO GIRL IN THE PRESS WITH BEEP LIKE THAT. SHIT, WE KNEW ALL ABOUT HER.
IT'S SHIT WE ALL KNEW ABOUT HER, BUT LIKE I SAID TO HER-- I SAID: "YO, THE BITCH AIN'T EVEN COLD YET. LET IT GO." BUT YOU NEVER KNOW WHAT THAT GIRL'S GONNA DO FROM ONE MINUTE TO THE NEXT, BECAUSE NEITHER DOES SHE.
TSSH. FUCK YOU, WAZZ.

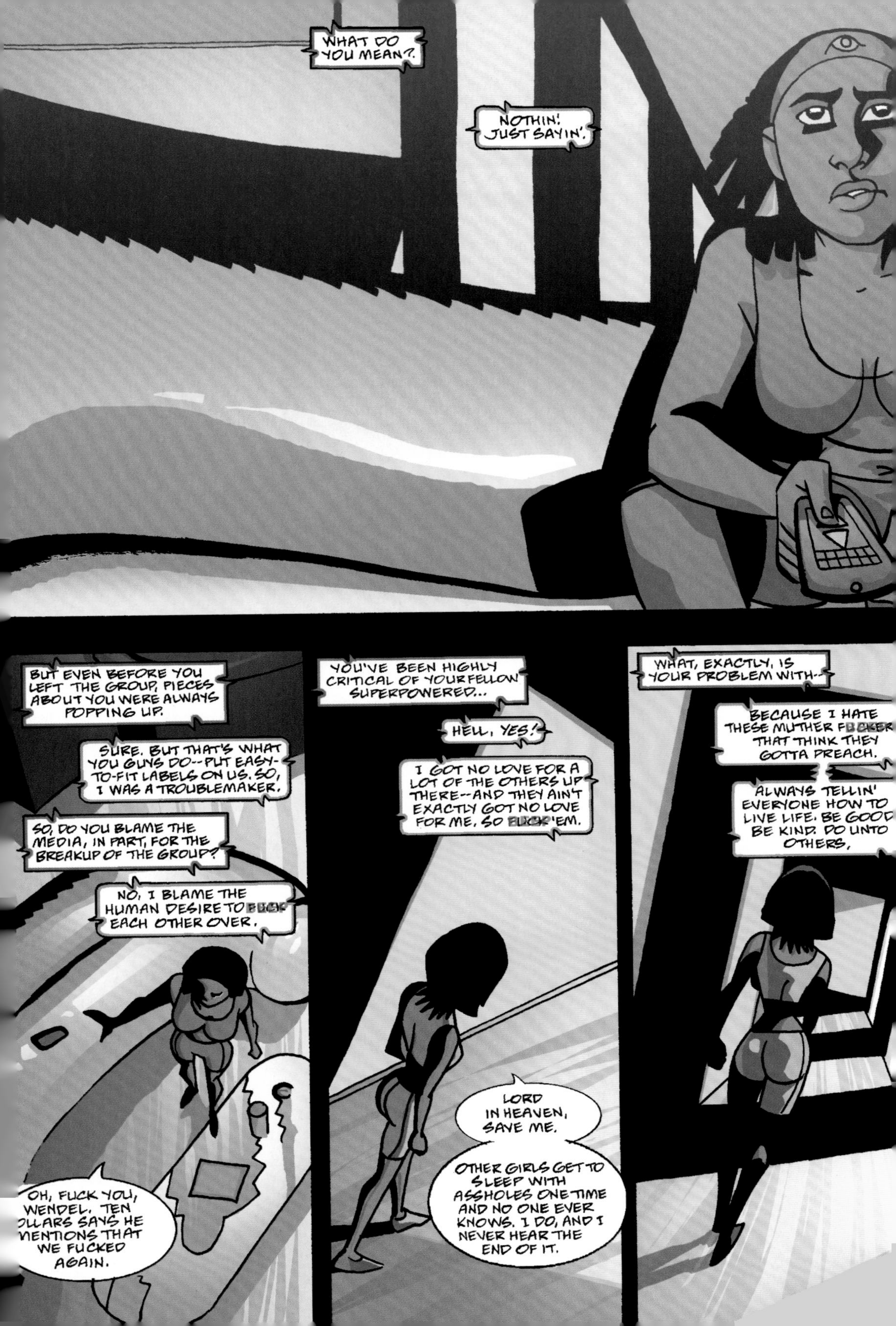
WHAT DO YOU MEAN?
NOTHIN! JUST SAYIN'.
BUT EVEN BEFORE YOU LEFT THE GROUP, PIECES ABOUT YOU WERE ALWAYS POPPING UP.
SURE. BUT THAT'S WHAT YOU GUYS DO--PUT EASY-TO-FIT LABELS ON US. SO, I WAS A TROUBLEMAKER.
SO, DO YOU BLAME THE MEDIA, IN PART, FOR THE BREAKUP OF THE GROUP?
NO, I BLAME THE HUMAN DESIRE TO FUCK EACH OTHER OVER.
OH, FUCK YOU, WENDEL. TEN DOLLARS SAYS HE MENTIONS THAT WE FUCKED AGAIN.
YOU'VE BEEN HIGHLY CRITICAL OF YOUR FELLOW SUPERPOWERED...
HELL, YES!
I GOT NO LOVE FOR A LOT OF THE OTHERS UP THERE--AND THEY AIN'T EXACTLY GOT NO LOVE FOR ME, SO FUCK 'EM.
LORD IN HEAVEN, SAVE ME.
OTHER GIRLS GET TO SLEEP WITH ASSHOLES ONE TIME AND NO ONE EVER KNOWS. I DO, AND I NEVER HEAR THE END OF IT.
WHAT, EXACTLY, IS YOUR PROBLEM WITH--
BECAUSE I HATE THESE MUTHER FUCKERS THAT THINK THEY GOTTA PREACH.
ALWAYS TELLIN' EVERYONE HOW TO LIVE LIFE. BE GOOD. BE KIND. DO UNTO OTHERS.

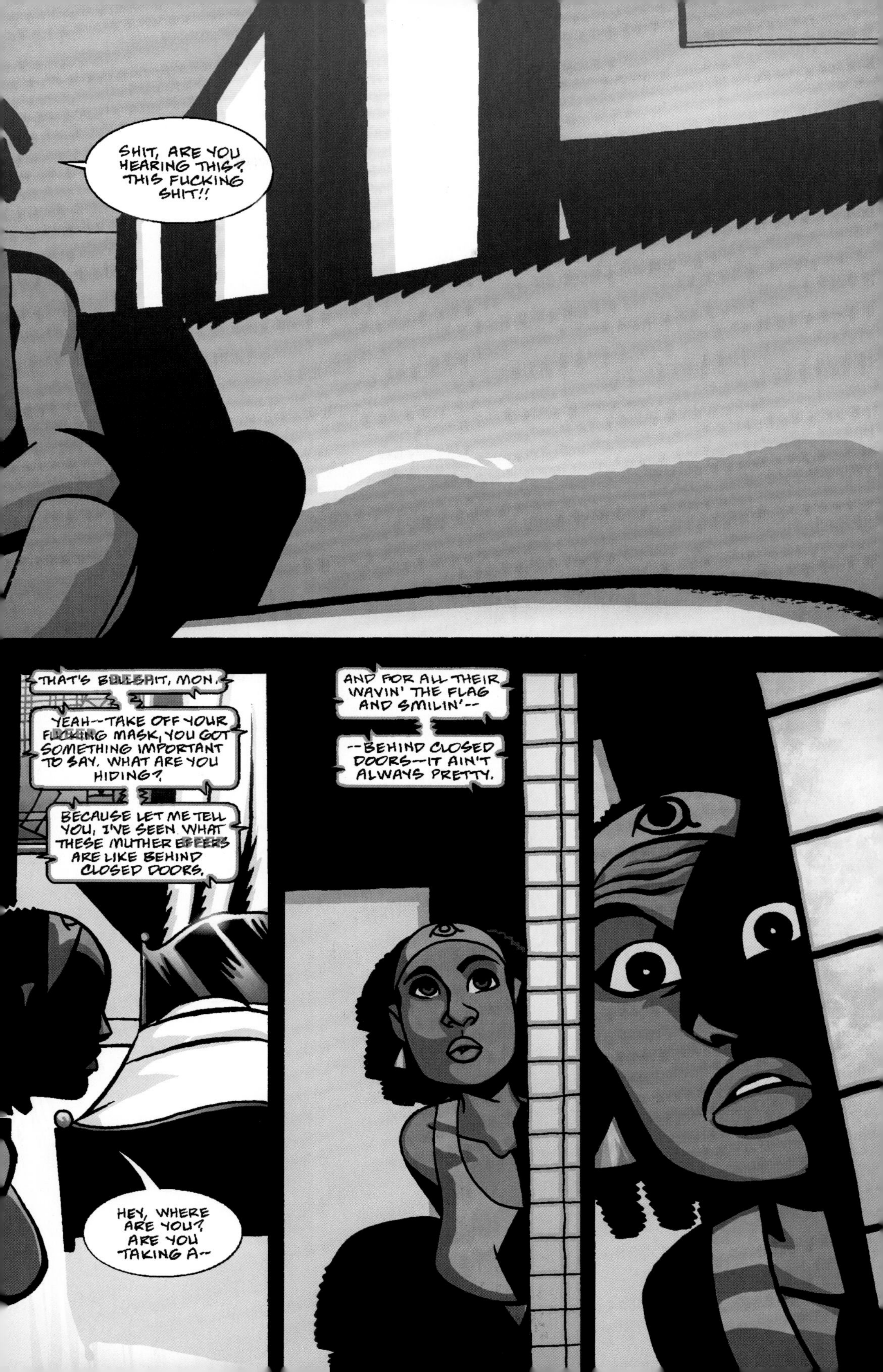
SHIT, ARE YOU HEARING THIS? THIS FUCKING SHIT!!
THAT'S BULLSHIT, MON.
YEAH--TAKE OFF YOUR FUCKING MASK, YOU GOT SOMETHING IMPORTANT TO SAY. WHAT ARE YOU HIDING?
BECAUSE LET ME TELL YOU, I'VE SEEN WHAT THESE MUTHER EFFERS ARE LIKE BEHIND CLOSED DOORS.
HEY, WHERE ARE YOU? ARE YOU TAKING A--
AND FOR ALL THEIR WAVIN' THE FLAG AND SMILIN'--
--BEHIND CLOSED DOORS--IT AIN'T ALWAYS PRETTY.

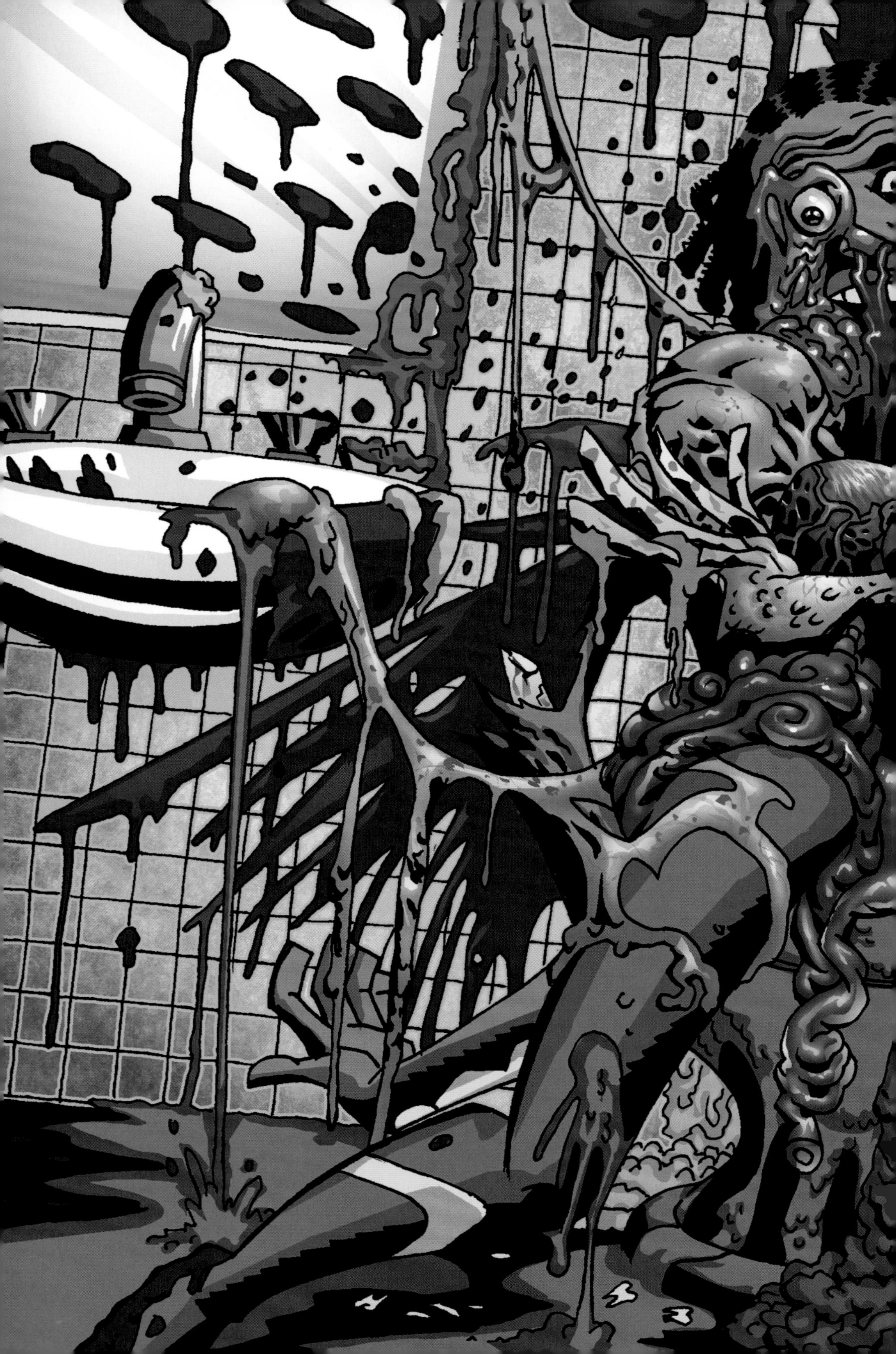

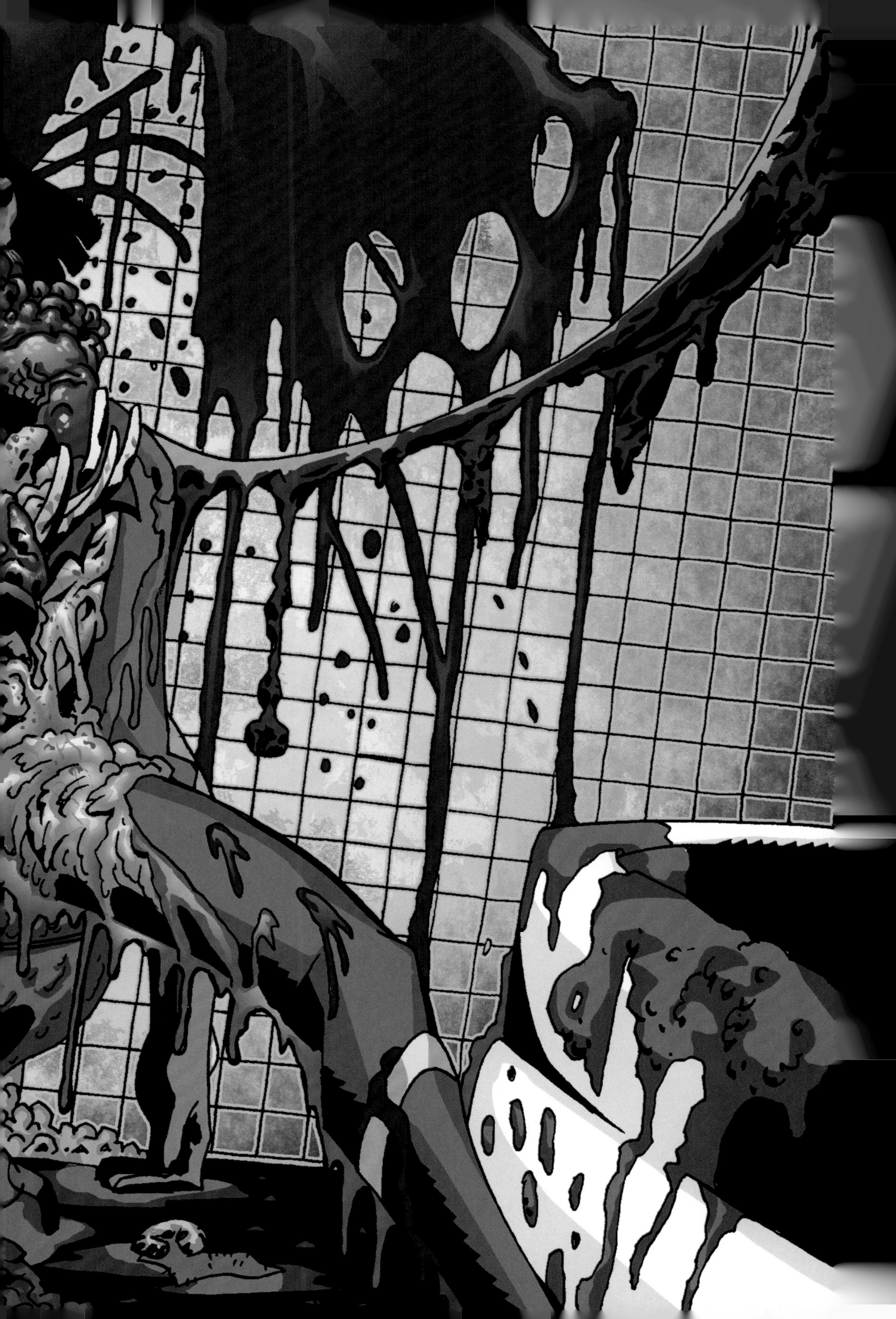

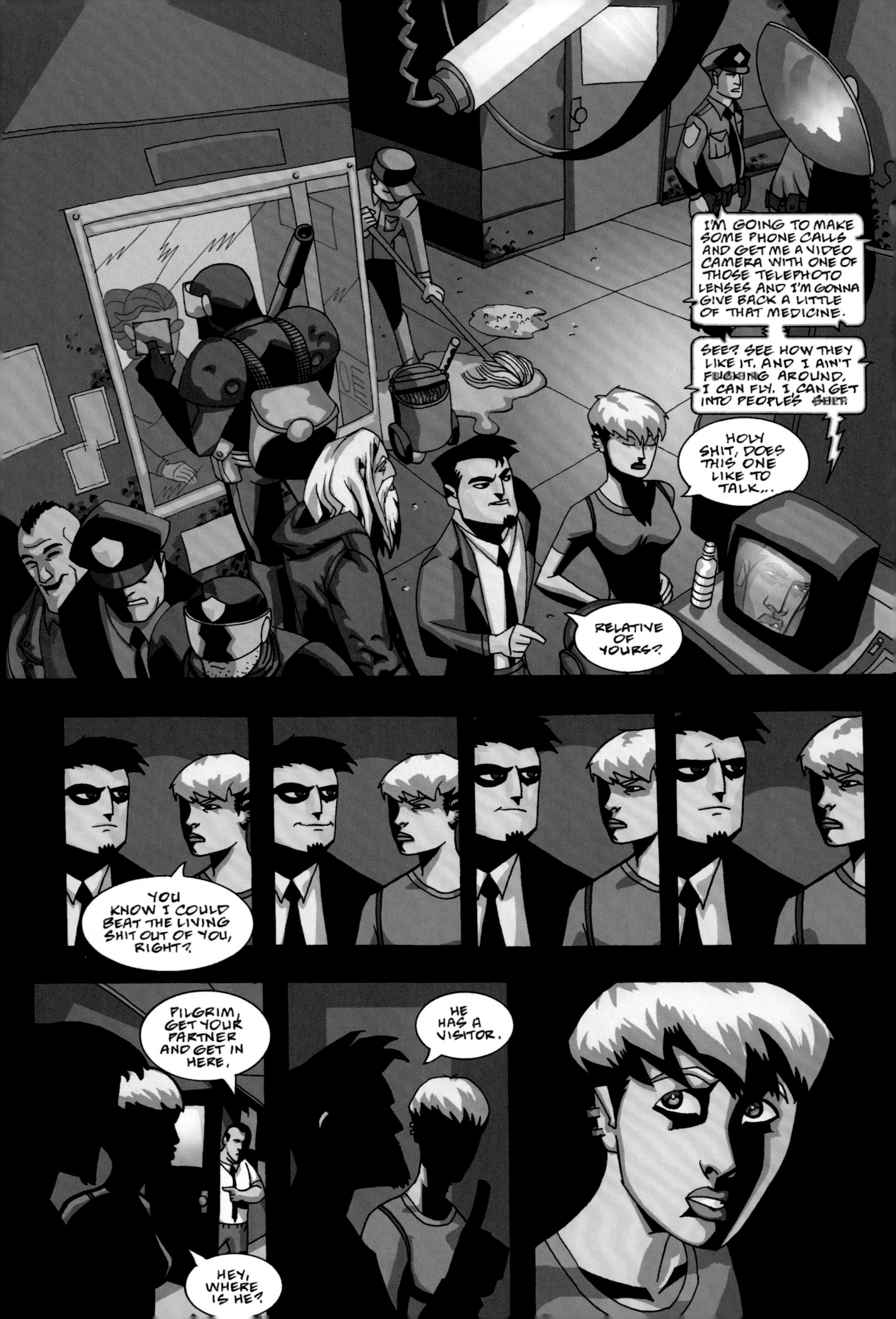
I'M GOING TO MAKE SOME PHONE CALLS AND GET ME A VIDEO CAMERA WITH ONE OF THOSE TELEPHOTO LENSES AND I'M GONNA GIVE BACK A LITTLE OF THAT MEDICINE.
SEE? SEE HOW THEY LIKE IT. AND I AIN'T FUCKING AROUND. I CAN FLY. I CAN GET INTO PEOPLE'S SHIT.
HOLY SHIT, DOES THIS ONE LIKE TO TALK...
RELATIVE OF YOURS?
YOU KNOW I COULD BEAT THE LIVING SHIT OUT OF YOU, RIGHT?
PILGRIM, GET YOUR PARTNER AND GET IN HERE.
HEY, WHERE IS HE?
HE HAS A VISITOR.

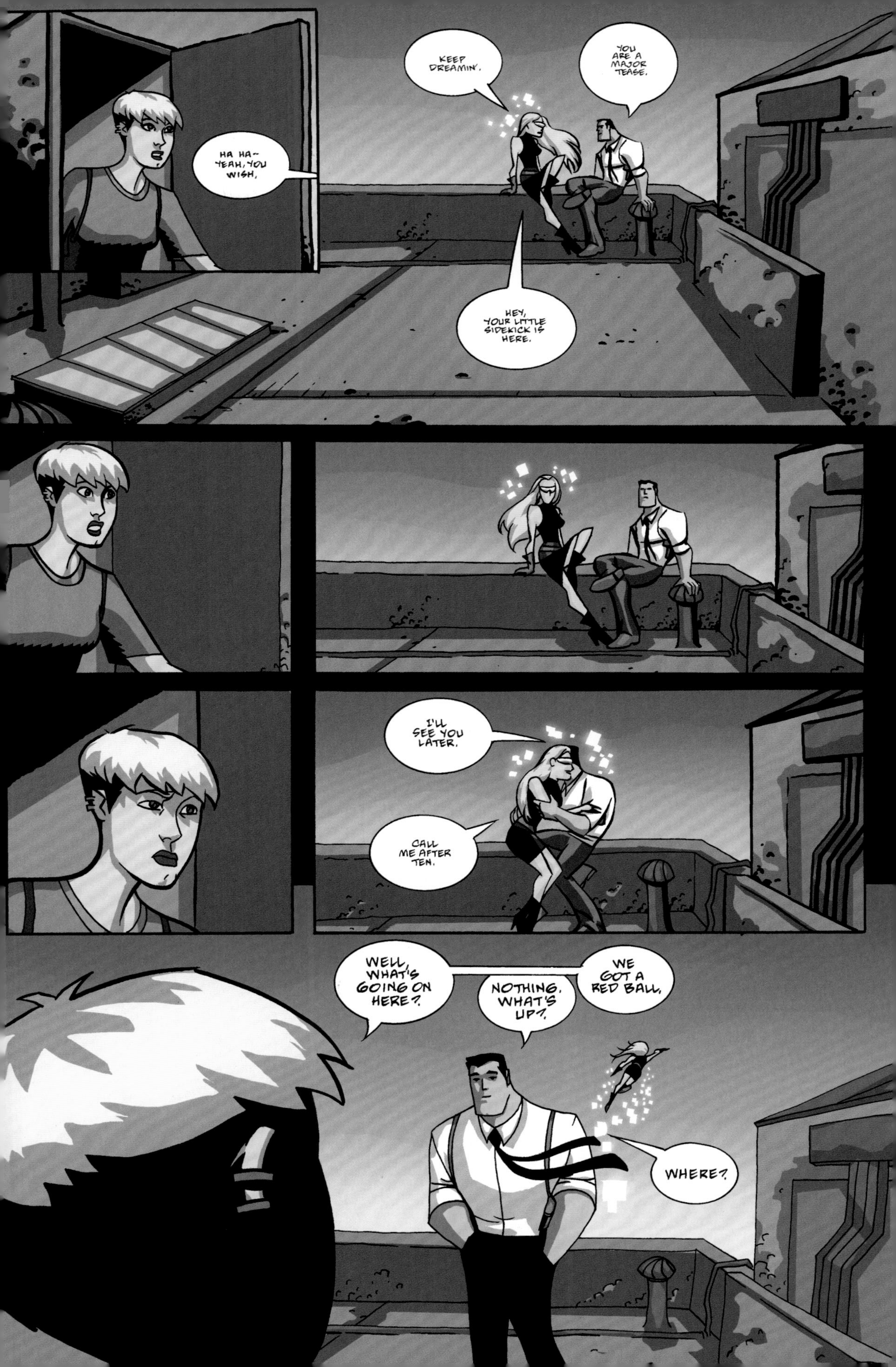
HA HA--
YEAH, YOU WISH.
KEEP DREAMIN'.
YOU ARE A MAJOR TEASE.
HEY, YOUR LITTLE SIDEKICK IS HERE.
I'LL SEE YOU LATER.
CALL ME AFTER TEN.
WELL, WHAT'S GOING ON HERE?
NOTHING. WHAT'S UP?
WE GOT A RED BALL.
WHERE?

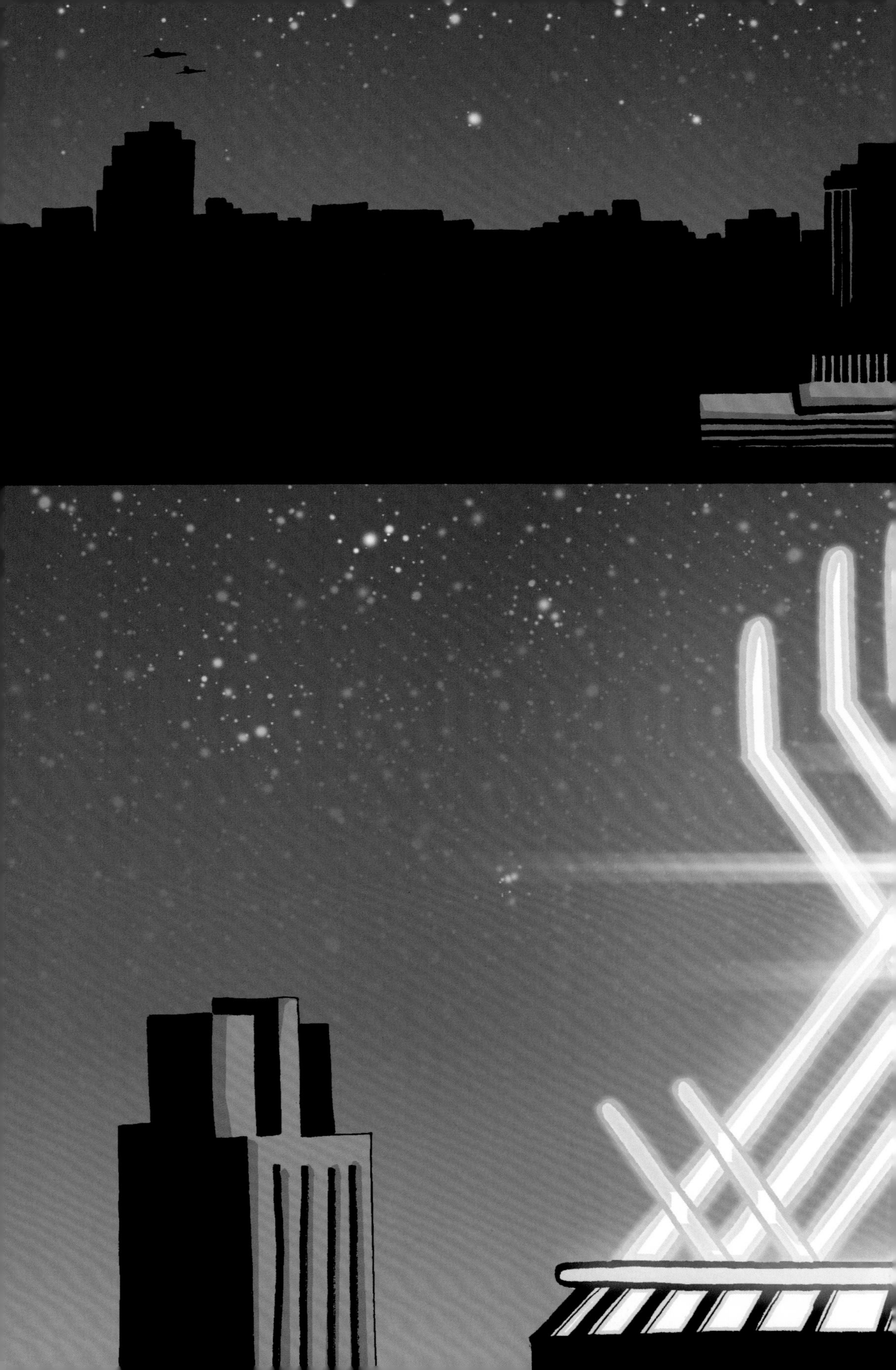

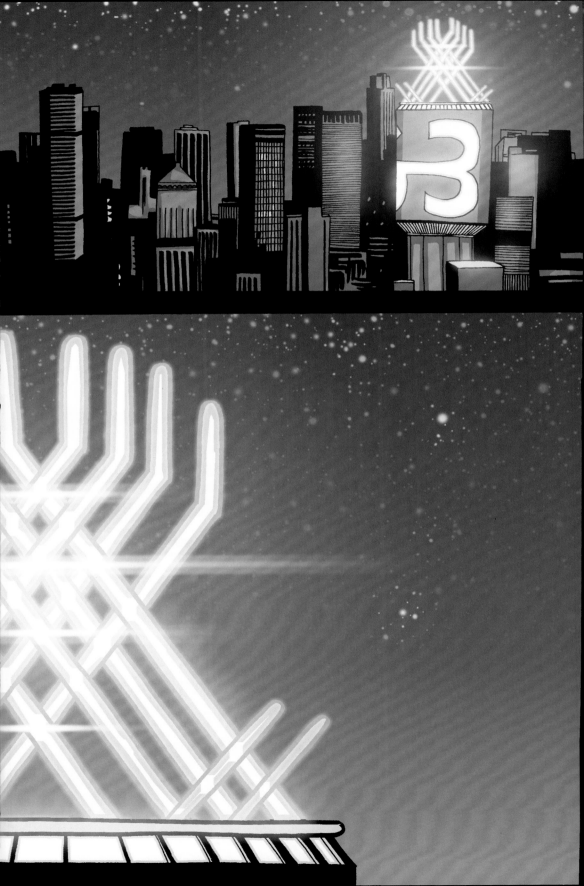

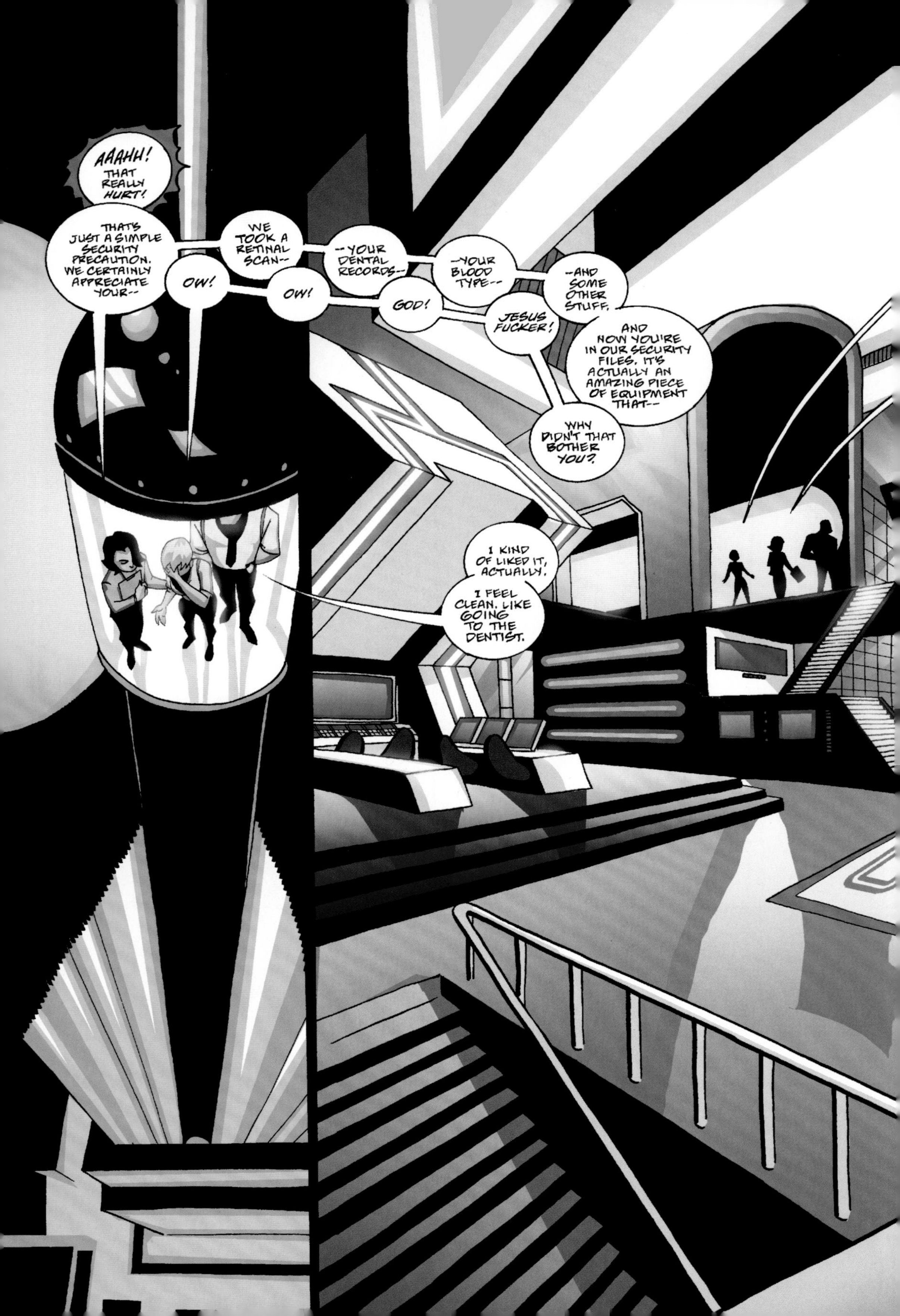
AAAHH! THAT REALLY HURT!
THAT'S JUST A SIMPLE SECURITY PRECAUTION. WE CERTAINLY APPRECIATE YOUR--
OW!
WE TOOK A RETINAL SCAN--
OW!
--YOUR DENTAL RECORDS--
GOD!
--YOUR BLOOD TYPE--
JESUS FUCKER!
--AND SOME OTHER STUFF.
AND NOW YOU'RE IN OUR SECURITY FILES. IT'S ACTUALLY AN AMAZING PIECE OF EQUIPMENT THAT--
WHY DIDN'T THAT BOTHER YOU?
I KIND OF LIKED IT, ACTUALLY.
I FEEL CLEAN. LIKE GOING TO THE DENTIST.

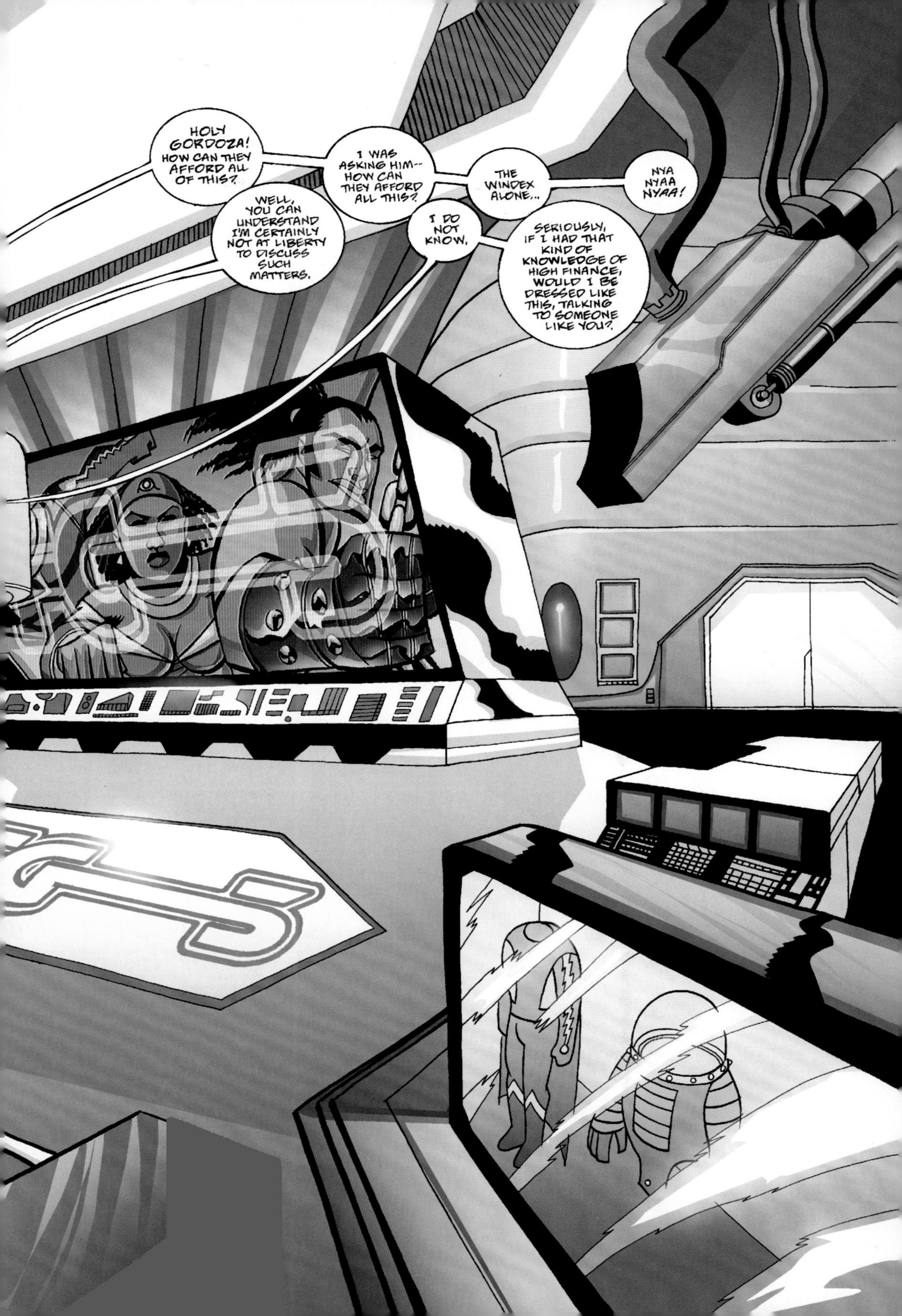

HOLY GORDOZA! HOW CAN THEY AFFORD ALL OF THIS?
WELL, YOU CAN UNDERSTAND I'M CERTAINLY NOT AT LIBERTY TO DISCUSS SUCH MATTERS.
I WAS ASKING HIM-- HOW CAN THEY AFFORD ALL THIS?
I DO NOT KNOW.
THE WINDEX ALONE...
SERIOUSLY, IF I HAD THAT KIND OF KNOWLEDGE OF HIGH FINANCE, WOULD I BE DRESSED LIKE THIS, TALKING TO SOMEONE LIKE YOU?
NYA NYAA NYAA!

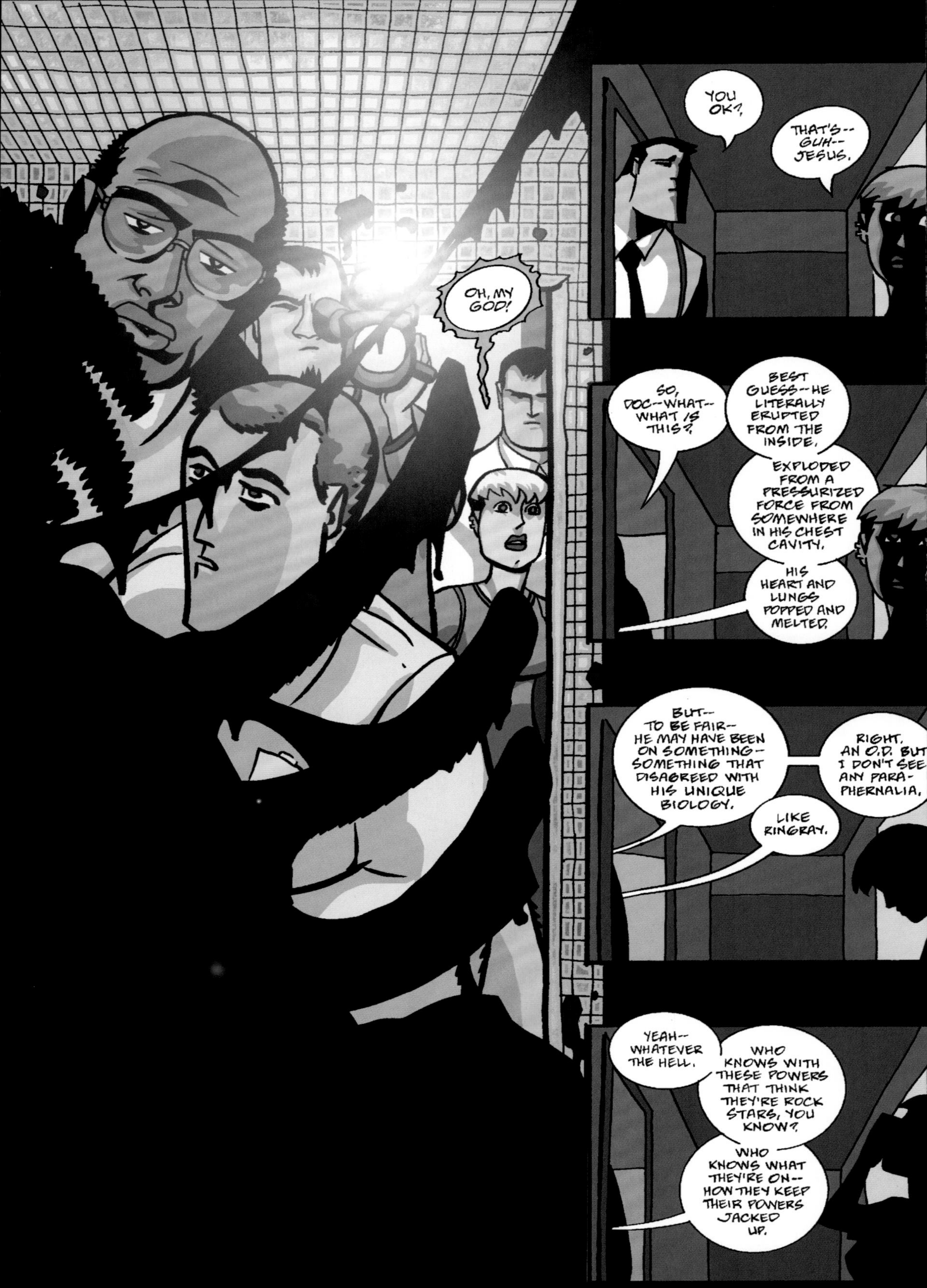
OH, MY GOD!
YOU OK?,
THAT'S--GUH--JESUS.
SO, DOC--WHAT--WHAT IS THIS?
BEST GUESS--HE LITERALLY ERUPTED FROM THE INSIDE,
EXPLODED FROM A PRESSURIZED FORCE FROM SOMEWHERE IN HIS CHEST CAVITY,
HIS HEART AND LUNGS POPPED AND MELTED.
BUT--TO BE FAIR--HE MAY HAVE BEEN ON SOMETHING--SOMETHING THAT DISAGREED WITH HIS UNIQUE BIOLOGY.
RIGHT, AN O.D. BUT I DON'T SEE ANY PARAPHERNALIA,
LIKE RINGRAY.
YEAH--WHATEVER THE HELL.
WHO KNOWS WITH THESE POWERS THAT THINK THEY'RE ROCK STARS, YOU KNOW?
WHO KNOWS WHAT THEY'RE ON--HOW THEY KEEP THEIR POWERS JACKED UP.

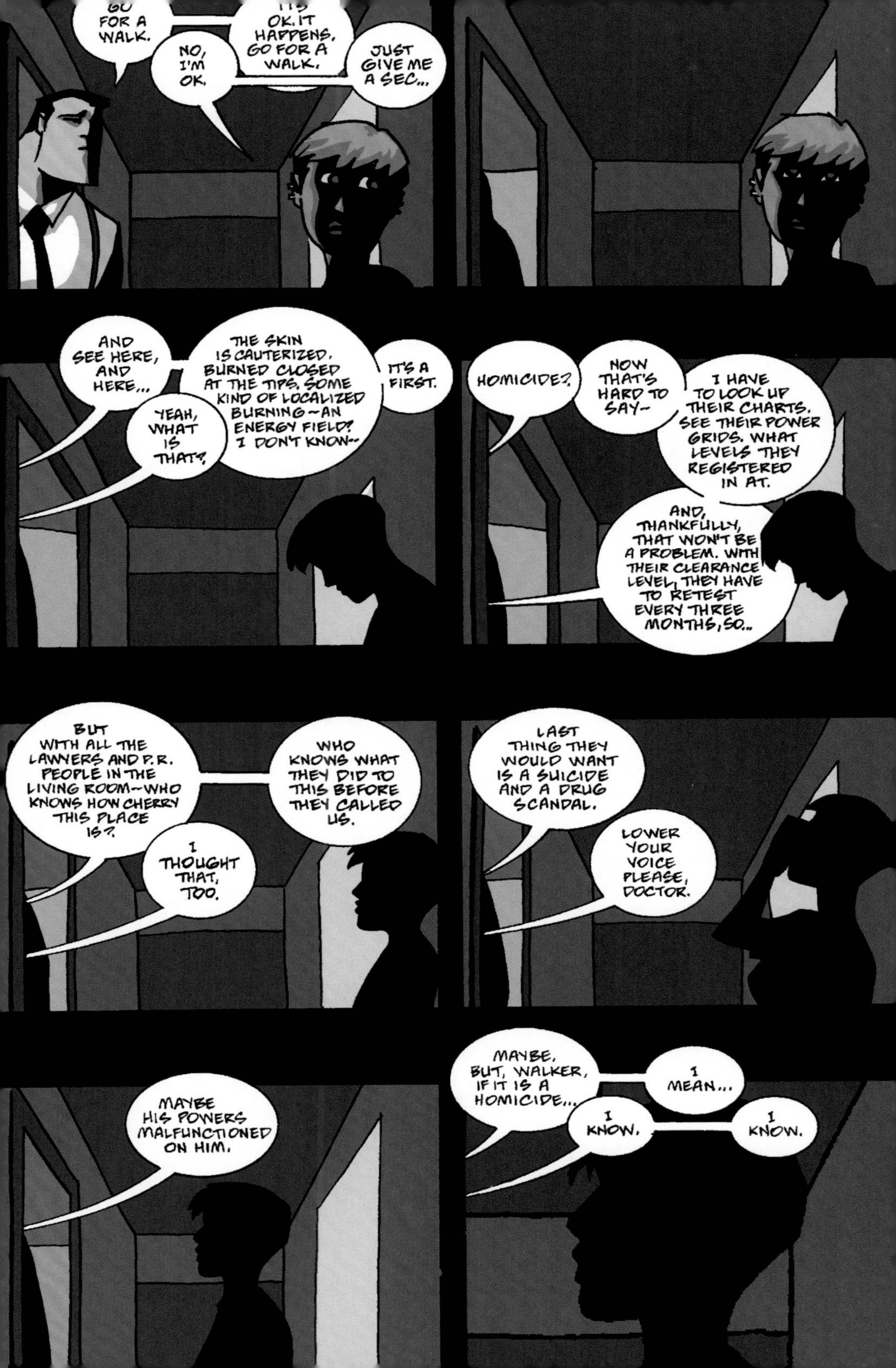
GO FOR A WALK.
NO, I'M OK.
OK. IT HAPPENS, GO FOR A WALK.
JUST GIVE ME A SEC...
AND SEE HERE, AND HERE...
YEAH, WHAT IS THAT?
THE SKIN IS CAUTERIZED. BURNED CLOSED AT THE TIPS. SOME KIND OF LOCALIZED BURNING--AN ENERGY FIELD? I DON'T KNOW--
IT'S A FIRST.
HOMICIDE?
NOW THAT'S HARD TO SAY--
I HAVE TO LOOK UP THEIR CHARTS. SEE THEIR POWER GRIDS. WHAT LEVELS THEY REGISTERED IN AT.
AND, THANKFULLY, THAT WON'T BE A PROBLEM. WITH THEIR CLEARANCE LEVEL, THEY HAVE TO RETEST EVERY THREE MONTHS, SO...
BUT WITH ALL THE LAWYERS AND P.R. PEOPLE IN THE LIVING ROOM--WHO KNOWS HOW CHERRY THIS PLACE IS?
I THOUGHT THAT, TOO.
WHO KNOWS WHAT THEY DID TO THIS BEFORE THEY CALLED US.
LAST THING THEY WOULD WANT IS A SUICIDE AND A DRUG SCANDAL.
LOWER YOUR VOICE PLEASE, DOCTOR.
MAYBE HIS POWERS MALFUNCTIONED ON HIM.
MAYBE, BUT, WALKER, IF IT IS A HOMICIDE...
I KNOW.
I MEAN...
I KNOW.

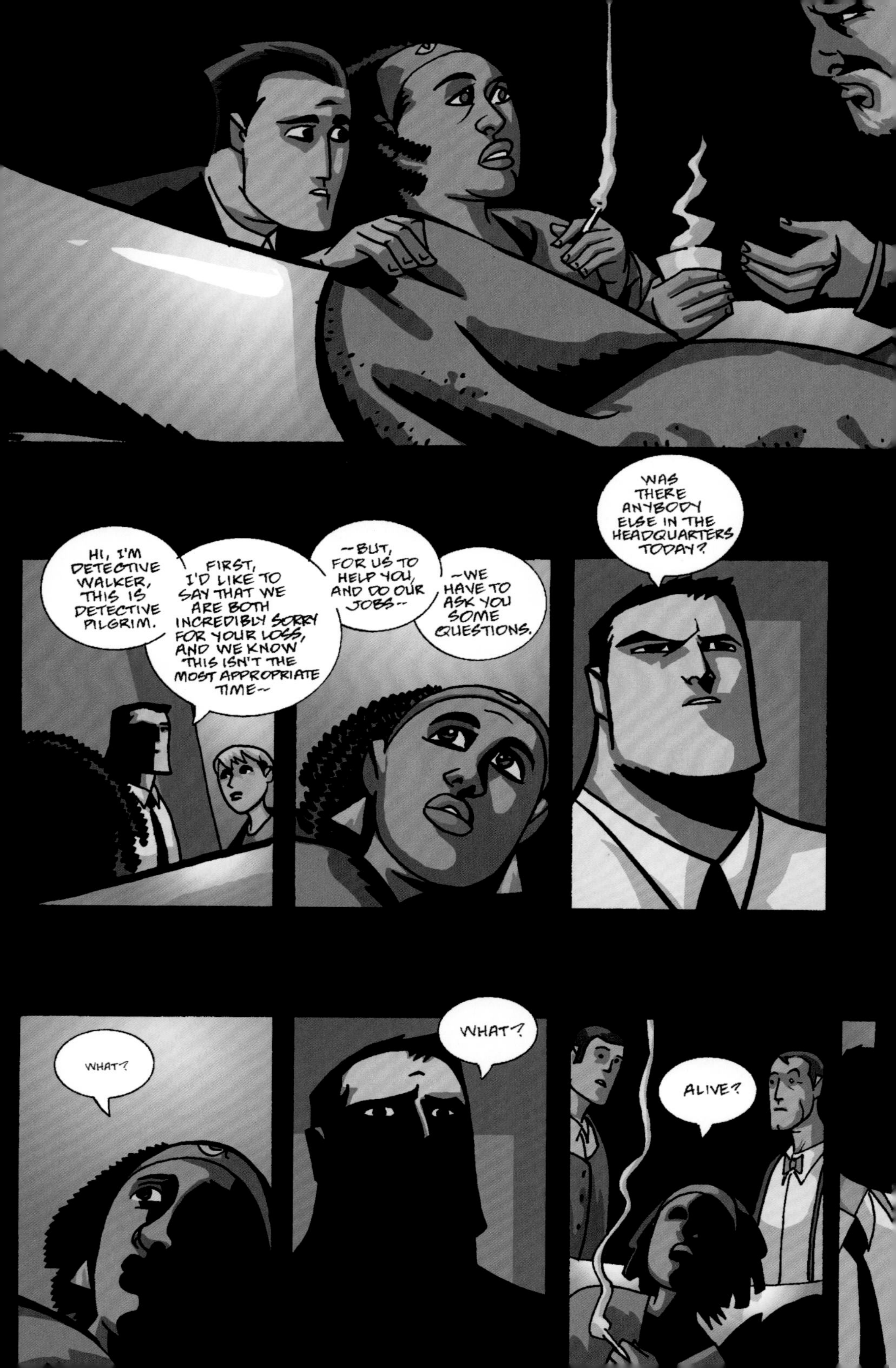
HI, I'M DETECTIVE WALKER, THIS IS DETECTIVE PILGRIM.
FIRST, I'D LIKE TO SAY THAT WE ARE BOTH INCREDIBLY SORRY FOR YOUR LOSS, AND WE KNOW THIS ISN'T THE MOST APPROPRIATE TIME--
--BUT, FOR US TO HELP YOU, AND DO OUR JOBS--
--WE HAVE TO ASK YOU SOME QUESTIONS.
WAS THERE ANYBODY ELSE IN THE HEADQUARTERS TODAY?
WHAT?
WHAT?
ALIVE?

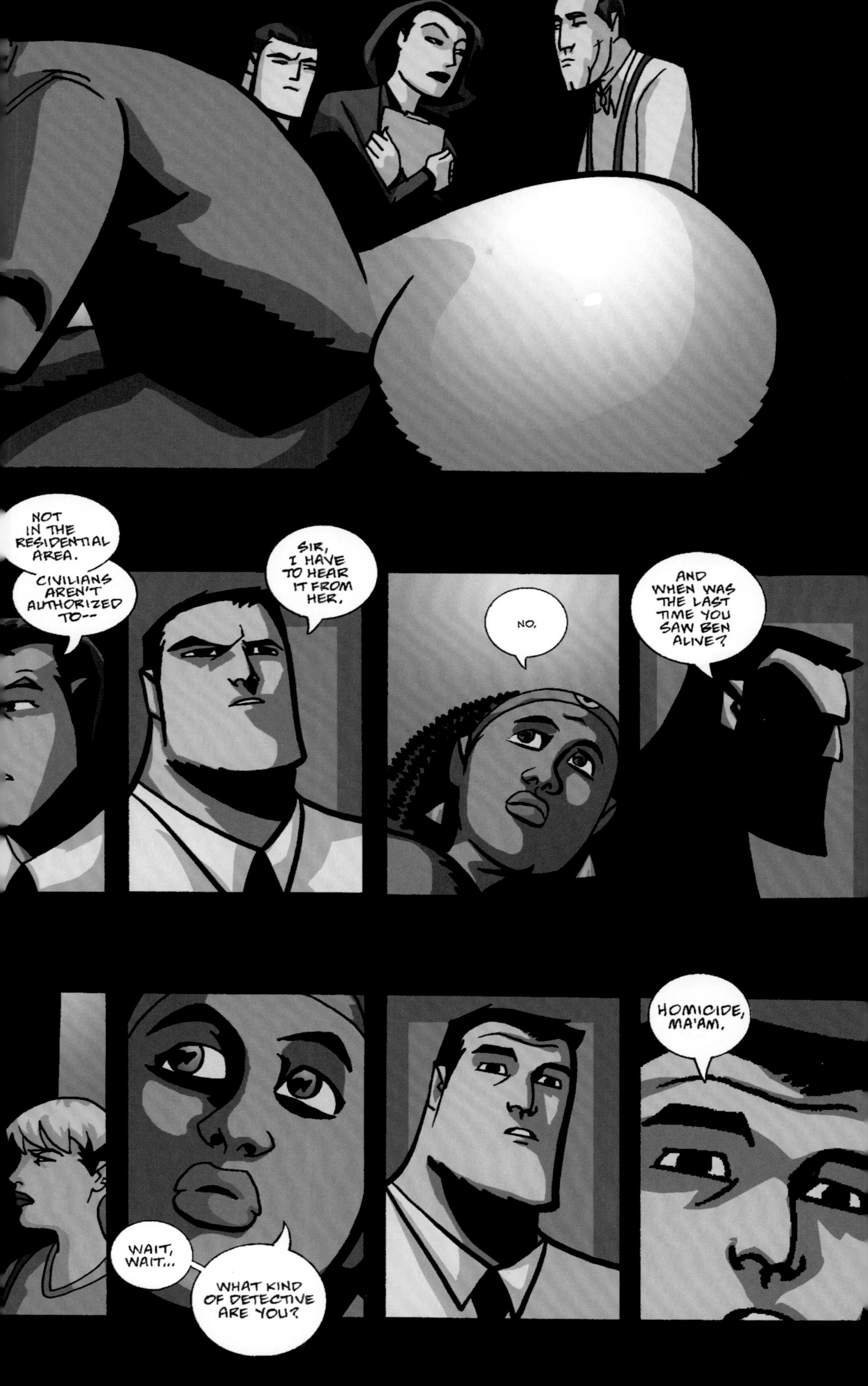
NOT IN THE RESIDENTIAL AREA.
CIVILIANS AREN'T AUTHORIZED TO--
SIR, I HAVE TO HEAR IT FROM HER.
NO.
AND WHEN WAS THE LAST TIME YOU SAW BEN ALIVE?
WAIT, WAIT...
WHAT KIND OF DETECTIVE ARE YOU?
HOMICIDE, MA'AM.

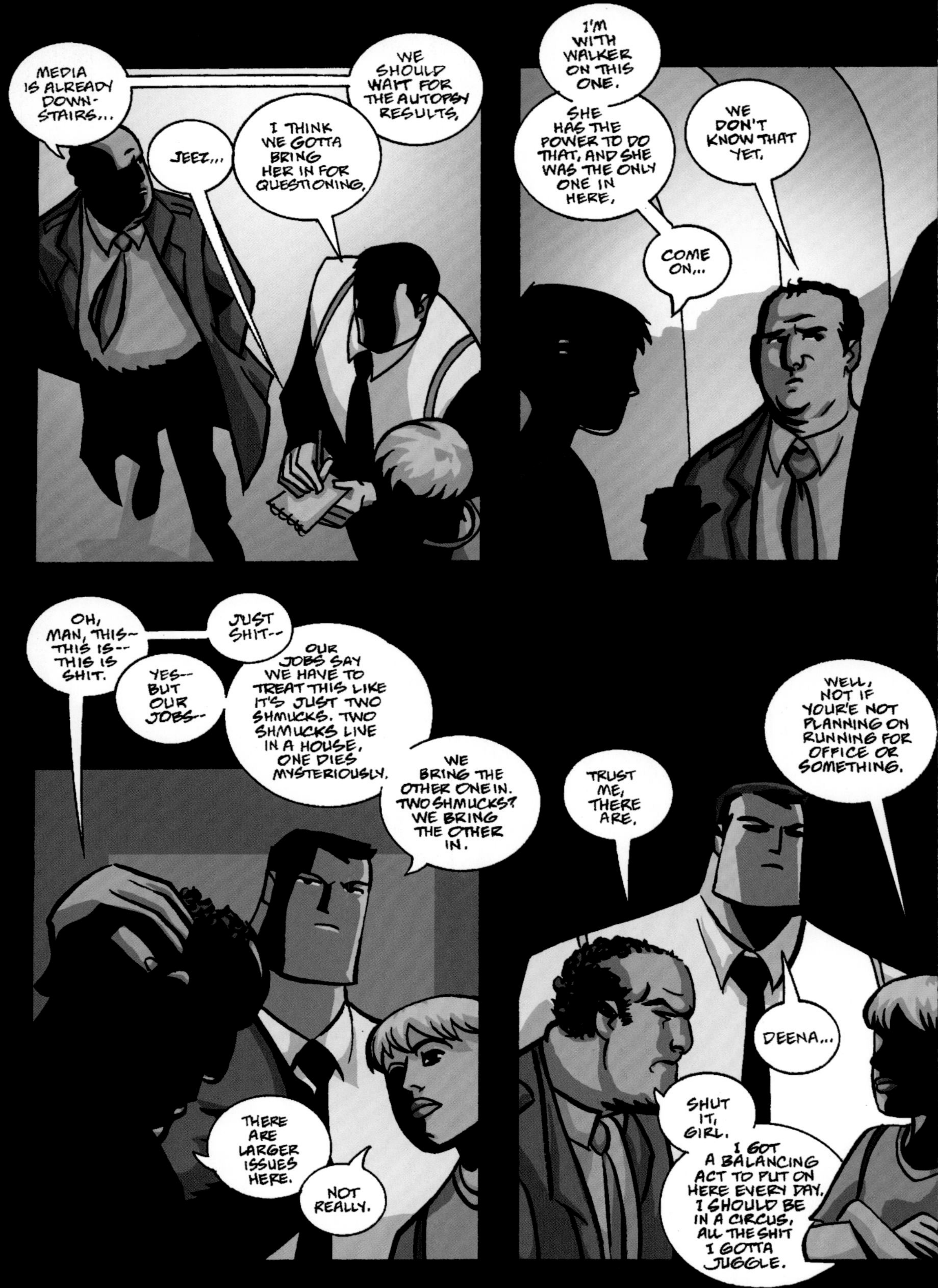
MEDIA IS ALREADY DOWN-STAIRS...
WE SHOULD WAIT FOR THE AUTOPSY RESULTS.
JEEZ...
I THINK WE GOTTA BRING HER IN FOR QUESTIONING.
I'M WITH WALKER ON THIS ONE.
SHE HAS THE POWER TO DO THAT, AND SHE WAS THE ONLY ONE IN HERE.
WE DON'T KNOW THAT YET.
COME ON...
OH, MAN, THIS-- THIS IS-- THIS IS SHIT.
JUST SHIT--
YES-- BUT OUR JOBS--
OUR JOBS SAY WE HAVE TO TREAT THIS LIKE IT'S JUST TWO SHMUCKS. TWO SHMUCKS LIVE IN A HOUSE, ONE DIES MYSTERIOUSLY.
WE BRING THE OTHER ONE IN. TWO SHMUCKS? WE BRING THE OTHER IN.
THERE ARE LARGER ISSUES HERE.
NOT REALLY.
WELL, NOT IF YOUR'E NOT PLANNING ON RUNNING FOR OFFICE OR SOMETHING.
TRUST ME, THERE ARE.
DEENA...
SHUT IT, GIRL.
I GOT A BALANCING ACT TO PUT ON HERE EVERY DAY. I SHOULD BE IN A CIRCUS, ALL THE SHIT I GOTTA JUGGLE.

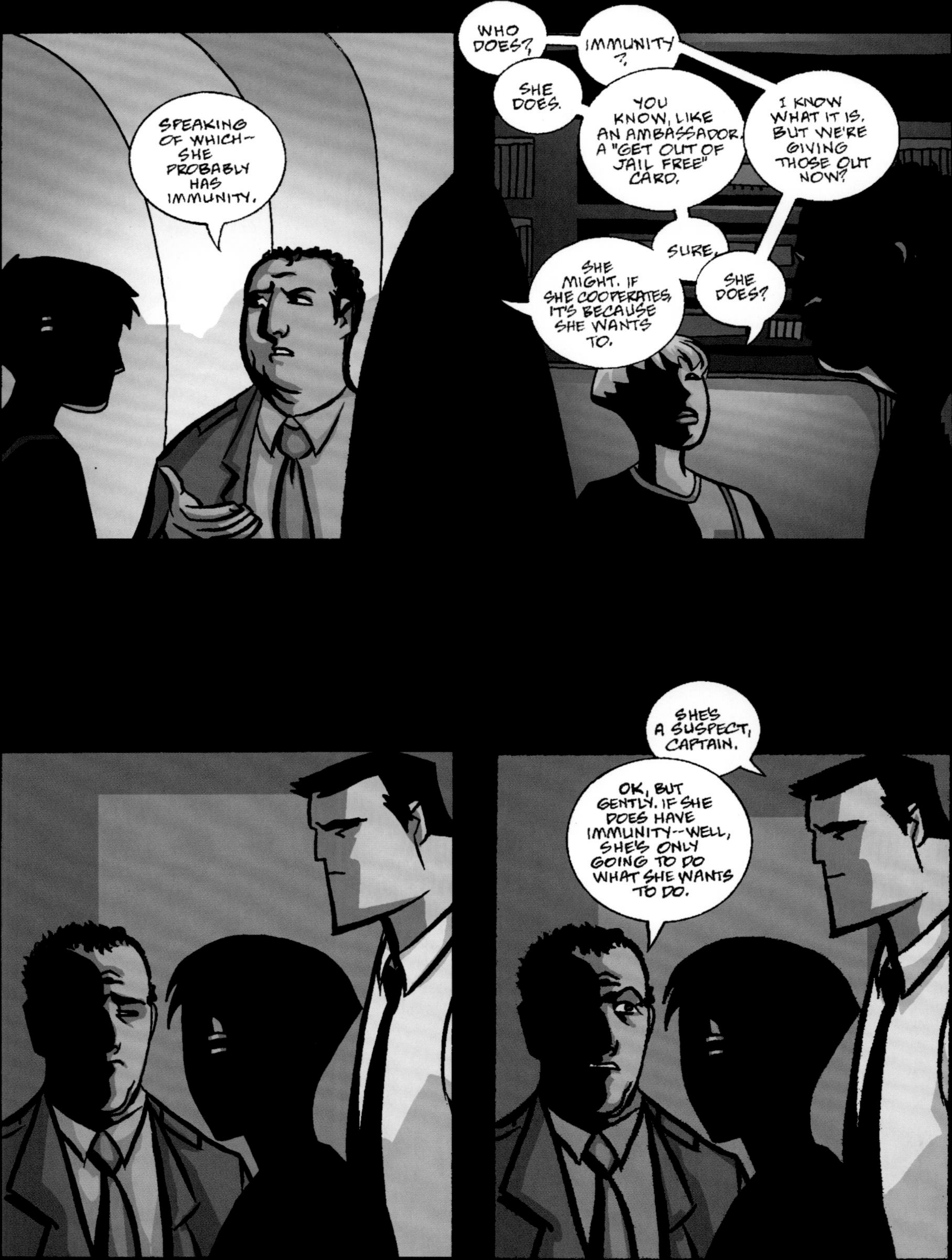
SPEAKING OF WHICH-- SHE PROBABLY HAS IMMUNITY.
WHO DOES?
IMMUNITY?
SHE DOES.
YOU KNOW, LIKE AN AMBASSADOR. A "GET OUT OF JAIL FREE" CARD.
I KNOW WHAT IT IS. BUT WE'RE GIVING THOSE OUT NOW?
SURE.
SHE DOES?
SHE MIGHT. IF SHE COOPERATES, IT'S BECAUSE SHE WANTS TO.
SHE'S A SUSPECT, CAPTAIN.
OK, BUT GENTLY. IF SHE DOES HAVE IMMUNITY--WELL, SHE'S ONLY GOING TO DO WHAT SHE WANTS TO DO.

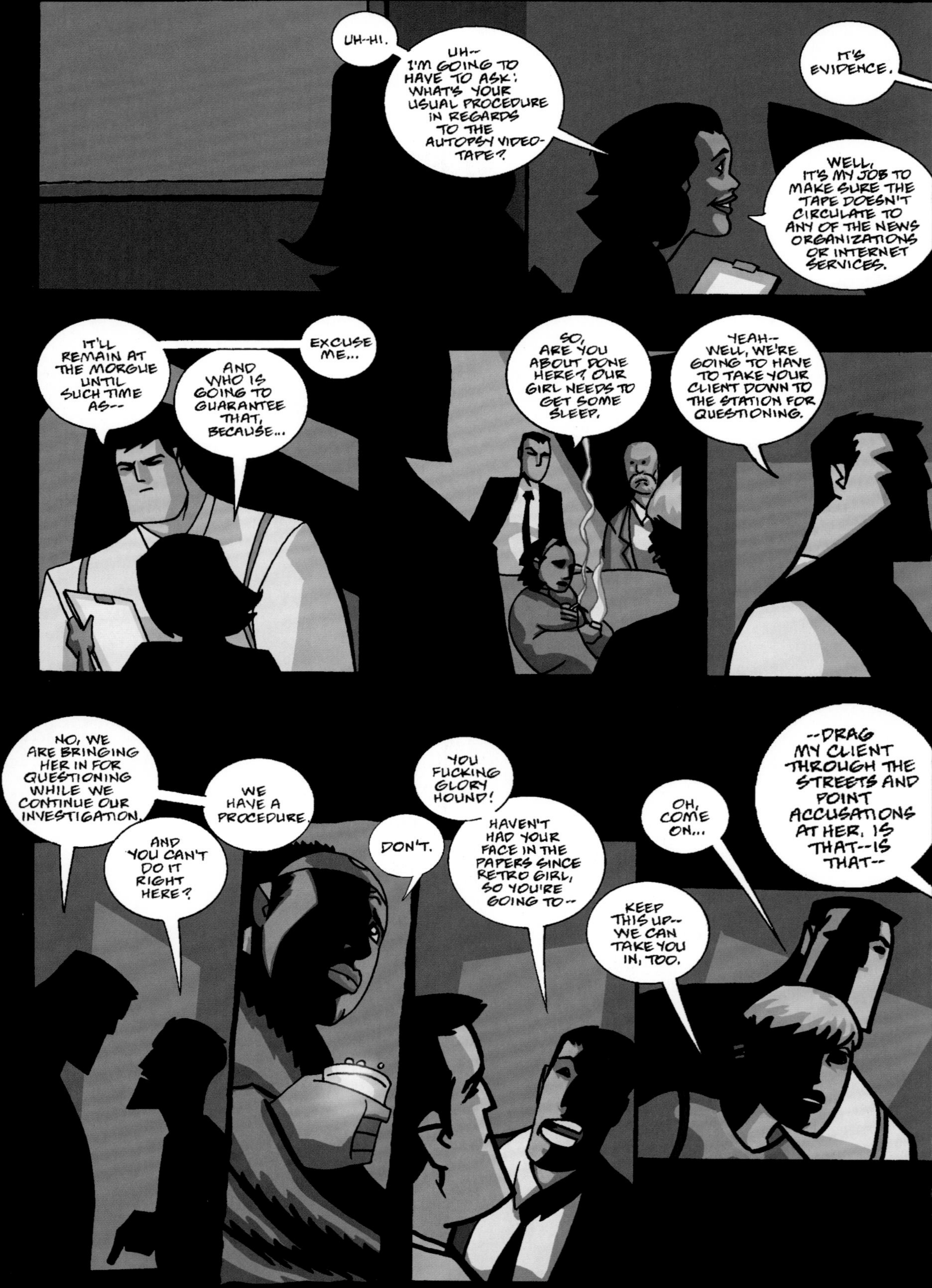

UH--HI.
UH-- I'M GOING TO HAVE TO ASK: WHAT'S YOUR USUAL PROCEDURE IN REGARDS TO THE AUTOPSY VIDEO-TAPE?
IT'S EVIDENCE.
WELL, IT'S MY JOB TO MAKE SURE THE TAPE DOESN'T CIRCULATE TO ANY OF THE NEWS ORGANIZATIONS OR INTERNET SERVICES.
IT'LL REMAIN AT THE MORGUE UNTIL SUCH TIME AS--
EXCUSE ME...
AND WHO IS GOING TO GUARANTEE THAT, BECAUSE...
SO, ARE YOU ABOUT DONE HERE? OUR GIRL NEEDS TO GET SOME SLEEP.
YEAH-- WELL, WE'RE GOING TO HAVE TO TAKE YOUR CLIENT DOWN TO THE STATION FOR QUESTIONING.
NO, WE ARE BRINGING HER IN FOR QUESTIONING WHILE WE CONTINUE OUR INVESTIGATION.
WE HAVE A PROCEDURE.
AND YOU CAN'T DO IT RIGHT HERE?
DON'T.
YOU FUCKING GLORY HOUND!
HAVEN'T HAD YOUR FACE IN THE PAPERS SINCE RETRO GIRL, SO YOU'RE GOING TO--
OH, COME ON...
KEEP THIS UP-- WE CAN TAKE YOU IN, TOO.
--DRAG MY CLIENT THROUGH THE STREETS AND POINT ACCUSATIONS AT HER. IS THAT--IS THAT--

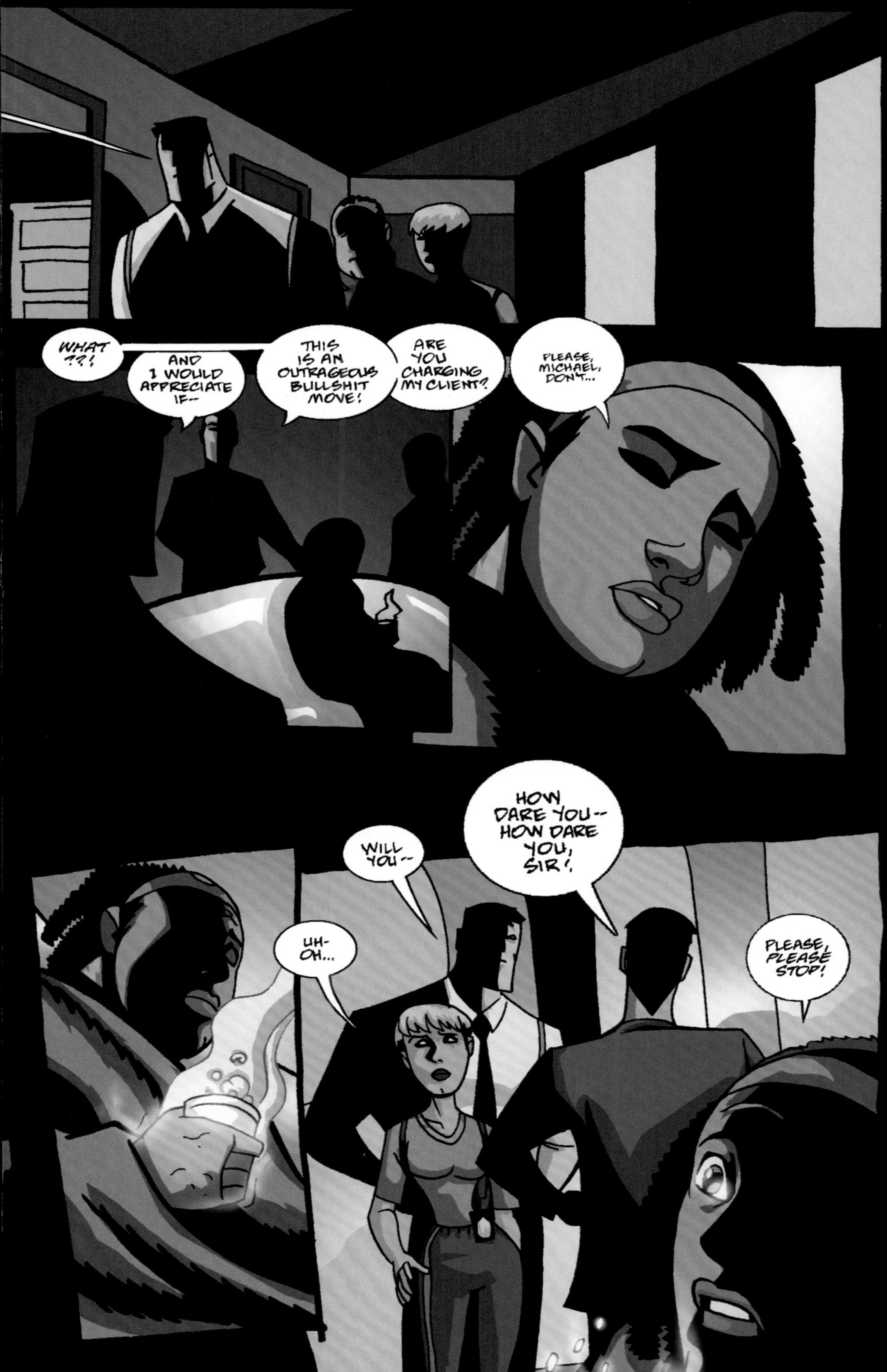
WHAT ??!
AND I WOULD APPRECIATE IF--
THIS IS AN OUTRAGEOUS BULLSHIT MOVE!
ARE YOU CHARGING MY CLIENT?
PLEASE, MICHAEL, DON'T...
WILL YOU--
HOW DARE YOU-- HOW DARE YOU, SIR!
UH-OH...
PLEASE, PLEASE STOP!

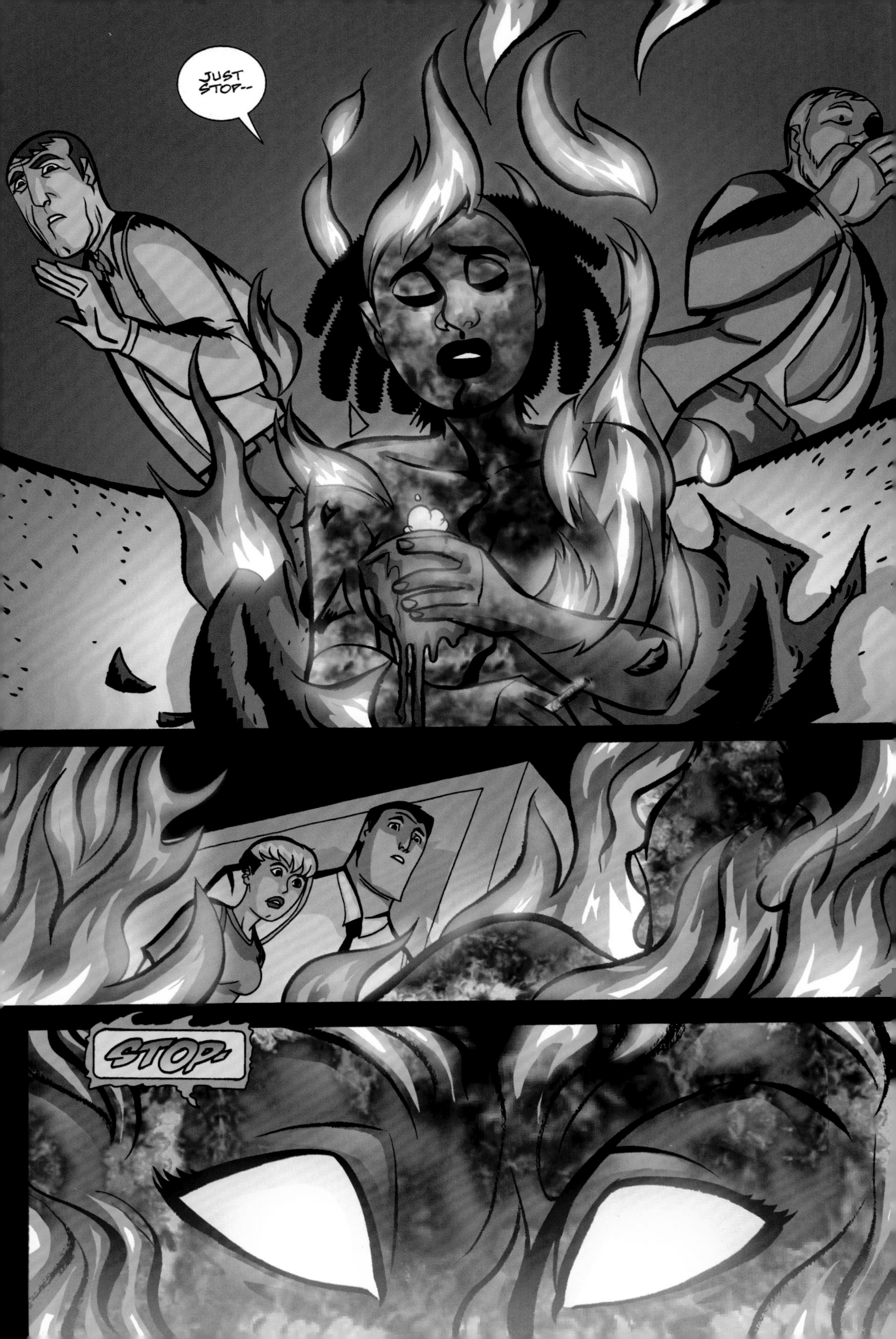
JUST STOP--
STOP-

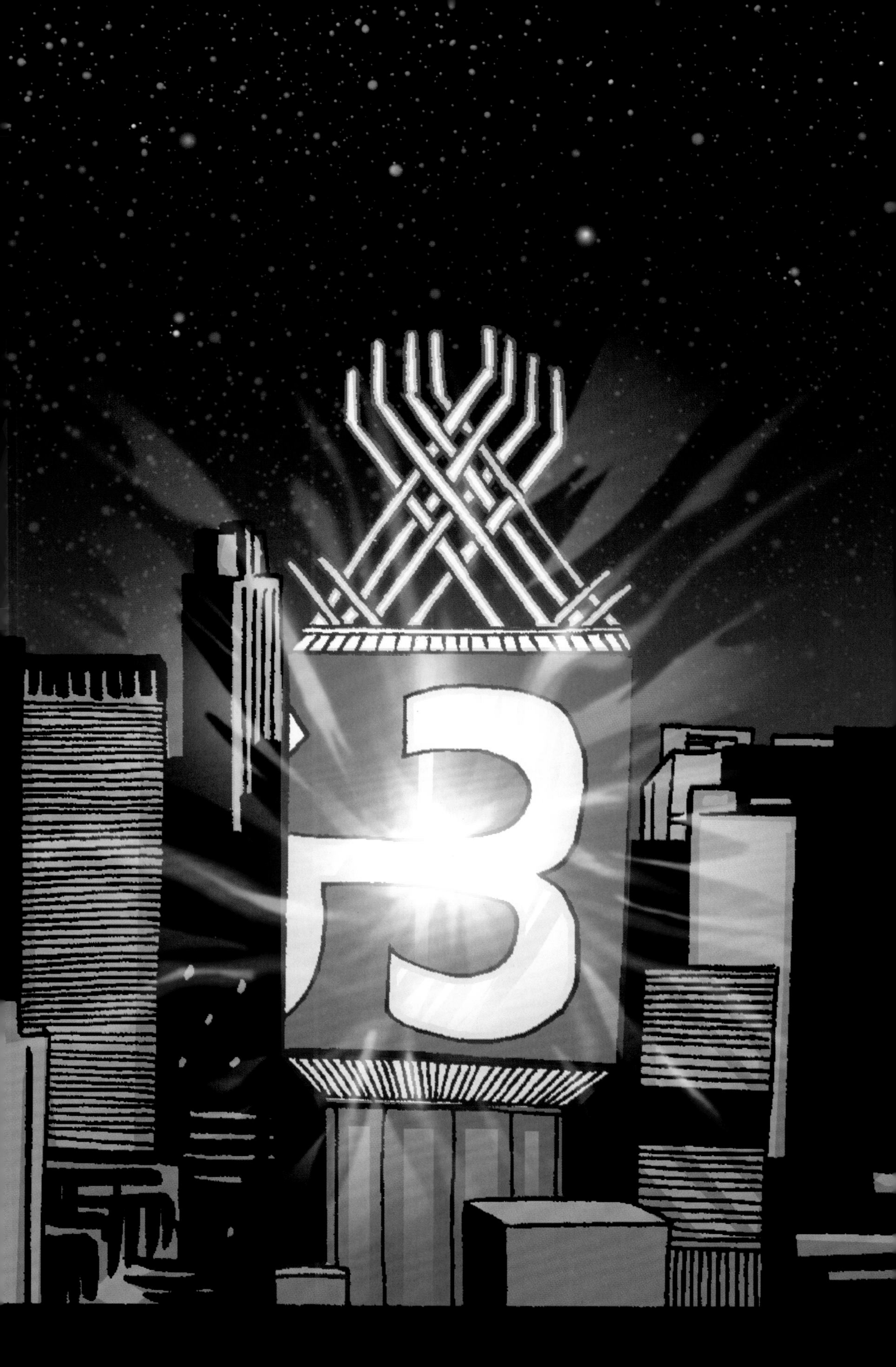

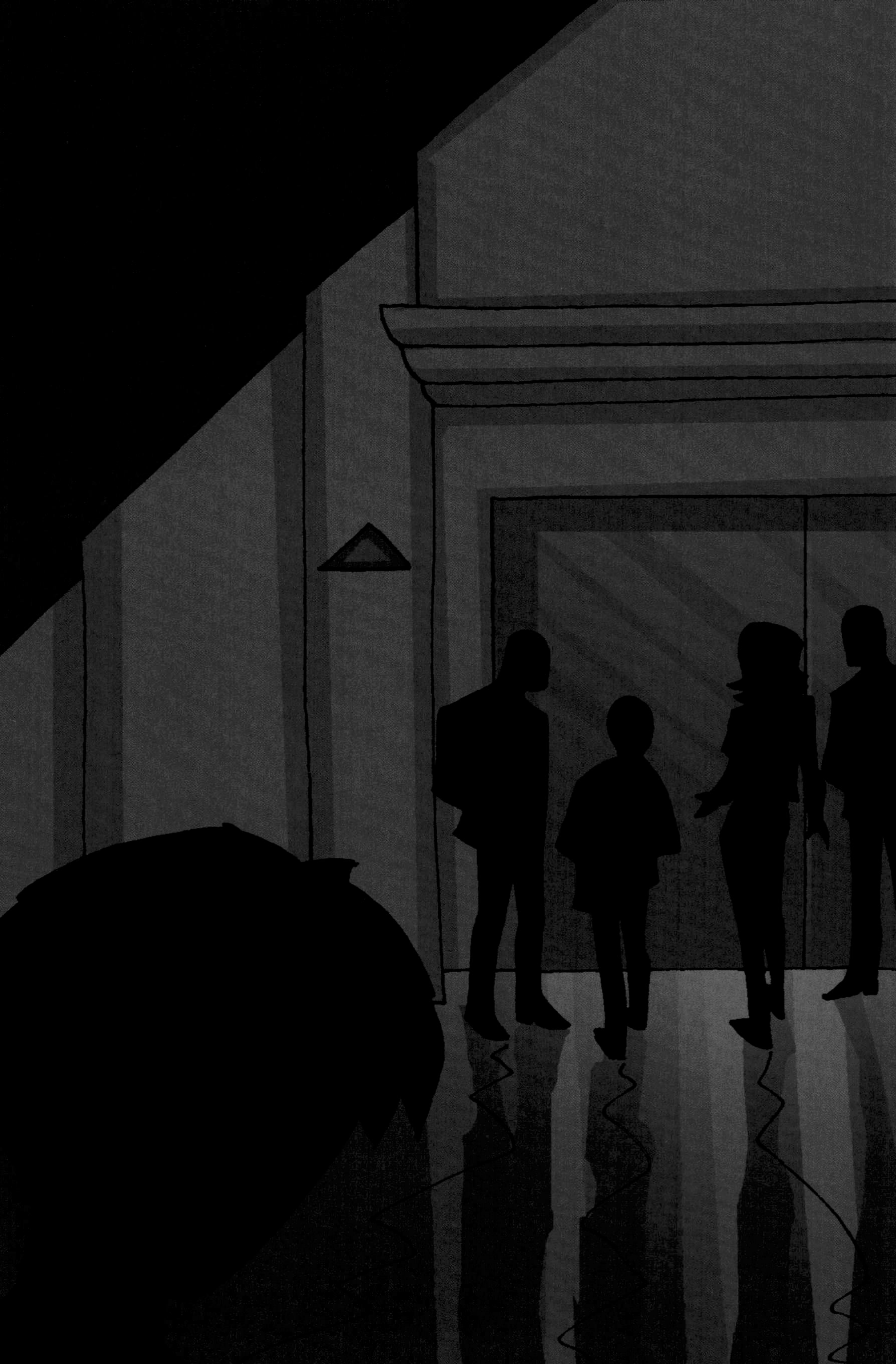

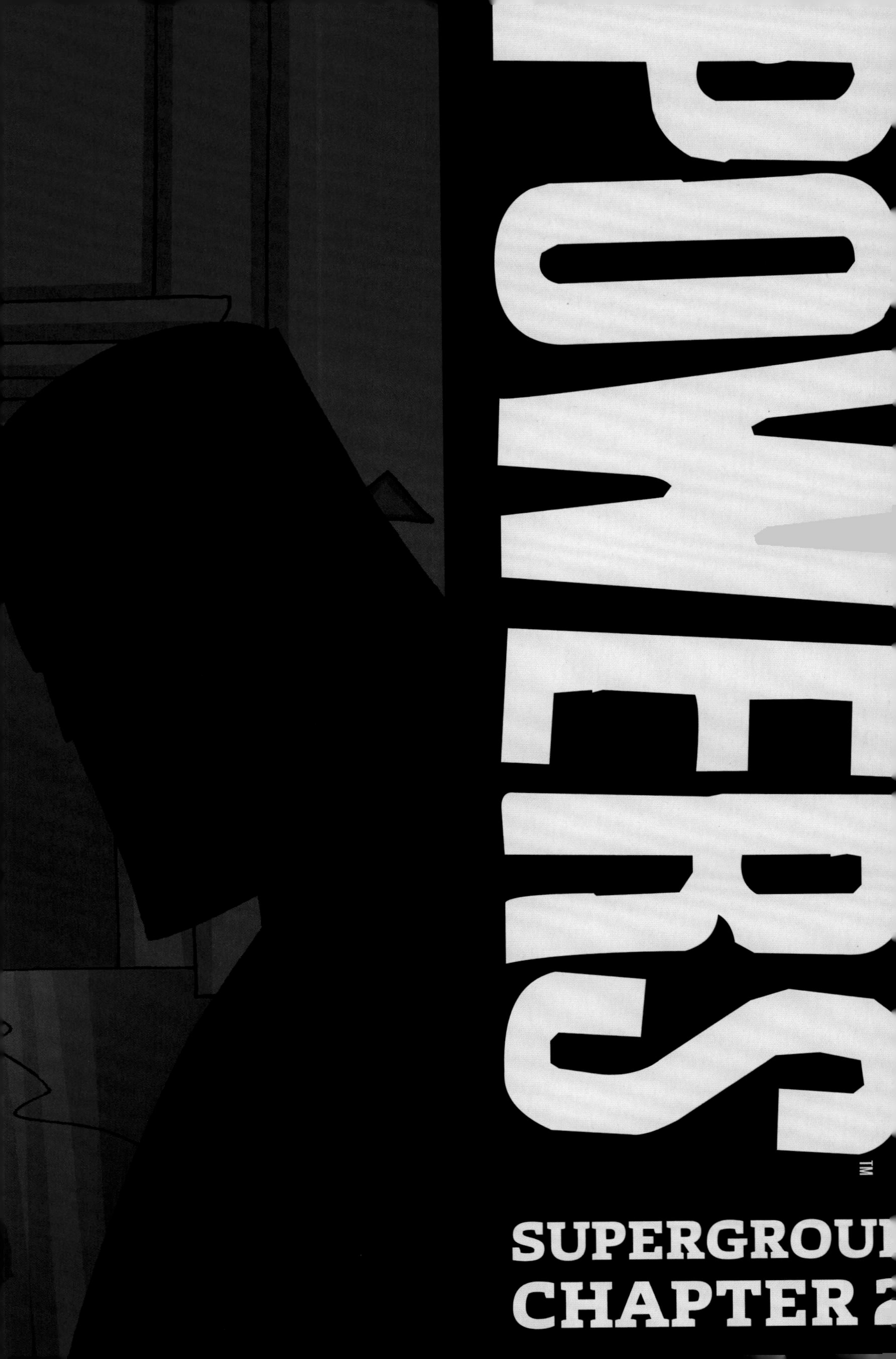

POWERS™

SUPERGROUP
CHAPTER 2

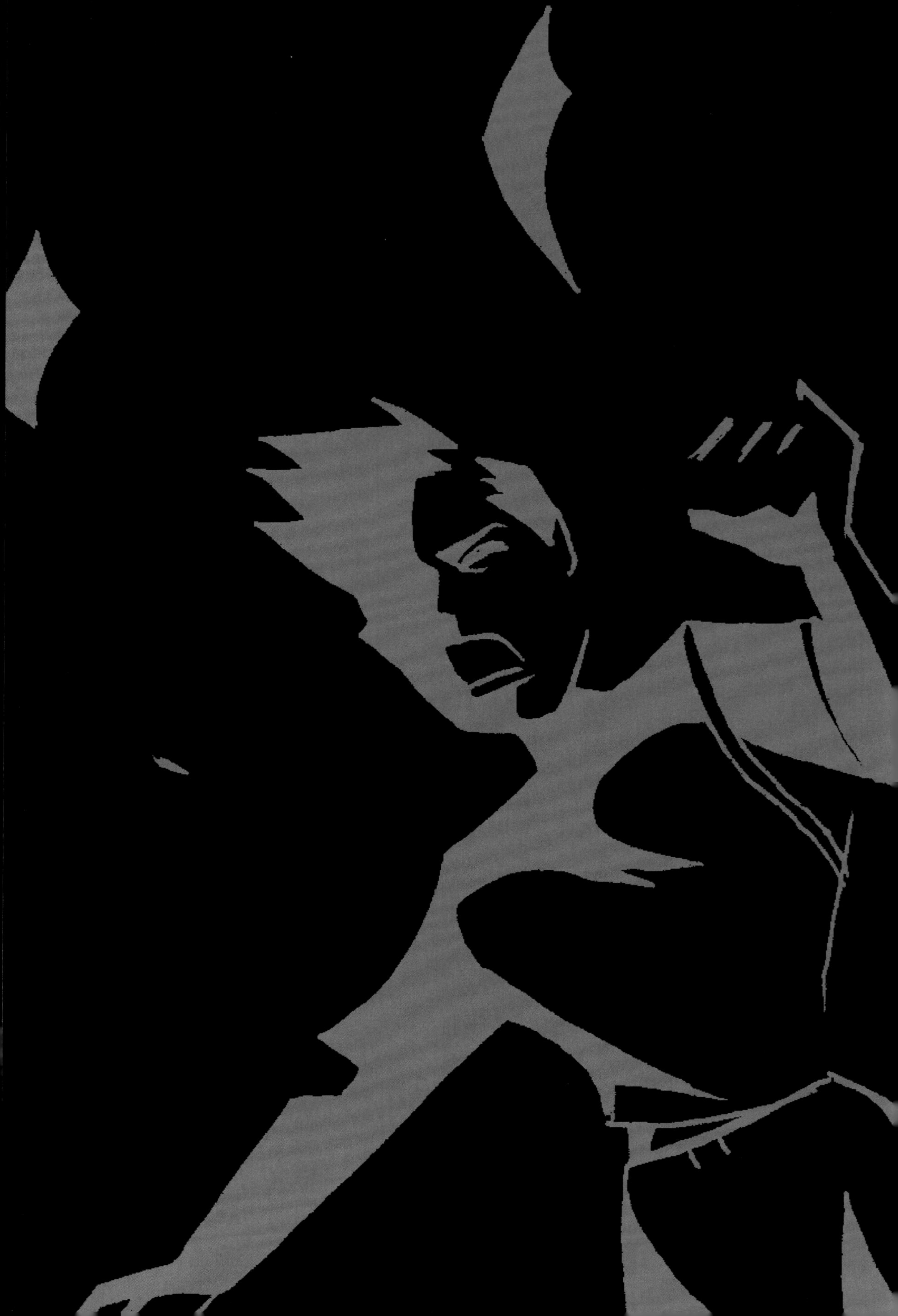

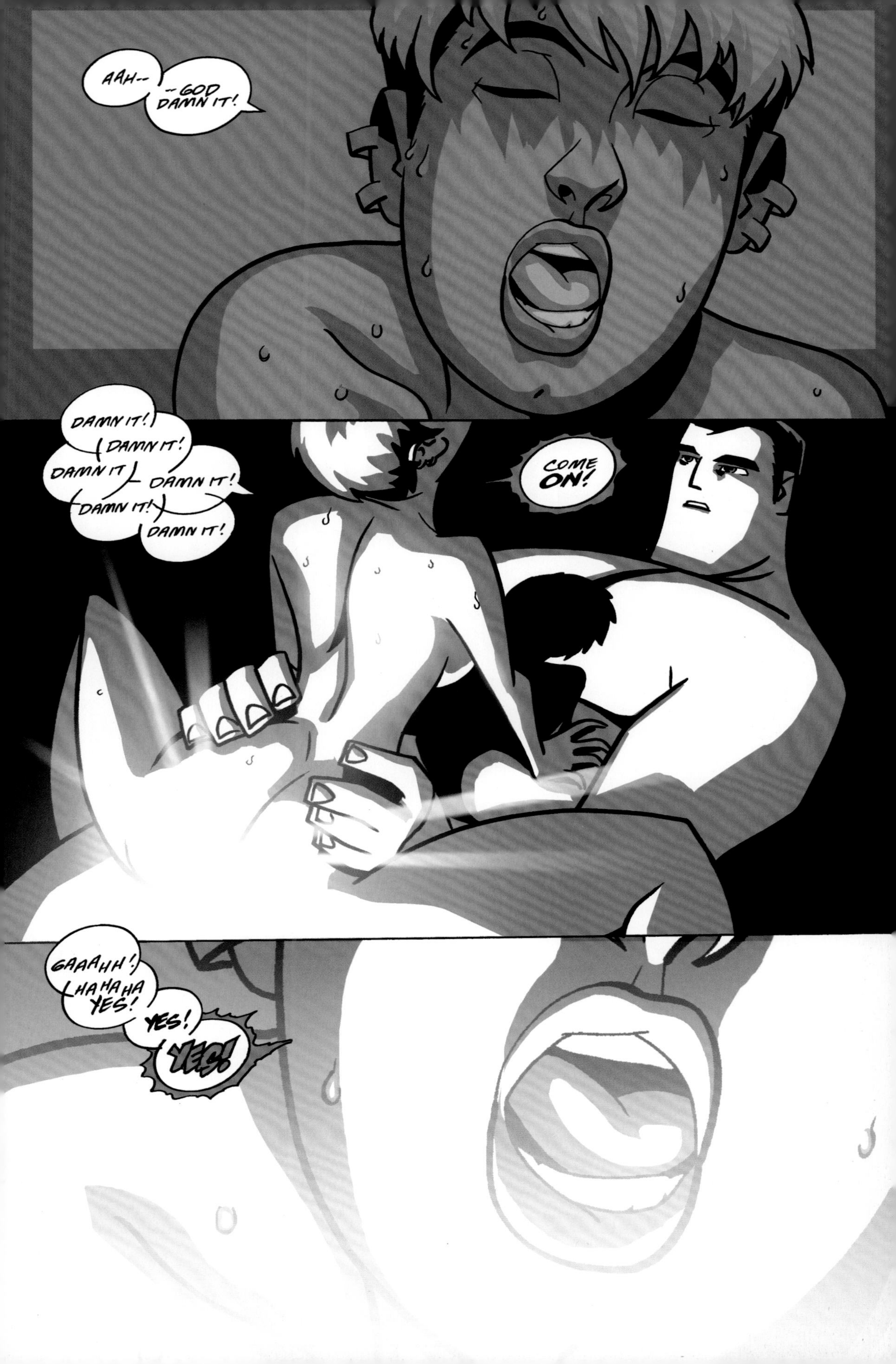
AAH--
--GOD DAMN IT!
DAMN IT!
DAMN IT!
DAMN IT
DAMN IT!
DAMN IT!
DAMN IT!
COME ON!
GAAAHH!
HA HA HA YES!
YES!
YES!

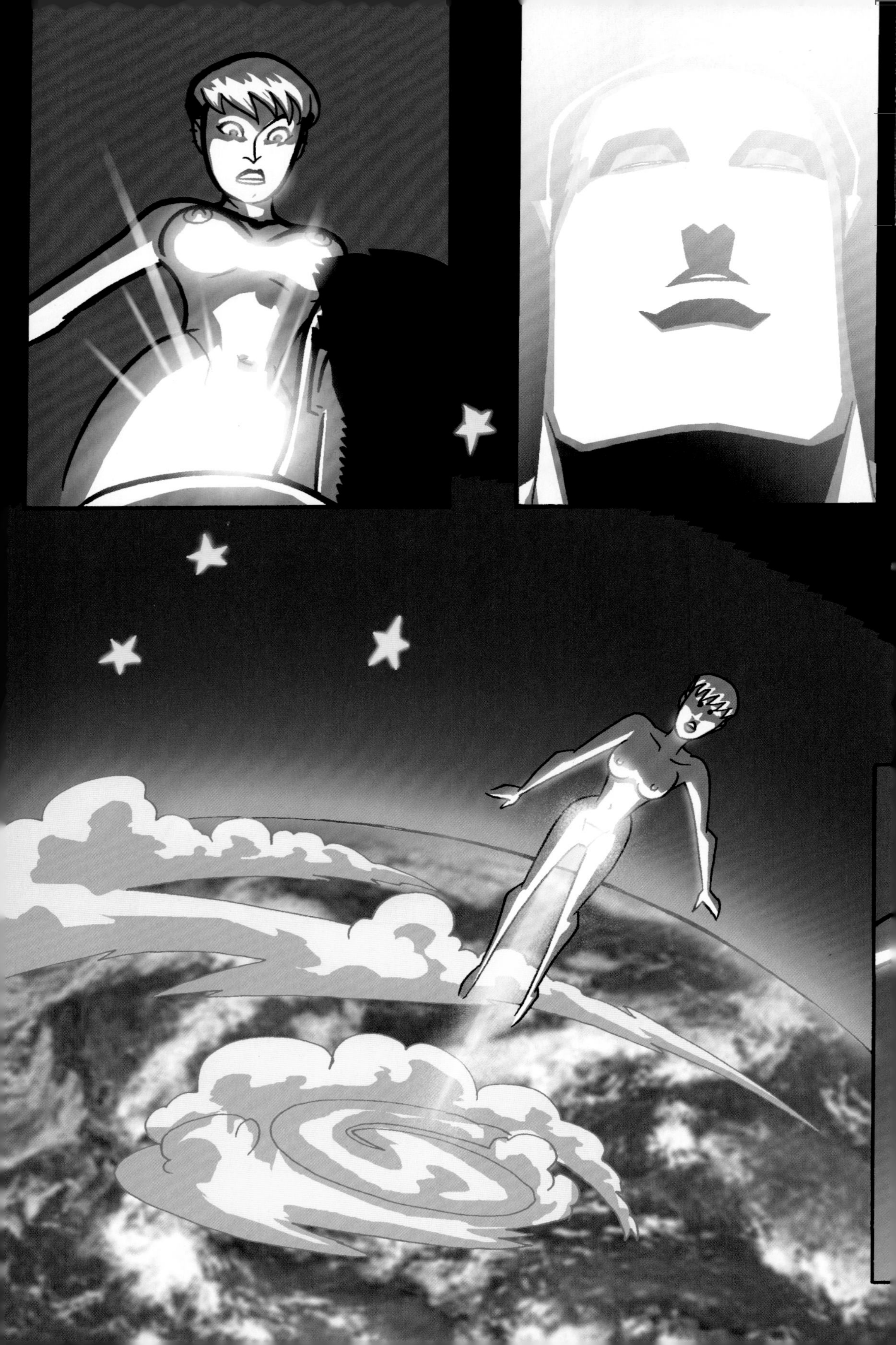

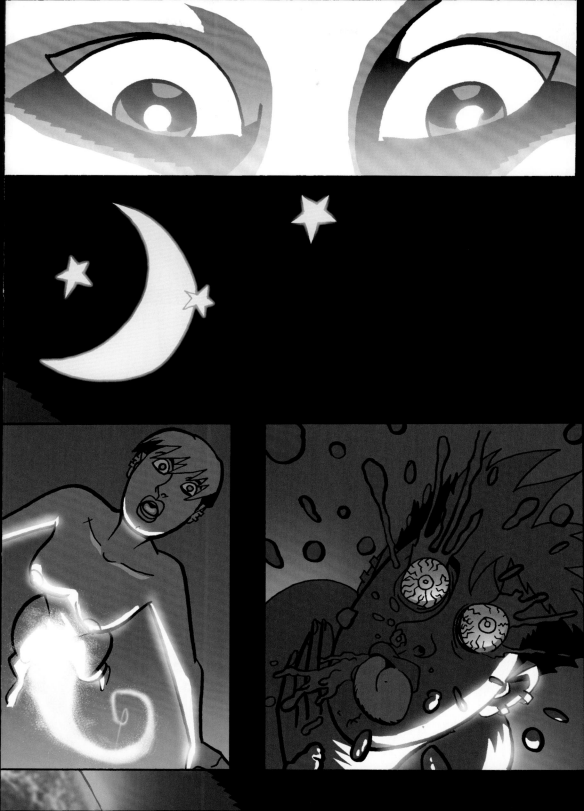

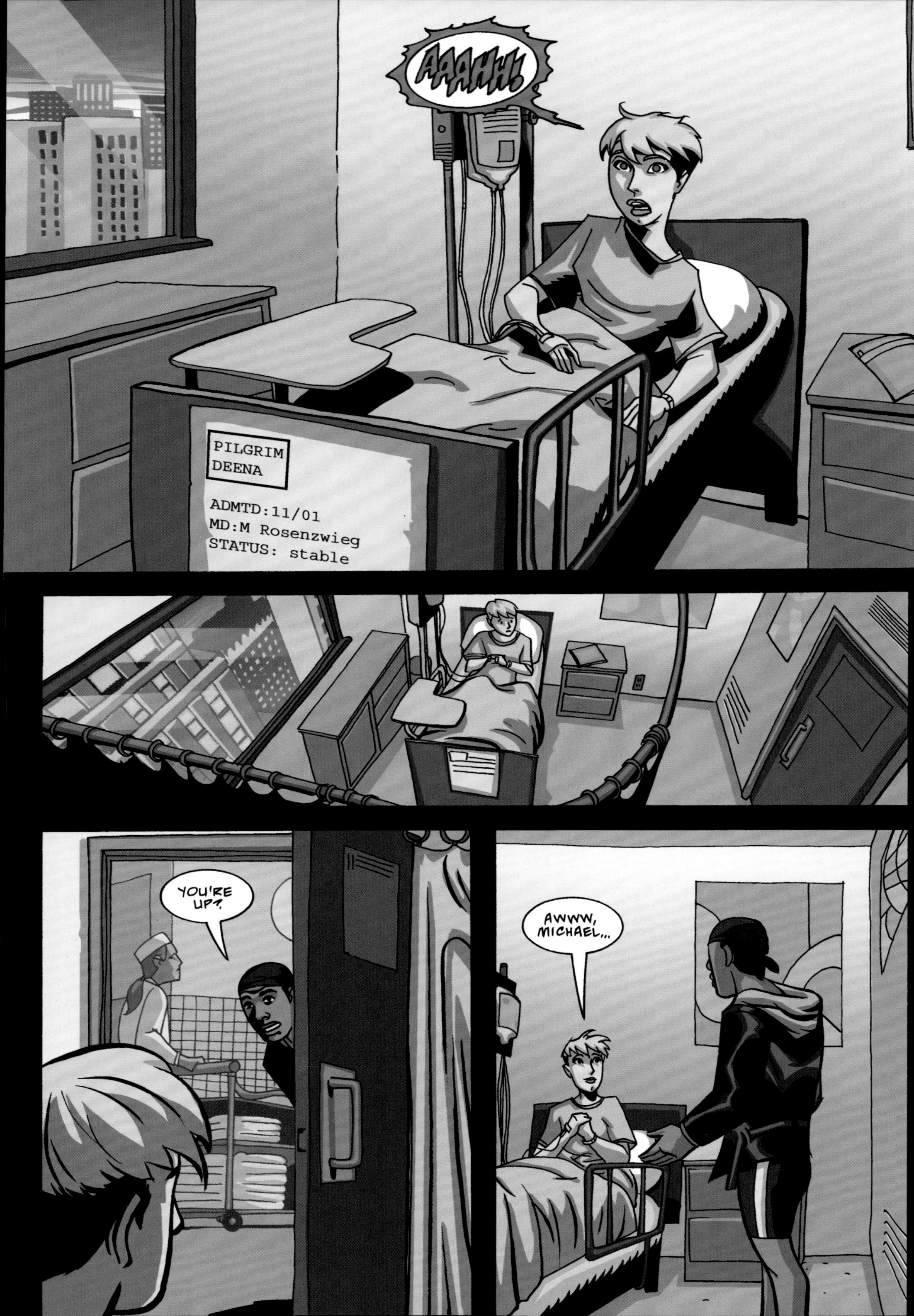
AAAHH!
PILGRIM
DEENA
ADMTD:11/01
MD:M Rosenzwieg
STATUS: stable
YOU'RE UP?
AWWW, MICHAEL...

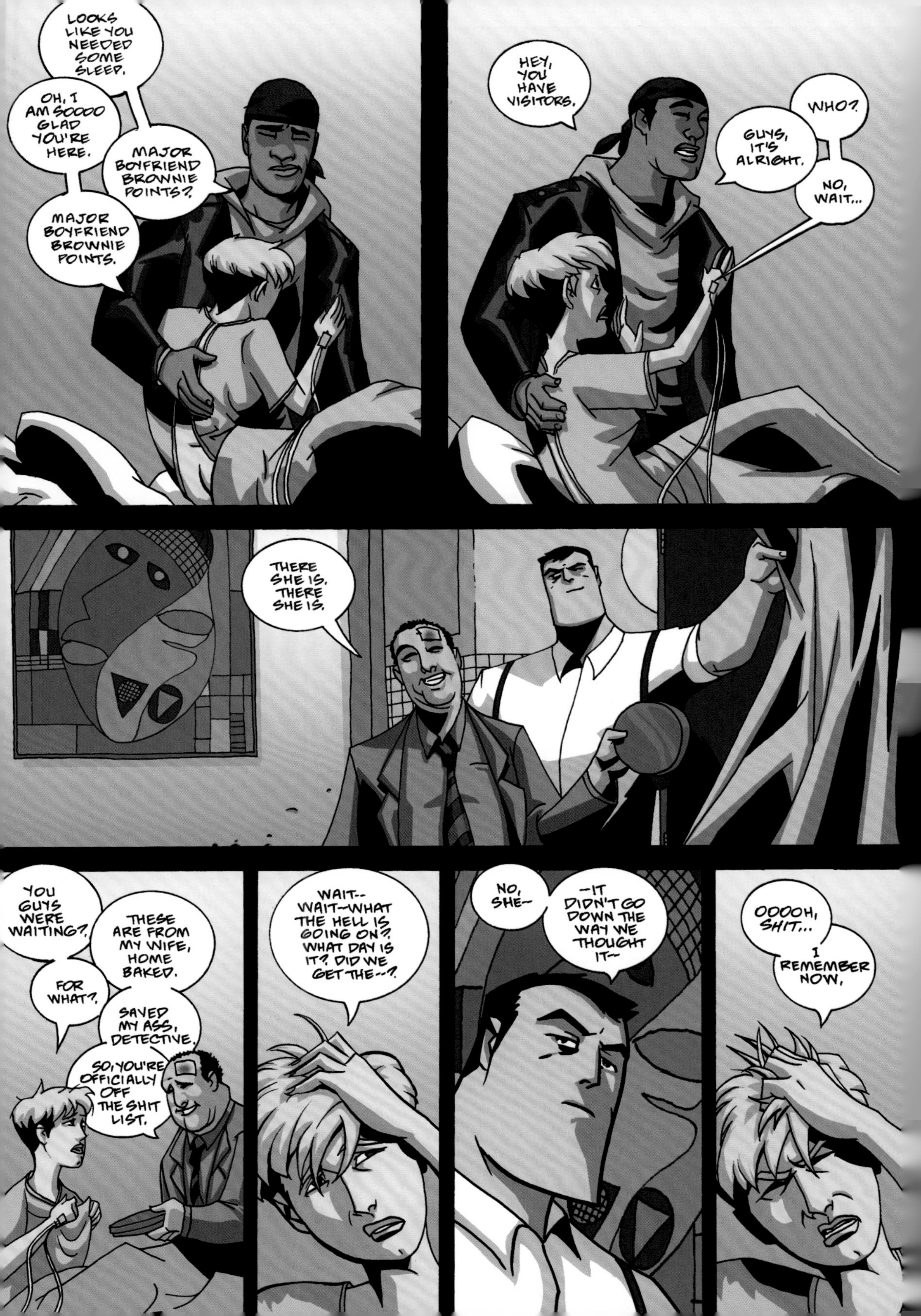
LOOKS LIKE YOU NEEDED SOME SLEEP.
OH, I AM SOOOO GLAD YOU'RE HERE.
MAJOR BOYFRIEND BROWNIE POINTS?
MAJOR BOYFRIEND BROWNIE POINTS.
HEY, YOU HAVE VISITORS.
WHO?
GUYS, IT'S ALRIGHT.
NO, WAIT...
THERE SHE IS. THERE SHE IS.
YOU GUYS WERE WAITING?
THESE ARE FROM MY WIFE, HOME BAKED.
FOR WHAT?
SAVED MY ASS, DETECTIVE.
SO, YOU'RE OFFICIALLY OFF THE SHIT LIST.
WAIT-- WAIT--WHAT THE HELL IS GOING ON? WHAT DAY IS IT? DID WE GET THE--?
NO, SHE--
--IT DIDN'T GO DOWN THE WAY WE THOUGHT IT--
OOOOH, SHIT...
I REMEMBER NOW.

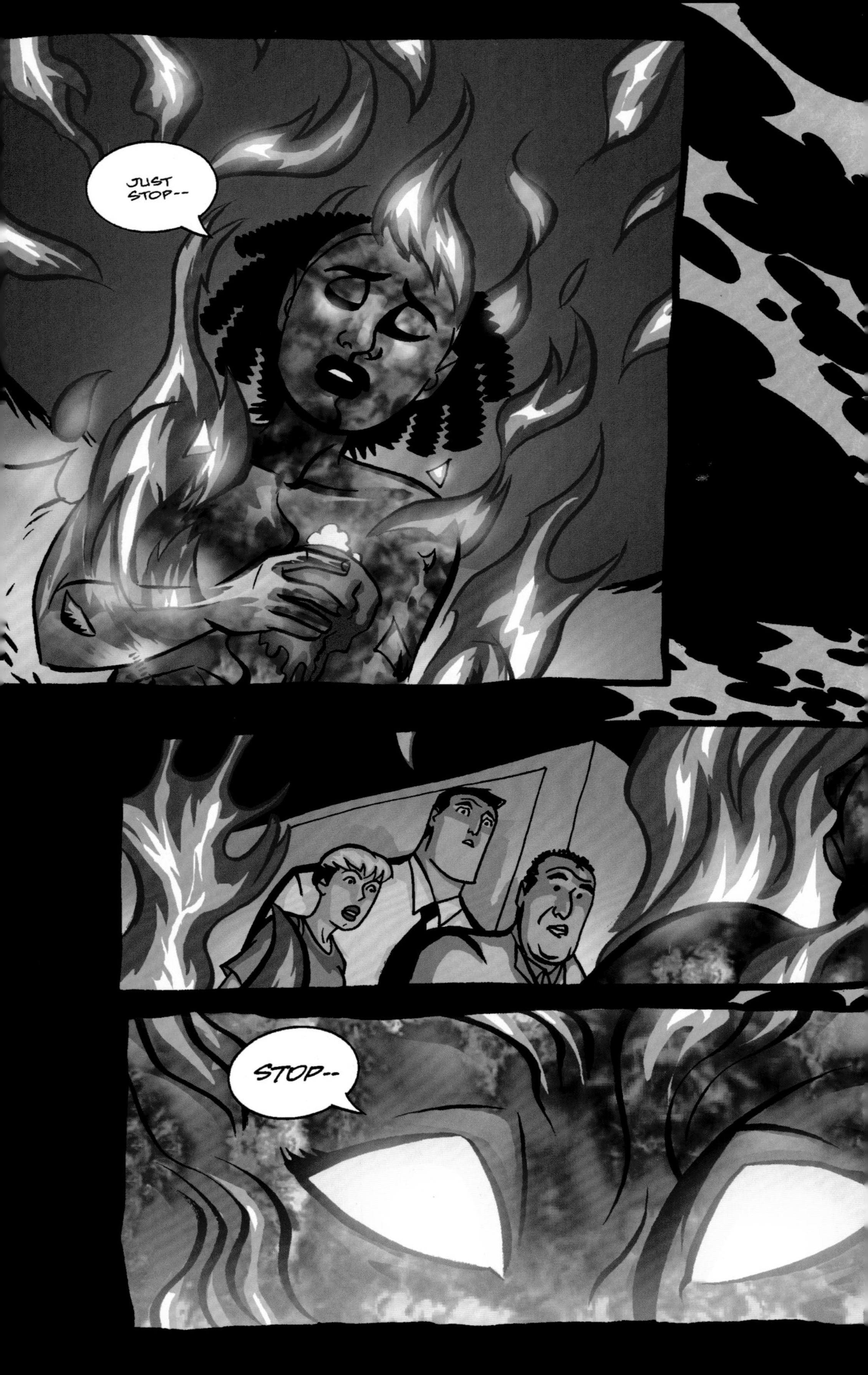
JUST STOP--
STOP--

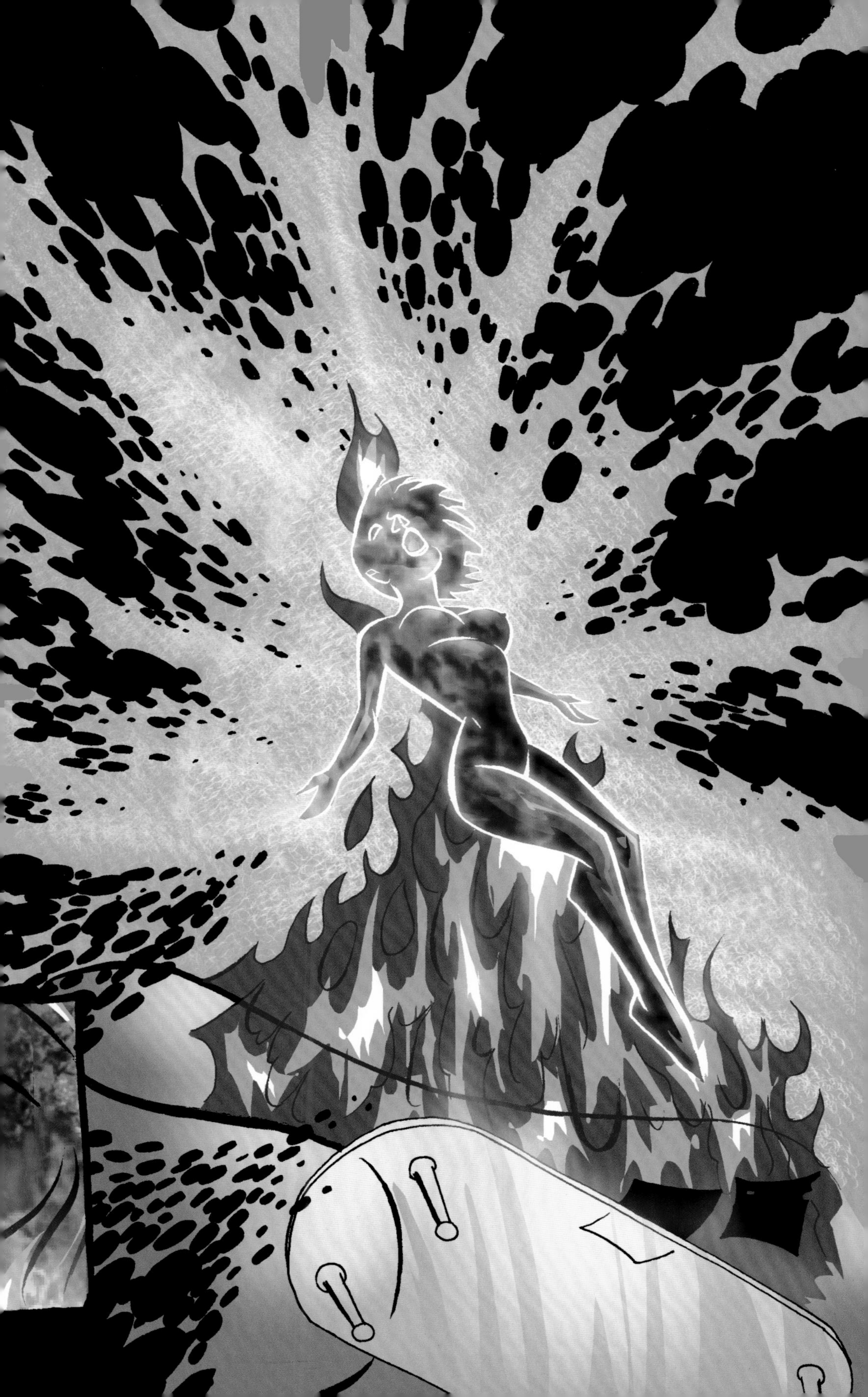

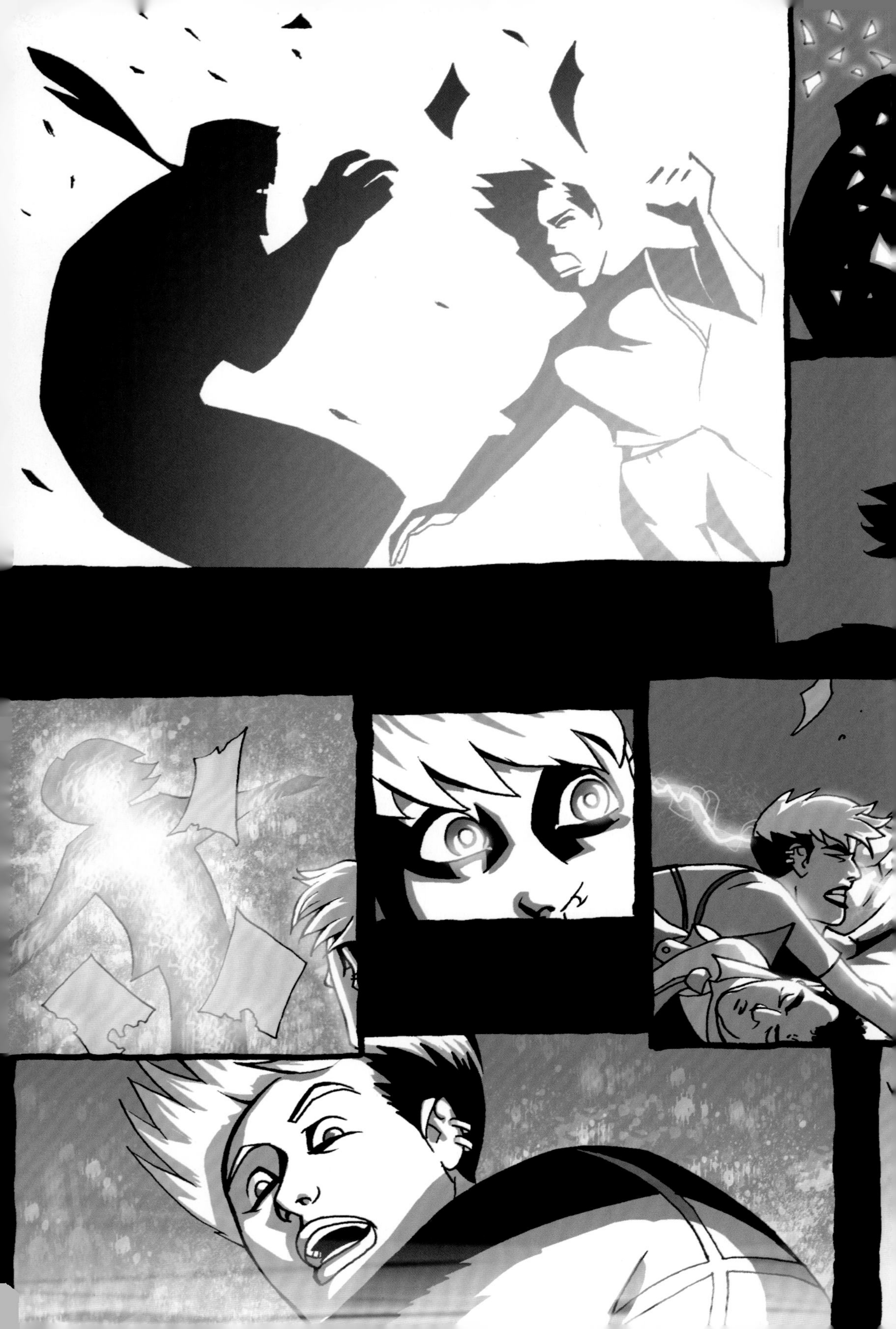

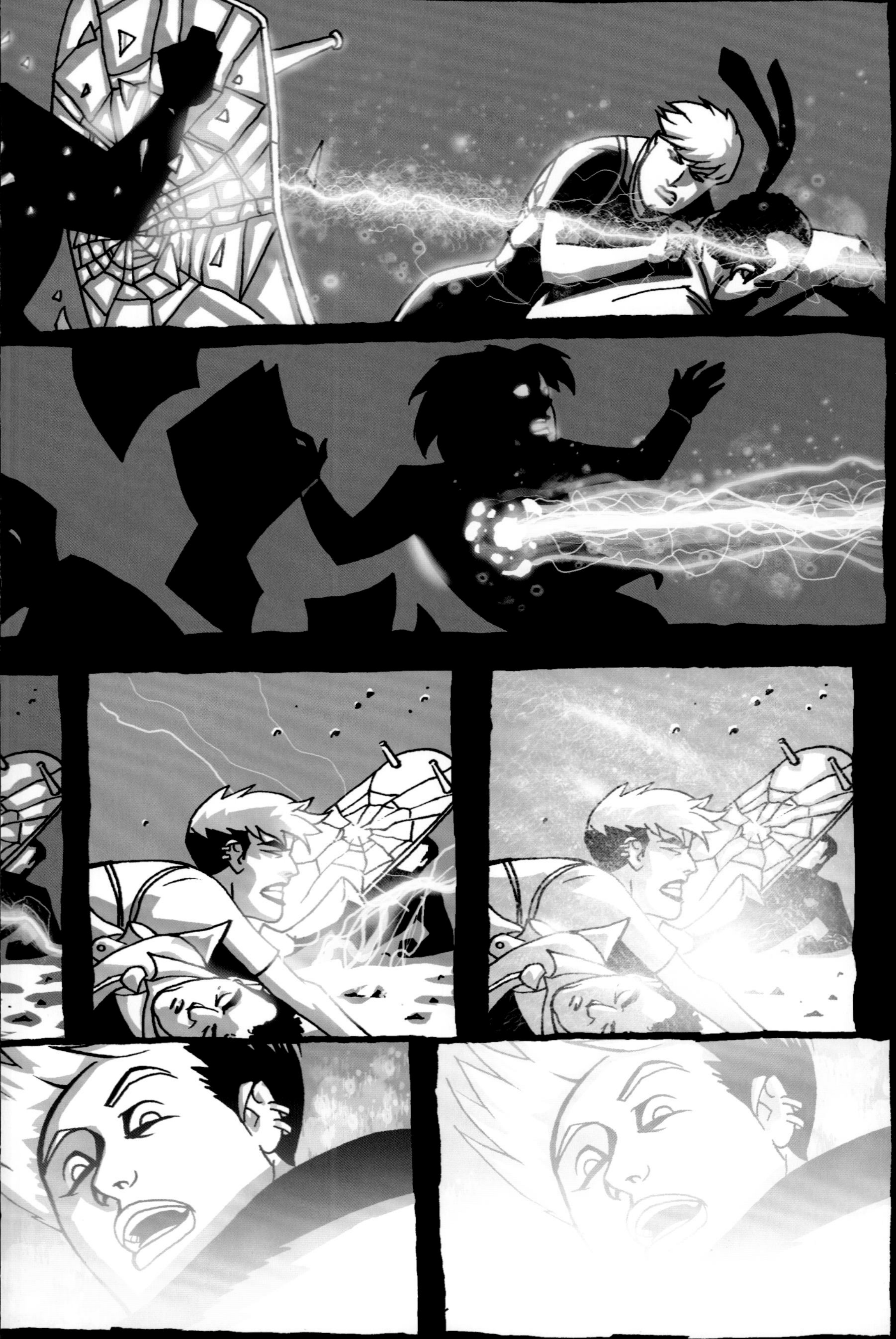

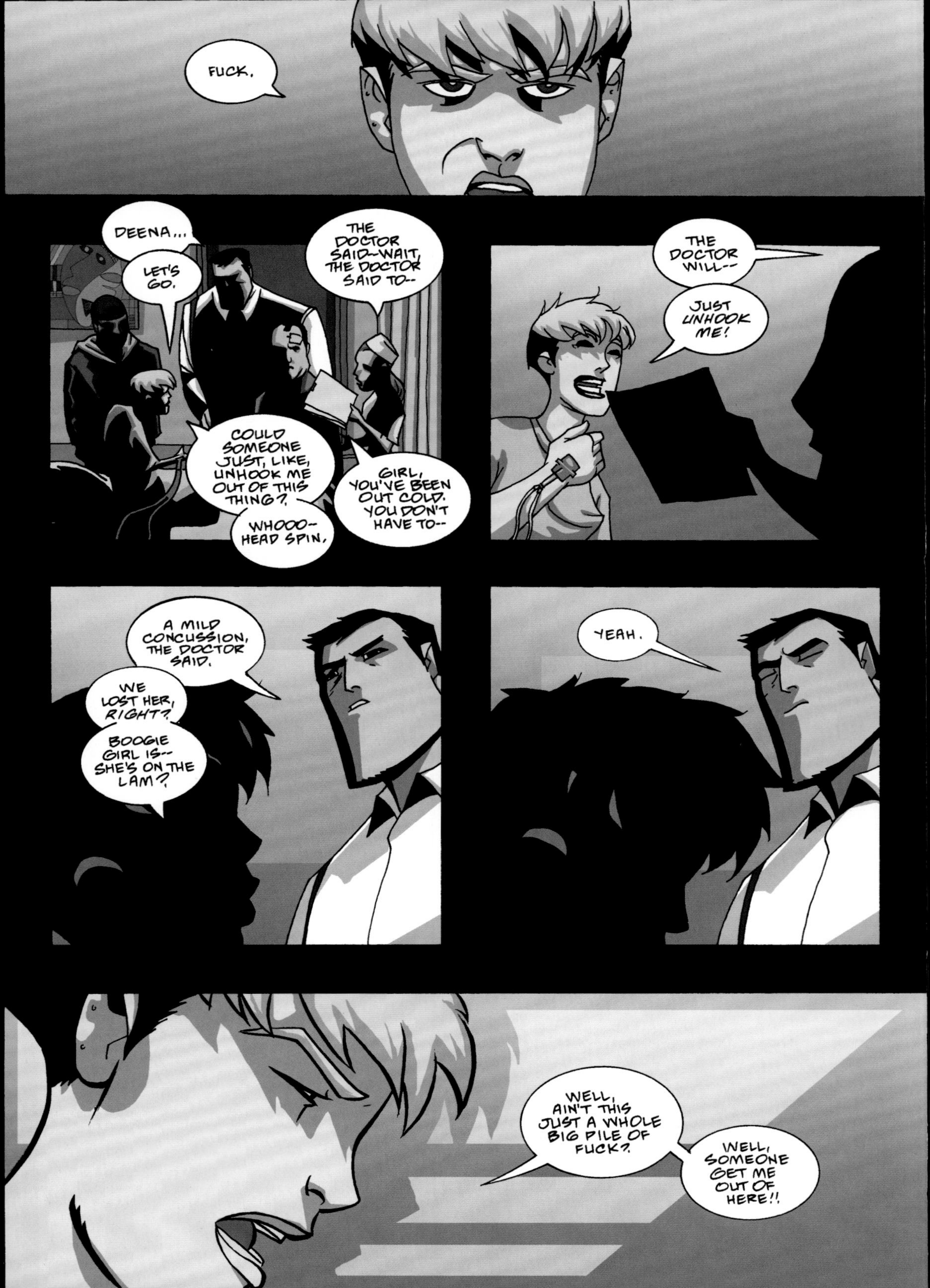
FUCK.
DEENA...
LET'S GO.
THE DOCTOR SAID--WAIT, THE DOCTOR SAID TO--
COULD SOMEONE JUST, LIKE, UNHOOK ME OUT OF THIS THING?.
WHOOO--HEAD SPIN.
GIRL, YOU'VE BEEN OUT COLD. YOU DON'T HAVE TO--
THE DOCTOR WILL--
JUST UNHOOK ME!
A MILD CONCUSSION, THE DOCTOR SAID.
WE LOST HER, RIGHT?
BOOGIE GIRL IS-- SHE'S ON THE LAM?
YEAH.
WELL, AIN'T THIS JUST A WHOLE BIG PILE OF FUCK?.
WELL, SOMEONE GET ME OUT OF HERE!!

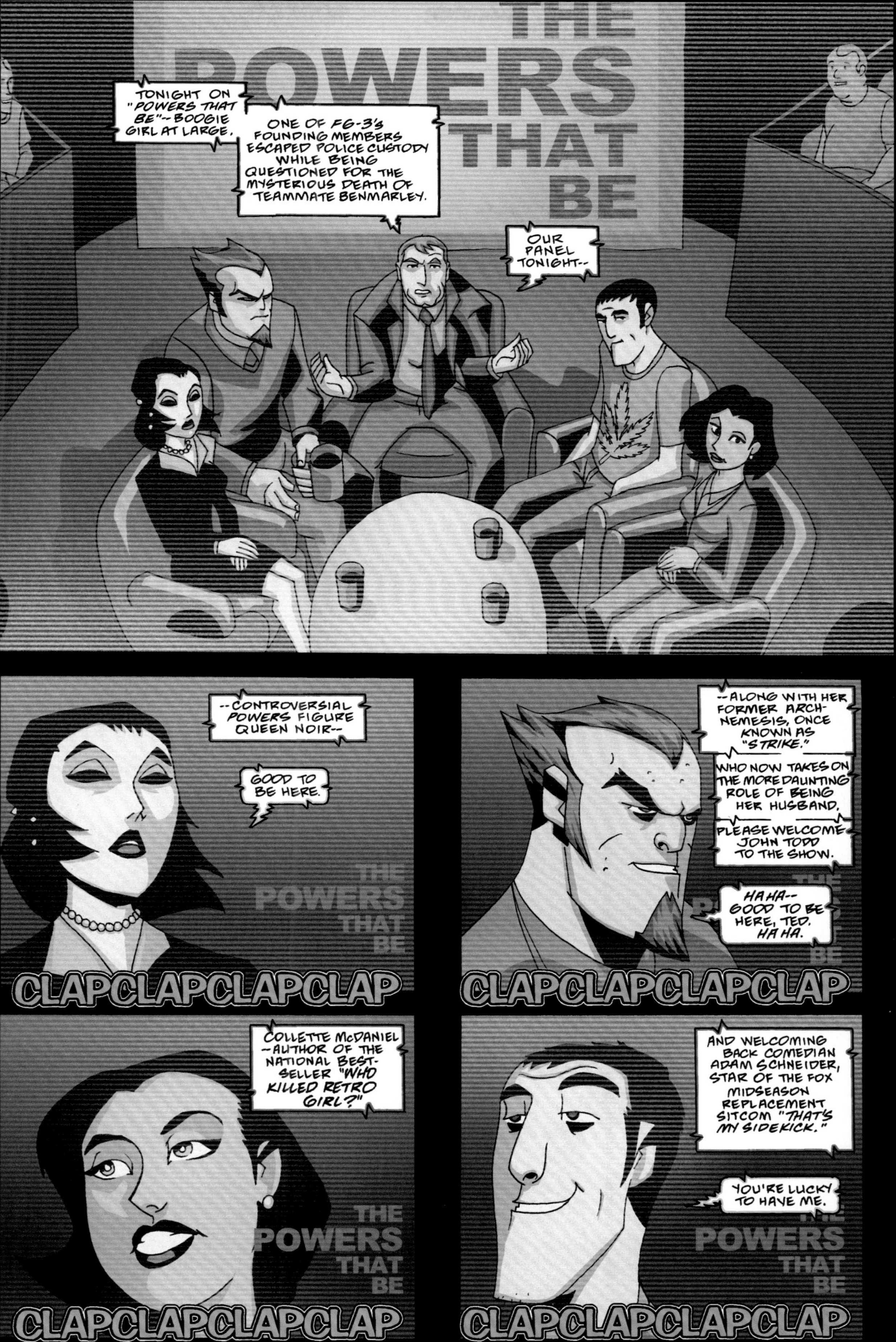
THE POWERS THAT BE
TONIGHT ON "POWERS THAT BE"-- BOOGIE GIRL AT LARGE.
ONE OF FG-3'S FOUNDING MEMBERS ESCAPED POLICE CUSTODY WHILE BEING QUESTIONED FOR THE MYSTERIOUS DEATH OF TEAMMATE BENMARLEY.
OUR PANEL TONIGHT--
--CONTROVERSIAL POWERS FIGURE QUEEN NOIR--
GOOD TO BE HERE.
THE POWERS THAT BE
CLAPCLAPCLAPCLAP
--ALONG WITH HER FORMER ARCH-NEMESIS, ONCE KNOWN AS "STRIKE."
WHO NOW TAKES ON THE MORE DAUNTING ROLE OF BEING HER HUSBAND.
PLEASE WELCOME JOHN TODD TO THE SHOW.
HA HA-- GOOD TO BE HERE, TED. HA HA.
CLAPCLAPCLAPCLAP
COLLETTE McDANIEL --AUTHOR OF THE NATIONAL BEST-SELLER "WHO KILLED RETRO GIRL?"
THE POWERS THAT BE
CLAPCLAPCLAPCLAP
AND WELCOMING BACK COMEDIAN ADAM SCHNEIDER, STAR OF THE FOX MIDSEASON REPLACEMENT SITCOM "THAT'S MY SIDEKICK."
YOU'RE LUCKY TO HAVE ME.
POWERS THAT BE
CLAPCLAPCLAPCLAP

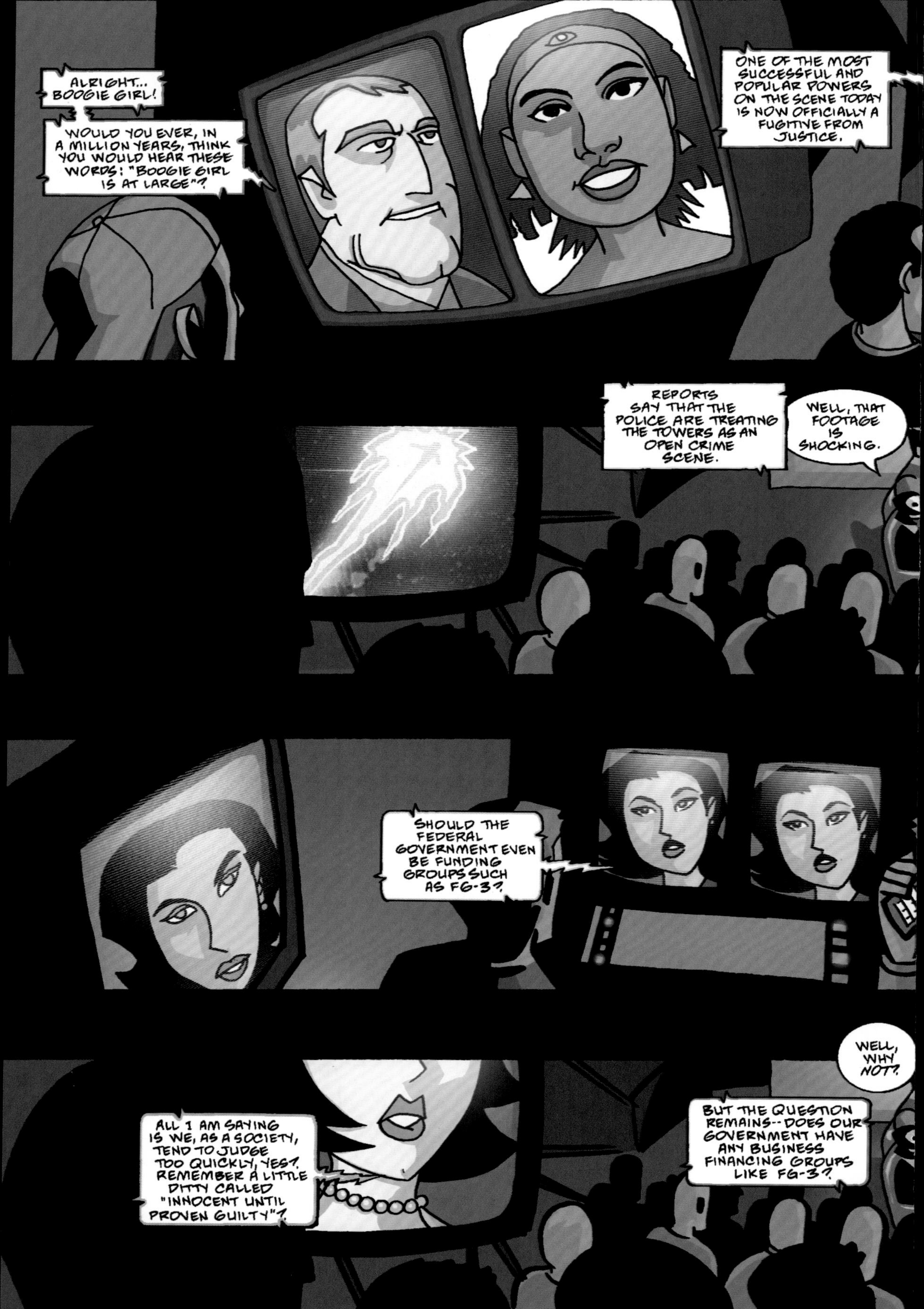
ALRIGHT... BOOGIE GIRL!
WOULD YOU EVER, IN A MILLION YEARS, THINK YOU WOULD HEAR THESE WORDS: "BOOGIE GIRL IS AT LARGE"?
ONE OF THE MOST SUCCESSFUL AND POPULAR POWERS ON THE SCENE TODAY IS NOW OFFICIALLY A FUGITIVE FROM JUSTICE.
REPORTS SAY THAT THE POLICE ARE TREATING THE TOWERS AS AN OPEN CRIME SCENE.
WELL, THAT FOOTAGE IS SHOCKING.
SHOULD THE FEDERAL GOVERNMENT EVEN BE FUNDING GROUPS SUCH AS FG-3?
WELL, WHY NOT?
ALL I AM SAYING IS WE, AS A SOCIETY, TEND TO JUDGE TOO QUICKLY, YES? REMEMBER A LITTLE DITTY CALLED "INNOCENT UNTIL PROVEN GUILTY"?
BUT THE QUESTION REMAINS--DOES OUR GOVERNMENT HAVE ANY BUSINESS FINANCING GROUPS LIKE FG-3?

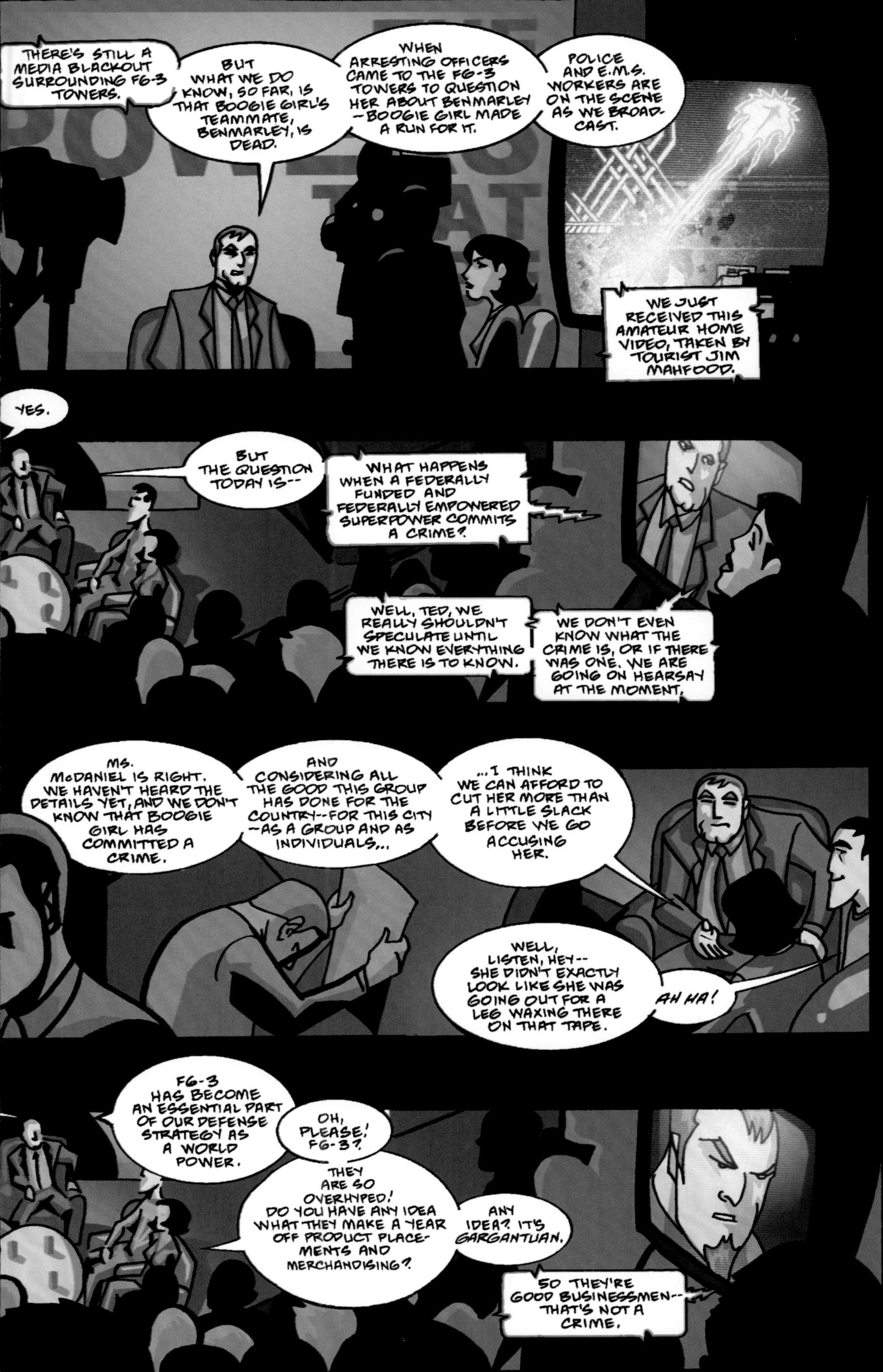
THERE'S STILL A MEDIA BLACKOUT SURROUNDING FG-3 TOWERS.
BUT WHAT WE DO KNOW, SO FAR, IS THAT BOOGIE GIRL'S TEAMMATE, BENMARLEY, IS DEAD.
WHEN ARRESTING OFFICERS CAME TO THE FG-3 TOWERS TO QUESTION HER ABOUT BENMARLEY --BOOGIE GIRL MADE A RUN FOR IT.
POLICE AND E.M.S. WORKERS ARE ON THE SCENE AS WE BROADCAST.
WE JUST RECEIVED THIS AMATEUR HOME VIDEO, TAKEN BY TOURIST JIM MAHFOOD.
YES.
BUT THE QUESTION TODAY IS--
WHAT HAPPENS WHEN A FEDERALLY FUNDED AND FEDERALLY EMPOWERED SUPERPOWER COMMITS A CRIME?
WELL, TED, WE REALLY SHOULDN'T SPECULATE UNTIL WE KNOW EVERYTHING THERE IS TO KNOW.
WE DON'T EVEN KNOW WHAT THE CRIME IS, OR IF THERE WAS ONE. WE ARE GOING ON HEARSAY AT THE MOMENT.
MS. McDANIEL IS RIGHT. WE HAVEN'T HEARD THE DETAILS YET, AND WE DON'T KNOW THAT BOOGIE GIRL HAS COMMITTED A CRIME.
AND CONSIDERING ALL THE GOOD THIS GROUP HAS DONE FOR THE COUNTRY--FOR THIS CITY --AS A GROUP AND AS INDIVIDUALS...
...I THINK WE CAN AFFORD TO CUT HER MORE THAN A LITTLE SLACK BEFORE WE GO ACCUSING HER.
WELL, LISTEN, HEY-- SHE DIDN'T EXACTLY LOOK LIKE SHE WAS GOING OUT FOR A LEG WAXING THERE ON THAT TAPE.
AH HA!
FG-3 HAS BECOME AN ESSENTIAL PART OF OUR DEFENSE STRATEGY AS A WORLD POWER.
OH, PLEASE! FG-3?
THEY ARE SO OVERHYPED! DO YOU HAVE ANY IDEA WHAT THEY MAKE A YEAR OFF PRODUCT PLACEMENTS AND MERCHANDISING?
ANY IDEA? IT'S GARGANTUAN.
SO THEY'RE GOOD BUSINESSMEN-- THAT'S NOT A CRIME.

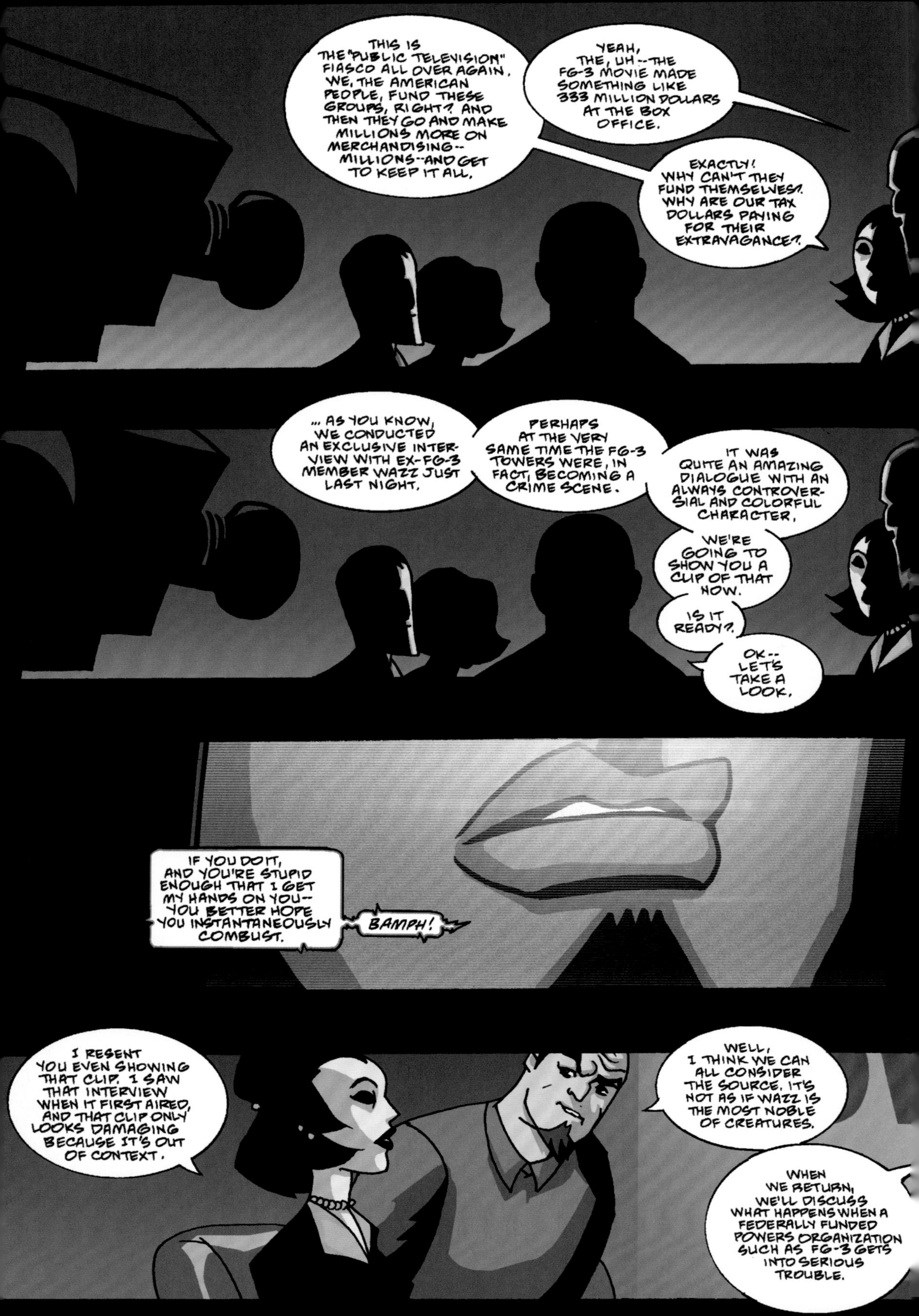
THIS IS THE "PUBLIC TELEVISION" FIASCO ALL OVER AGAIN. WE, THE AMERICAN PEOPLE, FUND THESE GROUPS, RIGHT? AND THEN THEY GO AND MAKE MILLIONS MORE ON MERCHANDISING-- MILLIONS--AND GET TO KEEP IT ALL.
YEAH, THE, UH--THE FG-3 MOVIE MADE SOMETHING LIKE 333 MILLION DOLLARS AT THE BOX OFFICE.
EXACTLY! WHY CAN'T THEY FUND THEMSELVES?! WHY ARE OUR TAX DOLLARS PAYING FOR THEIR EXTRAVAGANCE?!
...AS YOU KNOW, WE CONDUCTED AN EXCLUSIVE INTERVIEW WITH EX-FG-3 MEMBER WAZZ JUST LAST NIGHT.
PERHAPS AT THE VERY SAME TIME THE FG-3 TOWERS WERE, IN FACT, BECOMING A CRIME SCENE.
IT WAS QUITE AN AMAZING DIALOGUE WITH AN ALWAYS CONTROVERSIAL AND COLORFUL CHARACTER.
WE'RE GOING TO SHOW YOU A CLIP OF THAT NOW.
IS IT READY?!
OK-- LET'S TAKE A LOOK.
IF YOU DO IT, AND YOU'RE STUPID ENOUGH THAT I GET MY HANDS ON YOU-- YOU BETTER HOPE YOU INSTANTANEOUSLY COMBUST.
BAMPH!
I RESENT YOU EVEN SHOWING THAT CLIP. I SAW THAT INTERVIEW WHEN IT FIRST AIRED, AND THAT CLIP ONLY LOOKS DAMAGING BECAUSE IT'S OUT OF CONTEXT.
WELL, I THINK WE CAN ALL CONSIDER THE SOURCE. IT'S NOT AS IF WAZZ IS THE MOST NOBLE OF CREATURES.
WHEN WE RETURN, WE'LL DISCUSS WHAT HAPPENS WHEN A FEDERALLY FUNDED POWERS ORGANIZATION SUCH AS FG-3 GETS INTO SERIOUS TROUBLE.

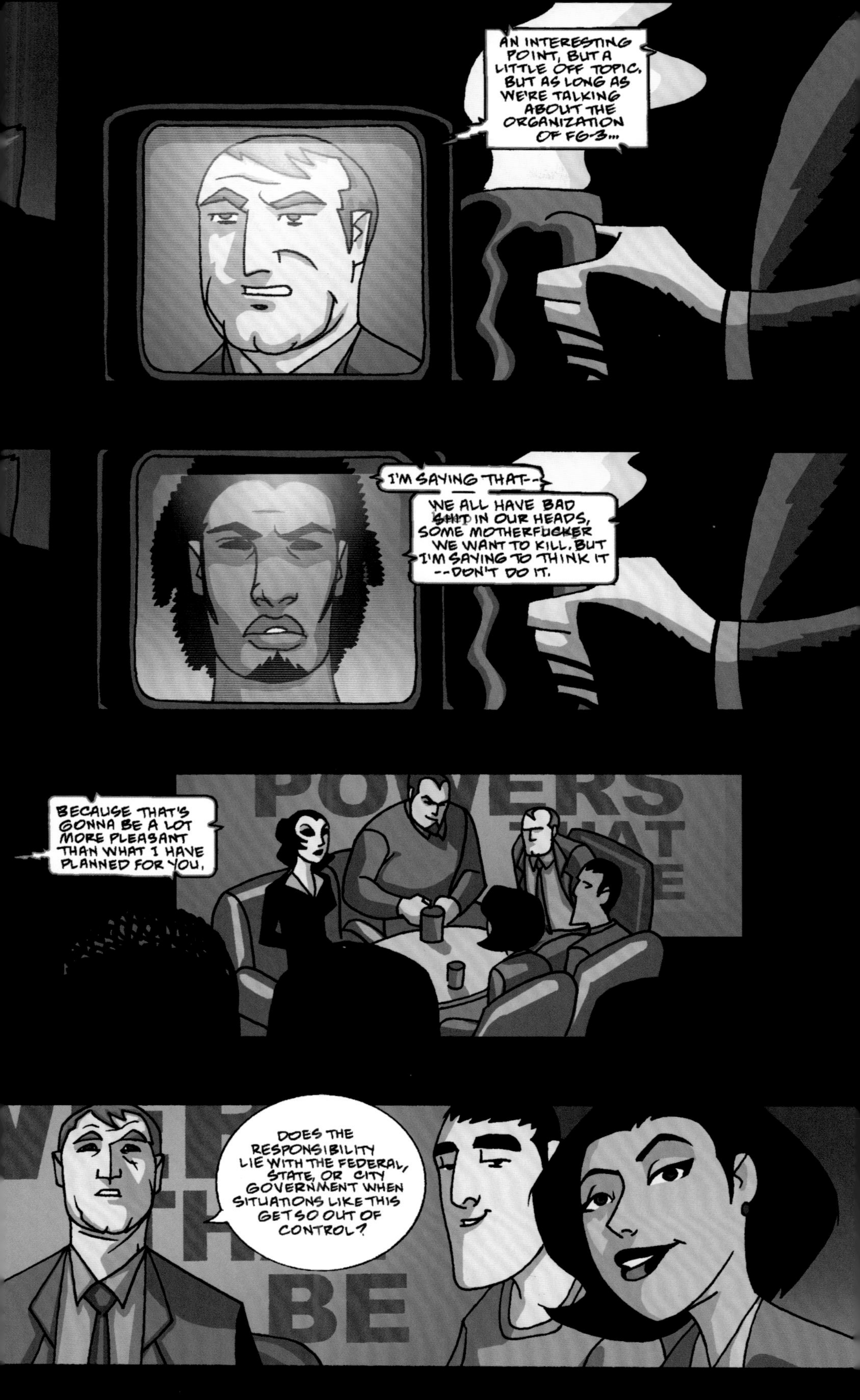
AN INTERESTING POINT, BUT A LITTLE OFF TOPIC, BUT AS LONG AS WE'RE TALKING ABOUT THE ORGANIZATION OF FG-3...
I'M SAYING THAT--
WE ALL HAVE BAD ~~SHIT~~ IN OUR HEADS, SOME MOTHERFUCKER WE WANT TO KILL. BUT I'M SAYING TO THINK IT --DON'T DO IT.
POWERS
BECAUSE THAT'S GONNA BE A LOT MORE PLEASANT THAN WHAT I HAVE PLANNED FOR YOU.
DOES THE RESPONSIBILITY LIE WITH THE FEDERAL, STATE, OR CITY GOVERNMENT WHEN SITUATIONS LIKE THIS GET SO OUT OF CONTROL?
BE

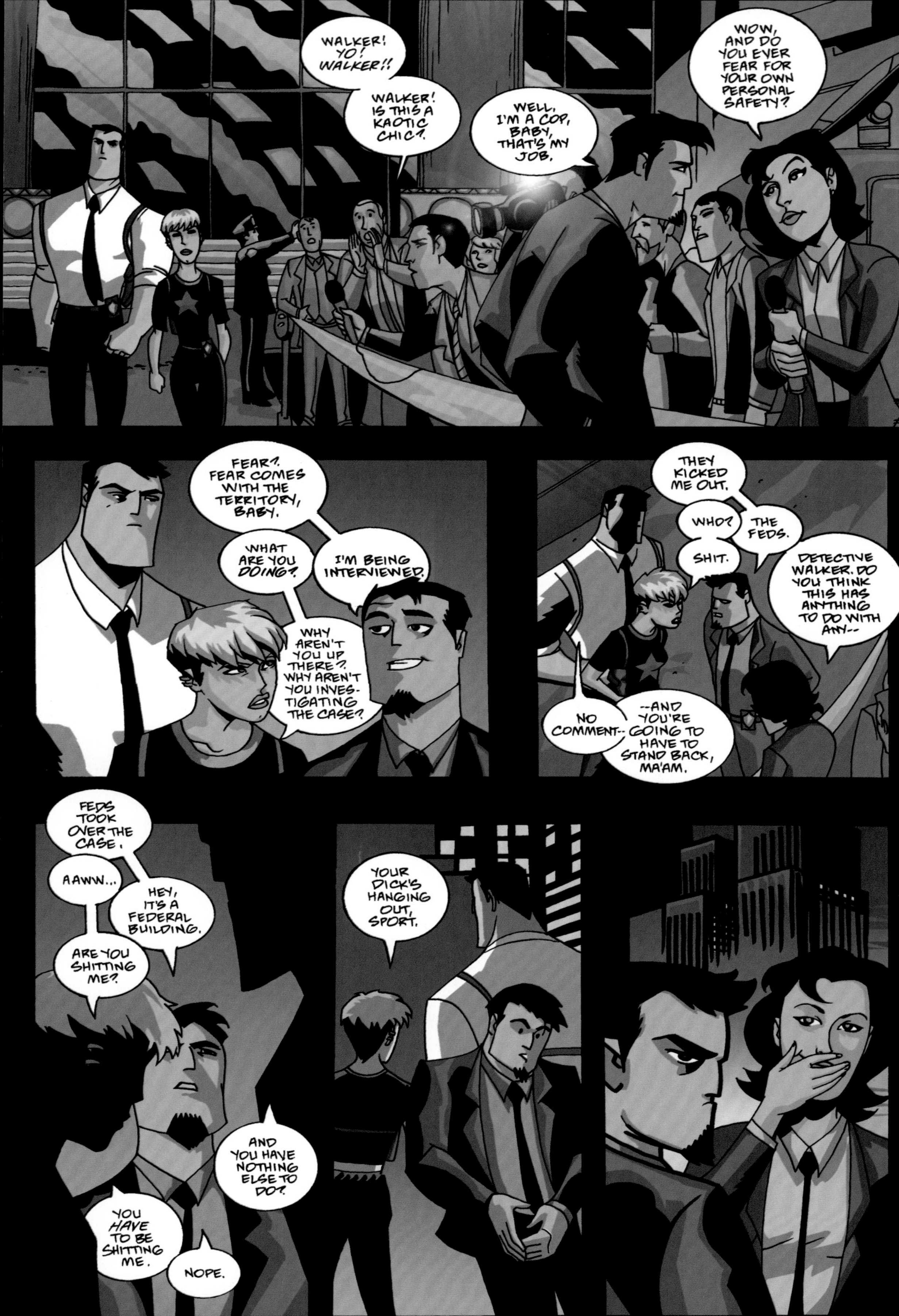
WALKER! YO! WALKER!!
WALKER! IS THIS A KAOTIC CHIC?.
WELL, I'M A COP, BABY, THAT'S MY JOB.
WOW, AND DO YOU EVER FEAR FOR YOUR OWN PERSONAL SAFETY?
FEAR?. FEAR COMES WITH THE TERRITORY, BABY.
WHAT ARE YOU DOING?.
I'M BEING INTERVIEWED.
WHY AREN'T YOU UP THERE?. WHY AREN'T YOU INVESTIGATING THE CASE?
THEY KICKED ME OUT.
WHO?
THE FEDS.
SHIT.
DETECTIVE WALKER, DO YOU THINK THIS HAS ANYTHING TO DO WITH ANY--
NO COMMENT--
--AND YOU'RE GOING TO HAVE TO STAND BACK, MA'AM.
FEDS TOOK OVER THE CASE.
AAWW...
HEY, IT'S A FEDERAL BUILDING.
ARE YOU SHITTING ME?
AND YOU HAVE NOTHING ELSE TO DO?
YOU HAVE TO BE SHITTING ME.
NOPE.
YOUR DICK'S HANGING OUT, SPORT.

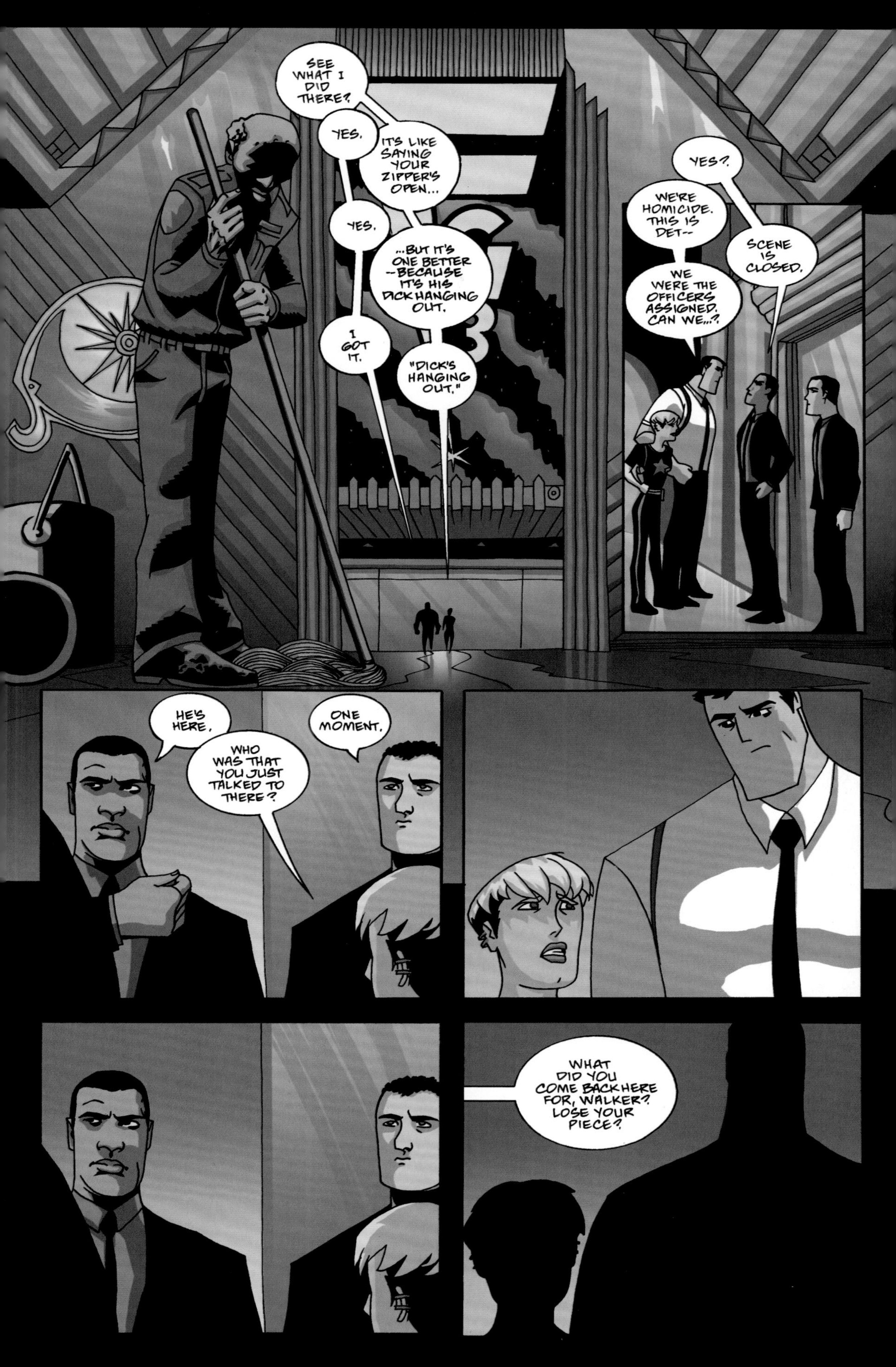
SEE WHAT I DID THERE?
YES.
IT'S LIKE SAYING YOUR ZIPPER'S OPEN...
YES.
...BUT IT'S ONE BETTER --BECAUSE IT'S HIS DICK HANGING OUT.
I GOT IT.
"DICK'S HANGING OUT."
YES?.
WE'RE HOMICIDE. THIS IS DET--
SCENE IS CLOSED.
WE WERE THE OFFICERS ASSIGNED. CAN WE...?
HE'S HERE.
ONE MOMENT.
WHO WAS THAT YOU JUST TALKED TO THERE?
WHAT DID YOU COME BACK HERE FOR, WALKER? LOSE YOUR PIECE?

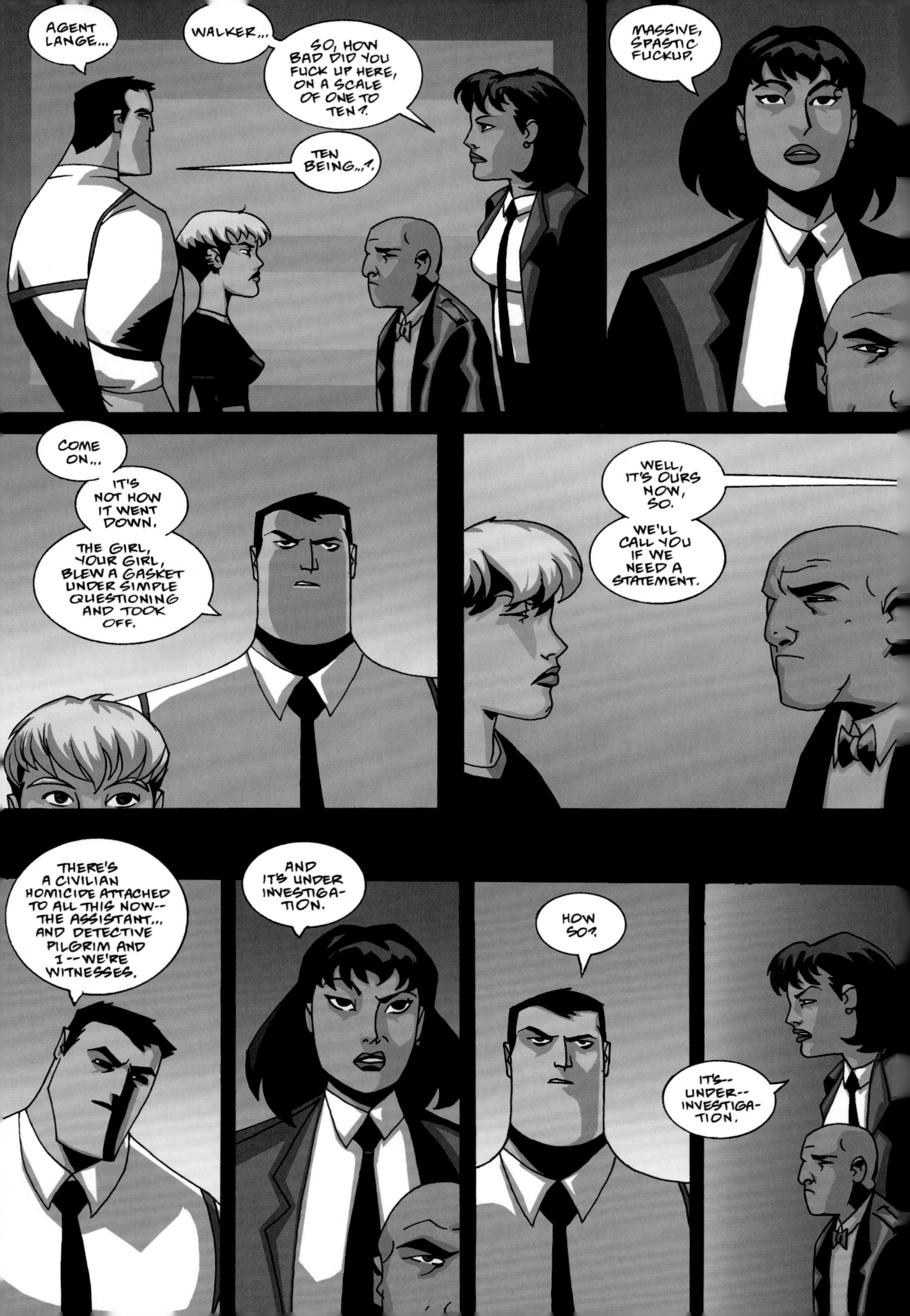
AGENT LANGE...
WALKER...
SO, HOW BAD DID YOU FUCK UP HERE, ON A SCALE OF ONE TO TEN?.
TEN BEING...?.
MASSIVE, SPASTIC FUCKUP.
COME ON...
IT'S NOT HOW IT WENT DOWN.
THE GIRL, YOUR GIRL, BLEW A GASKET UNDER SIMPLE QUESTIONING AND TOOK OFF.
WELL, IT'S OURS NOW, SO.
WE'LL CALL YOU IF WE NEED A STATEMENT.
THERE'S A CIVILIAN HOMICIDE ATTACHED TO ALL THIS NOW-- THE ASSISTANT... AND DETECTIVE PILGRIM AND I--WE'RE WITNESSES.
AND IT'S UNDER INVESTIGATION.
HOW SO?
IT'S-- UNDER-- INVESTIGATION.

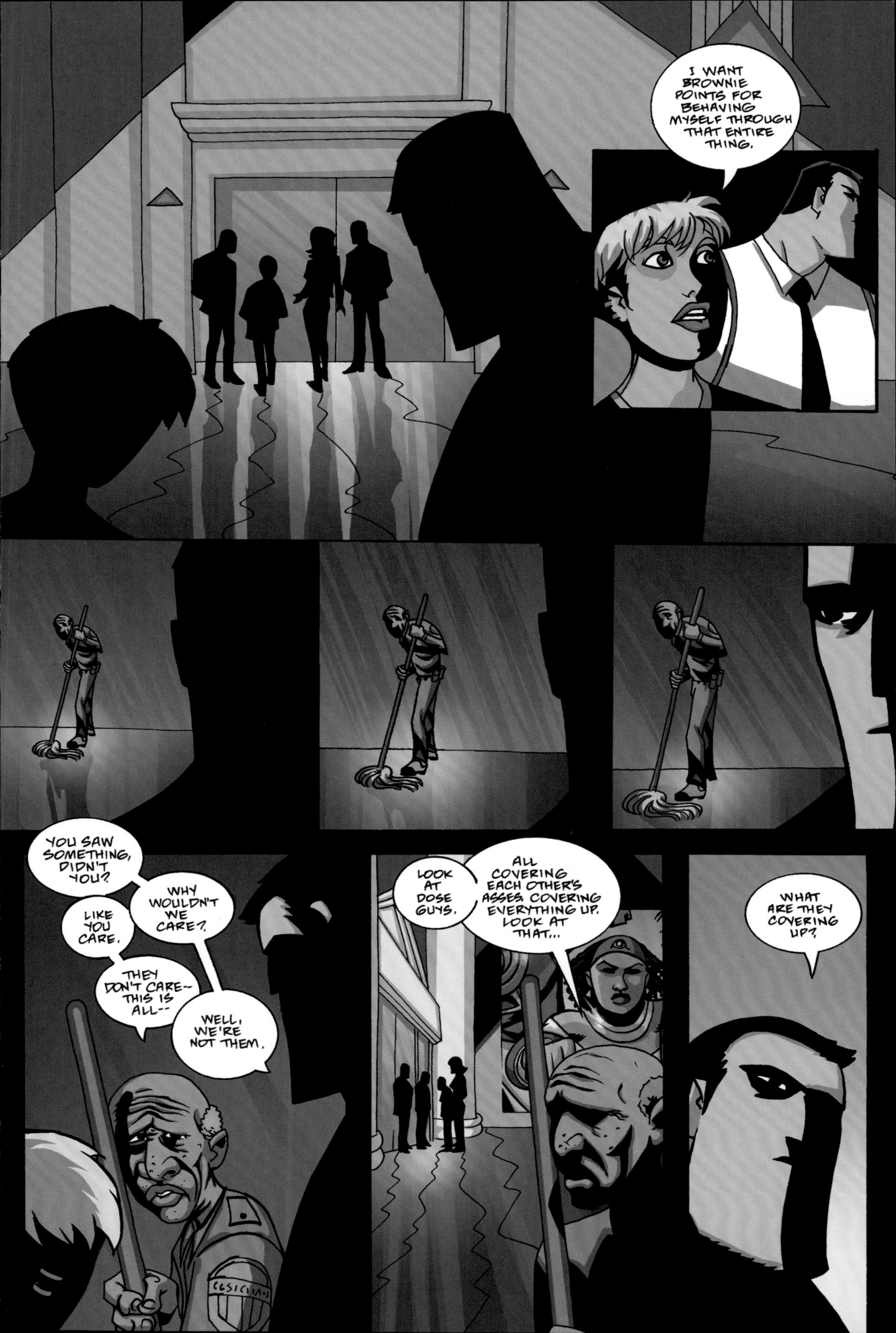
I WANT BROWNIE POINTS FOR BEHAVING MYSELF THROUGH THAT ENTIRE THING.
YOU SAW SOMETHING, DIDN'T YOU?
LIKE YOU CARE.
WHY WOULDN'T WE CARE?
THEY DON'T CARE-- THIS IS ALL--
WELL, WE'RE NOT THEM.
LOOK AT DOSE GUYS.
ALL COVERING EACH OTHER'S ASSES. COVERING EVERYTHING UP. LOOK AT THAT...
WHAT ARE THEY COVERING UP?

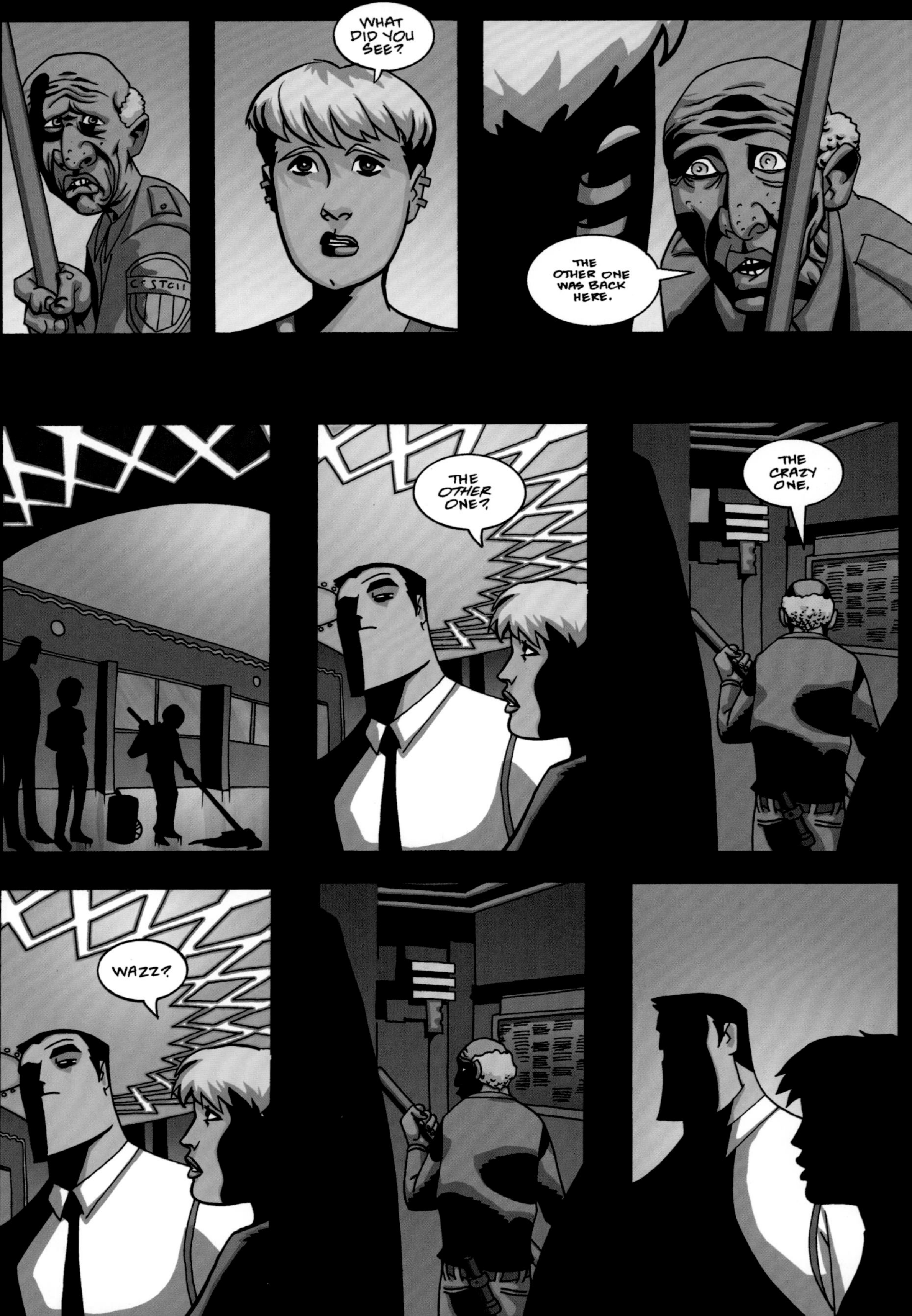
WHAT DID YOU SEE?
THE OTHER ONE WAS BACK HERE.
THE OTHER ONE?
THE CRAZY ONE.
WAZZ?

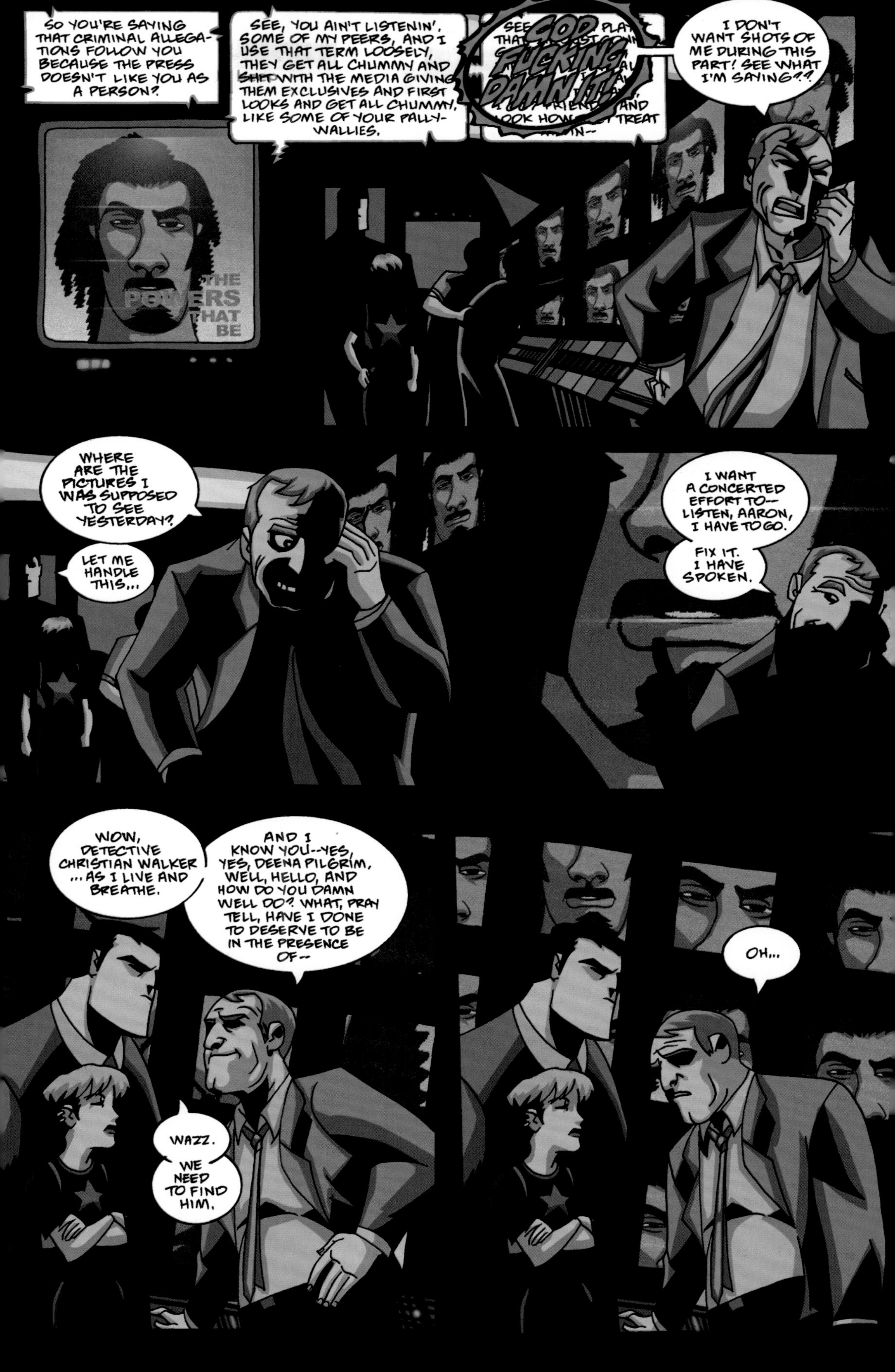
SO YOU'RE SAYING THAT CRIMINAL ALLEGATIONS FOLLOW YOU BECAUSE THE PRESS DOESN'T LIKE YOU AS A PERSON?
SEE, YOU AIN'T LISTENIN', SOME OF MY PEERS, AND I USE THAT TERM LOOSELY, THEY GET ALL CHUMMY AND SHIT WITH THE MEDIA GIVING THEM EXCLUSIVES AND FIRST LOOKS AND GET ALL CHUMMY, LIKE SOME OF YOUR PALLY-WALLIES.
GOD FUCKING DAMN IT!
I DON'T WANT SHOTS OF ME DURING THIS PART! SEE WHAT I'M SAYING?!?
THE POWERS THAT BE
WHERE ARE THE PICTURES I WAS SUPPOSED TO SEE YESTERDAY?
LET ME HANDLE THIS...
I WANT A CONCERTED EFFORT TO-- LISTEN, AARON, I HAVE TO GO.
FIX IT. I HAVE SPOKEN.
WOW, DETECTIVE CHRISTIAN WALKER ...AS I LIVE AND BREATHE.
AND I KNOW YOU--YES, YES, DEENA PILGRIM, WELL, HELLO, AND HOW DO YOU DAMN WELL DO? WHAT, PRAY TELL, HAVE I DONE TO DESERVE TO BE IN THE PRESENCE OF--
WAZZ.
WE NEED TO FIND HIM.
OH...

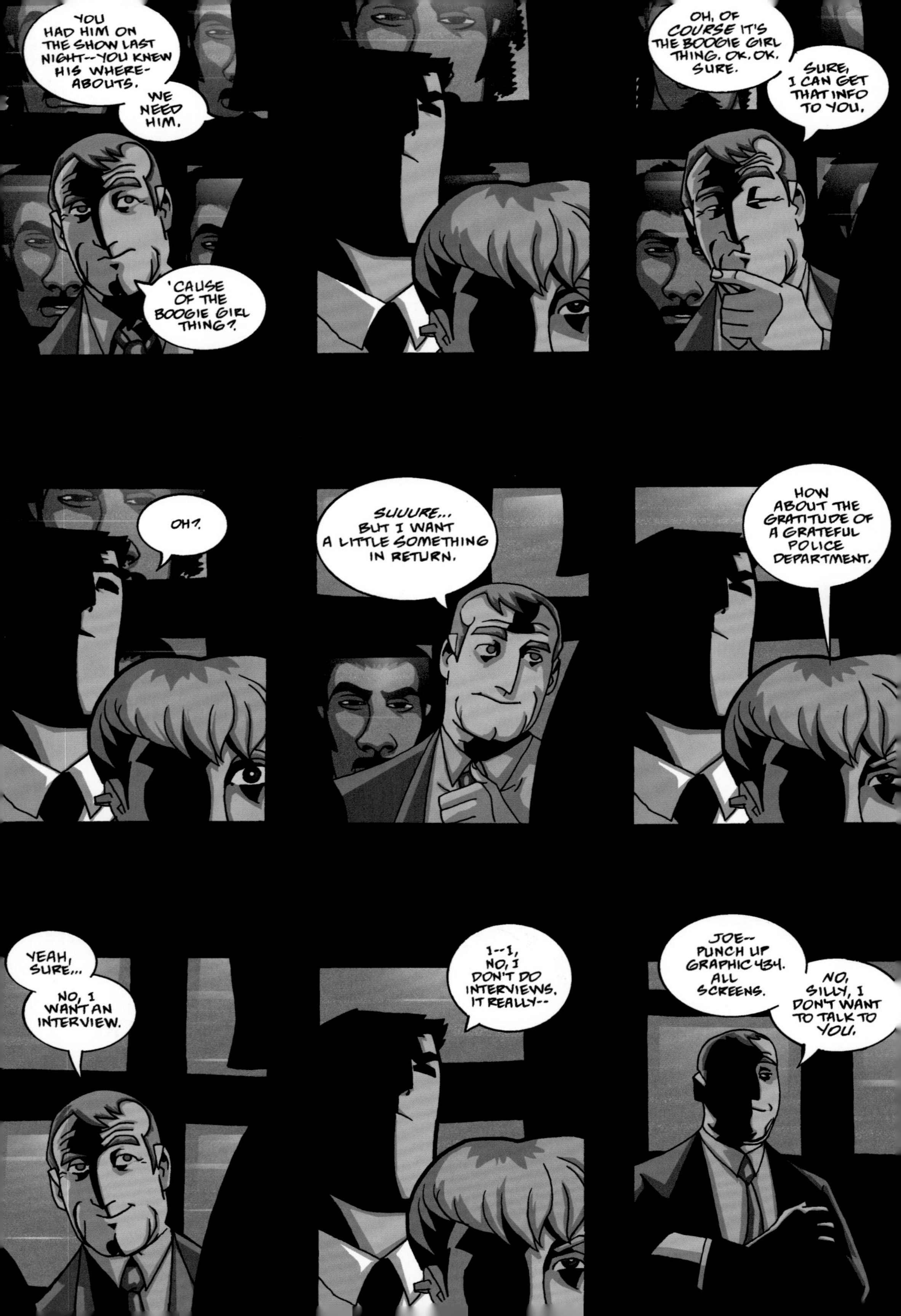
YOU HAD HIM ON THE SHOW LAST NIGHT--YOU KNEW HIS WHERE-ABOUTS.
WE NEED HIM.
'CAUSE OF THE BOOGIE GIRL THING?
OH, OF COURSE IT'S THE BOOGIE GIRL THING. OK. OK. SURE.
SURE, I CAN GET THAT INFO TO YOU.
OH?
SUUURE... BUT I WANT A LITTLE SOMETHING IN RETURN.
HOW ABOUT THE GRATITUDE OF A GRATEFUL POLICE DEPARTMENT.
YEAH, SURE...
NO, I WANT AN INTERVIEW.
I--I, NO, I DON'T DO INTERVIEWS. IT REALLY--
JOE-- PUNCH UP GRAPHIC 434. ALL SCREENS.
NO, SILLY, I DON'T WANT TO TALK TO YOU.

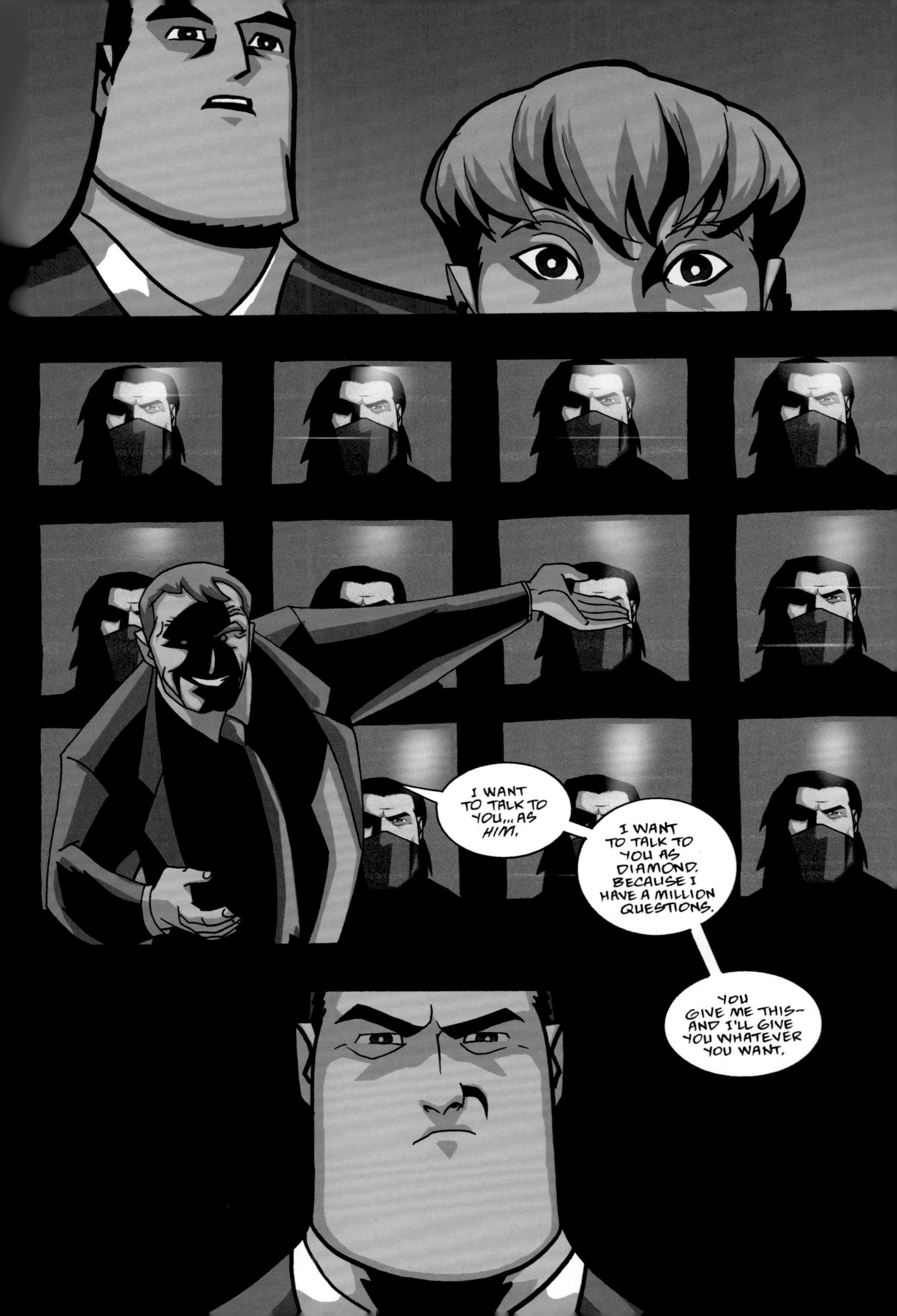
I WANT TO TALK TO YOU... AS *HIM*.
I WANT TO TALK TO YOU AS DIAMOND. BECAUSE I HAVE A MILLION QUESTIONS.
YOU GIVE ME THIS-- AND I'LL GIVE YOU WHATEVER YOU WANT.

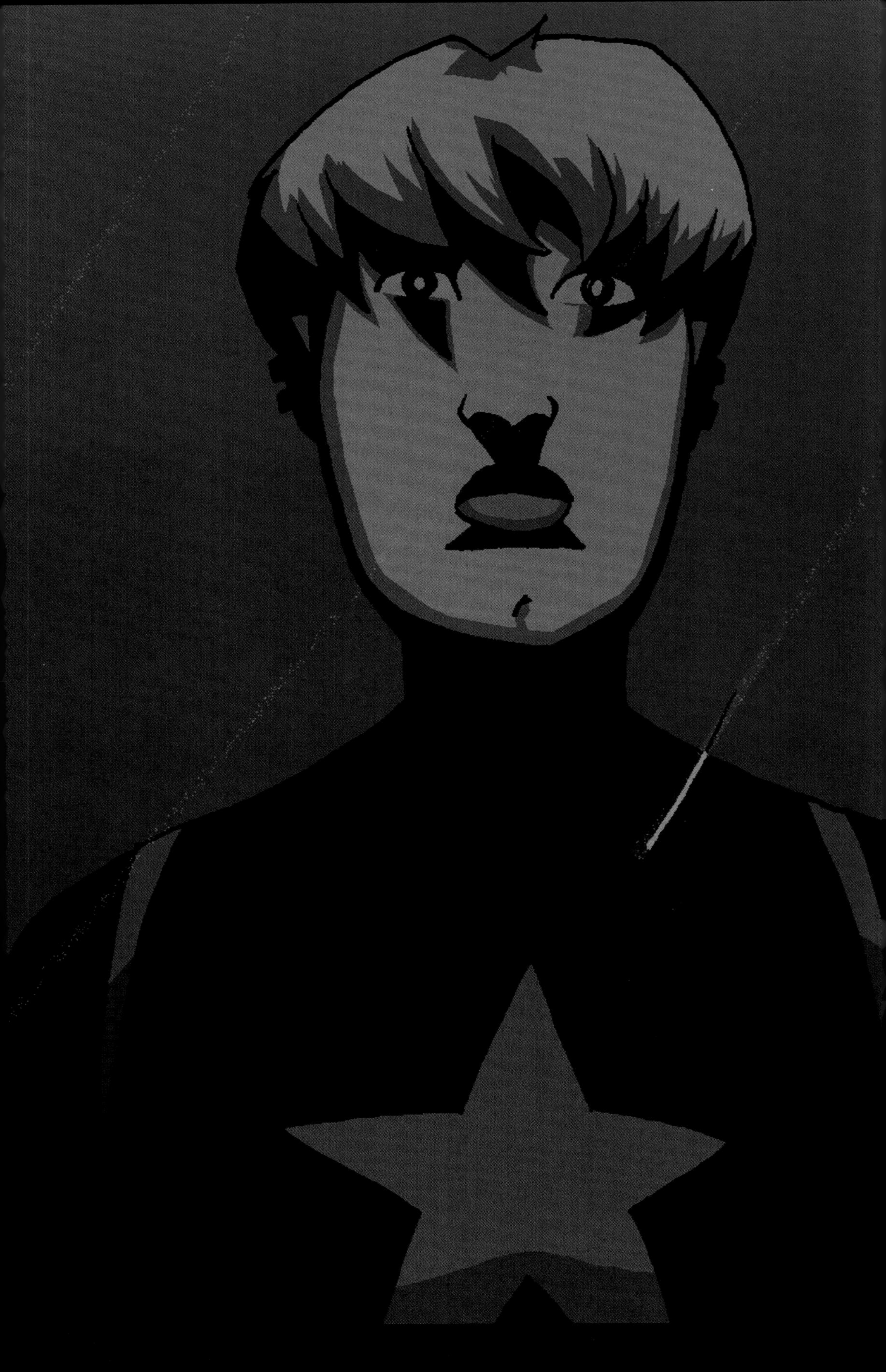

POWERS ™

SUPERGROUP
CHAPTER 3

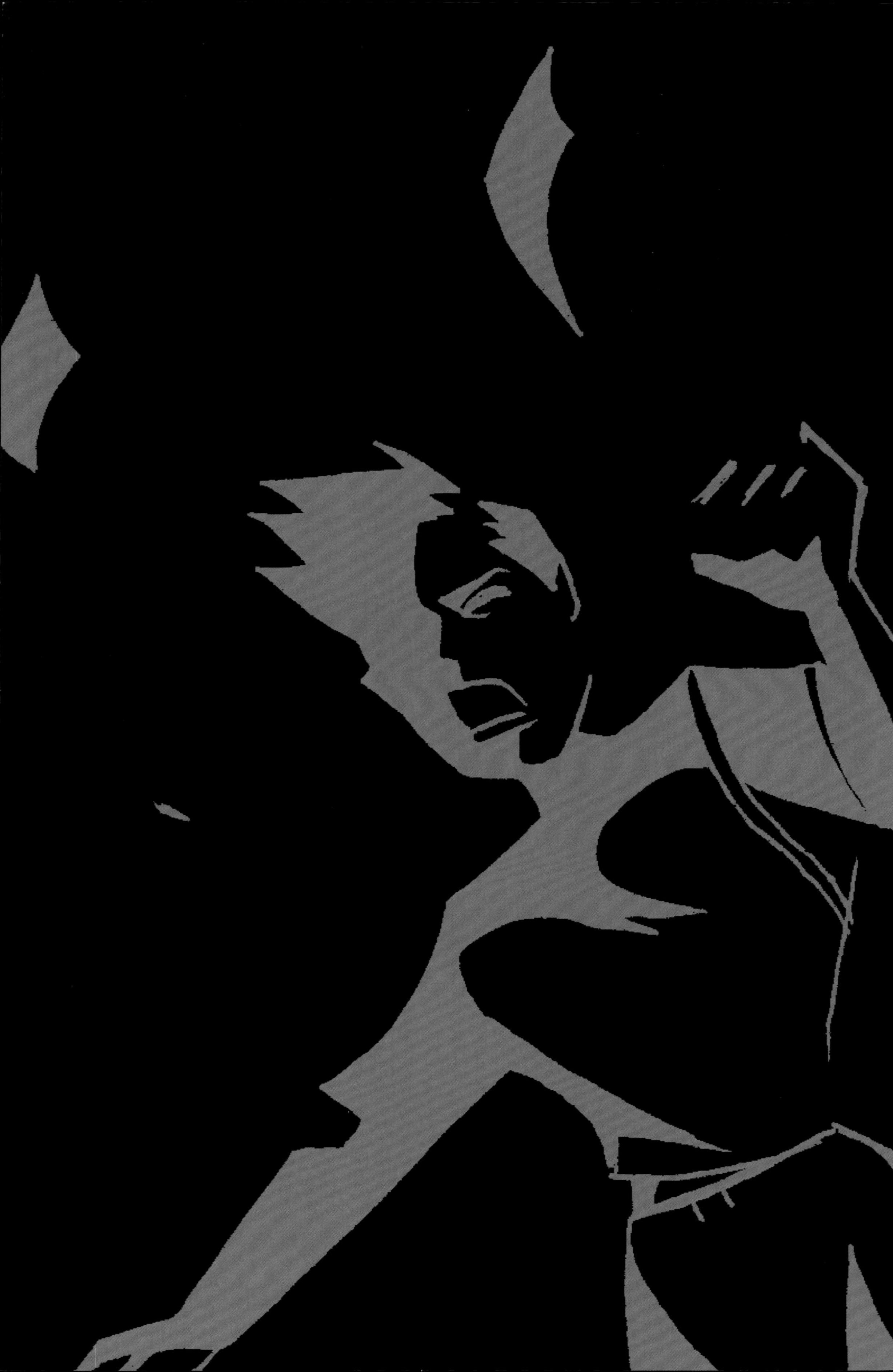

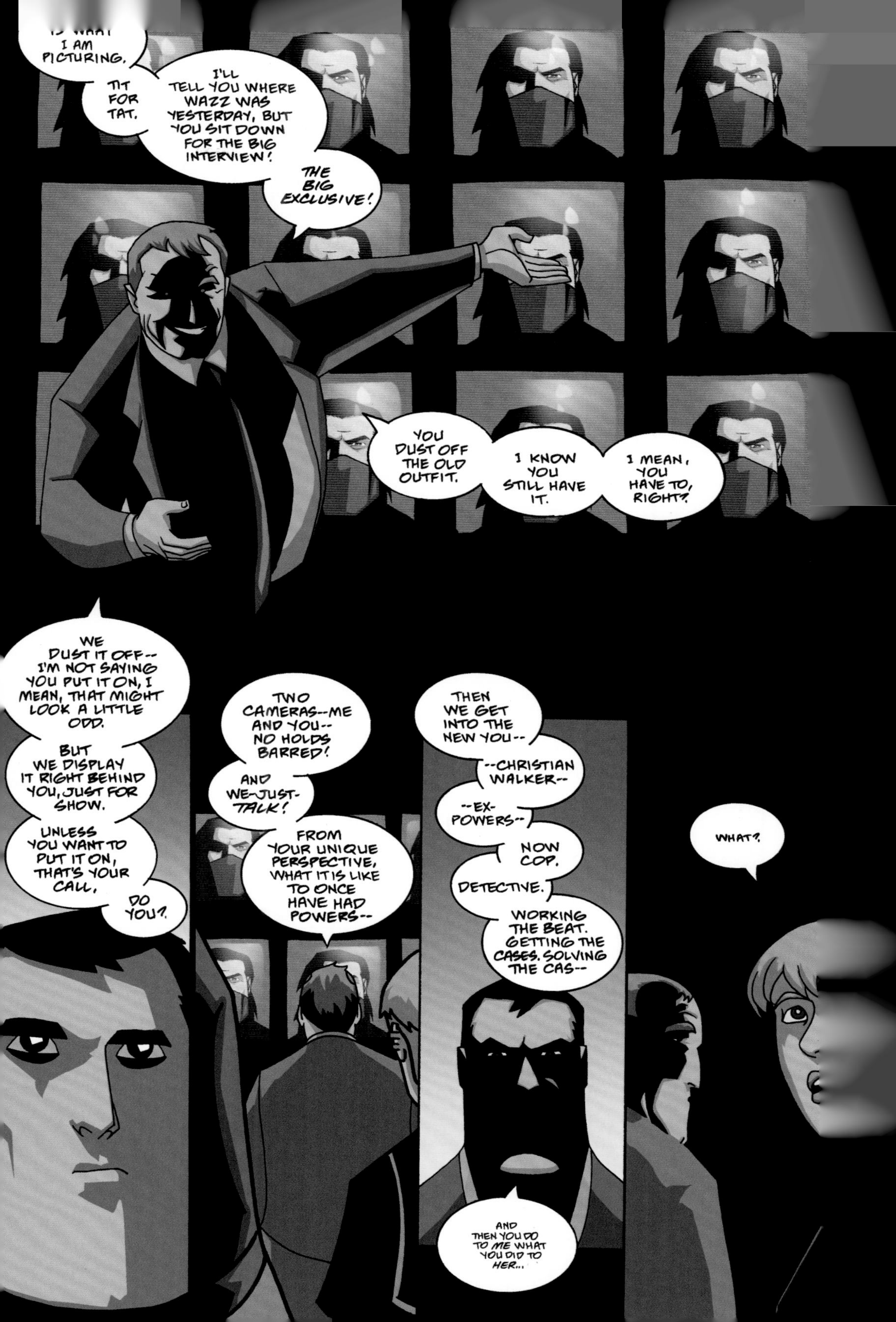
I AM PICTURING.
TIT FOR TAT.
I'LL TELL YOU WHERE WAZZ WAS YESTERDAY, BUT YOU SIT DOWN FOR THE BIG INTERVIEW!
THE BIG EXCLUSIVE!
YOU DUST OFF THE OLD OUTFIT.
I KNOW YOU STILL HAVE IT.
I MEAN, YOU HAVE TO, RIGHT?
WE DUST IT OFF-- I'M NOT SAYING YOU PUT IT ON, I MEAN, THAT MIGHT LOOK A LITTLE ODD.
BUT WE DISPLAY IT RIGHT BEHIND YOU, JUST FOR SHOW.
UNLESS YOU WANT TO PUT IT ON, THAT'S YOUR CALL.
DO YOU?
TWO CAMERAS--ME AND YOU-- NO HOLDS BARRED!
AND WE-JUST-TALK!
FROM YOUR UNIQUE PERSPECTIVE, WHAT IT IS LIKE TO ONCE HAVE HAD POWERS--
THEN WE GET INTO THE NEW YOU--
--CHRISTIAN WALKER--
--EX-POWERS--
NOW COP.
DETECTIVE.
WORKING THE BEAT. GETTING THE CASES. SOLVING THE CAS--
AND THEN YOU DO TO ME WHAT YOU DID TO HER...
WHAT?

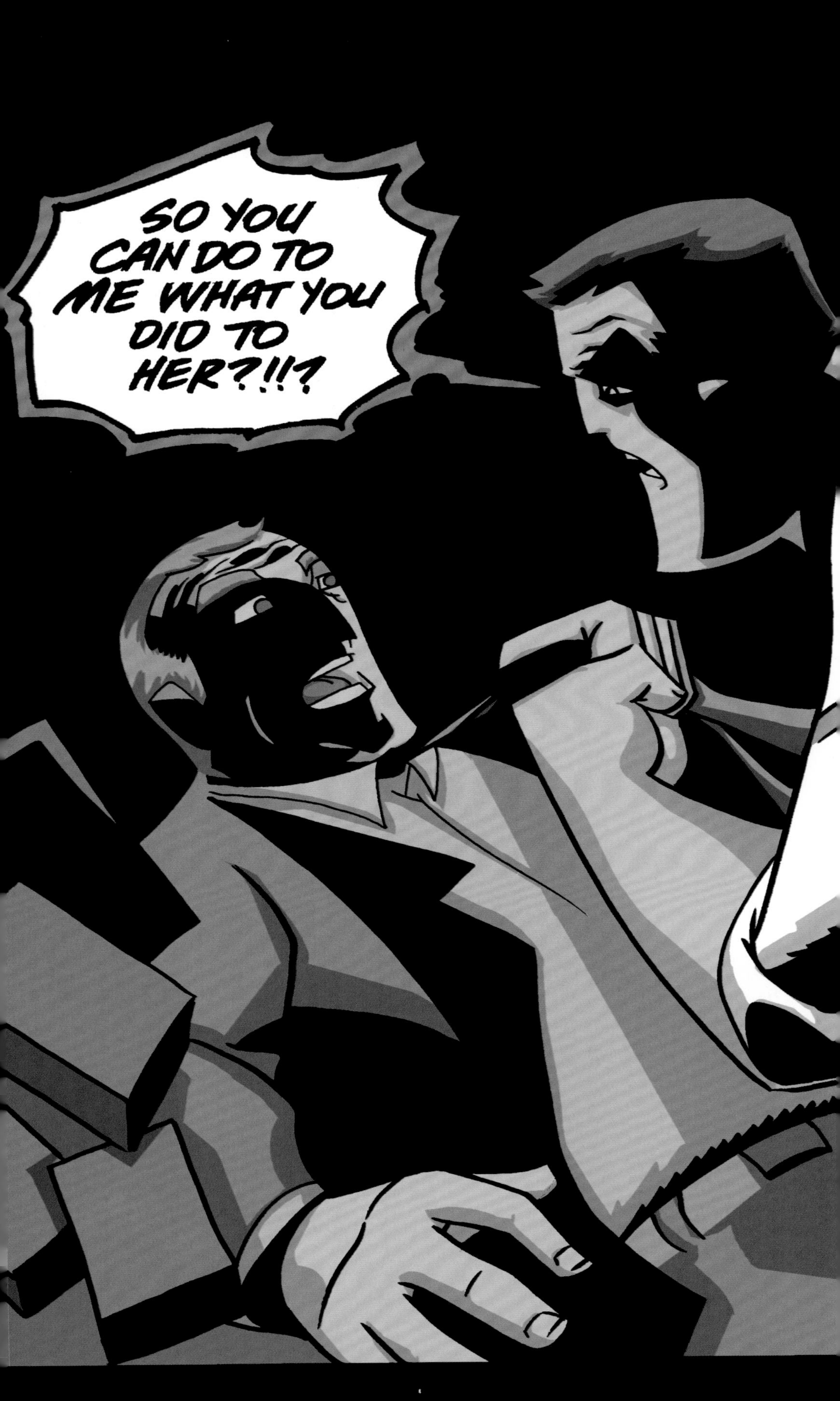
SO YOU CAN DO TO ME WHAT YOU DID TO HER?!!?

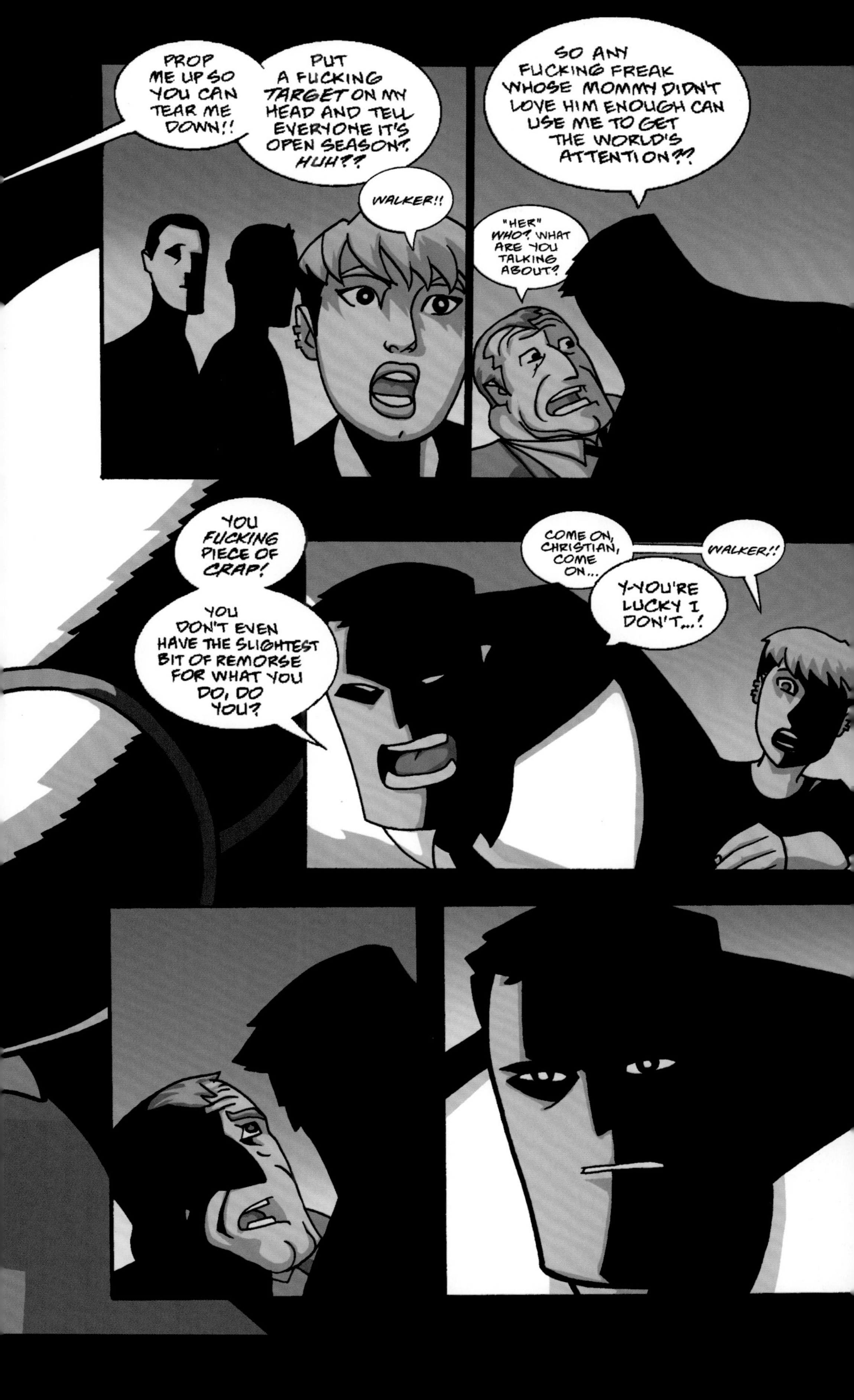
PROP ME UP SO YOU CAN TEAR ME DOWN!!
PUT A FUCKING TARGET ON MY HEAD AND TELL EVERYONE IT'S OPEN SEASON? HUH??
WALKER!!
SO ANY FUCKING FREAK WHOSE MOMMY DIDN'T LOVE HIM ENOUGH CAN USE ME TO GET THE WORLD'S ATTENTION??
"HER" WHO? WHAT ARE YOU TALKING ABOUT?
YOU FUCKING PIECE OF CRAP!
YOU DON'T EVEN HAVE THE SLIGHTEST BIT OF REMORSE FOR WHAT YOU DO, DO YOU?
COME ON, CHRISTIAN, COME ON...
WALKER!!
Y-YOU'RE LUCKY I DON'T...!

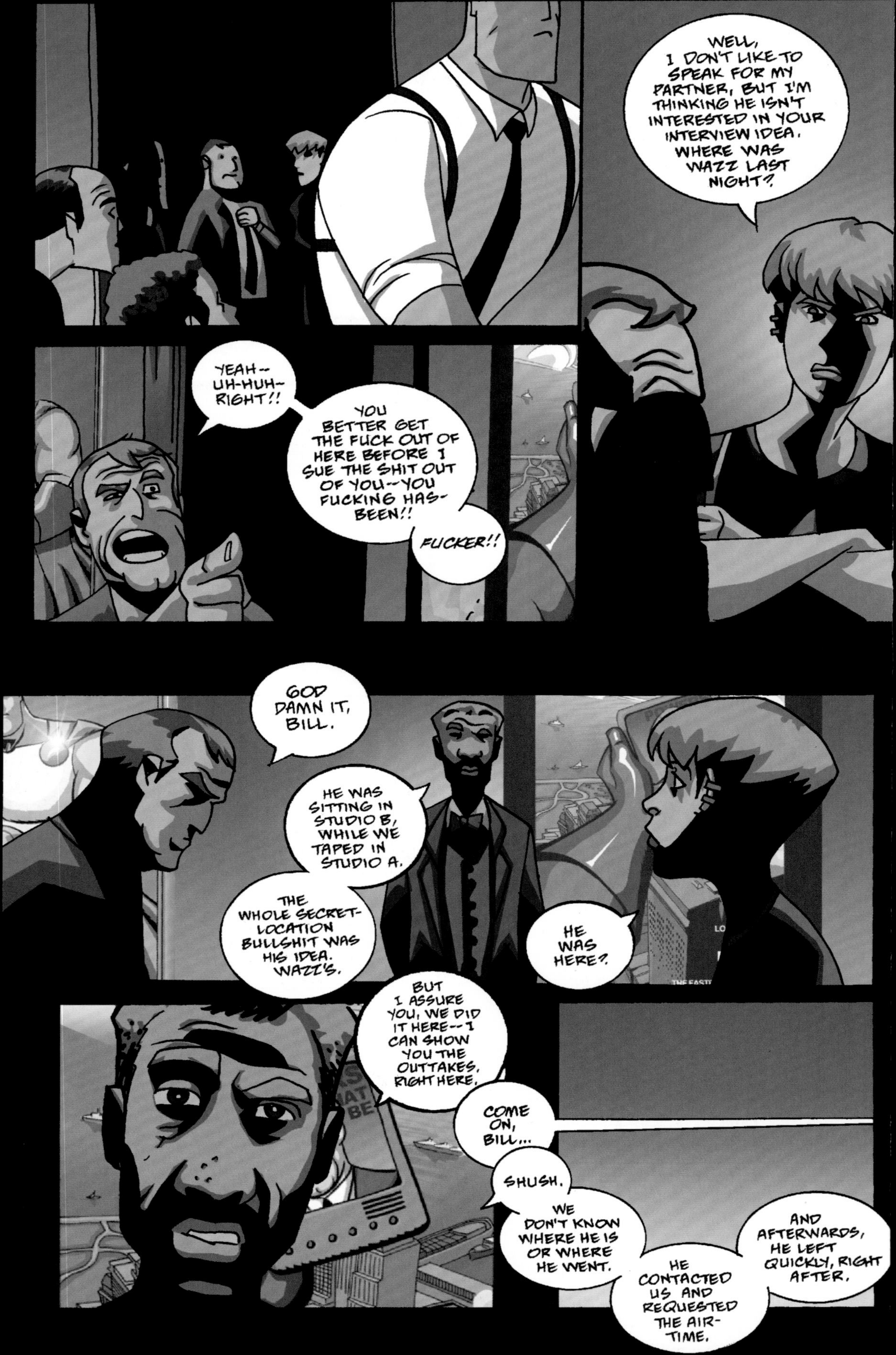
WELL, I DON'T LIKE TO SPEAK FOR MY PARTNER, BUT I'M THINKING HE ISN'T INTERESTED IN YOUR INTERVIEW IDEA. WHERE WAS WAZZ LAST NIGHT?
YEAH-- UH-HUH-- RIGHT!!
YOU BETTER GET THE FUCK OUT OF HERE BEFORE I SUE THE SHIT OUT OF YOU--YOU FUCKING HAS-BEEN!!
FUCKER!!
GOD DAMN IT, BILL.
HE WAS SITTING IN STUDIO B, WHILE WE TAPED IN STUDIO A.
THE WHOLE SECRET-LOCATION BULLSHIT WAS HIS IDEA. WAZZ'S.
HE WAS HERE?
BUT I ASSURE YOU, WE DID IT HERE--I CAN SHOW YOU THE OUTTAKES, RIGHT HERE.
COME ON, BILL...
SHUSH.
WE DON'T KNOW WHERE HE IS OR WHERE HE WENT.
HE CONTACTED US AND REQUESTED THE AIR-TIME.
AND AFTERWARDS, HE LEFT QUICKLY, RIGHT AFTER.

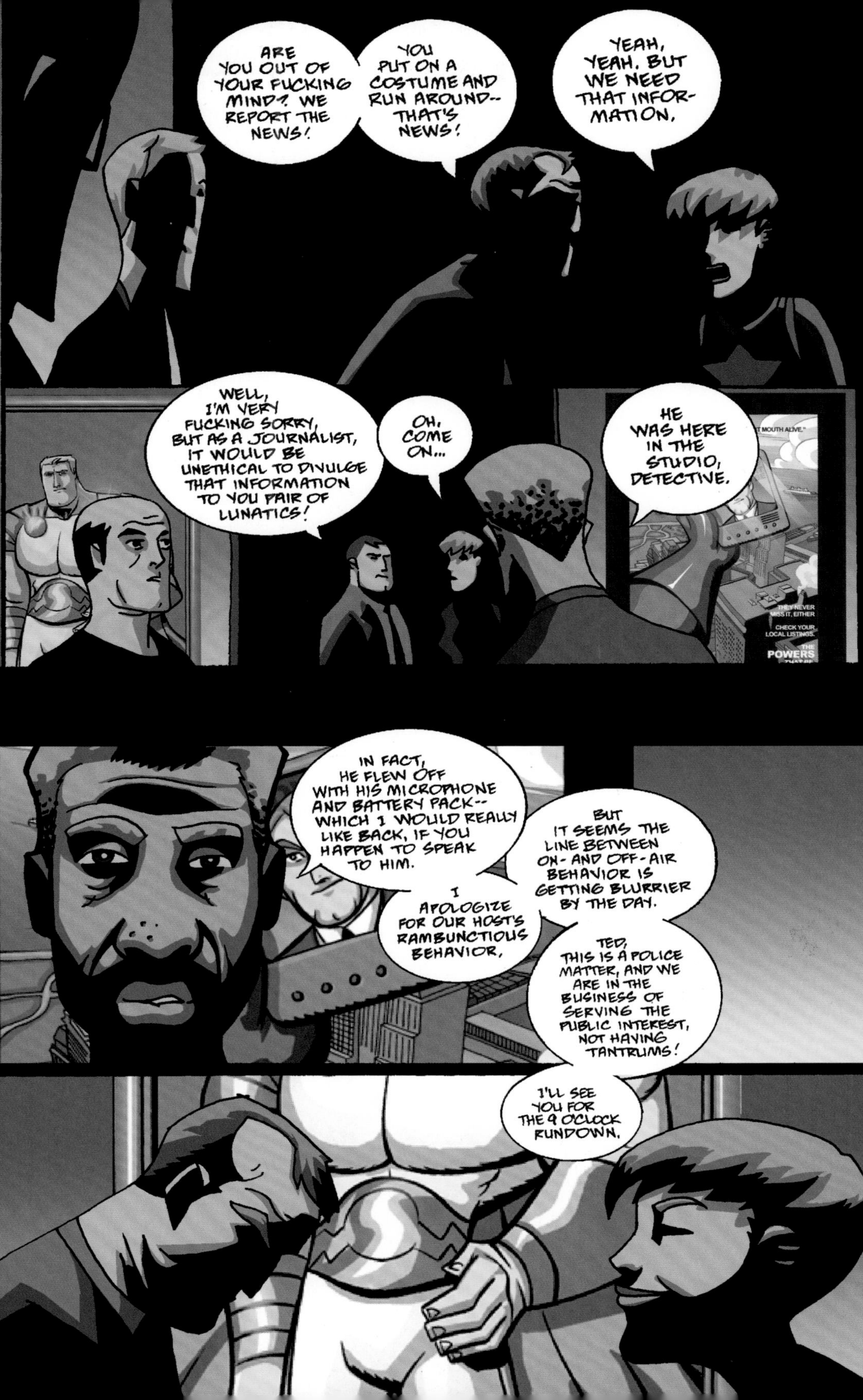
ARE YOU OUT OF YOUR FUCKING MIND? WE REPORT THE NEWS!
YOU PUT ON A COSTUME AND RUN AROUND-- THAT'S NEWS!
YEAH, YEAH. BUT WE NEED THAT INFORMATION.
WELL, I'M VERY FUCKING SORRY, BUT AS A JOURNALIST, IT WOULD BE UNETHICAL TO DIVULGE THAT INFORMATION TO YOU PAIR OF LUNATICS!
OH, COME ON...
HE WAS HERE IN THE STUDIO, DETECTIVE.
THEY NEVER MISS IT, EITHER
CHECK YOUR LOCAL LISTINGS.
POWERS
IN FACT, HE FLEW OFF WITH HIS MICROPHONE AND BATTERY PACK-- WHICH I WOULD REALLY LIKE BACK, IF YOU HAPPEN TO SPEAK TO HIM.
I APOLOGIZE FOR OUR HOST'S RAMBUNCTIOUS BEHAVIOR.
BUT IT SEEMS THE LINE BETWEEN ON- AND OFF-AIR BEHAVIOR IS GETTING BLURRIER BY THE DAY.
TED, THIS IS A POLICE MATTER, AND WE ARE IN THE BUSINESS OF SERVING THE PUBLIC INTEREST, NOT HAVING TANTRUMS!
I'LL SEE YOU FOR THE 9 O'CLOCK RUNDOWN.

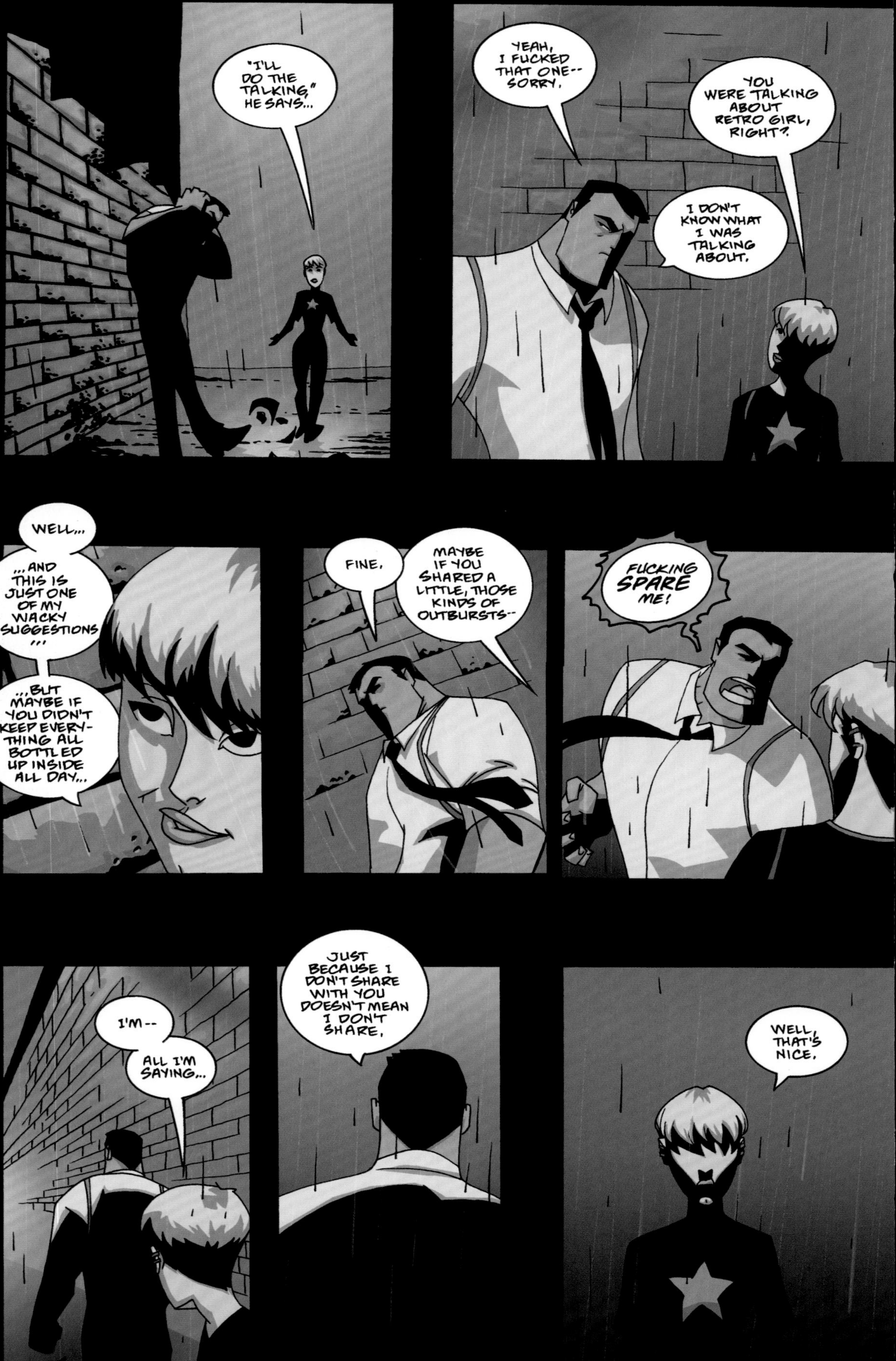
"I'LL DO THE TALKING," HE SAYS...
YEAH, I FUCKED THAT ONE-- SORRY.
YOU WERE TALKING ABOUT RETRO GIRL, RIGHT?
I DON'T KNOW WHAT I WAS TALKING ABOUT.
WELL...
...AND THIS IS JUST ONE OF MY WACKY SUGGESTIONS...
...BUT MAYBE IF YOU DIDN'T KEEP EVERY-THING ALL BOTTLED UP INSIDE ALL DAY...
FINE.
MAYBE IF YOU SHARED A LITTLE, THOSE KINDS OF OUTBURSTS--
FUCKING SPARE ME!
I'M--
ALL I'M SAYING...
JUST BECAUSE I DON'T SHARE WITH YOU DOESN'T MEAN I DON'T SHARE.
WELL, THAT'S NICE.

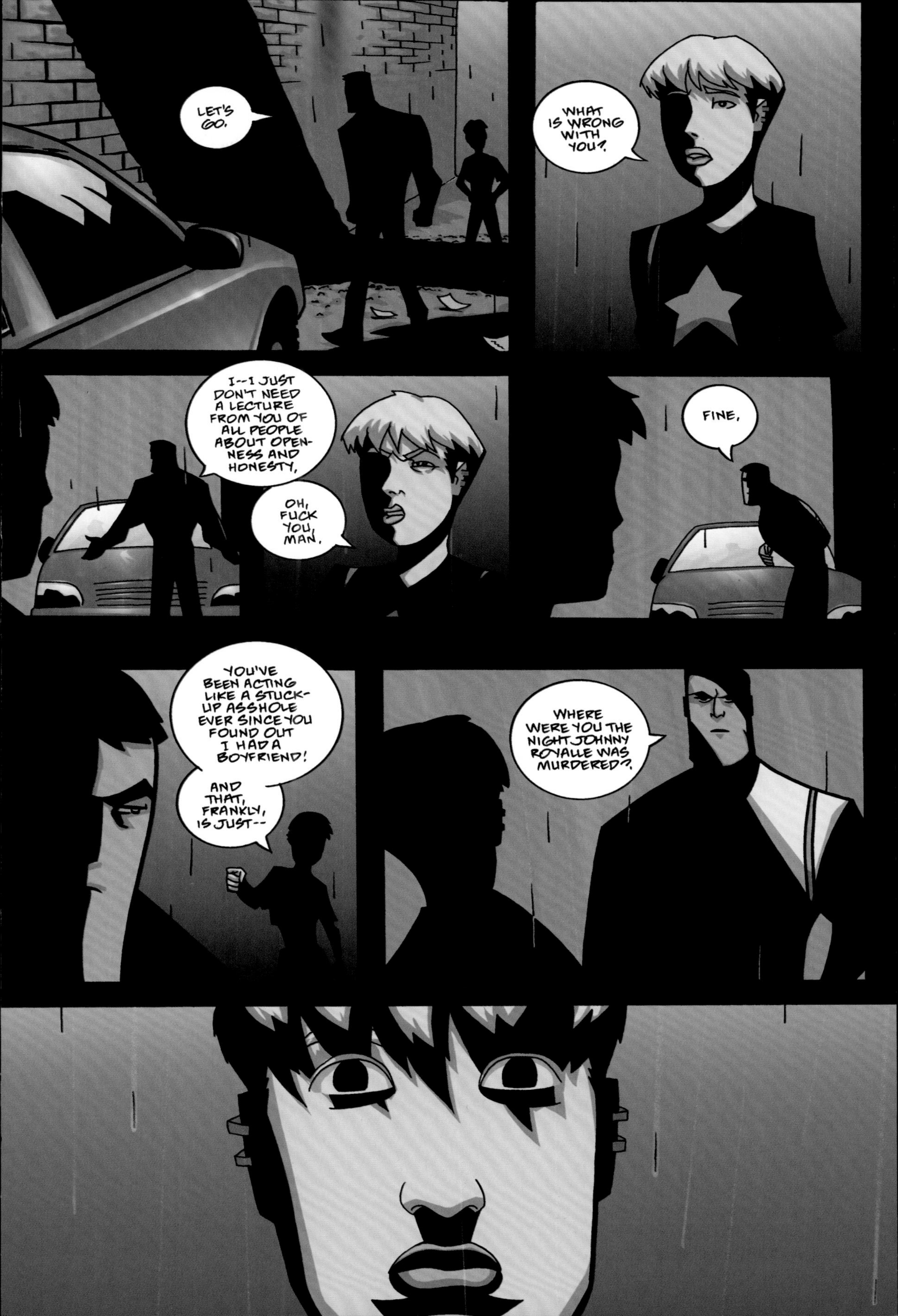
LET'S GO.
WHAT IS WRONG WITH YOU?
I--I JUST DON'T NEED A LECTURE FROM YOU OF ALL PEOPLE ABOUT OPENNESS AND HONESTY.
OH, FUCK YOU, MAN.
FINE.
YOU'VE BEEN ACTING LIKE A STUCK-UP ASSHOLE EVER SINCE YOU FOUND OUT I HAD A BOYFRIEND!
AND THAT, FRANKLY, IS JUST--
WHERE WERE YOU THE NIGHT JOHNNY ROYALLE WAS MURDERED?

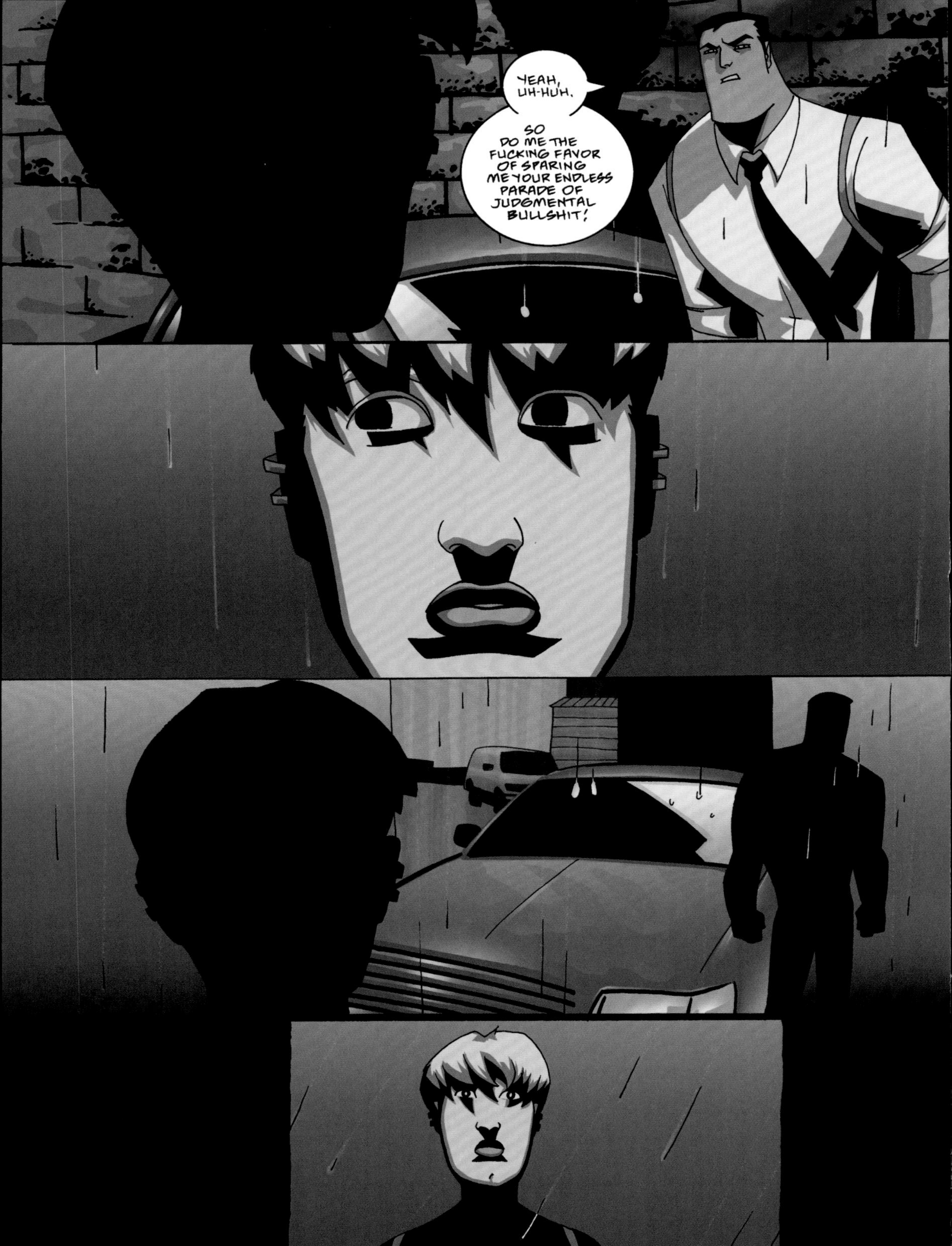
YEAH, UH-HUH.
SO DO ME THE FUCKING FAVOR OF SPARING ME YOUR ENDLESS PARADE OF JUDGMENTAL BULLSHIT!

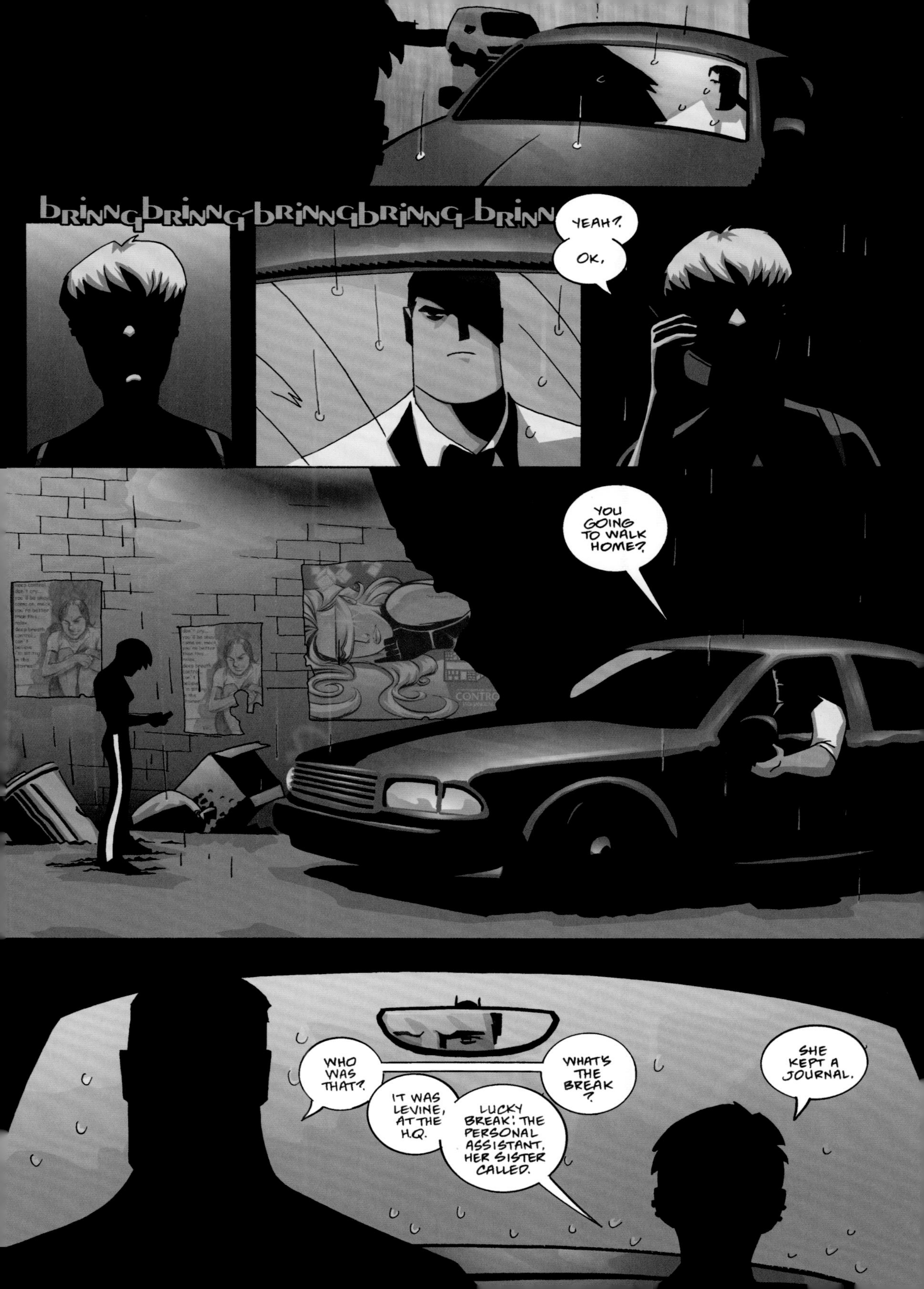
bringbring bringbring brinn
YEAH?.
OK.
YOU GOING TO WALK HOME?
WHO WAS THAT?
IT WAS LEVINE, AT THE H.Q.
WHAT'S THE BREAK?
LUCKY BREAK: THE PERSONAL ASSISTANT, HER SISTER CALLED.
SHE KEPT A JOURNAL.

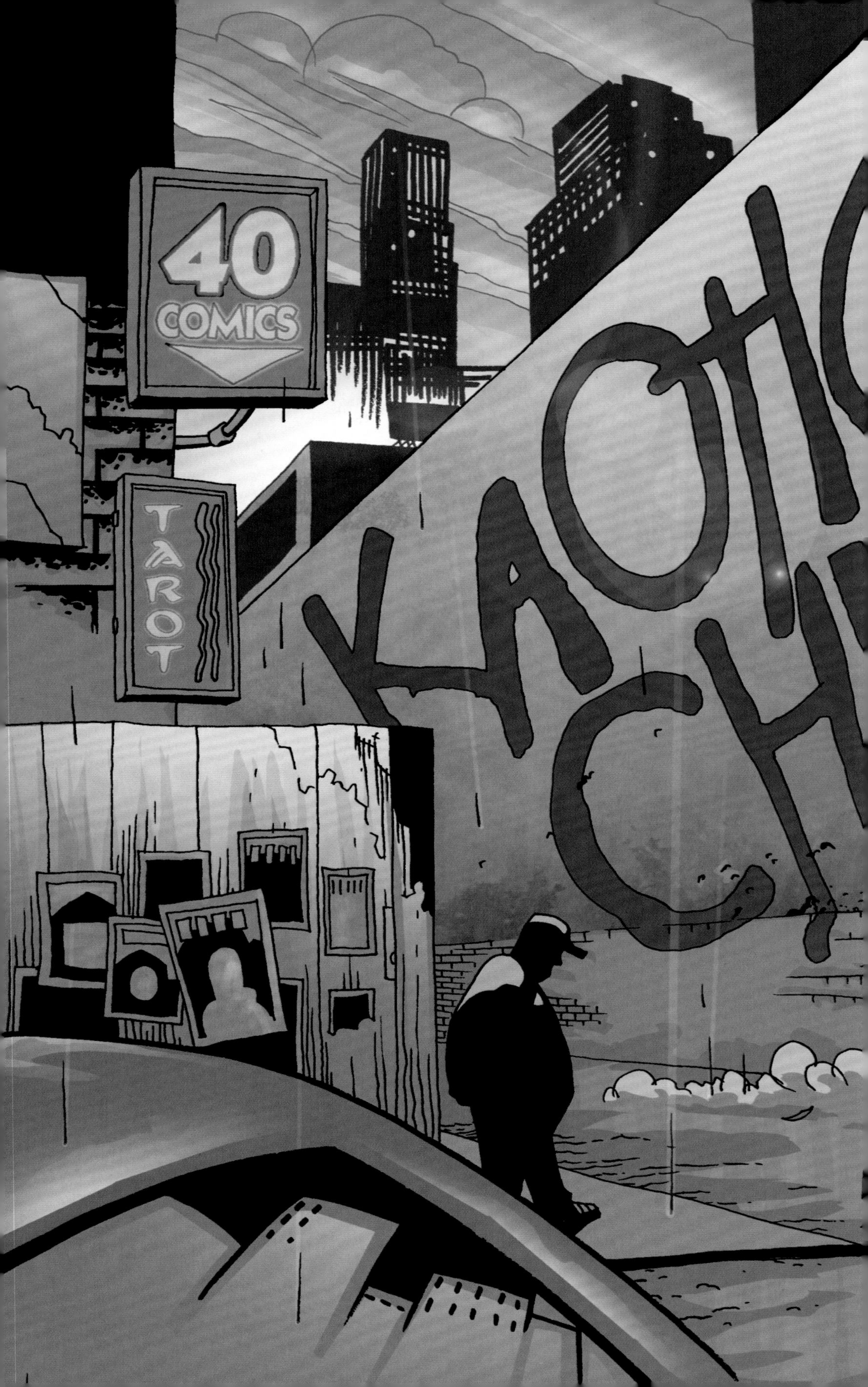
40
COMICS
TAROT

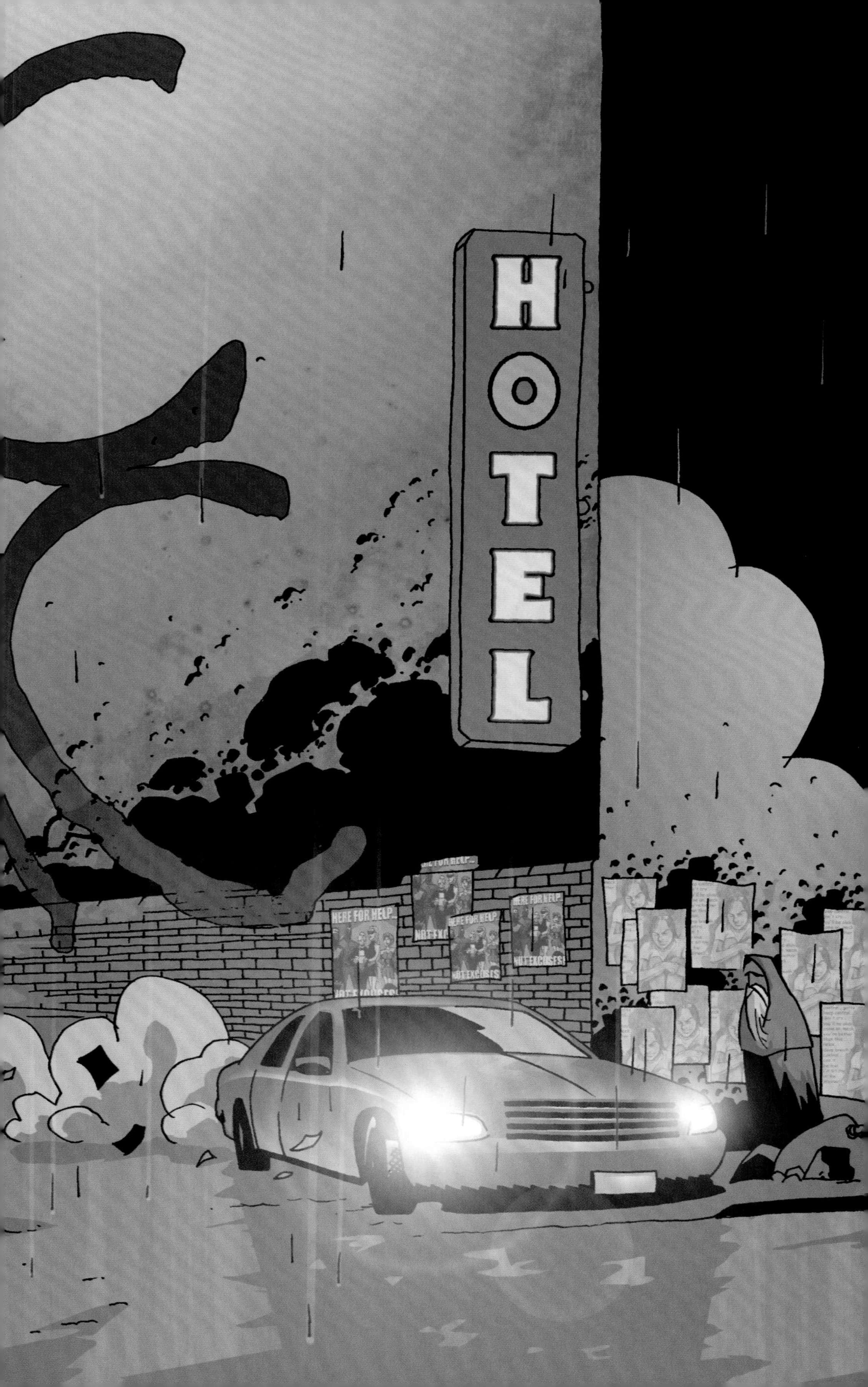
HOTEL
HERE FOR HELP.
NOT EXCUSES!

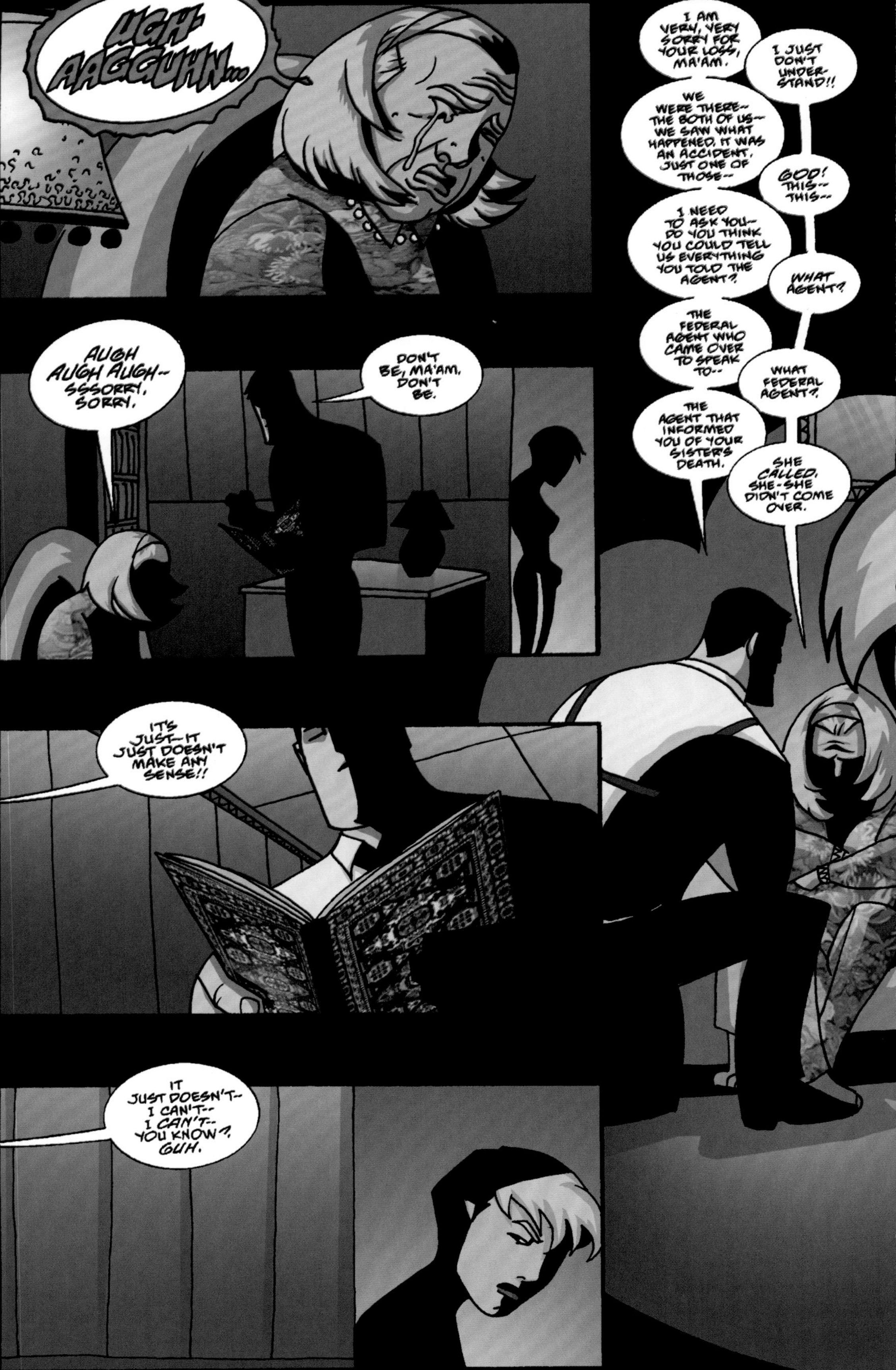
UGH-AAGGUHN...
I AM VERY, VERY SORRY FOR YOUR LOSS, MA'AM.
I JUST DON'T UNDERSTAND!!
WE WERE THERE-- THE BOTH OF US-- WE SAW WHAT HAPPENED. IT WAS AN ACCIDENT. JUST ONE OF THOSE--
GOD! THIS-- THIS--
I NEED TO ASK YOU-- DO YOU THINK YOU COULD TELL US EVERYTHING YOU TOLD THE AGENT?
WHAT AGENT?
THE FEDERAL AGENT WHO CAME OVER TO SPEAK TO--
WHAT FEDERAL AGENT?
THE AGENT THAT INFORMED YOU OF YOUR SISTER'S DEATH.
SHE CALLED. SHE-SHE DIDN'T COME OVER.
AUGH AUGH AUGH-- SSSORRY. SORRY.
DON'T BE, MA'AM. DON'T BE.
IT'S JUST-- IT JUST DOESN'T MAKE ANY SENSE!!
IT JUST DOESN'T-- I CAN'T-- I CAN'T-- YOU KNOW? GUH.

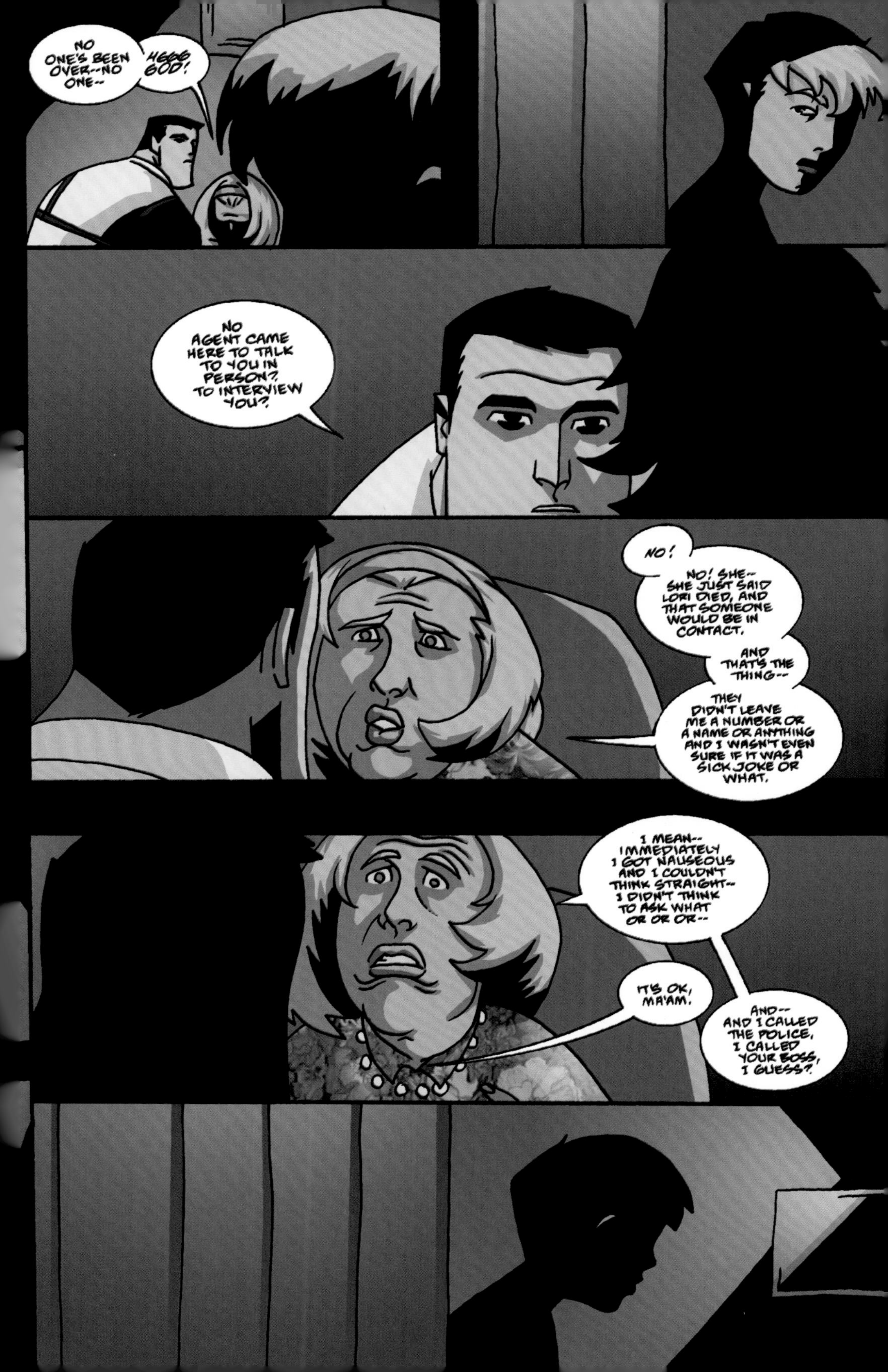
NO ONE'S BEEN OVER--NO ONE--
HGGG GOD!
NO AGENT CAME HERE TO TALK TO YOU IN PERSON? TO INTERVIEW YOU?
NO!
NO! SHE-- SHE JUST SAID LORI DIED, AND THAT SOMEONE WOULD BE IN CONTACT.
AND THAT'S THE THING--
THEY DIDN'T LEAVE ME A NUMBER OR A NAME OR ANYTHING AND I WASN'T EVEN SURE IF IT WAS A SICK JOKE OR WHAT.
I MEAN-- IMMEDIATELY I GOT NAUSEOUS AND I COULDN'T THINK STRAIGHT-- I DIDN'T THINK TO ASK WHAT OR OR OR--
IT'S OK, MA'AM.
AND-- AND I CALLED THE POLICE, I CALLED YOUR BOSS, I GUESS?

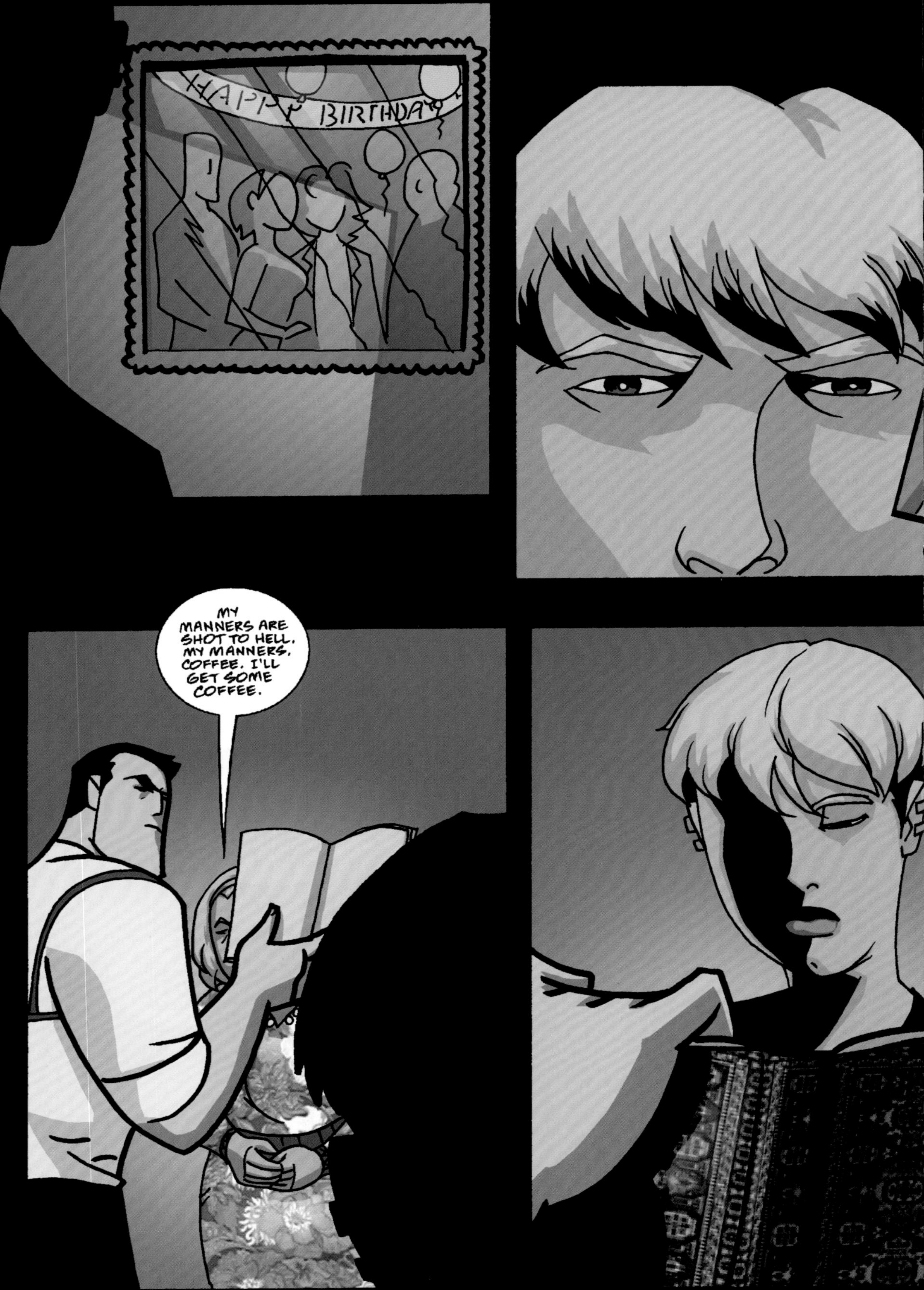

HAPPY BIRTHDAY
MY MANNERS ARE SHOT TO HELL. MY MANNERS. COFFEE. I'LL GET SOME COFFEE.

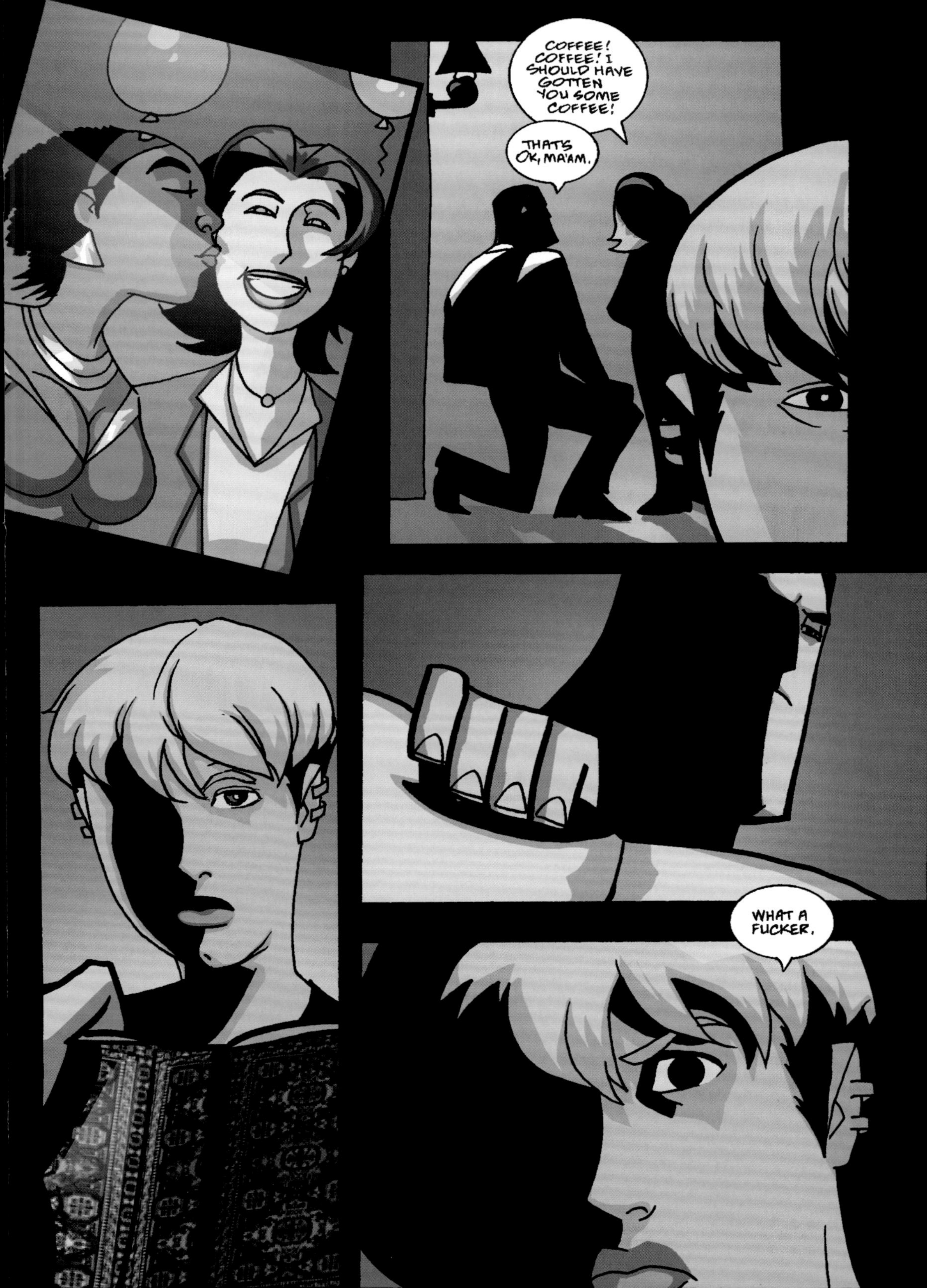
COFFEE! COFFEE! I SHOULD HAVE GOTTEN YOU SOME COFFEE!
THAT'S OK, MA'AM.
WHAT A FUCKER.

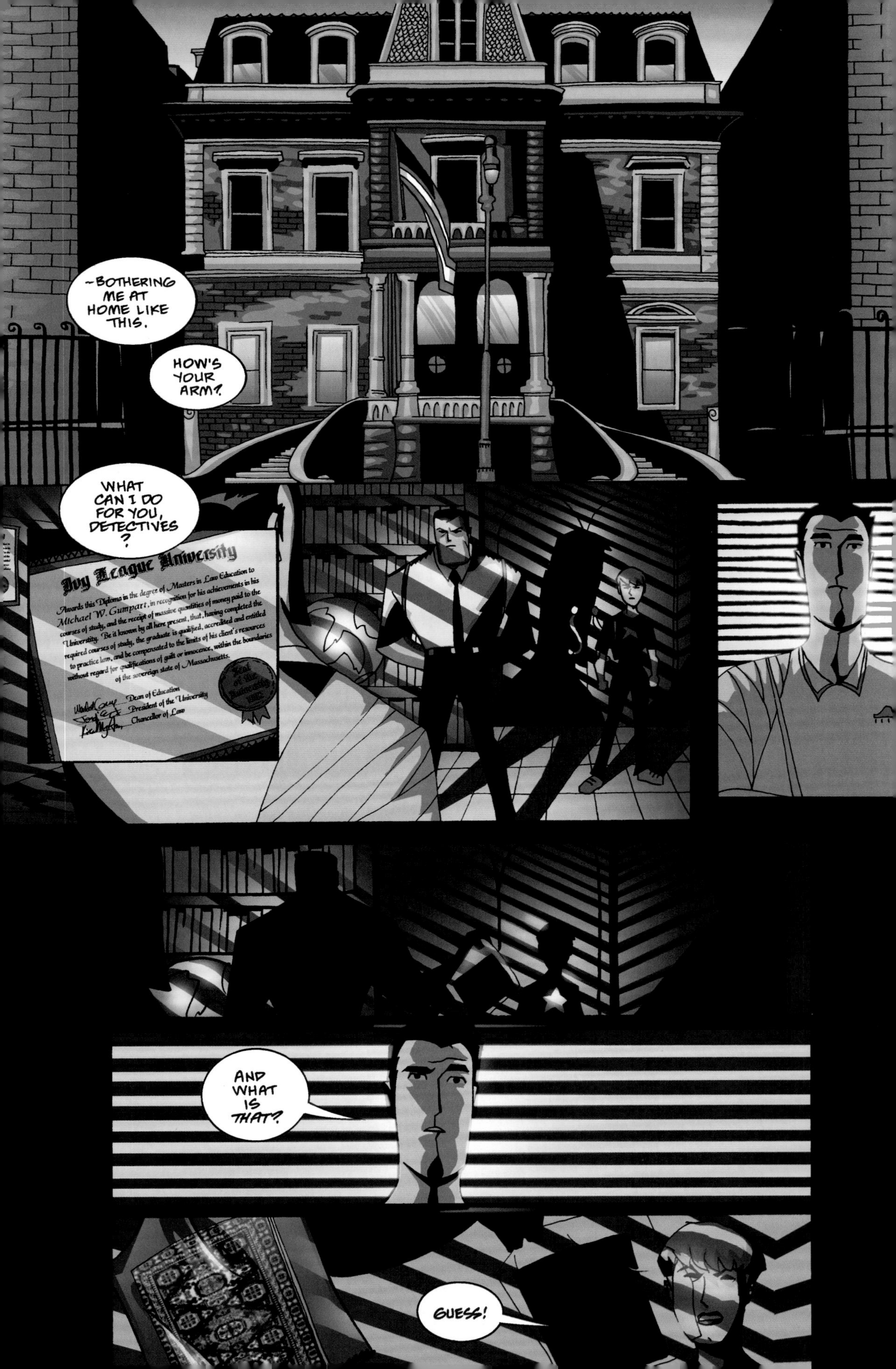
~BOTHERING ME AT HOME LIKE THIS.
HOW'S YOUR ARM?
WHAT CAN I DO FOR YOU, DETECTIVES?
Ivy League University
Awards this Diploma in the degree of Masters in Law Education to Michael W. Gumpart, in recognition for his achievements in his courses of study, and the receipt of massive quantities of money paid to the Universtity. Be it known by all here present, that, having completed the required courses of study, the graduate is qualified, accredited and entitled to practice law, and be compensated to the limits of his client's resources without regard for qualifications of guilt or innocence, within the boundaries of the sovereign state of Massachusetts.
Dean of Education
President of the University
Chancellor of Law
AND WHAT IS THAT?
GUESS!

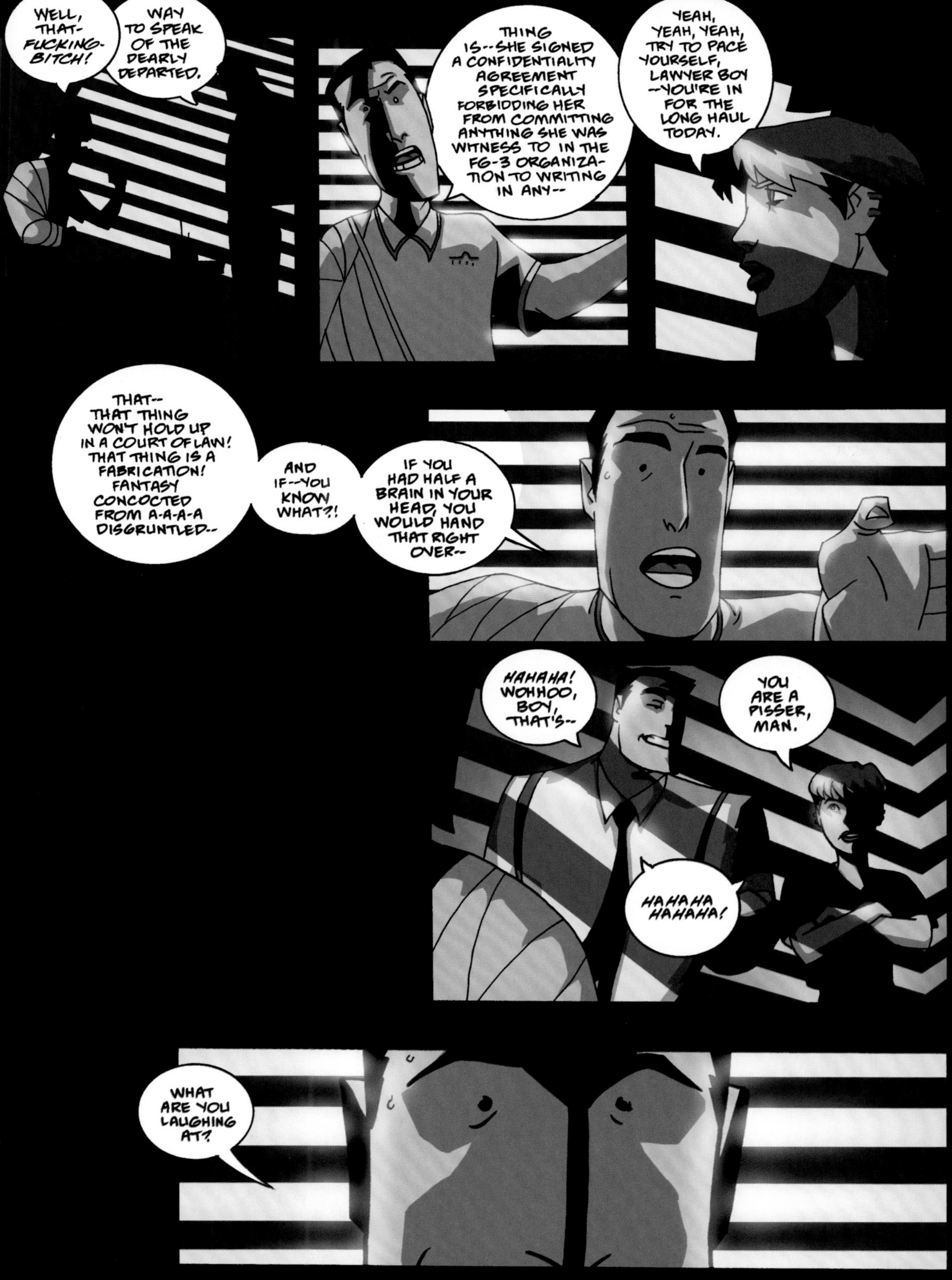
WELL, THAT- FUCKING- BITCH!
WAY TO SPEAK OF THE DEARLY DEPARTED.
THING IS--SHE SIGNED A CONFIDENTIALITY AGREEMENT SPECIFICALLY FORBIDDING HER FROM COMMITTING ANYTHING SHE WAS WITNESS TO IN THE FG-3 ORGANIZATION TO WRITING IN ANY--
YEAH, YEAH, YEAH, TRY TO PACE YOURSELF, LAWYER BOY --YOU'RE IN FOR THE LONG HAUL TODAY.
THAT-- THAT THING WON'T HOLD UP IN A COURT OF LAW! THAT THING IS A FABRICATION! FANTASY CONCOCTED FROM A-A-A-A DISGRUNTLED--
AND IF--YOU KNOW WHAT?!
IF YOU HAD HALF A BRAIN IN YOUR HEAD, YOU WOULD HAND THAT RIGHT OVER--
HAHAHA! WOHHOO, BOY, THAT'S--
YOU ARE A PISSER, MAN.
HAHAHA HAHAHA!
WHAT ARE YOU LAUGHING AT?

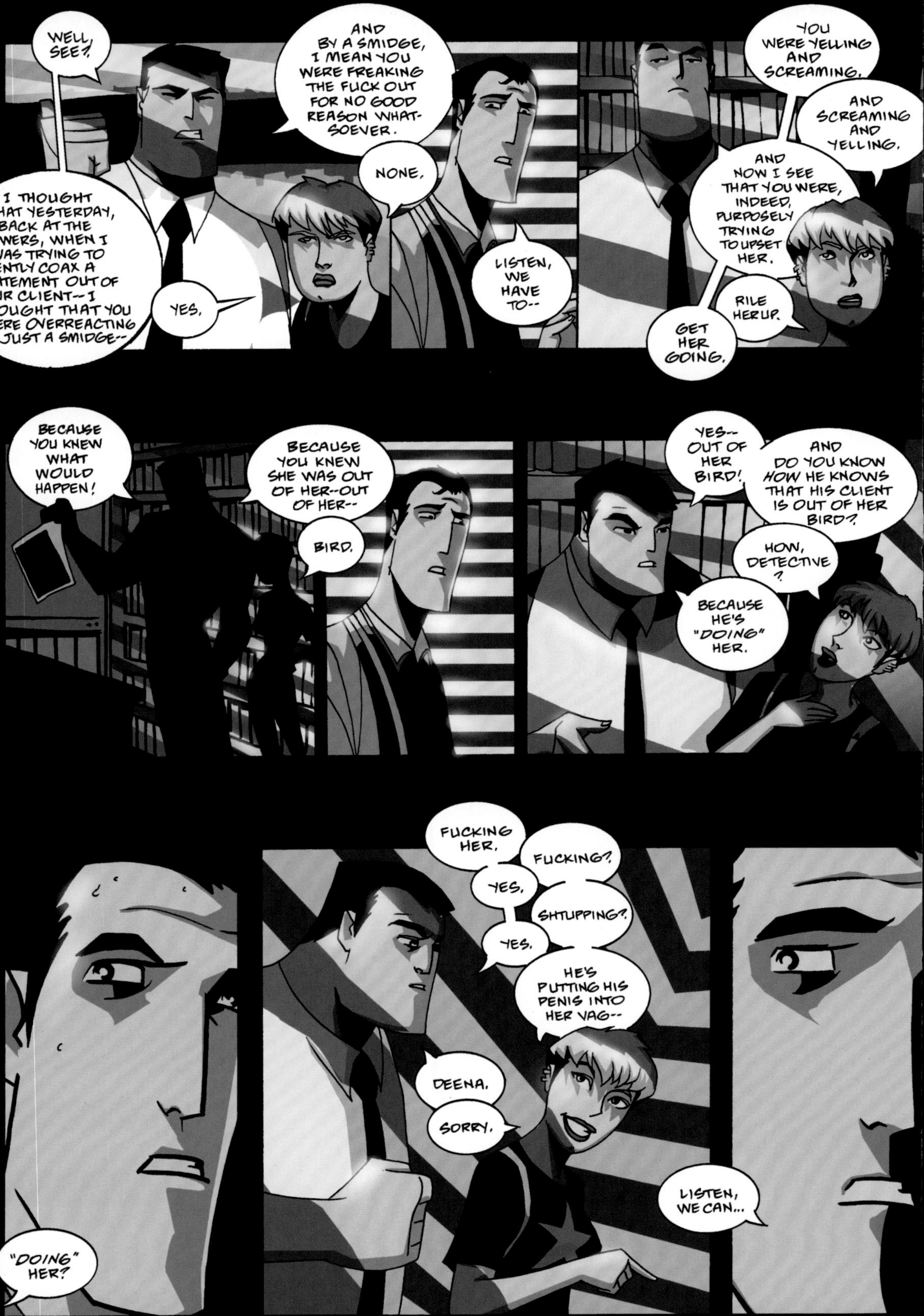
WELL, SEE?
I THOUGHT THAT YESTERDAY, BACK AT THE TOWERS, WHEN I WAS TRYING TO GENTLY COAX A STATEMENT OUT OF YOUR CLIENT-- I THOUGHT THAT YOU WERE OVERREACTING JUST A SMIDGE--
YES.
AND BY A SMIDGE, I MEAN YOU WERE FREAKING THE FUCK OUT FOR NO GOOD REASON WHATSOEVER.
NONE.
LISTEN, WE HAVE TO--
YOU WERE YELLING AND SCREAMING.
AND SCREAMING AND YELLING.
AND NOW I SEE THAT YOU WERE, INDEED, PURPOSELY TRYING TO UPSET HER.
RILE HER UP.
GET HER GOING.
BECAUSE YOU KNEW WHAT WOULD HAPPEN!
BECAUSE YOU KNEW SHE WAS OUT OF HER--OUT OF HER--
BIRD.
YES-- OUT OF HER BIRD!
AND DO YOU KNOW *HOW* HE KNOWS THAT HIS CLIENT IS OUT OF HER BIRD?
HOW, DETECTIVE?
BECAUSE HE'S "DOING" HER.
"DOING" HER?
FUCKING HER.
FUCKING?
YES.
SHTUPPING?
YES.
HE'S PUTTING HIS PENIS INTO HER VAG--
DEENA.
SORRY.
LISTEN, WE CAN...

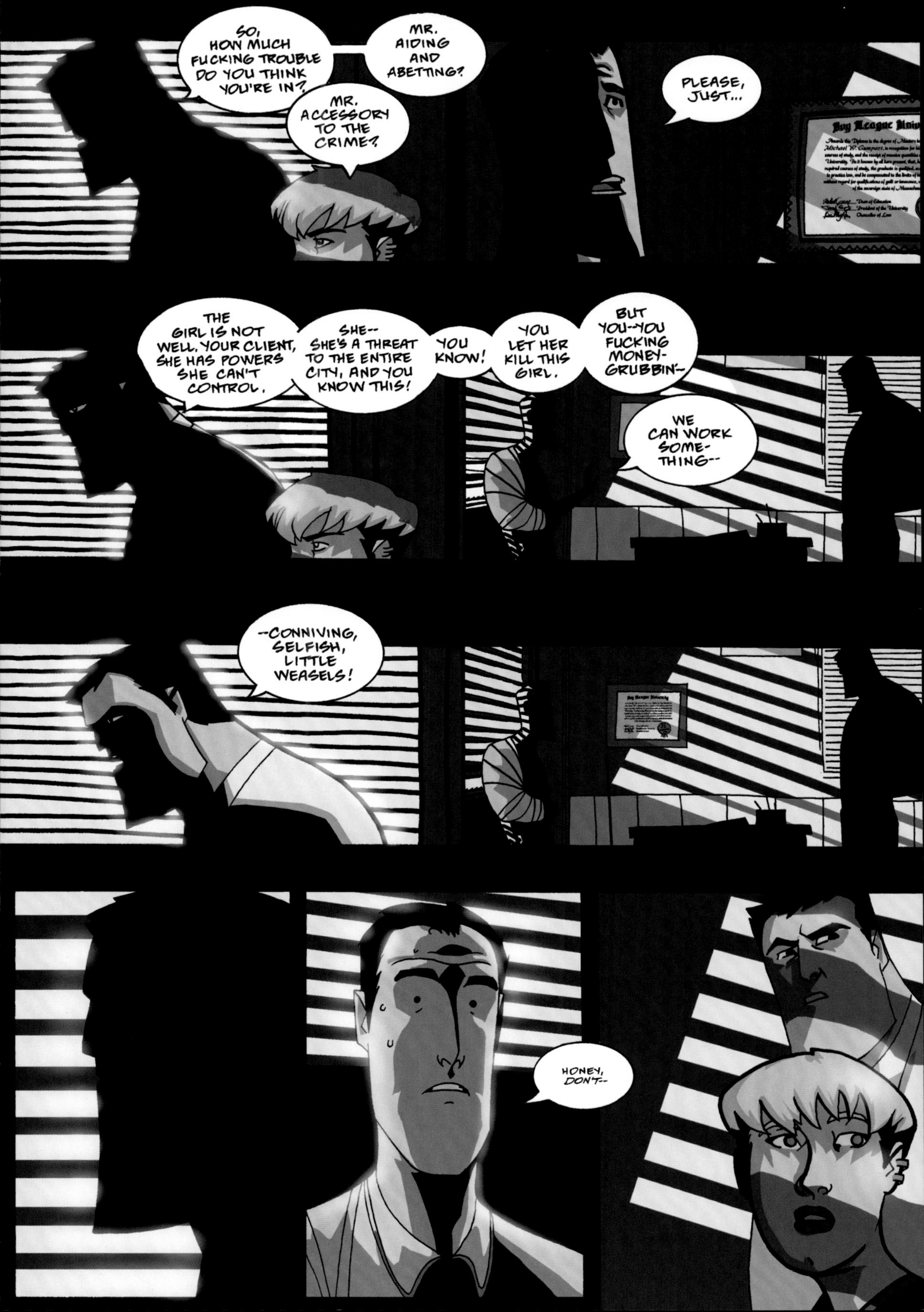
SO, HOW MUCH FUCKING TROUBLE DO YOU THINK YOU'RE IN?
MR. AIDING AND ABETTING?
MR. ACCESSORY TO THE CRIME?
PLEASE, JUST...
THE GIRL IS NOT WELL, YOUR CLIENT, SHE HAS POWERS SHE CAN'T CONTROL.
SHE-- SHE'S A THREAT TO THE ENTIRE CITY, AND YOU KNOW THIS!
YOU KNOW!
YOU LET HER KILL THIS GIRL.
BUT YOU--YOU FUCKING MONEY-GRUBBIN'--
WE CAN WORK SOME-THING--
--CONNIVING, SELFISH, LITTLE WEASELS!
HONEY, DON'T--

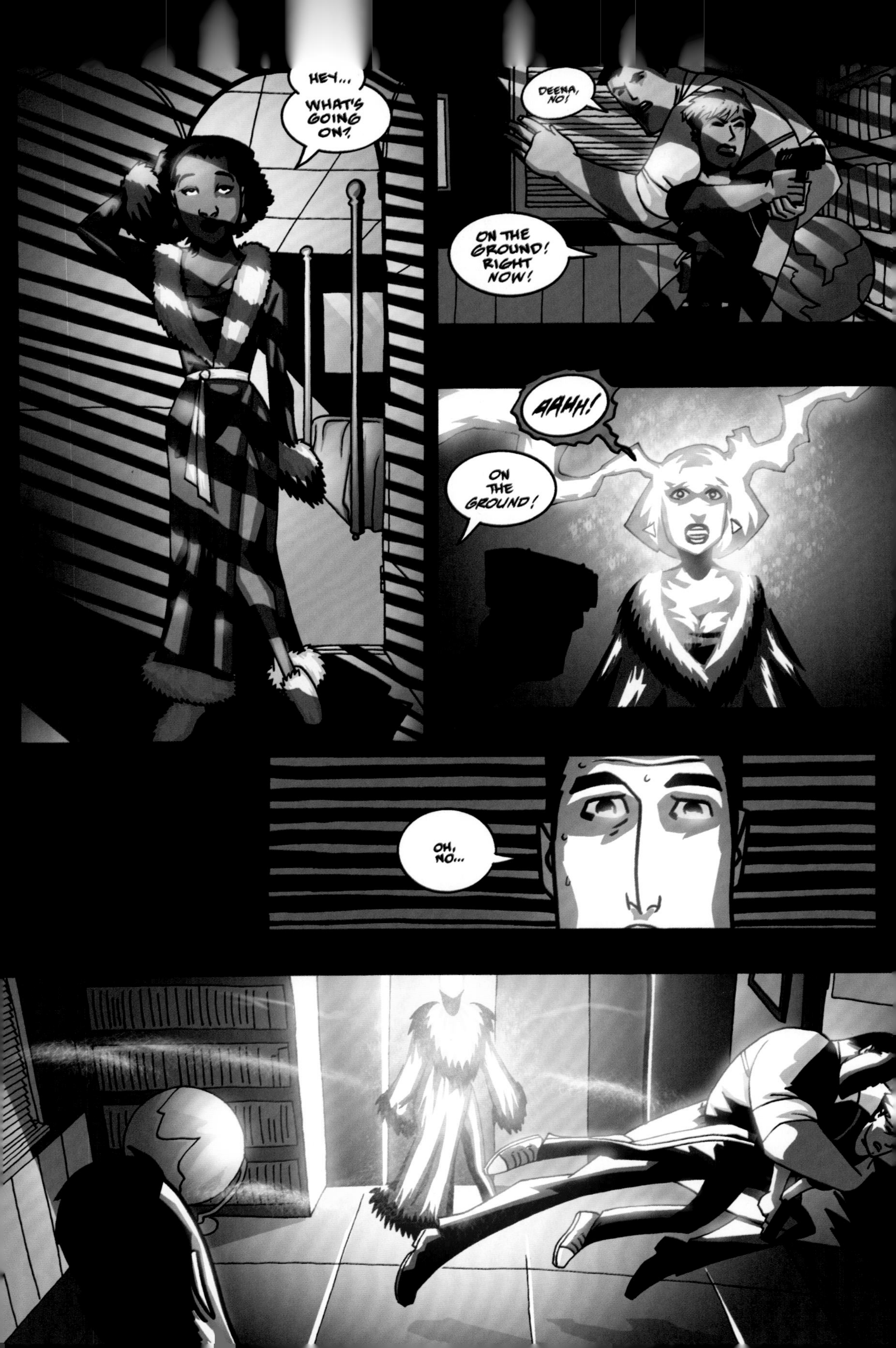
HEY... WHAT'S GOING ON?
DEENA, NO!
ON THE GROUND! RIGHT NOW!
AAHH!
ON THE GROUND!
OH, NO...

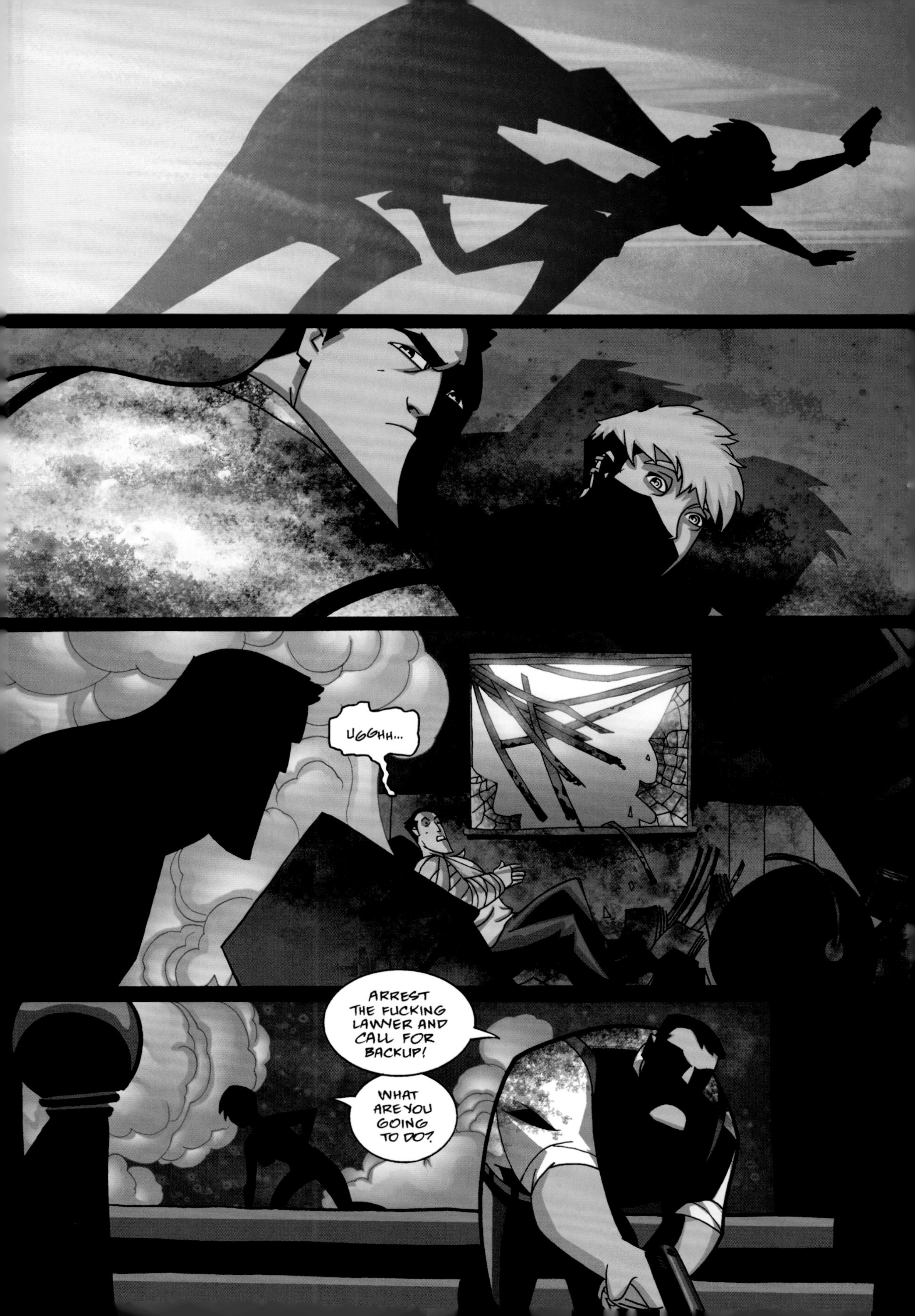
UGGHH...
ARREST THE FUCKING LAWYER AND CALL FOR BACKUP!
WHAT ARE YOU GOING TO DO?

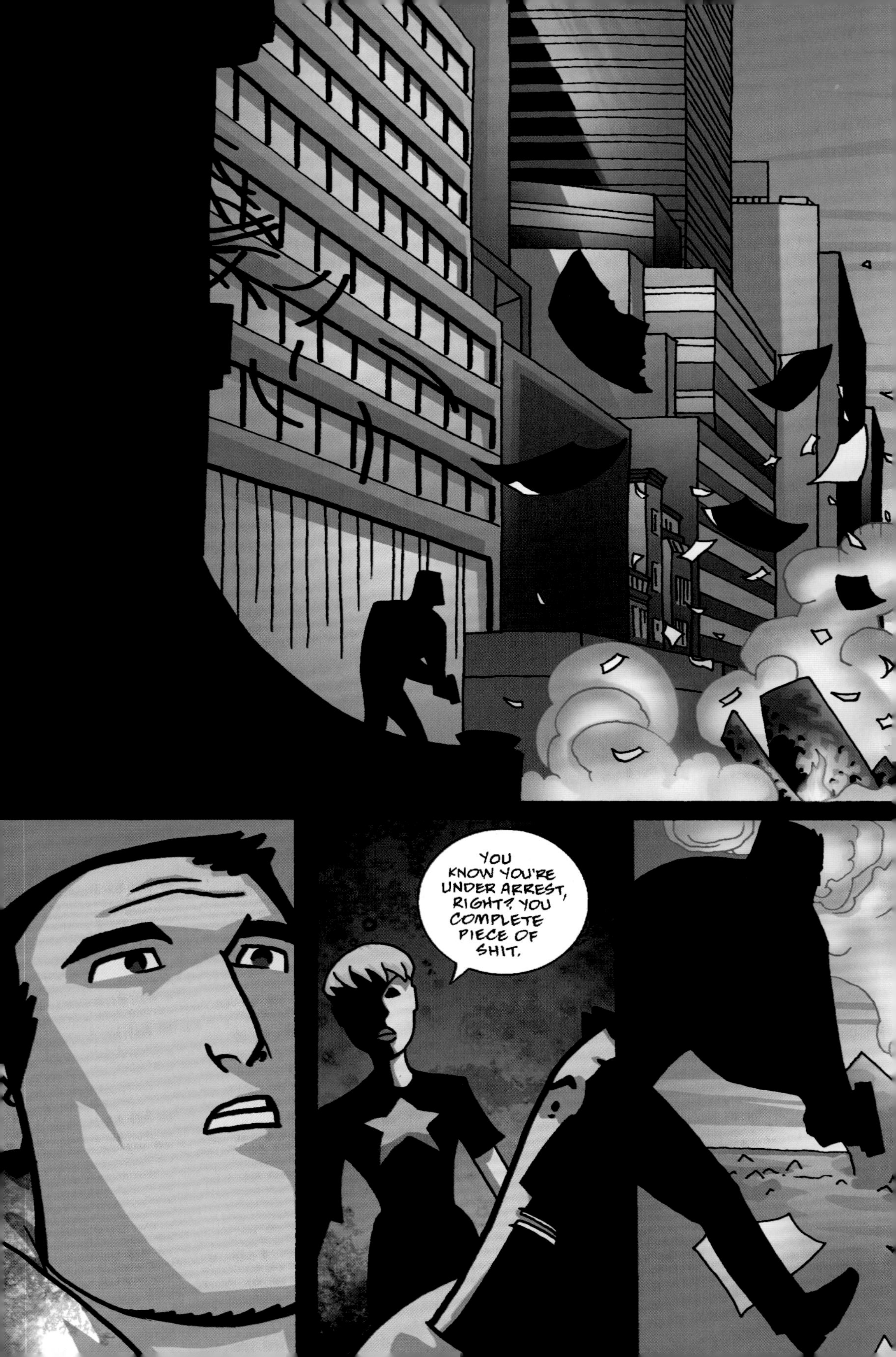
YOU KNOW YOU'RE UNDER ARREST, RIGHT? YOU COMPLETE PIECE OF SHIT.

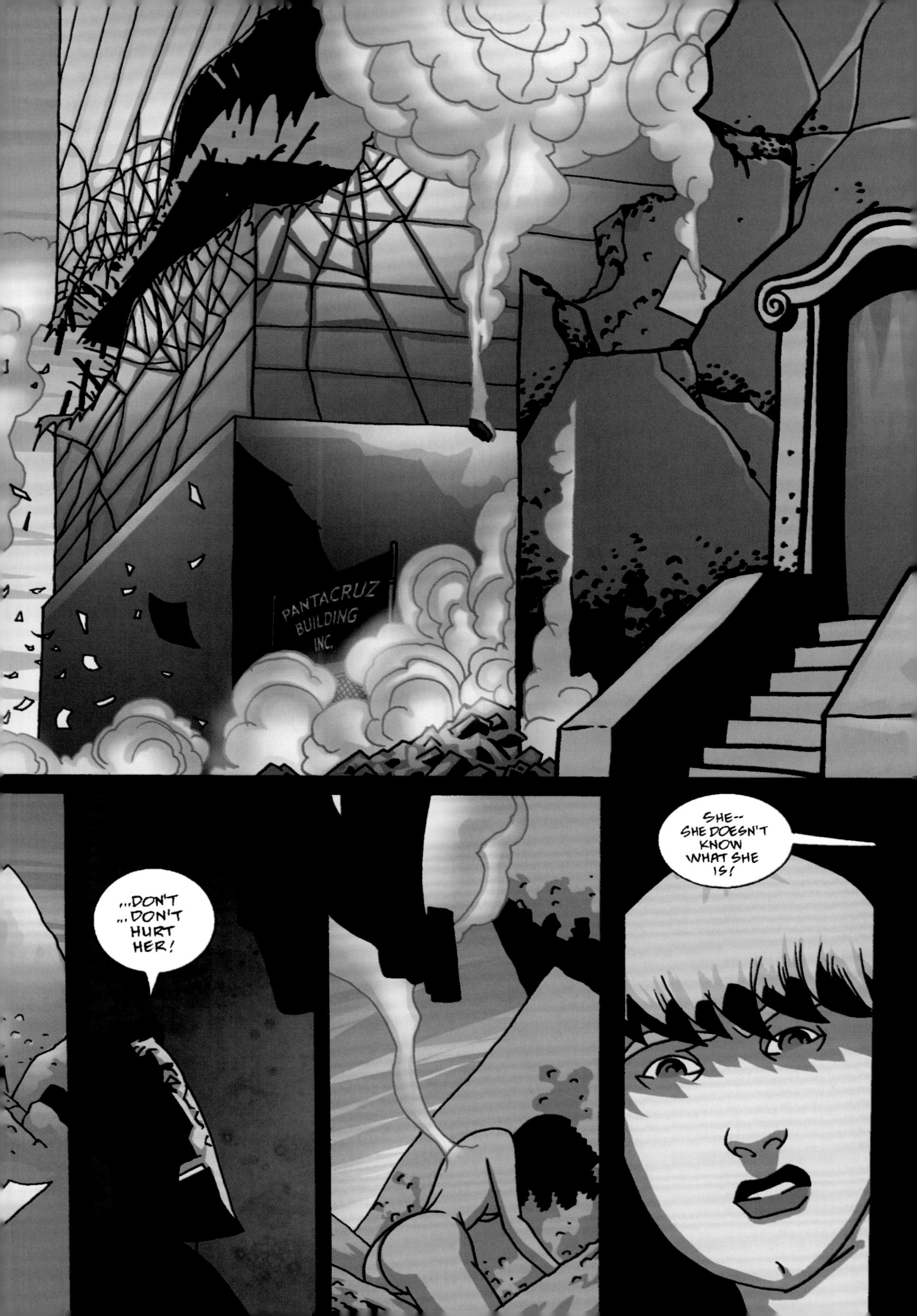
PANTACRUZ BUILDING INC.
...DON'T ...DON'T HURT HER!
SHE-- SHE DOESN'T KNOW WHAT SHE IS!

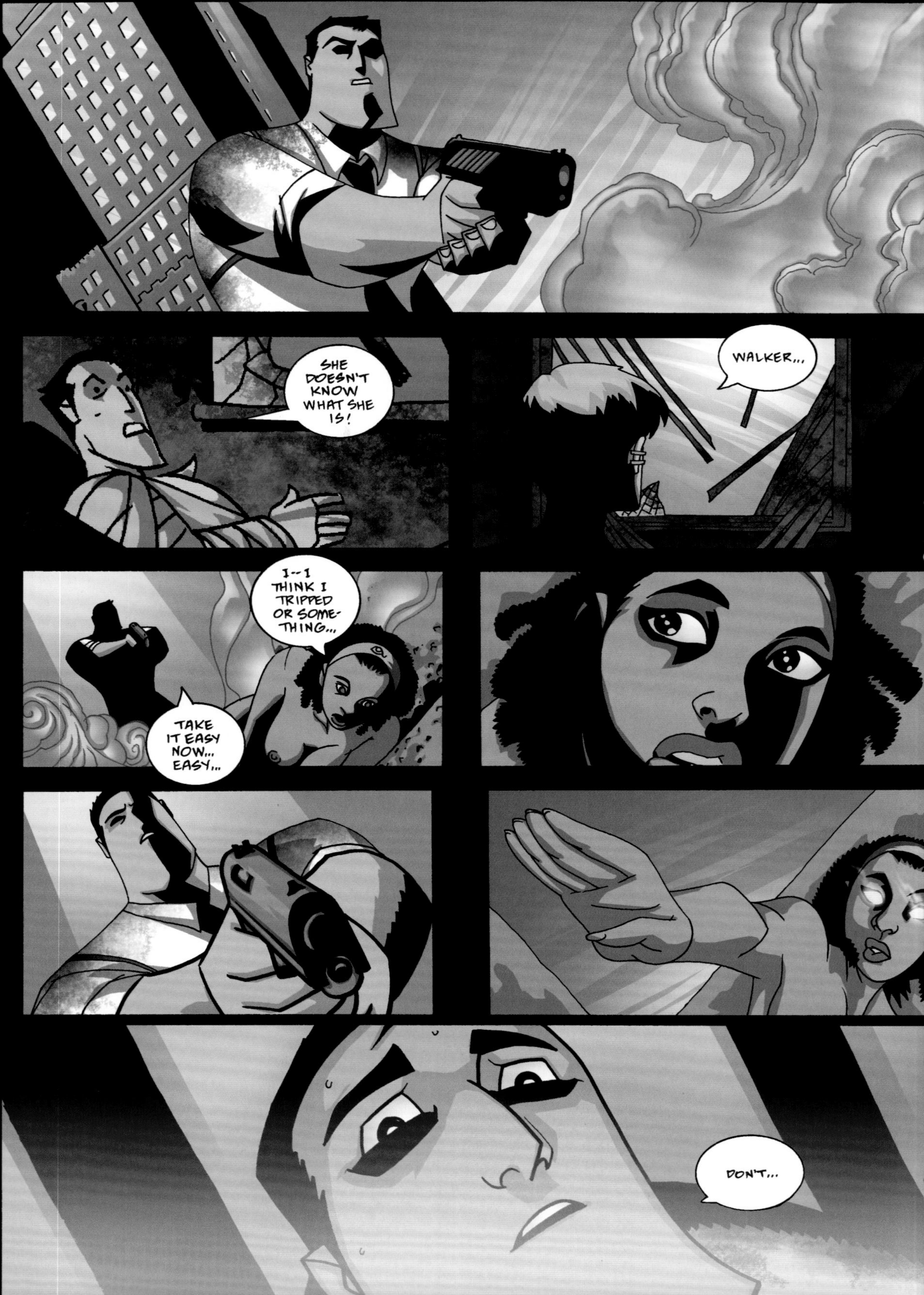
SHE DOESN'T KNOW WHAT SHE IS!
WALKER...
I--I THINK I TRIPPED OR SOME-THING...
TAKE IT EASY NOW... EASY...
DON'T...

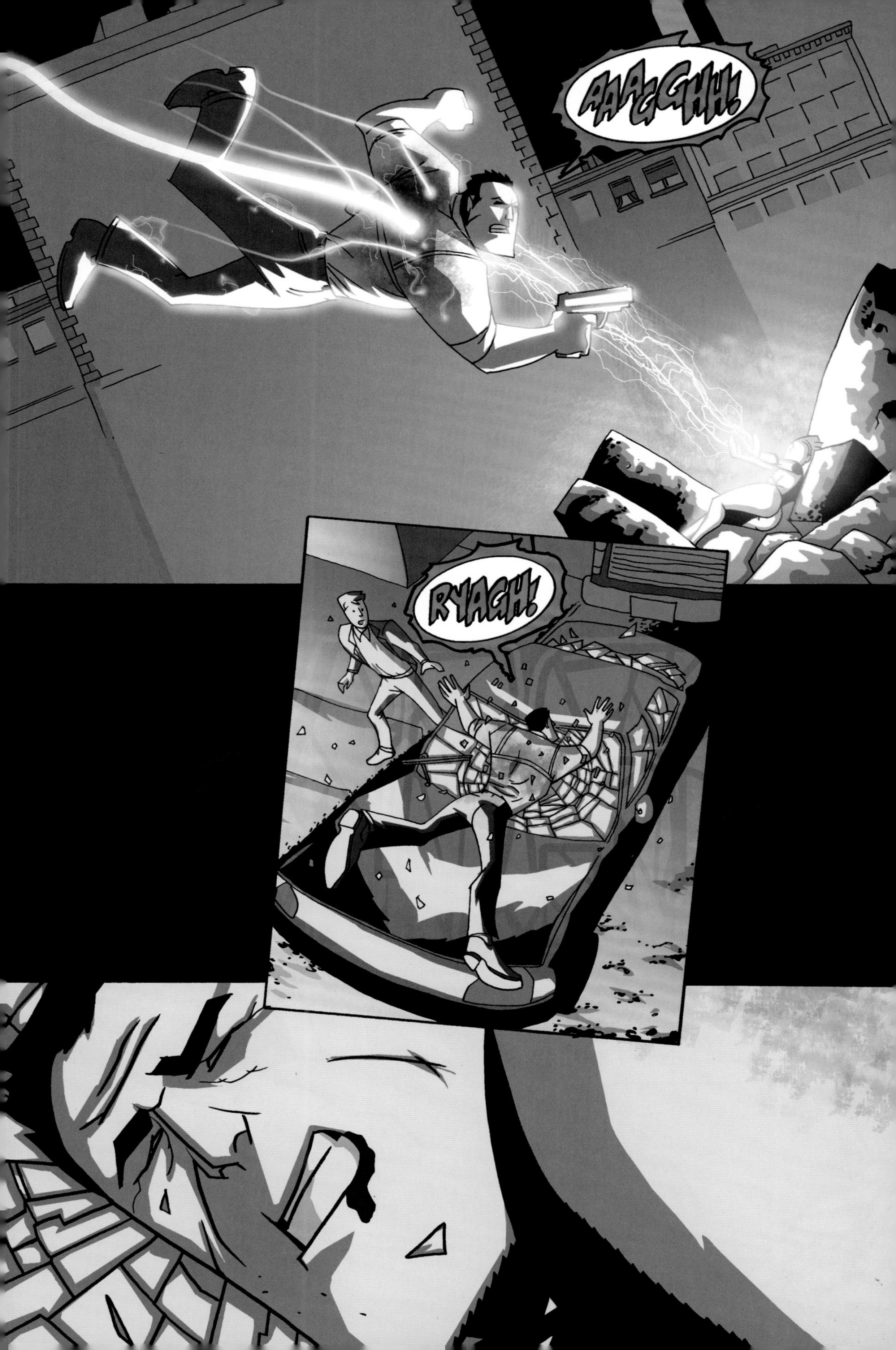
AAAGGHH!
RYAGH!

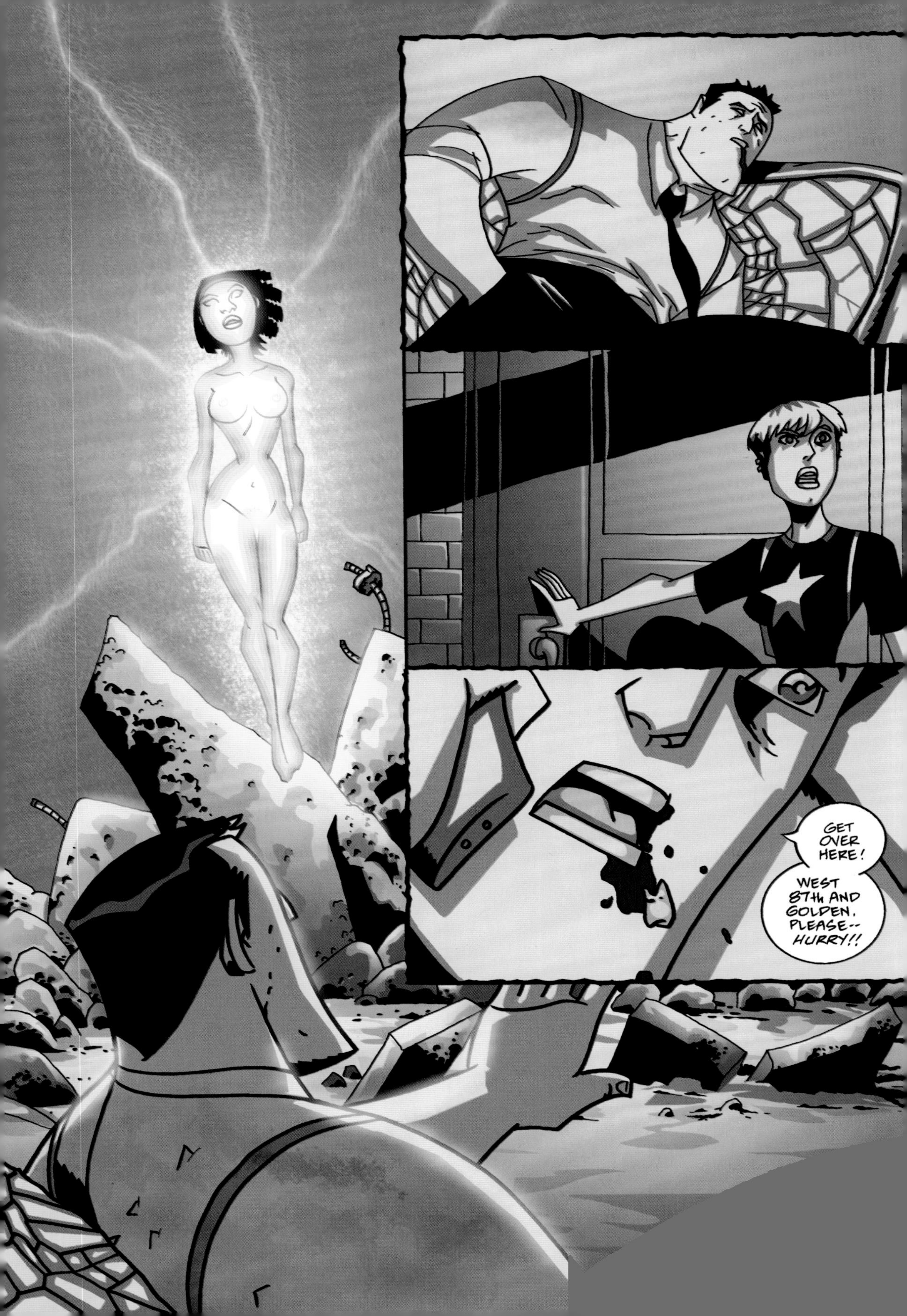
GET OVER HERE!
WEST 87th AND GOLDEN. PLEASE-- HURRY!!

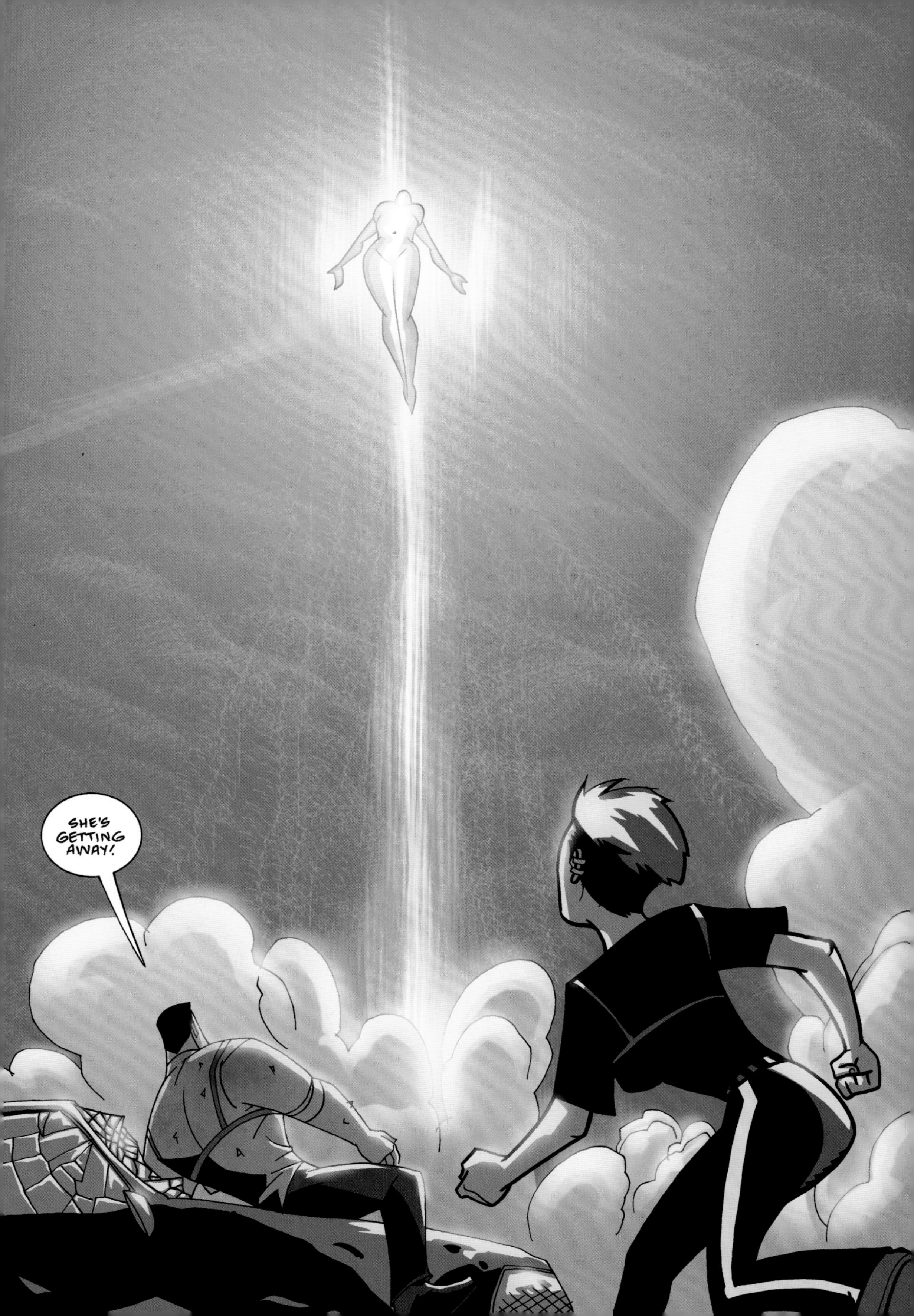
SHE'S GETTING AWAY!

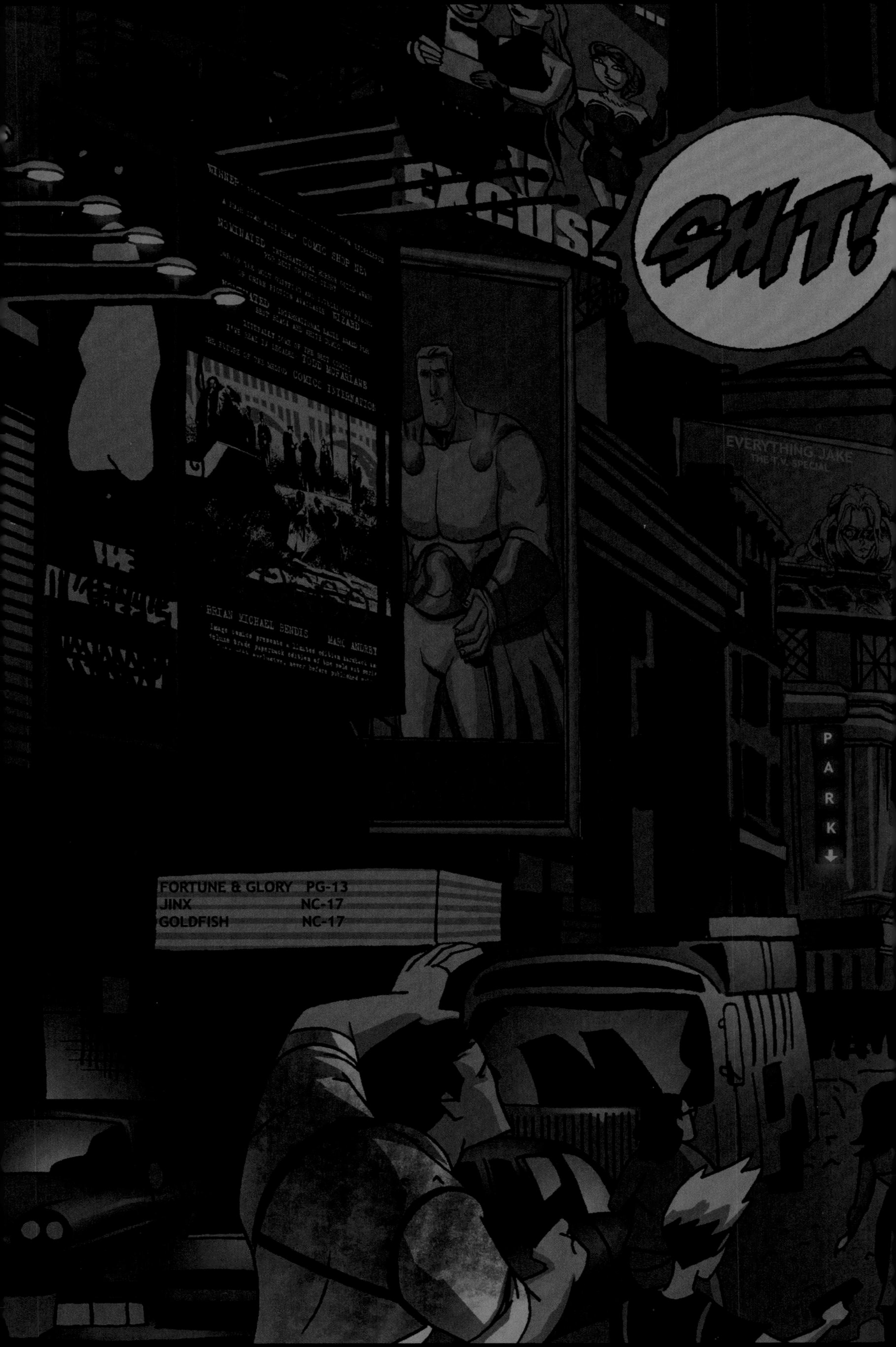
SHIT!
EVERYTHING JAKE
THE T.V. SPECIAL
PARK
FORTUNE & GLORY PG-13
JINX NC-17
GOLDFISH NC-17
BRIAN MICHAEL BENDIS

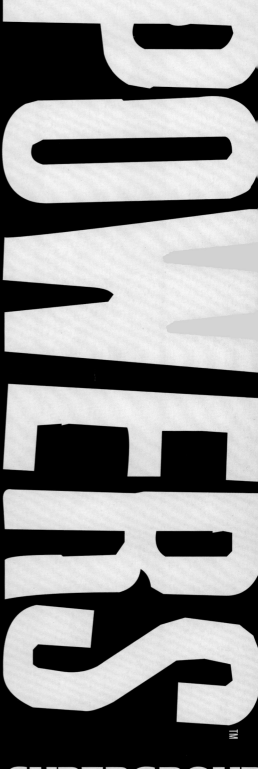

POWERS

™

SUPERGROUP
CHAPTER 4

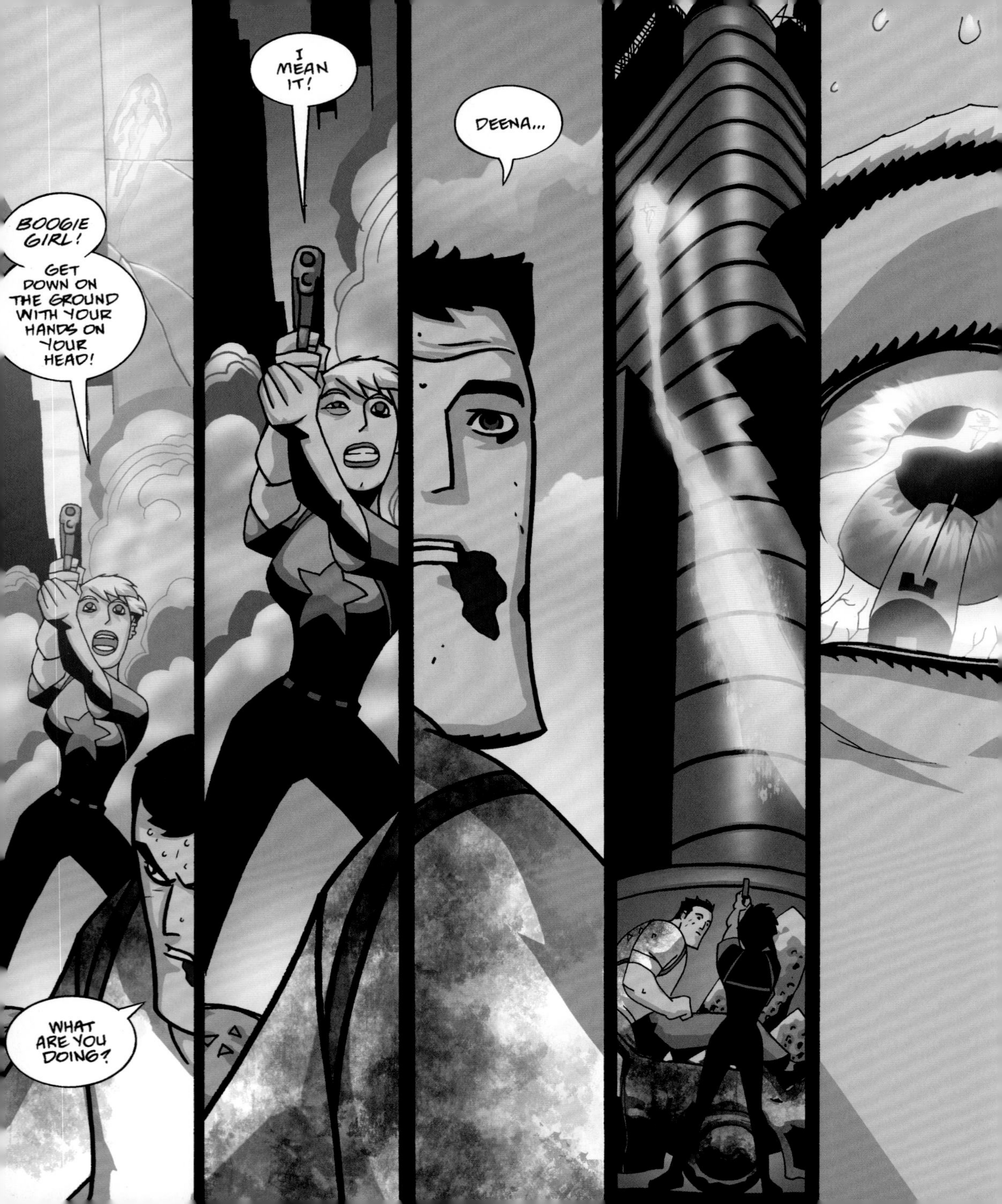
BOOGIE GIRL!
GET DOWN ON THE GROUND WITH YOUR HANDS ON YOUR HEAD!
I MEAN IT!
DEENA...
WHAT ARE YOU DOING?

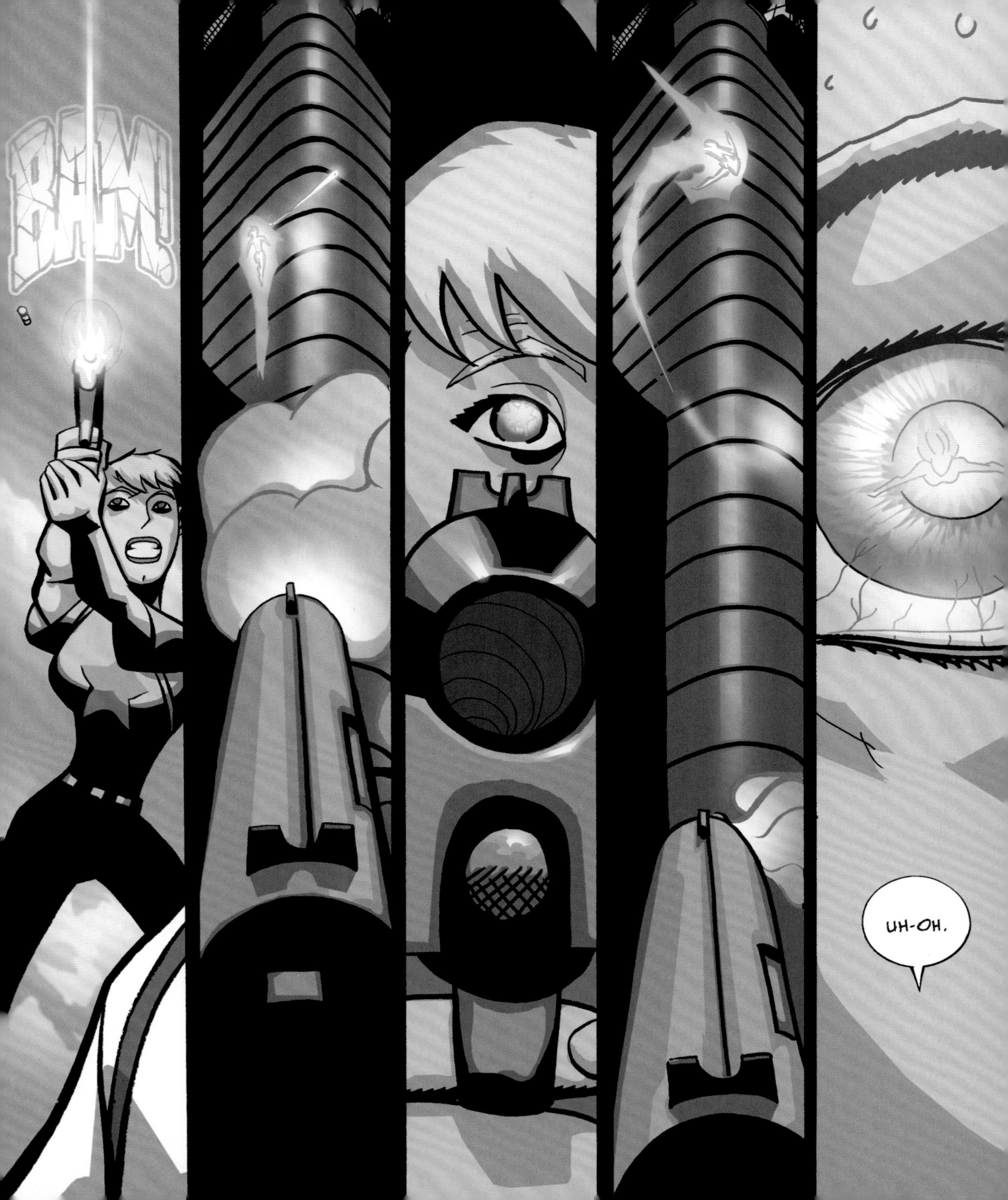
BAM!
UH-OH.

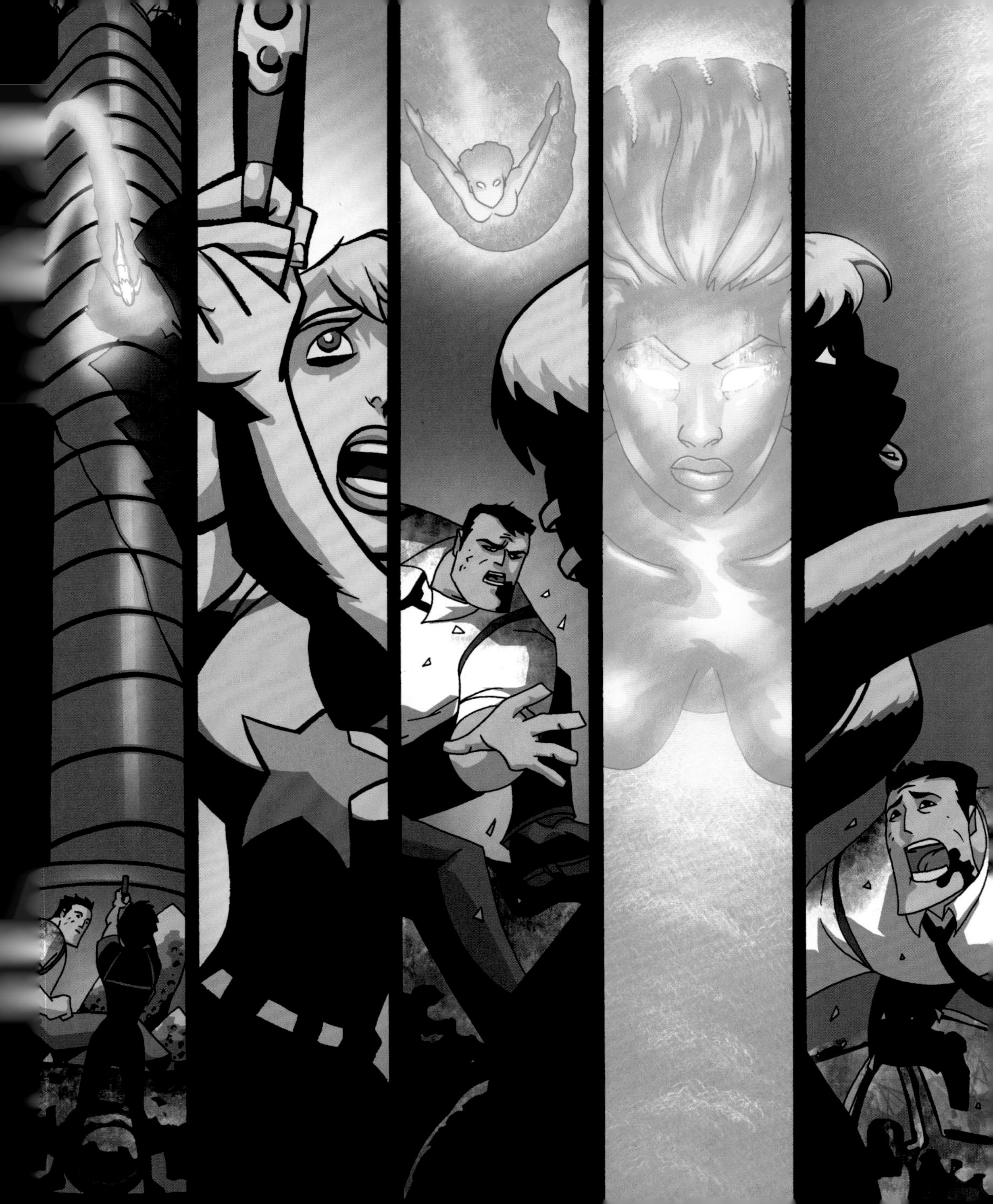

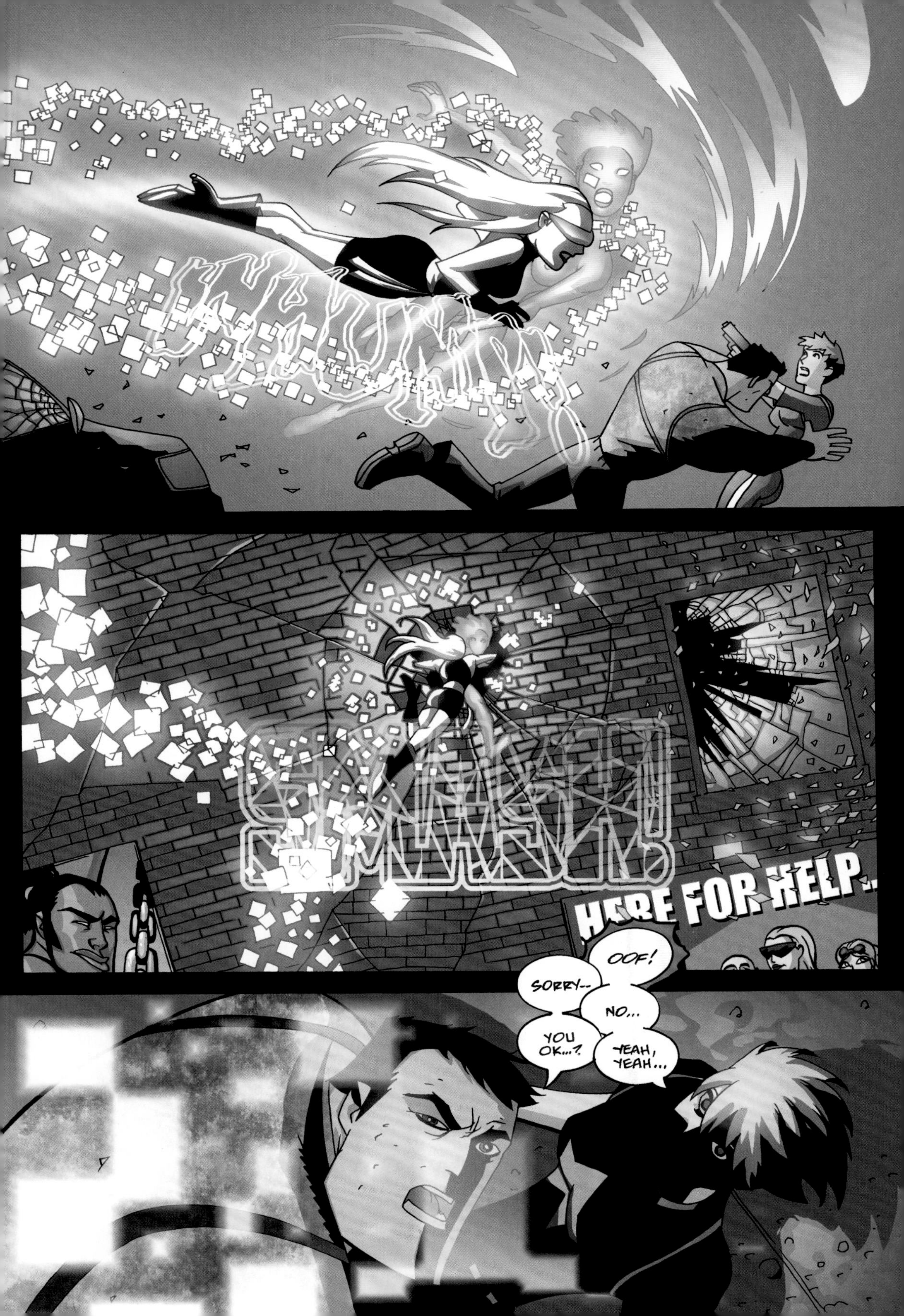

HERE FOR HELP..
OOF!
SORRY--
NO...
YOU OK...?
YEAH, YEAH...

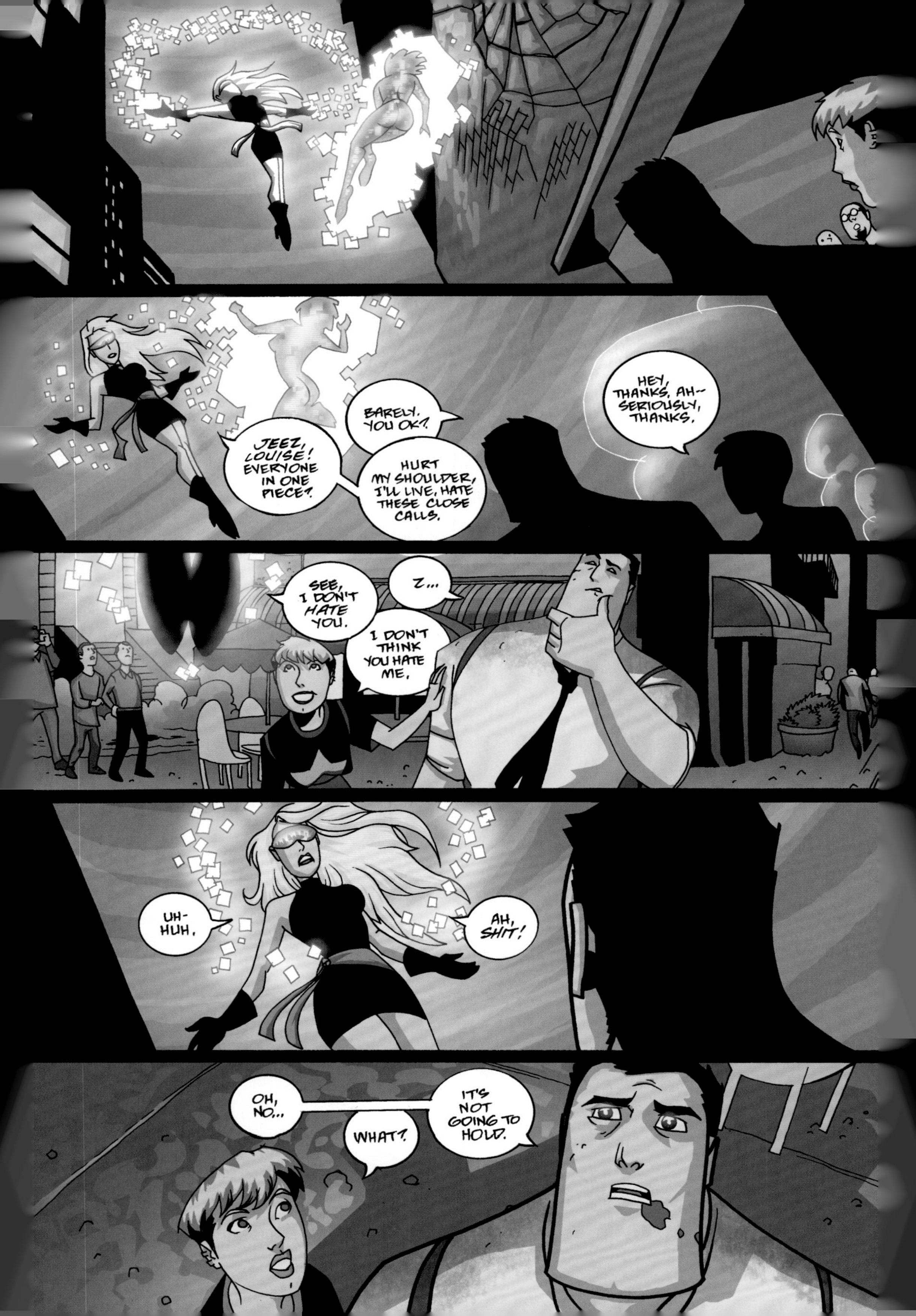

JEEZ, LOUISE! EVERYONE IN ONE PIECE?
BARELY. YOU OK?
HURT MY SHOULDER, I'LL LIVE. HATE THESE CLOSE CALLS.
HEY, THANKS, AH-- SERIOUSLY, THANKS.
SEE, I DON'T HATE YOU.
I...
I DON'T THINK YOU HATE ME.
UH-HUH.
AH, SHIT!
OH, NO...
WHAT?
IT'S NOT GOING TO HOLD.

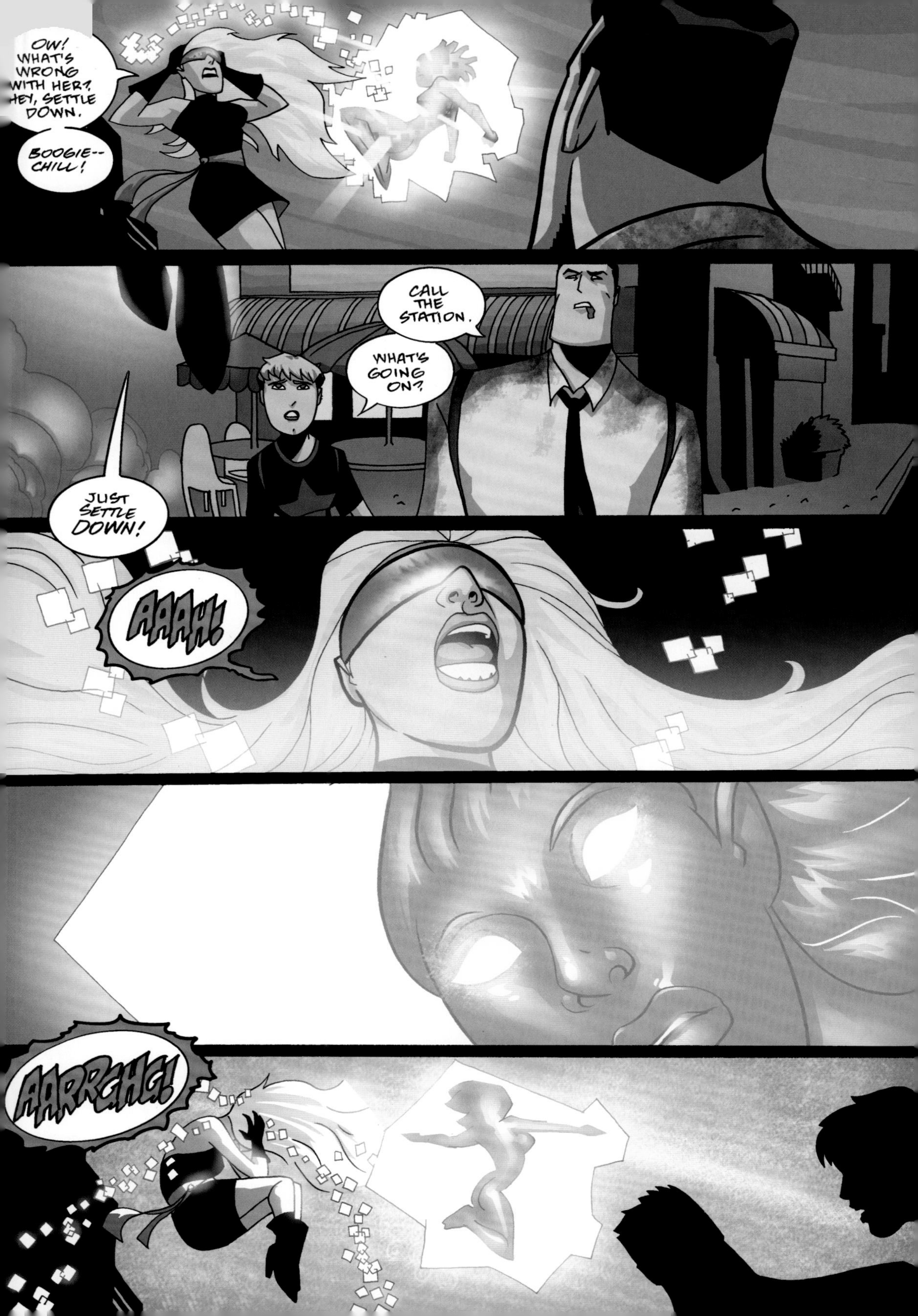
OW! WHAT'S WRONG WITH HER? HEY, SETTLE DOWN.
BOOGIE-- CHILL!
CALL THE STATION.
WHAT'S GOING ON?
JUST SETTLE DOWN!
AAAH!
AARRGHG!

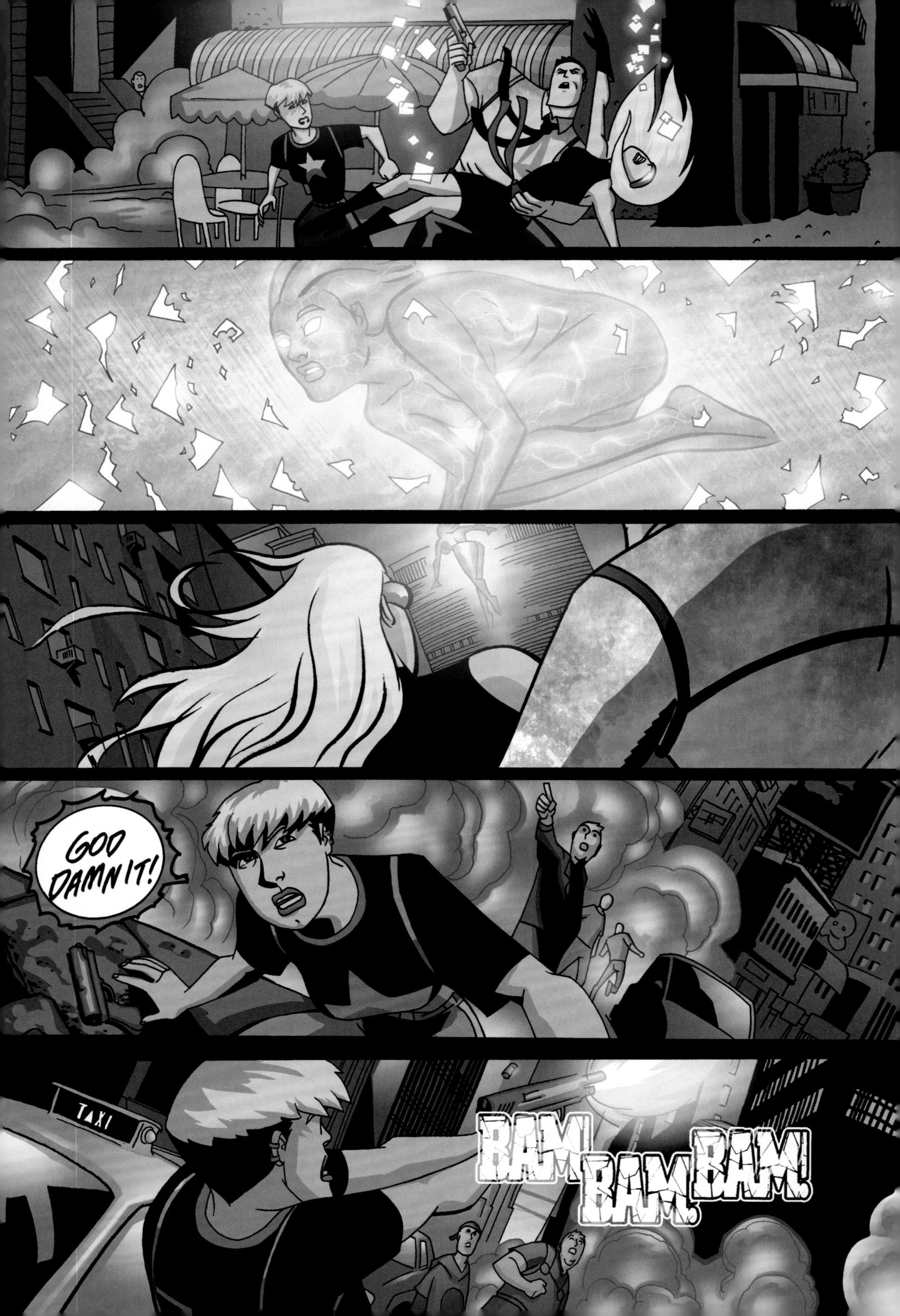
GOD DAMN IT!
TAXI
BAM! BAM! BAM!

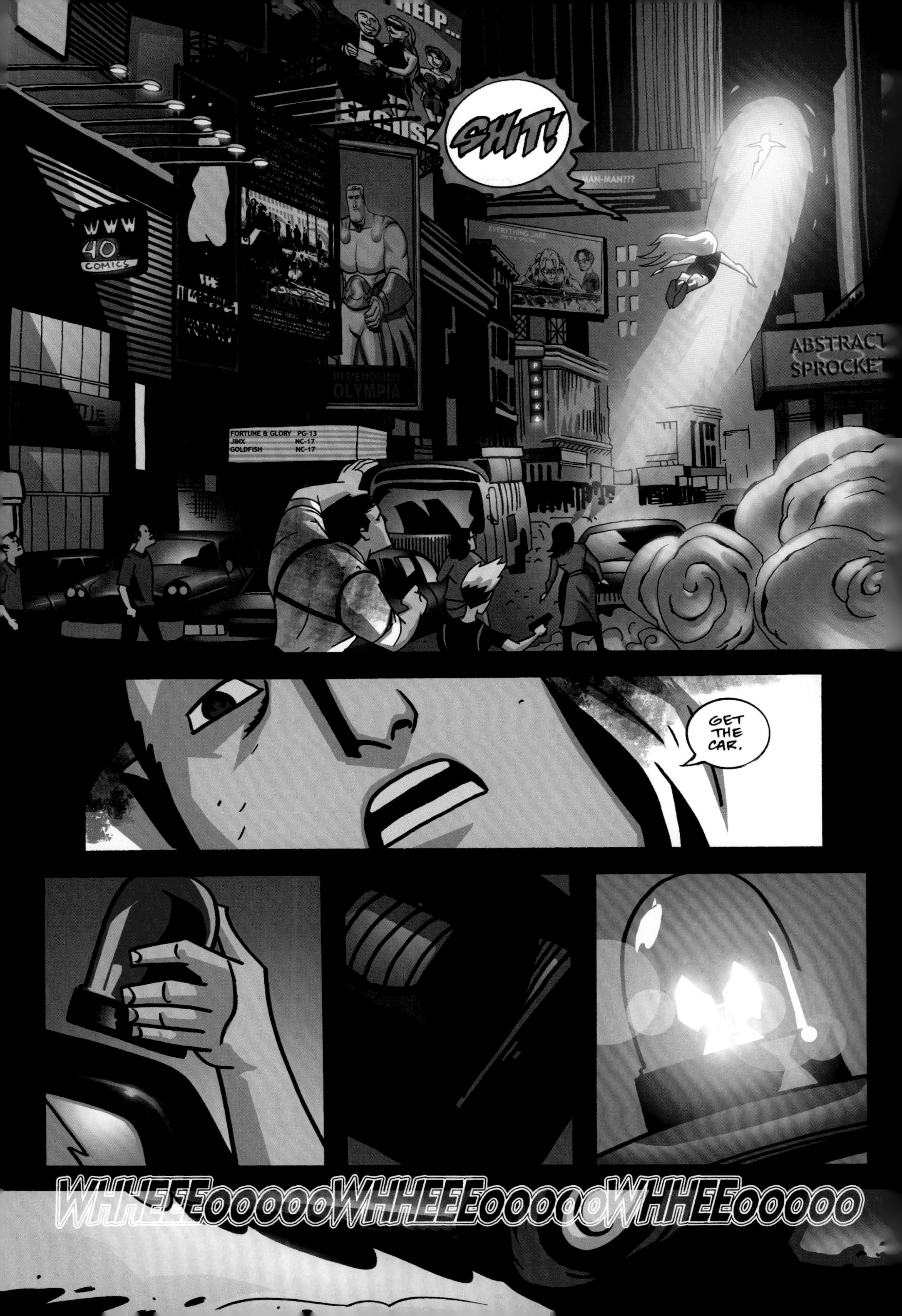
HELP...
WWW 40. COMICS
TORSO
IN MEMORIAM OLYMPIA
FORTUNE & GLORY PG-13
JINX NC-17
GOLDFISH NC-17
EVERYTHING JAKE
PARK
ABSTRACT SPROCKET
SHIT!
MAN-MAN???
GET THE CAR.
WHHEEEooooooWHHEEEooooooWHHEEoooooo

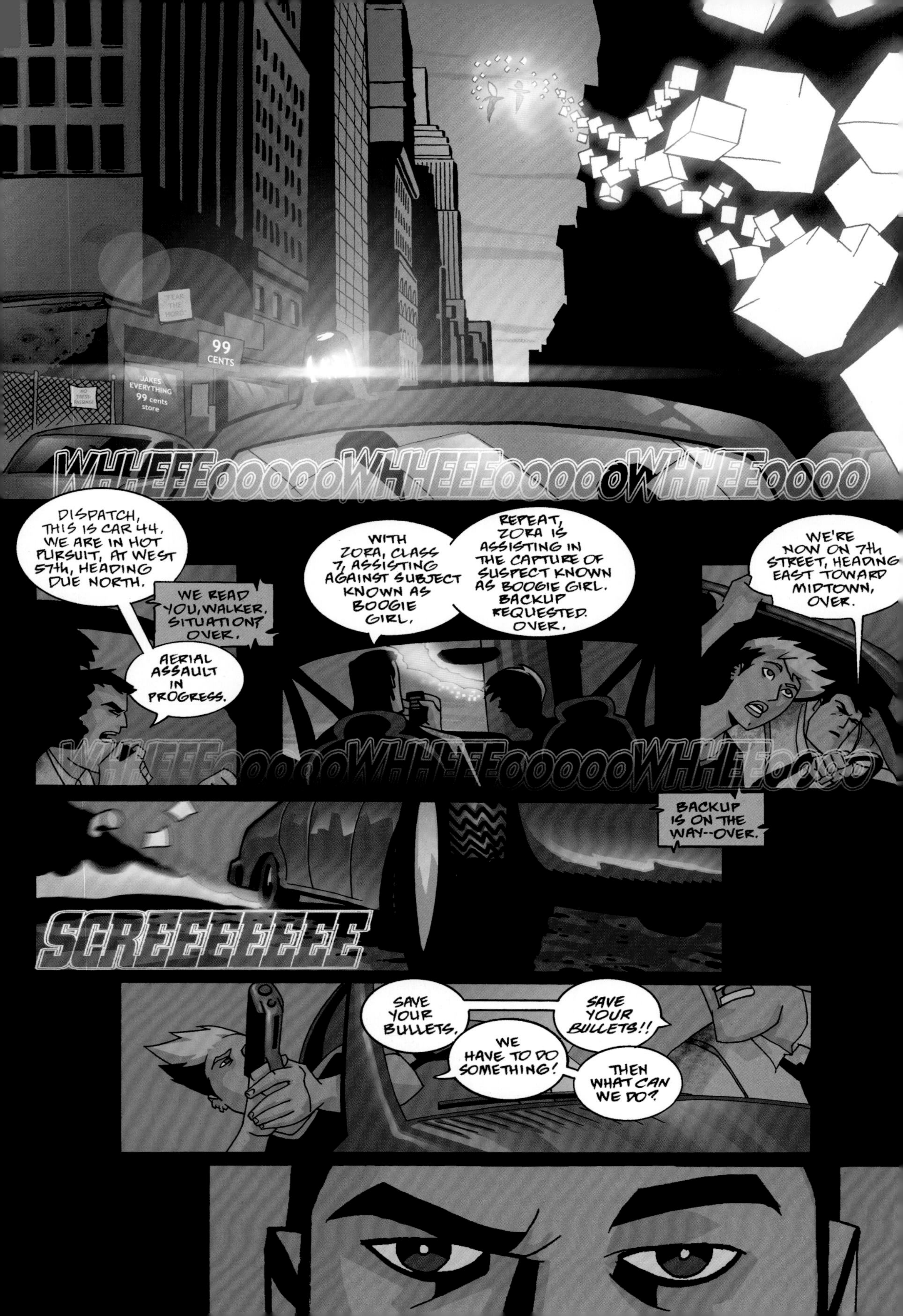
"FEAR THE HORD"
99 CENTS
JAKES EVERYTHING 99 cents store
NO TRESPASSING!
WHHEEEOOOOOOWHHEEEOOOOOOWHHEEOOOO
DISPATCH, THIS IS CAR 44. WE ARE IN HOT PURSUIT, AT WEST 57th, HEADING DUE NORTH.
WE READ YOU, WALKER. SITUATION? OVER.
AERIAL ASSAULT IN PROGRESS.
WITH ZORA, CLASS 7, ASSISTING AGAINST SUBJECT KNOWN AS BOOGIE GIRL.
REPEAT, ZORA IS ASSISTING IN THE CAPTURE OF SUSPECT KNOWN AS BOOGIE GIRL. BACKUP REQUESTED. OVER.
WE'RE NOW ON 7th STREET, HEADING EAST TOWARD MIDTOWN, OVER.
WHHEEEOOOOOOWHHEEOOOOOOWHHEEOOOO
BACKUP IS ON THE WAY--OVER.
SCREEEEEEEE
SAVE YOUR BULLETS.
SAVE YOUR BULLETS!!
WE HAVE TO DO SOMETHING!
THEN WHAT CAN WE DO?

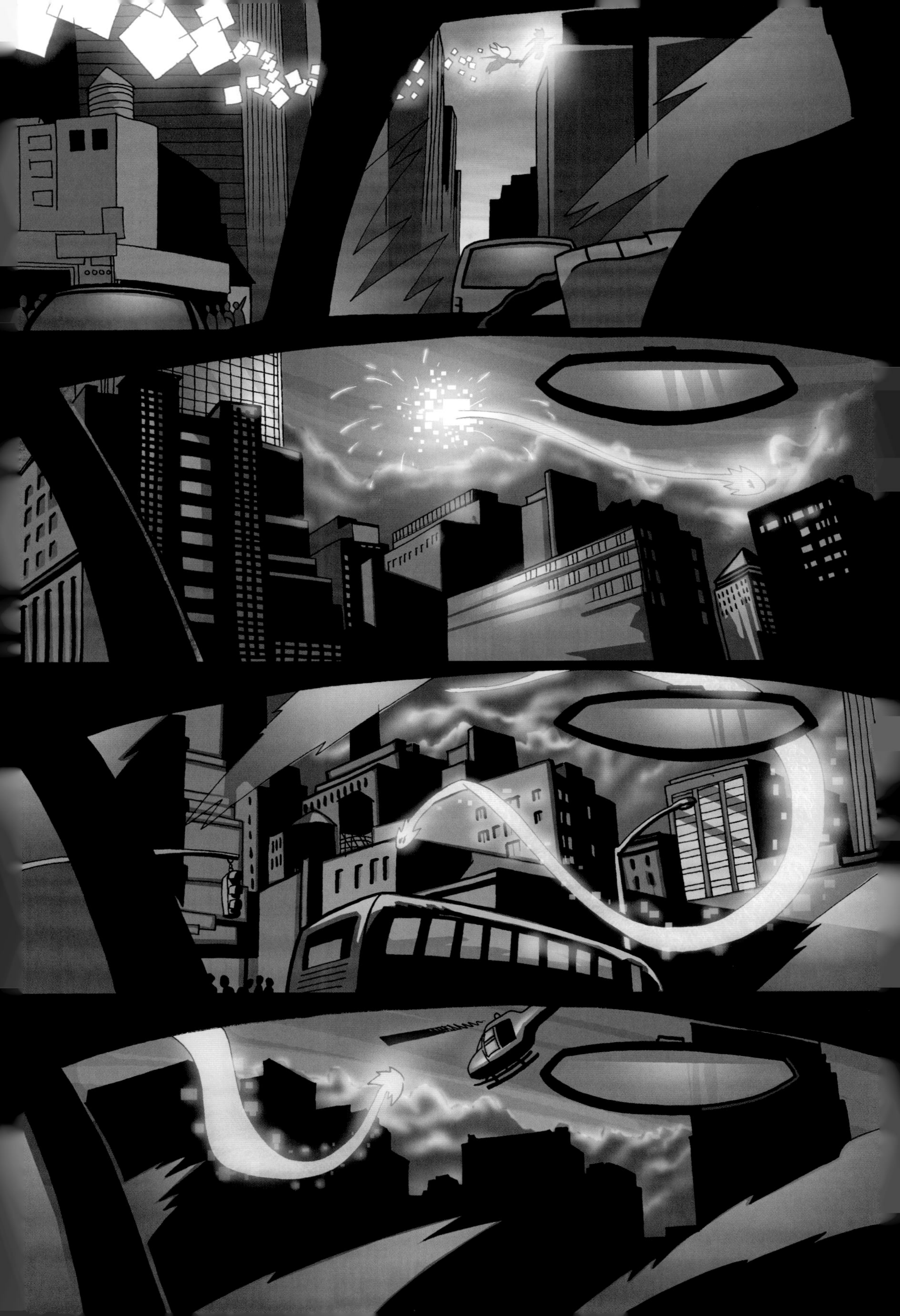

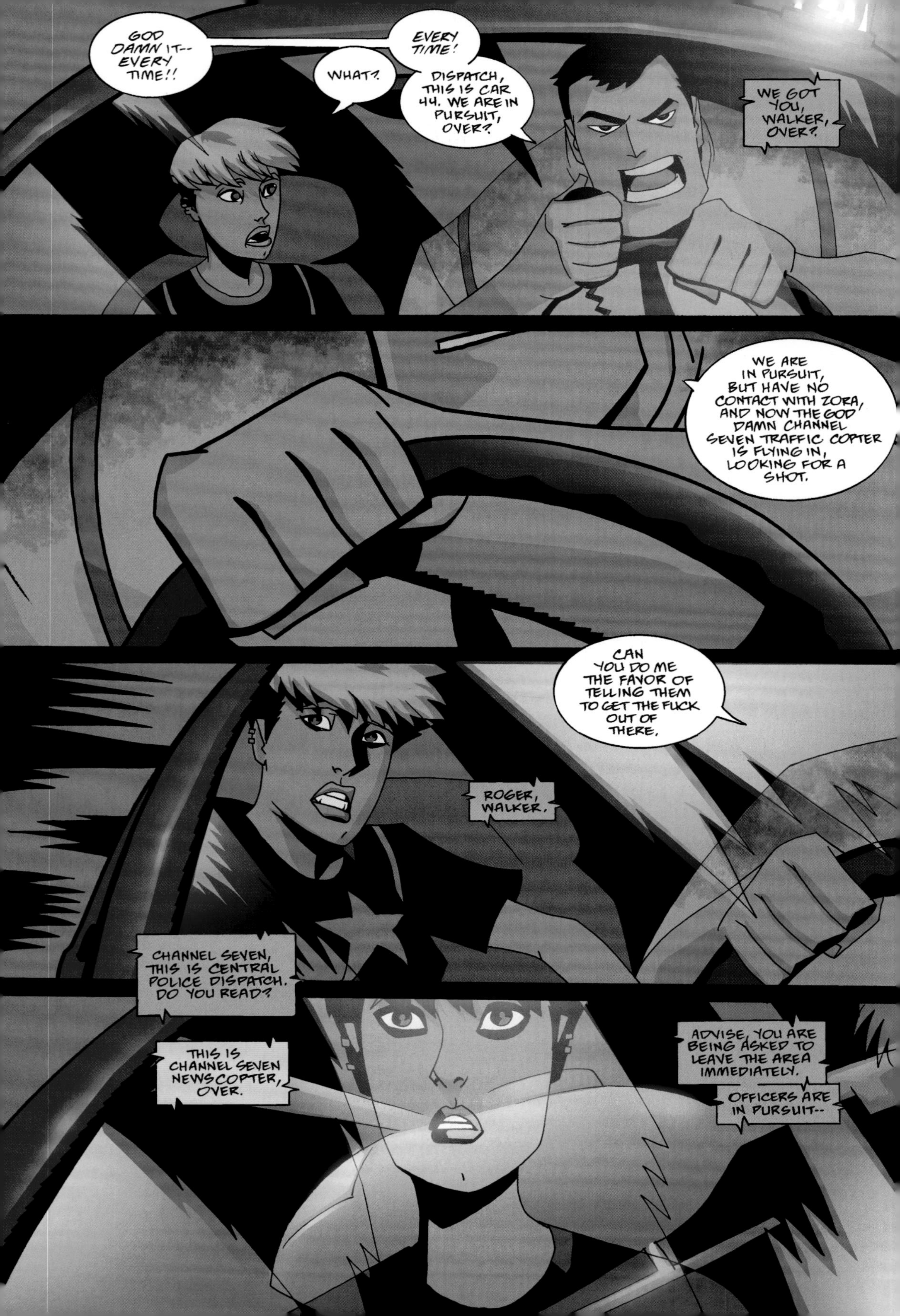
GOD DAMN IT-- EVERY TIME!!
EVERY TIME!
WHAT?
DISPATCH, THIS IS CAR 44. WE ARE IN PURSUIT, OVER?
WE GOT YOU, WALKER, OVER?
WE ARE IN PURSUIT, BUT HAVE NO CONTACT WITH ZORA, AND NOW THE GOD DAMN CHANNEL SEVEN TRAFFIC COPTER IS FLYING IN, LOOKING FOR A SHOT.
CAN YOU DO ME THE FAVOR OF TELLING THEM TO GET THE FUCK OUT OF THERE.
ROGER, WALKER.
CHANNEL SEVEN, THIS IS CENTRAL POLICE DISPATCH. DO YOU READ?
THIS IS CHANNEL SEVEN NEWSCOPTER, OVER.
ADVISE, YOU ARE BEING ASKED TO LEAVE THE AREA IMMEDIATELY.
OFFICERS ARE IN PURSUIT--

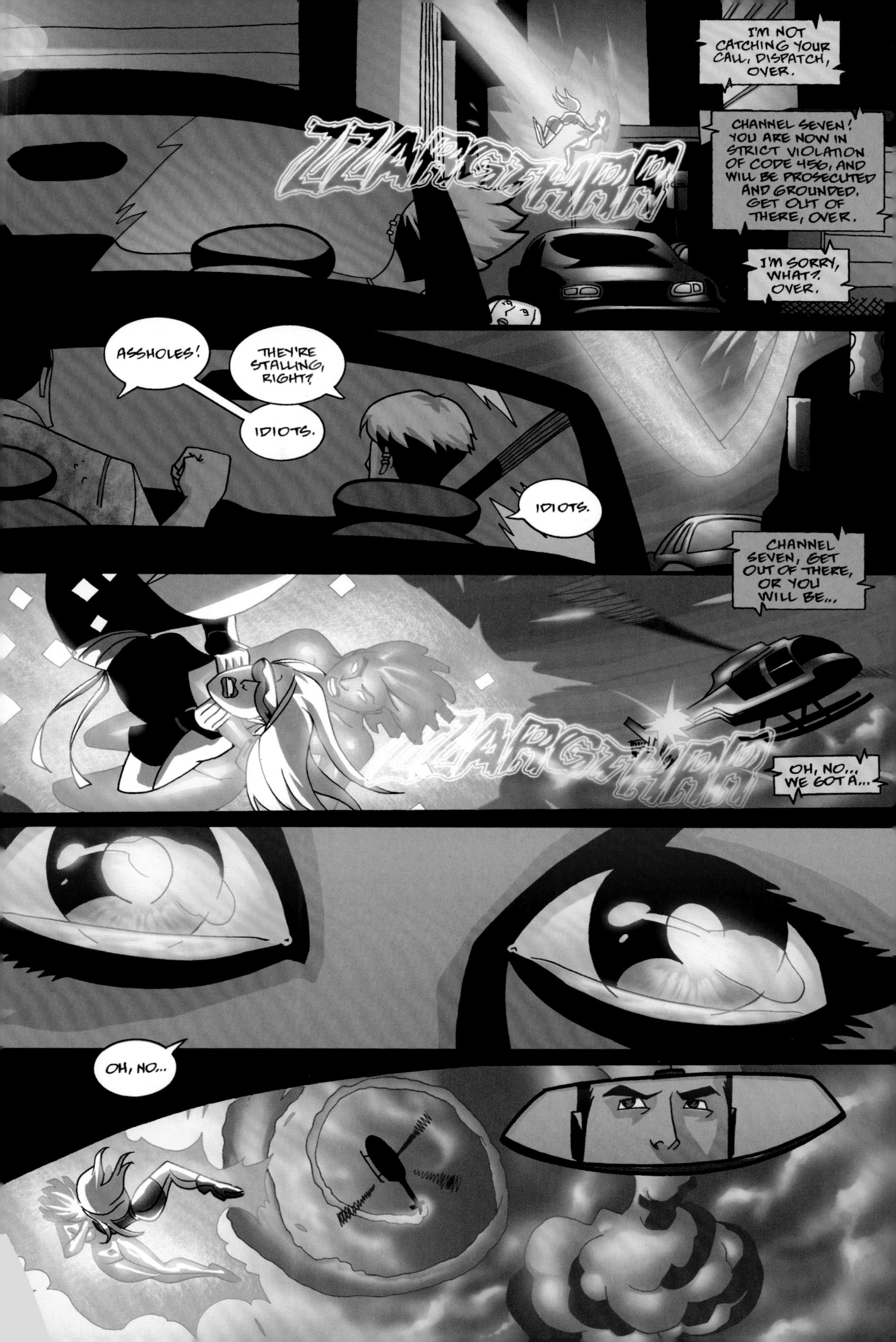
I'M NOT CATCHING YOUR CALL, DISPATCH, OVER.
ZZARGHRR
CHANNEL SEVEN! YOU ARE NOW IN STRICT VIOLATION OF CODE 456, AND WILL BE PROSECUTED AND GROUNDED. GET OUT OF THERE, OVER.
I'M SORRY, WHAT? OVER.
ASSHOLES!
THEY'RE STALLING, RIGHT?
IDIOTS.
IDIOTS.
CHANNEL SEVEN, GET OUT OF THERE, OR YOU WILL BE...
ZZARGHRR
OH, NO... WE GOT A...
OH, NO...

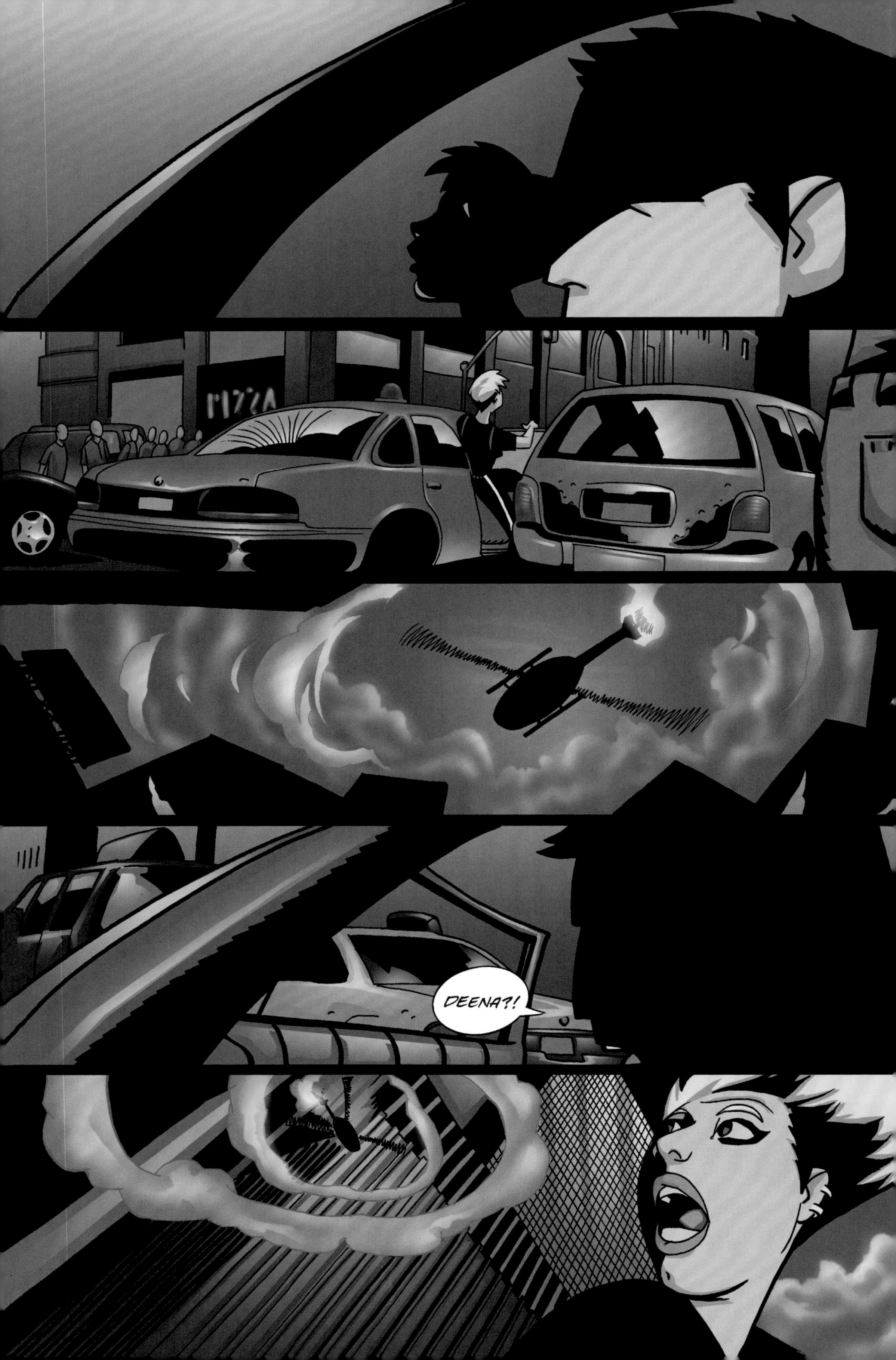
PIZZA
DEENA?!

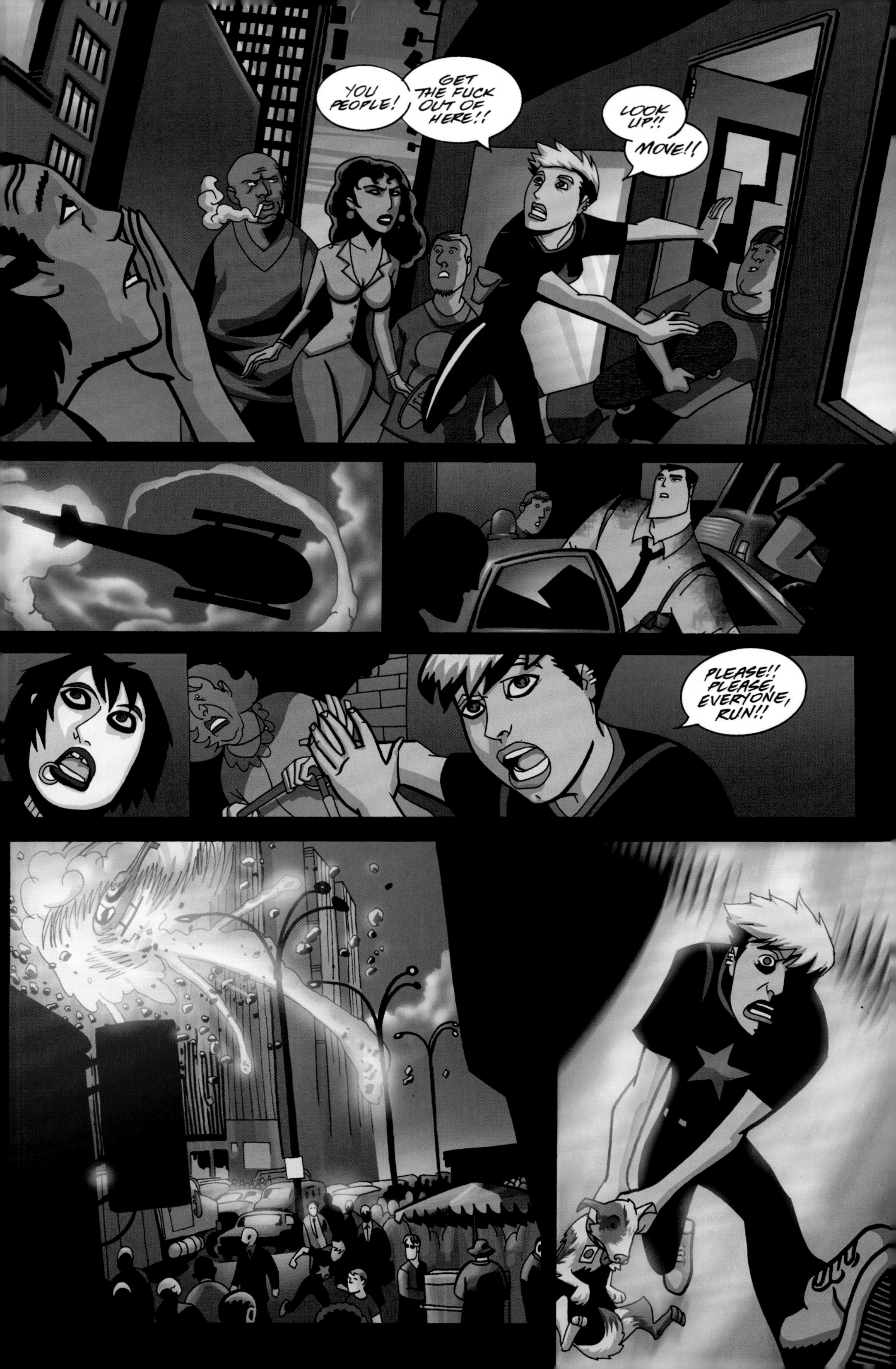
YOU PEOPLE!
GET THE FUCK OUT OF HERE!!
LOOK UP!!
MOVE!!
PLEASE!! PLEASE, EVERYONE, RUN!!

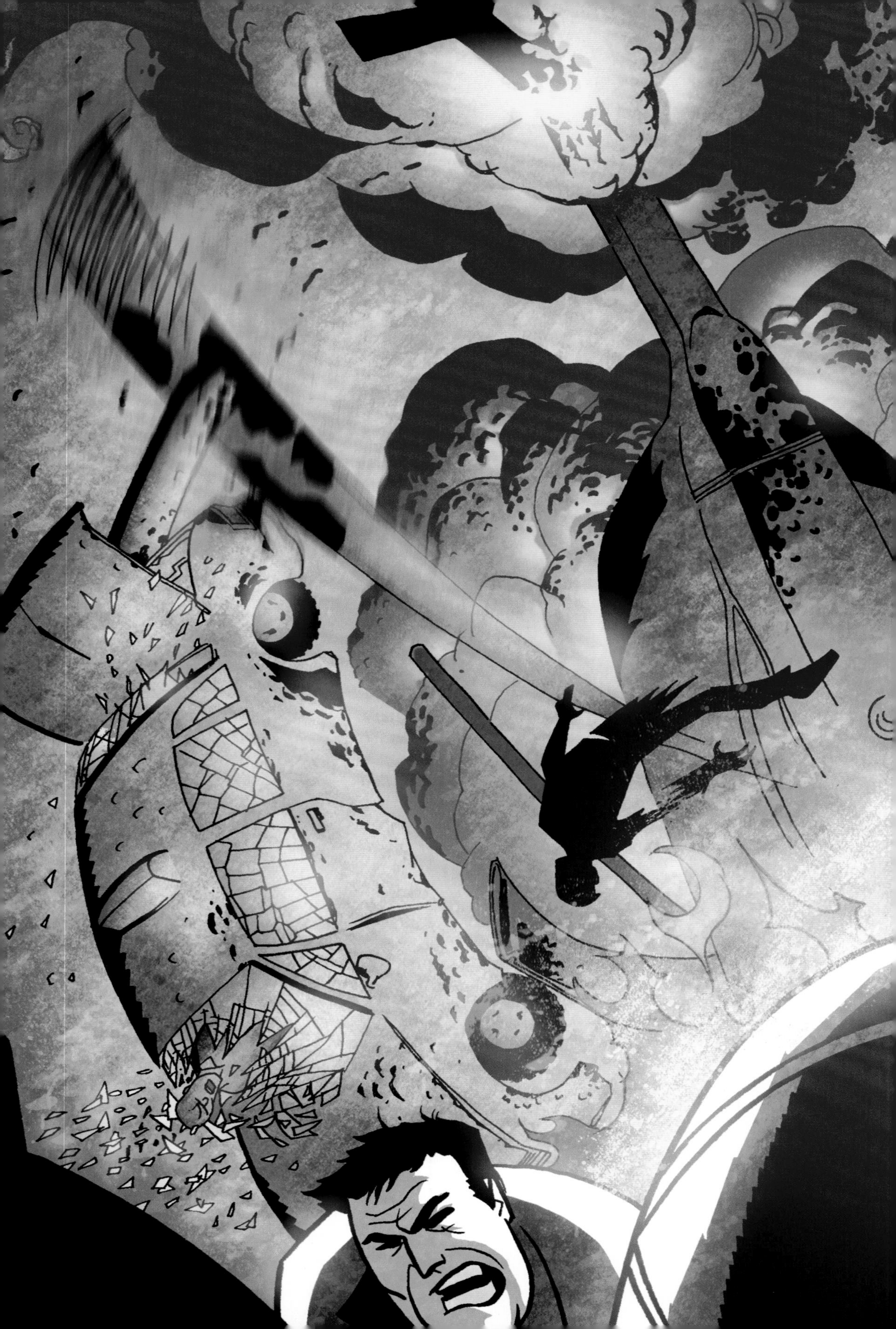

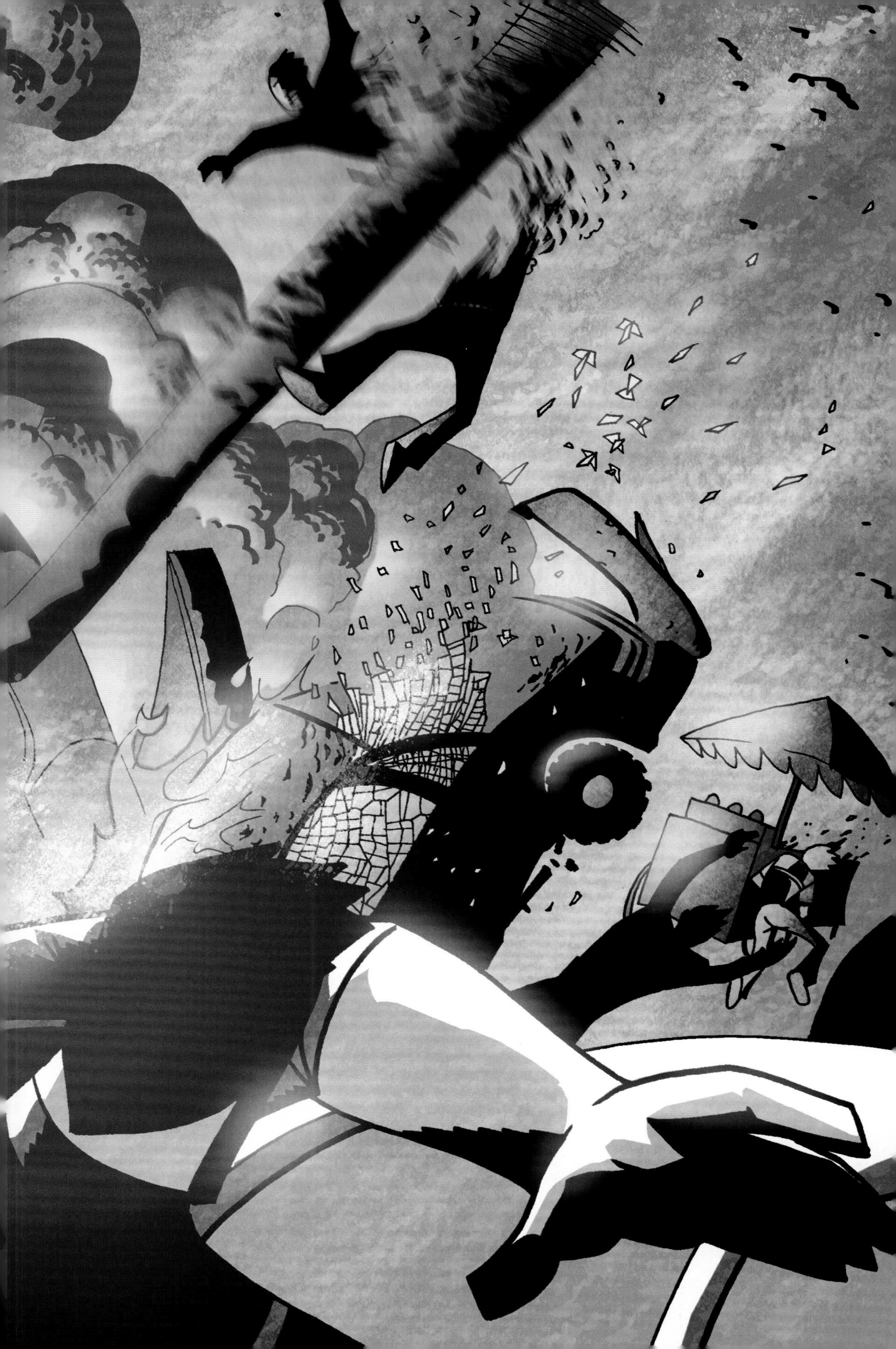

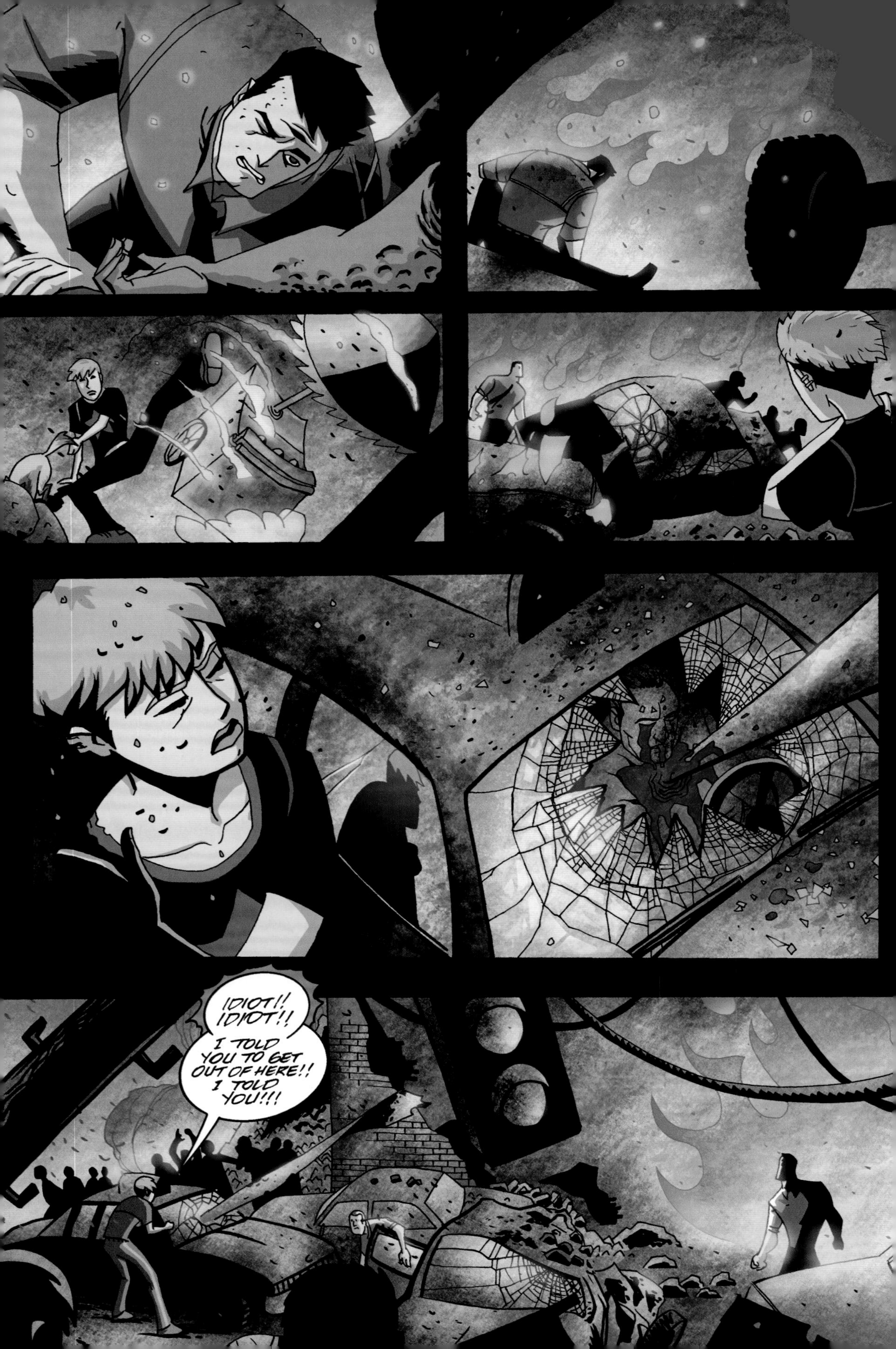
IDIOT!! IDIOT!!
I TOLD YOU TO GET OUT OF HERE!! I TOLD YOU!!!

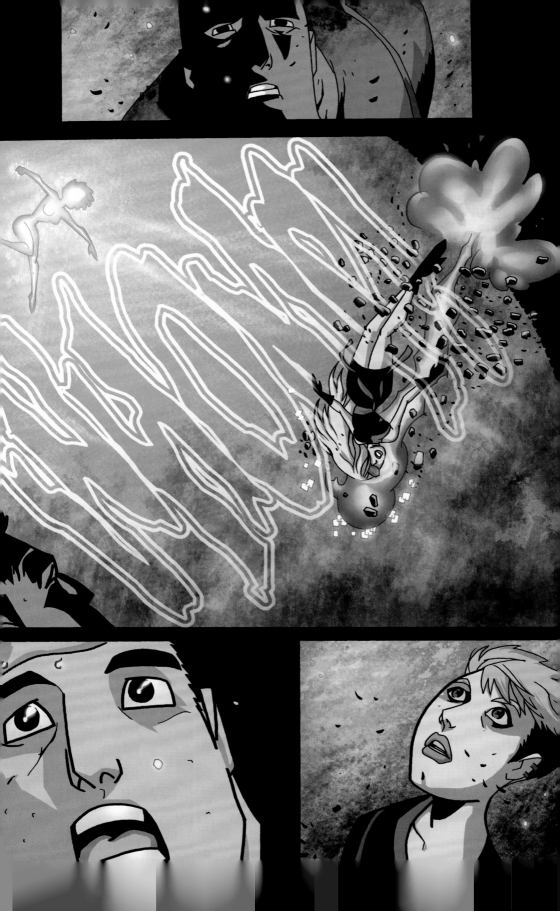

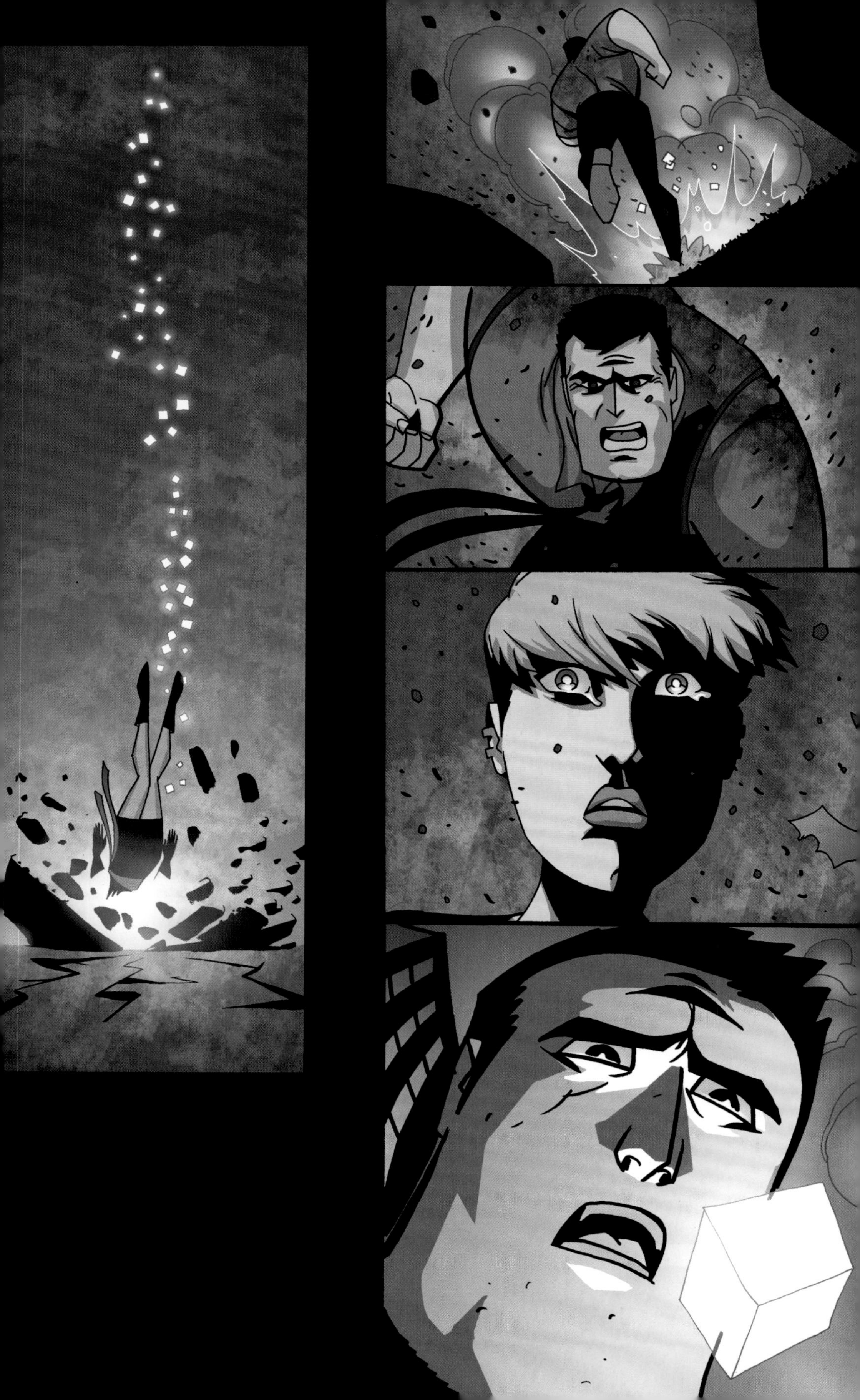

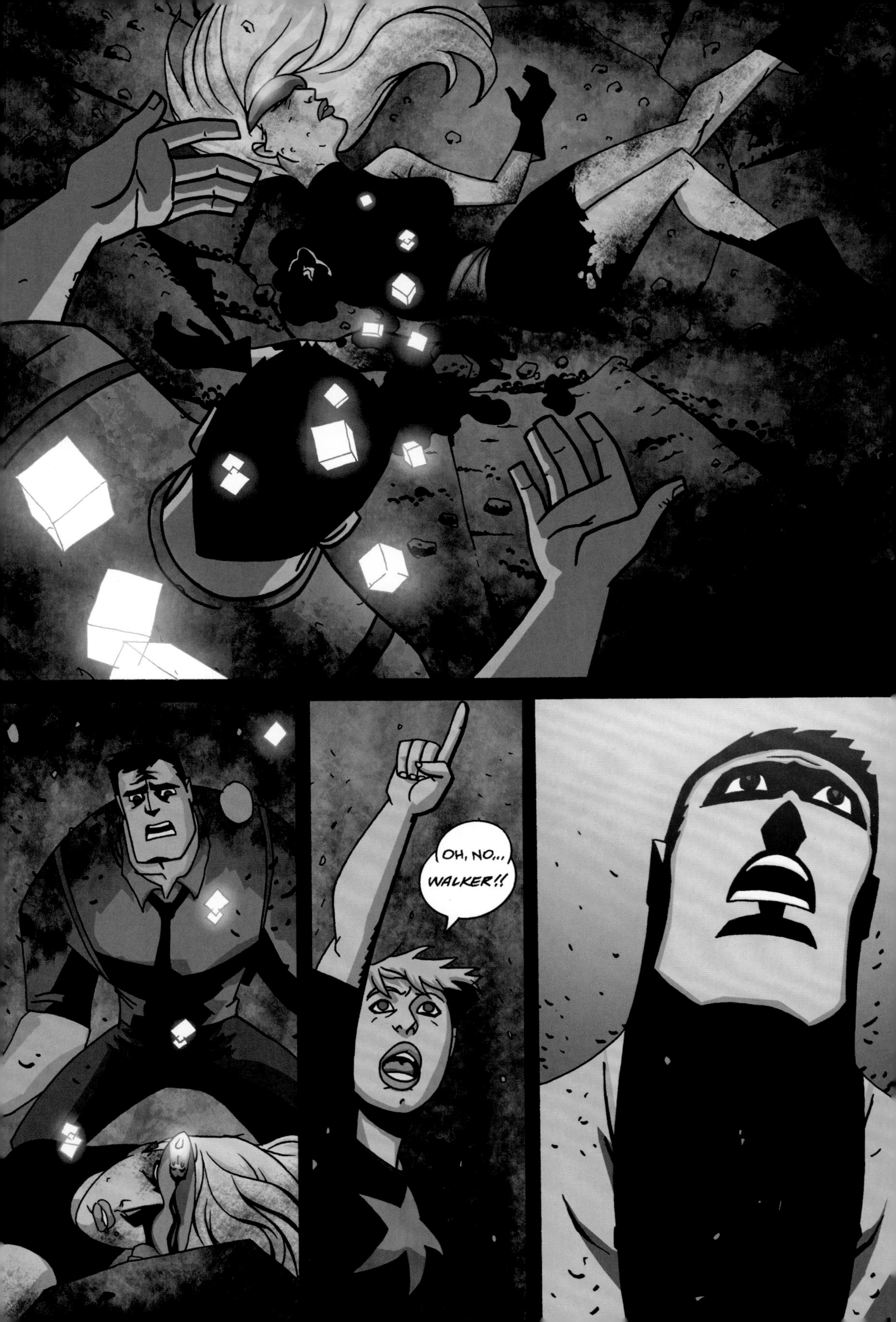
OH, NO... WALKER!!

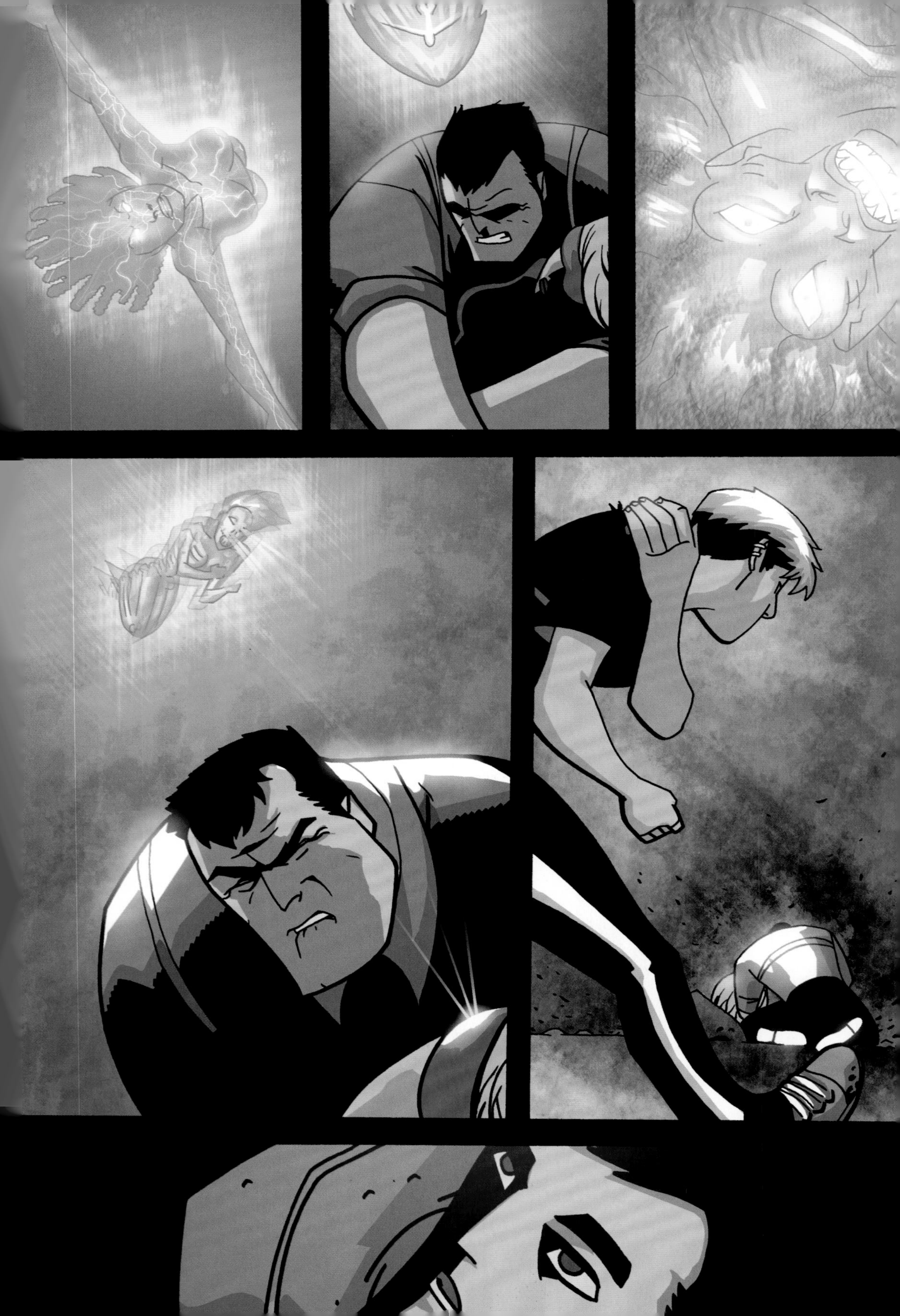

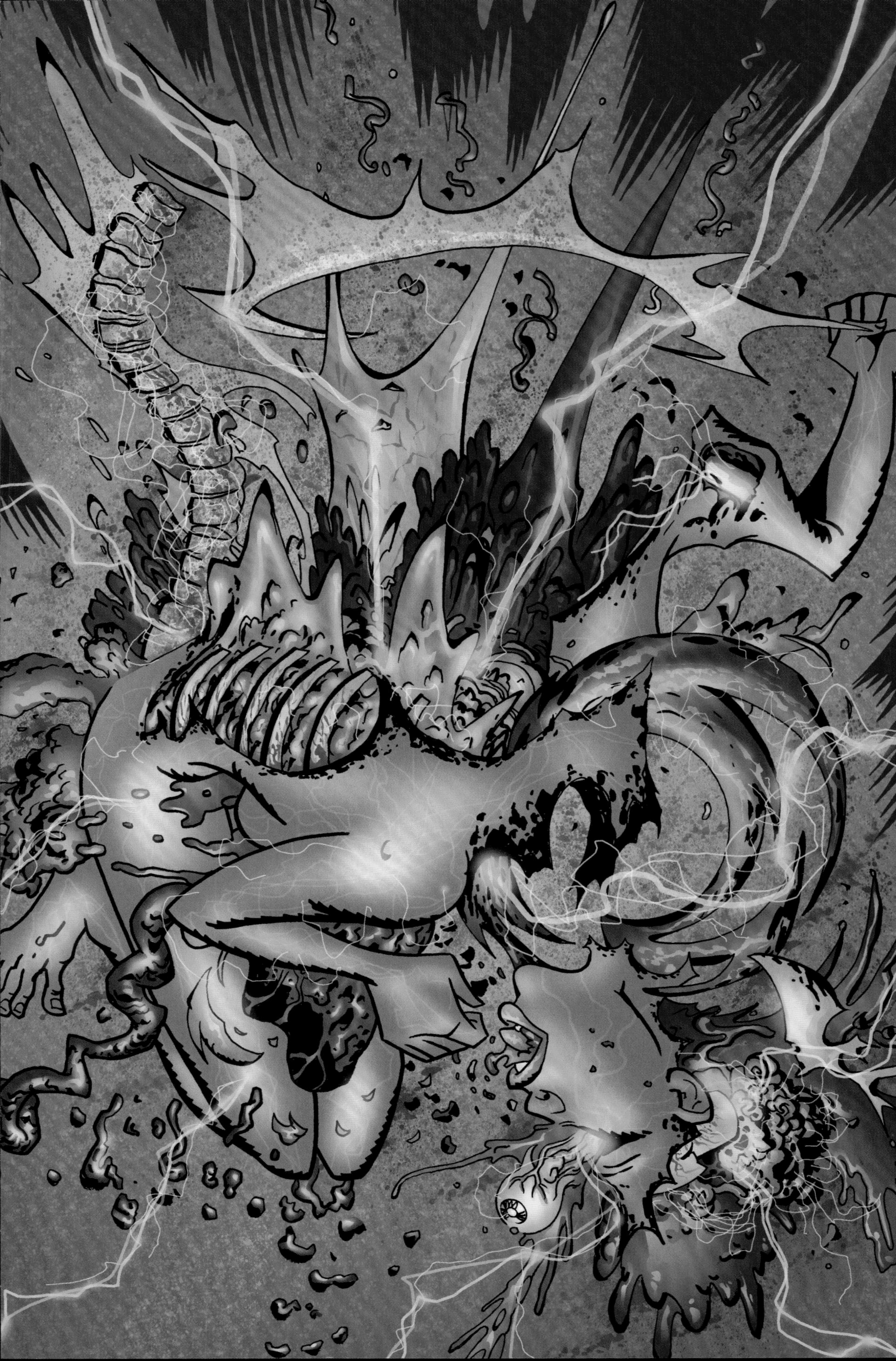

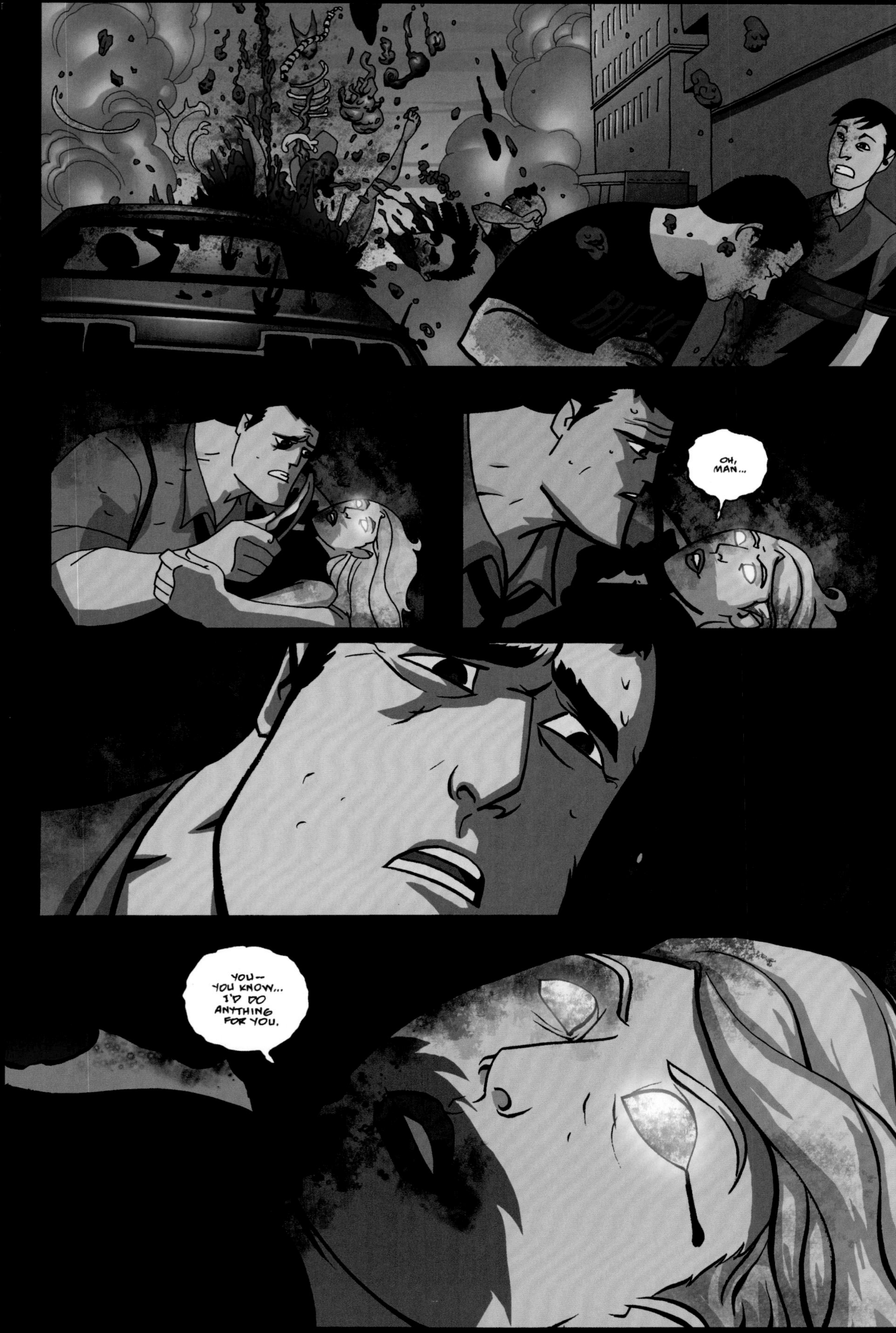
OH, MAN...
YOU-- YOU KNOW... I'D DO ANYTHING FOR YOU.

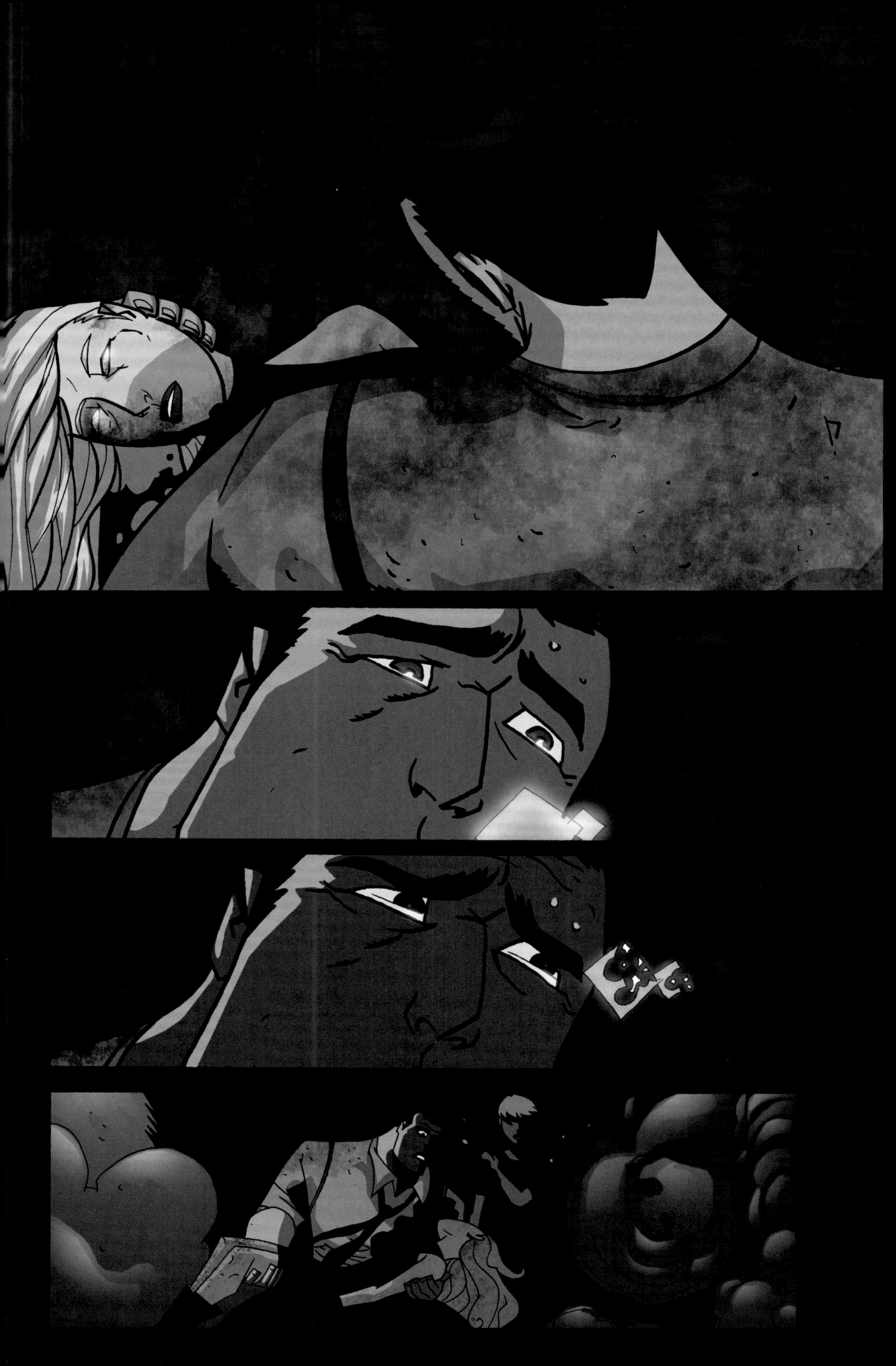

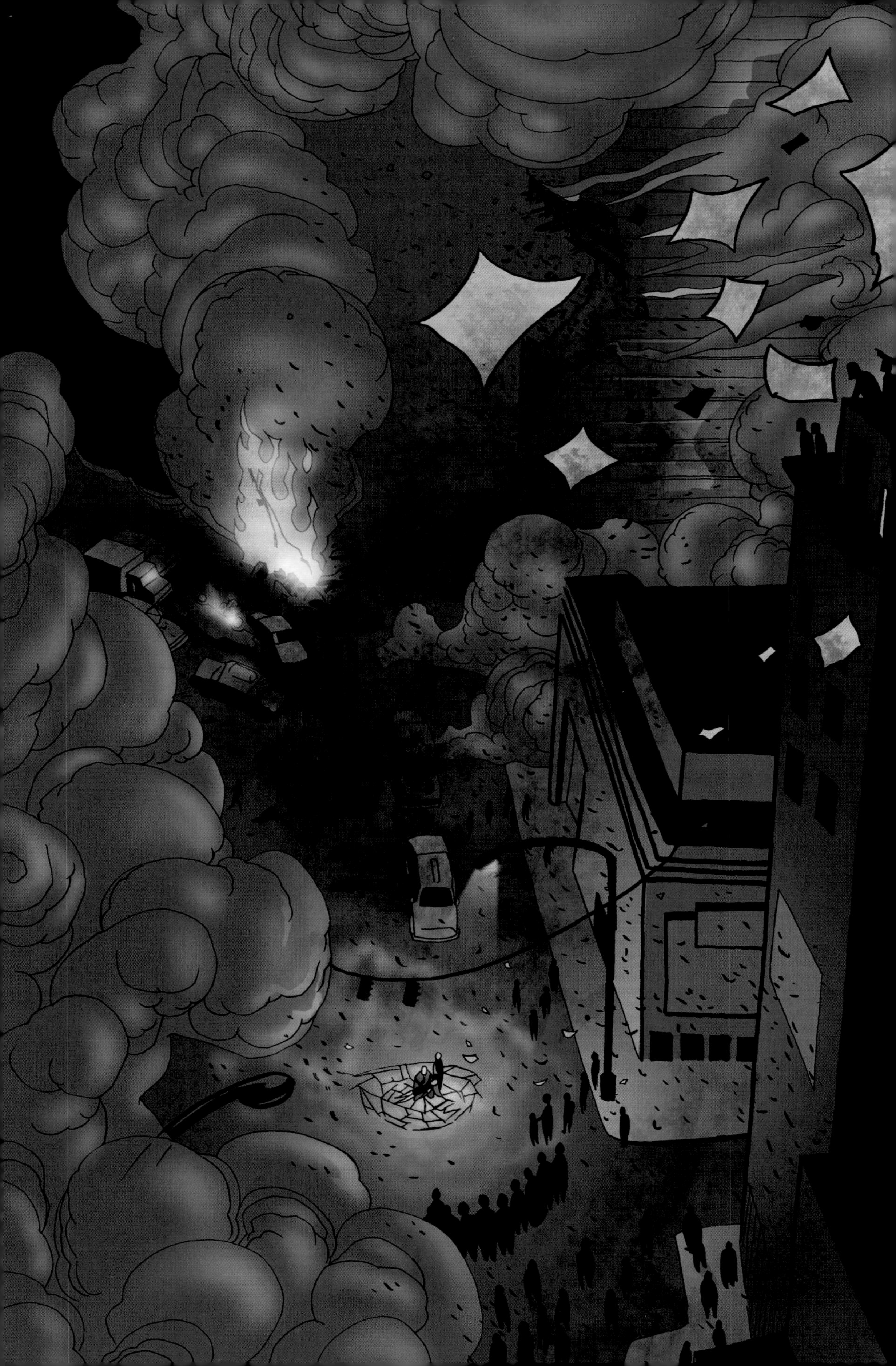

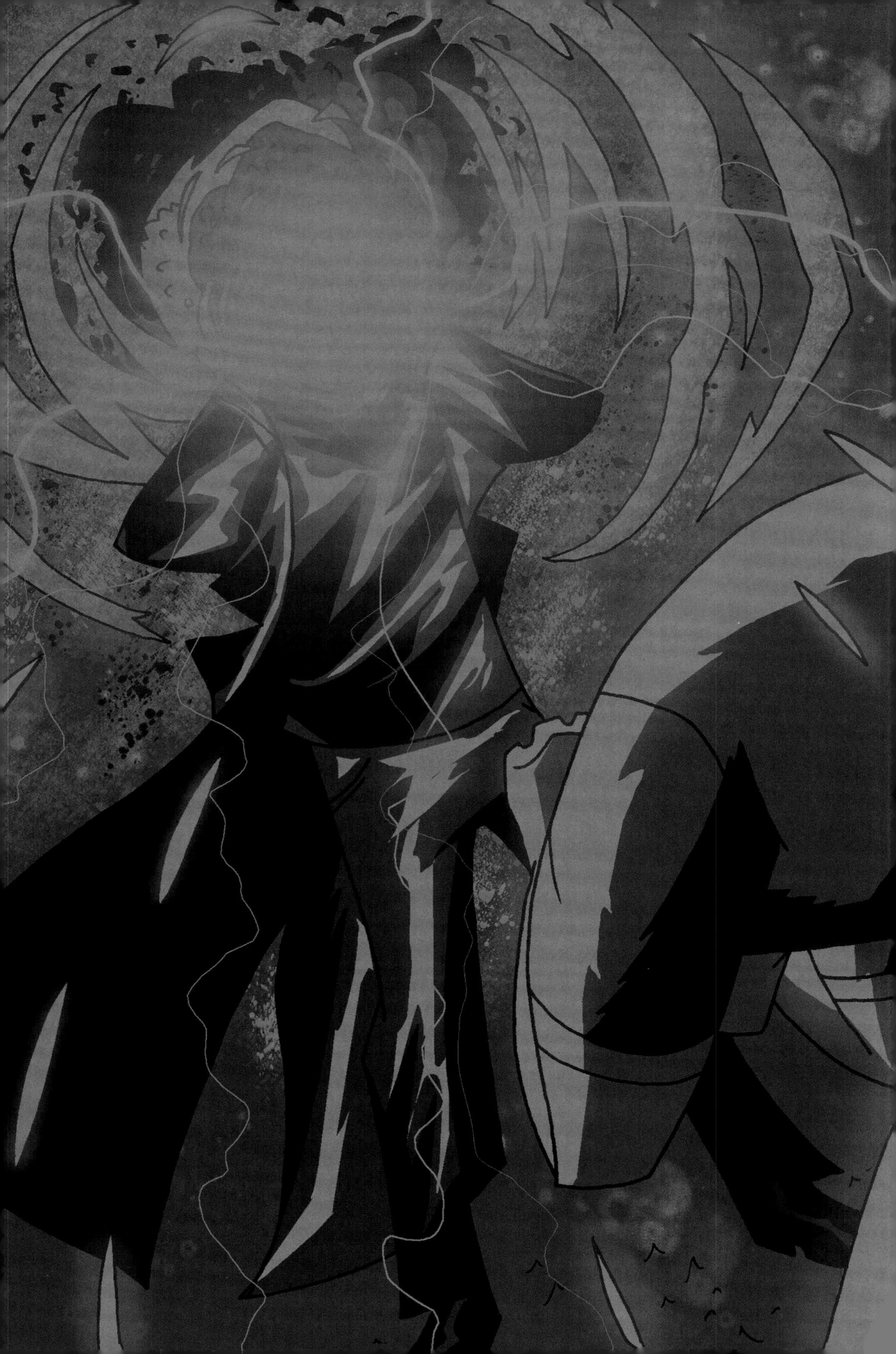

POWERS

™

SUPERGROUP
CHAPTER 5

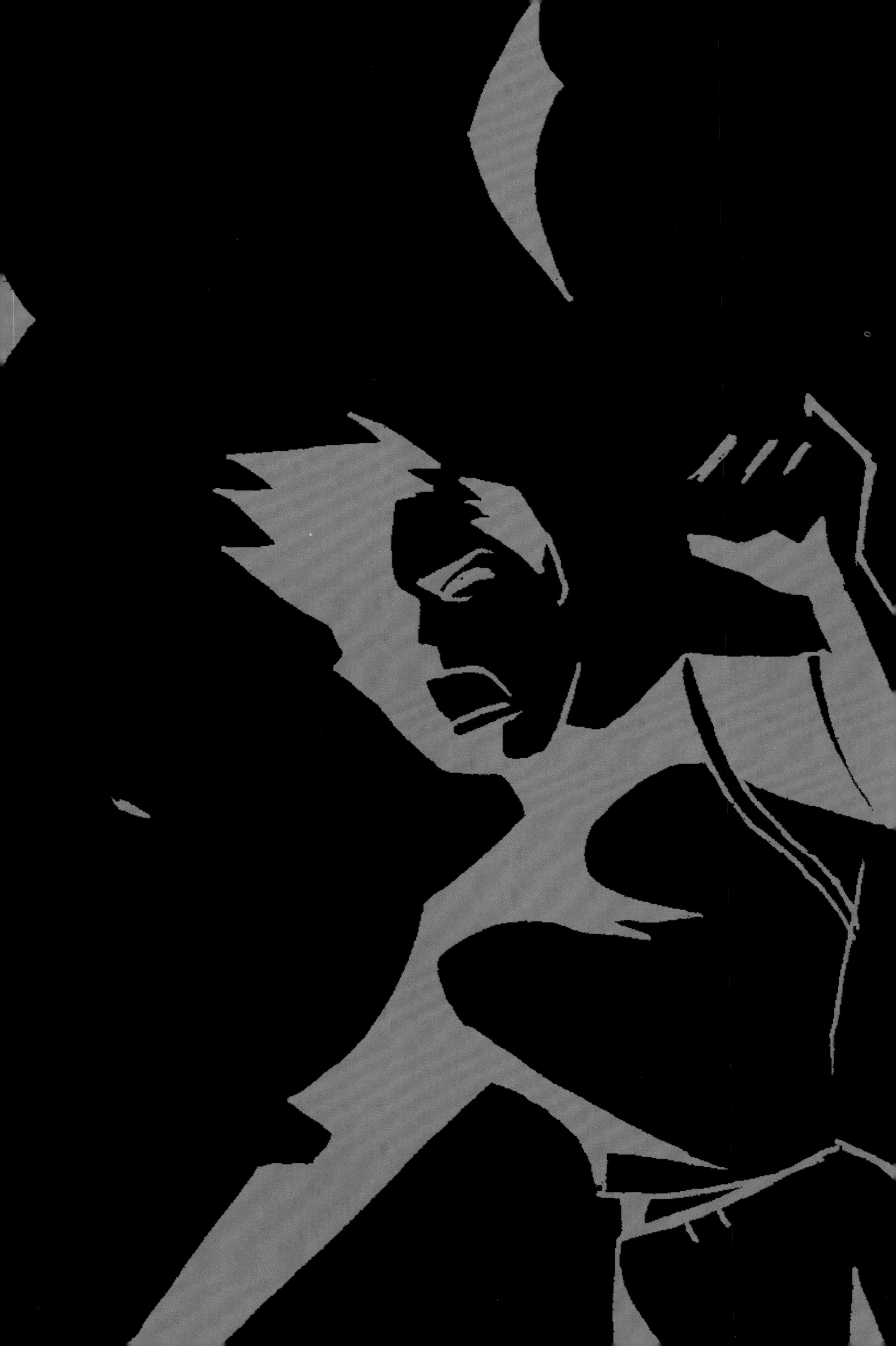

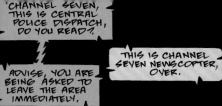

CHANNEL SEVEN, THIS IS CENTRAL POLICE DISPATCH, DO YOU READ?
ADVISE, YOU ARE BEING ASKED TO LEAVE THE AREA IMMEDIATELY.
OFFICERS ARE IN PURSUIT.
THIS IS CHANNEL SEVEN NEWSCOPTER, OVER.
WHO IS THAT?
IT'S THE POLICE CALLING US OUT OF HERE.
OH, FUCK THEM.
I GOTTA LISTEN TO THEM.
NO, NO. THIS IS KILLER FOOTAGE. JUST STALL THEIR STUPID--
HBC NEWS 69
HBC NEWS 69
UH-- I'M NOT CATCHING YOUR CALL, DISPATCH. OVER.
CHANNEL SEVEN! YOU ARE NOW IN STRICT VIOLATION OF CODE 456 AND WILL BE PROSECUTED AND GROUNDED! GET OUT OF THERE!! OVER.
OH, MY GOD!!
HBC NEWS 69
GY'AAHHH!
HBC NEWS 69

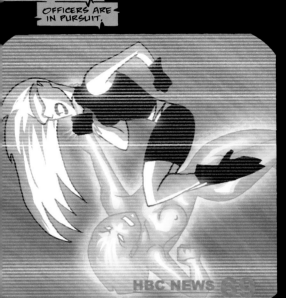

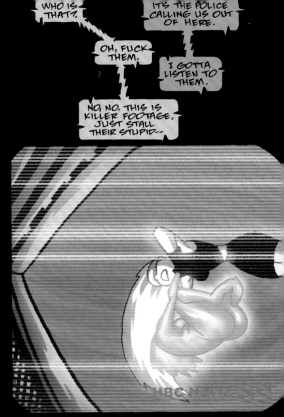

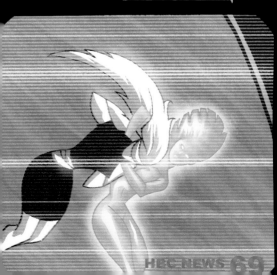

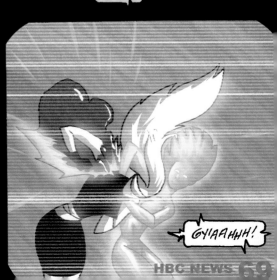

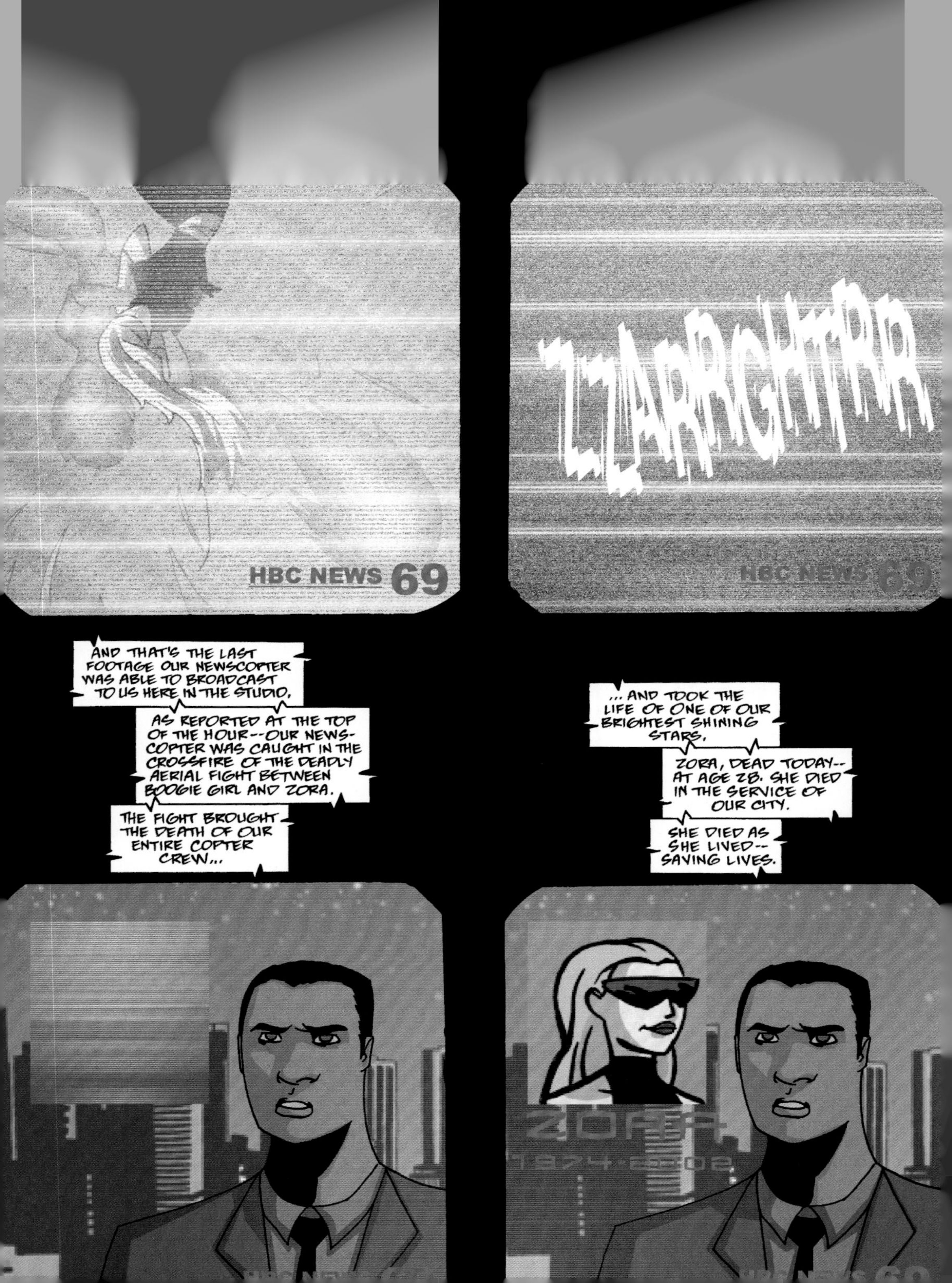
HBC NEWS 69
ZZARRGHTRR
HBC NEWS 69
AND THAT'S THE LAST FOOTAGE OUR NEWSCOPTER WAS ABLE TO BROADCAST TO US HERE IN THE STUDIO.
AS REPORTED AT THE TOP OF THE HOUR--OUR NEWS-COPTER WAS CAUGHT IN THE CROSSFIRE OF THE DEADLY AERIAL FIGHT BETWEEN BOOGIE GIRL AND ZORA.
THE FIGHT BROUGHT THE DEATH OF OUR ENTIRE COPTER CREW...
...AND TOOK THE LIFE OF ONE OF OUR BRIGHTEST SHINING STARS.
ZORA, DEAD TODAY--AT AGE 28. SHE DIED IN THE SERVICE OF OUR CITY.
SHE DIED AS SHE LIVED--SAVING LIVES.
ZORA
1974-2002

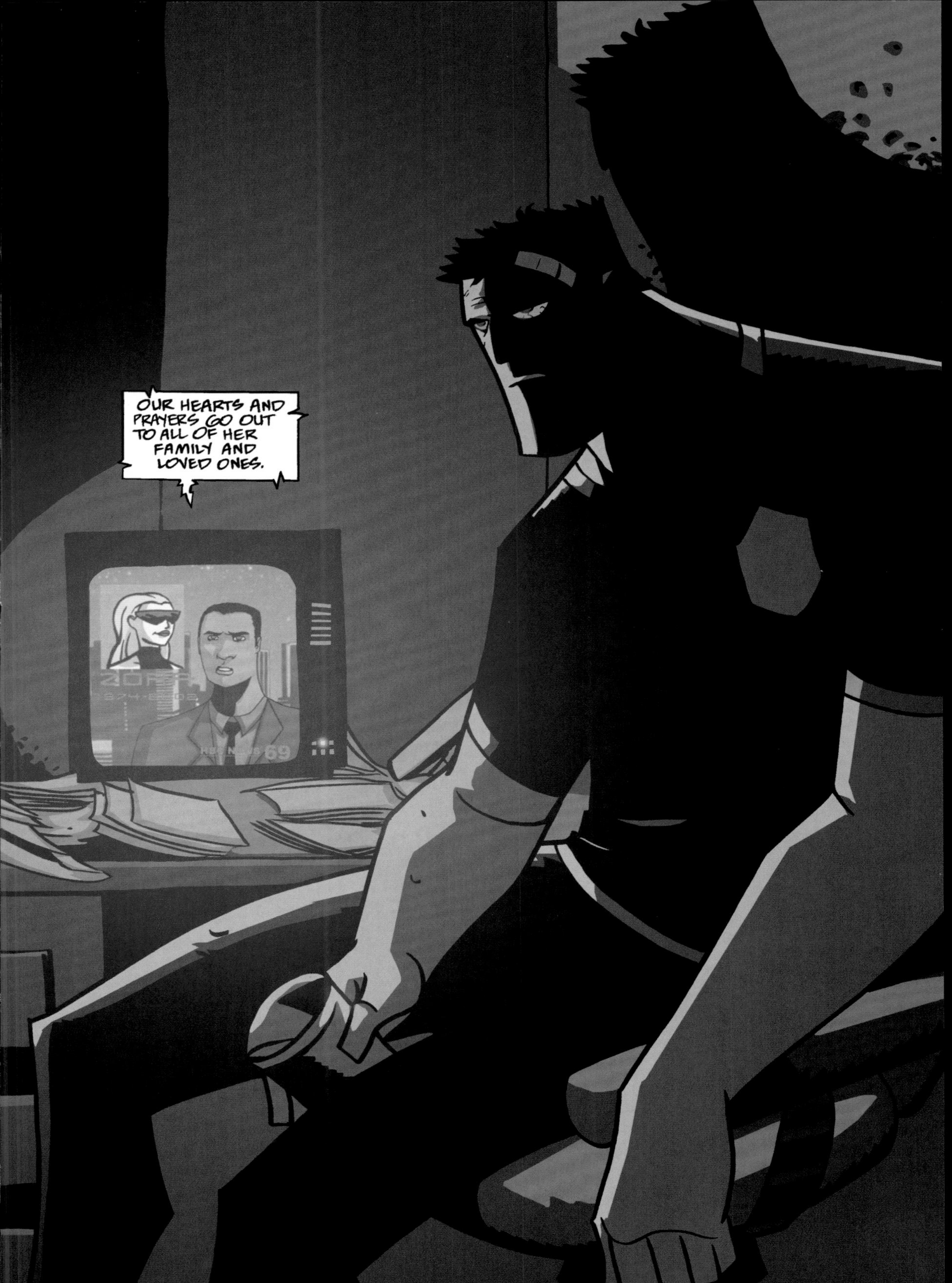
OUR HEARTS AND PRAYERS GO OUT TO ALL OF HER FAMILY AND LOVED ONES.

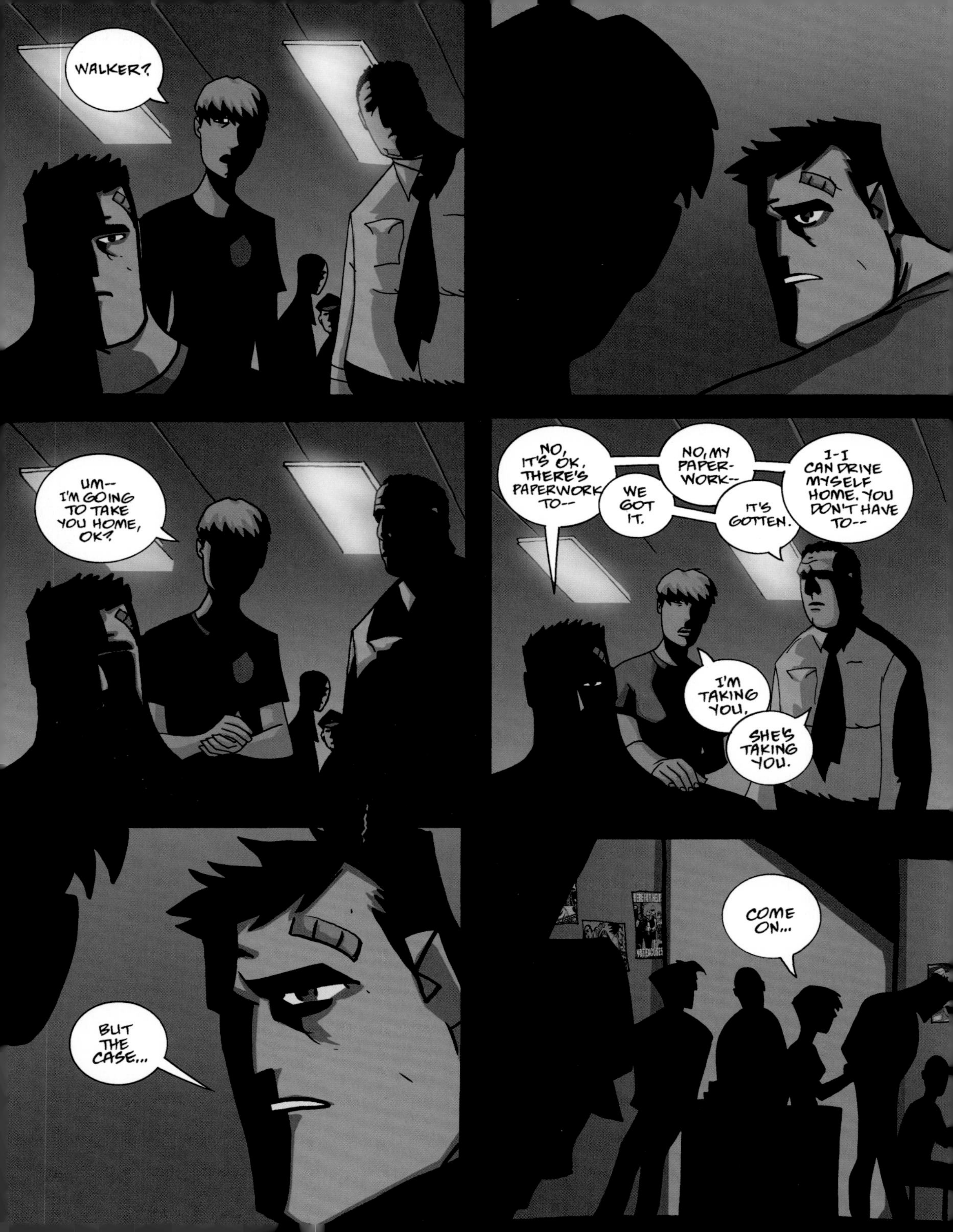
WALKER?
UM-- I'M GOING TO TAKE YOU HOME, OK?
NO, IT'S OK, THERE'S PAPERWORK TO--
WE GOT IT.
NO, MY PAPER-WORK--
IT'S GOTTEN.
I-I CAN DRIVE MYSELF HOME. YOU DON'T HAVE TO--
I'M TAKING YOU.
SHE'S TAKING YOU.
BUT THE CASE...
COME ON...

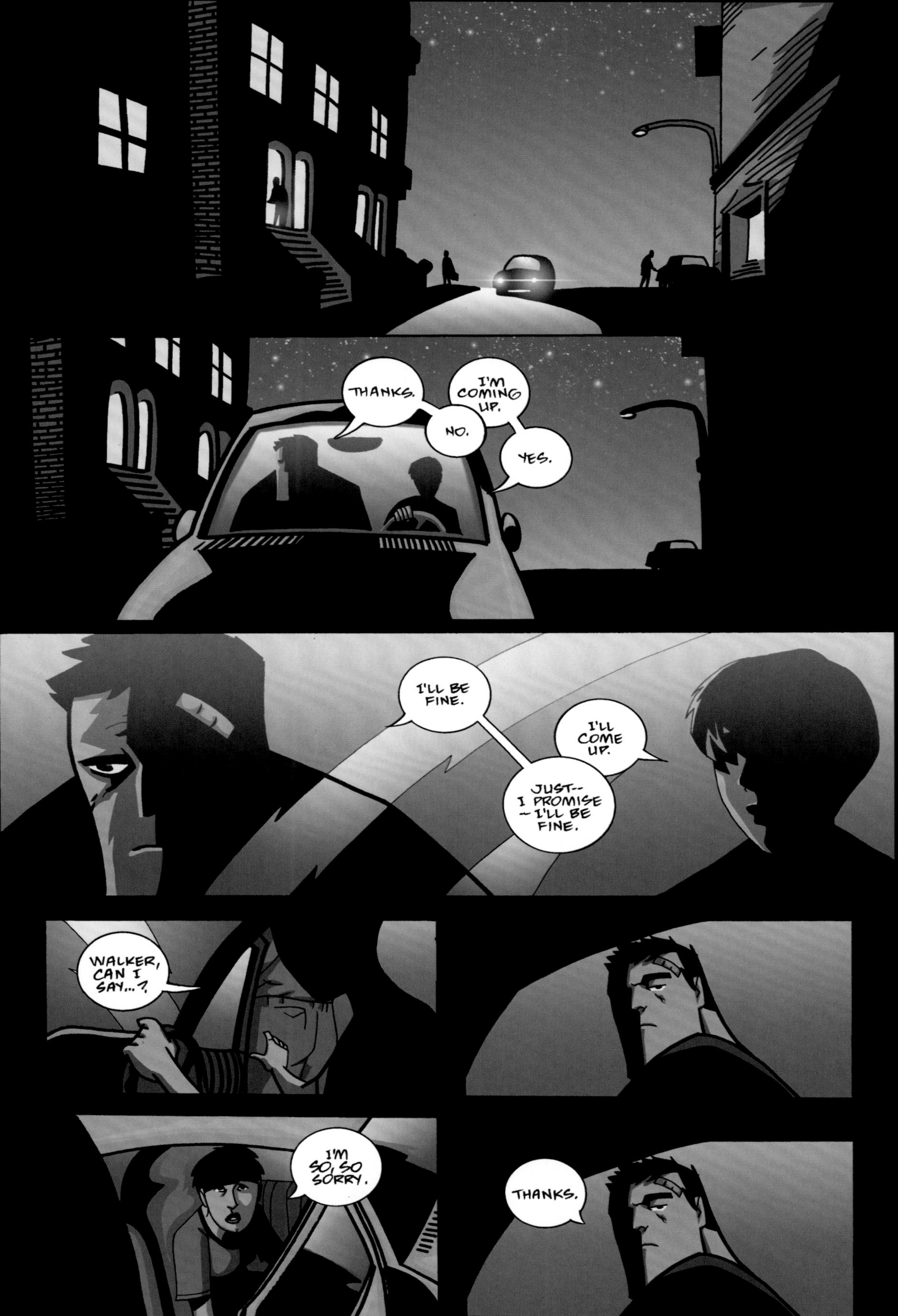
THANKS.
I'M COMING UP.
NO.
YES.
I'LL BE FINE.
I'LL COME UP.
JUST-- I PROMISE ~ I'LL BE FINE.
WALKER, CAN I SAY...?
I'M SO, SO SORRY.
THANKS.

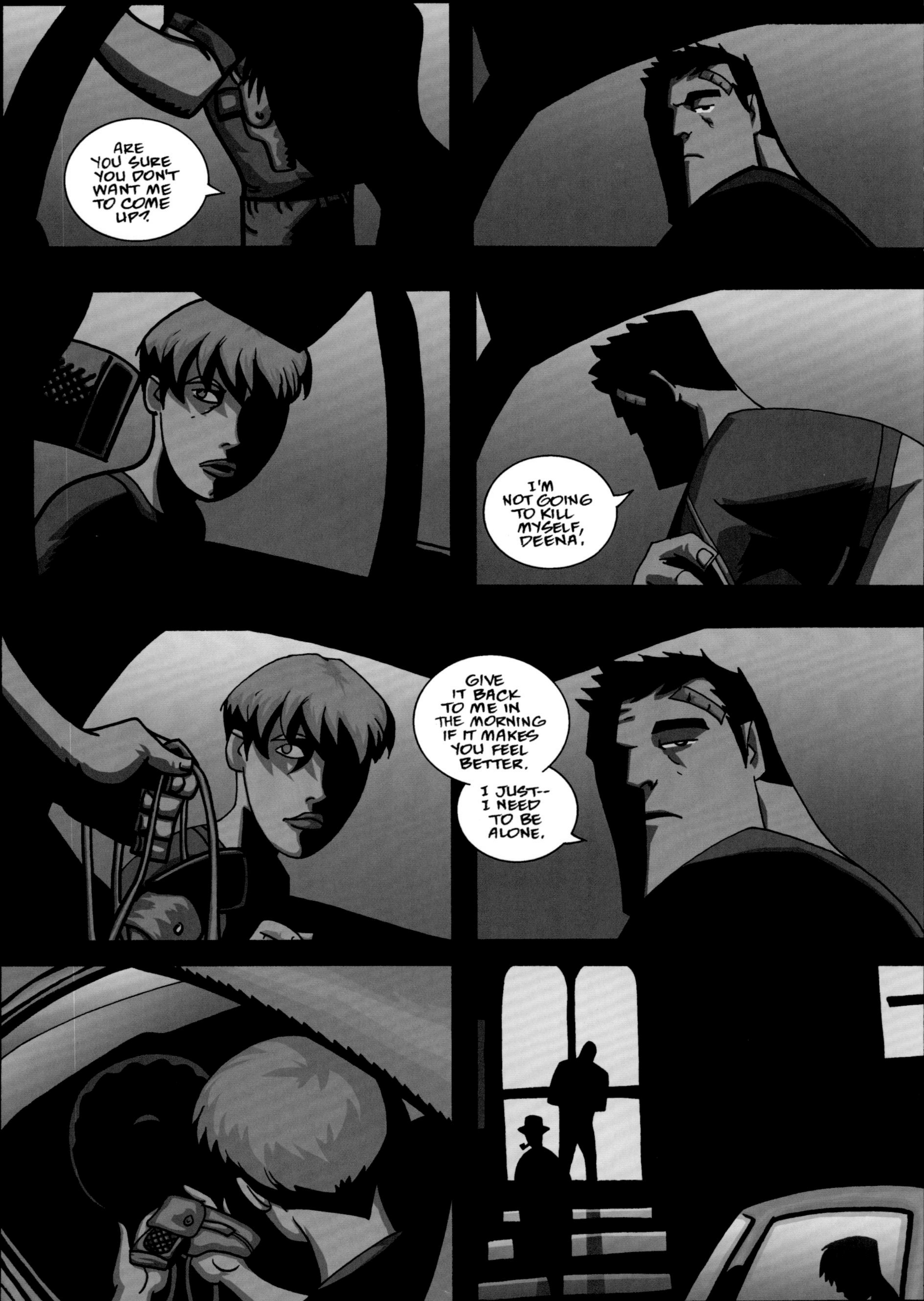
ARE YOU SURE YOU DON'T WANT ME TO COME UP?
I'M NOT GOING TO KILL MYSELF, DEENA!
GIVE IT BACK TO ME IN THE MORNING IF IT MAKES YOU FEEL BETTER.
I JUST-- I NEED TO BE ALONE.

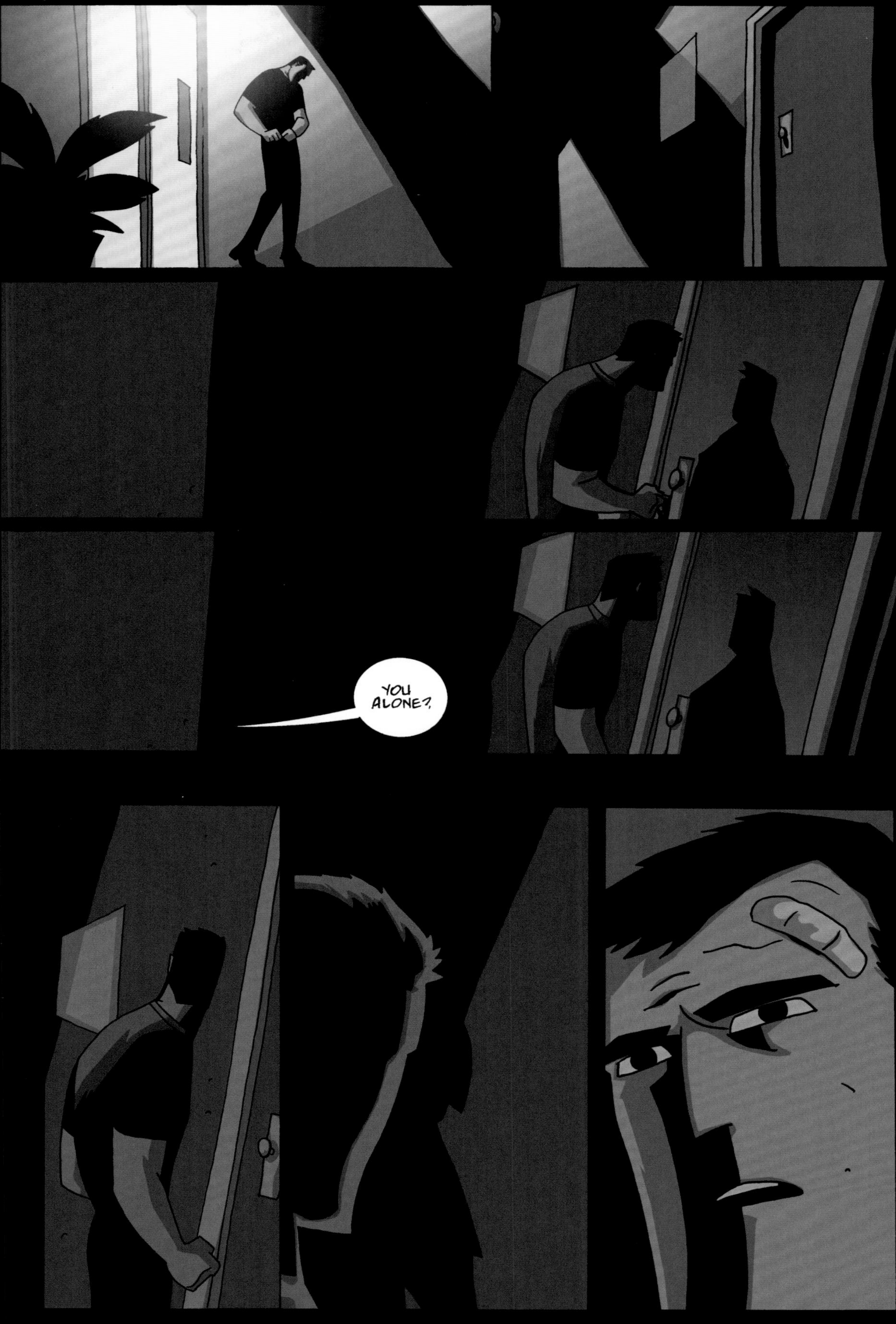
YOU ALONE?

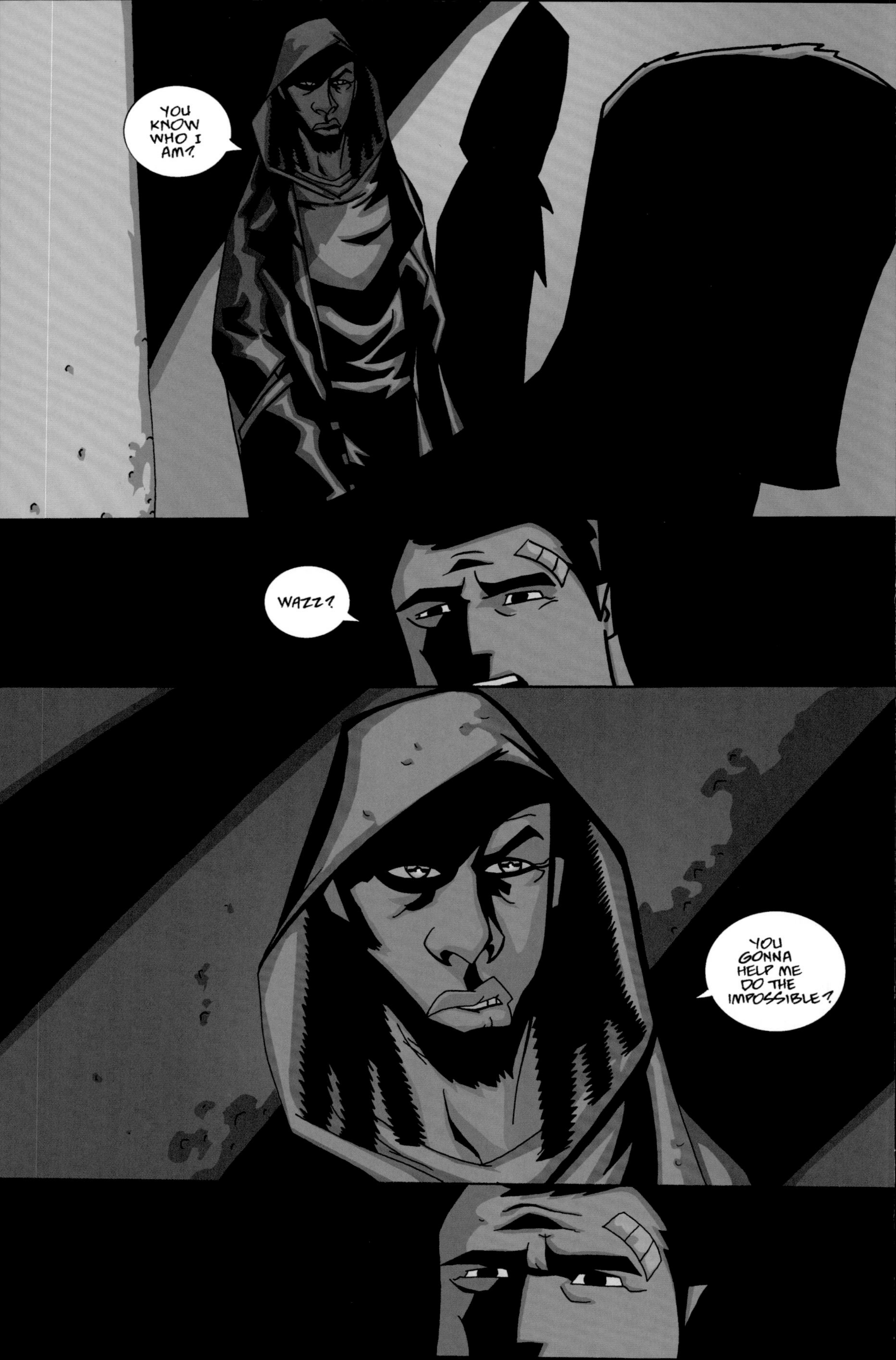
YOU KNOW WHO I AM?
WAZZ?
YOU GONNA HELP ME DO THE IMPOSSIBLE?

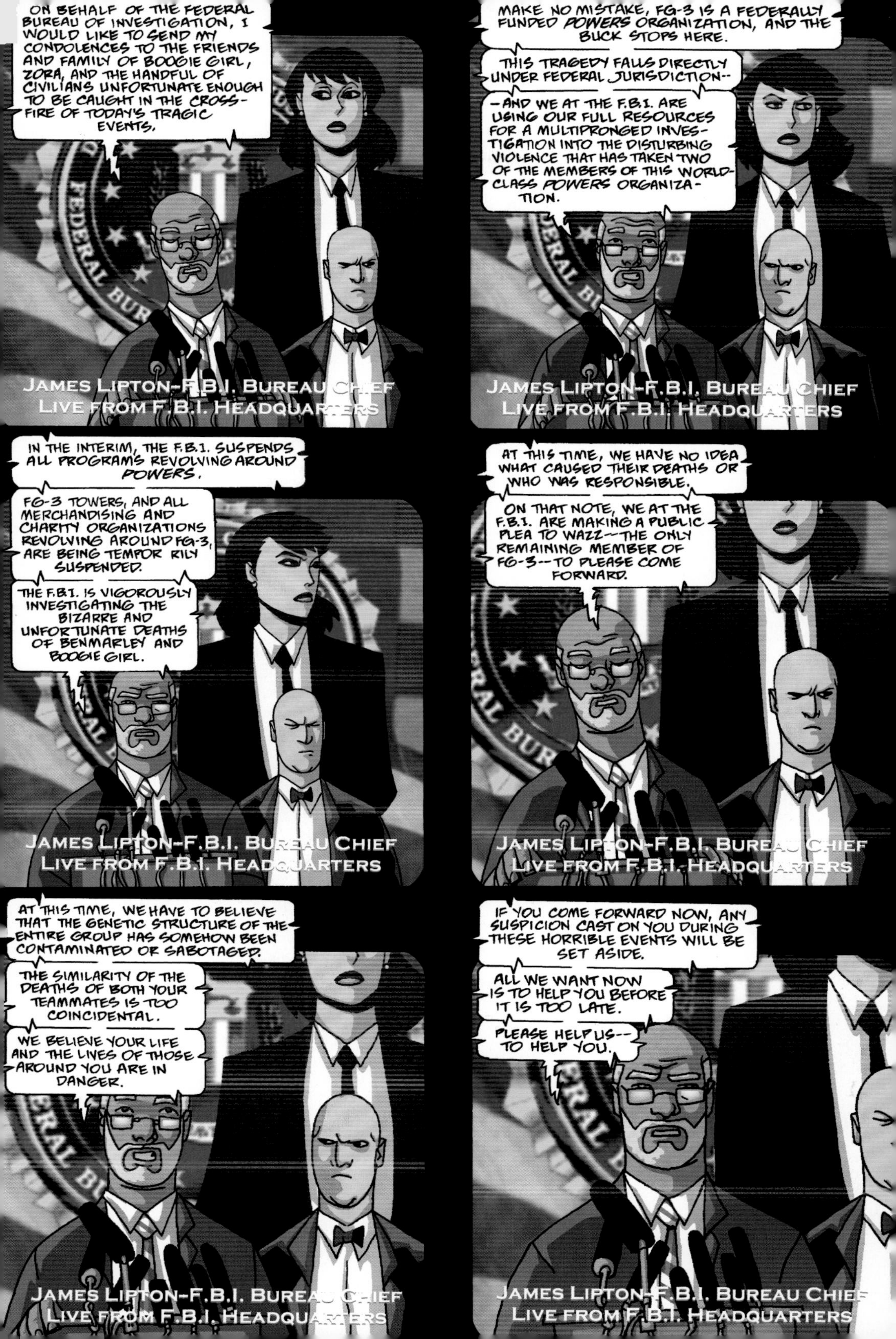
ON BEHALF OF THE FEDERAL BUREAU OF INVESTIGATION, I WOULD LIKE TO SEND MY CONDOLENCES TO THE FRIENDS AND FAMILY OF BOOGIE GIRL, ZORA, AND THE HANDFUL OF CIVILIANS UNFORTUNATE ENOUGH TO BE CAUGHT IN THE CROSS-FIRE OF TODAY'S TRAGIC EVENTS.
JAMES LIPTON-F.B.I. BUREAU CHIEF
LIVE FROM F.B.I. HEADQUARTERS
MAKE NO MISTAKE, FG-3 IS A FEDERALLY FUNDED POWERS ORGANIZATION, AND THE BUCK STOPS HERE.
THIS TRAGEDY FALLS DIRECTLY UNDER FEDERAL JURISDICTION--
--AND WE AT THE F.B.I. ARE USING OUR FULL RESOURCES FOR A MULTIPRONGED INVESTIGATION INTO THE DISTURBING VIOLENCE THAT HAS TAKEN TWO OF THE MEMBERS OF THIS WORLD-CLASS POWERS ORGANIZATION.
JAMES LIPTON-F.B.I. BUREAU CHIEF
LIVE FROM F.B.I. HEADQUARTERS
IN THE INTERIM, THE F.B.I. SUSPENDS ALL PROGRAMS REVOLVING AROUND POWERS.
FG-3 TOWERS, AND ALL MERCHANDISING AND CHARITY ORGANIZATIONS REVOLVING AROUND FG-3, ARE BEING TEMPOR RILY SUSPENDED.
THE F.B.I. IS VIGOROUSLY INVESTIGATING THE BIZARRE AND UNFORTUNATE DEATHS OF BENMARLEY AND BOOGIE GIRL.
JAMES LIPTON-F.B.I. BUREAU CHIEF
LIVE FROM F.B.I. HEADQUARTERS
AT THIS TIME, WE HAVE NO IDEA WHAT CAUSED THEIR DEATHS OR WHO WAS RESPONSIBLE.
ON THAT NOTE, WE AT THE F.B.I. ARE MAKING A PUBLIC PLEA TO WAZZ--THE ONLY REMAINING MEMBER OF FG-3--TO PLEASE COME FORWARD.
JAMES LIPTON-F.B.I. BUREAU CHIEF
LIVE FROM F.B.I. HEADQUARTERS
AT THIS TIME, WE HAVE TO BELIEVE THAT THE GENETIC STRUCTURE OF THE ENTIRE GROUP HAS SOMEHOW BEEN CONTAMINATED OR SABOTAGED.
THE SIMILARITY OF THE DEATHS OF BOTH YOUR TEAMMATES IS TOO COINCIDENTAL.
WE BELIEVE YOUR LIFE AND THE LIVES OF THOSE AROUND YOU ARE IN DANGER.
JAMES LIPTON-F.B.I. BUREAU CHIEF
LIVE FROM F.B.I. HEADQUARTERS
IF YOU COME FORWARD NOW, ANY SUSPICION CAST ON YOU DURING THESE HORRIBLE EVENTS WILL BE SET ASIDE.
ALL WE WANT NOW IS TO HELP YOU BEFORE IT IS TOO LATE.
PLEASE HELP US--TO HELP YOU.
JAMES LIPTON-F.B.I. BUREAU CHIEF
LIVE FROM F.B.I. HEADQUARTERS

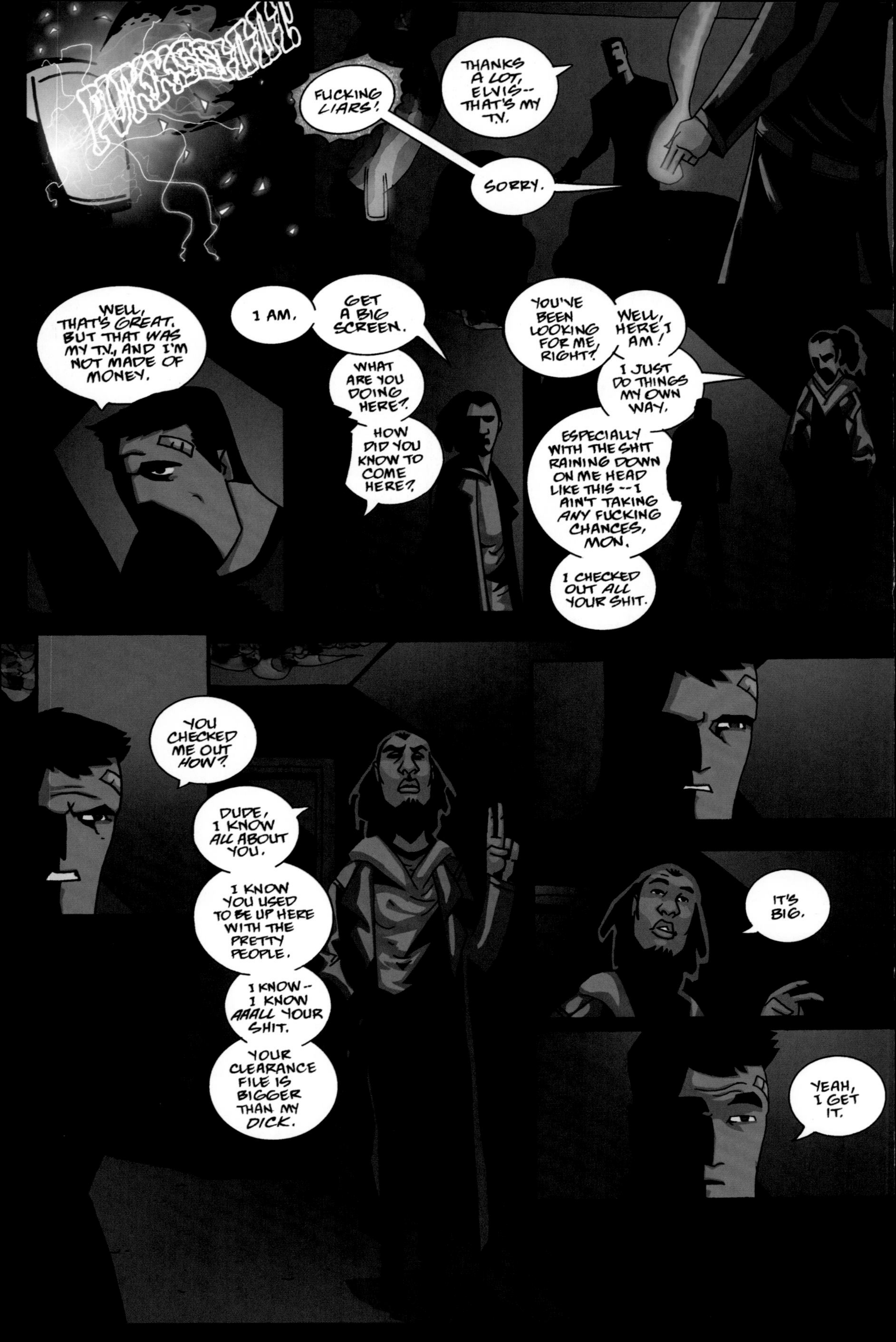
FUCKING LIARS!
THANKS A LOT, ELVIS-- THAT'S MY T.V.
SORRY.
WELL, THAT'S GREAT. BUT THAT WAS MY T.V., AND I'M NOT MADE OF MONEY.
GET A BIG SCREEN.
I AM.
WHAT ARE YOU DOING HERE?
HOW DID YOU KNOW TO COME HERE?
YOU'VE BEEN LOOKING FOR ME, RIGHT?
WELL, HERE I AM!
I JUST DO THINGS MY OWN WAY.
ESPECIALLY WITH THE SHIT RAINING DOWN ON ME HEAD LIKE THIS -- I AIN'T TAKING ANY FUCKING CHANCES, MON.
I CHECKED OUT ALL YOUR SHIT.
YOU CHECKED ME OUT HOW?
DUDE, I KNOW ALL ABOUT YOU.
I KNOW YOU USED TO BE UP HERE WITH THE PRETTY PEOPLE.
I KNOW-- I KNOW AAALL YOUR SHIT.
YOUR CLEARANCE FILE IS BIGGER THAN MY DICK.
IT'S BIG.
YEAH, I GET IT.

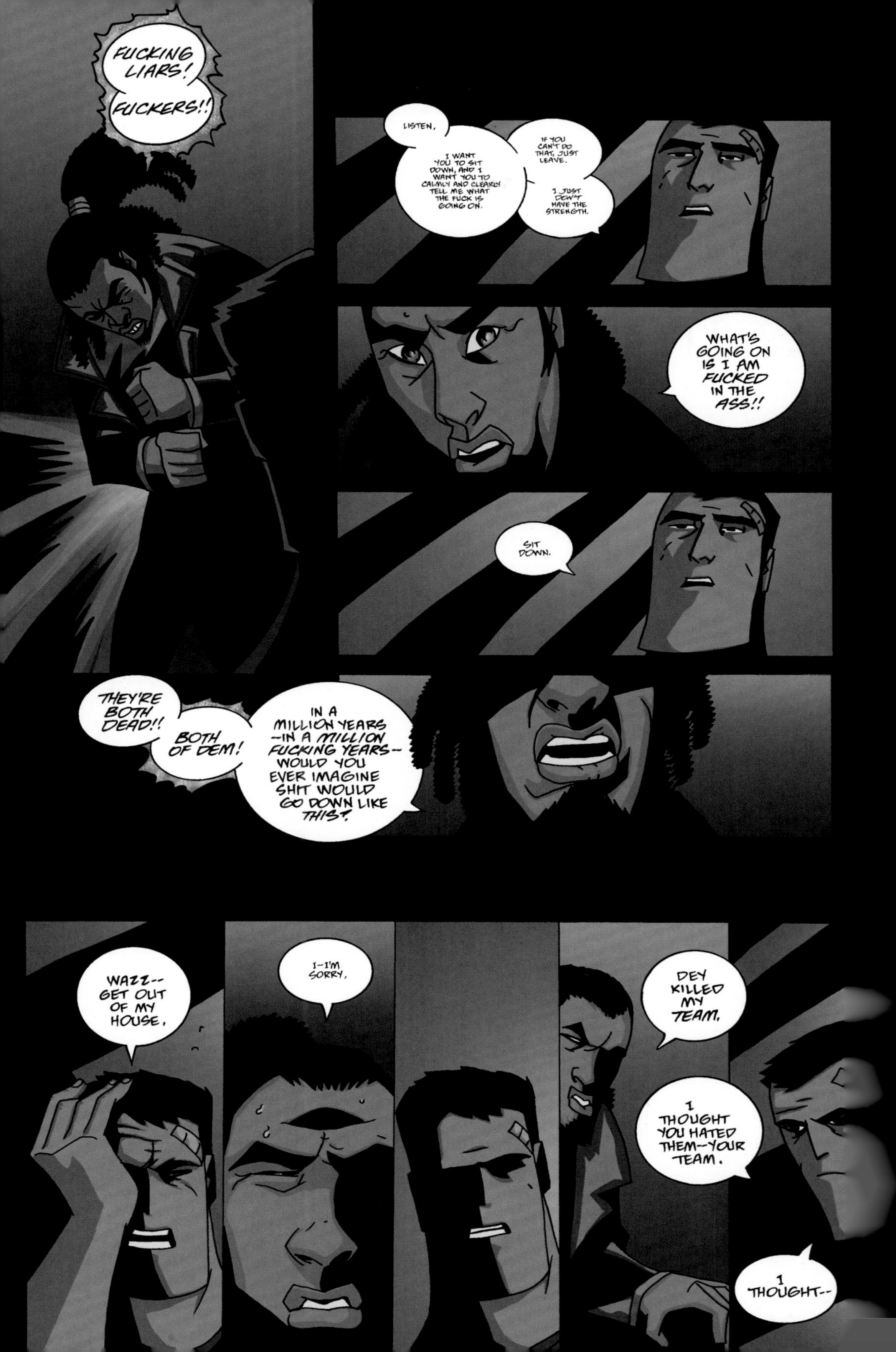
FUCKING LIARS!
FUCKERS!!
LISTEN,
I WANT YOU TO SIT DOWN, AND I WANT YOU TO CALMLY AND CLEARLY TELL ME WHAT THE FUCK IS GOING ON.
IF YOU CAN'T DO THAT, JUST LEAVE.
I JUST DON'T HAVE THE STRENGTH.
WHAT'S GOING ON IS I AM FUCKED IN THE ASS!!
SIT DOWN.
THEY'RE BOTH DEAD!!
BOTH OF DEM!
IN A MILLION YEARS --IN A MILLION FUCKING YEARS-- WOULD YOU EVER IMAGINE SHIT WOULD GO DOWN LIKE THIS?
WAZZ-- GET OUT OF MY HOUSE.
I--I'M SORRY.
DEY KILLED MY TEAM.
I THOUGHT YOU HATED THEM--YOUR TEAM.
I THOUGHT--

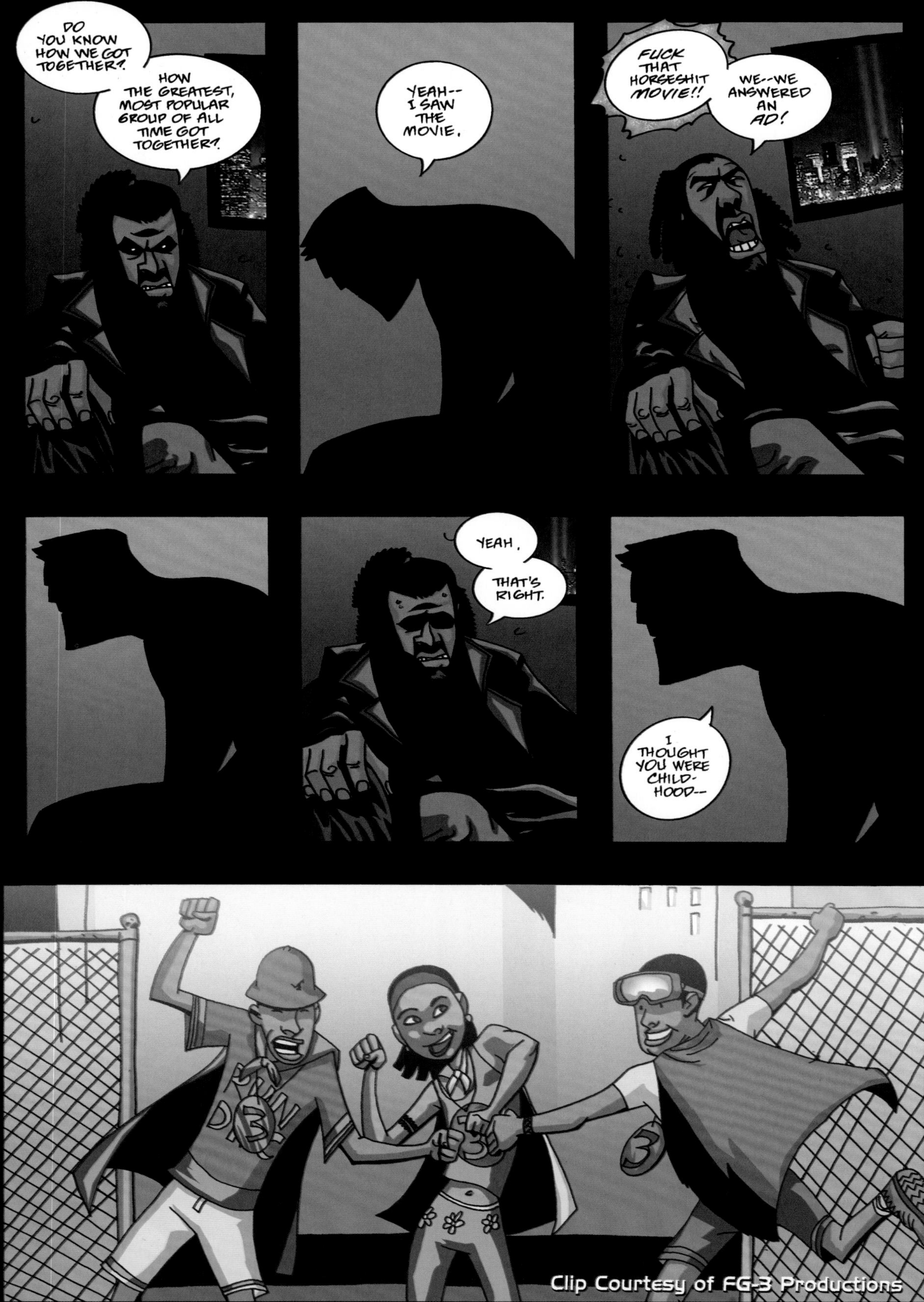
DO YOU KNOW HOW WE GOT TOGETHER?
HOW THE GREATEST, MOST POPULAR GROUP OF ALL TIME GOT TOGETHER?
YEAH-- I SAW THE MOVIE.
FUCK THAT HORSESHIT MOVIE!!
WE--WE ANSWERED AN AD!
YEAH,
THAT'S RIGHT.
I THOUGHT YOU WERE CHILD-HOOD--
Clip Courtesy of FG-3 Productions

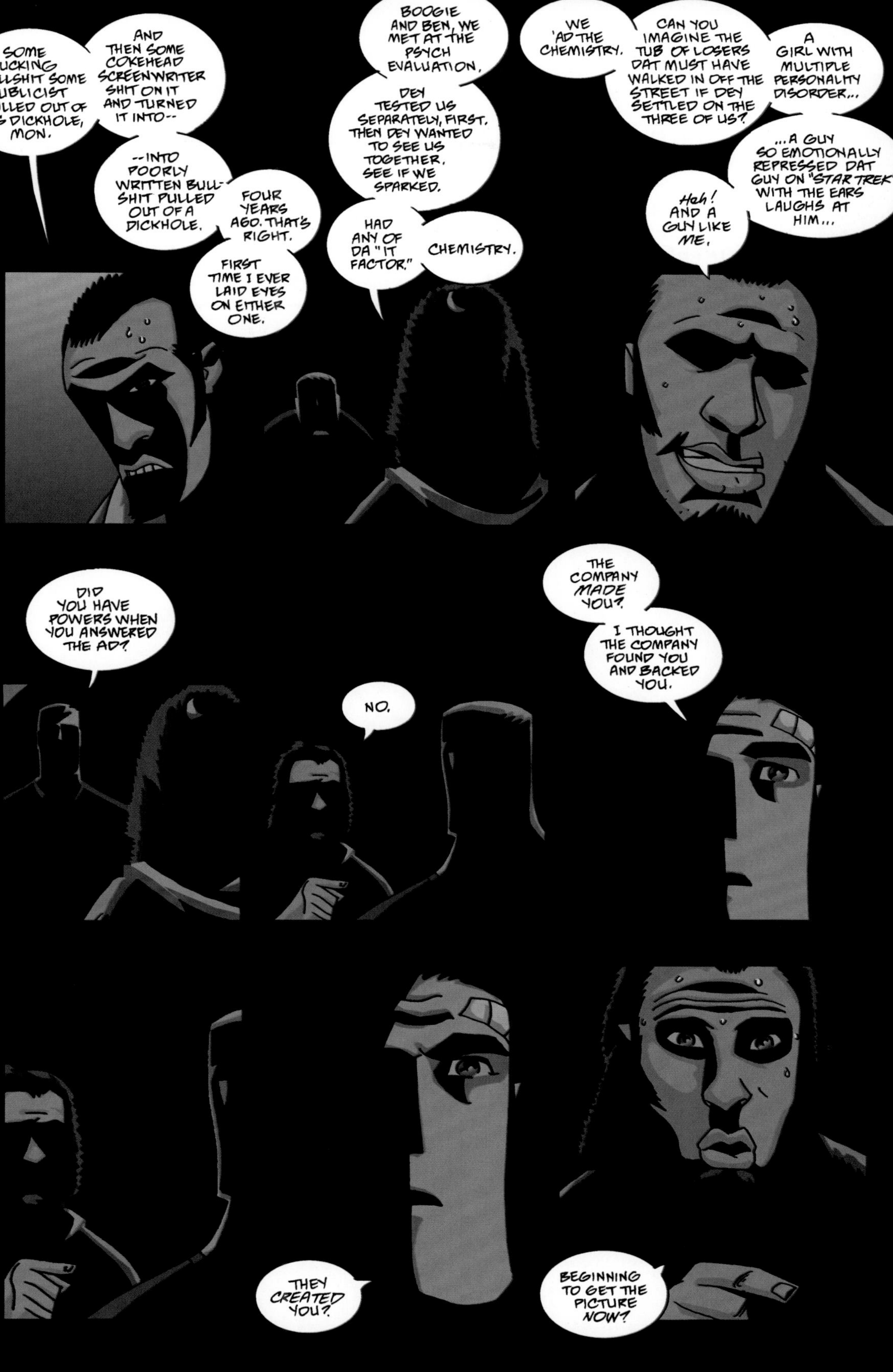
SOME FUCKING BULLSHIT SOME PUBLICIST PULLED OUT OF HIS DICKHOLE, MON.
AND THEN SOME COKEHEAD SCREENWRITER SHIT ON IT AND TURNED IT INTO--
--INTO POORLY WRITTEN BULL-SHIT PULLED OUT OF A DICKHOLE.
FOUR YEARS AGO. THAT'S RIGHT.
FIRST TIME I EVER LAID EYES ON EITHER ONE.
BOOGIE AND BEN, WE MET AT THE PSYCH EVALUATION.
DEY TESTED US SEPARATELY, FIRST. THEN DEY WANTED TO SEE US TOGETHER. SEE IF WE SPARKED.
HAD ANY OF DA "IT FACTOR."
CHEMISTRY.
WE 'AD THE CHEMISTRY.
CAN YOU IMAGINE THE TUB OF LOSERS DAT MUST HAVE WALKED IN OFF THE STREET IF DEY SETTLED ON THE THREE OF US?
A GIRL WITH MULTIPLE PERSONALITY DISORDER...
...A GUY SO EMOTIONALLY REPRESSED DAT GUY ON "STAR TREK" WITH THE EARS LAUGHS AT HIM...
Heh! AND A GUY LIKE ME.
DID YOU HAVE POWERS WHEN YOU ANSWERED THE AD?
NO.
THE COMPANY MADE YOU?
I THOUGHT THE COMPANY FOUND YOU AND BACKED YOU.
THEY CREATED YOU?
BEGINNING TO GET THE PICTURE NOW?

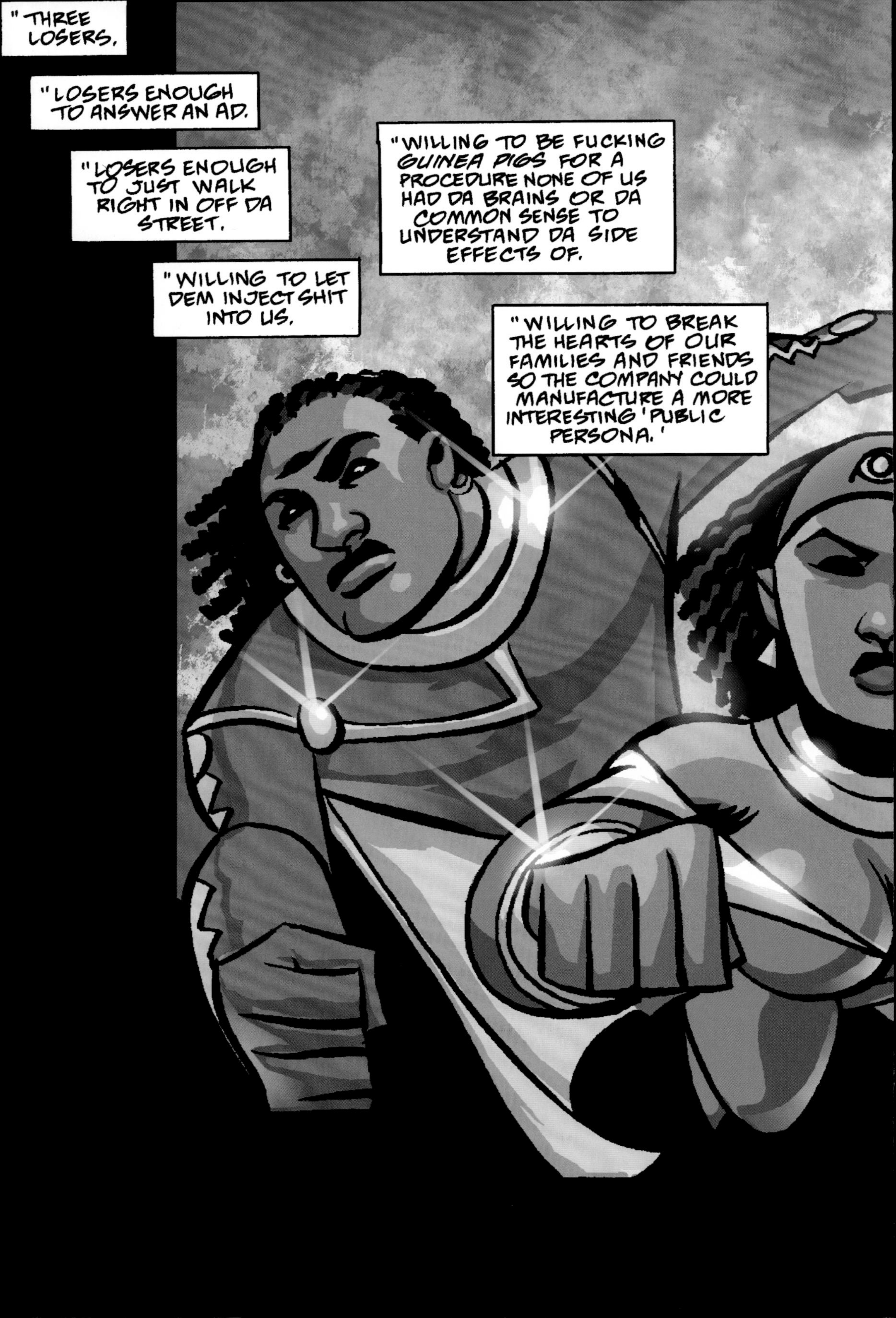
"THREE LOSERS.
"LOSERS ENOUGH TO ANSWER AN AD.
"LOSERS ENOUGH TO JUST WALK RIGHT IN OFF DA STREET.
"WILLING TO LET DEM INJECT SHIT INTO US.
"WILLING TO BE FUCKING GUINEA PIGS FOR A PROCEDURE NONE OF US HAD DA BRAINS OR DA COMMON SENSE TO UNDERSTAND DA SIDE EFFECTS OF.
"WILLING TO BREAK THE HEARTS OF OUR FAMILIES AND FRIENDS SO THE COMPANY COULD MANUFACTURE A MORE INTERESTING 'PUBLIC PERSONA.'

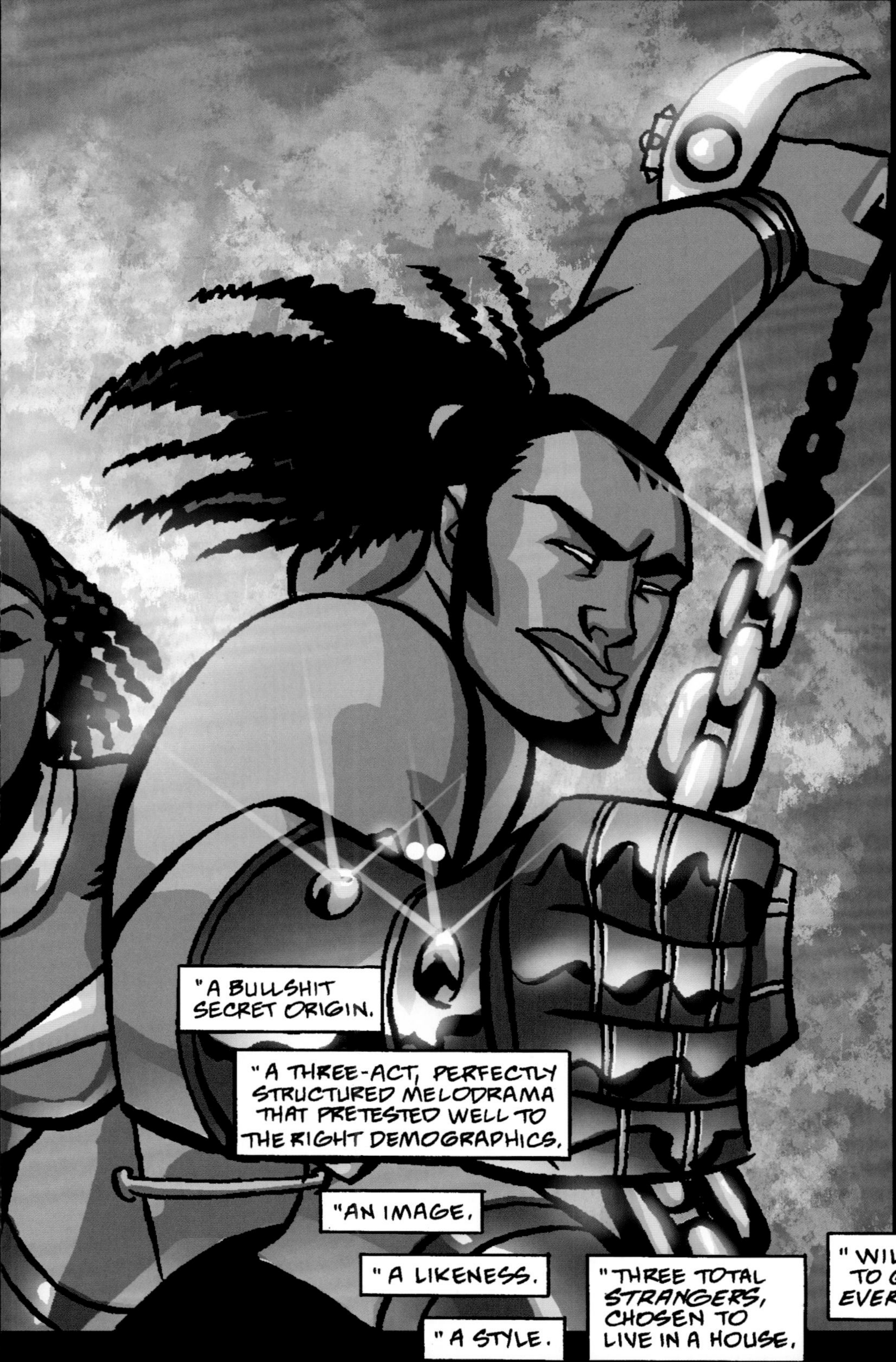
"A BULLSHIT SECRET ORIGIN.
"A THREE-ACT, PERFECTLY STRUCTURED MELODRAMA THAT PRETESTED WELL TO THE RIGHT DEMOGRAPHICS.
"AN IMAGE.
"A LIKENESS.
"A STYLE.
"THREE TOTAL STRANGERS, CHOSEN TO LIVE IN A HOUSE.
"WILLING TO GIVE UP EVERYTHING."

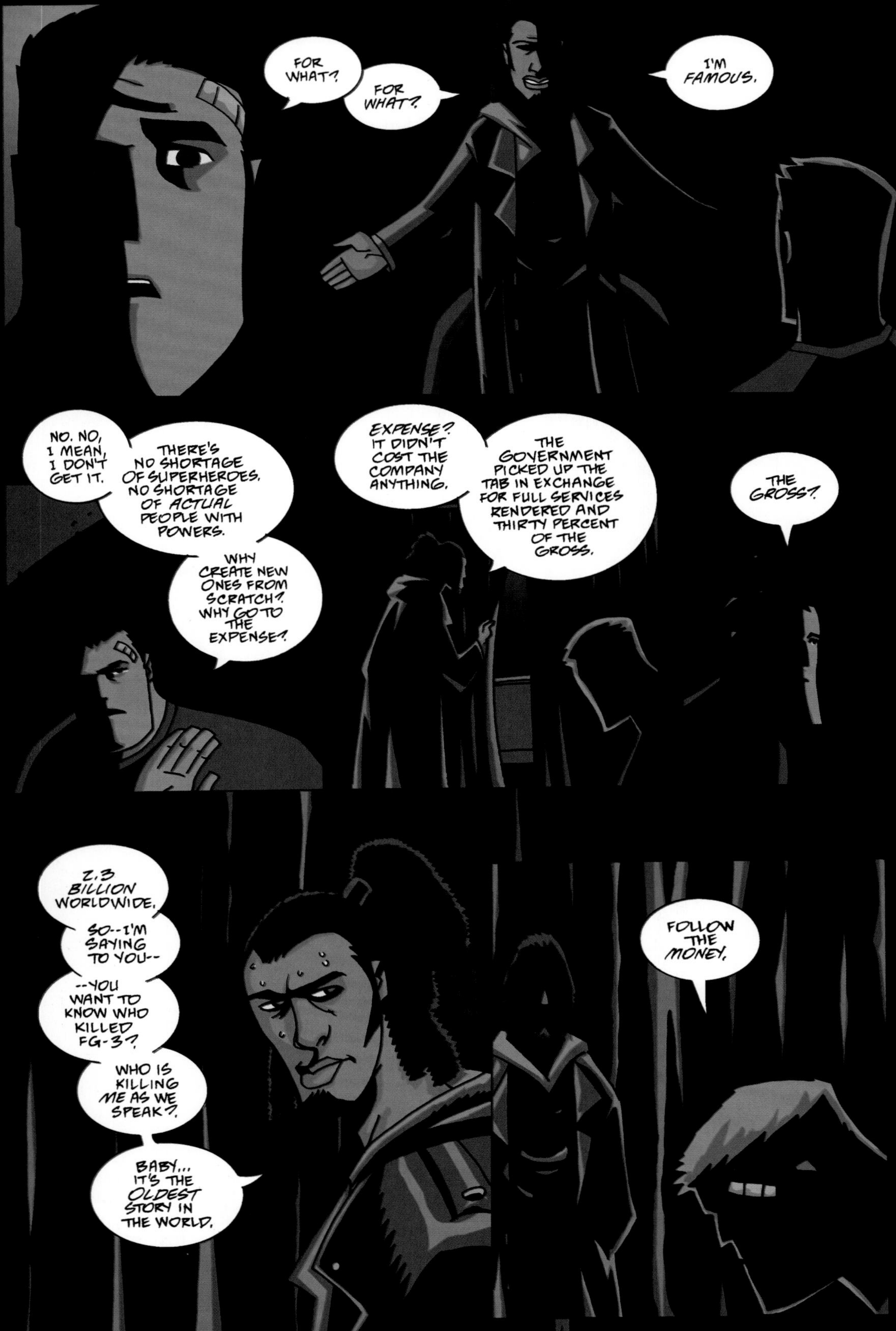
FOR WHAT?
FOR WHAT?
I'M FAMOUS.
NO. NO, I MEAN, I DON'T GET IT.
THERE'S NO SHORTAGE OF SUPERHEROES. NO SHORTAGE OF ACTUAL PEOPLE WITH POWERS.
WHY CREATE NEW ONES FROM SCRATCH? WHY GO TO THE EXPENSE?
EXPENSE? IT DIDN'T COST THE COMPANY ANYTHING.
THE GOVERNMENT PICKED UP THE TAB IN EXCHANGE FOR FULL SERVICES RENDERED AND THIRTY PERCENT OF THE GROSS.
THE GROSS?
2.3 BILLION WORLDWIDE.
SO--I'M SAYING TO YOU--
--YOU WANT TO KNOW WHO KILLED FG-3?
WHO IS KILLING ME AS WE SPEAK?
BABY... IT'S THE OLDEST STORY IN THE WORLD.
FOLLOW THE MONEY.

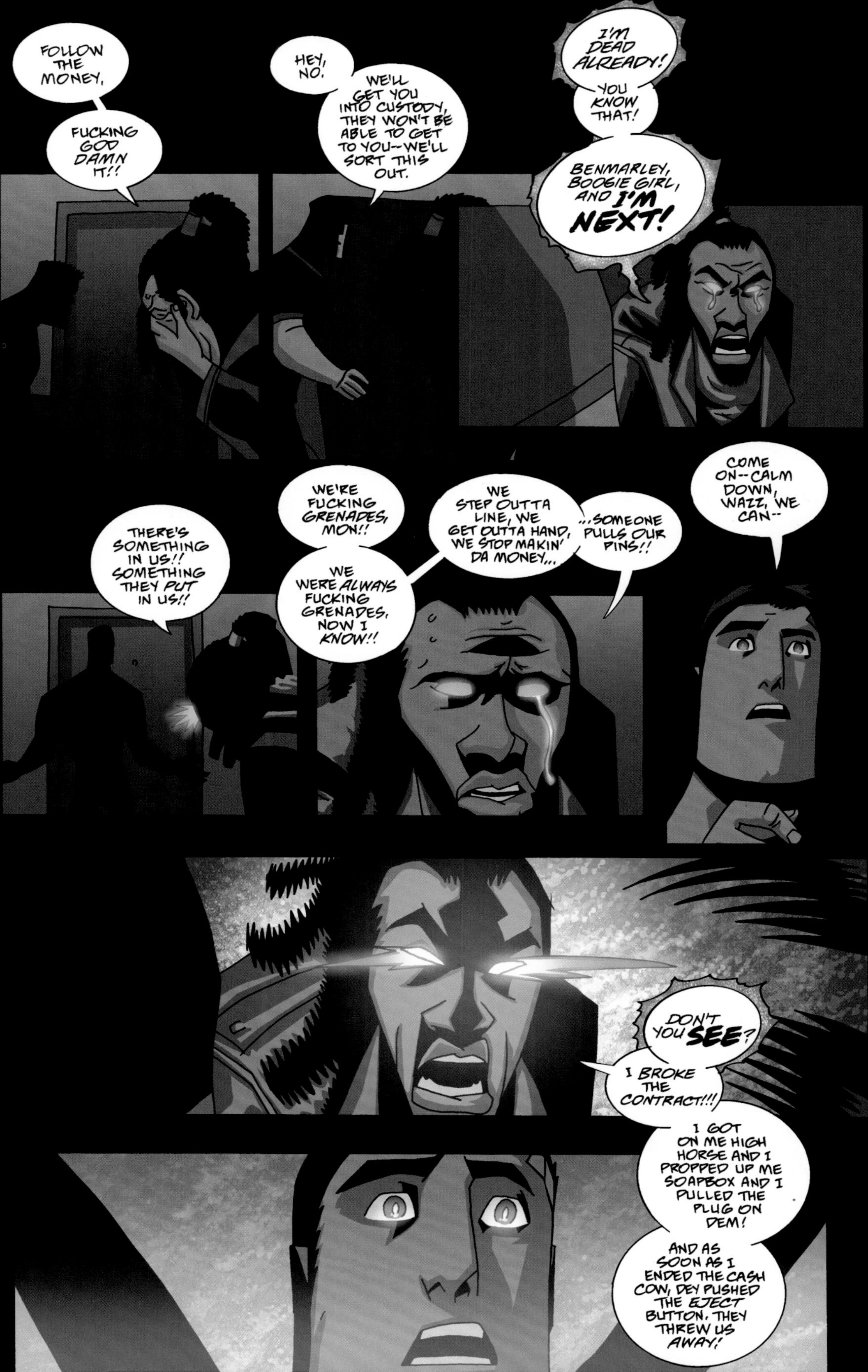

FOLLOW THE MONEY.
FUCKING GOD DAMN IT!!
HEY, NO.
WE'LL GET YOU INTO CUSTODY, THEY WON'T BE ABLE TO GET TO YOU--WE'LL SORT THIS OUT.
I'M DEAD ALREADY!
YOU KNOW THAT!
BENMARLEY, BOOGIE GIRL, AND I'M NEXT!
THERE'S SOMETHING IN US!! SOMETHING THEY PUT IN US!!
WE'RE FUCKING GRENADES, MON!!
WE WERE ALWAYS FUCKING GRENADES, NOW I KNOW!!
WE STEP OUTTA LINE, WE GET OUTTA HAND, WE STOP MAKIN' DA MONEY...
...SOMEONE PULLS OUR PINS!!
COME ON--CALM DOWN, WAZZ, WE CAN--
DON'T YOU SEE?
I BROKE THE CONTRACT!!!
I GOT ON ME HIGH HORSE AND I PROPPED UP ME SOAPBOX AND I PULLED THE PLUG ON DEM!
AND AS SOON AS I ENDED THE CASH COW, DEY PUSHED THE EJECT BUTTON. THEY THREW US AWAY!

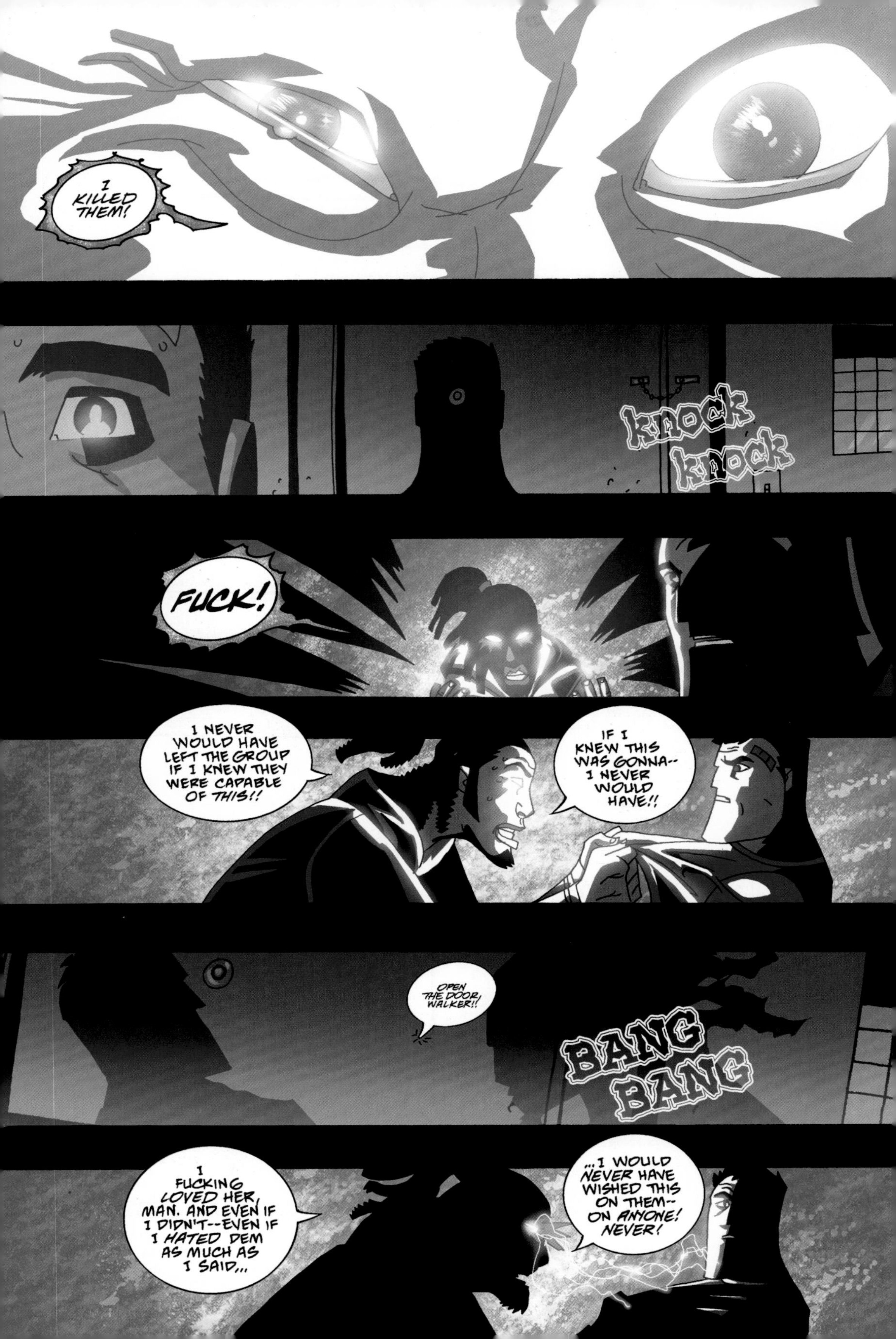
I KILLED THEM!
KNOCK KNOCK
FUCK!
I NEVER WOULD HAVE LEFT THE GROUP IF I KNEW THEY WERE CAPABLE OF THIS!!
IF I KNEW THIS WAS GONNA-- I NEVER WOULD HAVE!!
OPEN THE DOOR, WALKER!!
BANG BANG
I FUCKING LOVED HER, MAN. AND EVEN IF I DIDN'T--EVEN IF I HATED DEM AS MUCH AS I SAID...
...I WOULD NEVER HAVE WISHED THIS ON THEM-- ON ANYONE! NEVER!

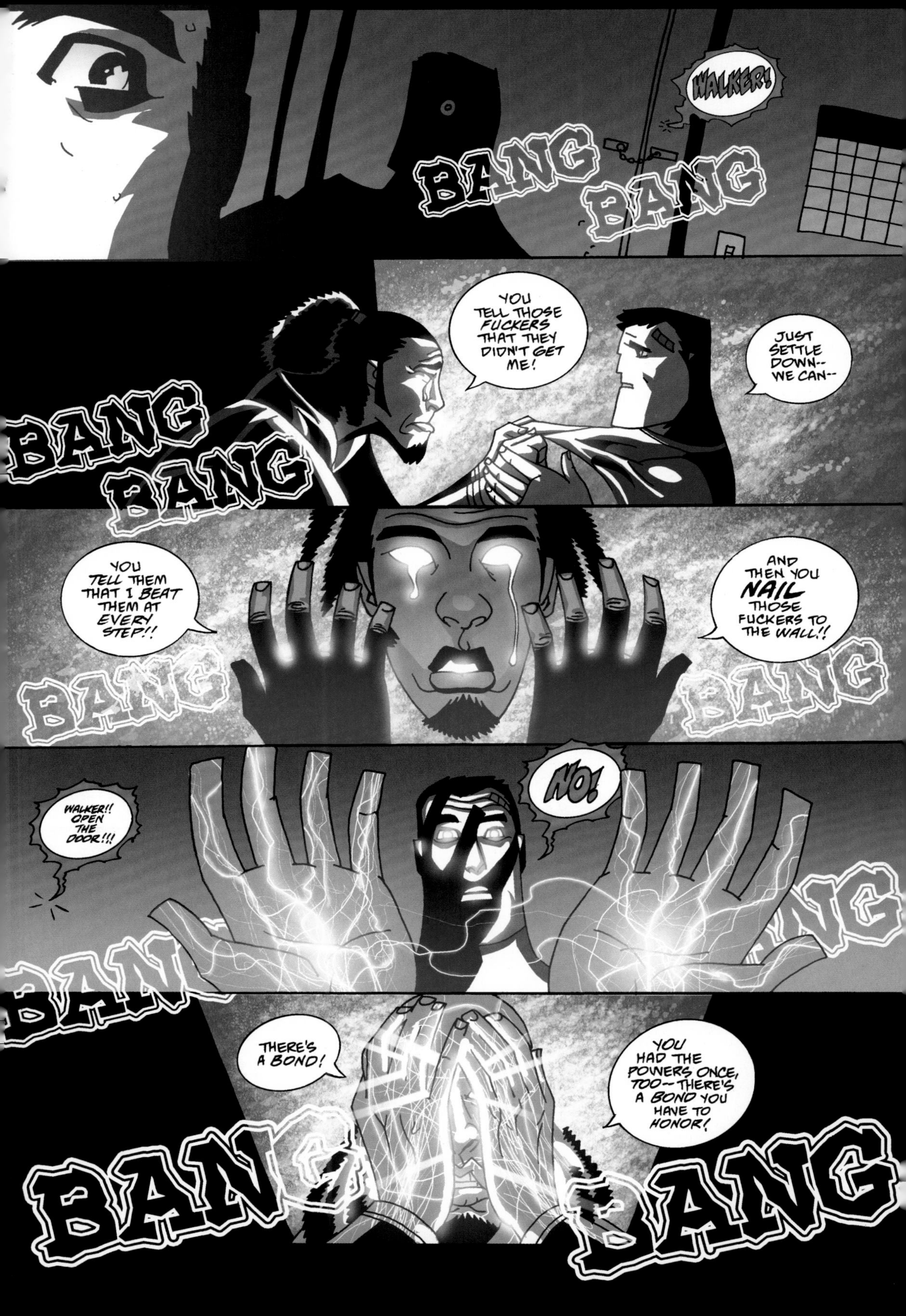
WALKER!
BANG BANG
BANG BANG
YOU TELL THOSE FUCKERS THAT THEY DIDN'T GET ME!
JUST SETTLE DOWN-- WE CAN--
YOU TELL THEM THAT I BEAT THEM AT EVERY STEP!!
AND THEN YOU NAIL THOSE FUCKERS TO THE WALL!!
BANG BANG
WALKER!! OPEN THE DOOR!!!
NO!
THERE'S A BOND!
YOU HAD THE POWERS ONCE, TOO-- THERE'S A BOND YOU HAVE TO HONOR!
BANG BANG

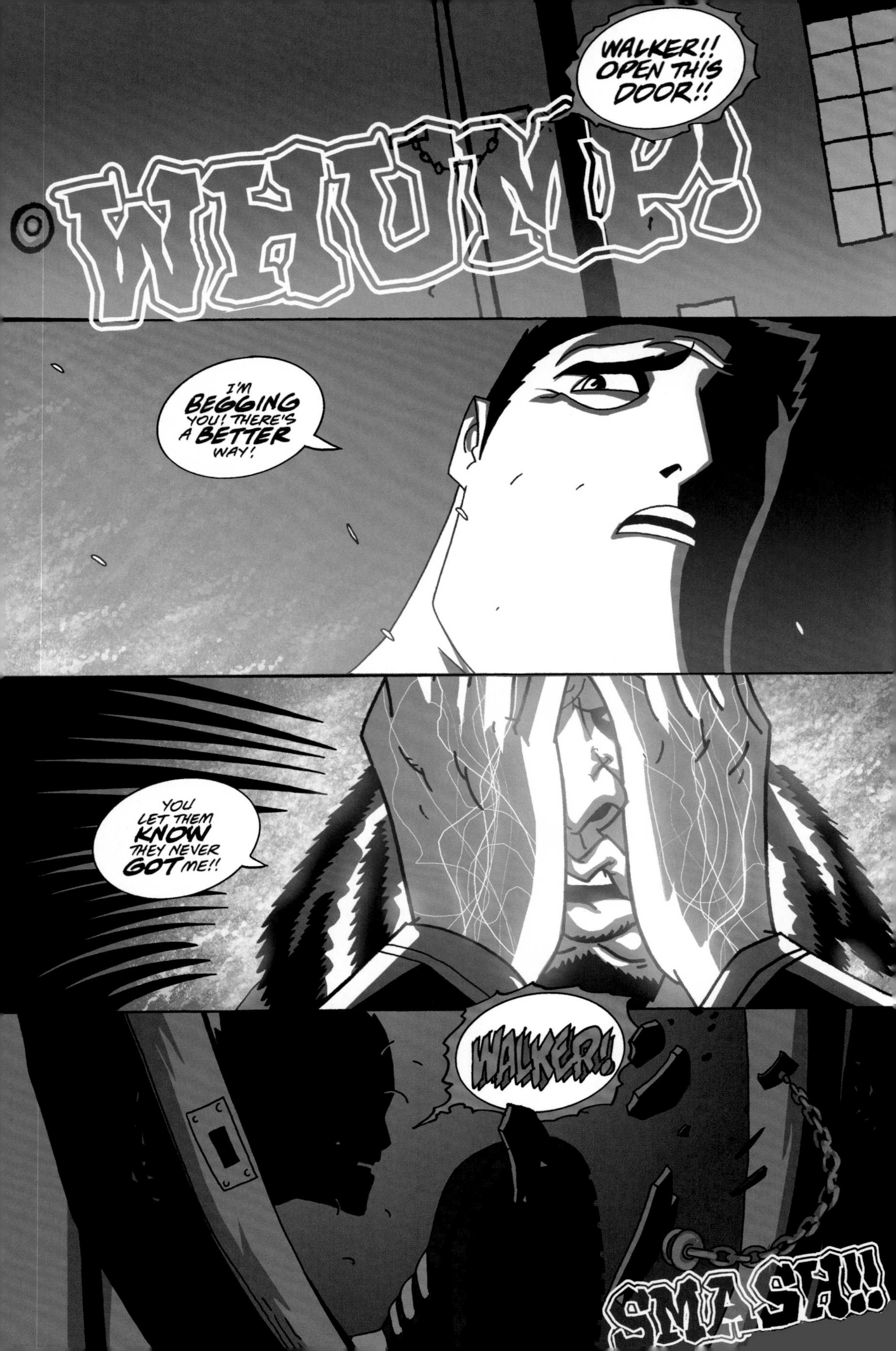
WALKER!! OPEN THIS DOOR!!
WHUMP!
I'M BEGGING YOU! THERE'S A BETTER WAY!
YOU LET THEM KNOW THEY NEVER GOT ME!!
WALKER!!
SMASH!!

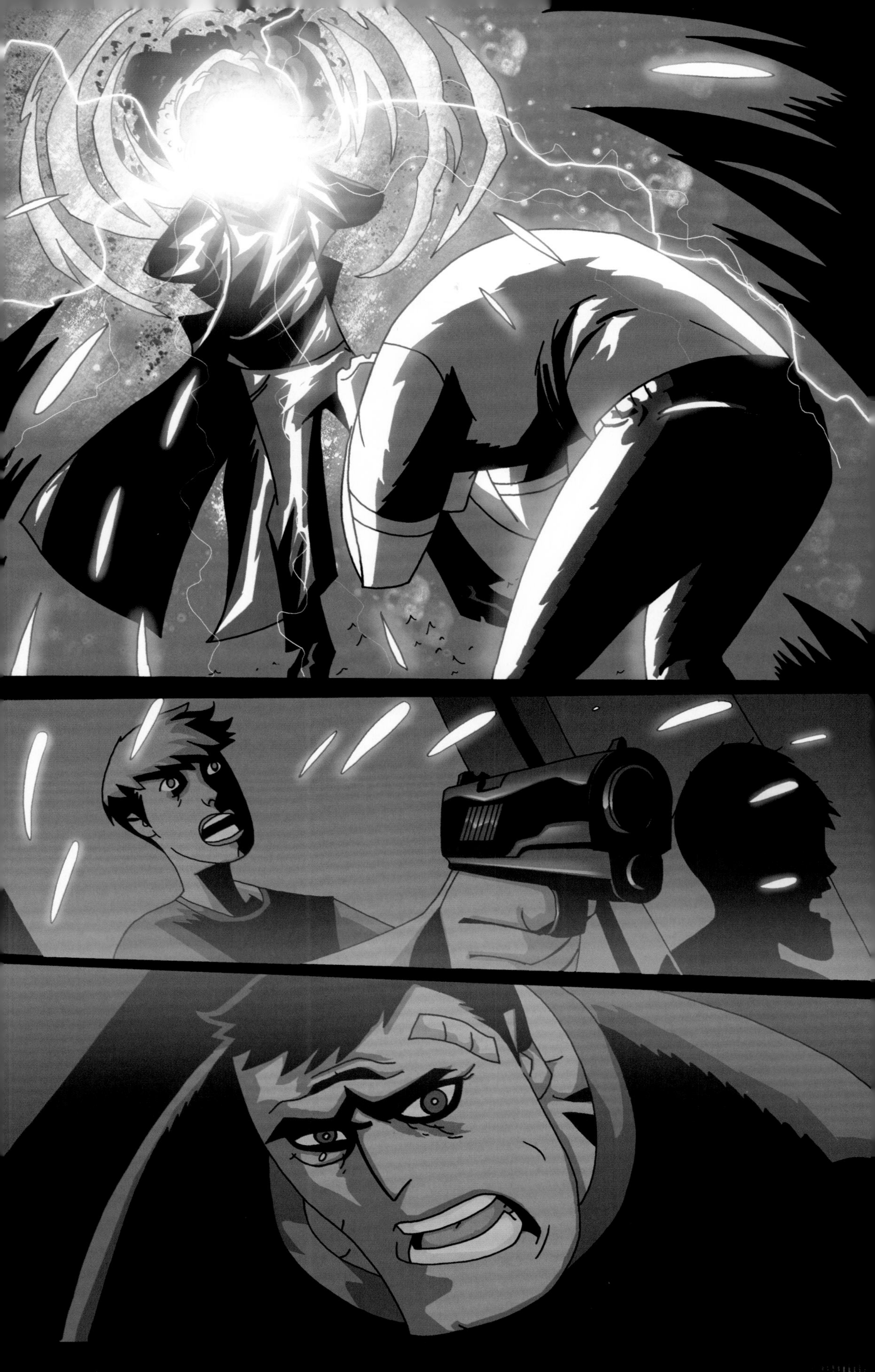

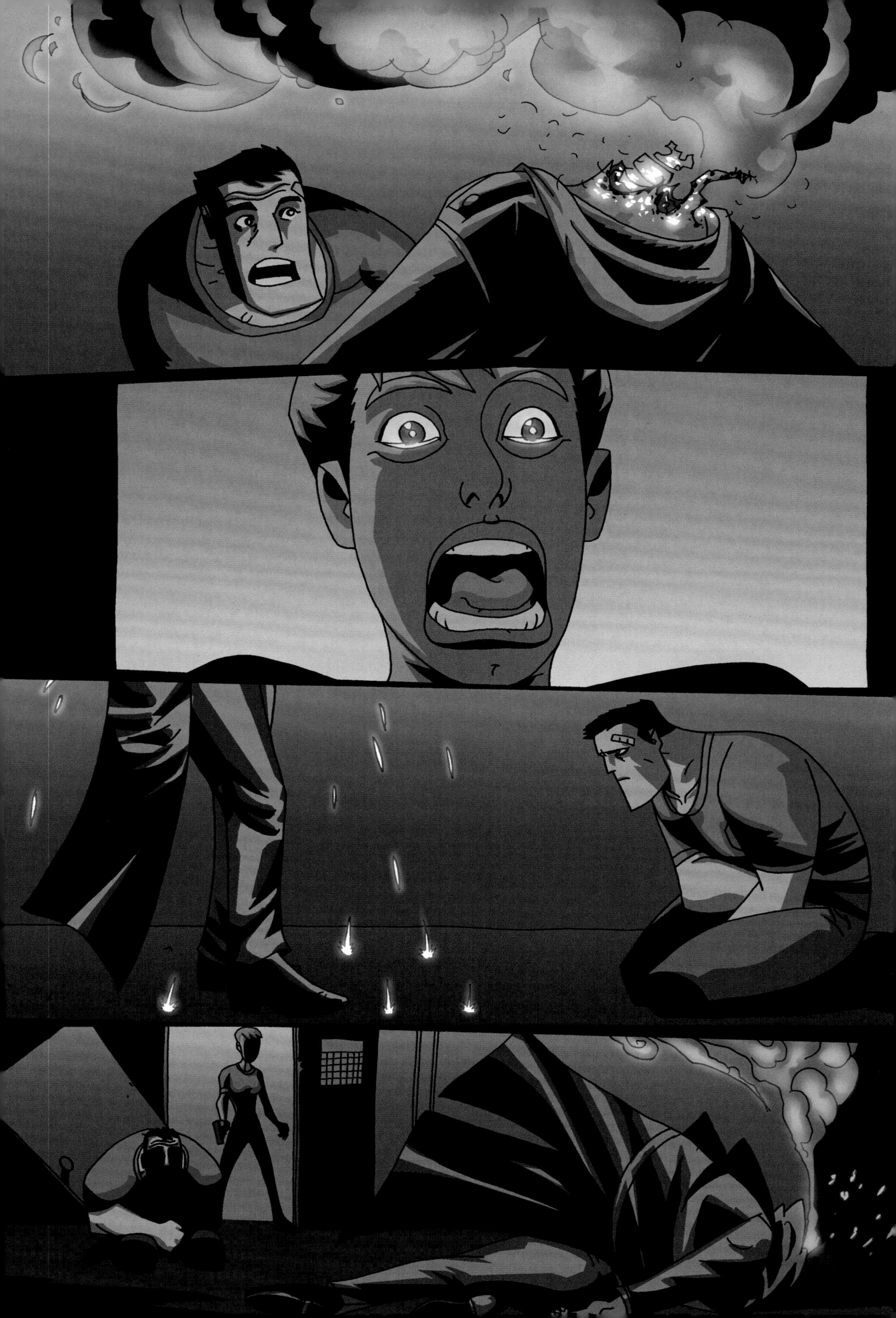

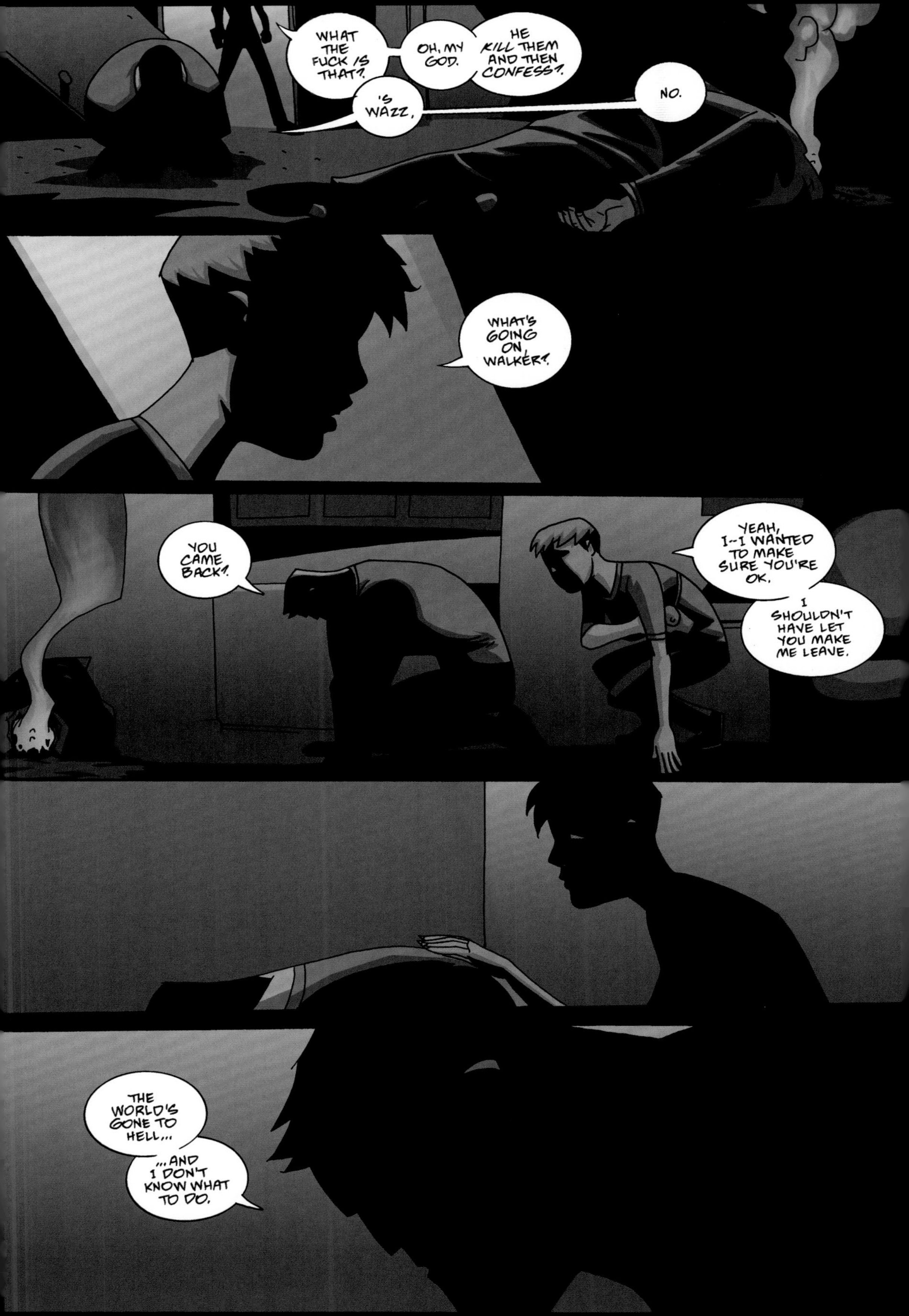

WHAT THE FUCK IS THAT?
OH, MY GOD.
HE KILL THEM AND THEN CONFESS?
'S WAZZ,
NO.
WHAT'S GOING ON, WALKER?
YOU CAME BACK?
YEAH, I--I WANTED TO MAKE SURE YOU'RE OK.
I SHOULDN'T HAVE LET YOU MAKE ME LEAVE.
THE WORLD'S GONE TO HELL...
...AND I DON'T KNOW WHAT TO DO.

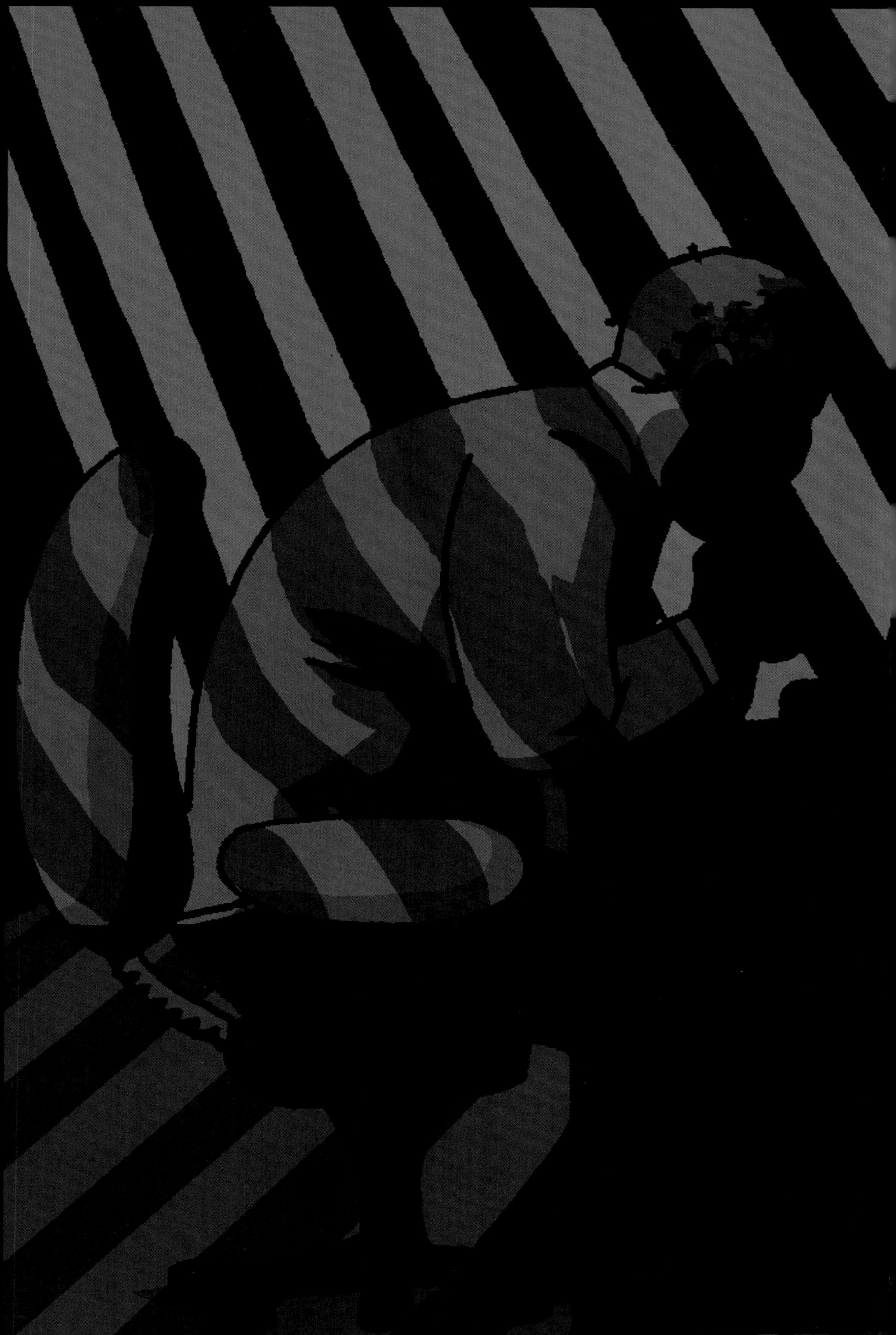

POWERS™

SUPERGROUP
CHAPTER 6

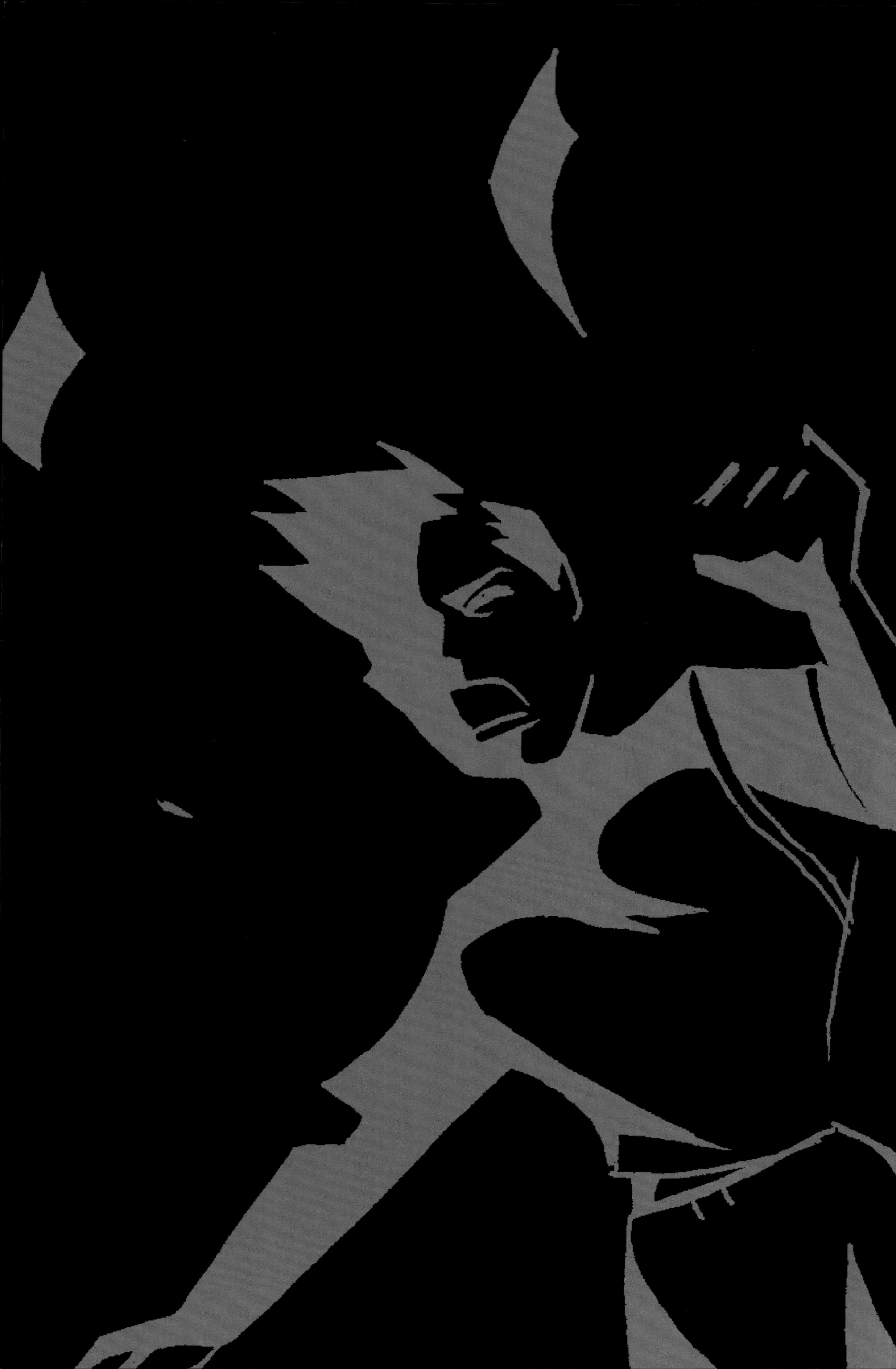

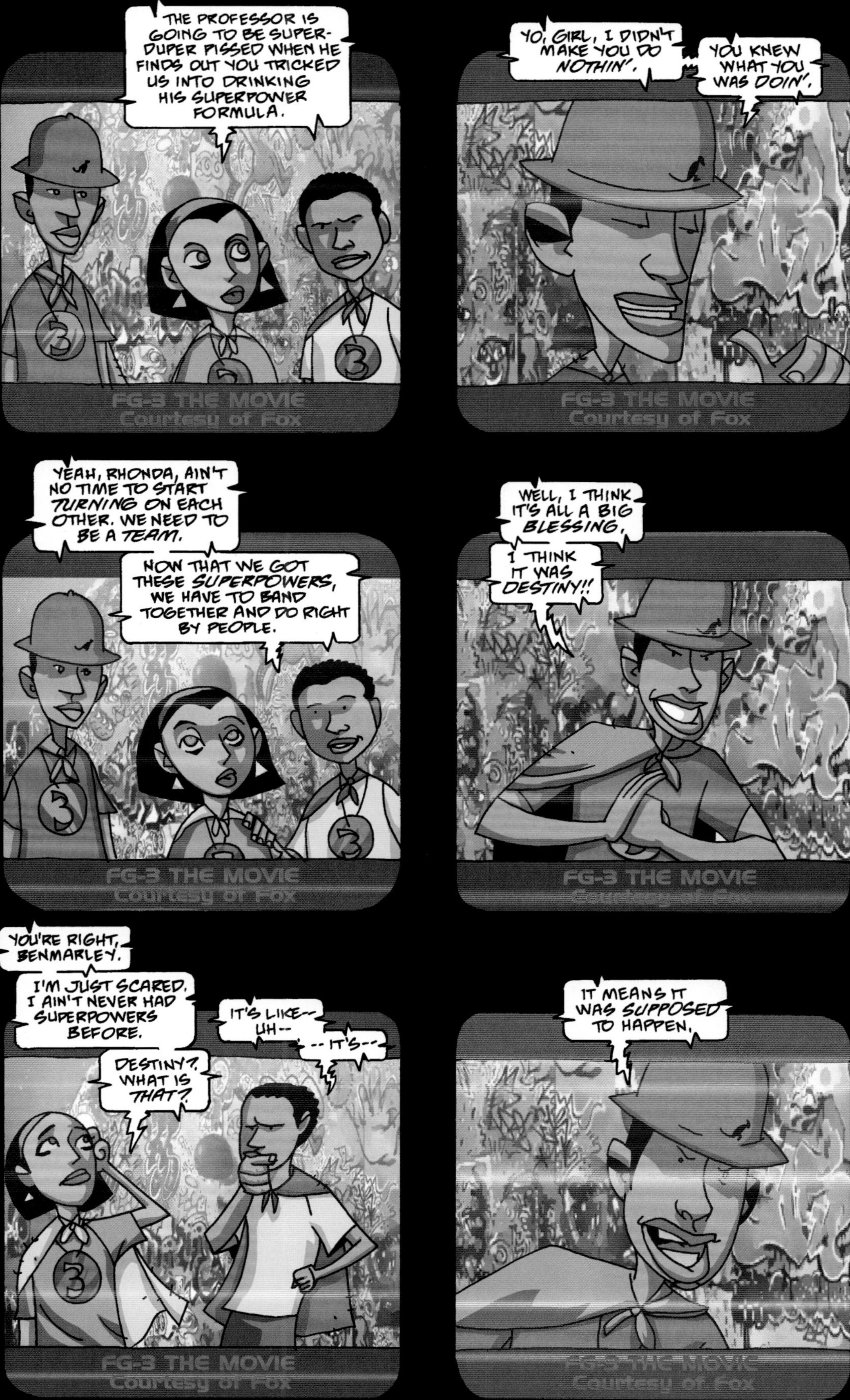
THE PROFESSOR IS GOING TO BE SUPER-DUPER PISSED WHEN HE FINDS OUT YOU TRICKED US INTO DRINKING HIS SUPERPOWER FORMULA.
FG-3 THE MOVIE
Courtesy of Fox
YO, GIRL, I DIDN'T MAKE YOU DO *NOTHIN'.*
YOU KNEW WHAT YOU WAS *DOIN'.*
FG-3 THE MOVIE
Courtesy of Fox
YEAH, RHONDA, AIN'T NO TIME TO START *TURNING* ON EACH OTHER. WE NEED TO BE A *TEAM.*
NOW THAT WE GOT THESE *SUPERPOWERS,* WE HAVE TO BAND TOGETHER AND DO RIGHT BY PEOPLE.
FG-3 THE MOVIE
Courtesy of Fox
WELL, I THINK IT'S ALL A BIG *BLESSING.*
I THINK IT WAS *DESTINY!!*
FG-3 THE MOVIE
YOU'RE RIGHT, BENMARLEY.
I'M JUST SCARED. I AIN'T NEVER HAD SUPERPOWERS BEFORE.
IT'S LIKE-- UH--
-- IT'S--
DESTINY? WHAT IS *THAT?*
FG-3 THE MOVIE
Courtesy of Fox
IT MEANS IT WAS *SUPPOSED* TO HAPPEN.
FG-3 THE MOVIE
Courtesy of Fox

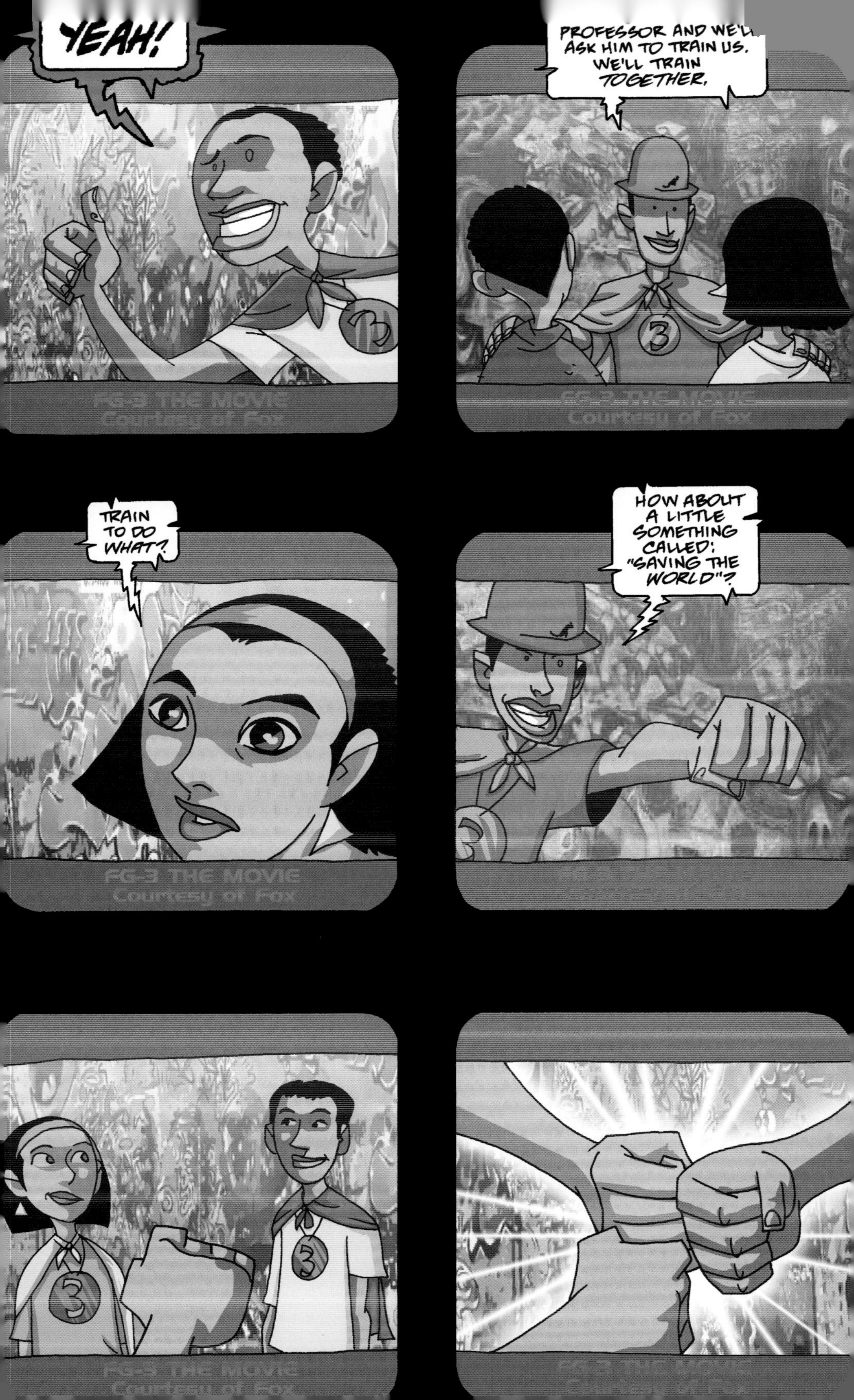
YEAH!
FG-3 THE MOVIE Courtesy of Fox
PROFESSOR AND WE'L ASK HIM TO TRAIN US. WE'LL TRAIN TOGETHER.
FG-3 THE MOVIE Courtesy of Fox
TRAIN TO DO WHAT?
FG-3 THE MOVIE Courtesy of Fox
HOW ABOUT A LITTLE SOMETHING CALLED: "SAVING THE WORLD"?
FG-3 THE MOVIE

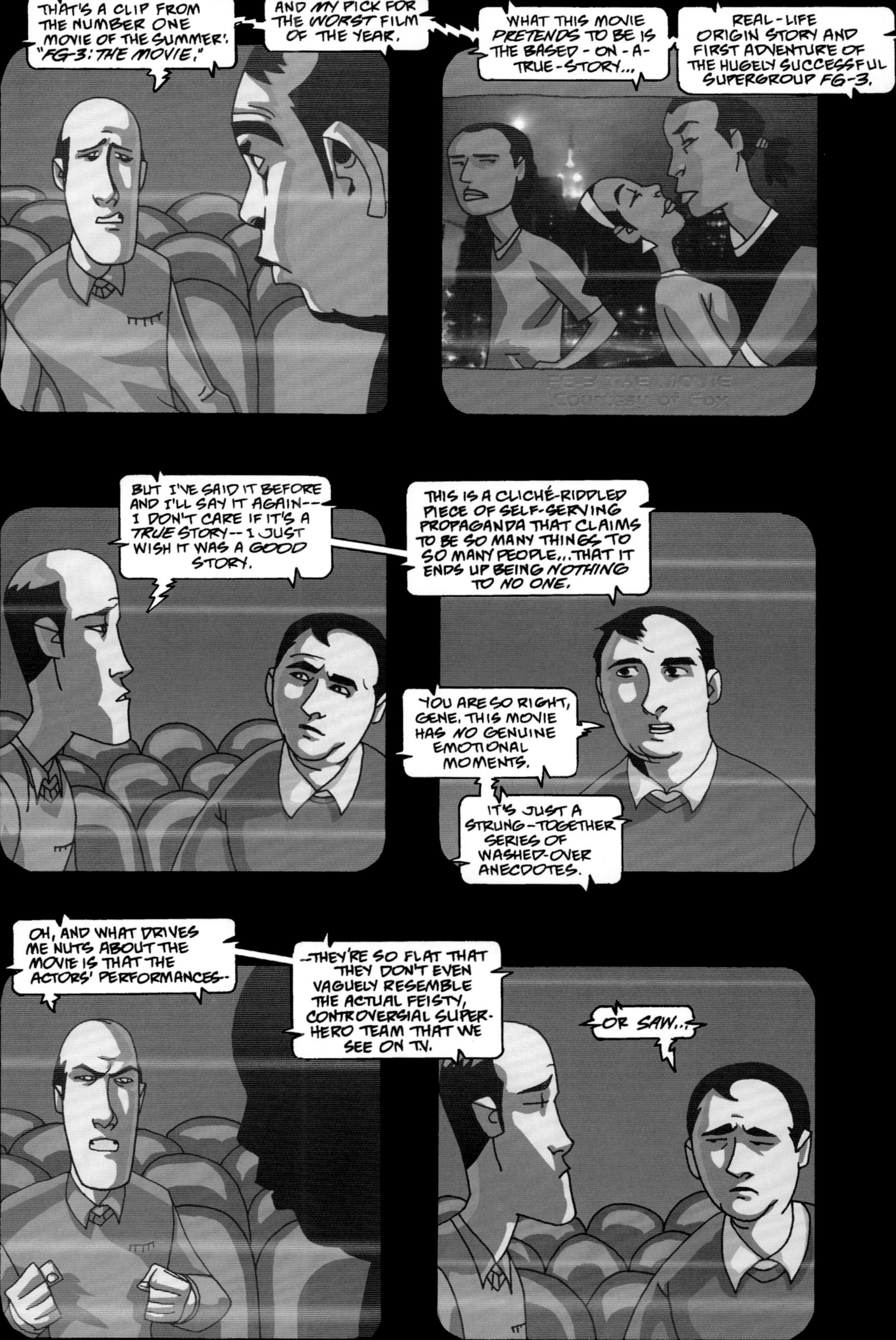

THAT'S A CLIP FROM THE NUMBER ONE MOVIE OF THE SUMMER: "FG-3: THE MOVIE,"
AND MY PICK FOR THE WORST FILM OF THE YEAR.
WHAT THIS MOVIE PRETENDS TO BE IS THE BASED-ON-A-TRUE-STORY...
REAL-LIFE ORIGIN STORY AND FIRST ADVENTURE OF THE HUGELY SUCCESSFUL SUPERGROUP FG-3.
BUT I'VE SAID IT BEFORE AND I'LL SAY IT AGAIN-- I DON'T CARE IF IT'S A TRUE STORY-- I JUST WISH IT WAS A GOOD STORY.
THIS IS A CLICHÉ-RIDDLED PIECE OF SELF-SERVING PROPAGANDA THAT CLAIMS TO BE SO MANY THINGS TO SO MANY PEOPLE... THAT IT ENDS UP BEING NOTHING TO NO ONE.
YOU ARE SO RIGHT, GENE. THIS MOVIE HAS NO GENUINE EMOTIONAL MOMENTS.
IT'S JUST A STRUNG-TOGETHER SERIES OF WASHED-OVER ANECDOTES.
OH, AND WHAT DRIVES ME NUTS ABOUT THE MOVIE IS THAT THE ACTORS' PERFORMANCES--
--THEY'RE SO FLAT THAT THEY DON'T EVEN VAGUELY RESEMBLE THE ACTUAL FEISTY, CONTROVERSIAL SUPER-HERO TEAM THAT WE SEE ON T.V.
--OR SAW...

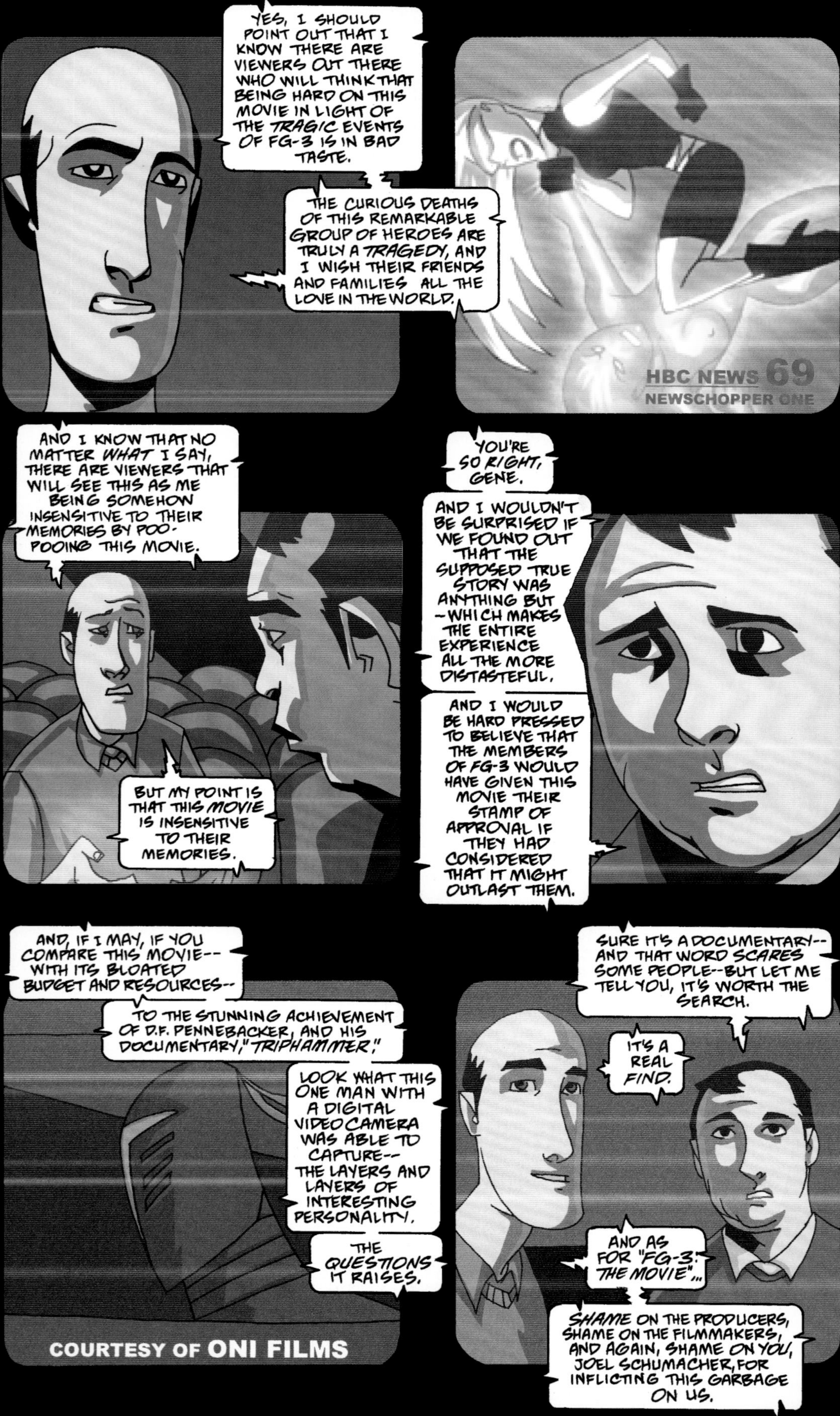
YES, I SHOULD POINT OUT THAT I KNOW THERE ARE VIEWERS OUT THERE WHO WILL THINK THAT BEING HARD ON THIS MOVIE IN LIGHT OF THE TRAGIC EVENTS OF FG-3 IS IN BAD TASTE.
THE CURIOUS DEATHS OF THIS REMARKABLE GROUP OF HEROES ARE TRULY A TRAGEDY, AND I WISH THEIR FRIENDS AND FAMILIES ALL THE LOVE IN THE WORLD.
HBC NEWS 69
NEWSCHOPPER ONE
AND I KNOW THAT NO MATTER WHAT I SAY, THERE ARE VIEWERS THAT WILL SEE THIS AS ME BEING SOMEHOW INSENSITIVE TO THEIR MEMORIES BY POO-POOING THIS MOVIE.
BUT MY POINT IS THAT THIS MOVIE IS INSENSITIVE TO THEIR MEMORIES.
YOU'RE SO RIGHT, GENE.
AND I WOULDN'T BE SURPRISED IF WE FOUND OUT THAT THE SUPPOSED TRUE STORY WAS ANYTHING BUT --WHICH MAKES THE ENTIRE EXPERIENCE ALL THE MORE DISTASTEFUL.
AND I WOULD BE HARD PRESSED TO BELIEVE THAT THE MEMBERS OF FG-3 WOULD HAVE GIVEN THIS MOVIE THEIR STAMP OF APPROVAL IF THEY HAD CONSIDERED THAT IT MIGHT OUTLAST THEM.
AND, IF I MAY, IF YOU COMPARE THIS MOVIE--WITH ITS BLOATED BUDGET AND RESOURCES--
TO THE STUNNING ACHIEVEMENT OF D.F. PENNEBACKER, AND HIS DOCUMENTARY, "TRIPHAMMER,"
LOOK WHAT THIS ONE MAN WITH A DIGITAL VIDEO CAMERA WAS ABLE TO CAPTURE--THE LAYERS AND LAYERS OF INTERESTING PERSONALITY.
THE QUESTIONS IT RAISES.
COURTESY OF ONI FILMS
SURE IT'S A DOCUMENTARY--AND THAT WORD SCARES SOME PEOPLE--BUT LET ME TELL YOU, IT'S WORTH THE SEARCH.
IT'S A REAL FIND.
AND AS FOR "FG-3: THE MOVIE"...
SHAME ON THE PRODUCERS, SHAME ON THE FILMMAKERS, AND AGAIN, SHAME ON YOU, JOEL SCHUMACHER, FOR INFLICTING THIS GARBAGE ON US.

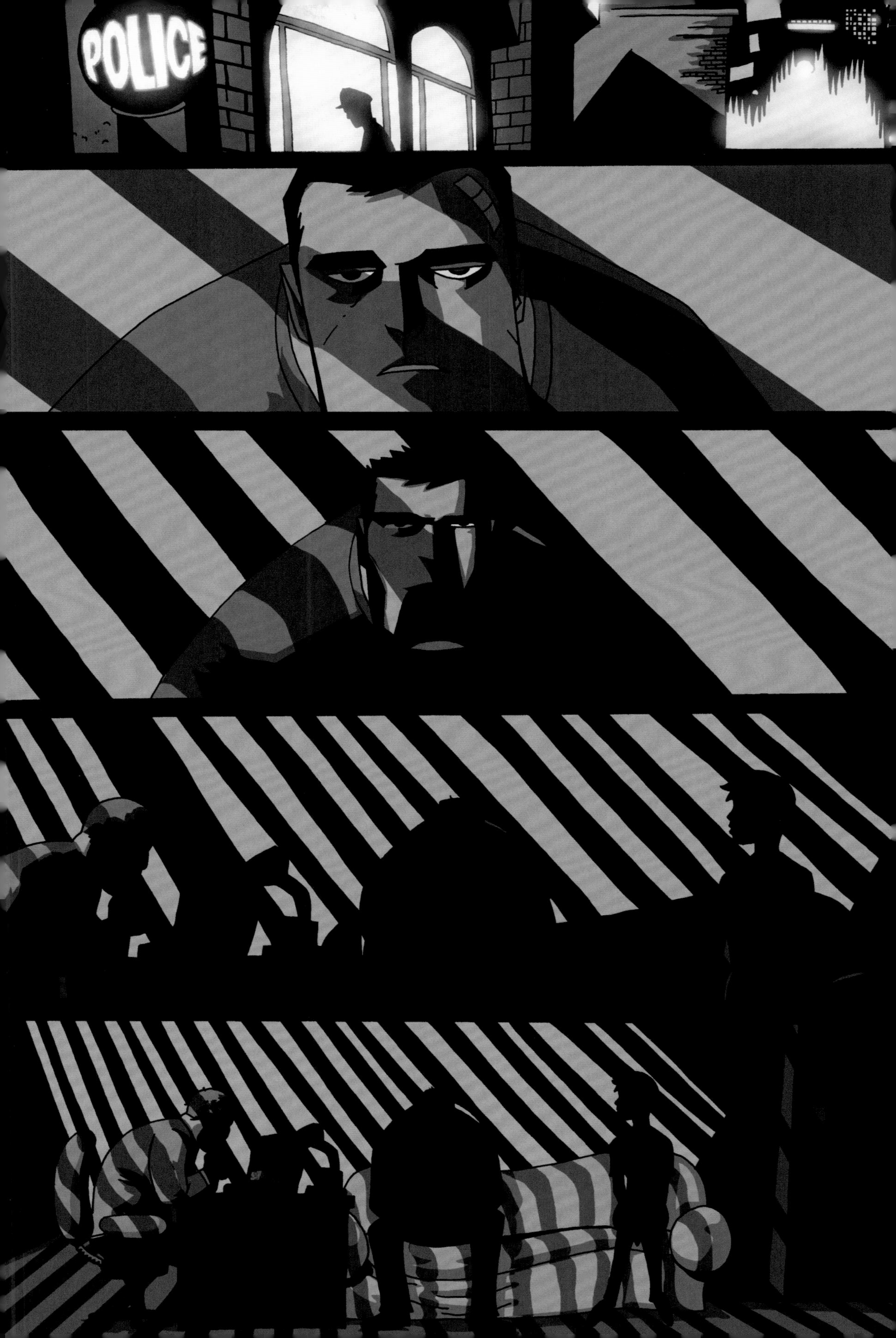
POLICE

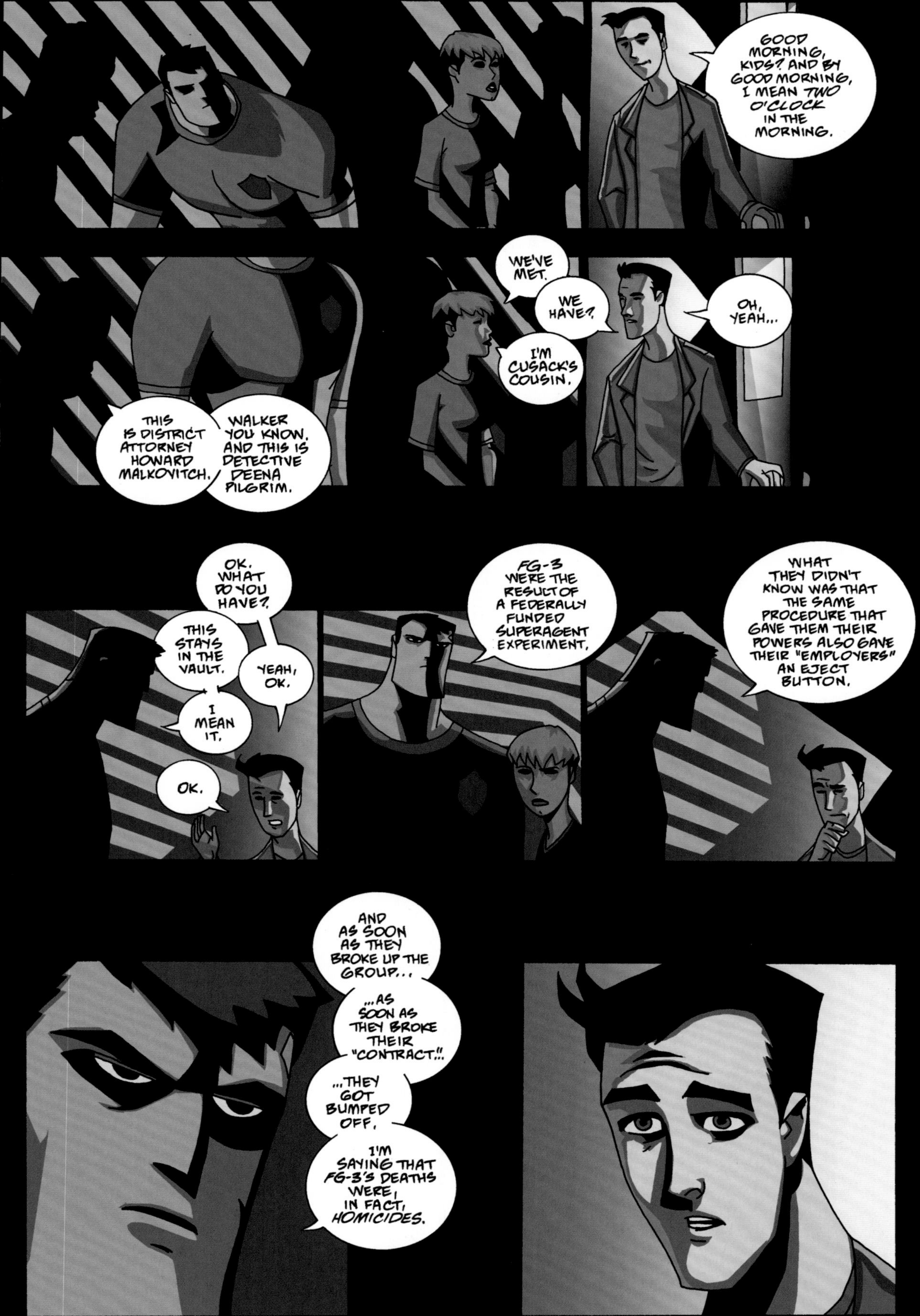

GOOD MORNING, KIDS? AND BY GOOD MORNING, I MEAN TWO O'CLOCK IN THE MORNING.
WE'VE MET.
WE HAVE?
I'M CUSACK'S COUSIN.
OH, YEAH...
THIS IS DISTRICT ATTORNEY HOWARD MALKOVITCH.
WALKER YOU KNOW. AND THIS IS DETECTIVE DEENA PILGRIM.
OK. WHAT DO YOU HAVE?
THIS STAYS IN THE VAULT.
YEAH, OK.
I MEAN IT.
OK.
FG-3 WERE THE RESULT OF A FEDERALLY FUNDED SUPERAGENT EXPERIMENT.
WHAT THEY DIDN'T KNOW WAS THAT THE SAME PROCEDURE THAT GAVE THEM THEIR POWERS ALSO GAVE THEIR "EMPLOYERS" AN EJECT BUTTON.
AND AS SOON AS THEY BROKE UP THE GROUP...
...AS SOON AS THEY BROKE THEIR "CONTRACT,"...
...THEY GOT BUMPED OFF.
I'M SAYING THAT FG-3'S DEATHS WERE, IN FACT, HOMICIDES.

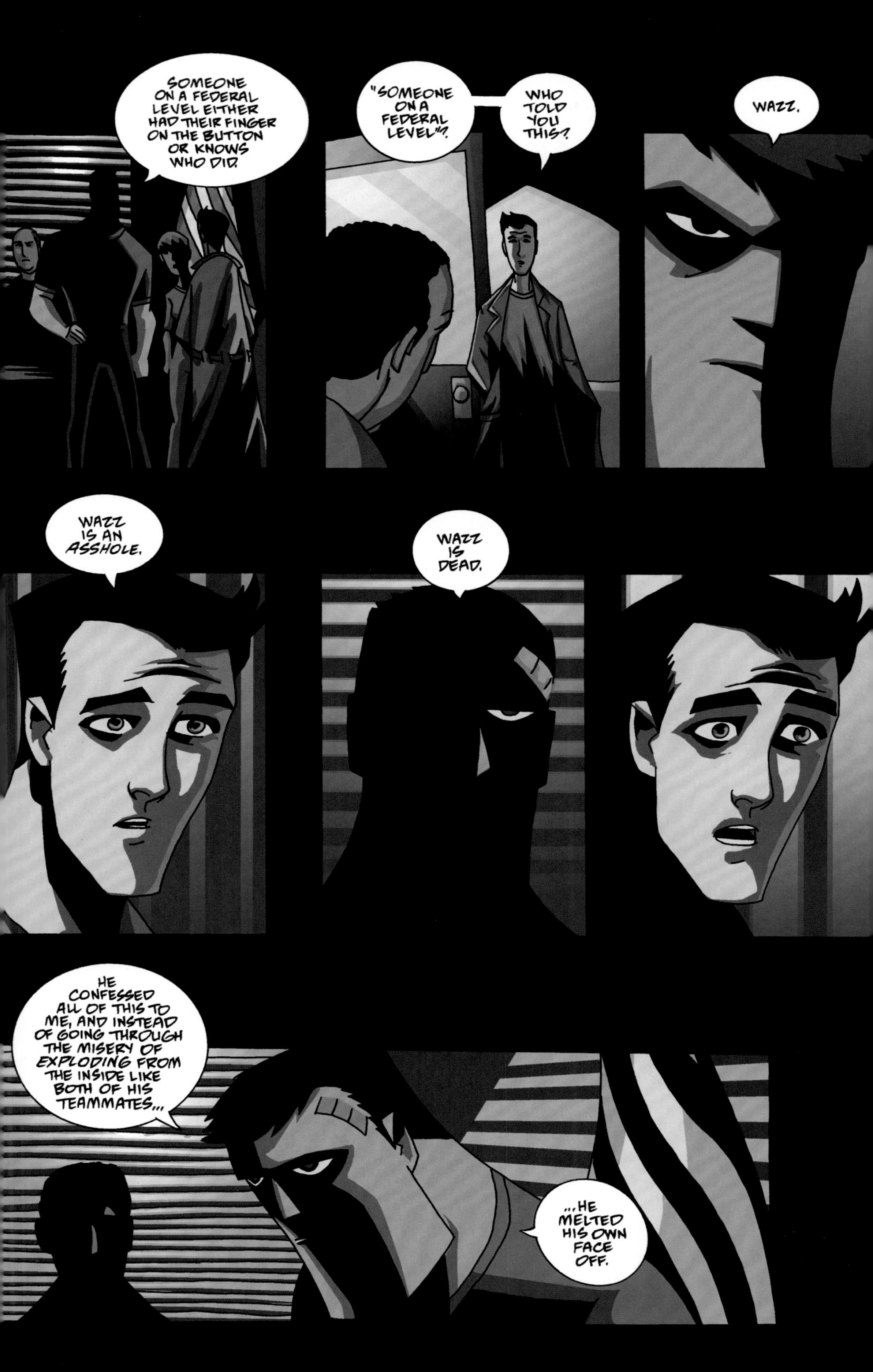
SOMEONE ON A FEDERAL LEVEL EITHER HAD THEIR FINGER ON THE BUTTON OR KNOWS WHO DID.
"SOMEONE ON A FEDERAL LEVEL"?
WHO TOLD YOU THIS?
WAZZ.
WAZZ IS AN ASSHOLE.
WAZZ IS DEAD.
HE CONFESSED ALL OF THIS TO ME, AND INSTEAD OF GOING THROUGH THE MISERY OF EXPLODING FROM THE INSIDE LIKE BOTH OF HIS TEAMMATES...
...HE MELTED HIS OWN FACE OFF.

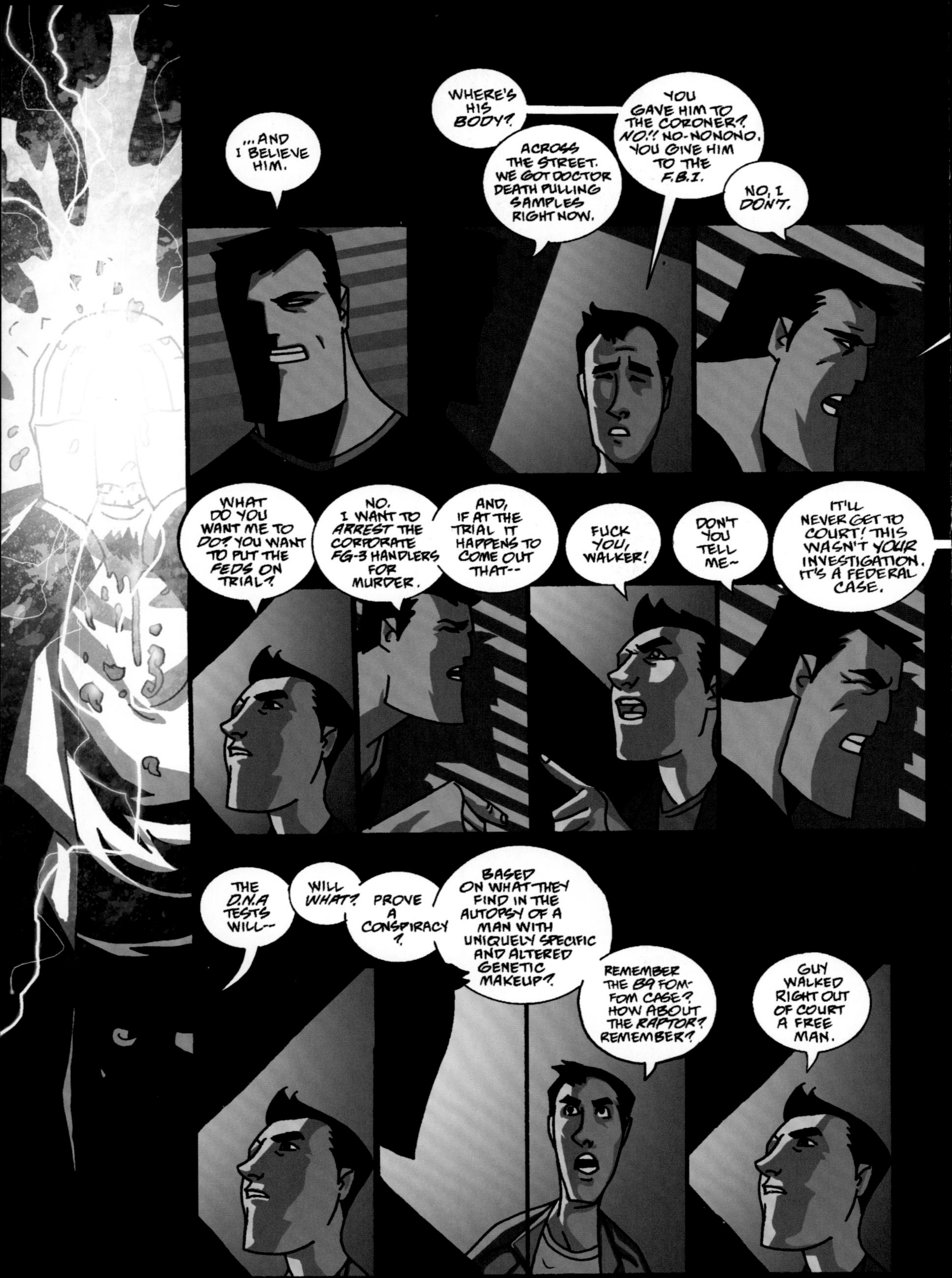
...AND I BELIEVE HIM.
WHERE'S HIS BODY?
ACROSS THE STREET. WE GOT DOCTOR DEATH PULLING SAMPLES RIGHT NOW.
YOU GAVE HIM TO THE CORONER? NO!! NO-NONONO. YOU GIVE HIM TO THE F.B.I.
NO, I DON'T.
WHAT DO YOU WANT ME TO DO? YOU WANT TO PUT THE FEDS ON TRIAL?
NO. I WANT TO ARREST THE CORPORATE FG-3 HANDLERS FOR MURDER.
AND, IF AT THE TRIAL IT HAPPENS TO COME OUT THAT--
FUCK YOU, WALKER!
DON'T YOU TELL ME~
IT'LL NEVER GET TO COURT! THIS WASN'T YOUR INVESTIGATION. IT'S A FEDERAL CASE.
THE D.N.A TESTS WILL--
WILL WHAT?
PROVE A CONSPIRACY?
BASED ON WHAT THEY FIND IN THE AUTOPSY OF A MAN WITH UNIQUELY SPECIFIC AND ALTERED GENETIC MAKEUP?
REMEMBER THE B9 FOM-FOM CASE? HOW ABOUT THE RAPTOR? REMEMBER?
GUY WALKED RIGHT OUT OF COURT A FREE MAN.

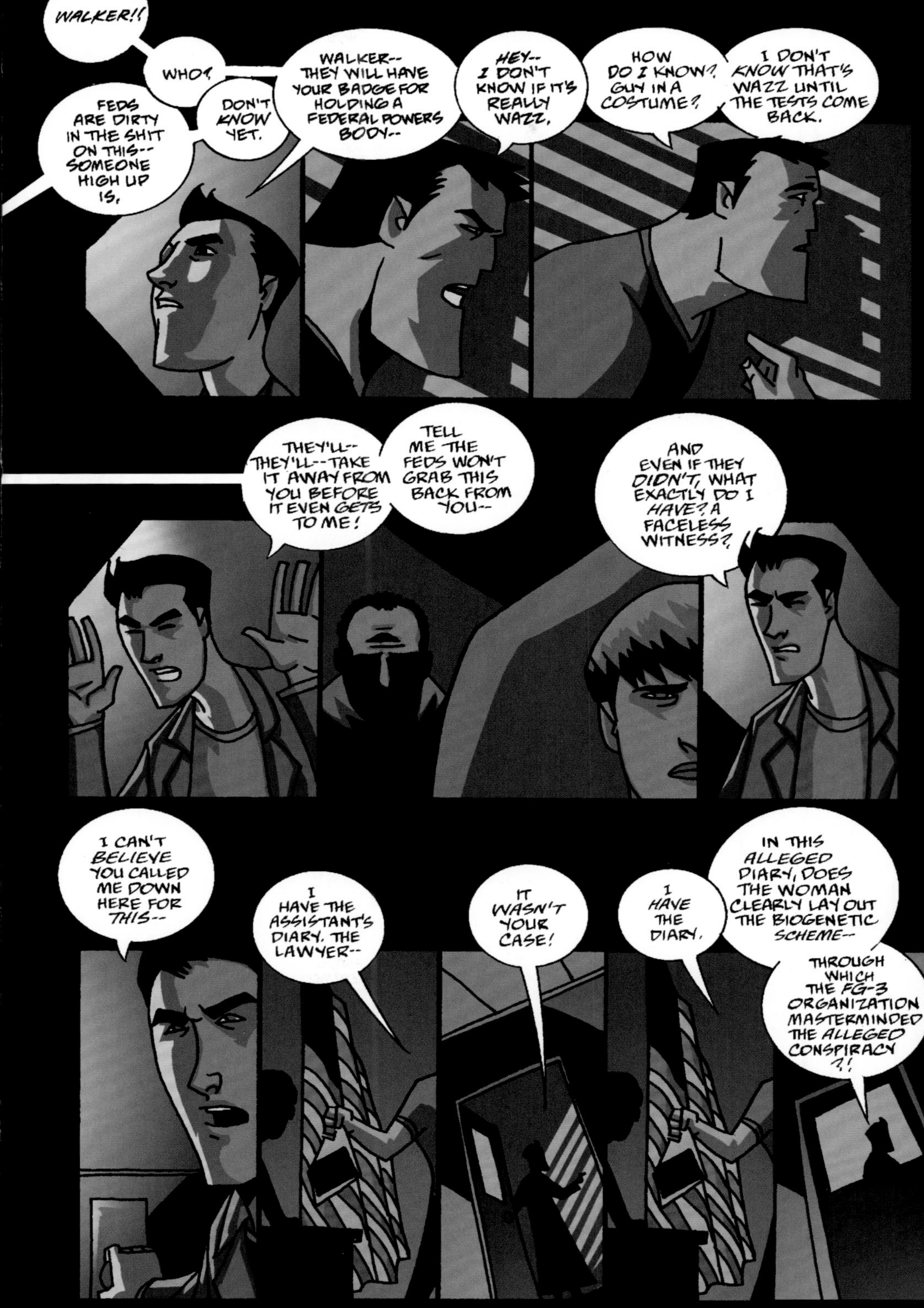
WALKER!!
WHO?
FEDS ARE DIRTY IN THE SHIT ON THIS-- SOMEONE HIGH UP IS.
DON'T KNOW YET.
WALKER-- THEY WILL HAVE YOUR BADGE FOR HOLDING A FEDERAL POWERS BODY--
HEY-- I DON'T KNOW IF IT'S REALLY WAZZ.
HOW DO I KNOW? GUY IN A COSTUME?
I DON'T KNOW THAT'S WAZZ UNTIL THE TESTS COME BACK.
THEY'LL-- THEY'LL--TAKE IT AWAY FROM YOU BEFORE IT EVEN GETS TO ME!
TELL ME THE FEDS WON'T GRAB THIS BACK FROM YOU--
AND EVEN IF THEY DIDN'T, WHAT EXACTLY DO I HAVE? A FACELESS WITNESS?
I CAN'T BELIEVE YOU CALLED ME DOWN HERE FOR THIS--
I HAVE THE ASSISTANT'S DIARY. THE LAWYER--
IT WASN'T YOUR CASE!
I HAVE THE DIARY.
IN THIS ALLEGED DIARY, DOES THE WOMAN CLEARLY LAY OUT THE BIOGENETIC SCHEME--
THROUGH WHICH THE FG-3 ORGANIZATION MASTERMINDED THE ALLEGED CONSPIRACY?!

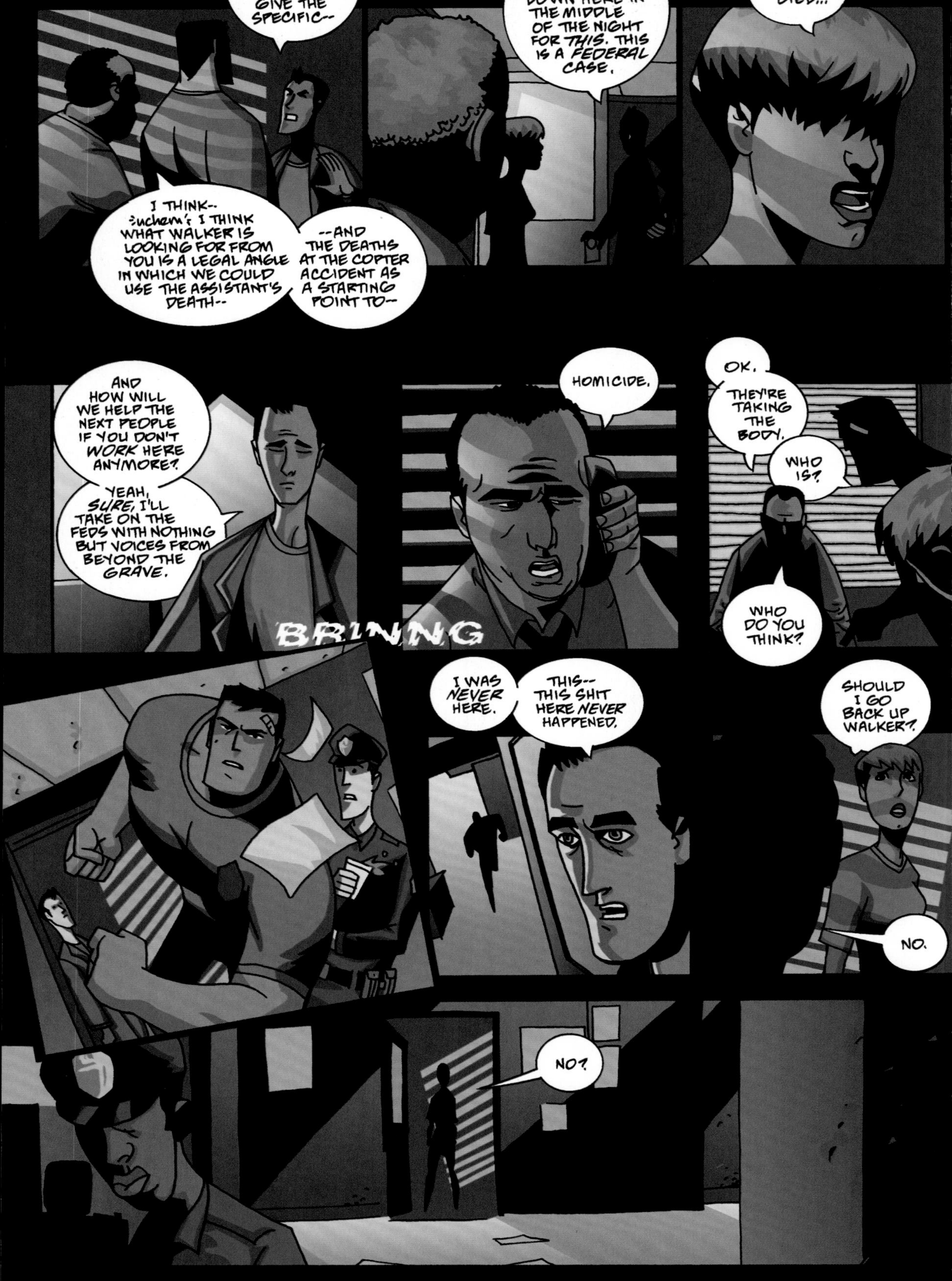
DID SHE NAME NAMES? DOES SHE GIVE THE SPECIFIC--
I CAN'T BELIEVE YOU CALLED ME DOWN HERE IN THE MIDDLE OF THE NIGHT FOR THIS. THIS IS A FEDERAL CASE.
PEOPLE DIED...
I THINK-- uchem: I THINK WHAT WALKER IS LOOKING FOR FROM YOU IS A LEGAL ANGLE IN WHICH WE COULD USE THE ASSISTANT'S DEATH--
--AND THE DEATHS AT THE COPTER ACCIDENT AS A STARTING POINT TO--
AND HOW WILL WE HELP THE NEXT PEOPLE IF YOU DON'T WORK HERE ANYMORE?
YEAH, SURE, I'LL TAKE ON THE FEDS WITH NOTHING BUT VOICES FROM BEYOND THE GRAVE.
BRINNG
HOMICIDE.
OK.
THEY'RE TAKING THE BODY.
WHO IS?
WHO DO YOU THINK?
I WAS NEVER HERE.
THIS-- THIS SHIT HERE NEVER HAPPENED.
SHOULD I GO BACK UP WALKER?
NO.
NO?

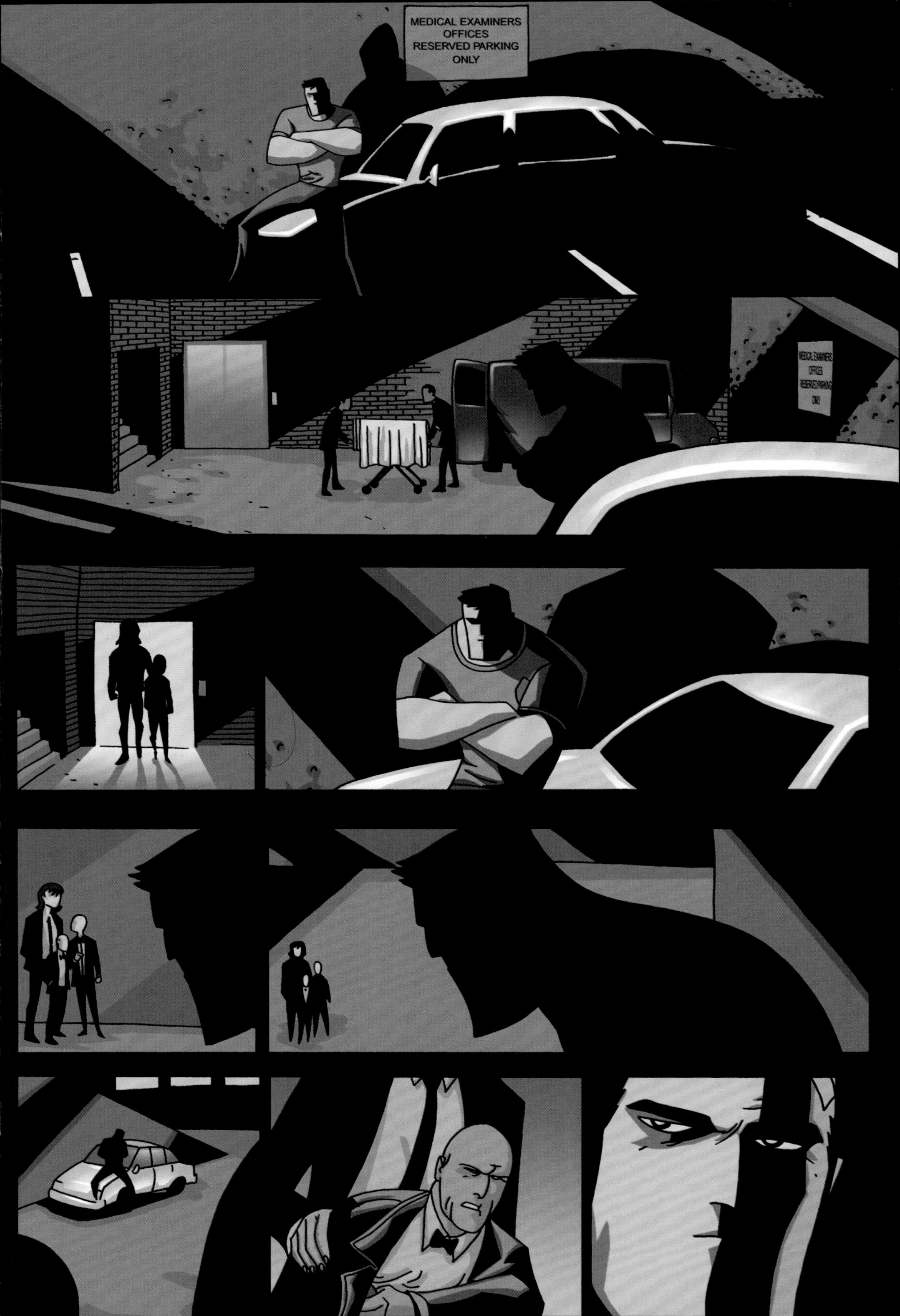
MEDICAL EXAMINERS
OFFICES
RESERVED PARKING
ONLY

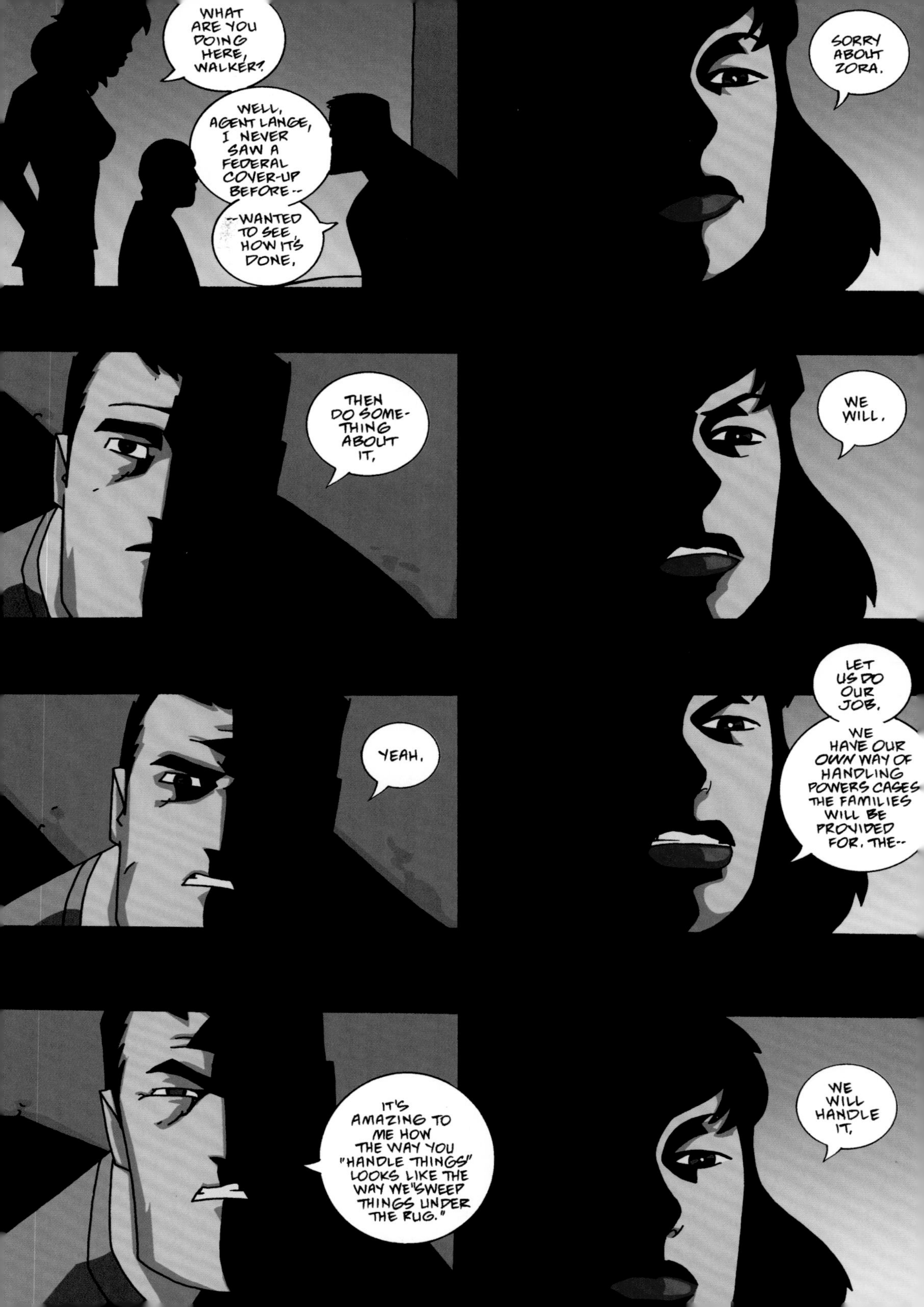
WHAT ARE YOU DOING HERE, WALKER?
WELL, AGENT LANGE, I NEVER SAW A FEDERAL COVER-UP BEFORE--
--WANTED TO SEE HOW IT'S DONE.
SORRY ABOUT ZORA.
THEN DO SOMETHING ABOUT IT.
WE WILL.
YEAH.
LET US DO OUR JOB.
WE HAVE OUR OWN WAY OF HANDLING POWERS CASES. THE FAMILIES WILL BE PROVIDED FOR. THE--
IT'S AMAZING TO ME HOW THE WAY YOU "HANDLE THINGS" LOOKS LIKE THE WAY WE "SWEEP THINGS UNDER THE RUG."
WE WILL HANDLE IT.

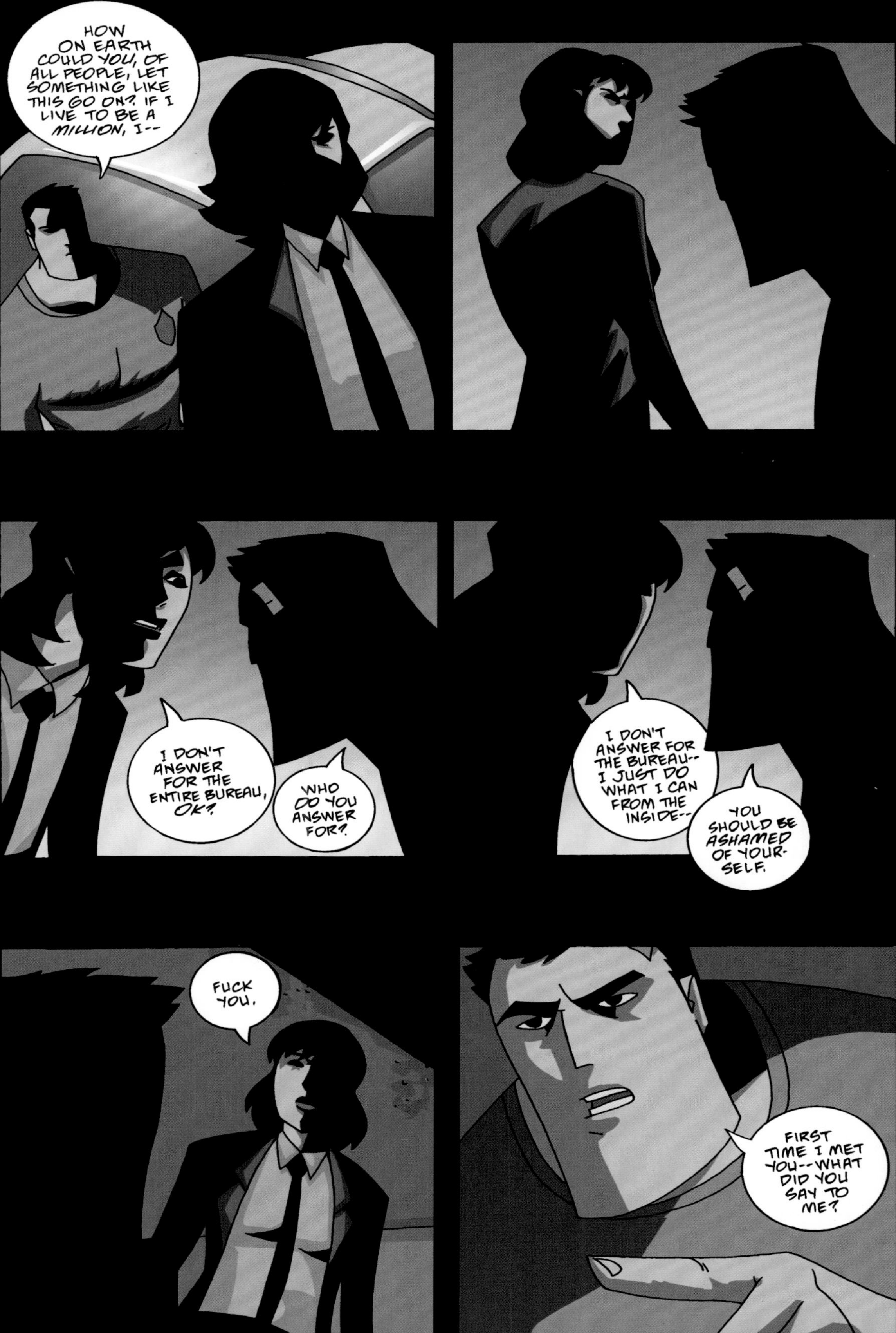
HOW ON EARTH COULD YOU, OF ALL PEOPLE, LET SOMETHING LIKE THIS GO ON? IF I LIVE TO BE A MILLION, I--
I DON'T ANSWER FOR THE ENTIRE BUREAU, OK?
WHO DO YOU ANSWER FOR?
I DON'T ANSWER FOR THE BUREAU-- I JUST DO WHAT I CAN FROM THE INSIDE--
YOU SHOULD BE ASHAMED OF YOURSELF.
FUCK YOU.
FIRST TIME I MET YOU--WHAT DID YOU SAY TO ME?

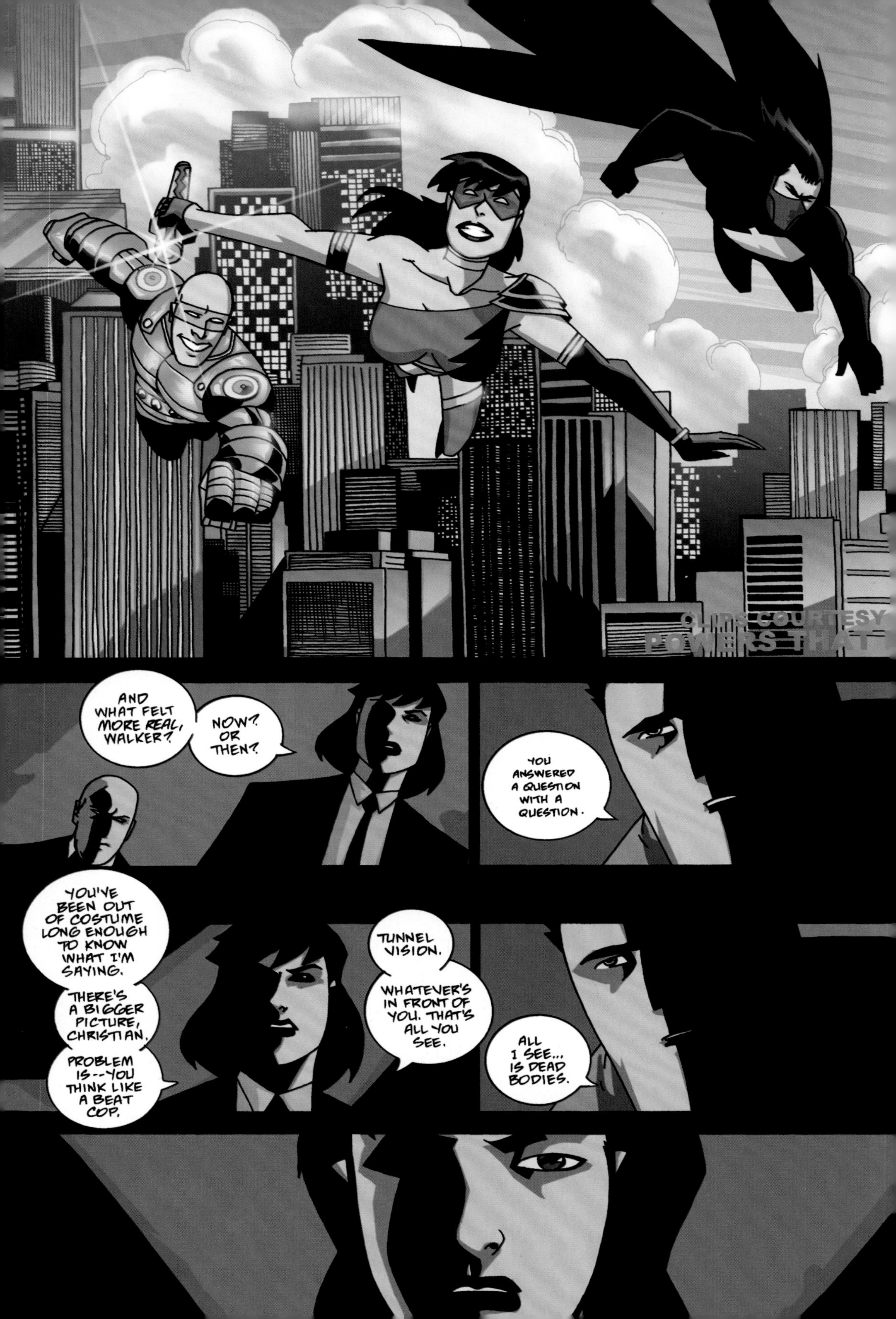
CLIPS COURTESY
POWERS THAT
AND WHAT FELT MORE REAL, WALKER?
NOW? OR THEN?
YOU ANSWERED A QUESTION WITH A QUESTION.
YOU'VE BEEN OUT OF COSTUME LONG ENOUGH TO KNOW WHAT I'M SAYING.
THERE'S A BIGGER PICTURE, CHRISTIAN.
PROBLEM IS--YOU THINK LIKE A BEAT COP.
TUNNEL VISION.
WHATEVER'S IN FRONT OF YOU. THAT'S ALL YOU SEE.
ALL I SEE... IS DEAD BODIES.

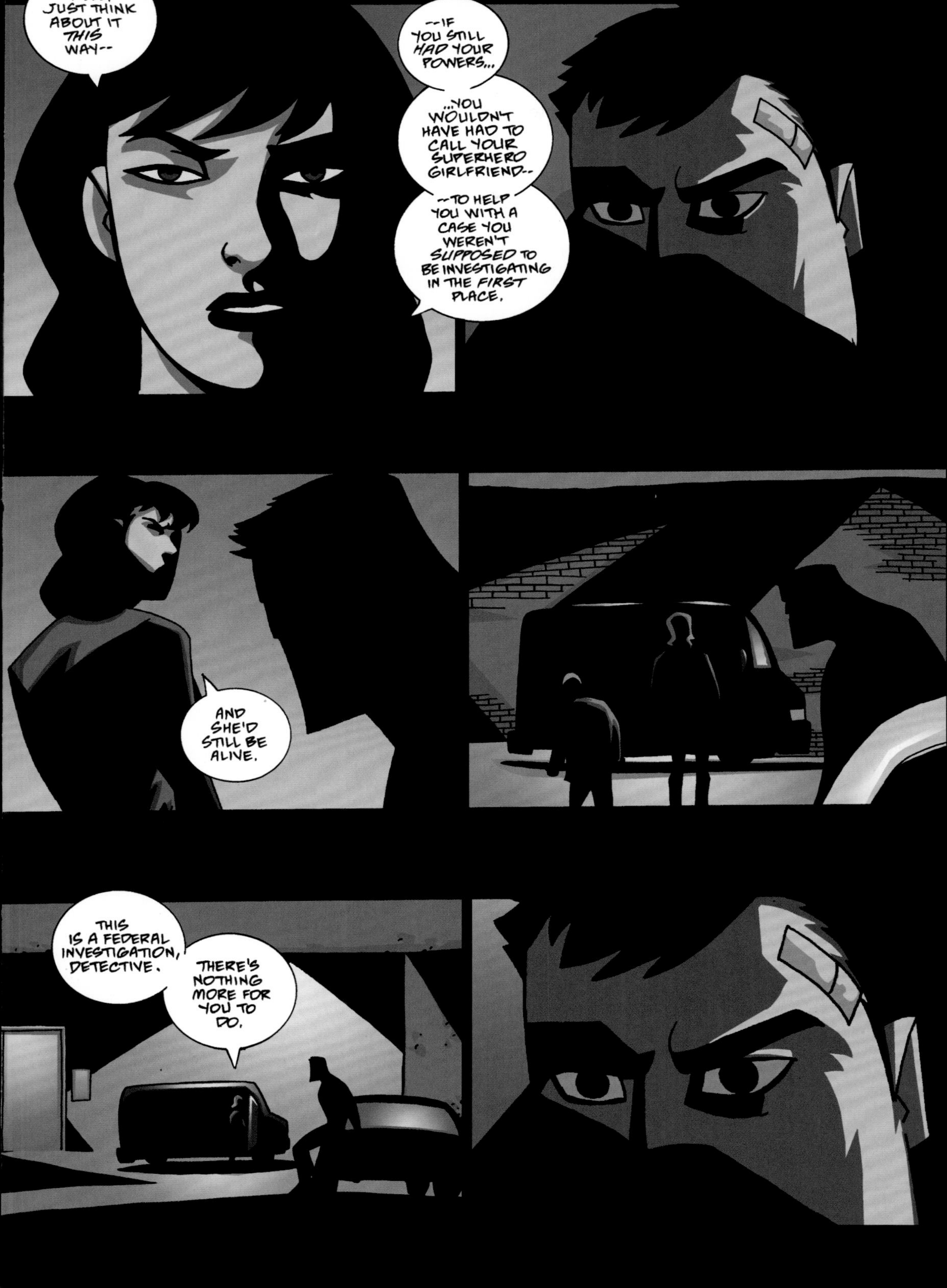
WELL, JUST THINK ABOUT IT THIS WAY--
--IF YOU STILL HAD YOUR POWERS...
...YOU WOULDN'T HAVE HAD TO CALL YOUR SUPERHERO GIRLFRIEND--
--TO HELP YOU WITH A CASE YOU WEREN'T SUPPOSED TO BE INVESTIGATING IN THE FIRST PLACE.
AND SHE'D STILL BE ALIVE.
THIS IS A FEDERAL INVESTIGATION, DETECTIVE.
THERE'S NOTHING MORE FOR YOU TO DO.

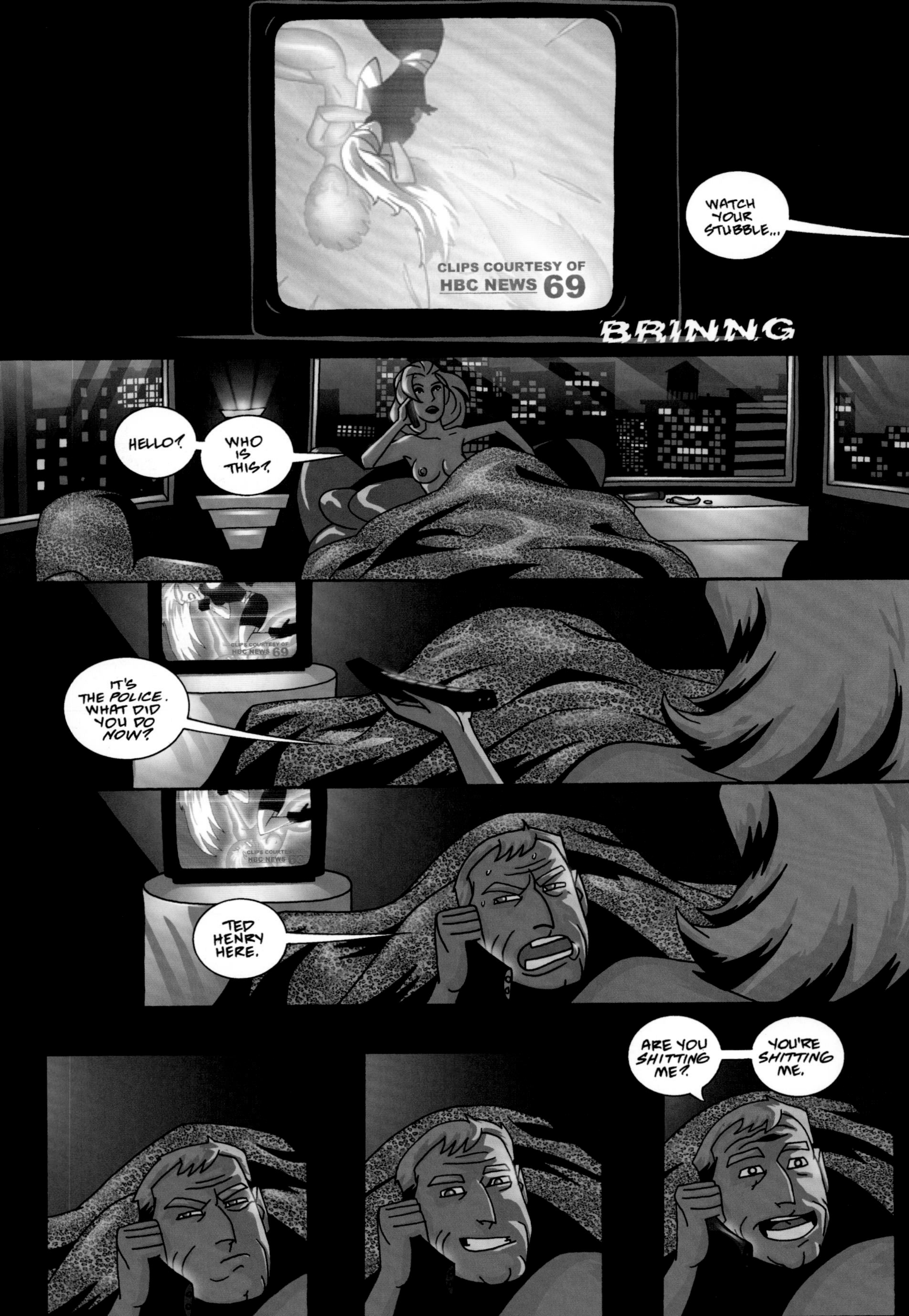
CLIPS COURTESY OF
HBC NEWS 69
WATCH YOUR STUBBLE...
BRINNG
HELLO?
WHO IS THIS?
CLIPS COURTESY OF
HBC NEWS 69
IT'S THE POLICE. WHAT DID YOU DO NOW?
TED HENRY HERE.
ARE YOU SHITTING ME?
YOU'RE SHITTING ME.

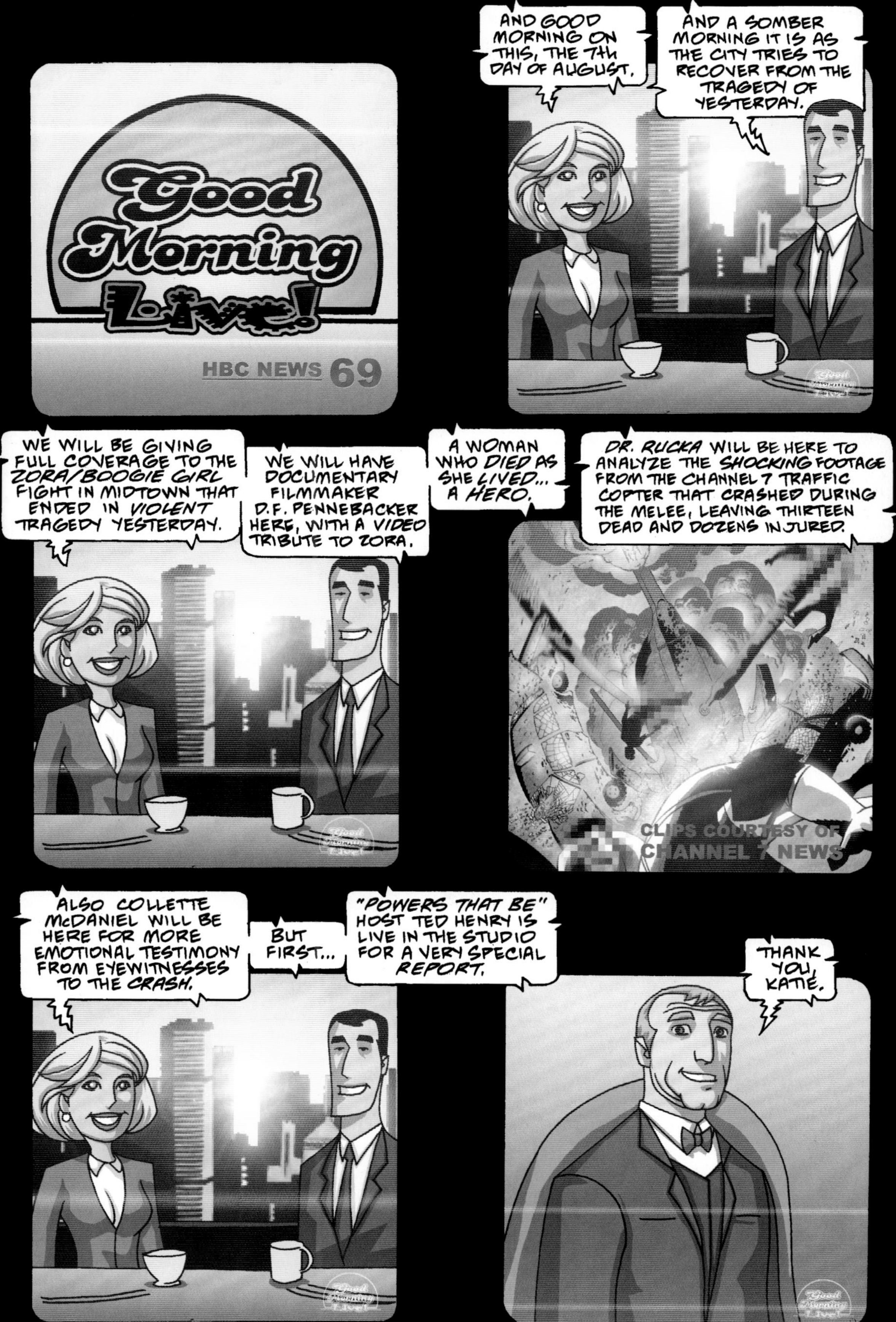
Good Morning Live!
HBC NEWS 69
AND GOOD MORNING ON THIS, THE 7th DAY OF AUGUST.
AND A SOMBER MORNING IT IS AS THE CITY TRIES TO RECOVER FROM THE TRAGEDY OF YESTERDAY.
WE WILL BE GIVING FULL COVERAGE TO THE ZORA/BOOGIE GIRL FIGHT IN MIDTOWN THAT ENDED IN VIOLENT TRAGEDY YESTERDAY.
WE WILL HAVE DOCUMENTARY FILMMAKER D.F. PENNEBACKER HERE, WITH A VIDEO TRIBUTE TO ZORA.
A WOMAN WHO DIED AS SHE LIVED... A HERO.
DR. RUCKA WILL BE HERE TO ANALYZE THE SHOCKING FOOTAGE FROM THE CHANNEL 7 TRAFFIC COPTER THAT CRASHED DURING THE MELEE, LEAVING THIRTEEN DEAD AND DOZENS INJURED.
CLIPS COURTESY OF CHANNEL 7 NEWS
ALSO COLLETTE McDANIEL WILL BE HERE FOR MORE EMOTIONAL TESTIMONY FROM EYEWITNESSES TO THE CRASH.
BUT FIRST...
"POWERS THAT BE" HOST TED HENRY IS LIVE IN THE STUDIO FOR A VERY SPECIAL REPORT.
THANK YOU, KATIE.

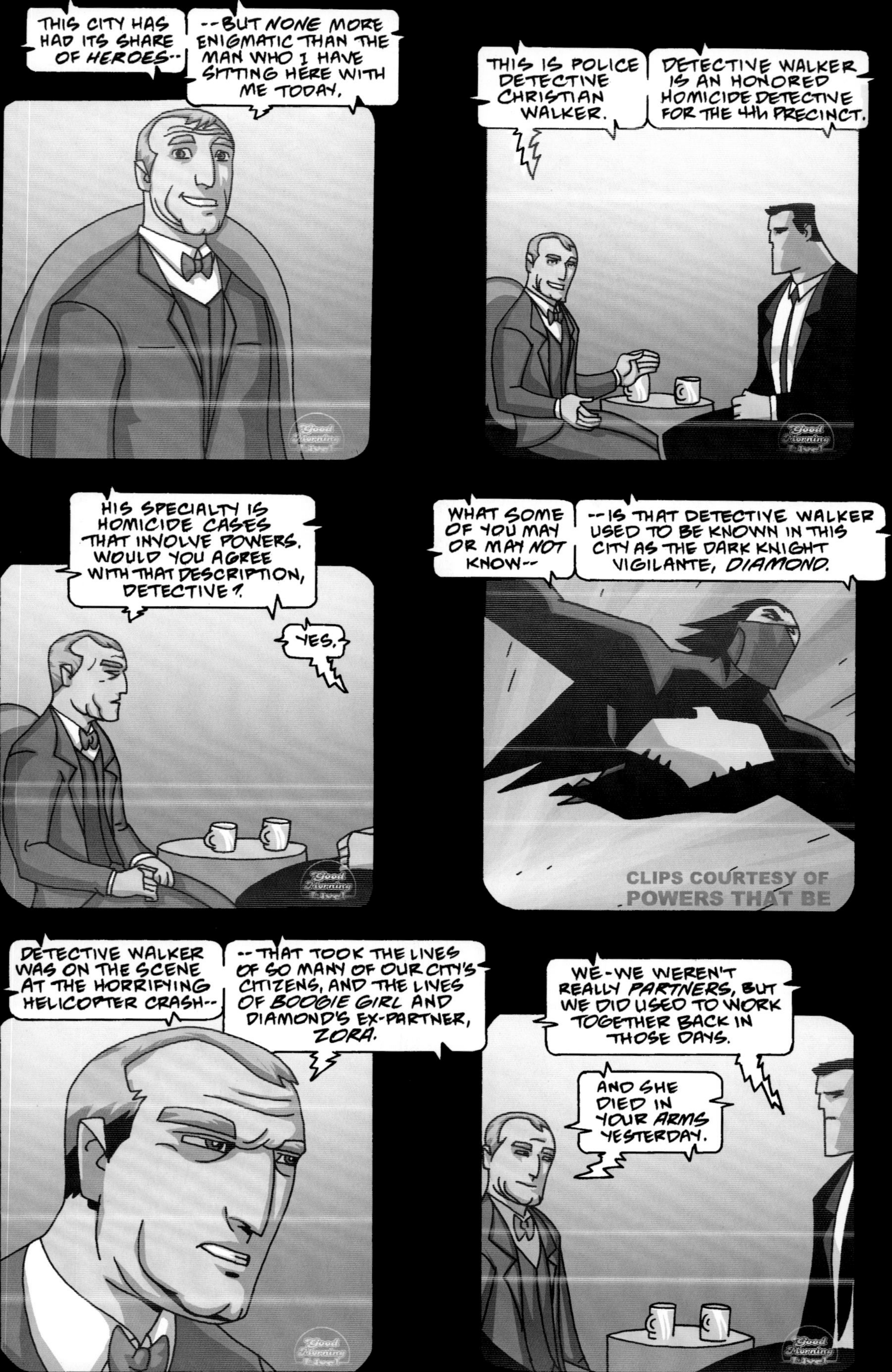
THIS CITY HAS HAD ITS SHARE OF *HEROES*--
--BUT *NONE* MORE ENIGMATIC THAN THE MAN WHO I HAVE SITTING HERE WITH ME TODAY.
THIS IS POLICE DETECTIVE CHRISTIAN WALKER.
DETECTIVE WALKER IS AN HONORED HOMICIDE DETECTIVE FOR THE 4th PRECINCT.
HIS SPECIALTY IS HOMICIDE CASES THAT INVOLVE POWERS. WOULD YOU AGREE WITH THAT DESCRIPTION, DETECTIVE?
YES.
WHAT SOME OF YOU MAY OR MAY *NOT* KNOW--
--IS THAT DETECTIVE WALKER USED TO BE KNOWN IN THIS CITY AS THE DARK KNIGHT VIGILANTE, *DIAMOND*.
CLIPS COURTESY OF
POWERS THAT BE
DETECTIVE WALKER WAS ON THE SCENE AT THE HORRIFYING HELICOPTER CRASH--
--THAT TOOK THE LIVES OF SO MANY OF OUR CITY'S CITIZENS, AND THE LIVES OF *BOOGIE GIRL* AND DIAMOND'S EX-PARTNER, *ZORA*.
WE-WE WEREN'T REALLY *PARTNERS*, BUT WE DID USED TO WORK TOGETHER BACK IN THOSE DAYS.
AND SHE DIED IN YOUR *ARMS* YESTERDAY.

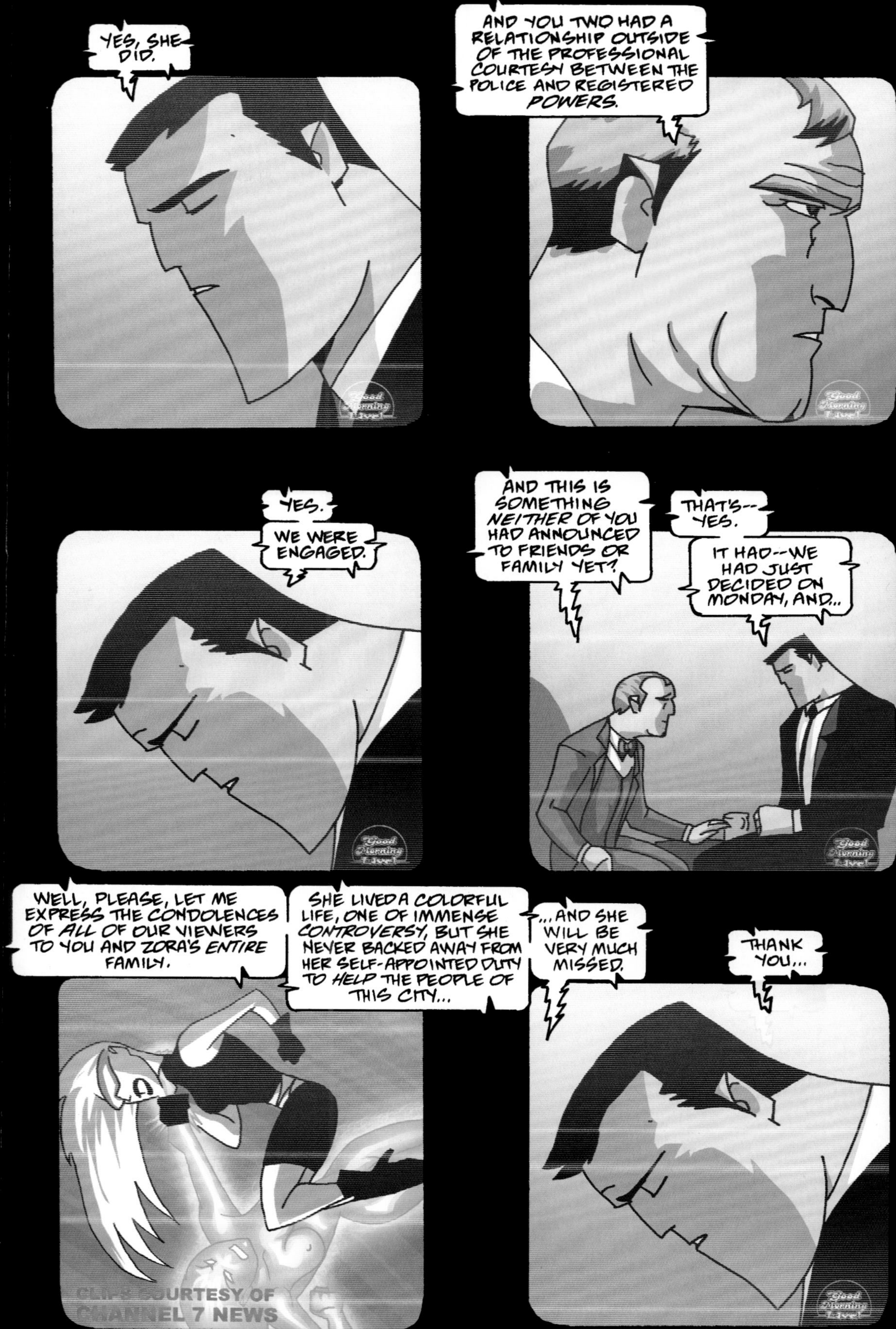
YES, SHE DID.
AND YOU TWO HAD A RELATIONSHIP OUTSIDE OF THE PROFESSIONAL COURTESY BETWEEN THE POLICE AND REGISTERED POWERS.
YES.
WE WERE ENGAGED.
AND THIS IS SOMETHING NEITHER OF YOU HAD ANNOUNCED TO FRIENDS OR FAMILY YET?
THAT'S-- YES.
IT HAD--WE HAD JUST DECIDED ON MONDAY, AND...
WELL, PLEASE, LET ME EXPRESS THE CONDOLENCES OF ALL OF OUR VIEWERS TO YOU AND ZORA'S ENTIRE FAMILY.
SHE LIVED A COLORFUL LIFE, ONE OF IMMENSE CONTROVERSY, BUT SHE NEVER BACKED AWAY FROM HER SELF-APPOINTED DUTY TO HELP THE PEOPLE OF THIS CITY...
...AND SHE WILL BE VERY MUCH MISSED.
THANK YOU...
CLIPS COURTESY OF
CHANNEL 7 NEWS

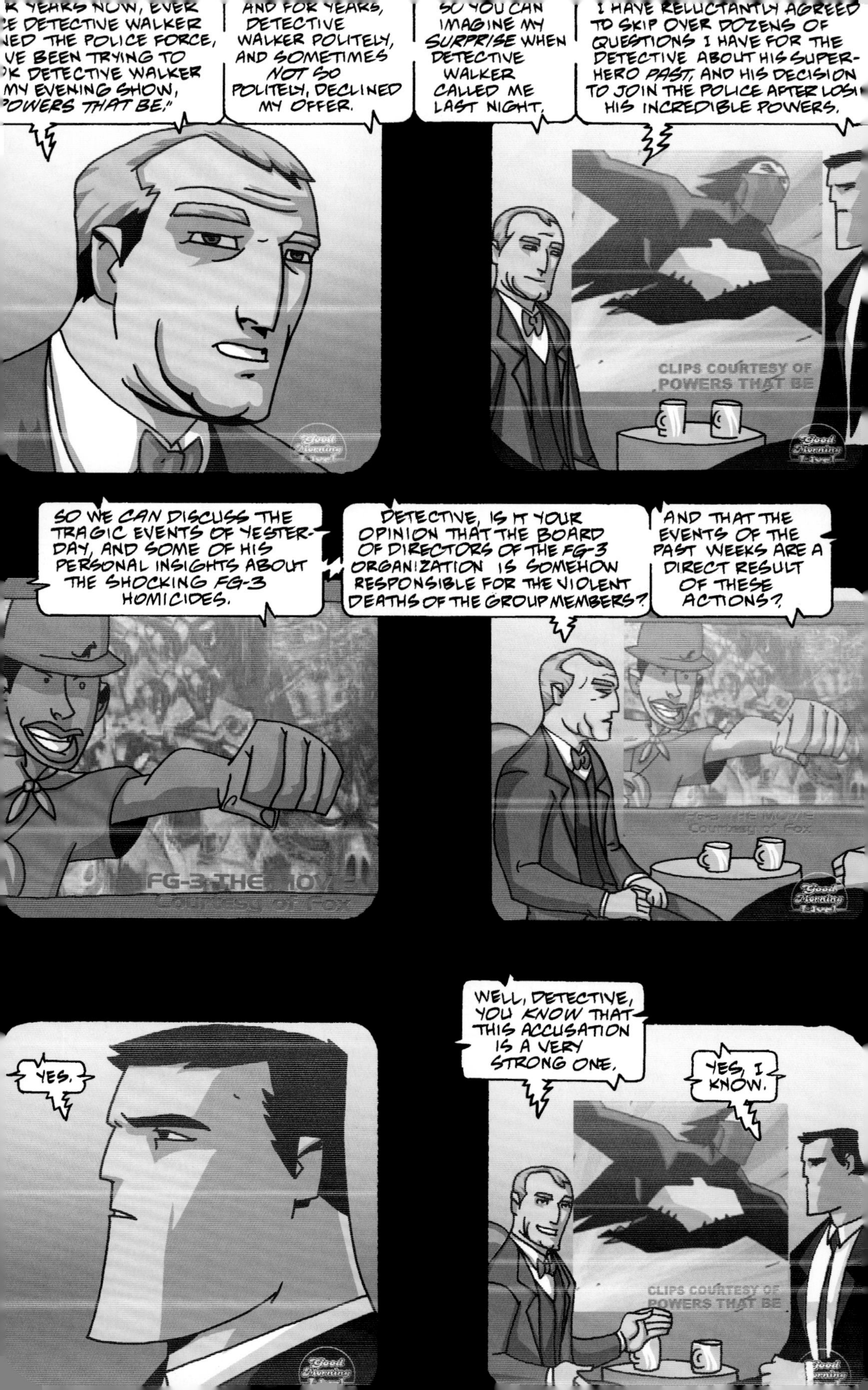
R YEARS NOW, EVER CE DETECTIVE WALKER NED THE POLICE FORCE, VE BEEN TRYING TO OK DETECTIVE WALKER MY EVENING SHOW, POWERS THAT BE."
AND FOR YEARS, DETECTIVE WALKER POLITELY, AND SOMETIMES *NOT SO* POLITELY, DECLINED MY OFFER.
SO YOU CAN IMAGINE MY *SURPRISE* WHEN DETECTIVE WALKER CALLED ME LAST NIGHT.
I HAVE RELUCTANTLY AGREED TO SKIP OVER DOZENS OF QUESTIONS I HAVE FOR THE DETECTIVE ABOUT HIS SUPER-HERO *PAST*, AND HIS DECISION TO JOIN THE POLICE AFTER LOSI HIS INCREDIBLE POWERS.
CLIPS COURTESY OF POWERS THAT BE
SO WE *CAN* DISCUSS THE TRAGIC EVENTS OF YESTER-DAY, AND SOME OF HIS PERSONAL INSIGHTS ABOUT THE SHOCKING *FG-3* HOMICIDES.
FG-3 THE MOVIE Courtesy of Fox
DETECTIVE, IS IT YOUR OPINION THAT THE BOARD OF DIRECTORS OF THE *FG-3* ORGANIZATION IS SOMEHOW RESPONSIBLE FOR THE VIOLENT DEATHS OF THE GROUP MEMBERS?
AND THAT THE EVENTS OF THE PAST WEEKS ARE A DIRECT RESULT OF THESE ACTIONS?
YES.
WELL, DETECTIVE, YOU *KNOW* THAT THIS ACCUSATION IS A VERY STRONG ONE.
YES, I KNOW.
CLIPS COURTESY OF POWERS THAT BE

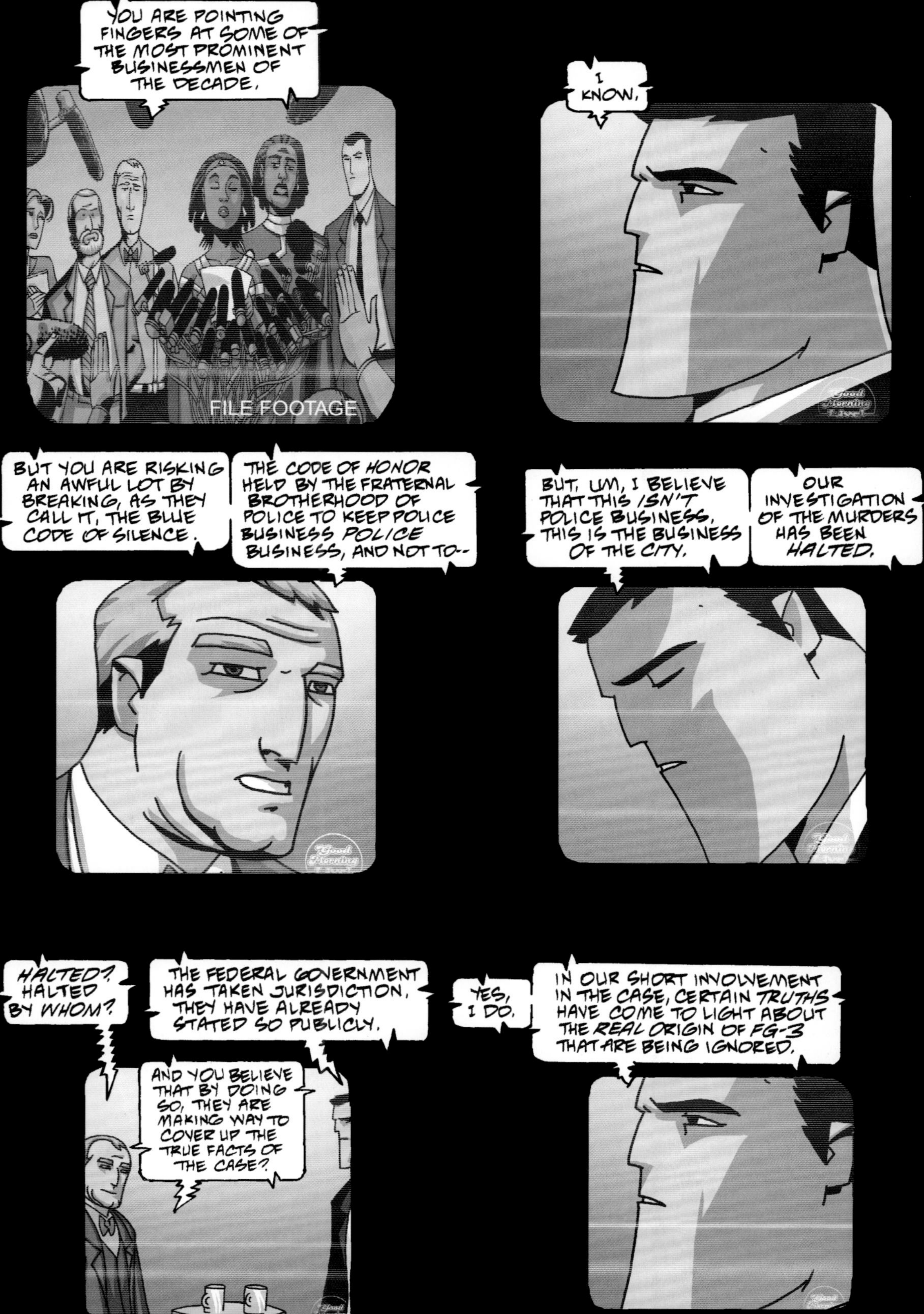
YOU ARE POINTING FINGERS AT SOME OF THE MOST PROMINENT BUSINESSMEN OF THE DECADE.
FILE FOOTAGE
I KNOW.
BUT YOU ARE RISKING AN AWFUL LOT BY BREAKING, AS THEY CALL IT, THE BLUE CODE OF SILENCE.
THE CODE OF *HONOR* HELD BY THE FRATERNAL BROTHERHOOD OF POLICE TO KEEP POLICE BUSINESS *POLICE* BUSINESS, AND NOT TO--
BUT, UM, I BELIEVE THAT THIS *ISN'T* POLICE BUSINESS. THIS IS THE BUSINESS OF THE CITY.
OUR INVESTIGATION OF THE MURDERS HAS BEEN *HALTED*.
HALTED? HALTED BY *WHOM?*
THE FEDERAL GOVERNMENT HAS TAKEN JURISDICTION. THEY HAVE ALREADY STATED SO PUBLICLY.
AND YOU BELIEVE THAT BY DOING SO, THEY ARE MAKING WAY TO COVER UP THE TRUE FACTS OF THE CASE?
YES, I DO.
IN OUR SHORT INVOLVEMENT IN THE CASE, CERTAIN *TRUTHS* HAVE COME TO LIGHT ABOUT THE *REAL* ORIGIN OF FG-3 THAT ARE BEING IGNORED.

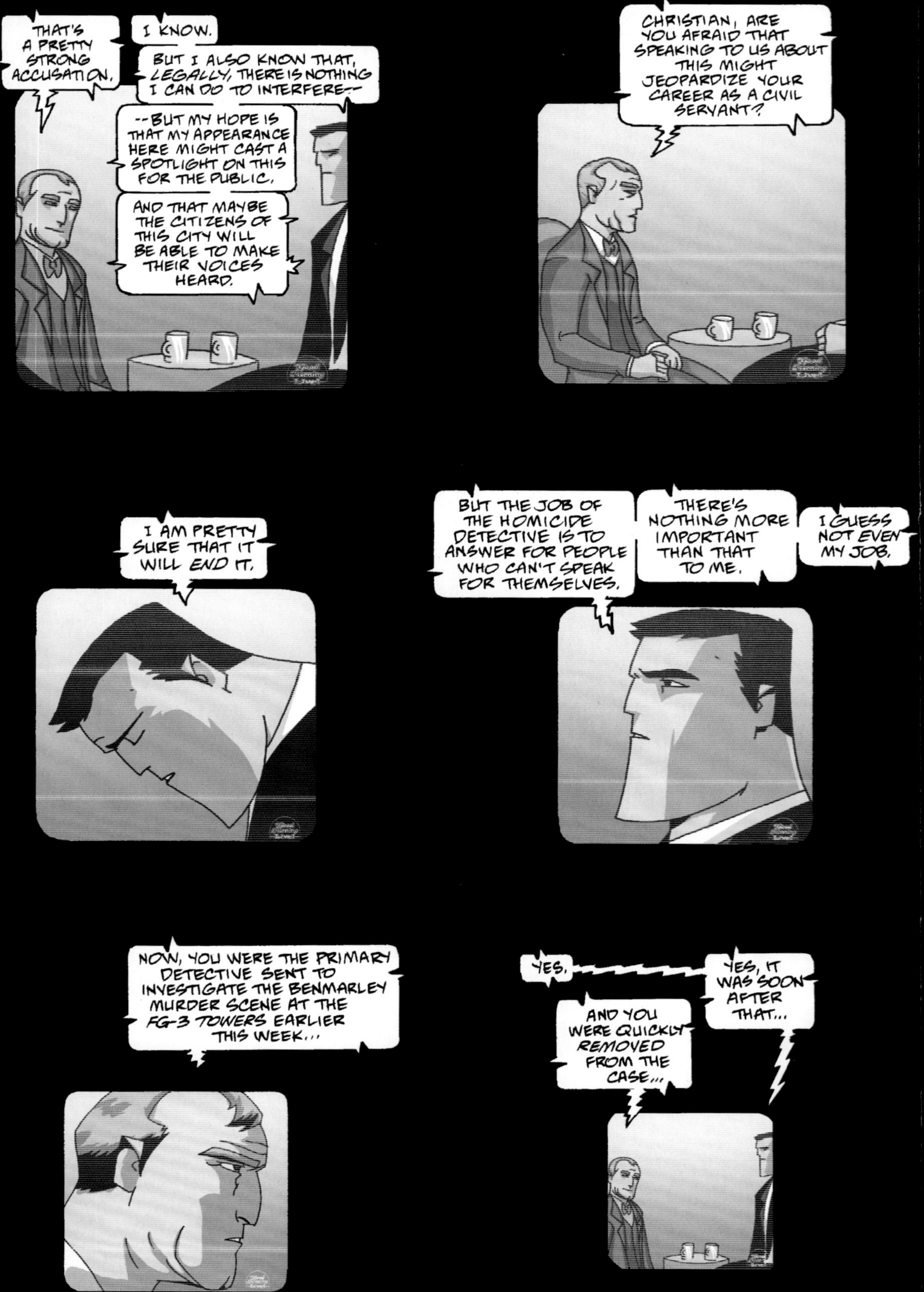
THAT'S A PRETTY STRONG ACCUSATION.
I KNOW.
BUT I ALSO KNOW THAT, LEGALLY, THERE IS NOTHING I CAN DO TO INTERFERE--
--BUT MY HOPE IS THAT MY APPEARANCE HERE MIGHT CAST A SPOTLIGHT ON THIS FOR THE PUBLIC.
AND THAT MAYBE THE CITIZENS OF THIS CITY WILL BE ABLE TO MAKE THEIR VOICES HEARD.
CHRISTIAN, ARE YOU AFRAID THAT SPEAKING TO US ABOUT THIS MIGHT JEOPARDIZE YOUR CAREER AS A CIVIL SERVANT?
I AM PRETTY SURE THAT IT WILL END IT.
BUT THE JOB OF THE HOMICIDE DETECTIVE IS TO ANSWER FOR PEOPLE WHO CAN'T SPEAK FOR THEMSELVES.
THERE'S NOTHING MORE IMPORTANT THAN THAT TO ME.
I GUESS NOT EVEN MY JOB.
NOW, YOU WERE THE PRIMARY DETECTIVE SENT TO INVESTIGATE THE BENMARLEY MURDER SCENE AT THE FG-3 TOWERS EARLIER THIS WEEK...
YES.
AND YOU WERE QUICKLY REMOVED FROM THE CASE...
YES, IT WAS SOON AFTER THAT...

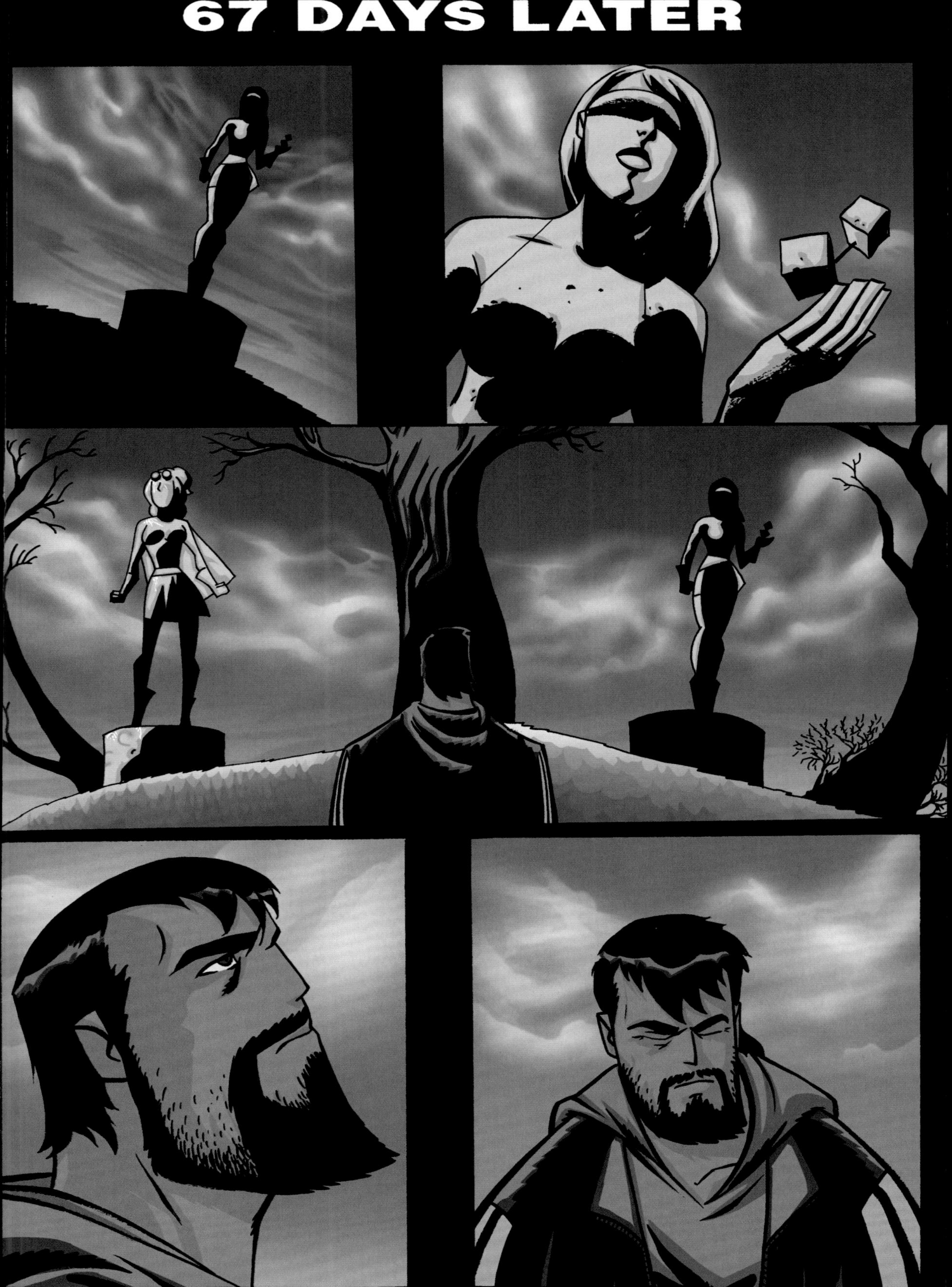
67 DAYS LATER

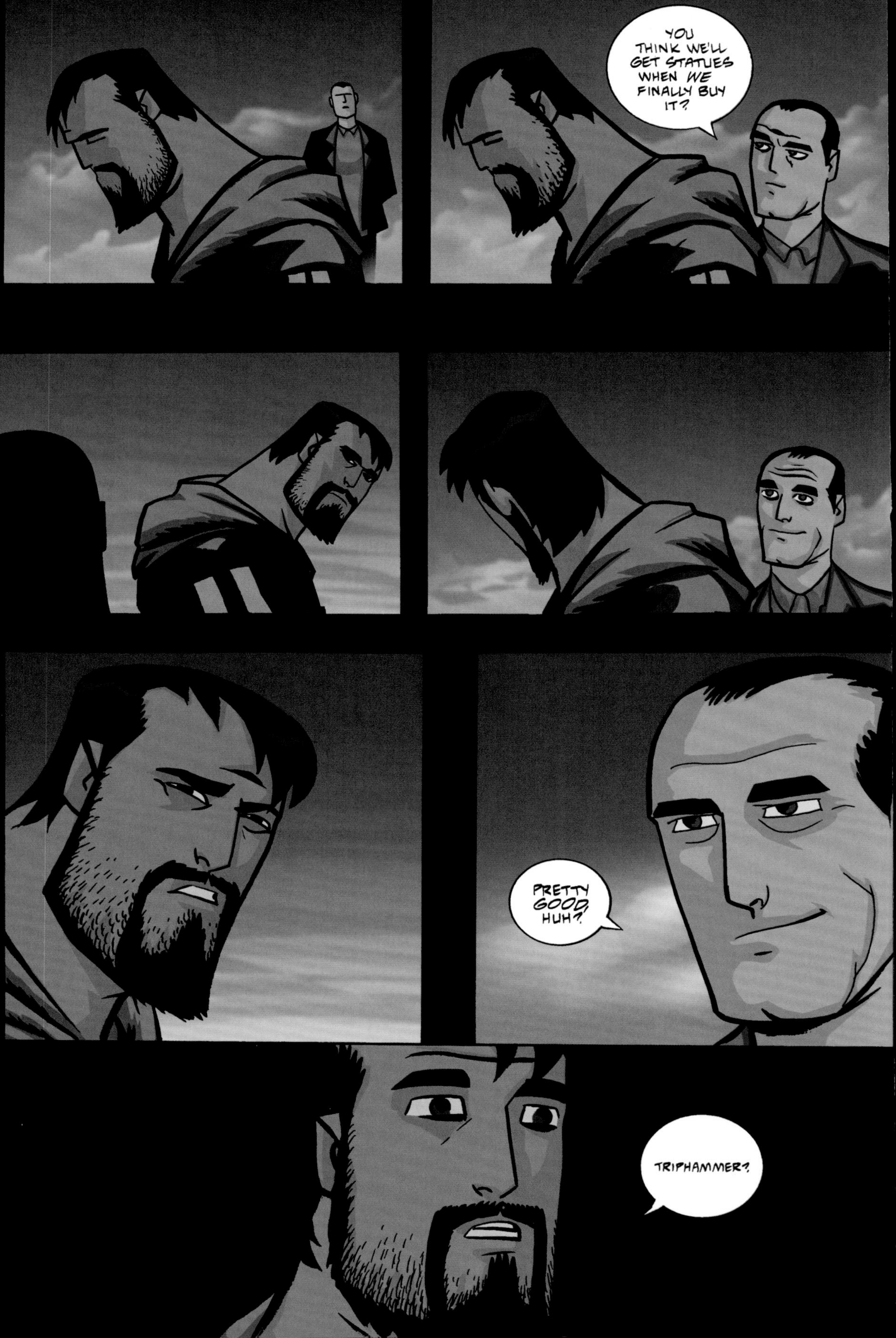
YOU THINK WE'LL GET STATUES WHEN WE FINALLY BUY IT?
PRETTY GOOD, HUH?
TRIPHAMMER?

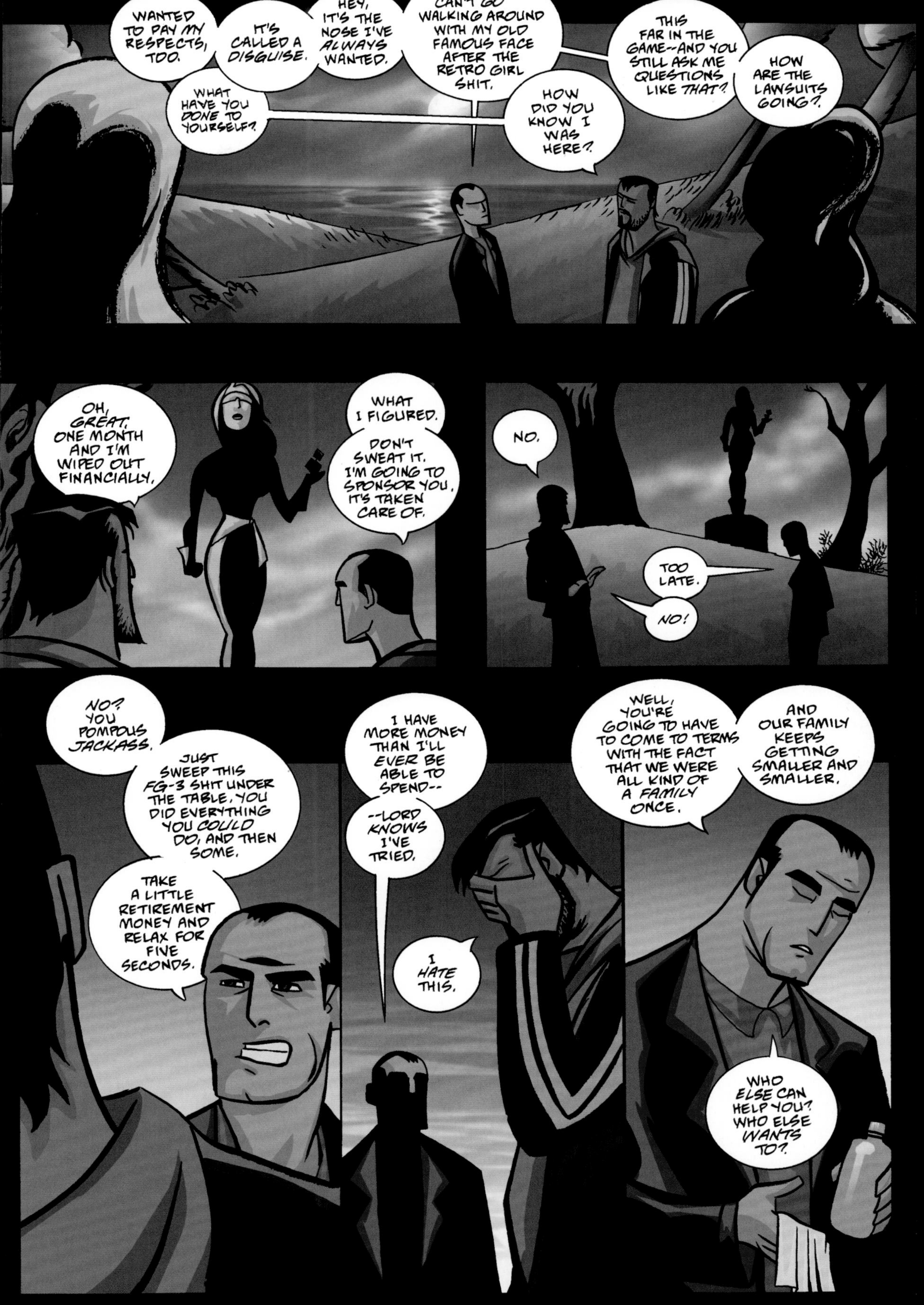

WANTED TO PAY MY RESPECTS, TOO.
WHAT HAVE YOU DONE TO YOURSELF?
IT'S CALLED A DISGUISE.
HEY, IT'S THE NOSE I'VE ALWAYS WANTED.
CERTAINLY CAN'T GO WALKING AROUND WITH MY OLD FAMOUS FACE AFTER THE RETRO GIRL SHIT.
HOW DID YOU KNOW I WAS HERE?
THIS FAR IN THE GAME--AND YOU STILL ASK ME QUESTIONS LIKE THAT?
HOW ARE THE LAWSUITS GOING?
OH, GREAT. ONE MONTH AND I'M WIPED OUT FINANCIALLY.
WHAT I FIGURED.
DON'T SWEAT IT. I'M GOING TO SPONSOR YOU, IT'S TAKEN CARE OF.
NO.
TOO LATE.
NO!
NO? YOU POMPOUS JACKASS.
JUST SWEEP THIS FG-3 SHIT UNDER THE TABLE, YOU DID EVERYTHING YOU COULD DO, AND THEN SOME.
TAKE A LITTLE RETIREMENT MONEY AND RELAX FOR FIVE SECONDS.
I HAVE MORE MONEY THAN I'LL EVER BE ABLE TO SPEND--
--LORD KNOWS I'VE TRIED.
I HATE THIS.
WELL, YOU'RE GOING TO HAVE TO COME TO TERMS WITH THE FACT THAT WE WERE ALL KIND OF A FAMILY ONCE.
AND OUR FAMILY KEEPS GETTING SMALLER AND SMALLER.
WHO ELSE CAN HELP YOU? WHO ELSE WANTS TO?

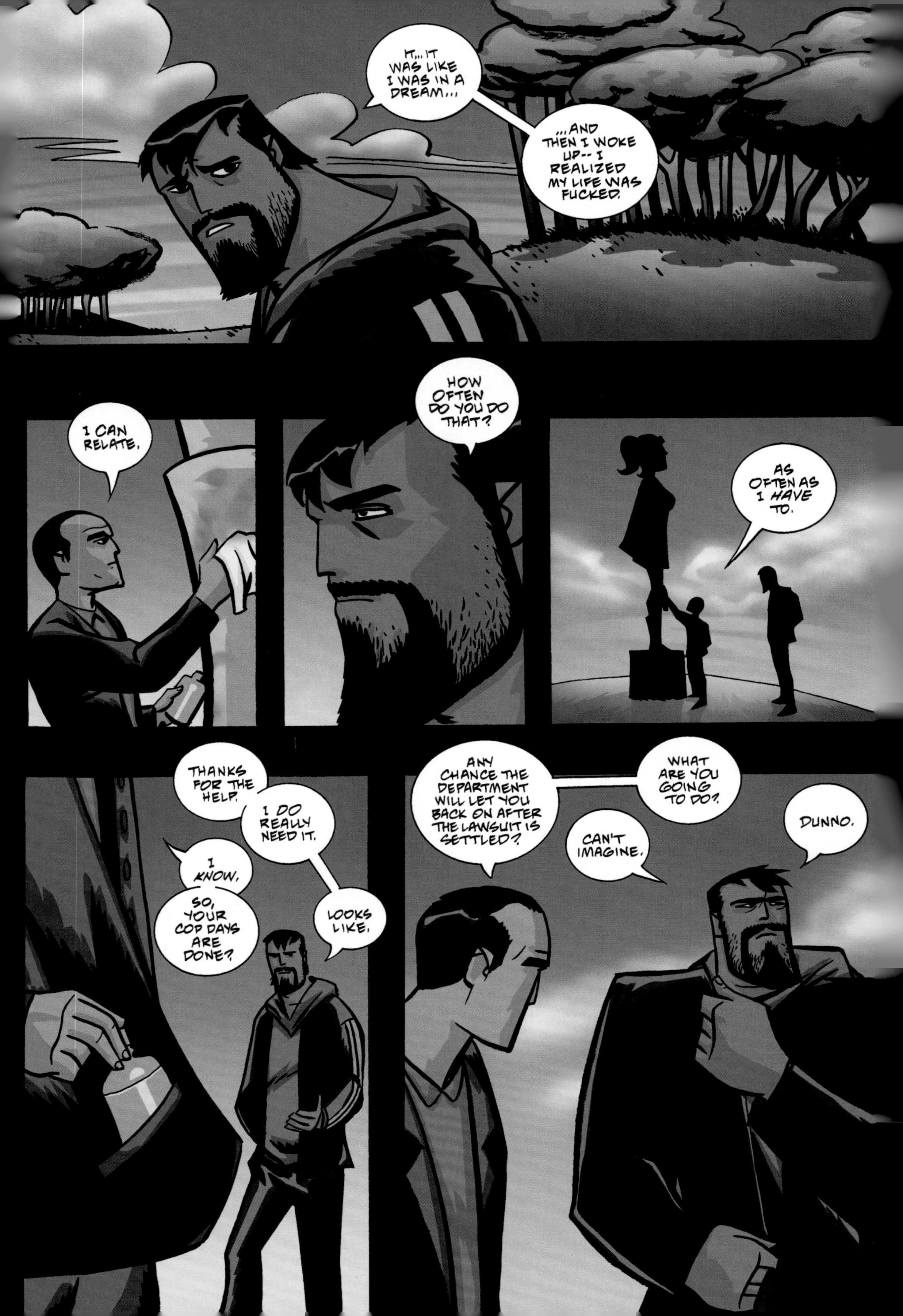
IT... IT WAS LIKE I WAS IN A DREAM...
...AND THEN I WOKE UP-- I REALIZED MY LIFE WAS FUCKED.
I CAN RELATE.
HOW OFTEN DO YOU DO THAT?
AS OFTEN AS I HAVE TO.
THANKS FOR THE HELP.
I DO REALLY NEED IT.
I KNOW.
SO, YOUR COP DAYS ARE DONE?
LOOKS LIKE.
ANY CHANCE THE DEPARTMENT WILL LET YOU BACK ON AFTER THE LAWSUIT IS SETTLED?
CAN'T IMAGINE.
WHAT ARE YOU GOING TO DO?
DUNNO.

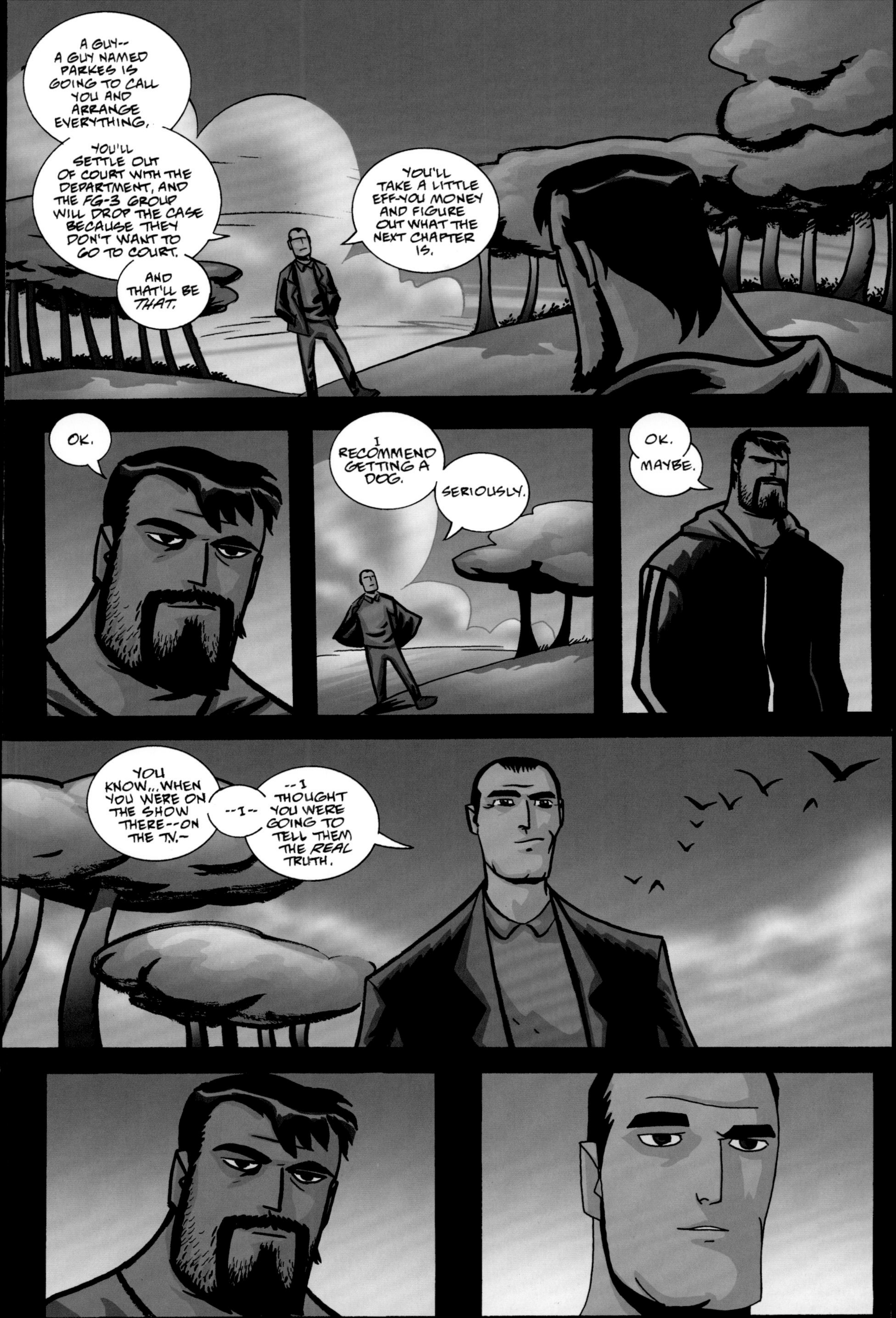
A GUY--
A GUY NAMED PARKES IS GOING TO CALL YOU AND ARRANGE EVERYTHING.
YOU'LL SETTLE OUT OF COURT WITH THE DEPARTMENT, AND THE FG-3 GROUP WILL DROP THE CASE BECAUSE THEY DON'T WANT TO GO TO COURT.
AND THAT'LL BE *THAT*.
YOU'LL TAKE A LITTLE EFF-YOU MONEY AND FIGURE OUT WHAT THE NEXT CHAPTER IS.
OK.
I RECOMMEND GETTING A DOG.
SERIOUSLY.
OK.
MAYBE.
YOU KNOW... WHEN YOU WERE ON THE SHOW THERE--ON THE T.V.--
--I--
--I THOUGHT YOU WERE GOING TO TELL THEM THE *REAL* TRUTH.

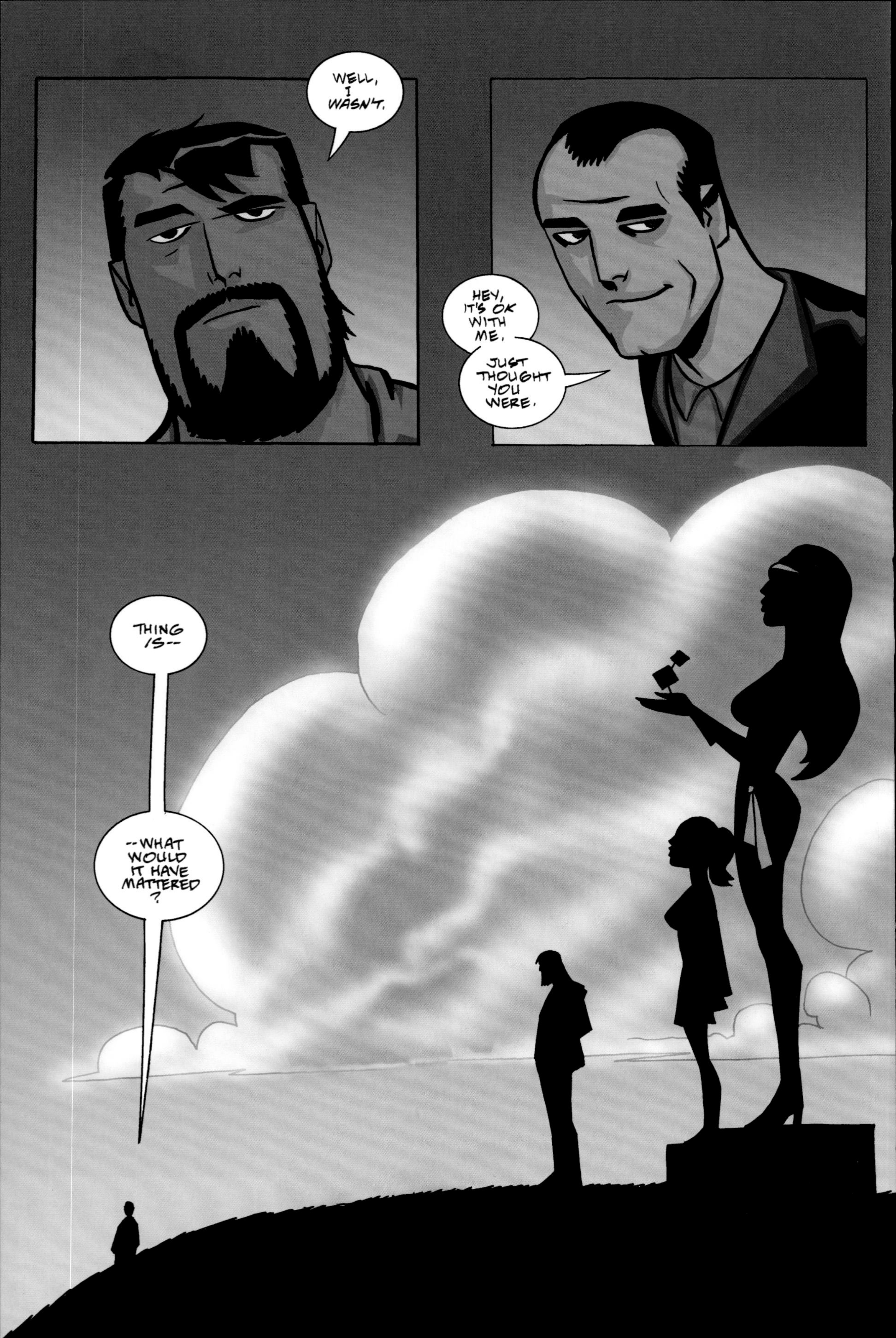
WELL, I WASN'T.
HEY, IT'S OK WITH ME.
JUST THOUGHT YOU WERE.
THING IS--
--WHAT WOULD IT HAVE MATTERED?

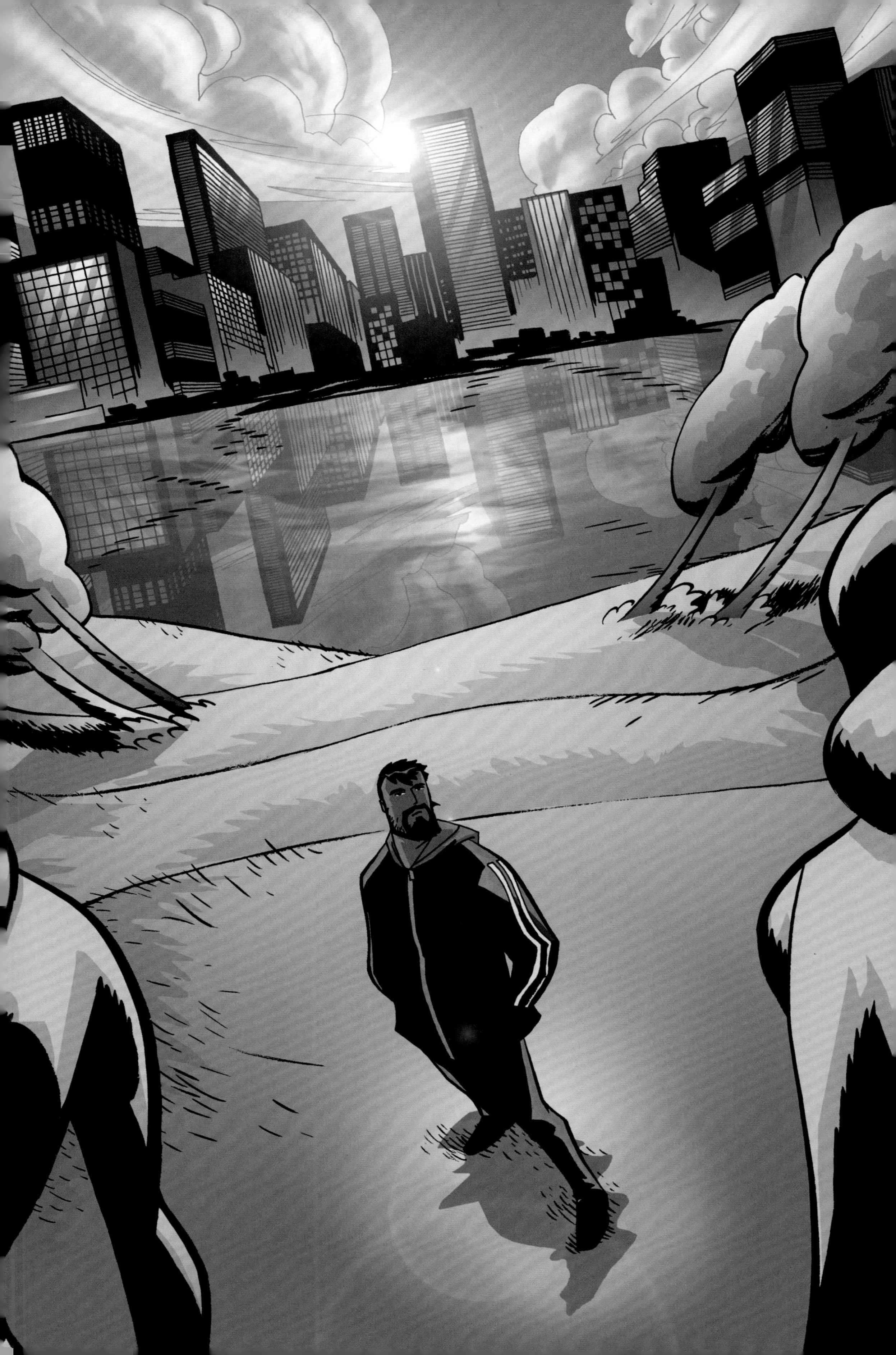

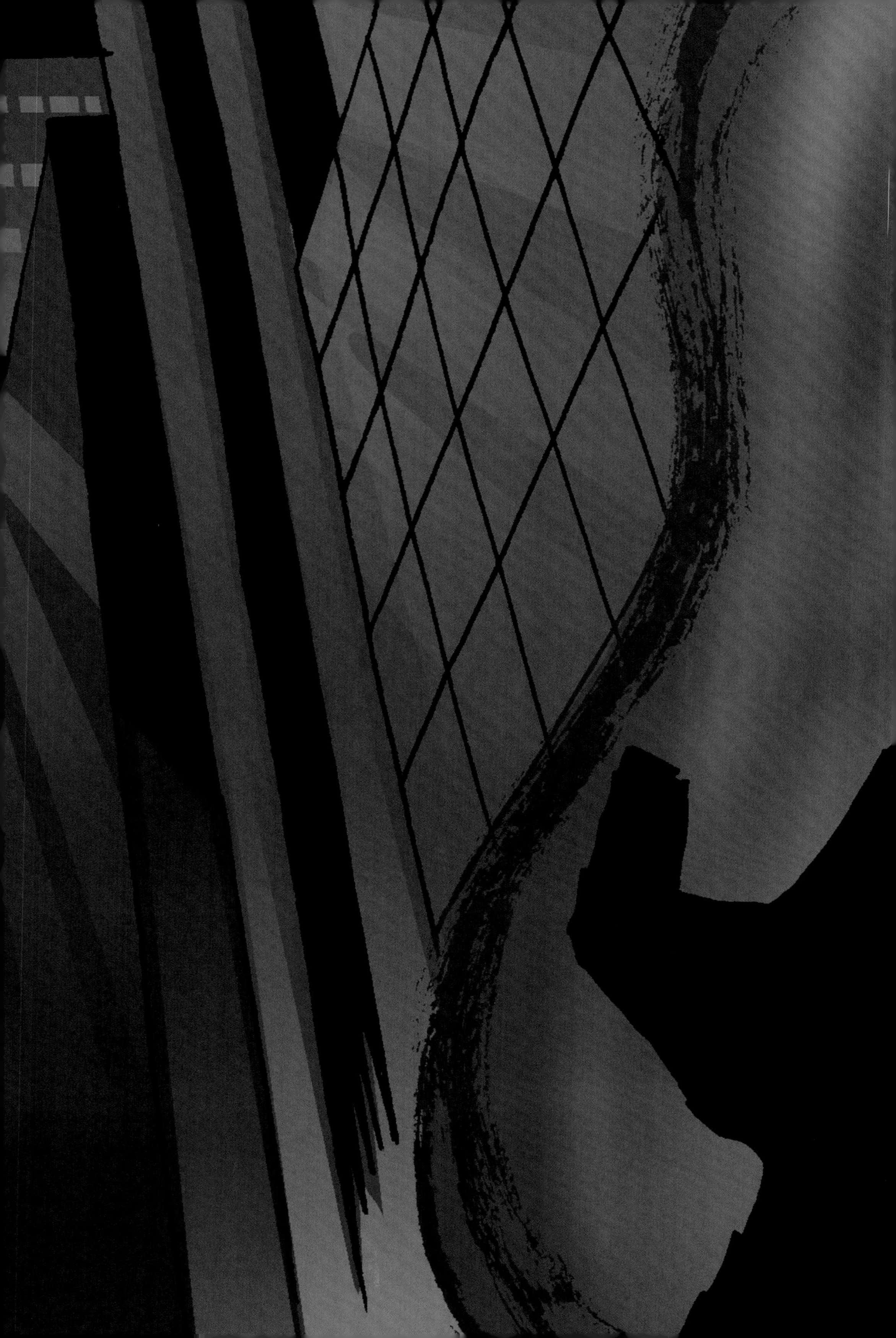

POWERS ™

ANARCHY
CHAPTER 1

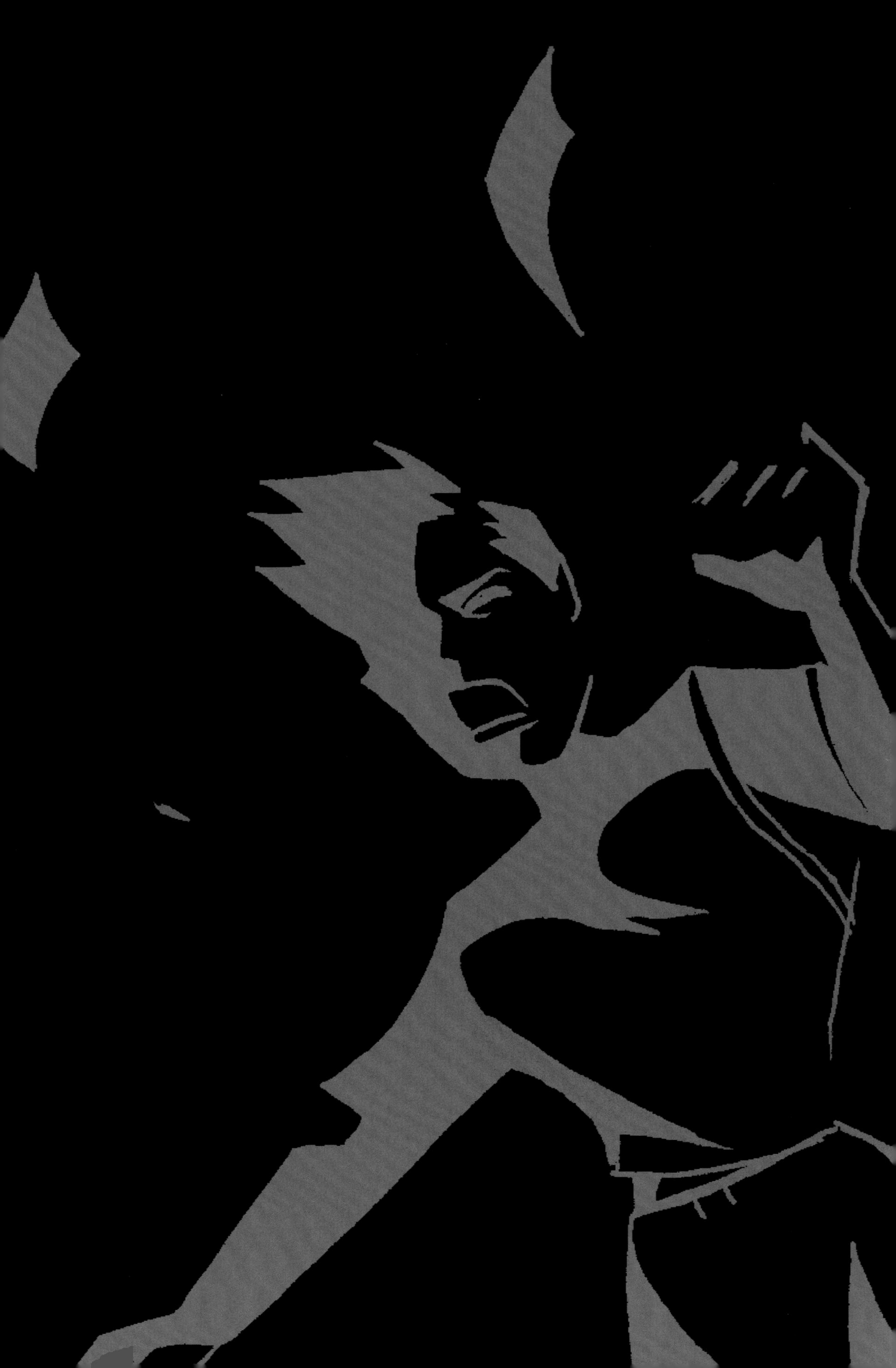

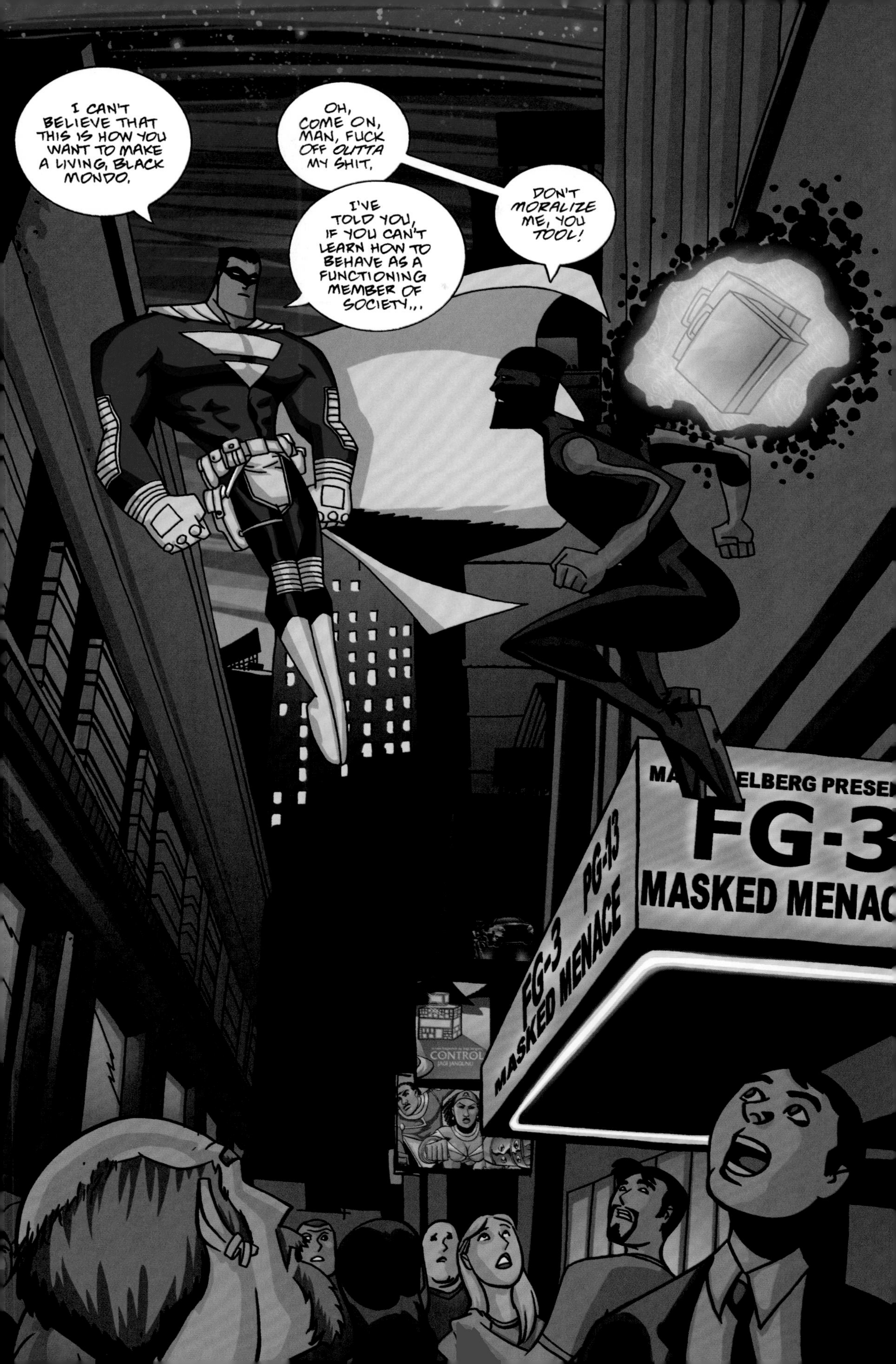
I CAN'T BELIEVE THAT THIS IS HOW YOU WANT TO MAKE A LIVING, BLACK MONDO.
OH, COME ON, MAN, FUCK OFF OUTTA MY SHIT.
DON'T MORALIZE ME, YOU TOOL!
I'VE TOLD YOU, IF YOU CAN'T LEARN HOW TO BEHAVE AS A FUNCTIONING MEMBER OF SOCIETY...
FG-3
MASKED MENACE
PG-13
FG-3
MASKED MENACE
CONTROL

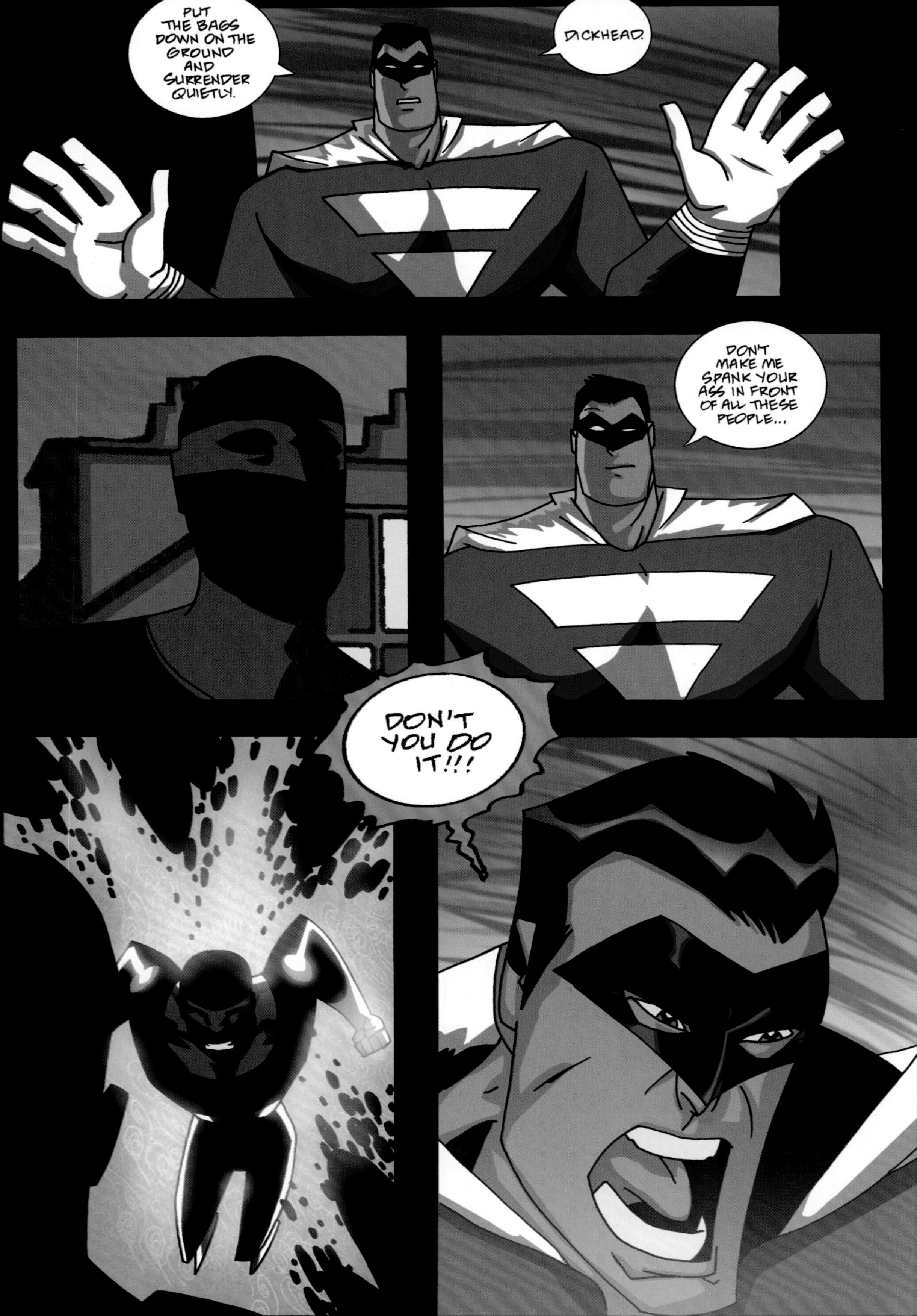
PUT THE BAGS DOWN ON THE GROUND AND SURRENDER QUIETLY.
DICKHEAD.
DON'T MAKE ME SPANK YOUR ASS IN FRONT OF ALL THESE PEOPLE...
DON'T YOU DO IT!!!

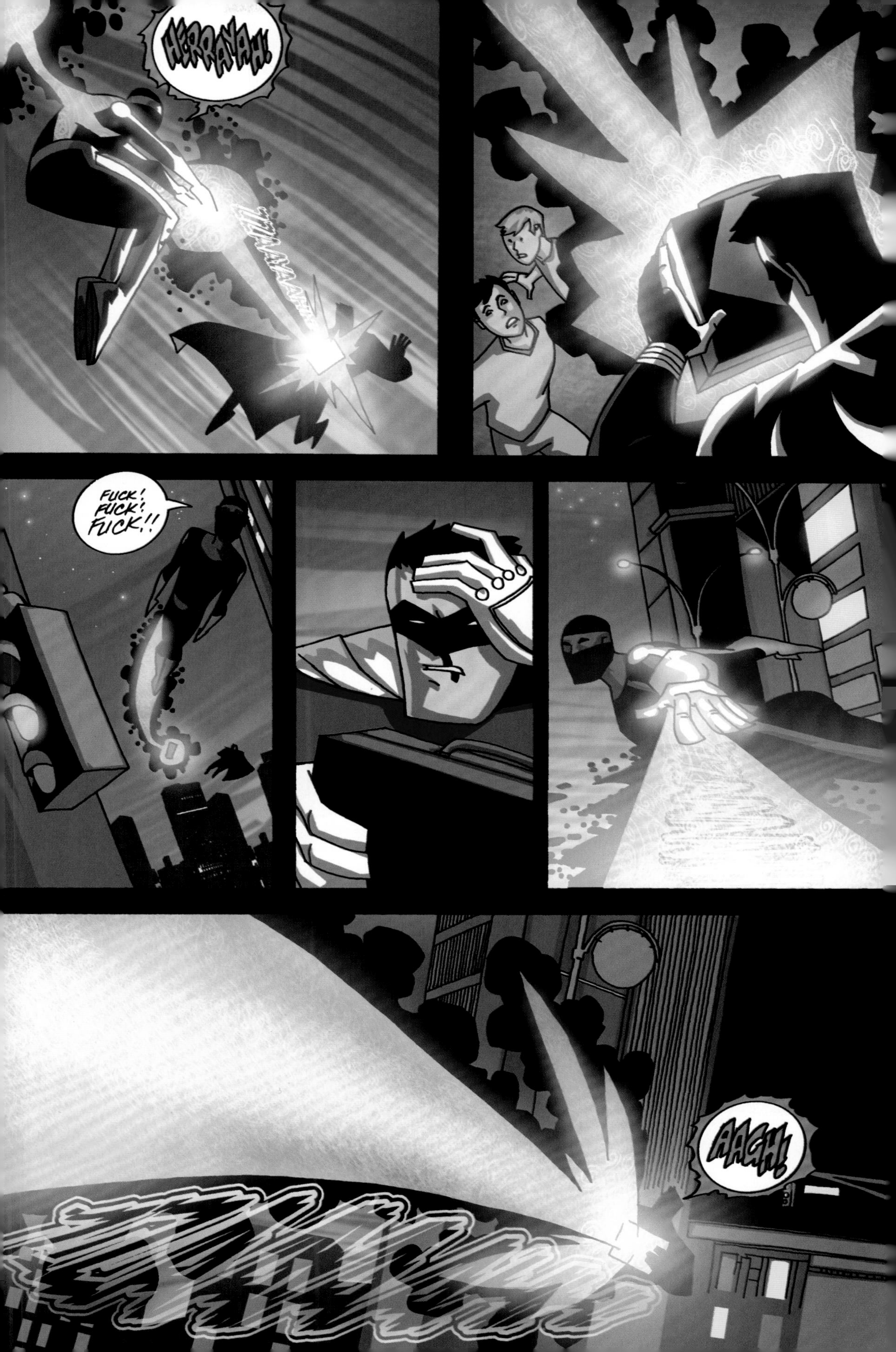
HERRAYAH!
TZZAAAAH!!
FUCK! FUCK! FUCK!!
AAGH!

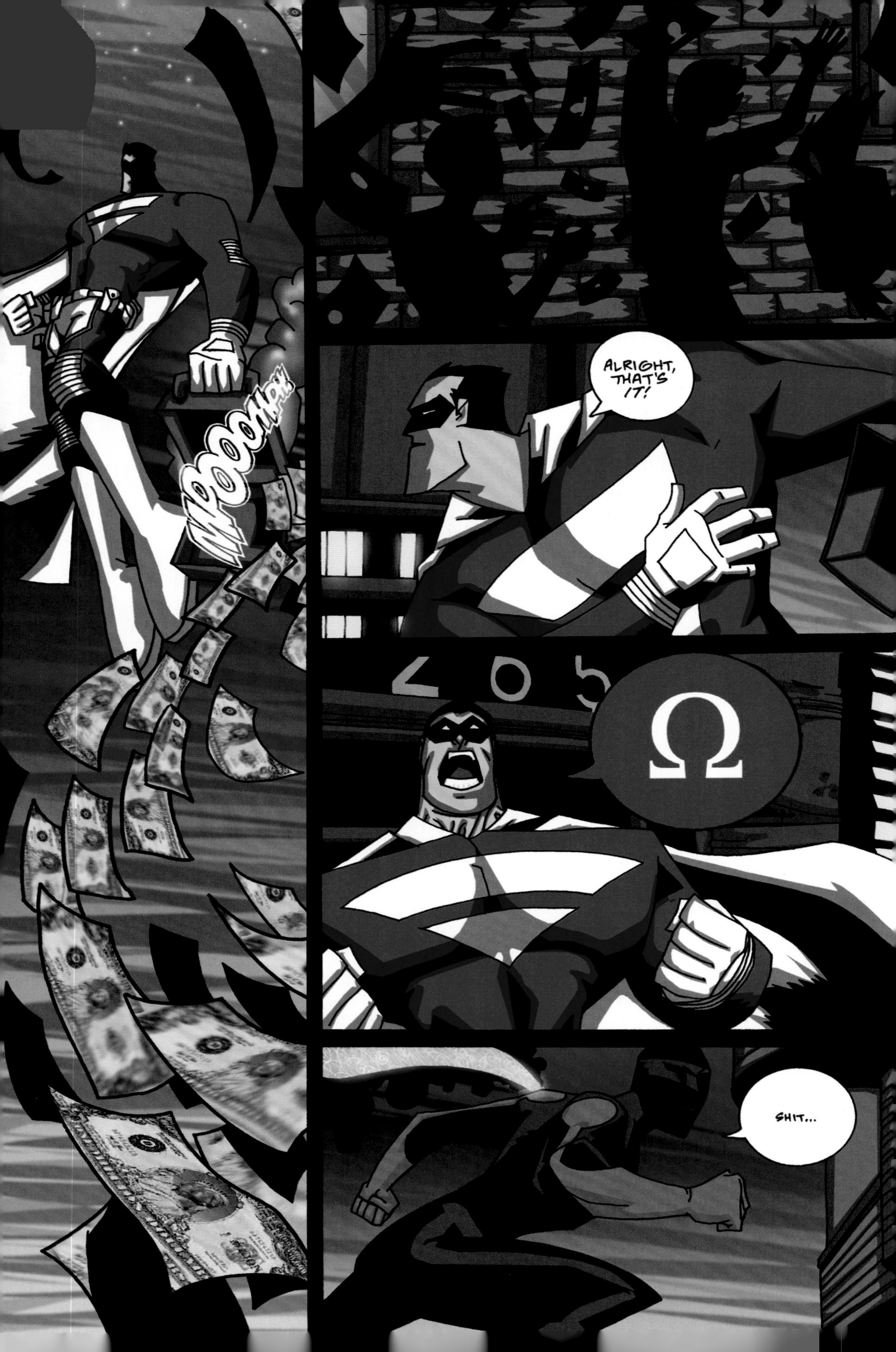
ALRIGHT, THAT'S IT!
Ω
SHIT...

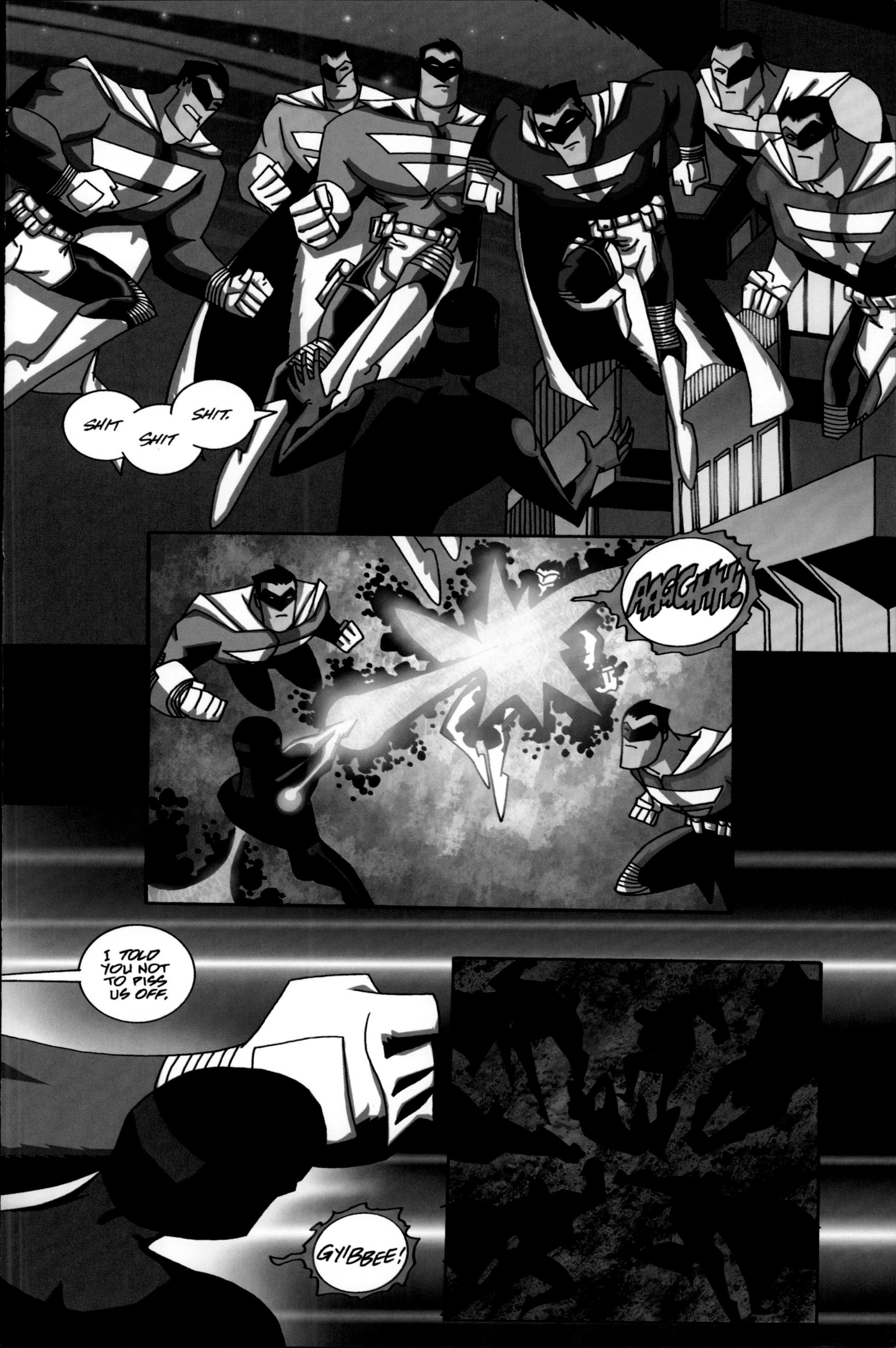
SHIT SHIT SHIT.
AAAGHHH!
I TOLD YOU NOT TO PISS US OFF.
GYIBBEE!

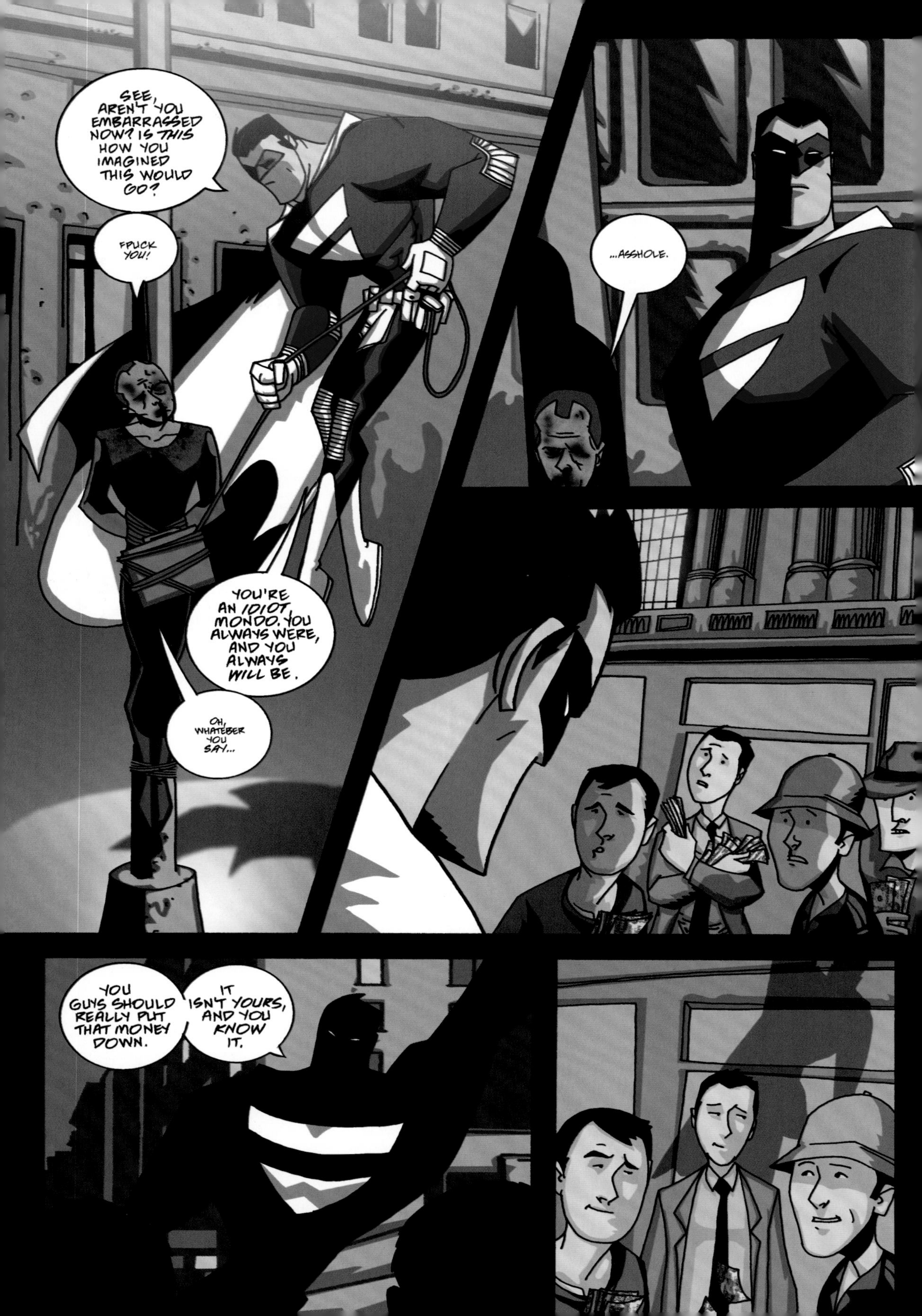
SEE, AREN'T YOU EMBARRASSED NOW? IS THIS HOW YOU IMAGINED THIS WOULD GO?
FFUCK YOU!
...ASSHOLE.
YOU'RE AN IDIOT, MONDO. YOU ALWAYS WERE, AND YOU ALWAYS WILL BE.
OH, WHATEBER YOU SAY...
YOU GUYS SHOULD REALLY PUT THAT MONEY DOWN.
IT ISN'T YOURS, AND YOU KNOW IT.

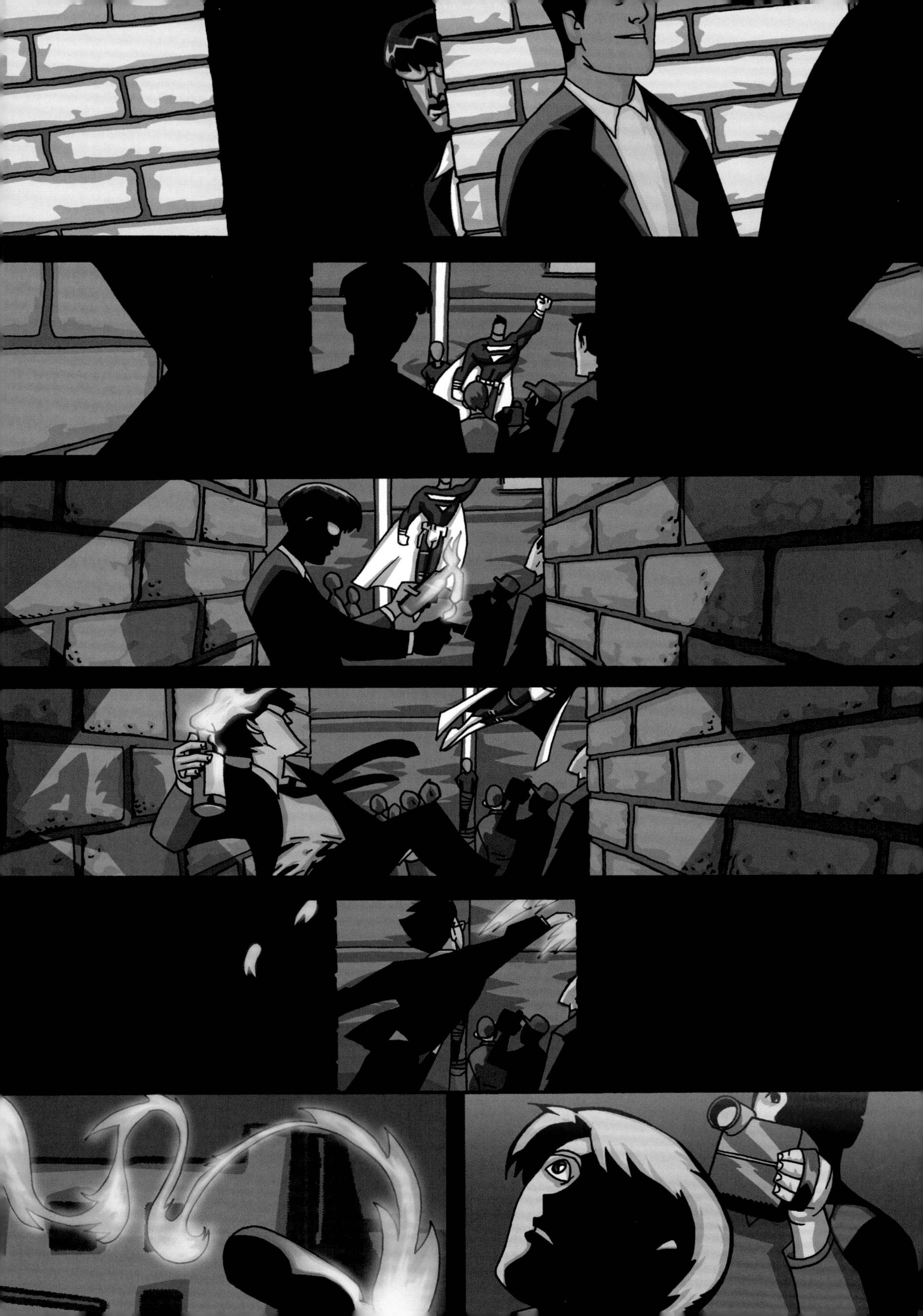

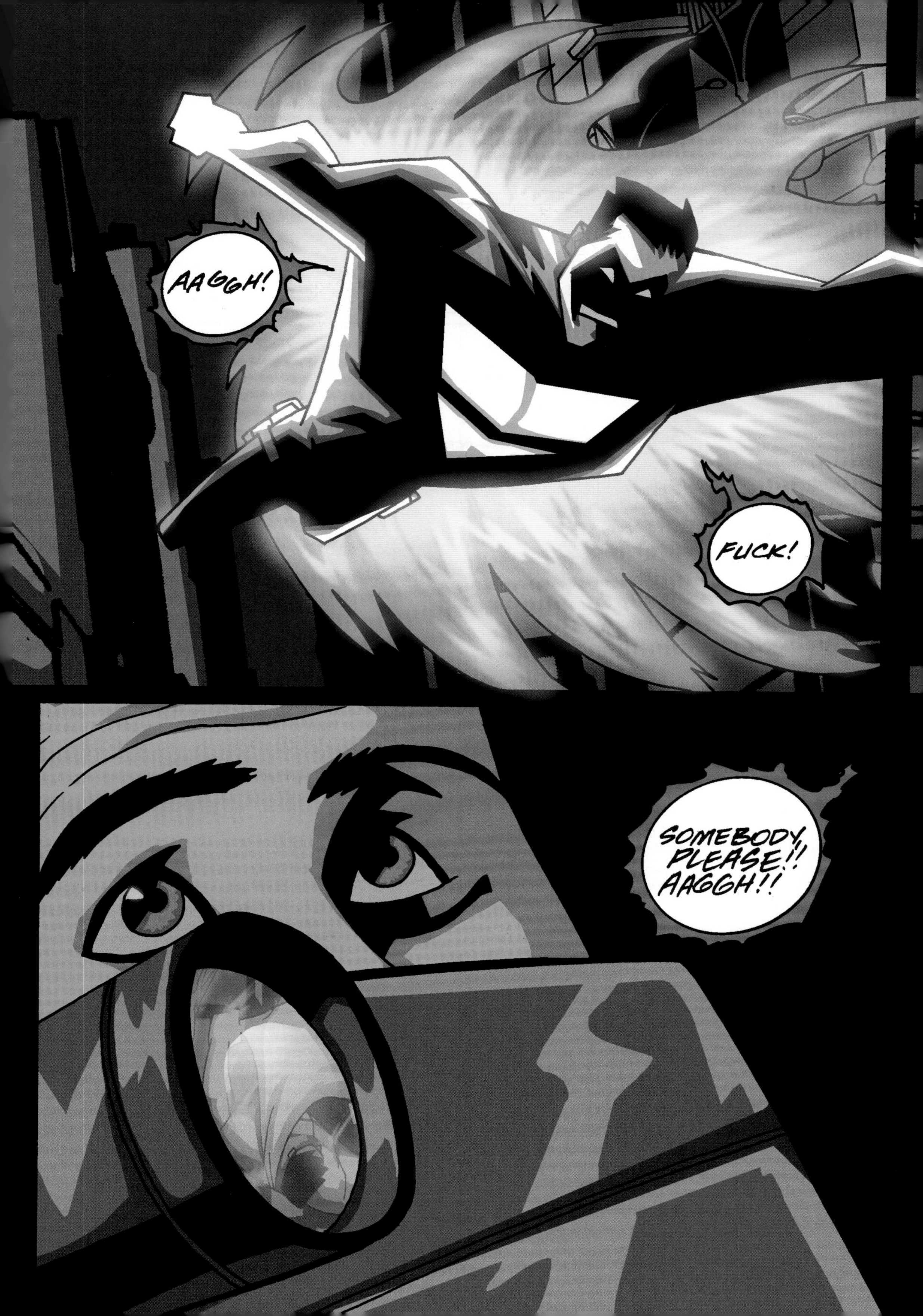
AAGGH!
FUCK!
SOMEBODY, PLEASE!! AAGGH!!

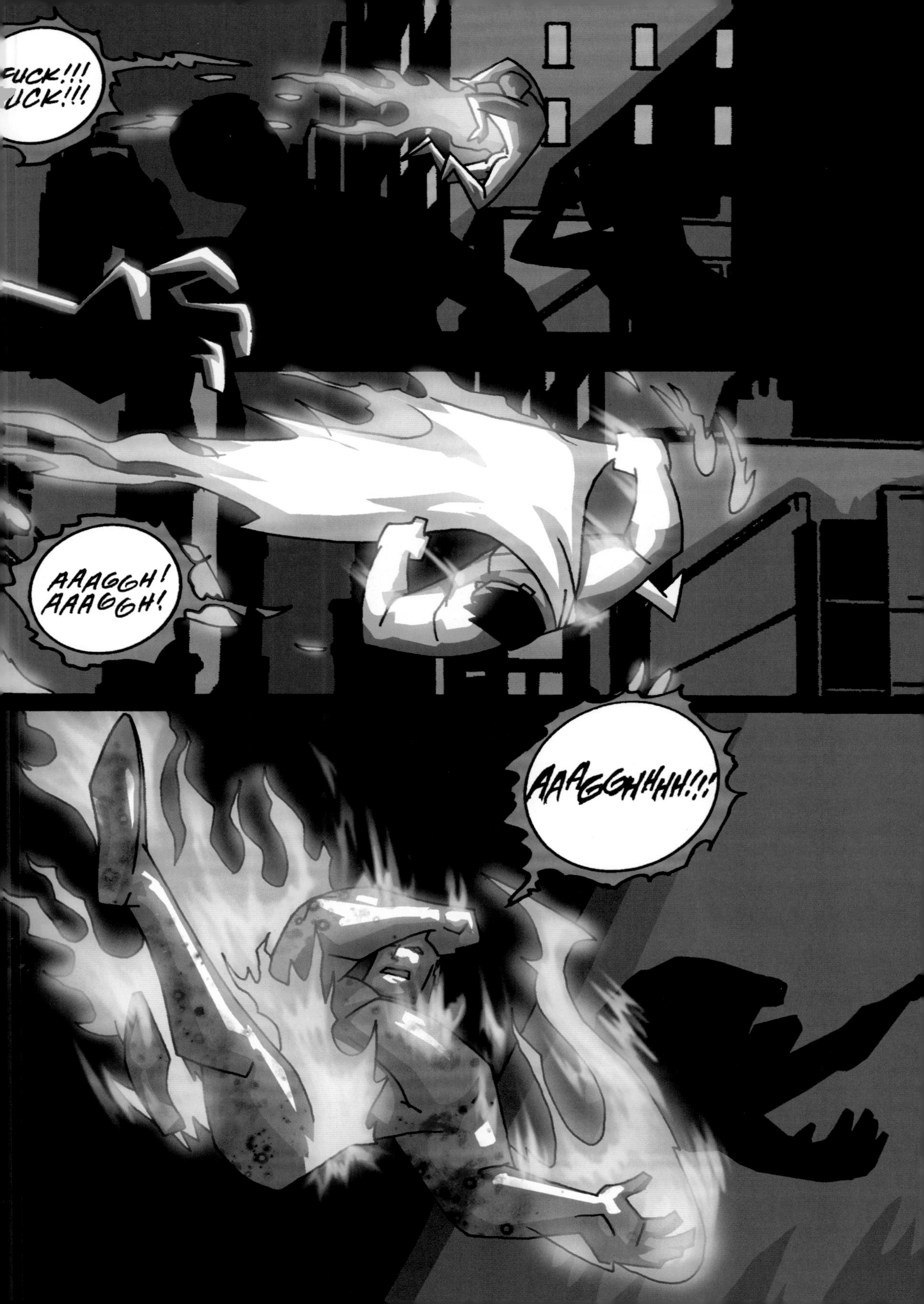

FUCK!!!
UCK!!!
AAAGGH! AAAGGH!
AAAGGHHHH!!!

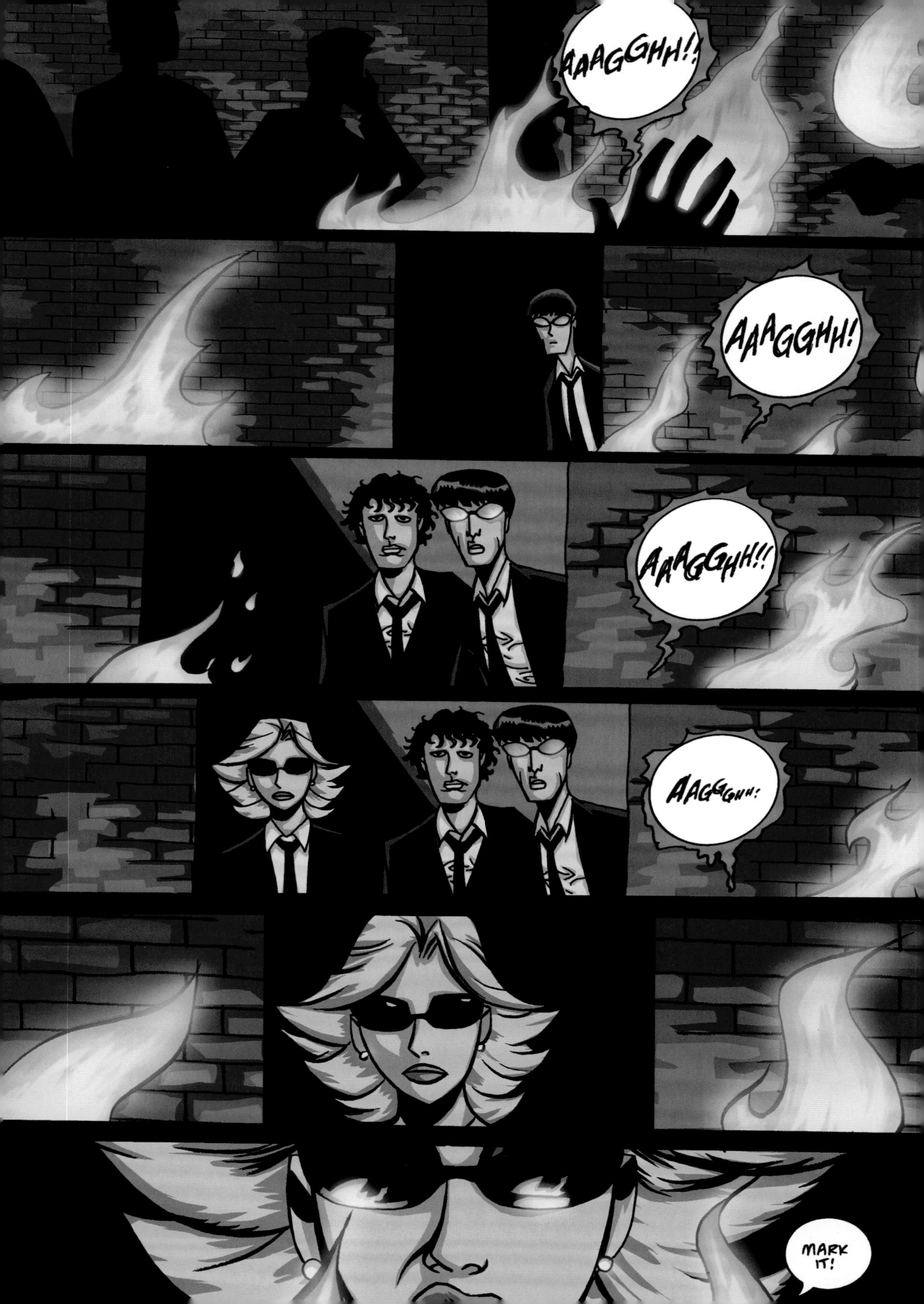
AAAGGHH!!
AAAGGHH!
AAAGGHH!!
AAGGGHH!
MARK IT!

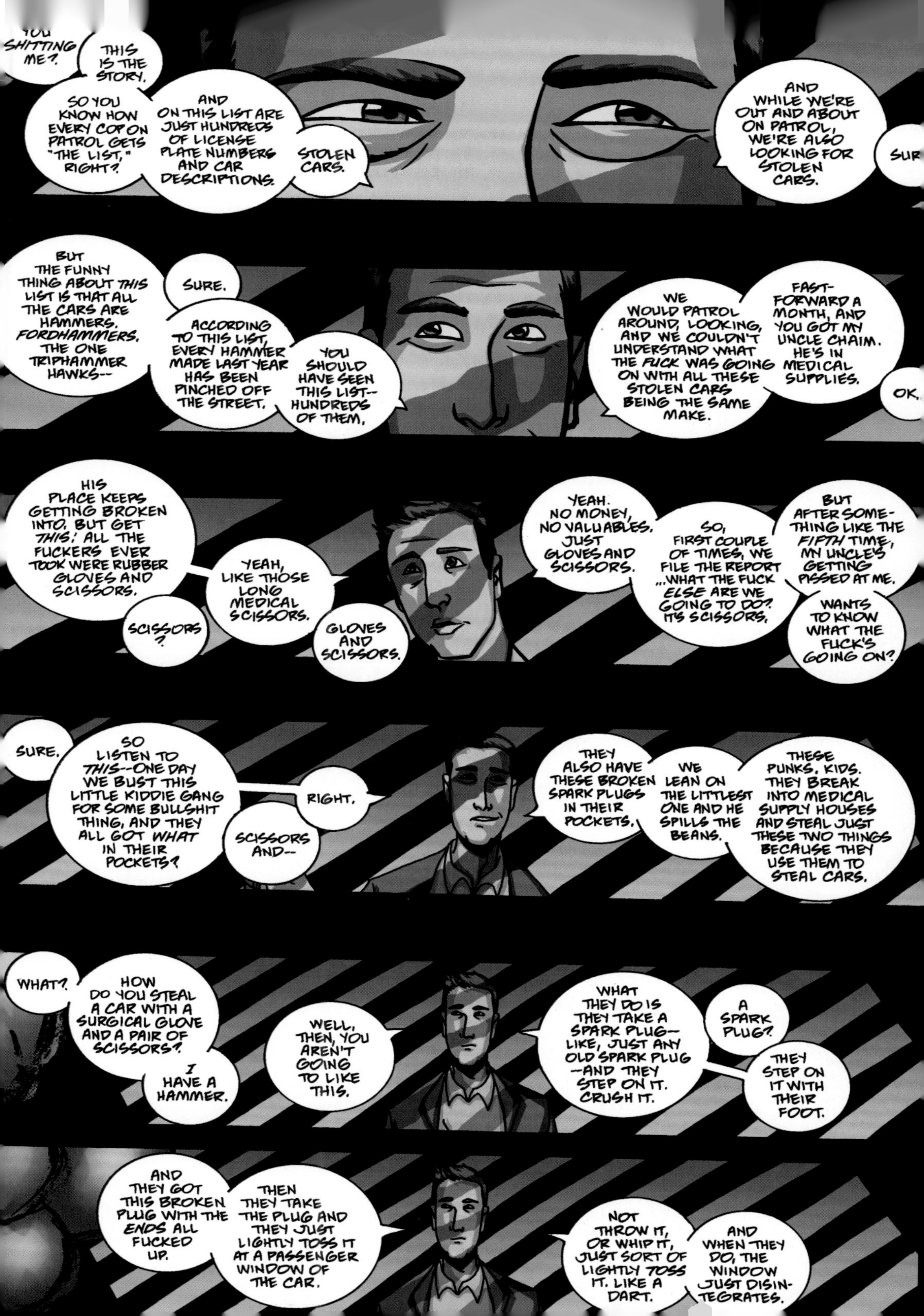
YOU SHITTING ME?
THIS IS THE STORY.
SO YOU KNOW HOW EVERY COP ON PATROL GETS "THE LIST," RIGHT?
AND ON THIS LIST ARE JUST HUNDREDS OF LICENSE PLATE NUMBERS AND CAR DESCRIPTIONS.
STOLEN CARS.
AND WHILE WE'RE OUT AND ABOUT ON PATROL, WE'RE ALSO LOOKING FOR STOLEN CARS.
SUR
BUT THE FUNNY THING ABOUT *THIS* LIST IS THAT ALL THE CARS ARE HAMMERS. *FORDHAMMERS*. THE ONE TRIPHAMMER HAWKS--
SURE.
ACCORDING TO THIS LIST, EVERY HAMMER MADE LAST YEAR HAS BEEN PINCHED OFF THE STREET.
YOU SHOULD HAVE SEEN THIS LIST-- HUNDREDS OF THEM.
WE WOULD PATROL AROUND, LOOKING, AND WE COULDN'T UNDERSTAND WHAT THE *FUCK* WAS GOING ON WITH ALL THESE STOLEN CARS BEING THE SAME MAKE.
FAST-FORWARD A MONTH, AND YOU GOT MY UNCLE CHAIM. HE'S IN MEDICAL SUPPLIES.
OK.
HIS PLACE KEEPS GETTING BROKEN INTO. BUT GET *THIS*: ALL THE FUCKERS EVER TOOK WERE RUBBER GLOVES AND SCISSORS.
SCISSORS?
YEAH, LIKE THOSE LONG MEDICAL SCISSORS.
GLOVES AND SCISSORS.
YEAH. NO MONEY, NO VALUABLES. JUST GLOVES AND SCISSORS.
SO, FIRST COUPLE OF TIMES, WE FILE THE REPORT ...WHAT THE FUCK *ELSE* ARE WE GOING TO DO? IT'S SCISSORS.
BUT AFTER SOME-THING LIKE THE *FIFTH* TIME, MY UNCLE'S GETTING PISSED AT ME.
WANTS TO KNOW WHAT THE FUCK'S GOING ON?
SURE.
SO LISTEN TO *THIS*--ONE DAY WE BUST THIS LITTLE KIDDIE GANG FOR SOME BULLSHIT THING, AND THEY ALL GOT *WHAT* IN THEIR POCKETS?
RIGHT.
SCISSORS AND--
THEY ALSO HAVE THESE BROKEN SPARK PLUGS IN THEIR POCKETS.
WE LEAN ON THE LITTLEST ONE AND HE SPILLS THE BEANS.
THESE PUNKS. KIDS. THEY BREAK INTO MEDICAL SUPPLY HOUSES AND STEAL JUST THESE TWO THINGS BECAUSE THEY USE THEM TO STEAL CARS.
WHAT?
HOW DO YOU STEAL A CAR WITH A SURGICAL GLOVE AND A PAIR OF SCISSORS?
I HAVE A HAMMER.
WELL, THEN, YOU AREN'T GOING TO LIKE THIS.
WHAT THEY DO IS THEY TAKE A SPARK PLUG-- LIKE, JUST ANY OLD SPARK PLUG --AND THEY STEP ON IT. CRUSH IT.
A SPARK PLUG?
THEY STEP ON IT WITH THEIR FOOT.
AND THEY GOT THIS BROKEN PLUG WITH THE *ENDS* ALL FUCKED UP.
THEN THEY TAKE THE PLUG AND THEY JUST LIGHTLY TOSS IT AT A PASSENGER WINDOW OF THE CAR.
NOT THROW IT, OR WHIP IT, JUST SORT OF LIGHTLY *TOSS* IT. LIKE A DART.
AND WHEN THEY DO, THE WINDOW JUST DISIN-TEGRATES.

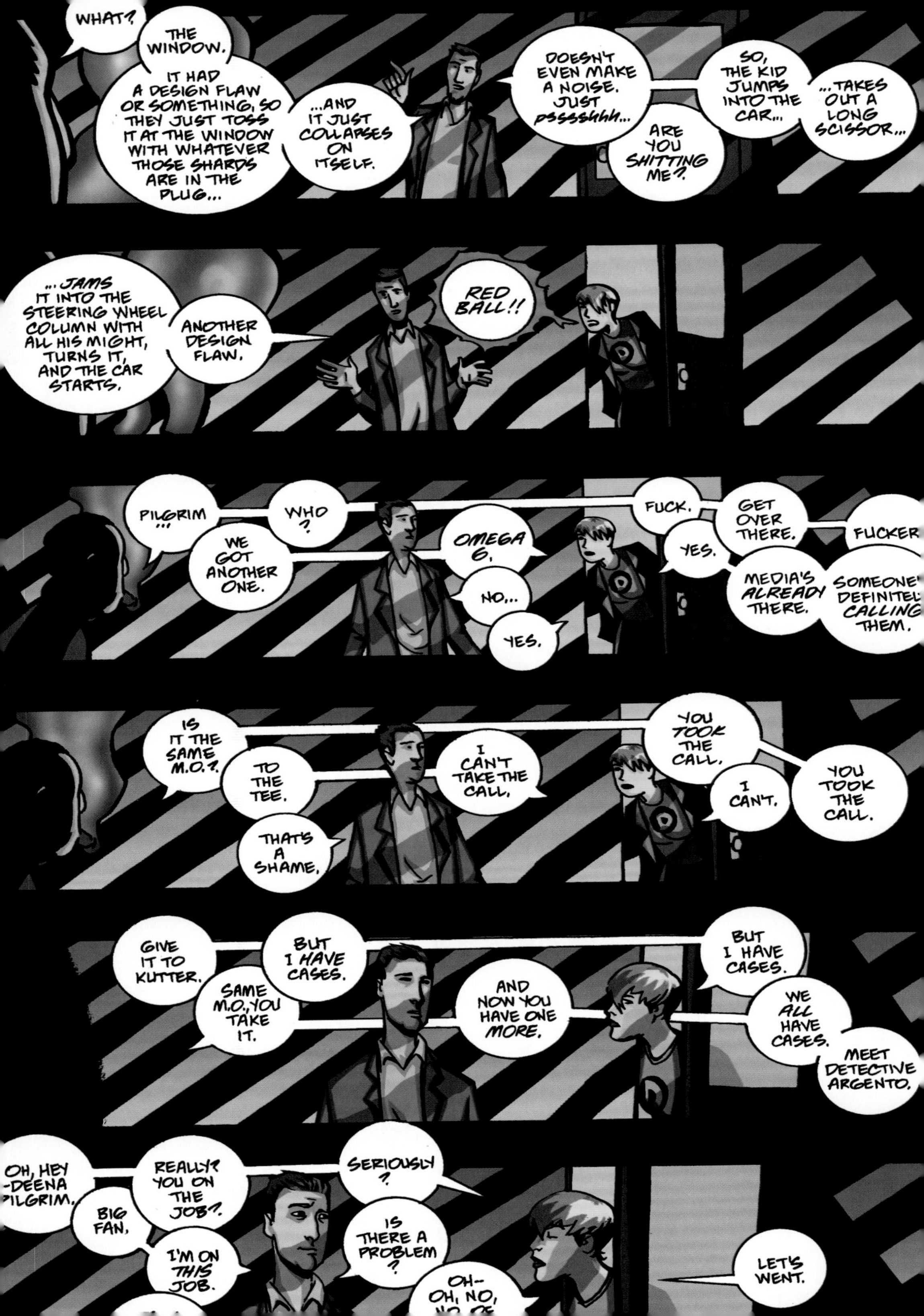
WHAT?
THE WINDOW.
IT HAD A DESIGN FLAW OR SOMETHING, SO THEY JUST TOSS IT AT THE WINDOW WITH WHATEVER THOSE SHARDS ARE IN THE PLUG...
...AND IT JUST COLLAPSES ON ITSELF.
DOESN'T EVEN MAKE A NOISE. JUST *pssssshhh*...
ARE YOU SHITTING ME?
SO, THE KID JUMPS INTO THE CAR...
...TAKES OUT A LONG SCISSOR...
...*JAMS* IT INTO THE STEERING WHEEL COLUMN WITH ALL HIS MIGHT, TURNS IT, AND THE CAR STARTS.
ANOTHER DESIGN FLAW.
RED BALL!!
PILGRIM...
WHO?
WE GOT ANOTHER ONE.
OMEGA 6.
NO...
YES.
FUCK.
YES.
GET OVER THERE.
MEDIA'S *ALREADY* THERE.
FUCKER
SOMEONE' DEFINITEL *CALLING* THEM.
IS IT THE SAME *M.O.?*
TO THE TEE.
THAT'S A SHAME.
I CAN'T TAKE THE CALL.
YOU *TOOK* THE CALL.
I CAN'T.
YOU TOOK THE CALL.
GIVE IT TO KUTTER.
BUT I *HAVE* CASES.
SAME M.O., YOU TAKE IT.
AND NOW YOU HAVE ONE *MORE.*
BUT I HAVE CASES.
WE *ALL* HAVE CASES.
MEET DETECTIVE ARGENTO.
OH, HEY -DEENA PILGRIM.
BIG FAN.
REALLY? YOU ON THE JOB?
I'M ON *THIS* JOB.
SERIOUSLY?
IS THERE A PROBLEM?
OH- OH, NO,
LET'S WENT.

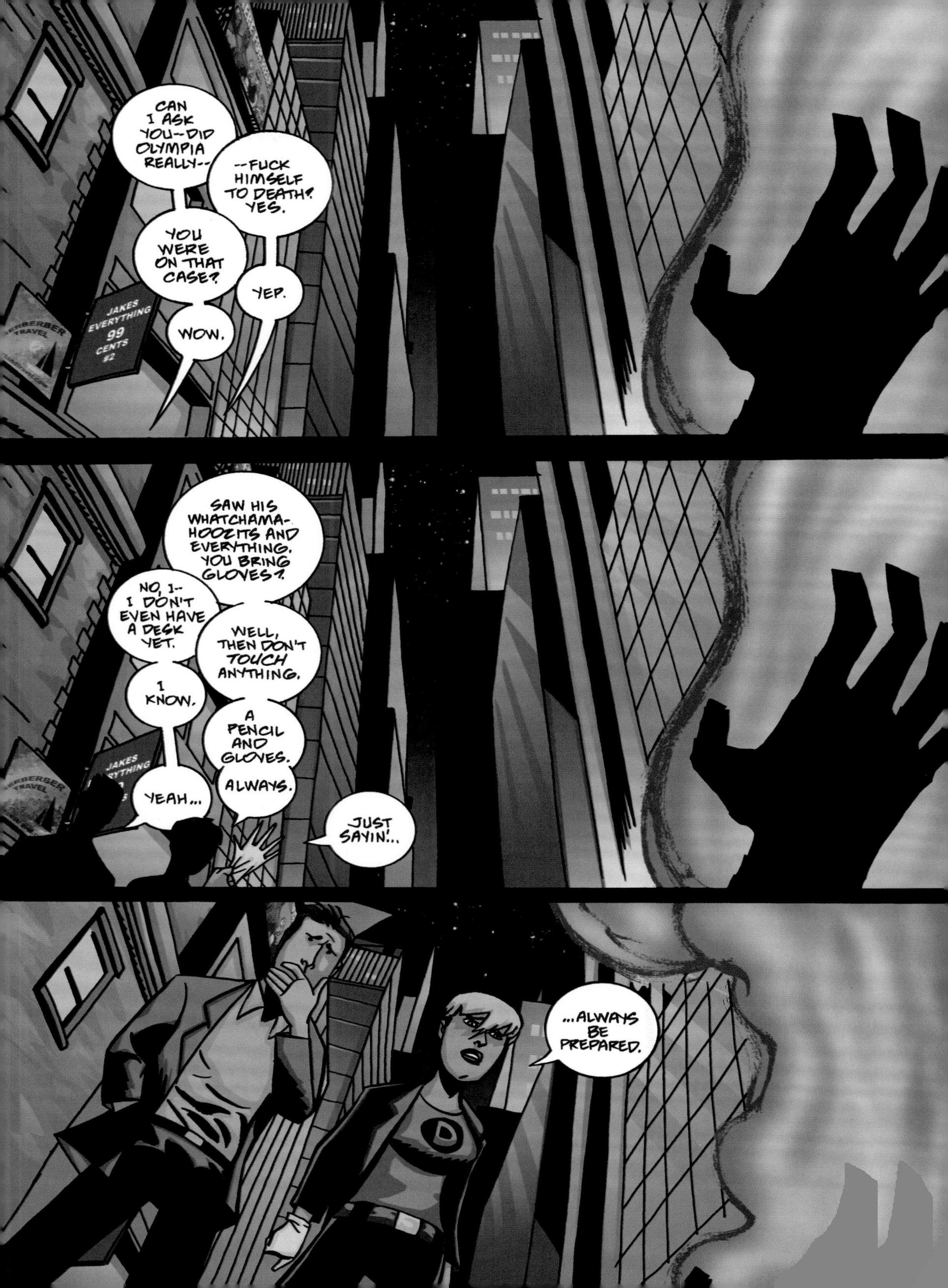
CAN I ASK YOU--DID OLYMPIA REALLY--
--FUCK HIMSELF TO DEATH? YES.
YOU WERE ON THAT CASE?
YEP.
WOW.
JAKES EVERYTHING 99 CENTS #2
SAW HIS WHATCHAMA-HOOZITS AND EVERYTHING. YOU BRING GLOVES?
NO, I-- I DON'T EVEN HAVE A DESK YET.
WELL, THEN DON'T TOUCH ANYTHING.
I KNOW.
A PENCIL AND GLOVES.
ALWAYS.
YEAH...
JUST SAYIN'...
...ALWAYS BE PREPARED.

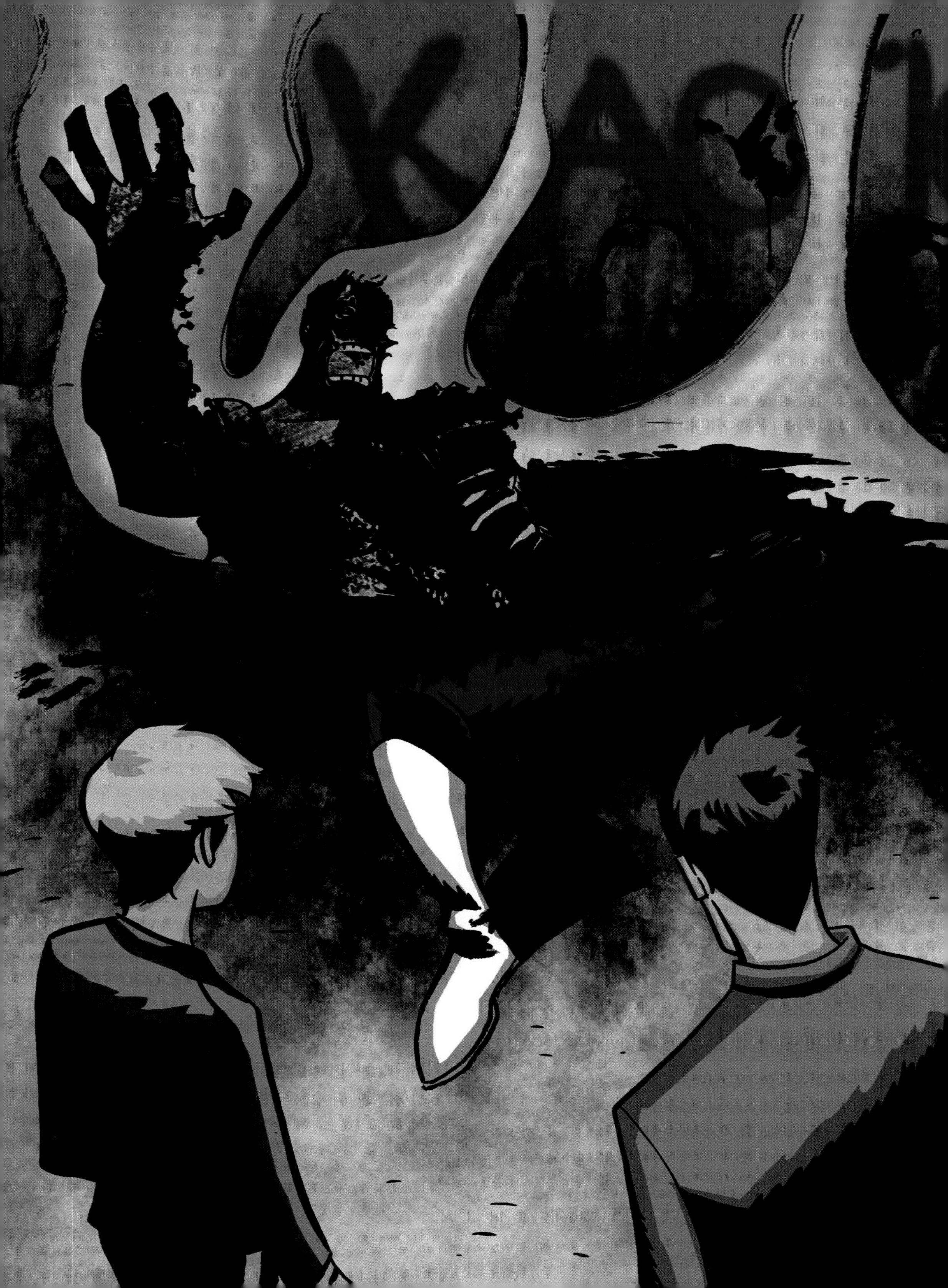

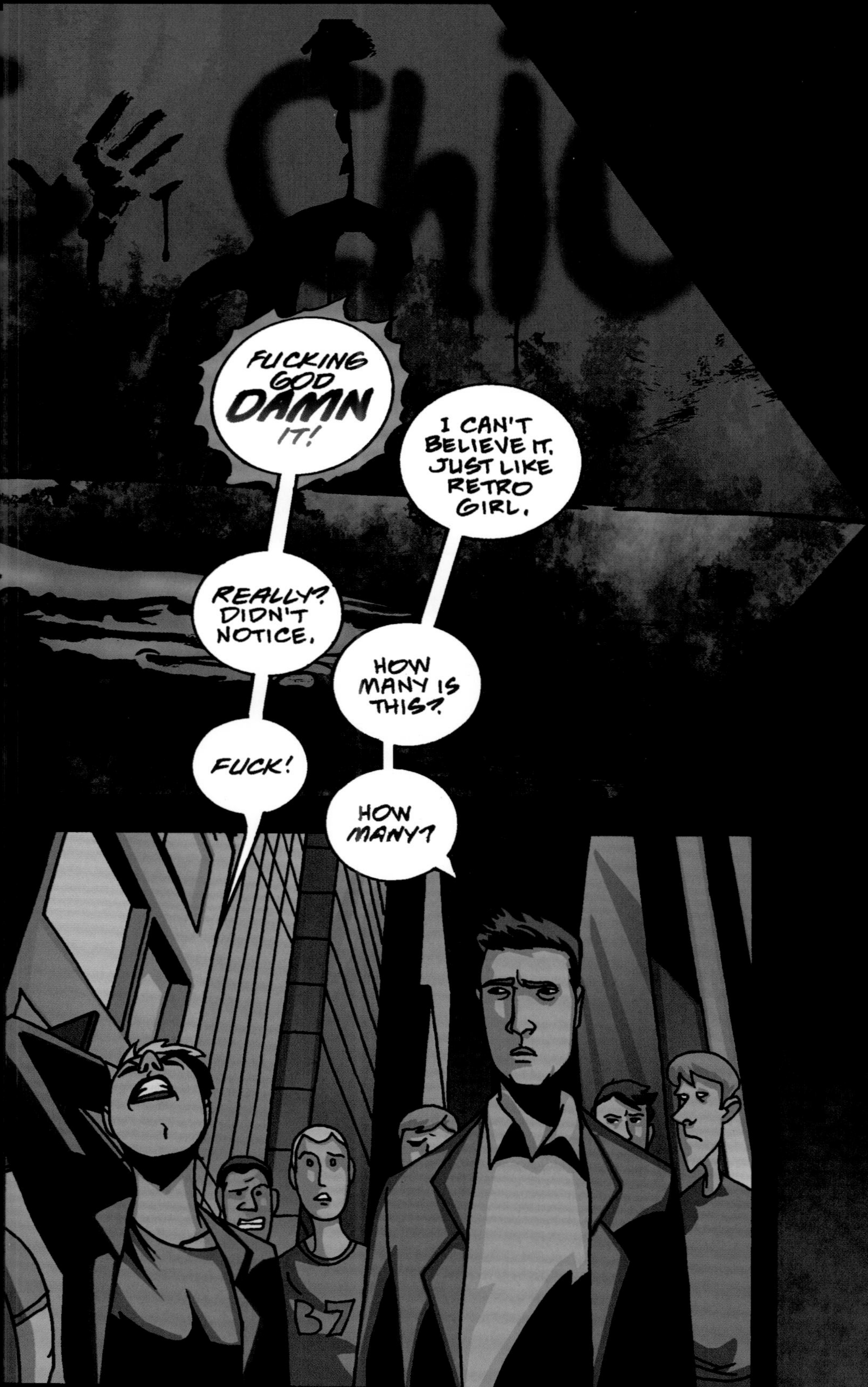

FUCKING GOD DAMN IT!
I CAN'T BELIEVE IT. JUST LIKE RETRO GIRL.
REALLY? DIDN'T NOTICE.
HOW MANY IS THIS?
FUCK!
HOW MANY?

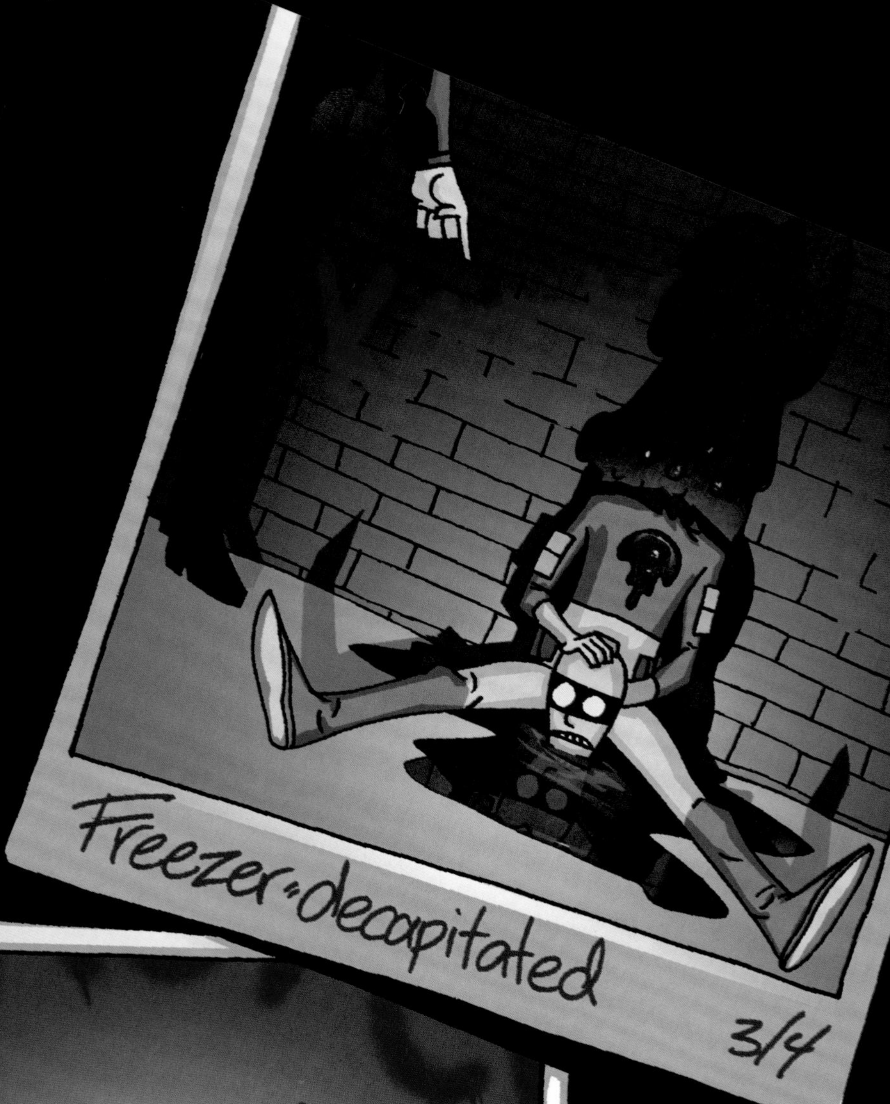
Freezer=decapitated
3/4

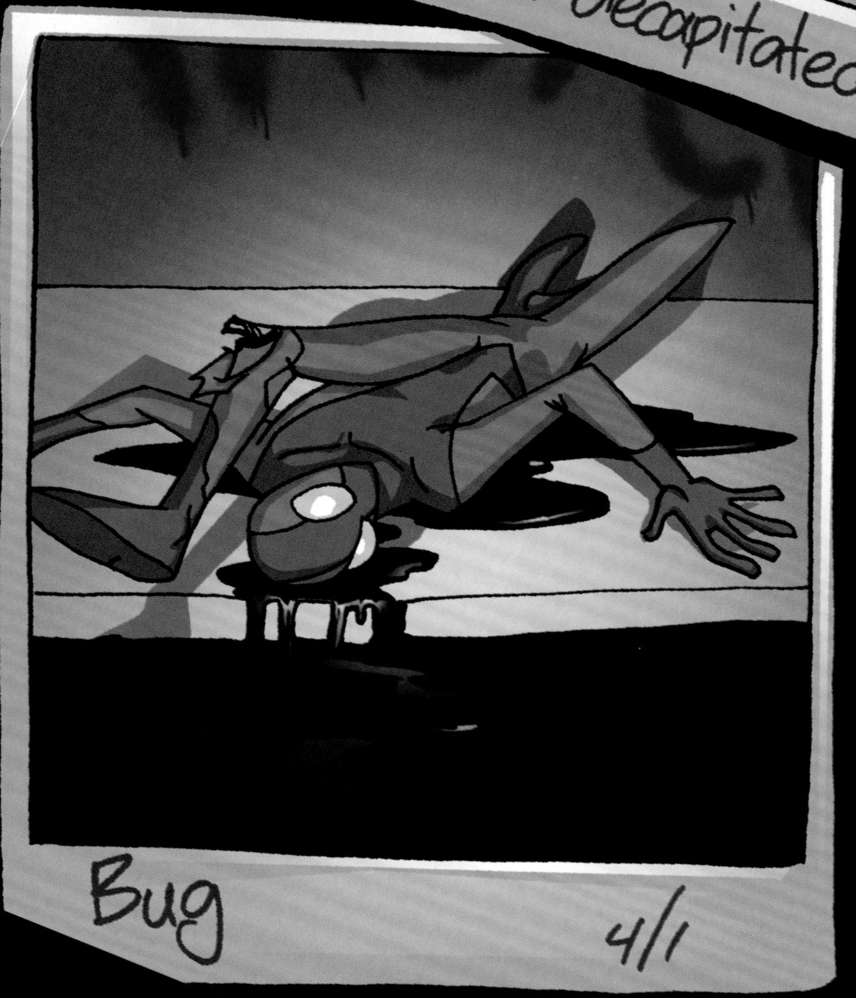
Bug
4/1

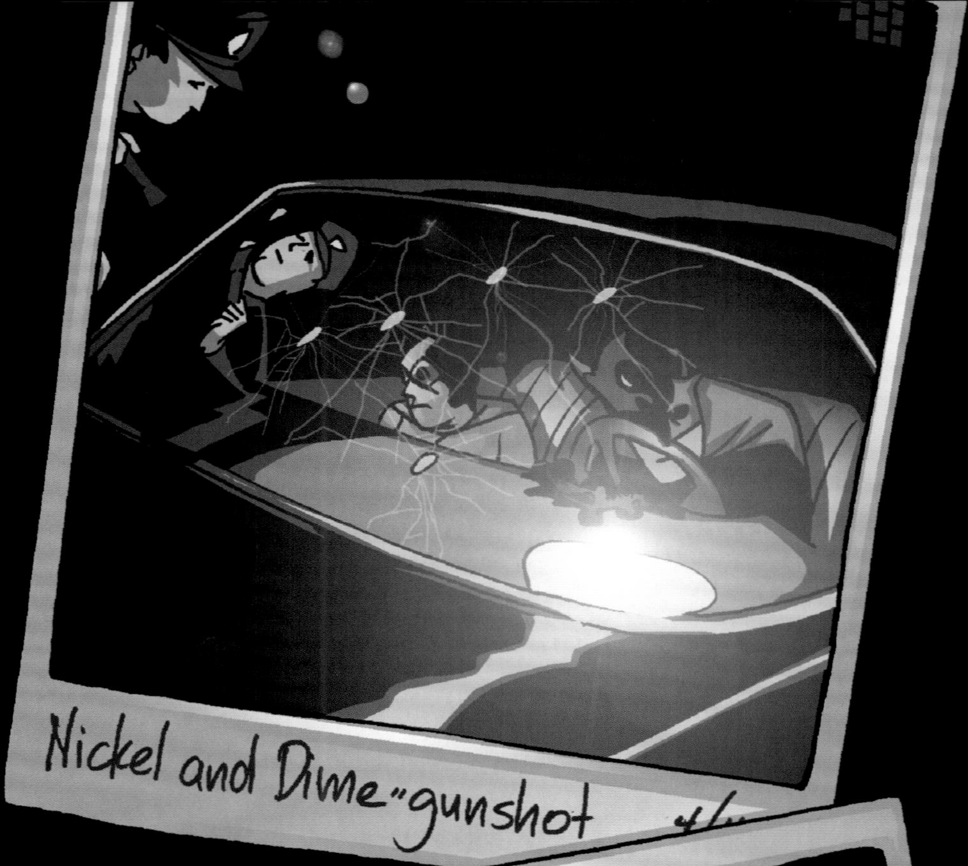
Nickel and Dime" gunshot

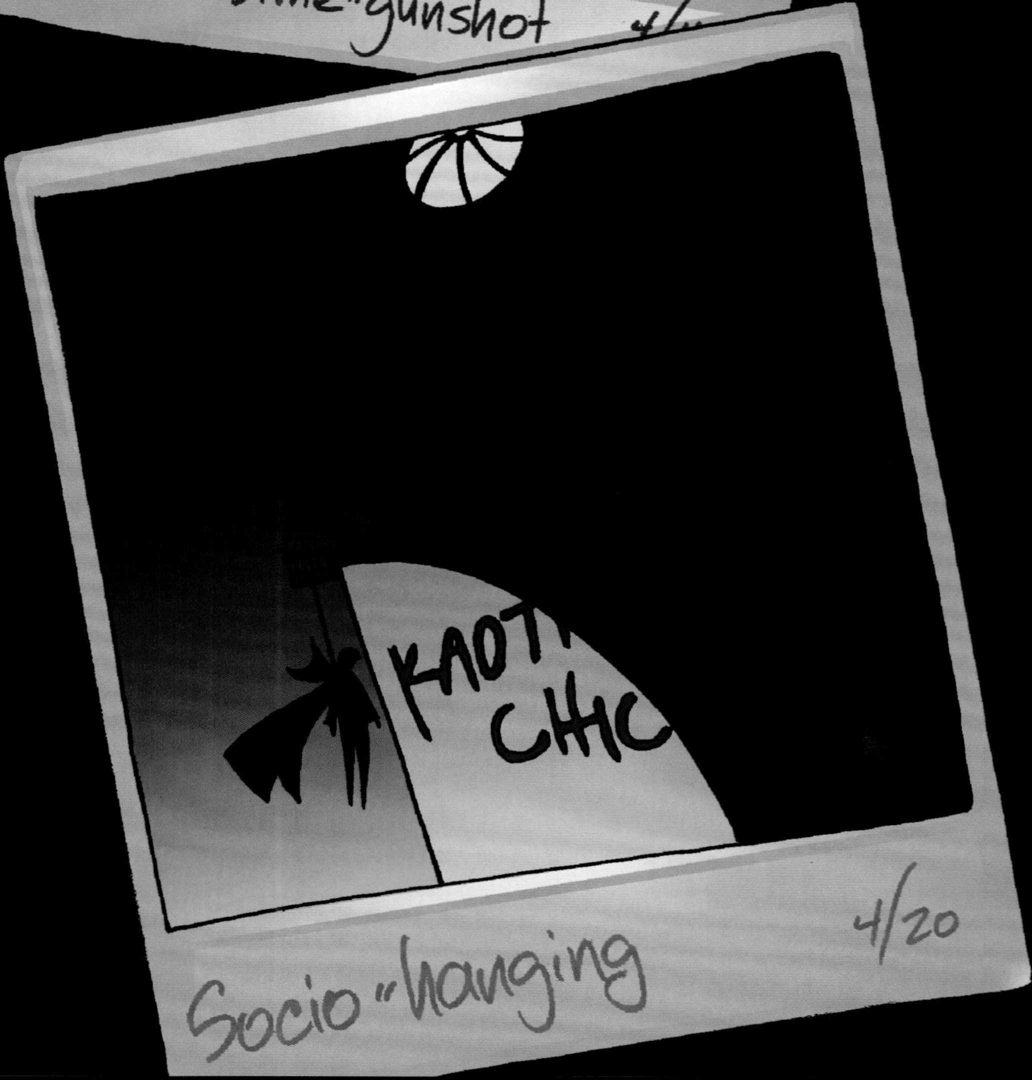
CHIC
4/20
Socio" hanging

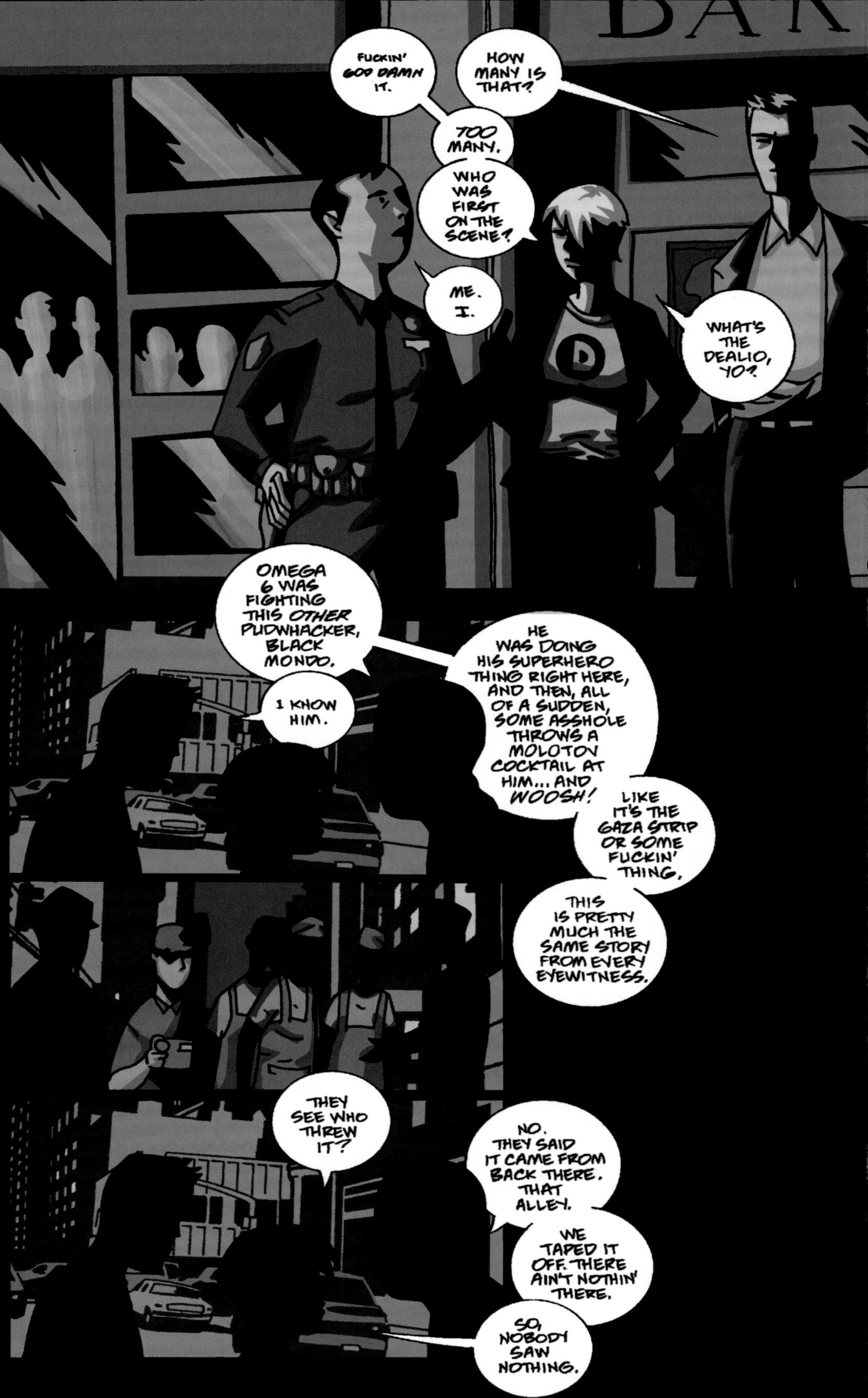
BAR
FUCKIN' GOD DAMN IT.
HOW MANY IS THAT?
TOO MANY.
WHO WAS FIRST ON THE SCENE?
ME. I.
WHAT'S THE DEALIO, YO?
OMEGA 6 WAS FIGHTING THIS OTHER PUDWHACKER, BLACK MONDO.
I KNOW HIM.
HE WAS DOING HIS SUPERHERO THING RIGHT HERE, AND THEN, ALL OF A SUDDEN, SOME ASSHOLE THROWS A MOLOTOV COCKTAIL AT HIM... AND WOOSH!
LIKE IT'S THE GAZA STRIP OR SOME FUCKIN' THING.
THIS IS PRETTY MUCH THE SAME STORY FROM EVERY EYEWITNESS.
THEY SEE WHO THREW IT?
NO. THEY SAID IT CAME FROM BACK THERE. THAT ALLEY.
WE TAPED IT OFF. THERE AIN'T NOTHIN' THERE.
SO, NOBODY SAW NOTHING.

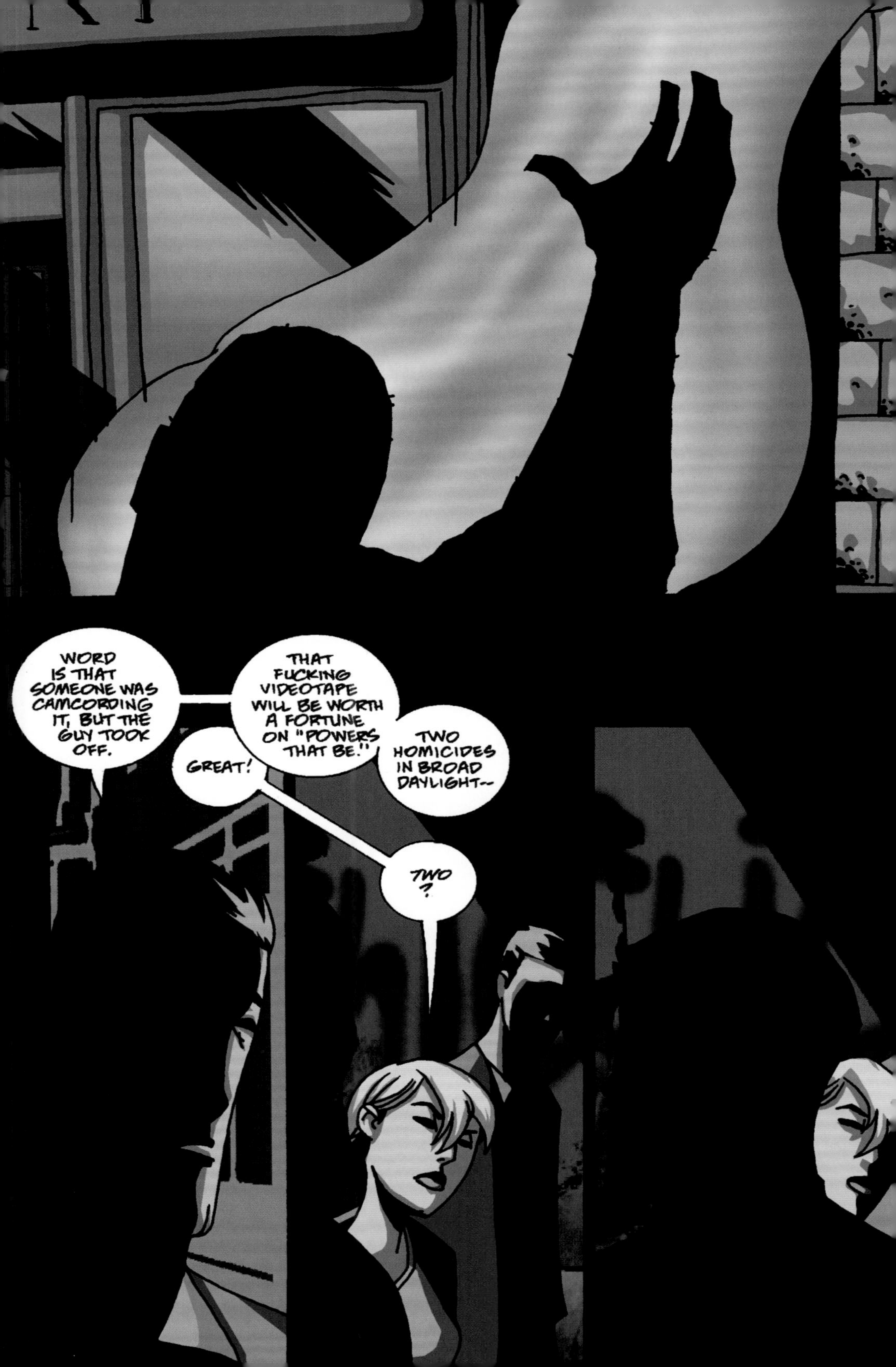
WORD IS THAT SOMEONE WAS CAMCORDING IT, BUT THE GUY TOOK OFF.
THAT FUCKING VIDEOTAPE WILL BE WORTH A FORTUNE ON "POWERS THAT BE."
GREAT!
TWO HOMICIDES IN BROAD DAYLIGHT--
TWO?

FUCK ME IN THE EAR.

WHAT IS THIS?

SOME-BODY CUT OFF HIS HEAD.

NO WITNESSES TO *THIS*, EITHER.

WE DON'T KNOW *WHAT* HAPPENED, EXCEPT OMEGA 6 TIED HIM TO THE POLE HERE, FOR US, I GUESS, BUT...

NO WITNESSES? IT'S RIGHT IN THE MIDDLE OF--

THEY WERE ALL WATCHING OMEGA 6 BURN.

NOBODY EVEN NOTICED IT 'TIL WE GOT HERE.

...DY ...ED ...ODY ...OFF

...ONE ?.

...OW, ...AT'S A ...ADED ...UCKING...

WAIT...

WHERE'S ...

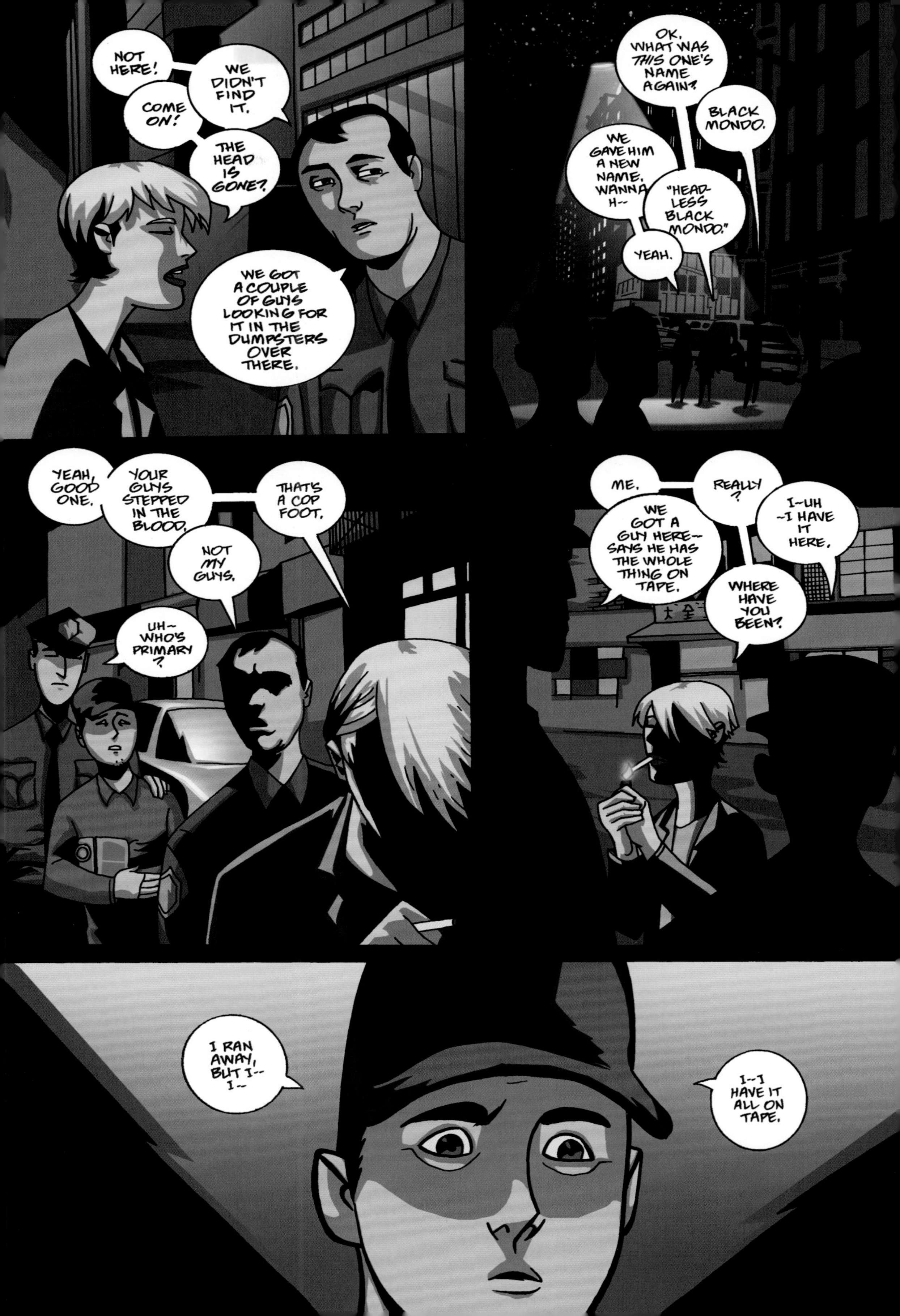
NOT HERE!
WE DIDN'T FIND IT.
COME ON!
THE HEAD IS GONE?
WE GOT A COUPLE OF GUYS LOOKING FOR IT IN THE DUMPSTERS OVER THERE.
OK, WHAT WAS THIS ONE'S NAME AGAIN?
BLACK MONDO.
WE GAVE HIM A NEW NAME, WANNA H--
"HEADLESS BLACK MONDO."
YEAH.
YEAH, GOOD ONE.
YOUR GUYS STEPPED IN THE BLOOD.
THAT'S A COP FOOT.
NOT MY GUYS.
UH-- WHO'S PRIMARY?
ME.
REALLY?
WE GOT A GUY HERE-- SAYS HE HAS THE WHOLE THING ON TAPE.
I--UH --I HAVE IT HERE.
WHERE HAVE YOU BEEN?
I RAN AWAY, BUT I-- I--
I--I HAVE IT ALL ON TAPE.

AAAGGHHH!!

MAN, THAT'S FUCKING INSANE!

OOF!

YEAH, DON'T STOP AND HELP HIM, YOU RETARDS!

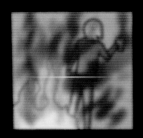

SHE LOOK FAMILIAR TO ANY OF YOU?

NOPE.

FUCK!

NOPE.

NO.

CAN WE RUN IT THROUGH THE COMPUTER?

THIS ISN'T "STAR TREK."

I WAS JUST ASKING.

IT DOESN'T WORK THAT WAY- FUCK!

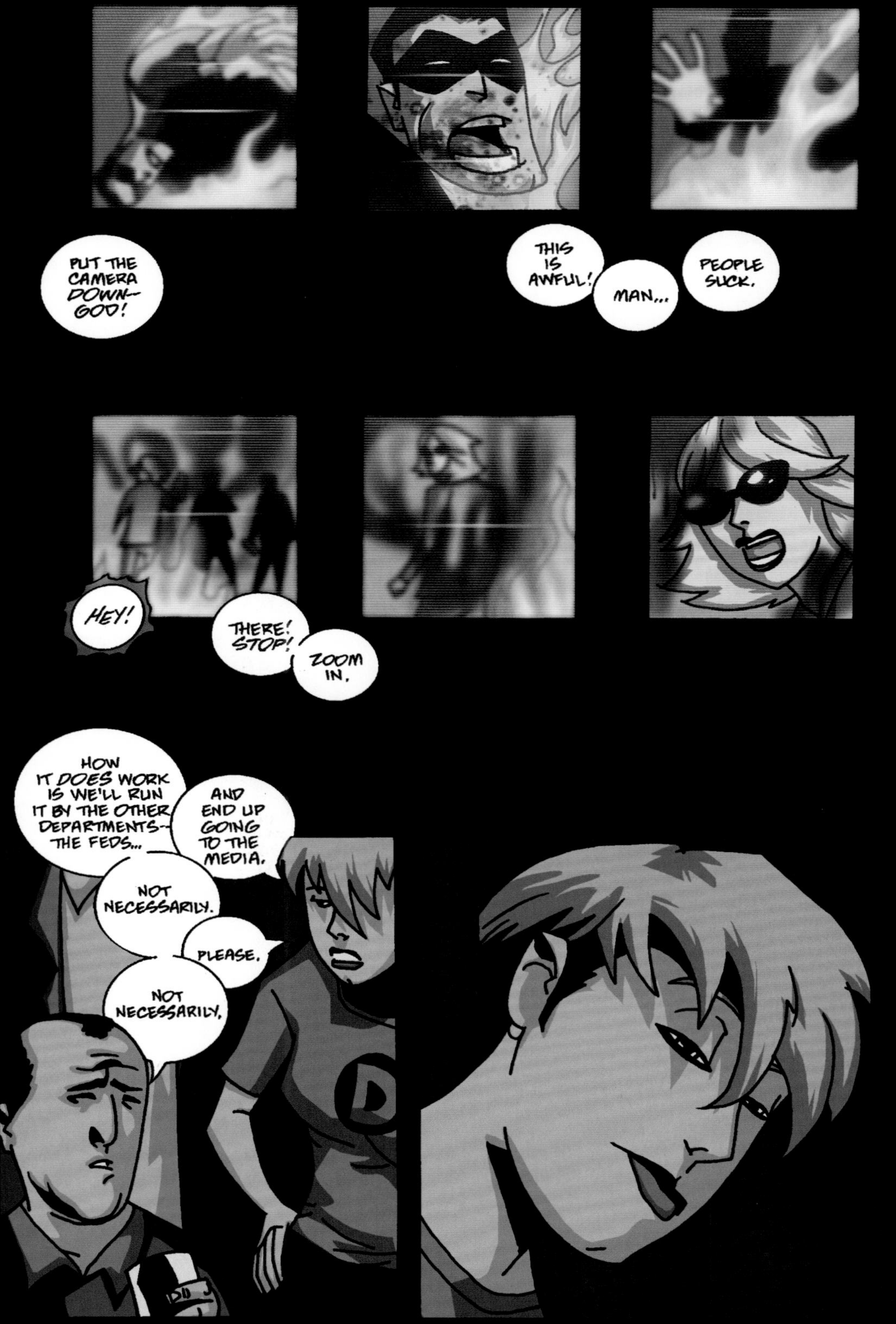
PUT THE CAMERA DOWN-- GOD!
THIS IS AWFUL!
MAN...
PEOPLE SUCK.
HEY!
THERE! STOP!
ZOOM IN.
HOW IT DOES WORK IS WE'LL RUN IT BY THE OTHER DEPARTMENTS-- THE FEDS...
AND END UP GOING TO THE MEDIA.
NOT NECESSARILY.
PLEASE.
NOT NECESSARILY.

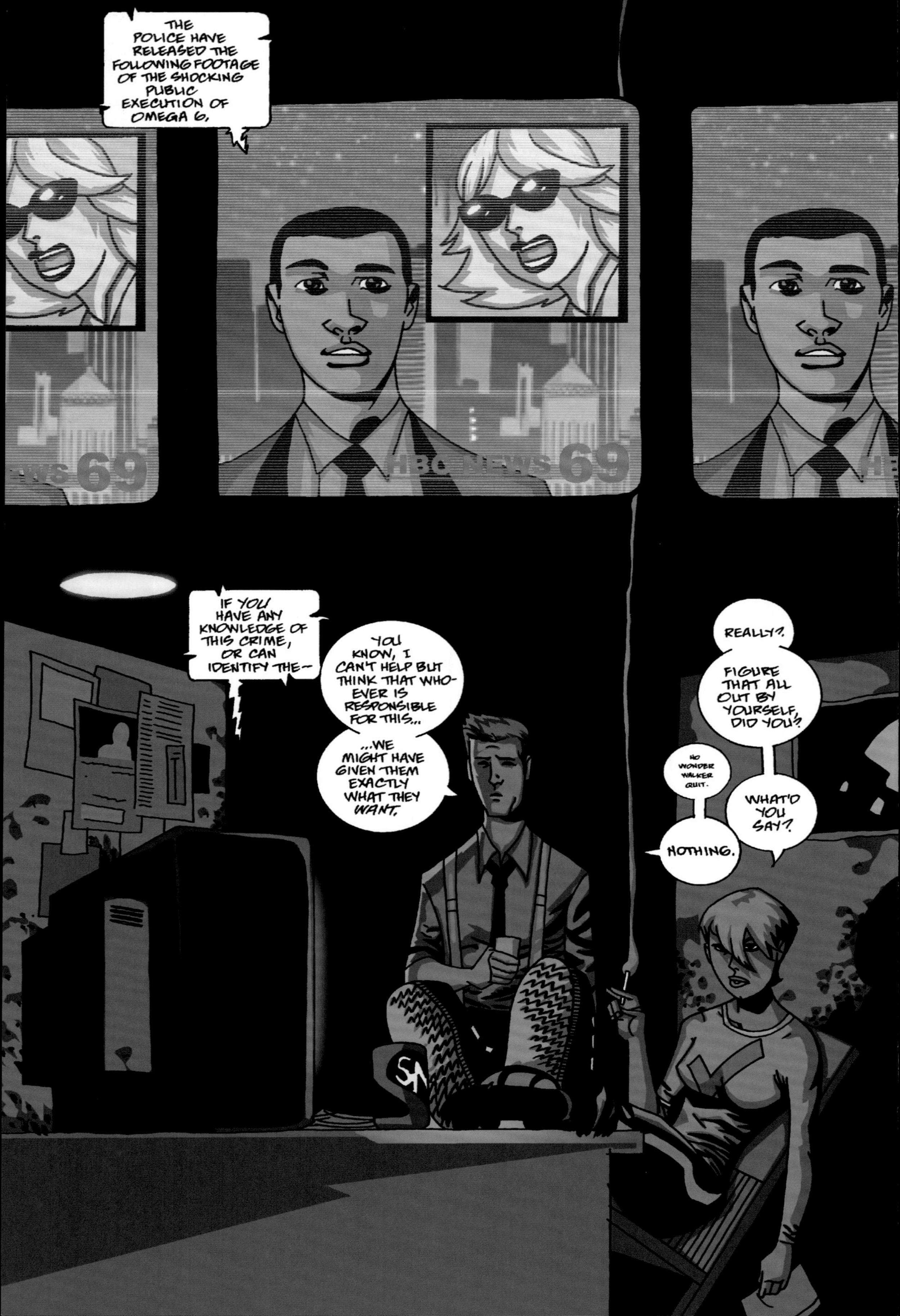
THE POLICE HAVE RELEASED THE FOLLOWING FOOTAGE OF THE SHOCKING PUBLIC EXECUTION OF OMEGA 6,
HBC NEWS 69
IF YOU HAVE ANY KNOWLEDGE OF THIS CRIME, OR CAN IDENTIFY THE--
YOU KNOW, I CAN'T HELP BUT THINK THAT WHOEVER IS RESPONSIBLE FOR THIS...
...WE MIGHT HAVE GIVEN THEM EXACTLY WHAT THEY WANT.
REALLY?.
FIGURE THAT ALL OUT BY YOURSELF, DID YOU?
NO WONDER WALKER QUIT.
WHAT'D YOU SAY?
NOTHING.

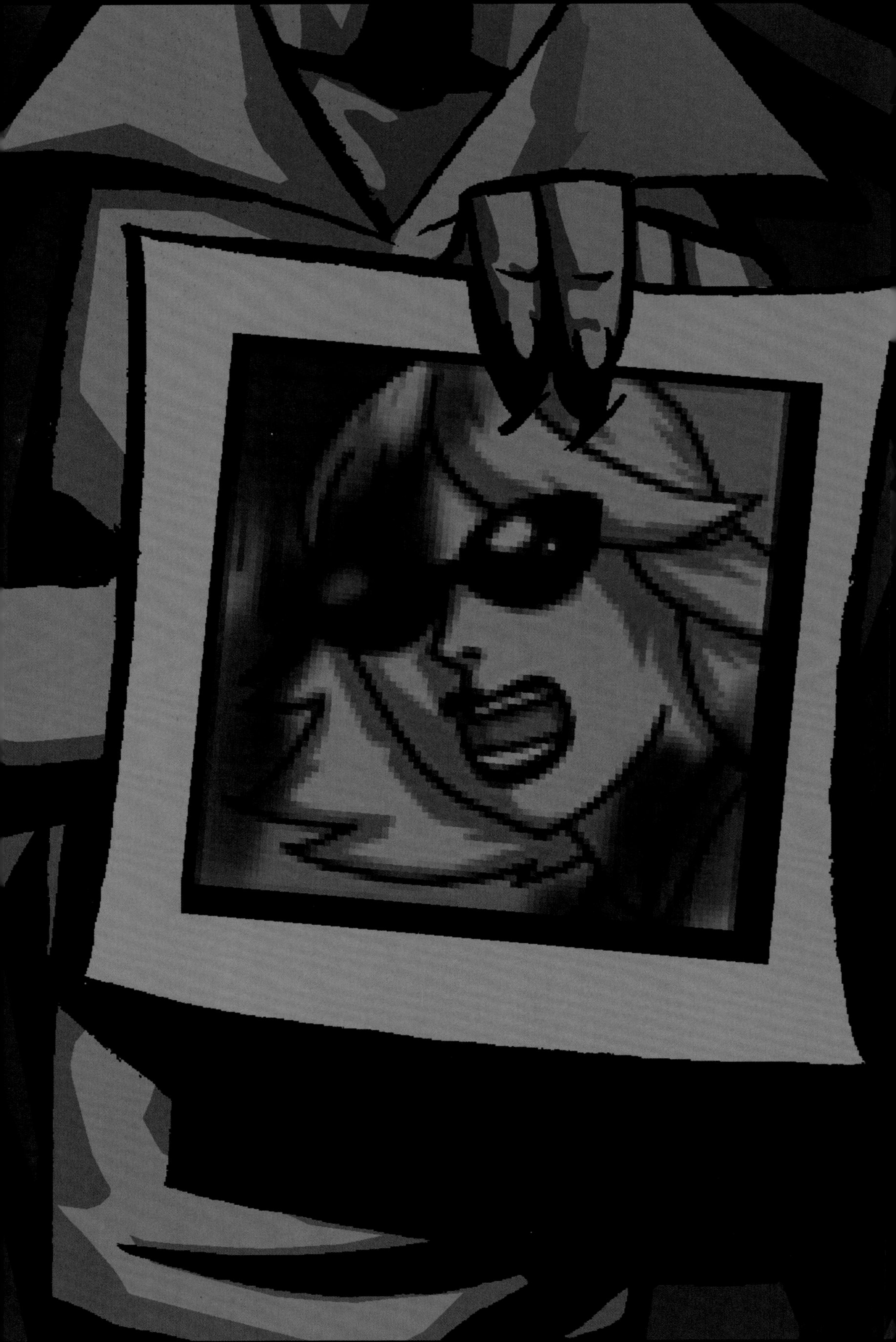

POWERS™

ANARCHY
CHAPTER 2

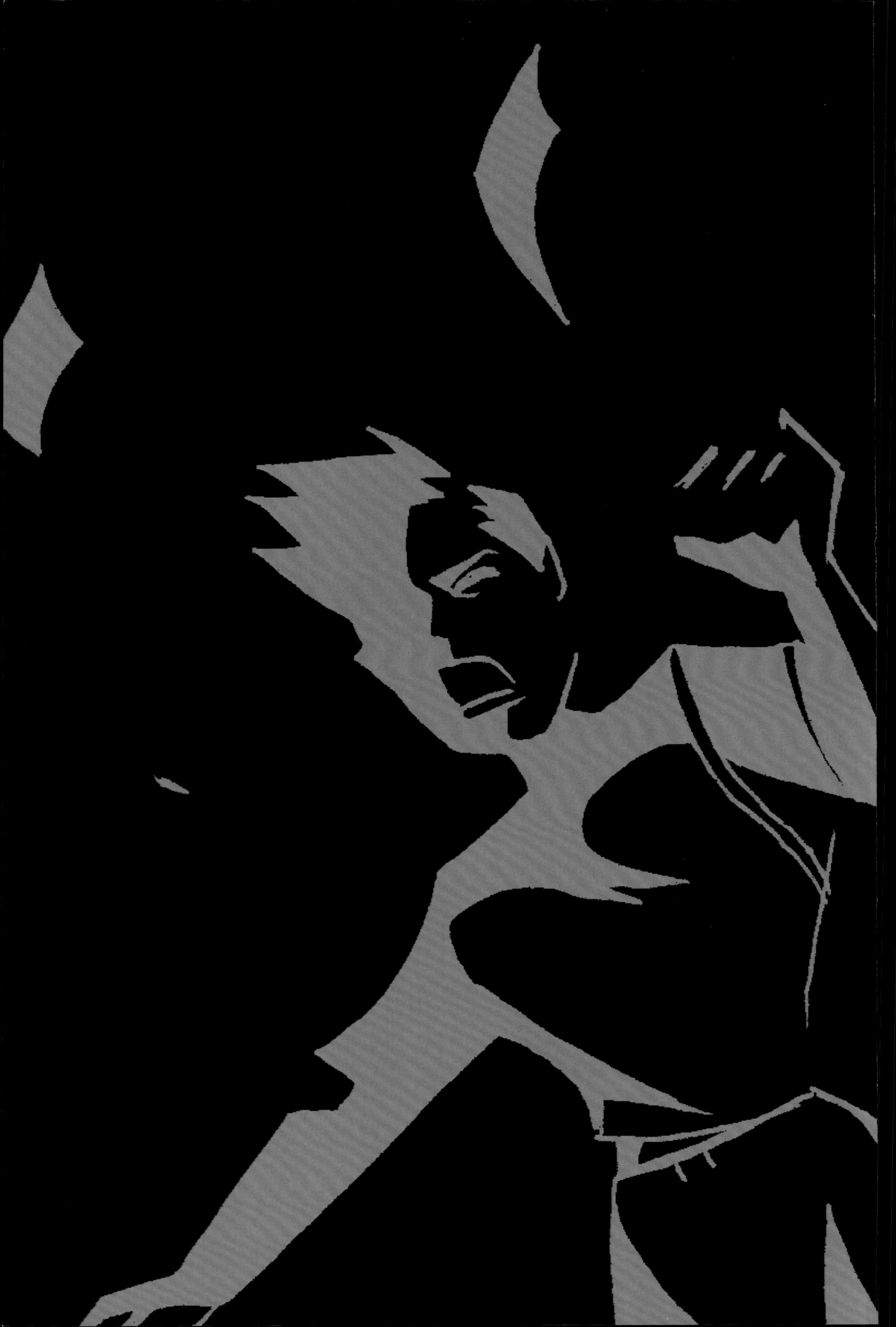

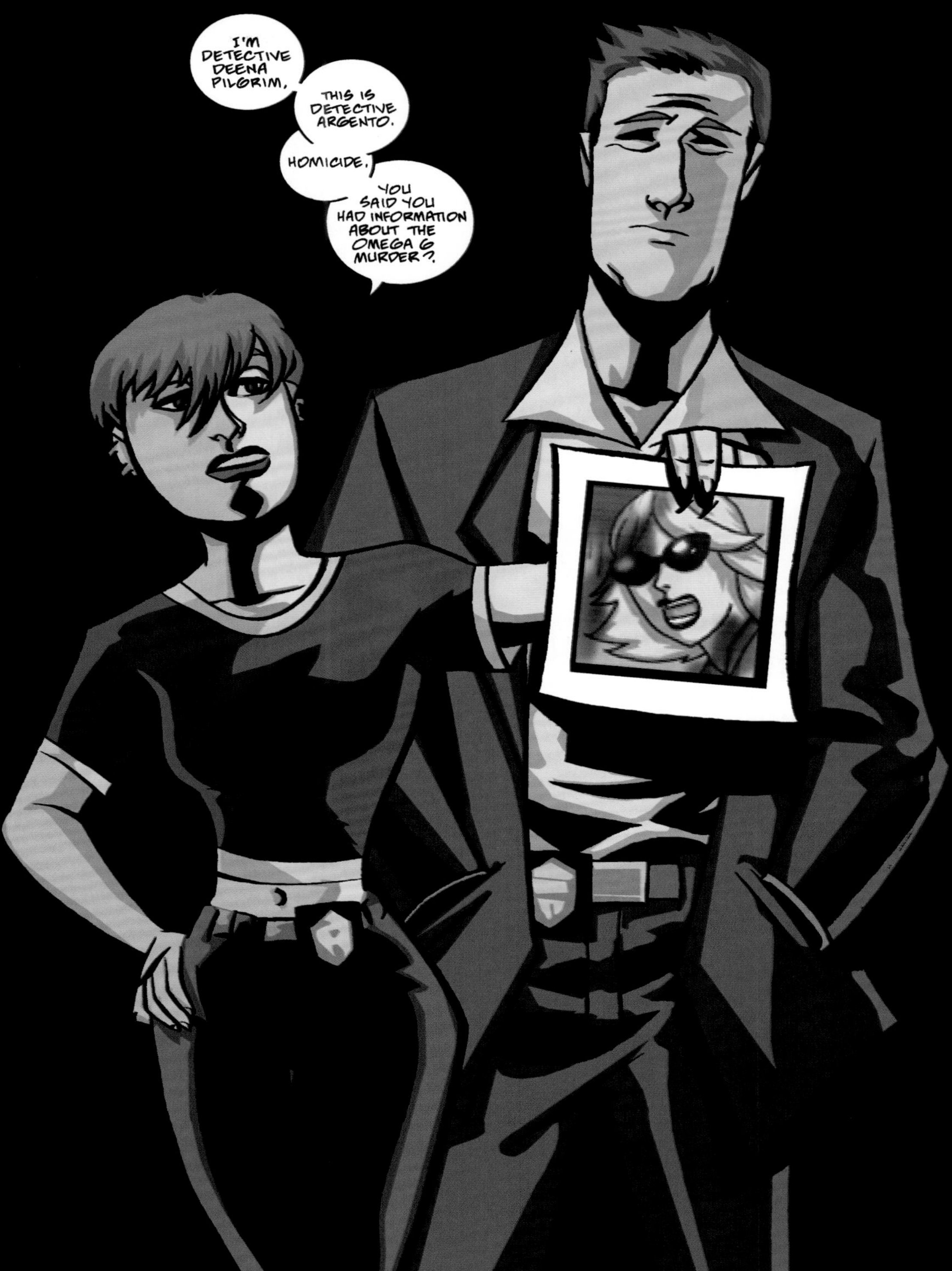
I'M DETECTIVE DEENA PILGRIM,
THIS IS DETECTIVE ARGENTO.
HOMICIDE.
YOU SAID YOU HAD INFORMATION ABOUT THE OMEGA 6 MURDER?

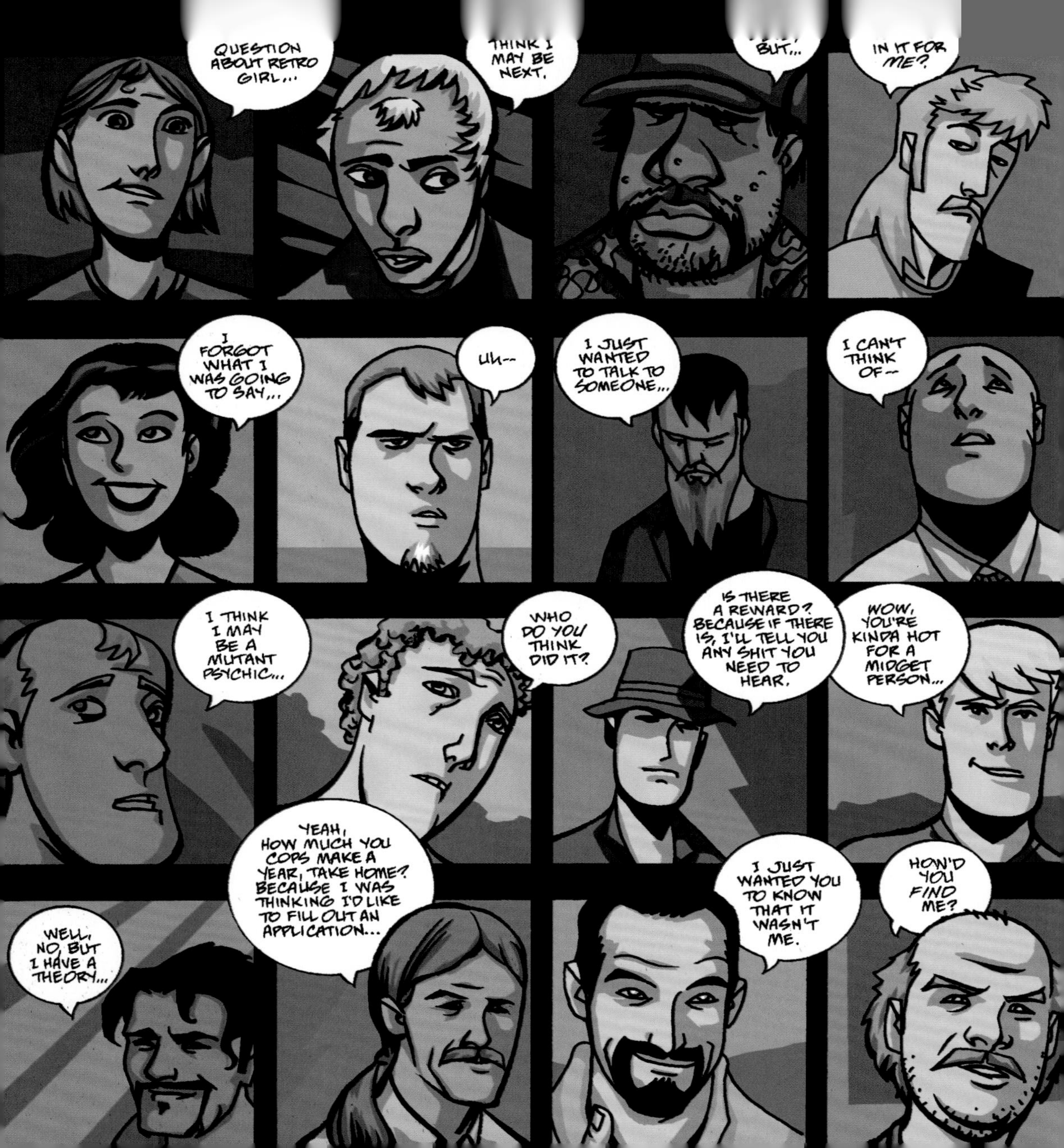
QUESTION ABOUT RETRO GIRL...
THINK I MAY BE NEXT.
BUT...
IN IT FOR ME?
I FORGOT WHAT I WAS GOING TO SAY...
UH--
I JUST WANTED TO TALK TO SOMEONE...
I CAN'T THINK OF--
I THINK I MAY BE A MUTANT PSYCHIC...
WHO DO YOU THINK DID IT?
IS THERE A REWARD? BECAUSE IF THERE IS, I'LL TELL YOU ANY SHIT YOU NEED TO HEAR.
WOW, YOU'RE KINDA HOT FOR A MIDGET PERSON...
WELL, NO, BUT I HAVE A THEORY...
YEAH, HOW MUCH YOU COPS MAKE A YEAR, TAKE HOME? BECAUSE I WAS THINKING I'D LIKE TO FILL OUT AN APPLICATION...
I JUST WANTED YOU TO KNOW THAT IT WASN'T ME.
HOW'D YOU FIND ME?

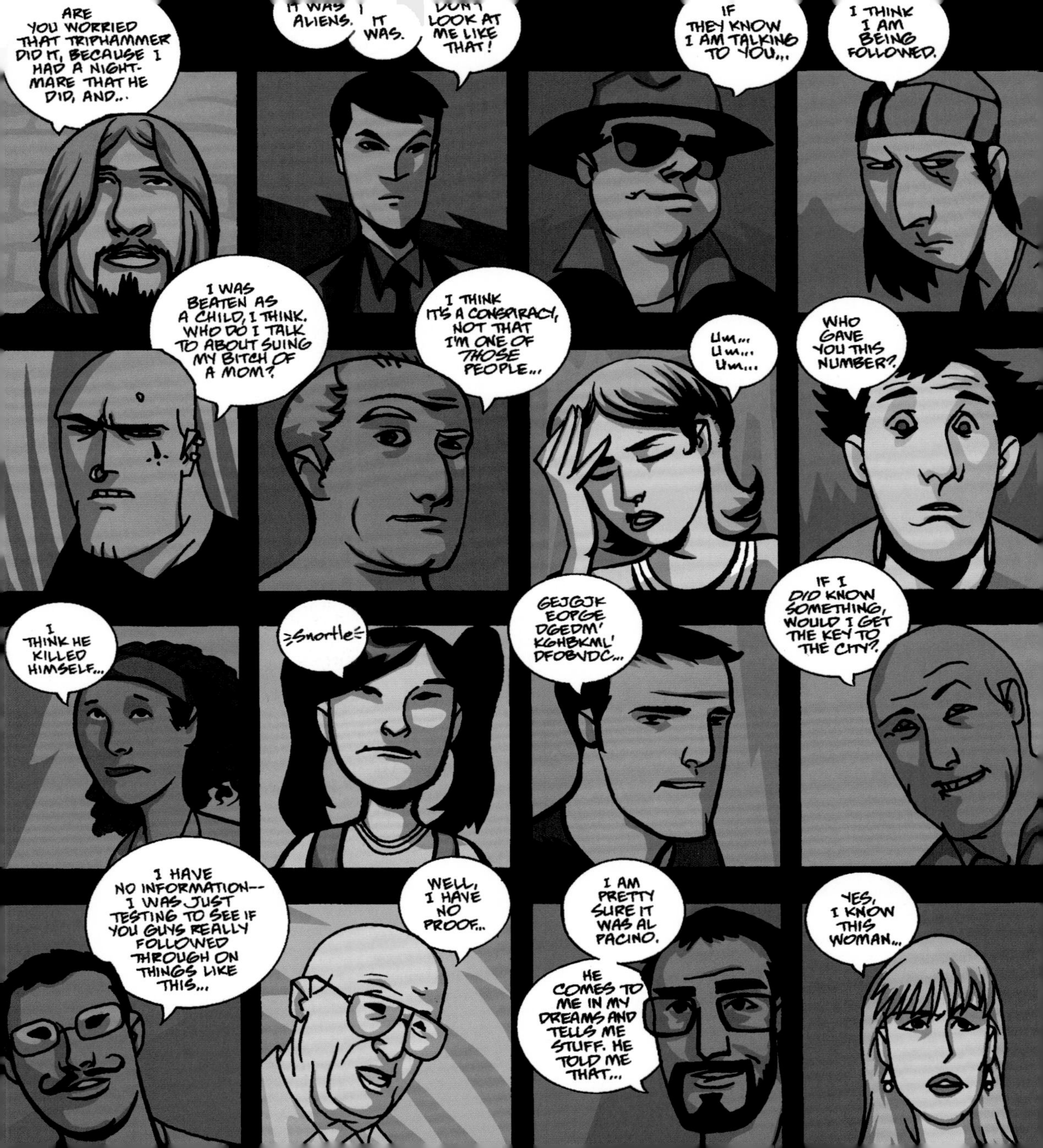
ARE YOU WORRIED THAT TRIPHAMMER DID IT, BECAUSE I HAD A NIGHT-MARE THAT HE DID, AND...
IT WAS ALIENS.
IT WAS.
LOOK AT ME LIKE THAT!
IF THEY KNOW I AM TALKING TO YOU...
I THINK I AM BEING FOLLOWED.
I WAS BEATEN AS A CHILD, I THINK. WHO DO I TALK TO ABOUT SUING MY BITCH OF A MOM?
I THINK IT'S A CONSPIRACY, NOT THAT I'M ONE OF THOSE PEOPLE...
UM... UM... UM...
WHO GAVE YOU THIS NUMBER?
I THINK HE KILLED HIMSELF...
Snortle
GEJGJK EOPGE DGEDM' KGHBKML' DFOBVDC...
IF I DID KNOW SOMETHING, WOULD I GET THE KEY TO THE CITY?
I HAVE NO INFORMATION-- I WAS JUST TESTING TO SEE IF YOU GUYS REALLY FOLLOWED THROUGH ON THINGS LIKE THIS...
WELL, I HAVE NO PROOF...
I AM PRETTY SURE IT WAS AL PACINO.
HE COMES TO ME IN MY DREAMS AND TELLS ME STUFF. HE TOLD ME THAT...
YES, I KNOW THIS WOMAN...

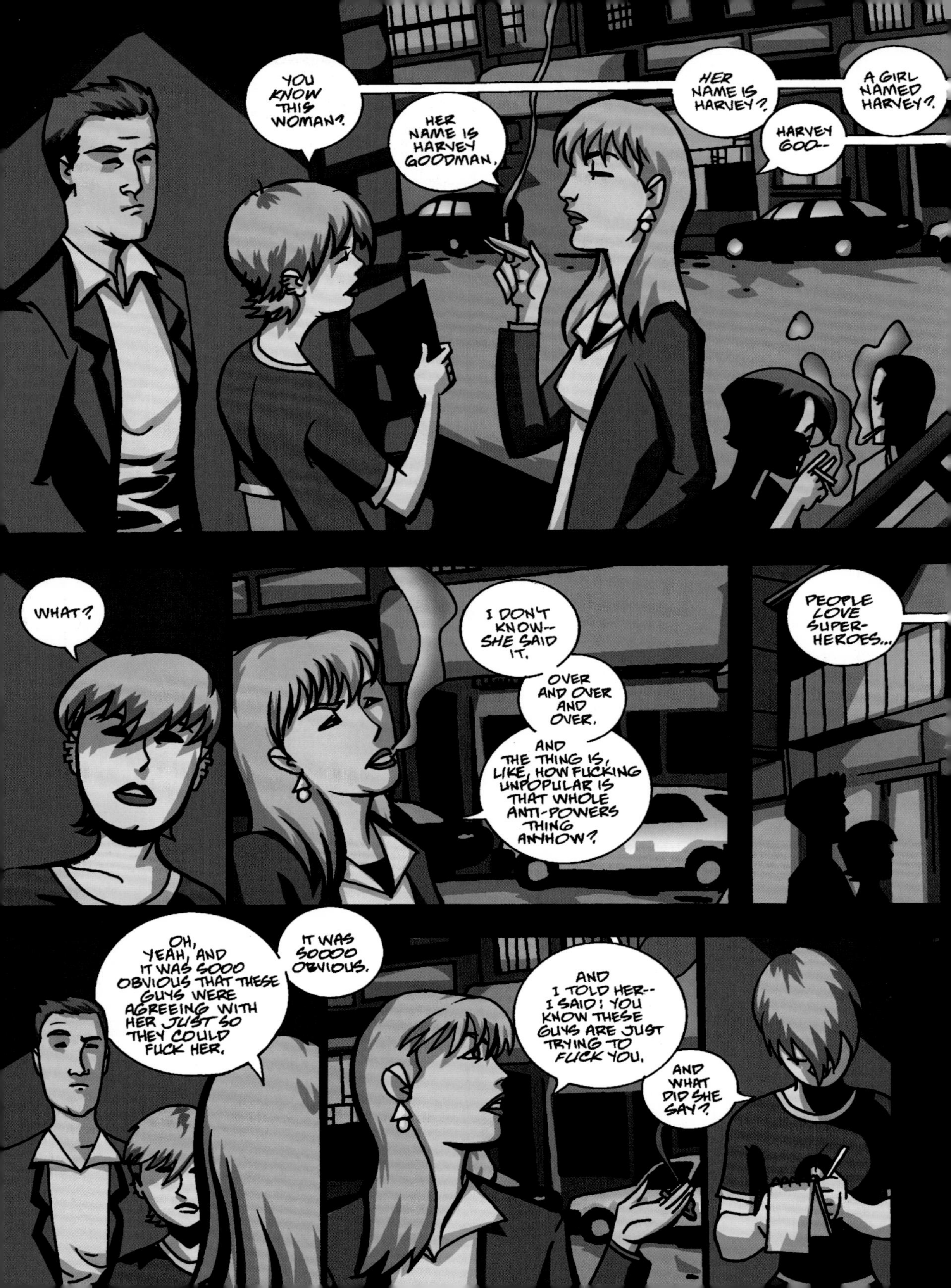
YOU KNOW THIS WOMAN?
HER NAME IS HARVEY GOODMAN.
HER NAME IS HARVEY?
A GIRL NAMED HARVEY?
HARVEY GOO--
WHAT?
I DON'T KNOW-- SHE SAID IT.
OVER AND OVER AND OVER.
AND THE THING IS, LIKE, HOW FUCKING UNPOPULAR IS THAT WHOLE ANTI-POWERS THING ANYHOW?
PEOPLE LOVE SUPER-HEROES...
OH, YEAH, AND IT WAS SOOO OBVIOUS THAT THESE GUYS WERE AGREEING WITH HER JUST SO THEY COULD FUCK HER.
IT WAS SOOOO OBVIOUS.
AND I TOLD HER-- I SAID: YOU KNOW THESE GUYS ARE JUST TRYING TO FUCK YOU.
AND WHAT DID SHE SAY?

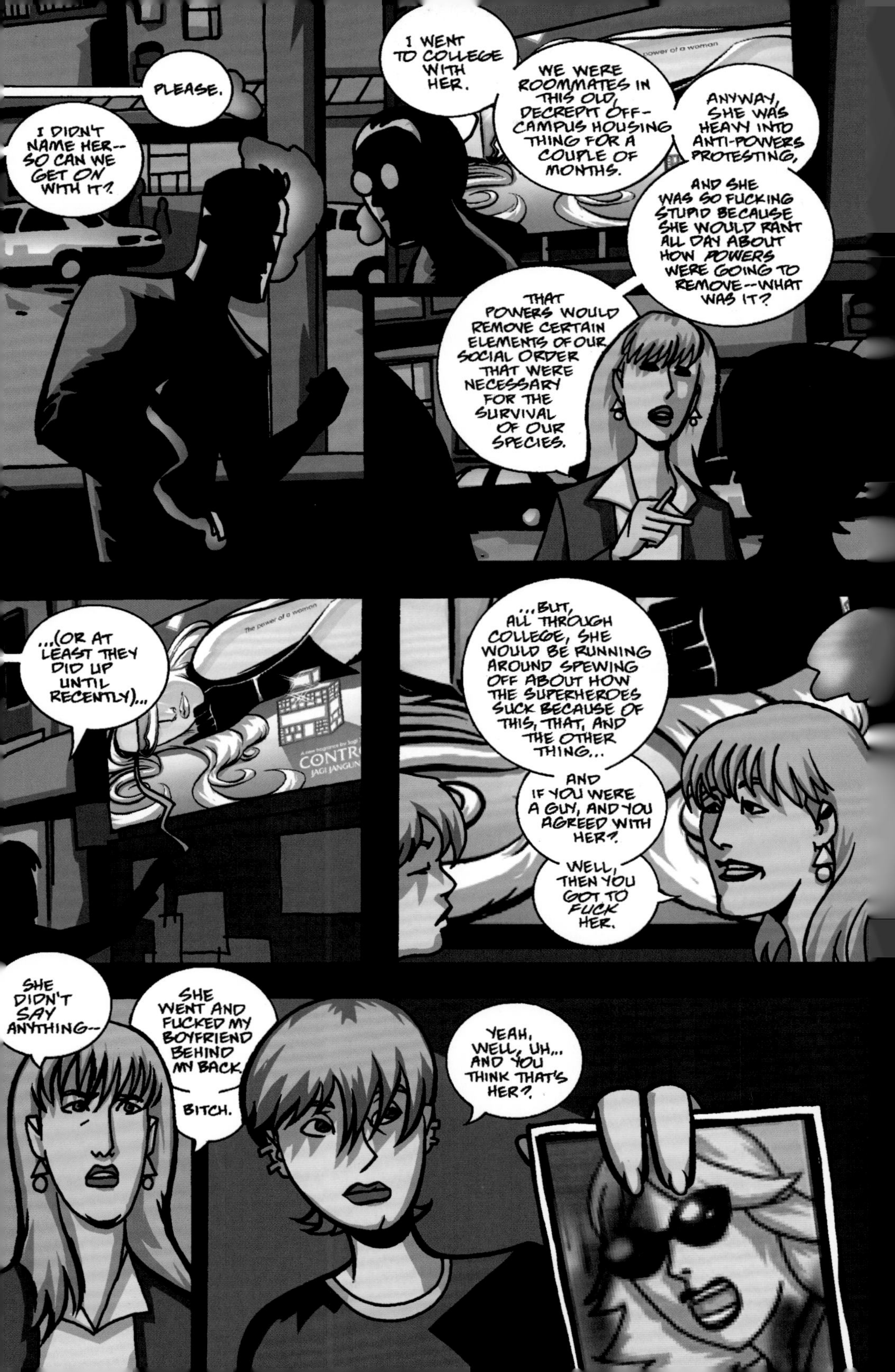
PLEASE.
I DIDN'T NAME HER-- SO CAN WE GET ON WITH IT?
I WENT TO COLLEGE WITH HER.
WE WERE ROOMMATES IN THIS OLD, DECREPIT OFF-CAMPUS HOUSING THING FOR A COUPLE OF MONTHS.
ANYWAY, SHE WAS HEAVY INTO ANTI-POWERS PROTESTING,
AND SHE WAS SO FUCKING STUPID BECAUSE SHE WOULD RANT ALL DAY ABOUT HOW POWERS WERE GOING TO REMOVE--WHAT WAS IT?
THAT POWERS WOULD REMOVE CERTAIN ELEMENTS OF OUR SOCIAL ORDER THAT WERE NECESSARY FOR THE SURVIVAL OF OUR SPECIES.
The power of a woman
...(OR AT LEAST THEY DID UP UNTIL RECENTLY)...
...BUT, ALL THROUGH COLLEGE, SHE WOULD BE RUNNING AROUND SPEWING OFF ABOUT HOW THE SUPERHEROES SUCK BECAUSE OF THIS, THAT, AND THE OTHER THING...
AND IF YOU WERE A GUY, AND YOU AGREED WITH HER?
WELL, THEN YOU GOT TO FUCK HER.
SHE DIDN'T SAY ANYTHING--
SHE WENT AND FUCKED MY BOYFRIEND BEHIND MY BACK.
BITCH.
YEAH, WELL, UH... AND YOU THINK THAT'S HER?

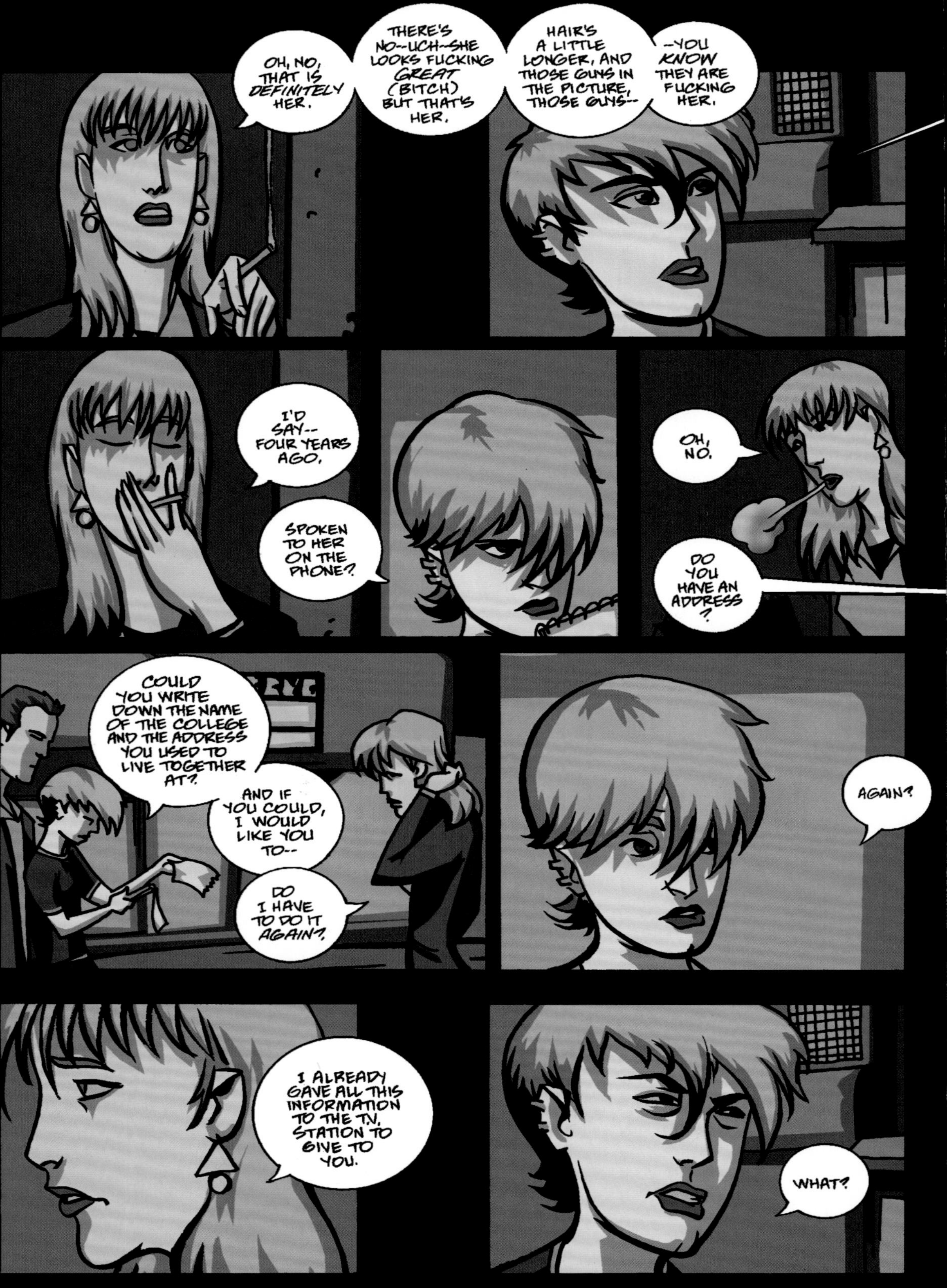
OH, NO, THAT IS DEFINITELY HER.
THERE'S NO--UCH--SHE LOOKS FUCKING GREAT (BITCH) BUT THAT'S HER.
HAIR'S A LITTLE LONGER, AND THOSE GUYS IN THE PICTURE, THOSE GUYS--
--YOU KNOW THEY ARE FUCKING HER.
I'D SAY-- FOUR YEARS AGO.
SPOKEN TO HER ON THE PHONE?
OH, NO.
DO YOU HAVE AN ADDRESS?
COULD YOU WRITE DOWN THE NAME OF THE COLLEGE AND THE ADDRESS YOU USED TO LIVE TOGETHER AT?
AND IF YOU COULD, I WOULD LIKE YOU TO--
DO I HAVE TO DO IT AGAIN?
AGAIN?
I ALREADY GAVE ALL THIS INFORMATION TO THE T.V. STATION TO GIVE TO YOU.
WHAT?

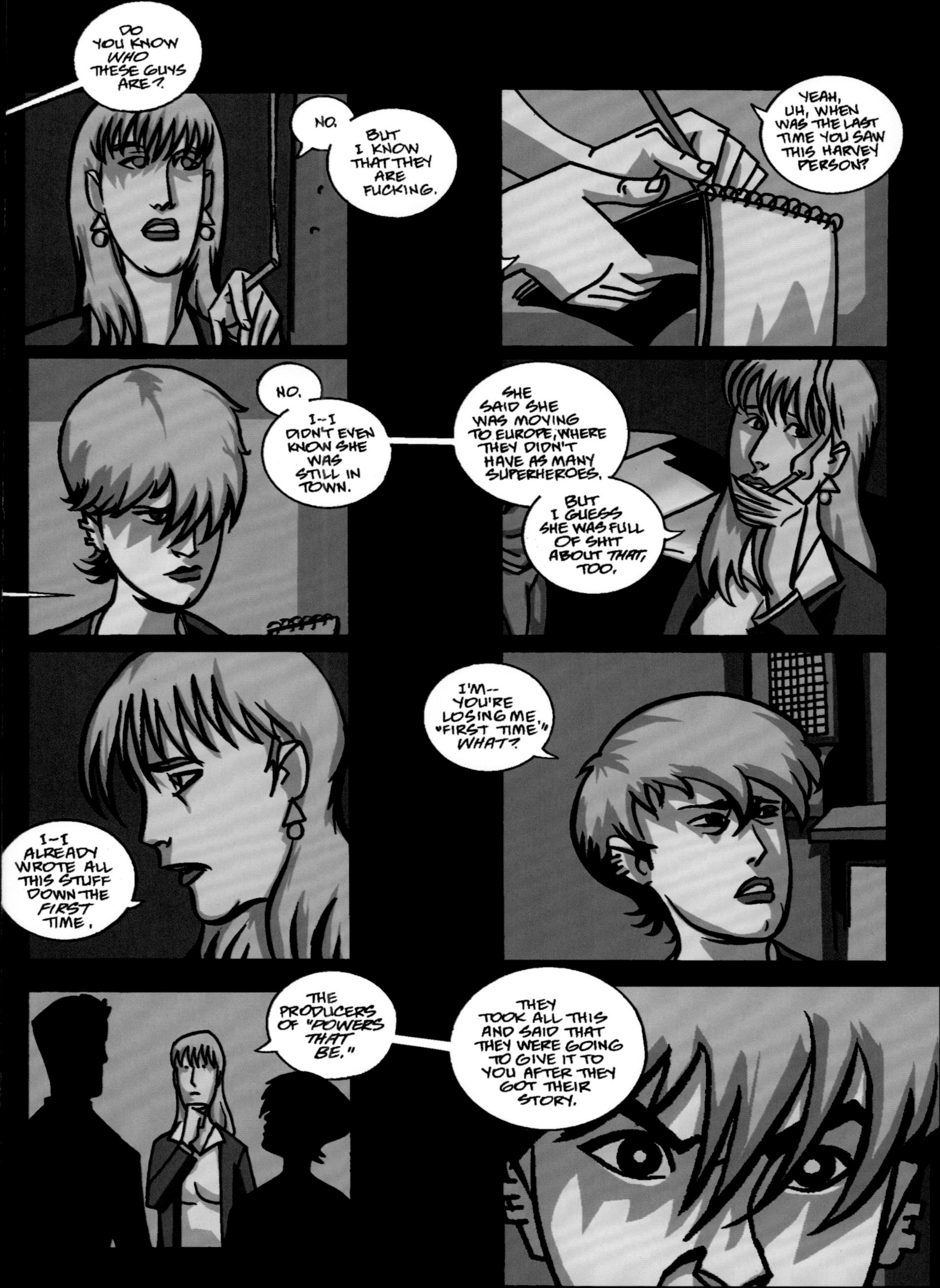

DO YOU KNOW *WHO* THESE GUYS ARE?
NO.
BUT I KNOW THAT THEY ARE FUCKING.
YEAH, UH, WHEN WAS THE LAST TIME YOU SAW THIS HARVEY PERSON?
NO.
I--I DIDN'T EVEN KNOW SHE WAS STILL IN TOWN.
SHE SAID SHE WAS MOVING TO EUROPE, WHERE THEY DIDN'T HAVE AS MANY SUPERHEROES.
BUT I GUESS SHE WAS FULL OF SHIT ABOUT *THAT*, TOO.
I--I ALREADY WROTE ALL THIS STUFF DOWN THE *FIRST* TIME.
I'M-- YOU'RE LOSING ME. "FIRST TIME" *WHAT?*
THE PRODUCERS OF *"POWERS THAT BE."*
THEY TOOK ALL THIS AND SAID THAT THEY WERE GOING TO GIVE IT TO YOU AFTER THEY GOT THEIR STORY.

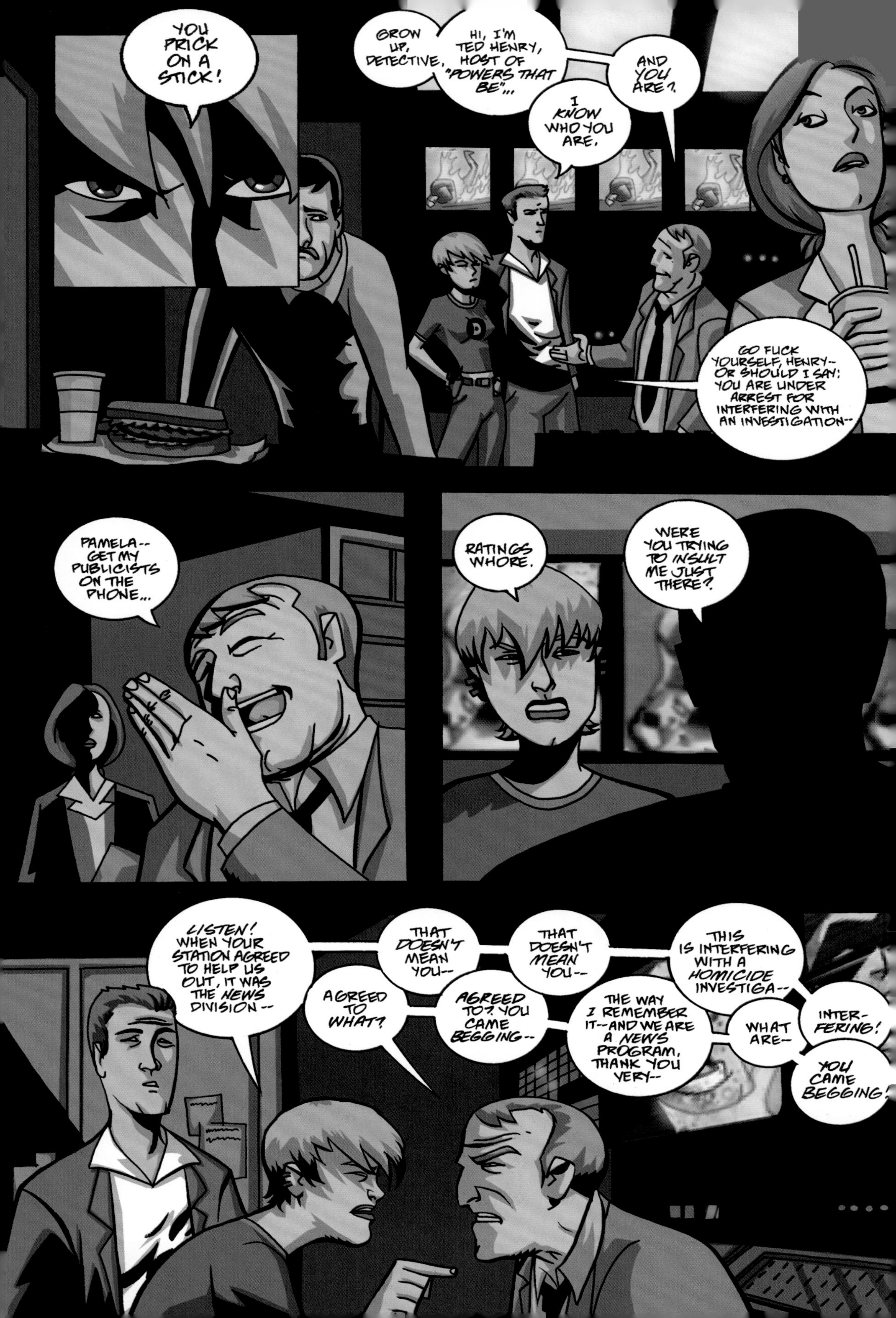

YOU PRICK ON A STICK!
GROW UP, DETECTIVE.
HI, I'M TED HENRY, HOST OF "POWERS THAT BE"...
AND YOU ARE?
I KNOW WHO YOU ARE.
GO FUCK YOURSELF, HENRY-- OR SHOULD I SAY: YOU ARE UNDER ARREST FOR INTERFERING WITH AN INVESTIGATION--
PAMELA-- GET MY PUBLICISTS ON THE PHONE...
RATINGS WHORE.
WERE YOU TRYING TO INSULT ME JUST THERE?
LISTEN! WHEN YOUR STATION AGREED TO HELP US OUT, IT WAS THE NEWS DIVISION--
AGREED TO WHAT?
THAT DOESN'T MEAN YOU--
AGREED TO? YOU CAME BEGGING--
THAT DOESN'T MEAN YOU--
THE WAY I REMEMBER IT--AND WE ARE A NEWS PROGRAM, THANK YOU VERY--
THIS IS INTERFERING WITH A HOMICIDE INVESTIGA--
WHAT ARE--
INTER-FERING!
YOU CAME BEGGING!

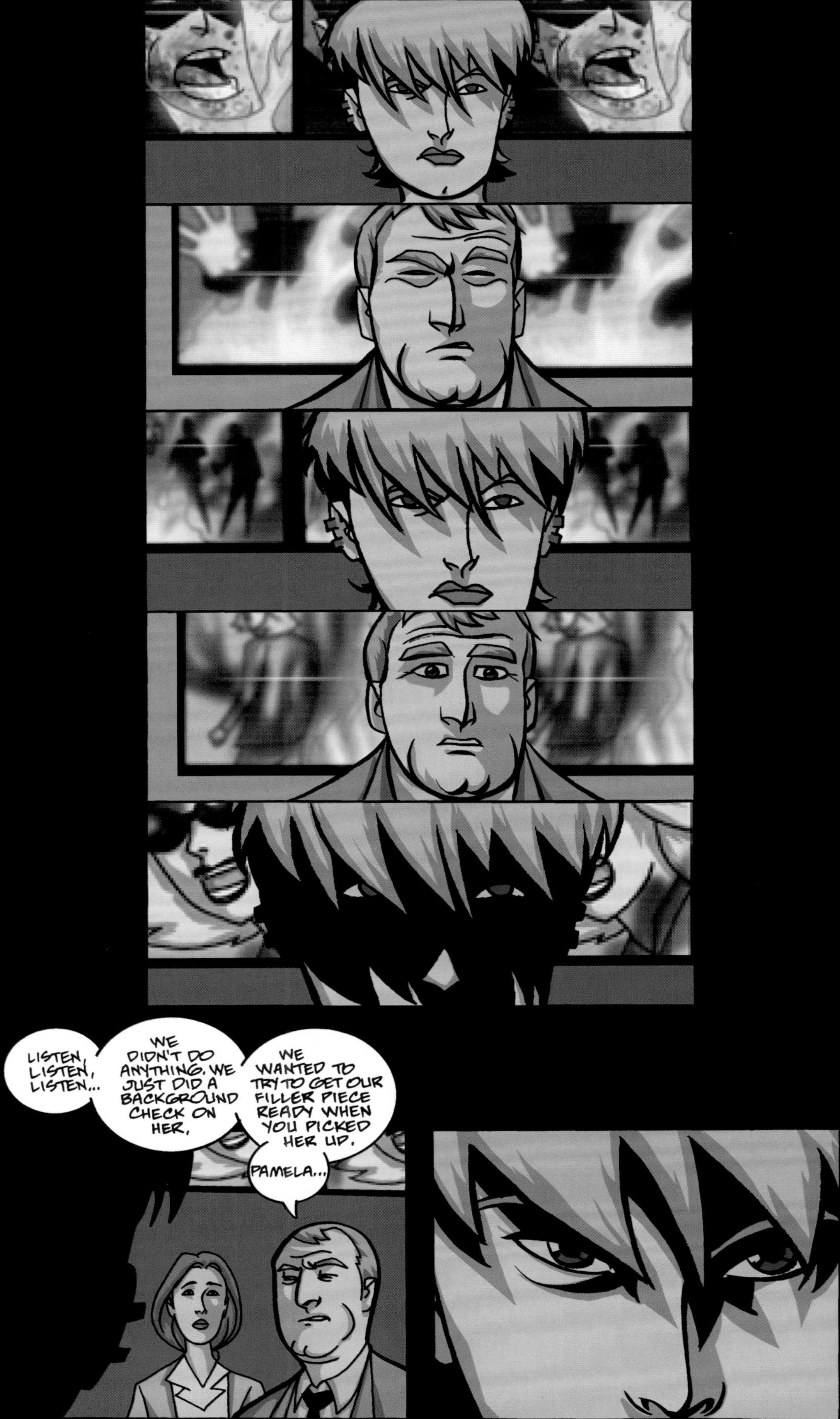
LISTEN, LISTEN, LISTEN...
WE DIDN'T DO ANYTHING. WE JUST DID A BACKGROUND CHECK ON HER.
WE WANTED TO TRY TO GET OUR FILLER PIECE READY WHEN YOU PICKED HER UP.
PAMELA...

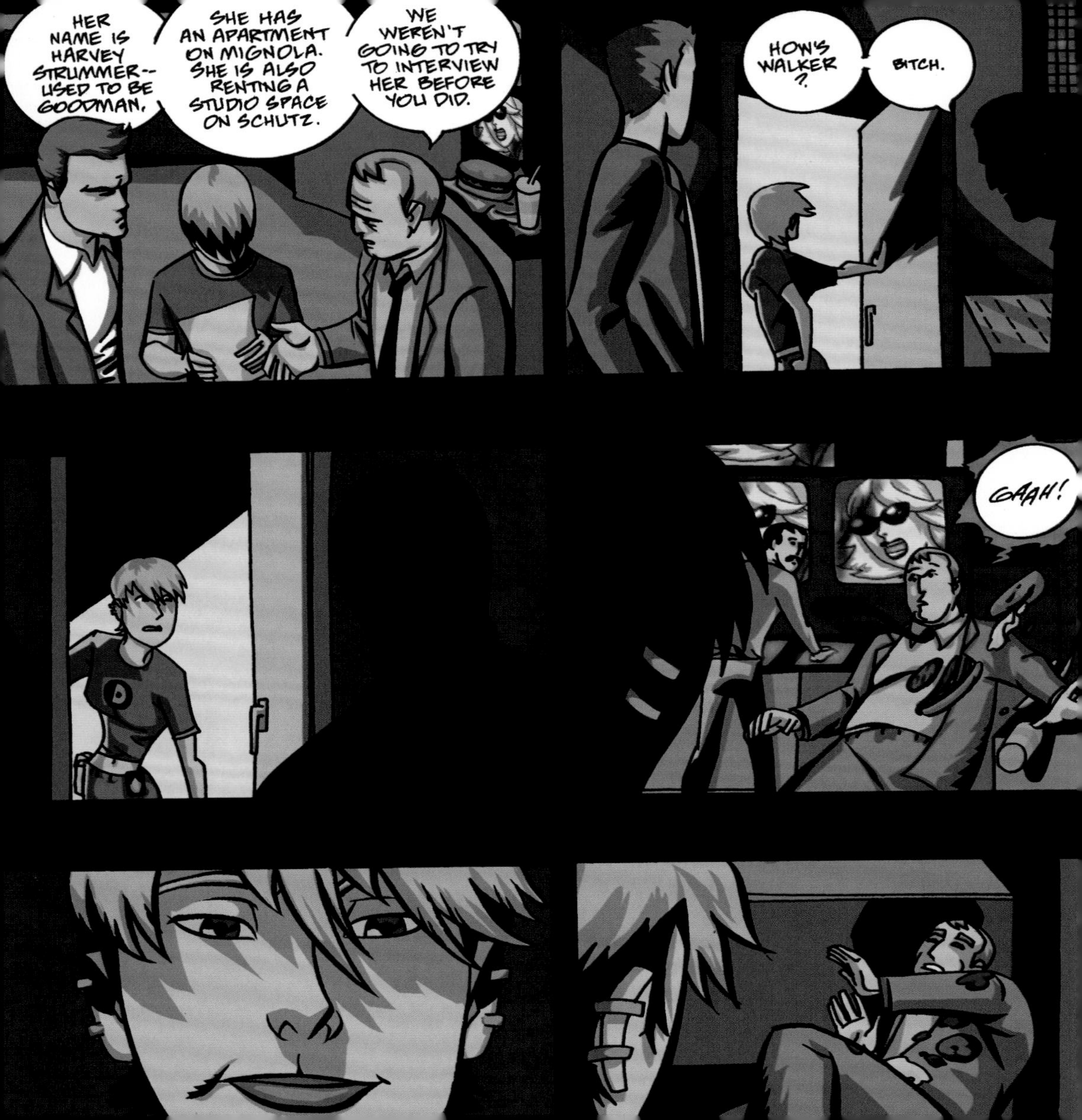
HER NAME IS HARVEY STRUMMER-- USED TO BE GOODMAN.
SHE HAS AN APARTMENT ON MIGNOLA. SHE IS ALSO RENTING A STUDIO SPACE ON SCHUTZ.
WE WEREN'T GOING TO TRY TO INTERVIEW HER BEFORE YOU DID.
HOW'S WALKER?
BITCH.
GAAH!

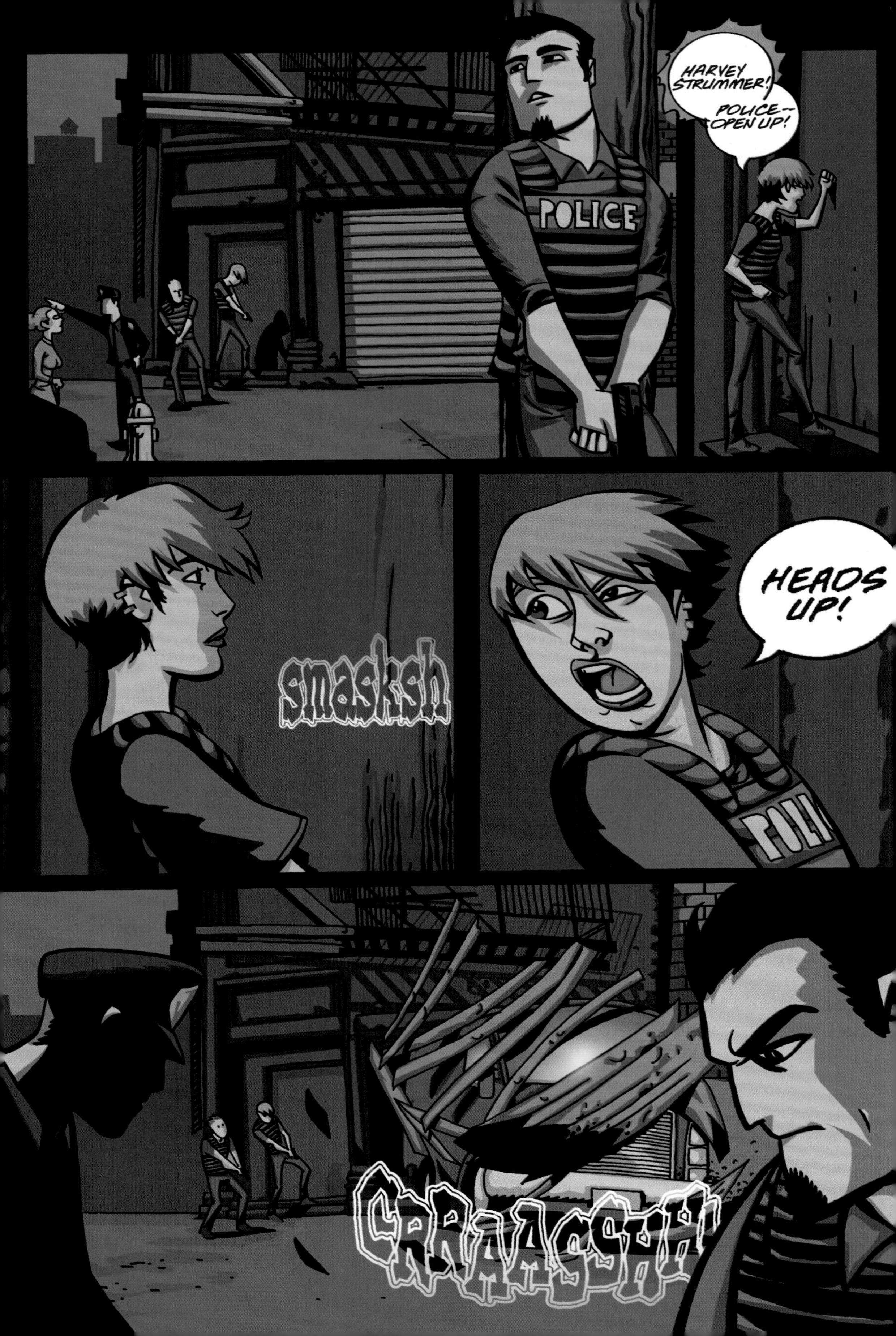

HARVEY STRUMMER!
POLICE-- OPEN UP!
POLICE
smasksh
HEADS UP!
POLI
CRRAAGSHH

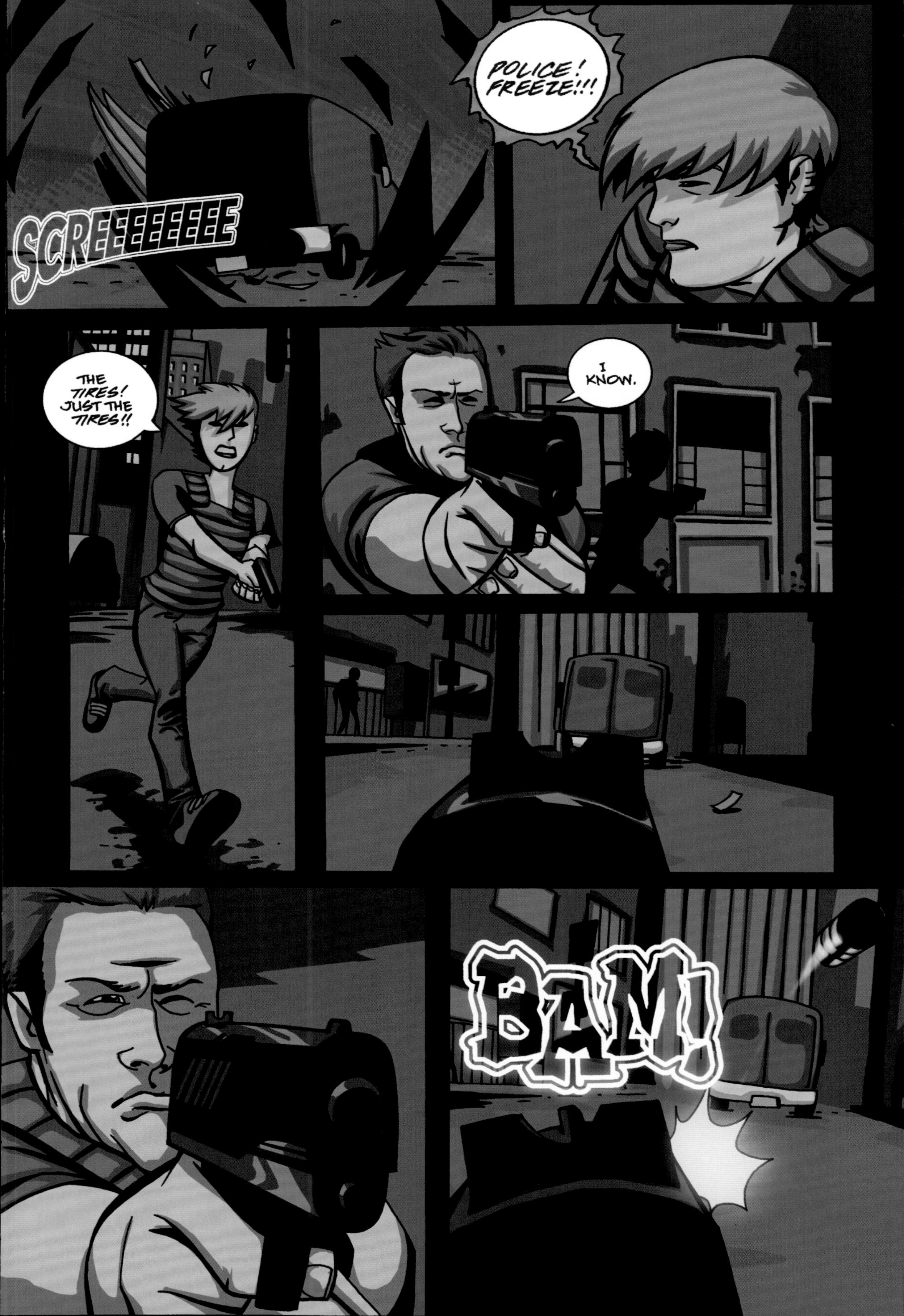
SCREEEEEEEE
POLICE! FREEZE!!!
THE TIRES! JUST THE TIRES!!
I KNOW.
BAM!

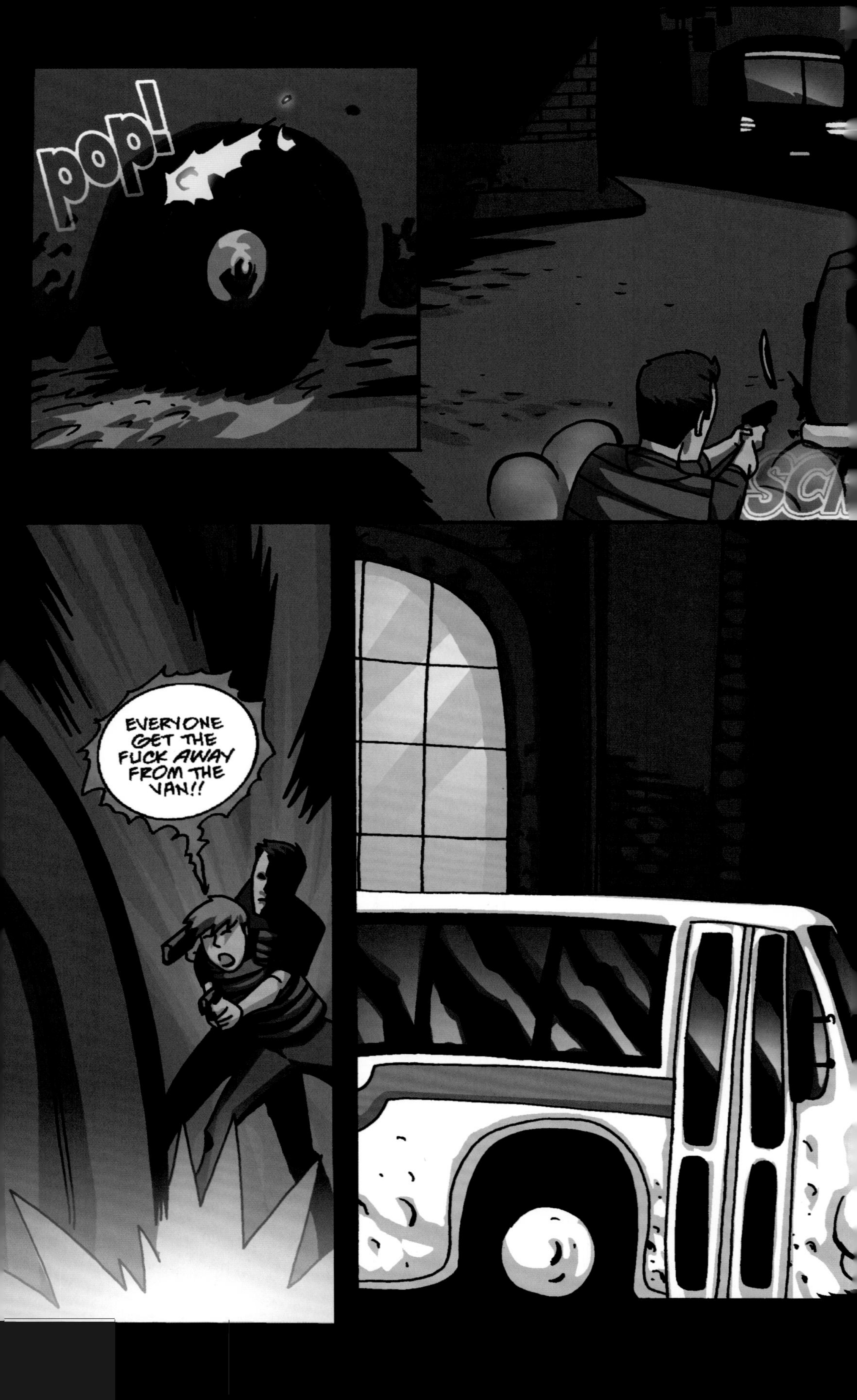
pop!
EVERYONE GET THE FUCK AWAY FROM THE VAN!!

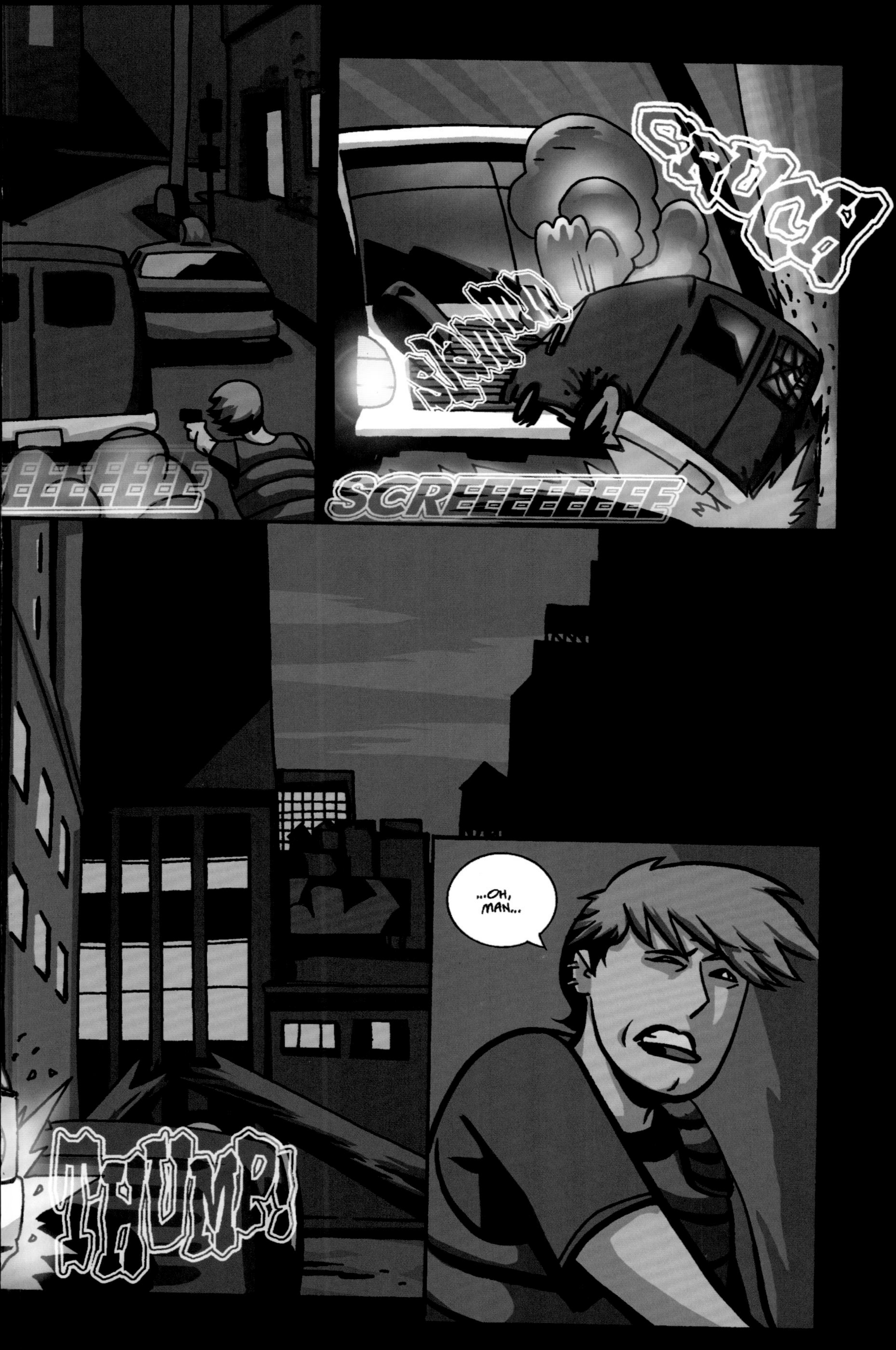
SCREEEEEEEEE
THUMP!
...OH, MAN...

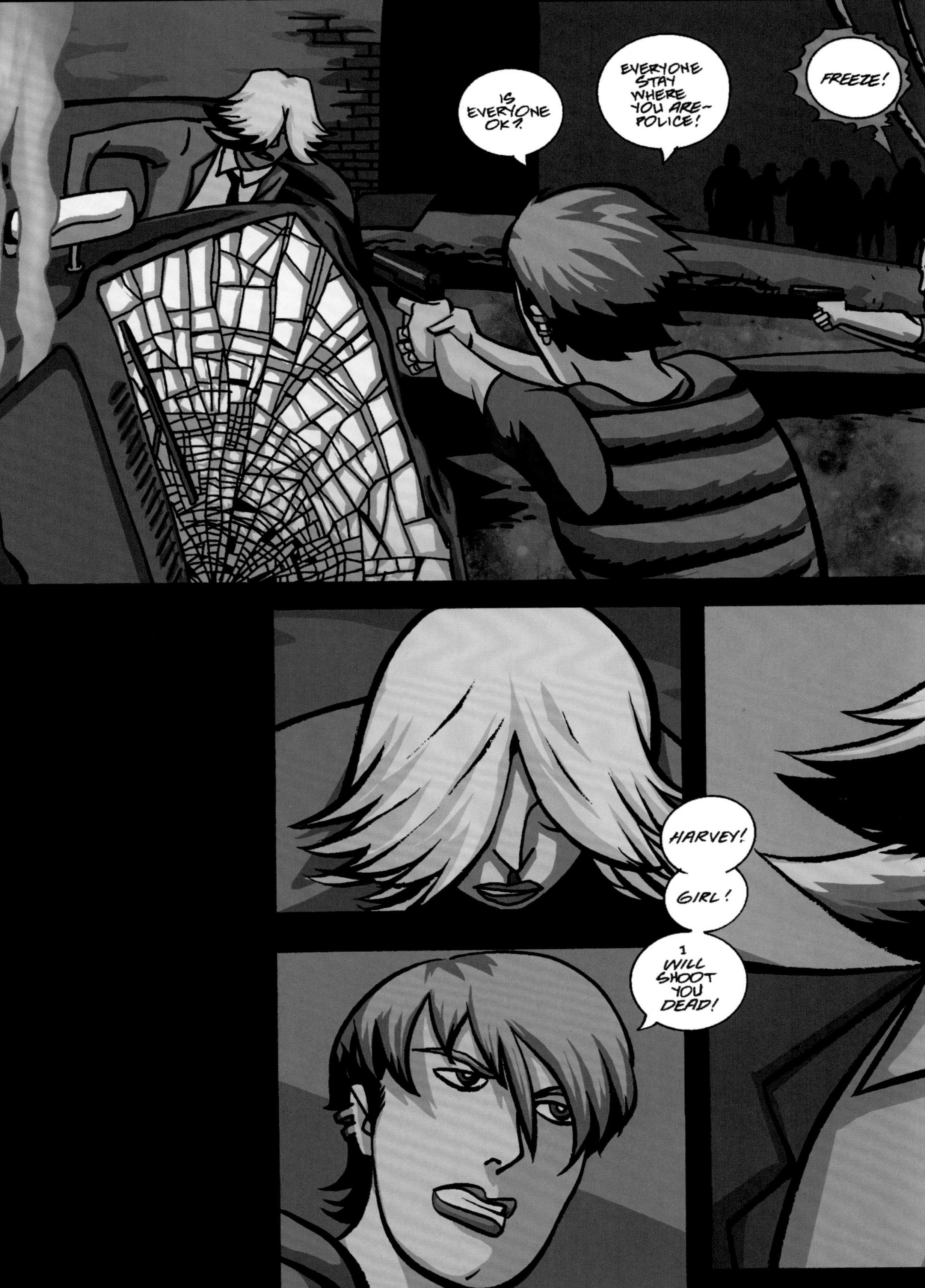
IS EVERYONE OK?
EVERYONE STAY WHERE YOU ARE- POLICE!
FREEZE!
HARVEY!
GIRL!
I WILL SHOOT YOU DEAD!

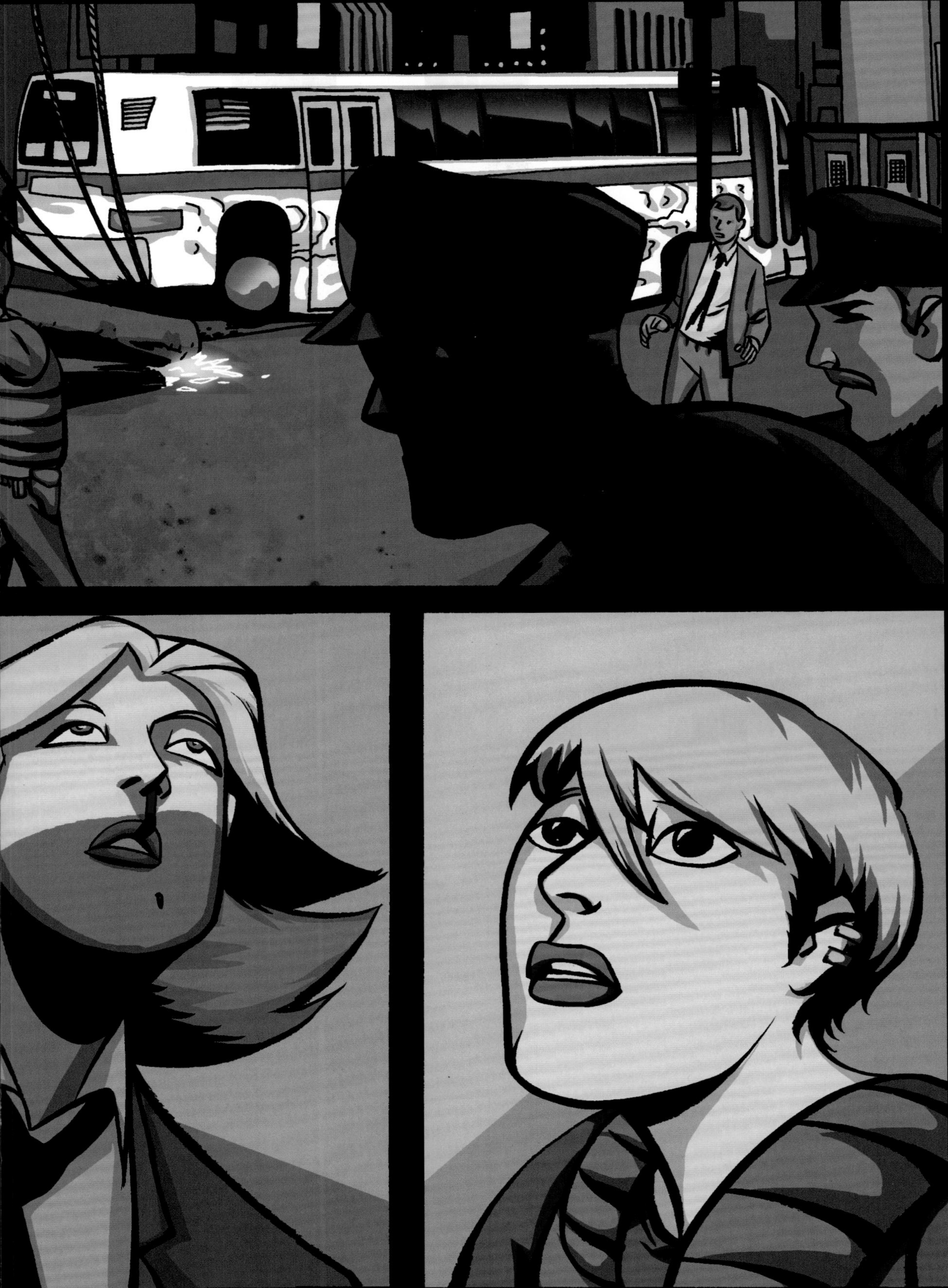

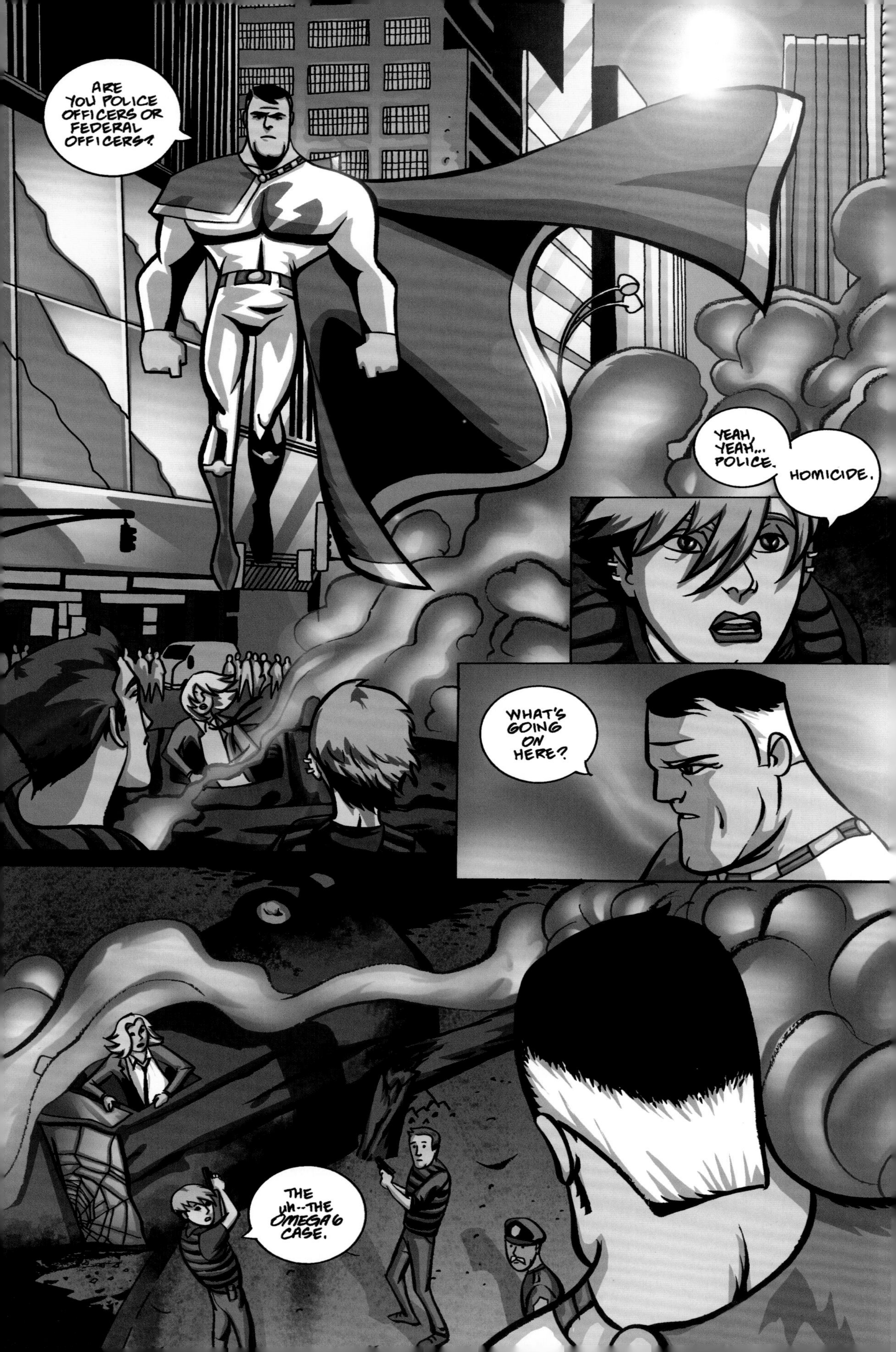
ARE YOU POLICE OFFICERS OR FEDERAL OFFICERS?
YEAH, YEAH... POLICE.
HOMICIDE.
WHAT'S GOING ON HERE?
THE uh--THE OMEGA 6 CASE.

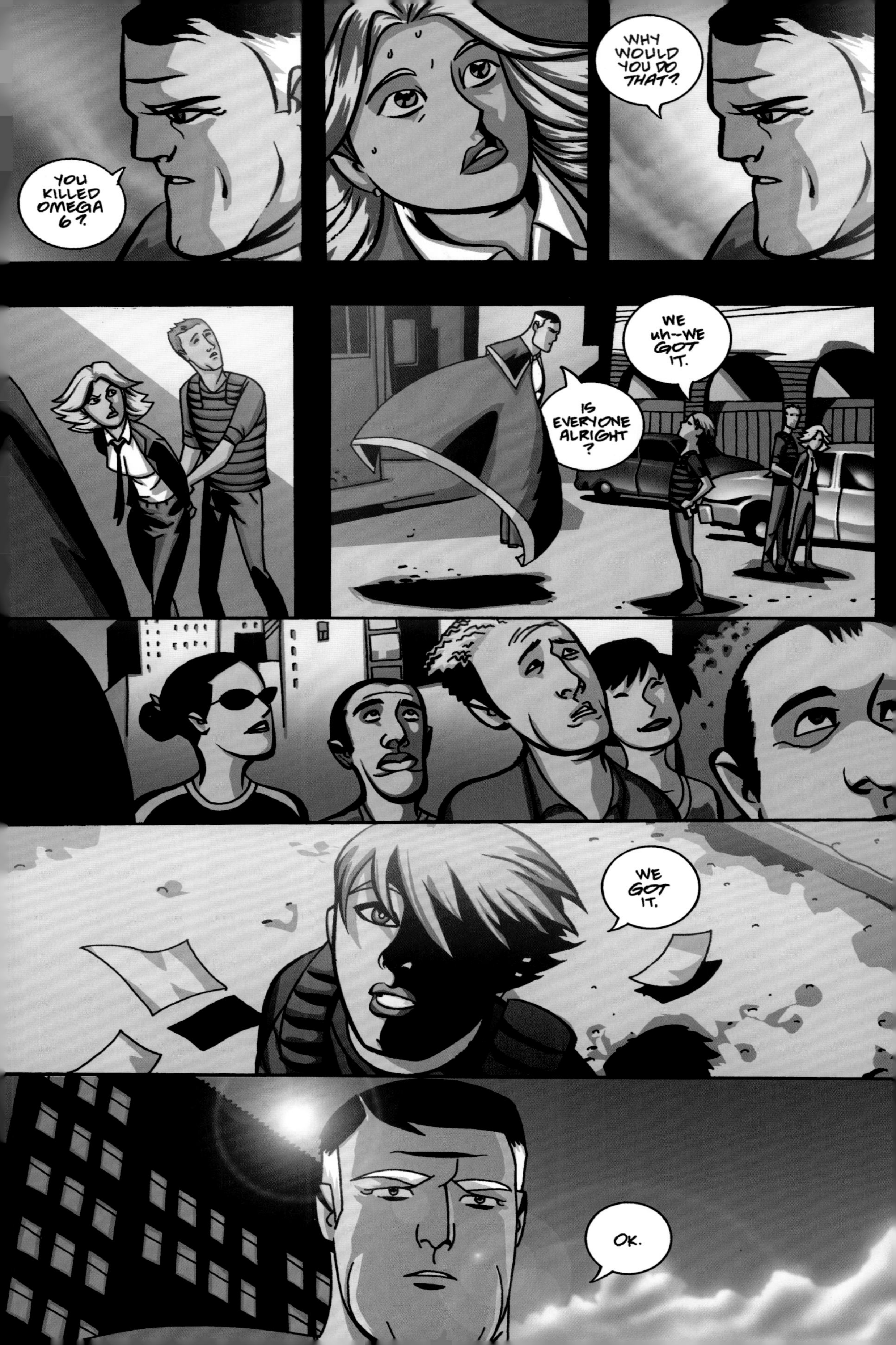

YOU KILLED OMEGA 6?
WHY WOULD YOU DO THAT?
IS EVERYONE ALRIGHT?
WE uh--WE GOT IT.
WE GOT IT.
OK.

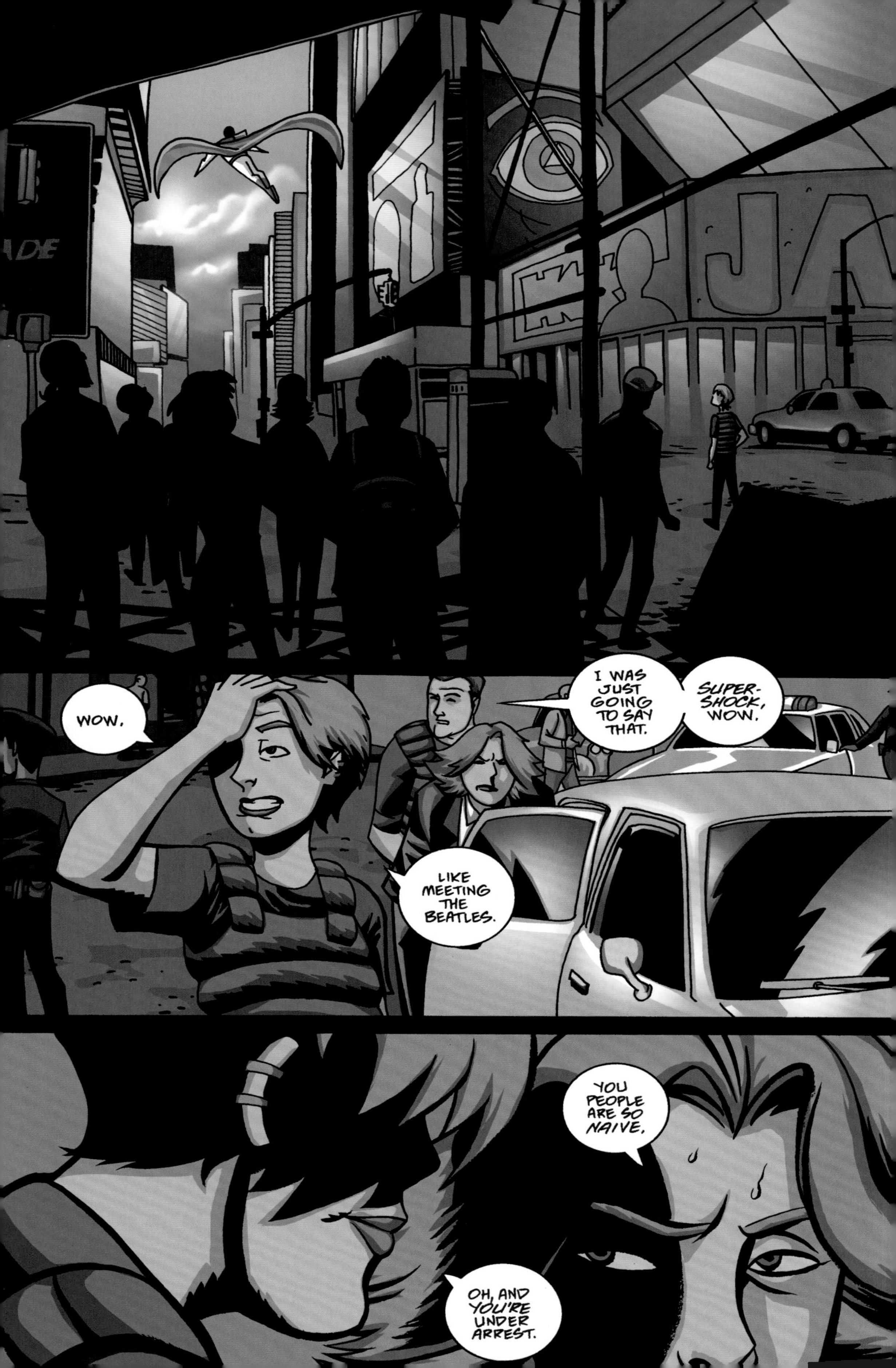
ADE
WOW.
I WAS JUST GOING TO SAY THAT.
SUPER-SHOCK, WOW.
LIKE MEETING THE BEATLES.
YOU PEOPLE ARE SO NAIVE.
OH, AND YOU'RE UNDER ARREST.

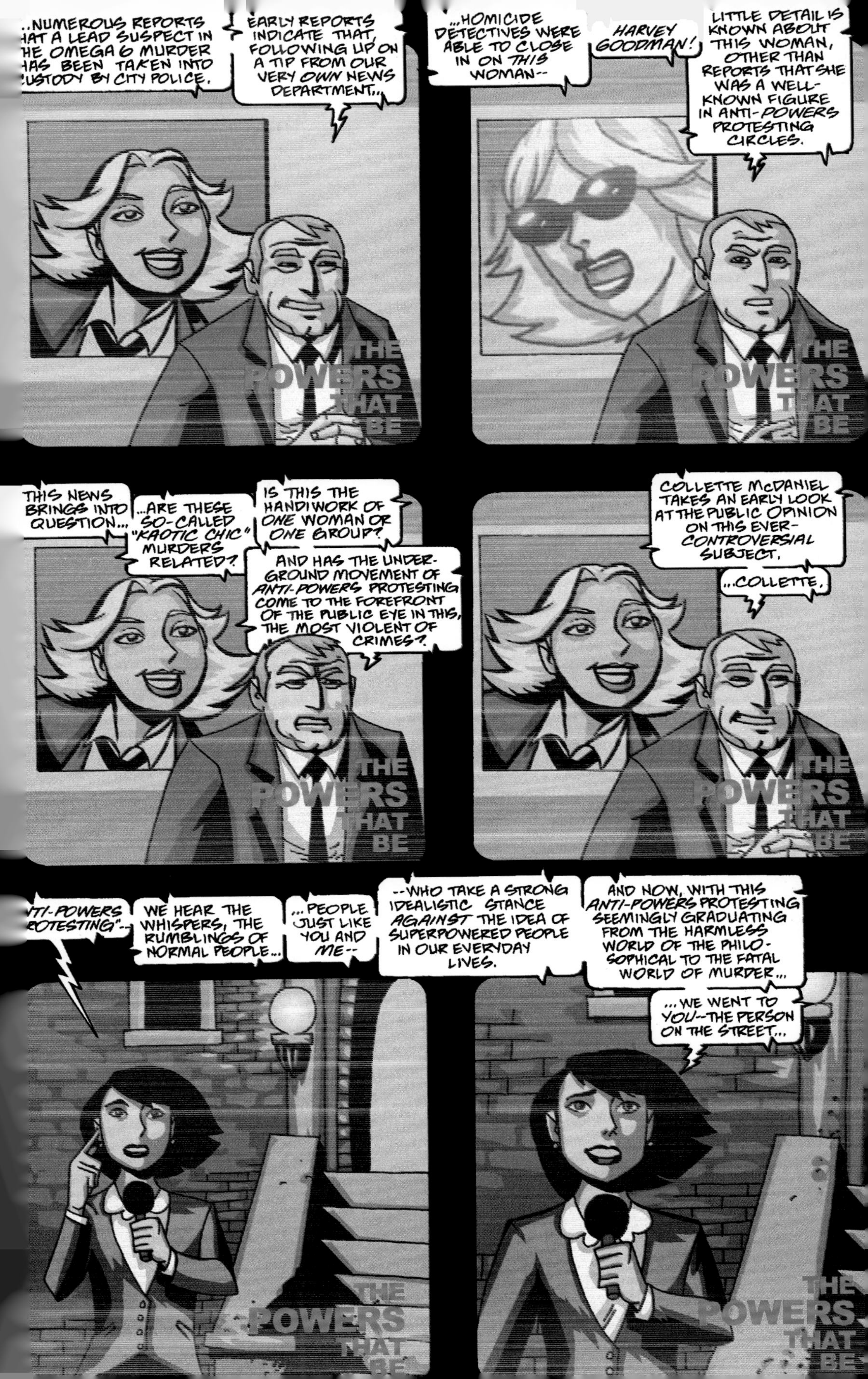

...NUMEROUS REPORTS THAT A LEAD SUSPECT IN THE OMEGA 6 MURDER HAS BEEN TAKEN INTO CUSTODY BY CITY POLICE.
EARLY REPORTS INDICATE THAT, FOLLOWING UP ON A TIP FROM OUR VERY OWN NEWS DEPARTMENT...
...HOMICIDE DETECTIVES WERE ABLE TO CLOSE IN ON THIS WOMAN--
HARVEY GOODMAN!
LITTLE DETAIL IS KNOWN ABOUT THIS WOMAN, OTHER THAN REPORTS THAT SHE WAS A WELL-KNOWN FIGURE IN ANTI-POWERS PROTESTING CIRCLES.
THE POWERS THAT BE
THIS NEWS BRINGS INTO QUESTION...
...ARE THESE SO-CALLED "KAOTIC CHIC" MURDERS RELATED?
IS THIS THE HANDIWORK OF ONE WOMAN OR ONE GROUP?
AND HAS THE UNDERGROUND MOVEMENT OF ANTI-POWERS PROTESTING COME TO THE FOREFRONT OF THE PUBLIC EYE IN THIS, THE MOST VIOLENT OF CRIMES?
COLLETTE McDANIEL TAKES AN EARLY LOOK AT THE PUBLIC OPINION ON THIS EVER-CONTROVERSIAL SUBJECT.
...COLLETTE.
"ANTI-POWERS PROTESTING"...
WE HEAR THE WHISPERS, THE RUMBLINGS OF NORMAL PEOPLE...
...PEOPLE JUST LIKE YOU AND ME--
--WHO TAKE A STRONG IDEALISTIC STANCE AGAINST THE IDEA OF SUPERPOWERED PEOPLE IN OUR EVERYDAY LIVES.
AND NOW, WITH THIS ANTI-POWERS PROTESTING SEEMINGLY GRADUATING FROM THE HARMLESS WORLD OF THE PHILOSOPHICAL TO THE FATAL WORLD OF MURDER...
...WE WENT TO YOU--THE PERSON ON THE STREET...

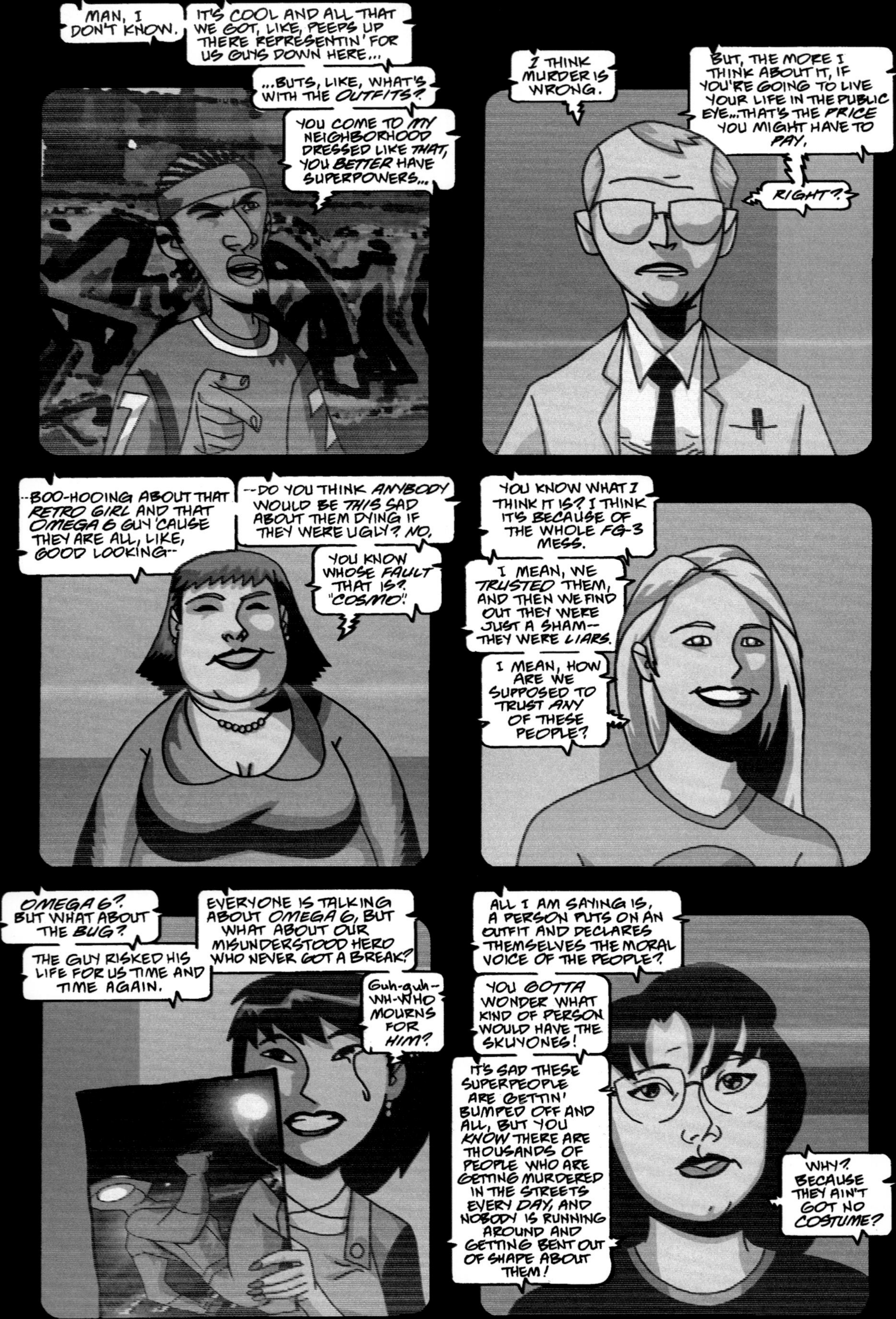
MAN, I DON'T KNOW.
IT'S COOL AND ALL THAT WE GOT, LIKE, PEEPS UP THERE REPRESENTIN' FOR US GUYS DOWN HERE...
...BUTS, LIKE, WHAT'S WITH THE OUTFITS?
YOU COME TO MY NEIGHBORHOOD DRESSED LIKE THAT, YOU BETTER HAVE SUPERPOWERS...
I THINK MURDER IS WRONG.
BUT, THE MORE I THINK ABOUT IT, IF YOU'RE GOING TO LIVE YOUR LIFE IN THE PUBLIC EYE...THAT'S THE PRICE YOU MIGHT HAVE TO PAY,
RIGHT?
--BOO-HOOING ABOUT THAT RETRO GIRL AND THAT OMEGA 6 GUY 'CAUSE THEY ARE ALL, LIKE, GOOD LOOKING--
--DO YOU THINK ANYBODY WOULD BE THIS SAD ABOUT THEM DYING IF THEY WERE UGLY? NO.
YOU KNOW WHOSE FAULT THAT IS? "COSMO".
YOU KNOW WHAT I THINK IT IS? I THINK IT'S BECAUSE OF THE WHOLE FG-3 MESS.
I MEAN, WE TRUSTED THEM, AND THEN WE FIND OUT THEY WERE JUST A SHAM-- THEY WERE LIARS.
I MEAN, HOW ARE WE SUPPOSED TO TRUST ANY OF THESE PEOPLE?
OMEGA 6? BUT WHAT ABOUT THE BUG?
EVERYONE IS TALKING ABOUT OMEGA 6, BUT WHAT ABOUT OUR MISUNDERSTOOD HERO WHO NEVER GOT A BREAK?
THE GUY RISKED HIS LIFE FOR US TIME AND TIME AGAIN.
Guh-guh-- WH-WHO MOURNS FOR HIM?
ALL I AM SAYING IS, A PERSON PUTS ON AN OUTFIT AND DECLARES THEMSELVES THE MORAL VOICE OF THE PEOPLE?
YOU GOTTA WONDER WHAT KIND OF PERSON WOULD HAVE THE SKUYONES!
IT'S SAD THESE SUPERPEOPLE ARE GETTIN' BUMPED OFF AND ALL, BUT YOU KNOW THERE ARE THOUSANDS OF PEOPLE WHO ARE GETTING MURDERED IN THE STREETS EVERY DAY, AND NOBODY IS RUNNING AROUND AND GETTING BENT OUT OF SHAPE ABOUT THEM!
WHY? BECAUSE THEY AIN'T GOT NO COSTUME?

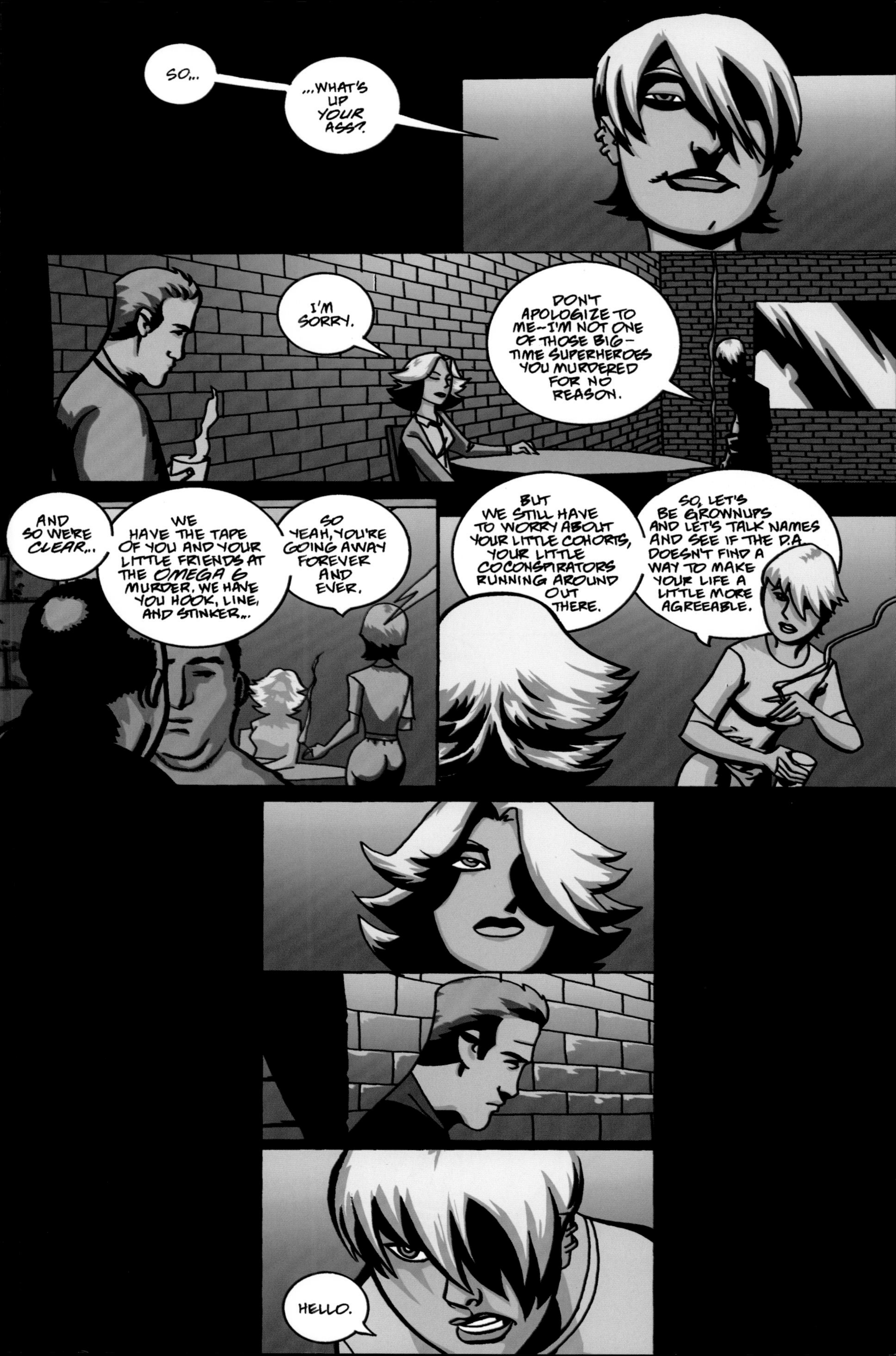
SO...
...WHAT'S UP YOUR ASS?
I'M SORRY.
DON'T APOLOGIZE TO ME--I'M NOT ONE OF THOSE BIG-TIME SUPERHEROES YOU MURDERED FOR NO REASON.
AND SO WE'RE CLEAR...
WE HAVE THE TAPE OF YOU AND YOUR LITTLE FRIENDS AT THE OMEGA 6 MURDER. WE HAVE YOU HOOK, LINE, AND STINKER...
SO YEAH, YOU'RE GOING AWAY FOREVER AND EVER.
BUT WE STILL HAVE TO WORRY ABOUT YOUR LITTLE COHORTS, YOUR LITTLE COCONSPIRATORS RUNNING AROUND OUT THERE.
SO, LET'S BE GROWNUPS AND LET'S TALK NAMES AND SEE IF THE D.A. DOESN'T FIND A WAY TO MAKE YOUR LIFE A LITTLE MORE AGREEABLE.
HELLO.

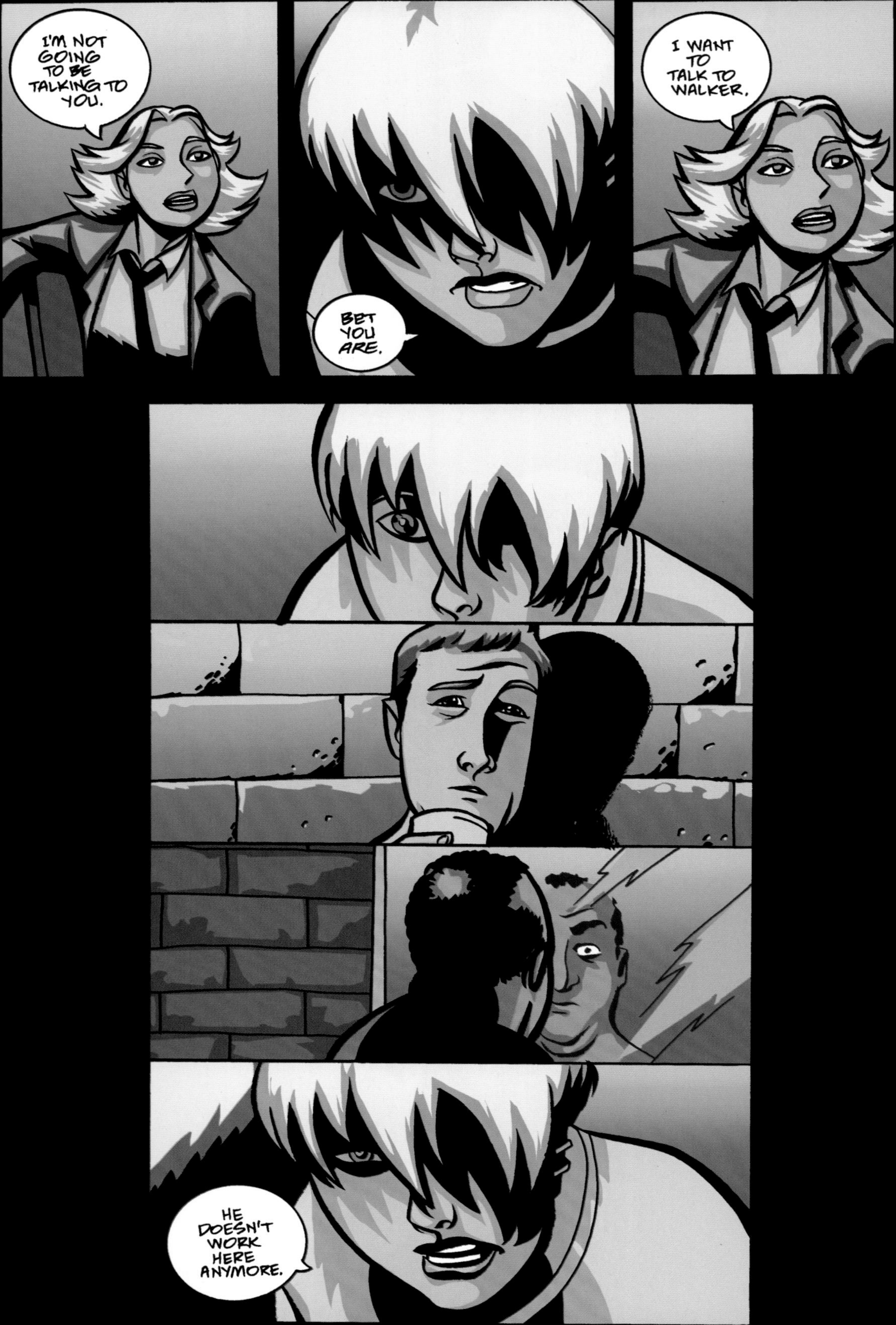
I'M NOT GOING TO BE TALKING TO YOU.
BET YOU ARE.
I WANT TO TALK TO WALKER.
HE DOESN'T WORK HERE ANYMORE.

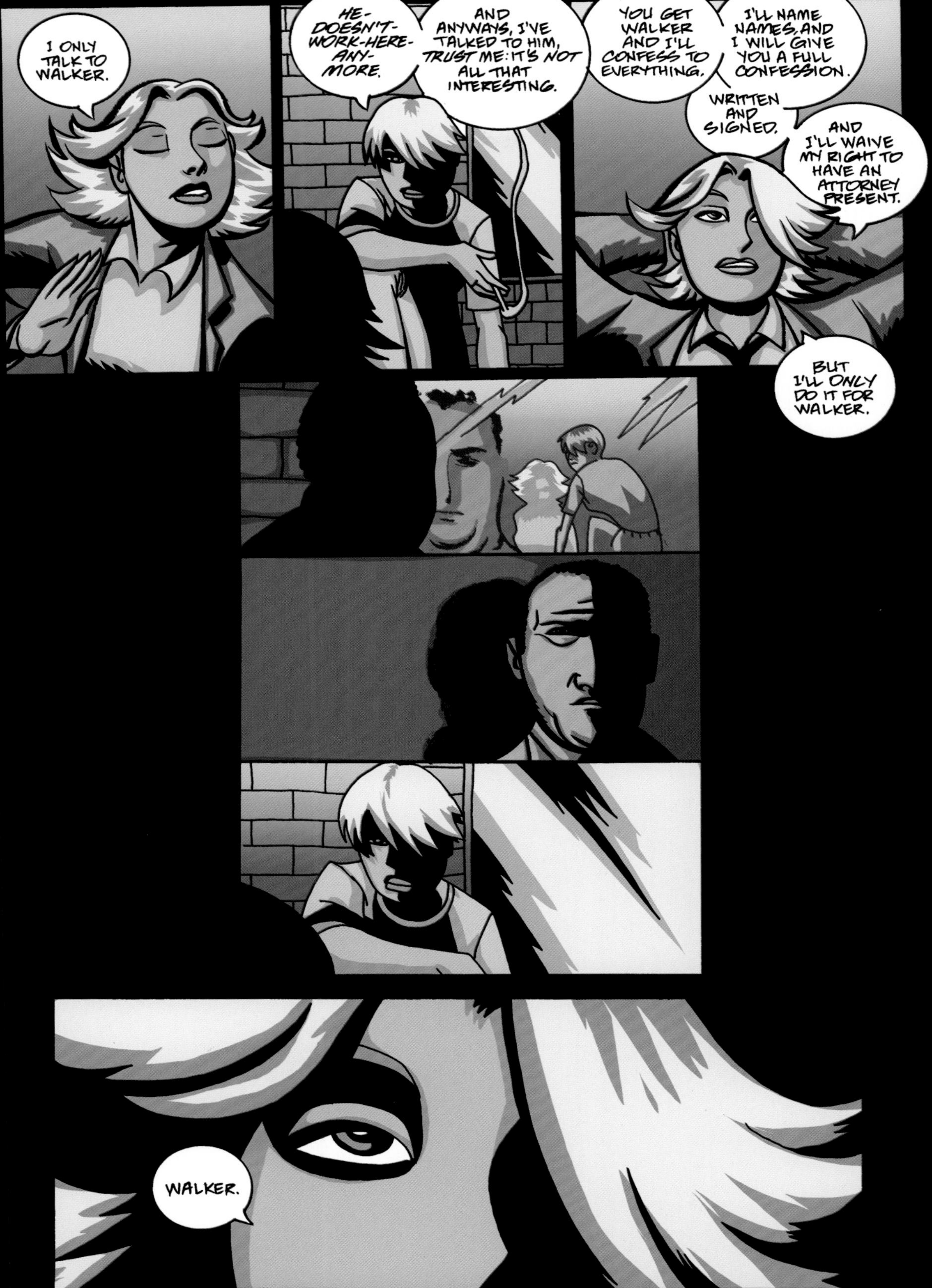
I ONLY TALK TO WALKER.
HE-DOESN'T-WORK-HERE-ANY-MORE.
AND ANYWAYS, I'VE TALKED TO HIM, TRUST ME: IT'S NOT ALL THAT INTERESTING.
YOU GET WALKER AND I'LL CONFESS TO EVERYTHING.
I'LL NAME NAMES, AND I WILL GIVE YOU A FULL CONFESSION.
WRITTEN AND SIGNED.
AND I'LL WAIVE MY RIGHT TO HAVE AN ATTORNEY PRESENT.
BUT I'LL ONLY DO IT FOR WALKER.
WALKER.

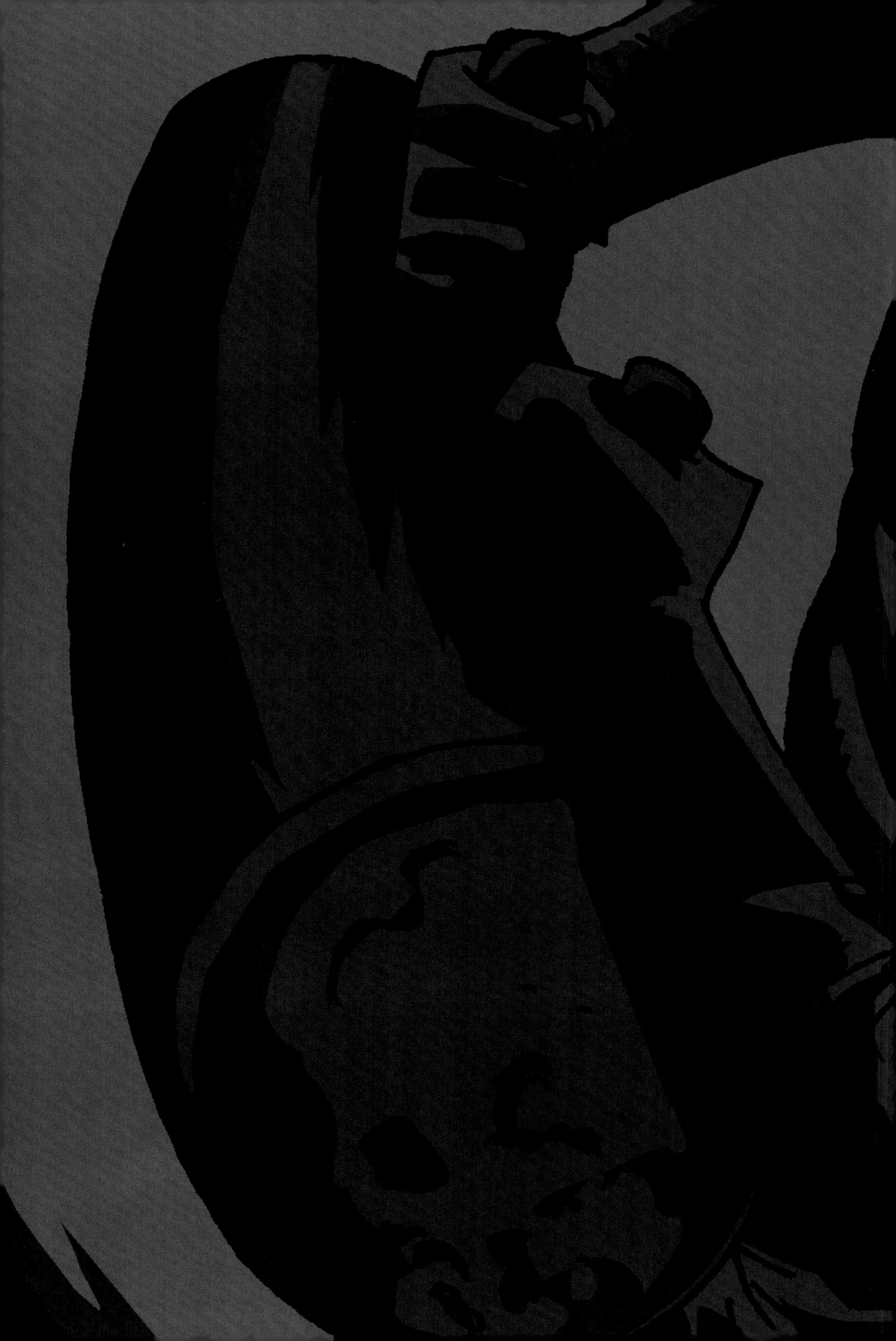

POWERS™

ANARCHY
CHAPTER 3

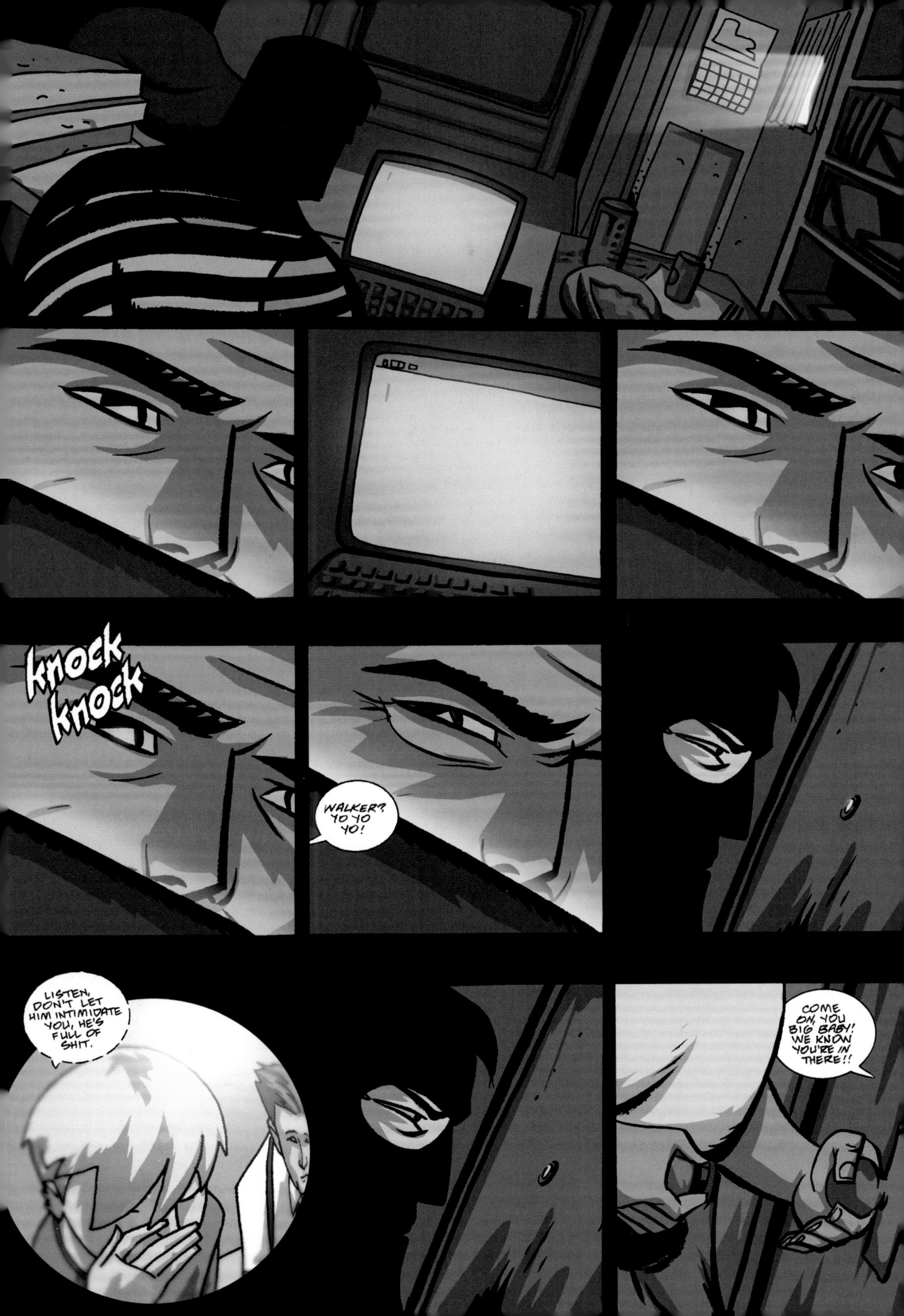

knock
knock
WALKER? YO YO YO!
LISTEN, DON'T LET HIM INTIMIDATE YOU, HE'S FULL OF SHIT.
COME ON, YOU BIG BABY! WE KNOW YOU'RE IN THERE!!

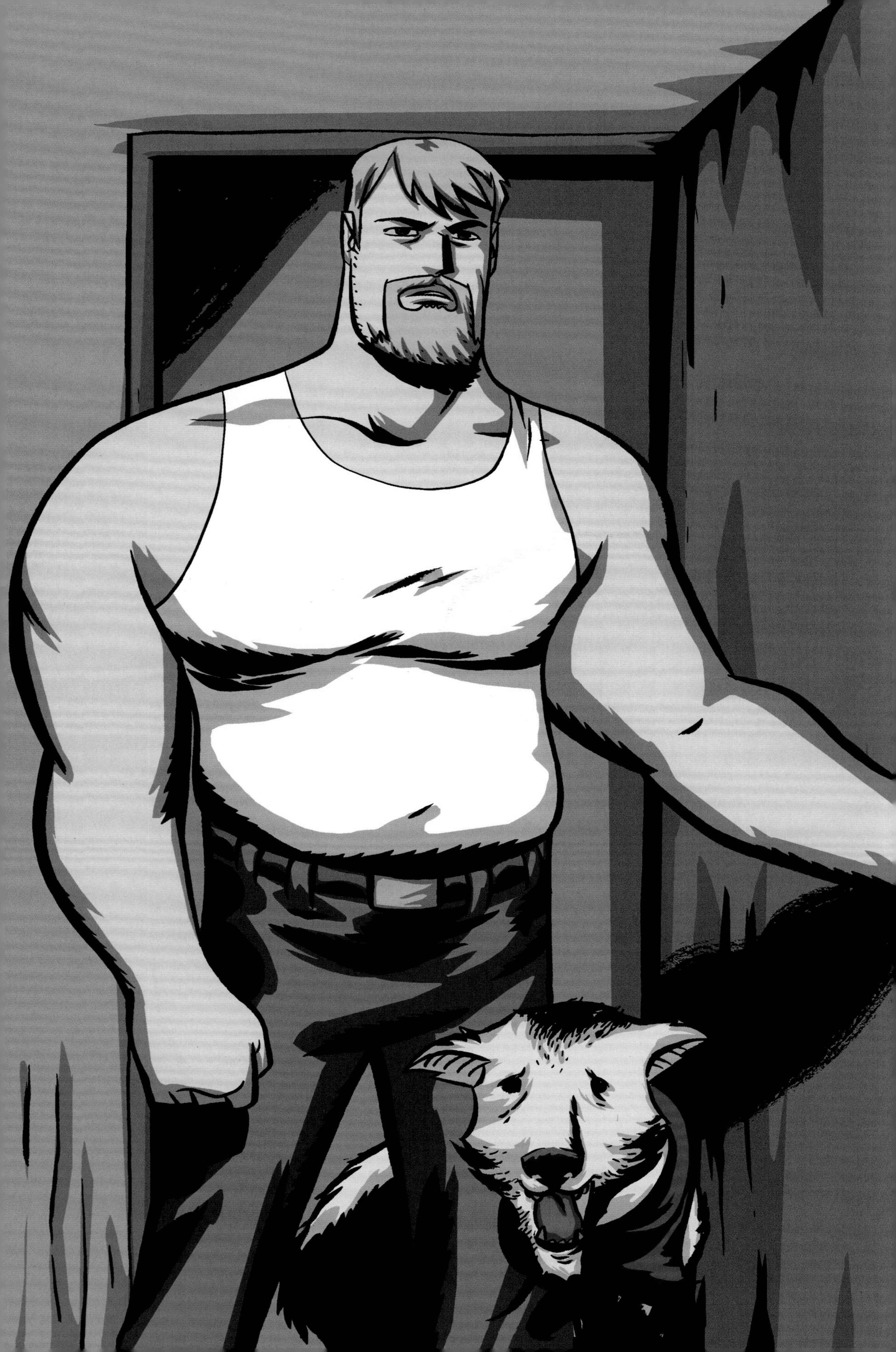

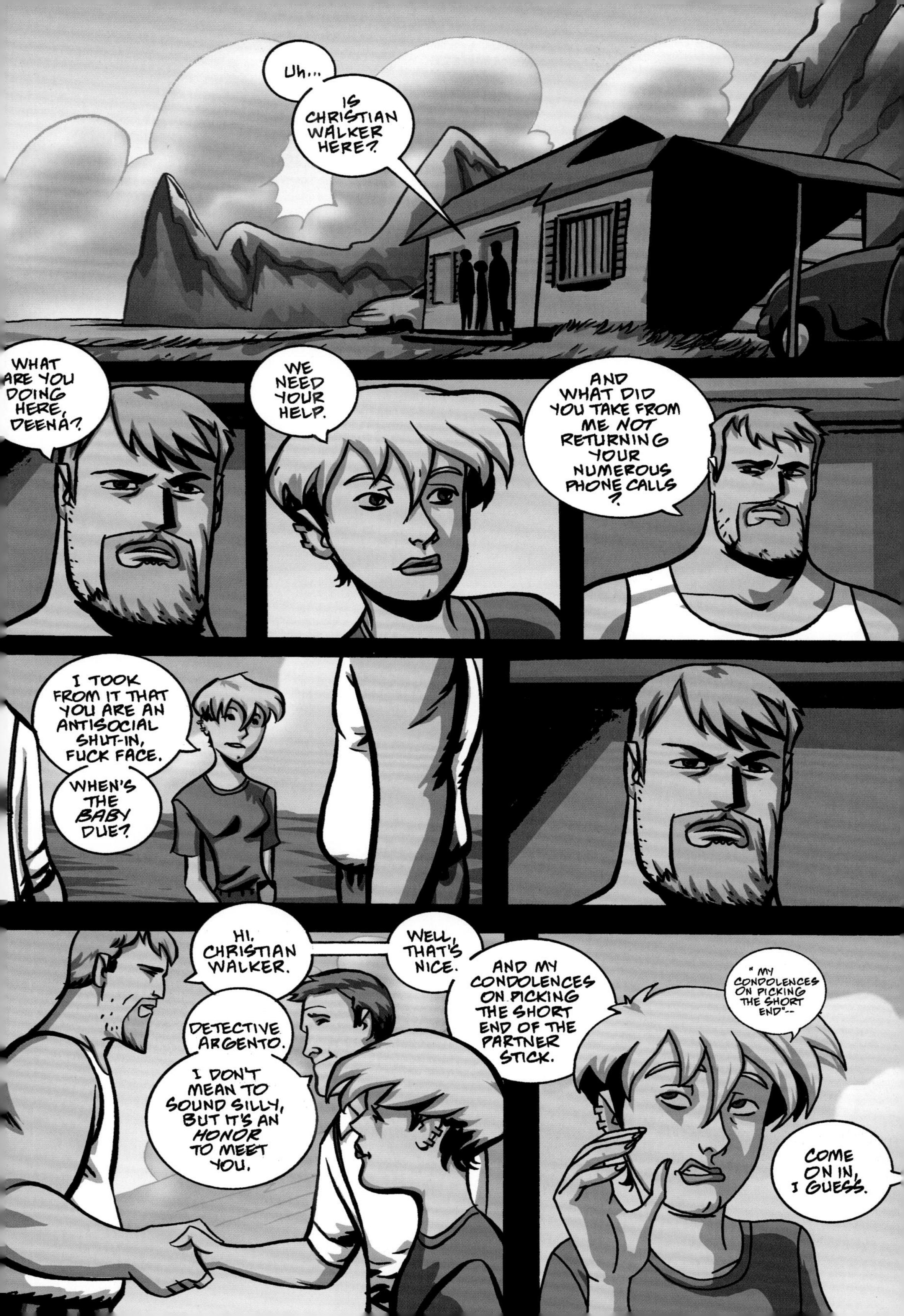
Uh...
IS CHRISTIAN WALKER HERE?
WHAT ARE YOU DOING HERE, DEENA?
WE NEED YOUR HELP.
AND WHAT DID YOU TAKE FROM ME NOT RETURNING YOUR NUMEROUS PHONE CALLS?
I TOOK FROM IT THAT YOU ARE AN ANTISOCIAL SHUT-IN, FUCK FACE.
WHEN'S THE BABY DUE?
HI, CHRISTIAN WALKER.
DETECTIVE ARGENTO.
I DON'T MEAN TO SOUND SILLY, BUT IT'S AN HONOR TO MEET YOU.
WELL, THAT'S NICE.
AND MY CONDOLENCES ON PICKING THE SHORT END OF THE PARTNER STICK.
"MY CONDOLENCES ON PICKING THE SHORT END"--
COME ON IN, I GUESS.

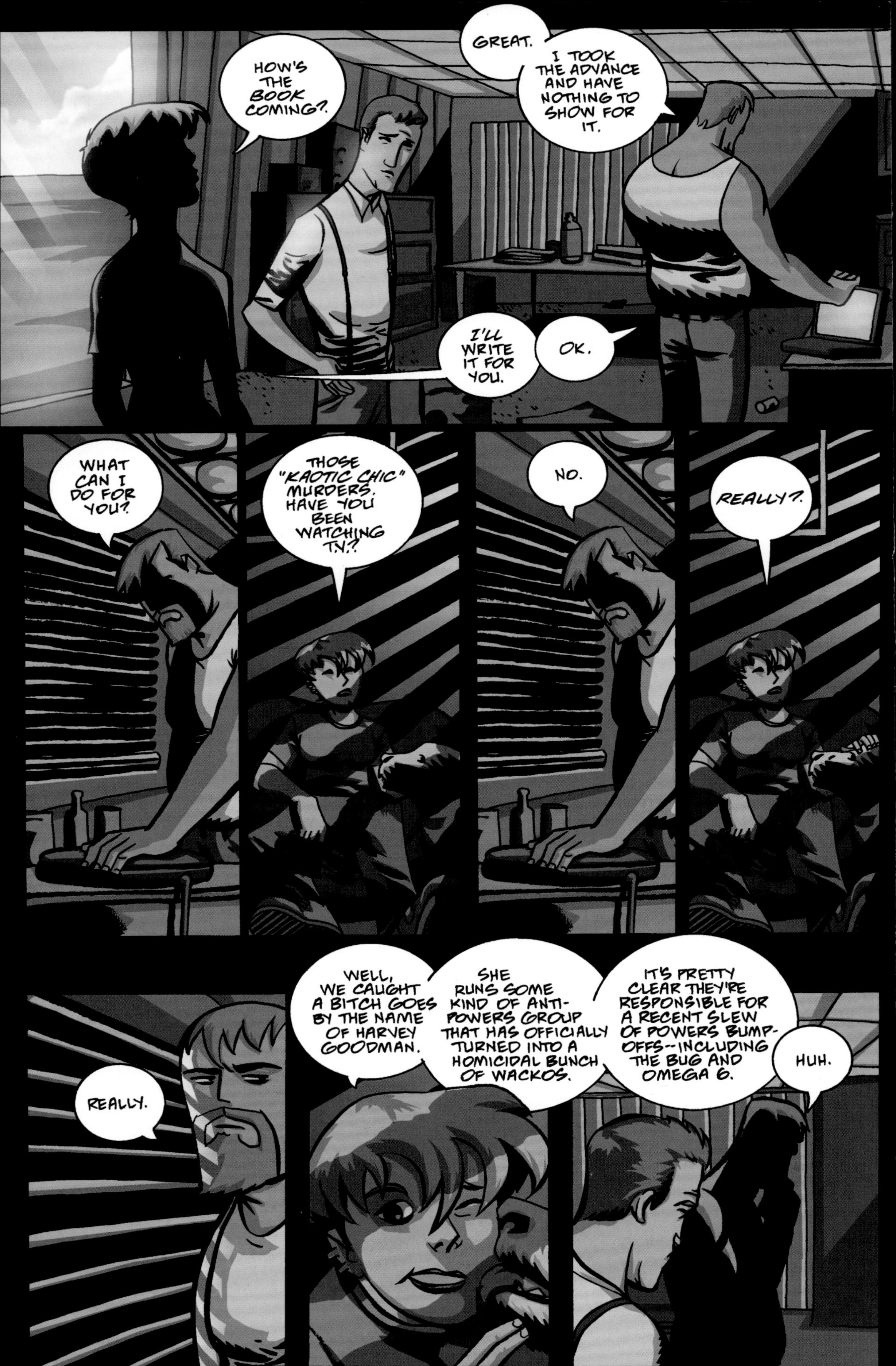
HOW'S THE BOOK COMING?
GREAT.
I TOOK THE ADVANCE AND HAVE NOTHING TO SHOW FOR IT.
I'LL WRITE IT FOR YOU.
OK.
WHAT CAN I DO FOR YOU?
THOSE "KAOTIC CHIC" MURDERS. HAVE YOU BEEN WATCHING T.V.?
NO.
REALLY?
REALLY.
WELL, WE CAUGHT A BITCH GOES BY THE NAME OF HARVEY GOODMAN.
SHE RUNS SOME KIND OF ANTI-POWERS GROUP THAT HAS OFFICIALLY TURNED INTO A HOMICIDAL BUNCH OF WACKOS.
IT'S PRETTY CLEAR THEY'RE RESPONSIBLE FOR A RECENT SLEW OF POWERS BUMP-OFFS--INCLUDING THE BUG AND OMEGA 6.
HUH.

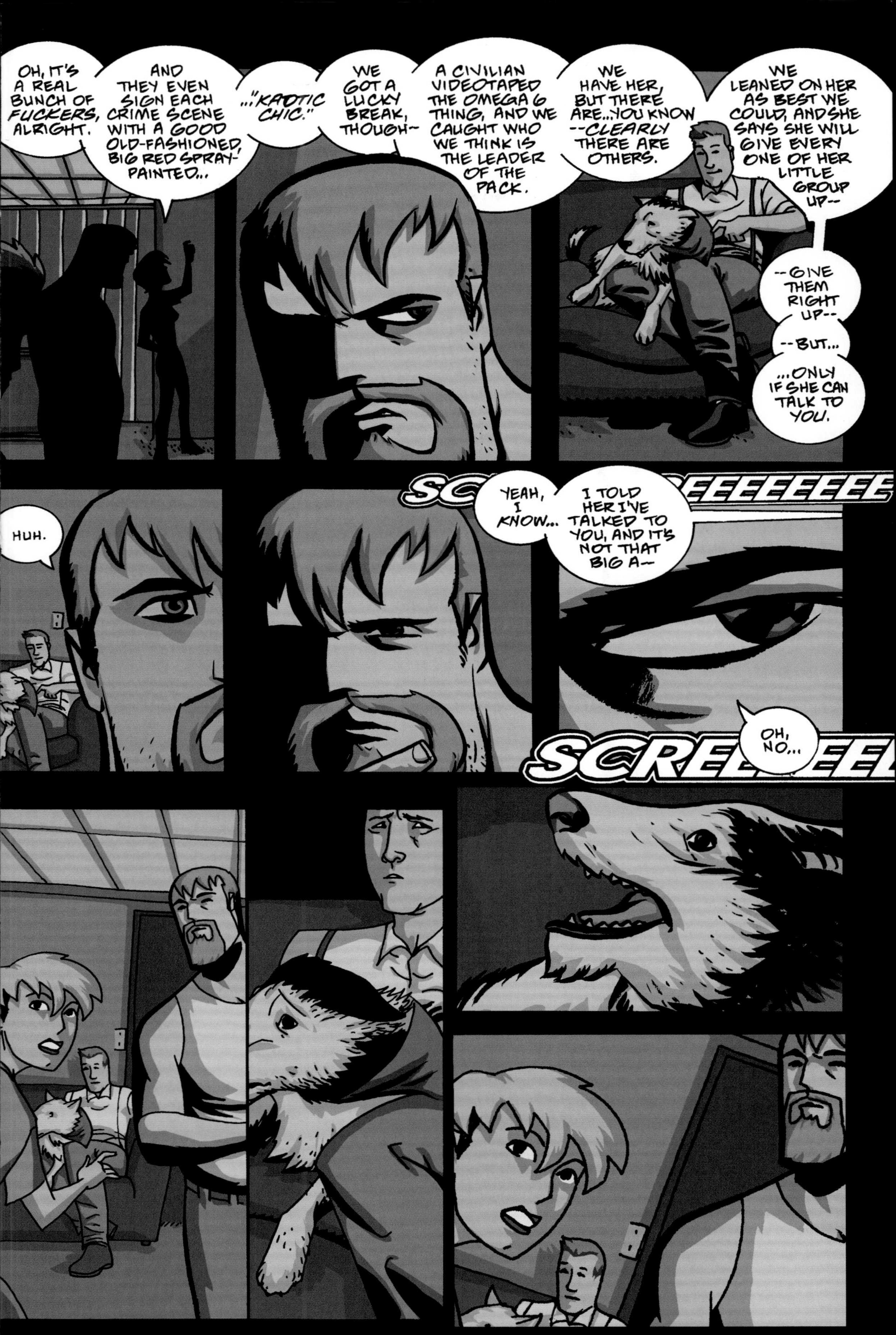
OH, IT'S A REAL BUNCH OF FUCKERS, ALRIGHT.
AND THEY EVEN SIGN EACH CRIME SCENE WITH A GOOD OLD-FASHIONED, BIG RED SPRAY-PAINTED...
..."KAOTIC CHIC."
WE GOT A LUCKY BREAK, THOUGH--
A CIVILIAN VIDEOTAPED THE OMEGA 6 THING, AND WE CAUGHT WHO WE THINK IS THE LEADER OF THE PACK.
WE HAVE HER, BUT THERE ARE...YOU KNOW --CLEARLY THERE ARE OTHERS.
WE LEANED ON HER AS BEST WE COULD, AND SHE SAYS SHE WILL GIVE EVERY ONE OF HER LITTLE GROUP UP--
--GIVE THEM RIGHT UP--
--BUT...
...ONLY IF SHE CAN TALK TO YOU.
HUH.
SCREEEEEEEEEE
YEAH, I KNOW...
I TOLD HER I'VE TALKED TO YOU, AND IT'S NOT THAT BIG A--
OH, NO...
SCREEEEEL

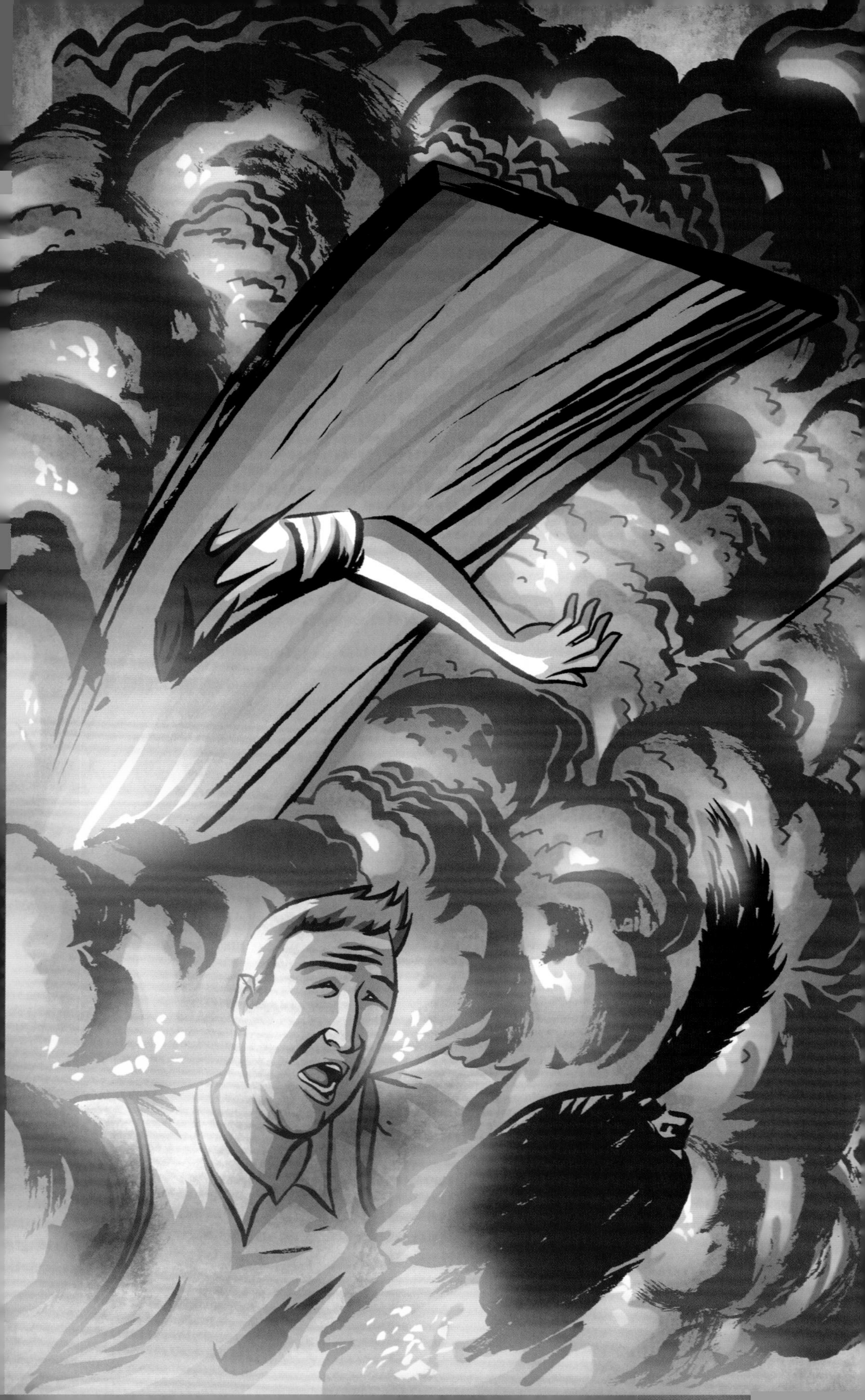

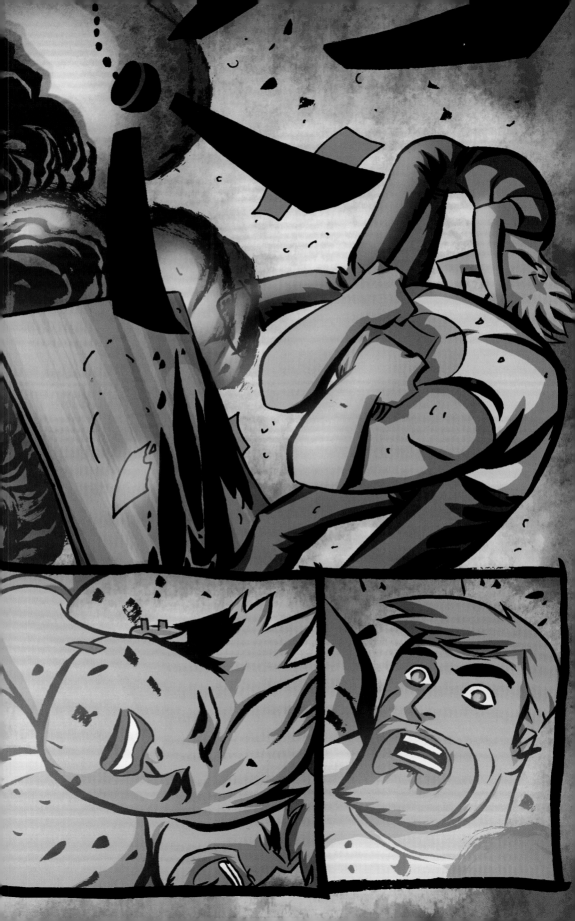

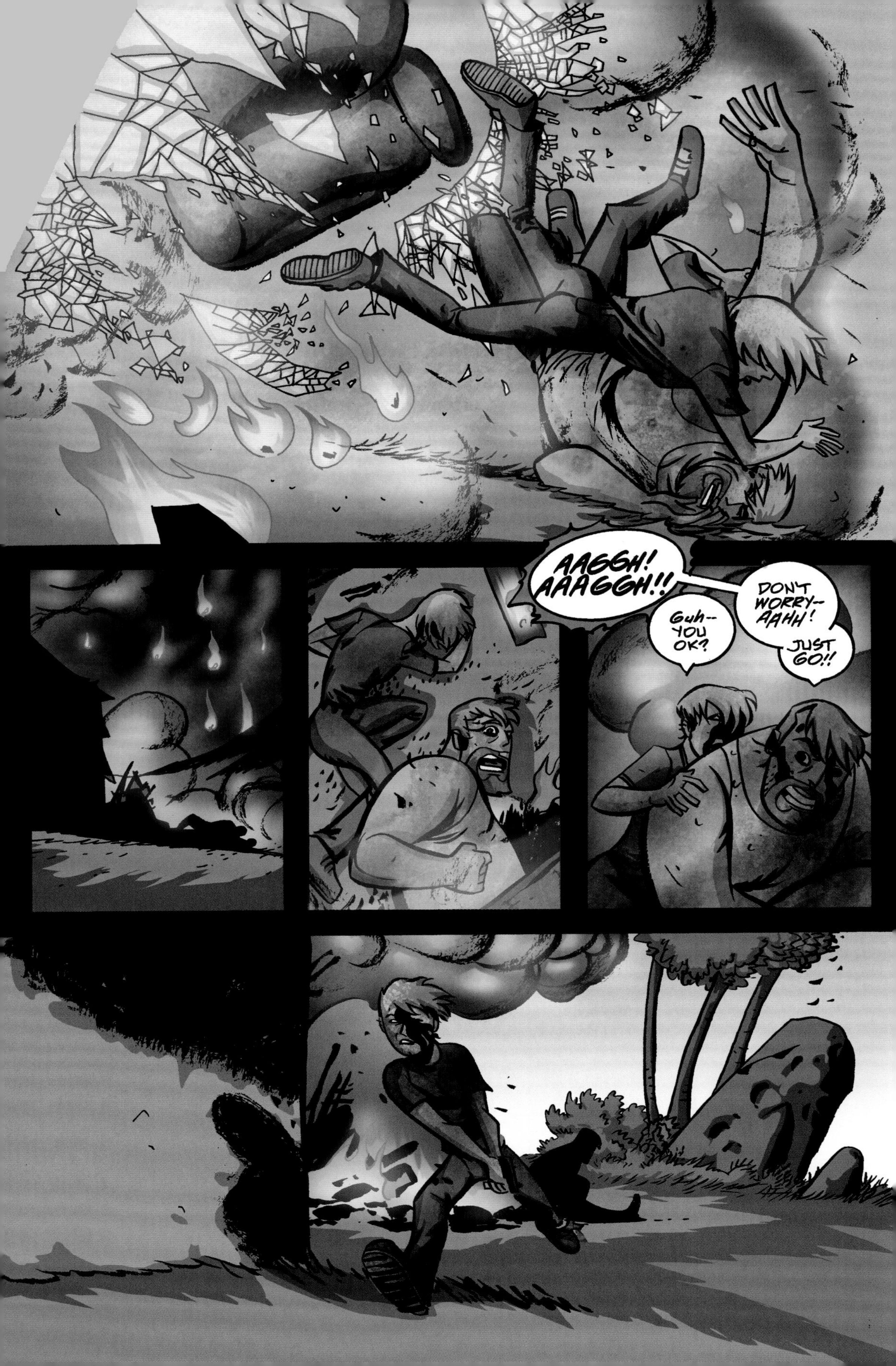
AAGGH! AAAGGH!!
Guh-- YOU OK?
DON'T WORRY-- AAHH!
JUST GO!!

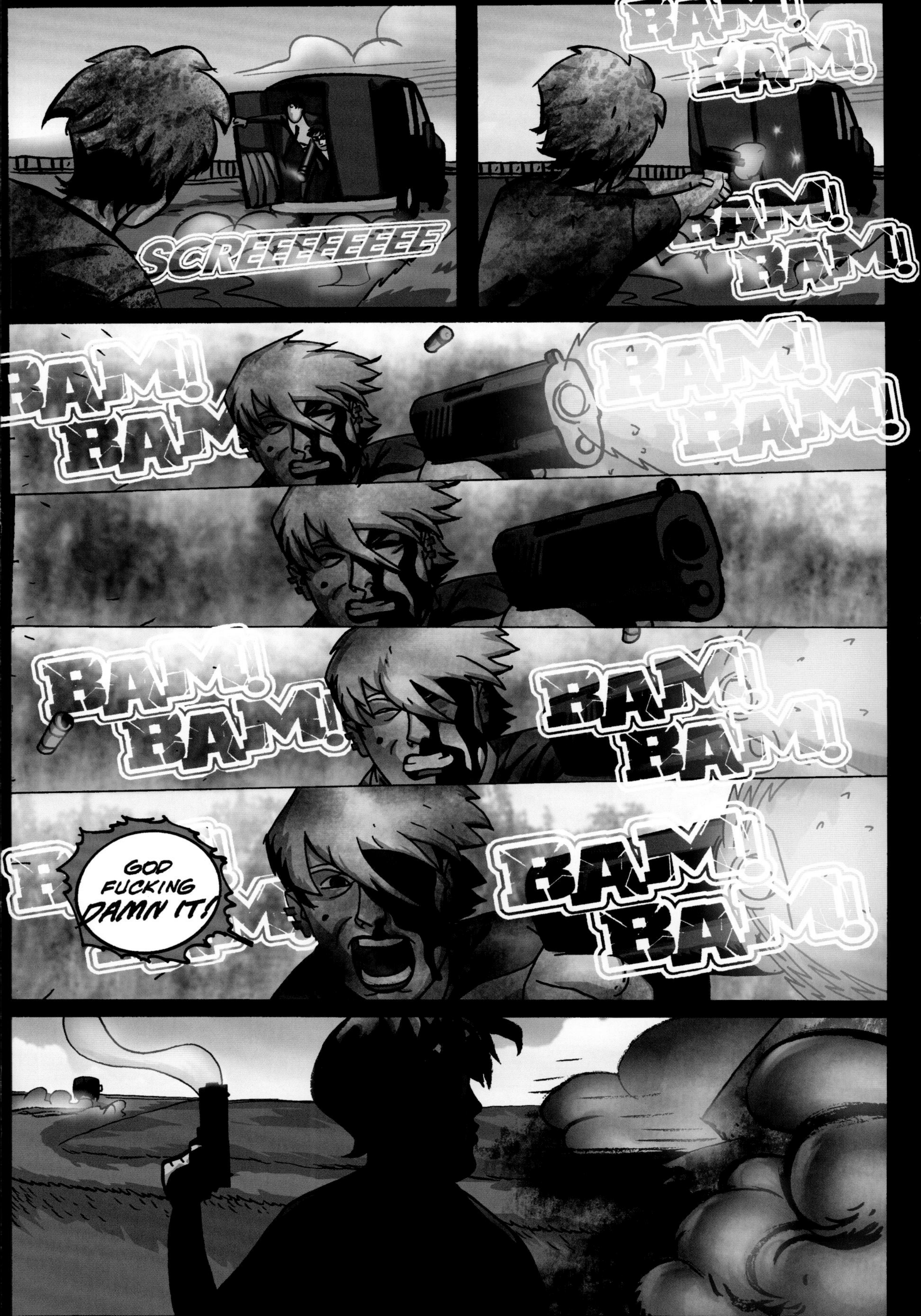
SCREEEEEEEE
BAM! BAM!
BAM! BAM!
BAM! BAM!
BAM! BAM!
BAM! BAM!
BAM! BAM!
GOD FUCKING DAMN IT!
BAM! BAM!

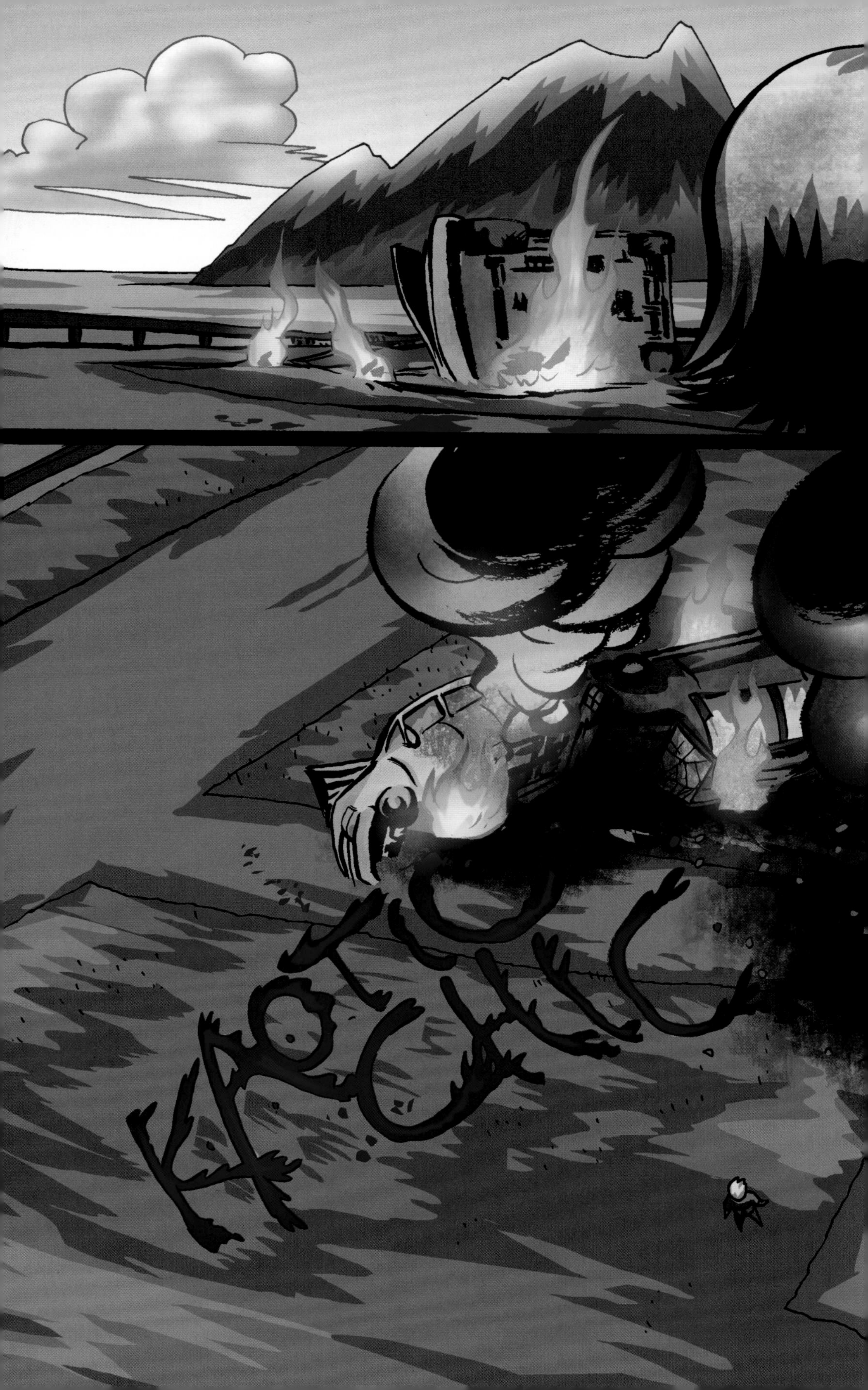

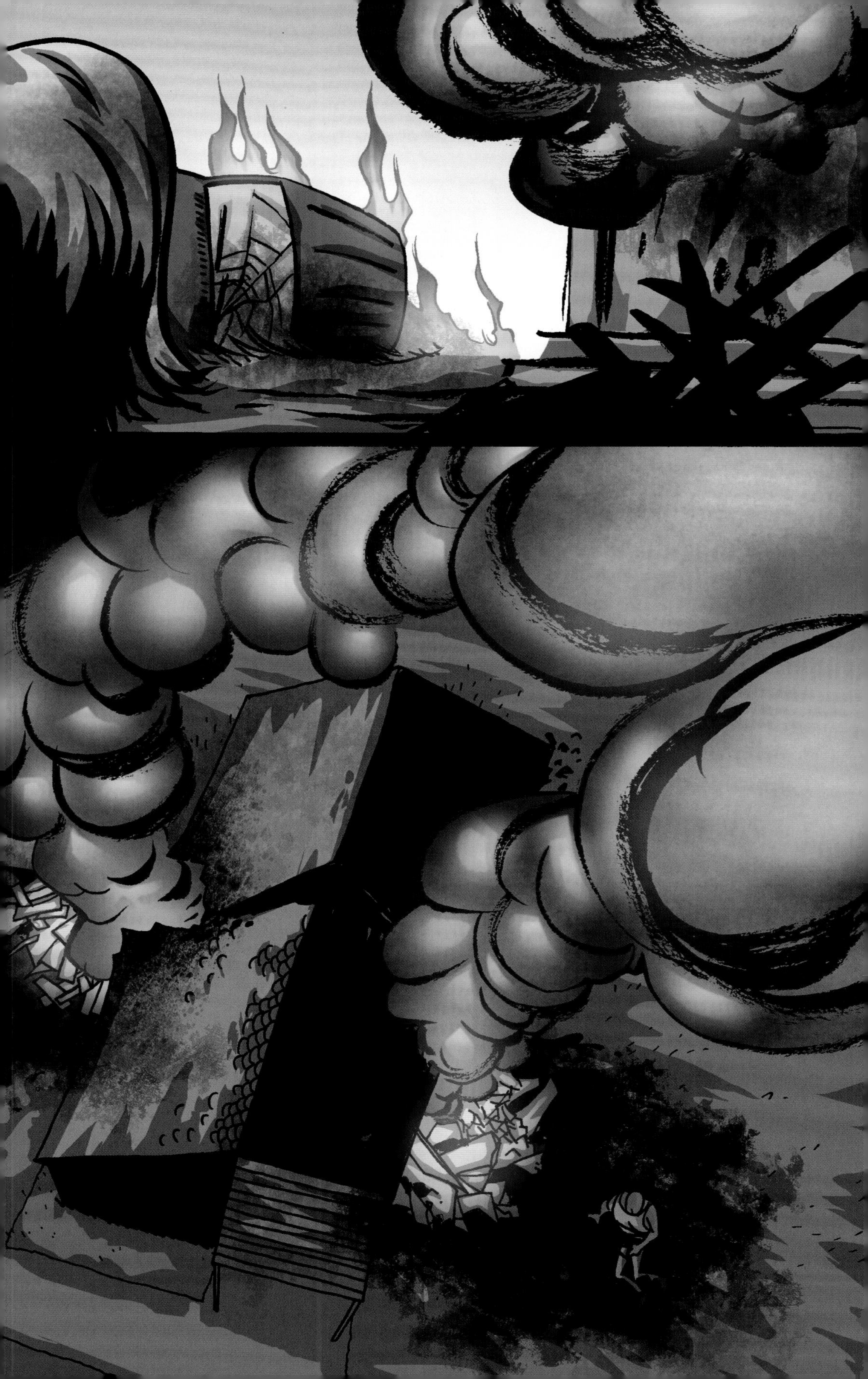

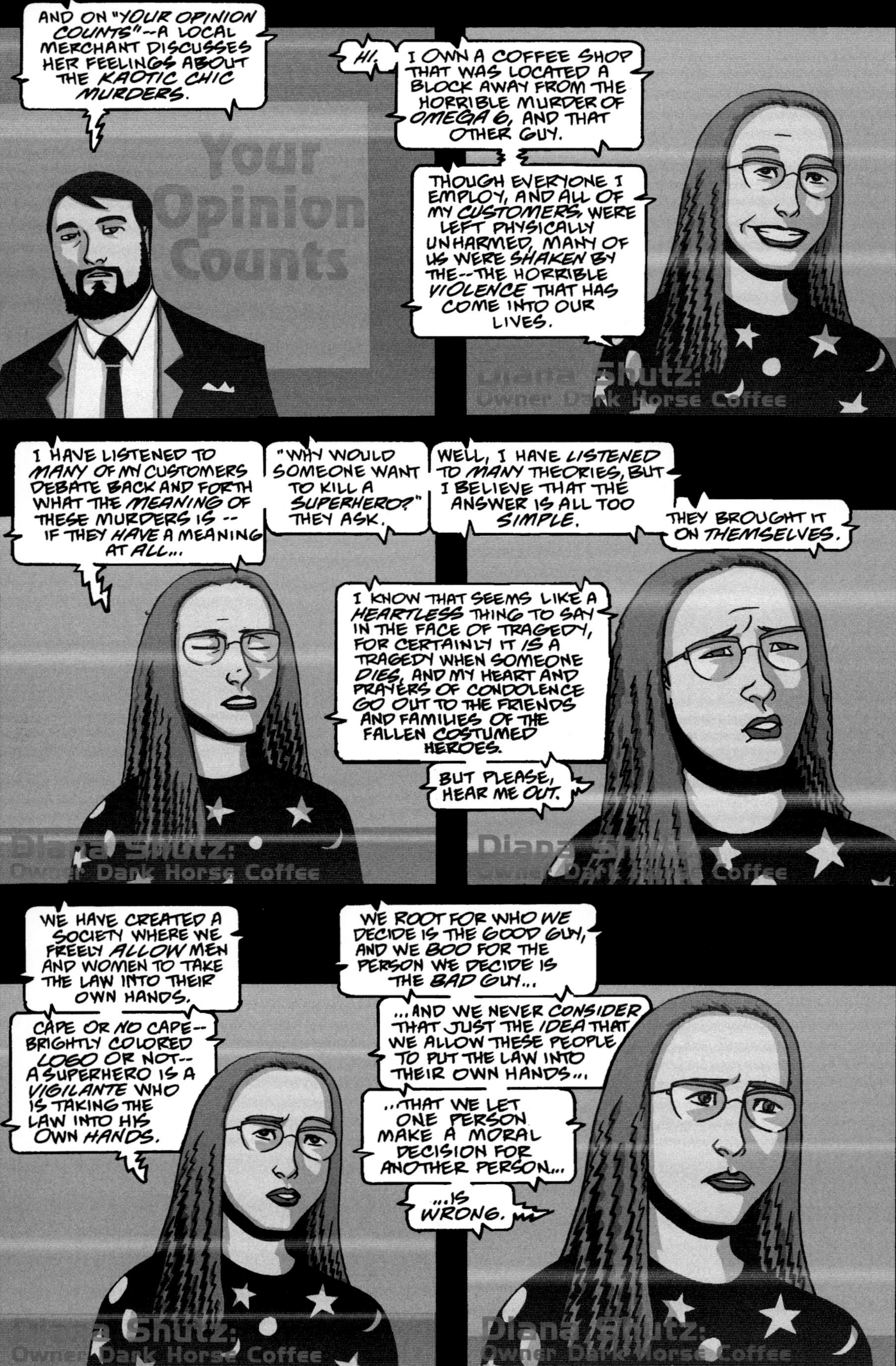
AND ON "YOUR OPINION COUNTS"--A LOCAL MERCHANT DISCUSSES HER FEELINGS ABOUT THE KAOTIC CHIC MURDERS.
Your Opinion Counts
HI.
I OWN A COFFEE SHOP THAT WAS LOCATED A BLOCK AWAY FROM THE HORRIBLE MURDER OF OMEGA 6, AND THAT OTHER GUY.
THOUGH EVERYONE I EMPLOY, AND ALL OF MY CUSTOMERS, WERE LEFT PHYSICALLY UNHARMED, MANY OF US WERE SHAKEN BY THE--THE HORRIBLE VIOLENCE THAT HAS COME INTO OUR LIVES.
Diana Shutz:
Owner Dark Horse Coffee
I HAVE LISTENED TO MANY OF MY CUSTOMERS DEBATE BACK AND FORTH WHAT THE MEANING OF THESE MURDERS IS -- IF THEY HAVE A MEANING AT ALL...
"WHY WOULD SOMEONE WANT TO KILL A SUPERHERO?" THEY ASK.
Diana Shutz:
Owner Dark Horse Coffee
WELL, I HAVE LISTENED TO MANY THEORIES, BUT I BELIEVE THAT THE ANSWER IS ALL TOO SIMPLE.
THEY BROUGHT IT ON THEMSELVES.
I KNOW THAT SEEMS LIKE A HEARTLESS THING TO SAY IN THE FACE OF TRAGEDY, FOR CERTAINLY IT IS A TRAGEDY WHEN SOMEONE DIES, AND MY HEART AND PRAYERS OF CONDOLENCE GO OUT TO THE FRIENDS AND FAMILIES OF THE FALLEN COSTUMED HEROES.
BUT PLEASE, HEAR ME OUT.
Diana Shutz:
Owner Dark Horse Coffee
WE HAVE CREATED A SOCIETY WHERE WE FREELY ALLOW MEN AND WOMEN TO TAKE THE LAW INTO THEIR OWN HANDS.
CAPE OR NO CAPE--BRIGHTLY COLORED LOGO OR NOT--A SUPERHERO IS A VIGILANTE WHO IS TAKING THE LAW INTO HIS OWN HANDS.
Diana Shutz:
Owner Dark Horse Coffee
WE ROOT FOR WHO WE DECIDE IS THE GOOD GUY, AND WE BOO FOR THE PERSON WE DECIDE IS THE BAD GUY...
...AND WE NEVER CONSIDER THAT JUST THE IDEA THAT WE ALLOW THESE PEOPLE TO PUT THE LAW INTO THEIR OWN HANDS...
...THAT WE LET ONE PERSON MAKE A MORAL DECISION FOR ANOTHER PERSON...
...IS WRONG.
Diana Shutz:
Owner Dark Horse Coffee

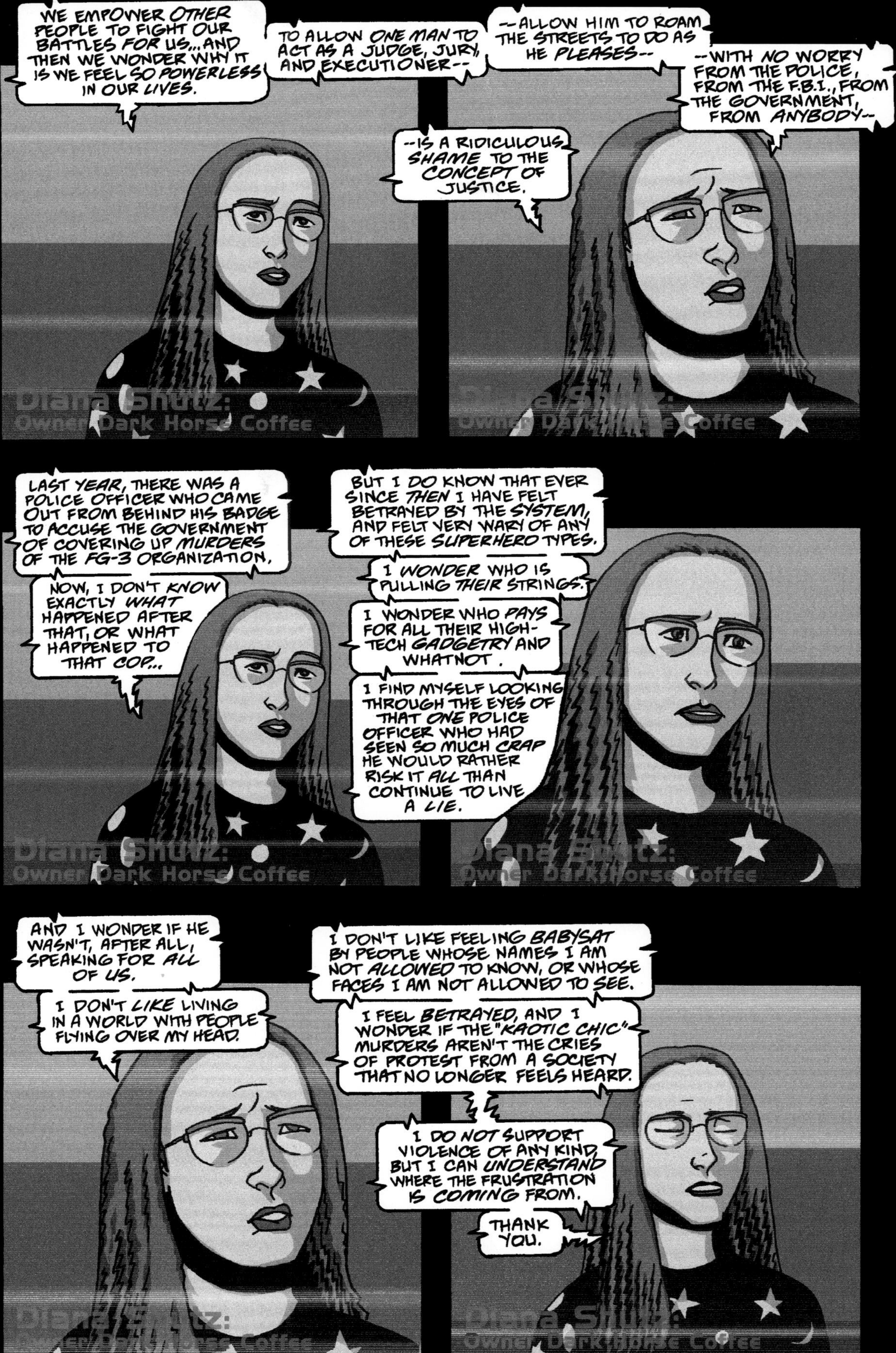
WE EMPOWER OTHER PEOPLE TO FIGHT OUR BATTLES FOR US...AND THEN WE WONDER WHY IT IS WE FEEL SO POWERLESS IN OUR LIVES.
Diana Shutz:
Owner Dark Horse Coffee
TO ALLOW ONE MAN TO ACT AS A JUDGE, JURY, AND EXECUTIONER--
--ALLOW HIM TO ROAM THE STREETS TO DO AS HE PLEASES--
--WITH NO WORRY FROM THE POLICE, FROM THE F.B.I., FROM THE GOVERNMENT, FROM ANYBODY--
--IS A RIDICULOUS SHAME TO THE CONCEPT OF JUSTICE.
LAST YEAR, THERE WAS A POLICE OFFICER WHO CAME OUT FROM BEHIND HIS BADGE TO ACCUSE THE GOVERNMENT OF COVERING UP MURDERS OF THE FG-3 ORGANIZATION.
NOW, I DON'T KNOW EXACTLY WHAT HAPPENED AFTER THAT, OR WHAT HAPPENED TO THAT COP...
BUT I DO KNOW THAT EVER SINCE THEN I HAVE FELT BETRAYED BY THE SYSTEM, AND FELT VERY WARY OF ANY OF THESE SUPERHERO TYPES.
I WONDER WHO IS PULLING THEIR STRINGS.
I WONDER WHO PAYS FOR ALL THEIR HIGH-TECH GADGETRY AND WHATNOT.
I FIND MYSELF LOOKING THROUGH THE EYES OF THAT ONE POLICE OFFICER WHO HAD SEEN SO MUCH CRAP HE WOULD RATHER RISK IT ALL THAN CONTINUE TO LIVE A LIE.
AND I WONDER IF HE WASN'T, AFTER ALL, SPEAKING FOR ALL OF US.
I DON'T LIKE LIVING IN A WORLD WITH PEOPLE FLYING OVER MY HEAD.
I DON'T LIKE FEELING BABYSAT BY PEOPLE WHOSE NAMES I AM NOT ALLOWED TO KNOW, OR WHOSE FACES I AM NOT ALLOWED TO SEE.
I FEEL BETRAYED, AND I WONDER IF THE "KAOTIC CHIC" MURDERS AREN'T THE CRIES OF PROTEST FROM A SOCIETY THAT NO LONGER FEELS HEARD.
I DO NOT SUPPORT VIOLENCE OF ANY KIND, BUT I CAN UNDERSTAND WHERE THE FRUSTRATION IS COMING FROM.
THANK YOU.

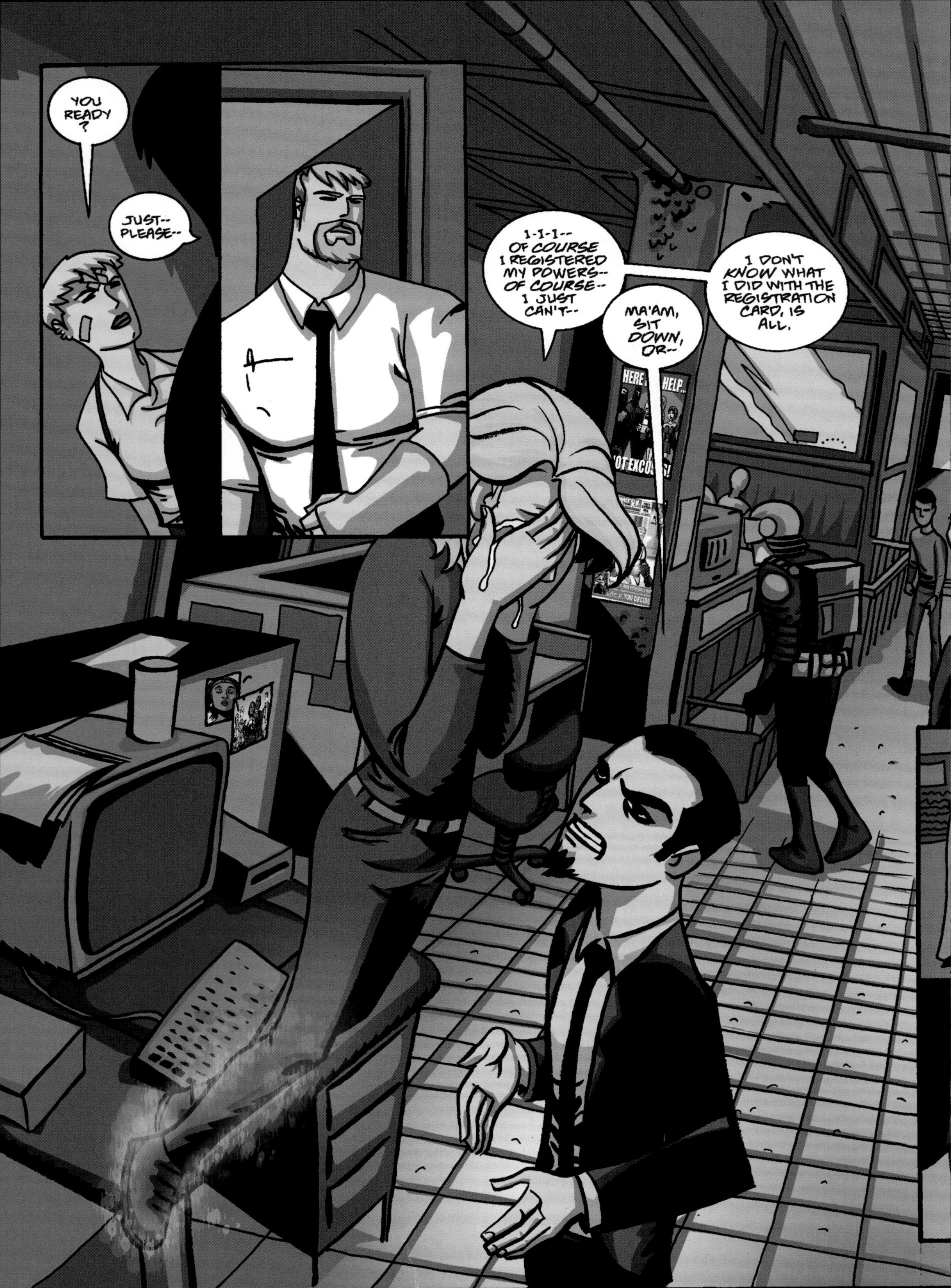
YOU READY?
JUST-- PLEASE--
I-I-I-- OF COURSE I REGISTERED MY POWERS-- OF COURSE-- I JUST CAN'T--
I DON'T KNOW WHAT I DID WITH THE REGISTRATION CARD, IS ALL.
MA'AM, SIT DOWN, OR--

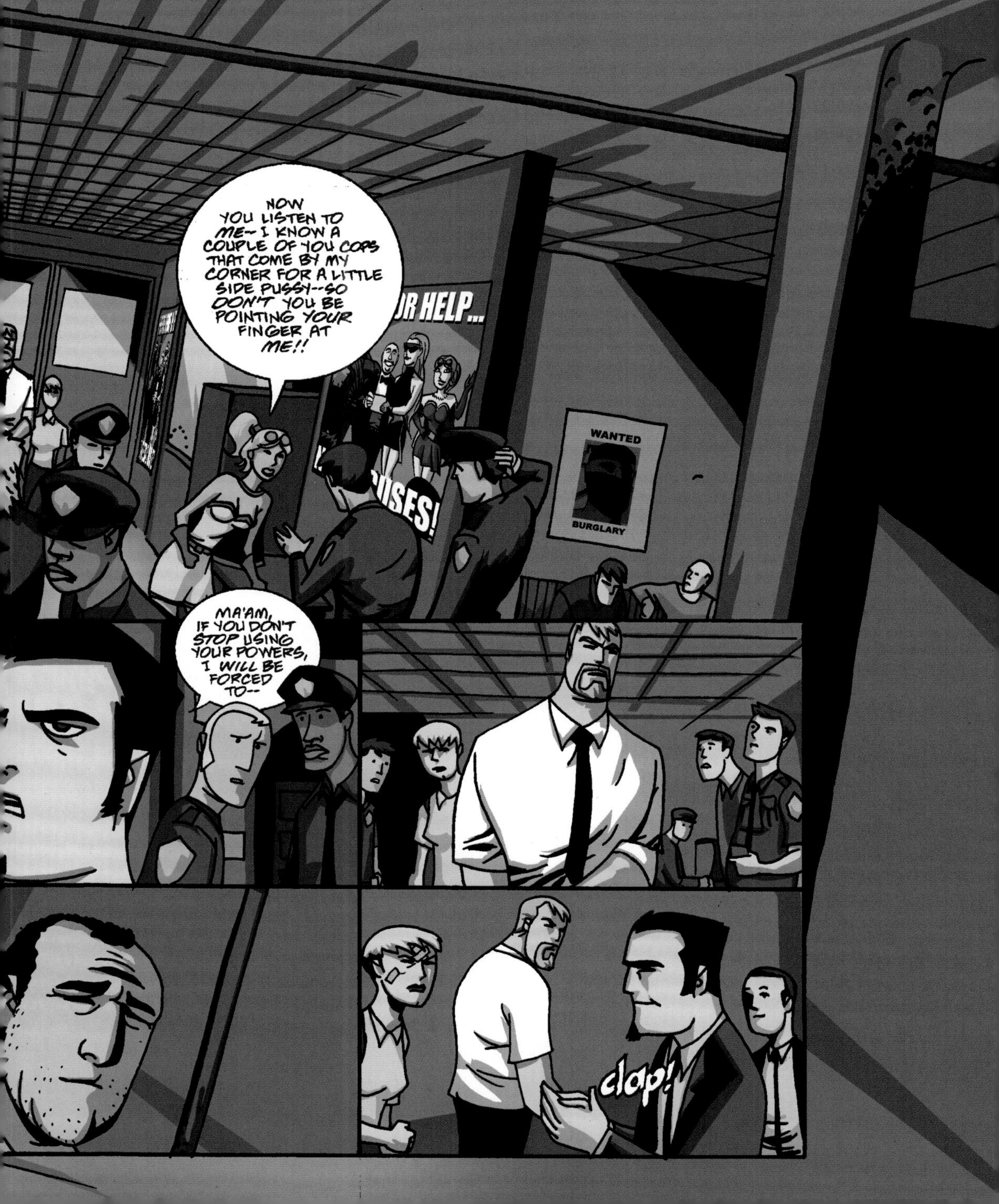
NOW YOU LISTEN TO ME-- I KNOW A COUPLE OF YOU COPS THAT COME BY MY CORNER FOR A LITTLE SIDE PUSSY--SO DON'T YOU BE POINTING YOUR FINGER AT ME!!
...R HELP...
...USES!
WANTED
BURGLARY
MA'AM, IF YOU DON'T STOP USING YOUR POWERS, I WILL BE FORCED TO--
clap!

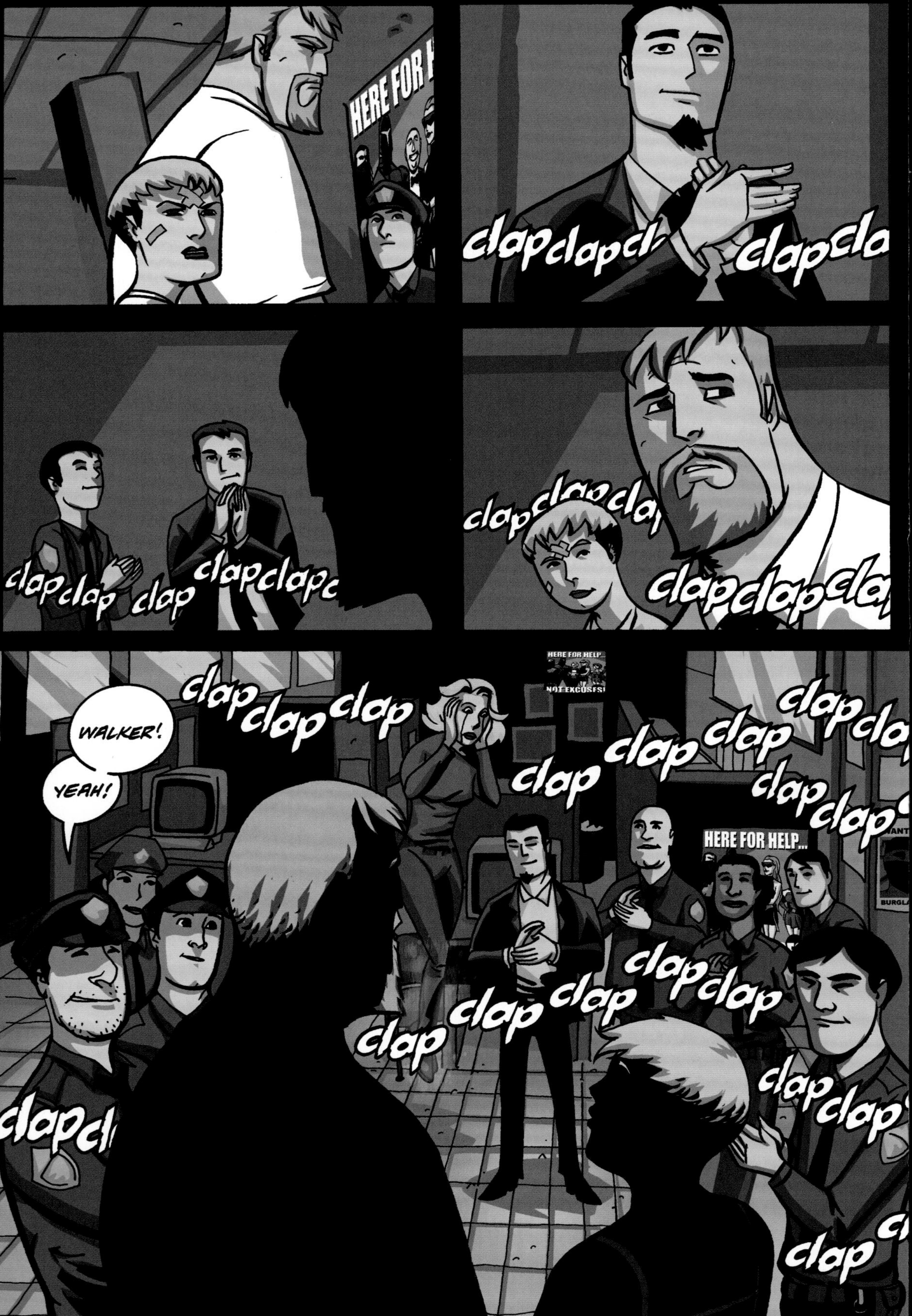
HERE FOR
clapclapcl
clapcla
clapclap clap clapclapc
clapclapclap
clapclapcla
HERE FOR HELP...
NOT EXCUSES!
clap clap clap
WALKER!
YEAH!
clap clap clap
clap clap
HERE FOR HELP...
clap clap clap clap clap
clapcl
clap clap
clap

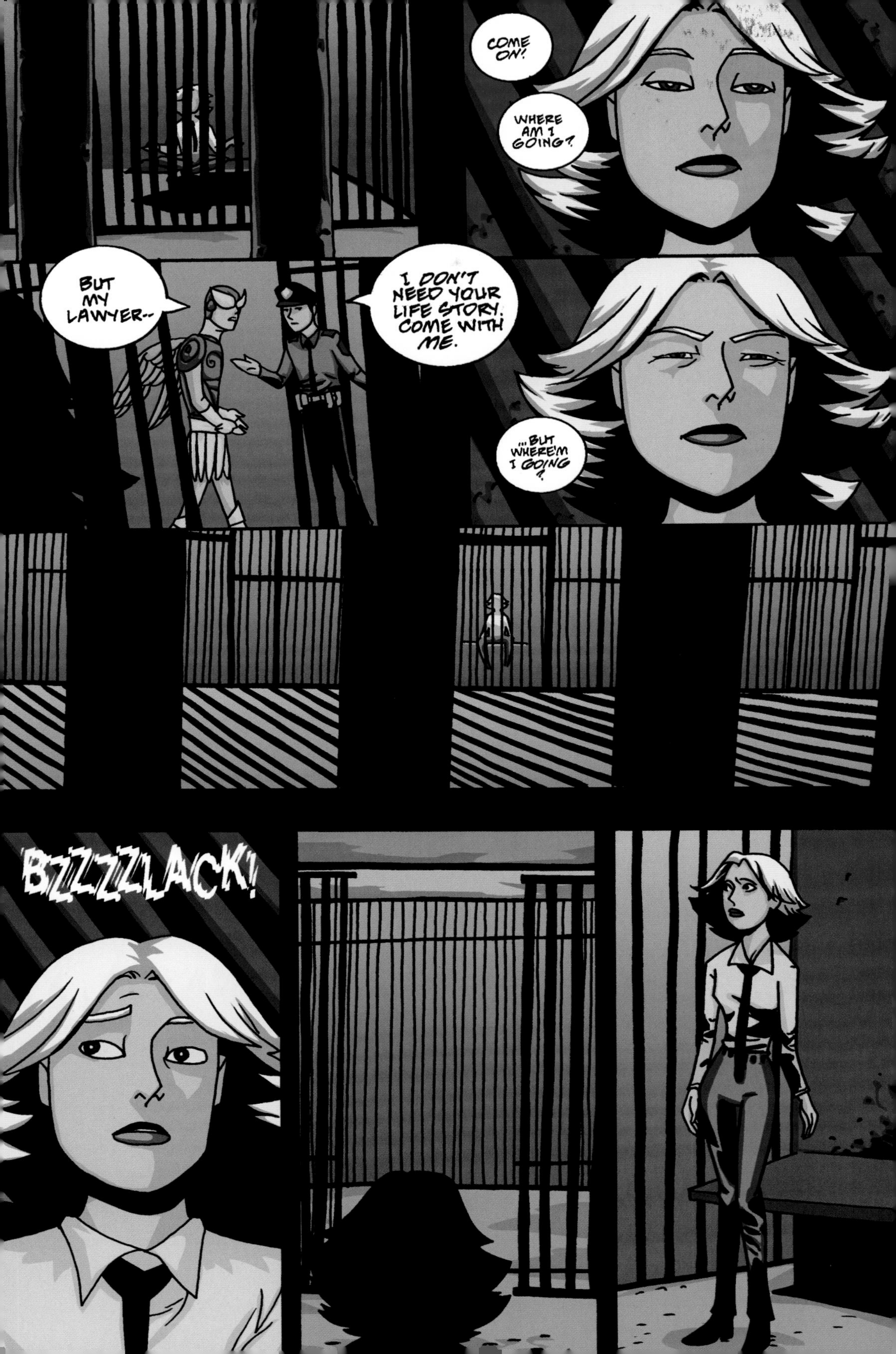

COME ON!
WHERE AM I GOING?
BUT MY LAWYER--
I DON'T NEED YOUR LIFE STORY. COME WITH ME.
...BUT WHERE'M I GOING?
BZZZLACK!

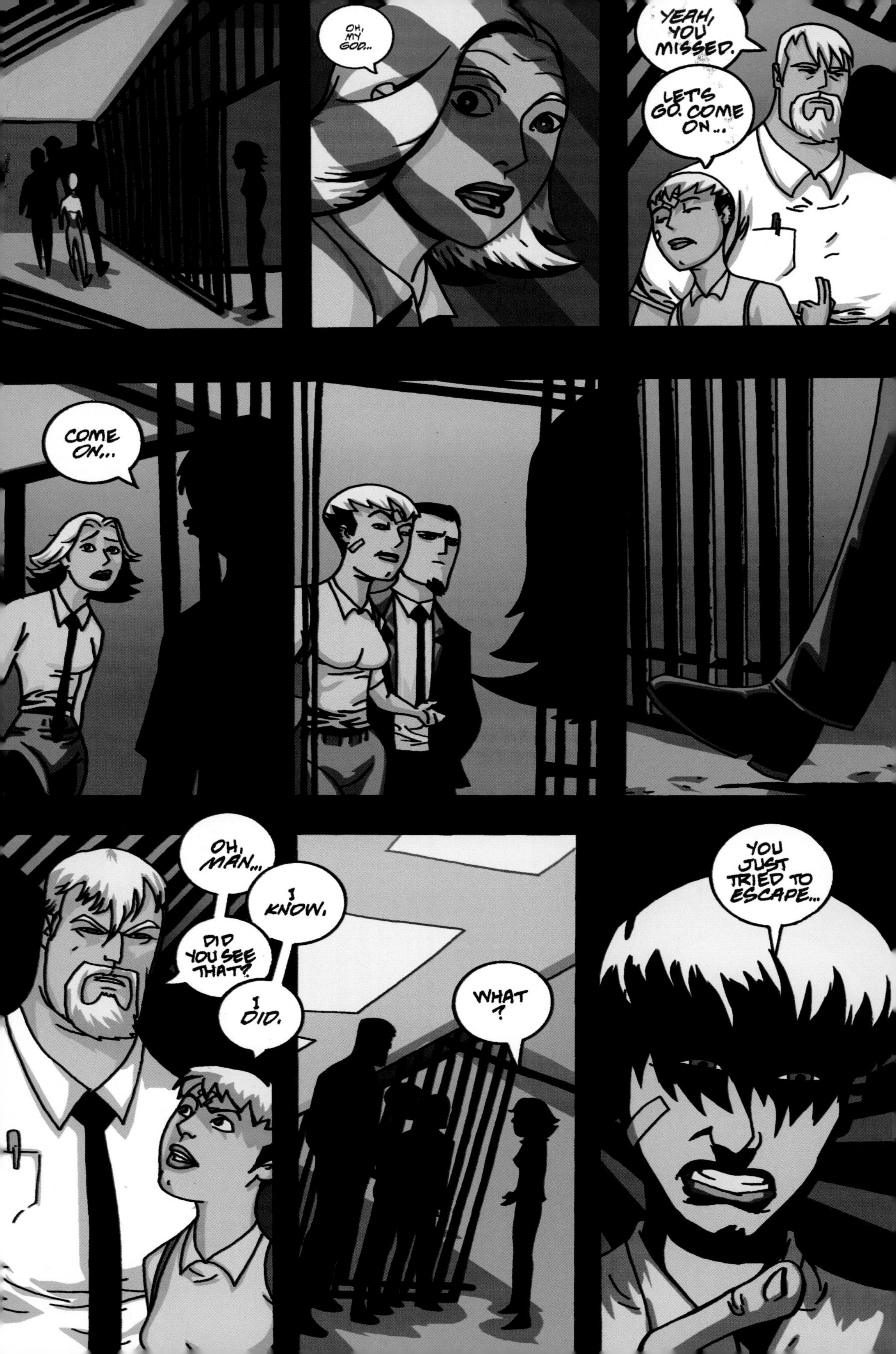
OH, MY GOD...
YEAH, YOU MISSED.
LET'S GO. COME ON...
COME ON...
OH, MAN...
I KNOW.
DID YOU SEE THAT?
I DID.
WHAT?
YOU JUST TRIED TO ESCAPE...

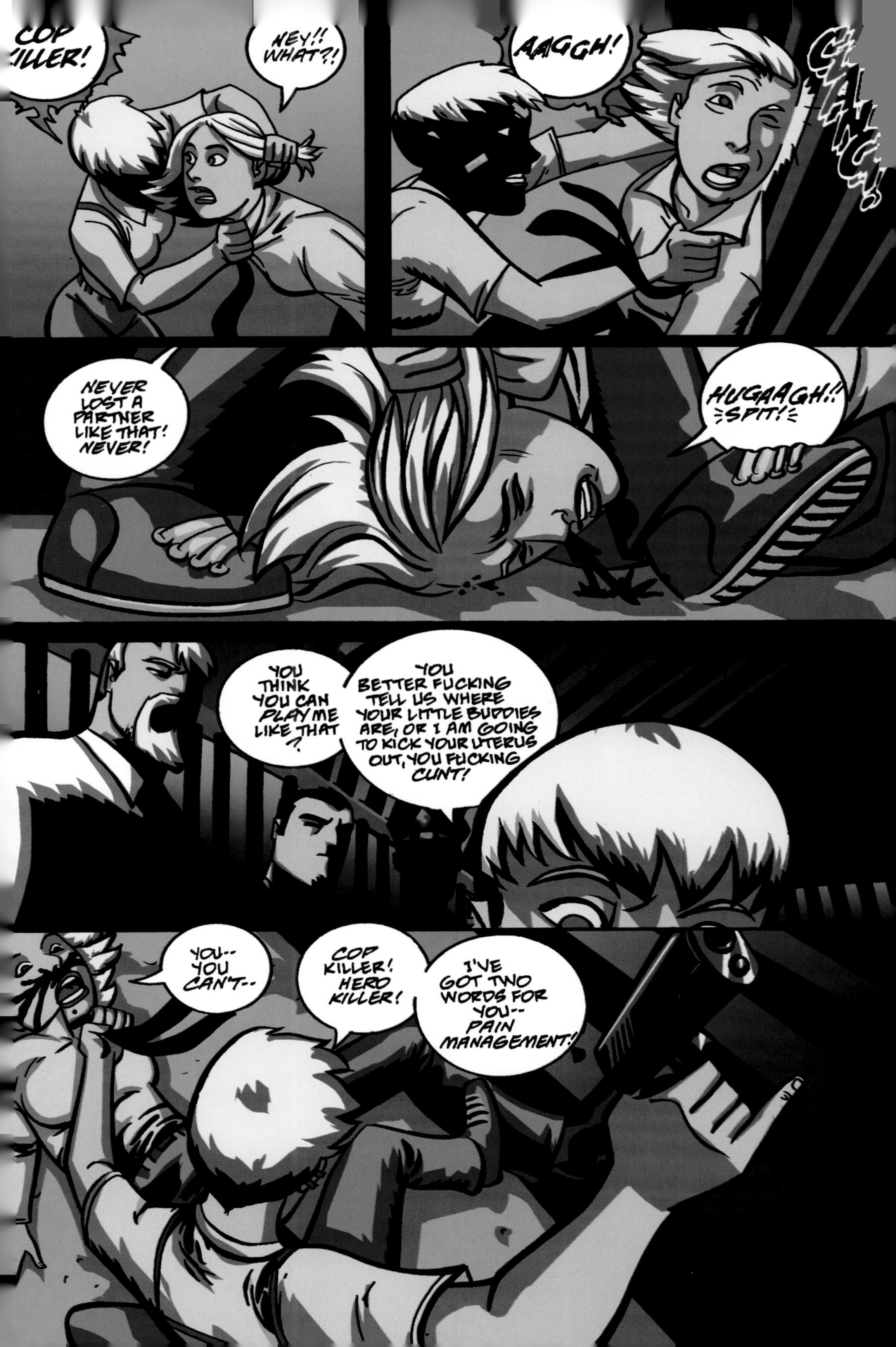
COP KILLER!
HEY!! WHAT?!
AAGGH!
CLANG!
NEVER LOST A PARTNER LIKE THAT! NEVER!
HUGAAGH!! SPIT!
YOU THINK YOU CAN PLAY ME LIKE THAT?
YOU BETTER FUCKING TELL US WHERE YOUR LITTLE BUDDIES ARE, OR I AM GOING TO KICK YOUR UTERUS OUT, YOU FUCKING CUNT!
YOU-- YOU CAN'T--
COP KILLER! HERO KILLER!
I'VE GOT TWO WORDS FOR YOU-- PAIN MANAGEMENT!

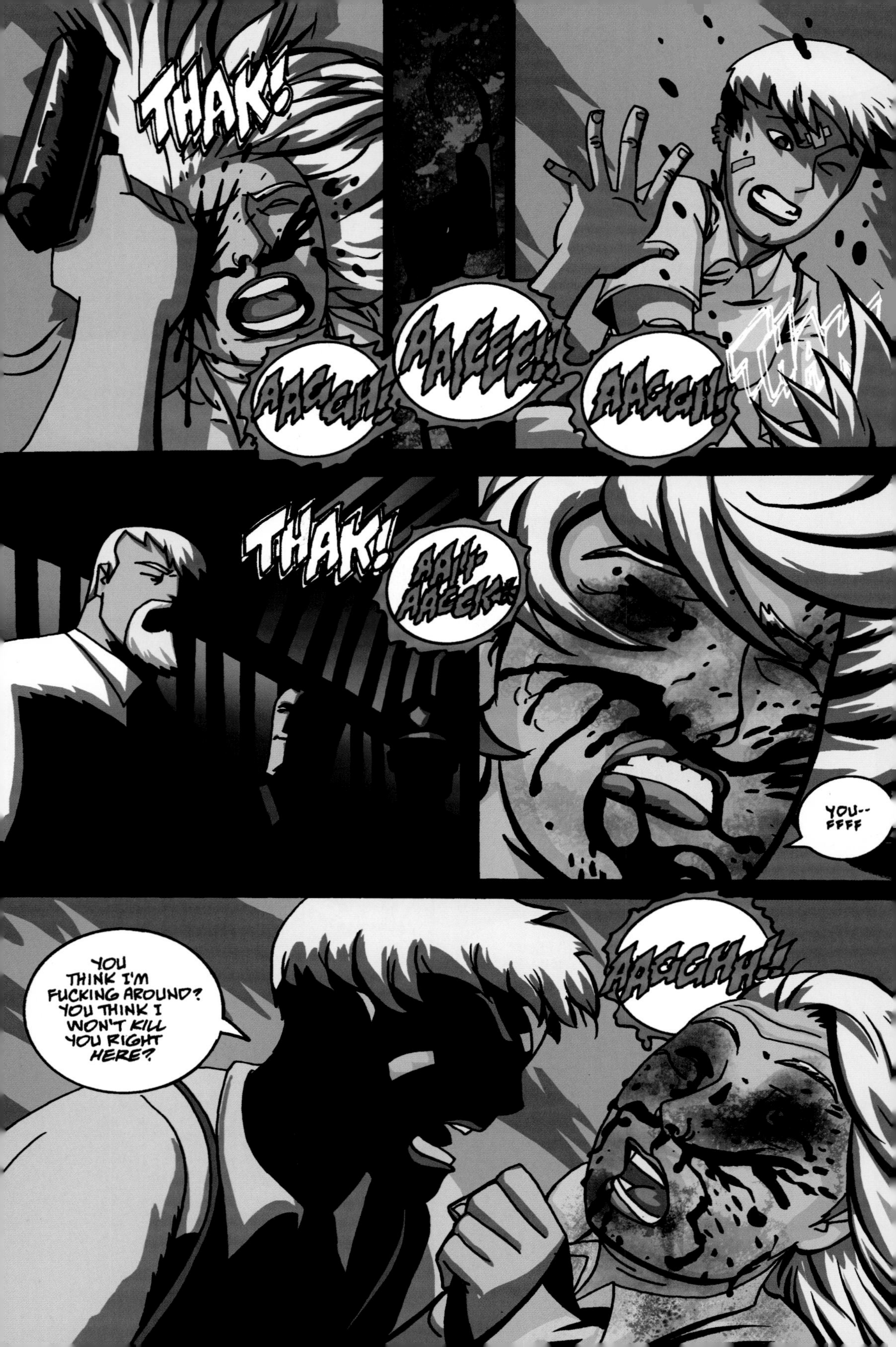
THAK!
AAGGH!
AAIEEE!!
AAGGH!
THAK!
AAH-AAECK!!
YOU--FFFF
YOU THINK I'M FUCKING AROUND? YOU THINK I WON'T KILL YOU RIGHT HERE?
AAGGHH!!

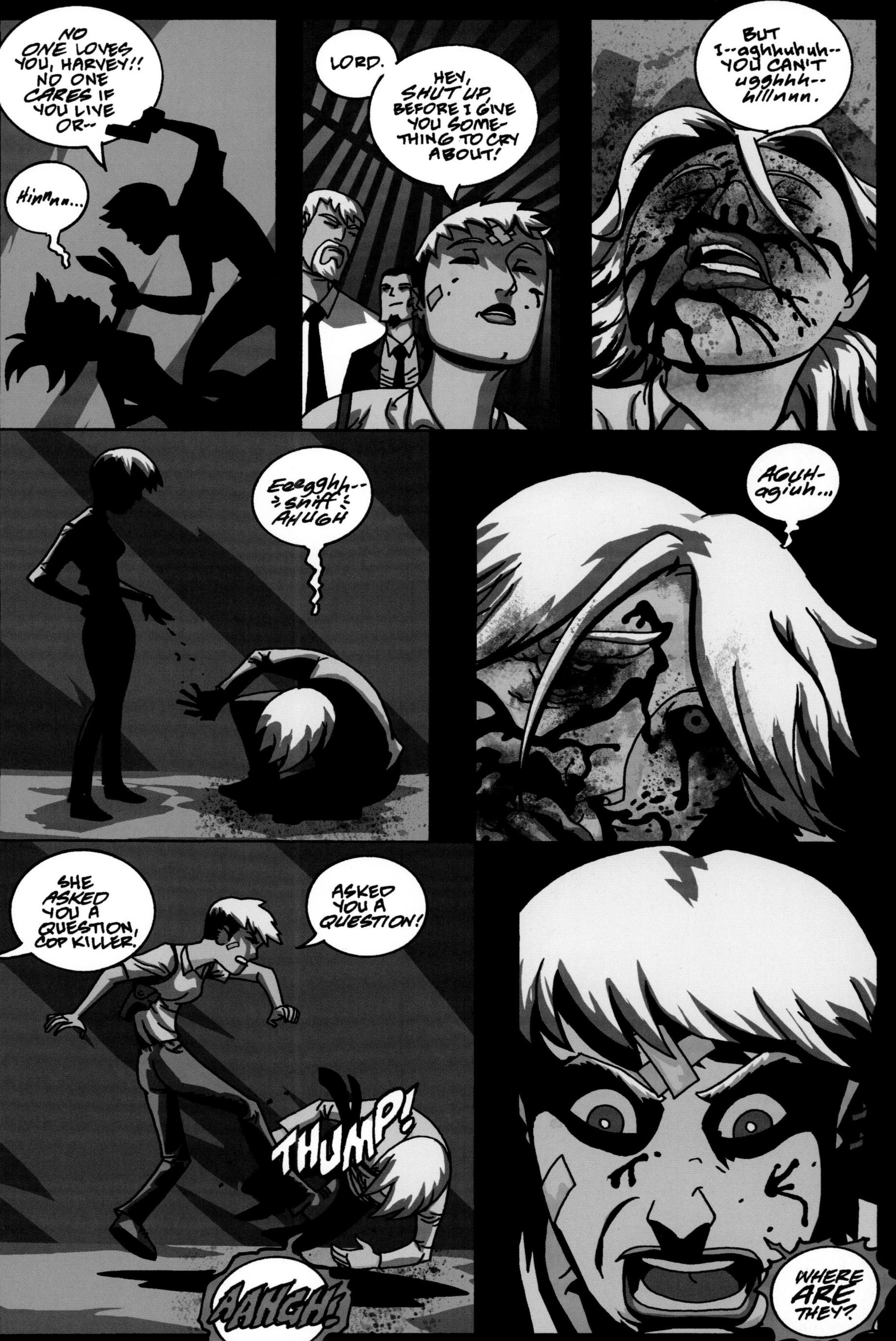
NO ONE LOVES YOU, HARVEY!! NO ONE CARES IF YOU LIVE OR--
Hinnnn...
LORD.
HEY, SHUT UP, BEFORE I GIVE YOU SOMETHING TO CRY ABOUT!
BUT I--aghhuhuh-- YOU CAN'T ugghhh-- hlllnnn.
Eeegghh-- sniff AHUGH
AGUH-agiuh...
SHE ASKED YOU A QUESTION, COP KILLER.
ASKED YOU A QUESTION!
THUMP!
AAHGH!
WHERE ARE THEY?

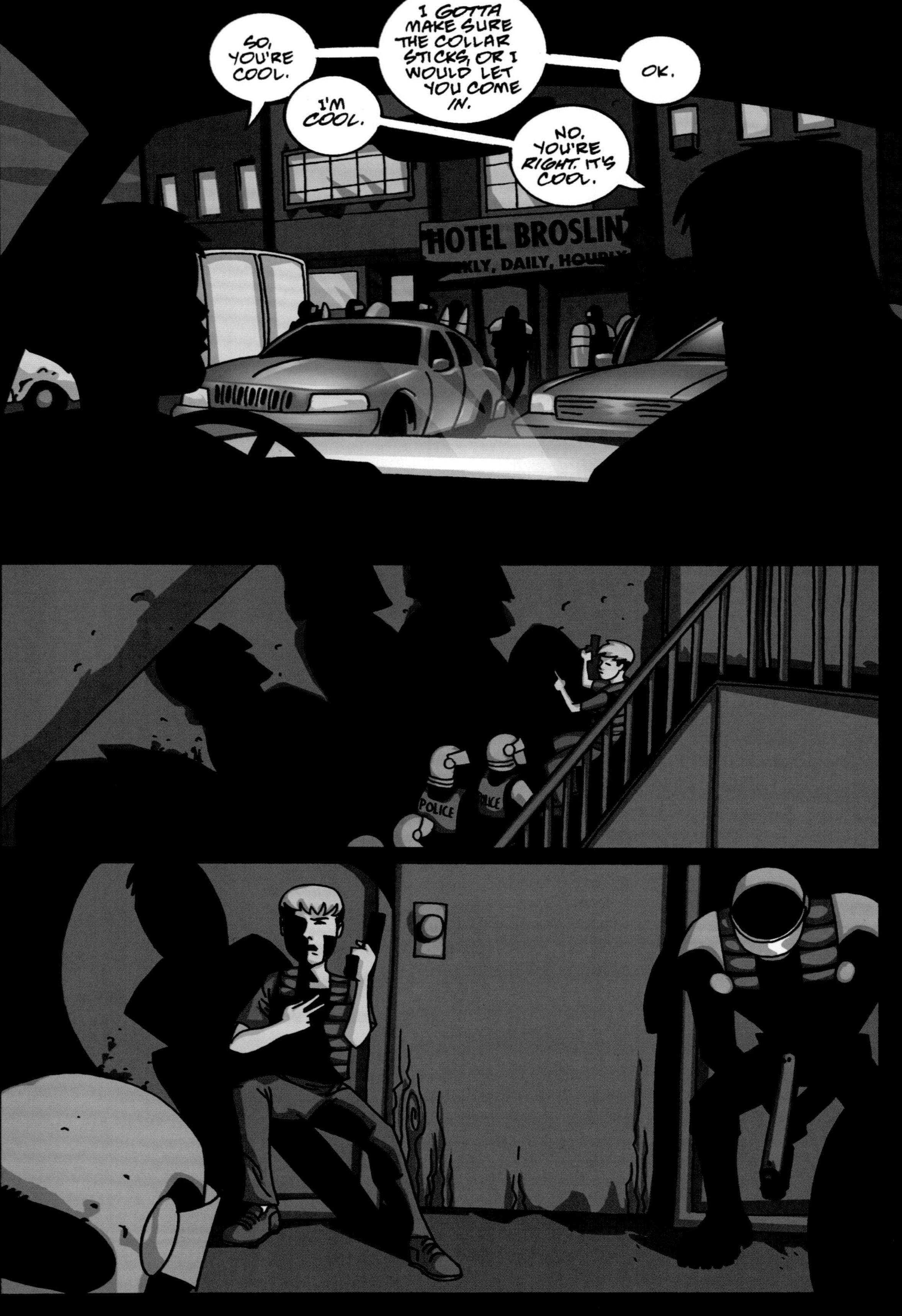
SO, YOU'RE COOL.
I GOTTA MAKE SURE THE COLLAR STICKS, OR I WOULD LET YOU COME IN.
OK.
I'M COOL.
NO. YOU'RE RIGHT. IT'S COOL.
HOTEL BROSLIN
POLICE

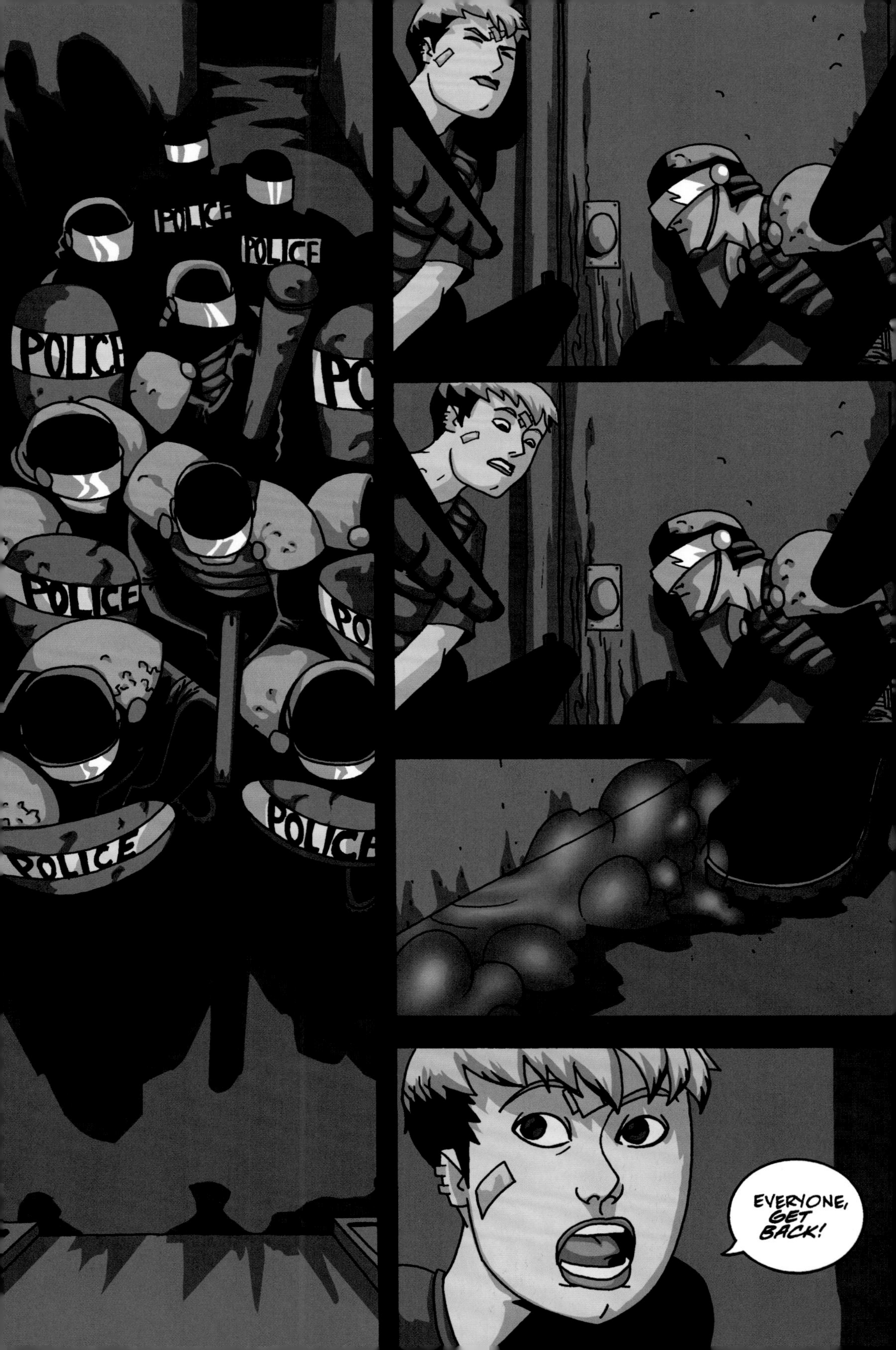
POLICE
EVERYONE, GET BACK!

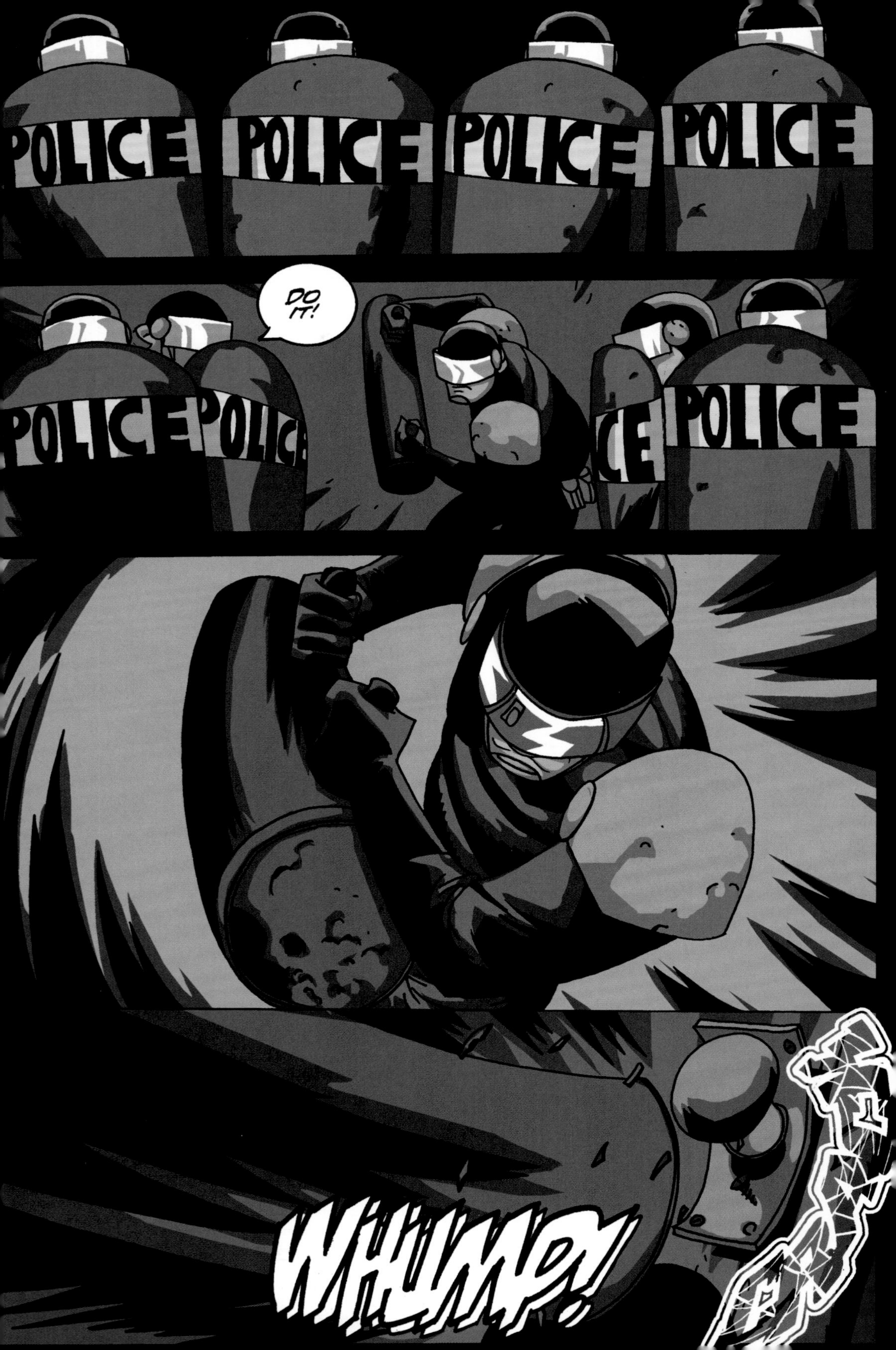
POLICE
POLICE
POLICE
POLICE
POLICE
POLICE
DO IT!
CE
POLICE
WHUMP!

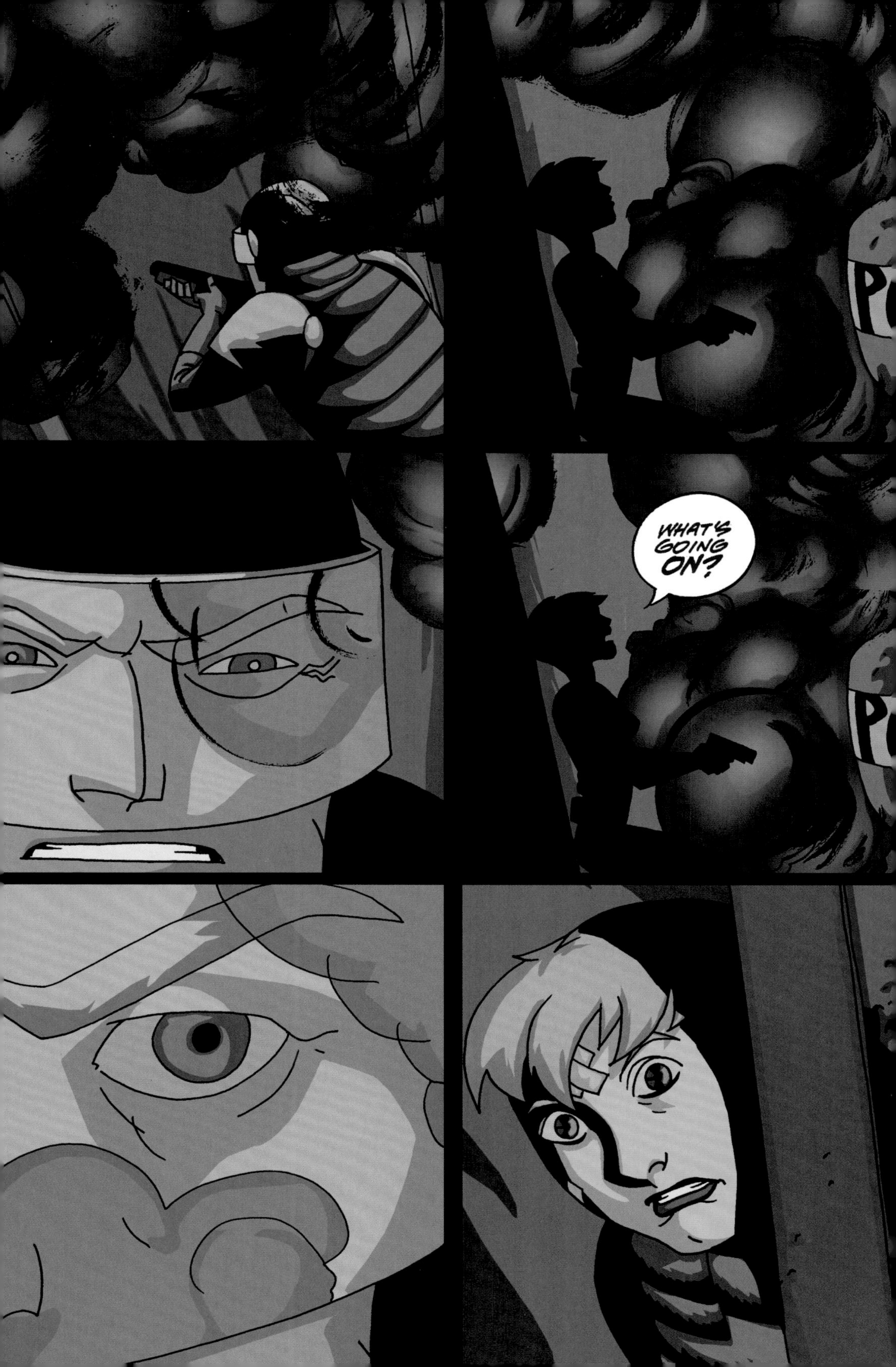
WHAT'S GOING ON?

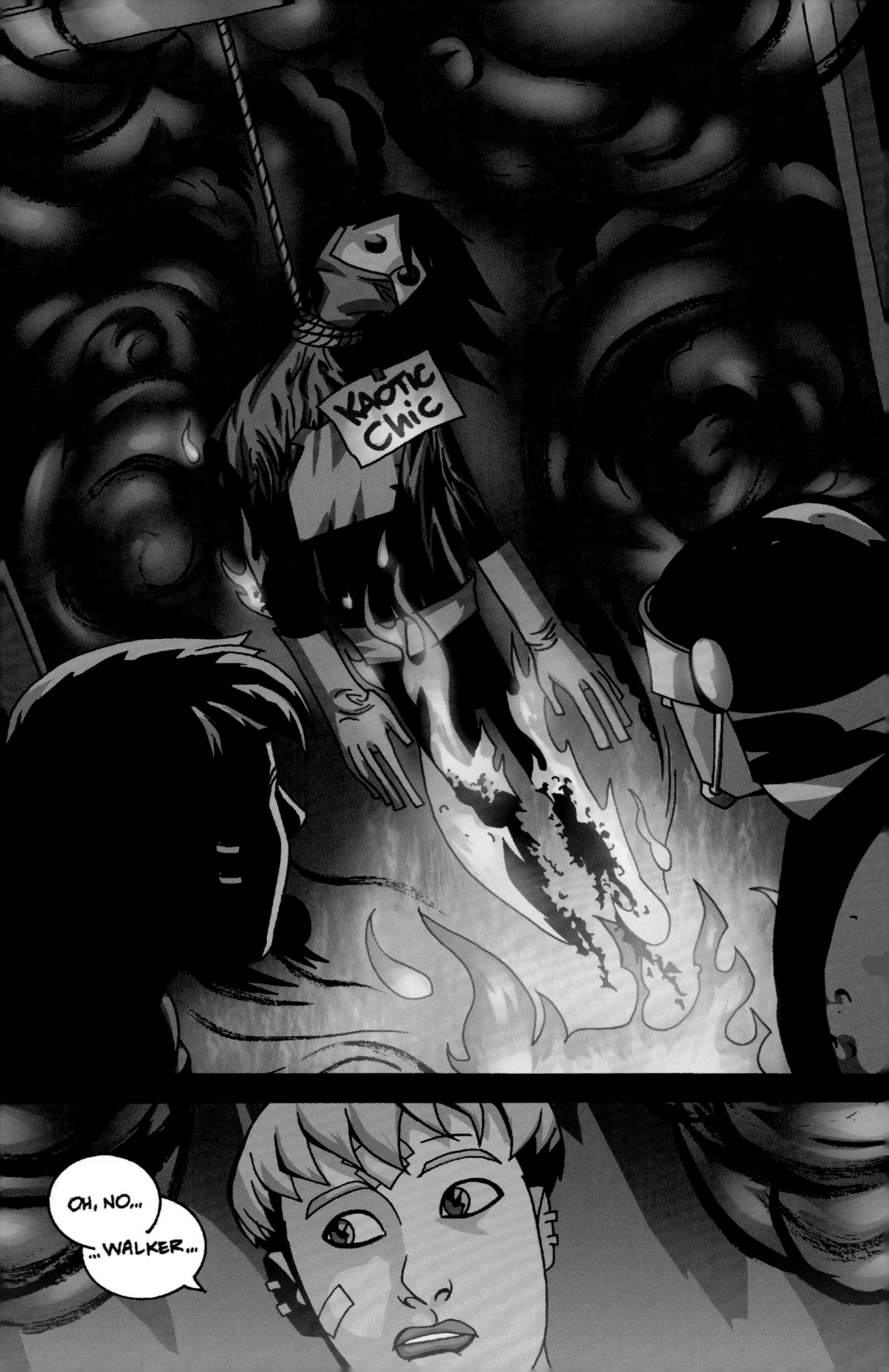
KAOTIC CHIC
OH, NO...
...WALKER...

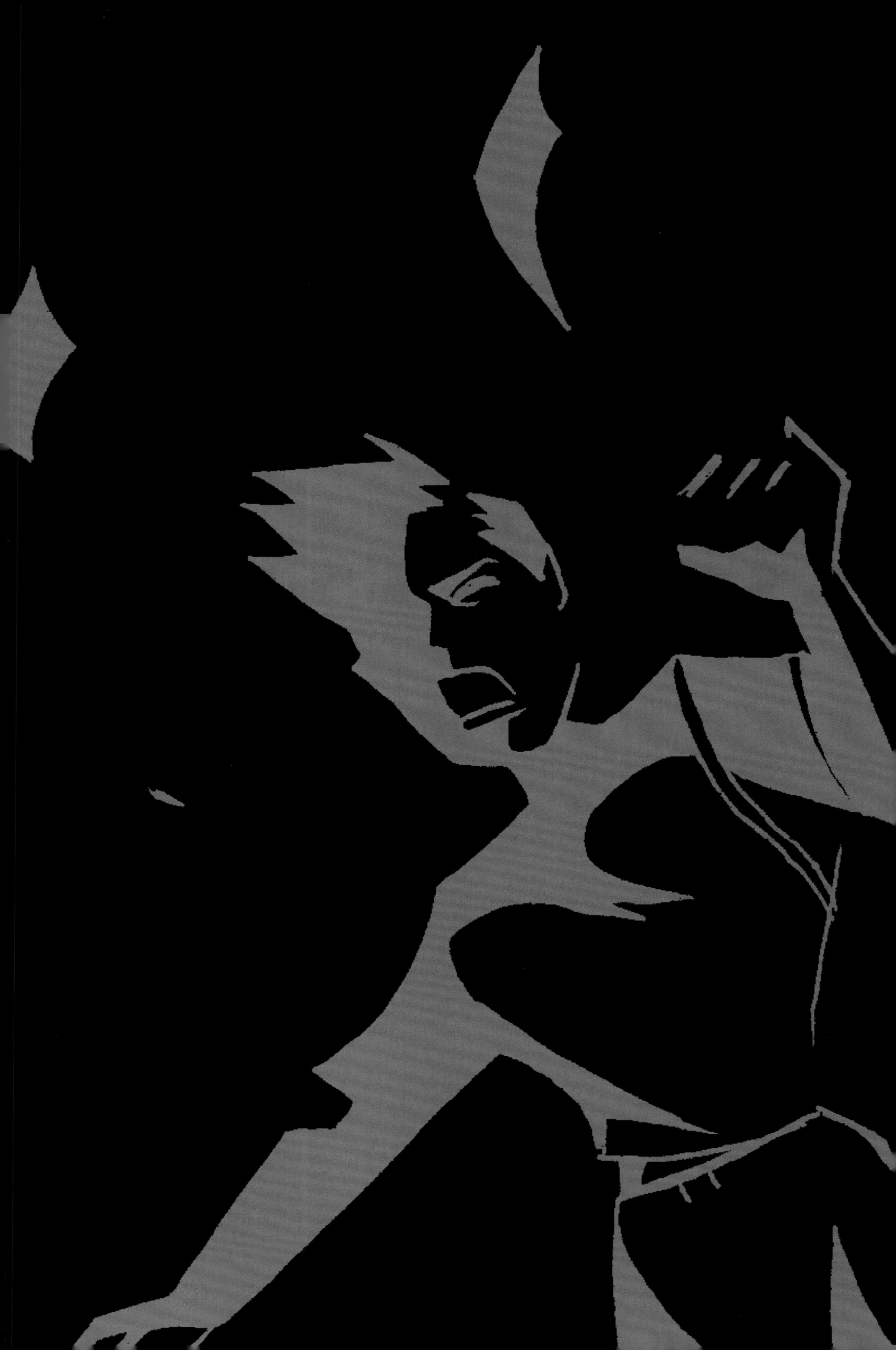

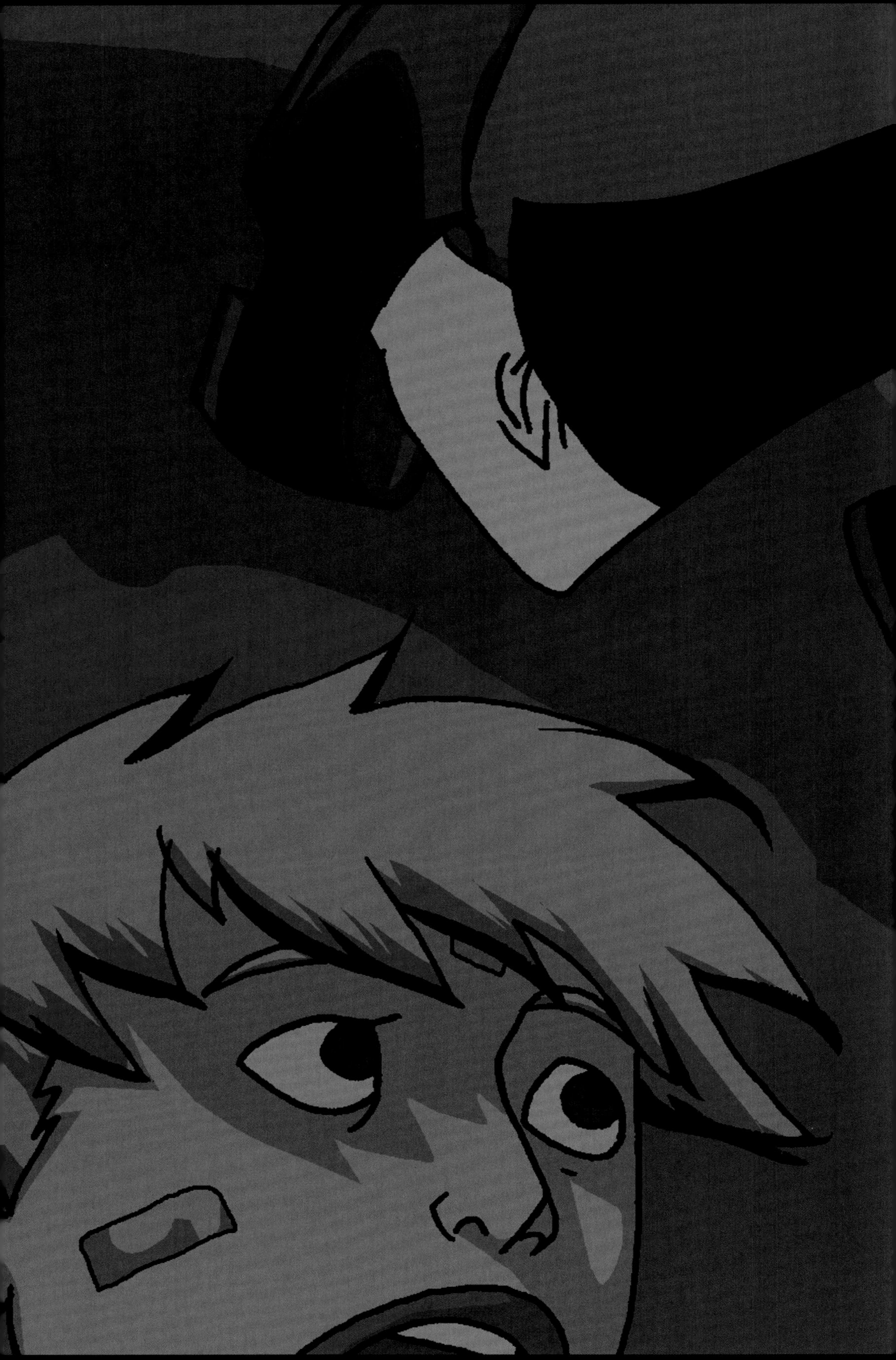

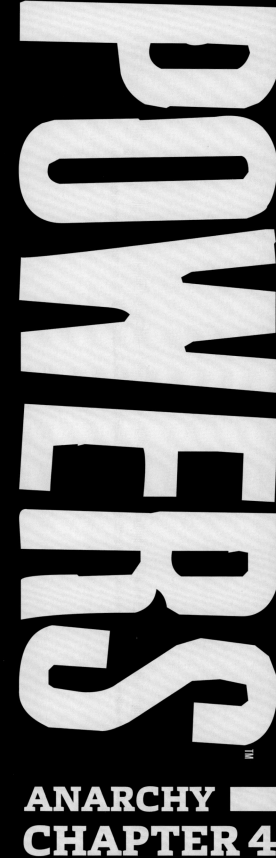

POWERS™

ANARCHY
CHAPTER 4

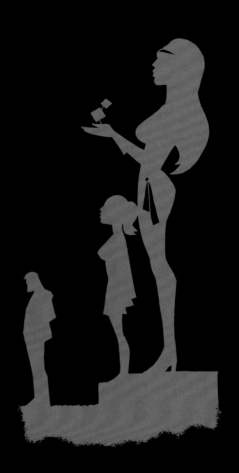

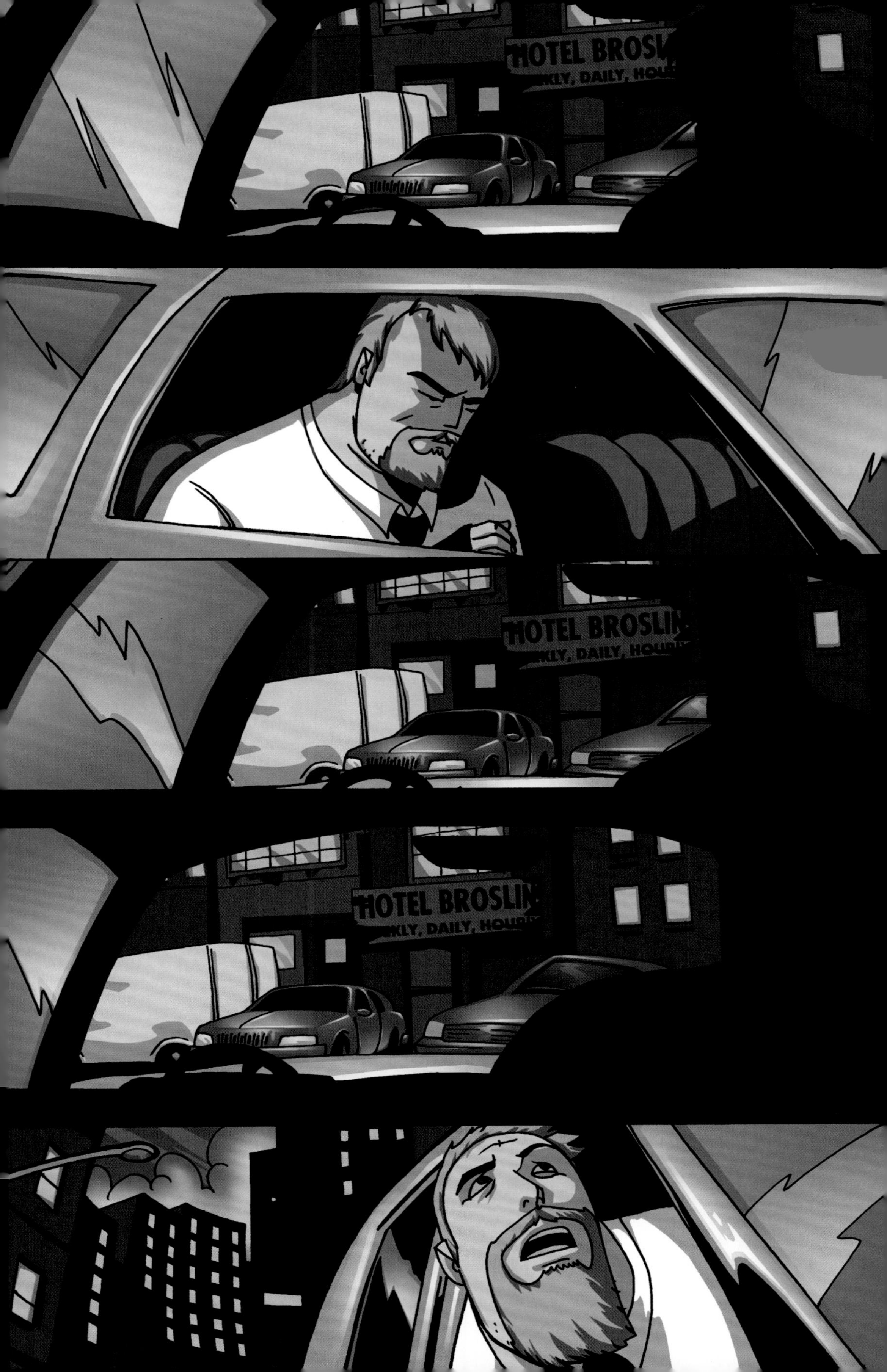
HOTEL BROSLIN
DAILY,

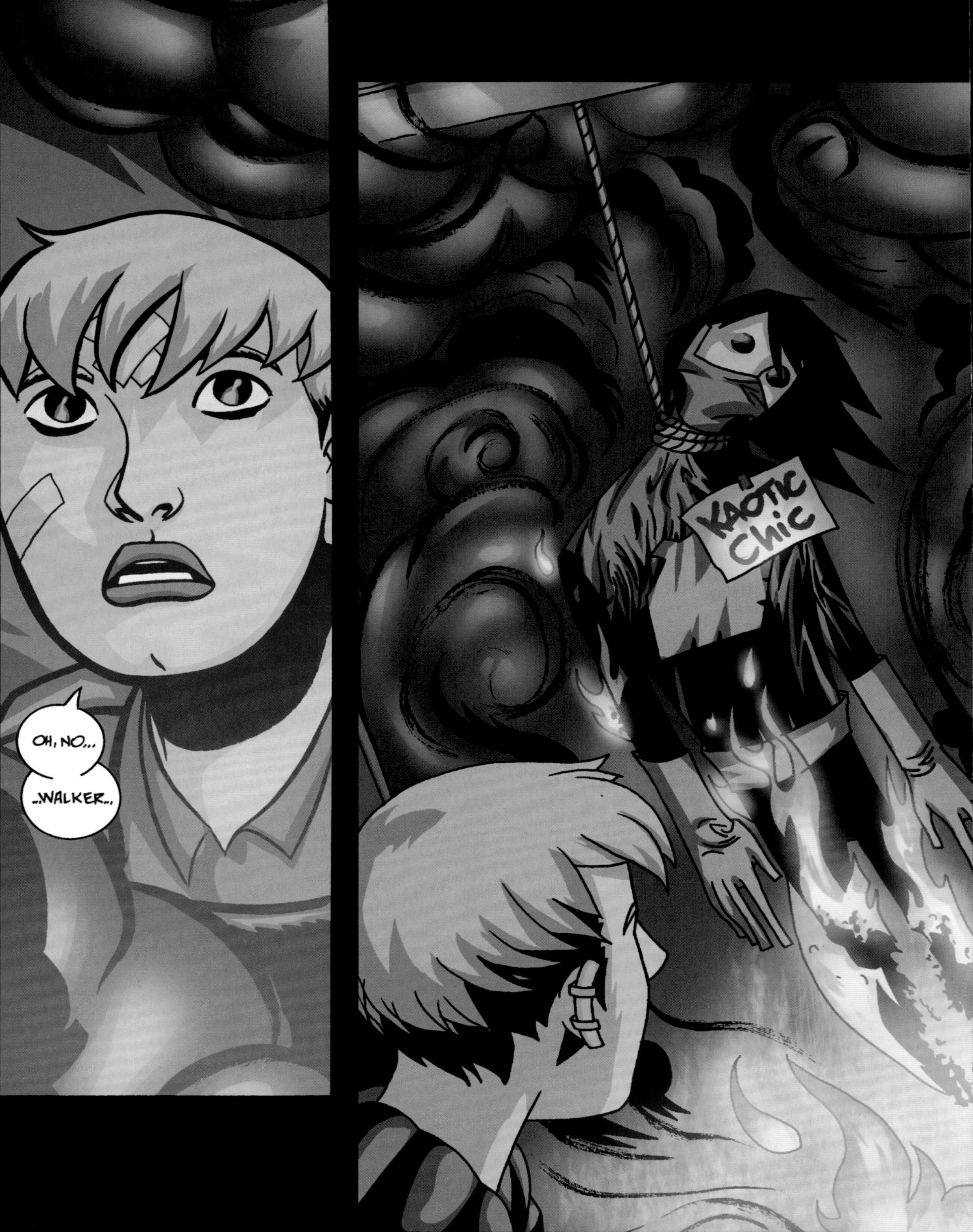
OH, NO...
..WALKER..
KAOTIC Chic

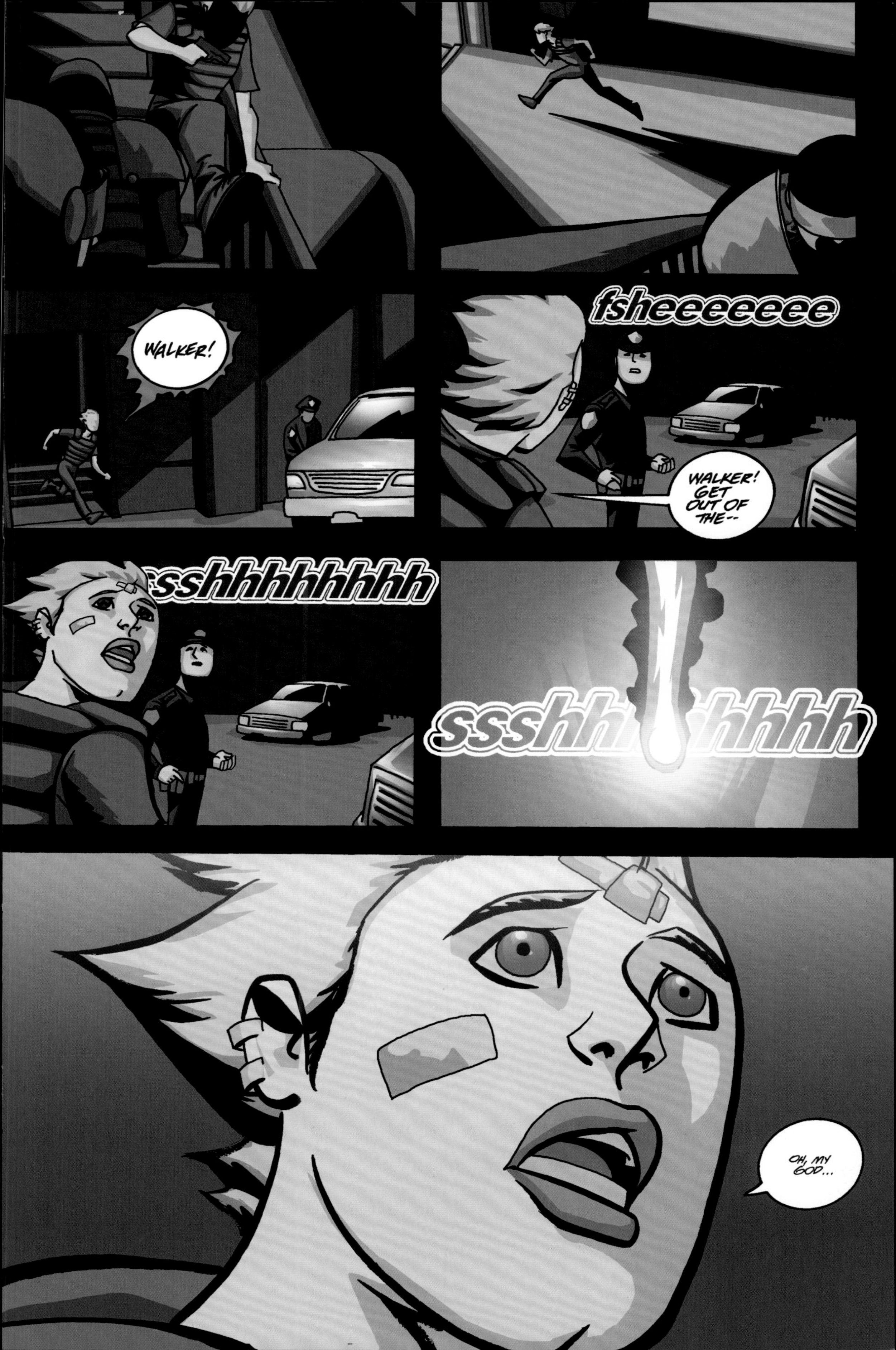
WALKER!
fsheeeeeeee
WALKER! GET OUT OF THE--
ssshhhhhhhh
ssshhhhhhh
OH, MY GOD...

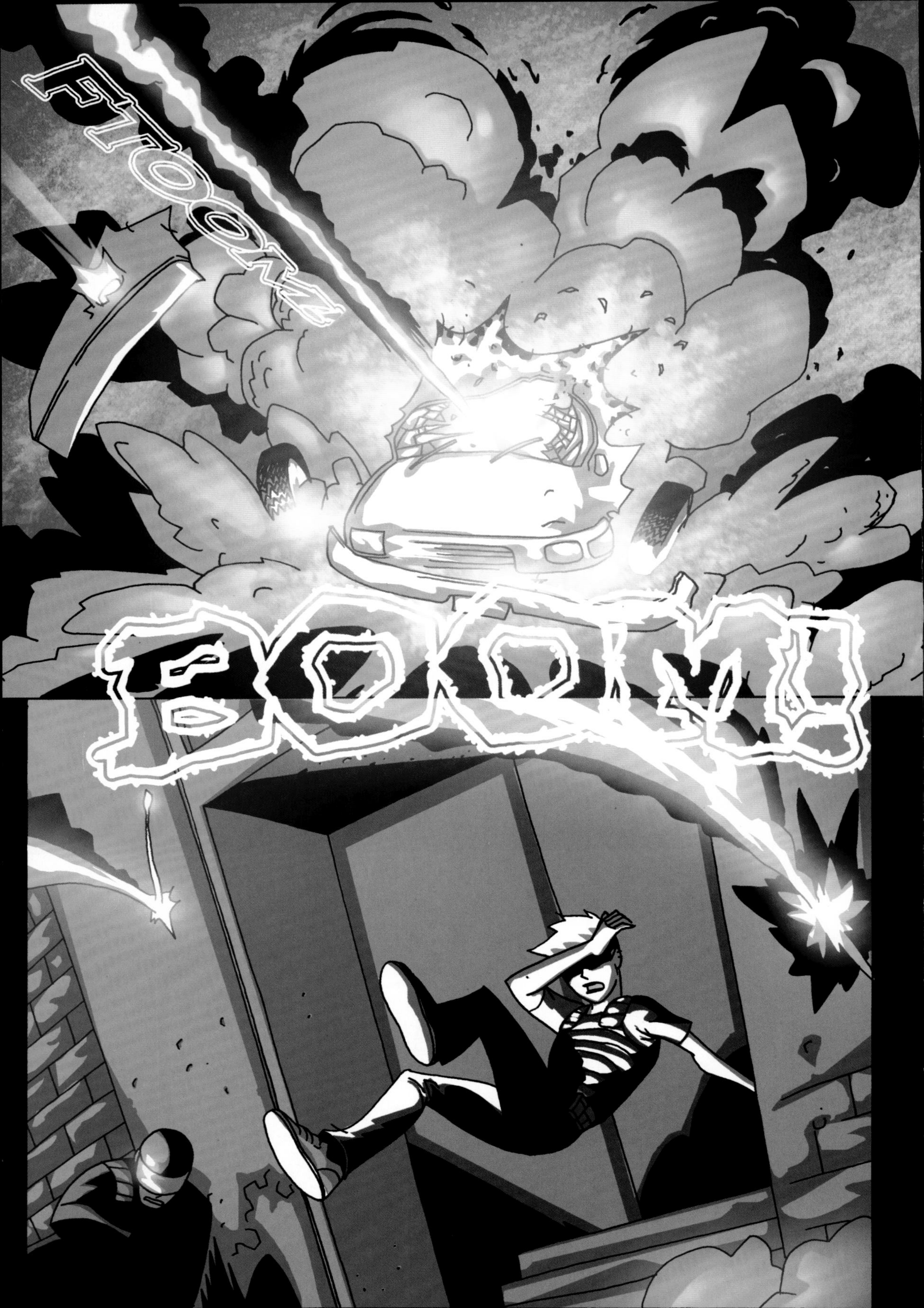
FTOOM
BOOM!

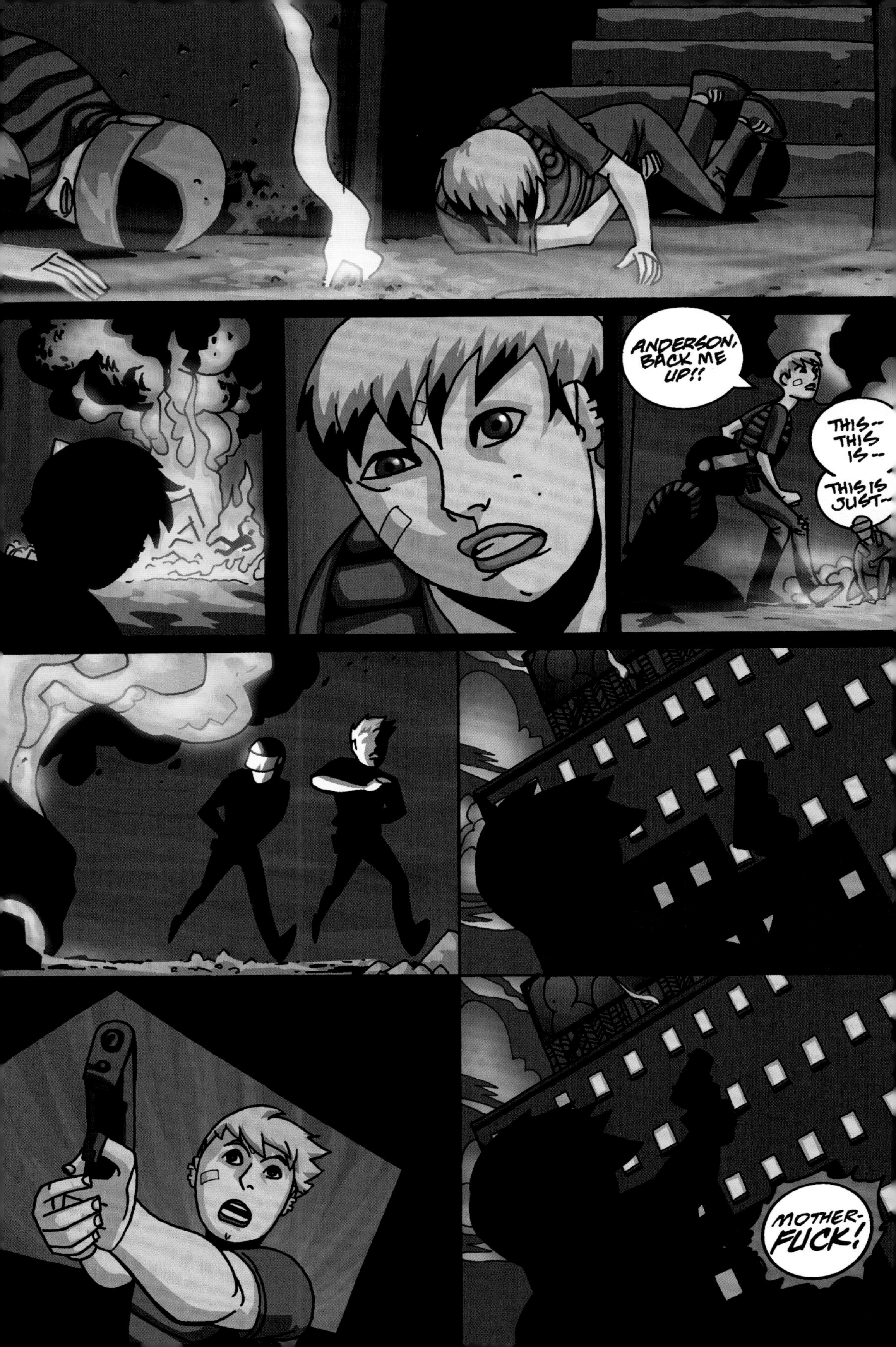
ANDERSON, BACK ME UP!!
THIS-- THIS IS--
THIS IS JUST--
MOTHER-FUCK!

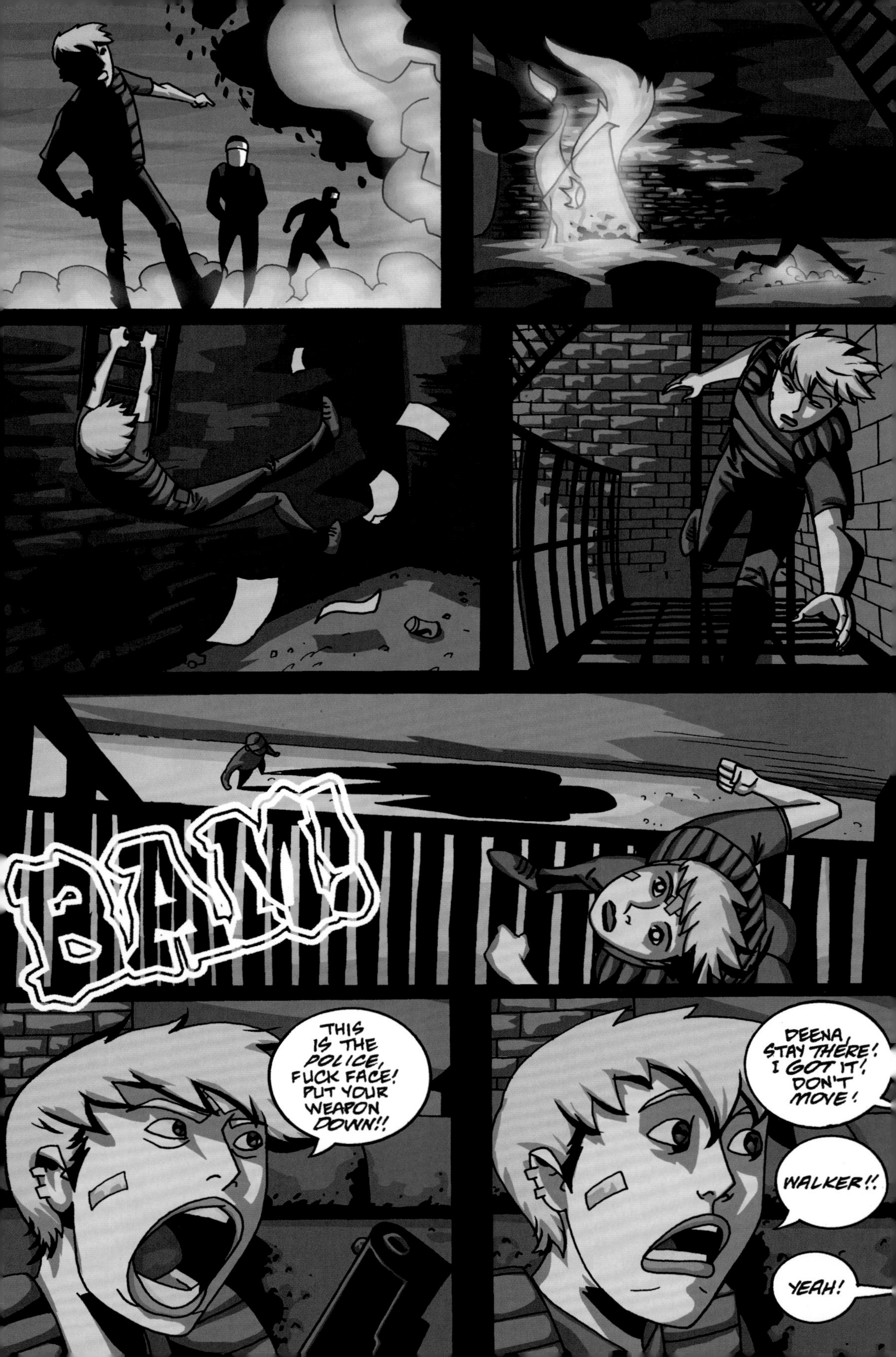
BAM!
THIS IS THE POLICE, FUCK FACE! PUT YOUR WEAPON DOWN!!
DEENA, STAY THERE! I GOT IT! DON'T MOVE!
WALKER!!
YEAH!

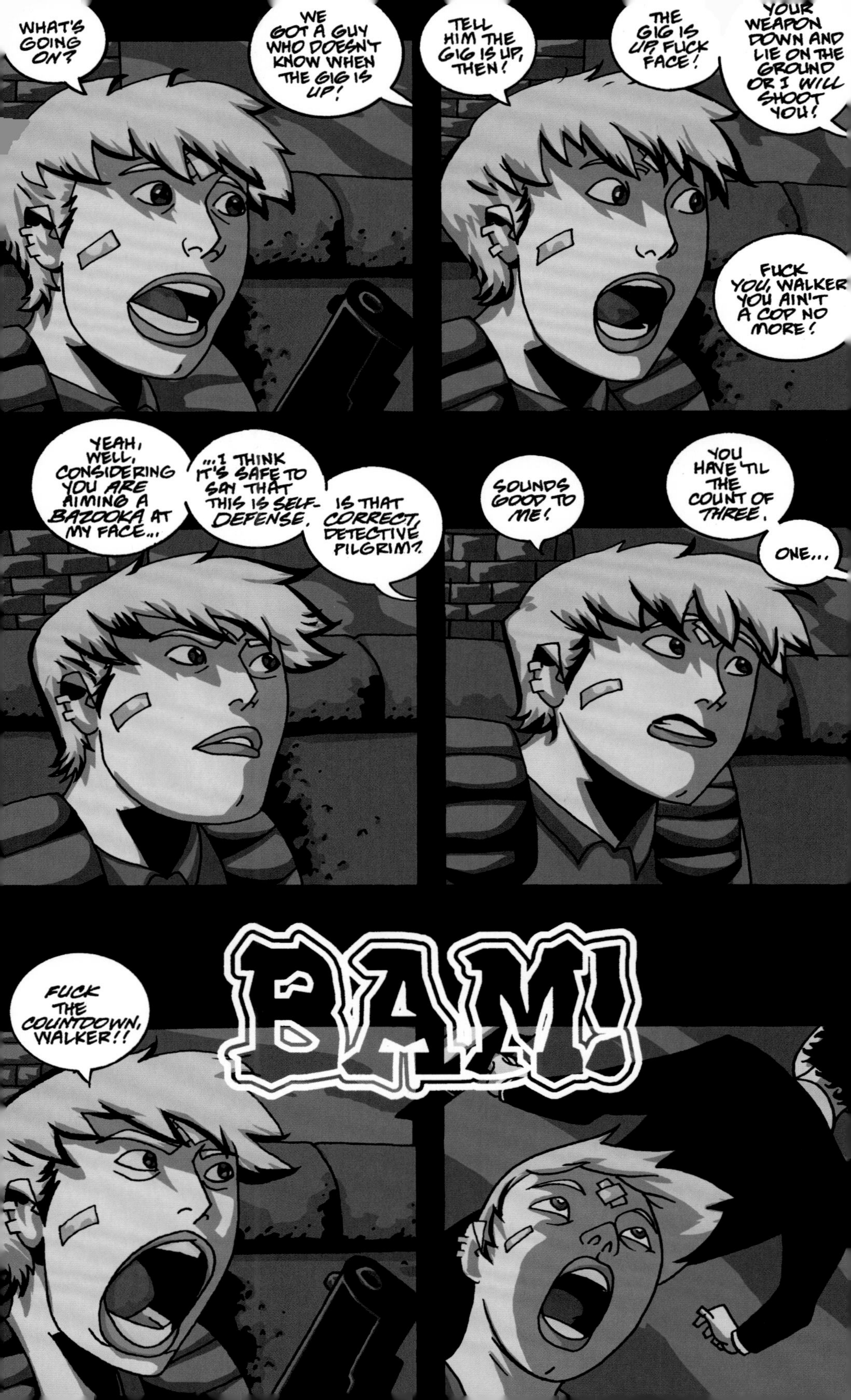
WHAT'S GOING ON?
WE GOT A GUY WHO DOESN'T KNOW WHEN THE GIG IS UP!
TELL HIM THE GIG IS UP, THEN!
THE GIG IS UP, FUCK FACE!
YOUR WEAPON DOWN AND LIE ON THE GROUND OR I WILL SHOOT YOU!
FUCK YOU, WALKER YOU AIN'T A COP NO MORE!
YEAH, WELL, CONSIDERING YOU ARE AIMING A BAZOOKA AT MY FACE...
...I THINK IT'S SAFE TO SAY THAT THIS IS SELF-DEFENSE.
IS THAT CORRECT, DETECTIVE PILGRIM?
SOUNDS GOOD TO ME!
YOU HAVE 'TIL THE COUNT OF THREE.
ONE...
FUCK THE COUNTDOWN, WALKER!!
BAM!

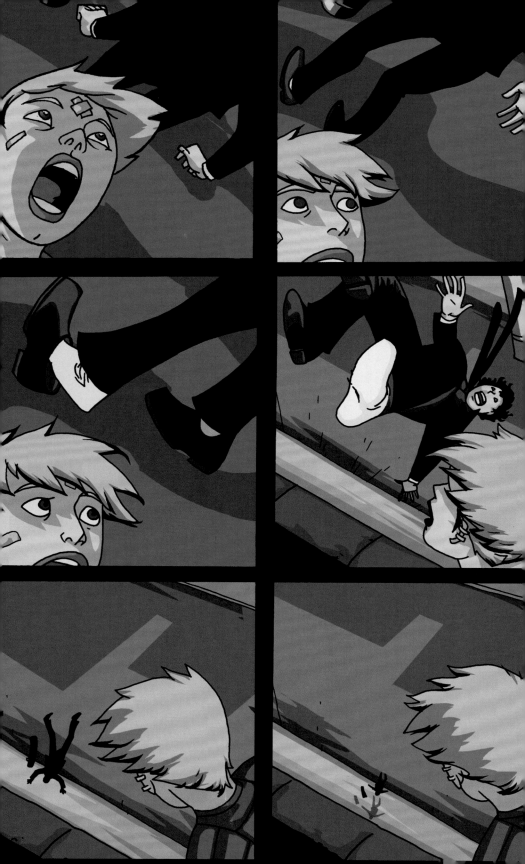

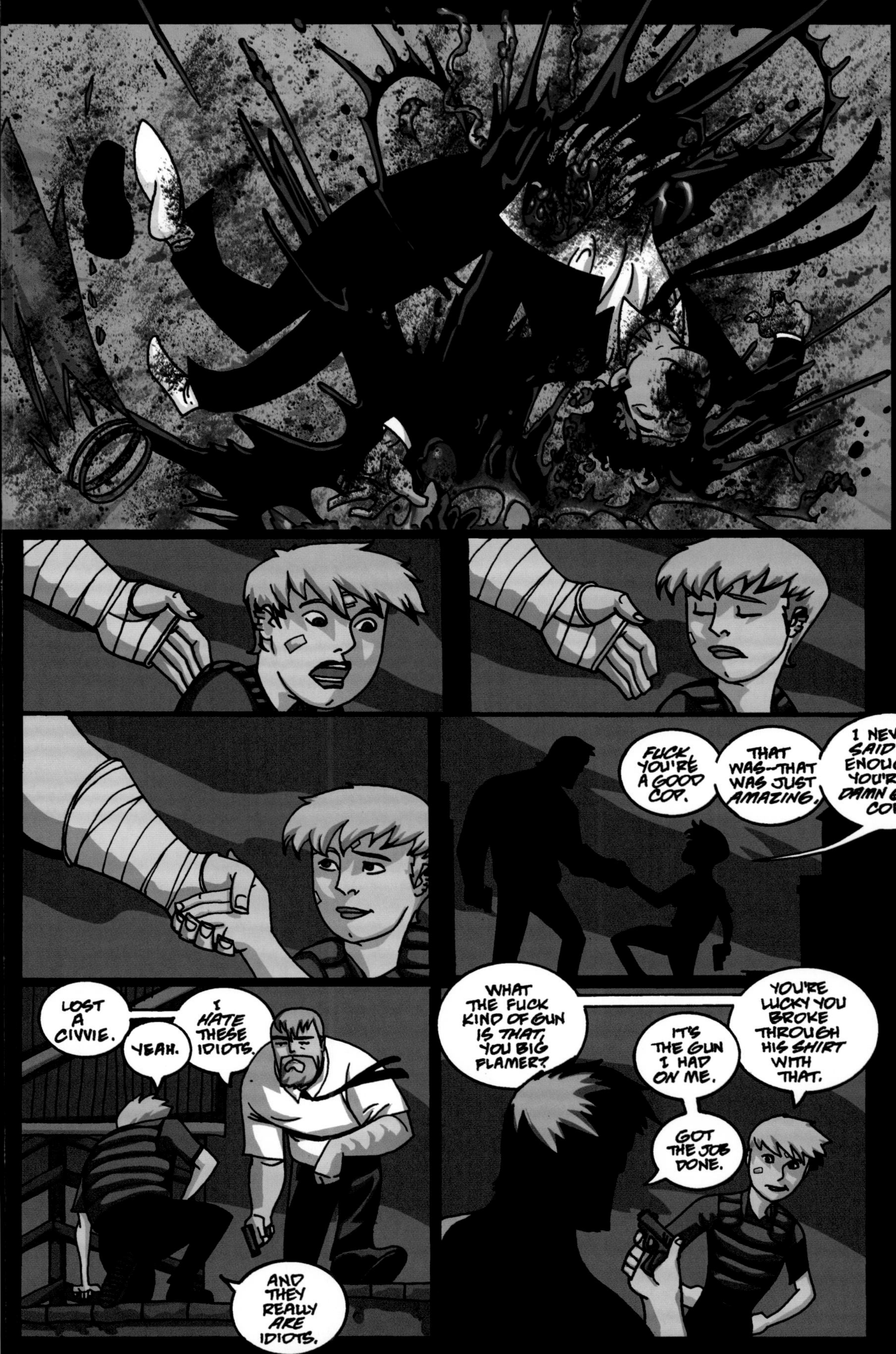
FUCK, YOU'RE A GOOD COP.
THAT WAS--THAT WAS JUST AMAZING.
I NEVER SAID IT ENOUGH-- YOU'RE A DAMN GOOD COP.
LOST A CIVVIE.
YEAH.
I HATE THESE IDIOTS.
AND THEY REALLY ARE IDIOTS.
WHAT THE FUCK KIND OF GUN IS THAT, YOU BIG FLAMER?
IT'S THE GUN I HAD ON ME.
GOT THE JOB DONE.
YOU'RE LUCKY YOU BROKE THROUGH HIS SHIRT WITH THAT.

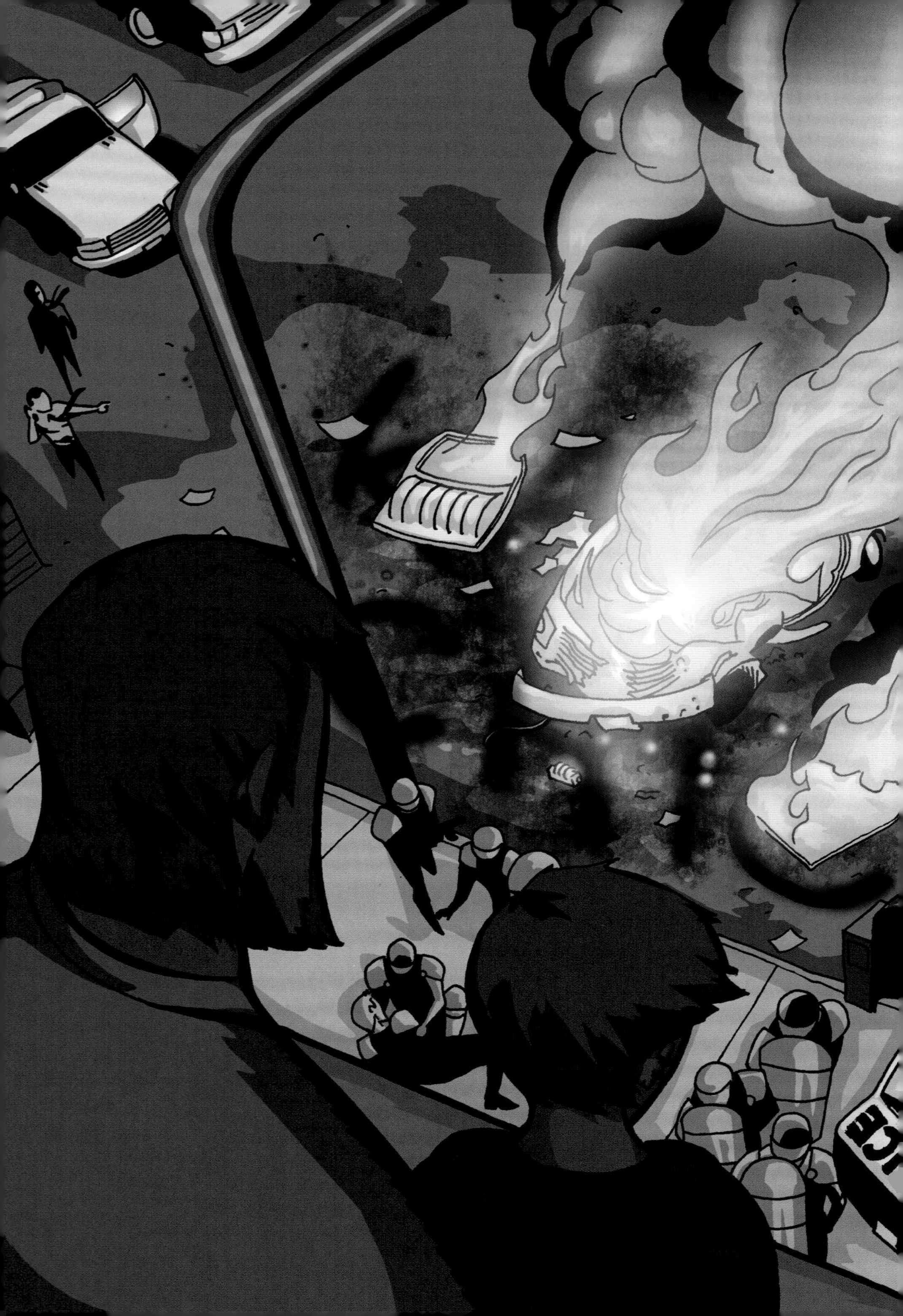

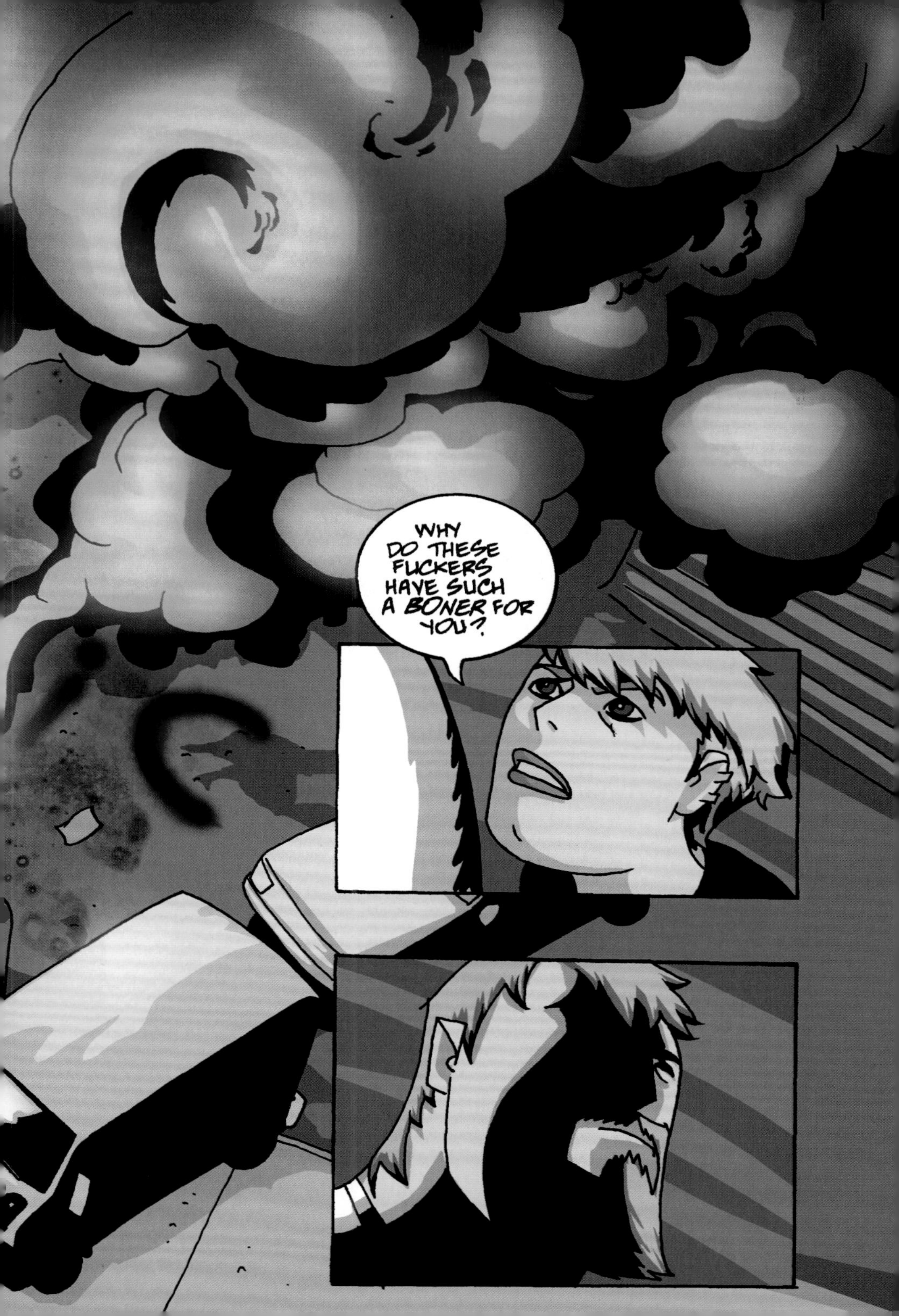
WHY DO THESE FUCKERS HAVE SUCH A *BONER* FOR YOU?

UPSIDE
by COLLETTE McDANIEL

COLLETTE McDANIEL
Author of "Who Killed Retro Girl?"

COLLETTE McDANIEL
Author of "Who Killed Retro Girl?"

...RDS SPRAY-PAINTED OVER ...CORPSE OF RETRO GIRL AS ...DREW HER FINAL BREATH THAT ...FUL DAY AT MORRISON ...EMENTARY SCHOOL.

HER KILLER, JON JACKSON STEVENS, TOOK THE MEANING OF THOSE CRYPTIC WORDS TO HIS GRAVE.

RETRO GIRL

JON JACKSON STEVENS

...EN THERE'S ...GOODMAN.

...ER THIS FOOTAGE WAS SHOT ...R AND HER PARTNERS IN ...E DESECRATING THE SITE ...OMEGA 6'S VIOLENT ...PUBLIC BURNING...

... A HALF DOZEN MURDERS WERE PINNED ON HARVEY AND HER GROUP, NOW KNOWN AS "THE KAOTIC CHIC MURDERS."

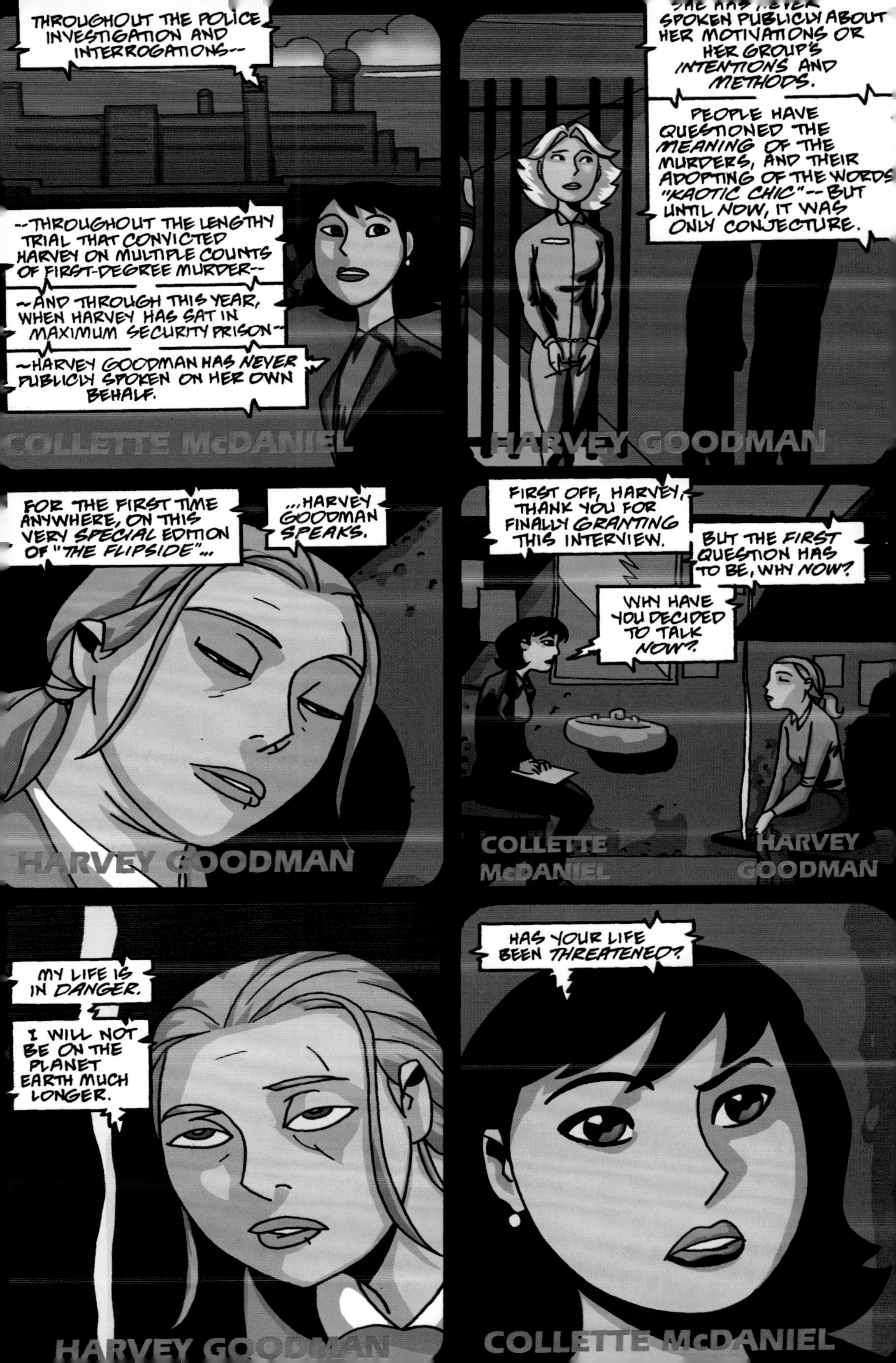

THROUGHOUT THE POLICE INVESTIGATION AND INTERROGATIONS--
--THROUGHOUT THE LENGTHY TRIAL THAT CONVICTED HARVEY ON MULTIPLE COUNTS OF FIRST-DEGREE MURDER--
--AND THROUGH THIS YEAR, WHEN HARVEY HAS SAT IN MAXIMUM SECURITY PRISON--
--HARVEY GOODMAN HAS NEVER PUBLICLY SPOKEN ON HER OWN BEHALF.
COLLETTE McDANIEL
SPOKEN PUBLICLY ABOUT HER MOTIVATIONS OR HER GROUP'S INTENTIONS AND METHODS.
PEOPLE HAVE QUESTIONED THE MEANING OF THE MURDERS, AND THEIR ADOPTING OF THE WORDS "KAOTIC CHIC"-- BUT UNTIL NOW, IT WAS ONLY CONJECTURE.
HARVEY GOODMAN
FOR THE FIRST TIME ANYWHERE, ON THIS VERY SPECIAL EDITION OF "THE FLIPSIDE"...
...HARVEY GOODMAN SPEAKS.
HARVEY GOODMAN
FIRST OFF, HARVEY, THANK YOU FOR FINALLY GRANTING THIS INTERVIEW.
BUT THE FIRST QUESTION HAS TO BE, WHY NOW?
WHY HAVE YOU DECIDED TO TALK NOW?
COLLETTE McDANIEL
HARVEY GOODMAN
MY LIFE IS IN DANGER.
I WILL NOT BE ON THE PLANET EARTH MUCH LONGER.
HARVEY GOODMAN
HAS YOUR LIFE BEEN THREATENED?
COLLETTE McDANIEL

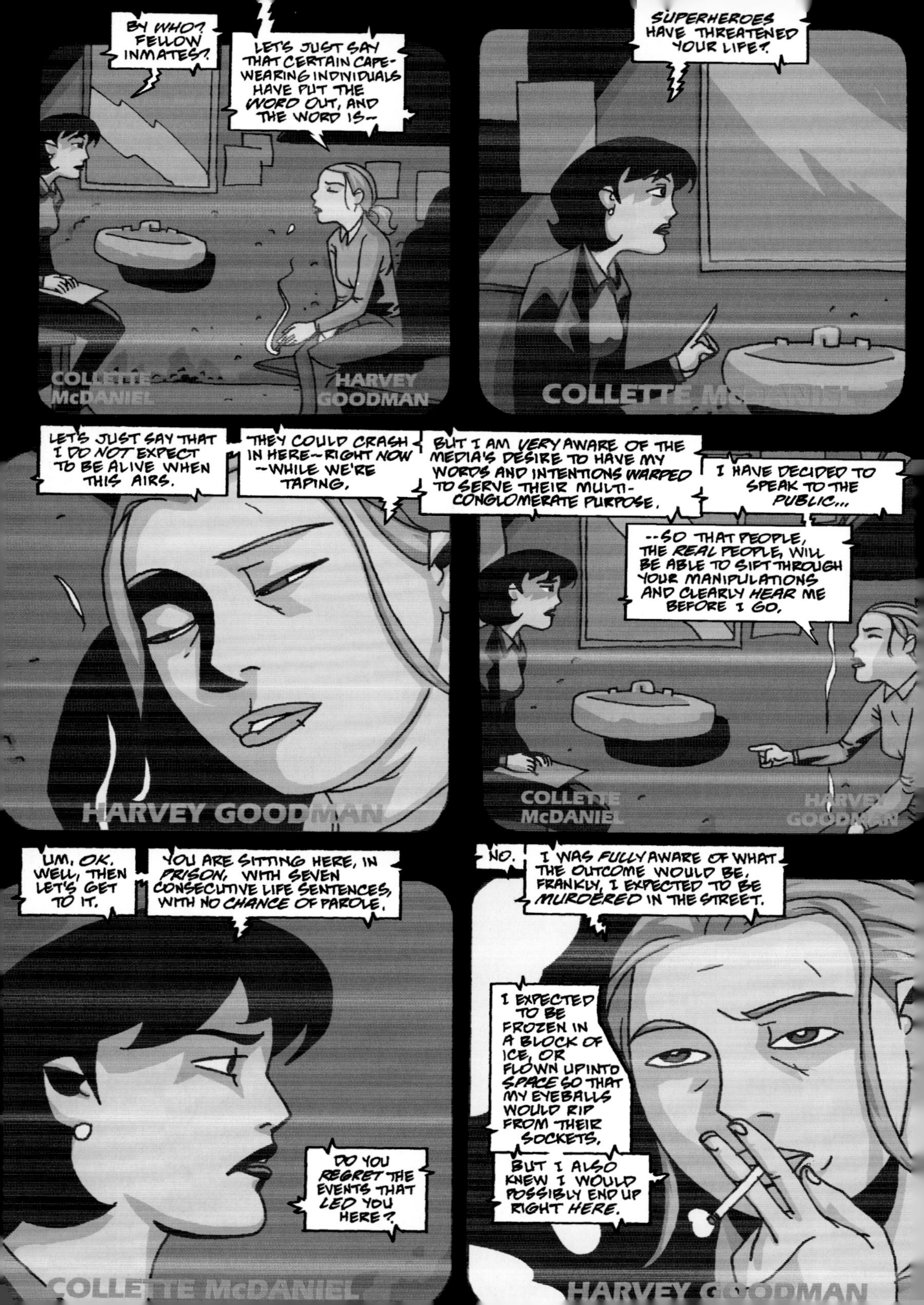
BY *WHO*? FELLOW INMATES?
LET'S JUST SAY THAT CERTAIN CAPE-WEARING INDIVIDUALS HAVE PUT THE *WORD* OUT, AND THE WORD IS--
COLLETTE McDANIEL
HARVEY GOODMAN
SUPERHEROES HAVE THREATENED YOUR LIFE?
COLLETTE McDANIEL
LET'S JUST SAY THAT I DO *NOT* EXPECT TO BE ALIVE WHEN THIS AIRS.
THEY COULD CRASH IN HERE--RIGHT *NOW* --WHILE WE'RE TAPING.
BUT I AM *VERY* AWARE OF THE MEDIA'S DESIRE TO HAVE MY WORDS AND INTENTIONS *WARPED* TO SERVE THEIR MULTI-CONGLOMERATE PURPOSE.
HARVEY GOODMAN
I HAVE DECIDED TO SPEAK TO THE *PUBLIC*...
--SO THAT PEOPLE, THE *REAL* PEOPLE, WILL BE ABLE TO SIFT THROUGH YOUR MANIPULATIONS AND CLEARLY *HEAR* ME BEFORE I GO.
COLLETTE McDANIEL
HARVEY GOODMAN
UM, *OK*. WELL, THEN LET'S GET TO IT.
YOU ARE SITTING HERE, IN *PRISON*, WITH SEVEN CONSECUTIVE LIFE SENTENCES, WITH NO *CHANCE* OF PAROLE.
DO YOU *REGRET* THE EVENTS THAT *LED* YOU HERE?
COLLETTE McDANIEL
NO.
I WAS *FULLY* AWARE OF WHAT THE OUTCOME WOULD BE. FRANKLY, I EXPECTED TO BE *MURDERED* IN THE STREET.
I EXPECTED TO BE FROZEN IN A BLOCK OF ICE, OR FLOWN UP INTO *SPACE* SO THAT MY EYEBALLS WOULD RIP FROM THEIR SOCKETS.
BUT I ALSO KNEW I WOULD POSSIBLY END UP RIGHT *HERE*.
HARVEY GOODMAN

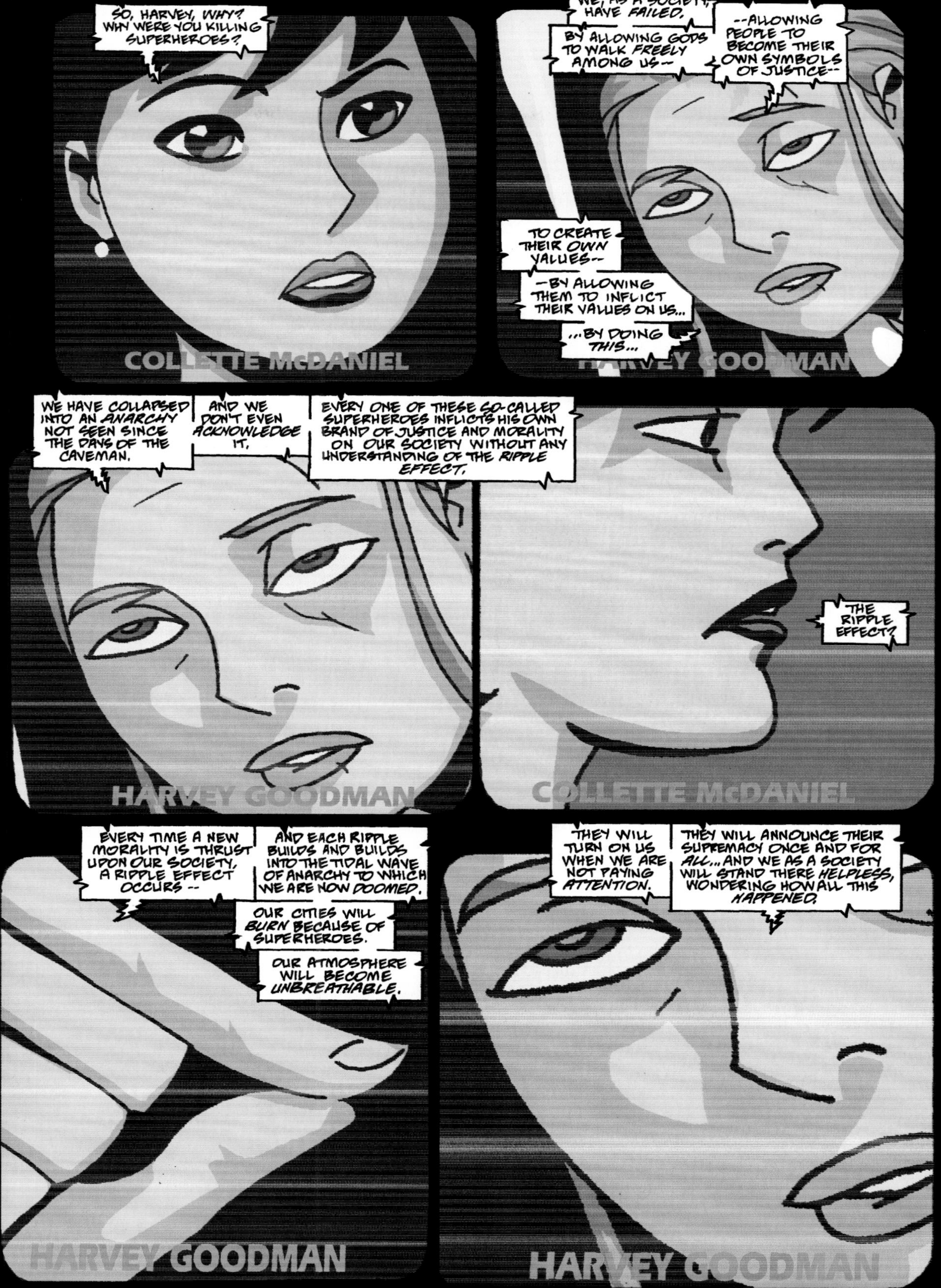

SO, HARVEY, WHY? WHY WERE YOU KILLING SUPERHEROES?
COLLETTE McDANIEL
WE, AS A SOCIETY, HAVE FAILED,
BY ALLOWING GODS TO WALK FREELY AMONG US--
--ALLOWING PEOPLE TO BECOME THEIR OWN SYMBOLS OF JUSTICE--
TO CREATE THEIR OWN VALUES--
--BY ALLOWING THEM TO INFLICT THEIR VALUES ON US...
...BY DOING THIS...
HARVEY GOODMAN
WE HAVE COLLAPSED INTO AN ANARCHY NOT SEEN SINCE THE DAYS OF THE CAVEMAN.
AND WE DON'T EVEN ACKNOWLEDGE IT,
EVERY ONE OF THESE SO-CALLED SUPERHEROES INFLICTS HIS OWN BRAND OF JUSTICE AND MORALITY ON OUR SOCIETY WITHOUT ANY UNDERSTANDING OF THE RIPPLE EFFECT.
HARVEY GOODMAN
THE RIPPLE EFFECT?
COLLETTE McDANIEL
EVERY TIME A NEW MORALITY IS THRUST UPON OUR SOCIETY, A RIPPLE EFFECT OCCURS --
AND EACH RIPPLE BUILDS AND BUILDS INTO THE TIDAL WAVE OF ANARCHY TO WHICH WE ARE NOW DOOMED.
OUR CITIES WILL BURN BECAUSE OF SUPERHEROES.
OUR ATMOSPHERE WILL BECOME UNBREATHABLE.
HARVEY GOODMAN
THEY WILL TURN ON US WHEN WE ARE NOT PAYING ATTENTION.
THEY WILL ANNOUNCE THEIR SUPREMACY ONCE AND FOR ALL... AND WE AS A SOCIETY WILL STAND THERE HELPLESS, WONDERING HOW ALL THIS HAPPENED.
HARVEY GOODMAN

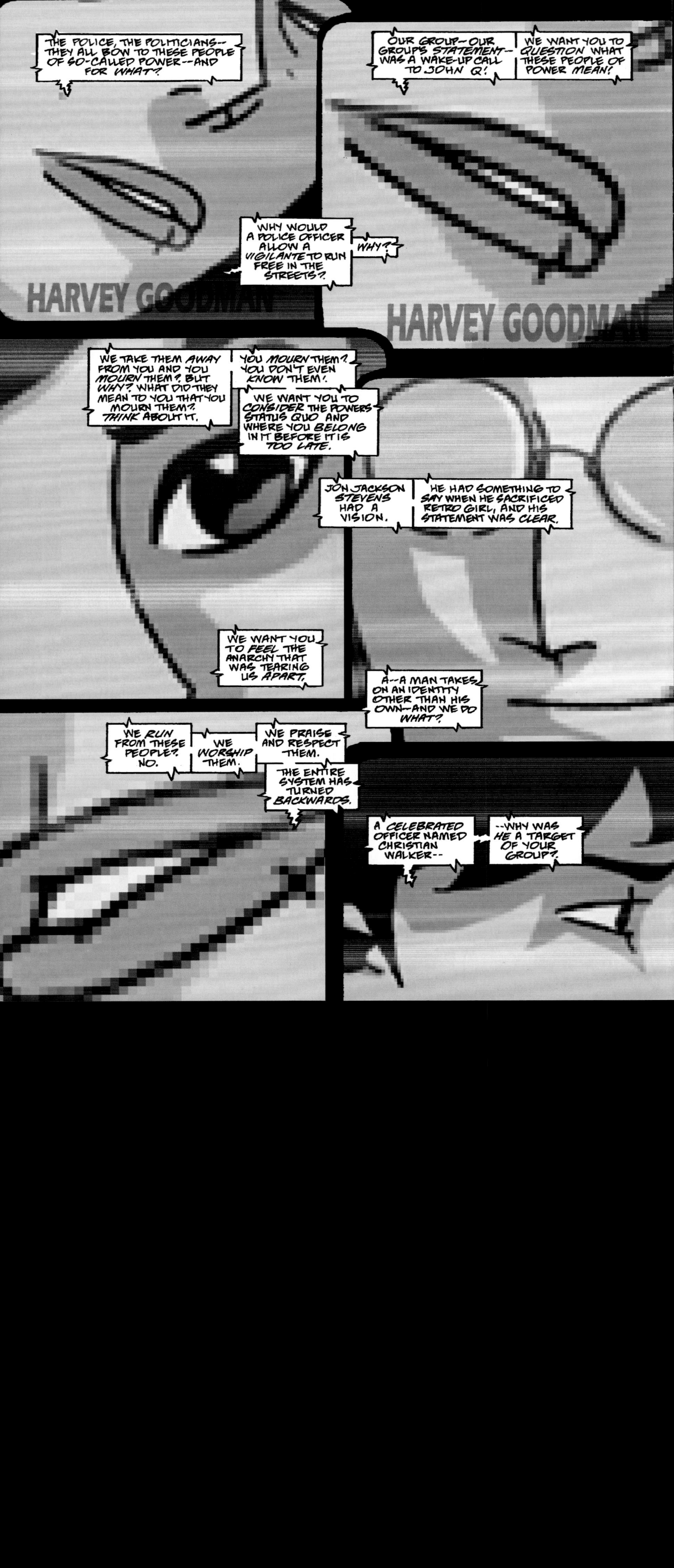
THE POLICE, THE POLITICIANS-- THEY ALL BOW TO THESE PEOPLE OF SO-CALLED POWER--AND FOR WHAT?
OUR GROUP--OUR GROUP'S STATEMENT--WAS A WAKE-UP CALL TO JOHN Q!
WE WANT YOU TO QUESTION WHAT THESE PEOPLE OF POWER MEAN!
WHY WOULD A POLICE OFFICER ALLOW A VIGILANTE TO RUN FREE IN THE STREETS?
WHY?
HARVEY GOODMAN
HARVEY GOODMAN
WE TAKE THEM AWAY FROM YOU AND YOU MOURN THEM? BUT WHY? WHAT DID THEY MEAN TO YOU THAT YOU MOURN THEM? THINK ABOUT IT.
YOU MOURN THEM? YOU DON'T EVEN KNOW THEM!
WE WANT YOU TO CONSIDER THE POWERS STATUS QUO AND WHERE YOU BELONG IN IT BEFORE IT IS TOO LATE.
JON JACKSON STEVENS HAD A VISION.
HE HAD SOMETHING TO SAY WHEN HE SACRIFICED RETRO GIRL, AND HIS STATEMENT WAS CLEAR.
WE WANT YOU TO FEEL THE ANARCHY THAT WAS TEARING US APART.
A--A MAN TAKES ON AN IDENTITY OTHER THAN HIS OWN--AND WE DO WHAT?
WE RUN FROM THESE PEOPLE? NO.
WE WORSHIP THEM.
WE PRAISE AND RESPECT THEM.
THE ENTIRE SYSTEM HAS TURNED BACKWARDS.
A CELEBRATED OFFICER NAMED CHRISTIAN WALKER--
--WHY WAS HE A TARGET OF YOUR GROUP?

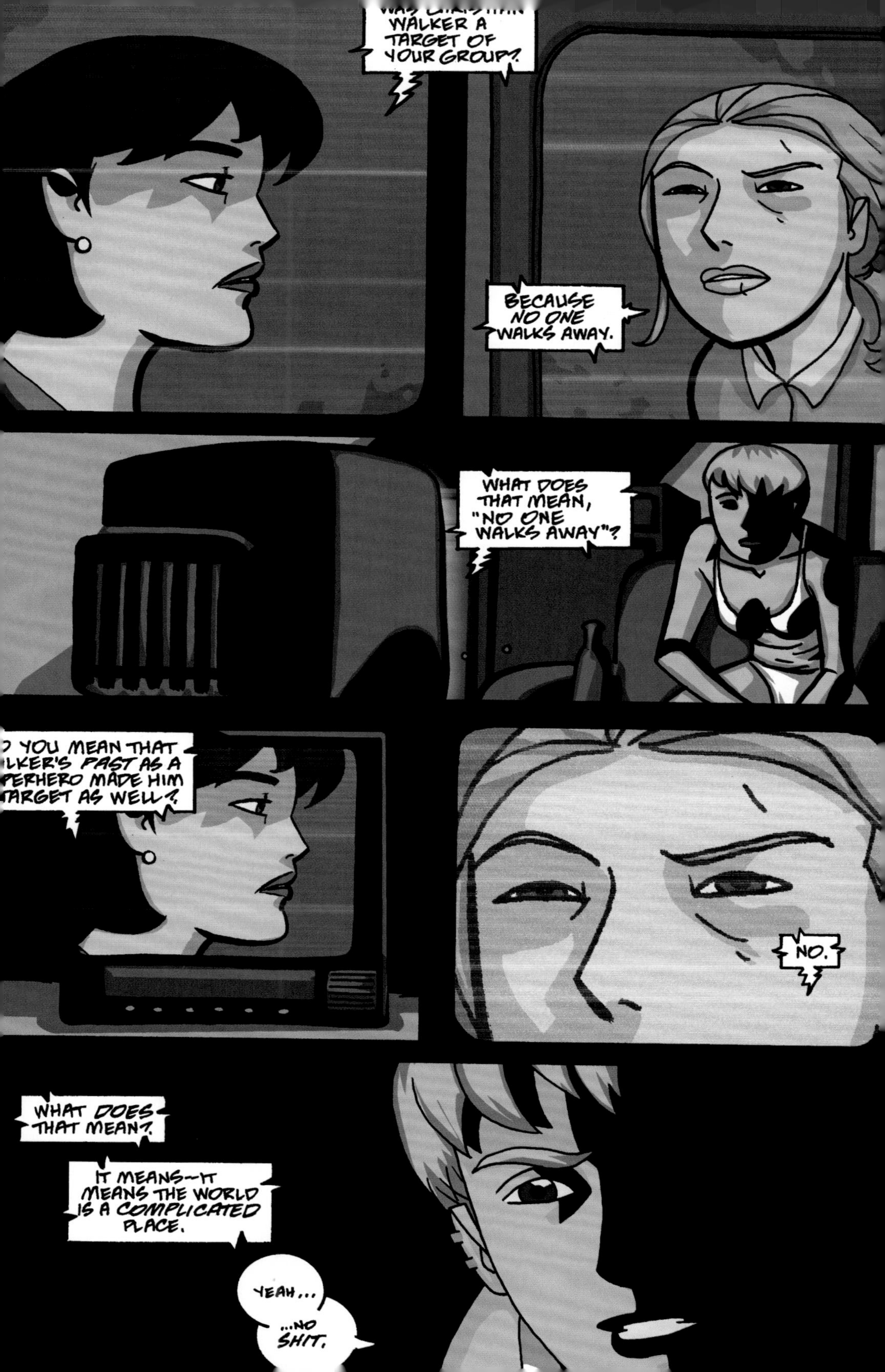
WALKER A TARGET OF YOUR GROUP?
BECAUSE NO ONE WALKS AWAY.
WHAT DOES THAT MEAN, "NO ONE WALKS AWAY"?
YOU MEAN THAT
LKER'S PAST AS A
PERHERO MADE HIM
TARGET AS WELL?
NO.
WHAT DOES THAT MEAN?
IT MEANS--IT MEANS THE WORLD IS A COMPLICATED PLACE.
YEAH...
...NO SHIT.

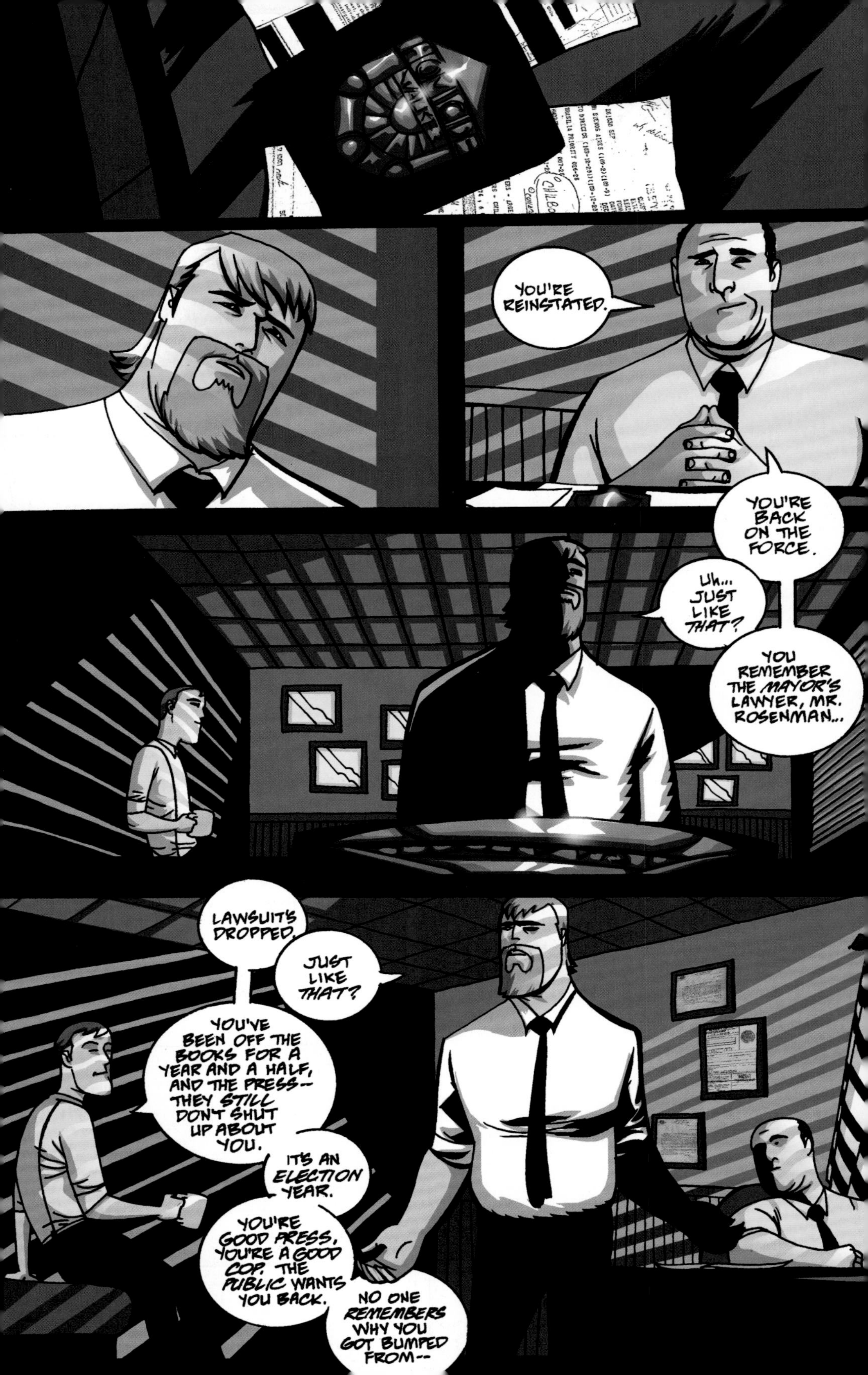
YOU'RE REINSTATED.
YOU'RE BACK ON THE FORCE.
Uh... JUST LIKE THAT?
YOU REMEMBER THE MAYOR'S LAWYER, MR. ROSENMAN...
LAWSUIT'S DROPPED.
JUST LIKE THAT?
YOU'VE BEEN OFF THE BOOKS FOR A YEAR AND A HALF, AND THE PRESS-- THEY STILL DON'T SHUT UP ABOUT YOU.
IT'S AN ELECTION YEAR.
YOU'RE GOOD PRESS, YOU'RE A GOOD COP. THE PUBLIC WANTS YOU BACK.
NO ONE REMEMBERS WHY YOU GOT BUMPED FROM--

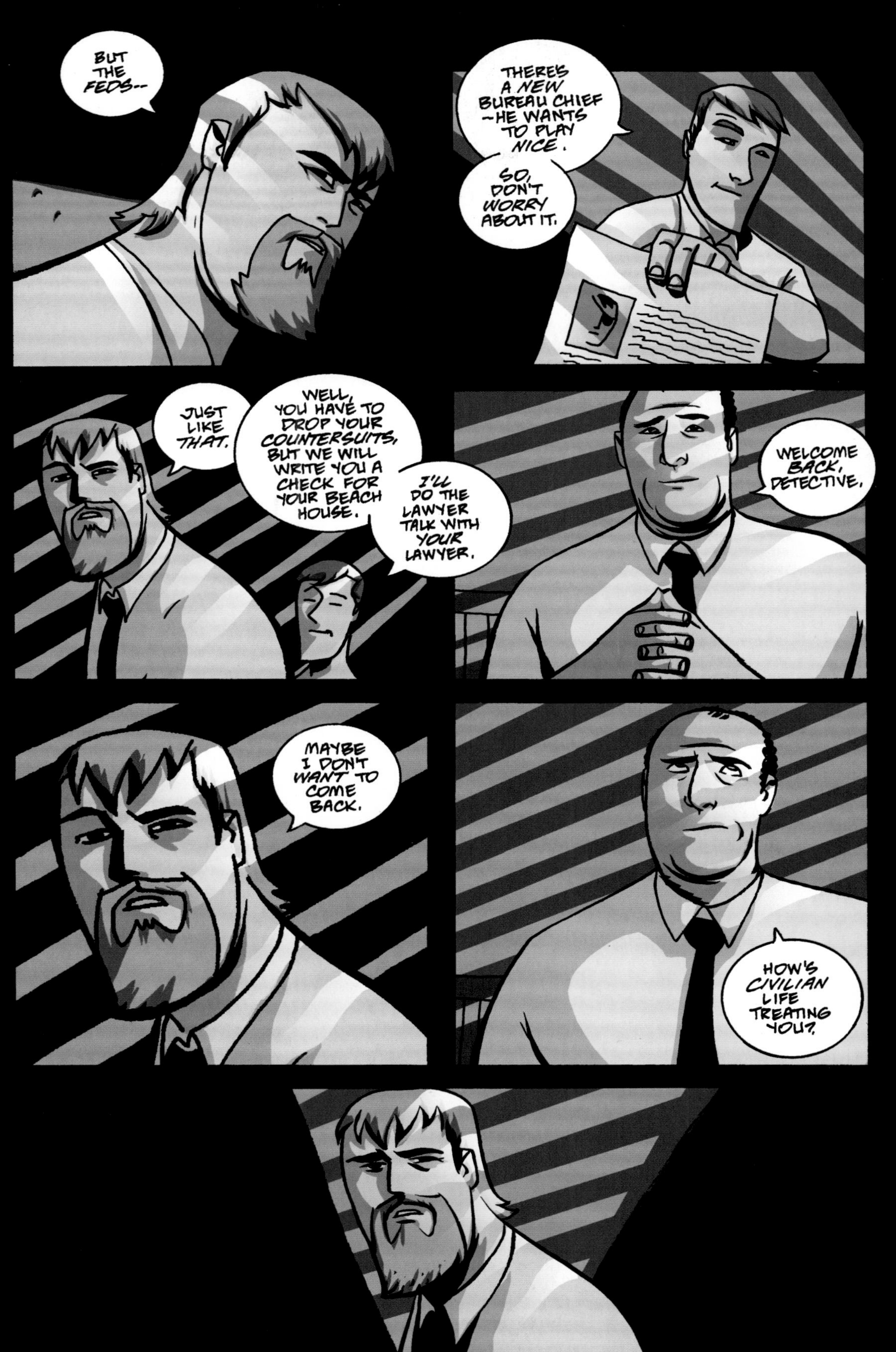
BUT THE FEDS--
THERE'S A NEW BUREAU CHIEF --HE WANTS TO PLAY NICE.
SO, DON'T WORRY ABOUT IT.
JUST LIKE THAT.
WELL, YOU HAVE TO DROP YOUR COUNTERSUITS, BUT WE WILL WRITE YOU A CHECK FOR YOUR BEACH HOUSE.
I'LL DO THE LAWYER TALK WITH YOUR LAWYER.
WELCOME BACK, DETECTIVE.
MAYBE I DON'T WANT TO COME BACK.
HOW'S CIVILIAN LIFE TREATING YOU?

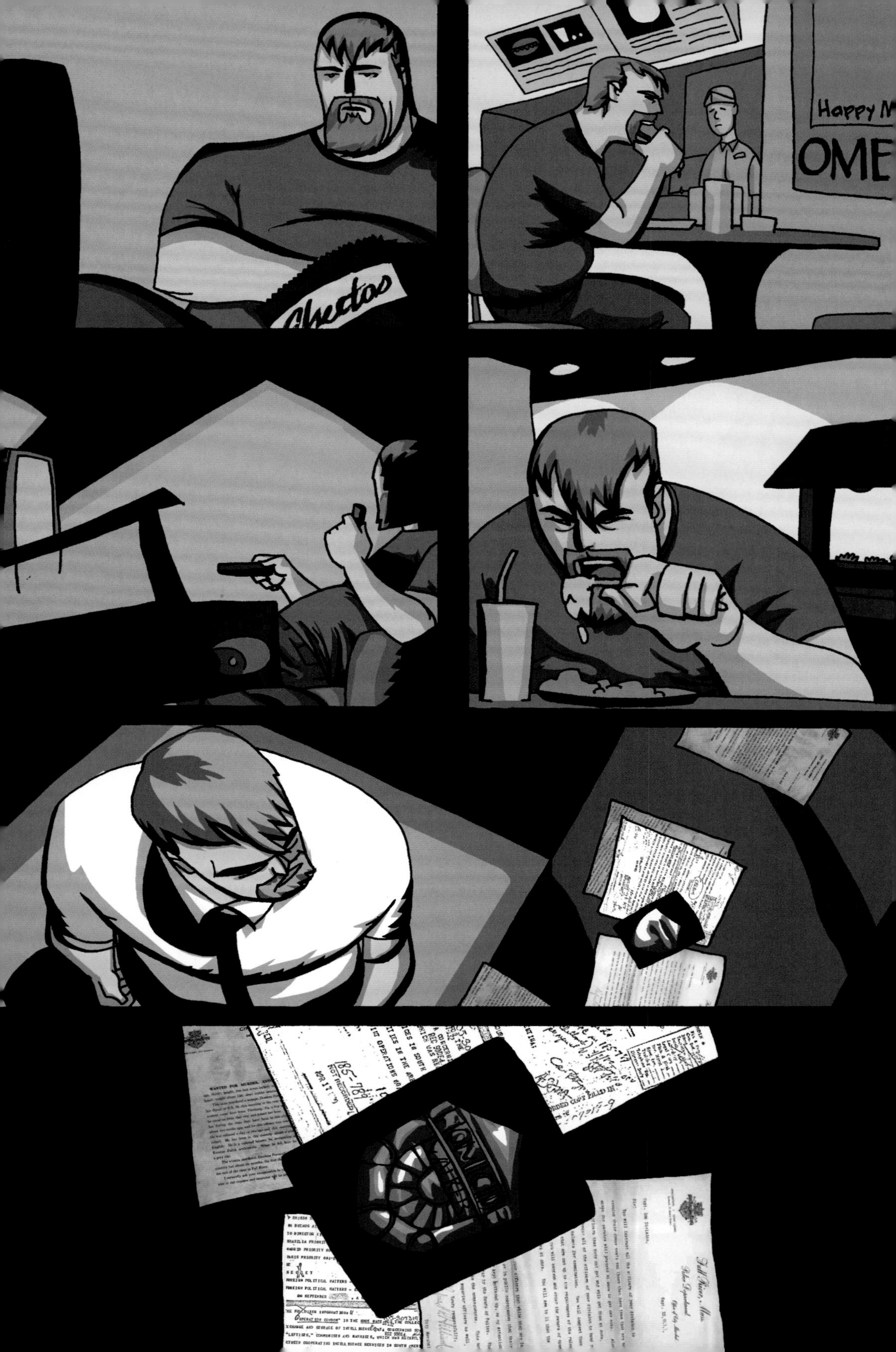

Happy M
OME
WANTED FOR MURDER
SECRET
FOREIGN POLITICAL MATTERS
OPERATION CONDOR

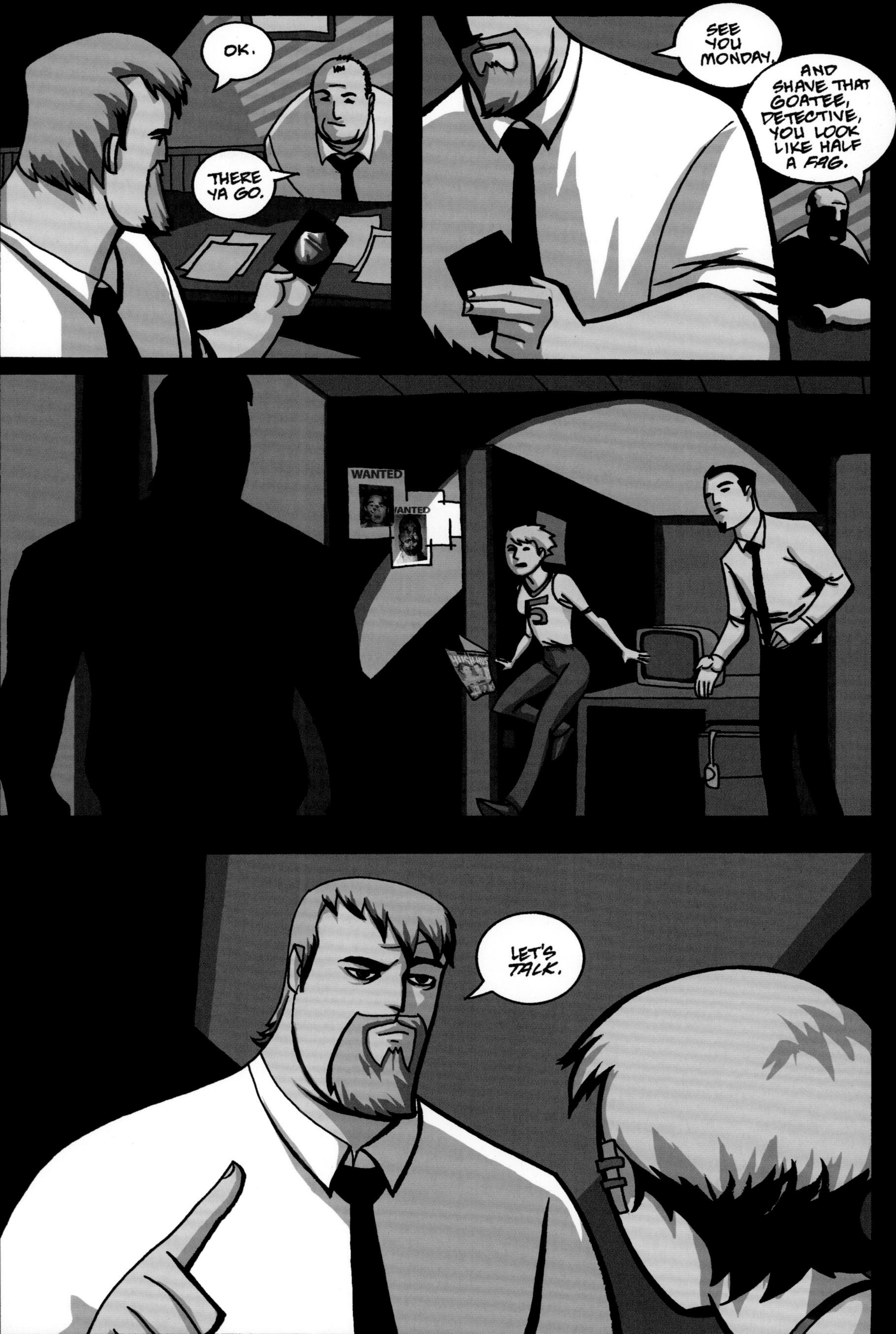
OK.
THERE YA GO.
SEE YOU MONDAY.
AND SHAVE THAT GOATEE, DETECTIVE, YOU LOOK LIKE HALF A FAG.
WANTED
WANTED
LET'S TALK.

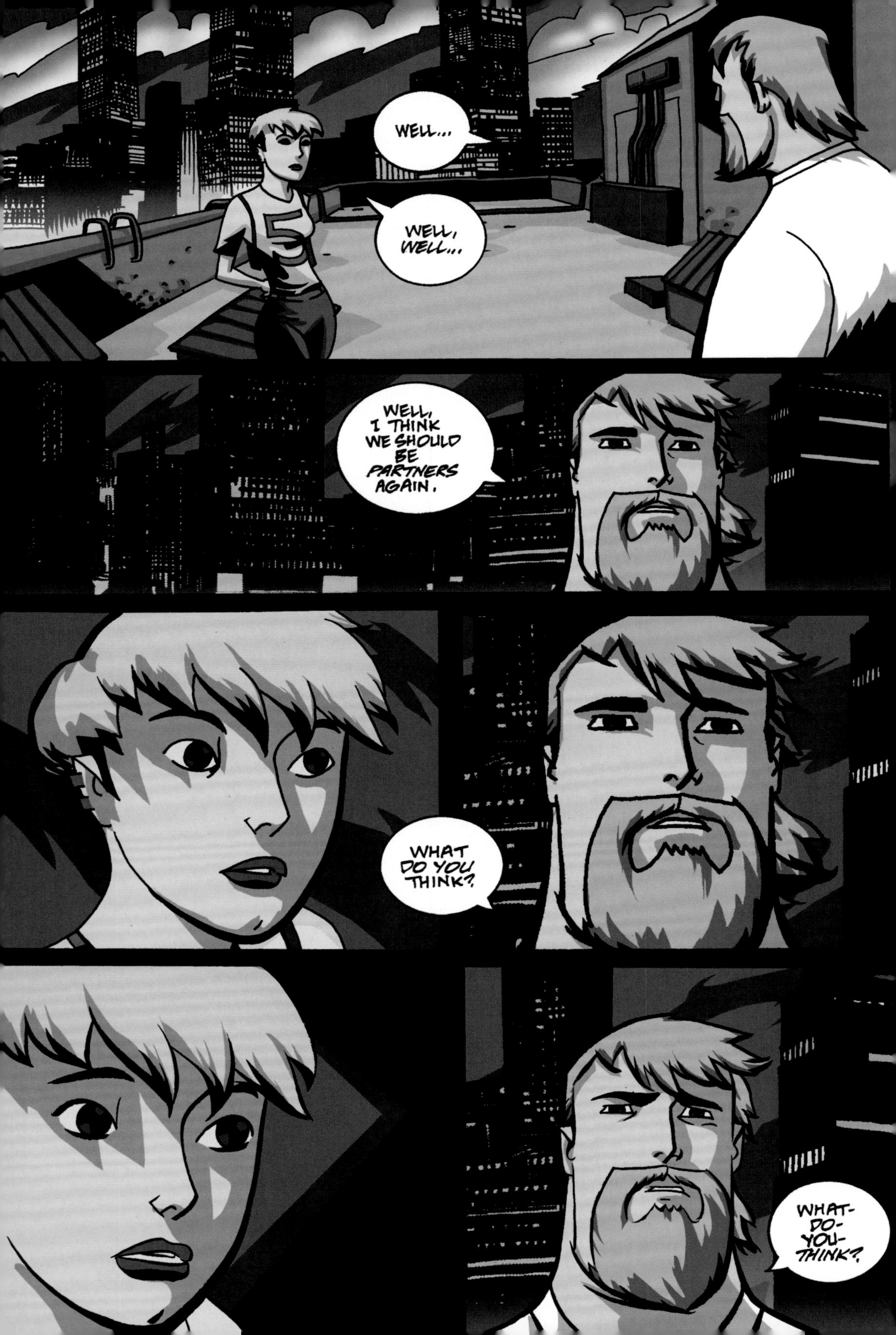
WELL...
WELL, WELL...
WELL, I THINK WE SHOULD BE PARTNERS AGAIN.
WHAT DO YOU THINK?
WHAT-DO-YOU-THINK?

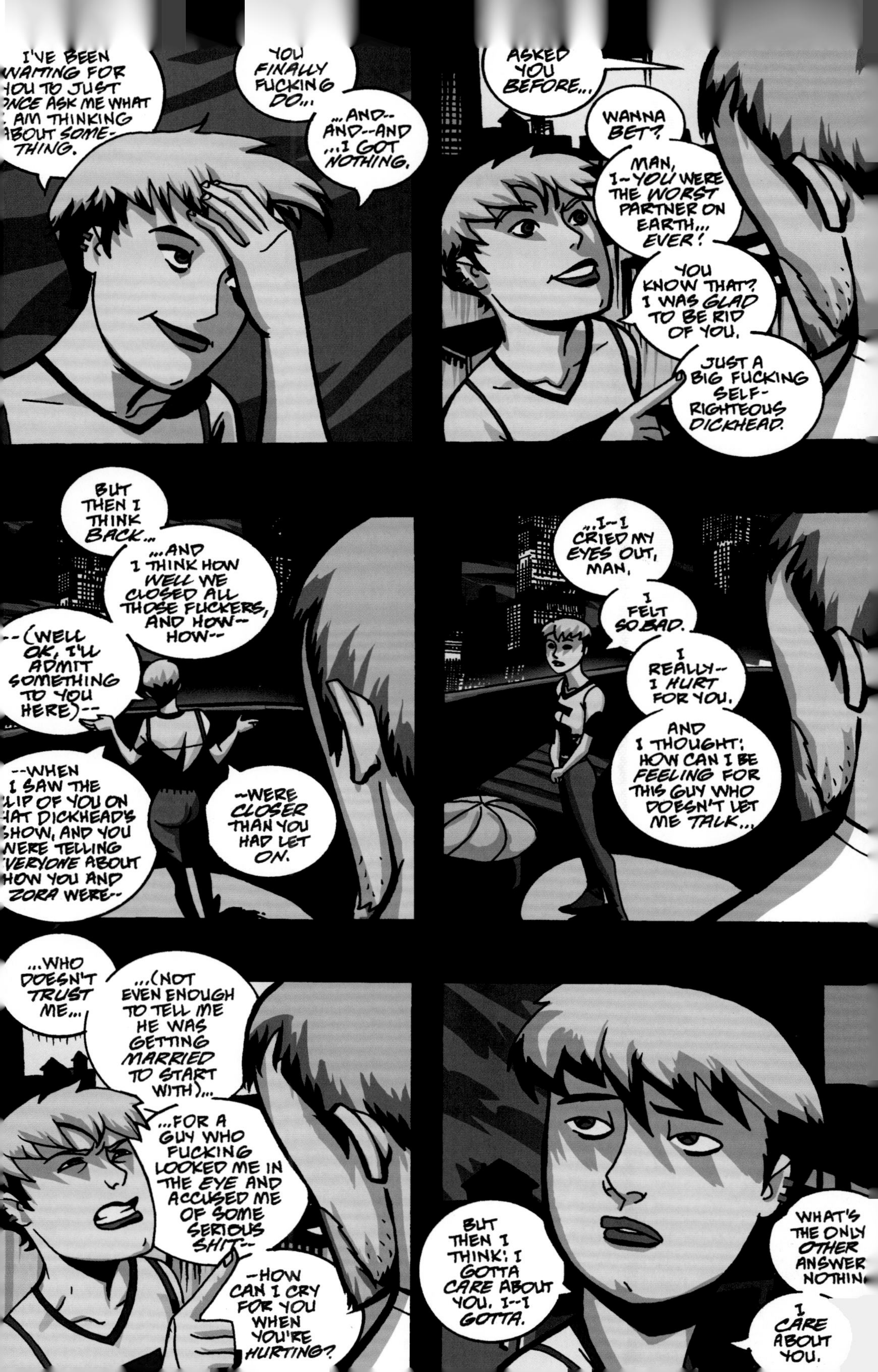

I'VE BEEN WAITING FOR YOU TO JUST ONCE ASK ME WHAT I AM THINKING ABOUT SOMETHING.
YOU FINALLY FUCKING DO...
...AND--AND--AND ...I GOT NOTHING.
ASKED YOU BEFORE...
WANNA BET?
MAN, I--YOU WERE THE WORST PARTNER ON EARTH... EVER!
YOU KNOW THAT? I WAS GLAD TO BE RID OF YOU.
JUST A BIG FUCKING SELF-RIGHTEOUS DICKHEAD.
BUT THEN I THINK BACK...
...AND I THINK HOW WELL WE CLOSED ALL THOSE FUCKERS, AND HOW--HOW--
--(WELL OK, I'LL ADMIT SOMETHING TO YOU HERE)--
--WHEN I SAW THE CLIP OF YOU ON THAT DICKHEAD'S SHOW, AND YOU WERE TELLING EVERYONE ABOUT HOW YOU AND ZORA WERE--
--WERE CLOSER THAN YOU HAD LET ON.
...I--I CRIED MY EYES OUT, MAN.
I FELT SO BAD.
I REALLY--I HURT FOR YOU.
AND I THOUGHT: HOW CAN I BE FEELING FOR THIS GUY WHO DOESN'T LET ME TALK...
...WHO DOESN'T TRUST ME...
...(NOT EVEN ENOUGH TO TELL ME HE WAS GETTING MARRIED TO START WITH)...
...FOR A GUY WHO FUCKING LOOKED ME IN THE EYE AND ACCUSED ME OF SOME SERIOUS SHIT--
--HOW CAN I CRY FOR YOU WHEN YOU'RE HURTING?
BUT THEN I THINK: I GOTTA CARE ABOUT YOU. I--I GOTTA.
WHAT'S THE ONLY OTHER ANSWER NOTHIN
I CARE ABOUT YOU.

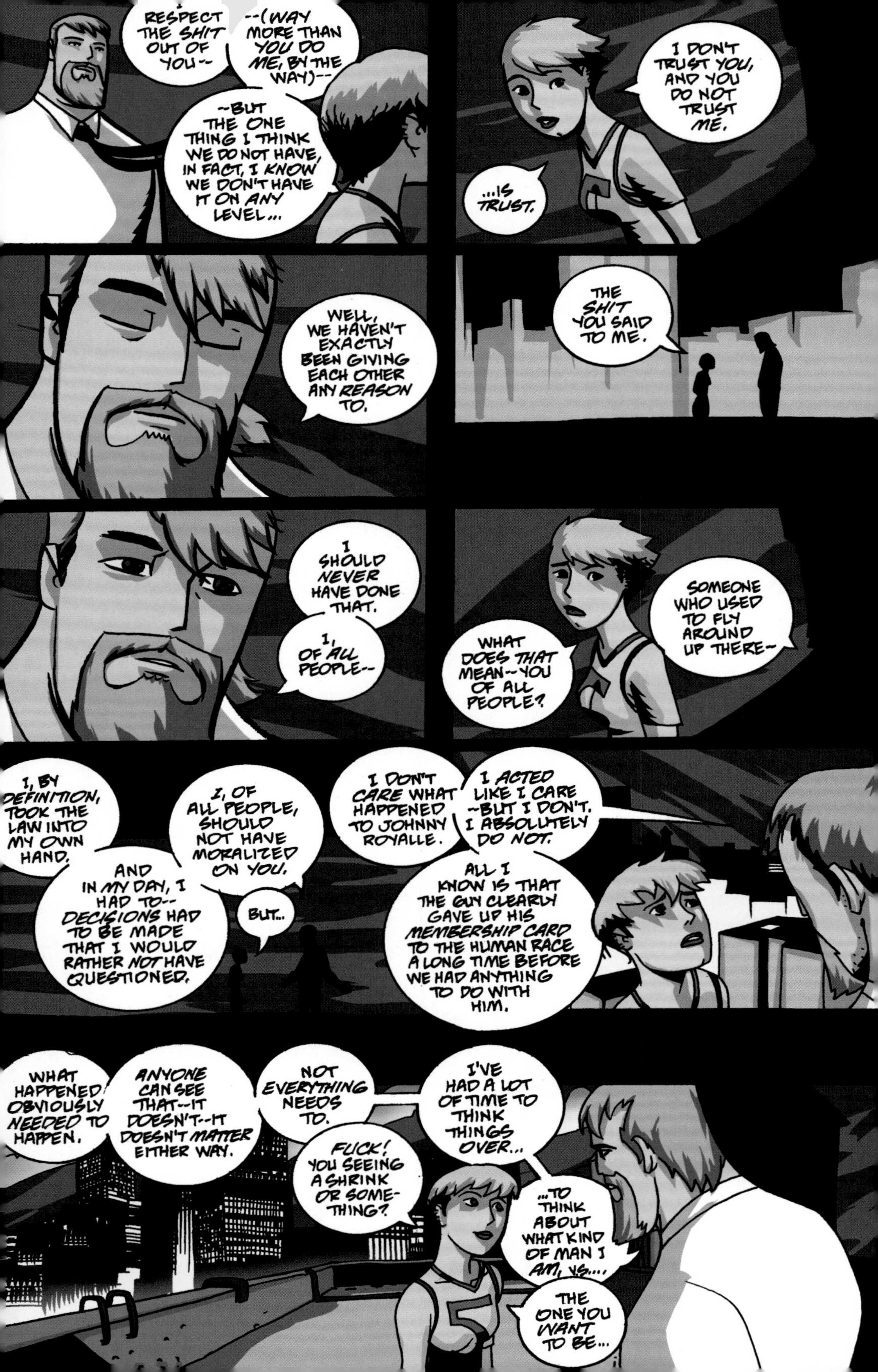
RESPECT THE SHIT OUT OF YOU--
--(WAY MORE THAN YOU DO ME, BY THE WAY)--
--BUT THE ONE THING I THINK WE DO NOT HAVE, IN FACT, I KNOW WE DON'T HAVE IT ON ANY LEVEL...
...IS TRUST.
I DON'T TRUST YOU, AND YOU DO NOT TRUST ME.
WELL, WE HAVEN'T EXACTLY BEEN GIVING EACH OTHER ANY REASON TO.
THE SHIT YOU SAID TO ME.
I SHOULD NEVER HAVE DONE THAT.
I, OF ALL PEOPLE--
WHAT DOES THAT MEAN--YOU OF ALL PEOPLE?
SOMEONE WHO USED TO FLY AROUND UP THERE--
I, BY DEFINITION, TOOK THE LAW INTO MY OWN HAND.
AND IN MY DAY, I HAD TO-- DECISIONS HAD TO BE MADE THAT I WOULD RATHER NOT HAVE QUESTIONED.
I, OF ALL PEOPLE, SHOULD NOT HAVE MORALIZED ON YOU.
BUT...
I DON'T CARE WHAT HAPPENED TO JOHNNY ROYALLE.
I ACTED LIKE I CARE --BUT I DON'T. I ABSOLULTELY DO NOT.
ALL I KNOW IS THAT THE GUY CLEARLY GAVE UP HIS MEMBERSHIP CARD TO THE HUMAN RACE A LONG TIME BEFORE WE HAD ANYTHING TO DO WITH HIM.
WHAT HAPPENED OBVIOUSLY NEEDED TO HAPPEN.
ANYONE CAN SEE THAT--IT DOESN'T--IT DOESN'T MATTER EITHER WAY.
NOT EVERYTHING NEEDS TO.
I'VE HAD A LOT OF TIME TO THINK THINGS OVER...
FUCK! YOU SEEING A SHRINK OR SOME-THING?
...TO THINK ABOUT WHAT KIND OF MAN I AM, VS....
THE ONE YOU WANT TO BE...

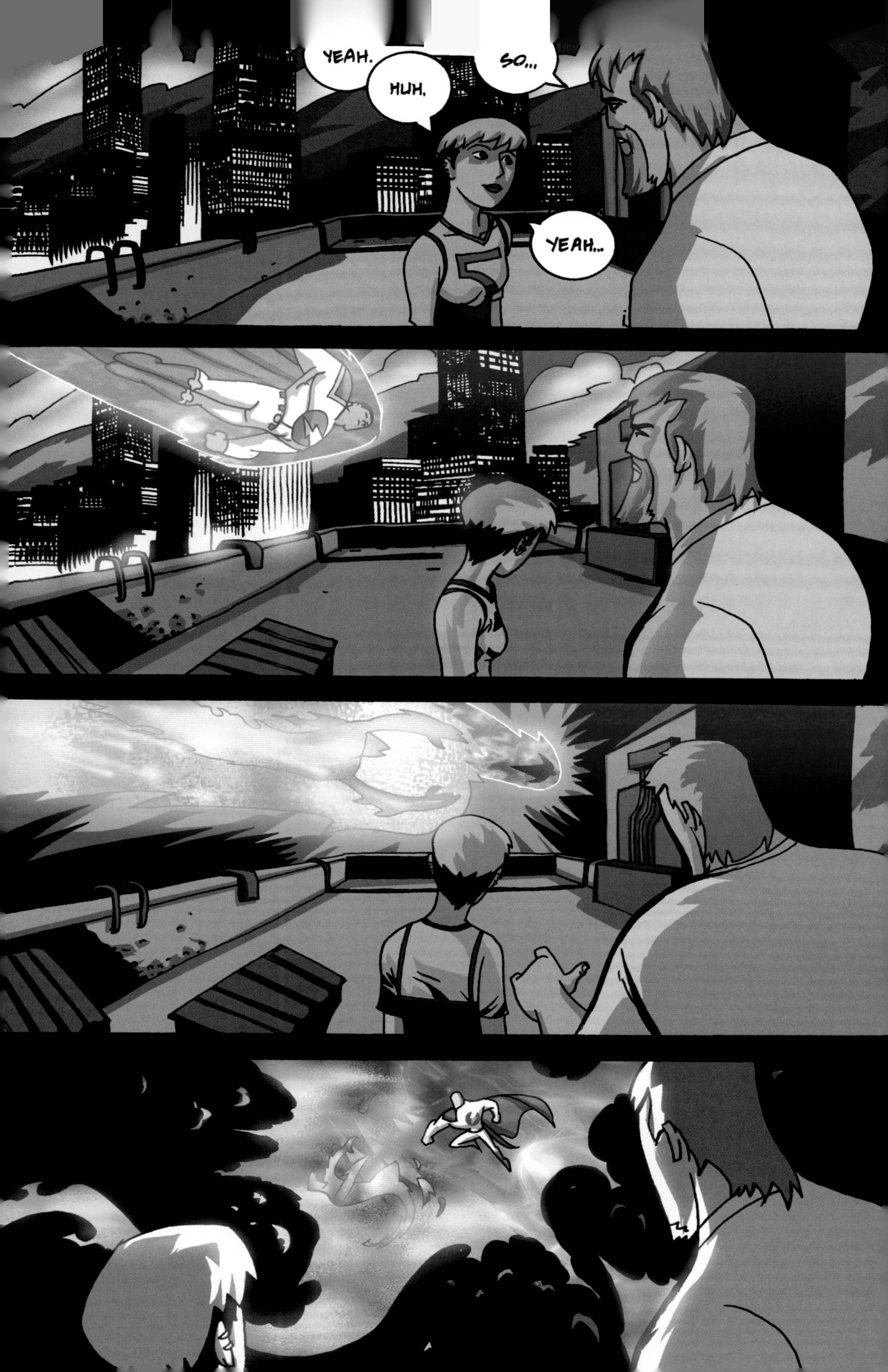
YEAH.
HUH.
SO...
YEAH...

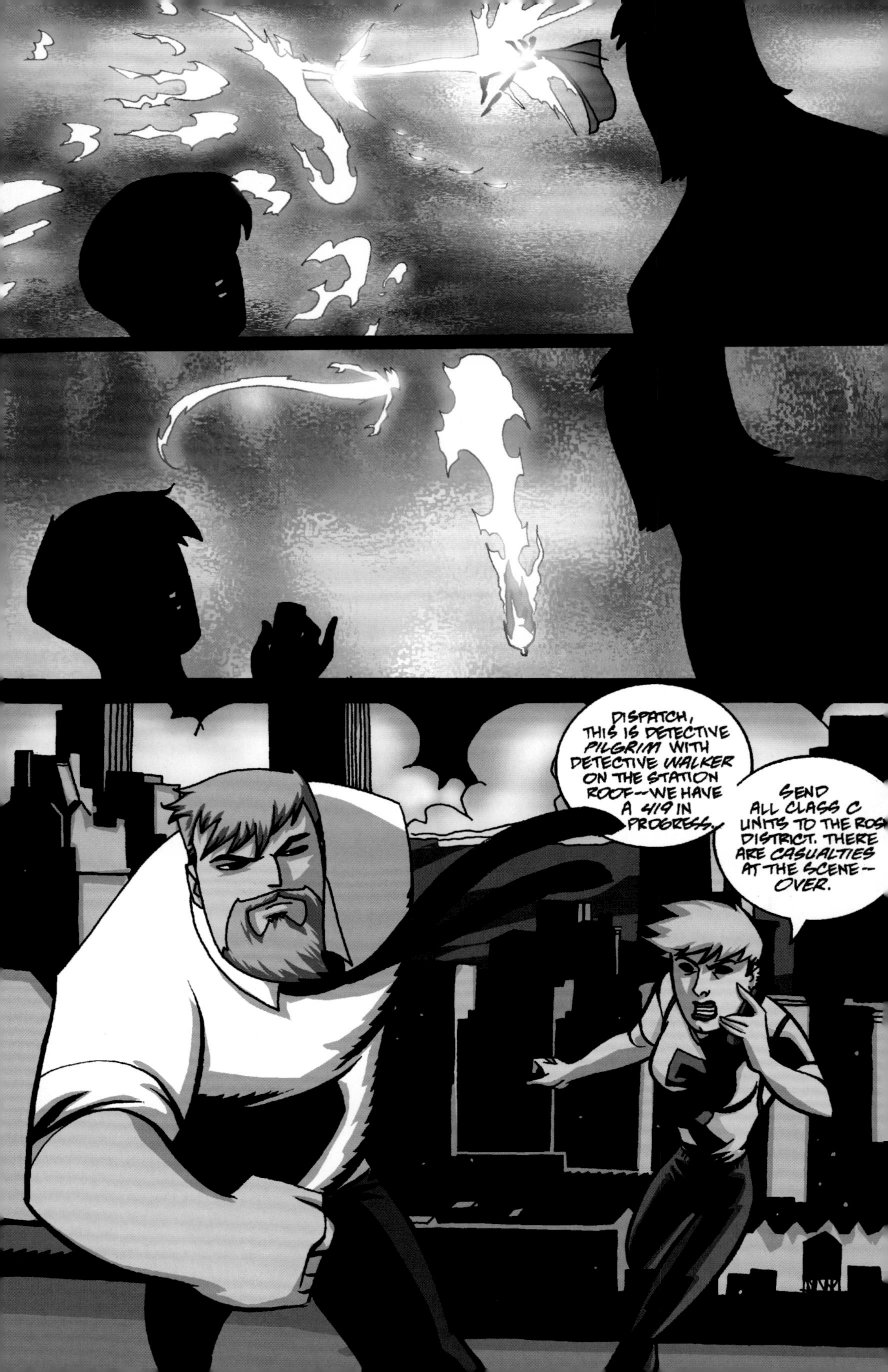
DISPATCH, THIS IS DETECTIVE PILGRIM WITH DETECTIVE WALKER ON THE STATION ROOF--WE HAVE A 419 IN PROGRESS.
SEND ALL CLASS C UNITS TO THE ROS DISTRICT. THERE ARE CASUALTIES AT THE SCENE--OVER.

POWERS

™

COVER
GALLERY

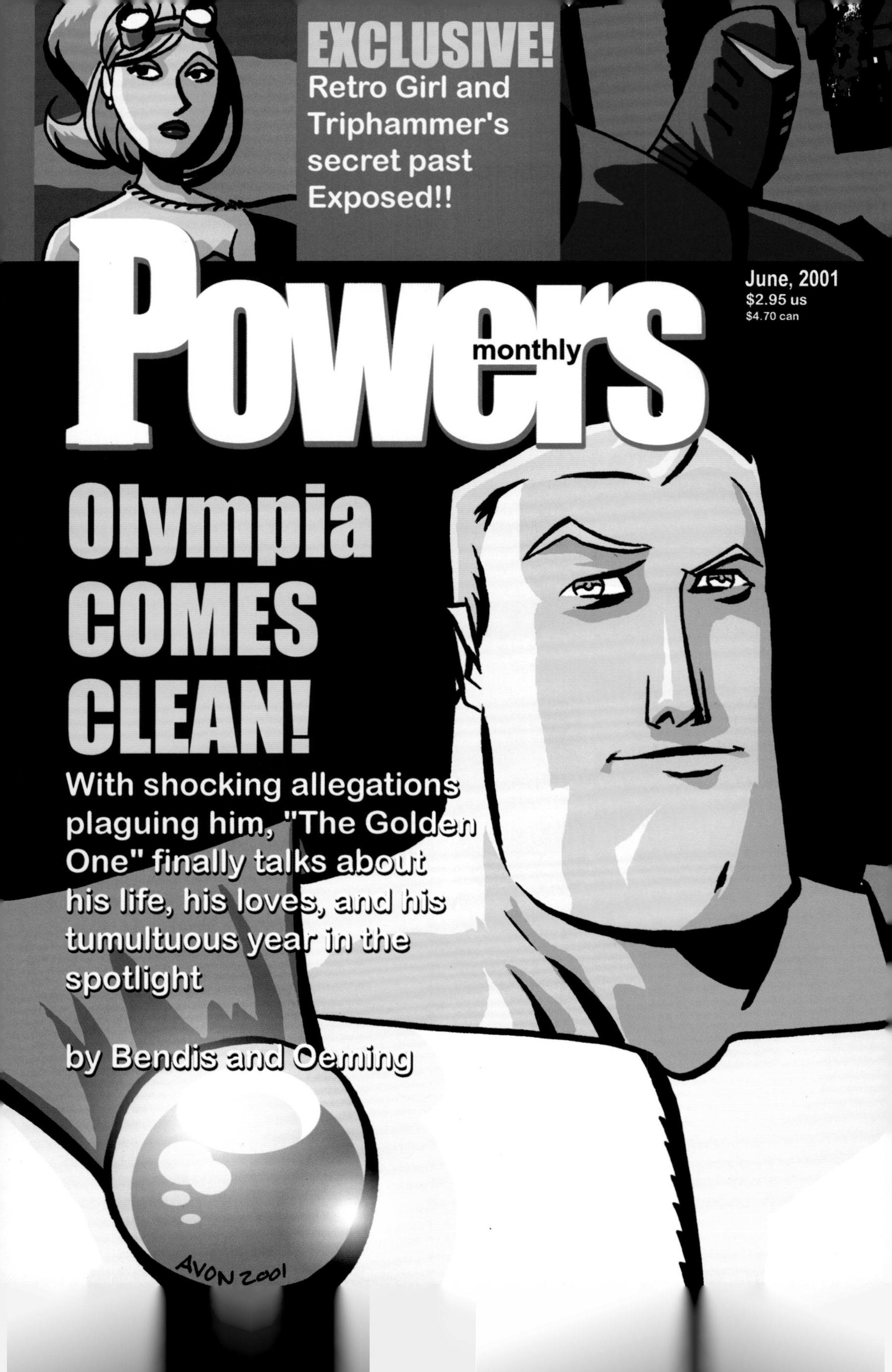
EXCLUSIVE!
Retro Girl and Triphammer's secret past Exposed!!
Powers monthly
June, 2001
$2.95 us
$4.70 can
Olympia COMES CLEAN!
With shocking allegations plaguing him, "The Golden One" finally talks about his life, his loves, and his tumultuous year in the spotlight
by Bendis and Oeming
AVON 2001

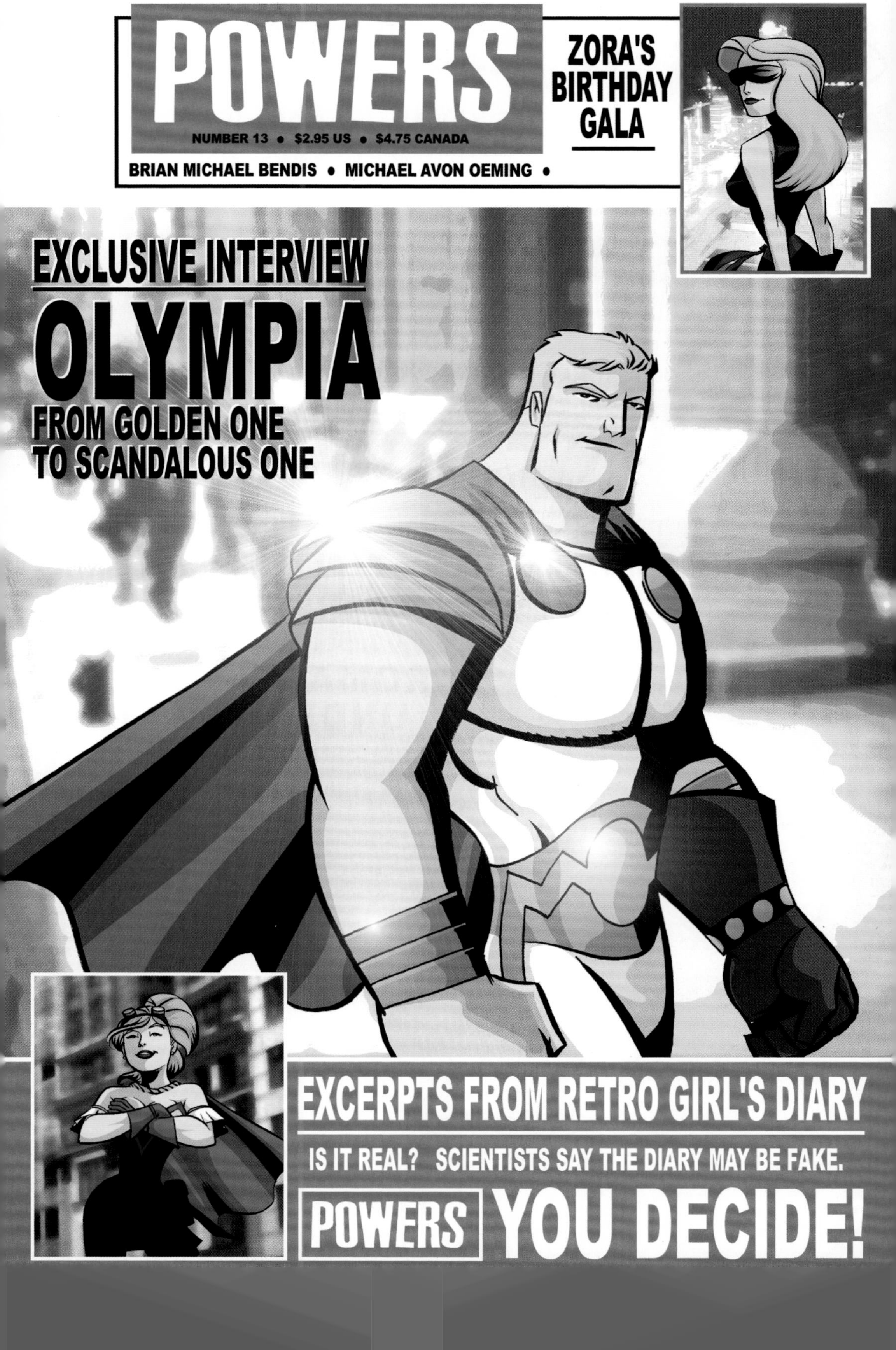

POWERS
NUMBER 13 • $2.95 US • $4.75 CANADA
BRIAN MICHAEL BENDIS • MICHAEL AVON OEMING •
ZORA'S BIRTHDAY GALA
EXCLUSIVE INTERVIEW
OLYMPIA
FROM GOLDEN ONE TO SCANDALOUS ONE
EXCERPTS FROM RETRO GIRL'S DIARY
IS IT REAL? SCIENTISTS SAY THE DIARY MAY BE FAKE.
POWERS
YOU DECIDE!

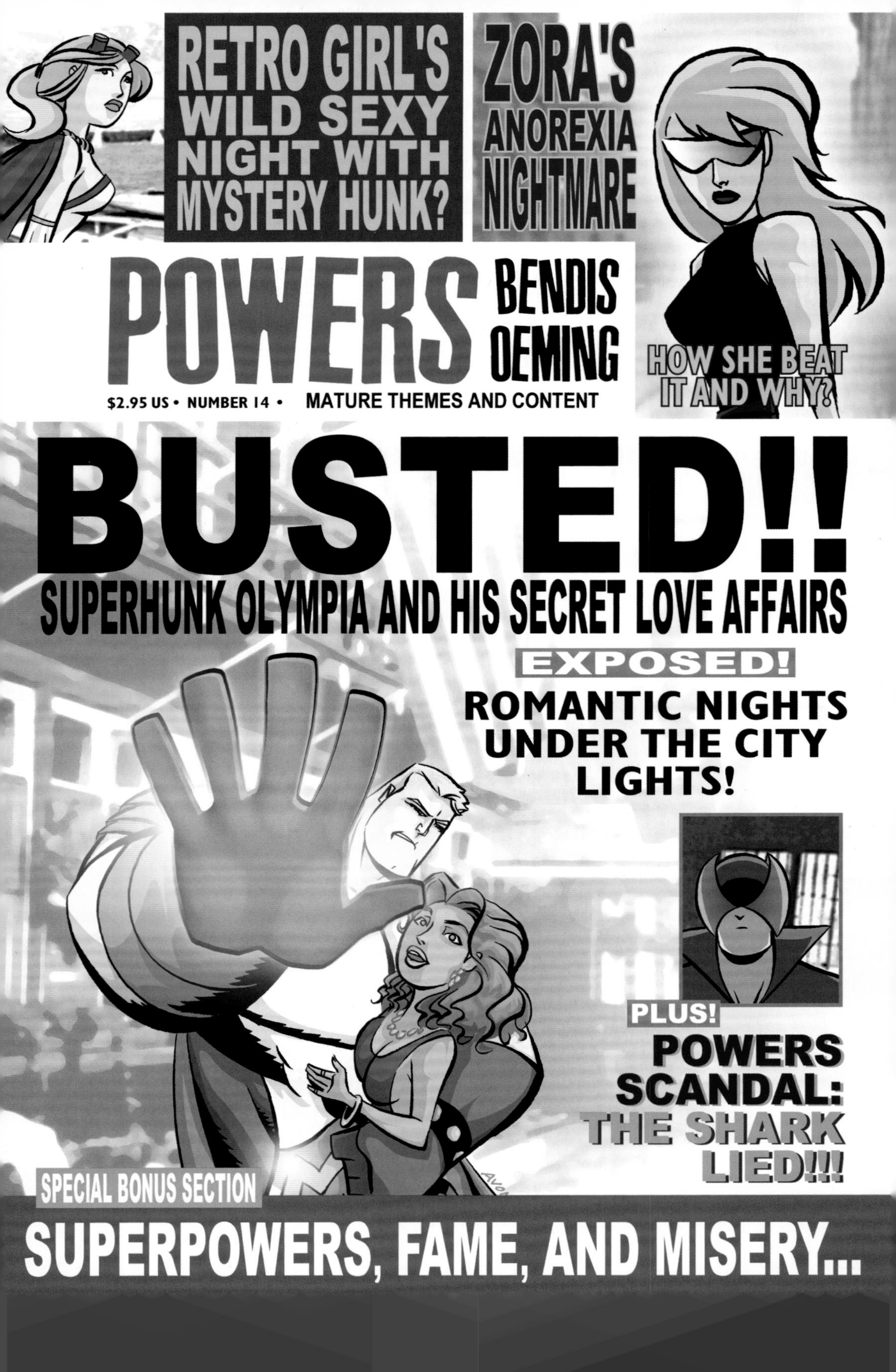

RETRO GIRL'S WILD SEXY NIGHT WITH MYSTERY HUNK?
ZORA'S ANOREXIA NIGHTMARE
POWERS
BENDIS OEMING
HOW SHE BEAT IT AND WHY?
$2.95 US • NUMBER 14 • MATURE THEMES AND CONTENT
BUSTED!!
SUPERHUNK OLYMPIA AND HIS SECRET LOVE AFFAIRS
EXPOSED!
ROMANTIC NIGHTS UNDER THE CITY LIGHTS!
PLUS!
POWERS SCANDAL: THE SHARK LIED!!!
SPECIAL BONUS SECTION
SUPERPOWERS, FAME, AND MISERY...

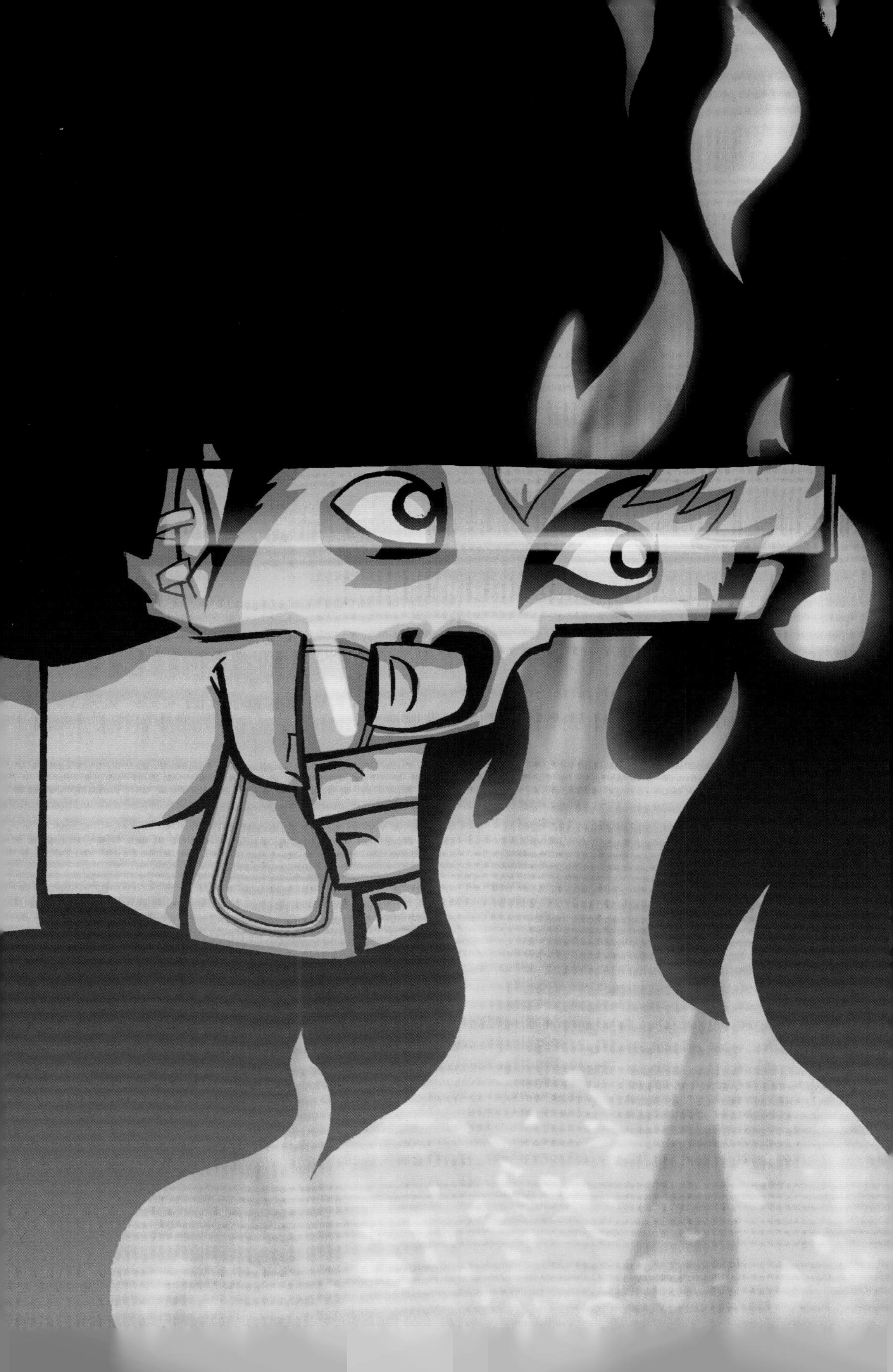

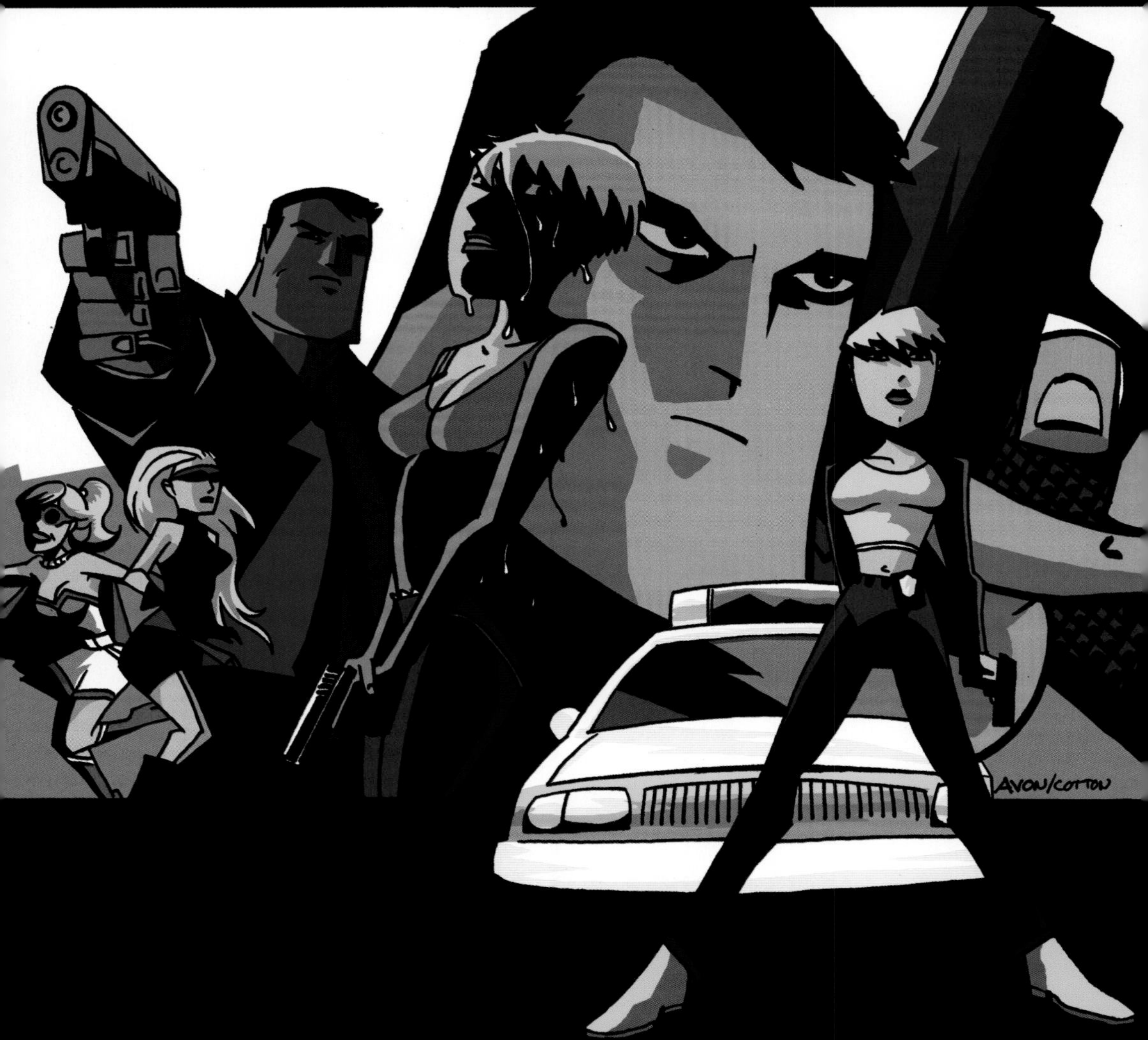
AVON/COTTON

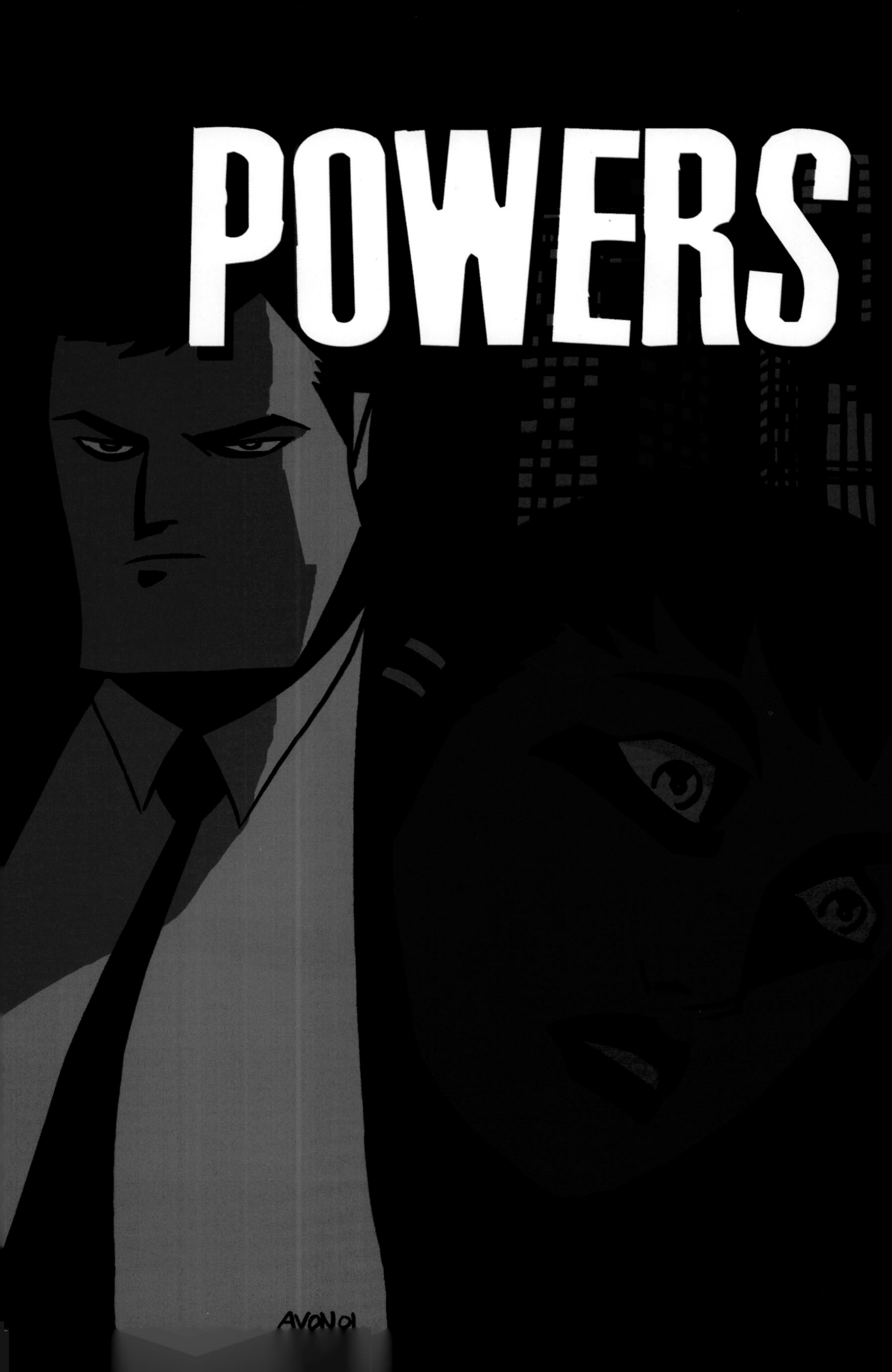
POWERS
AVON 01

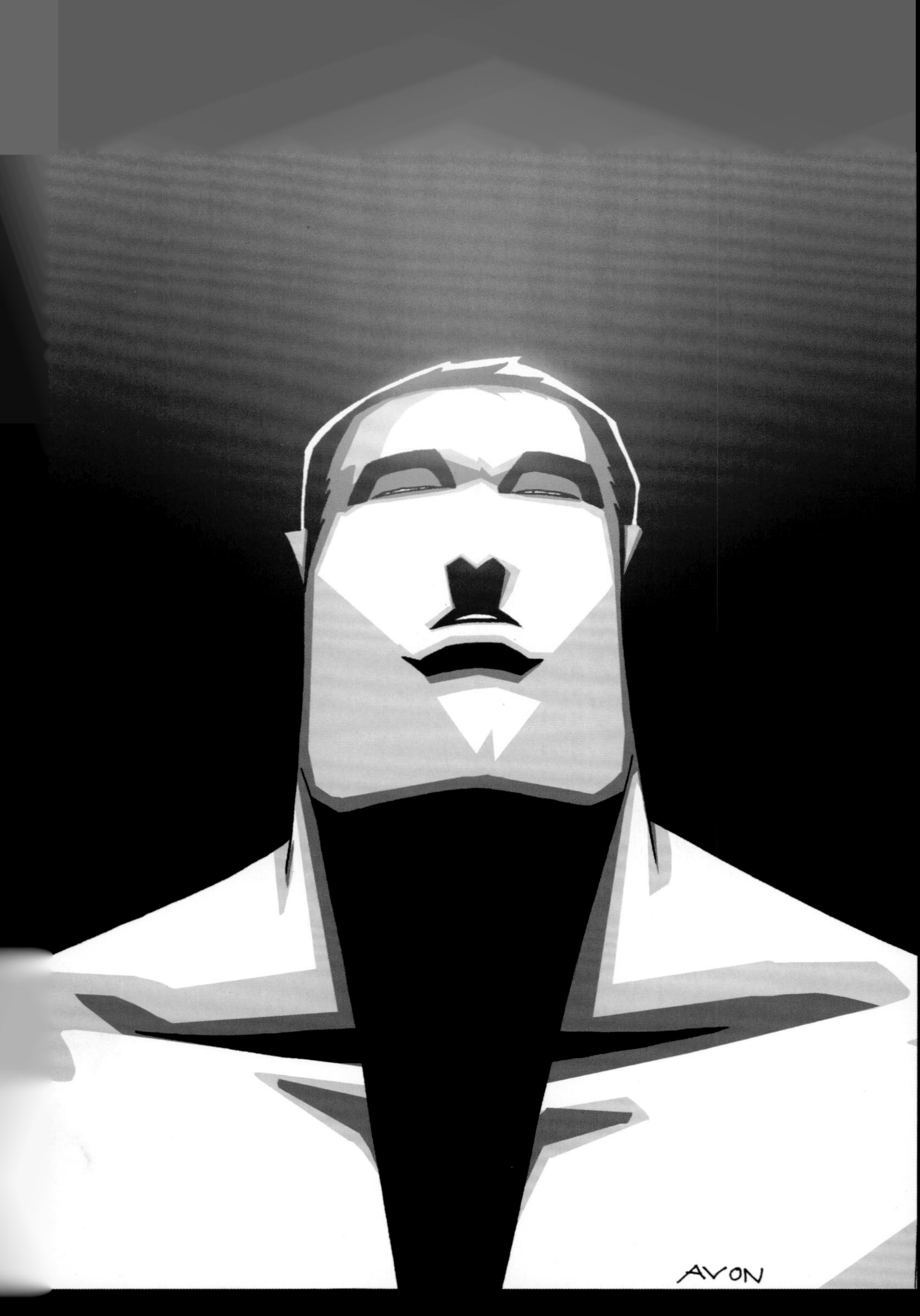
AVON

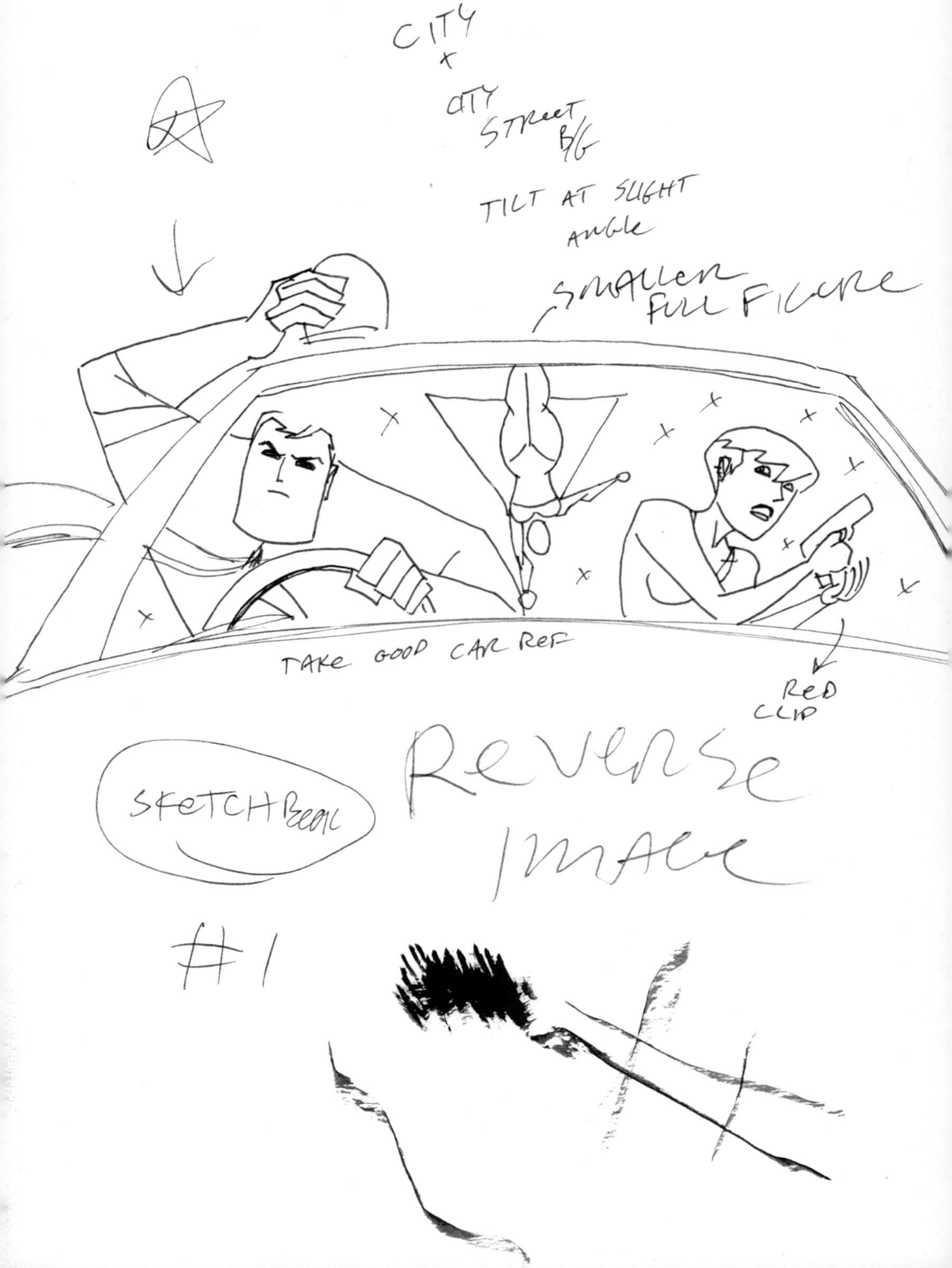

CITY
+
CITY
STREET
B/G
TILT AT SLIGHT
ANGLE
SMALLER
FULL FIGURE
TAKE GOOD CAR REF
RED
CLIP
SKETCHBOOK
REVERSE
IMAGE
#1

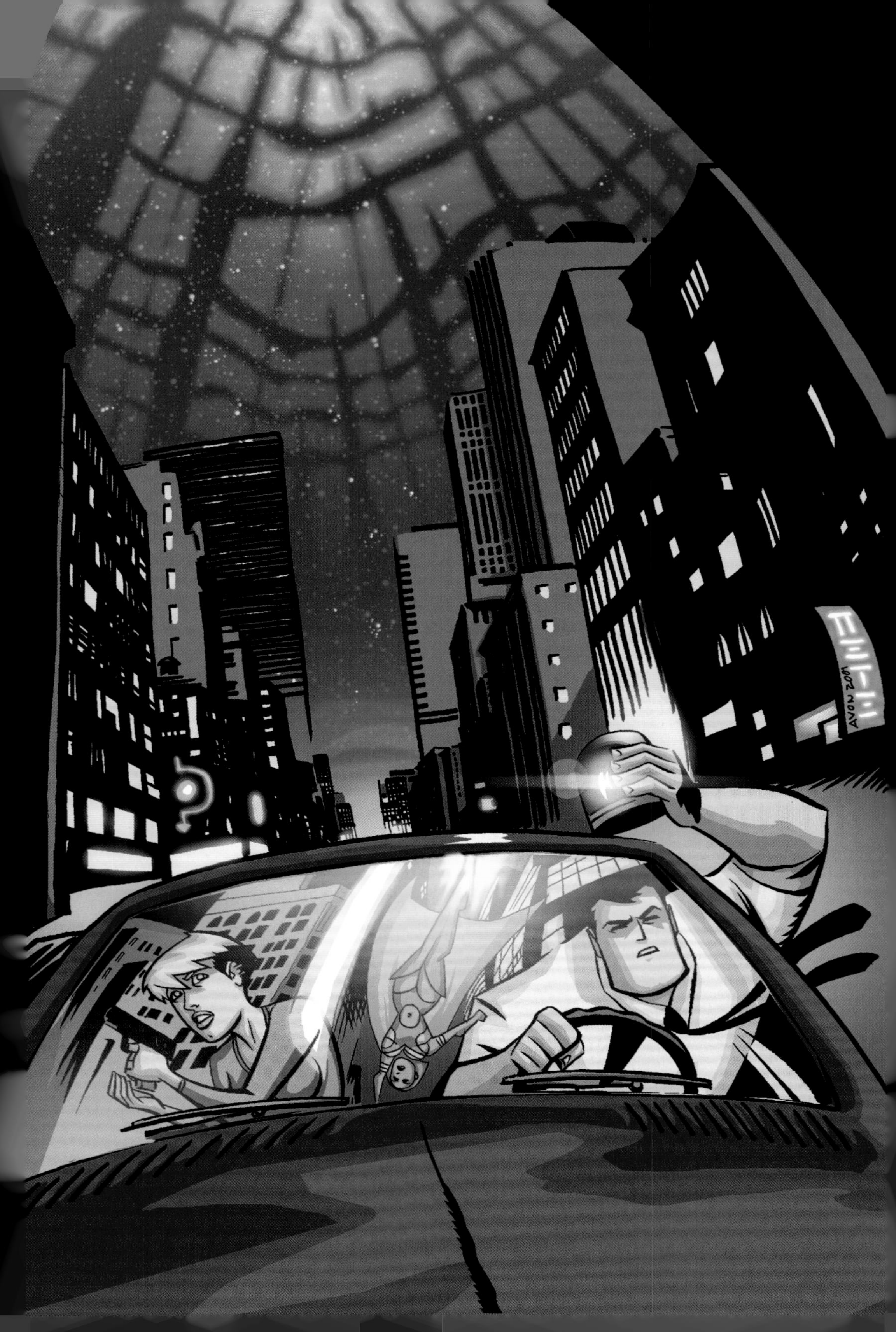

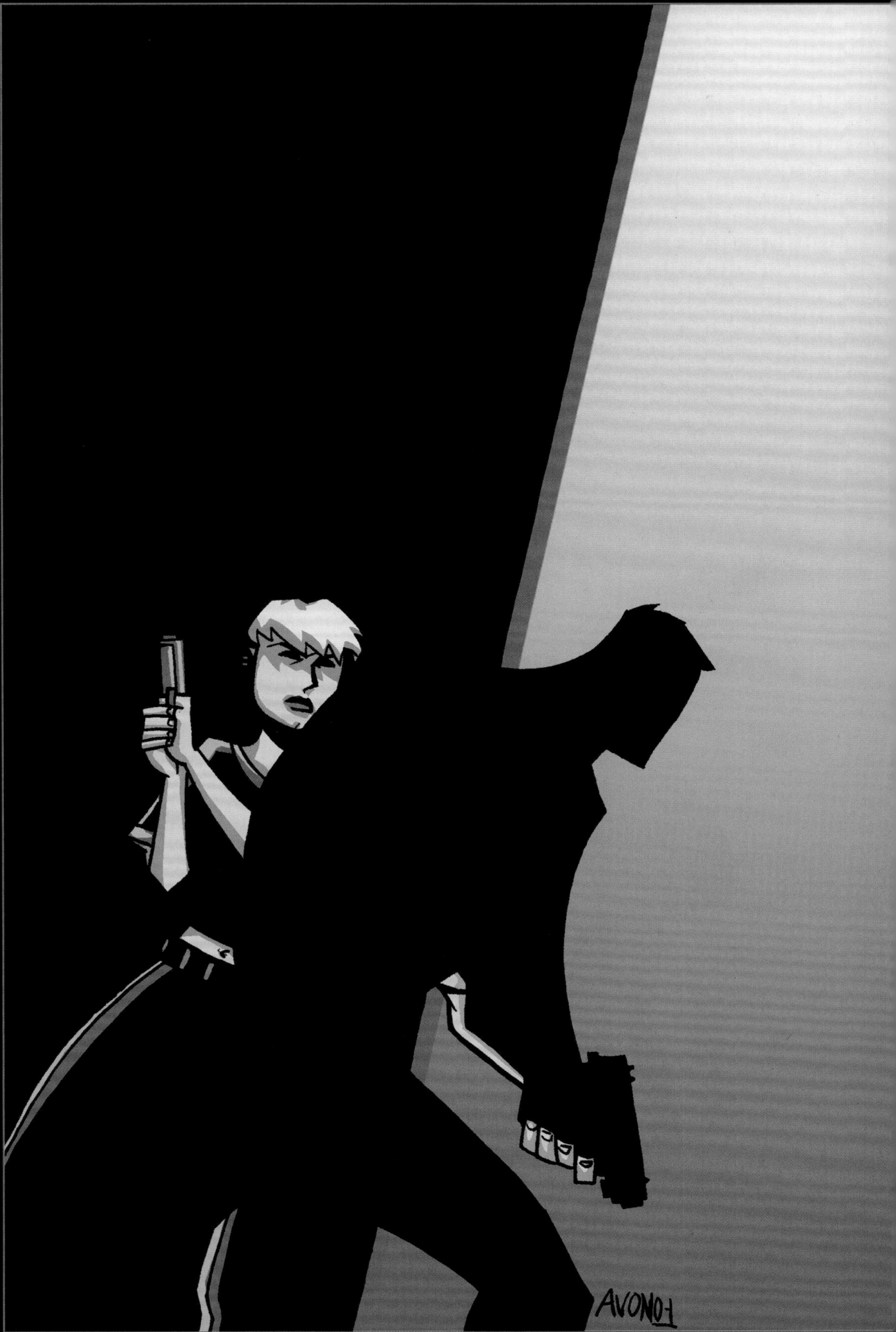

Powers #19 cover

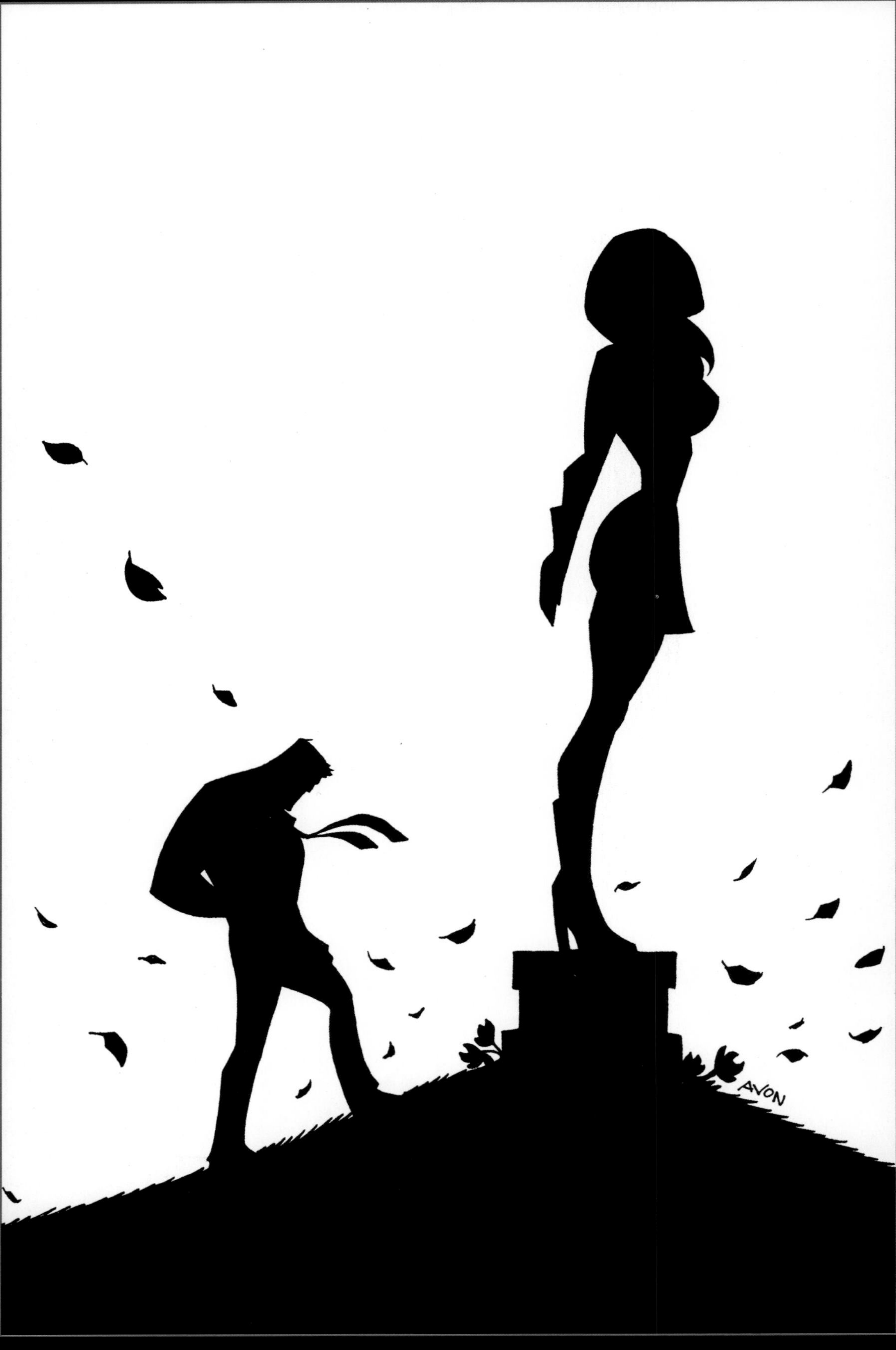
AVON

Powers #20 cover

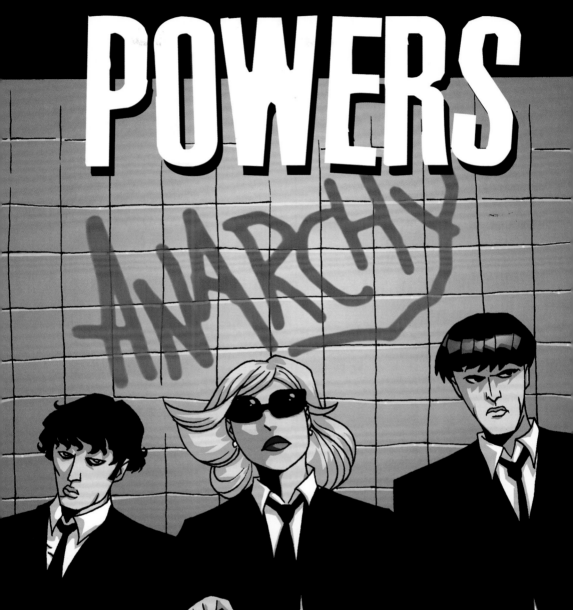

BRAND NEW STORY ARC!

POWERS

ANARCHY

BRIAN MICHAEL BENDIS
MICHAEL AVON OEMING

POWERS

KAOTIC CHIC

"POWERS IS A WORK DESERVING OF THE RARELY JUSTIFIABLE TITLE...
MASTERPIECE!"- GRADE: A!
-COMIC BUYER'S GUIDE

BRIAN MICHAEL BENDIS
MICHAEL AVON OEMING

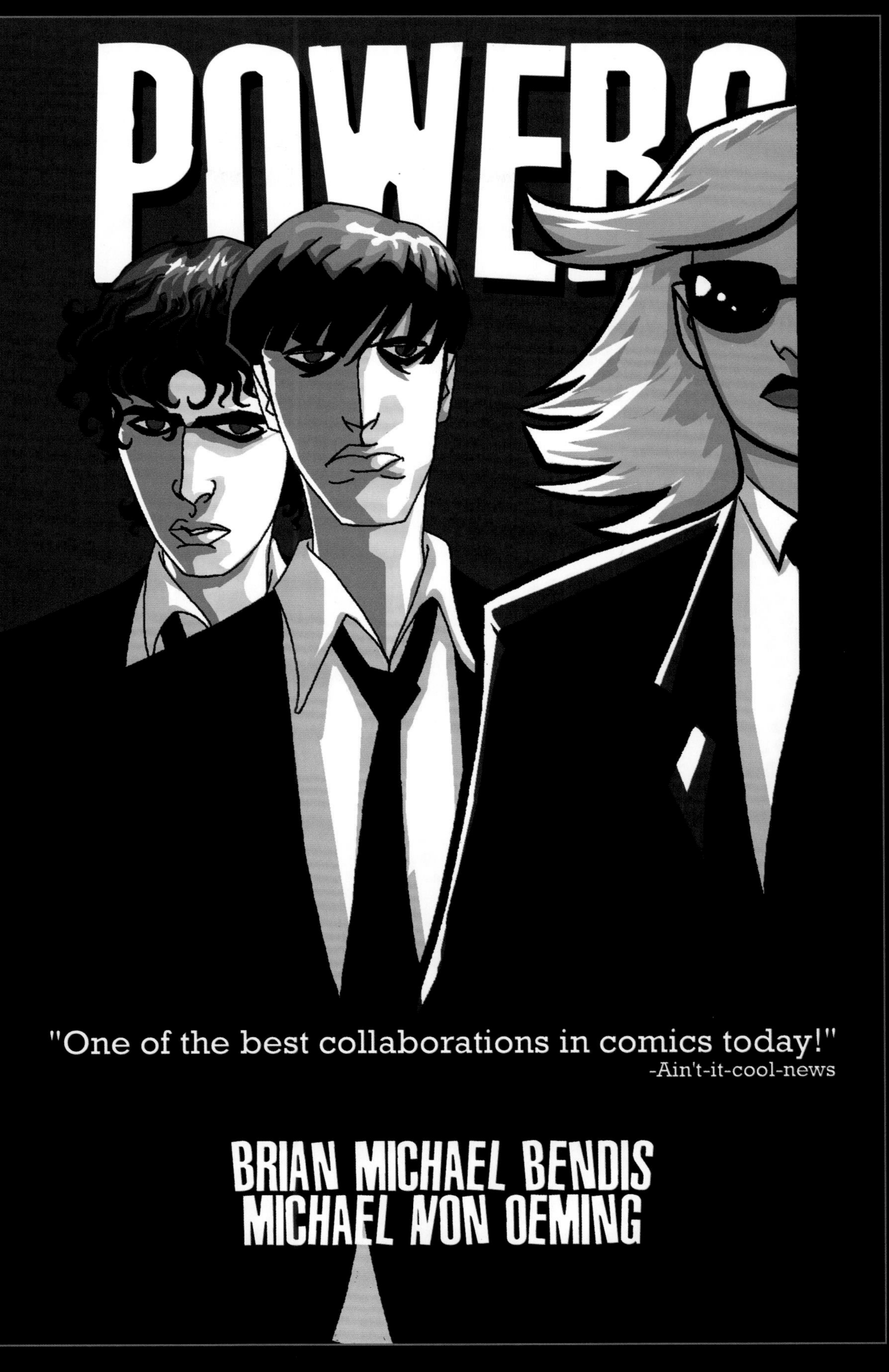
POWERS
"One of the best collaborations in comics today!"
-Ain't-it-cool-news
BRIAN MICHAEL BENDIS
MICHAEL AVON OEMING

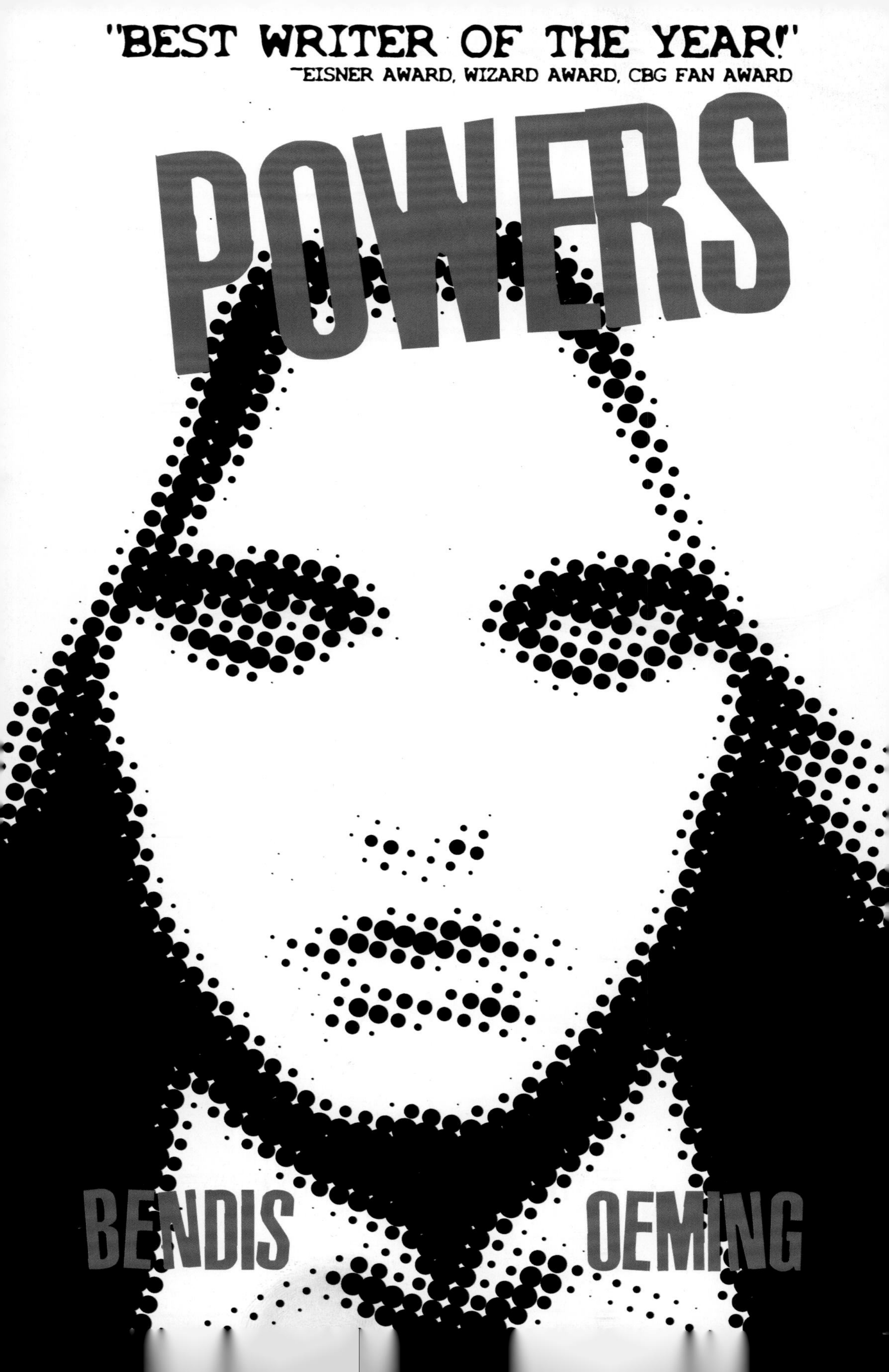
"BEST WRITER OF THE YEAR!"
—EISNER AWARD, WIZARD AWARD, CBG FAN AWARD
POWERS
BENDIS
OEMING

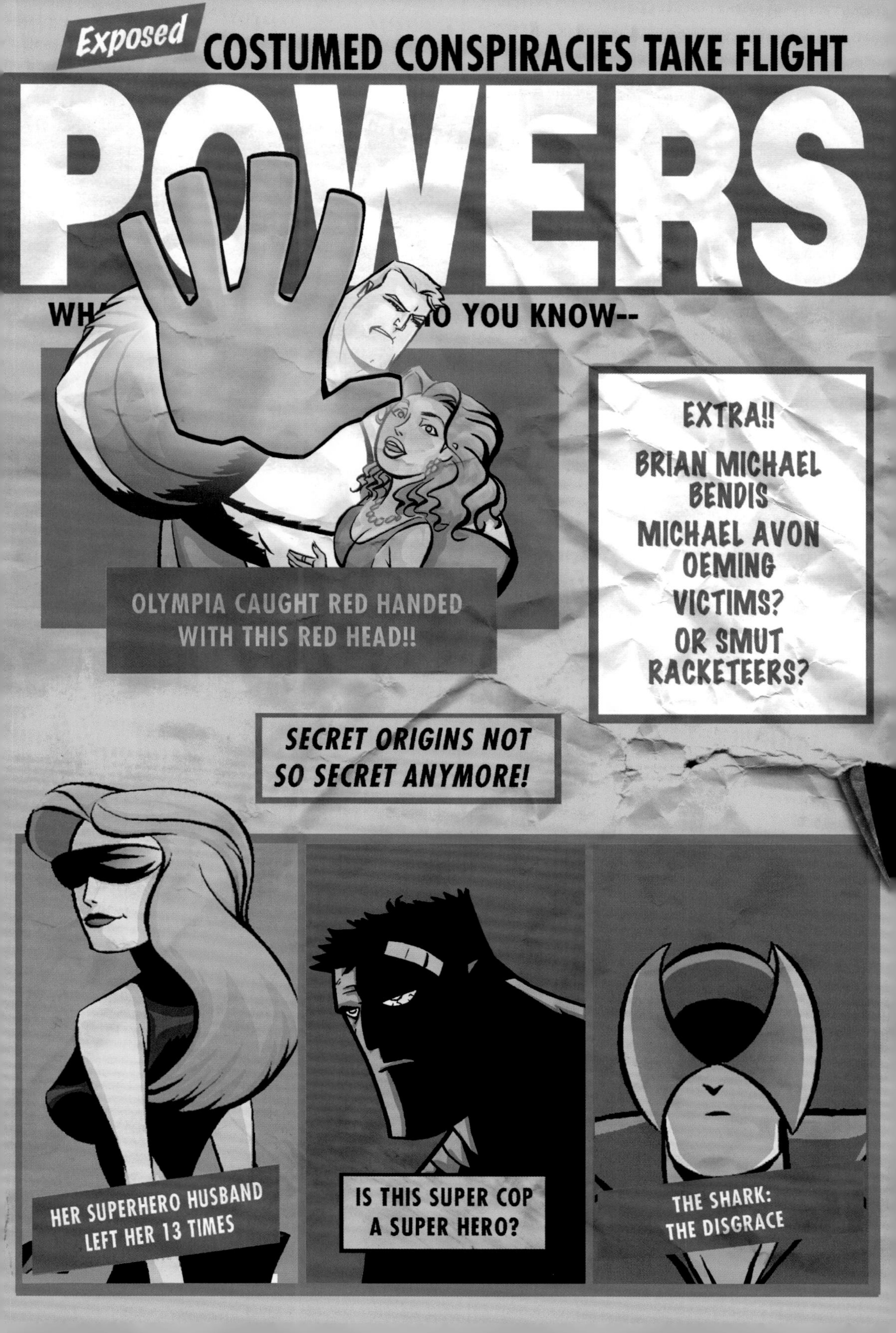

Exposed
COSTUMED CONSPIRACIES TAKE FLIGHT
POWERS
WHA
O YOU KNOW--
OLYMPIA CAUGHT RED HANDED
WITH THIS RED HEAD!!
EXTRA!!
BRIAN MICHAEL BENDIS
MICHAEL AVON OEMING
VICTIMS?
OR SMUT RACKETEERS?
SECRET ORIGINS NOT SO SECRET ANYMORE!
HER SUPERHERO HUSBAND LEFT HER 13 TIMES
IS THIS SUPER COP A SUPER HERO?
THE SHARK: THE DISGRACE

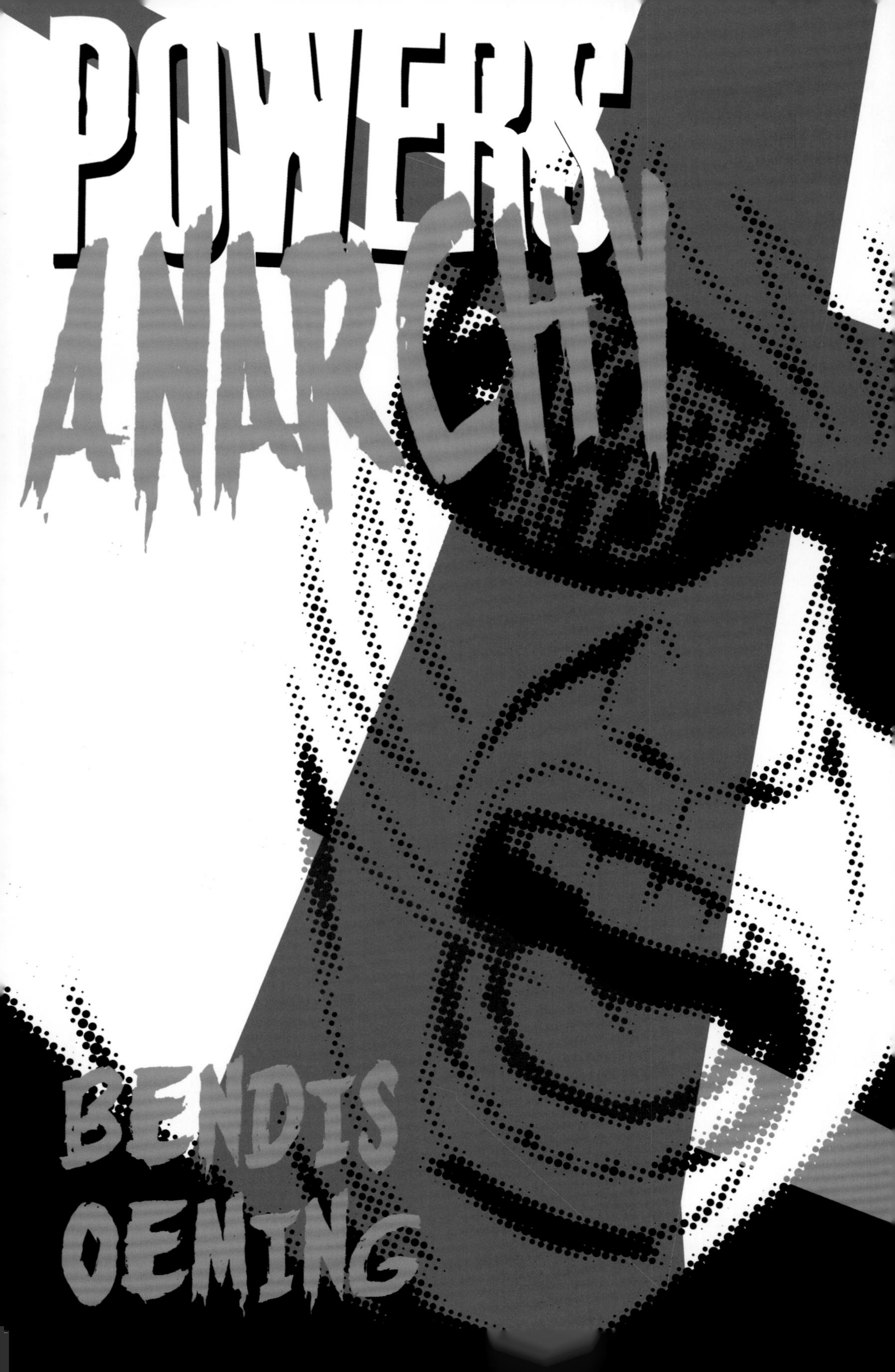
POWERS
ANARCHY
BENDIS
OEMING

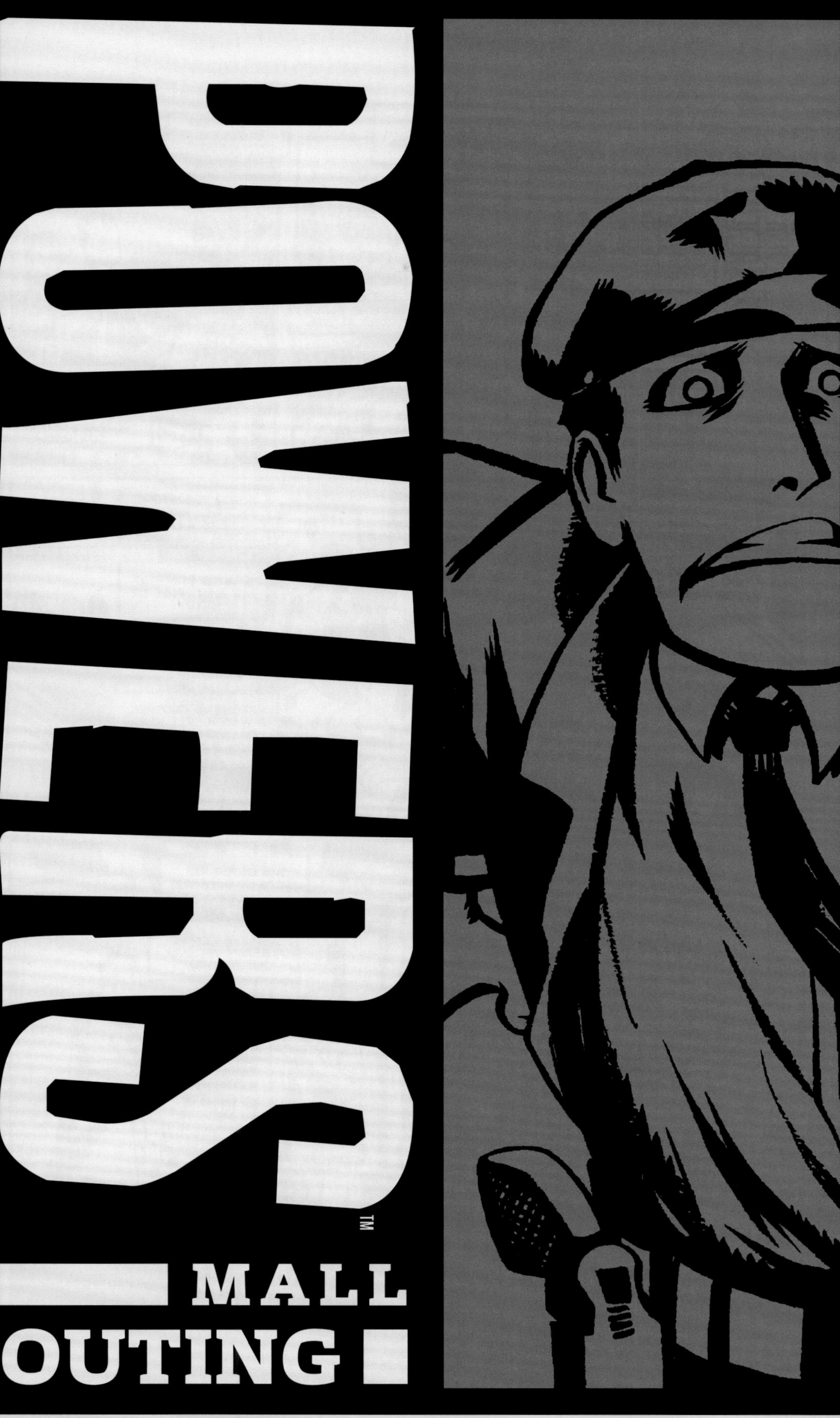
POWERS™
MALL
OUTING

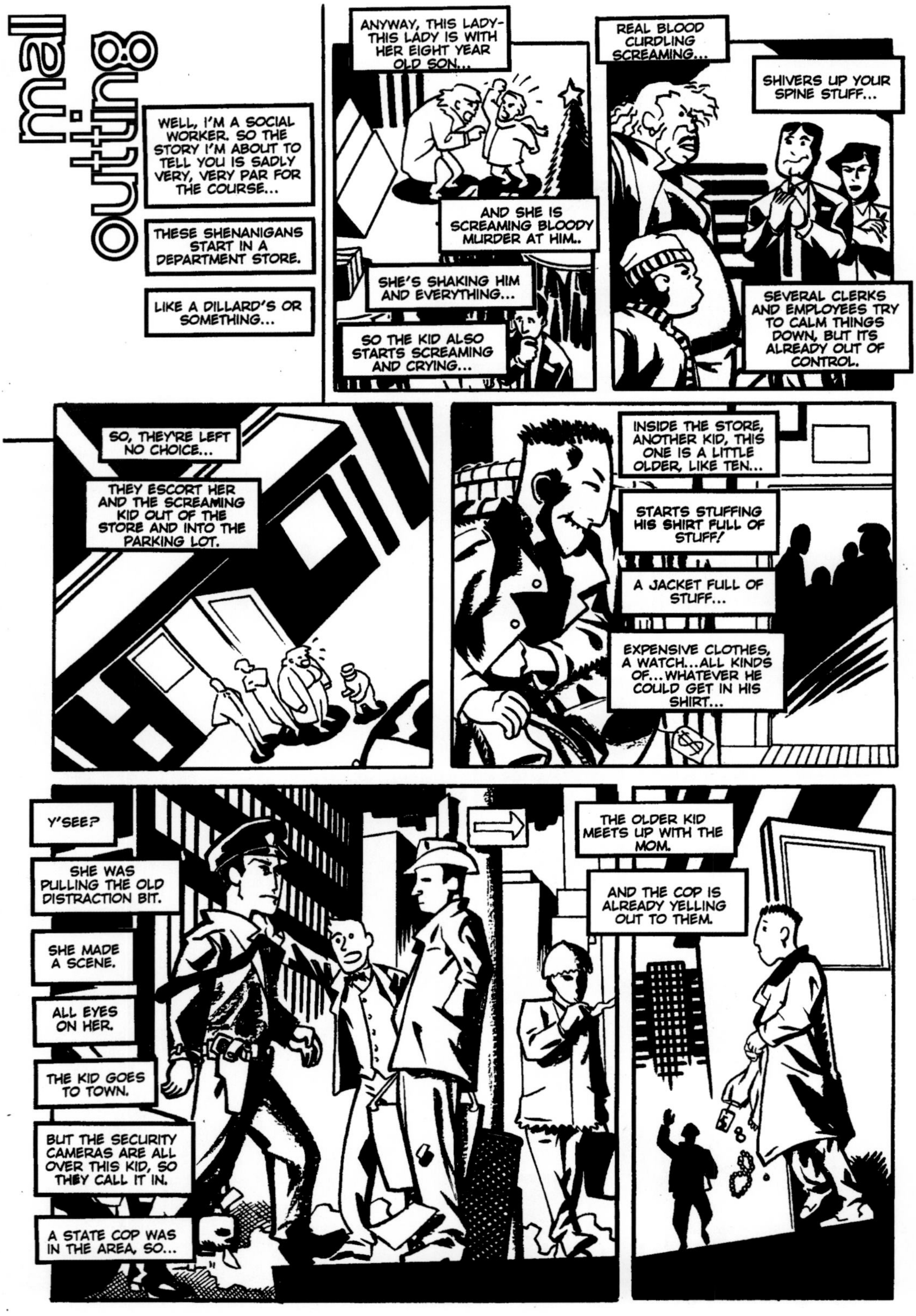
mall outing
WELL, I'M A SOCIAL WORKER. SO THE STORY I'M ABOUT TO TELL YOU IS SADLY VERY, VERY PAR FOR THE COURSE...
THESE SHENANIGANS START IN A DEPARTMENT STORE.
LIKE A DILLARD'S OR SOMETHING...
ANYWAY, THIS LADY- THIS LADY IS WITH HER EIGHT YEAR OLD SON...
AND SHE IS SCREAMING BLOODY MURDER AT HIM..
SHE'S SHAKING HIM AND EVERYTHING...
SO THE KID ALSO STARTS SCREAMING AND CRYING...
REAL BLOOD CURDLING SCREAMING...
SHIVERS UP YOUR SPINE STUFF...
SEVERAL CLERKS AND EMPLOYEES TRY TO CALM THINGS DOWN, BUT ITS ALREADY OUT OF CONTROL.
SO, THEY'RE LEFT NO CHOICE...
THEY ESCORT HER AND THE SCREAMING KID OUT OF THE STORE AND INTO THE PARKING LOT.
INSIDE THE STORE, ANOTHER KID, THIS ONE IS A LITTLE OLDER, LIKE TEN...
STARTS STUFFING HIS SHIRT FULL OF STUFF!
A JACKET FULL OF STUFF...
EXPENSIVE CLOTHES, A WATCH...ALL KINDS OF...WHATEVER HE COULD GET IN HIS SHIRT...
Y'SEE?
SHE WAS PULLING THE OLD DISTRACTION BIT.
SHE MADE A SCENE.
ALL EYES ON HER.
THE KID GOES TO TOWN.
BUT THE SECURITY CAMERAS ARE ALL OVER THIS KID, SO THEY CALL IT IN.
A STATE COP WAS IN THE AREA, SO...
THE OLDER KID MEETS UP WITH THE MOM.
AND THE COP IS ALREADY YELLING OUT TO THEM.

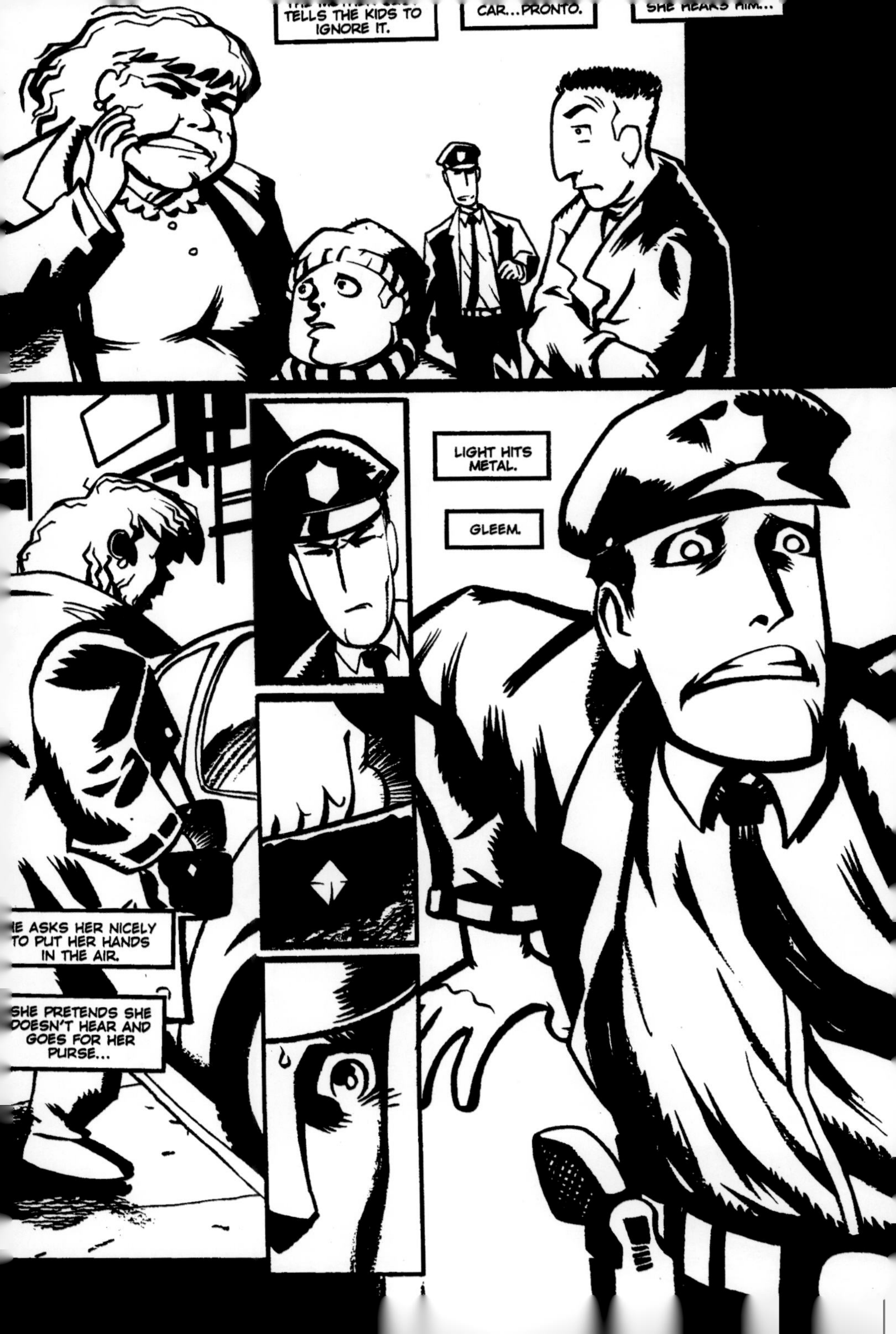
TELLS THE KIDS TO IGNORE IT.
CAR...PRONTO.
SHE HEARS HIM...
E ASKS HER NICELY TO PUT HER HANDS IN THE AIR.
SHE PRETENDS SHE DOESN'T HEAR AND GOES FOR HER PURSE...
LIGHT HITS METAL.
GLEEM.

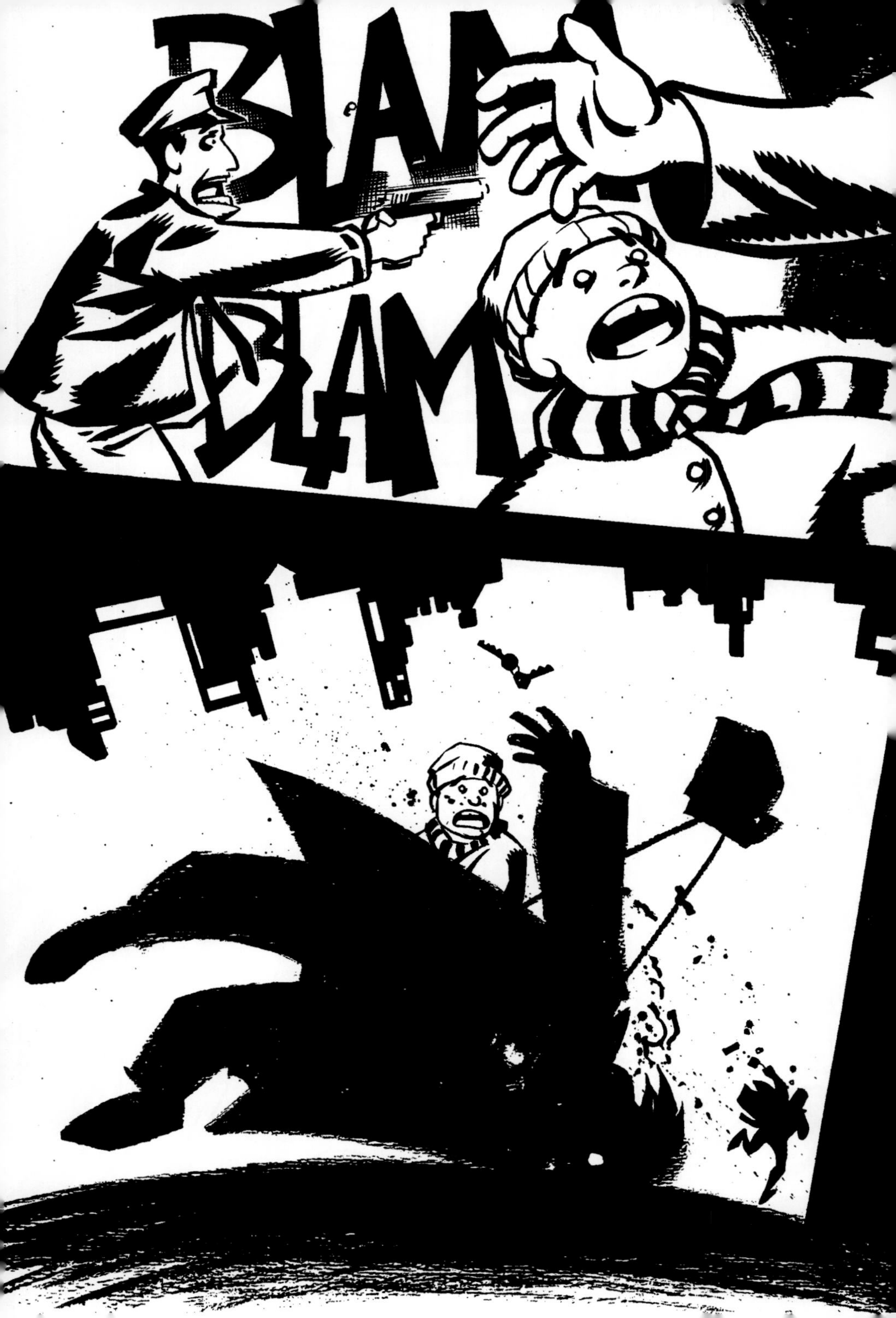
BLAM
BLAM

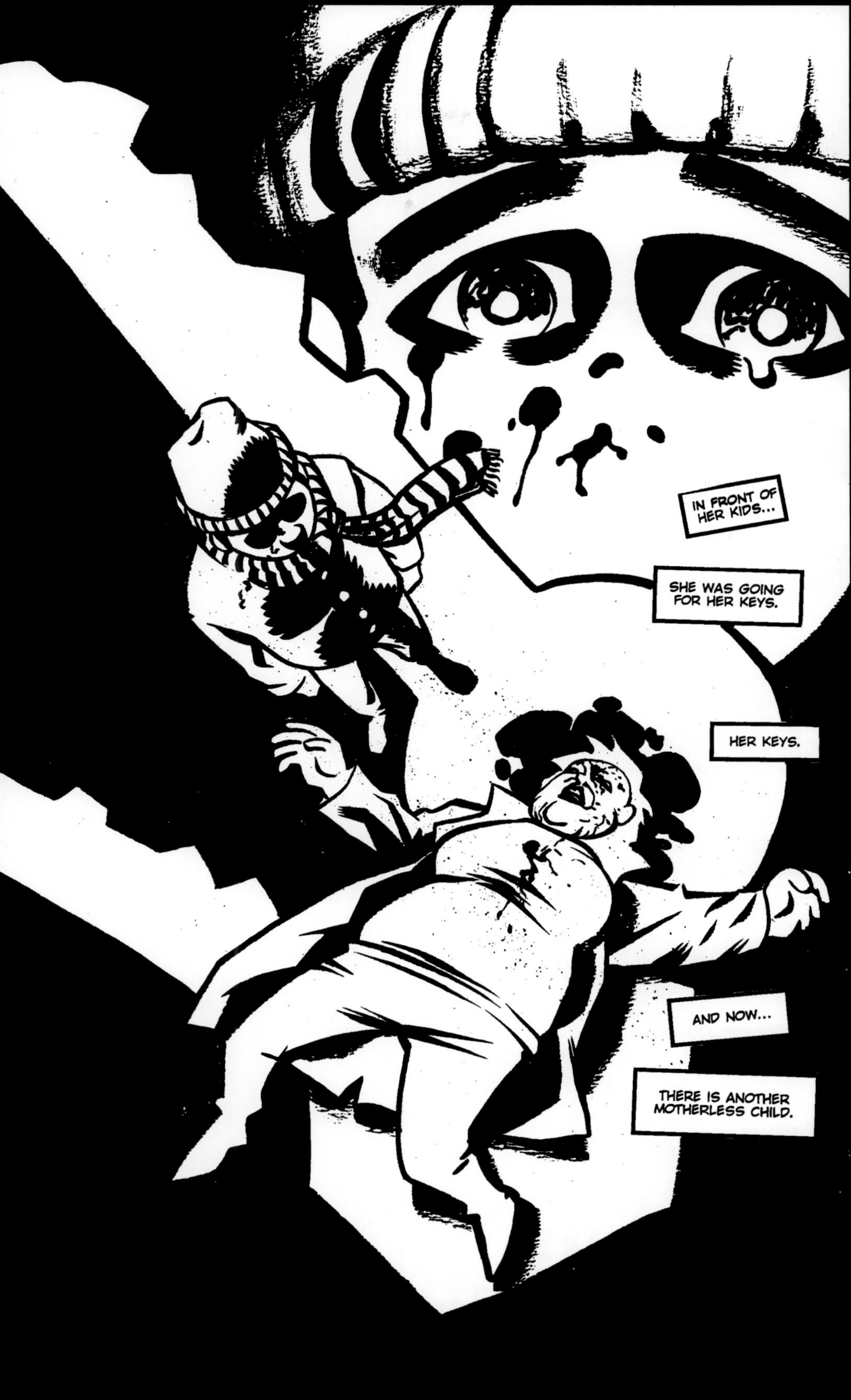
IN FRONT OF HER KIDS...
SHE WAS GOING FOR HER KEYS.
HER KEYS.
AND NOW...
THERE IS ANOTHER MOTHERLESS CHILD.

POWERS

BENDIS INTERVIEW

The following is part of a very lengthy interview conducted by the rascals at HeroRealm.com.

For a complete transcript of the interview, visit their site.

INTERVIEW BY ALEX HAMBY
MARCH 27, 2002

ALEX: I'm a big fan of *Powers*. Where did that idea come from?

BRIAN: It's hard to put a thing on it . . .

It was a mixture of Mike [Oeming] and me becoming better friends through the years. He'd always show David Mack and me these drawings he was doing. He started doing drawings in the *Powers* style of *Kabuki*, *Jinx*, and *Goldfish* because that's what we were working on at the time. They excited both of us but they excited me to such a degree that I couldn't even stand it. At the same time, I started analyzing why it was that I never attempted to write a superhero comic but I loved them so much. I really loved the genre—and I realized that a lot of my generation of comic writers, if you weren't assigned one of the heroes, *Dark Knight* and *Watchmen* kind of screwed it up for us.

We were raised on the ultimate (not to use *Ultimate* without getting a royalty) superhero stories in *Dark Knight* and *Watchmen*. It's sort of like everything had been said. So, I just moved on to another genre where I thought I had something to say. Then here we come, years later, and I analyze what I like about the genre and what I would have to say about it. I started thinking about the VH1 *Behind the Music* look at superheroes. Then I started mashing together my love of crime fiction, love of the police procedural—then I started thinking about what the police procedure would be for superheroes but really get into it.

I had just read *Homicide*, the book that the TV show is based on, which is an amazing procedural. Then Mike started doing drawings, then I told him the idea, and then he started doing drawings based on the idea. Then BOOM you got the whole thing.

Then I read Janis Joplin's biography and for some reason that made it click. I can't tell you why.

ALEX: Ah, you're a Janis Joplin fan. We've got something in common. How do your goals differ from *Powers* and all of your other work?

BRIAN: They don't. Anything with my name on it has the exact same goal, which is to craft a book that I would buy. That's the goal. My personal goals are very, very high. Higher than anyone has got for me, be it my employers or my readers. If my name is on it—there are very few things in this world that you get to leave behind.

I just read Gil Kane's biography and I'm sitting there going, "You know what, man? There are very few things that will outlive you and comics will outlive me." Clearly we see that they will.

So, kick ass on them. At least make them something you would buy. People will like them, not like them, at least make sure that you will buy them. So, every decision I've made, jobs I take, that's the first test. Would I buy this book? Would I buy *Daredevil* with Alex Maleev drawing it? Hell yeah! Absolutely.

That's the goal.

As far as *Powers* is concerned, the only difference is that we get to kill everybody. We get to kill anyone we want, whereas that is the one thing we wouldn't be able to do at Marvel. Marvel's not going to let me do a homicide book where I get to kill Captain America. So, we get to analyze the genre from that unique perspective.

ALEX: You went through that whole starving artist thing.

BRIAN: Nine years of it, thank you. [*Laughs*]

ALEX: You did a lot of stuff that people are retroactively talking about.

BRIAN: I don't care when they bought it as long as they bought it.

ALEX: What do you think finally sparked the attention of Todd McFarlane and then Marvel?

BRIAN: Well, I actually know this. I was at Image and I had been there for many years before the founders even knew there was an Image central.

We all got comps. Todd was at Top Cow, saw the *Goldfish* trade, and took it. He read it on the way home to Arizona. When he got back he said to Beau Smith, "Hey, find me this guy, I think he's at Image." [*Laughs*]

He just really liked *Goldfish*, he really liked that kind of storytelling, and he offered me a couple of projects. He goes, "I got two projects for you. One is a modern-day *Frankenstein* . . ."

And I'm like, "Is this really Todd McFarlane on the phone?" It was really surreal, right?

". . . it's about a giant monkey robot . . ." I don't want to do a giant monkey robot book.

Then he goes, "My other one's about two detectives." That sounds good! Then we started talking about *Sam and Twitch* and it was right up my alley. It wasn't a *Spawn* book and it was something I could do. That worked out real well.

Exactly at the same time, my friend David Mack started working at Marvel Knights with Joe Quesada. I was absolutely in love with Marvel Knights, what it meant, what they were trying to do, and how they were treating David. I think David slipped them a couple, I think, *Jinx*—and I think Joe just loved *Jinx*. Loved my writing, not my drawing, which he made very clear.

He called me—you get the Marvel Knights call, which is, "If you came to Marvel what would you do?" And I laundry listed stories I've been writing in my head since I was eleven. We were going to do Nick Fury but that didn't work out. Then *Daredevil* became a scheduling mess and he asked if David and I would do *Daredevil*. I was like, "Er, yeah . . . okay."

That was a book I was actually scared of. It meant so much to me in my youth that I didn't know. But I had a story I had been working on for quite a while and to work with David also was very important to me. David and I have been best friends since we both got into comics and I wanted one time for us to do something worthy of that friendship. So, that was a very personal thing for me.

Then I literally handed in *Daredevil* scripts and that day Bill Jemas had plopped into Joe's office and said, "Gee, we've been working on this *Ultimate Spider-Man* but it's not coming together. Who would you hire?" And shockingly Joe said me. We took it from there.

Joe calls me and says, "You're going to get a call to start *Spider-Man* over again."

ALEX: So, it happened all because you took on *Daredevil*?

BRIAN: If anything this says—and we're talking nine years into my comic book career this is happening—it's literally being in the right place at the right time. Finally one of my trades is on someone's desk at the right moment and finally I handed in a script and I was on someone's mind at the time when something I was qualified to do came around the pike.

I get this email every day, every hour, that's like "Help me. I can't break in."

I'm like, "Dude, I'm the last person to ask." I mean I Forrest Gumped my way through this like no one's business. I am eager to be here and I am so happy but meanwhile I sent in 4,000 submissions between the age of 20 and 25—I just stopped. I thought no one's interested. It's a lottery anyhow. Finally someone who could do something put me on a book like that.

It was fun and I didn't get fired right away, which I assumed was going to happen. So that was fun too.

I handed in a script for *Ultimate* two days after I got the gig. There was no Spider-Man, there's no costume. Either they're going to shit on this or they're going to love it. Thankfully they loved it or I would have been kill-feed. You would have never heard my name again.

ALEX: Here's the ego question: do you think your taking the Marvel gig led to the company's regaining some of the momentum it had lost?

BRIAN: I think decisions like hiring people like me, David, Paul Jenkins, and Straczynski—there's a thought process there that I am very proud to be a part of. I am one of a few things that worked out pretty well. My goals are pure and so are those of my friends who I just mentioned. We all just want to make really good comics with a unique voice. People really wanted that.

David and I kinda joke that we had to wait till everyone else left comics before we got our shot. Everyone from the early nineties left. They made their money, or they didn't, and they left. We stayed because we were going to stay either way. I would have just made my black-and-white comics and I would have been fine. So, we finally got our shot because there was nobody else left to hire.

don't think it's me, but I think there's a decision-making process that is very forward thinking. I like working for forward-thinking people. I like it in comics, when I'm working on stuff outside of comics—I like it when people are thinking outside the box.

ALEX: Here's a long one: now that you are with Marvel doing *Alias*, *Daredevil*, *Ultimate Spider-Man*, and you're producing a Spider-Man cartoon, are you an independent writer working for a mainstream company or a mainstream writer who happens to do an indie comic in the form of *Powers*?

BRIAN: I run a company and one of the services that I provide Marvel is a big client for. Jinxworld is a company and it produces *Powers* and out of there comes my work for Marvel.

It's really weird because I don't put labels on any of this stuff. I treat it all the same. Just because it has my name on it, it has to be treated as if it is the last book I am going to write. As if it is the only shot I am going to get at this. I give it everything I've got.

ALEX: Good answer.

BRIAN: I don't want it to suck. Even if you don't like it you can at least say, "It's an interesting decision process. It's not my cup of tea but at least I can see the people behind it gave it a shot."

ALEX: Now, with working on so many books, how do you manage to give them each a unique voice?

BRIAN: (A) I don't drink. [*Laughs*] There are traps of this business that I've learned wisely from the generations before me.

I have always admired and respected the work of people who produced a lot of work like Jack Kirby and John Romita. I think that them producing a lot of work made the work a lot better. I think that when they were using all of their steam, it wasn't the volume of the work that mattered; it was the quality that mattered. I always aspired to be that kind of comic creator. On the same note, I don't want to be, "Oh look, look, he can write fifty titles." I have no interest in being that guy. It's just I can.

So, I don't drink and I don't play video games, which is the more horrible thing to happen to mainstream comics—the creation of PlayStation. If they would take them away from comic creators, you wouldn't even hear about a late book.

So, there's that and I am way, way ahead of schedule. I am six months ahead on all of my books. That means whatever mood I'm in when I wake up, that's the book I'll write. There's no deadline emergency. If I wake up and I'm in a *Daredevil* mood—usually when the book comes out and Alex [Maleev] and I are talking I am in a *Daredevil* mood I'll write *Daredevil* because I'm in a mood to write it. I can be in a *Powers* mood for two solid weeks and write tons of it.

ALEX: So, how long does it take you to turn out a book?

BRIAN: I don't know. Sometimes it takes a long time and sometimes you have a creative orgasm and it comes out of you. Not to be gross but sometimes it comes out of you. Don't you ever get to typing and you know, it just builds and comes right out of you. I don't know, it's just very organic. When the organic thing's happening it's a lot of fun.

Sometimes I type something that ends up looking like an Alan Moore script. Then I go back on a day when I am less of a fanatic and I format it so it looks normal. [*Laughs*]

That's the thing. If you stay ahead of schedule deadline is not an issue. It's all pure. So, anytime have to write something under a crunch, I always hate it. I just don't want that feeling. That's just spoiling myself but it works for me.

ALEX: Let's switch gears. This will be where things turn a little bit. I read in the back of an issue of *Powers* where you spoke about continuity. It was a transcript from a convention where you spoke about continuity. Can you give me a couple highlights regarding your beliefs regarding continuity?

BRIAN: What did I say? [*Laughs*]

ALEX: All right, I'll tell you. I can't quote it verbatim, I'll just get the basic gist . . .

BRIAN: Yeah, fine.

ALEX: Your idea regarding continuity was respect for creators who came before you: that you didn't want to contradict someone else's work.

BRIAN: Yeah.

ALEX: So, you hold true to that statement?

BRIAN: Yeah, pretty much. That's not the only thing but yeah.

ALEX: I would think that this comes from the fact that the comic industry, as a standard rule, treats itself like a mini Hollywood.

BRIAN: Not really. It may be perceived that way by you but a lot of the people I know in comics don't treat it like the be all, end all of human existence. They are so happy to be doing comics.

ALEX: Errrr . . .

BRIAN: I know. There are people in this business but they come and go so quickly that they don't even count to me. They are making properties so they can sell them. That sort of stuff.

ALEX: But there are people in the industry who still act like that. We've been in and around the industry since the '90s. There's still that fan perception of creators thinking they are above the fans.

BRIAN: Are you saying that there are comic creators who act above the fans?

ALEX: Yes. There's a lot of them.

BRIAN: There are a few of them. I would call those people assholes. Let's refer to them as assholes and there are assholes everywhere. That's not just in comics. That's everywhere! You leave the house and you're going to bump into an asshole.

There are people, say you walk around the small-press alley, and you find people who are acting like they are royalty deserving some sort of entitlement and they're shocked that you don't see it. They're just waiting for a mainstream break so they can be assholes to everyone. That guy is just waiting for a reason.

My thing is: I don't choose to view comics that way because there are so many people who don't act that way.

ALEX: Can I ask you a question?

BRIAN: Yeah.

ALEX: Based on the internet, based on simply typewritten words on a screen, how is anyone supposed to make an accurate judgment call on anyone else?

BRIAN: Here's an idea: just read the books and enjoy them.

END.

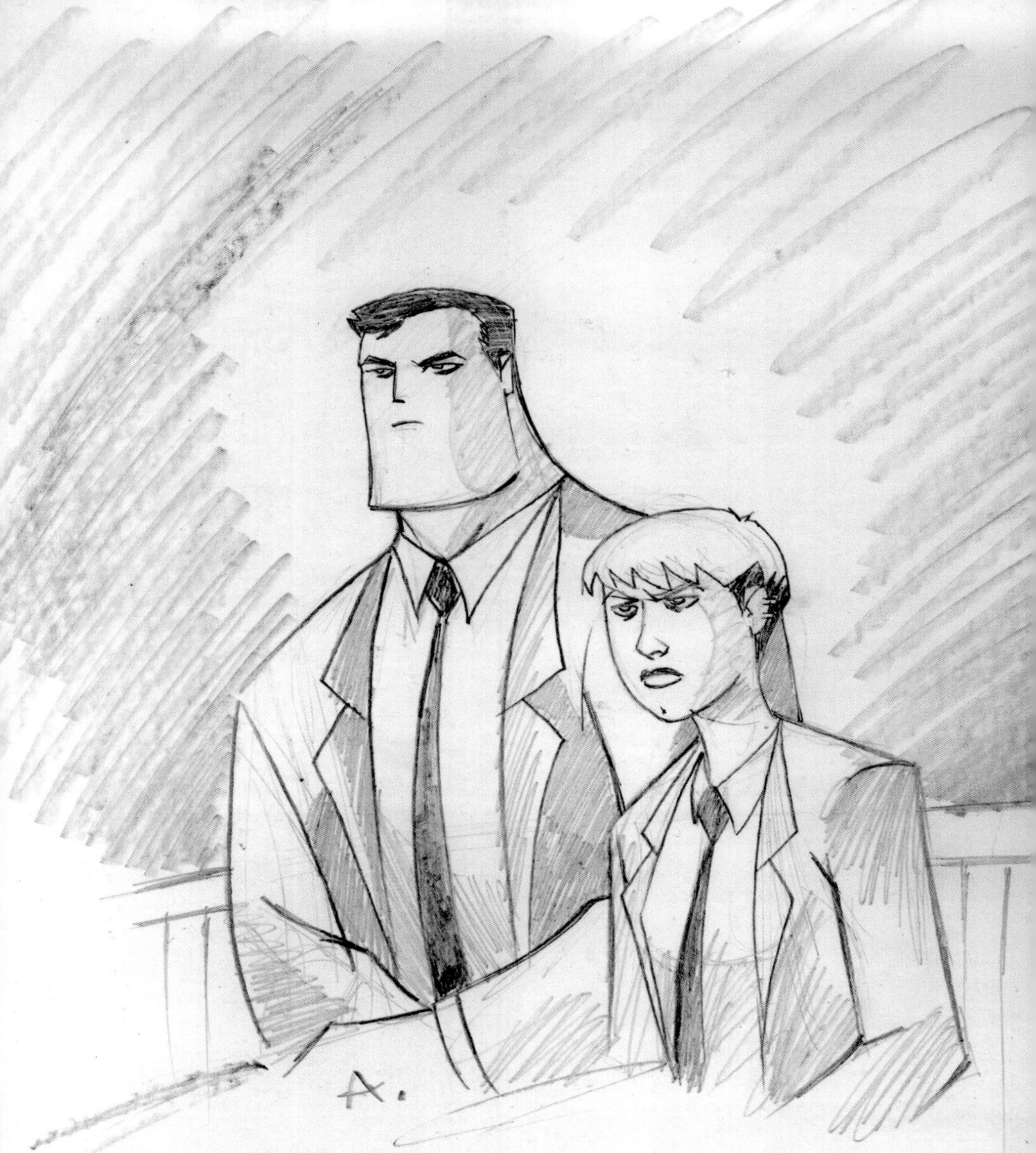
A.

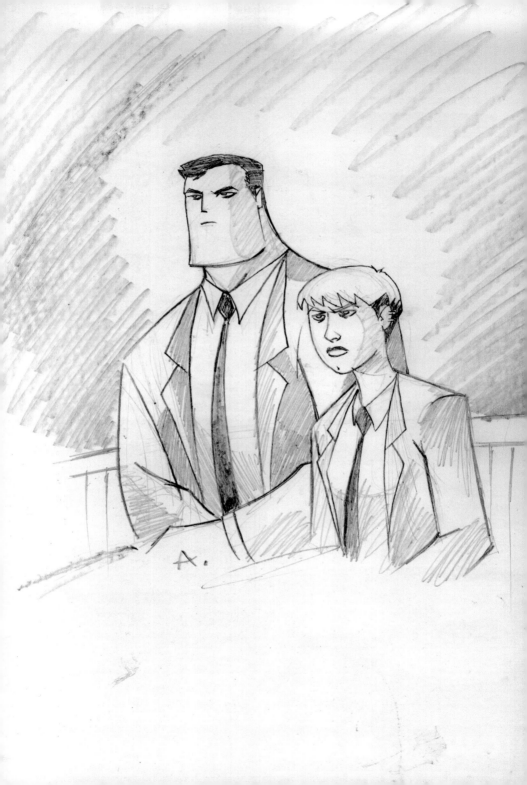

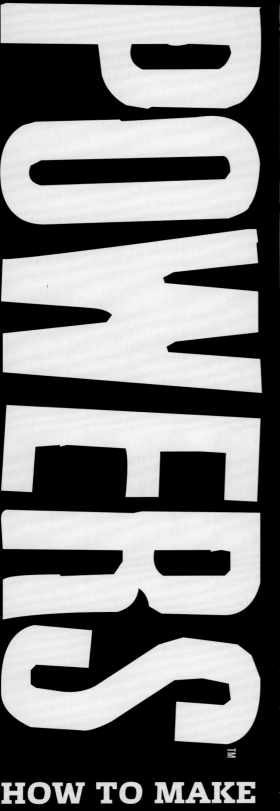

POWERS

HOW TO MAKE
POWERS

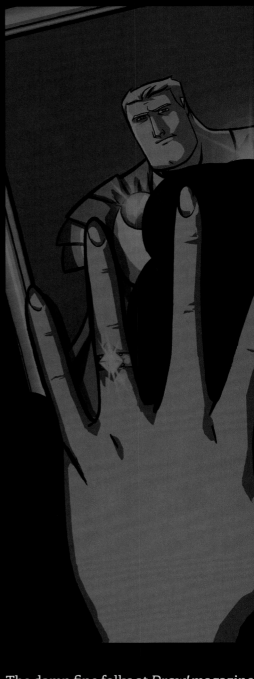

The damn fine folks at *Draw!* magazine asked Mike and the gang to put together this intensive behind-the-scenes look at the creation of *Powers*, the monthly comic. We are presenting it here as it originally appeared in the magazine.

A very special thank-you to *Draw!* magazine for their attention and generosity.

—Brian Michael Bendis

POWERS™

Wow, *Draw!* magazine is one of the *Powers* team most favorite mags. In just a short time *Draw!* ha proven to bring insightful lessons from the land c comics and animation to the people, and we hop to do the same here—shed a little light on how w go about our process of work.

It all begins with the script from Brian Bendis. S without further hype (doesn't he get enough? here is my partner and good friend, Brian Bendi with a few words on how he builds his scripts.

—Mike Avon Oeming,
***Powers* artist and cocreator**

I don't know anything.

I'm not being modest or taking my usual bat in the water of self-loathing. I really don't knov anything. I'm self-taught. I learned as I wen And what I learned was that there are no hard set "rules" for writing. There is no one pearl c wisdom that will open the door to the univers of writing. Anytime someone tells me what th "rules" are, my eyes roll up in my head and I los consciousness. So, I can't promise you'll fin anything even remotely resembling that here.

Any technical writing technique or theory tha I hold to—and I definitely do hold to some vita techniques and theories—I got from a boo called *Story* by Robert McKee. Actually, I picke up a lot from pop-culture osmosis, as I am sur many of you have, but this book put names an labels on it. It organized what I had learne into a formidable and essential text. *Story* i absolutely essential reading for all professe storytellers and lovers of the craft of storytellin no matter what medium. It gets you thinking an keeps you on course, and really, what's mor important than that?

BUILDING ■
■ THE PAGE
WITH THE 2003 *POWERS* TEAM

of the storytelling with dialogue attached. It's very similar to a movie screenplay with each word of scene description picked for maximum impact. I'm brief but I am to the point.

Other styles include the "Marvel house style," in which the writer gives the artist a page or two of story description. The artist then interprets the story the way he or she wants, then the writer comes back and constructs the dialogue to accentuate the art. Alan Moore is famous for writing complicated stream-of-consciousness scripts for artists to approach like cryptographers. Paul Jenkins is known to fill scripts with personal anecdotes to accentuate the kinds of emotions he wants to convey in his scenes. Mark Millar drinks himself into a coma and wakes up three days later to find all of his scripts for the year neatly typed up and ready to go.

learned how to write from two things: practice and reading other people's scripts. I love to read a good script more than I love going to a movie or reading a book or comic. I love reading scripts to movies before they are released so that when I do finally get to see them, I can compare the movie I directed in my head to the movie I am watching.

The only advice I can give is to write honestly. Don't write what you think people want. All people want is to not be insulted. They want to be entertained. They want to know the person writing to them has something honest and interesting to say.

If you write something you think people want, you will always fail. Let's say that everyone loves blue this year—blue is all the rage. So you sit down and write something blue. Well, by the time you get your blue out for people to see, people will have moved on to pink and won't want blue anymore. And now you're stuck with this blue thing that no one wants, including you.

The best thing you can offer the world as a writer is something you'd like to read, something that you would buy. Then, if someone else wants to buy it too, that's great news for you. It's all gravy after that. But bare minimum, having something you wrote be something you would want to read is really the reason anyone in any medium writes. That's why we made *Powers*: we wanted to buy the comic.

But—there is no standard script format used in the comic book industry. People just kind of find their ways around the unique concept of collaboration with artists to tell a story.

My style is referred to in "the biz" as full script, which means there's a panel-by-panel description

(That last one, of course, is a joke. Mark Millar doesn't do that . . . Ed Brubaker does.)

One of the hardest things storytellers have to accept is that they can't control the environment in which their work is read or their readers' mindsets, so they have to try to control the flow and timing as best they can. This is so important to me and it's probably the thing that drives my editors the craziest about me.

This balloon placement and final polish is my favorite part of writing comics. It's so much fun to have a pile of finished art to craft your words around. It's a beautiful feeling to see the work of an artist who is on the same page as you. I imagine it must feel quite similar to a film director and his editor when they have piles of really good footage to put together.

What I'm saying is: I'm a picker. I know some of my peers are not. Many of them hand in their scripts and look forward. That's fine . . . but I pick. I pick scripts to death, but in doing so I usually find the best one-liners, my best moments. On the flip side it's also where I make the most typos.

For the up-and-coming writers out there: if questions about craft and theory still bounce around your brain, visit me and my comic-creator peers at the jinxworld.com message board. Feel free to ask any questions and discuss it.

Also, for more information, I have a behind-the-scenes look at the creation of the *Jinx* graphic novel both in the graphic novel and on my website.

I don't have any advice on breaking into the business. If I'd known how, it wouldn't have taken me forever to get in. I do know one thing, though:

REPEAT 6
TILT EYES + HAND
REPEAT EYE BROW UP

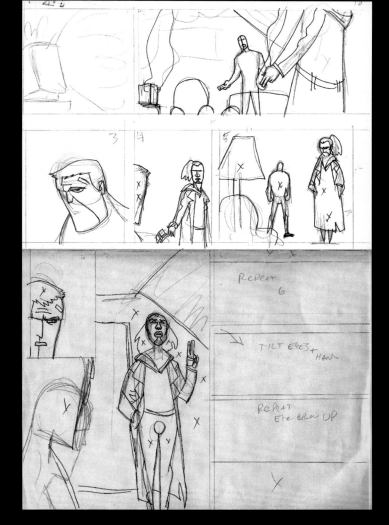

Writers write! They don't sit around wishing they were writing or talking about what they're thinking of writing. They write! Because while you're sitting around and talking about it, someone is out there writing their fucking ass off. Someone is out there kicking your ass and stealing your dream job.

So read this while you're on the toilet, but when you're done, write something. I will be.

—Brian Michael Bendis,
***Powers* writer and cocreator**

THE "PENCILS"

I say "pencils" because I rarely actually pencil. I go right from my breakdown to inking the page, with as little pencil as possible. When I get Brian's fat script, I'll usually scribble a very small panel layout, with no figures or composition. Then, I'll use an 11" x 17" photocopy paper and, very lightly with pencil, do a very loose breakdown. Many of our pages have a good amount of dialogue, so I've taken to leaving large tear areas to hold the words, and in this way, I can prevent most of my art being covered. From that stage, I break out my pen. Usually a ballpoint pen and that's when most of the drawing actually happens. I use as few lines as I can, always thinking of animation, using the "line of action" to make figures fluid. Often, I'll use the much-dreaded TANGENT line to move the eye.

I try and keep a continuous line on the exterior of figures, imagining each figure as a silhouette, a simple image.

You can see here where I've indicated repeating panels. Even if I'm changing a figure or expression within the panel, I will wait to photocopy the finished figure I'm repeating and then trace it. I don't paste down the repeats as often.

That effect works best when someone is shocked or taken off guard. I worry about all the drawn detail in the next stage.

The fun part for me is here. All my thought process happens in the layout, so now I can relax, toss on a DVD to listen to, and half watch while I draw. I work on a light box, lay down the breakdowns and place my drawing paper, which is not comic paper, but 11" x 17" laser copy paper. It's thicker than photocopy, but thinner than Bristol, so it's much easier to light box. I use two or three things to ink with—most of the page is inked with a rollerball pen. Just a black pen. I think it's called Uniball and it moves very fast, doesn't fade or change color, doesn't snag the paper or smudge. It's great. I can move really fast with this, and I'd say 90 percent of the page is done with that. Sometimes, for smaller faces, I use a Pigma Micron, number 001. I also use the number 1 Micron, which is big and broad, for panel borders and sometimes close-ups, or silhouette outlines like in panel 5 here.

Sometimes, I break out the brush, but the brush has a very distinct look from the pen. You can see the shift in brush to pen in the newer issues of

Powers. Sometimes I will use a combination of both, and some stories will call for just the brush. You may also notice I don't use a ruler. I only use straight lines for panel borders, but everything within the panels is freehand to give it a loose, alive feeling. I like the sketchiness of fast inking. For me, it helps give the energy you can find in sketches but rarely in pages.

Check out the repeated panels. You can see where I chose to shift or redraw expressions. I think the "acting" is where my strength is on the page. When my characters hurt, so do I a little. I love characters like Wazz or Triphammer who seem to be one thing, but are truly another. Just like most people you meet, they are not all they seem. This too, I think, is the strength in *Powers*. We show you that everything has a layer, a meaning. Everything from story, character, plot, art, colors to letters—all have layers and meaning.

—Mike Avon Oeming,
***Powers* artist and cocreator**

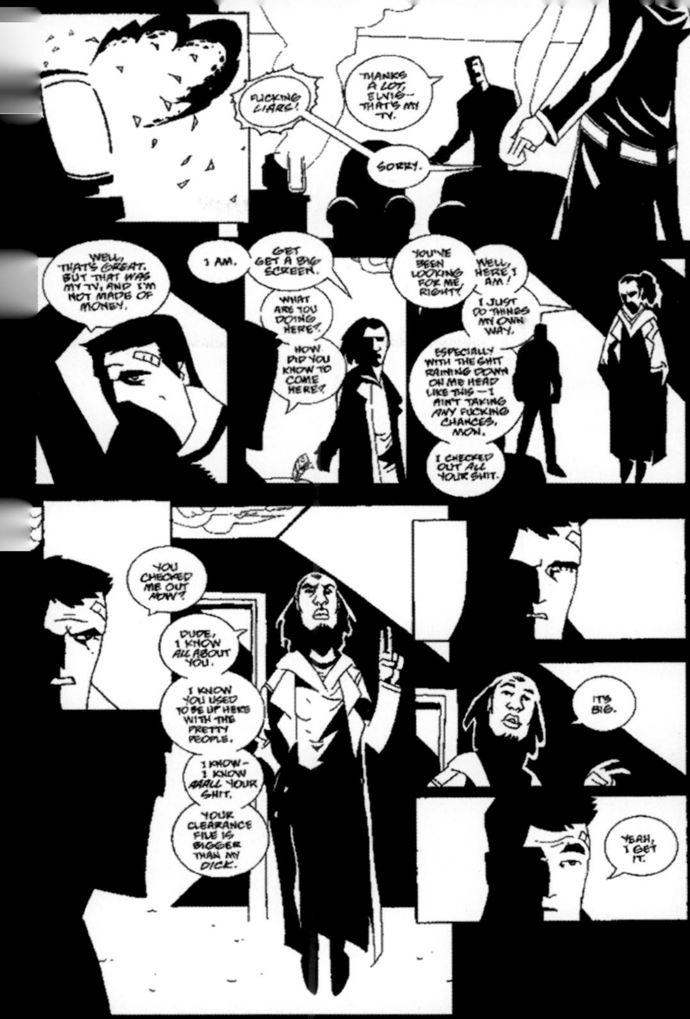
FUCKING LIARS!
THANKS A LOT, ELVIS—THAT'S MY TV.
SORRY.
WELL, THAT'S GREAT. BUT THAT WAS MY TV, AND I'M NOT MADE OF MONEY.
I AM.
GET A BIG SCREEN.
WHAT ARE YOU DOING HERE?
HOW DID YOU KNOW TO COME HERE?
YOU'VE BEEN LOOKING FOR ME, RIGHT?
WELL, HERE I AM!
I JUST DO THINGS MY OWN WAY.
ESPECIALLY WITH THE SHIT RAINING DOWN ON ME HEAD LIKE THIS—I AIN'T TAKING ANY FUCKING CHANCES, MON.
I CHECKED OUT ALL YOUR SHIT.
YOU CHECKED ME OUT MON?
DUDE, I KNOW ALL ABOUT YOU.
I KNOW YOU USED TO BE UP HERE WITH THE PRETTY PEOPLE.
I KNOW— I KNOW AAALL YOUR SHIT.
YOUR CLEARANCE FILE IS BIGGER THAN MY DICK.
IT'S BIG.
YEAH, I GET IT.

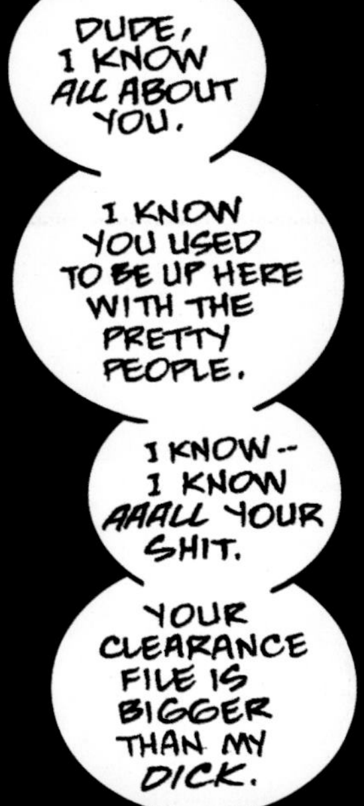
DUDE, I KNOW ALL ABOUT YOU.
I KNOW YOU USED TO BE UP HERE WITH THE PRETTY PEOPLE.
I KNOW-- I KNOW AAALL YOUR SHIT.
YOUR CLEARANCE FILE IS BIGGER THAN MY DICK.

THE LETTERS

Brian emails the script to me a month or two early, but I don't even open the file until I get the FedEx package of pages from Mike. Since most of the double-page spreads are drawn smaller, at printed size, I pull and photocopy them larger, to match the rest of the single (11" x 17") pages. (I really can't letter that tiny.) Then I tape the page to my board and attach an overlay sheet of 14" x 17" Canson Pro Layout Marker paper. Using a nonreproducing blue lead pencil, I make light circles on the overlay to "spot" the balloons, making sure they all fit, interconnect correctly, and somehow link to the right characters. Next, I use an Ames lettering guide and a T-square to blue-pencil rule my guidelines.

I've been working with Foundation Pentels on *Powers*. An X-Acto cut gives me the slight chisel tip I need—no cut for bold italics. I letter by hand to approximate the innate organic handicraft of the comic artwork. Visually repetitive computer fonts are fine for robots, public address announcements and politicians—mechanical constructs—but I think real comic people (with two-dimensional black outlines around them) need a more bouncy quirky freehand approach to simulate human speech. I draw the balloon outlines with oval templates, and French curve the tails to complement the geometric formatting of the rectangular page and panels (plus I draw ugly, bumpy, lopsided balloons freehand).

Some pages are silent (God bless you, Brian) but most are very wordy, and I usually have to completely redo two to three pages per issue to get a cleaner fit. I try hard to keep the words behind the figure work, tracing the overlapping outlines with a red pen, which reproduces as a trap line in scanning and complicates the colorist's job (sorry, Peter). This keeps focus on the characters, who can struggle through their story without being stabbed in the ear by balloon pointers, or sliced through the boobs or forehead by a big white ellipse full of dialogue.

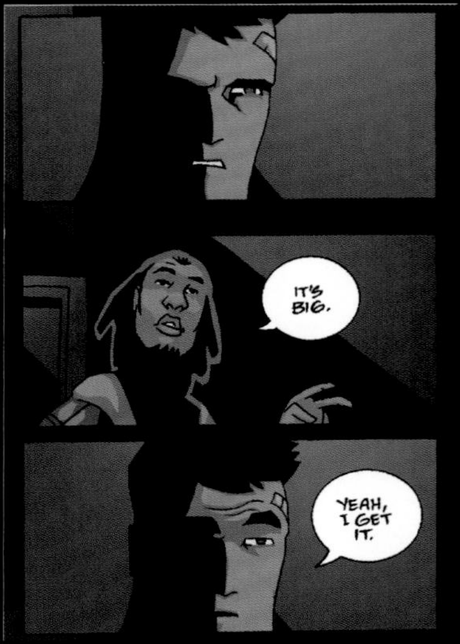
IT'S BIG.
YEAH, I GET IT.

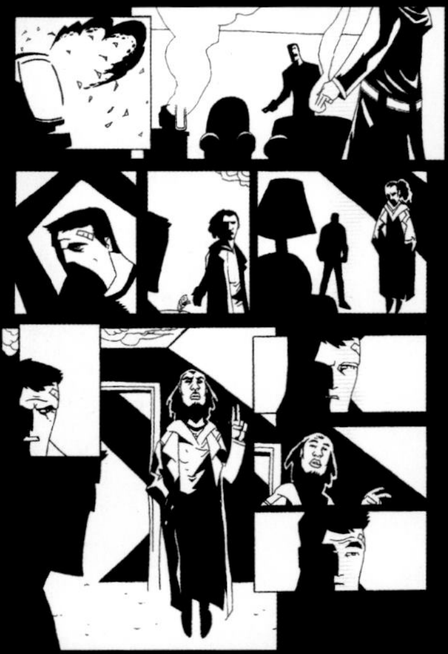

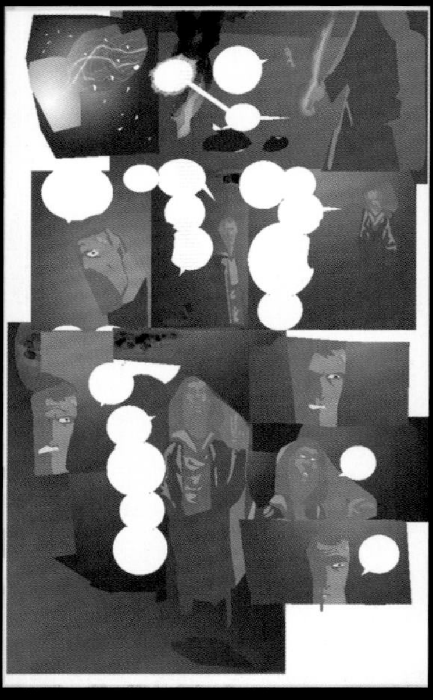

This is what the colors look like underneath Mike's lines.

Sound effects are computer generated for conceptually uniform, hard-edged, and repetitive sources, like gunshots, sirens, helicopters, and signage. I also design all those little TV logos and superscripts. Printed out, these CG sounds and signs are rubber cemented on the overlay, in position, so that Peter can scan everything in one pass. Death screams, orgasms, and demented laughter—noises made by people, nature, and God—get kinetic SFX done by hand directly on the overlay. I may make notes for suggestions about color holds or show-through on the outer edges of the page. Then, everything gets shipped off to California.

—Ken Bruzenak, *Powers* letterer

I'M A COLORIST/ INKER/LETTERER . . .

Let me explain . . .

As a colorist, I start the process by first receiving Brian's script via email, and Mike's pages with Ken's letters attached from Ken, who had his hands on 'em last.

From there, I scan in each page at 300 dpi, and I don't own one of those huge scanners that take a whole page, so it takes two passes to get one page of *Powers* actually scanned. I then scan in Ken's letters, which also end up in two parts. After all the scanning is complete, I put all the images together in Photoshop.

I then proceed to my semi-inking phase, by popping in all the blacks that Mike has nicely marked with an *X* . . . I then clean up any specks or marks that possibly appeared in the scan.

Finally the coloring begins. I set up each page with what we colorists call channels; there are a few of 'em: RGB (red, green, blue) and LINE ART.

That last one is the key. It acts like an overlay: that channel holds all of Mike's wondrous art. While I see the art, I'm actually working underneath it, not touching a thing . . . yet . . . I set up each page with what is called flats, and that is a basic color laid down, to separate the skin from clothing and all that is in between. Most of the time, I get the help of my amazing wife for this part. It can be tedious at times . . .

Okay, when all the setup is complete, I can finally get down to rendering each page. I add lighting and shadows as necessary. I closely read Brian's script as I color each page and decide what the mood of the particular scene would be. For this page, if you've noticed, Walker's skin tone (actually throughout the issue) is very muted, almost gray. This is because I chose to reflect the fact that Zora, his ill-fated wife-to-be, has been killed and it has taken its toll. The scene takes place in Walker's apartment at night and pretty much dictates that the colors should also be muted and very downplayed.

Well, after I go through rendering the page, I go into special effects mode, where I go in and add any type of lighting or glowing effects. These are my personal favorite things to do. I get to turn on the lights, create textures for certain powers, and add stuff into the background like on billboards and street signs.

There are basically two popular ways of achieving these effects: the "normal" way and the "layers" way. Normal is basically taking the actual art and pasting it down to the channel that I have been working on, and doing the effect right on the art. The layers way (which I prefer) actually adds another layer on top of the art, where I can do any type of effect, and if necessary, very easily retouch it.

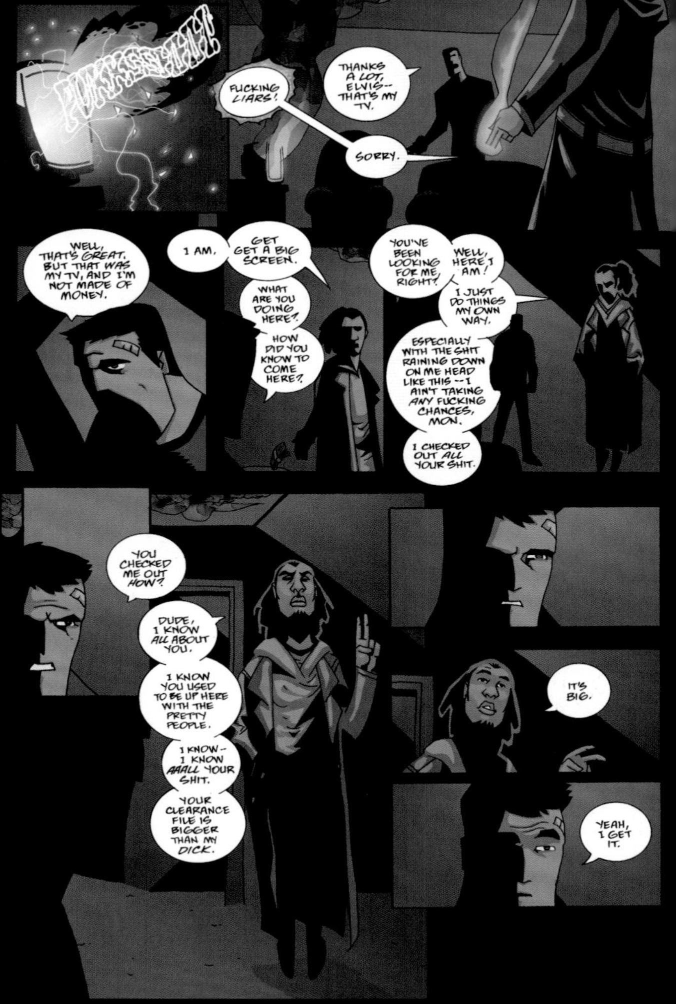

FUCKING LIARS!
THANKS A LOT, ELVIS-- THAT'S MY TV.
SORRY.
WELL, THAT'S GREAT. BUT THAT WAS MY TV, AND I'M NOT MADE OF MONEY.
I AM.
GET A BIG SCREEN.
WHAT ARE YOU DOING HERE?
HOW DID YOU KNOW TO COME HERE?
YOU'VE BEEN LOOKING FOR ME, RIGHT?
WELL, HERE I AM!
I JUST DO THINGS MY OWN WAY.
ESPECIALLY WITH THE SHIT RAINING DOWN ON ME HEAD LIKE THIS -- I AIN'T TAKING ANY FUCKING CHANCES, MON.
I CHECKED OUT ALL YOUR SHIT.
YOU CHECKED ME OUT HOW?
DUDE, I KNOW ALL ABOUT YOU.
I KNOW YOU USED TO BE UP HERE WITH THE PRETTY PEOPLE.
I KNOW-- I KNOW AAALL YOUR SHIT.
YOUR CLEARANCE FILE IS BIGGER THAN MY DICK.
IT'S BIG.
YEAH, I GET IT.

This is page 10 as it actually appeared in #19.

Once all the special effects are done and I'm happy with the page, I then put on my letterer's cap and proceed with placing Ken's scanned letters exactly where they belong on the page, also in Photoshop. Once that is done, I send off a JPEG to Brian and Mike, they give me their input on anything that might need tweaking, and I go about correcting it. I also go in and change any noticed typos that happen to be pointed out. Whew! After all that is done, the page is ready to be "trapped," which is the word I use for setting it up for print. I then either burn the issue onto a CD and FedEx it to Studio Color Group or I FTP it via cable modem, depending on the amount of time I have to get them the pages. And then I sleep for a week.

—Pete Pantazis, *Powers* colorist

Well, that's it, take it as you will—this is how we put *Powers* together. It's not traditional, it's not the best or right way to do things, but it's how we do it and how we feel most comfortable with it. Just like art, the process is done in such a way to best please the creators. You've heard from Brian, me, Ken, and Pete, but there are several other people behind the scenes. The Image control crew, who take care of everything from here; Brian's wife, Alisa, who takes care of all things legal; Pat Garrahy, who colored and did production on the first dozen or so issues; the websites and magazines who promote the book; and of course, the readers. Thanks to *Draw!* for giving us this chance to show you what's under our skirt.

Thanks,
Mike, Brian, Ken, and Pete, the *Powers* crew

POWERS

™

EMING INTERVIEWS BENDIS AND VICE VERSA

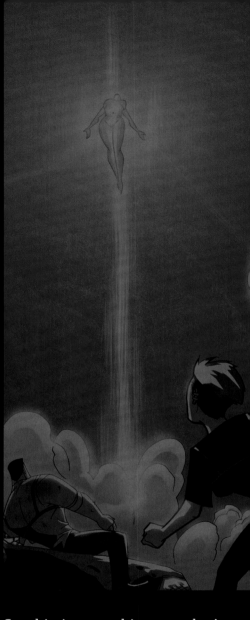

So, this is something you don't see every day: the creative team of the comic you just read raking each other over the coals a bit. We always thought our private talks were more interesting than the interviews we gave, so here, exclusively for you, is an unedited discussion between Mike and me on everything that we could think of at the time we thought to do this.

—Brian Michael Bendis

This section also includes original layouts from *Powers*.

OEMING: Why writing? Why have you chosen writing over art? I know one comes more naturally to you than the other and you never had a commercial style, but clearly you could be drawing some of your own stories, if not on a monthly basis, as a special issue or so. I could clearly see you drawing an *Alias* issue.

BENDIS: Life is opportunities. I took the art gigs when they came, both in comics and outside of comics. And now it's the writing gigs that are coming. I just read a great quote: "A career is about what you say no to." That is so true. I think about what I have decided not to do and why and wipe my brow in relief, you know? I supported myself as a graphic artist for almost twelve years. I will draw again. I love to do it. Plus, I am so much more successful as a writer, it's almost sad.

OEMING: You started as an artist, doing work for local mags and papers. Even doing caricatures. At what point did you want to start writing?

BENDIS: The first time I drew a caricature at someone's fucking nightmare bar mitzvah. That did pay well, and it funded all my crime graphic novels, but it has to be the lowest form of artistic expression on the planet. I really hated it. And as I hated it more and more, my caricatures got meaner and meaner.

What is the worst job you ever took for money? And don't say *Powers*, ass.

OEMING: It was last year. I did the cover to a children's book called *Blue Avenger*. I thought it would be fun. Hey, this is a "real book" I'd be doing a cover to. It pays really well, too. But nothing on this earth is worse than a book editor. They know everything about words, but nothing about pictures. Example: They say they want a zebra, so I give them a zebra, but then they ask for no stripes. I say, then it will look like a horse. No, they say, they want a zebra, just no stripes. So I do it . . . then they say it doesn't look like a zebra. This story had something to do with a donut. So I drew one in the background like they wanted. Well, I put sprinkles on it, because without sprinkles or something, it just looks like a tire. They say, "Make it glazed," so I do, and it looks like a tire. I assure them with colors, it will look like it's glazed. Then they say it looks too literal; it should be a "cosmic donut." No shit. So I made it look like there was space swirling out of the fucking thing like it's giving birth to the universe. In the end, I don't think any of us were happy with it. This was worse than doing porn comics in the early '90s, because at least then I could get excited, jerk off, and get something out of it. But this was pure torture.

When did writing really click for you, meaning you went beyond writing stuff to facilitate your art to where the art was there to facilitate your writing?

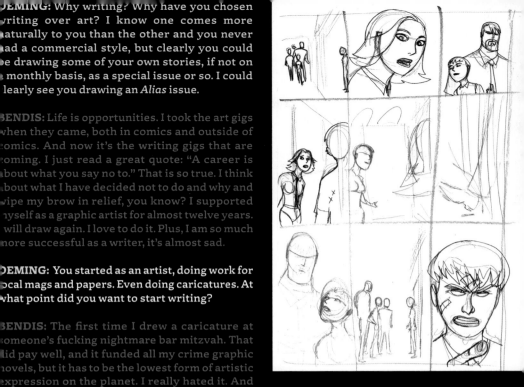

BENDIS: It was never about writing only to facilitate my art. It was more about just overall storytelling. The only thing odd about the whole thing is how natural the expression of writing is for me and what a struggle drawing is and was, and yet I wasn't even considering the idea of writing for a living, because that seemed just insane to me.

Why did you start drawing? Not when, why?

OEMING: I'd always drawn because of my mom. She would draw a lot. She had a drinking problem (well, actually, drinking wasn't the problem—she did that fine—but the rest of her life went to shit) and I had to be raised by my aunt and uncle for about seven years. For the first five, she didn't live with us; she was trying to get sober, but still drinking. Anyway, she'd write me letters with drawings in them. I've always associated art with life, I guess, because of that. I remember once getting a letter from her with some happy clown on it she drew. For the most part, I was patient—knew what was wrong with her, and it was just a waiting game until she got better. But when I got that letter, it set me off. Usually she drew flowers and butterflies, but this had happy clowns on it, and I guess a happy clown was the last thing I felt like. I remember ripping it up. I was about five. The only thing worse than the happy clowns was ripping them apart. We kept drawing though, and it became a cheap pastime.

I stopped drawing shortly after Mom came to live with us. I think I didn't "need" it anymore most importantly, I remember a teacher telling me a drawing I did wasn't very good and that I was much better than that. So I stopped. I didn't really draw for a long time after that. A few times, but not all the time like I had been. Then I moved from Jersey to Texas (Mom and I did this once before, when I was younger and she first got custody of me, but we came back to Jersey) in about the sixth grade, and it was terrible for me. I didn't adjust at all. It was actually traumatic. I locked myself in my room. I learned to jerk off properly and read comics. Funny how those two go together so well.

Anyway, I found comics at a flea market and fell in love with Spider-Man all over again. I started tracing and tracing. We moved back to Jersey. I went from tracing to copying to drawing. Then X-Men Annual #9 came out, and it was all over for me. Art Adams made me want to be a comic book artist for sure, and I've been on that path ever since.

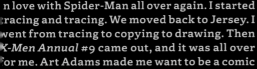

Before Robert McKee's _Story_, what was your major writing influence? Was it simply reading other writers that turned you on, or was there a specific school of thought that you worked on? Or was it mostly instinctual?

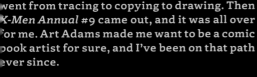

BENDIS: I was taken away by three writers: Richard Price, David Mamet, and Woody Allen. The three best dialogue writers in the history of any medium. Characters that talk to each other and not at each other. I studied their work, and it sent me on a quest for the work they loved, and I started reading that, and then I started making my own decisions as a writer. People hate when I say this, but I am totally self-taught. Never took a class.

You write, as well. What are your influences other than _Penthouse Forum_?

OEMING: Well, not to kiss your ass, because I've already got the _Powers_ gig, but at this point, it's you. Not so much what or how you write, but the things we discuss through the making of _Powers_ have become the new tools I carry with me in writing and storytelling. There are writers and books you've introduced me to and ways to study a story that have equipped me with new writing skills. So you can only blame yourself when I'm off writing and not drawing _Powers_!

Before you, I was into superficial writing. I wrote stories around cool things, not around story. That was one problem with _Ship of Fools_. I gave Bryan Glass ideas to write around—a bunch of disjointed, weird shit he had to try and put together in a story—so in the end it had no focus. We plan on reissuing _Ship of Fools_ slightly rewritten and some art moved around to open up the story and give it focus. At that point, my main writing influences were Mike Baron from _Nexus_, which I feel is the best overall series ever written, and Douglas Adams of _Hitchhiker's Guide_. I still love that stuff.

BENDIS: Also, not many people know how many things you can do and how varied your art and line work can be. What got you on the road you are on now?

OEMING: Shortly before _Powers_, I think I had finally started on a good "realistic style." I did a short _Kabuki_ story like that. But then at the same time, that's when my career hit a dead end (like a lot of pros in the mid-'90s crash), and I had to get a "real job." My son, Ethan, was born, so I needed to bring in money on a regular basis. So, with the new job and baby came less time to work, so I needed to focus on a more simple, less time-consuming drawing style. It had really started about a year earlier, when I was really trying to be Alex Toth, but then I found Bruce Timm and married the two in a way that worked and was less time consuming. Don't think you can just jump into a simple style; it's actually very difficult at first stripping the work down like that. It really makes your weaknesses shine through; it takes a long time to develop. So I eased into it. I tried working on *Batman Adventures*, but I still couldn't do the style. I think I got real comfortable with it just as I started *Hammer of the Gods*. Then *Powers* happened, and by that time I was really into it. Look at the first trade of *Powers* and the work coming out now—you can still see a progression. While it's still there, I've gotten pretty far away from Timm and Toth, almost more into general animation, especially during the *Supergroup* and *Anarchy* story arcs, when I was using the mono dead lines. They look like animation cels.

Was there a genre you were into before crime stories?

BENDIS: Marvel superhero comics.

DEMING: At what point did those crime stories really take hold of you?

BENDIS: Yeah, this is still odd to me, because I didn't know that this is what I wanted as a writer until I started writing. Everything that came out of me were these poppy Jim Thompson graphic novels, and I didn't even know who he was. No one was more surprised than me. It's the idea that in crime fiction you can examine a character by really throwing him into a corner and seeing what he will do.

DEMING: Do you think that interest in crime comics, the idea of someone being thrown into a corner emotionally, is a reflection of your own experiences? I know, like many people, you didn't have a perfectly happy childhood. Do you think any residual anger from when you were younger is what attracted you to crime stories?

You really introduced me to crime stories and noir. Who introduced it to you, or did you discover it consciously or subconsciously? I've always been into European mythology, but it wasn't until recently that it became conscious. I can trace it back to my childhood. How far does a fascination with crime stories go back for you?

BENDIS: Hmm . . . I started my love of the genre in comic form. All those crime comics like Steranko's and all the Muñoz novels really got under my skin. Then, like my writer heroes, I backtracked to find Jim Thompson and Hammett. I read every Thompson novel in a three-week period, like I was taking a course in it.

...hen I saw the *Visions of Light* documentary, and they started talking about the rules of film noir. I knew them, but I had never heard them spoken out loud before, and when I heard them I literally stood up in the theater and yelled, "Hallelujah!" I knew that this was for me.

OEMING: When a story comes to you, what part of it comes first—the overall idea or specifics of the story?

BENDIS: Could be anything. Sometimes it's just an image, like a dead superhero lying in a playground, or a one-liner that you think is so good you start constructing a story about it for the sole purpose of publishing that one line.

When you read the script, what do you do—just read it through and take it in, or start thinking as the artist immediately? What goes on in that head of yours? We have never discussed that.

OEMING: I think I'm lucky, because images come to my head immediately. I really mean immediately—sometimes before I finish the sentence, I know what the panel is going to be. I rarely even do a second layout or change a panel when I first draw it, unless it doesn't fit the story and you ask me to, which is fine. But images come to me like an attack, to the point that it's distracting. I think that comes from my childhood. My aunt and uncle always had the radio on—if the TV wasn't on, the radio was, and when we slept, we slept with the radio on. It was always easy listening—that '70s and '80s singer-songwriter stuff, like Crosby, Stills, and Nash; James Taylor; Billy Joel; Cat Stevens; Carly Simon; Simon and Garfunkel; Gary Numan; Harry Chapin, that sort of stuff. All those songs had stories. So I'm sleeping there, or trying to sleep, and listening to these songs. Each of them told a loose story, and with my eyes closed, I saw the stories or played them out in my head. I'd have to say that singer-songwriters may have been the single most important writing influence on me—artistically as well, because that's where the immediate imagery comes from.

To this day, I hear a song and I can build a story around it. That's where *Hammer of the Gods* came from—Led Zeppelin's "Immigrant Song": "We come from the land of the ice and snow, from the midnight sun where the hot springs flow, the Hammer of the Gods will drive our ships to new lands, to fight the horde, sing and cry, 'Valhalla, I am coming!'"

Those words made me write what became *Hammer of the Gods*, although it has little to do with the words of the song . . . well, except the last line—that's almost the plot!

Do you think in terms of the themes, then the story builds around that, or do you have an idea you bring the themes to?

BENDIS: After I decide on the story, I start questioning what the purpose of it is. I really don't think enough people do this—ask themselves why they are writing what they are writing. It needs to say something other than just being cool. And sometimes I clearly state the purpose in the material, and other times I don't—I just let it hang there. And sometimes the theme can derail the original story and take it in another direction. You have to be open to it. You've seen me do that, do a 180 on what I told you the story was going to be, because the characters or theme dictate it.

OEMING: That's awesome. I try to do that, too. I either have the meaning and build the story around that, or have a cool story with no meaning and then find that meaning and go back and work it in. Like in *Powers*, it's a superhero universe seen through the eyes of police. The theme is how it is observed by the media and everyday man. What came first—was it the media seeing heroes, or a superhero universe seen through the eyes of cops?

BENDIS: At first it was the clichés of the superhero genre through the harder eyes of the cops. And then we both decided to add the VH1 *Behind the Music* twist to it—that every arc has some footing in a famous rock-star story—and that's when it became magic to us. That's when I knew it was worth publishing, because now it was about a lot of things.

OEMING: How do you structure a story? I think now you mull it over in your head and then go straight to writing, but was there a time when you wrote step-by-step outlines and built it around that?

BENDIS: I think I learned how to do that, so now I am much more interested in fucking around with the three-act structure. Like, with you I have shorthand, so I can be more open about how I write the script. I write a list of scenes and what each scene's point is or what the big image of the scene is—the moment—and then I let the characters go for a ride.

OEMING: In *Powers*, we tend to stay away from the big exploding ending. We are more comfortable with a character-driven or psychological ending than a Jerry Bruckheimer explosion—action through character rather than spectacle. I've always felt it was because spectacle endings are, well, not that smart. I love simple stories, like how in *Bastard Samurai*, it's a basic revenge story.

BENDIS: Boy, I really liked that plug you just tossed in like that, all casual and shit. I am proud of you; you've come a long way.

OEMING: I'm not calling my own ending dumb, but where I like to chop the head off of my villain...

You would tend to have the villain be defeated through character rather than physical action. Is that because you find the physical ending too simple?

BENDIS: Um, no. Basically anyone can blow up the set James Bond-style at the end. A chimp could do that. Doesn't mean it isn't satisfying, but I always look for the smarter or unexpected route.

OEMING: Are you afraid of writing an ending that doesn't engage enough thought from the reader? Zhang Yimou's movie *Hero* really struck me as having a Bendis ending.

BENDIS: Hmm, that's nice, I saw this Jenna Jameson movie that I thought ended a lot like one of your books. Ha!

Well, no. I mean, it's all about that particular story. I love a big action scene, but I also think a person hitting another person is a big damn deal, you know? You ever get slapped? It fucks up your whole day. So, I try to write the action with that in mind, and as endings go, I like to leave it a little vague—let the audience think about it for a second, maybe.

OEMING: What bothers you most about writers today in comics? I don't mean outside of the page, but what is the most common problem you see in their works?

BENDIS: Other than the lazy, alcoholic poseurs that are more into their image than their work, I think what really bums me out is I see a lot of comics that were failed movie pitches, or people writing comics to sell as properties. Now, we both have had the luck of selling movie properties, including *Powers*—but we never, ever, ever consciously created something for that purpose. Comics are a vital medium, form of expression and entertainment, not a steppingstone or a slum for your shit *Aliens* knockoffs. I really hate all the clutter that is thrown into *Previews* that is so clearly made to get Hollywood's attention.

OEMING: What is it specifically about the writers you admire? The work, not the person. Greg Rucka, for instance.

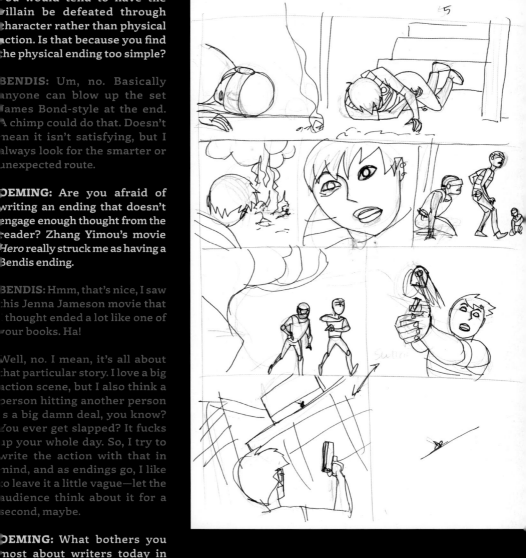

BENDIS: He is a real writer. He is the best technical writer I have ever met or talked to. And he isn't afraid to talk about the craft, like so many are. Many writers are afraid to talk about it because they think people will find out how full of shit they are.

OEMING: Mamet.

BENDIS: There's so much I couldn't even type it here. He is my guru. I have a huge book of interviews by him that I keep on my nightstand. Like the Bible, I go to it if I am lost. Seriously.

OEMING: Alan Moore.

BENDIS: He's the gold standard. He's like our De Niro. He is so good so often that he is often taken for granted.

I won two consecutive Best Writer Eisners, and I don't think I did anything as inventive as anything he did in one double-page spread of *Promethea*. It seems insane to me that his books aren't higher on the charts. But listen, he's a witch living in the blue dimension, so he's fine. Okay, I got some for you. Mike Mignola.

OEMING: He's my Mamet. Honestly, when I am lost or uninspired, I flip through his work. The looseness, especially. He's not afraid of the line, he's not a slave to it, he rules it! I love tight artists, I really do, but the tight lines often suck the life out of their work. Mike's lines are so loose they can be sloppy and abstract and still work. Besides the lines, Mike's work exudes a mood I find almost hypnotic. He is mythology on the page, his work evokes the subconscious.

BENDIS: Alex Toth.

OEMING: Storytelling and black spotting. While he doesn't do storytelling like I do—I like a much more "in-between" feel to the panels—he cuts to the chase. He's the master of simplicity, and yet his work is more complex than most. He's a genius and a master of the medium. His black spotting and composition is just something few, if any, can compare to. My favorite work of his is the late '60s into the early '80s. I still write him from time to time and he writes back.

BENDIS: Bruce Timm.

OEMING: He actually helped me understand Alex Toth's work better. From Timm, I learned a lot about form, keeping the exterior of a body simple, smooth lines on the outside that make the character flow, not interrupted by lines that break the form. Timm flows better than any artist I know of.

BENDIS: Adam Hughes.

OEMING: Adam taught me a lot, hands on. I worked with him when we lived in the same town. We met just before he broke into comics. He introduced me to Steve Rude's work (Neil Vokes showed him Rude; Neil showed me Toth and Timm; Neil is another big influence on me) and taught me a lot about storytelling. There is a panel in a *Star Trek* novel he did where there are guys running off a ship in line. He drew them as if it were animation, each guy in the next pose a person would be in, as if running, left foot, right foot, and in-betweens. We talked a lot about art and artists. He tends to like more refined artists, while I like them looser and sloppy. Adam is also a very close friend.

BENDIS: Steranko.

OEMING: I've never been into Steranko's work. If you see any there, it's the Jack Kirby influence probably, or the influences of others. I love Jim's work, but didn't discover it until recently.

BENDIS: David Mack. In fact, let's gossip about all the shit we know about David Mack.

OEMING: I happen to know that David is a great wrestler and can fart really loud. Thankfully, he never farted on me when we wrestled. His design sense, the lack of respect for the borders of a page, really influenced me! You can see that a lot in *Bulletproof Monk* and in the *Oni Press Color Special* issue with the *Powers* story we goofed around on. All done in love. He's also in need of Ritalin.

What is something you see in your favorite writers (not one I mentioned above) that you like the least?

BENDIS: Well, I think I get annoyed at how criticized they are by people who don't get it. I get very annoyed at how much shit Aaron Sorkin gets from critics when his work is so vastly superior to everything else on television; it's amazing to me.

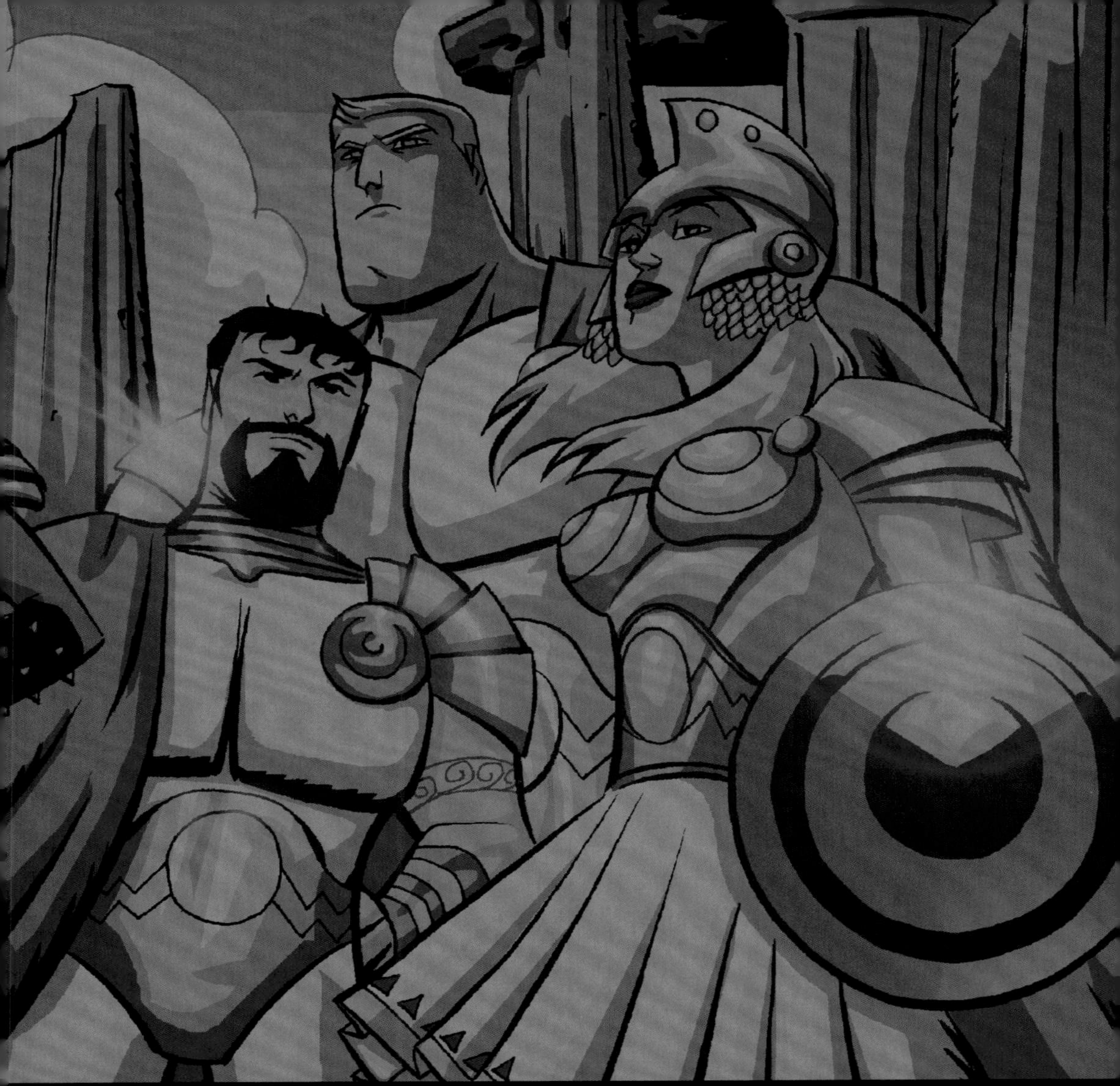

You hate *Watchmen*? Explain this travesty.

OEMING: I don't hate it, it just doesn't get me. I think it's because it's been so influential on other books that when I try reading it, all those lessons have been used in good and bad ways so the effect is watered down when I read the original. I've tried reading it three times, and not once did it interest me. Now don't get me wrong, I love Alan Moore. I even love his music. In fact, there are ways I like his music more than the writing. I love most of his work. *Parliament of Justice* is very influenced by *V for Vendetta*. I just don't "get" *Watchmen*. It's just a mental shortcoming on my part. I'd die to work with Moore.

BENDIS: For a lifelong comic professional, you don't seem very into comics on a monthly basis. Do you read a lot of comics? What do you read, what's your favorite comic? Why are you s standoffish to the business on some levels?

OEMING: It's odd, but it's like this with a lot c comics people I know. The more you make comic the less you read them. Nothing makes me mor happy than writing or drawing comics, but readin them doesn't hold my interest. In fact, I rarel read the finished product of my own book. I thin the last issue of *Powers* I read when it was dor is like issue #7. No shit. Same with *Hammer*. Bu with *Bastard*, I did read those when it was don to measure if we went too far in not explainin everything, or *Parliament* because it was Neil an me, and that was a goal to meet. But for the mos part I don't read my own comics. I enjoy makin them, not reading them.

I've been reading the *Daredevil* trades, and fucking love those. I've read Rucka's *Whitec*

OEMING: When you read a story or watch a movie, and you are trying to analyze it, what are the things you are looking for?

BENDIS: Why it works or why it doesn't. I am mostly examining how scenes work juxtaposed against each other. There's where the magic is. How about you?

OEMING: Mostly it's visuals, but in stories, I look for truth. It can be a super-wacky film, but it has to have its own truth. I just saw *Kill Bill*, and there are ridiculous things going on, but for this film, it's all true and works. I'm still learning to learn.

What's one of the newest things you've learned about writing? Where did you learn it from—watching a film, reading a book?

BENDIS: Well, I am very inter-ested in breaking out of my comfort zone. There are things I know I do well, and there are things I do not know if I do well, so I am trying to do them to experience it and see if it works. In *Powers*, particularly, I have attempted styles and genres I never thought I would

recently. Other than *Hellboy*, I don't read monthly comics. I also stay away from the business in general—who's doing what, what new books are out, who is running what company. I feel that if it's not my business, I'm not going to waste my energy on it. All my energy goes into my work and family. There's a war between Marvel and DC these days, and I couldn't be less interested. Also, I just don't understand a lot of it; I'm not business minded.

Don't get me wrong—I love comics, but I love making them more than anything else. It's like that a lot in life for me. I'm about the journey, not the destination.

What do you see in, say, a Scorsese film that repeats itself as a flaw in storytelling? I know the aforementioned Robert McKee hates *Goodfellas*, but he didn't elaborate, he simply laughed at it. What do you think it was?

BENDIS: Sour grapes. *Goodfellas* didn't hold to his predetermined structure values and it worked. So he shits on it. Though I wholeheartedly recommend his book, I am not a slave to it. Bitchy is bitchy; cranking on *Goodfellas* is bitchy.

try, specifically to see why.

What's the one thing about your art that you think you need to improve and why? And why haven't you tried it yet? And what are you waiting for?

OEMING: Ha, taking my time! I'd really love to have a project where I can slow down and think the shit out of each page and the story as a whole. Right now, it's largely instinct built from years of hands-on work, but I'd like to approach a project with no time constraints and really work it. I'd also like to work on my backgrounds more. I think taking my time would help, but I'm a speed freak.

In *Powers*, we have total freedom to do whatever we want or what the story wants us to do. At Marvel, you don't have that freedom. You have editors and bosses and characters that have to maintain continuity. I've found that what you've done with *Daredevil* is amazing—you actually found room for character growth there, something rare and hard to do in a mainstream, established series. How much does that hold you back? Especially on *Ultimate Spider-Man*, I imagine there's much less you can do. Shouldn't Mary Jane be smoking pot and having sex with Peter?

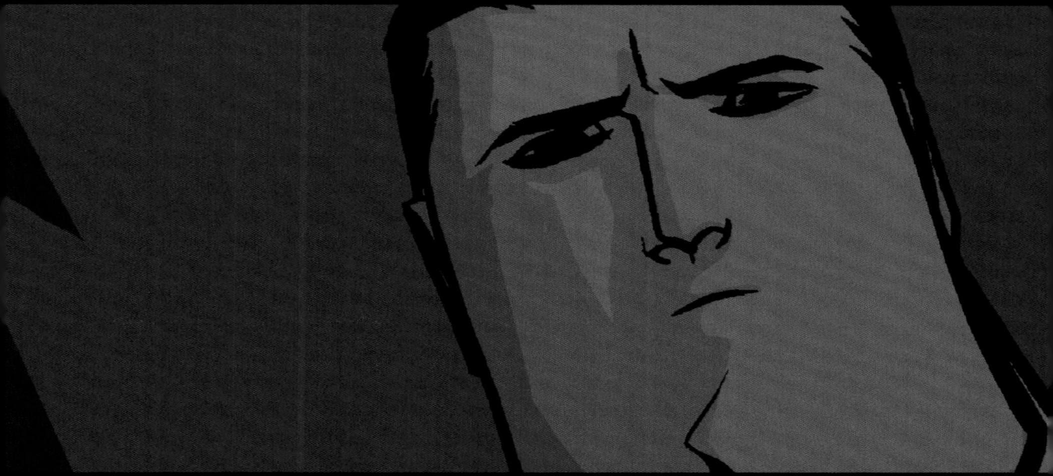

BENDIS: Who says she doesn't? Well, I don't see the limitations at Marvel as limitations. I see them as opportunities to be creative. I read this interview with Ridley Scott recently, and he said nothing makes him more inspired than a budget. He said every limitation put before him has created a situation where he forced himself to be more creative than he would have been otherwise. I have the same feeling. Also, it's the juxtaposition of creator owned and work for hire that has made my work so fulfilling to me. Both experiences have pros and cons, and I find they feed off each other. I think it has a lot to do with the way a lot of people have responded to my work.

Also, Marvel is pretty damn trusting of me, and I have been allowed to go out on the plank many a time. Anal, anyone? And I will forever be the guy who used the F-word in a Marvel comic first. See, you have had some unfulfilling work-for-hire experiences; you need a fulfilling one, and I am going to make you do one so you can experience how awesome it could be.

OEMING: Great! I can't wait. Maybe that's the one I can take my time on. Obviously drawing an issue of a comic takes longer than writing an issue of a comic—or at least it should. *Powers* is my love but also a monthly gig, which can be hard at times, grinding work.

BENDIS: Boo-hoo, wahh-wahh.

OEMING: I do my "side projects" really to keep me sane. Even though you write several books at a time, how do you keep any of those gigs from becoming stale?

BENDIS: If they got stale, I would bail in two seconds. Life is too short, and it's my name on the cover. Also, I stay ahead of schedule, so sometimes I don't write, let's say, *Powers* for months at a time, and then write it constantly for weeks. I write it when I am inspired to. That's the real key to everything.

You have the attention span of a ferret full of Snickers bars, so it's harder for you to focus but you're also a martial arts master, so it's odd. You are a conundrum wrapped in a package of contradiction.

OEMING: Thanks! How much longer do you see *Powers* going?

BENDIS: It's over. Bye, Mike.

OEMING: We know the ending, and we've talked it over. Not in terms of issues or years, but how many story lines do you see coming up? We've promised to never write or draw *Powers* beyond the amount of fresh ideas we have.

BENDIS: Exactly—we'll know when it's time to wrap it up. I think both of us were surprised at how challenging this year was creatively; we really pushed each other. I don't feel like we're even near the end.

OEMING: We've done less police procedurals, which are my favorite stories.

BENDIS: Me, too. They're fun to write. Why are you so into them?

OEMING: The pacing. I have trouble mixing noir and heroes. Sometimes you have Pete darken and thicken the lines because I have that problem. When I see cops walk into a room with a dead superhero, however, it's all mood and shadows. People are in danger in the *Powers* universe; you never know when Deena, Walker, the captain, whoever might get killed. I like the dirtiness of the work.

They do, unfortunately, have repeating conventions to the story that people think are tired of

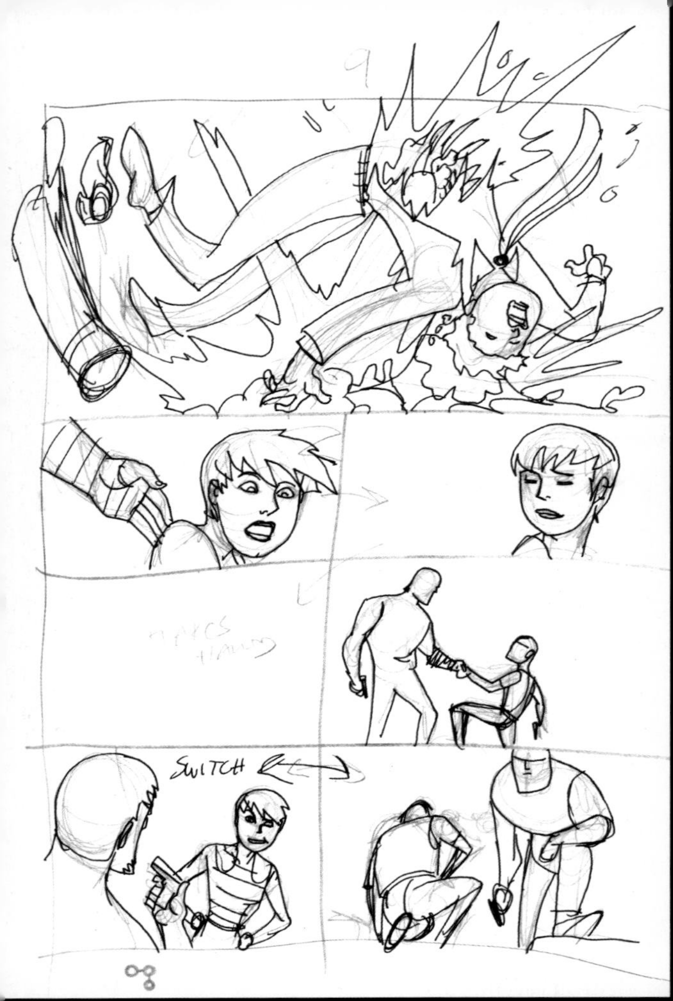
SWITCH

predictable. Like there must be a murder in a murder investigation, there must be a body, it must be a hero, etc. How do we continue to do those in such a way that our more astute readers won't perceive it as repetitious? *Homicide* and *Law and Order* do it every week.

BENDIS: Also, at this point, there are tons of *Powers* knockoffs. I know I sound like Howard Stern, but man, I look through *Previews* and I get a nosebleed. It's flattering and I welcome it, but a lot of these publishers fucking rejected *Powers*, so it's funny. But I think we have the freedom and the vision to stay ahead of the pack, so that's not that much of a concern. I think that we certainly shocked people with the last couple of stories. I think most people know for certain that even if the story starts with a body, they don't know how it's going to end. But yeah, it's my favorite part, too. We'll get back to it very soon.

But you just like drawing the talking heads.

DEMING: How much do you listen to your detractors? I know we get tons of mail saying how great we are, but it's always the few that tell us we suck that bug us, or even worse, the shrug-off. At what point do we take that into account? If we continually laugh it off, we can become one of the many burned-out creators who only listen to the cheerleaders who think they are still doing great work when it's actually crap.

BENDIS: That's a very good question. I don't know if I have an answer yet, because there's also the fact that it is absolutely impossible to make everyone happy. Every book I have ever been involved with has been someone's favorite and someone's least favorite; one person cried, the other person was bored. I don't know what the answer is. But a lot of times the critic tells you where he or she is coming from, which qualifies the critique. In the review they will say, "I wish *Powers* was more photorealistic." And we have to look at that and say "Well, it's not, so what's your point?" That's like saying, "I wish *The Matrix* was funnier." They weren't trying to be funny, so why even analyze it like that? Or a critic will say, "I have been reading comics for fifty-five years, and Stan Lee could have told that story in six pages." Like somehow I don't know I am taking a different approach to the scenes than they did in the '60s; like somehow that idea totally eludes me. So, I don't know. Our approval rating is pretty high, and people do vote with their wallets, so I guess that's really what you have to listen to. But even then, how much do you give people what they think they want versus what you need to say as a storyteller? See? No easy answer; I do not know.

I think the best thing we both have done is not spend our time online arguing with people that disagree with us aesthetically. We let the work speak for itself. A lot of our peers bury themselves with online arguments when they should be working on the book. What it does do for me is it makes me work harder, because I know there's no bullshit that will fly—the people speak out. You know? But I know that sometimes my critics annoy you a lot more than they do me. Also, people don't even get when they are reacting exactly how we want them to, like with a tease or a cliffhanger. Some people get so fucking angry about a cliffhanger and they don't even see how much fun they are having. I'm like, "See, you care. It's fun."

I know in your porn chatrooms, you get a lot of criticism for your flowery metaphors. How do you deal with it?

OEMING: I deal with it in a big pink bunny suit . . .

Anyway, often in *Powers*, I'm running against deadlines and can take shortcuts, such as not doing a full background or keeping the camera too close too often to avoid drawing more. Aside from that, what do you think I have to work on the most in my work?

BENDIS: I think you need to be more photorealistic. My only concern with you has always been style consistency—you have so many things you can do, and so many tools at your disposal, that you often forget the power of a consistent line through a story arc. We talk about that a lot. But this is a problem of you being too talented and eating too much sugar more than anything else.

OEMING: That's true. I especially think you see that in this compilation. As of *Forever*, however, I've decided to stay with the brush. I think I got the pen out of my *Powers* system. What about yourself, what is your biggest weakness? I don't mean the stuff you stay away from writing, like fantasy or group books, but in the work that you do, what is your weakest ability?

BENDIS: Clearly I have trouble with the format of a comic. I have trouble keeping to my page count and have for years. I either go over my page count or take a scene that could be a nice four-pager and I cram it into two pages because I have no wiggle room. It bothers me. Also, I can't spell almost to the point of learning disability. Like when I won all those nice awards this summer, I felt like a fake or something. Why don't I know the difference between "their" and "they're"? I mean, I know the difference, but I don't do it.

OEMING: If I had to name one weakness in your work, I'd have to say it is your inability to self-edit. I'm sure you see how much you actually cut out, but sometimes I look at the amount of words on a page and it goes beyond a wordy page to an impossibly wordy page. Sometimes I can't understand why there are so many words on a page. Sometimes there's as many words as there is art. Why can't you look at a page and say, "I have to cut this way down"? I'm not complaining—hey, it's less for me to fucking draw! But on a scale of one to ten, sometimes you're on a twelve or thirteen when it comes to a page with too much dialogue.

BENDIS: See, that was a very wordy response, Mr. Blah Blah Blah! I agree in theory, and often I think you are surprised by what I yank off the page at the last minute.

OEMING: Wait a minute—you "yank off" on the page? No, that doesn't surprise me . . .

Anyway, I know comics are limited in space, but instead of cramming lots of words into one place, why not change the pacing of the story so you end an issue on a different climax in order to pan out those dialogue scenes to make them fit without overcrowding the page? Just move the events

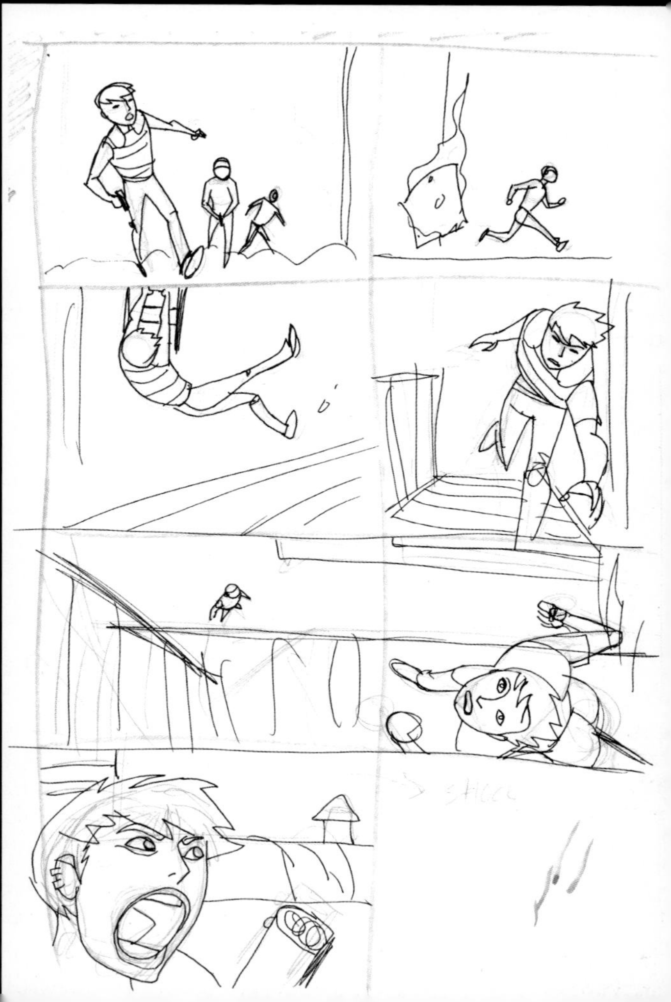

...own and find new climaxes if there's not enough room that issue.

BENDIS: See, I know I just gave you a bitch of a script this week and you are reeling, but, honestly, I fall in love with a particular cliffhanger, or decide that this amount of story is worth the $2.95 we have to charge. I hate that comics are so expensive, so I try to cram a lot in. I feel very beholden to people to give them a good read. But if I didn't write all those balloons, you'd have to draw backgrounds, so why are you pulling at this string?

OEMING: Hey, you said we had to ask the hard questions! Other than asking mean ones, like why you eat so much candy, I'm asking professional ones like this.

A major shift had happened in comics, where the art was more important than the story, to the point we had no stories. Erik Larsen even announced that writers were no longer needed! Now the shift has gone, thankfully, to the writers, but do you think in mainstream comics that's gone too far? Sometimes people just want to see shit blow up and men fight men. By sometimes, I mean once an issue.

BENDIS: And honestly, 90 percent of comics still do that. Only a few are allowed the arrogance/ luxury to do whatever they want storywise. It's just, to my shock above all others—there is a big audience for story-driven comics, and most can wait for the fight scene; they don't need it.

OEMING: I know you're big into politics, but I never see it in your work. Why is that? And please, don't change; I hate that whole world and those who drag it into their writing.

BENDIS: Oh, my politics—or I should say my feelings about politics—are all over my books. When you say politics, people think that means I'm like Susan Sarandon and I'm protesting and shit. No, I am aware and obsessed with the murky water that is our political process and how our government works, and more importantly how it affects us on a day-to-day basis, and that is all over my work. All my characters are oppressed by the man, as they are by your puritanical view of women.

OEMING: We love people talking about *Powers*, about the character stuff. At what point should we spell things out for people? Maybe long after we're done? People keep asking me if Deena killed Johnny Stomps, and I just ask them what they think. They also ask me why if Walker suspects she did it, why he doesn't really do anything about it.

BENDIS: As far as I can tell, most people get it, and then there's all the fun everyone has talking about it online. I say we let them have the fun...

...Why are you trying to spoil their fun, Mike? Fun spoiling Nazi!

OEMING: I love when you write a character as an asshole and then we learn they are more valiant than most of the characters in that same world. *Powers* characters have a real depth. Do you find that in real life very often?

BENDIS: Yes and no. Often I hope that this asshole I am talking to has some depth, only to find out that they don't. I guess that is what art is for, so we can have what we want in life.

OEMING: While it's not your thing, do you think you will ever want to write a sci-fi story or fantasy based story? You have been branching out more into group books, which you swore off once . . . I think you could write a really intelligent sci-fi or fantasy book, something much needed in that genre and a challenge that I think would bring out new dimensions in your work.

BENDIS: Well, technically all Marvel comics are sci-fi comics. I mean, they all have that sci-fi element. I'm writing *Ultimate Fantastic Four*, and that's about as sci-fi as it gets. You probably can't tell because of all the talking.

OEMING: Looking over the issues of *Powers*, what would you have done differently in any given issue? Dig deep; find something.

BENDIS: Well, if we felt we told the perfect *Powers* story, we wouldn't have to keep doing them. How about you?

OEMING: Just art stuff. Walker not being consistent physically in the first four issues; the line work changing midstory in *Anarchy*; not pulling the camera back often enough. When I look at my art, I just look for the bad things—my eye is drawn right to it.

What about your mainstream work? Is there anything you wish you had written or addressed differently given hindsight? Something you look back on and say, "Shit, I missed this aspect of the story," or "I didn't emphasize enough of such and such."

BENDIS: If I did *Elektra* again, I would just go all hot-chick kung fu and not try to be all brainy with it. I like the story we told, but if I did it again I would save that story for another time and just deliver the ass-kicking Elektra I and everyone else wanted.

Also, *Daredevil: Ninja* was a textbook example of the artist and writer having no ability to communicate with each other. Marvel offered me a parachute, and I didn't take it; I should have taken it. I felt I could save it, but I couldn't. There's...

good stuff in there, but it could have been great. Thank God for Alex Maleev.

OEMING: Yeah, that was a good example of communication breakdown. Another great Zeppelin song . . .

BENDIS: You got a pretty sordid comics past, Mr. Edward Penis-hands; how about you?

OEMING: Actually, I don't have any problems with those early porn books; they were goofy. But everything until *Powers*, with the exception of *Bulletproof Monk*, part of *Ship of Fools*, and *Foot Soldiers*, hurts my eyes to look at. I wish I had just gotten a real job and let my art grow out of the public eye!

What are the top five questions you hate being asked the most in interviews? We get a lot of repeat questions, to the point it seems like the interviewer has put no thought into it.

BENDIS: Well, listen—being asked a question over and over is better than not being asked anything by anyone. Speaking of which, I both admire and am annoyed by how much you don't know you're a big deal in comics. You are one of the best artists in comics—you have won awards, all of your projects are successful, you have sold all kinds of stuff. Yet you seem to think you're the grunt artist of *Judge Dredd*. So, my question is, do you ever think you'll take a second and step outside yourself and look around and go, "Oh, hey—okay, I made it"? I'm not saying be an asshole rock-star fuckhead, because I hate that, too, but many times I wish you knew your place in the biz.

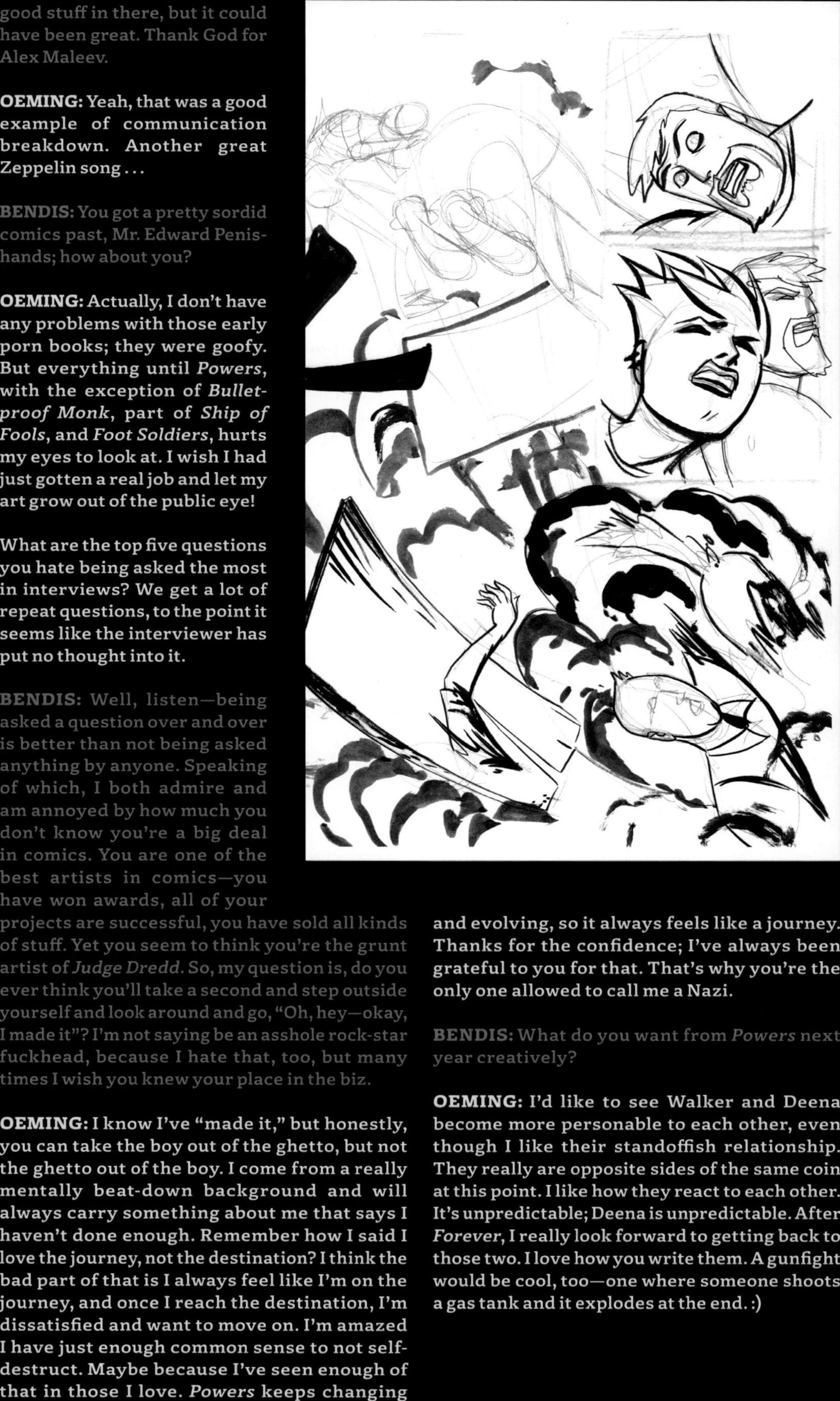

OEMING: I know I've "made it," but honestly, you can take the boy out of the ghetto, but not the ghetto out of the boy. I come from a really mentally beat-down background and will always carry something about me that says I haven't done enough. Remember how I said I love the journey, not the destination? I think the bad part of that is I always feel like I'm on the journey, and once I reach the destination, I'm dissatisfied and want to move on. I'm amazed I have just enough common sense to not self-destruct. Maybe because I've seen enough of that in those I love. *Powers* keeps changing and evolving, so it always feels like a journey. Thanks for the confidence; I've always been grateful to you for that. That's why you're the only one allowed to call me a Nazi.

BENDIS: What do you want from *Powers* next year creatively?

OEMING: I'd like to see Walker and Deena become more personable to each other, even though I like their standoffish relationship. They really are opposite sides of the same coin at this point. I like how they react to each other. It's unpredictable; Deena is unpredictable. After *Forever*, I really look forward to getting back to those two. I love how you write them. A gunfight would be cool, too—one where someone shoots a gas tank and it explodes at the end. :)

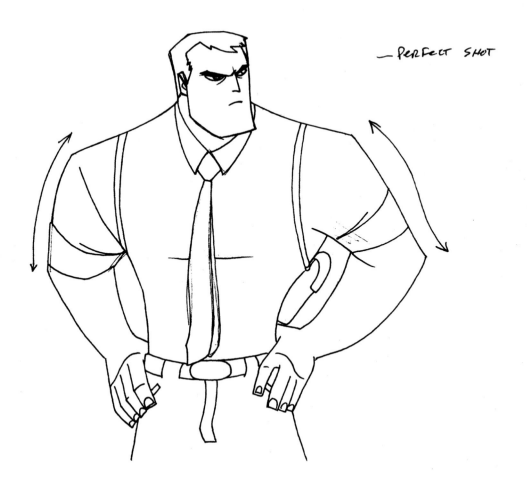

— PERFECT SHOT

WALKER / FRONT / AVON 12-31-01

WALKER
STATUE DESIGNS

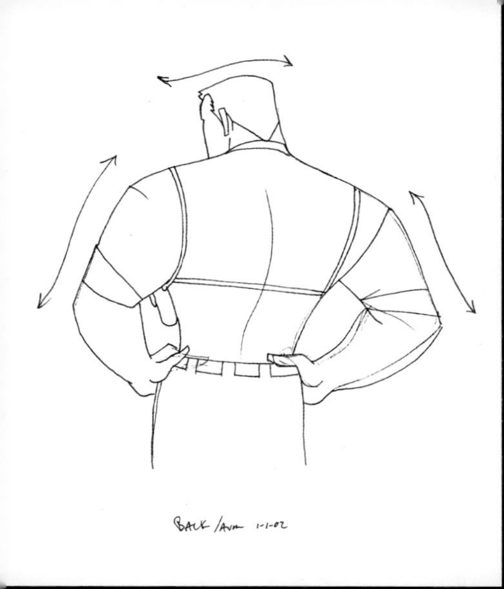
BACK / 1-1-02

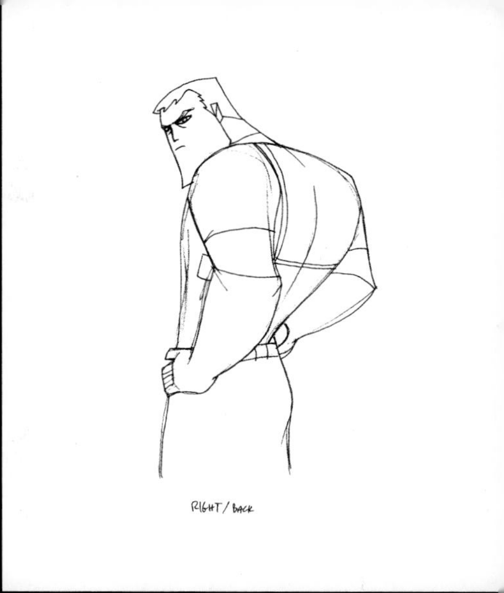
RIGHT / BACK

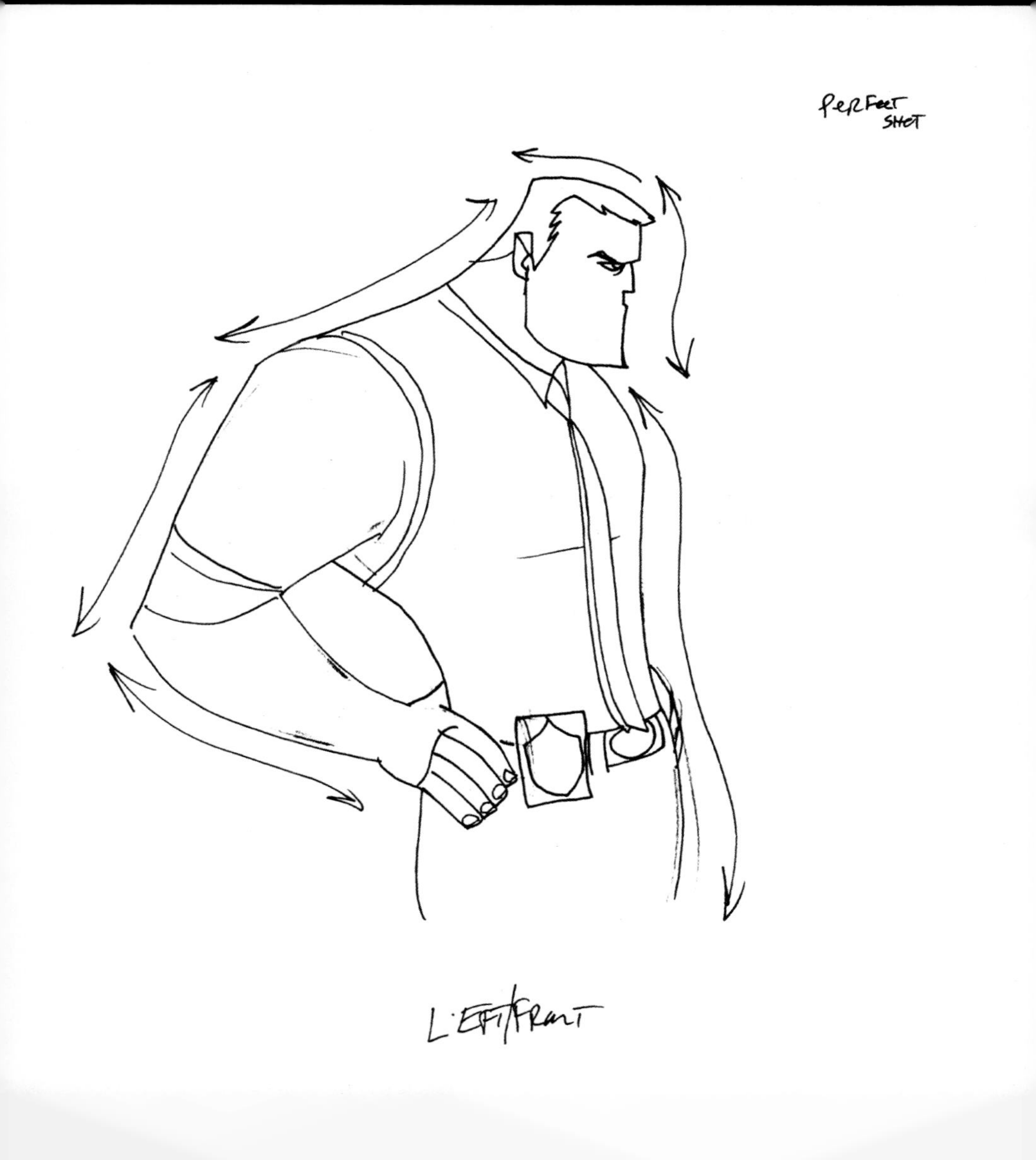
PERFECT SHOT
LEFT/FRONT

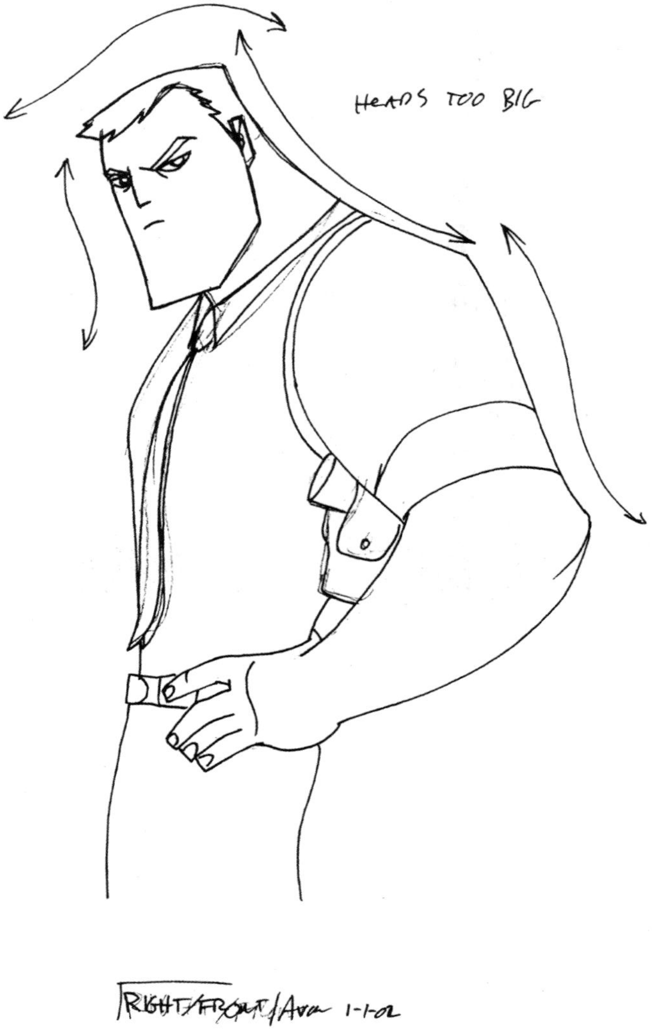
HEADS TOO BIG
RIGHT/FRONT/ARM 1-1-02

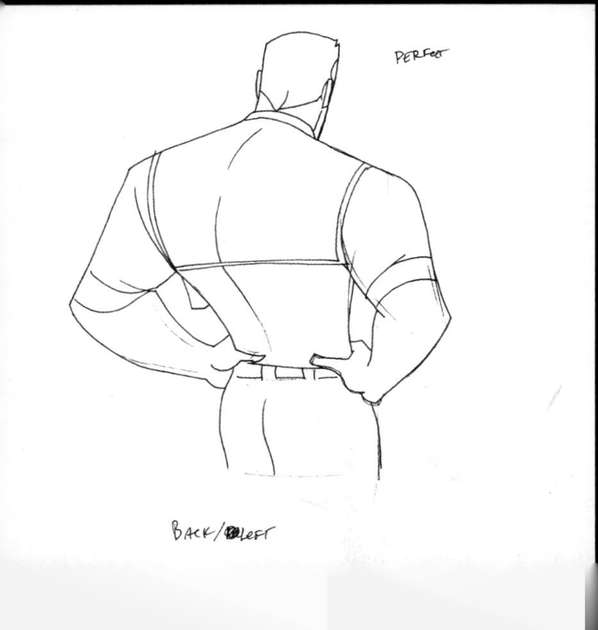
PERFECT
BACK/LEFT

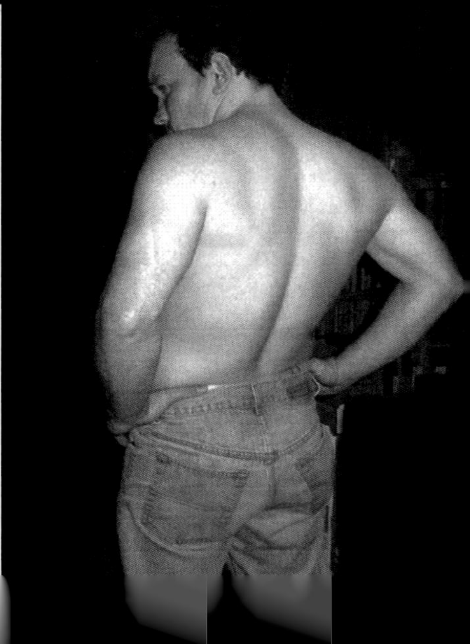

Brian Michael Bendis...

is a Peabody Award–winning comics creator and Amazon and *New York Times* bestseller most known for cocreating Miles Morales, Jessica Jones, Maria Hill, Naomi, Ironheart, and dozens of other characters and stories that populate the Marvel, DC, and all-new original universes.

The Jinxworld line of creator-owned comics can be found at the legendary Dark Horse Comics. These titles include the new sci-fi epic *Joy Operations* (with cocreator Stephen Byrne), the yakuza romance *Pearl* (with Jessica Jones cocreator Michael Gaydos), the comic book industry spy thriller *Cover* (with award-winning multimedia sensation David Mack), *Scarlet* (with cocreator Alex Maleev), and the alternate history mob story *Murder Inc.* (with *Powers* cocreator Mike Avon Oeming).

Phenomena, a new YA graphic novel series by Brian and artist André Lima Araújo, will debut from Abrams Comic-Arts in 2022.

Cover has been ordered for animation pilot presentation from HBO Max with Rooster Teeth producing. Brian is also developing *Legion of Super-Heroes* for HBO Max / WB Animation.

Brian is executive producer and consultant for the Academy Award–winning hit Sony feature *Spider-Man: Into the Spider-Verse* (and its sequels, coming in 2023 and 2024). Miles Morales was cocreated by Brian and Sara Pichelli.

Brian won a Peabody Award for his work as the cocreator of *Jessica Jones* on Netflix from Marvel TV.

The announcement of Brian's multifaceted move to DC Entertainment after a nearly twenty-year run at Marvel made international headlines and trended worldwide. Brian made his DC debut in the landmark *Action Comics* #1,000 and currently writes *Justice League vs. The Legion of Super-Heroes* after finishing his years-long runs on *Superman*, *Action Comics*, *Batman: Universe*, and *Legion of Super-Heroes* and on curating Wonder Comics, featuring the return of *Young Justice*, *Dial H for Hero*, *Wonder Twins*, and the breakout original new character . . . Naomi. *Naomi* was adapted by Ava DuVernay and Array into a show on the CW.

Brian's release from Random House entitled *Words for Pictures* is an intricate look at the creation of comic books and graphic novels based on the college-level graphic novel class he teaches at Portland State University. It shot to number one on its Amazon chart.

Over the years at Marvel Entertainment, Brian completed historic runs on *Spider-Man* (eighteen years), *Avengers* (nine years), *Iron Man*, and *Guardians of the Galaxy*; a hundred-issue run on the *X-Men* franchise; and the wildly successful "event" projects *Avengers vs. X-Men*, *House of M*, *Secret War*, *Secret Invasion*, *Age of Ultron*, *Civil War II*, and *Siege*. as

Brian was one of the premiere architects of Marvel's Ultimate line of comics.

Previously, Brian was part of the Marvel creative committee which helped set the foundation of the MCU. He consulted for all of the Marvel movies from the first *Iron Man* all the way through to *Guardians of the Galaxy Volume 2*.

Brian is the creator of the Jinx line of crime comics. This line has spawned the graphic novels *Goldfish*, *Fire*, *Jinx*, *Torso* (with Marc Andreyko), and *Total Sell Out*.

Brian received an honorary doctorate in the arts from the Cleveland Institute of Art and a certificate of excellence from the Central Intelligence Agency for his work on diversity issues. Brian has won five Eisner Awards, including Best Writer two years in a row, and was honored with the prestigious Inkpot Award for comic art excellence. Brian is the recipient of the Press Club of Cleveland's Excellence in Journalism Award.

He lives in Portland, Oregon, with his wife, Alisa; his daughters, Olivia, Tabatha, and Sabrina; his son, London; and his dogs, Splenda and Bowie.

Brian's TED Talk, MIT lecture, and appearances on *Late Night with Seth Meyers* are available for viewing at Jinxworld.com.

Michael Avon Oeming...

is best known as the Eisner and Harvey Award–winning co-creator of *Powers*. He began his comics career as an inker, breaking in early at the age of fourteen. By his late teens, he had already worked on titles such as Daredevil and Justice League. A fan of mythology, Oeming often bases his writing on fantasy, as in *Thor: Ragnaroks*, *Ares*, and *Red Sonja*. He has collaborated with longtime friend Brian Michael Bendis on *Powers*, *United States of Murder Inc.*, and *Takio*. Oeming is also well known for creator-owned work he's written and/or drawn, such as *Batman*, *Thor*, *Superman*, *Judge Dredd*, *The Spirit*, *Black Panther*, and *The Avengers*.

In 2009 he began working on video games at Valve Corp., where for several years he contributed on *Portal 2*, *Left 4 Dead*, and *Team Fortress 2*.

Since then, much of Oeming's work has focused on creator-owned projects, such as his *Victories* series, *Sinergy* (with wife Taki Soma), and the occasional superhero story for the "Big Two." He recently finished a two-year run on *Cave Carson Has a Cybernetic Eye* from DC's Young Animal. Oeming also works in film and television production, serving as executive producer on *Powers*, *Them*, and *The Mice Templar* for Gaumont Animation, and is working on more TV projects in development.

CHECK OUT MORE BOOKS FROM THE *NEW YORK TIMES* BESTSELLING AND EISNER AWARD-WINNING

JINXWORLD LINE FROM DARK HORSE COMICS!

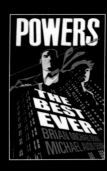

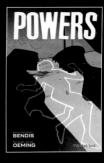

GOLDFISH
BRIAN MICHAEL BENDIS
TORSO
BRIAN MICHAEL BENDIS
MARC ANDREYKO
JINX
BRIAN MICHAEL BENDIS
JOY OPERATIONS
SCARLET
BENDIS
MALEEV
COVER

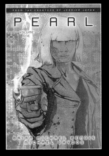

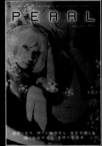

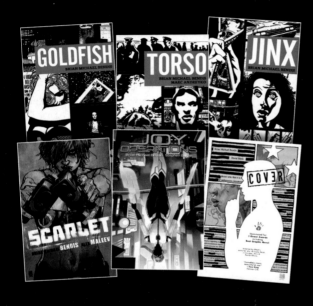

GOLDFISH
ISBN 978-1-50673-014-1
$19.99
Brian Michael Bendis

TORSO
ISBN 978-1-50673-025-7
$19.99
Brian Michael Bendis

JINX
ISBN 978-1-50673-015-8
$24.99
Brian Michael Bendis

SCARLET
ISBN 978-1-50673-024-0
$29.99
Brian Michael Bendis, Alex Maleev

JOY OPERATIONS
ISBN 978-1-50672-946-6
$24.99
Brian Michael Bendis, Stephen Byrne

COVER VOLUME 1
ISBN 978-1-50673-055-4
$19.99
Brian Michael Bendis, David Mack

AVAILABLE AT YOUR LOCAL COMICS SHOP OR BOOKSTORE TO FIND A COMICS SHOP IN YOUR AREA, VISIT COMICSHOPLOCATOR.COM
For more information or to order direct, visit darkhorse.com

POWERS
THE BEST EVER
BRIAN MICHAEL BENDIS
MICHAEL AVON OEMING

POWERS
BENDIS
OEMING
VOLUME ONE

POWERS: THE BEST EVER
ISBN 978-1-50673-016-5 | $29.99
Brian Michael Bendis, Michael Avon Oeming

POWERS VOLUME 1
ISBN 978-1-50673-017-2 | $29.99
Brian Michael Bendis, Michael Avon Oeming

PEARL

PEARL

PEARL VOLUME 1
ISBN 978-1-50672-932-9 | $19.99
Brian Michael Bendis, Alex Maleev

PEARL VOLUME 2
ISBN 978-1-50672-933-6 | $19.99
Brian Michael Bendis, Alex Maleev

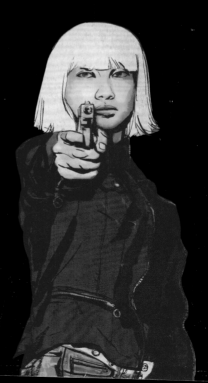